Annotated Teacher's Edition

Prentice Hall WRITING and GRAMMAR

Communication in Action

PEARSON Prentice Hall

Grade 6-Copper ISBN: 0-13-037496-2
Grade 7-Bronze ISBN: 0-13-037497-0
Grade 8-Silver ISBN: 0-13-037499-7

1 2 3 4 5 6 7 8 9 10 07 06 05 04 03

Experience the power of language!

Also Available!

Handbook Edition

All the power of *Writing and Grammar* in a portable, compact size.

iText

INTERACTIVE STUDENT TEXT ONLINE AND ON CD-ROM WITH E-RATER™

(See p. T12.)

NEW!
INTEGRATED LESSON PLANNING ASSISTANT
seamlessly integrates instruction with *Prentice Hall Literature.*

Also Available!

Everyday Spelling

Look for cross-references in this teacher's edition that allow you to integrate spelling lessons!

3-Part Organization

Prentice Hall Writing and Grammar: Communication in Action is conveniently divided into the following three sections for ease of use:

- **Writing** guides students through each step of the writing process with an emphasis on revision.
- **Grammar, Usage, and Mechanics** provides more grammar practice than any other program and includes unique hands-on grammar activities.
- **Academic and Workplace Skills** focuses on practical, real-world skills for today's multimedia generation.

Motivate all your students!

Make the connections that give students a purpose for learning.

Connect to the language arts.

Connections to literature, writing, and grammar show students the relevance of what they learn.

10.1 **Model From Literature**

In this how-to essay, science writer Janice VanCleave (1942–) lets readers see how erosion moves mountains.

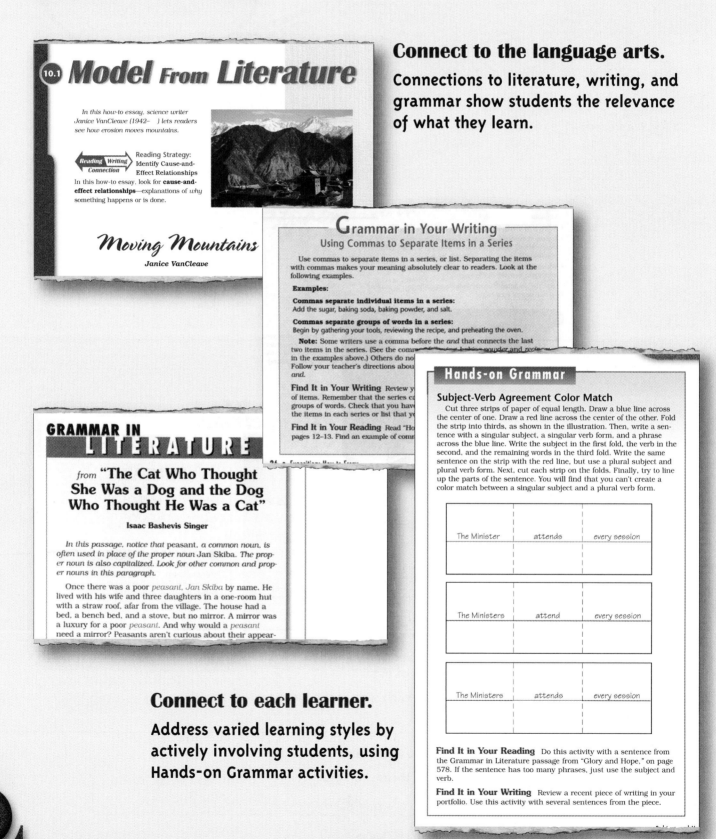

Reading Writing Connection — Reading Strategy: Identify Cause-and-Effect Relationships

In this how-to essay, look for **cause-and-effect relationships**—explanations of *why* something happens or is done.

Moving Mountains

Janice VanCleave

Grammar in Your Writing

Using Commas to Separate Items in a Series

Use commas to separate items in a series, or list. Separating the items with commas makes your meaning absolutely clear to readers. Look at the following examples.

Examples:

Commas separate individual items in a series:
Add the sugar, baking soda, baking powder, and salt.

Commas separate groups of words in a series:
Begin by gathering your tools, reviewing the recipe, and preheating the oven.

Note: Some writers use a comma before the *and* that connects the last two items in the series. (See the comm... in the examples above.) Others do no... Follow your teacher's directions abou... *and*.

Find It in Your Writing Review y... of items. Remember that the series ca... groups of words. Check that you hav... the items in each series or list that y...

Find It in Your Reading Read "Ho... pages 12–13. Find an example of comm...

GRAMMAR IN LITERATURE

from **"The Cat Who Thought She Was a Dog and the Dog Who Thought He Was a Cat"**

Isaac Bashevis Singer

In this passage, notice that peasant, *a common noun, is often used in place of the proper noun* Jan Skiba. *The proper noun is also capitalized. Look for other common and proper nouns in this paragraph.*

Once there was a poor *peasant, Jan Skiba* by name. He lived with his wife and three daughters in a one-room hut with a straw roof, afar from the village. The house had a bed, a bench bed, and a stove, but no mirror. A mirror was a luxury for a poor *peasant*. And why would a *peasant* need a mirror? Peasants aren't curious about their appear-

Hands-on Grammar

Subject-Verb Agreement Color Match

Cut three strips of paper of equal length. Draw a blue line across the center of one. Draw a red line across the center of the other. Fold the strip into thirds, as shown in the illustration. Then, write a sentence with a singular subject, a singular verb form, and a phrase across the blue line. Write the subject in the first fold, the verb in the second, and the remaining words in the third fold. Write the same sentence on the strip with the red line, but use a plural subject and plural verb form. Next, cut each strip on the folds. Finally, try to line up the parts of the sentence. You will find that you can't create a color match between a singular subject and a plural verb form.

The Minister	attends	every session

The Ministers	attend	every session

The Ministers	attends	every session

Find It in Your Reading Do this activity with a sentence from the Grammar in Literature passage from "Glory and Hope," on page 578. If the sentence has too many phrases, just use the subject and verb.

Find It in Your Writing Review a recent piece of writing in your portfolio. Use this activity with several sentences from the piece.

Connect to each learner.

Address varied learning styles by actively involving students, using Hands-on Grammar activities.

EXPOSITION
Comparison-and-Contrast Essay

What Is a Comparison-and-Contrast Essay?

A **comparison-and-contrast essay** analyzes the similarities and differences between two or more things. It can help you to decide which bicycle to buy. A good comparison-and-contrast essay can even change your perspective—as when a reviewer compares the latest hit song with an old album, letting you hear the startling similarities. A comparison-and-contrast essay includes

- a topic involving two or more things that are neither nearly identical nor extremely different.
- details illustrating both similarities and differences.
- clear organization that highlights the points of comparison.

To learn the criteria on which your essay may be evaluated, see the Rubric for Self-Assessment on page 166.

Writers in ACTION

In his books and articles, Richard Lederer compares English to other languages and different English words to each other. He knows the value of saying more in fewer words: "... writing is hard work, and writing concisely is even more difficult."

Types of Comparison-and-Contrast Essays

In addition to an ordinary comparison-and-contrast essay, some specialized essays also use comparison and contrast:

- **Product comparisons** compare two or more products, providing up-to-date information on each and discussing the advantages and disadvantages of purchasing each one.
- **Plan evaluations** compare two or more alternative plans or decisions, discussing the circumstances and comparing the advantages and disadvantages of each plan.

PREVIEW Student Work IN PROGRESS

To develop your comparison-and-contrast writing skills, follow the work of Dylan Parker of Carr Lane VPA Middle School in St. Louis, Missouri. In this chapter, Dylan uses featured prewriting, drafting, and revising techniques to develop the comparison-and-contrast essay "Skateboards for Success." At the end of the lesson, you can read Dylan's completed essay.

Comparison-and-Contrast Essay • 151

Connect to students' lives.

An authentic student model in every writing chapter tracks the development of one student's writing through a specific writing mode.

Connect to the latest technology.

Media and Technology Skills workshops teach students relevant, real-world skills and offer a full array of online and multimedia resources. (See p. T12.)

Media and Technology Skills

Using Computer Technology

Activity: Getting Help On-line

Computer programs typically come with built-in "how-to's"—on-line help the user can access while using the program. On-line help lets you learn as you work. It is as though the computer were a teacher and a tool rolled into one! By mastering Help, you can turn problems with computers into opportunities to learn.

Computer Help
Built-in Help
- Balloon Help
- On-line manuals

Other Kinds of Help
- "Read Me" files
- Printed manuals

Learn About It

Balloon Help Turn Balloon Help on or off through a program's menu bar. With Balloon Help on, a balloon appears whenever you roll your mouse pointer over a button, dialogue box, or other feature. Each balloon contains a brief description identifying the function of the feature on which the pointer is resting.

On-line Manuals To consult the on-line manual for a program, select "Help" from the menu bar. "Contents" lists topics by category. "Index" lists topics alphabetically and often provides a Search feature that allows you to search for a particular subject.

Other Kinds of Help Often, the best troubleshooting tips come from the program's "Read Me" file. You may open a "Read Me" file in a text-editor program. Software also comes with a printed manual, which offers detailed information on operating the program.

Apply It Choose an application, such as a ...processing program, to which you ... Think of a difficulty you have ... program or a question you ... program's use. Use ... to solve the prob... Take notes in a ... the one to the ... manual explaining ... ways of getting

My Question or Problem ______
Type of Help ______

How to Use This Kind of Help
Step 1 ______
Step 2 ______
Step 3 ______

Did I Get an Answer to My Question? y__/n__

Easy/Hard to Use (Explain)

Media and Technology Skills • 219

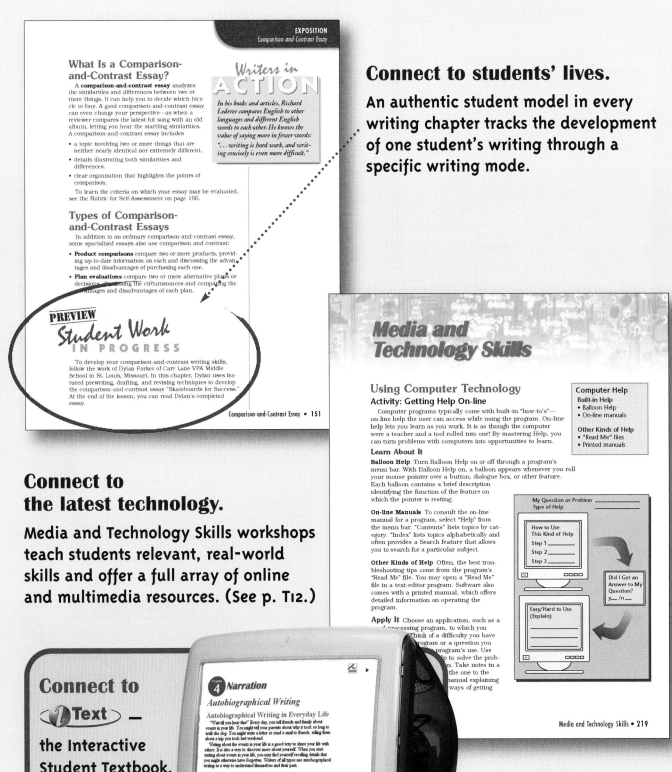

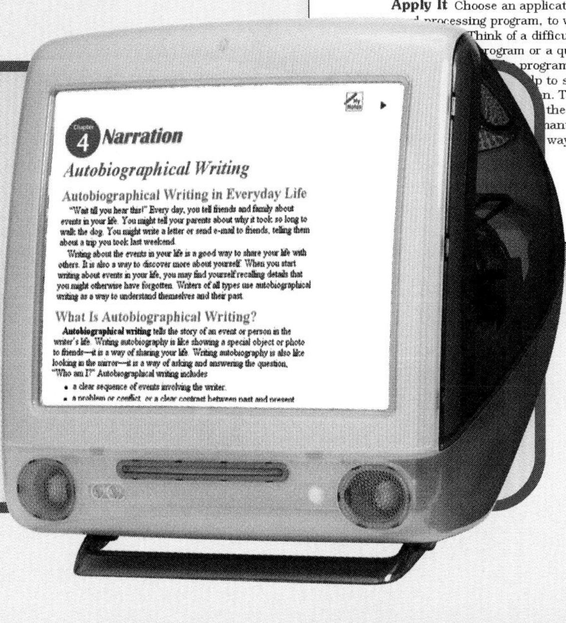

Connect to iText —

the Interactive Student Textbook, online and on CD-ROM.
(See p. T12.)

More practice and revision support!

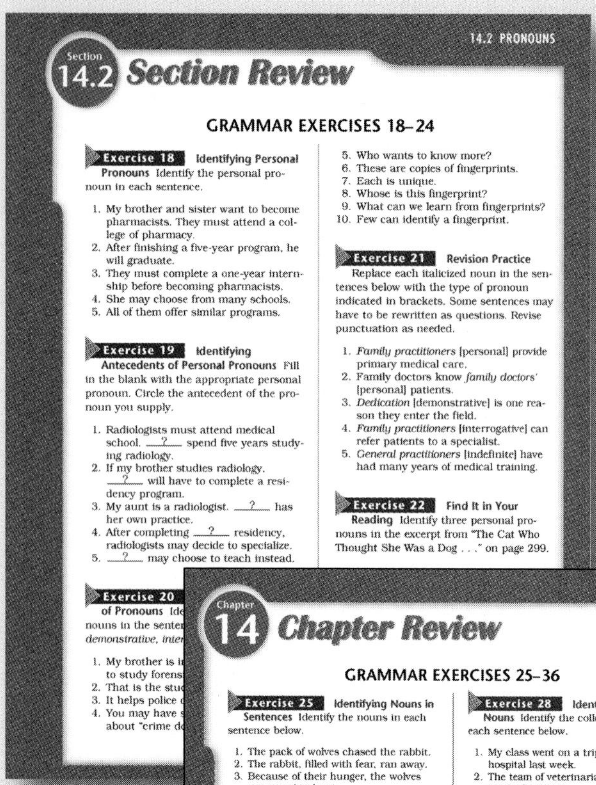

Section 14.2 **Section Review**

GRAMMAR EXERCISES 18–24

Exercise 18 **Identifying Personal Pronouns** Identify the personal pronoun in each sentence.

1. My brother and sister want to become pharmacists. They must attend a college of pharmacy.
2. After finishing a five-year program, he will graduate.
3. They must complete a one-year internship before becoming pharmacists.
4. She may choose from many schools.
5. All of them offer similar programs.
6. Who wants to know more?
7. These are copies of fingerprints.
8. Each is unique.
9. Whose is this fingerprint?
10. What can we learn from fingerprints?
11. Few can identify a fingerprint.

Exercise 19 **Identifying Antecedents of Personal Pronouns** Fill in the blank with the appropriate personal pronoun. Circle the antecedent of the pronoun you supply.

1. Radiologists must attend medical school. __?__ spend five years studying radiology.
2. If my brother studies radiology, __?__ will have to complete a residency program.
3. My aunt is a radiologist. __?__ has her own practice.
4. After completing __?__ residency, radiologists may decide to specialize.
5. __?__ may choose to teach instead.

Exercise 20 ... of Personal Pronouns Ide... nouns in the senter... *demonstrative, inter*...

1. My brother is i... to study forens...
2. That is the stu...
3. It helps police ...
4. You may have ... about "crime d...

Exercise 21 **Revision Practice** Replace each italicized noun in the sentences below with the type of pronoun indicated in brackets. Some sentences may have to be rewritten as questions. Revise punctuation as needed.

1. *Family practitioners* [personal] provide primary medical care.
2. Family doctors know *family doctors'* [personal] patients.
3. *Dedication* [demonstrative] is one reason they enter the field.
4. *Family practitioners* [interrogative] can refer patients to a specialist.
5. *General practitioners* [indefinite] have had many years of medical training.

Exercise 22 **Find It in Your Reading** Identify three personal pronouns in the excerpt from "The Cat Who Thought She Was a Dog . . ." on page 299.

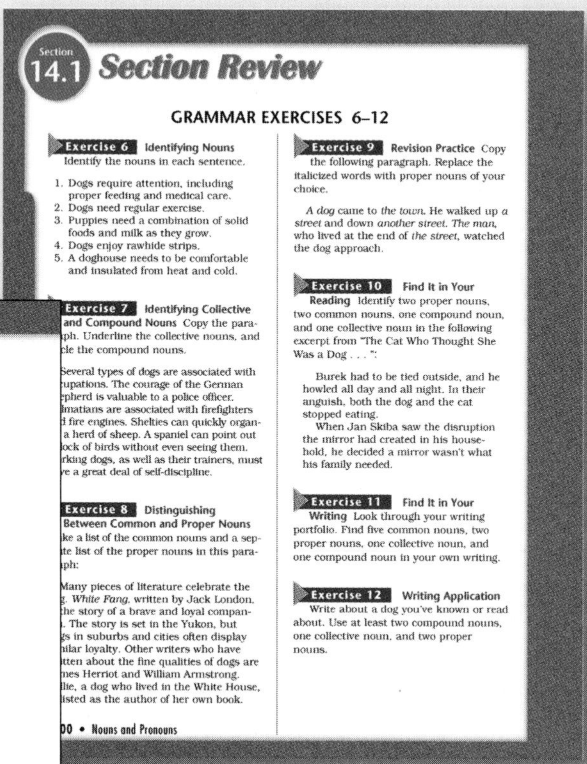

Section 14.1 **Section Review**

GRAMMAR EXERCISES 6–12

Exercise 6 **Identifying Nouns** Identify the nouns in each sentence.

1. Dogs require attention, including proper feeding and medical care.
2. Dogs need regular exercise.
3. Puppies need a combination of solid foods and milk as they grow.
4. Dogs enjoy rawhide strips.
5. A doghouse needs to be comfortable and insulated from heat and cold.

Exercise 7 **...and Compound Nouns** Copy the para...ph. Underline the collective nouns, and ...cle the compound nouns.

...everal types of dogs are associated with ...upations. The courage of the German ...epherd is valuable to a police officer. ...lmatians are associated with firefighters ...d fire engines. Shelties can quickly organ... a herd of sheep. A spaniel can point out ...ock of birds without even seeing them. ...rking dogs, as well as their trainers, must ...e a great deal of self-discipline.

Exercise 8 **Distinguishing Between Common and Proper Nouns** ...ke a list of the common nouns and a sep...te list of the proper nouns in this para...ph:

...Many pieces of literature celebrate the ...g. *White Fang*, written by Jack London, ...he story of a brave and loyal compan... . The story is set in the Yukon, but ...s in suburbs and cities often display ...ilar loyalty. Other writers who have ...tten about the fine qualities of dogs are ...nes Herriot and William Armstrong. ...llie, a dog who lived in the White House, ...listed as the author of her own book.

Exercise 9 **Revision Practice** Copy the following paragraph. Replace the italicized words with proper nouns of your choice.

A dog came to *the town*. He walked up *a street* and down *another street*. *The man*, who lived at the end of *the street*, watched the dog approach.

Exercise 10 **Find It in Your Reading** Identify two proper nouns, two common nouns, one compound noun, and one collective noun in the following excerpt from "The Cat Who Thought She Was a Dog . . .":

Burek had to be tied outside, and he howled all day and all night. In their anguish, both the dog and the cat stopped eating.

When Jan Skiba saw the disruption the mirror had created in his household, he decided a mirror wasn't what his family needed.

Exercise 11 **Find It in Your Writing** Look through your writing portfolio. Find five common nouns, two proper nouns, one collective noun, and one compound noun in your own writing.

Exercise 12 **Writing Application** Write about a dog you've known or read about. Use at least two compound nouns, one collective noun, and two proper nouns.

...00 • Nouns and Pronouns

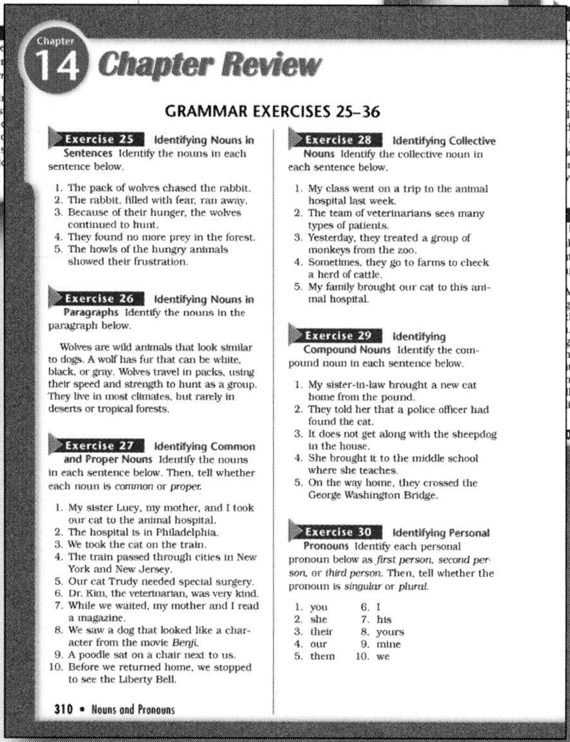

Chapter 14 **Chapter Review**

GRAMMAR EXERCISES 25–36

Exercise 25 **Identifying Nouns in Sentences** Identify the nouns in each sentence below.

1. The pack of wolves chased the rabbit.
2. The rabbit, filled with fear, ran away.
3. Because of their hunger, the wolves continued to hunt.
4. They found no more prey in the forest.
5. The howls of the hungry animals showed their frustration.

Exercise 26 **Identifying Nouns in Paragraphs** Identify the nouns in the paragraph below.

Wolves are wild animals that look similar to dogs. A wolf has fur that can be white, black, or gray. Wolves travel in packs, using their speed and strength to hunt as a group. They live in most climates, but rarely in deserts or tropical forests.

Exercise 27 **Identifying Common and Proper Nouns** Identify the nouns in each sentence below. Then, tell whether each noun is *common* or *proper*.

1. My sister Lucy, my mother, and I took our cat to the animal hospital.
2. The hospital is in Philadelphia.
3. We took the cat on the train.
4. The train passed through cities in New York and New Jersey.
5. Our cat Trudy needed special surgery.
6. Dr. Kim, the veterinarian, was very kind.
7. While we waited, my mother and I read a magazine.
8. We saw a dog that looked like a character from the movie *Benji*.
9. A poodle sat on a chair next to us.
10. Before we returned home, we stopped to see the Liberty Bell.

Exercise 28 **Identifying Collective Nouns** Identify the collective noun in each sentence below.

1. My class went on a trip to the animal hospital last week.
2. The team of veterinarians sees many types of patients.
3. Yesterday, they treated a group of monkeys from the zoo.
4. Sometimes, they go to farms to check a herd of cattle.
5. My family brought our cat to this animal hospital.

Exercise 29 **Identifying Compound Nouns** Identify the compound noun in each sentence below.

1. My sister-in-law brought a new cat home from the pound.
2. They told her that a police officer had found the cat.
3. It does not get along with the sheepdog in the house.
4. She brought it to the middle school where she teaches.
5. On the way home, they crossed the George Washington Bridge.

Exercise 30 **Identifying Personal Pronouns** Identify each personal pronoun below as *first person*, *second person*, or *third person*. Then, tell whether the pronoun is *singular* or *plural*.

1. you	6. I
2. she	7. his
3. their	8. yours
4. our	9. mine
5. them	10. we

310 • Nouns and Pronouns

Practice, practice, practice . . .

More grammar exercises than any other program provide the practice your students need to improve their grammar skills and apply them in writing and speaking.

. . . and even MORE practice!

Hundreds of additional grammar exercises!

Prentice Hall
WRITING and GRAMMAR
Communication in Action
Bronze Level
Grammar Exercise Workbook
•Two practice pages for each grammar concept

HUNDREDS OF ADDITIONAL GRAMMAR EXERCISES!

Interactive grammar exercises provide instant feedback on iText.

iText contains thousands of grammar exercises in a variety of formats.

More strategic revision

Systematic, hands-on revision strategies help students examine what they write and how to improve it.

10.4 Revising

Looking at Overall Structure

Add an Introduction and Conclusion

After writing your first draft, reread your how-to essay, looking for ways to improve and polish it. You will probably recognize that you don't want to jump right in with step one and end abruptly at the last step. Instead, give a general overview of your topic in an introduction. Then, explain the different steps in the body of the essay and review, summarize, or briefly comment on the procedures in a conclusion.

Revision Strategy
◆ Write a Strong Lead

Begin with an image or idea that "leads" your reader into the essay. Look through your prewriting notes to find details that remind you why you enjoy the activity or why you decided to write about your topic. The detail that grabbed your interest may spark your audience's interest as well. Use one of these details to make that first sentence an attention grabber!

Student Work IN PROGRESS

A Strong Lead

Felix reviewed his prewriting notes and found that his class party gave him the idea for the topic "How to Make Banana Cake." He used an exaggerated image of hungry students to write an attention-grabbing lead.

Our seventh-grade teacher, Mrs. Flood, knows that it takes more than an ordinary cake to feed twenty ravenous seventh-graders. That's why she always asks Mike or me to make our famous Banana Cake. Making Banana Cake takes a little more time than making a cake from a box, but you will find that every bite of the finished product is worth the time it takes. By following the steps outlined here, you can learn how to make this delicious dessert.

Felix introduces his topic with details that make it appealing.

Analyzing Your Paragraphs

Identify Paragraph Purpose

Once you're comfortable with the general structure of your paper, carefully focus on each individual paragraph. The purpose of each paragraph will determine the words or phrases that may need to be added to make your meaning clearer.

Revision Strategy
◆ Use Steps, Stacks, Chains, and Balances

- **Steps** If the paragraph is explaining a step or several related steps for which time order is important, make sure you have indicated the sequence. Use words such as *first*, *next*, and *finally*.
- **Stacks** If the paragraph explains how one part of a process contributes to another, show the connection between ideas with words such as *and*, *furthermore*, and *for instance*.
- **Chains** If the paragraph explains the cause-and-effect relationship between steps, use words such as *so*, *because*, and *consequently*.
- **Balance** If the paragraph shows choice or contrast, use words such as *but*, *however*, *on the other hand*, and *rather*.

▶ Critical Viewing Do you think these boys successfully followed the directions for making a cake? **[Evaluate]**

Authentic modeling

Real student models help illustrate revision techniques in action.

Student Work IN PROGRESS

A Strong Lead

Felix reviewed his prewriting notes and found that his class party gave him the idea for the topic "How to Make Banana Cake." He used an exaggerated image of hungry students to write an attention-grabbing lead.

Our seventh-grade teacher, Mrs. Flood, knows that it takes more than an ordinary cake to feed twenty ravenous seventh-graders. That's why she always asks Mike or me to make our famous Banana Cake. Making Banana Cake takes a little more time than making a cake from a box, but you will find that every bite of the finished product is worth the time it takes. By following the steps outlined here, you can learn how to make this delicious dessert.

Felix introduces his topic with details that make it appealing.

20 • Exposition: How-to Essay

Comprehensive assessment preparation!

Thorough preparation guarantees student success.

Standardized Test Preparation Workshops

Standardized Test Preparation Workshops after each chapter provide comprehensive preparation for PSAT, SAT, ACT, AP*, state, and local standardized tests.

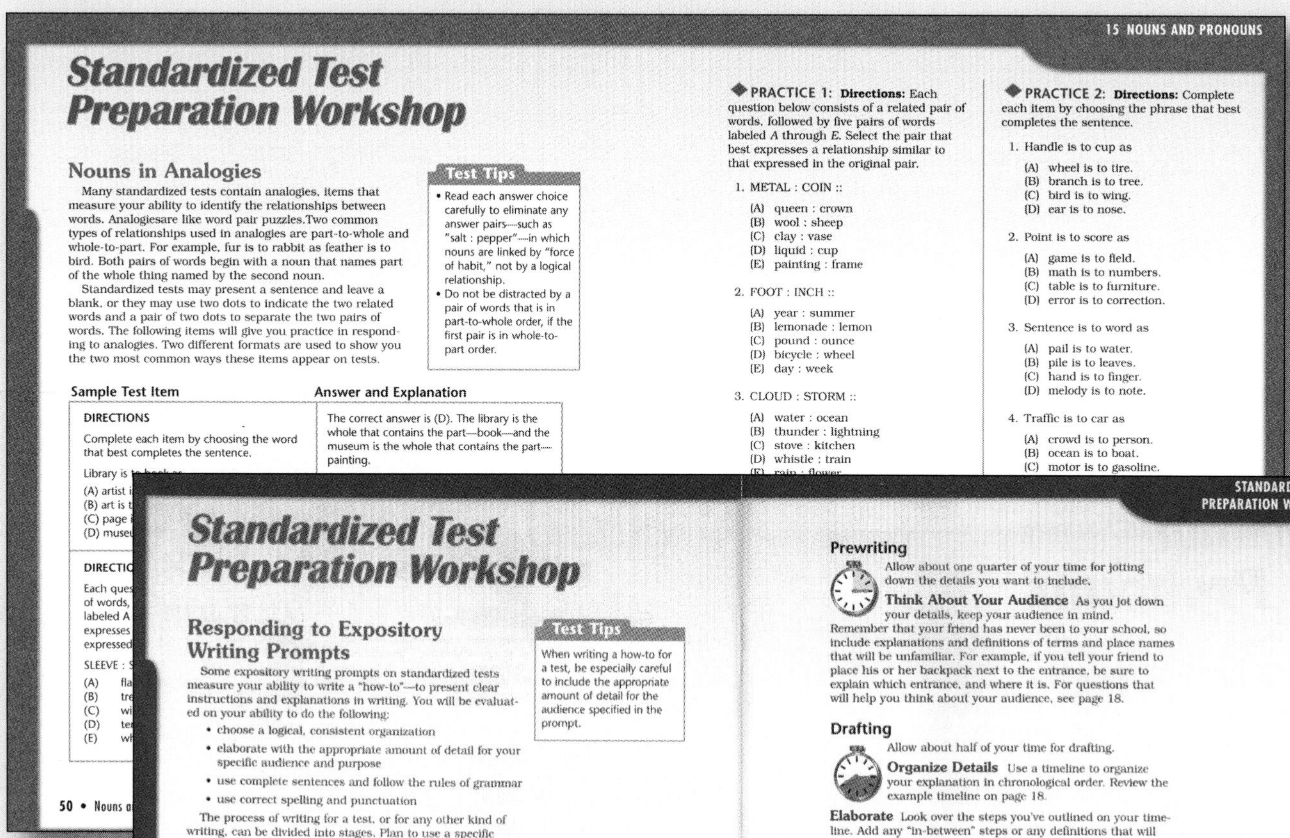

15 NOUNS AND PRONOUNS

Standardized Test Preparation Workshop

Nouns in Analogies

Many standardized tests contain analogies, items that measure your ability to identify the relationships between words. Analogiesare like word pair puzzles.Two common types of relationships used in analogies are part-to-whole and whole-to-part. For example, fur is to rabbit as feather is to bird. Both pairs of words begin with a noun that names part of the whole thing named by the second noun.

Standardized tests may present a sentence and leave a blank, or they may use two dots to indicate the two related words and a pair of two dots to separate the two pairs of words. The following items will give you practice in responding to analogies. Two different formats are used to show you the two most common ways these items appear on tests.

Test Tips

- Read each answer choice carefully to eliminate any answer pairs—such as "salt : pepper"—in which nouns are linked by "force of habit," not by a logical relationship.
- Do not be distracted by a pair of words that is in part-to-whole order, if the first pair is in whole-to-part order.

Sample Test Item

DIRECTIONS

Complete each item by choosing the word that best completes the sentence.

Library is

(A) artist
(B) art is
(C) page
(D) muse

DIRECTI

Each ques of words, labeled A expresses expressed

SLEEVE :

(A) fla
(B) tre
(C) wi
(D) te
(E) wh

Answer and Explanation

The correct answer is (D). The library is the whole that contains the part—book—and the museum is the whole that contains the part—painting.

◆ PRACTICE 1: **Directions:** Each question below consists of a related pair of words, followed by five pairs of words labeled *A* through *E*. Select the pair that best expresses a relationship similar to that expressed in the original pair.

1. METAL : COIN ::
   (A) queen : crown
   (B) wool : sheep
   (C) clay : vase
   (D) liquid : cup
   (E) painting : frame
2. FOOT : INCH ::
   (A) year : summer
   (B) lemonade : lemon
   (C) pound : ounce
   (D) bicycle : wheel
   (E) day : week
3. CLOUD : STORM ::
   (A) water : ocean
   (B) thunder : lightning
   (C) stove : kitchen
   (D) whistle : train

◆ PRACTICE 2: **Directions:** Complete each item by choosing the phrase that best completes the sentence.

1. Handle is to cup as
   (A) wheel is to tire.
   (B) branch is to tree.
   (C) bird is to wing.
   (D) ear is to nose.
2. Point is to score as
   (A) game is to field.
   (B) math is to numbers.
   (C) table is to furniture.
   (D) error is to correction.
3. Sentence is to word as
   (A) pail is to water.
   (B) pile is to leaves.
   (C) hand is to finger.
   (D) melody is to note.
4. Traffic is to car as
   (A) crowd is to person.
   (B) ocean is to boat.
   (C) motor is to gasoline.

50 • Nouns a

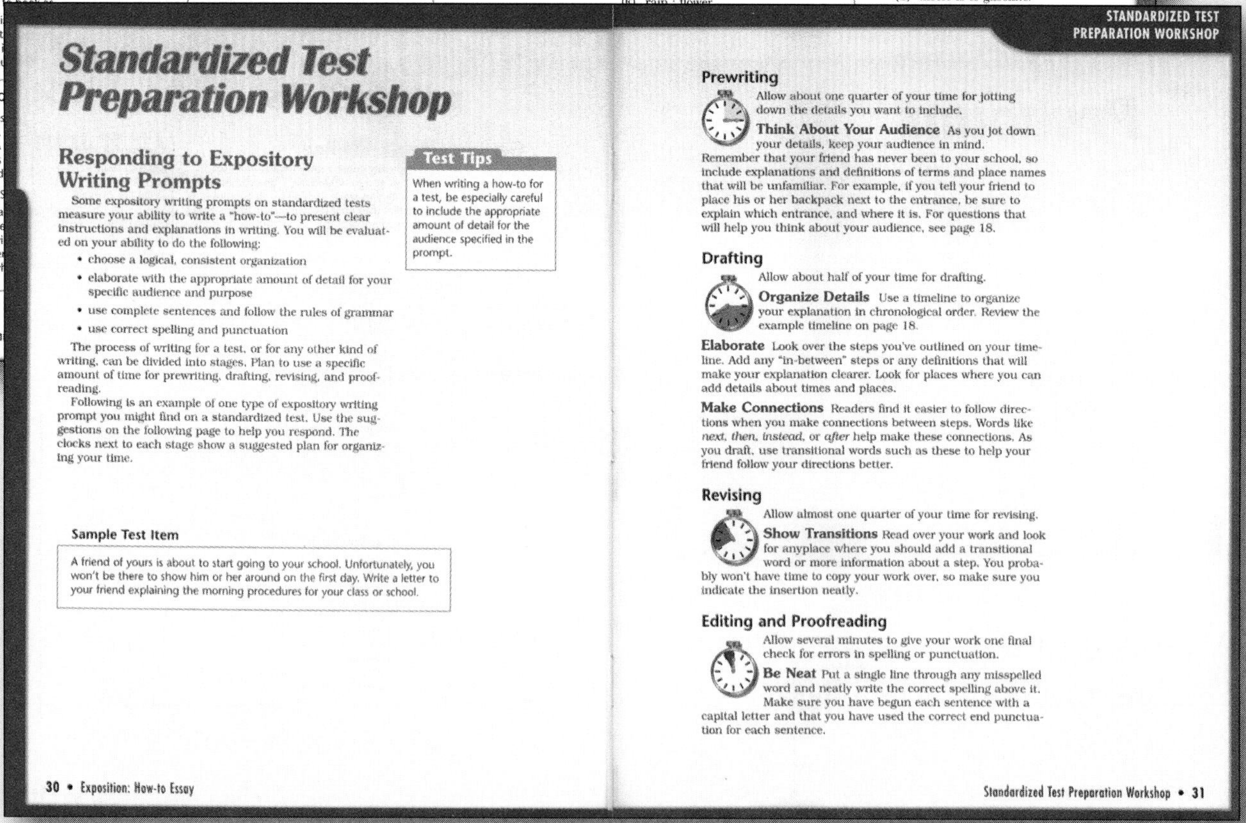

STANDARDIZED TEST PREPARATION WORKSHOP

Standardized Test Preparation Workshop

Responding to Expository Writing Prompts

Some expository writing prompts on standardized tests measure your ability to write a "how-to"—to present clear instructions and explanations in writing. You will be evaluated on your ability to do the following:

- choose a logical, consistent organization
- elaborate with the appropriate amount of detail for your specific audience and purpose
- use complete sentences and follow the rules of grammar
- use correct spelling and punctuation

The process of writing for a test, or for any other kind of writing, can be divided into stages. Plan to use a specific amount of time for prewriting, drafting, revising, and proofreading.

Following is an example of one type of expository writing prompt you might find on a standardized test. Use the suggestions on the following page to help you respond. The clocks next to each stage show a suggested plan for organizing your time.

Test Tips

When writing a how-to for a test, be especially careful to include the appropriate amount of detail for the audience specified in the prompt.

Sample Test Item

A friend of yours is about to start going to your school. Unfortunately, you won't be there to show him or her around on the first day. Write a letter to your friend explaining the morning procedures for your class or school.

Prewriting

Allow about one quarter of your time for jotting down the details you want to include.

Think About Your Audience As you jot down your details, keep your audience in mind. Remember that your friend has never been to your school, so include explanations and definitions of terms and place names that will be unfamiliar. For example, if you tell your friend to place his or her backpack next to the entrance, be sure to explain which entrance, and where it is. For questions that will help you think about your audience, see page 18.

Drafting

Allow about half of your time for drafting.

Organize Details Use a timeline to organize your explanation in chronological order. Review the example timeline on page 18.

Elaborate Look over the steps you've outlined on your timeline. Add any "in-between" steps or any definitions that will make your explanation clearer. Look for places where you can add details about times and places.

Make Connections Readers find it easier to follow directions when you make connections between steps. Words like *next, then, instead,* or *after* help make these connections. As you draft, use transitional words such as these to help your friend follow your directions better.

Revising

Allow almost one quarter of your time for revising.

Show Transitions Read over your work and look for anyplace where you should add a transitional word or more information about a step. You probably won't have time to copy your work over, so make sure you indicate the insertion neatly.

Editing and Proofreading

Allow several minutes to give your work one final check for errors in spelling or punctuation.

Be Neat Put a single line through any misspelled word and neatly write the correct spelling above it. Make sure you have begun each sentence with a capital letter and that you have used the correct end punctuation for each sentence.

30 • Exposition: How-to Essay

Standardized Test Preparation Workshop • 31

*AP and Advanced Placement Program are registered trademarks of the College Entrance Examination Board, which was not involved in the production of, and does not endorse, this product.

Diagnostic Test

Skill Check A. Identify the nouns in each sentence. Explain why each word is a noun.

1. Dogs can be purchased from a breeder.
2. Good pets can also be found at the shelter.
3. Preparations—such as getting food, dishes, toys, a collar, and a bed—need to be made before the arrival of a new puppy.
4. A veterinarian gives the dog shots for rabies and distemper.
5. All dogs must wear licenses, which ensure identification and immunization.

Skill Check B. Identify the collective or compound noun in each sentence. Tell whether the noun you identify is collective or compound.

1. The whole family should share in taking care of a pet.
2. Dogs need shelter, such as a doghouse, in which to sleep.
3. Supplies can be purchased at a pet shop.
4. Use caution when introducing the new pet to a large group.
5. Avoid packs of stray dogs when walking your pet.

Skill Check C. Identify each italicized noun as common or proper.

The *American Kennel Club* was started in 1884. This *organization* is associated with more than 4,000 *clubs* throughout the *United States*. *Frances* belongs to a group in her *town*. She goes to *shows* in *Austin* with her cousin *Sarah*.

Skill Check D. Identify the pronouns in each sentence. Then, identify each pronoun's antecedent. You may need to refer to previous sentences to find the antecedent.

1. Martin loves dogs. He has three German shepherds.
2. They are very gentle.
3. His sister, Tanya, helps him care for them.
4. She trained them to sit and stay.
5. All the neighbors admire their dogs.

Skill Check E. Identify the italicized pronoun in each sentence as personal, demonstrative, interrogative, or indefinite.

1. *We* went to the pound to see puppies.
2. *My* mother asked, "*Which* do you want?"
3. *That* was a difficult decision.
4. *Those* pups were so cute I wanted them all.
5. *Each* had *its* special qualities.

phschool.com

Rubric for Self-Assessment

Use these criteria to evaluate your comparison-and-contrast essay.

	Score 4	Score 3	Score 2	Score 1
Audience and Purpose	Clearly provides a reason for a comparison-contrast analysis	Adequately provides a reason for a comparison-contrast analysis	Provides a reason for a comparison-contrast analysis	Does not provide a reason for a comparison-contrast analysis
Organization	Clearly presents information in a consistent organization best suited to the topic	Presents information using an organization suited to the topic	Chooses an organization not suited to comparison and contrast	Shows a lack of organizational strategy
Elaboration	Elaborates most ideas with facts, details, or examples; links all information to comparison and contrast	Elaborates many ideas with facts, details, or examples; links most information to comparison and contrast	Does not elaborate all ideas; does not link some details to comparison and contrast	Does not provide facts or examples to support a comparison and contrast
Use of Language	Demonstrates excellent sentence and vocabulary variety; includes very few mechanical errors	Demonstrates adequate sentence and vocabulary variety; includes few mechanical errors	Demonstrates repetitive use of sentence structure and vocabulary; includes many mechanical errors	Demonstrates poor use of language; generates confusion; includes many mechanical errors

2 • Comparison-and-Contrast Essay

Self-Assessment

Rubrics for Self-Assessment with each writing lesson help build critical thinking skills as students evaluate their own work.

Diagnostic Tests

Diagnostic Tests before each grammar chapter help you assess students' skill levels and identify areas for improvement.

Flexible assessment options

A variety of assessment options help develop confident and successful test-takers.

The right tools when you need them!

Well-organized teaching resources make for better instruction.

Success for all students

Accommodate your students' diverse needs by customizing instruction with assignments that address different ability levels and learning styles.

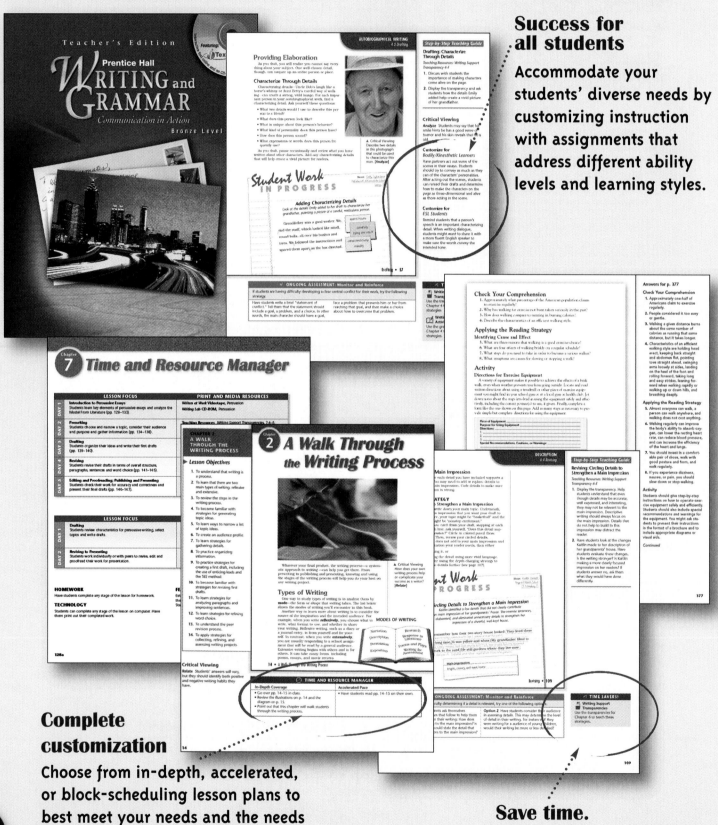

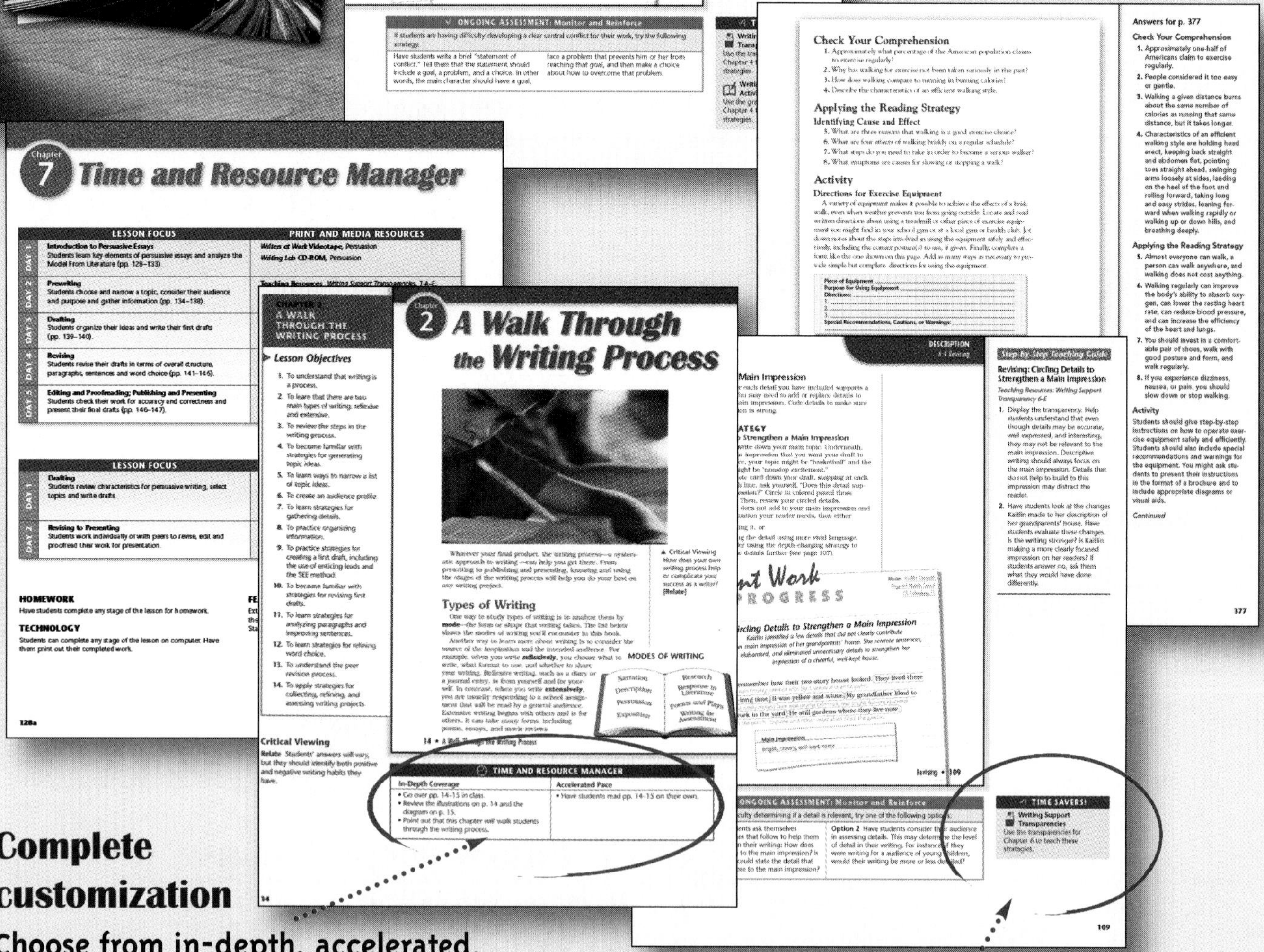

Complete customization

Choose from in-depth, accelerated, or block-scheduling lesson plans to best meet your needs and the needs of your students.

Save time.

Access point-of-use support.

Make planning easier.

Select from a wealth of integrated ancillary support for all of the language arts.

The future is here!

Prentice Hall delivers on the promise of technology with the entire student text online.

PH SuccessNet™ featuring iText

Where your *Writing and Grammar* text comes alive!

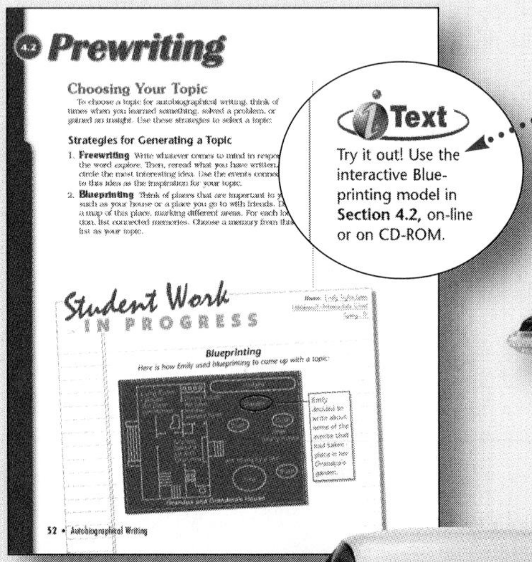

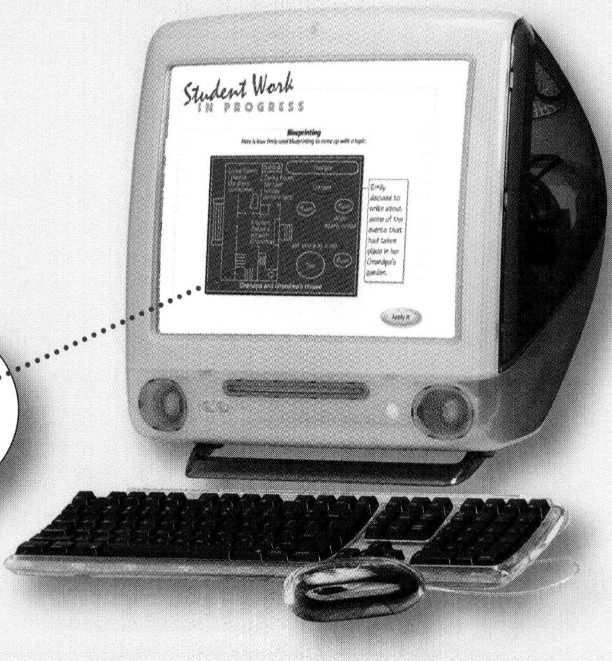

Web references

Take your students beyond the text!

Prentice Hall's *Writing and Grammar* Companion Web Site

Go to PHSchool.com to bring the world of writing to your students through support, extension activities, and a wealth of extra grammar activities.

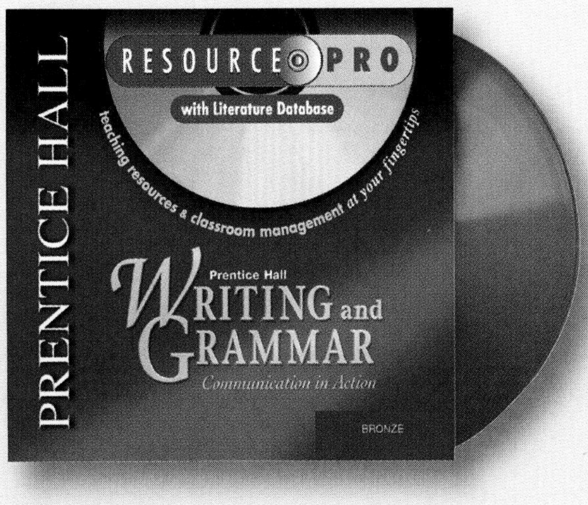

Resource Pro

All of your teaching support is just a mouse-click away.

Formal Assessment Book with Test Bank CD-ROM

Allows you to gauge your students' ability levels and establish your own skills objectives.

TEACHING RESOURCES

Writing

Writing Support Activity Book
Topic Bank for Heterogeneous Classes
Multigenre Research Project

Grammar, Usage, and Mechanics

Grammar Exercise Workbook, Teacher's Edition
Daily Language Practice
Hands-on Grammar Activity Book
Extra Grammar and Writing Exercises

Academic and Workplace Skills

Academic and Workplace Skills Activity Book, Teacher's Edition
Vocabulary and Spelling Practice Book, Teacher's Edition
Reading Support Practice Book, Teacher's Edition

Assessment

Standardized Test Preparation Workbook, Teacher's Edition
Writing Assessment and Portfolio Management
Formal Assessment/Assessment Resources Software CD-ROM

Professional Resources

Integrated Lesson Planning Assistant
How to Manage Instruction in the Block
How to Assess Student Work
Putting Patterns to Work
Kick Off for Success: Organizing for School
Hearing All Sides: Resolving Conflict

ADDITIONAL ANCILLARIES

Workbooks

Hands-on Grammar Activity Book
Writing Support Activity Book
Grammar Exercise Workbook
Reading Support Practice Book
Vocabulary and Spelling Workbook
Academic and Workplace Skills Workbook
Standardized Test Preparation Workbook

Transparencies

Writing Support Transparencies
Daily Language Practice Transparencies
Grammar Exercises Answers on Transparencies
Scoring Rubrics on Transparencies

Technology

iText Interactive Textbook, online and on CD-ROM
Writing and Grammar Companion Web Site
Test Bank CD-ROM
Writers at Work Videotape
Resource Pro CD-ROM

Looking for more spelling support?
EVERYDAY SPELLING NOW AVAILABLE

Correlation to the Six Traits Analytical Model

Chapter	Ideas	Organization	Voice	Word Choice	Sentence Fluency	Conventions
1 The Writer in You	p. 7	p. 7	p. 7	p. 7	p. 7	p. 7
2 A Walk Through the Writing Process						
2.1	pp. 14–17					
2.2	p. 18	p. 18				
2.3	p. 20	p. 19		p. 21	p. 20	
2.4						p. 22
Spot/Hum.	p. 24					
3 Sentences, Paragraphs, and Compositions						
3.1				p. 32	pp. 29–32	pp. 31, 32
3.2	pp. 33–36					
3.3	p. 37	pp. 38–39, 41				
3.4			p. 42	pp. 42–43	p. 42	
Spot/Hum.	p. 44					
4 Narration: Autobiography						
4.1	pp. 50–53					
4.2	pp. 54–57					
4.3	p. 59	p. 58				
4.4		pp. 60–62		p. 64	p. 63	p. 65
4.5						p. 66
4.7	pp. 68–69	pp. 68–69				
Spot/Hum.	p. 72					
5 Narration: Short Story						
5.1	pp. 78–83	pp. 78–83				
5.2	pp. 84–87					
5.3	pp. 88–89					
5.4	pp. 90–91			p. 93	p. 92	
5.5						p. 95
5.7	pp. 97–99	pp. 97–99				
Spot/Hum.	p. 102					
6 Description						
6.1	pp. 108–111	pp. 108–111		pp. 108–111		
6.2	pp. 112–115					
6.3	p. 117	p. 116				
6.4	pp. 119–120	pp. 118, 120		p. 122	p. 121	p. 123
6.5						p. 124
6.7	pp. 126–127	pp. 126–127		pp. 126–129		
Spot/Hum.	p. 130					
7 Persuasion						
7.1	pp. 136–139	pp. 136–139				
7.2	pp. 140–143					
7.3	p. 145	p. 144		p. 145	p. 145	
7.4	pp. 146–148	p. 148		p. 150	p. 149	p. 149
7.5						p. 151
7.7	pp. 153–157	pp. 153–155				
Spot/Hum.	p. 158					
8 Exposition: Comparison and Contrast						
8.1	pp. 163–165	pp. 163–165				
8.2	pp. 166–169					
8.3	pp. 170–171	pp. 170–171				
8.4	pp. 173–174	p. 172			p. 174	p. 175
8.5	p. 176					
8.7	pp. 178–181	pp. 178–181				
Spot/Hum.	p. 182					
9 Exposition: Cause and Effect						
9.1	pp. 188–189	pp. 188–189				
9.2	pp. 190–193					
9.3	pp. 194–195	pp. 194–195				
9.4		pp. 196–198		p. 200		p. 199
9.5						p. 201
9.7	p. 205	pp. 203–204				
Spot/Hum.	p. 206					

Chapter	Ideas	Organization	Voice	Word Choice	Sentence Fluency	Conventions
10 Exposition: How-to Essay						
10.1	pp. 212–213	pp. 212–213				
10.2	pp. 214–217					
10.3	p. 219	p. 218				
10.4		pp. 220–221		p. 223	p. 222	
10.5						p. 225
10.7	pp. 227–229	pp. 227–228				
Spot/Hum.	p. 230					
11 Research Report						
11.1	pp. 235–237					
11.2	pp. 238–241					
11.3	pp. 242–243					
11.4		pp. 244–245		p. 248	p. 246	p. 247
11.5						p. 250
11.7	pp. 252–255	p. 255				
Spot/Hum.	p. 256					
12 Response to Literature						
12.1	pp. 262–263	pp. 262–263		pp. 262–263		
12.2	pp. 264–265, pp. 267–268	pp. 266, 269				
12.3	pp. 270–271					
12.4	pp. 272–273			p. 276	p. 274	p. 275
12.5						p. 278
12.7	pp. 280–283	p. 283				
Spot/Hum.	p. 284					
13 Writing for Assessment						
13.1	pp. 290–291					
13.2	p. 293	p. 292				
13.3	p. 294	p. 294		p. 295		
13.4						p. 296
13.5	pp. 298–299	pp. 298–299	pp. 298–299			
Spot/Hum.	p. 302					
14 Nouns and Pronouns						
14.1						pp. 310–315
14.2						pp. 316–325
15 Verbs						
15.1				pp. 330–333		pp. 330–333
15.2				pp. 334–347		pp. 334–337
15.3						pp. 338–343
16 Adjectives and Adverbs						
16.1						pp. 348–359
16.2						pp. 360–368
17 Prepositions						pp. 372–378
18 Conjunctions and Interjections						
18.1						pp. 384–389
18.2						pp. 390–394
19 Basic Sentence Parts						
19.1						pp. 398–401
19.2						pp. 402–405
19.3						pp. 406–409
19.4						pp. 410–415
19.5						pp. 416–427
20 Phrases and Clauses						
20.1						pp. 432–447
20.2						pp. 448–461

Correlation to the Six Traits Analytical Model

Chapter	Ideas	Organization	Voice	Word Choice	Sentence Fluency	Conventions
21 Effective Sentences						
21.1						pp. 466–468
21.2					pp. 469–475	
21.3					pp. 476–479	
21.4						pp. 480–499
22 Using Verbs						
22.1						pp. 506–515
22.2						pp. 516–527
22.3						pp. 528–535
23 Using Pronouns						pp. 540–549
24 Making Words Agree						
24.1						pp. 554–561
24.2						pp. 562–569
25 Using Modifiers						
25.1						pp. 574–583
25.2						pp. 584–589
26 Punctuation						
26.1						pp. 596–599
26.2						pp. 600–609
26.3						pp. 610–613
26.4						pp. 614–622
26.5						pp. 623–633
27 Capitalization						pp. 638–653
Sentence Diagraming Workshop						pp. 658–669
28 Speaking, Listening, Viewing, and Representing						
28.1	pp. 674, 678	p. 675		p. 678		
29 Vocabulary and Spelling						
29.1				pp. 696–698		
29.2				pp. 699–701		
29.3				pp. 702–705		
29.4						pp. 706–715
30 Reading Skills						
30.1	pp. 723–724	pp. 723–724				
30.2	pp. 725–728, 730	p. 730	p. 729	p. 729		
30.3			p. 731	p. 734		p. 733
31 Study, Reference, and Test-Taking Skills						

Silver Level

PEARSON
Prentice Hall

Upper Saddle River, New Jersey
Needham, Massachusetts

Writing and Grammar

Communication in Action

Copper
Bronze
Silver
Gold
Platinum
Ruby
Diamond

PEARSON
Prentice Hall

ISBN 0-13-037493-8

1 2 3 4 5 6 7 8 9 10 07 06 05 04 03

Go Online
PHSchool.com

Use iText *Writing and Grammar*, the interactive textbook!

- instant feedback on interactive grammar exercises
- interactive writing tools and writing tutorials
- access to e-rater™, the electronic essay-scoring tool

iText is also available on CD-ROM.

Go on-line to get instant help on the Writing and Grammar Web site!

- additional grammar practice opportunities
- scoring rubrics with scored student models for different modes of writing

Here's how to use the Writing and Grammar Web site:

Look for these Web Codes in your book:

eck-8001
eck-8002

Here's how to use Web Codes:

1. Go on-line. Enter URL: PHSchool.com
2. If you want instant feedback on interactive grammar exercises, enter Web Code: eck-8002
   Choose the appropriate chapter from the menu that appears.
3. If you want to review writing rubrics and scored student models, enter Web Code: eck-8001
   Choose the appropriate chapter from the menu that appears.

iii

Program Authors

The program authors guided the direction and philosophy of *Prentice Hall Writing and Grammar: Communication in Action.* Working with the development team, they contributed to the pedagogical integrity of the program and to its relevance to today's teachers and students.

Joyce Armstrong Carroll

In her forty-year career, Joyce Armstrong Carroll, Ed.D., has taught on every grade level from primary to graduate school. In the past twenty years, she has trained teachers in the teaching of writing. A nationally known consultant, she has served as president of TCTE and on NCTE's Commission on Composition. More than fifty of her articles have appeared in journals such as *Curriculum Review, English Journal, Media & Methods, Southwest Philosophical Studies, Ohio English Journal, English in Texas,* and the *Florida English Journal.* With Edward E. Wilson, Dr. Carroll co-authored *Acts of Teaching: How to Teach Writing* and co-edited *Poetry After Lunch: Poems to Read Aloud.* Beyond her direct involvement with the writing pedagogy presented in this series, Dr. Carroll guided the development of the Hands-on Grammar feature. She co-directs the New Jersey Writing Project in Texas.

Edward E. Wilson

A former editor of *English in Texas*, Edward E. Wilson has served as a high-school English teacher and a writing consultant in school districts nationwide. Wilson has served on the Texas Teacher Professional Practices Commission and on NCTE's Commission on Composition. With Dr. Carroll, he co-wrote *Acts of Teaching: How to Teach Writing* and co-edited the award-winning *Poetry After Lunch: Poems to Read Aloud.* In addition to his direct involvement with the writing pedagogy presented in this series, Wilson provided inspiration for the Spotlight on Humanities feature. Wilson's poetry appears in Paul Janeczko's anthology *The Music of What Happens.* Wilson co-directs the New Jersey Writing Project in Texas.

Gary Forlini

Gary Forlini, a nationally known education consultant, developed the grammar, usage, and mechanics instruction and exercises in this series. After teaching in the Pelham, New York, schools for many years, he established Research in Media, an educational research agency that provides information for product developers, school staff developers, media companies, and arts organizations, as well as private-sector corporations and foundations. Mr. Forlini was co-author of the *S.A.T. Home Study* program and has written numerous industry reports on elementary, secondary, and post-secondary education markets.

iv

National Advisory Panel

The teachers and administrators serving on the National Advisory Panel provided ongoing input into the development of *Prentice Hall Writing and Grammar: Communication in Action.* Their valuable insights ensure that the perspectives of teachers and students throughout the country are represented within the instruction in this series.

Dr. Pauline Bigby-Jenkins
Coordinator for Secondary English Language Arts
Ann Arbor Public Schools
Ann Arbor, Michigan

Lee Bromberger
English Department Chairperson
Mukwonago High School
Mukwonago, Wisconsin

Mary Chapman
Teacher of English
Free State High School
Lawrence, Kansas

Jim Deatherage
Language Arts Department Chairperson
Richland High School
Richland, Washington

Luis Dovalina
Teacher of English
La Joya High School
La Joya, Texas

JoAnn Giardino
Teacher of English
Centennial High School
Columbus, Ohio

Susan Goldberg
Teacher of English
Westlake Middle School
Thornwood, New York

Jean Hicks
Director, Louisville Writing Project
University of Louisville
Louisville, Kentucky

Karen Hurley
Teacher of Language Arts
Perry Meridian Middle School
Indianapolis, Indiana

Karen Lopez
Teacher of English
Hart High School
Newhall, California

Marianne Minshall
Teacher of Reading and Language Arts
Westmore Middle School
Columbus, Ohio

Nancy Monroe
English Department Chairperson
Bolton High School
Alexandria, Louisiana

Ken Spurlock
Assistant Principal
Boone County High School
Florence, Kentucky

Cynthia Katz Tyroff
Staff Development Specialist and Teacher of English
Northside Independent School District
San Antonio, Texas

Holly Ward
Teacher of Language Arts
Campbell Middle School
Daytona Beach, Florida

Grammar Review Team

The following teachers reviewed the grammar instruction in this series to ensure accuracy, clarity, and pedagogy.

Kathy Hamilton
Paul Hertzog
Daren Hoisington
Beverly Ladd
Karen Lopez
Dianna Louise Lund
Sean O'Brien

CONTENTS IN BRIEF

Chapters 1–13

Part 1: Writing 1

Chapters 14–27

Part 2: Grammar, Usage, and Mechanics 306

Chapters 28–31

Part 3: Academic and Workplace Skills 670

Resources

CONTENTS
PART 1: WRITING

Chapter 1 The Writer in You 2

Chapter 2 A Walk Through the Writing Process 12

Chapter 3 Sentences, Paragraphs, and Compositions
Structure and Style 28

INTEGRATED SKILLS

INTEGRATED SKILLS

INTEGRATED SKILLS

Chapter 4

Narration

Autobiographical Writing

Student Work IN PROGRESS

Featured Work:
"Zermatt or Bust!"
by Evan Twohy
Prospect Sierra School
El Cerrito, California

INTEGRATED SKILLS

Chapter 5

Narration

Chapter 6

Description 106

Student Work IN PROGRESS

Featured Work:
"My Home Sweet Wet Home"
by Victoria Kilinskis
St. Francis Xavier School
La Grange, Illinois

INTEGRATED SKILLS

Chapter 7 Persuasion

Student Work IN PROGRESS

Featured Work:
"I Will Be Drug Free"
by Ryan Caparella
Chain of Lakes Middle School
Orlando, Florida

INTEGRATED SKILLS

xii

Chapter 8 Exposition: *Comparison-and-Contrast Essay* 162

Student Work IN PROGRESS

Featured Work:
"Small Town, Big City"
by Mindy Glasco
Los Alamos Middle School
Los Alamos, New Mexico

INTEGRATED SKILLS

Chapter 9 Exposition

Student Work IN PROGRESS

Featured Work:
"The Dust Bowl"
by Emily Meade
Ingersoll Middle School
Canton, Illinois

INTEGRATED SKILLS

Chapter

10 Exposition

How-to Essay 210

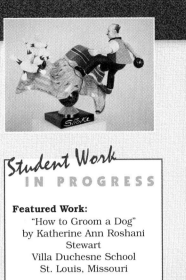

Student Work IN PROGRESS

Featured Work:
"How to Groom a Dog"
by Katherine Ann Roshani Stewart
Villa Duchesne School
St. Louis, Missouri

INTEGRATED SKILLS

Chapter 11 Research

Student Work IN PROGRESS

Featured Work:
"Ben Franklin: Man of Many Talents"
by Joseph Hochberger
Gotha Middle School
Windermere, Florida

INTEGRATED SKILLS

Chapter 12 Response to Literature

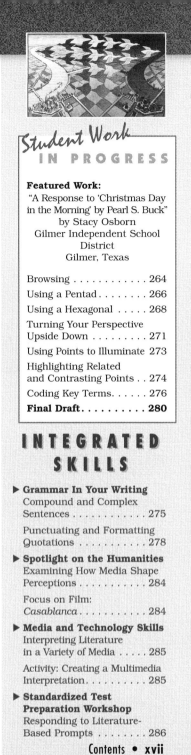

Student Work IN PROGRESS

Featured Work:
"A Response to 'Christmas Day in the Morning' by Pearl S. Buck"
by Stacy Osborn
Gilmer Independent School District
Gilmer, Texas

INTEGRATED SKILLS

Chapter 13

Writing for Assessment 288

Student Work IN PROGRESS

Featured Work:
"A Letter to His Majesty, King George III"
by Paul Keller
Roosevelt Middle School
Oceanside, California

INTEGRATED SKILLS

PART 2: GRAMMAR, USAGE, AND MECHANICS

Chapter 19

Basic Sentence Parts 396

Chapter 20

Phrases and Clauses 430

Chapter 21

Chapter 22

Chapter 23

Chapter 24

PART 3: ACADEMIC AND WORKPLACE SKILLS

Chapter 28

Speaking, Listening, Viewing, and Representing . . . 672

Chapter 29

Vocabulary and Spelling 694

Resources

PART 1
WRITING

Lesson Objectives

1. To understand writing as a recursive process and to develop ownership of their own writing processes
2. To write in a variety of forms, including narrative, descriptive, persuasive, expository, and literary texts, and to develop skills in writing for assessment
3. To analyze works of literature and student drafts as models and examples of specific writing strategies
4. To develop voice and adjust their writing to various audiences and purposes
5. To develop research skills and to use writing as a tool for learning
6. To apply specific prewriting strategies for generating and narrowing writing topics
7. To use graphic organizers and other methods for organizing and supporting ideas in drafting
8. To approach revision in a systematic way in terms of overall structure, paragraphs, sentences, and word choice
9. To edit and proofread drafts to ensure appropriate usage and accuracy in spelling and the conventions and mechanics of written English
10. To understand rubrics and to use them to evaluate their own writing and the writing of others

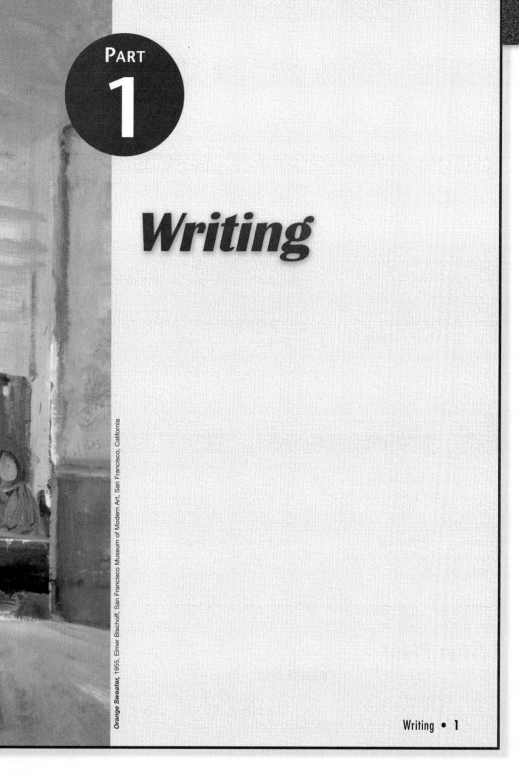

Orange Sweater, 1955, Elmer Bischoff, San Francisco Museum of Modern Art, San Francisco, California

Part 1

Writing

Step-by-Step Teaching Guide

Responding to Fine Art

Orange Sweater
by Elmer Bischoff

Use this painting to start a discussion about the process of writing.

1. Have students examine the painting on these pages. You might use the following questions to prompt discussion:

   Where do you think this scene takes place? How do you know? What do you think the figure is doing?

2. Have students provide a brief story that explains why this person is writing. Encourage them to use as many details from the painting as they can.

Chapter 1 Time and Resource Manager

In-Depth Lesson Plan

	LESSON FOCUS	PRINT AND MEDIA RESOURCES
DAY 1	**Introduction to Writing** Students are introduced to ideas about writing (p. 2).	***Writing and Grammar iText*** **(Interactive Text),** Ch. 1
DAY 2	**Introduction to Writing** *(continued)* Students learn prewriting and writing strategies. They are introduced to strategies for sharing and publishing their work (pp. 3–6).	**Teaching Resources** *Writing Support Transparencies,* 1-A; *Writing Support Activity Book,* 1-1 ***Writing and Grammar iText*** **(Interactive Text),** Ch. 1
DAY 3	**Qualities of Good Writing; Reflecting on Your Writing** Students identify qualities of good writing and write a reflective response on their own writing practices (p. 7).	***Writing and Grammar iText*** **(Interactive Text),** Ch. 1

Accelerated Lesson Plan

	LESSON FOCUS	PRINT AND MEDIA RESOURCES
DAY 1	**The Writer in You** Students are introduced to ideas about writing. They learn strategies for developing, sharing, and publishing their work (pp. 2–6).	***Writing and Grammar iText*** **(Interactive Text),** Ch. 1
DAY 2	**Qualities of Good Writing; Reflecting on Your Writing** Students identify qualities of good writing and write a reflective response on their own writing practices (p. 7).	***Writing and Grammar iText*** **(Interactive Text),** Ch. 1

Options for Adapting Lesson Plans

HOMEWORK

Have students complete any stage of the lesson for homework.

SPELLING

To teach spelling skills in conjunction with writing skills, work through *Prentice Hall Everyday Spelling,* Grade 8, Chapter 1, as you cover this *Writing and Grammar* chapter.

FEATURES

Extend coverage with Spotlight on the Humanities (p. 8), Media and Technology Skills (p. 9), and Standardized Test Preparation Workshop (p. 10).

TECHNOLOGY

Students can complete any stage of the lesson on the computer, using *Writing and Grammar iText* or a word-processing program. Have them print out their completed work.

INTEGRATED SKILLS COVERAGE

Viewing and Representing
Critical Viewing, SE pp. 2, 4, 6, 8
Describing a Work of Art, SE p. 8
ATE p. 8

Real-World Connection
ATE p. 5

ASSESSMENT SUPPORT

Standardized Test Preparation Workshop SE pp. 10–11

Standardized Test Preparation Workbook, pp. 1–2

Formal Assessment, *Ch. 1*

MEETING INDIVIDUAL NEEDS

Less Advanced Students ATE p. 11. See also Ongoing Assessments ATE pp. 4, 5.

More Advanced Students ATE pp. 3, 11

Logical/Mathematical Learners ATE p. 9

Musical/Auditory Learners ATE p. 6

BLOCK SCHEDULING

Pacing Suggestions
For 90-minute Blocks
- Have students read and discuss the complete chapter in one 90-minute class period.

Professional Development Support
- ***How to Manage Instruction in the Block*** This teaching resource provides management and activity suggestions.

MEDIA AND TECHNOLOGY

For the Teacher
- ***Writing and Grammar iText*** **(Interactive Text),** Ch.1

WRITING AND GRAMMAR ON-LINE

iText Interactive Text (On-line or on CD-ROM)
- Easily navigable instruction with interactive Revision Checkers
- Full use of e-rater™, the essay-scoring system (on-line only)

Companion Web Site PHSchool.com
- Scoring rubrics with models (use Web Code eck-8001)

See the Go On-line! feature, SE p. iii.

Lesson Objectives

1. To understand the writing process.
2. To develop a writing life.
3. To share work with others.

Critical Viewing

Speculate Students' answers will vary. Most will say he is writing a report for school, basing their answer on the fact that two books are open before him, books that appear to feature maps or other informational graphics.

Chapter 1 The Writer in You

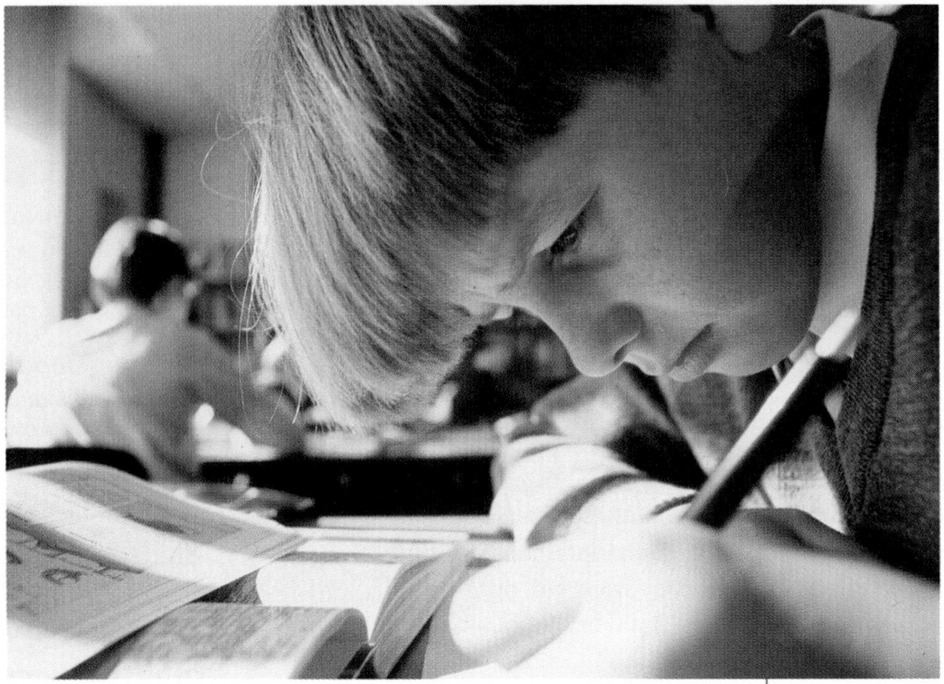

▲ Critical Viewing
For what purpose do you think this boy might be writing? **[Speculate]**

Writing in Everyday Life

A writer writes—it's as simple as that. Every time you use a pen or type on a keyboard, you are a writer. There is no big mystery about being a writer. However, being an effective and powerful writer takes time, practice, and self-awareness.

You have already grown a great deal as a writer. You have advanced from writing your name, using newly learned alphabet letters, to composing thoughtful essays for school. Today, you use writing for a wide variety of important daily tasks. Your writing takes many forms: phone messages, a journal, business letters, e-mail, stories, reports, invitations, and more. Sometimes, you write a quick note or a sign in just a few minutes. Other times, you take weeks to plan and complete a larger project, such as a persuasive essay or a short story.

TIME AND RESOURCE MANAGER

Resources
Technology: Writing and Grammar iText, Ch. 1

In-Depth Coverage	Accelerated Pace
• Cover pp. 2–7 in class.	• Assign pp. 2–7 for independent student reading.

Why Write?

Countless situations require you to communicate clearly with others. Writing is one of the most important tools for achieving that communication. Of course, speaking is a vital part of communication, too. Unless it is recorded, though, a discussion disappears except in memory. Writing leaves a permanent record of your ideas.

Developing Your Writing Life

Writing has an advantage over speaking. As a writer, you can collect and focus your thoughts before you share them with others. Writing helps you explore and develop your thoughts. Author Joan Didion explains that she writes "entirely to find out what I'm thinking, what I'm looking at, what I see and what it means. What I want and what I fear." Writing can help you identify your own strengths and reach your own goals.

For example, when you begin to write a remembrance, your guiding memory might be vague or unclear. As you write, you will discover specific details that help you bring your memory to life. The process of writing actually sharpens and refines your remembrance.

Writers in ACTION

Poet Maya Angelou prefers to write in hotel rooms where she is "surrounded by no distractions. . . . No milkmaids, no flowers, nothing. I just want to feel. . . ."

To get started, she often reads something by a favorite author. Reading reminds her of "how beautiful, how pliable, the language is, how it will lend itself. If you pull it, it says, 'Okay.' I remember that, and I start to write."

Keep Track of Your Ideas

Uncovering ideas is the first part of a writer's work. Jack London said, "You can't wait for inspiration. You have to go after it with a club." You must hunt for good ideas and develop reliable methods for keeping them once you find them.

Writer's Notebook or Journal Carrying a small notebook is a great way to be ready when inspiration strikes. You can jot down all sorts of ideas in your writer's notebook. Copy down a few lines of a conversation you have had with a teacher. Write down an advertising slogan that makes you think or makes you laugh.

Researcher File Many of your most unusual ideas will come from doing some research in a library or on the Web. Writer Zora Neale Hurston explained that "research is formalized curiosity. It is poking and prying with a purpose." You can create a research file to keep track of interesting articles, Web pages, and other resources. You can also include note cards that you create while researching a specific topic. Each note card might contain a quotation or fact and its source.

PREPARE and ENGAGE

Interest GRABBER Offer these examples of how some professional writers tap into the writer in them.

- Amy Tan uses people and experiences in her own life.
- Laurence Yep couldn't find books to read about Chinese Americans, so he spent his life writing them.
- Sandra Cisneros uses her memories of her childhood and her Mexican heritage.

Activate Prior Knowledge

Ask students whether any of them ever write for pleasure or any reason apart from schoolwork. (Students may keep journals, write letters, send e-mail, or even write poetry or stories.) Then have students share some difficulties they encounter when writing. Do they have trouble finding a quiet, private place at home to write? Do they constantly have to stop to look up the spelling of words? Do they find it difficult to write on certain subjects? Tell them that in this chapter, they will learn some ways to help themselves write more easily.

TEACH

Step-by-Step Teaching Guide

Keep Track of Your Ideas

1. The American novelist Henry James found the inspiration for many of his novels and stories in dinner conversations with friends. Like James, many other writers keep notes of casual conversations that they think are good material for writing. Tell students that keeping a notebook ensures that a writer won't forget these stories and conversations.
2. Mystery writer Mark Graham finds inspiration in old newspaper articles. Historical novels such as Alexander Dumas's *The Three Musketeers* and E. L. Doctorow's *Ragtime* are partly based on historical research, as are many of the plays of William Shakespeare. Many writers have found history and research to be a wonderful source of material for stories.

More About the Writer

Maya Angelou's best-known work is her multivolume autobiography, which began in 1970 with *I Know Why the Caged Bird Sings.* Angelou became an adult in the free atmosphere of the 1960's, when she attended college, became a professional dancer, and traveled to Africa.

Customize for *More Advanced Students*

Challenge students to extend the Interest Grabber and find out what any writer of their choice has said about the art of writing. Have students read these comments to the class.

Step-by-Step Teaching Guide

Keep Track of Your Writing and Reading

1. Urge each student to tell one thing he or she wrote about last year and where the idea came from. Try to elicit 20 or 30 sources of information. Students who have trouble finding ideas may want to use some of the hints that worked for classmates.
2. Male students may think writing—especially keeping a journal—is not cool. Their journals can be private. They don't have to show them to anyone, and they can write secretly if they want to. Mention some male writers—Garrison Keillor, Arthur Clarke, Gary Soto, Ray Bradbury, for example. Aren't they cool?

Critical Viewing

Analyze Students may suggest that a person should keep all of his or her writing, however rough, because there is always something to be learned from it.

1

Keep Track of Your Writing and Reading

Writing Portfolio Monitoring your writing progress is an essential part of growing as a writer. To assemble a writing portfolio, collect final versions of your favorite writing. You can also include earlier drafts to show your progress.

An effective writing portfolio is a living record. Review your work regularly in order to monitor your writing accomplishments and challenges. Update your portfolio's contents, removing work you no longer want to highlight or adding a new work that makes you feel particularly proud.

▲ Critical Viewing What advice would you give to a student creating a writing portfolio for the first time? **[Analyze]**

Reader's Journal Reading the works of other writers will often stimulate ideas of your own. Keep a journal to comment or reflect on what you read. Copy quotations that capture a writer's style. Describe unique points of view or organizational methods. You might even include notes about how articles or books could be translated into films or documentaries.

Try Different Approaches

All writers develop their own favorite writing habits. The more you write, the better you will be able to make writing decisions that work for you.

Getting Started Some writers get their best ideas while sitting quietly in a place they know well. Others gain inspiration from observing an active public place, reading a favorite author, or listening to particular music. Experiment with strategies that help you find new and interesting ideas. When you get an idea, make a note about how you got it: Where were you? What triggered the idea? Soon, you will have a good idea about which places and events are likely to inspire you.

Writing a Draft The author John Steinbeck gave this advice to writers about drafting: "Write freely and as rapidly as possible and throw the whole thing on paper. Never correct or rewrite until the whole thing is down. 'Rewrite in process' is usually found to be an excuse for not going on." Not all writers agree. Some prefer to make their changes as they draft.

Improving Your Work You will discover preferences for editing and revising, too. Even if you did some crossing out and rewriting while you drafted, you will probably want to make more changes. You may want to take a break and then return to the draft by yourself. Or, you may prefer to ask a peer reviewer to help you look for sections to improve.

ONGOING ASSESSMENT: Monitor and Reinforce

If students have trouble finding ideas to write about or have trouble remembering their ideas, try the following option.

Have students keep small notebooks with them at all times for one week. Students can note down any stories they hear or come across that sound like good ideas for essays or articles. Remind them that everything that happens around them is potential material for a story. At the end of the week, have students discuss the experiment. Did anyone gather good material for a story or an essay? What kinds of things did people record in their notebooks?

Plan to Write

Some types of writing feel almost automatic. You might not have to think very hard to fill out an application or write down a phone message. Other writing requires considerably more time and attention. If you are writing a complex video script, taking an essay test, or drafting a business letter, you are juggling many parts of a large writing project. You can make it easier to keep track of everything you want to say by organizing your writing life.

Organize Your Environment

Writing is both a mental and a physical process. Your writing environment must suit both aspects. The physical process is supported by choosing a constructive setting and appropriate materials. Your mental process requires support, too. Set up an environment that is encouraging and creative.

Choose the Right Spot The setting in which you write can greatly affect your productivity. Find a place where you won't be interrupted. Background sounds can be annoying or inspiring. Some writers work best to the sounds of music or birds. Customize your environment to suit your tastes.

Prepare Your Materials Choose writing materials that you find comfortable. Also, make sure that you have enough materials before you begin. You don't want to run out of paper or ink once you're writing.

Budget Your Time A schedule can help you stay on track while completing a long writing project. Begin with the final deadline and work backward. Write the due date on a calendar. Then, choose a date on which to begin or complete each stage in the writing process.

NOVEMBER

	1	2 Choose biography subject and begin research	3	4	5	6
7	8	9 Draft biography	10	11	12 Review draft with peer review team	13 Revise
14 Finish revising	15	16 Proofread biography	17	18 Biography due	19	20

Step-by-Step Teaching Guide

Organize Your Environment

1. Share a description of your own writing environment. Ask students whether there are specific places or times of day in which they like to write. Ask whether there are particular books they like to have for reference, such as a dictionary.
2. Many writers have created masterpieces under adverse conditions. Harriet Beecher Stowe wrote the novel *Uncle Tom's Cabin* at her kitchen table, supervising her children and watching the stove at the same time. As a child, Gary Paulsen created his own space in the basement in a small, warm area behind the furnace. Many writers have found a haven in the library. Tell students not to be discouraged if they have little peace, quiet, or privacy at home. However, any writer who is able to do so will set up a comfortable place to work. Urge students to find the best places for themselves to work.

Real-World Connection

Teaching Resources: Writing Support Transparency, 1-A; Writing Support Activity Book, 1-1

Point out the paragraph headed "Budget Your Time." Explain that professional writers always have to meet deadlines. Journalists often have daily deadlines. The writers of this textbook had to meet weekly deadlines. Even writers of long novels work on a schedule.

ONGOING ASSESSMENT: Monitor and Reinforce

If students do not have the right writing environment, try one of the following options.

Option 1 Remind students to use the facilities of the school. The school library should be comfortable and quiet and provide a good working atmosphere. It certainly has books that students do not have at home. And it has a librarian who is eager to help them. Urge students who need a quiet place to write to try the school library.

Option 2 Some students may write best in a public place because they concentrate better with lively activity in the background. Students may want to try writing in local diners or at the public library. Urge them to experiment until they find the perfect place for writing.

Step-by-Step Teaching Guide

Sharing Your Work

1. Students share ideas all the time. They talk about what to wear, what to eat, where to go, what to do. They listen to what others have to say. There is very little difference between sharing ideas aloud and sharing written ideas.
2. Emphasize that in a peer review process, students should treat one another with respect. Students should always try to use tact when pointing out areas of a classmate's writing they think could use improvement. Remind students that a peer critic should point out not only problems; he or she should also express approval and admiration of clever ideas and well-written passages. Students need to learn to recognize and take pride in their strengths as writers.

Critical Viewing

Analyze Possible answers: Agree on plans and outlines before starting to write. Read each other's final drafts and incorporate any changes they agree on.

Customize for *Musical/Auditory Learners*

Much popular music is sung by groups, and often the lyrics are written by two or more group members. Have students do some research in the periodicals section of the public library to find out how and why these songwriters work together.

Step-by-Step Teaching Guide

Publishing

1. Share any knowledge you have of forums in which students can publish their work. Encourage them to submit their work to the school literary magazine or newspaper if your school has either.
2. Students may be interested in founding a literary magazine if the school does not have one. Help them to get faculty sponsorship and whatever else they need.

1

Sharing Your Work

Work With Others

Your personal writing process can and should be adapted to include other people. You will find many opportunities to cooperate during writing.

Group Brainstorming

The expression "the more, the merrier" often applies to generating new ideas. Group brainstorming is an excellent strategy for breaking through writer's block—the feeling that you just don't have any ideas. Brainstorming involves freely suggesting ideas without stopping to judge them. Bouncing ideas off other people in a group can help you fill a page with topics and ideas that might deserve further exploration.

▲ Critical Viewing Name two guidelines that these students should follow while writing collaboratively. **[Analyze]**

Collaborative and Cooperative Writing

You can tackle almost any writing project with a partner or a team. Team members can share the writing tasks. For example, when working on a video script, one teammate might create the storyboard and write descriptions of locations; another might write interview questions; still another might prepare the narrative voice-over text. Writing with others can inspire you to break old habits and try new strategies, too.

Peer Reviewers A peer reviewer can help you review a draft and look for passages that are particularly strong, as well as those that need work. A good rule of thumb to follow when working with others on your writing is this: Consider their comments and then make up your own mind.

Publishing

Sharing your work through publication can be a satisfying conclusion to your writing process. Many magazines, Web sites, and contests accept student submissions. Look through your portfolio for work you would like to share with a wider audience. Consult with your teacher or a librarian for suggestions regarding places to publish, or see page 783 for a list of student publications.

What Are the Qualities of Good Writing?

Ideas Many writers choose the same topics to write about—but each writer has his or her own ideas about each topic. Your ideas are what will make your writing different from the writing of others. Don't simply offer readers information they already have; share your unique ideas and insights.

Organization If writing is to be effective, it must be understood. Organize your writing so that readers can follow its internal structure. Give information in the right amount and in the right order.

Voice When you call friends on the telephone, many of them probably recognize your voice even before you identify yourself. As a writer, too, you have a distinctive voice. Learn to develop your writing voice. Let your personality show in the way you express yourself, while still observing the conventions of written English.

Word Choice If you just asked a waiter to "bring food," you could end up with any one of a wide variety of dishes. You are probably more precise when you order something to eat—you use precise words with precise meanings. As a writer, help your readers understand exactly what you mean by using the most precise word for your purpose. Consider the connotations, or associations, of words as well as their denotations, or dictionary meanings.

Sentence Fluency Good writing contains a variety of sentence patterns and lengths. Sentence variety creates a flow that sounds smooth and polished.

Conventions When people share a language, certain rules or conventions make it possible for everyone to communicate effectively. When you write, follow the conventions for English—the rules of grammar, usage, and mechanics.

Reflecting on Your Writing

As you review your writing portfolio, or before you begin a new project, spend some time thinking about your accomplishments and goals. Ask yourself these questions:

- Of what piece of writing am I the most proud? Why?
- What specific types of writing would I like to try?
- Did I ever feel intimidated by a blank piece of paper? How did I conquer my fear? What strategy might I try next time?

You may find it useful to share your responses with a partner and to note your ideas in your writer's journal.

Step-by-Step Teaching Guide

What Are the Qualities of Good Writing?

1. Discuss with the class the six aspects of writing listed on page 7. Have students discuss which categories are essential to any successful communication. (Possible answer: organization; precise word choice)
2. Have students name favorite writers and describe the distinctive features of their work, identifying the category to which each feature belongs.

Step-by-Step Teaching Guide

Reflecting on Your Writing

1. Have volunteers share answers to the last Reflecting on Your Writing question on page 7.
2. Point out that techniques such as keeping a journal, freewriting, and brainstorming can all help students feel freer in generating ideas for writing: They "oil the engine" of the imagination.

PRENTICE HALL
Everyday Spelling

If you have taught the spelling skills in *Prentice Hall Everyday Spelling,* Grade 8, Chapter 1, in conjunction with this *Writing and Grammar* chapter, review and assess students' mastery of the skills before concluding the chapter.

ONGOING ASSESSMENT: Assess Mastery

Use one of the following options to assess students' understanding of the writing process.

Self-Assessment Have students write a short paragraph describing what they have learned from this chapter. Have them consider how they can improve their writing, which areas they think need work, and how the ideas in this chapter will help them.

Teacher Assessment Monitor students' writing assignments throughout the year. Meet with students individually as needed to discuss their work and give them any necessary guidance.

Lesson Objectives

1. To interpret and evaluate the various ways image makers represent meanings.
2. To write a response to a work of art.

Step-by-Step Teaching Guide

Analyzing How Meaning Is Communicated Through the Arts

1. Choose a Spotlight element for class discussion, or have students work independently or in groups on the element of their choice. Give students the opportunity to find the necessary books and recordings.
2. Discuss with the class the various forms of artistic expression mentioned on this page and discuss some of their similarities and differences. Help students appreciate that paintings, photographs, recorded music, and films can last a long time and be appreciated again and again. Live performances are unique. When they are captured on film, their quality of excitement and immediacy is inevitably lost. Ask your students which forms of art they generally enjoy most and whether they know why they prefer those forms.
3. Help your students choose a work of art to write about. Caution students to be sure they will be able to locate their choice easily in the school or local library, at home, or on the Internet.
4. Remind students that journal entries are not formal pieces of writing but rather quick, impressionistic responses.

Spotlight on the Humanities

Analyzing How Meaning Is Communicated Through the Arts

Introducing the Spotlight on the Humanities

Whether broadcast in a playwright's words upon a stage, written in the words of a poet on the page, or revealed in the brushstrokes of a painter, self-expression can take form in several different media. In the Spotlight on the Humanities features, you will discover how all art is connected—layer upon layer—and how the inspiration that moved the hearts and minds of creative artists in the past continues to touch artists of today. As artists experiment and challenge boundaries, definitions of various art forms grow and change. However, to give you a framework for a study of the humanities, consider these broad categories:

- **Fine art** creates meaning through color, line, texture, and subject. Paintings, sketches, sculpture, and collage can convey literal or abstract ideas.
- **Photography** uses still images to create meaning. A photograph captures still images on film, but photographers express ideas through subject, composition, and lighting.
- **Theater** is designed to be performed by actors on a stage. Using props, scenery, sound effects, and lighting, drama brings a story to life. In some cases, music and dance are incorporated into the story line. For example, in an opera, the story is told completely through song.
- **Film** captures sound and motion to convey an idea. Like dramatic theater, most film is narrative and uses setting, costumes, and characterization to develop a story. A filmmaker can create a unique point of view using camera angles, as well as lighting and sound techniques.
- **Music** uses sound to create meaning. Whether presented as an oboe solo, an operatic aria, or a symphony, music can create moods or present variations on a theme.
- **Dance** creates meaning through organized movement. It can be performed by a single person, a pair, or larger groups.

Writing Activity

Select a work from one of the categories above. Write a brief journal response describing your chosen work of art. Explain its characteristics and why you like or dislike the work.

▲ Critical Viewing The Parthenon is located in Greece, where drama originated. Based on what you see in this picture, what other form of artistic expression may have been important to the ancient Greeks? **[Infer]**

Viewing and Representing

Activity Let students display reproductions of the works they wrote about or play music CDs quietly in the background as they read their journal entries to the class. Students who wrote about theater or dance may be able to show photographs of the performances. Students might display film stills reproduced in books or articles.

Critical Viewing

Infer Most students will state that monumental architecture was probably an art form important to the ancient Greeks, judging from the stately appearance of this building.

Media and Technology Skills

Making Technology Work for You

Activity: Identify Appropriate Technology

One important way to grow as a writer is to share your work with others. You have a variety of technologies from which to choose to help you prepare and present your work. The type of technology you use with any given work depends on the content you are communicating.

Learn About It Familiarize yourself with the varieties of available technology. Ask a librarian to help you find out what's available at your school or community library.

- **Writing tools** Computer *word-processing programs* allow you to store, edit, and retrieve text. *Desktop-publishing programs* let you add pictures to your writing and customize the layout (appearance and arrangement) of your work.
- **Virtual resources** The *Internet* is an extensive computer network that allows individuals to access and post information, pictures, and so on. *E-mail* is a way to send and receive messages nearly instantaneously over the Internet.
- **Audiovisual tools** Several tools allow you to record images and sound. A *video camera* captures moving images as well as sound. A *still camera* records still images, which can be displayed on their own or projected in a series with a *slide projector.* A *tape recorder* preserves and plays back sound.

TOPICS	Writing Tools	Virtual Resources	Audiovisual Tools
Exercise			
Pet Care			
Study Skills			

Evaluate It Review the topics for reports or presentations listed in the chart above. With a group, discuss how you might utilize different technological tools to create an effective report or presentation for each topic. Copy the chart in your notebook, and record the results of the group discussion.

Uses of Technology

Writing Tools

- **Writing software** allows easy revisions; some feature prompts that help you to organize the writing process
- **Desktop-publishing programs** enable you to present your work with a professional touch

Virtual Resources

- **Internet** lets you present your work to a wide audience; permits easy research
- **E-mail** allows students to share work and get fast feedback on it

Audiovisual Tools

- **Video camera** makes it easy to demonstrate complicated procedures
- **Still camera** can show something that is hard to describe
- **Slide projector** adds visual interest to oral presentations
- **Tape recorder** helps in taking complete notes during interviews

Lesson Objectives

1. To evaluate the purposes and effects of various media.
2. To assess how the medium and presentation contribute to the message.
3. To write to record and reflect on ideas.

Step-by-Step Teaching Guide

Making Technology Work for You

Teaching Resources: Writing Support Transparency 1-A; Writing Support Activity Book 1-1

1. Discuss the various tools and resources mentioned on this page of the textbook. If time permits, ask student experts in your class to demonstrate some of the features of these resources.
2. Display the transparency. Use the chart to begin recording a discussion of how the various tools may be used.
3. Give students copies of the blank organizer. Ask them to use the chart to finish recording the discussion of how the various tools can be used for different kinds of presentations.

Customize for *Logical/Mathematical Learners*

Students may enjoy making a chart that lists all the various types of technological tools down one side and the purposes to which they can be put across the top. They can use the charts to see at a glance how each technological tool can be used and which ones are most universally useful.

Lesson Objectives

1. To produce cohesive and coherent written texts by organizing ideas, using effective transitions, and choosing precise wording.
2. To develop, draft, revise, and proofread an essay.
3. To use correct grammar, spelling, and punctuation.

Step-by-Step Teaching Guide

Responding to Writing Prompts

Teaching Resources: Standardized Test Preparation Workbook, pp. 1–2

1. Discuss the six evaluation points on this page of the textbook. Stress the importance of taking the time to reread test instructions. When students are asked to respond to a quotation, as in the sample writing prompt on this page, they should restate the quotation in their own words to make sure they understand it.
2. Students should jot down a few examples that support or refute the premise about which they are asked to write.
3. Stress the importance of organizing the structure of their essay by developing a list, a formal or informal outline, a chart, or some sort of graphic organizer. They may want to list introductory ideas for a beginning paragraph and conclusions for a final paragraph and several points to include in between.
4. Assign the sample writing prompt to students. Give them the amount of time they will have on your state's standardized writing tests.

Standardized Test Preparation Workshop

Responding to Writing Prompts

As shown in this chapter, writing is an integral part of your everyday life. Because writing is one of the most powerful communication tools you will ever use, it is important that you express your ideas clearly. Your ability to communicate through writing is often measured when you respond to a writing prompt on a standardized test. When scorers evaluate your writing, they will look for evidence that you can

- respond directly to the prompt.
- make your writing thoughtful and interesting.
- organize your ideas so that they are clear and easy to follow.
- develop your ideas thoroughly by using appropriate details and precise language.
- stay focused on your purpose for writing by making sure that each sentence you write contributes to your composition as a whole.
- communicate effectively by using correct spelling, capitalization, punctuation, grammar, usage, and sentence structure.

The process of writing for a test, or any kind of writing, can be divided into stages. Plan to use a specific amount of time for prewriting, drafting, revising, and proofreading.

Following is an example of one type of writing prompt that you might find on a standardized test. Use the suggestions on the following page to help you respond. The clocks next to each stage show a suggested plan for organizing your time.

Test Tip

Some tests limit the time or space allowed for a response. Know the rules of the test before you begin responding so that you can plan the best way to use your time and space.

Sample Writing Situation

Read the following quotation. In an essay, explain why you agree or disagree with the quotation. To support your position, use examples from literature as well as from personal experience.

> "It is neither wealth nor splendor, but tranquility and occupation, which give happiness."
>
> —Thomas Jefferson

TEST-TAKING TIP

A common error made by test takers is overlooking part of the writing assignment. To avoid this problem, students can underline each task they are asked to do in the directions and number the tasks in the margin of their paper. In the sample prompt, for example, the students are asked to do four things: read the quotation, write an essay of agreement or disagreement, use examples from literature, and use examples from personal experience.

Prewriting

Allow about one fourth of your time for prewriting.

Identify Key Words Look over the prompt, and identify exactly what you are being asked to do. In this case, you are being asked to explain why you agree or disagree. You are being asked to take a position. Further, the prompt specifically asks you to use examples from literature as well as personal experience.

Use an Organizer Jot down notes in an easy-to-read format. Use a cluster diagram or a two-column chart to lay out your position and several examples. Then, jot down details around each of the examples. Finally, use numbers or letters to identify which ideas and points you will use at the beginning, middle, and end.

Drafting

Allow almost half of your time for drafting.

Begin With a Strong Introduction In your introduction, express in your own words how you will address the prompt. However, avoid falling into the trap of simply restating the prompt. For example, if you agree with the quotation, you might begin by writing, "I think I would have gotten along very well with Thomas Jefferson if I had lived during his time. Although he himself was wealthy, his words reveal his understanding that other factors are more important in achieving happiness." Beginning with such a statement addresses the prompt, and it shows a little more thought than if you simply restate the prompt by beginning "I agree with the quotation from Thomas Jefferson."

Follow the Directions In the body of your response, make sure that you follow the directions given in the prompt. If examples from literature are called for, include them. If you don't have any examples jotted down in your prewriting notes, look over your key points, and identify at least one character or situation from literature that illustrates those points.

Revising, Editing, and Proofreading

Allow a little more than one fourth of your time to revise, edit, and proofread your work.

Fine-Tune Your Work After drafting, review your response to make sure that your ideas flow logically. Neatly insert transitions if the connection between one paragraph and the next is not clear. Finally, check that you have used complete sentences and that you have observed the conventions of spelling and mechanics.

Customize for *Less Advanced Students*

Discuss the Thomas Jefferson quotation with the group. Have several volunteers interpret the quotation and give examples. (You might begin by retelling the story of King Midas, if no one has any ideas.) After everyone in the group understands the quotation and can give examples, use the sample prompt to model the various ways to organize ideas for writing that are mentioned on this page of the textbook.

Customize for *More Advanced Students*

Challenge these students to use examples from literature they have read both in class and outside the classroom to support their opinions. Students who have taken opposite positions may enjoy reading their test papers to an audience and asking which arguments were most persuasive.

Chapter 2 Time and Resource Manager

In-Depth Lesson Plan

	LESSON FOCUS	PRINT AND MEDIA RESOURCES
DAY 1	**Introduction to the Writing Process** Students are introduced to the writing process (pp. 12–13).	***Writing and Grammar iText* (Interactive Text)**, Ch. 2, Introduction
DAY 2	**What Is Prewriting?** Students discuss the process of choosing and narrowing a topic, considering audience and purpose, and gathering information (pp. 14–17).	**Teaching Resources** *Writing Support Transparencies,* 2-A–D; *Writing Support Activity Book,* 2.1–4 ***Writing and Grammar iText* (Interactive Text)**, Section 2.1
DAY 3	**What Is Drafting?** Students discuss the process of organizing ideas and writing first drafts (p. 18).	***Writing and Grammar iText* (Interactive Text)**, Section 2.2
DAY 4	**What Is Revising?** Students discuss the process of revising drafts in terms of overall structure, paragraphs, sentences, and word choice (pp. 19–21).	**Teaching Resources** *Writing Support Transparencies,* 2-F ***Writing and Grammar iText* (Interactive Text)**, Section 2.3
DAY 5	**What Are Editing, Proofreading, Publishing, and Presenting?** Students discuss the process of checking their work for accuracy and correctness and presenting final drafts (pp. 22–23).	***Writing and Grammar iText* (Interactive Text)**, Sections 2.4–5

Accelerated Lesson Plan

	LESSON FOCUS	PRINT AND MEDIA RESOURCES
DAY 1	**Introduction Through Drafting** Students review characteristics of the writing process. They discuss selecting topics and writing drafts (pp. 12–18).	***Writing and Grammar iText* (Interactive Text)**, Ch. 2, Introduction Through Section 2.2
DAY 2	**Revising Through Presenting** Students review and discuss the process of revising, editing, and proofreading their work for presentation (pp. 19–23).	**Teaching Resources** *Writing Support Transparencies,* 2-F ***Writing and Grammar iText* (Interactive Text)**, Sections 2.3–5

Options for Adapting Lesson Plans

HOMEWORK

Have students complete any stage of the lesson for homework.

SPELLING

To teach spelling skills in conjunction with writing skills, work through *Prentice Hall Everyday Spelling,* Grade 8, Chapter 2, as you cover this *Writing and Grammar* chapter.

FEATURES

Extend coverage with Spotlight on the Humanities (p. 24), Media and Technology Skills (p. 25), and Standardized Test Preparation Workshop (p. 26).

TECHNOLOGY

Students can complete any stage of the lesson on the computer, using *Writing and Grammar iText* or a word-processing program. Have them print out their completed work.

INTEGRATED SKILLS COVERAGE

Viewing and Representing
Critical Viewing, SE pp. 12, 24
Using Movies to Spark Ideas, SE p. 24
ATE p. 24

Real-World Connection
ATE p. 18

Integrating Workplace Skills
Narrowing Topics for Writing, ATE p. 15

ASSESSMENT SUPPORT

Standardized Test Preparation Workshop SE pp. 26–27; ATE p. 23

Standardized Test Preparation Workbook, pp. 3–4

Writing Assessment and Portfolio Management

MEETING INDIVIDUAL NEEDS

Less Advanced Students See Ongoing Assessments, ATE pp. 15, 21.

ESL Students ATE pp. 14, 22, 27

More Advanced Students ATE p. 13

Musical/Auditory Learners ATE p. 17

BLOCK SCHEDULING

Pacing Suggestions
For 90-minute Blocks
- Have students discuss the complete chapter in a single class period.

Professional Development Support
- ***How to Manage Instruction in the Block*** This teaching resource provides management and activity suggestions.

MEDIA AND TECHNOLOGY

For the Teacher
- ***Writing and Grammar iText*** **(Interactive Text),** Ch.2

WRITING AND GRAMMAR ON-LINE

iText Interactive Text (On-line or on CD-ROM)
- Easily navigable instruction with interactive Revision Checkers
- Full use of e-rater™, the essay-scoring system (on-line only)

Companion Web Site PHSchool.com
- Scoring rubrics with models (use Web Code eck-8001)

See the Go On-line! feature, SE p. iii.

CHAPTER 2
A WALK THROUGH THE WRITING PROCESS

Lesson Objectives

1. To understand the writing process.
2. To choose and narrow a writing topic.
3. To consider audience and purpose in developing a writing topic.
4. To apply strategies for gathering and organizing details.
5. To draft a text with an introduction, body, and conclusion.
6. To evaluate and revise the overall structure of a draft.
7. To benefit from the peer review process in the revision process.
8. To edit, proofread, and publish a text.

Critical Viewing

Connect Students' responses will vary, but they may say that the more formal the type of writing they do, the more careful and extensive their habits are.

Chapter 2 A Walk Through the Writing Process

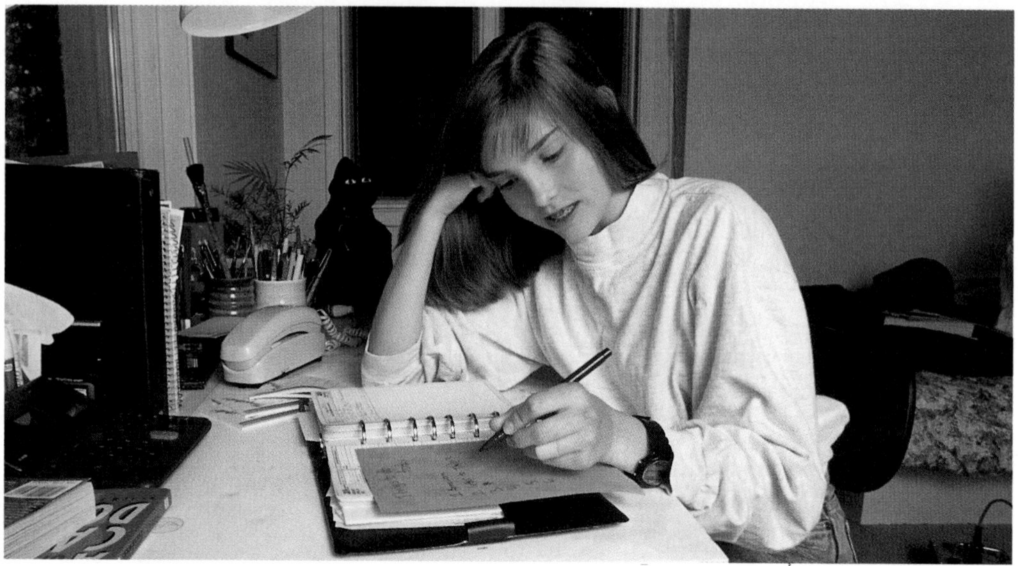

▲ Critical Viewing
How do your writing habits reflect the type of writing you do? **[Connect]**

The **writing process**—a systematic approach to writing—can help you achieve your writing goals. From prewriting through publishing and presenting, understanding the stages of the writing process will help you to be a better writer.

Types of Writing

Writing can be categorized in terms of **modes,** the form or shape that the writing takes. The chart at right shows the modes you'll encounter in this book.

Writing may also be divided into two broader categories: *reflexive* and *extensive,* according to the inspiration and intended audience of your work. When you write **reflexively,** you choose the subject and the format and you decide whether to share your writing with others. Reflexive writing—such as a journal or diary entry—is *for* you and *from* you. In contrast, when you write **extensively,** you follow guidelines set by others. This type of writing, which includes a report or an essay assigned in school, is *for* others and *from* others.

The Modes of Writing

Narration
Description
Persuasion
Exposition
Research Writing
Response to Literature
Poetry and Drama
Writing for Assessment

TIME AND RESOURCE MANAGER

Resources
Technology: Writing and Grammar iText, Ch. 2

In-Depth Coverage	Accelerated Pace
• Cover pp. 12–13 in class. • Review with students the types of writing with which they are familiar.	• Assign pp. 12–13 for independent student review.

The Process of Writing

These are the stages of the writing process:

- **Prewriting** is the process of freely exploring ideas, choosing a topic, and gathering and organizing details before you write.
- **Drafting** is a way to get your ideas down on paper in roughly the format you intend.
- **Revising** gives you the opportunity to correct any errors and improve your writing's form and content.
- **Editing and Proofreading** let you polish your writing, fixing errors in grammar, spelling, and mechanics.
- **Publishing and Presenting** allow you to share your writing.

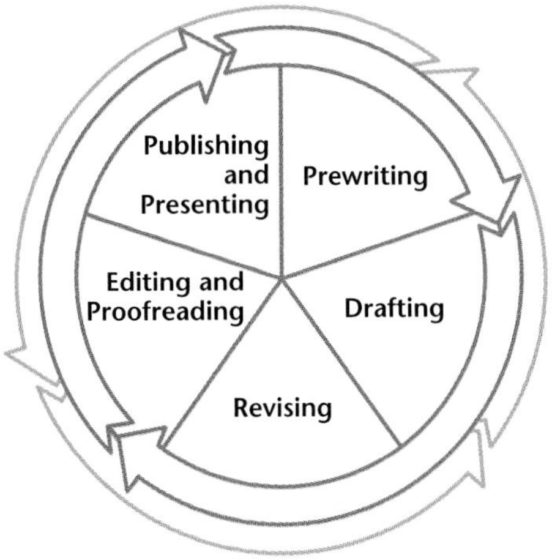

These steps may seem to suggest a progression from one to the next, but writers often return to earlier writing stages as they work. For example, when you are drafting, you may discover that you need to do some additional investigation of your topic. When you are revising, you may decide to include more information from your prewriting stage.

A Guided Tour

You can use this chapter as an introduction to the stages of the writing process. Look closely at the steps of the process presented here. Consider some of the strategies used by effective writers, and experiment with them in your own writing. By applying these strategies to your own writing process, you can improve the quality of your final draft.

PREPARE and ENGAGE

Interest GRABBER Give students this example of a process—how to housebreak a dog.

- Think about the parts of the process that are important. Narrow them down to the most relevant to the task. (This is like prewriting.)
- Try these steps with your dog. Note what is working and what isn't. (drafting)
- Change your plan, adding more of what works and removing what doesn't work. (revising; anything the dog likes or rejects can be considered the peer review!)
- Practice with your dog every day until it is housebroken. (publishing and presenting)

Activate Prior Knowledge

Ask volunteers to suggest topics for each mode of writing listed in the chart.

Customize for *More Advanced Students*

Ask students how they think reflexive writing might differ from extensive writing. (Students may suggest that reflexive writing is rougher, its grammar is not perfect, or that it is often fragmentary.) Point out that reflexive writing, like the notes and ideas in a writer's notebook or journal, is often excellent material for extensive writing.

TEACH

Step-by-Step Teaching Guide

Prewriting: Choosing Your Topic

1. Have students tell about times when they have been faced with a blank sheet of paper. How do they begin writing? Do they feel challenged or nervous? Do they draw pictures to help get themselves started?
2. Ask students to describe their magazine- or newspaper-reading habits. Do they skim through and look at headlines and pictures, or do they stop to read the articles? When they read editorials, do they feel the urge to respond? What kind of inspiration for students' own thinking and writing do magazines and newspapers provide?
3. A good topic is any topic students are interested in. It can be something they know about or something they want to learn. A bad topic is something they chose just to impress the teacher or something they know interests the teacher but bores them.

Customize for *ESL Students*

Tells students that reviewing newspapers is not only a good way to find topics for writing, but it also is a useful tool for familiarizing oneself with a particular culture's language.

2.1 What Is Prewriting?

All writers can experience moments of uncertainty when faced with a blank sheet of paper. Often, writers are not sure what to write about or how much to write. The prewriting stage provides preparation for writing by helping you flex and stretch your creative muscles. Prewriting consists of routines and strategies for getting started; it's a mental warm-up for writing. Each writing chapter will offer you several techniques for getting started, including choosing a topic, narrowing a topic, considering audience and purpose, and gathering details before you draft.

Learn More

For additional Prewriting strategies suited to specific writing tasks, see Chapters 4–13.

Choosing Your Topic

In order to write, you must first choose a topic. You'll find that you do your best writing when you address a topic that you find meaningful. Prewriting strategies allow you to explore issues, ideas, and experiences that are significant to you. Try the sample strategies to help generate a topic for writing.

SAMPLE STRATEGY

Reviewing Newspapers and Magazines To find a topic that is contemporary and interesting, flip through articles and advertisements in newspapers and magazines. For each subject or image that catches your eye, write a key word that summarizes what you found. Then, using this key word to direct your thinking, jot down a few ideas for writing. Review your notes to find a topic.

In this example, the writer found several compelling subjects and images in a newsmagazine. After reading an article on family reunions, the writer decided to write an essay about her aunt and uncle.

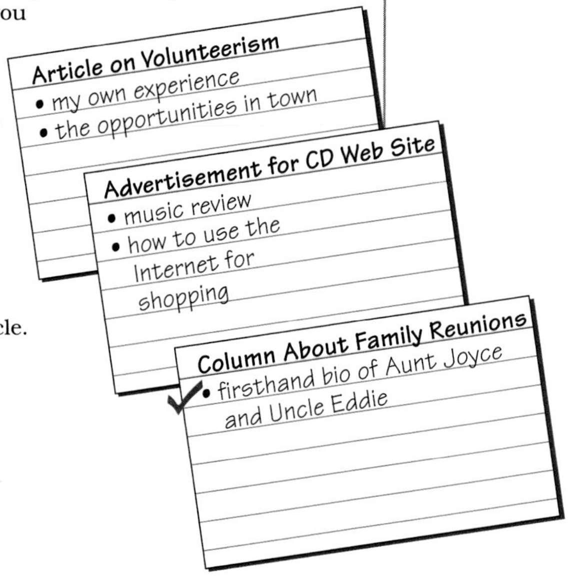

Article on Volunteerism
• my own experience
• the opportunities in town
Advertisement for CD Web Site
• music review
• how to use the Internet for shopping
Column About Family Reunions
• firsthand bio of Aunt Joyce and Uncle Eddie

TIME AND RESOURCE MANAGER

In-Depth Coverage	Accelerated Pace
• Cover pp. 14–17 in class. • Have students apply the prewriting strategies they have learned (p. 17).	• Assign pp. 14–17 for independent student reading. • Have students apply the prewriting strategies they have learned (p. 17).

Narrowing Your Topic

Once you have chosen a topic to write about, make sure it is not so general or broad that it becomes unmanageable. For example, in a short paper, it would be difficult to address the benefits of all competitive sports. However, by narrowing your focus to show the benefits of joining a school soccer team, you will be able to treat the subject thoroughly. Look at these sample broad and narrowed topics:

BROAD:	Pets
NARROW:	Bringing a new pet home
NARROWER:	How to house-train a puppy
BROAD:	Cities
NARROW:	Hollywood
NARROWER:	Spotting celebrities in the city of stars

SAMPLE STRATEGY

Using a Topic Web One way to narrow a topic that is too broad is to create a topic web. Start by placing a broad topic at the top of the web. Next, divide the broad topic into two or more subtopics. Then, divide each subtopic into even narrower topics, drawing lines to connect each topic with its subtopics. The following model shows how you might narrow the broad topic "Television Shows" by using this strategy.

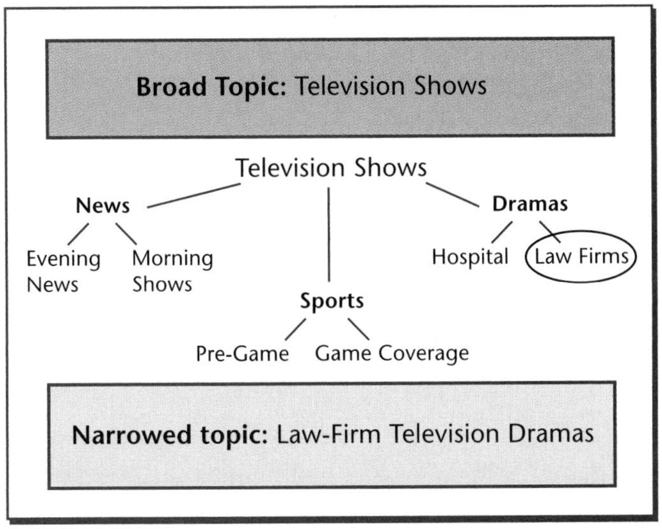

Step-by-Step Teaching Guide

Prewriting: Narrowing Your Topic

Teaching Resources: Writing Support Transparency 2-A; Writing Support Activity Book, 2-1

1. On the chalkboard, write a sample topic of interest to most students, such as baseball or movies. These topics are much too broad for a short writing assignment. Ask students to suggest subtopics they would be interested in writing about, such as Mark McGwire's 70-Home Run Season or Special Effects in *Galaxy Quest.* Point out that a writer can cover a specific topic like these entertainingly and in depth in a fairly short paper but would have to write a whole library to cover a general topic.
2. Practice the topic web strategy. Have students suggest a few very broad topics. Write them on the chalkboard and have the class work together to narrow each one in turn. This will give students the confidence to apply the strategy on their own.

Integrating Workplace Skills

Explain to students that many jobs require people to narrow topics for writing. A newspaper reporter, for instance, must decide what aspect he or she will focus on when writing a story. A doctor delivering a paper at a medical conference must also decide what aspects of the study he or she will focus on for the presentation.

ONGOING ASSESSMENT: Monitor and Reinforce

If students have difficulty with the concepts of choosing and narrowing topics, try one of the following options.

Option 1 Have students choose partners with whom to discuss topics. Each student should already have a broad topic in mind. Students can interview each other, asking questions that will help focus on a specific area of interest.

Option 2 Have each student say his or her main idea in one sentence. The student can then write an outline that lists all the aspects of this main idea that he or she wants to discuss. Students must be sure that all the steps in the outline are relevant to the main idea.

Step-by-Step Teaching Guide

Prewriting: Considering Your Audience and Purpose

Teaching Resources: Writing Support Transparency 2-B; Writing Support Activity Book, 2-2

1. Choose a sample topic, such as baseball, with which to demonstrate the different approaches a writer might take, depending on his or her audience. Someone writing for Little League beginners might describe the different positions, the rules of the game, and the mechanics of pitching. Someone writing for lifelong fans might reminisce about great or unusual games he or she has seen. This writer would assume that readers already knew the rules of the game and would not need to describe them.
2. Point out the link between audience and purpose. People read for different reasons. Those who read to learn often look for informative writing. Those who read to be entertained usually look for humorous, dramatic, or descriptive writing that does not instruct but assumes readers already have the background knowledge necessary to understand the topic being discussed.

2.1

Considering Your Audience and Purpose

To increase the effectiveness of your writing, analyze your audience, or the people you hope to reach. Then, refine your purpose by focusing on your reason for writing.

Considering Your Audience Before you begin to draft, consider the audience you want your writing to reach. For example, teenagers have different concerns from those of business executives; writers should take such differences into account when writing for a particular audience. A profile like the one shown here can help you identify the interests and knowledge level of your readers. Use your answers to guide the language and details you include in your writing.

AUDIENCE PROFILE

- What is the average age of my audience?
- What do they know about my topic?
- What details will be most interesting to my audience?
- What background do I need to provide?

Considering Your Purpose Your purpose, or your reason for writing, will influence the kinds of details you include. If you want to praise a restaurant for its varied menu, include examples of the range of dishes available. In contrast, if you want to entertain readers with a description of the bumbling service, include humorous examples that re-create your dining experience. Consider these tips for achieving specific purposes:

- **To inform—**include facts, details, and examples that show your subject in a new light.
- **To reflect—**summarize an experience, but focus on showing what you have learned from it.
- **To persuade—**include reasons and arguments to support a position.

Gathering Details

Just as a gardener gathers seeds, bulbs, gloves, and tools before planting, you must gather the details and materials you will need before you write your first draft. Collecting relevant ideas and facts at this stage makes writing easier.

SAMPLE STRATEGY

Preparing a Parts-of-Speech Word Web A parts-of-speech word web can help you gather the right words to describe your subject. In this example, a writer identifies details to describe a rainstorm.

PARTS-OF-SPEECH WORD WEB

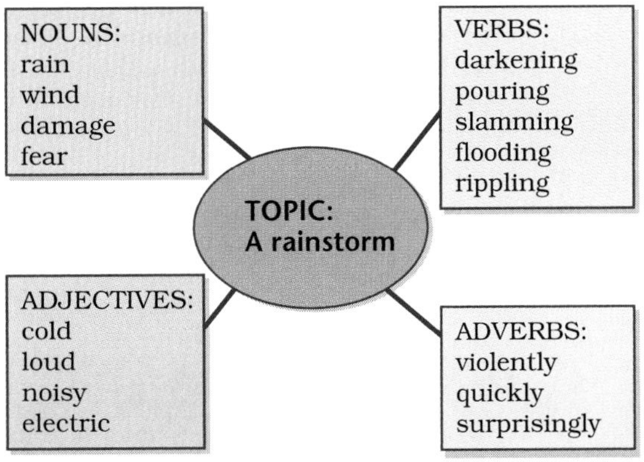
NOUNS:
rain
wind
damage
fear
VERBS:
darkening
pouring
slamming
flooding
rippling
TOPIC:
A rainstorm
ADJECTIVES:
cold
loud
noisy
electric
ADVERBS:
violently
quickly
surprisingly

SAMPLE STRATEGY

Using Hexagonal Writing The hexagonal writing technique can be helpful for writing about literature. Hexagonal writing allows you to focus on different aspects of a piece of literature and to prepare to write an organized, thorough analysis. Complete each side of a hexagon according to the directions in the sample shown.

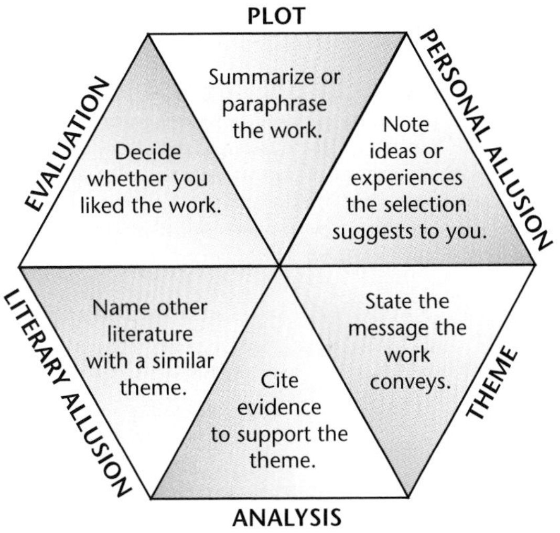
PLOT
Summarize or paraphrase the work.
PERSONAL ALLUSION
Note ideas or experiences the selection suggests to you.
THEME
State the message the work conveys.
ANALYSIS
Cite evidence to support the theme.
LITERARY ALLUSION
Name other literature with a similar theme.
EVALUATION
Decide whether you liked the work.

DIRECTIONS FOR USING A HEXAGON

APPLYING THE PREWRITING STRATEGIES

1. Find three magazine articles or images that interest you. For each, identify a potential writing topic.
2. Narrow the subject "Leisure Time" into a topic that you would be able to address in an essay.
3. Create two different audience profiles for a report you might write about bicycles. Identify two unique audiences.
4. Create a parts-of-speech word web to describe your best friend.
5. Complete a hexagon for a short story you have recently read.

Step-by-Step Teaching Guide

Prewriting: Gathering Details

Teaching Resources: Writing Support Transparencies 2-C and 2-D; Writing Support Activity Book, 2-3 and 2-4

1. Write the word *dance* on the chalkboard. Have students think of specific images this brings to mind—a school dance they attended, a ballet performance they saw on TV, a group of kids they saw dancing on a street corner. Have them complete part-of-speech word webs about this dance that they remember. Then have them discuss the results as a whole class. Ask students to explain how they think the word webs can help them get started on a descriptive essay about a dance.
2. Display on an overhead projector a poem from *Prentice Hall Literature: Timeless Voices, Timeless Themes,* Silver. Have the class work together to apply the hexagonal writing strategy to it. Point out that this strategy works well for all types of literary writing—fiction or nonfiction, filled with imagery or straightforward.

Customize for *Musical/Auditory Learners*

Have students listen to a piece of music. They can use its title for the center of a parts-of-speech word web and then fill in the web with nouns, verbs, adjectives, and adverbs that come to mind while listening to the music.

Step-by-Step Teaching Guide

Drafting: Shaping Your Writing

1. Emphasize the importance of a good opening sentence. Writers need to grab the reader's attention early.
2. Analyze the opening sentences in two selections in *Prentice Hall Literature: Timeless Voices, Timeless Themes,* Silver. Have students explain what qualities make the leads interesting.

Real-World Connection

Bring in the front page of a newspaper and have students examine it. Point to the major headlines, noting that they are in bolder and larger type than the text of the articles. Invite students to consider ways in which the lead of an essay is like a newspaper headline. (Sample response: Like a newspaper headline, a lead is the first thing readers will read; it must "pull them into" the work.)

Step-by-Step Teaching Guide

Drafting: Providing Elaboration

1. Elaboration in writing is like evidence in a courtroom. In court, the defense and the prosecution cannot just make assertions; they have to back them up with facts and details. When arguing a point in writing, a writer cannot expect to be persuasive unless he or she elaborates on the point. A writer must add details that will convince the reader.
2. Ask a volunteer to make up an opening sentence for a story. Write this sentence on the chalkboard. Ask another student to extend the opening, and have a third elaborate on it. As students have fun with this exercise, they will begin to see how a paragraph and a whole story can grow from the development of one idea.
3. You might want students to apply the drafting strategies in small groups, having one student begin, the second extend, and the third elaborate. Then, have students change roles so that each one gets to try each step.

2.2 What Is Drafting?

Shaping Your Writing

Focusing on the Form Readers bring expectations to every type of writing they encounter. They expect persuasion to convince, narration to tell a story, and comparison-and-contrast writing to show similarities and differences. Keep these expectations in mind as you draft.

Pulling Readers In With an Enticing Lead Your opening sentences should introduce your topic, show off your writing style, and encourage your audience to keep reading. Start with a compelling quotation or a vivid description. Then, link your opening sentences to your topic and main idea.

Providing Elaboration

Whether you are writing a letter of complaint or a short story, the details and explanations you include can enhance your writing. Add facts and descriptions to help readers imagine the action or understand your ideas. The SEE method is one strategy that can help you strengthen your writing.

SAMPLE STRATEGY

Using the SEE Method You strengthen your writing by providing greater depth of information when you use the SEE method—Statement, Extension, Elaboration. Start with a statement of the main idea. Then, write an extension by restating or explaining the first sentence. Elaborate further by providing even more detail about the main idea. Think of the SEE method as a way to shed more light on your subject:

STATEMENT:	After a long day, Andy was ready to leave.
EXTENSION:	At eleven o'clock, he cleared his desk and grabbed his keys.
ELABORATION:	As he walked out, he waved to the night guard and headed for the deserted parking lot.

APPLYING THE DRAFTING STRATEGIES

1. Write an interest-grabbing lead for a description of a busy train station.
2. Complete the sentences below. Then, using the SEE method, elaborate on each one.
   (a) My favorite season is __?__.
   (b) __?__ played an important role in history.

TIME AND RESOURCE MANAGER

In-Depth Coverage	Accelerated Pace
• Cover p. 18 in class. • Have students apply the drafting strategies they have learned (p. 18).	• Assign p. 18 for independent student reading. • Have students apply the drafting strategies they have learned (p. 18).

2.3 What Is Revising?

Revision can be a challenging process, especially when you are looking at several aspects of your writing at once. To make the task easier, use a system called **ratiocination** (rash´ ē äs ə nā´ shen). This method of applying logical thinking to your writing helps you focus on one element at a time. For example, by marking your draft with brackets, highlighting, circles, or other clues, you can make informed decisions about revising. The revision sections of each writing chapter provide strategies to guide your analysis of structure, paragraphs, sentences, and word choice.

Writers in ACTION

"After a lifetime of writing, I still revise every sentence many times and still worry that I haven't caught every ambiguity; I don't want anyone to have to read a sentence of mine twice to find out what it means."

—William Zinsser

Revising Your Overall Structure

Whether you are revising a story, a response to literature, or another type of writing, a logical first step in revision is to review the overall structure of your writing. Make sure your draft is well-organized and that your main idea is clearly communicated. Here is one technique to focus your evaluation:

SAMPLE STRATEGY

REVISION STRATEGY
Scanning the Sequence

Review the sequence of ideas in your draft to be sure the organization is logical. Using an index card for each paragraph in your writing, jot down a summarizing word or phrase to identify the main idea developed. Then, review your cards and evaluate their sequence. If the presentation of ideas does not support your main idea effectively, consider reordering the paragraphs. Move the cards until you find an order that works. You might also add transitional words, phrases, or sentences to make the writing flow more smoothly. In the model shown here, the writer reorders her essay on baseball.

EVALUATING SEQUENCE

Main idea: Baseball is popular for many reasons.

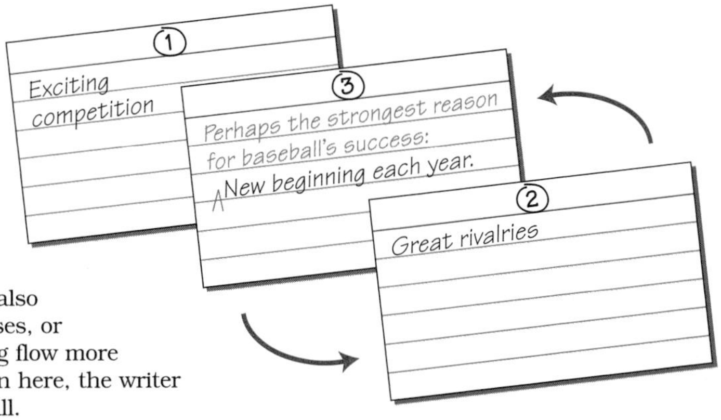

1
Exciting competition
3
Perhaps the strongest reason for baseball's success:
New beginning each year.
2
Great rivalries

Step-by-Step Teaching Guide

Revising: Revising Your Overall Structure

1. Read students these comments about revising by children's writer Bruce Brooks. With the right attitude, revising does not have to be a chore.

   I think "revision" is badly named. The "re" prefix implies that you are going back over something you've already done. But you're not going back. You are going on with the writing process. It's all just part of getting it right. A friend of mine who played basketball once said that he envied me because he had just missed a foul shot that would have tied the score at the end of an important game. He said, "But you can write that foul shot until you make it."

2. If students work on word processors, they may want to try a variation on the scanning strategy. Students can print out their work, read it over, mark changes in the sequence by hand on the pages, and then cut and paste the text on screen to follow the new order. Encourage students who have access to technology to use it to improve their writing.

TIME AND RESOURCE MANAGER

In-Depth Coverage	Accelerated Pace
• Cover pp. 19–21 in class. • Have students apply the revision strategies they have learned (p. 21).	• Assign pp. 19–21 for independent student reading. • Have students apply the revision strategies they have learned (p. 21).

Step-by-Step Teaching Guide

Revising: Revising Your Paragraphs and Sentences

1. Even interesting details in a paragraph should be removed if they are not relevant to the point you are trying to make in the paragraph as a whole. If students find interesting details that don't support the paragraphs in which they appear, they need not delete the details altogether. They may be able to move them to a new paragraph or possibly use them in some future piece of writing.
2. Long sentences are no better or worse than short ones. Ernest Hemingway favored short, simple sentences; William Faulkner preferred long ones. Both were great writers.
3. Encourage students to reread their writing carefully as they consider sentence length. They should be as objective as possible. Do the sentences they have written express exactly what they mean to say? Do they convey the intended tone? Does the writing seem too simple or too complex? Students should vary sentence length only if they feel that it will improve their work.

2.3

Revising Your Paragraphs

Take a closer look at each paragraph in your writing. To allow each part of your writing to contribute successfully to the draft, you may need to change some of your paragraphs.

SAMPLE STRATEGY

REVISION STRATEGY
Comparing Body Paragraphs to Purpose

To be sure your draft achieves the purpose you had planned, write your specific purpose on a sticky note. As you review each paragraph in your draft, slide the note down the paper. Highlight details that address your purpose. If you notice that some paragraphs do not have highlights, add or revise a sentence to strengthen your work.

COMPARING PARAGRAPH TO PURPOSE

My aunt went to college to study nursing. ^This was a good career choice for her because she has a caring personality and likes to make people feel at ease. Later, she married my uncle and started to work at Barnabas Hospital, where she worked steadily for twenty years. Everyone who meets her at the hospital is struck by her good humor. She always tells patients jokes or finds the humor in a situation.

Aunt Elaine finds ways to spend time with my brothers and sisters . . .

Purpose: to praise

Revising Your Sentences

When you focus on your writing at the sentence level, try to enliven it by breaking repetitive patterns. One way to do this is to take a closer look at the lengths of the sentences in your draft.

SAMPLE STRATEGY

REVISION STRATEGY
Tracking Sentence Lengths

To reveal problems with sentence length in any writing you do, track a word count. For each sentence in your draft, count the words and note the number in the side margin. Use these tips for revision.

Evaluate	Revise
• Do you notice a series of short or long sentences?	• Break the pattern by combining short sentences or breaking down long ones.

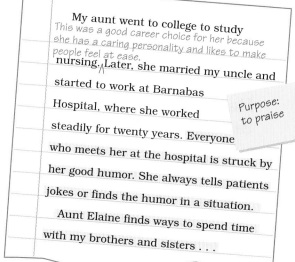

Revising Your Word Choice

Get the most mileage out of the words you use by taking a closer look at the language in your draft. Every complete sentence has a verb, so verbs are a good candidate for your review.

SAMPLE STRATEGY

REVISION STRATEGY
Circling "Be" Verbs

Verbs are the action words and state-of-being words that bring a sentence to life. Using a red pen, circle the *be* verbs in your draft. Locate every use of *am, is, are, was, were, be, being,* and *been.* While you may occasionally need to use a verb that expresses being, challenge yourself to eliminate some of these verbs by replacing them with precise action verbs. Look at the example at right.

EVALUATING "BE" VERBS

As one of the most famous dance teams, Fred Astaire and Ginger Rogers ~~are an~~ *danced their way into* American legend. They ~~were~~ *starred* in ten films together, and their graceful style made it look so easy!

Peer Review

When you invite other people to respond to your writing, you get the chance to see your work from a reader's point of view. Use these ideas to take advantage of a classmate's perspective.

Focusing Peer Review

Purpose	Ask
Evaluate description	What words helped you see the subject I described?
Analyze organization Summarize the main idea	Which details seemed unrelated to my main idea?

Evaluate the Feedback You have the authority to say what your final draft will include. Consider your reviewers' suggestions, and ask further questions to get more specific directions. Then, decide how you want to revise your work.

APPLYING THE REVISION STRATEGY

Choose a recent draft you have written, and try the revision strategies shown here. Then, identify and explain four improvements you have made.

Step-by-Step Teaching Guide

Revising: Revising Your Word Choice

1. Write a few sentences with forms of the verb *be* on the chalkboard. Challenge students to try to express the same ideas with vivid action verbs.

   The music was loud.

   The volume of the music almost blew me out of my seat.

   In the second sentence, the reader has an idea of how loud loud really was.

2. Students need not seek to delete every use of the verb *be* in a piece of writing. Sometimes this verb is the appropriate one. Students should keep in mind, however, that this verb conveys a state of being rather than an action taken. Substituting action verbs for linking verbs automatically makes their writing more alive.

Step-by-Step Teaching Guide

Revising: Peer Review

Teaching Resources: Writing Support Transparency 2-F

1. When a writer shows his or her work to another person, this is an act of trust and respect. Anyone asked to review someone else's writing should feel honored by the request and make every effort to give the writer good, helpful, constructive feedback.

2. A reviewer should read an essay or story once straight through, then go back and reread more slowly and carefully. On the second reading, the reviewer should make notes of any questions. Reviewers should look for issues such as unclear transitions, irrelevant details, ideas that seem to be out of sequence, and arguments that fail to persuade. Critics should always give reasons for their comments.

ONGOING ASSESSMENT: Monitor and Reinforce

If students have trouble with the peer review process, try the following option.

Have partners exchange stories or articles they have written. Each student should review the other's work. Afterward, partners can go over their questions and comments together.

Students whose work is being reviewed should ask questions that clarify and focus the partner's comments.

Step-by-Step Teaching Guide

Editing and Proofreading

1. Explain to students that no one enjoys reading a piece of writing that contains errors in grammar, usage, and mechanics. Such errors can seriously detract from a writer's credibility.
2. Review with students the categories they should focus on as they proofread their work.
3. Students who write on word processors probably rely on spell check. Remind them that spell-checkers can catch only misspelled words. Write the following sentence on the board, as an example of a sentence that spell check will think is perfect.

   They're was a paws in the TV show, sew I went two the kitchen to get eyes cream.
4. Encourage students to read their final drafts after they run the spell check.

Customize for *ESL Students*

Students learning English can work with more fluent partners for the proofreading process. They can work together on grammar and spelling problems.

2.4 What Are Editing and Proofreading?

All forms of writing—from a letter to a friend to a research paper—are more effective when they are error-free. Once you are satisfied with the content of your writing, polish the grammar, usage, and mechanics.

Learn More

For extensive instruction on grammar, usage, and mechanics issues that affect your writing, see Chapters 14–27.

Focusing on Proofreading

Challenge yourself to learn and apply the skills of proofreading to everything you write. While the writing chapters in this book offer a specific focus to help you develop these skills, review your writing carefully to find and correct all errors. These are the broad categories that should direct your proofreading work:

Check Your Spelling Check every word in your draft and consult a dictionary to confirm any spelling of which you are unsure. Be especially mindful of the presentation of the names of people, places, and organizations.

Check Your Grammar and Usage Use a dictionary and a usage handbook to correct problems in language and grammatical structures. For example, review subject-verb agreement, check that you have not included sentence fragments unintentionally, and confirm the usage of such problem word pairs as *further* and *farther, accept* and *except,* and *can* and *may.*

Review Capitalization and Punctuation Review your draft to be sure you've begun each sentence with a capital letter and used proper end punctuation.

Double-Check the Facts When your writing includes facts gathered from outside sources or makes claims that you believe are true, take the time to confirm the accuracy of your work. Consult reference material to double-check these items:

- names
- dates
- statistics
- direct quotations

APPLYING THE EDITING AND PROOFREADING STRATEGIES

To focus your proofreading on the types of errors you make, start a list of the mistakes you often make. Compare your list with that of a partner, and discuss techniques for finding and correcting these errors. Keep the list in your portfolio, and use it to guide your proofreading this year.

TIME AND RESOURCE MANAGER

In-Depth Coverage	Accelerated Pace
• Cover pp. 22–23 in class. • Have students apply the Editing and Proofreading and Publishing and Presenting strategies.	• Assign pp. 22–23 for independent student reading. • Have students apply the Editing and Proofreading and Publishing and Presenting strategies.

2.5 What Are Publishing and Presenting?

Moving Forward

This chapter has provided you with an introduction to the techniques and strategies you can use at every stage of the writing process. Each of the writing chapters in this book will teach you specific strategies to help you write in the mode or type of writing discussed. Take note of the ones that are especially effective for you, and apply them to other writing you complete.

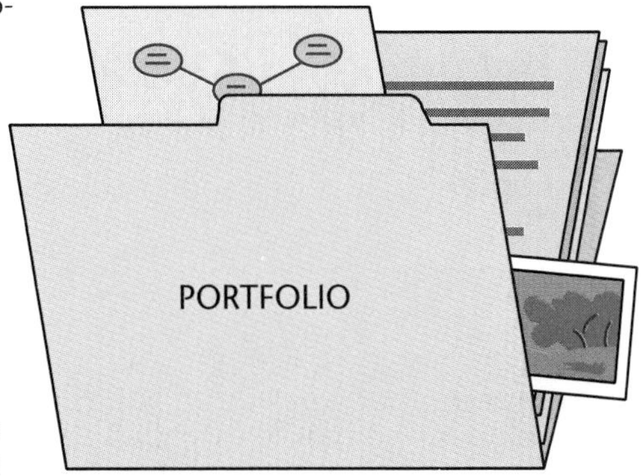

Building Your Portfolio Keep your finished writing products in an organized container, such as a folder, a binder, or a box. This portfolio can help you see your progress as a writer. In addition to the final drafts you keep, you may also want to use your portfolio as a place to store drafts, save peer review notes, and keep ideas for future writing projects.

Reflecting on Your Writing To help yourself become a better writer, take the time to learn from each of your writing experiences. In each writing chapter, a *Reflecting on Your Writing* feature provides questions to encourage you to think about your writing process.

Assessing Your Writing All writing should meet standards of clarity; however, each type of writing should also meet requirements unique to its form. For example, descriptive writing should convey a central image, but a narrative should tell a story. Use the *Rubric for Self-Assessment* in each writing chapter to be sure that you address the key features of each writing form you create.

APPLYING THE PUBLISHING AND PRESENTING STRATEGIES

1. The activities you completed during this chapter may serve as inspirations for later writing. Choose one prewriting activity, and save it in your portfolio. Discuss with a partner why you chose the activity you did.
2. To begin reflecting on your writing process, jot down a response to one of the following questions. Add your reflection to your portfolio.
   - Which of the revision strategies or activities did you find most useful? Why?
   - What are your strengths as a writer?

Step-by-Step Teaching Guide

Publishing and Presenting

1. Remind students to date all the written work that goes into their portfolios. This way they will be able to observe their progress.
2. Students should take self-assessment seriously. Urge them to reread their own work as objectively as possible, thinking about its best qualities and also noting ways it might be improved.
3. Discuss any options your school or community provides for the publication of outstanding student work, such as a school literary magazine, the school newspaper, the yearbook, national young-adult magazines, and the Internet. If any students are eager to publish their work, give them any help they need.

PRENTICE HALL
Everyday Spelling

If you have taught the spelling skills in *Prentice Hall Everyday Spelling,* Grade 8, Chapter 2, in conjunction with this *Writing and Grammar* chapter, review and assess students' mastery of the skills before concluding the chapter.

STANDARDIZED TEST PREPARATION WORKSHOP

Editing and Proofreading Standardized tests frequently measure students' ability to identify errors in grammar, usage, and mechanics in a given passage. Share the following sample test item with students:

Choose the letter of the type of error in the underlined portion of the following passage. If there is no error, choose "No error."

Many people believe that physical exercise not only provides benifits to the body, but also to the mind.

A Spelling error
B Capitalization error
C Punctuation error
D No error

The correct choice is item **A**. *Benefits* is the correct spelling.

Lesson Objectives

1. To analyze the process that leads to the creation of works of art.
2. To make connections between a variety of artistic works and sources of information.
3. To write a journal entry based on multimedia research.

Step-by-Step Teaching Guide

Recognizing Connections Among the Arts

1. Choose one of the Spotlight elements for class discussion, or have students work individually or in groups on the element of their choice. Give students the opportunity to find the necessary books, videotapes, or pictures.
2. Explain to students that finding connections among the arts is a way to expand their knowledge and pursue their own interests. Ask them, for example, if they have ever watched a movie or play that led them to want to find out more about a particular subject. Tell them that becoming conscious of their own reactions and questions while enjoying a work of art will help them seek out such connections.
3. Point out that *Hello, Dolly!* is a musical whose history brings together the work of a great writer, a jazz legend, and the careers of at least two major female musical theater performers, Pearl Bailey and Carol Channing.

Spotlight on the Humanities

Recognizing Connections Among the Arts

Focus on Theater: *Hello, Dolly!*

When you draft a story or an essay, you revise or fine-tune your draft until it meets your expectations. Similarly, in the theater, actors study and rehearse their roles until they are ready for opening night. From 1964 to 1971, the Broadway musical *Hello, Dolly!* ran for 2,844 performances, making it one of Broadway's longest-running shows. Starring Carol Channing in the role of Dolly Levi, the musical won ten Tony Awards, including Best Musical and Best Leading Actress. With music and lyrics by Jerry Herman and book by Michael Stewart, the play is based on the Thornton Wilder play *The Matchmaker.* Set in 1880, both shows tell the story of matchmaker Dolly Levi, who, in trying to find romantic matches for others, finds true love herself.

▲ **Critical Viewing** Which details of Carol Channing's costume help develop the 1880's setting? **[Interpret]**

Music Connection The 1967 Broadway production of *Hello, Dolly!* starred Pearl Bailey (1918–1990) and the legendary jazz singer and bandleader Cab Calloway (1907–1994). In 1930, Calloway's swing band caught the eye of the owner of the prestigious Cotton Club in New York City's Harlem, and they were hired to replace Duke Ellington's renowned band. By the late 1930's, Calloway had one of the top jazz bands in the world. In 1931, Calloway's famous signature song, "Minnie the Moocher," sold over one million copies.

Literature Connection In addition to the play that inspired *Hello, Dolly!*, Thornton Wilder (1897–1975) compiled a portfolio of work that would become classic, winning Pulitzer Prizes for his plays *Our Town* (1938) and *The Skin of Our Teeth* (1942), as well as for his novel *The Bridge of San Luis Rey* (1927).

Writing Process Activity: Using Movies to Spark Ideas

If possible, watch the film version of *Hello, Dolly!* starring Barbra Streisand. As you watch, jot down several writing ideas that the movie inspires. For example, you may want to learn more about an actor, an actress, or the time period depicted, or you may find another inspiration in the work. Save this list in your portfolio for later development.

Viewing and Representing

Activity Encourage students to take notes as they watch the movie. Tell them that these notes can record their own reactions, questions, confusions, and other thoughts. Point out that visual artists often draw sketches in their journals to remind them of an image or an idea. Tell them that they can take visual notes in this way as well.

Critical Viewing

Interpret Students may note particular details of Carol Channing's costume, such as her oversized hat, long, elaborate dress, and upswept hairstyle. Ask them about clothing styles of the past and the periods when they were current.

Media and Technology Skills

Using Technology for Aspects of the Writing Process

Activity: Setting Up Your Portfolio

When you write using a computer and a printer, you can revise your drafts, see your changes clearly, and keep copies of all stages of your writing process. In addition to helping you create a tracking system of your works in progress, an electronic portfolio can store copies of your writing in several subject areas. When you review the works you have completed, you can evaluate your progress as a writer. Consider building and maintaining an electronic portfolio.

Learn About It Most computer operating systems, or platforms, make the storage and organization of files simple. The first level of organization is the desktop, which holds folders that the user names. Within each of these folders, a series of subfolders allows users to devise systematized filing plans. For example, a folder labeled "Writing Projects, September–June" might contain all of the writing work you do in a school year.

Structure It Create a directory structure to help you find your work quickly. For example, for every project you undertake, make a folder to hold all the related work. Look at this example:

Name	Date Modified
▽ 10/15—Science-fiction story	Oct 15
a–prewriting notes	Oct 5
b–first draft	Oct 8
c–revision	Oct 9
d–final draft	Oct 14
e–reflection	Oct 15
▷ 11/11—comparing radio stations	Nov 11
▷ 01/02—student council notes	Jan 2

Maintain It As you use your portfolio, you may choose to make revisions to the system you've developed. For example, you might decide to place early drafts in a separate folder or to create a separate file for all your writing ideas. To keep the system efficient, devote some time each month to cleaning it up.

Computer Tips

- Use the SAVE AS function to generate revised drafts. For example, if your first file is "biography," name the first revision "biography2" and the next one "biography3".
- If you share your computer with others, keep your files separate by using appropriately labeled desktop folders.
- If you store your portfolio on a hard drive, regularly back it up on a floppy disk. Then, protect these disks by keeping them away from heat and magnetic sources.
- Label disks clearly. Use felt-tip pens to write on floppy disks.

Lesson Objectives

1. To become proficient at navigating and creating organization within a variety of technology resources.
2. To evaluate the effectiveness and organization of technology resources.
3. To use writing processes to develop and revise drafts.

Step-by-Step Teaching Guide

Using Technology for Aspects of the Writing Process

Teaching Resources: Writing Support Transparency 2-G

1. Ask students how they think writers developed manuscripts before the widespread use of computers. Explain to or elicit from students that writers worked by hand or on a typewriter, which meant that making changes could be a laborious process.
2. Have a class discussion about the advantages and disadvantages of being a writer before and after the advent of personal computers. Discuss such issues as revising, editing, and proofreading documents, as well as storing, saving, and transporting them.
3. Ask students how they store their own work at home or at school. Have student volunteers share their approach to using and creating directories. Point out that people develop different systems for naming and storing files.
4. Explain to students that they should become familiar with the ways in which the programs they're using store files, so that they can develop simple, efficient systems that work well within those programs.

Lesson Objectives

1. To use writing processes to develop and revise drafts.
2. To use prewriting strategies to generate ideas.
3. To organize and present information to ensure support for ideas.
4. To develop writing by categorizing ideas and using effective transitions.

Step-by-Step Teaching Guide

Using the Writing Process to Address Writing Prompts

Teaching Resources: Standardized Test Preparation Workbook, pp. 3–4

1. Emphasize to students that the basic steps of the writing process still apply, even when they are under the strict limitations of a standardized test. Review the importance of prewriting, drafting, revising, editing, and proofreading.
2. Point out that during standardized tests, they may have to combine or blur the lines between several stages of the writing process. Drafting and revision, for example, often occur simultaneously when a writer responds to a writing prompt on a standardized test.
3. Explain that prewriting techniques, such as outlining and using charts that help writers organize their ideas, are especially important because students usually won't have time to write second drafts. Tell them that having a clear idea about what they want to say in each section of their essay will focus and strengthen the one draft they develop during the test.
4. Reassure students that while neatness counts, examiners understand that time constraints prevent most standardized tests of this kind from being perfect finished products. Emphasize, however, that following the rules of grammar, punctuation, and spelling will make their writing clearer for their audience.

Standardized Test Preparation Workshop

Using the Writing Process to Address Writing Prompts

Using the writing process helps writers create well-organized, interesting, and coherent works. When responding to a test prompt for a standardized test, you can use a time-limited version of the writing process to construct an effective response. You will be evaluated on your ability to do the following:

- choose a logical, consistent organization
- elaborate with the appropriate amount of detail for your specific audience and purpose
- use appropriate transitions so ideas flow together coherently
- use complete sentences
- use correct spelling and grammar

Following is an example of one type of writing prompt that you might find on a standardized test.

Use the suggestions on the following page to help you respond. The clocks next to each stage show a suggested plan for organizing your time.

Test Tip

When you want to be persuasive, logic is of the utmost importance. Unless your argument makes sense, you will have no basis for persuasion.

Sample Test Item

In some schools, both in the United States and abroad, boys and girls are educated in separate classes. Some educators and parents believe that children will learn more and be less distracted in a boys- or girls-only classroom. Do you agree or disagree with this? Choose a side. Then, write a speech defending your stance to be presented to the local Board of Education. Use facts, details, examples, or personal experience to support your position.

TEST-TAKING TIP

Tell students that one of the most common errors people make when responding to writing prompts on standardized tests is that they start writing immediately, without organizing their ideas and opinions. Point out that the sample writing prompt above might provoke strong reactions in people taking the test. Convinced that they should simply follow the flow of their thoughts and opinions, writers might write themselves into a corner. Point out that they can usually ask for scratch paper or use one part of their test booklet to outline or organize their thoughts. Explain that listing out all of their supporting facts, details, and examples ahead of time will give them a better sense of how their essay will be structured and how it will conclude.

Prewriting

Allow one fourth of your time for prewriting.

Consider the Issue Before you dive into writing, take the time to think about the issue. Jot down several ideas that separate schools inspire. Note the positive and negative aspects of such an educational system. Then, review your notes to decide what your position will be.

Understand the Opposing View Once you decide where you stand on separate classes for males and females, try to understand why someone would believe the opposite. Write down one or two of the strongest reasons for that side. Thinking about the arguments of the opposing view will help you determine how to strengthen your own position.

Draw an Outline Create an outline for the presentation of your argument. This will organize your ideas, identify areas of weakness, and serve as a rough sketch for your draft.

Drafting

Allow half your time for drafting.

Consider Your Audience While turning your outline and notes into your draft, keep in mind the audience you are trying to persuade. Since you will be addressing the Board of Education, you should use polite, formal language and avoid all use of slang.

Write an Attention-Grabbing Introduction Start off your speech with something that will make your audience immediately interested. For example, you might provide insight into your own personal experience or describe a scene at a school like the ones described in the prompt. Then, link your lead to your main idea and state your opinion clearly.

Provide Supporting Paragraphs Your body paragraphs should each develop a main sentence that supports your main idea. Include details, anecdotes, or examples to elaborate your position. Be sure to use persuasive language that will make your argument more effective.

Revising, Editing, and Proofreading

Allow one fourth of your time for revising, editing, and proofreading.

If Possible, Take a Short Break Close your eyes for just a minute. Then, look back at your speech. A quick break will help you take a fresh look at your words and allow you to see your writing more clearly. Read your draft and decide whether it offers convincing evidence to support your position. Wherever possible, add more details, stronger words, or transitional sentences to make your speech more persuasive.

Proofread Your Essay Use the last few minutes to check your writing for errors in spelling, grammar, and punctuation. Add words or phrases neatly in the space above the text, using a caret (^) to indicate exact placement.

Customize for *ESL Students*

Students who speak English as a second language may get overwhelmed by the time constraints imposed by a standardized test. In addition, ESL students are often accustomed to checking and re-checking their work before handing it in because they are sometimes unsure of their writing skills. Encourage ESL students to choose a thesis statement about which they have strong thoughts and opinions. Emphasize the importance of selecting very specific supporting details. Explain that supporting one or two points clearly is better than presenting many all at once, hoping one of them sounds correct.

Chapter 3

Time and Resource Manager

In-Depth Lesson Plan

	LESSON FOCUS	PRINT AND MEDIA RESOURCES
DAY 1	**Sentence Combining; Writing Effective Paragraphs** Students practice sentence combining and build unified, coherent paragraphs from main ideas, topic sentences, and supporting sentences (pp. 28–38).	**Teaching Resources** *Writing Support Transparencies,* 3-A ***Writing and Grammar iText* (Interactive Text),** Ch. 3, Introduction through Section 3.1; Section 21.2
DAY 2	**Paragraphs in Essays and Other Compositions** Students are introduced to the parts of a composition and the different functions of paragraphs (pp. 39–41).	**Teaching Resources** *Writing Support Transparencies,* 3-B ***Writing and Grammar iText* (Interactive Text),** Section 3.2
DAY 3	**Writing Style** Students work with various aspects of style, including tone and diction (pp. 42–43).	***Writing and Grammar iText* (Interactive Text),** Section 3.3

Accelerated Lesson Plan

	LESSON FOCUS	PRINT AND MEDIA RESOURCES
DAY 1	**Sentence Combining; Writing Effective Paragraphs** Students practice sentence combining for sentence variety and review characteristics of effective paragraphs (pp. 28–38).	**Teaching Resources** *Writing Support Transparencies,* 3-A ***Writing and Grammar iText* (Interactive Text),** Ch. 3, Introduction through Section 3.1; Section 21.2
DAY 2	**Writing Effective Compositions; Writing Style** Students review characteristics of effective compositions, concentrating on structure and style (pp. 39–43).	**Teaching Resources** *Writing Support Transparencies,* 3-B ***Writing and Grammar iText* (Interactive Text),** Sections 3.2–3

Options for Adapting Lesson Plans

HOMEWORK

Have students complete any stage of the lesson for homework.

SPELLING

To teach spelling skills in conjunction with writing skills, work through *Prentice Hall Everyday Spelling,* Grade 8, Chapter 3, as you cover this *Writing and Grammar* chapter.

FEATURES

Extend coverage with Spotlight on the Humanities (p. 44), Media and Technology Skills (p. 45), and Standardized Test Preparation Workshop (p. 46).

TECHNOLOGY

Students can complete any stage of the lesson on the computer, using *Writing and Grammar iText* or a word-processing program. Have them print out their completed work.

INTEGRATED SKILLS COVERAGE

Viewing and Representing
Critical Viewing, SE pp. 28, 30, 31, 35, 37, 43, 44
Analyzing Composition, SE p. 44
ATE p. 44

Speaking and Listening
Formal/Informal English, ATE p. 43

Real-World Connection
ATE p. 38

ASSESSMENT SUPPORT

Standardized Test Preparation Workshop SE pp. 46–47; ATE p. 40

Standardized Test Preparation Workbook, pp. 5–6

Writing Assessment and Portfolio Management

MEETING INDIVIDUAL NEEDS

Less Advanced Students ATE p. 47. See also Ongoing Assessments ATE pp. 34, 37, 41.

ESL Students ATE pp. 40, 47

More Advanced Students ATE pp. 42, 45

BLOCK SCHEDULING

Pacing Suggestions
For 90-minute Blocks
- Have students complete the chapter in a single period.

Professional Development Support
- ***How to Manage Instruction in the Block*** This teaching resource provides management and activity suggestions.

MEDIA AND TECHNOLOGY

For the Student
- ***Writing and Grammar iText*** **(Interactive Text),** Ch.3; Section 21.2

WRITING AND GRAMMAR ON-LINE

iText Interactive Text (On-line or on CD-ROM)
- Easily navigable instruction with interactive Revision Checkers
- Full use of e-rater™, the essay-scoring system (on-line only)

Companion Web Site PHSchool.com
- Scoring rubrics with models (use Web Code eck-8001)

See the Go On-line! feature, SE p. iii.

CHAPTER 3
SENTENCES, PARAGRAPHS, AND COMPOSITIONS

Lesson Objectives

1. To practice sentence-combining skills to achieve smooth and varied sentence style.
2. To organize paragraphs.
3. To write effective topic sentences.
4. To write effective supporting sentences.
5. To maintain the unity of a paragraph.
6. To create coherence within a paragraph.
7. To write different types of paragraphs.
8. To use formal and informal English where appropriate.

Critical Viewing

Analyze Students may say that the people are using construction skills. Like the skills needed to "build" a paragraph or composition, construction skills involve an ability to put together the right materials in the right way to achieve the best result.

Chapter 3

Sentences, Paragraphs, and Compositions

Structure and Style

▲ Critical Viewing What skills are the people in this picture using? Compare the skills they are using to the skills needed to "build" a paragraph or composition. **[Analyze]**

What Are Sentences, Paragraphs, and Compositions?

Like houses, sentences, paragraphs, and compositions are built from pieces that are planned, that fit together logically, and that provide solid support. A **sentence** is a group of words with a subject and a predicate that expresses a complete thought. A **paragraph** is a group of sentences that function as a unit to express a single focus or point. A **composition** is a group of paragraphs that are logically arranged to develop and support a single main idea. Each sentence supports the topic of the paragraph. Each paragraph contributes to the main idea of the composition.

TIME AND RESOURCE MANAGER

Resources
Technology: Writing and Grammar iText, Section 21.2

In-Depth Coverage	Accelerated Pace
• Cover pp. 28–32 in class. • Have students complete Exercises 1–4 in class. Work through the first two items in each exercise with the class as a group.	• Assign pp. 28–32 for independent student review. • Assign Exercises 1–4 for homework.

3.1 Sentence Combining

Controlling Your Sentences

You use sentences every day—to ask questions, make statements, express emotion, or share information. In order to hold your reader's interest in your writing, it is necessary to vary your sentence structure. Too many short sentences may make your writing choppy and disconnected. One way to avoid the excessive use of short sentences is to combine sentences—to express two or more related ideas or pieces of information in a single sentence.

Inserting Words and Phrases

Sentences may be combined by changing one of them into a phrase that adds information to the other. (In some cases, the information may be added with the insertion of just one word.) Sometimes, you may have to change the form of words and use additional punctuation.

EXAMPLE: In 1848, gold was discovered at Sutter's Mill in California. James Marshall found the gold.

COMBINED: In 1848, gold was discovered **by James Marshall** at Sutter's Mill in California.

EXAMPLE: San Francisco grew from a village to a city as a result of the Gold Rush. San Francisco was the port closest to Sutter's Mill.

COMBINED: San Francisco**, the port closest to Sutter's Mill,** grew from a village to a city as a result of the Gold Rush.

Exercise 1 **Combining With Words and Phrases** Combine each pair of sentences by inserting key information from one sentence into the other. Add commas as necessary.

1. More than 80,000 people rushed to California in 1849. They were known as *forty-niners*.
2. Some early miners were able to dig for gold with a knife. The gold was near the surface.
3. Some miners made fortunes in a few weeks. They were lucky.
4. Miners came from the United States, Mexico, and Canada. They traveled overland or by sea.
5. Sacramento became a mining center in 1849. Sacramento is now the capital of California.

Answer Key

Exercise 1

Possible answers:

1. More than 80,000 people, known as *forty-niners,* rushed to California in 1849.
2. Some early miners were able to dig for gold near the surface with a knife.
3. Some lucky miners made fortunes in a few weeks.
4. Miners traveled overland or by sea from the United States, Mexico, and Canada.
5. Sacramento, now the capital of California, became a mining center in 1849.

PREPARE and ENGAGE

Interest GRABBER Bring in one book written for beginning readers, one book for third- or fourth-grade readers, and one book for young-adult readers. On the board, write down a sentence or two from each book that show the different sentence structures used, demonstrating the predominance of simple sentences in the beginners' book and the varied sentence structure in the young-adult book. Tell students that writers who write for older, more sophisticated readers vary their sentence structure to create smoother, more interesting reading.

Activate Prior Knowledge

Write the following sentence:

She sang Spanish songs about love.

Have students identify the modifiers in the sentence. (*Spanish*—adjective, modifies *songs; about love*—prepositional phrase, modifies *songs)* Tell students that both the adjective *Spanish* and the prepositional phrase *about love* answer the question *what kind of songs?* By taking modifiers from one sentence and adding them to another, writers can combine sentences.

TEACH

Step-by-Step Teaching Guide

Inserting Words and Phrases

1. On the board, write the uncombined sentences in the first example on the page, explaining that they give information about *how* and *where* gold was discovered.
2. Underscore the name *James Marshall* in the second sentence. Explain that the underscored information can be made into a phrase and added to the first sentence. Write the combined sentence as shown:

   In 1848, gold was discovered by James Marshall at Sutter's Mill in California.
3. Go over the second example in the same way. Have students read the combined sentence aloud. Discuss why the combined sentences are better. (They flow smoothly; they hold the reader's interest.)

Step-by-Step Teaching Guide

Using Compound Subjects, Verbs, and Objects

1. Explain to students that a compound subject is two or more subjects that have the same verb and are joined by the conjunction *and* or *or*. Then, write the following sentences on the board:

   Denise wants to go for a walk.

   Ralph wants to go for a walk.

2. Explain to students that these sentences may be combined using a compound subject. Write the combined sentence on the board, underlining the compound subject.

   Ralph and Denise want to go for a walk.

3. Explain that verbs and objects can be combined as well. Write the following sentences on the board and have students identify the compound verbs and the compound objects:

   The boys ate lunch and swam in the river. (compound verb: *ate and swam*)

   Jessica sings and plays the piano. (compound verb: *sings and plays*)

   Rudy plays football and basketball. (compound object: *football and basketball*)

Critical Viewing

Possible response: The miners and their dog find gold in the stream.

Answer Key

Exercise 2

Possible answers:

1. The miners needed food and housing.
2. Sam Brannan bought all the carpet tacks in California and sold them for huge amounts of money to the miners.
3. Samuel Clemens came to California during the Gold Rush and wrote for the *San Francisco Call.*
4. Samuel Clemens, who wrote under the name Mark Twain, and his boss at the *Call,* Bret Harte, became famous authors.
5. During the Gold Rush, Levi Strauss and John Studebaker started businesses that later had nationwide success.

3.1

Using Compound Subjects, Verbs, and Objects

Two or more short sentences may have elements in common—they may have the same subject, verb, or object. Such sentences may be combined into a single sentence that uses a compound subject, a compound verb, or a compound object.

COMMON VERB AND OBJECT:	Trading ships spread the news of the gold strike in California. Newspapers spread the news of the gold strike, too.
COMPOUND SUBJECT:	**Trading ships and newspapers** spread the news of the gold strike in California.
COMMON SUBJECT:	People walked to the gold fields. People rode in covered wagons to the gold fields. People traveled by ship to the gold fields.
COMPOUND VERB:	People **walked, rode** in covered wagons, or **traveled** by ship to the gold fields.
COMMON SUBJECT AND VERB:	The forty-niners discovered hardships in California. They also discovered disease and loneliness.
COMPOUND OBJECT:	The forty-niners discovered **hardships, disease,** and **loneliness** in California.

Learn More

For additional information about compound subjects and verbs, see Section 19.3.

Exercise 2 **Using Compound Subjects, Verbs, and Objects**

Combine each pair of sentences by creating compound subjects, compound verbs, or compound objects.

1. The miners needed food. They also needed housing.
2. Sam Brannan bought all the carpet tacks in California. He sold them for huge amounts of money to the miners.
3. Samuel Clemens came to California during the Gold Rush. He wrote for the *San Francisco Call.*
4. Samuel Clemens, who wrote under the name Mark Twain, became a famous author. His boss at the *Call,* Bret Harte, became a famous author, too.
5. During the Gold Rush, Levi Strauss started a business that later had nationwide success. During the Gold Rush, John Studebaker also started a business that later had nationwide success.

Critical Viewing ▼ Using a compound subject, write a sentence that describes this picture. **[Apply]**

ONGOING ASSESSMENT: Monitor and Reinforce

Use one of the following options to diagnose students' current level of proficiency in combining sentences.

Option 1 Have students review recent written work and identify any passages that are repetitive or lacking sentence variety. Have them revise these passages. Then, hold conferences with individual students, reviewing the passages they have revised. Prepare to give extra help to students who have difficulty with the assignment.	**Option 2** Ask students to write a brief paragraph about a character in a story or movie whom they find inspiring or intriguing. Have them then revise their paragraphs to ensure that they have used both short and long sentences. Plan extra help for students whose revised paragraphs are repetitive, unclear, or lacking in sentence variety.

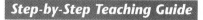

Forming Compound Sentences

You can combine two sentences by rewriting each as an independent clause in a **compound sentence.** An **independent clause** is a group of words that contains a subject and verb and can stand on its own. Independent clauses may be combined by using a comma and a coordinating conjunction such as *and, but, or,* or *nor* or by using a semicolon.

EXAMPLE: Georgia became a state in 1788. Atlanta became the capital in 1868.

COMPOUND SENTENCE: Georgia became a state in 1788, **and** Atlanta became the capital in 1868.

EXAMPLE: New York is called the Empire State. Georgia is called the Empire State of the South.

COMPOUND SENTENCE: New York is called the Empire State**;** Georgia is called the Empire State of the South.

Note that each conjunction expresses a different relationship between ideas. For example, *and* indicates similarity or addition, *but* indicates contrast, and *or* indicates an alternative.

Exercise 3 **Forming Compound Sentences** Combine each pair of sentences in a compound sentence by using a comma and a coordinating conjunction or by using a semicolon.

1. The Okefenokee Swamp is located in southeastern Georgia. It covers 700 square miles.
2. In 1540, Hernando de Soto led a group of explorers through Georgia in search of gold. They did not find any.
3. In colonial times, England and Spain could not peacefully settle their disagreements about the border between Georgia and Florida. They went to war.
4. Georgia was the last of the original thirteen colonies founded. It became the fourth state in 1788.
5. Settlers were eager to move into Georgia's western regions. Land companies were eager to sell them land there.
6. In the 1795 Yazoo Fraud, land companies used bribery to gain lands from the state. The outraged citizens of Georgia voted to stop them.
7. Northern Georgia was the site of a gold rush that began in 1828. This gold rush was not as extensive as the one in California in 1849.
8. Much of the gold was located on Cherokee land. The government forced the relocation of the Cherokees soon after the discovery.
9. In the 1800's, cotton was the state's main product. In the 1870's, industry in the state began to grow.
10. I might write my paper about Georgia in colonial times. I might change my mind and write about Georgia after the Revolutionary War.

Learn More

For additional information about compound sentences, see Section 20.2

▼ Critical Viewing
Write a compound sentence describing how a gold seeker might have reacted to nuggets in his or her pan, such as those shown. **[Speculate]**

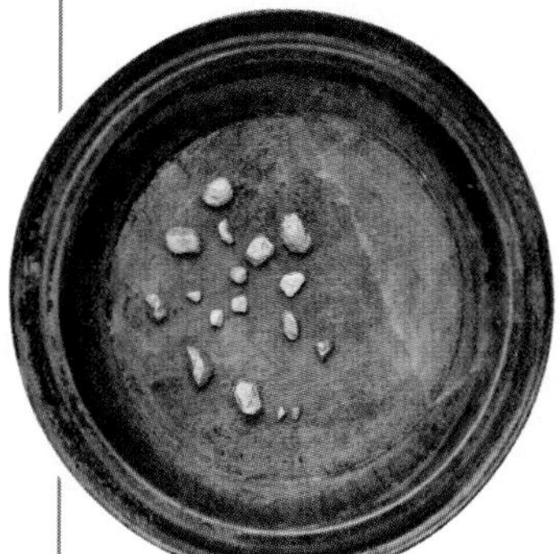

Step-by-Step Teaching Guide

Forming Compound Sentences

1. Explain to students that two independent clauses that are related can be combined to form a compound sentence. Write the following sentences on the board:

   The snow came down steadily.

   The roads became slippery.

2. Then, write the combined sentence on the board and underscore the comma and the conjunction:

   The snow came down steadily, and the roads became slippery.

   Point out to students that a comma always comes before the coordinating conjunction joining clauses in a compound sentence.

3. Explain to students that the two sentences could also have been joined with a semicolon. Write the compound sentence on the board:

   The snow came down steadily; the roads became slippery.

4. Emphasize that a semicolon is correct only when there is a close relationship between the clauses.

Critical Viewing

Speculate Sample response: He tilted the pan into the sun, and he gave a whoop of joy.

Customize for *More Advanced Students*

Give more advanced students a copy of a brief article from a newspaper or magazine. Ask them to identify compound sentences.

Answer Key

Exercise 3

Possible answers:

1. The Okefenokee Swamp is located in southeastern Georgia; it covers 700 square miles.
2. In 1540, Hernando de Soto led a group of explorers through Georgia in search of gold, but they did not find any.
3. In colonial times, England and Spain could not peacefully settle their disagreements about the border between Georgia and Florida, so they went to war.

Answer Key continued

4. Georgia was the last of the original thirteen colonies founded, but it became the fourth state in 1788.
5. Settlers were eager to move into Georgia's western regions; land companies were eager to sell them land there.
6. In the 1795 Yazoo Fraud, land companies used bribery to gain lands from the state, but the outraged citizens of Georgia voted to stop them.
7. Northern Georgia was the site of a gold rush that began in 1828, but this gold rush was not as extensive as the one in California in 1849.
8. Much of the gold was located on Cherokee land, and the government forced the relocation of the Cherokees soon after the discovery.
9. In the 1800's, cotton was the state's main product, but in the 1870's, industry in the state began to grow.
10. I might write my paper about Georgia in colonial times, or I might change my mind and write about Georgia after the Revolutionary War.

Step-by-Step Teaching Guide

Using Subordination

1. Write the following subordinate clause on the board:

   (S) (V)

   If the weather clears

   Point out the subject and the verb. Then, ask students if the clause expresses a complete thought. (no) Explain that a subordinate clause has a subject and verb but, unlike an independent clause, does not express a complete thought.
2. Have students give you suggestions for using the clause in a complete sentence. (Possible response: *If the weather clears, we will go swimming.)*
3. Point out that when a subordinate clause begins a sentence, it is followed by a comma.
4. Explain to students that *If the weather clears* is an adverb clause because it answers the question *when?*
5. Explain that an adjective clause answers the questions *which one?* or *what kind?* Review the example in the text with students. The adjective clause *whose full name is James Earl Carter, Jr.* helps to answer the question *which Jimmy Carter?*

Answer Key

Exercise 4

Possible answers:

1. Jimmy Carter, who became governor of Georgia in 1971, was born in Plains, Georgia, in 1924.
2. When he was five years old, Jimmy Carter sold boiled peanuts to passers-by in Plains, Georgia.
3. In 1942, Jimmy Carter was appointed to the Naval Academy at Annapolis, which he entered in 1943.
4. In 1946, Jimmy Carter married Rosalynn Smith, who was his sister's best friend.
5. After leaving the presidency in 1981, Jimmy Carter received the Nobel Peace Prize in 2002.

3.1

Using Subordination

You can combine two sentences by rewriting one as a subordinate clause and adding it to the other. A **subordinate clause** is a group of words that contains a subject and a verb but does not express a complete thought. One type of subordinate clause is an **adjective clause**—a subordinate clause that begins with *who, whom, whose, which,* or *that.*

EXAMPLE: Jimmy Carter was the thirty-ninth president of the United States. His full name is James Earl Carter, Jr.

COMBINED: Jimmy Carter, **whose full name is James Earl Carter, Jr.,** was the thirty-ninth president of the United States.

You can also combine two sentences by rewriting one as an **adverb clause**—a subordinate clause that begins with a subordinating conjunction such as *although, after, because,* or *until.*

EXAMPLE: Davy Crockett was against the removal of the Cherokees from Georgia. The Indian Removal Act of 1830 was passed.

COMBINED: ***Although* Davy Crockett was against the removal of the Cherokees from Georgia,** the Indian Removal Act of 1830 was passed.

This chart lists a few important subordinating conjunctions.

Time	Cause	Purpose	Condition
after	as	in order that	although
before	because	so that	provided that
until	unless	that	though
when			
while			

Exercise 4 **Combining by Using Clauses** Combine paired sentences by rewriting one as indicated in parentheses.

1. Jimmy Carter was born in Plains, Georgia, in 1924. In 1971, he became governor of Georgia. (adjective clause)
2. Jimmy Carter sold boiled peanuts to passers-by in Plains, Georgia. He was five years old at the time. (adverb clause)
3. In 1942, Jimmy Carter was appointed to the Naval Academy at Annapolis. He entered the Academy in 1943. (adjective clause)
4. Rosalynn Smith was Jimmy's sister's best friend. In 1946, Jimmy Carter married Rosalynn Smith. (adjective clause)
5. In 2002, Jimmy Carter received the Nobel Peace Prize. He left the presidency in 1981. (adverb clause)

Learn More

For additional information about adjective and adverb clauses, see Section 20.2.

ONGOING ASSESSMENT: Monitor and Reinforce

If students have difficulty understanding subordination, try the following option.

On the board, write the following sentence:

John will read the book.

Then, list several subordinating conjunctions: *after, although, because, before, if, when, where,* and *while.* Ask students to add information to the sentence using each of these conjunctions. Each student should write eight sentences, using a different subordinating conjunction in each. Then, have volunteers read their sentences aloud. Point out the subordinate clause in each sentence presented. Remind students that if their sentences begin with a subordinating clause, they should insert a comma following the clause.

3.2 Writing Effective Paragraphs

Main Idea and Topic Sentence

Many of the paragraphs that you will use in compositions are topical paragraphs. *Topical paragraphs* contain a **topic sentence,** a sentence that expresses the key point or main idea of the paragraph. The topic sentence is supported or developed by the facts, details, restatements, and explanations provided in the other sentences in the paragraph.

In some paragraphs, the **main idea** is directly stated. One sentence provides the main idea around which the other sentences are organized. Some paragraphs, however, may have an **implied main idea**—the sentences in the paragraph work together to suggest, without directly stating, the main idea of the paragraph.

WRITING MODELS

from The Trouble with Television
Robert MacNeil

It is difficult to escape the influence of television. If you fit the statistical averages, by the age of 20 you will have been exposed to at least 20,000 hours of television. You can add 10,000 hours for each decade you have lived after the age of 20. The only things Americans do more than watch television are work and sleep.

In this passage, the stated topic sentence is shown in blue italics. This sentence refers to the inescapable influence of television. The rest of the paragraph supports and illustrates the opening sentence.

from Harriet Tubman: Guide to Freedom
Ann Petry

They stumbled along behind her, half-dead for sleep, and she urged them on, though she was as tired and as discouraged as they were. She had never been in Canada but she kept painting wondrous word pictures of what it would be like. She managed to dispel their fear of pursuit, so that they would not become hysterical, panic-stricken. Then she had to bring some of the fear back, so that they would stay awake and keep walking though they drooped with sleep.

In this paragraph, all the sentences work together to support the implied main idea: Tubman must make the slaves feel afraid as well as encouraged. She must not let her group lose hope, and she must urge them on, despite her personal feelings.

PREPARE and ENGAGE

Interest GRABBER Write the following paragraph on the chalkboard and read it aloud with gusto:

When Bruno came to America from Italy, he was shocked—shocked!—to discover the weird toppings people put on pizza. Salsa, for goodness' sake, and cheddar cheese. But the worst was pineapple. Mamma mia!

Ask students what the paragraph is about and how they know. (Bruno's shock at American pizza toppings; the first sentence tells the topic.)

Activate Prior Knowledge

Ask students to use the paragraph in the Interest Grabber to define a paragraph. (It has a main idea and supporting details. It is about a single idea.)

Teaching from the Models

Have volunteers read aloud the literature excerpts on their own. Point out that both paragraphs share an important quality: Each is about only one main idea.

TIME AND RESOURCE MANAGER

In-Depth Coverage	Accelerated Pace
• Cover pp. 33 to 38 in class. • Read and discuss the Writing Models, p. 33. • Have students complete Exercises 5–11 in class.	• Assign pp. 33 to 38 for independent student review. • Assign Exercises 5–11 for homework.

Step-by-Step Teaching Guide

Writing a Topic Sentence

1. The topic is what a paragraph is mostly about. It is the main idea. The topic can be implied or directly stated, as in the writing models on the previous page. If a paragraph has an implied main idea, a reader can give it a topic sentence in his or her own words.
2. For homework, have each student find one paragraph from a book, magazine article, or anything else and bring it to class. Tell students to be sure their paragraphs are five or six sentences long. Have some volunteers read their paragraphs aloud. Have the class identify the topic sentences and put implied main ideas into words.

Answer Key

Exercise 5

The first sentence is the topic sentence.

Exercise 6

The implied main idea is that the writer enjoyed everything about being at the beach.

Exercise 7

Answers will vary. Samples are given.

1. It was the low point of the war.
2. This story has a wonderful main character.

3.2

Exercise 5 **Identifying a Stated Topic Sentence** Identify the stated topic sentence of the following paragraph.

In the 1920's, New York City's Harlem, which had a large African American population, was a vital social, political, and cultural center. Black artists, writers, and musicians came from all over. The writers wrote poetry and novels, the artists painted, and the musicians played music in Harlem's renowned theaters and clubs. Reminded of the Renaissance in Europe, people called this period the Harlem Renaissance.

Exercise 6 **Identifying an Implied Main Idea** Identify the implied topic sentence of the following paragraph.

I collapse on the towel and remain there, immobilized, like a beached whale. The warmth of the summer sand sinks into my bones. The gulls cry overhead. The sun beats down. The waves lap at the shore. I drift off into a peaceful, mindless slumber.

Writing a Topic Sentence

A topic sentence expresses the main point in a paragraph. As you plan your essay, you will already have some of your main points in mind. Other points may occur to you as you gather details. To write a topic sentence, consider the point you want to make and the details you have or will find. Then, write a single sentence that covers the details and expresses your point.

EXAMPLE:	The lake is icy cold. The shoreline is rocky. A strange film floats on the surface. Snapping turtles have been seen patrolling the murky water.
TOPIC SENTENCE:	The lake is unfit for swimming.

Exercise 7 **Writing Topic Sentences** Write a topic sentence for each group of sentences below.

1. Supplies were low, and the soldiers were discouraged. Although the snow had stopped, the temperature remained below freezing. Across the river was the enemy. As soon as the river froze, the enemy would attack.
2. Max, the main character in the story, always has a plan. No matter what goes wrong, he comes up with an idea for solving the problem. Sometimes, he makes clever gadgets; other times, he just has an idea that no one else has.

ONGOING ASSESSMENT: Monitor and Reinforce

If students have difficulty identifying and writing topic sentences, use one of the following options.

Option 1 Before they begin writing, have students ask themselves, "What do I want to say? How can I summarize my ideas in one sentence?" Have them write the sentence that answers the second question. It should serve as the topic sentence for the paragraph.

Option 2 Have students read paragraphs carefully, looking for the topic sentence or implied main idea. If students cannot identify it, have them ask themselves, "What is this paragraph mostly about?" The answer will be the main idea.

Writing Supporting Sentences

A topic sentence, whether stated or implied, contains a paragraph's main idea. The remaining sentences in the paragraph are called **supporting sentences.** They develop, explain, or illustrate the main idea or topic sentence.

You can use one or more of the following strategies to support or develop the main idea:

Use Facts Facts are statements that are provable. They support your main idea by offering proof.

TOPIC SENTENCE: Our soccer team will probably make it to this season's championship game.

SUPPORTING FACT: The team has won all of the games it played this season.

Use Statistics A statistic is a fact, usually stated with numbers.

TOPIC SENTENCE: Our soccer team will probably make it to this season's championship game.

SUPPORTING STATISTIC: The team's record so far is 8–0.

Use Examples, Illustrations, or Instances An example, illustration, or instance is a specific person, thing, or event that demonstrates a point.

TOPIC SENTENCE: Our soccer team will probably make it to this season's championship game.

ILLUSTRATION: The team has beaten all of its opponents, including the Wolverines, who hadn't lost a game in the three previous seasons.

Use Details Details are the specifics—the parts of the whole.

TOPIC SENTENCE: Our soccer team will probably make it to this season's championship game.

DETAIL: In last week's game, there were only seconds left in the final quarter when the striker scored the winning goal.

Exercise 8 **Writing Supporting Sentences** Write two supporting sentences for each of the following topic sentences. Use a variety of types of support.

1. Good nutrition is important for good health.
2. Hiking is a great way to exercise and to get in touch with nature.
3. Life is full of unexpected adventures.
4. Caring for a pet can be a rewarding experience.
5. Playing team sports teaches responsibility and cooperation.

▲ Critical Viewing In what way might this soccer player need support from teammates? **[Connect]**

Step-by-Step Teaching Guide

Writing Supporting Sentences

1. A support is something that holds something else up. Supporting details hold up the main idea and/or topic sentence. They keep a paragraph from collapsing into a jumble of pieces.
2. Give students a sample topic sentence, such as *The New York Yankees are the greatest team in baseball history.* Ask whether this is a statement of fact or an opinion. (opinion) Ask how a writer might convince readers that this opinion is valid. (by adding facts to support the claim) Write a few sentences, such as *The Yankees have won more than twice as many World Series as any other team,* on the board. Show students that the main idea plus the details equals the paragraph.

Critical Viewing

Connect Students may say that soccer is a game that involves team effort. No one player can win a game on his or her own.

Answer Key

Exercise 8

Answers will vary.

Step-by-Step Teaching Guide

Placing Your Topic Sentence

Teaching Resources: Writing Support Transparency 3-A

1. Most students instinctively make the first sentence of a paragraph the topic sentence. This keeps them focused on what they want to say. There is nothing wrong with this, but it is not the only way to organize a paragraph.
2. Go over the variations on the TRI pattern and point out the variety they allow. A paragraph might begin with an illustration and then make a generalization that serves as the paragraph's main idea.

Customize for *More Advanced Students*

Have students extend Exercise 8 on page 35 by writing a whole paragraph around each topic sentence. Remind students to use a variety of details. Challenge them to position the topic sentence of the five different paragraphs in different places.

Answer Key

Exercise 9

Topic sentence: "The key to a good pizza is the toppings." Arrangements will vary. Make sure students support their responses regarding the most effective arrangement with details.

3.2

Placing Your Topic Sentence

Often, the most effective placement for your topic sentence is at the beginning of a paragraph, where it introduces the subject of the paragraph. Sometimes, however, you may choose to place your topic sentence in the middle or at the end of a paragraph. You might place the topic sentence in the middle when you need to lead up to it or provide background. You might place the topic sentence at the end to create emphasis or to summarize the details you've provided.

Paragraph Patterns By identifying the function of different sentences within a paragraph, you can analyze the arrangement of sentences and choose the pattern that is most effective. One way to look at the paragraph pattern is through TRI (Topic, Restatement, Illustration). With these basic elements, you "construct" a paragraph.

TOPIC SENTENCE:	State your key idea.
RESTATEMENT:	Interpret your key idea—put it into other words.
ILLUSTRATION:	Support your key idea with an illustration or an example.

After you have identified the basic parts of your paragraph, try variations of the TRI pattern, such as TIR, TII, or ITR, until you are satisfied with the results.

T	It's fun to watch movies on a bleak and rainy weekend.
R	Comedies are especially entertaining and can brighten an otherwise dreary day.
I	Last Saturday it was pouring. We rented two hilarious videos and had a great time watching them with our friends Jake and Rebecca.

Exercise 9 **Placing a Topic Sentence** Arrange the following sentences in a paragraph. First, identify the topic sentence. Next, rearrange the sentences using the TRI pattern. Then, rearrange the sentences in a variation of TRI. Evaluate which arrangement is most effective.

A layer of cheese provides the foundation for a medley of olives, peppers, and onions. These ingredients turn pizza into pizzazz! They add color, texture, and taste to the pie. They turn dough and cheese into a smorgasbord of tasty treats. The key to a good pizza is the toppings.

Maintaining Unity and Coherence

Achieving Unity

A paragraph or composition has **unity** when all of its parts relate to the main idea. Every sentence supports, explains, or develops the main idea of the paragraph. Every paragraph supports or develops the main idea, or **thesis statement,** of the composition. Details that are not related to the main points can undermine the unity of your writing and should be deleted.

In the following paragraph, one sentence is marked for deletion because it interferes with the unity of the paragraph.

The ancient Romans were successful in gaining territory and building an empire for many reasons. First of all, the Romans had a fine military organization. More important, the government of Rome could adapt to new situations. ~~Ancient Roman ruins are fascinating~~. Probably the most important reason of all was that the Romans treated captured people fairly.

Exercise 10 **Revising for Unity** On a separate sheet of paper, copy the following paragraph. Mark for deletion any sentences that interfere with the unity of the paragraph.

Pompeii was an ancient Roman city founded in the eighth century B.C. The city was located less than one mile from Mount Vesuvius, a volcanic mountain. In A.D. 79, Mount Vesuvius erupted violently. Volcanic mountains exist throughout the world. The volcanic eruption showered Pompeii with hot ashes and stones. Pompeii was soon completely buried in ashes. Pompeii remained buried until 1748, when a peasant digging in a vineyard accidentally struck a wall of the city. Italian vineyards are known for their fine grapes. After the chance discovery, archaeologists began to excavate the city. Today, about one fourth of Pompeii is uncovered, and tourists can now walk the ancient streets.

▶ Critical Viewing What details from this ruin suggest that it was once part of a unified whole? **[Connect]**

ONGOING ASSESSMENT: Monitor and Reinforce

If students have trouble writing unified paragraphs, try the following strategy.

Have students trade first drafts with partners. Each student should highlight details that don't support the main idea of the paragraphs in which they appear. Partners can give specific reasons that a detail does not belong in a particular paragraph. They can help each other decide whether to move the details to new paragraphs or to eliminate them.

Step-by-Step Teaching Guide

Maintaining Unity and Coherence

1. Ask if students have ever objected "But that's not the point!" in a conversation. Irrelevant details are as frustrating and annoying in a paragraph as they are in an argument. The organizing rule for every paragraph is to stick to the point.
2. Details that do not fit in one paragraph may be relevant in another one. If a writer wants to develop a description or give readers certain information that does not support the main idea of one paragraph, he or she can move this information to a new paragraph. Making sure that all details are relevant is sometimes a matter of reorganizing rather than deleting.

Answer Key

Exercise 10

Pompeii was an ancient Roman city founded in the eighth century B.C. The city was located less than one mile from Mount Vesuvius, a volcanic mountain. In A.D. 79, Mount Vesuvius erupted violently. ~~Volcanic mountains exist throughout the world~~. The volcanic eruption showered Pompeii with hot ashes and stones. Pompeii was soon completely buried in ashes. Pompeii remained buried until 1748, when a peasant digging in a vineyard accidentally struck a wall of the city. ~~Italian vineyards are known for their fine grapes~~. After the chance discovery, archaeologists began to excavate the city. Today, about one fourth of Pompeii is uncovered, and tourists can now walk the ancient streets.

Critical Viewing

Connect Students may say that the columns suggest there was a larger structure.

Real-World Connection

When a playwright gives a character a lengthy speech, every line of the speech must support its main idea. In a play, every word and line is important, and there is no room for unnecessary or vague statements. Ask students how an audience would react to speeches full of irrelevant details and lacking in logical progression. (The audience would be confused; the play would be irritating and dull.)

Step-by-Step Teaching Guide

Establishing Coherence

1. Review the different types of organization with students and the corresponding transitional words and phrases they can use to signal the connections between ideas in their work.
2. Explain that transitions do not create connections between ideas. Instead, they help the reader anticipate and so better understand these connections. You might offer the following analogy: Two roads must be connected if a driver is to turn from one onto the other. A good road sign, however, helps the driver make the turn smoothly instead of passing it, slamming on the brakes, and backing up. Similarly, a transition in writing helps readers turn smoothly from one idea to the next.

3.2

Establishing Coherence

A paragraph or composition has **coherence** when the ideas are logically connected and the reader can see how one idea is related to another. To establish coherence, choose and maintain a *logical organization* and connect sentences and paragraphs with *transitional words and phrases.*

Organization	Transitional Words and Phrases	Common Purposes
Chronological	first, next, last, then, meanwhile, finally	Process explanations Narratives
Spatial	near, above, below, beyond, next to	Descriptions Directions
Comparison and Contrast	however, on the other hand, likewise, similarly	Comparison-and-contrast essays Evaluations
Cause and Effect	therefore, as a result, due to, because	Cause-and-effect essays Analyses

Exercise 11 **Revising for Coherence** On a separate sheet of paper, rewrite the following paragraph. Establish coherence by reorganizing details with one of the organizational patterns explained above. Use transitional words and phrases to show connections. Add details or make other changes as needed.

The English language contains many words that have been borrowed from other languages. Some words come from French, which had been influenced by the classical languages of Greek and Latin. French was the language of the rulers, so words like *government* and *legal* became part of the language used by the conquered Anglo-Saxons. Early American settlers borrowed some words from Native American languages to name things for which they had no names. In 1066, France invaded England. Modern scientists borrow directly from Latin or Greek to name new discoveries. Prefixes and suffixes that are used in English also come from Greek and Latin. Explorers of the fifteenth and sixteenth centuries who traveled from England to far-off places often incorporated words from the places they visited.

Answer Key

Exercise 11

Rewrites will vary. Sample is given.

The English language contains many words that have been borrowed from other languages. Explorers of the fifteenth and sixteenth centuries who traveled from England to far-off places often incorporated words from the places they visited. Early American settlers borrowed some words from Native

Answer Key continued

American languages to name things for which they had no names. Some words come from French, which had been influenced by the classical languages of Greek and Latin. In 1066, France invaded England. French was the language of the rulers, so words like *government* and *legal* became part of the language used by the conquered Anglo-Saxons. Modern scientists borrow directly from Latin or Greek to name new discoveries. Prefixes and suffixes that are used in English also come from Greek and Latin.

3.3 Paragraphs in Essays and Other Compositions

Understanding the Parts of a Composition

A **composition** is something that consists of—or is put together from—a number of parts. Musical compositions are made up of notes of music. Written compositions are made up of sentences and paragraphs that are organized in a logical order to develop a main idea or thesis. Most compositions have three basic parts, or sections.

Introduction

The **introduction** of a composition indicates the focus of the composition. This focus is expressed in a sentence called the **thesis statement**. The introduction usually serves the additional purpose of capturing readers' interest with a strong **lead.** This lead may take the form of a quotation that is related to the topic or a surprising statement that makes readers curious and eager to read more.

Body Paragraphs

The **body paragraphs** of a composition develop the thesis statement with supporting facts, details, and examples. The paragraphs in the body are organized in a logical order, such as time order, order of importance, or spatial order. The chart on the previous page shows some common methods of organization and the kinds of writing for which they are most often used.

Conclusion

The **conclusion**, as its name suggests, "wraps up," or closes, the composition. In this part of the composition, a few sentences sum up the thesis statement and the overall support. An effective conclusion ends memorably. A memorable ending might be a strong statement, an interesting quotation, or a call to action.

Exercise 12 **Planning a Composition** On a separate sheet of paper, outline the parts of a how-to essay on an activity or skill you know well. Write a lead that will make your readers want to try the activity. Identify the most logical organization for your body paragraphs. Then, select the information you will include in each body paragraph, and write preliminary topic sentences. Finally, decide how you will conclude in a memorable way.

Step-by-Step Teaching Guide

Understanding the Parts of a Composition

1. Explain to students that most compositions have the same basic structure.
2. After reviewing each of the three parts, have students discuss why they think the parts occur in the order they do. How would changing the order affect someone's comprehension of the composition?

Exercise 12

Answers will vary.

TIME AND RESOURCE MANAGER

In-Depth Coverage	Accelerated Pace
• Cover pp. 39–41 in class. • Read and discuss the Writing Model, p. 40.	• Assign pp. 39–41 for independent student review.

Step-by-Step Teaching Guide

Types of Paragraphs

1. Write the words *topical paragraph* and *functional paragraph* on the chalkboard. Underline *topic* and *function* in each phrase to help students remember the purpose of each type.
2. Review the three purposes of functional paragraphs. You may want to bring in examples of each kind to show students.

Customize for *ESL Students*

Different languages punctuate dialogue in different ways. In Spanish, for example, dialogue is often set off with dashes. Use a story containing dialogue that the students have read to review the rules for using quotation marks in dialogue in English. Remind students that if a character speaks for more than one paragraph, each paragraph opens with quotation marks, but only the last paragraph ends with quotation marks.

3.3

Types of Paragraphs

Topical Paragraphs

A **topical paragraph** consists of a group of sentences containing one main idea or sentence and several sentences that support or illustrate that main idea.

Functional Paragraphs

Functional paragraphs are used for specific purposes. Although a functional paragraph may not contain a topic sentence, it is unified and coherent because the sentences are clearly connected and logically ordered. Functional paragraphs can serve the following purposes:

To Arouse or Sustain Interest A few vivid sentences can work together to capture the reader's attention.

To Indicate Dialogue One of the conventions of written dialogue is that a new paragraph begins each time the speaker changes.

To Make a Transition A short paragraph can help readers move between the main ideas in two topical paragraphs.

WRITING MODEL

from **Animal Craftsmen**

Bruce Brooks

I scrambled down the ladder, leaping from the third rung and landing in the frosty salad of . . . leaves and windswept grass that collected at the foot of the barn wall. I looked down and saw that my left boot had, by no more than an inch, just missed crushing the very thing I was rushing off to seek. There, lying dry and separate on the leaves, was the wasp house.

I looked up. Yes. I was standing directly beneath the spot where the sphere had hung—it was a straight fall. I picked up the wasp house, gave it a shake to see if any insects were inside, and, discovering none, took it home.

My awe of the craftsman grew as I unwrapped the layers of the nest. Such beautiful paper! It was much tougher than any I had encountered. . . .

This paragraph indicates the transition from the narration of the preceding paragraph to the description in the one that follows.

STANDARDIZED TEST PREPARATION WORKSHOP

Grammar and Usage Standardized tests often ask students to identify a particular type of grammatical error. Ask students which of the following sentences contains an error in punctuation.

A "Holmes, how do you do it?" I asked, amazed.

B "It is the habit of observation, Watson, answered my friend."

C "You see the same clues that I see, but you do not observe."

D "But how," I demanded, "will this help our client?"

Students should choose **B.** Quotation marks should surround only the spoken words, not phrases such as "answered my friend" or "he said."

Paragraph Blocks

Occasionally, you may have too much information about a single idea to include in one manageable paragraph. When this occurs, you can devote several paragraphs to the development of that single idea. These "blocks" of paragraphs all support the same main idea or topic sentence. By separating the contributing ideas into blocks, you make your ideas more understandable.

PARAGRAPH BLOCKS

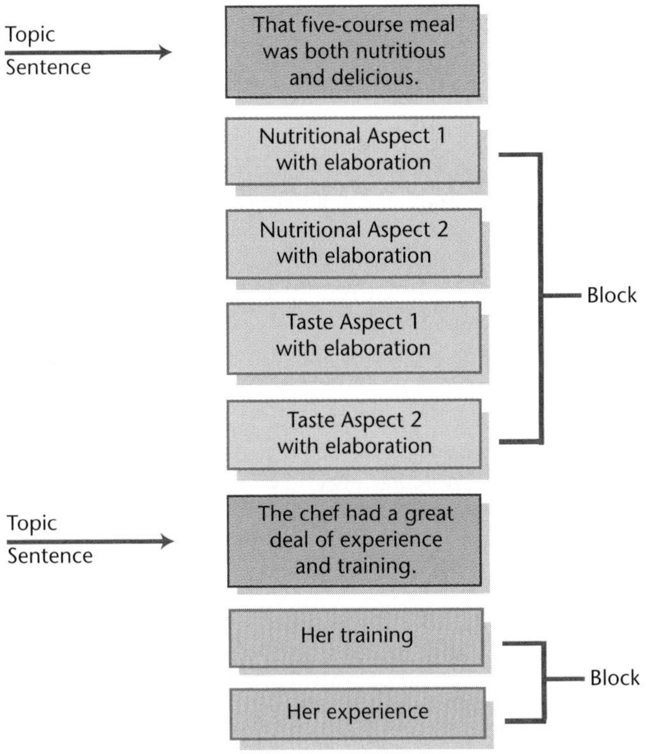

Exercise 13 **Analyzing Types of Paragraphs** Choose an article from a magazine that focuses on a hobby or interest of yours. Make a photocopy of the article. Then, identify and color-code the different types of paragraphs you find. Draw a box around each topical paragraph and underline the topic sentence. Bracket the margin to show paragraph blocks. Finally, use a red star to indicate functional paragraphs, and note in the margin the function that each performs.

Step-by-Step Teaching Guide

Paragraph Blocks

Teaching Resources: Writing Support Transparency 3-B

1. Paragraph length is largely a matter of judgment. Some writers express themselves best in very long paragraphs; others prefer very short ones. Students should always read over their work and think carefully about whether each sentence in a paragraph really relates to its main idea or whether the paragraph includes more than one main idea. If students find a change of subject in a paragraph, they should rework it into two paragraphs.
2. Paragraph blocking really means organizing an essay into subtopics. For instance, a paragraph might ask why Mozart became such a successful composer while still very young. Instead of giving all the reasons for Mozart's early fame (extraordinary talent, a determined father, his own love of music) in one paragraph, a writer can develop each reason into a paragraph of its own. This allows the writer to include more detail.

Answer Key

Exercise 13

Answers will vary.

ONGOING ASSESSMENT: Monitor and Reinforce

If students have trouble identifying types of paragraphs, try the following strategy.

Give pairs of students a set of paragraphs from *Prentice Hall Literature: Timeless Voices, Timeless Themes,* Silver, to read and identify by type. Partners can identify the function of each paragraph and explain their reasoning.

Step-by-Step Teaching Guide

Developing Your Style

1. No one paragraph style is better than another. Different styles are appropriate for different subjects and situations. Students have individual preferences; writing is a form of self-expression, and all students have different ideas about appropriate paragraph length.
2. Go over the different aspects of paragraph style. Encourage students to keep these points in mind when rereading first drafts of writing assignments.

Customize for *More Advanced Students*

Have students form a reading group and compare paragraphs from their favorite writers. Students can read their chosen paragraphs aloud and compare and contrast the styles of the different writers. Students should describe the styles and decide what makes them effective.

Answer Key

Exercise 14

Answers will vary.

PRENTICE HALL

Everyday Spelling

If you have taught the spelling skills in *Prentice Hall Everyday Spelling,* Grade 8, Chapter 3, in conjunction with this *Writing and Grammar* chapter, review and assess students' mastery of the skills before concluding the chapter.

3.4 *Writing Style*

Developing Your Style

Your clothing, your hairstyle, and the activities you prefer are expressions of your personal style. Style also refers to the way you express yourself in writing. Several qualities that contribute to your writing style are shown below:

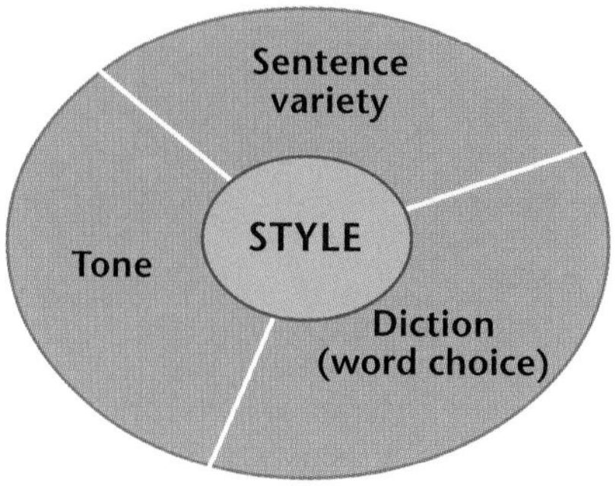

Creating Sentence Variety You have a variety of options to contribute to your writing style as well. When you write a paragraph, try to vary your sentence lengths, types, and structures.

Choosing Words The words you choose add to the style, or overall effect, of a paragraph. Think about your choice of words when planning how to achieve a particular effect. For instance, if you are writing a description, you'll employ vivid details to convey a powerful image. The clarity of your description will be aided when you use specific, rather than general, nouns. The way words sound can also contribute to a paragraph's style.

Setting a Tone Your attitude toward your subject is conveyed in the tone of your writing. You may view your subject in many ways, such as with scorn, appreciation, or awe. The paragraphs of an e-mail to a classmate will probably have a casual tone, while the paragraphs of a cause-and-effect essay assignment will probably have a more serious and formal tone.

Exercise 14 **Choosing a Paragraph Style** Read the two Writing Models on page 33. Study the sentence lengths and structures, the word choice, and the tone of each. Discuss with a partner how the styles of the two paragraphs are similar and different. Then, write a paragraph of your own, modeled on the style of one of the paragraphs you have read. See if your partner can tell which style you used as a model.

TIME AND RESOURCE MANAGER

In-Depth Coverage	Accelerated Pace
• Cover pp. 42–43 in class.	• Assign pp. 42–43 for independent student review.

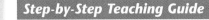

Using Formal and Informal English

Standard English can be either formal or informal. Formal English is appropriate for serious and academic purposes. Use informal English for casual writing or when you want your writing to have a conversational tone.

The Conventions of Formal English

Formal English is the standard language of written communication. You will use formal English for most of your school assignments. It is appropriate for reports, speeches, biographies, instructional manuals, articles, presentations, and job and school applications. When writing in formal English, you should observe these conventions:

- Avoid contractions.
- Do not use slang.
- Follow standard English usage and grammar.
- Use a serious tone and sophisticated vocabulary.

Informal English

Informal English is the language of everyday speech. You can also use informal English when you write humorous essays, dialogue, letters to friends, personal reminders, journal entries, and some stories. When you use informal English, you can

- use contractions.
- use slang and popular expressions, especially to capture the natural sounds of speech.

FORMAL ENGLISH: He said he will discount the price of the next compact disc that I purchase.

INFORMAL ENGLISH: He said he'll give me a break on the next CD I buy.

▼ Critical Viewing
Would you and your friends use formal or informal English to talk about CD's? **[Connect]**

Exercise 15 **Using Formal and Informal English** Rewrite the following sentences on a separate sheet of paper. Use formal English for those written in informal English. Use informal English for those written in formal English.

1. That was the coolest movie ever!
2. I thought the director did a superb job.
3. All the actors delivered outstanding performances.
4. The skiing footage was awesome!
5. The final scene was a total shocker—it blew us all away!

ONGOING ASSESSMENT: Assess Mastery

Use one of the following options to assess students' paragraphs in final draft.

Self-Assessment Have students read their own paragraphs to identify the topic sentence or main idea, make sure it is supported, make sure all details are relevant, and evaluate the style. Students should note any areas in which they feel they need improvement.	**Teacher Assessment** Meet with students individually to go over their writing assignments. Ask students where they feel they need improvement and give them any necessary advice or guidance in these areas.

Step-by-Step Teaching Guide

Using Formal and Informal English

Suggest the following situations. Ask whether formal or informal English is more appropriate.

- *dinner at home* (I)
- *dinner with a friend's family* (F)
- *job interview at a local fast-food restaurant* (F)
- *dealing with customers after getting the job* (F)
- *talking with principal in school hallway* (F)
- *talking with principal you ran into in line at a movie theater* (I)

Integrating Speaking Skills

Have two students prepare brief speeches on the same topic for the class. Students should meet to agree on the topic. They can review a movie, explain the steps in making a triple-decker sandwich, or anything else they like. One student should speak in formal English, the other in informal English. After listening to the speeches, the class should compare and contrast them, discussing which style was more appropriate and why.

Answer Key

Exercise 15

Answers will vary. Samples are given.

1. That was a splendid film.
2. I thought the director really nailed it.
3. The actors were amazing.
4. The skiing footage was stunning.
5. The final scene was breathtaking.

Critical Viewing

Connect Students should say that they would use informal English.

Lesson Objectives

1. To evaluate the way a visual image maker represents meanings.
2. To write an analysis of a work of art.

Step-by-Step Teaching Guide

Analyzing Composition

1. Choose one of the Spotlight elements for class discussion, or have students work individually or in groups on the element of their choice. Give students the opportunity to find the necessary books, videotapes, or pictures.
2. You may want to choose the Spotlight activity that ties in most closely to your curriculum or the one for which you can locate the necessary resources.
3. Show the class a book of Bravo's photographs. Compare various examples from the book with the image on this page of the textbook.
4. You might want to explain to students that Surrealism was a literary and art movement that went beyond conventional art of the time to explore the unconscious, often expressed through dreams. Surrealism was founded in the early 1920's and was influenced by the famous psychoanalyst Sigmund Freud's ideas about the unconscious.
5. Make examples of Kahlo's art available for students to study.
6. You may wish to elicit students' general reaction to the photograph on this page before they begin writing their analyses of the composition.

Spotlight on the Humanities

Analyzing Composition

Focus on Photography: Manuel Bravo

In art and photography, composition refers to the way visual elements are put together to achieve a particular effect. Many photographers plan the composition of a photograph before they take it.

Born in Mexico City, Manuel Alvarez Bravo (1902–2002) gained fame as a photographer during the Mexican art movement of the 1930's. His work focused on the details of the lives of ordinary people. While Bravo had an interest in Surrealism, he was never a part of that art movement. In 1930–1931, Bravo served as a cameraman on the film *Que Viva Mexico,* a documentary filmed by Russian director Sergei Eisenstein.

▲ Critical Viewing Do you think this photograph would be more or less effective if it were in color? Explain. **[Support]**

Film Connection Known for his experiments with montage and progression of scenes, Russian film director Sergei Eisenstein (1898–1948) is renowned as one of the greatest film directors of all time. Trained as an architect and civil engineer, Eisenstein created such films as *Battleship Potemkin* (1925), which contains a now-classic scene on the Odessa steps where Cossack troops confront civilians friendly to the *Potemkin*'s crew.

Art Connection In the 1930's, Mexican artist Frida Kahlo (1907–1954) sat for photographer Manuel Alvarez Bravo in his studio. Kahlo, who was born in Mexico, was a painter known for the deep expression of thought and feeling in her work, and she became one of the most respected artists of her day. She spent much of her time with her students, who called themselves *Los Fridos*, inspiring them to use their Mexican heritage in their work. Kahlo, who loved to use bright colors, was a member of the Surrealist art movement. In 1929, she married another popular Surrealist painter, Diego Rivera.

Writing Activity: Analyzing Composition

Analyze the composition of the photograph above by answering the following questions: What is the subject of the photograph? Where is the subject placed in relation to other objects? What is the second-most important object in the photograph? Why do you think it is included? Which parts of the photograph are very light? Which parts are very dark? Then, for each question, write a paragraph explaining your answer and your reaction to the photograph.

Viewing and Representing

Activity Small groups of students may work in teams to analyze the photograph for the class. Each team member can answer one or more of the questions posed in the Writing Activity.

Critical Viewing

Support Most students will feel that the composition would be less effective if the photograph were in color because the careful balance of shades of gray would disappear in color. Accept students' responses that the photograph would be more effective in color if they can give reasons to support their opinions.

Media and Technology Skills

Recognizing the Varieties of Media

Activity: Compare and Contrast Print and Electronic Media

We experience firsthand only a tiny part of what happens in the world. The major part of our experience of the world is shaped by the media. The **media** are all the forms of communication used to deliver information and entertainment to the public.

Think About It In Shakespeare's time, if you wanted to see a play, you had to be there. Today, you can watch a performance live on stage, on television, or on video. Afterward, you might hear about it on the radio or read about it in the paper. Your choice is a matter of preference and accessibility.

- **Print media** Although a newspaper cannot deliver information as quickly as a television newscast, it often allows writers to develop stories and provide fuller coverage. Print media are also easily accessible. Electronic media are programmed to be broadcast at specific times. A newspaper or magazine, while published at a specific time, can be read at your convenience. Because print media are intended to be read, more complex words and sentence structures may be used than are used in broadcast media.
- **Electronic media** Information can usually be shared more quickly through electronic means than through print. However, because listeners or viewers may move on to another activity, electronic media usually depend on short, catchy sentences. Coverage in general may also be more superficial than it is in print media. (Some exceptions include documentaries and investigative reporting.)

Types of Media

Print
- Books
- Magazines
- Newspapers
- Photography
- Print advertisements
- Cartoons

Electronic
- Film
- Radio
- Television
- News wire services
- Internet
- Commercials

Analyze It Choose one print medium and one electronic medium. Use a Venn diagram to explore the similarities and differences in the coverage and treatment that each gives a particular topic. For each category shown on this sample Venn diagram, provide specific examples from the medium you choose.

COMPARISON OF MEDIA

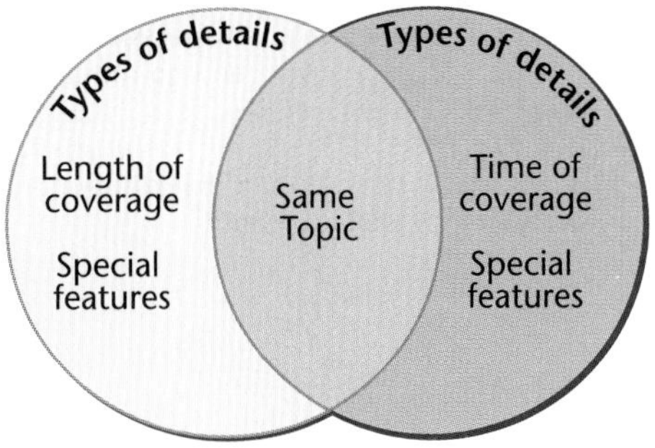

Lesson Objectives

1. To evaluate the purposes and effects of various media.
2. To evaluate how different forms of media influence and inform.
3. To write to record ideas and reflect on them.

Step-by-Step Teaching Guide

Recognizing the Varieties of Media

Teaching Resources: Writing Support Transparency 3-C; Writing Support Activity Book 3-1

1. Compare with your students the variety of media available today with the media available in Shakespeare's time. Then have students speculate about forms of media that people in the year 3000 might enjoy.
2. List on the board several current news stories your students suggest. Choose one and display the transparency. Record a couple of similarities and differences between print and electronic media on the diagram.
3. Give students copies of the blank organizer. Let them decide whether they want to continue recording ideas about the news story the class discussed or choose another news topic. Have students complete the Venn diagram showing similarities and differences between the two types of media.
4. Have students compare their Venn diagrams.

Customize for *More Advanced Students*

Expect a sophisticated nuanced treatment of the differences between print and electronic media from these students. Have them write analyses and include visuals (photocopies of ads and cartoons, magazines and newspapers, computer screen shots, and so on) to support their theses.

Lesson Objectives

1. To analyze writing for strategy, organization, and style.
2. To read test items.

Step-by-Step Teaching Guide

Analyzing Strategy, Organization, and Style

Teaching Resources: Standardized Test Preparation Workbook, pp. 5–6

1. Make sure all your students understand why the sentence *I also have a cute cat that enjoys playing* does not fit with the rest of the passage.
2. Read aloud several paragraphs to your class. As you read, make up a sentence that doesn't fit the paragraph. Ask volunteers to identify the sentence that doesn't fit and explain why it is out of place.
3. Remind students that standardized tests are timed and they must try to answer all the questions on the test. When they are about halfway through the test, they should check the time and see whether they need to try to read more quickly.

Standardized Test Preparation Workshop

Analyzing Strategy, Organization, and Style

Standardized tests frequently measure your knowledge of writing skills. In these types of tests, items include a passage in which part of a sentence is marked for your analysis. You will be asked to analyze strategy, organization, sequence of sentences, and style within a passage. The following are three types of questions that you may encounter:

- **Strategy questions** ask whether a given revision is appropriate in the context of the passage.
- **Organization questions** ask you to choose the most logical sequence of ideas or to decide whether a sentence should be added, deleted, or moved.
- **Style questions** focus on your ability to identify the writer's point of view or evaluate the use of language for an intended audience.

The sample test item that follows will give you practice in answering these types of questions.

Test Tips

- As you read a paragraph, think about how the writer could clarify it by deleting or adding information.
- If a passage sounds awkward or illogical, think about how sentences could be rearranged to make the passage more logical.

Sample Test Item	Answer and Explanation
Directions: Read the passage, and then answer the questions that follow. 1 There are so many things I love about 2 my dog. He always greets me at the 3 door and seems so happy to see me. 4 I also have a cute cat that enjoys playing. 5 My dog also loves to play outside and 6 keeps me company when I go running.	
1 Which of the following draws attention away from the main focus? A Line 2 B Line 3 C Line 4 D Line 5	The correct answer is C. Since the passage is about a dog, Line 4 is out of place because it mentions a cat.

TEST-TAKING TIP

Advise students to make a guess about questions they are unsure of. They might make a tick mark next to those questions and if time permits at the end of the test, return to those items, reread them, and decide whether they want to change their answers. Remind students that if they read carefully, their first guess stands a good chance of being correct.

Practice 1 **Directions:** Read the passage, and then answer the questions that follow. Choose the letter of the best answer.

Those of us who live in the northeastern region of the United States live through four distinct seasons. When asked to choose my favorite season, it's not easy for me to make a decision, because each season has aspects that I appreciate. I like the fall because it's an amazing time to see the leaves turn vibrant colors on the trees. In the winter, I can go sleigh riding and ice skating, and when I'm inside I can warm up with a cup of hot chocolate.

Both of my sisters' birthdays are in the winter. I also like the spring because it's a hopeful time when we first see signs of birds and flowers, and the temperature outside always feels comfortable. However, even with all of the great qualities of the other seasons, I would have to say that summer is my favorite season.

There are so many reasons why I anticipate the arrival of summer. First, summer is warm enough to wear shorts and a T-shirt, which is much more comfortable than wearing big sweaters and jackets in the winter. I spend most of the summer wearing sandals, and whenever possible, I walk around in my bare feet. I live near the ocean. I spend a large part of my summer swimming at the beach. In the summer, I also ride my bike outside and take long walks, which I find very relaxing. Another one of my favorite aspects of summer is having barbecues. I love when my family cooks on an outdoor grill, and then we eat outside. I guess the greatest part of summer is the ability to do so much outside in the warm, fresh air.

Therefore, I welcome each season and find something new and pleasant about each one.

1 If the writer wanted to add more information about the benefits of summer, which of the following statements would be suitable?

A Since I love to fish, summer provides me with lots of opportunities to spend time next to the water with my fishing pole.

B Although it's a fun time, summer can be very hot and humid.

C There are so many things to do in the summer, but most of my friends go away on vacation in the summer, so I often end up by myself.

D In the spring, the temperature feels very comfortable.

2 Which of the following draws attention away from the main focus?

F Line 9

G Line 13

H Line 22

J Line 31

3 Which is the BEST sentence to add to the conclusion?

A It is summer, however, that brings me the most joy and contentment.

B Everyone should try to do the same.

C Autumn, however, is my favorite.

D Everyone knows, though, that winter is the coldest.

4 Which identifies the author's purpose?

F To entertain

G To persuade

H To criticize

J To evaluate

Answer Key

Practice 1

1. A
2. G
3. A
4. J

Customize for *Less Advanced Students*

To provide additional practice for these students, write your own examples of simple strategy, organization, and style questions; use the Standardized Test Preparation Workshop on pages 132–133; or look for examples in test practice books. Have small groups of students practice answering these items together so that they will have more confidence when they are called on to complete these types of items in actual testing conditions.

Customize for *ESL Students*

Students whose first language is not English will find standardized tests especially challenging. Scan the test and write the meaning of each difficult word on the chalkboard. Ask students to check the board as they take the test if they don't know the meaning of any of the words.

Chapter 4 Time and Resource Manager

In-Depth Lesson Plan

	LESSON FOCUS	PRINT AND MEDIA RESOURCES
DAY 1	**Introduction to Autobiographical Writing** Students learn key elements of autobiographical writing and analyze the Model From Literature (pp. 48–53).	***Writers at Work* Videotape,** Narration ***Writing and Grammar iText* (Interactive Text),** Ch. 4, Introduction
DAY 2	**Prewriting** Students choose and narrow a topic, consider their audience and purpose, and gather information (pp. 54–57).	**Teaching Resources** *Writing Support Transparencies,* 4-A–C; *Topic Bank for Heterogeneous Classes,* Ch. 4 ***Writing and Grammar iText* (Interactive Text),** Section 4.2
DAY 3	**Drafting** Students organize their ideas and write their first drafts (pp. 58–59).	**Teaching Resources** *Writing Support Transparencies,* 4-D–E; *Writing Support Activity Book,* 4-1 ***Writing and Grammar iText* (Interactive Text),** Section 4.3
DAY 4	**Revising** Students revise their drafts in terms of overall structure, paragraphs, sentences, and word choice (pp. 60–65).	**Teaching Resources** *Writing Support Transparencies,* 4-F–I; *Writing Support Activity Book,* 4-2 ***Writing and Grammar iText* (Interactive Text),** Section 4.4
DAY 5	**Editing and Proofreading; Publishing and Presenting** Students check their work for accuracy and correctness and present their final drafts (pp. 66–67).	**Teaching Resources** *Scoring Rubrics on Transparency,* Ch. 4; *Formal Assessment,* Ch. 4 ***Writing and Grammar iText* (Interactive Text),** Sections 4.5–6

Accelerated Lesson Plan

	LESSON FOCUS	PRINT AND MEDIA RESOURCES
DAY 1	**Introduction Through Drafting** Students review the characteristics of autobiographical writing, select topics, and write drafts (pp. 48–59).	**Teaching Resources** *Writing Support Transparencies,* 4-A–E; *Writing Support Activity Book,* 4-1 ***Writing and Grammar iText* (Interactive Text),** Ch. 4, Introduction through Section 4.3
DAY 2	**Revising Through Presenting** Students work individually or with peers to revise, edit, and proofread their work for presentation (pp. 60–67).	**Teaching Resources** *Writing Support Transparencies,* 4-F–I; *Writing Support Activity Book,* 4-2; *Scoring Rubrics on Transparency,* Ch. 4; *Formal Assessment,* Ch. 4 ***Writing and Grammar iText* (Interactive Text),** Sections 4.4–6

Options for Adapting Lesson Plans

HOMEWORK

Have students complete any stage of the lesson for homework.

SPELLING

To teach spelling skills in conjunction with writing skills, work through *Prentice Hall Everyday Spelling,* Grade 8, Chapter 4, as you cover this *Writing and Grammar* chapter. At the Editing and Proofreading stage, remind students to apply the spelling skills to their autobiograpical narratives.

FEATURES

Extend coverage with Connected Assignment (p. 70), Spotlight on the Humanities (p. 72), Media and Technology Skills (p. 73), and Standardized Test Preparation Workshop (p. 74).

TECHNOLOGY

Students can complete any stage of the lesson on the computer, using *Writing and Grammar iText* or a word-processing program. Have them print out their completed work.

INTEGRATED SKILLS COVERAGE

Integrating Grammar
Punctuating Introductory Elements, ATE pp. 52, 66
General and Specific Nouns, SE p. 65

Reading/Writing Connection
Reading Strategy, SE p. 50
Writing Application, SE p. 53

Viewing and Representing
Critical Viewing, SE pp. 48, 50, 51, 52, 53, 57, 60, 62, 68, 70, 72
Interpreting Images, ATE p. 49
ATE p. 72

Real-World Connection
ATE p. 73

Technology
Technology Tip, SE p. 57

BLOCK SCHEDULING

Pacing Suggestions
For 90-minute Blocks
- Have students complete the Prewriting and Drafting stages in a single period.
- Focus one class period on Revising and Editing and Publishing and Presenting. Allow at least 30 minutes for peer revision.

Resources for Varying Instruction
- ***Writing and Grammar iText* (Interactive Text)** A 90-minute block provides an ideal opportunity for students to work on computer.
- ***Writers at Work* Videotape** Show the Narration segment in class.

Professional Development Support
- ***How to Manage Instruction in the Block*** This teaching resource provides management and activity suggestions.

ASSESSMENT SUPPORT

Standardized Test Preparation Workshop SE pp. 74–75; ATE p. 64

Standardized Test Preparation Workbook, pp. 7–8

Scoring Rubrics on Transparency, Ch. 4

Formal Assessment, Ch. 4

Writing Assessment and Portfolio Management

MEDIA AND TECHNOLOGY

For the Student
- ***Writing and Grammar iText* (Interactive Text)**, Ch. 4

For the Teacher
- ***Writers at Work* Videotape**, Narration
- ***Resource Pro* CD-ROM**

MEETING INDIVIDUAL NEEDS

Less Advanced Students ATE pp. 58, 71, 75. See also Ongoing Assessments ATE pp. 51, 55, 57, 62, 65, 67.

More Advanced Students ATE pp. 51, 59, 75

Visual/Spatial Learners ATE p. 58

Gifted/Talented Students ATE p. 71

WRITING AND GRAMMAR ON-LINE

iText Interactive Text (On-line or on CD-ROM)
- Easily navigable instruction with interactive Revision Checkers
- Full use of e-rater™, the essay-scoring system (on-line only)

Companion Web Site PHSchool.com
- Scoring rubrics with models (use Web Code eck-8001)

See the Go On-line! feature, SE p. iii.

LITERATURE CONNECTIONS

Related selections from *Prentice Hall Literature: Timeless Voices, Timeless Themes*, Silver:

Professional Model from *An American Childhood,* Annie Dillard, SE p. 53

Topic Bank Option "The Road Not Taken," Robert Frost, SE p. 55

CHAPTER 4
NARRATION: AUTOBIOGRAPHICAL WRITING

Lesson Objectives

1. To understand the characteristics of autobiographical writing.
2. To choose and narrow an autobiographical topic.
3. To consider audience and purpose in developing an autobiographical narrative topic.
4. To apply strategies for gathering and organizing details.
5. To draft an essay with an introduction, body, and conclusion.
6. To evaluate and revise the overall structure of an autobiographical narrative.
7. To analyze the structure of paragraphs.
8. To examine sentences to assure variety in nouns.
9. To edit, proofread, and publish an autobiographical narrative.

Critical Viewing

Speculate Students' responses will vary.

Chapter 4 Narration
Autobiographical Writing

▲ Critical Viewing
What do you think the boy is thinking? What story might he tell of his train ride? **[Speculate]**

Autobiographical Writing in Everyday Life

After you take a difficult test or play in a crucial game or spend a day out sick, people want to know: "So, what happened?!" The answer is a kind of story, a short autobiographical narrative you might create on the spot. These stories about what we did or wish we'd done remind us of who we are. They also bind us closer to others.

In **autobiographical writing,** you set down a story from life on paper, and you can tell it in as much detail as you wish. Don't be surprised, though, if the story changes a little in the telling—if past defeat turns into a kind of victory, or past disappointments become valuable lessons. In this chapter, you will learn ways to strengthen and improve your autobiographical writing.

TIME AND RESOURCE MANAGER

Resources
Technology: Writers at Work Videotape; Writing and Grammar iText, Ch. 4

In-Depth Coverage	Accelerated Pace
• Cover pp. 48–53 in class. • Show Narration: Autobiographical Writing section of the Writers at Work Videotape. • Read the Model From Literature (pp. 50–53) in class and use it to brainstorm for autobiographical ideas with students. • Discuss examples of autobiographical writing that students already know or do (journals, diaries, memoirs, letters).	• Discuss definitions and types of autobiographical writing in class. • Assign the Model From Literature (pp. 50–53) for independent reading.

What Is Autobiographical Writing?

Autobiographical writing tells the story of an event, period, or person in the writer's life. By writing autobiographically, you can share part of your life with others. You can also learn more about yourself. A good autobiographical piece usually includes

- true events from the writer's life presented in logical order and in such a way as to build the reader's interest.
- a central conflict, or problem, that the writer or another person has to resolve, or a shift between the writer's past and present views of events.
- the use of vivid details to give a clear sense of characters and places.

To learn the criteria on which your work may be assessed, see the Rubric for Self-Assessment on page 67.

Writers in ACTION

Rudolfo Anaya is the author of novels, short stories, and articles. He has also translated folk tales that are an important part of Mexican American culture. He understands that telling stories about ourselves is part of life.

"I think people sometimes think that storytelling is a time in our life that we go sit in a certain room and tell a story or write a story, but it's not. Storytelling goes on all day long."

Types of Autobiographical Writing

There are a few types of autobiographical writing:

- **Autobiographical incidents**, which are also called **personal narratives,** recount an event in which the writer played a central role.
- **Reflective essays** tell of an experience and give the writer's thoughts on its meaning.
- **Autobiographical narratives** relate memorable experiences, and frequently include information about the writer's early life and personal qualities.
- **Memoirs** are recollections of the writer's relationship with a particular person, place, animal, or thing.

PREVIEW Student Work IN PROGRESS

To tell a story from your own life, use the strategies and tips in this lesson. You will follow the prewriting, drafting, and revising techniques used by Evan Twohy, who attends Prospect Sierra School in El Cerrito, California, to develop his autobiographical essay, "Zermatt or Bust!"

PREPARE and ENGAGE

Interest GRABBER Read aloud the following opening sentences from autobiographical essays. Ask students which they would like to read and why.

I began working in journalism when I was eight years old. (Russell Baker)

Some boys taught me to play football. (Annie Dillard)

We loved to play baseball. (Lionel C. García)

For our family, moviegoing was rare. (Gary Soto)

Learning stamps you with its moments. (Eudora Welty)

Activate Prior Knowledge

Ask students to recall a time when they attended an important event. Did they share what happened with friends? How did they set the scene, and what techniques did they use in the retelling? After discussing these issues, refer students to the characteristics of autobiographical writing in the text.

More About the Writer

Rudolfo Anaya (born 1937) uses his Mexican American heritage as a springboard for his writing. He is also concerned with the past. As he puts it, "For those of us who listen to the Earth, and to the old legends and myths of the people, the whispers of the blood draw us to our past." He is the author of *Bless Me, Ultima, The Heart of Aztlan,* and *Tortuga.*

Integrating Viewing Skills

Have students view a painting or photograph, then describe the image and the effect it has on them. Ask students to write from an autobiographical perspective about the impact of the image.

TEACH

Reading\Writing Connection

Reading: Predict

One way to pay careful attention to the progress of a story is to stop now and then and predict what will happen. By keeping track of some of the narrative clues that suggest where the story may be heading, and predicting how these incidents might alter the story, students can read like detectives.

Teaching from the Model

You can use this model from literature to show students how to find a topic for autobiographical writing. Help students see that Kline's childhood jealousy of his brother, his affection for his pet, and his understanding about winning and losing made good topics because they revealed a great deal about the author.

Step-by-Step Teaching Guide

Engage Students Through Literature

1. Read this excerpt aloud, or have volunteers read it.
2. After the reading, ask students to discuss the excerpt. You can use questions such as these to prompt discussion.

   What do you think about Kline's childhood memories? Which details suggest what his childhood was like?

   How did winning the race change Kline's views about his brother? How did they change his views about Chubby? About himself?
3. Have students brainstorm and recall as many autobiographical details as they can about Kline from the passage.
4. Ask students to think about the autobiographical details that help readers identify writers. Which kind of autobiographical details are useful in creating a picture of the writer?

Critical Viewing

Interpret Students may say *"wild"* and *"energetic."*

4.1 Model From Literature

A pilot, sailor, and inventor as well as a writer, Larry Paul Kline (1951–) tells a story of his childhood love of animals in "The Star of the Rodeo."

▲ Critical Viewing What characteristics might this horse represent to a young boy in the West? **[Interpret]**

Reading Writing Connection Reading Strategy: **Predict** As you read this narrative, **make predictions**—ask yourself, "What will happen next?" Look for hints from the author. For example, Kline writes of his competition with his brother: "I wanted so badly to be the star for a change." By emphasizing this desire, he hints at what will happen next. You can predict that young Larry will get a chance to prove himself a star.

After you make a prediction, read on to see whether or not it comes true.

The Star of the Rodeo

Larry Paul Kline

As a very young child in Niagara Falls, New York, I was in and out of the hospital with serious asthma attacks. When I was six years old, the doctors told my parents that if they did not take me to a better climate, I would certainly die. And so my family moved to a tiny town high up in the mountains outside Denver. It was beautiful, but very remote. In the late '50s, there were far more animals than people in Conifer, Colorado.

In the opening sentence, Kline reports his ailment, and his doctors' dramatic announcement, to draw readers into the story.

We kids were in heaven. My older brother, Dan, and I would pack food and sleeping bags, take two horses and our dog, and go camping for the weekend in the wilderness around our home. We saw a lot of wildlife on our trips—including bears, bobcats and even a few elusive mountain lions. We learned to be silent and observe the life around us with respect. One time, I remember waking up and looking straight into the enormous nose of an elk. I lay perfectly still until the elk moved on. Blending with our surroundings, riding our horses for days at a time, we considered ourselves real mountain men. My parents knew that as long as the dog and the horses were with us, we would be safe and always find our way home.

Details about the animal population help Kline quickly characterize the setting of his story.

I remember that Dan, three years older and stronger, always beat me at everything. It became a burning passion with me to win. I wanted so badly to be the star for a change.

Here, Kline establishes the central conflict of his autobiographical story: his desire as a child to win against his brother.

When I was eight, Dad brought home a horse named Chubby. Chubby's owner had suffered a heart attack and was told to stop riding. The owner thought that we would give Chubby a good home, so he gave the sixteen-year-old gelding to my parents for free.

Chubby, a smallish, charcoal-gray horse, had been a tri-state rodeo champion in roping and bulldogging. Strong, intelligent and responsive, he had tremendous spirit, and my whole family loved him. Dan, of course, got first pick of the horses, so I was left with a slower, lazier horse named Stormy. Chubby was probably too much horse for a boy of eight anyway, but I envied my brother and wished fervently that Chubby were my horse.

He connects Chubby's arrival with the central conflict of the story. His brother's surprising decision increases the tension.

In those days, my brother and I entered 4-H Club gymkhanas with our horses every year. The year I was nine, I practiced the barrel race over and over in preparation for that year's competition. But Stormy was a plodding horse and even while I practiced, I knew it was a lost cause. It was the deep passion to win that kept me at it—urging Stormy on, learning the moves for getting around the barrels and back to the finish line.

On the day of the gymkhana, my older brother stunned me by offering to let me ride Chubby in the barrel race. I was beside myself with excitement and joy. Maybe this time, I could finally win.

When I mounted Chubby, I sensed immediately that I was in for a completely different barrel race. With Stormy, it was always a struggle to get her moving from a standing position, and then a chore to keep her going. As we waited for the start signal that day, Chubby was prancing in place, alert and obviously eager to be

▼ Critical Viewing
Would you take pride in an ability to perform this task? Explain. **[Relate]**

Customize for *More Advanced Students*

Have students read independently and write details from the writer's life that they have learned from this account of his childhood. Then ask students to write an alternate ending to the story.

Critical Viewing

Relate Students may say that they would take pride because it is a difficult thing to do.

ONGOING ASSESSMENT: Diagnose

Use one of the following options to diagnose students' current level of proficiency in autobiographical writing.

Option 1 Ask students to write an autobiographical paragraph about something they enjoy doing in their free time. Hold conferences to review each student's sample. Use the conference to determine which students will need extra support in developing an autobiographical narrative.

Option 2 Have students freewrite on the topic "How I spent last weekend" or "Where I see myself in 20 years." Review their work to determine whether students are comfortable freewriting on an autobiographical subject.

Integrating Grammar Skills

Kline uses introductory clauses in his writing: "As a very young child in Niagara Falls, New York," "When I was six years old," "When I mounted Chubby." Kline punctuates each with a comma, to indicate that it is separate from the rest of the sentence. Encourage students to incorporate this grammar principle in their own writing.

Critical Viewing

Evaluate Students will note that the horse is running at an extreme angle. A rider must be very skilled to stay on a horse running this way.

4.1

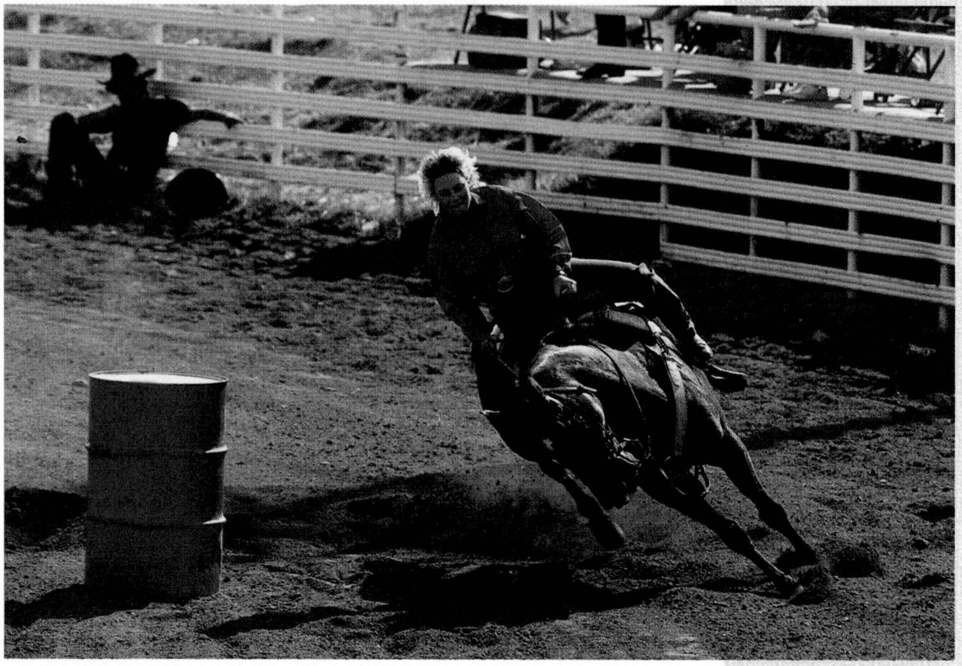

▲ Critical Viewing
Judging from this photograph of a barrel race, how skillful a rider must the young Kline have been? Explain your answer. **[Evaluate]**

running. When the signal came, Chubby was off like a rocket before I could react, and it was all I could do to hold on. We were around those barrels and back at the finish line in seconds. My adrenaline was still pumping as I slid off the horse and was surrounded by my cheering family. I won that blue ribbon by a mile and then some.

Kline has organized the story of the race logically, presenting events in sequence.

That night I went to bed worn out with the excitement and glory of it all. But as I lay there, I found myself feeling uneasy. What had *I* really done to earn that first place? All I could come up with was that I'd managed not to fall off and humiliate myself or Chubby. It was the horse that had won the blue ribbon, not me. I looked at the ribbon pinned to my lampshade and suddenly felt ashamed.

Instead of simply resolving the story's conflict, Kline deepens it. The conflict is no longer a rivalry between brothers—it is now Kline's own struggle to understand the meaning of victory.

The next morning, I woke early. I got out of bed, dressed quickly and crept out of the house toward the barn. I pinned the blue ribbon on the wall of Chubby's stall and stood rubbing his neck, feeling him lip my pockets, looking for the sugar cubes he loved so much. Then it hit me: this horse didn't care about ribbons, blue or otherwise. He preferred something he could eat. Chubby had run that way yesterday, not to win, but simply because he loved to run. He truly enjoyed the challenge and the fun of the game.

With a new respect, I got a bucket of rolled oats, his favorite grain, and let him eat it while I got out the currycomb and gave him a thorough brushing. This horse had given me my blue ribbon, but more important, Chubby had shown me what it means to give yourself to what you do with your entire mind, body, and soul.

My heart light once more, I vowed that for the rest of his days, I was going to make sure Chubby got his reward in *horse* currency: grain, sugar, brushing, the chance to run—and lots of love.

Kline resolves the conflict with a shift in perspective. Instead of needing to win, he now appreciates the value of doing something for its own sake.

Kline's statement of gratitude makes an effective conclusion, emphasizing the importance of the lesson Chubby has taught him.

Reading Writing Connection

Writing Application: **Help Readers Make Predictions** As you draft and revise your autobiographical piece, give readers hints that will encourage them to predict what will happen next.

LITERATURE

To read another selection in which a writer recalls a lesson learned in childhood, read an excerpt from *An American Childhood* by Annie Dillard. You can find one in *Prentice Hall Literature: Timeless Voices, Timeless Themes,* Silver.

◀ Critical Viewing
Do you think feeding and brushing a horse are a fair reward for its winning a race? Explain. **[Evaluate]**

Responding to Literature

Like Kline, Dillard remembers something she learned in childhood. But Kline was pleased with his new knowledge about horses—it changed the way he looked at things. Dillard, on the other hand, preferred her old ideas of the strange lights to the reality that they were just cars.

Critical Viewing

Evaluate Students are likely to say yes. Brushing and feeding are things horses enjoy very much.

Reading\Writing Connection

Writing: Help Readers Make Predictions

Explain to students that hints can make reading a more enjoyable experience because readers will want to continue reading to find the answers to the questions.

Step-by-Step Teaching Guide

Prewriting: Freewriting

1. Freewriting about themselves should come naturally to students, and this is the opportunity to put whatever is on their minds onto the page.
2. Have students write for short bursts of time without letting their pens stop.
3. Remind students that freewriting is used to generate as much material as possible from which to choose a topic.
4. Ask students to select a topic from their freewriting to pursue in greater depth.

Step-by-Step Teaching Guide

Prewriting: Blueprinting

1. After students have chosen one place where they spend a great deal of time or that is meaningful to them, ask them to draw an outline or blueprint of the place for someone who has never seen it.
2. Encourage students to list any incidents associated with the location they have chosen that were memorable.
3. Have students choose one incident as the topic for their writing.

Step-by-Step Teaching Guide

Prewriting: Writing Round

Teaching Resources: Writing Support Transparency 4-A

1. Display the transparency to show how Evan used a writing round to help him choose a topic.
2. Group students in clusters of three or four.
3. Name one leader for each group and have that student write an original sentence telling something about himself or herself to launch the writing round.
4. Ask each student to contribute as many sentences about himself or herself as possible to the paragraph in a ten-minute period.
5. At the end of the time, ask each student to select a topic.

4.2 Prewriting

Choosing Your Topic

The first step in autobiographical writing is deciding on a topic. Think of incidents in your life that have special meaning for you—funny times, moving times, exciting times. Use the following strategies to select a topic you would like to develop:

Strategies for Generating a Topic

1. **Freewriting** Grab a pen, and start writing about special times in your life. Focus on getting down as many ideas as you can. After five minutes, read what you've written. Choose one of these memories as a topic.
2. **Blueprinting** Draw and label a blueprint of a place that is meaningful to you, such as your room, a friend's house, or the park. Then, study your map. List special incidents you associate with each area. Choose one as your topic.
3. **Writing Round** Form a group with classmates. Write a sentence in which you tell something about yourself. Pass the paper around until each person has added at least one new sentence connected to the previous ones. At the end, read the sentences aloud. Choose a topic suggested in the writing round.

iText

Try it out! Use the interactive Blueprinting activity in **Section 4.2,** on-line or on CD-ROM.

Student Work IN PROGRESS

Name: Evan Twohy
Prospect Sierra School
El Cerrito, CA

Holding a Writing Round

Evan chose his topic—a family vacation—from his notes on a writing round.

Evan: I am a big baseball fan.

Rita: Me, too! Last year, I visited my aunt who lives in New York, and she took me to the Baseball Hall of Fame in Cooperstown.

Harold: I went to New York once on vacation with my family, but we didn't go to Cooperstown. We stayed in New York City and had a great time. We even saw a Broadway play.

Evan: We did something different last summer, too—we went to the Alps!

Topic: My family's trip to the Alps.

TIME AND RESOURCE MANAGER

Resources
Print: Writing Support Transparencies, 4-A–C
Technology: Writing and Grammar iText, Section 4.2

In-Depth Coverage	Accelerated Pace
• Cover pp. 54–57 in class. • Work through the Freewriting, Blueprinting, or Writing Round strategy with the class (p. 54). • Use the Responding to Fine Art transparency to generate additional topics. • Do the Remember When We . . . ? activity in class.	• Discuss strategies for generating topics. • Have students work independently to choose and narrow their topics. • Have students work with partners to focus on audience, purpose, and gathering details.

TOPIC BANK

If you're having trouble finding a topic, consider the following possibilities:

1. **Remember When We . . . ?** Think of an unforgettable experience you shared with a friend. Tell the story of this experience, reflecting on your reactions to it then and now.
2. **Dream On** Think of a place other than the one in which you now live. It might be a place you visit occasionally or a place in which you used to live. Write a narrative about this place, telling of a significant incident that occurred there.

Responding to Fine Art

3. Interpret the mood of the woman in this painting, noting the colors used—are they bright and clashing or gentle and harmonious?—and the rhythm of the lines—are they jagged or smooth, straight or curving? Then, write about a time when you shared this mood.

Self-Portrait, 1889 Milly Childers, Leeds Museums and Galleries (City Art Gallery) U.K.

Responding to Literature

4. Read Robert Frost's poem "The Road Not Taken." Think of a time when you faced a choice like that described in the poem. Write a narrative telling the story of your decision. Explain the situation, your reasons for choosing as you did, and how you feel about the "road not taken." You can find Frost's poem in *Prentice Hall Literature: Timeless Voices, Timeless Themes,* Silver.

Cooperative Writing Opportunity

5. **Group Memoir** In a group, list teachers, librarians, custodians, and other school personnel who have helped you and your classmates last year. Each group member should choose one "personality" to write about, recording his or her memories of this person. Group members may also interview the person about whom they are writing to get the subject's viewpoint. Collect the memoirs in a binder, illustrate the collection, and display it in the library.

ONGOING ASSESSMENT: Monitor and Reinforce

If some students are having difficulty coming up with a topic, use one of the following options.

Option 1 Pair students and have them share topics: one partner asks questions about the other's topics to help generate additional topics while the other records new ideas.	**Option 2** Suggest that students choose an idea from the Topic Bank. If many students have difficulty, work with the whole class on one idea selected from the Topic Bank or from ideas suggested by students.

Step-by-Step Teaching Guide

Responding to Fine Art

Self Portrait, 1889 by Milly Childers (1882–1920)

Teaching Resources: Writing Support Transparency 4-B

1. Display the transparency and engage students in a discussion about it. You might use questions such as these to prompt discussion:

   Given that this is a self-portrait, what does the woman's pose suggest about her personality?

   Do you think she is happy with herself?

   What clues in the painting does she provide about herself?

2. Ask students to brainstorm for autobiographical elements suggested by this piece of art. Here are some possibilities:

   What do facial expressions or behaviors reveal about our personalities?

   What details (how old we are, what we do, where we are) indicate something about ourselves?

Responding to Literature

Students might use Robert Frost's "The Road Not Taken" as a starting point for an autobiographical narrative. Ask students whether they feel the poet fully explored his personal feelings about the decision he made to take the road less traveled. Then ask them if they have had to make difficult or unpopular decisions.

Spotlight on the Humanities

For additional topic suggestions, refer students to the Spotlight on the Humanities on page 72.

TIME SAVERS!

Writing Support Transparencies

Use the transparencies for Chapter 4 to teach these strategies.

Step-by-Step Teaching Guide

Prewriting: Use Looping to Narrow a Topic

Teaching Resources: Writing Support Transparency 4-C

1. Since students may be daunted by writing about themselves, ask them to think of their writing as a letter to a pen pal who wants to know everything about them.
2. Help students narrow their topics by giving the following examples:

   Too broad: My family

   Narrow enough: Last summer's family reunion

   Too broad: Cooking

   Narrow enough: How I learned to cook an egg
3. Display the transparency to illustrate how Evan used looping to help him narrow his topic.
4. If students find their topics are too broad after looping, have them write the words they circled and brainstorm for other ideas for topics.

4.2

Narrowing Your Topic

Narrow your topic by focusing on one strong story. For example, the topic "Growing Up in Brooklyn" would include a whirl of stories about your home, your relatives, and so on. By focusing on "The Day Uncle Sid Thought We Were Being Invaded," you can tell a solid, entertaining story. Use the strategy of looping to narrow your topic.

Use Looping to Narrow a Topic

These are the steps of looping:

1. Write freely on your topic for about five minutes.
2. Read what you've written, and circle the "center of gravity"—the idea you find most interesting or important.
3. Write freely for five minutes on this "center of gravity."
4. Review your writing, and find a new "center of gravity."

If this new "center" will make a focused, interesting topic for a narrative, use it as your narrowed topic. If not, continue looping until you arrive at such a topic.

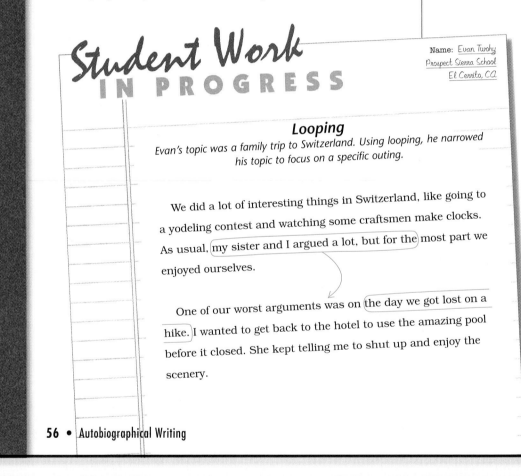

Student Work IN PROGRESS

Name: Evan Twohy
Prospect Sierra School
El Cerrito, CA

Looping

Evan's topic was a family trip to Switzerland. Using looping, he narrowed his topic to focus on a specific outing.

We did a lot of interesting things in Switzerland, like going to a yodeling contest and watching some craftsmen make clocks. As usual, my sister and I argued a lot, but for the most part we enjoyed ourselves.

One of our worst arguments was on the day we got lost on a hike. I wanted to get back to the hotel to use the amazing pool before it closed. She kept telling me to shut up and enjoy the scenery.

Considering Your Audience and Purpose

Knowing your **audience**—who your readers will be—will lead you to shape your writing in specific ways. For instance, if you are writing a letter to your grandparents about your vacation, you don't have to explain that Muffy is your sister's nickname. If you are writing about your vacation for class, you might have to explain this and other details.

Knowing your **purpose** will also help you shape your work. Before you draft, analyze your purpose.

Analyze Your Purpose

To decide on your purpose, ask yourself these questions:

- Is my topic funny, moving, or exciting? Is my purpose to **entertain** the reader?
  If so, focus on the amusing, moving, or adventurous aspects of your story.
- Does my topic involve a lesson I learned? Is my purpose to **instruct** the reader?
  If so, focus on the events that taught you the lesson and draw conclusions from them.
- Am I writing about a particularly interesting person? Can I **capture that character's personality** in words?
  If so, focus on details showing the person as he or she is.

▲ Critical Viewing Imagine that you were part of this scene. What might your purpose in writing about it be? Explain. **[Apply]**

Gathering Details

Once you've narrowed your topic and considered your purpose, gather details—events, descriptions, dialogue—to include in your narrative. If you are writing about an experience you shared with others, consider conducting an interview.

Interview Others

Jot down notes on the events about which you are writing. Then, using a different color for each participant in these events, draw rectangles around events on which a participant might have a special point of view. Circle places where your own memories of events are unclear. Reviewing your circled and boxed notes, make a list of questions for each interviewee.

Arrange to speak with each person for an uninterrupted stretch of time. During the interview, ask your questions and take notes on the interviewee's answers. Make sure your notes are accurate—you can ask the person to repeat himself or herself if necessary.

Technology Tip

Use a word processor to input your questions for your interview. Afterward, you can type in the interviewee's answer directly below each question.

Step-by-Step Teaching Guide

Prewriting: Considering Your Audience and Purpose

1. Remind students that their topic will, in some sense, define their audience. In their drafts, they should keep in mind who will read their story, and provide the necessary details.
2. Explain that some writing can be informal, like e-mail, while other writing requires more formality. By considering the purpose of their writing—what they are trying to say—and the audience—to whom they are trying to say it—students will be able to narrow their topics.

Step-by-Step Teaching Guide

Prewriting: Interview Others

1. Autobiographical writing requires good detective work—students need to interview the people involved in the events they choose as their topics.
2. Ask students to practice interviewing family, friends, and relatives by asking questions about events. "What do you recall . . . ?" and "How would you describe . . . ?" are good opening questions in an interview.

Critical Viewing

Apply Answers will vary. Students may say to entertain or instruct. They might want to tell how exciting it was to visit the Eiffel Tower or tell how they learned to appreciate a certain aspect of French culture.

ONGOING ASSESSMENT: Monitor and Reinforce

If students are having difficulty considering their purpose in their autobiographical narrative, use one of the following options.

Option 1 Suggest that students imagine that they are writing an account of an event for a person who is new to the community and needs to know what happened before he or she arrived. Have them use details that will make it clear that their purpose is to inform.

Option 2 Ask students to write an account of something that happened to them and imagine that it will be read over the school's public address system. Their account should be descriptive enough to make sense to someone who does not know all of the people involved.

TIME SAVERS!

Writing Support Transparencies
Use the transparencies for Chapter 4 to teach these strategies.

Step-by-Step Teaching Guide

Drafting: Order Events; Emphasize Tension

Teaching Resources: Writing Support Transparency 4-D, Writing Support Activity Book 4-1

1. Explain that the details in a narrative need to be arranged in a particular order. For example, if a student writes about the time she left a window open and the cat got out, it would make sense for her to order her details as follows:

   The cat is an indoor-only cat. (exposition)

   The student left the window open. (inciting incident)

   The cat noticed the window ajar. (development)

   The cat escaped through the open window. (climax)

   The student caught the cat before it disappeared. (resolution)

   If these details are told in a different order, the story might not make sense.
2. Now ask students to identify the exposition, inciting incident, development, climax, and resolution in their details. Caution students that not every story has all of those stages, but most good ones do.
3. Display the transparency and have students read the information in the chart. Give students copies of the blank organizer to help them emphasize tensions in their essays.

Customize for *Visual/Spatial Learners*

Have students draw pictures of what happened at each stage of the story. Then have them order the pictures according to the order of events of their autobiographical narratives. They can use their illustrations to focus their narratives.

Customize for *Less Advanced Students*

Encourage students to write down a few descriptive words to remind them of an event, then brainstorm for more words to describe it. Have students rewrite the words in the order in which the event occurred.

4.3 Drafting

Shaping Your Writing

Any well-told story, even a true one, has a **plot**—a sequence of events retold in a way that will sustain a reader's interest. After you've gathered your details, organize them into a plot.

Order Events

First, take notes on the **conflict** in your story. A conflict appears whenever a character wants something that another character or force stops him or her from getting. You may also create interest by showing how your view of an event changed. (For an example, read "The Star of the Rodeo" on page 50.)

After defining a conflict, organize events around it. In the first part of your story, introduce the characters, setting, and situation. Build to a **climax**—a turning point. End with a resolution that settles the conflict.

Emphasize Tension

Tension in your story keeps your reader turning the pages. To create tension, consider which events in your narrative build to a climax. Refer to the example in this chart:

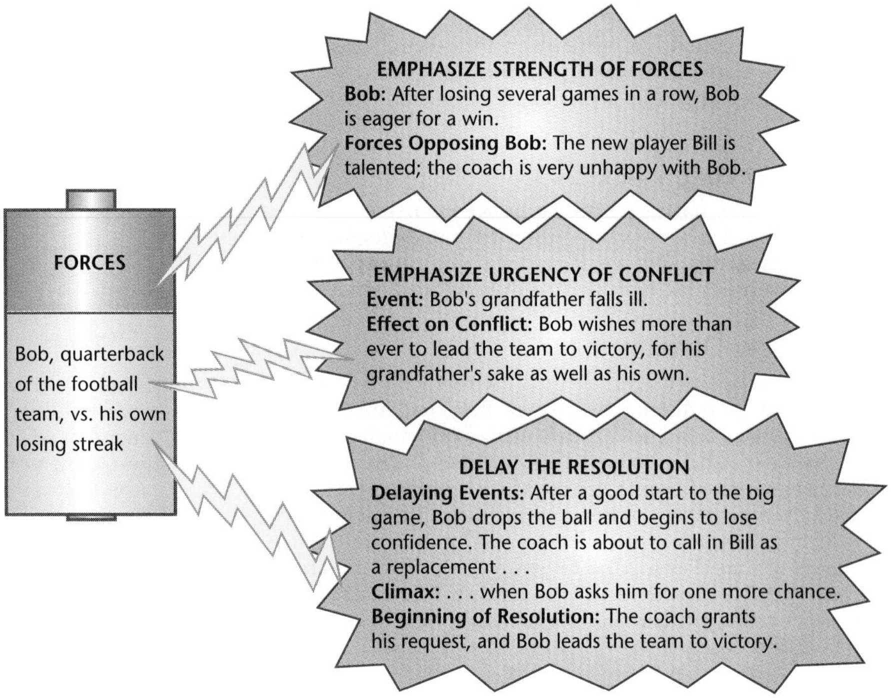

FORCES
Bob, quarterback of the football team, vs. his own losing streak
EMPHASIZE STRENGTH OF FORCES
Bob: After losing several games in a row, Bob is eager for a win.
Forces Opposing Bob: The new player Bill is talented; the coach is very unhappy with Bob.
EMPHASIZE URGENCY OF CONFLICT
Event: Bob's grandfather falls ill.
Effect on Conflict: Bob wishes more than ever to lead the team to victory, for his grandfather's sake as well as his own.
DELAY THE RESOLUTION
Delaying Events: After a good start to the big game, Bob drops the ball and begins to lose confidence. The coach is about to call in Bill as a replacement . . .
Climax: . . . when Bob asks him for one more chance.
Beginning of Resolution: The coach grants his request, and Bob leads the team to victory.

TIME AND RESOURCE MANAGER

Resources
Print: Writing Support Transparencies, 4-D–E; Writing Support Activity Book, 4-1
Technology: Writing and Grammar iText, Section 4.3

In-Depth Coverage	Accelerated Pace
• Cover pp. 58–59 in class. • Have students do their autobiographical writing draft in class. • Demonstrate the techniques of adding significant details using the transparency.	• Have students review pp. 58–59 independently, then write their first draft. • Respond to individual drafting issues as needed.

Providing Elaboration

Uncle Ed's twinkling eyes . . . The mall parking lot, as gray, pitted, and lonely as the surface of the moon . . . Details such as these convey the essence of a person or place in just a few words. As you write your autobiographical piece, add such significant details to create colorful, accurate pictures.

Add Significant Details

As you draft, pause at the end of a paragraph. Review it for references introducing an important character or place. For each reference, place a sticky note in the margin. On the note, write your answer to the following questions:

- When I think of the person or place, what feature first comes to mind?
- When I think of the person or place, what feeling first comes to mind?

After you have finished drafting, review your notes. Include any details from them that will enhance the picture you create for readers.

Student Work IN PROGRESS

Name: Evan Twohy
Prospect Sierra School
El Cerrito, CA

Adding Significant Details

As he drafted, Evan added details that capture the beauty of the Swiss mountains.

We strolled down the ^dusty, unpaved^ roads and gazed at ~~the~~ ^sunlit^ fields ^abundant with colorful flowers^. The scenery was exquisite, with ^trickling^ waterfalls and ^sheer^ cliffs, and the scent of fresh pine needles emanated from the moist soil.

dusty, unpaved

sunlit
abundant
with colorful
flowers

trickling

sheer

Step-by-Step Teaching Guide

Drafting: Providing Elaboration; Add Significant Details

Teaching Resources: Writing Support Transparency 4-E

1. Display the transparency to show students how adding significant details can enhance the pictures created in a story. Details make a story more memorable and, in some cases, more accurate.
2. Suggest that students imagine that they are telling their story to a distant relative or a reporter, someone who would want to know all of the details to set the scene.
3. Have students write their significant details to be added in the margins or at the end of each paragraph, then add them to their stories in the revision.

Customize for *More Advanced Students*

Suggest that students write their stories with as many details as possible, then eliminate the details that are unnecessary to the story. This exercise should help them discriminate between details that are crucial and enriching, and those that are superfluous to the plot.

TIME SAVERS!

Writing Support Transparencies
Use the transparencies for Chapter 4 to teach these strategies.

Writing Support Activity Book
Use the graphic organizers for Chapter 4 to facilitate these strategies.

Step-by-Step Teaching Guide

Revising: Revising Your Overall Structure

Teaching Resources: Writing Support Transparency 4-F; Writing Support Activity Book 4-2

1. Each part of a narrative has a function. The opening sentences, or lead, need to convince the reader to keep reading. For a narrative piece, this lead should hint at where the story is going without giving everything away.
2. Ask students to review their introductions. Does the introduction engage the reader and grab their attention?
3. Display the transparency and review the kinds of details students can use to create an effective lead.
4. Give students copies of the blank organizers. Have them add details that they can use to create an effective lead for their essays.

Critical Viewing

Interpret Students may say, "Will the juggler stay on the rope?" He might drop one of the pins and lose his balance.

4.4 Revising

Revising Your Overall Structure

Now that you have finished a first draft, your ideas are on the page. Next, make sure they will catch a reader's imagination. Revise to ensure that your opening engages readers and that your story continues to hold their interest.

▲ **Critical Viewing** What question does this photograph raise? What might happen next? **[Interpret]**

Create an Effective Lead

In a narrative, a good first sentence "hooks" the reader, leading him or her to ask, "What will happen next?" or "What's going on?" The next sentence or two should tie this "hook" to the rest of the story, as in this example:

HOOK: A sound like a garbage can full of chains rolling down the stairs woke me in the middle of the night.

TIE TO STORY: It took me a second to remember the "trap" my brother had set for me in the kitchen doorway. It took me another second to remember that my parents usually went straight for the kitchen after an evening out.

To create a good hook, you can use a few kinds of details:

an engaging description
On a winter's day, with a little luck, a hiker in the hills can catch sight of the sunset glinting off Graysmere's stained-glass windows.
a statement that hints at a story
It all started with Grandpa's hankering for fudge.
dialogue or a character's thoughts
From beneath the rusted-out hulk of an ancient sedan I heard a voice: "Just let me tighten this widget a smidge, and I'll be right with you."
an exciting action
Looking the opposing tackle straight in the eye, I took the hiked ball, faked a pass, and casually handed it off to a runner.
an interesting, apt quotation
When Shakespeare said, "Some have greatness thrust on them," he might have been thinking about the time my friend Fred "volunteered" me for the school play.

TIME AND RESOURCE MANAGER

Resources
Print: Writing Support Transparencies, 4-F–I; Writing Support Activity Book, 4-2
Technology: Writing and Grammar iText, Section 4.4

In-Depth Coverage	Accelerated Pace
• Cover pp. 60–65 in class. • Work through the Revision Strategies with the entire class. • Review Grammar in Your Writing.	• Have students review pp. 60–65 independently. • Have students revise their autobiographical narratives independently.

Build Tension

Once you've captured the reader's attention, hold it by building the excitement of your story. Use clues to ensure the tension builds before the climax (the turning point that will decide how the conflict ends).

REVISION STRATEGY
Using Clues to Take Your Story's "Temperature"

Mark the climax of your story with a large red triangle. Starting several paragraphs before the climax, circle each of the following "temperature-raising" details in the color indicated:

YELLOW:	details that establish facts basic to the conflict
ORANGE:	details connecting new events to the conflict
RED:	details adding to the urgency of the conflict

If you find a paragraph near your climax lacking circled details, consider adding details connected with the conflict.

Student Work IN PROGRESS

Name: Evan Twohy
Prospect Sierra School
El Cerrito, CA

Measuring Story "Temperature"

After identifying several "temperature-raising" details before his climax, Evan decided to add a few more.

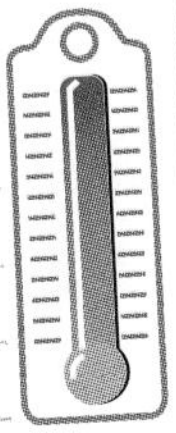

When we arrived at the place to which the signs were guiding us, it turned out that, "Z'mutt" was approximately four cow sheds and a café, all in a row.
"I knew it," I said. "Now we certainly won't be able to swim."
"Does this mean you'll relax and enjoy the scenery?" laughed my sister.

A good hour later, after going in the wrong direction more times than the right one, we began following signs for "Z'mutt." ~~"Z'mutt," it turned out, had nothing to do with "Zermatt."~~ Desperate for our hotel, we sped frantically through the tiny town. We stumbled onto yet another trail and began descending rapidly, until we finally rushed down a small, flat path and ended up, exhausted, in Zermatt.

Evan added his sister's response to relate this event to his conflict with his sister.

Evan replaced this sentence. The new sentence adds urgency to the conflict by creating a contrast between what they found and what they were looking for.

Step-by-Step Teaching Guide

Revising: Build Tension

Teaching Resources: Writing Support Transparency 4-G

1. Encourage students to make sure that they continue to hold the reader's attention in their storytelling. Ask them to identify various places in their narratives where the tension is rising toward the climax of their story. Have students build tension with additional details as needed.
2. Have students identify the climax of their narrative and verify that it is clearly set apart with rising and falling tension in the paragraphs before and after this central conflict.
3. Display the transparency. Using Evan's work as a model, have students take their stories' "temperatures" by identifying areas that might need revision and reorganizing as they see fit.

TIME SAVERS!

Writing Support Transparencies
Use the transparencies for Chapter 4 to teach these strategies.

Writing Support Activity Book
Use the graphic organizers for Chapter 4 to facilitate these strategies.

Step-by-Step Teaching Guide

Revising: Check-Marking for Coherence

1. Each paragraph in a narrative is a step that leads readers toward the end of the story. Missing steps, or steps that lead in other directions, make it difficult to follow the story to its end.
2. With this model in mind, ask students to go through their autobiographical narratives and check each paragraph to make sure that it is in the correct order and leads clearly to the end of the story.
3. Then have students examine each sentence in the context of each paragraph. Does each sentence belong in the paragraph it is in? Have students shift sentences to proper paragraphs if needed.

Critical Viewing

Apply Students may say that the girl's grandfather is teaching her how to play chess. Students' additional sentences will vary.

4.4

Revising Your Paragraphs

Strengthen Coherence

A paragraph is not a dump—don't throw just any old sentence in there! Like the features of a well-laid-out park, each sentence in a paragraph should have a clear relation to the others. Clean up the "litter" in your paragraphs. Check the connection of each sentence to the main idea of the paragraph.

iText

Get instant help! Use the check-marking tool in the Essay Builder, accessible from the menu bar, on-line or on CD-ROM.

REVISION STRATEGY
Check-Marking for Coherence

Follow these steps to check-mark for coherence.

1. For each paragraph in your draft, identify the main idea.
2. On a sticky note, jot a brief phrase summing up this main idea. Stick the note next to the paragraph.
3. Review each paragraph in your draft. For each sentence in a paragraph, first read the phrase on the sticky note and then read the sentence.
4. Place a check mark over any sentence that seems out of place when you read it after your main idea.
5. After you have finished, review each checked sentence. Eliminate any sentence that does not belong in the paragraph, or rewrite it to make its connection to other sentences clearer.

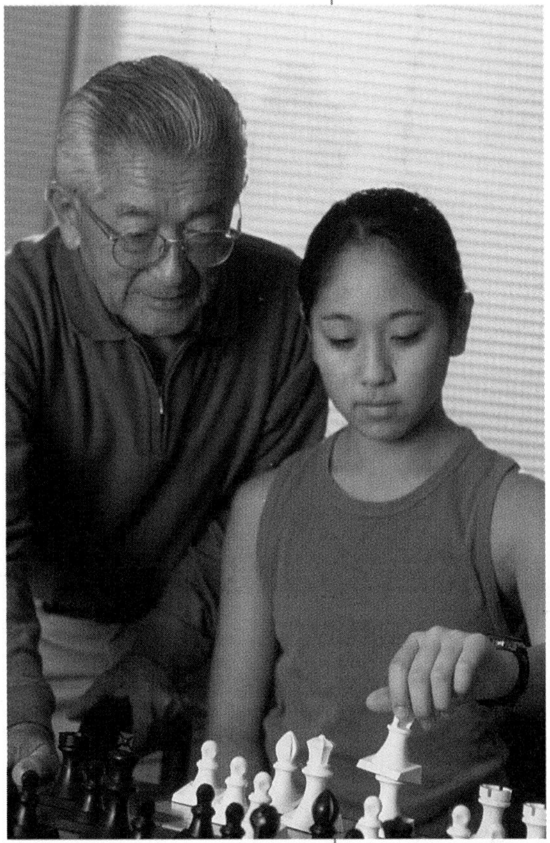

▶ Critical Viewing
Write a sentence describing the activity in this photograph. Then, add several related sentences, and organize them in the best order. **[Apply]**

ONGOING ASSESSMENT: Monitor and Reinforce

If some students are having difficulty revising, use one of the following options.

Option 1 Have students prepare an outline of their narrative, assigning a topic sentence to each paragraph and indicating how each sentence fits in each paragraph. If students have difficulty justifying sentences in paragraphs, they should revise accordingly.	**Option 2** Have partners work as editors of each other's work. Ask students to put checks next to sentences that do not fit well in paragraphs. Have students work together to revise the narratives, reorganizing sentences and paragraphs where necessary.

Revising Your Sentences

Vary the Sentence Structure

Even if you build tension, you can still write a dull story. Imagine a story in which every sentence started with *I*: "I did this. I did that. I did something else." This droning beat would put you to sleep! Color-code sentence beginnings to help create an interesting rhythm and vary sentence structure.

REVISION STRATEGY
Color-Coding Sentence Beginnings

Code the first word of each sentence in your draft with a colored shape, as follows:

Articles	include *the*, *a*, and *an*.
Nouns	name a person, place, or thing.
Pronouns	such as *I*, *you*, *he*, *she*, *it*, *we*, and *they* stand in place of nouns.
Adjectives	tell more about something named by a noun. *Blue*, *envious*, and *difficult* are all adjectives.
Adverbs	tell more about a verb, an adjective, or another adverb. *Quickly*, *brightly*, and *less* are adverbs.
Prepositions	show the relationship between things. *In*, *out*, *off*, *on*, *toward*, and *away* are prepositions.

Find groups of circles in the same color. Rewrite sentences in these groups so that some begin with another kind of word.

Collaborative Writing Tip

In a group, read aloud some of the sentences that you want to structure differently. Group members should take turns suggesting other ways in which you might say the same thing.

Student Work IN PROGRESS

Name: Evan Twohy
Prospect Sierra School
El Cerrito, CA

Color-Coding Sentence Beginnings

When Evan saw the number of red rectangles in this paragraph, he rewrote several sentences so that they began with different kinds of words.

[As our car rattled out of the little log station,] ~~We~~ peered excitedly out the blue plastic windows ~~as our car rattled out of the little log station~~. Despite the fact that it was almost impossible to see through the white scratches on the pane, my mom snapped photo after photo. We were looking forward to an enjoyable afternoon on the mountain. ~~We planned~~ [Our plan was] to do some hiking and then return to Zermatt. . . .

Step-by-Step Teaching Guide

Revising: Vary the Sentence Structure

Teaching Resources: Writing Support Transparency 4-H

1. Display the transparency. Have students discuss how Evan's revisions improved his paragraph.
2. Have students underline the verbs in their sentences. Ask students to replace forms of the verb *be (am, is, was, are, were, be, being, been)* with action verbs.
3. Ask students to read their sentences aloud and listen for repetitious phrasing. Encourage them to replace similar sentences with new ones that use a varied pattern of subject and verb. For example:

   Boring: She ate cake. He ate cake.

   Revised: First, she ate cake. Then he devoured what was left.
4. Emphasize that writing is like anything else—the same old thing will not keep the attention of the reader. If a student ate ketchup every day for lunch, eventually the ketchup would cease to be interesting or good. Students should think of their writing as a recipe—the more varied the ingredients used, or the more interesting the interpretation of familiar ingredients, the more lasting the impression their work will have on their readers.

TIME SAVERS!

Writing Support Transparencies

Use the transparencies for Chapter 4 to teach these strategies.

Step-by-Step Teaching Guide

Revising: Use Precise Nouns

Teaching Resources: Writing Support Transparency 4-I

1. Display the transparency to show students how using more precise language can improve one's writing.
2. Ask students to go through their narratives and look critically at the nouns they use. Do they repeat "Julio" ten times when they could say "he," or do they write "the bird" instead of "the eagle" to describe what they saw on a trip? Have them reword their narratives with new nouns as necessary.
3. Have partners read through each other's work, looking for words that could be replaced with more precise nouns.
4. Have students use a thesaurus to find synonyms for nouns that seem repetitive or dull.

4.4

Revising Your Word Choice

Use Precise Nouns

The story you tell unfolds for readers as a series of pictures in their imagination. The more precise your words, the clearer the pictures your readers will form. For instance, if you are writing about a vehicle, the precise word *minivan or hatchback* will give your readers a clearer picture than *car.* A single precise noun also has more impact than a lengthy, though precise, explanation. For example, "person who likes biking" is not as effective as "cyclist."

Highlight nouns to help you use precise words.

REVISION STRATEGY
Highlighting Nouns

Highlight the first five and the last five nouns in your draft. For each, ask yourself:

- What picture do I want to paint with this noun?
- Does my reader need more information to form this picture?
- What precise noun, used by itself, will provide most of this information?

Replace nouns that do not paint a clear picture, or that need additional explanation, with precise nouns.

Research Tip

Use a thesaurus to help you find precise nouns to replace vague or general ones. Always check the meaning of an unfamiliar word in a dictionary before using it.

Student Work IN PROGRESS

Name: Evan Tuohy
Prospect Sierra School
El Cerrito, CA

Highlighting Nouns

After reviewing nouns in his draft, Evan replaced a few general nouns with precise nouns to help the reader envision Zermatt.

... Zermatt is a quaint ~~place~~ town that consists of a ~~small church~~ chapel, a pathetic mini golf course, a children's cemetery, an old-fashioned ~~store~~ bakery, many tourist shops, and more than fifteen ~~hotels~~ chalets . . .

STANDARDIZED TEST PREPARATION WORKSHOP

Vocabulary Standardized test questions may require students to recognize multiple meanings of words. Ask students to choose the word that fits in both of the following sentences.

The winter ____ felled some oak trees in our front yard.

Dad needed to ____ the clock each morning when he woke up.

A gust
B smoke
C wind
D adjust

C is the only word that fits both sentences, as a noun meaning "a gust of air" and as a verb meaning "to turn or twist."

Grammar in Your Writing
General and Specific Nouns

A **noun** is a word that names a person, place, or thing. Nouns can be more or less specific. The most general nouns include a wide variety of persons, places, or things. For instance, the word *animal* can be used for giraffes, zebras, turtles, and ants. The more specific the noun, the smaller the variety of things it includes. For instance, the word *apes* names a group of animals that are similar to one another. The word *chimp* is even more specific. **Proper nouns**—nouns naming an individual person, place, or thing—are quite specific. Here are some examples of general and specific nouns:

People		Places		Things	
General:	child	General:	building	General:	clothes
Specific:	infant	Specific:	skyscraper	Specific:	overalls
	toddler		factory		suit
General:	relative	General:	beach	General:	feeling
Specific:	brother	Specific:	seashore	Specific:	tenderness
	Aunt Sue		boardwalk		frustration

Find It in Your Reading Review "The Star of the Rodeo" by Larry Paul Kline on page 50. Find three examples of specific nouns, and describe the picture each creates.

Find It in Your Writing Find three general nouns in your draft. For each, determine whether it captures the precise picture you mean to give readers or whether you should replace it with a more specific noun.

To learn more about nouns, see Chapter 14.

Peer Review
"Say Back"

In a group of four or five students, read your whole story aloud while the others listen closely. Pause briefly, and then read it again. This time, listeners should quickly jot down (1) what they liked and (2) what they want to know more about. Afterward, listeners will "say back" to you what they've jotted down. Use their comments to guide you as you work on your final revision.

Step-by-Step Teaching Guide

Grammar in Your Writing: General and Specific Nouns

1. Discuss the differences between general and specific nouns and proper nouns.
2. Ask students to bring in a magazine or newspaper article that interests them. Have them work in pairs, underlining general nouns, circling specific nouns, and starring proper nouns.
3. Ask them to rewrite a paragraph from the article using more specific nouns where general nouns are used, if they feel it is necessary.
4. Encourage students to reexamine their narratives and insert specific and proper nouns where they are needed. Explain that narrative clarity can be achieved by greater specificity in language.

Find It in Your Reading

Some of the specific nouns students may identify are *mountain lion, passion,* and *heart attack.*

Find It in Your Writing

Have students replace any general nouns with more specific ones. Encourage students to share examples from their writing with the class.

ONGOING ASSESSMENT: Prerequisite Skills

If students have difficulty with nouns and proper nouns, you may find it helpful to review the following to ensure coverage of prerequisite knowledge.

In the Textbook	Print Resources	Technology
Nouns and Pronouns, pp. 310–313	Grammar Exercise Workbook, pp. 1–6	Writing and Grammar iText, Section 14.1; On-Line Exercise Bank, Section 14.1

Step-by-Step Teaching Guide

Editing and Proofreading

1. Explain that careless errors may make it hard for readers to understand their work.
2. Have students review their writing for errors in grammar, spelling, and punctuation, including errors in comma use.

Step-by-Step Teaching Guide

Grammar in Your Writing: Using Commas After Introductory Elements

1. Write the following sentence:

   When my sister visited my aunt, Jane went also.

   Ask students to say the sentence quietly to themselves and listen for the pause (after *aunt*). Explain that the comma prevents confusion in this example. It makes clear that my sister did not visit "Aunt Jane," but that Jane went along.
2. Review phrases and clauses. Then have students look for introductory phrases and clauses in their narratives and punctuate them with commas.

Find It in Your Reading

Possible responses: *1) As a very young child in Niagara Falls, New York, . . . 2) When I was six years old, . . . 3) In the late '50s, . . .*

Find It in Your Writing

Have students exchange drafts and check each other's use of commas.

PRENTICE HALL
Everyday Spelling

If you have taught the spelling skills in *Prentice Hall Everyday Spelling*, Grade 8, Chapter 4, in conjunction with this *Writing and Grammar* chapter, review and assess students' mastery of the skills before concluding the chapter. Remind students to apply the spelling skills as they edit and proofread their autobiographical narratives.

4.5 Editing and Proofreading

Errors in your narrative can distract readers. Proofread carefully for errors in spelling, punctuation, and grammar.

Focusing on Commas

Check your work for the incorrect use of commas. Make sure you have included a comma after every introductory clause.

Proofreading in Pairs

Exchange drafts with another student for proofreading. Correct all the errors you find with an erasable red or blue pencil.

Grammar in Your Writing

Using Commas After Introductory Elements

A **phrase** is a group of words that work together like a single word to modify a word in a sentence. A **clause** is a group of words with a subject and a verb. Phrases and clauses can be used to add information at the beginning of a sentence. These introductory elements should be separated from the rest of the sentence by commas, as in these examples:

INTRODUCTORY PHRASES: Humming softly to myself, I walked down the street.
For many reasons, it is a good idea to eat vegetables.

INTRODUCTORY CLAUSES: Before he went to bed, he said "good night" to his hamster.
When I carry an umbrella, I often leave it someplace.

Find It in Your Reading Review "The Star of the Rodeo" by Larry Paul Kline on page 50. Find three examples of introductory elements followed by commas.

Find It in Your Writing Review your draft, and circle any introductory elements. Make sure that each is separated by a comma from the rest of the sentence. If you do not find any introductory elements, consider rewriting some sentences to begin with an introductory clause.

To learn more about using commas, see Chapter 26.

TIME AND RESOURCE MANAGER

Resources
Print: Scoring Rubrics on Transparency, Chapter 4; Writing Assessment: Scoring Rubric and Scoring Models in Autobiographical Writing
Technology: Writing and Grammar iText, Sections 4.5–6

In-Depth Coverage	Accelerated Pace
• Cover pp. 66–69 in class. • Review the Rubric for Self-Assessment in class. • Analyze in class the final draft on p. 68. • Allow students to edit and proofread their essays in class. • Have students present their final drafts.	• Have students review pp. 66–69 independently. • Have students edit and proofread their narratives independently. • Respond to individual editing issues as needed.

4.6 Publishing and Presenting

Consider these possibilities for publishing and presenting your work.

Building Your Portfolio

1. **Publish Your Memoirs** Get together with other students to publish a book of memoirs. Work as a team to create a cover and to illustrate the pieces. Finally, write a paragraph that states the purpose of the collection.
2. **Video Collection** Make a video "documentary" in which each member of the class reads his or her narrative, followed by a brief interview with the student about his or her work. Students should take turns introducing and interviewing each other.

Reflecting on Your Writing

Jot down your thoughts on writing autobiographically. Begin by answering the following questions:

- As you wrote about what happened to you, did you gain any fresh insights into yourself?
- How did thinking about the conflict help you structure your work?

Internet Tip

To see autobiographical narratives scored with this rubric, go on-line: PHSchool.com
Enter Web Code: eck-8001

Rubric for Self-Assessment

Evaluate your autobiographical narrative using the following criteria:

	Score 4	Score 3	Score 2	Score 1
Audience and Purpose	Contains an engaging introduction; successfully entertains or presents a theme	Contains a somewhat engaging introduction; entertains or presents a theme	Contains an introduction; attempts to entertain or to present a theme	Begins abruptly or confusingly; leaves purpose unclear
Organization	Creates an interesting, clear narrative; told from a consistent point of view	Presents a clear sequence of events; told from a specific point of view	Presents a mostly clear sequence of events; contains inconsistent points of view	Presents events without logical order; lacks a consistent point of view
Elaboration	Provides insight into character; develops plot; contains dialogue	Contains details and dialogue that develop character and plot	Contains details that develop plot; contains some dialogue	Contains few or no details to develop characters or plot
Use of Language	Uses word choice and tone to reveal story's theme; contains no errors in grammar, punctuation, or spelling	Uses interesting and fresh word choices; contains few errors in grammar, punctuation, and spelling	Uses some clichés and trite expressions; contains some errors in grammar, punctuation, and spelling	Uses uninspired word choices; has many errors in grammar, punctuation, and spelling

ONGOING ASSESSMENT: Assess Mastery

Use one of the following options to assess final drafts of students' essays.

Self Assessment Ask students to score their essay using the rubric provided. Then have students write a single paragraph reflecting on the most valuable thing they learned in completing this essay.

Teacher Assessment You may wish to use the rubric and the scoring models provided in Writing Assessment, Silver Level, to score the essays.

Step-by-Step Teaching Guide

Publishing and Presenting

1. Publishing students' writing can be as simple as posting it on an Internet bulletin board or sending it out to friends on an e-mail distribution list.
2. In preparing their narratives for publication, students may want to incorporate supplemental material (family trees, photographs, diagrams, illustrations) that would enhance their final product. Have them integrate those materials into their final draft.
3. Students may especially want to share their autobiographies with people who are mentioned in the narratives or who knew them at the time the events occurred.

ASSESS

Step-by Step Teaching Guide

Assessment

Teaching Resources: Scoring Rubrics on Transparency 4; Formal Assessment, Chapter 4

1. Display the Scoring Rubric transparency and review the criteria in class.
2. Before students proceed with self-assessment, you may wish to review the Final Draft of the Student Work in Progress on pages 68–69. Have students score the Final Draft in one or more of the rubric categories. For example, how would students score the piece in terms of audience and purpose?
3. In addition to students self-assessment, you may wish to use the following assessment options:
   - score student essays yourself, using the rubric and scoring models from Writing Assessment.
   - review the Standardized Test Preparation Workshop on pages 74–75 and have students respond to a autobiographical writing prompt within a time limit.
   - administer the Chapter 4 Test from Formal Assessment in Teaching Resources to assess students' grasp of concepts presented.

Step-by-Step Teaching Guide

Teaching From the Final Draft

1. Help students see that "Zermatt or Bust" incorporates key elements of autobiographical narrative.
   - The topic is well chosen; the interesting episode described is discrete in length.
   - Audience and purpose are established carefully. The essay sets out to answer the question the reader might have about why Evan and his family need to return to Zermatt before eight.
   - The introduction is captivating and grabs the reader's attention. It also sets the scene dramatically and gives an idea of what is to come.
   - The body of the essay sets up the tensions in the story, and tension builds evenly throughout.
   - A short conclusion revisits the central conflict of the story and its resolution.
2. Ask students if they think that the way the essay is constructed helps them understand what happened to Evan and his family on their trip.
3. Ask students if they would revise the essay in any way, or how they would change it to make it more or less suspenseful. How might they apply these ideas to their own writing?

Critical Viewing

Relate Answers will vary. Students may say the Matterhorn, the café, the Swiss people, etc.

4.7 Student Work IN PROGRESS

FINAL DRAFT

▶ Critical Viewing
If you were writing an autobiographical narrative about a visit to this place, on what aspect of this scene would you focus? **[Relate]**

Zermatt or Bust!

Evan Twohy
Prospect Sierra School
El Cerrito, California

One by one, we leaped into our *sesselbahn*, a sky ride that runs precariously up to the peak of the Matterhorn mountain in the Swiss Alps. The door slammed shut after us, and the tram began to move. As our car rattled out of the little log station, we peered excitedly out the blue plastic windows. Despite the fact that it was almost impossible to see through the white scratches on the pane, my mom snapped photo after photo. We were looking forward to an enjoyable afternoon on the mountain. Our plan was to do some hiking and then return to Zermatt—the small, touristy town where we were staying—before eight. It was now four.

Evan creates an effective beginning by starting in the middle of an action that is already going on.

What was the rush to get back to Zermatt, you may ask. It's true that Zermatt is a quaint town that consists of a chapel, a mini golf course, a children's cemetery, an old-fashioned bakery, many tourist shops, and more than fifteen chalets, but its chief attraction for me was the pool at the hotel where my family was staying. The pool was extravagant. It had a waterfall and blasts of water shooting up from the floor. And it closed at eight.

In his exposition, Evan explains what he wants—the first step in creating a conflict or problem.

Our sesselbahn jolted to a stop, and the doors slid open. My family and I hopped out happily and made our way outside. We strolled down the dusty, unpaved roads and gazed at sunlit fields abundant with colorful flowers. The scenery was exquisite, with trickling waterfalls and sheer cliffs, and the scent of fresh pine needles emanated from the moist soil. We were so wrapped up in the beauty of the Alps that we completely forgot the time. It was almost six-fifteen, and we hadn't reached our final destination.

Notice that Evan includes vivid details to help the reader picture the scene.

"Maybe we should just turn back," I whined. "The sesselbahn won't take as long. At the rate we're going, we'll probably have enough time to dip our toes in the water."

"Shh," my sister quickly snapped. "This is once-in-a-lifetime scenery. Can't you just relax? There are more than a billion swimming pools back in America, anyway."

"Not as good as this one."

"Oh, shush!"

"Oh, stop bickering, you two!" my mom called from up ahead. "What's the problem?"

My sister and I explained the controversy. My mom sided with me, whereas my dad agreed with my sister. We finally decided that it would take just as long to get back to Zermatt via the sesselbahn as by foot, so we continued walking. I reluctantly trudged on behind my family, looking at my watch.

Evan mentions his watch to maintain tension, reminding the reader of the fast-approaching deadline.

I got really nervous about the pool when we found that all the trails led us in the opposite direction from where we wanted to go.

"I knew it," I said. "Now we certainly won't be able to swim."

"Does this mean you'll relax and enjoy the scenery?" laughed my sister.

A good hour later, after going in the wrong direction more times than the right one, we began following signs for "Z'mutt." When we arrived at the place to which the signs were guiding us, it turned out that "Z'mutt" was approximately four cow sheds and a café, all in a row. Desperate for our hotel, we sped frantically through the tiny town. We stumbled onto yet another trail and began descending rapidly, until we finally rushed down a small, flat path and ended up, exhausted, in Zermatt.

In the half hour I was able to relax in the pool, I thought about the day's events and what I had seen. Under the soothing influence of the water jets, I began to think my sister was right. I could go to a pool anywhere, but hiking in the Alps was a unique experience that I would not trade for anything. Of course, I might never have had that thought if we hadn't made it back in time!

Evan ties up his story nicely by concluding with a realization.

Teaching From the Final Draft

Explain to students that a beginning, a middle, and an end are important features of a piece of writing. Using the conclusion of "Zermatt or Bust" as an example, have students examine the conclusions of their narratives to see if their endings solve or satisfy a problem taken up in the beginning or middle of their narratives.

Lesson Objectives

1. To write a firsthand biography.
2. To choose an appropriate topic for a firsthand biography.
3. To draft, revise, and edit a firsthand biography.
4. To publish a firsthand biography for an audience.

Step-by-Step Teaching Guide

Firsthand Biography

Teaching Resources: Writing Support Transparency 4-J; Writing Support Activity Book 4-3

1. Invite students to bring a favorite snapshot of a friend or family member to class and bring in a photograph of your own. Briefly discuss some of the photos. What personality traits do they reveal? What events do they bring to mind? Encourage students to use photos of the subjects of their firsthand biographies as memory aids.
2. Suggest that students review writing strategies from Chapter 4.
3. To help them choose subjects for their firsthand biographies, students can compile lists of people they admire and friends who have shared exciting times as described in the textbook.
4. Use the transparency to model, charting significant moments in one's relationship with a subject.
5. Give each student a copy of the blank organizer. Ask students to record significant interactions with the subject of their biography on the chart.
6. Encourage students to submit their firsthand biographies to your school's literary magazine or to collect the firsthand biographies and assemble them into a class anthology.

Connected Assignment
Firsthand Biography

You've probably seen posed, formal photographs of a friend or family member. You may hardly recognize the person—hair done up just for the occasion, head turned at an odd angle, a forced smile on his or her face. Compare a posed photograph with one you've taken of the person yourself. Your photograph probably shows the person as he or she really is.

Like a photograph you take of a friend, a firsthand biography offers unique insights into its subject. A **firsthand biography** is a true account of the life of someone whom the writer knows or knew personally, focusing on one event or period in the subject's life. A firsthand biography includes

- a subject other than the narrator.
- an organized retelling of events from the life of the subject.
- a first-person point of view—the work is narrated using the pronoun *I*.
- an insight into the subject only the writer could provide.

▲ Critical Viewing Which side of the actor shown in the photograph is likelier to be explored in a firsthand biography? Explain. **[Hypothesize]**

Prewriting To find a subject for your firsthand biography, put your life on the line—create a timeline of important parts of your life. Use these memories to choose your subject. You might choose a subject who falls into one of the following categories:

- **Firsthand Biography of Someone You Admire** Write about a person you know and admire, such as an accomplished family member or friend, a coach, or a teacher.
- **Firsthand Biography of a Fellow Adventurer** Think back to an adventure in your life—an exciting baseball game, a visit to a new place, or your first trip to the zoo. Who was with you? What impact did his or her presence have?

Once you have selected the person about whom you wish to write, focus on a specific event involving him or her or on a special characteristic he or she has. Remember that the strength of your biography lies in your perspective on the person. Concentrate on the lessons the person has taught you or a side of the person that only you might see.

Create a graphic organizer to record and arrange the details you will use to show the most important aspects of your relationship with the person. Use a chart like the one shown.

Critical Viewing

Hypothesize Most students will believe that the private side of the actor is more likely to be explored in a firsthand biography rather than the public face he reveals as the character on the movie poster.

Last Fall	Early Spring	Late Spring	Summer	This Fall
I meet coach Groznik. He scares me a little because of his loud voice.	The coach suprises me by picking me to pitch.	After a few months of working with him, I was able to pitch more accurately than ever before.	I went to hear the town orchestra play Beethoven's *Third* and was shocked to see Coach playing in the viola section.	I had a long talk with coach about Beethoven (one of my heroes) and the difference between sports and music.

Gather details that reveal your subject's personality and special qualities. Include the following kinds of details:

- things he or she has said
- major accomplishments
- personal quirks
- incidents that reveal how he or she has influenced you
- incidents that reveal how he or she has shaped events in which you were both involved.

Drafting As you draft, make sure that you narrate events in the first person (use the pronoun *I*). Focus on painting a clear picture of your subject, relating each detail to your central impression of the person. Elaborate on your story by including your own impressions and reactions to events.

Revising and Editing After you have completed a draft, review its overall structure. Make the following kinds of revisions:

- **Check Sequence** Make sure that you have presented events and descriptions in a logical sequence.
- **Add Transitions** Use transitional words such as *afterward, before, during*, and *as a result* to show the order and relation of events clearly.
- **Build to a Point** If your biography reads like a recital of facts, find the moment in your draft that gives the strongest impression of your subject. Move this section to the end, and rewrite earlier sections to prepare the reader for it.
- **Add Your Reactions** Look for places in your draft where your reader will be most curious about the reactions of you or your subject. Add details about these reactions.

Publishing and Presenting After you have revised your biography, proofread your paper to make sure that there are no errors in spelling, grammar, or punctuation. Consider presenting a copy of your firsthand biography to its subject.

Customize for *Gifted/Talented Students*

Students may enjoy illustrating their firsthand biographies with portraits of the subjects. They should use the media of their choice, including photography. Encourage student cartoonists to present their firsthand biographies in comic book format, complete with four-color art, a flashy cover, and a riveting title.

Customize for *Less Advanced Students*

These students may need some help narrowing the scope of their firsthand biographies. Discuss the people about whom they have chosen to write. Guide them as they think of several very specific reasons they have chosen their subjects and urge them to keep these reasons in mind as they decide what to write. Have students focus their writing on one or two incidents they feel best reveal their subjects and their influence on them.

Lesson Objectives

1. To interpret and evaluate the various ways visual image makers represent meanings.
2. To evaluate the effects of varying media.
3. To select visuals to complement meanings.
4. To write a journal entry based on paintings and music.

Step-by-Step Teaching Guide

Understanding Meaning in the Arts

1. Show the class several other examples of Rubens's portraits. Discuss with students what the portraits reveal of the sitters' personalities and the fashions of the times. Keep the examples of Rubens's work available so your students can write about them as directed on this page of the textbook.
2. Interested students may wish to research Rubens's illustrious career and present what they have learned to the rest of the class.
3. You may wish to make several CDs of Bach's music available to your students so they can choose a piece to write about for the autobiographical writing activity assignment.

Viewing and Representing

Activity Ask volunteers to show reproductions of the paintings and play CDs of the music they chose for their Baroque journal for the rest of the class. They should sum up the reasons these works of art express their feelings about the events they describe in their journals.

Critical Viewing

Compare and Contrast Many students will believe that the dress of the sitters expresses their position in society rather than their individual personalities.

Spotlight on the Humanities

Understanding Meaning in the Arts

Focus on Painting: Peter Paul Rubens and the Baroque

In this painting, Flemish painter Peter Paul Rubens (1577–1640) has created an autobiography without words. Among all the ruffles, the painter's eyes hint at his skeptical, probing outlook on the world. Under the fancy hat, his wife Isabella's sense of humor, or even mischief, traces itself on her lips, about to open in smiles or laughter. In their hands lies a tale of their marriage.

The ruffles and fancy hats also tell the story of the times in which Rubens lived. During the seventeenth century, decorative flourishes and complicated lines characterized fashion as well as art. Rubens was one of the defining painters of this period, called the Baroque when one is referring to the arts.

Influenced by the Italian painters Carracci and Caravaggio, Rubens was known for luxurious color, sophisticated composition, and his use of shade and light. Like this portrait, many of his paintings are marked by a tension between complex composition and direct emotion. Rubens became a major influence on painters of the eighteenth and nineteenth centuries.

Rubens and his wife Isabella in the honeysuckle, Peter Paul Rubens

▲ **Critical Viewing** Contrast the expressions on the people's faces in this painting with their complicated dress. Then, explain whether their clothing "hides" their personalities or expresses them. **[Compare and Contrast]**

Music Connection The baroque spirit also blossomed in the music of the seventeenth and eighteenth century. Johann Sebastian Bach (1685–1750) of Germany was the foremost composer of baroque music. Just as baroque painting used complex designs, Bach's music elaborates on each musical theme with swirling phrases of mathematical complexity. Yet it is also a music of penetrating beauty and sharp feeling.

Autobiographical Writing Activity: Baroque Journal

Listen to several recording of Bach's music. Choose one as the "theme song" for an event in your life. Next, look through a collection of Ruben's paintings. Choose the one that comes closest to the mood of the event you have chosen. Then, write a journal entry narrating the event from your life, and explaining why you have chosen the music and the painting you have.

Media and Technology Skills

Produce Visuals to Make Meaning

Activity: Create an Autobiographical Photo Essay

Rubens's portrait of himself and his wife gives insight into the couple. You can use a camera to share an insight into yourself. Learn more about taking photographs, and create an autobiographical photo essay.

Learn About It Read the owner's manual of the camera you are using to familiarize yourself with its features. If you are using a 35mm camera, learn how to apply the concepts of film speed, f-stop, and aperture. If necessary, ask for the help of a more experienced photographer.

Keep a Log Take a few rolls of film in varying conditions of light and at various distances and angles. If you have access to different lenses, try using each. Keep a log of the conditions under which you took each shot and the results they produced.

Experiment With Different Effects Different uses of the camera create different meanings. For example, a picture taken with a wide-angle lens creates a different effect from one taken with an ordinary lens.

Apply It Using a chart like the one below, plan and take a series of photographs that reveal something about yourself. Choose people, objects, places, and events that show an aspect of your life, and photograph them in a way that reveals what is important about them to you. You might include a picture that you take of yourself in a mirror or using a timer. After you have completed your project, display it to the class.

Aspect of Myself	Type of Photograph	Special Considerations
I enjoy the band The Migraines.	Interior	• Take photo of my room showing posters on wall. • Use wide-angle lens to get more posters in and for cool effect. • Take in dim light with flash to add shadow for effects.

Types of Images

Portrait
A close-up of a person or his or her face. The person's dress and pose and the background to the portrait can imply much about the person.

Action Shot
A shot of a person performing a specific action. The photograph should include enough background to make the circumstances clear.

Still Life
A shot of a group of objects. In a still life, a photographer pays special attention to the arrangement of objects.

Landscape/Interior
A shot of a place that gives some sense of its dimensions, situation, and mood. (A landscape is an outdoor scene; an interior is indoors.) In landscapes and interiors, a photographer pays special attention to the composition created by features of the place.

Real-World Connection

Show students a few examples of your favorite magazine or newspaper photo essays and discuss the demands of careers in photo journalism. Emphasize that photo journalists usually have just one chance to capture a story. They must know the capabilities of their equipment and materials intimately and have extra cameras, lenses, and film on hand in case they need it. Photo editors cull the photos later in a newspaper or magazine office and editors and designers assemble the photographs into photo essays.

Lesson Objectives

1. To produce visuals to extend meanings.
2. To assess how the medium contributes to the message.

Step-by-Step Teaching Guide

Create an Autobiographical Photo Essay

Teaching Resources: Writing Support Transparency 4-K; Writing Support Activity Book 4-4

1. Select examples from magazines of the four types of photographic images described on this page. Display the examples and discuss them with the class. Which type of image do students like to look at most? Which one is the most fun to shoot? Explain that students will create autobiographical photo essays that include at least one of these types of photos and as many as all four.
2. You may want to read and explain sections of the owner's guide from your camera or a friend's camera to help students understand their own owner's guides. Urge students to ask parents or photographer friends for help with deciphering the parts of their guides that puzzle them.
3. Display the transparency. Use the chart to model how to plan a series of photographs.
4. Give each student copies of the blank organizer. Have students use the charts to plan their photo essays.
5. Display the completed photo essays in the classroom or a location in your school where everyone can enjoy them.

Lesson Objectives

1. To write to express and reflect on ideas.
2. To develop, draft, revise, and proofread an essay.
3. To use correct grammar, spelling, and punctuation.

Step-by-Step Teaching Guide

Supporting an Interpretation With Autobiographical Narrative

Teaching Resources: Standardized Test Preparation Workbook, pp. 7–8

1. Have students list the steps for responding to writing prompts on standardized tests on the board. Discuss the items on the list and modify and amplify them as necessary. Make sure to emphasize that test takers must understand exactly what to do before they proceed.
2. Clarify the meaning of Emerson's quotation on the sample test with students by having volunteers explain the quote in their own words.
3. Urge students to read the directions on tests at least twice to make sure they understand what to do. Note that the sample test does not ask if students agree with the quotation but only that they find examples that illustrate the quotation.
4. Assure students that the percent of the total time on the test to spend on each of the steps of the writing process is approximate. Students must remember to leave a few minutes near the end of the test for editing and proofreading,

Standardized Test Preparation Workshop

Supporting an Interpretation With Autobiographical Narrative

The writing prompts on standardized tests often ask for a narrative response in which you use personal experience as support for your main idea. The following are the criteria upon which your writing will probably be evaluated:

- Does your style and word choice suit the purpose and audience named in the prompt?
- Do you organize details in a meaningful sequence, such as chronological order or order of importance?
- Do you use appropriate transitions to connect ideas?
- Do you elaborate on your experience using sensory details, characterization, dialogue and other details?
- Do you use correct grammar, spelling, and punctuation?

When writing for a timed test, plan to devote a specified amount of time to prewriting, drafting, revising, and proofreading.

Test Tip

If you are having difficulty interpreting a quotation on a test, first identify the main topic of the quotation. Then, jot down a brief list of ideas on the subject. Reread the quotation to see if it fits any of these ideas. If the quotation does not fit any idea on your list, brainstorm for other ideas on the subject that it might fit.

Sample Writing Situation

Read the following quotation:

The reward of a thing well done is to have done it.

—Ralph Waldo Emerson

Then, respond to the following prompt.

Write an essay explaining what you think Emerson means in this quotation. Support your interpretation using stories from real life, books, movies, music, or television shows.

TEST-TAKING TIP

One good way to organize ideas for an essay test is to make an informal outline. Students can list the major points they intend to make and include supporting points under the main headings. They might list all their ideas and go back and highlight the major points and the supporting evidence in the same color marker. Then they can add supporting details to major points that lack them and cross off points that don't fit their topic.

Prewriting

Allow close to one fourth of your time for prewriting.

Gather Details Begin by writing a brief interpretation of Emerson's quotation. Restate, in your own words, what he means. Next, to support your interpretation, make a list of things you have done well and of examples illustrating Emerson's idea from books, songs, or movies. Review your interpretation. If the stories you have listed give you a new insight into Emerson's words, consider revising your interpretation. Then, choose the one or two personal experiences and the one or two other examples that best illustrate your interpretation.

Consider Your Audience No audience is specified in the prompt, so you should write for an adult audience of test evaluators. Use formal language, avoiding slang and contractions.

Drafting

Allow almost half of your time for drafting.

Organization Create a sentence outline for your essay. First, jot down a sentence for each of your main ideas. Then, underneath each main idea, outline the story that supports the idea. You may choose to organize story events in chronological order. Alternatively, you may choose to relate your story by beginning with the most important details.

Introduction, Body, and Conclusion After organizing details, write an introductory paragraph giving the quotation and your interpretation of it. Then, in each body paragraph, illustrate your interpretation by briefly retelling the stories you have chosen. In your conclusion, restate your interpretation.

Revising, Editing, and Proofreading

Allow almost one fourth of your time to revise and edit. Use the last few minutes to proofread your work.

Strengthen Your Case Review your draft. Neatly cross out any details that do not clearly illustrate your interpretation. Add transitions where necessary to make the order of events in the stories you retell clear.

Make Corrections Eliminate contractions and slang from your interpretation. Check for errors in spelling, grammar, and punctuation. When making changes, place one line through text that you want eliminated. Use a caret (^) to indicate the places where you want to add words.

Customize for *Less Advanced Students*

Help less advanced students succeed at writing essays on timed tests by going through the process with them. Choose a simple quotation and model restating the gist of the quote and completing each step of the writing process. Then give the students another quote and let them write essays on their own. Circulate among the group to answer questions and check progress. Stop the clock after about half the allotted time has passed to make sure students are completing their drafts. Answer questions and address any problems you have noticed. Then have students complete their essays as you check students' progress as they revise, edit, and proofread their work.

Customize for *More Advanced Students*

Students may enjoy challenging one another to interpret quotations they find in Bartlett's or other sources. They might find quotes with which they disagree and write essays refuting the quotes. Remind students to include real-life examples that support their opinions.

Chapter 5

Time and Resource Manager

In-Depth Lesson Plan

	LESSON FOCUS	PRINT AND MEDIA RESOURCES
DAY 1	**Introduction to the Short Story** Students learn key elements of the short story and analyze the Model From Literature (pp. 76–83).	***Writers at Work* Videotape**, Narration ***Writing and Grammar iText* (Interactive Text),** Ch. 5, Introduction
DAY 2	**Prewriting** Students choose and narrow a topic, consider their audience and purpose, and gather information (pp. 84–87).	**Teaching Resources** *Writing Support Transparencies,* 5-A–C; *Topic Bank for Heterogeneous Classes,* Ch. 5 ***Writing and Grammar iText* (Interactive Text),** Section 5.2
DAY 3	**Drafting** Students organize their ideas and write their first draft (pp. 88–89).	**Teaching Resources** *Writing Support Transparencies,* 5-D–E; *Writing Support Activity Book,* 5-1 ***Writing and Grammar iText* (Interactive Text),** Section 5.3
DAY 4	**Revising** Students revise their drafts in terms of overall structure, paragraphs, sentences, and word choice (pp. 90–94).	**Teaching Resources** *Writing Support Transparencies,* 5-F–G ***Writing and Grammar iText* (Interactive Text),** Section 5.4
DAY 5	**Editing and Proofreading; Publishing and Presenting** Students check their work for accuracy and correctness and present their final drafts (pp. 95–96).	**Teaching Resources** *Scoring Rubrics on Transparency,* Ch. 5; *Formal Assessment,* Ch. 5 ***Writing and Grammar iText* (Interactive Text),** Sections 5.5–6

Accelerated Lesson Plan

	LESSON FOCUS	PRINT AND MEDIA RESOURCES
DAY 1	**Introduction Through Drafting** Students review the characteristics of short stories, select topics, and write drafts (pp. 76–89).	**Teaching Resources** *Writing Support Transparencies,* 5-A–E; *Writing Support Activity Book,* 5-1 ***Writing and Grammar iText* (Interactive Text),** Ch. 5, Introduction through Section 5.3
DAY 2	**Revising Through Presenting** Students work individually or with peers to revise, edit, and proofread their work for presentation (pp. 90–96).	**Teaching Resources** *Writing Support Transparencies,* 5-F–G; *Scoring Rubrics on Transparency,* Ch. 5; *Formal Assessment,* Ch. 5 ***Writing and Grammar iText* (Interactive Text),** Sections 5.4–6

Options for Adapting Lesson Plans

HOMEWORK

Have students complete any stage of the lesson for homework.

SPELLING

To teach spelling skills in conjunction with writing skills, work through *Prentice Hall Everyday Spelling,* Grade 8, Chapter 5, as you cover this *Writing and Grammar* chapter. At the Editing and Proofreading stage, remind students to apply the spelling skills to their short stories.

FEATURES

Extend coverage with Connected Assignment (p. 100), Spotlight on the Humanities (p. 102), Media and Technology Skills (p. 103), and Standardized Test Preparation Workshop (p. 104).

TECHNOLOGY

Students can complete any stage of the lesson on the computer, using *Writing and Grammar iText* or a word-processing program. Have them print out their completed work.

INTEGRATED SKILLS COVERAGE

Integrating Grammar
Action Verbs and Linking Verbs, SE p. 93
Punctuating Dialogue, SE p. 95

Reading/Writing Connection
Reading Strategy, SE p. 78
Writing Application, SE p. 83

Viewing and Representing
Critical Viewing, SE pp. 76, 78, 80, 82, 86, 94, 97, 98, 102
Adapting a Scene, SE p. 102

Speaking and Listening
Reading Aloud, ATE p. 92

Vocabulary
Eponyms, ATE p. 79

Integrating Workplace Skills
Describing a Character, ATE p. 89

Real-World Connection
ATE p. 99

ASSESSMENT SUPPORT

Standardized Test Preparation Workshop SE pp. 104–105; ATE p. 79

Standarized Test Preparation Workbook, pp. 9–10

Scoring Rubrics on Transparency, Ch. 5

Formal Assessment, Ch. 5

Writing Assessment and Portfolio Management

MEETING INDIVIDUAL NEEDS

Less Advanced Students ATE pp. 101, 105. See also Ongoing Assessments ATE pp. 77, 80, 81, 85, 87, 93, 96.

ESL Students ATE pp. 81, 85

Bodily/Kinesthetic Learners ATE pp. 90, 95

BLOCK SCHEDULING

Pacing Suggestions
For 90-minute Blocks
- Have students complete the Prewriting and Drafting stages in a single period.
- Focus one class period on Revising and Editing and Publishing and Presenting. Allow at least 30 minutes for peer revision.

Resources for Varying Instruction
- ***Writing and Grammar iText* (Interactive Text)** A 90-minute block provides an ideal opportunity for students to work on computer.
- ***Writers at Work* Videotape** Show the Narration segment in class.

Professional Development Support
- ***How to Manage Instruction in the Block*** This teaching resource provides management and activity suggestions.

MEDIA AND TECHNOLOGY

For the Student
- ***Writing and Grammar iText* (Interactive Text),** Ch. 5

For the Teacher
- ***Writers at Work* Videotape,** Short Story
- ***Resource Pro* CD-ROM**

WRITING AND GRAMMAR ON-LINE

iText Interactive Text (On-line or on CD-ROM)
- Easily navigable instruction with interactive Revision Checkers
- Full use of e-rater™, the essay-scoring system (on-line only)

Companion Web Site PHSchool.com
- Scoring rubrics with models (use Web Code eck-8001)

See the Go On-line! feature, SE p. iii.

LITERATURE CONNECTIONS

Related selections from *Prentice Hall Literature: Timeless Voices, Timeless Themes,* Silver:

Professional Model "Raymond's Run," Toni Cade Bambara, SE p. 83

Topic Bank Option "The Tell-Tale Heart," Edgar Allan Poe, SE p. 85

CHAPTER 5
NARRATION: SHORT STORY

Lesson Objectives

1. To understand the characteristics of a short story.
2. To choose a topic for a short story and define its elements: characters and a conflict.
3. To consider audience and purpose for a short story.
4. To gather details about characters for a short story.
5. To draft a short story, incorporating plot and elaboration.
6. To revise a short story in order to create tension and surprise and to develop characters fully.
7. To analyze sentences to ensure that they show clear connections between ideas.
8. To energize writing by using vivid verbs.
9. To benefit from the peer review process in the revision of a short story.
10. To edit, proofread, and publish a short story.

Critical Viewing

Speculate Students' responses will vary. Accept all reasonable responses.

Chapter 5

Narration

Short Story

Illustration for the poem "Fog" by Carl Sandburg by John English

▲ Critical Viewing
What kind of story could you tell about this picture? What characters would be in the story? What conflict, or problem, might they face? **[Speculate]**

Short Stories in Everyday Life

Life, you might think, is what *happens* to people, not what they *say* about it. Yet think of your life without stories. No funny stories, like the one about math class you told your friend. No inspiring stories from your family history. No tall tales about why you were late! Without these stories, your life would go on—but what would you make of it? What would you see in it?

A short story is made up, so it probably won't give you many facts about events that have actually *happened.* Instead, it will show you the power of what we *say* about life. Using the right words, a short-story writer can turn life into adventure or comedy or tragedy.

In this chapter, you'll learn to use this power for yourself as you follow the strategies for writing your own short story.

TIME AND RESOURCE MANAGER

Resources
Technology: Writers at Work Videotape; Writing and Grammar iText, Ch. 5

In-Depth Coverage	Accelerated Pace
• Cover pp. 76–77 in class. • Show the Narration section of the Writers at Work Videotape. • Read the literature excerpt (pp. 78–83) in class and use it to brainstorm for short story ideas with students. • Discuss examples of short stories you or students know about or bring to class.	• Discuss definition and types of short stories in class. • Assign the Model From Literature for independent reading.

What Is a Short Story?

A **short story** is a brief, creative narrative—a retelling of events arranged to hold a reader's attention. By letting you enter the lives of its characters, a short story pushes you beyond the person you are today, reminding you of all the other possible *you*'s bustling under your skin. Most short stories have

- one or more characters, clearly developed through the course of the story.
- a **conflict,** or problem faced by the main characters.
- a clear structure—with a beginning, middle, and end—which develops the conflict and leads to a **climax** (turning point) and resolution.
- a **theme**, or question about life and human nature, expressed in the events of the story.

To learn the criteria on which your story may be judged, see the Rubric for Self-Assessment on page 96.

Types of Short Stories

There are a few different kinds of short story:

- **Realistic stories** try to reflect the everyday lives of ordinary people.
- **Character studies** reveal a deep truth about a character. They emphasize painting a portrait of the character over telling a series of events.
- **Genre stories,** such as science-fiction stories, detective stories, and horror stories, follow a few basic rules to create a specific effect, such as wonder, suspense, or horror.

Writers in ACTION

Eudora Welty published her first stories as a young woman and won the Pulitzer Prize for Fiction in 1973. On creating characters, she has said:

"I have been told . . . that I seem to love all my characters. What I do in writing of any character is to try to enter into the mind, heart, and skin of a human being who is not myself. Whether this happens to be a man or a woman, old or young, with skin black or white, the primary challenge lies in making the jump itself. It is the act of a writer's imagination that I set most high."

As you write, follow Welty's example: Get "inside" your characters.

PREVIEW Student Work IN PROGRESS

Robin Myers, a student at Maplewood Middle School in Maplewood, New Jersey, wrote a short story called "A Tear and a Smile." In this chapter, you'll see how she used featured strategies to come up with a topic, develop narrative elements, and revise her first draft. At the end of the chapter, you'll read her finished short story.

PREPARE and ENGAGE

Interest GRABBER Tell students the following joke:

A couple bought a chain saw to turn a fallen tree on their property into firewood. They worked hard all day but managed to cut only a few logs. Thinking that there was something wrong with the chain saw, they took it back to the store. The salesman looked over the chain saw and hit the switch. It started with a mighty roar, puzzling the customers. "What's that noise?" they shouted.

Explain that this joke is a very short story. It has characters and a plot. The plot contains a problem (the chain saw doesn't seem to work well) and a resolution in which the problem is solved (the salesman unwittingly shows the customers how to operate the chain saw).

Activate Prior Knowledge

Invite students to share jokes appropriate for the classroom. Have them identify the characters, problems, and resolutions.

More About the Writer

Eudora Welty once risked her life for reading by dashing into a burning house to rescue her beloved books. Welty's love of stories began even earlier. In her autobiography, she describes herself as a young girl who, at the start of a family outing, would eagerly climb into the backseat of the car. "Now, talk!" the other passengers would command. Welty would regale them with stories the whole trip.

ONGOING ASSESSMENT: Diagnose

Use one of the following options to diagnose students' current level of proficiency in narrative writing.

Option 1 Ask each student to select the strongest example of his or her narrative writing from last year. Hold conferences in which you review each student's sample. Use the conferences to determine which students will need extra support in developing a short story.

Option 2 Ask students to write a paragraph summarizing the plot of a short story they may or may not ever write.

TEACH

Reading\Writing Connection

Reading Strategy: Interpret

Interpreting helps students understand what they read. Readers can learn more about story characters by asking themselves what their words and actions tell about their personalities.

Teaching from the Model

Use this model from literature to help students generate a topic for their own short stories. As students read, they can think about whether something similar has happened to them. Have they ever felt that they were different from other people? How did it turn out?

Step-by-Step Teaching Guide

Engage Students Through Literature

1. Read the first paragraph of the story aloud, or have a volunteer read it.
2. Lead students in discussion by asking questions such as:
   - Although this story is set long ago, how does the problem the characters face seem contemporary?
   - What does the narrator's use of the word *delicious* to describe an impending upset tell you about her character?
3. Encourage students to brainstorm other topics for short stories that the passage brings to their minds. Here are some possibilities:
   - *Experiencing humorous mix-ups or misunderstandings at school*
   - *Experimenting with a new fad*
   - *Pursuing an unusual interest*
   - *Being surprised at finding out that parents and students share some opinions*

   Students can add the brainstormed ideas to their own banks of topics for short story writing. They can begin with a true incident and add their own embellishments to create a short story.

5.1 Model From Literature

In this humorous tale, short story writer, biographer, and journalist Emily Hahn (1905–1997) relates what happens when two sisters decide to wear knickerbockers to school. (Knickerbockers—short, loose trousers gathered at the knees—caused quite a sensation when women started wearing them in the 1920's.)

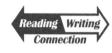

▲ Critical Viewing
Would the knickers pictured here create a stir in today's world? Explain why or why not. **[Speculate]**

Reading Writing Connection

Reading Strategy: Interpret Whenever you read, **interpret** what you have read by restating its significance. For example, when you read about an important event, ask yourself: What did this event show me about the characters or their situation? When the author emphasizes a detail, ask yourself: What does this detail show me? For example, in "New Clothes for School," Hahn writes that the mother's decision to have her daughters wear knickers is "a matter of deep calling to deep," and she notes that the mother had herself once "created a mild scandal" by her choice of clothes. These details show you that the mother and the daughters share a unique taste in clothes and take pleasure in stirring up trouble.

New Clothes for School

Emily Hahn

. . . When Mother saw an advertisement for knicker suits in the paper, she probably didn't realize what a delicious upset she was in for. Ostensibly, knickers for her two young daughters were just a good, practical idea. They seemed to settle the long-standing problem of how to dress us so that we could attend school and then go straight out to play rough games without ruining our clothes. Actually, it was a matter of deep calling to deep. Mother, in her young, office-going days, had created a mild scandal in St. Louis by wearing bloomers for bicycling, and she was hurt

Hahn's introduction gets the reader's attention by hinting at trouble to come.

Critical Viewing

Speculate Students may say that the answer depends on where the knickers are worn. If someone wore them to school, it may cause quite a stir.

and puzzled that Dauphine and I scorned bloomers. The knickers, however, met with our approval. They looked just like the clothes little boys wore before they graduated to long trousers, and, as successors to the comfortable rompers we had worn in childhood, they seemed pretty good. In 1920, remember, slacks had not yet been invented, and nobody wore pajamas in public except as Oriental fancy dress.

We were completely innocent about it, all three of us. Mother went downtown and bought the knicker suits, and one morning Dauphine and I put them on and started out for school.

On our way to the streetcar line, it began to be apparent that the public was going to consider the costume startling. A man driving a delivery truck reined in his horse and asked us if we had not forgotten something. It took us a little while to catch on. Then we flounced off indignantly, blushing. A group of street urchins followed us, making loud remarks. By the time the streetcar came, we were suffering badly from jitters.

Hahn begins to set up the main conflict in the story here: The girls' desire to wear knickers is opposed by public disapproval.

"Do you think maybe there's a law against it?" whispered Dauphine.

"Of course not, or Mother wouldn't have let us wear them," I said. "Why, they couldn't have sold them in the store. These crazy people!"

With this little speech by the narrator, Hahn quickly shows you that the narrator is Dauphine's leader and that she is brave.

The other passengers in the streetcar took a lively interest in our appearance. We stared ahead of ourselves with grim and rigid dignity. "Don't let them scare you," I counselled Dauphine. "I guess we've got a right to wear knickers if we want to."

Fortunately, a group of girls from school boarded the car a few stops along the line, and they broke the tension. They were squealingly enthusiastic about the innovation, making blithe, clearly insincere plans to convert their mothers to the idea. Though they weren't representatives of the bright young set, the support of anybody, however obscure and dull, meant a good deal just then. We clung to them with pathetic eagerness all the rest of the way.

By the end of that first morning, my sister and I had learned a lot. We had tasted the sweets as well as the bitterness of notoriety. There was now no doubt that the high school was aware of us. We knew what to expect from people approaching us in the narrow corridors. We became too well acquainted with the first startled jump, the second glance, the amused stare, the craned head, the animated discussion between bystanders, as each of us made her lonely way from class to class. It might have been less painful if we had been able to go together.

Most of my teachers, timid by nature, took the easy way out

Integrating Vocabulary Skills

Eponyms The word *bloomers* comes from the name of Amelia Bloomer. Bloomers were long, loose trousers gathered at the ankle. They were worn in the nineteenth century by women engaging in sports. Other eponyms that might interest students are *saxophone,* named for Adolphe Sax (1800s); *sideburns,* named for Civil War General Ambrose Burnside; and *jersey,* named after an island in the English Channel.

STANDARDIZED TEST PREPARATION WORKSHOP

Demonstrating Vocabulary Skills Many standardized tests require students to choose the correct definition of words and terms. Ask students to choose the word whose meaning is closest to that of the first word.

1. blithe
- **A** heavy
- **B** cheerful
- **C** mean
- **D** talented

2. innovation
- **A** change
- **B** machine
- **C** country
- **D** interior

3. indignant
- **A** poor
- **B** elegant
- **C** angry
- **D** proper

4. ordinance
- **A** idea
- **B** rule
- **C** noise
- **D** career

Answers: 1B, 2A, 3C, 4B

Critical Viewing

Compare and Contrast Students may say that the outfit shown on this page seems more outrageous because people today do not usually wear clothes made with so much fabric.

5.1

and ignored my knickered legs. Only one of them, an elderly spinster soured by too many years of teaching history, spoke about the costume when I entered her room. "What, Emily, is that extraordinary outfit?" she demanded. "What do you call it?"

In a husky voice I told her what it was called and where it had been bought. I really thought at first that she must want a pair.

"Looks completely ridiculous," she said in hearty tones. ". . . Tell your mother I said so."

"My mother likes knickers," I said. "She would like to wear them herself. She said she was sorry she's too old."

"Well, that settles it, of course," said the history teacher.

"Yes, Ma'am," I muttered, and buried my flaming face in a book. Neither Dauphine nor I had bargained on the teachers. We had never thought that teachers would have opinions about clothes.

There was a choice of two paths. We could give in and try to live down the knickers, or we could brazen it out by insisting on our rights and wearing the things again. On that first day two newspaper photographers lay in wait for us as we came off the school grounds. We should have gone over to the basketball field, for now was the moment to justify and vindicate those knickers by playing games with all the freedom and grace we were expected to feel. We didn't though. We made for home like scared rabbits.

"Are we going to tell Mother?" Dauphine asked on the streetcar.

"Tell her what?" I asked haughtily. "That a few fools looked twice at us? I guess she'd expect that, anyway. *She* wouldn't pay any attention to that."

"Oh," said Dauphine, and at her forlorn tone I looked sharply at her. "Then you're going to wear 'em tomorrow?" she asked.

"Aren't you?" I turned on her and she shrank back.

"I wanted to wear my pink dress," she faltered. "I never meant to stop skirts altogether. We've got a lot of dresses to wear out. . . . Well, all right. If you do, I guess I will, too."

The next day there was a piece in one of the evening papers, along with photographs. The Board of Education had refused to make any statement about knickers, and some enterprising reporter had tried to discover whether there was any ordinance on

▼ **Critical Viewing** The bloomers in this drawing were as outrageous in their day as the knickers pictured on page 78. Which would be the more outrageous fashion today? Explain. **[Compare and Contrast]**

Hahn develops the conflict further: The girls need to decide whether to defy public taste or give in to it. Their conversation also points at the theme of the story: When is standing up for your rights more important than being accepted by others?

ONGOING ASSESSMENT: Monitor and Reinforce

Students may be unclear about what knickers and bloomers are. Try these strategies to increase their understanding.

Option 1 Remind students that the illustrations that accompany stories often help clarify unfamiliar words and concepts.	**Option 2** Encourage students to point out words and phrases in the story's first paragraph that give clues about the meaning of *knickers* and *bloomers. (suits, dress us, without ruining our clothes, wearing bloomers for bicycling, clothes little boys wore, slacks)*

the subject of proper clothing for public-school students. He couldn't find any. There was only a vague city ruling about immodest attire.

"Immodest?" cried Mother, her face lighting up with the familiar glow of battle. "Do they dare to call these suits immodest? Why, the girls are covered from head to foot with good, thick wool! When I see some of those skimpy little things, with their rolled stockings and their low necks, I'm very proud of our girls. Isn't that so?"

With the phrase her face lighting up with the familiar glow of battle, *Hahn confirms the picture she is painting of the mother. The mother likes a conflict and enjoys defying public opinion.*

"Of course it's so," I said heartily. Dauphine did not reply, nor did my father, but then he wasn't listening.

Dauphine and I continued to wear our knickers to school. The excitement among the students soon died down, and the teachers managed to relax and pay attention to their jobs. A few girls in knicker suits were seen in the streets, and the newspapers worked up more and more interest in them. My Aunt Lillie made a trip from the suburbs to speak her mind to Mother about it. "I may be old-fashioned," she said, "but if . . . girls [were meant] to wear pants, they'd be born with 'em on."

Mr. Clarke, our principal, called an assembly one day, and, as usual, there was free speculation about its object. Mr. Clarke knew the authoritative value of the dark hint, and in the discharge of his duties he was always mysterious. I may be maligning him in saying his actions were the result of deliberate policy. They may have been the result of not quite knowing what to do next. In the *affaire des* knickers, for example, he was definitely up against it, because Mother had him on toast and we all knew it. Mr. Clarke had stuck his neck out; he had written her a letter signifying his disapproval of our costumes, and Mother was joyfully able to point out that his disapproval was purely private and personal. Besides, the newspapers had already made it clear that the Board of Education, upon due examination of its rights in the matter, had admitted that it couldn't expel Dauphine and me from class or dictate what we were to wear as long as we didn't come to school in a state suggesting nudity. Mr. Clarke didn't reply to the letter.

By explaining the legal position of the principal, Hahn heightens suspense—how will the school deal with the "outrageous" clothing worn by Dauphine and the narrator?

An assembly was a sort of emergency function in the auditorium, to which the entire school personnel (with the possible exception of the janitor) was peremptorily invited. In spite of the principal's cumbersome secrecy, I had a pretty good hunch that he intended to be pompous about knickers. It would be his only way to talk back to Mother.

Against Dauphine's protests, I dragged her down to the front

Customize for *ESL Students*

Students learning English may have trouble with the difficult words in this story, but they should instinctively understand the "music." They know what it is like to be—and often look—different from their classmates. Talk with students about Emily and Dauphine's feelings about wearing odd clothes. Does this story seem true?

ONGOING ASSESSMENT: Monitor and Reinforce

Students may find many unfamiliar words in the story. Try these strategies to increase reading comprehension and vocabulary.

Option 1 Have students make a list of unfamiliar words. Then have them read the sentences before and after each word and look for context clues, definitions, explanations, or synonyms.	**Option 2** If the story does not reveal a word's meaning, have students look it up in the dictionary.

Critical Viewing

Compare and Contrast Students may say that although the man in the photograph resembles the author's *physical* description of Mr. Clarke, his personality seems quite different.

5.1

row that afternoon and sat her next to me, directly below the rostrum. I was quite right in my hunch.

Mr. Clarke stood alone on the platform, a solid, stubby man with impressive thick white hair. After the rustling and whispering and the squeaking of folding seats had subsided, he still stood there in silence, solemn and awe-inspiring. He always started out that way, no matter what the occasion. He would lower his white head and stare at us fiercely, lips compressed and nostrils dilated, until our nerves were definitely strained. Then he would open his mouth and speak.

This day he was slow about opening his mouth, and from where I sat, bright-eyed and expectant in my knickers, I could detect a certain lack of assurance. Obviously, Mr. Clarke didn't quite know what he was going to say. At last he raised his head, placed his feet a little further apart, and declaimed, while avoiding our eyes.

"The immortal Shakespeare always has something pertinent to say," he began. "I cannot do better than to quote his deathless lines

> 'Be not the first by whom the new are tried,
> Nor yet the last to lay the old aside.'

I am grieved to tell you that our school's fair reputation has suffered. Owing to an ill-advised experiment made by two of our young women, who think themselves, no doubt, very modern. . . ."

Mr. Clarke loved to speak in a deep stern voice that could swell to a roar. On this occasion he let himself go, but he didn't really say anything in an entire half-hour except that knickers were immodest and that any girl wearing them rendered herself ludicrous and unwomanly. He did not, I marked with interest, forbid them. He didn't say anything that Dad would have to resent legally. He merely advised females against wearing pants, on the general grounds of morality, world civilization, and taste. Then he came to

▲ Critical Viewing
Using details from this photo, compare this man with Mr. Clarke. **[Compare and Contrast]**

Mr. Clarke's speech is the climax of the story. The reader's curiosity about how the story will end is at its greatest; the speech will determine how the conflict is resolved.

a stop, blew his nose, and started off the stage, with an avuncular wave of the hand to signify we could adjourn. An English teacher ran up the steps and whispered to him frantically. Mr. Clarke clapped his hands to call us back, and walked to the center of the platform.

"I have just been informed—that is, reminded," he said, "that it was not Shakespeare, as a matter of fact, who penned those immortal lines. It was Pope—Alexander Pope, Miss Jensen?" Miss Jensen, hovering offstage, nodded. "Yes," said Mr. Clarke, "it was Alexander Pope who wrote those words, as it happens. However, they are so wonderful that they might have been written by Shakespeare. And with that thought I will leave you."

"Well?" asked Dauphine as we walked out, last in the line of students. The others were looking back to see how we had taken it. My mouth was stiff from smiling carelessly.

"Well," I said, "what?"

"You wearing them tomorrow?" asked Dauphine.

"Sure," I said. "Aren't you?"

"Of course," she said savagely. "He doesn't give us any choice. Oh, dear, and I'm so tired of this color."

"Mine are wearing out," I said. There was a traitorous note in my voice, a note of hope.

At the resolution of the story's conflict, Mr. Clarke's waffling warning puts the decision about wearing knickers back on the girls. Instead of leading to victory or defeat, the resolution makes clear that the decision to wear knickers rests with the girls alone.

Reading Writing Connection

Writing Application: **Help Readers Interpret** As you write your short story, emphasize details that will help the readers **interpret** a character's personality and actions. You can emphasize a detail by discussing it at some length or by making sure it is the only detail of its kind that you include. For instance, Hahn spends a few sentences describing Mr. Clarke's return to the stage and his awkward way of excusing his error. By emphasizing these details, she invites you to see his foolishness.

LITERATURE

For another short story about a girl facing a challenge, see "Raymond's Run" by Toni Cade Bambara. You can find this short story in *Prentice Hall Literature: Timeless Voices, Timeless Themes,* Silver.

More About the Writer

Continuing her pattern of flouting convention, Emily Hahn became the first woman to graduate from the University of Wisconsin as a mining engineer. She once stated, "I have deliberately chosen the uncertain path whenever I had the chance." Hahn's "uncertain path" led her all over the world—to Hollywood, where she worked as a screenwriter; to Africa, where she worked in a hospital outpost and lived with a tribe of pygmies; and to China, where she worked as a correspondent. Hahn chronicled many of her adventures while a freelance writer for the *New Yorker* magazine. By the time of her death in 1997, she had written more than fifty books on such diverse topics as diamonds and apes.

Responding to Literature

In "Raymond's Run," Hazel Elizabeth Deborah Parker (aka Squeaky) wants to be different from others. Her beloved brother Raymond really is different. All he wants to do is to run just like his sister. Students may want to read the story and then write a story about someone they admire and want to be like.

Reading\Writing Connection

Writing: Help Readers Interpret

Have students find words and phrases from Hahn's story that help them understand the characters. Ask them what words and phrases they might use to help the reader understand the main character in a story about climbing Mount Everest.

Step-by-Step Teaching Guide

Prewriting: Freewriting

1. This exercise is meant to generate writing ideas in quantity, not necessarily in quality. Encourage students to jot down whatever comes into their heads, because even the silliest idea can be the germ of a good writing topic.
2. If students have difficulty getting started, suggest that they complete phrases like these:

   "The time I . . . ," "The best ____ on the planet," or "____s are always surprising."
3. As an alternative jump start, students could jot down a list of words that begin with each letter of the alphabet. Either of these approaches could give them new topic ideas.

Step-by-Step Teaching Guide

Prewriting: Periodical Flip-Through

1. Provide students with appropriate magazines or newspapers as well as sticky notes on which to jot down ideas about topics.
2. To generate additional topics, encourage students to relate some of the topics to one another. For example, a photo of a chimp and an advertisement for a bookstore called Big Ape Books might spark a unique story idea.

Step-by-Step Teaching Guide

Prewriting: Writing Round

Teaching Resource: Writing Support Transparency 5-A

1. Display the transparency to show students how Robin used a writing round to come up with a story idea.
2. As a variation of this strategy, students might write incomplete sentences that other students can add to. For example,

   Student 1: While hiking through the woods, I heard a . . .

   Student 2: . . . low whistle and a loud roar that seemed to come from . . .

   Student 3: . . . everywhere at once.

5.2 Prewriting

Choosing Your Topic

You may already have an idea for a story, but if not, here are a few strategies that might help you come up with a topic:

Strategies for Generating a Topic

1. **Freewriting** Spend five minutes writing down story topics. Focus on getting ideas down rather than on grammar or punctuation. Afterwards, choose one idea as a topic.
2. **Periodical Flip-Through** Flip through a stack of periodicals, and flag photographs, articles, headlines, cartoons, or ads you find intriguing, annoying, or outrageous. Choose a topic from among those suggested by your flagged items.
3. **Writing Round** In a group, have one student write the first sentence of a story. Then, have each student add a sentence. Afterwards, read the story aloud, and choose a topic suggested by it.

iText

Get instant help! Freewrite using the Essay Builder, accessible from the menu bar, on-line or on CD-ROM.

Student Work IN PROGRESS

Name: Robin Myers
Maplewood Middle School
Maplewood, NJ

Choosing a Topic From a Writing Round

These are the notes from a writing round session that helped Robin come up with a topic for her story—a character who discovers a secret.

(John) I knew there was something strange about our next-door neighbors the first day they moved in.

(Wendy) For one thing, why did the moving van arrive in the middle of the night?

(Joseph) The noise woke me up, so I went to the window.

(Heidi) That's when I noticed a man and a woman carrying dozens of large, heavy duffel bags into their new house.

(me) One of the bags was open slightly, and I could see something shiny inside.

My Topic: A character discovers a secret.

TIME AND RESOURCE MANAGER

Resources
Print: Writing Support Transparencies, 5-A–C
Technology: Writing and Grammar iText, Section 5.2

In-Depth Coverage	Accelerated Pace
• Cover pages 84–87 in class. • Guide students through the prewriting strategies for generating topics on pp. 84–85. • Have students use the Listing and Itemizing strategy on p. 86 to develop narrative elements in their stories. • Have students begin their stories. • Have students "interview" their characters to gather details about them.	• In class, discuss how to choose a good topic for a short story. • Have students list possible topics. • Ask students to submit topic proposals for your review.

TOPIC BANK

If you're having trouble coming up with a topic, consider these possibilities:

1. **An Arduous Journey** Write a story about a teenager who must make a long commute between home and school. (You might model your story after a myth, movie, or video game that involves a hero who faces an arduous journey.)
2. **A Small Tale** A number of stories chronicle the adventures of tiny people—fairy tales like "Tom Thumb," children's books like *The Borrowers*, and movies like *Fantastic Voyage*. Write a story about someone much smaller than his or her surroundings. Explain why this character is so tiny and what mishaps occur as a result.

Responding to Fine Art

3. Write a story based on this painting. Who is the sailor? Where is he going or returning from? Who is waiting for him, at home or at his destination? What is his conflict?

The Dory, Edward Hopper, The Nelson-Atkins Museum of Art, Kansas City, Missouri

Responding to Literature

4. Read the story "The Tell-Tale Heart" by Edgar Allan Poe. Then, write your own story from the point of view of one of the police officers who come to search the murderer's house (have your narrator use the first-person *I*). You can find "The Tell-Tale Heart" in *Prentice Hall Literature: Timeless Voices, Timeless Themes*, Silver.

Cooperative Writing Opportunity

5. **A Group Story** Working with two other students, discuss possible topics and collaborate on a story plan, outlining all of the events for a story and describing all of the characters. Then, have one student write the beginning of the story, another the middle, and one the end. When the first draft is finished, one group member should read it aloud. The group should agree on any changes that need to be made. Using the group's decisions, each writer should then revise his or her part of the story.

Step-by-Step Teaching Guide

Responding to Fine Art

The Dory, by Edward Hopper

Teaching Resources: Writing Support Transparency 5-B

1. Display the transparency and ask students what story the painting suggests to them.
2. Ask students to brainstorm some story elements suggested by the painting. Here are some possibilities:

   Character: an inexperienced sailor, a presidential candidate, or a jilted young man

   Conflict: an approaching storm, a threatening letter, or a jealous rival

Responding to Literature

In Poe's terrifying tale, a murderer mistakes the ticking of a watch for the beating of his victim's heart. His guilt drives him to confess. Students' stories should make one of the police officers the central character and show the problem he confronts.

Customize for *ESL Students*

Students learning English might benefit from working with two English speakers to write a group story.

Spotlight on the Humanities

For additional topic suggestions, refer students to the Spotlight on the Humanities on page 102.

ONGOING ASSESSMENT: Monitor and Reinforce

Students may benefit from reviewing the elements of a short story. Use the following strategies to help students generate topics. You may want to outline these items on the board.

1. The story has one or more well-developed characters.
2. The main characters face a conflict or problem.
3. The story has a beginning, a middle, and an end.
4. The story contains a turning point or climax and leads to a resolution.
5. The story has a theme that expresses a truth about human nature. The theme might be stated as a one-word answer to the question "What's it all about?" Possible answers: honesty, forgiveness, friendship, loyalty.

TIME SAVERS!

Writing Support Transparencies

Use the transparencies for Chapter 5 to teach these strategies.

Step-by-Step Teaching Guide

Prewriting: Developing Narrative Elements; Listing and Itemizing

Teaching Resources: Writing Support Transparency 5-C

1. Draw students' attention to the graphic organizer and the connections between the circled choices.
2. You can demonstrate the listing and itemizing strategy on the board, using the literature as a starting place. Tell students that the author of "New Clothes for School" might have followed a process similar to this one in choosing a topic.

   Possible main characters

   My sister and me

   My parents

   My classmates

   Possible conflicts

   Trouble at home

   Trouble at school

   Trouble at a show

   More specific possible conflict

   What we brought to school

   What we read

   What we wore
3. Have students indicate which items the writer may have chosen as she began to write "New Clothes for School."

Critical Viewing

Draw Conclusions Students may say that the owner of the room likes photography and painting because there are many images on the walls.

TIME SAVERS!

Writing Support Transparencies

Use the transparencies for Chapter 5 to teach these strategies.

5.2

Developing Narrative Elements

Once you've come up with a topic, define your story's basic elements. You need a **main character,** a person you can make vividly real to the reader. Next, you need to involve this character in a conflict. A **conflict** is a struggle between two opposing forces. A character's conflict may be **external,** as when a sheriff fights an outlaw, or **internal,** as when an outlaw struggles with his own conscience. Use the strategy of listing and itemizing to invent a main character and a central conflict.

▲ Critical Viewing
From this photo, what can you tell about the owner of this room? Explain which details support your conclusions. **[Draw Conclusions]**

List and Itemize

List choices about who your main character might be. Circle your most interesting choice, and create another list of ideas about that circled item. Review this list for the elements you need: a well-defined main character facing a particular conflict. If you do not find these elements, repeat the process.

Student Work IN PROGRESS

Name: Robin Myers
Maplewood Middle School
Maplewood, NJ

Listing and Itemizing

Robin used listing and itemizing to define her main character and conflict. She began with the topic from her writing round: A character discovers a secret.

a kid who uncovers a big mystery or crime
a kid who discovers that her neighbors are secret agents
(a kid who discovers a family secret) ①

kid discovers her parents are secret agents
kid discovers her parents are royalty
(kid discovers something about a parent who died) ②

thirteen-year-old girl (cross between me and Allie)
discovers a note her mom wrote before she died
finds note in the attic (own house? grandmother's?)
doesn't know her mother wrote it
wants to find out who wrote it and why (conflict)

Considering Your Audience and Purpose

An interesting main character and an exciting conflict will keep readers interested. You can't start telling your story, though, until you know your **audience**—who your readers are. Similarly, you need to know your **purpose** in writing. Consider these examples:

If your audience is made up of . . .

- **people like your friends:** You might quickly build a picture of a character by naming the music he or she likes.
- **older people:** If you mention that the character listens to the band Migraine, you should explain what that suggests about your character.

If your purpose is to . . .

- **entertain:** Include funny, moving, or scary details.
- **analyze a character:** Build a complex picture of the person by describing his or her habits, tastes, lifestyle, and motives.
- **present a theme (a question or message about life):** Use events that illustrate this question or message.

Gathering Details

To make characters come to life, you need to get to know them. "Interview" characters to gather details about them.

Interview Your Characters

"Ask" your characters questions, just as you would with someone you are getting know, and write down what you imagine their answers would be. Start with the list of questions shown.

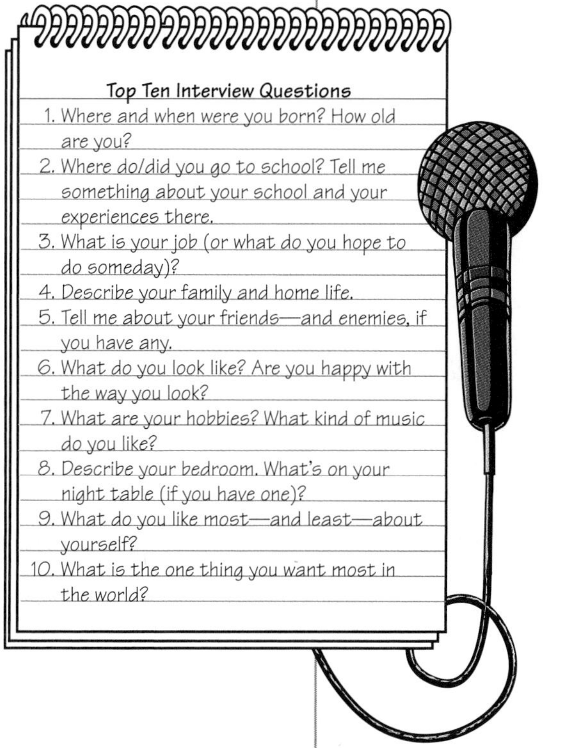

Top Ten Interview Questions
1. Where and when were you born? How old are you?
2. Where do/did you go to school? Tell me something about your school and your experiences there.
3. What is your job (or what do you hope to do someday)?
4. Describe your family and home life.
5. Tell me about your friends—and enemies, if you have any.
6. What do you look like? Are you happy with the way you look?
7. What are your hobbies? What kind of music do you like?
8. Describe your bedroom. What's on your night table (if you have one)?
9. What do you like most—and least—about yourself?
10. What is the one thing you want most in the world?

Step-by-Step Teaching Guide

Prewriting: Considering Your Audience and Purpose

1. Ask students how Emily Hahn might have written her story differently if she were writing for an audience of second graders. Ask volunteers to revise part of the story's first paragraph, using vocabulary and sentence length more appropriate for younger students.
2. Discuss whether the author's purpose in writing "New Clothes for School" was to entertain, to analyze a character, or to present a message about life. Help them understand that the author's purpose is to entertain. Encourage them to suggest additional details that would make the story more of a character analysis of Dauphine. (Answers may include her hobbies, the appearance of her bedroom, her friends, her favorite school subjects, and her thoughts.)

Step-by-Step Teaching Guide

Prewriting: Gathering Details; Interview Your Characters

1. Ask students to think of a potential story character and "interview" him or her to get answers to the ten questions.
2. As a warm-up to the above exercise, students may want to "interview" the main character in "New Clothes for School" or another story they have read. Explain that a story may not contain the answers to some of the questions and encourage students to make up appropriate answers.

ONGOING ASSESSMENT: Monitor and Reinforce

If some students are having difficulty coming up with a story topic, use one of the following options.

Option 1 Suggest that students choose a topic from the Topic Bank. If many students are having difficulty, work with the whole class on an idea from the Topic Bank or from ideas suggested by students.

Option 2 If Topic Bank ideas are too difficult, suggest that students try one of the assignments from the Topic Bank for Heterogeneous Classes in the Teaching Resources.

Step-by-Step Teaching Guide

Drafting: Shaping Your Writing; Create a Plot

Teaching Resources: Writing Support Transparency 5-D; Writing Support Activity Book 5-1

1. Display the transparency of a plot diagram. Invite students to look back at "New Clothes for School" and identify the exposition (the first paragraph, which introduces the main characters—a mother and two daughters), the conflict (whether or not knickers are appropriate for school wear), the climax (the school principal's criticism at the school assembly), the falling action (the principal's embarrassed correction about the source of his quote), and the resolution (the girls' decision about continuing to wear their knickers to school).
2. Explain that part of the setup in the story is the description of the school principal as someone who tries to inspire awe in the students and "loved to speak in a deep stern voice that could swell to a roar." Ask them when the payoff to this setup occurs. (when it is revealed that this pompous man who loves to speak and quote famous writers has attributed a quote to the wrong writer) Discuss with students how this payoff changes a reader's view of the principal. (from intimidating to rather ridiculous)
3. Have students map out their stories using the plot diagram.

5.3 Drafting

Shaping Your Writing

Now that you've gotten acquainted with your characters, it's time to begin your first draft. Start by mapping out your plot.

Create a Plot

A **plot** is the arrangement of actions and events in a story. In many stories, the plot follows this pattern:

- The **exposition** introduces the main characters and their basic situation, including the central conflict.
- This **conflict** develops during the rising action, leading to
- the **climax** (a high point of suspense, such as a startling revelation, a sudden insight, or a new twist), followed by
- the story's **falling action,** which leads to
- the **resolution,** in which the conflict is resolved in some way.

Using a Plot Diagram Map out the events in your story using a diagram like the one below. Refer to it as you draft.

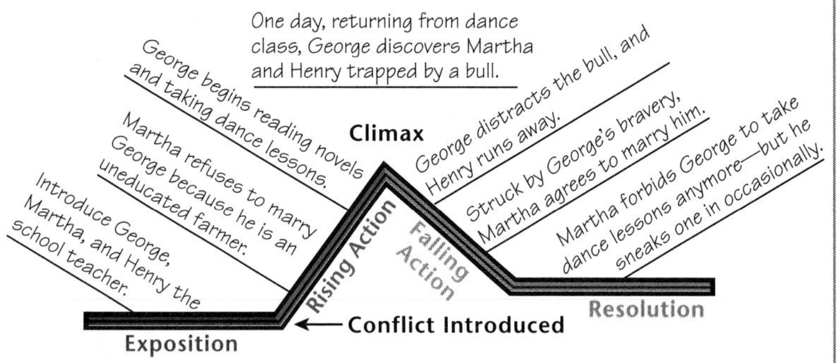

Build to a Climax

As you draft, make sure your plot builds toward the climax. Start by identifying the "setup" and the "payoff." The **setup** is the point at which you give facts that make the resolution possible. For example, you might explain at the beginning that a character speaks French. The **payoff** is the point at which the connection between the setup and the resolution becomes clear. For example, the character might surprise his friends by speaking French to get them out of a jam at the story's climax.

Pace your story effectively by introducing your setup and your payoff at the right times. If the setup is too close to the resolution, the resolution will seem forced. If the payoff comes too early, readers won't care how the story ends.

TIME SAVERS!

Writing Support Transparencies
Use the transparencies for Chapter 5 to teach these strategies.

Writing Support Activity Book
Use the graphic organizers for Chapter 5 to facilitate these strategies.

TIME AND RESOURCE MANAGER

Resources
Print: Writing Support Transparencies, 5-D–E; Writing Support Activity Book, 5-1
Technology: Writing and Grammar iText, Section 5.3

In-Depth Coverage	Accelerated Pace
• Cover pages 88–89 in class. • Discuss plot, climax, and characterization with students. • Ask students to begin shaping their stories.	• Ask students to start writing their stories.

Providing Elaboration

Use Details to Define Character

A driving plot that roars toward a climax will keep readers reading. Make sure, though, that your readers won't feel like people stuck on a roller coaster. If all you give them is a plot full of twists and turns, they may arrive at the end feeling dizzy and tired. If you give readers reasons to care about your characters, though, they will enjoy the ride.

Show, Don't Tell A character starts out like a stick figure. You can dress up this stick figure a bit by *telling* what the character is like ("Mitch was kind"). Or, you can turn your character into flesh and blood by *showing* what he or she is like. For example, you might describe the gentle tone of Mitch's voice and his quiet way of calming someone. You might also include descriptions of the warm way in which other characters respond to him.

As you draft your story, refer to your prewriting notes on your characters. Add details to your draft that show what each character is like.

Student Work IN PROGRESS

Name: Robin Myers
Maplewood Middle School
Maplewood, NJ

Showing Character

As she drafted, Robin included details showing her main character's thoughtfulness and curiosity, as in this paragraph from her draft.

Main Character: how will she react to an adventure?
↓
she is eager, curious
↓
heart beats fast, takes a deep breath

So here I am now, poised at the door of what could be an incredible adventure. I take a deep breath, step onto the landing, shut the heavy oak door with a creak, and ascend the attic stairs, armed with a flashlight and curiosity.

Robin added a physical detail to help readers understand her character.

Step-by-Step Teaching Guide

Drafting: Providing Elaboration

Teaching Resource: Writing Support Transparency 5-E

1. Display the transparency to show how Robin included details about her character's daring and sense of adventure. Encourage students to discuss how the details in Robin's paragraph help them understand the character much better than the simple statement "she is brave and adventurous" would have.
2. Have students look back at the list of questions to their "interviews." Encourage them to find two ways to describe their characters, by telling and by showing.

Integrating Workplace Skills

The ability to describe and define a character could prove useful in jobs that involve evaluating people. Teachers, lawyers, doctors, and social workers are just a few of the professionals that need to be able to describe people's conditions and capabilities. In addition, supervisors often must write evaluations of the workers who report to them. An evaluation that reads, "Tom readily takes on new responsibilities and is careful about his reports," is much more useful than one that reads simply, "Tom is a hard worker."

TIME SAVERS!

Writing Support Transparencies
Use the transparencies for Chapter 5 to teach these strategies.

Step-by-Step Teaching Guide

Revising: Create Tension and Surprise

1. Have students imagine that they are reading a story or watching a movie when they have one of these thoughts: I know what's going to happen, or I wonder what will happen. Discuss which thought is more likely to keep them reading or watching.
2. Ask students to describe their emotions when confronted with a suspenseful real-life situation (anxious, curious, afraid) and how their bodies react (tense muscles, increased heart rate, breathlessness). Explain that a milder form of these bodily reactions may result from reading a suspenseful story.
3. Invite students to tell why they think reading a suspenseful story can be an enjoyable experience.
4. Point out this example of foreshadowing in "New Clothes for School": "Mother, in her young, office-going days, had created a mild scandal in St. Louis by wearing bloomers for bicycling. . . ." Ask students what clue this gives about possible reactions to the girls' knickers. (People might criticize the knickers, too.)

Customize for *Bodily/Kinesthetic Learners*

Invite students to set up a literal explanation of the word *foreshadow*. For example, they could hold an object behind a large piece of paper, shine a flashlight on the object to create a shadow, and then have other students guess what the object is.

5.4 Revising

Revising Your Overall Structure

Once you have written a first draft, your story's basic plot—the sequence of actions—is on paper. Now, you must look at the way in which you retell this sequence.

Your story should be more than a list of events. It is an experience that you create for readers. Some short stories are like guided tours of a big city, with a clearly announced stop at each major landmark. Others are like the wild-goose chase on which you lead your brother at the mall while your family is preparing his surprise birthday party.

Your first step in revising your story is to make sure your plot builds toward an exciting climax—an emotional peak.

Create Tension and Surprise

Withholding Information Building to a climax is a matter of revealing information at just the right times. One technique for building to a climax is to create a nearly complete picture of a situation while holding back one crucial piece of information. Reveal the missing piece of information at or after the climax for impact.

One way to create tension as you build to your climax is to plant intriguing clues that will keep readers guessing what will happen next. These clues should hint at events without giving them away.

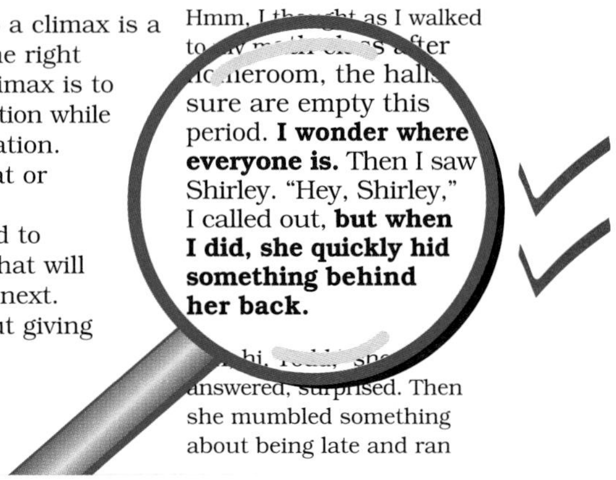
as I walked
sure are empty this
period. **I wonder where**
everyone is. Then I saw
Shirley. "Hey, Shirley,"
I called out, **but when**
I did, she quickly hid
something behind
her back.
she mumbled something
about being late and ran

REVISION STRATEGY
Magnifying Your Clues

Look through your draft for places where you've hinted at the story's climax or resolution. Place a check mark in the margin for every clue you find. Next, review each check-marked item. Ask yourself: Will this give too much away? If your answer is yes, consider rephrasing the clue to keep readers guessing.

Next, look for stretches of your draft where there are few check marks. Consider whether you should add hints to these sections. For each spot you choose, draw a magnifying glass in the margin. Afterward, go back and add a clue for each magnifying glass.

TIME AND RESOURCE MANAGER

Resources
Print: Writing Support Transparencies, 5-F–G
Technology: Writing and Grammar iText, Section 5.4

In-Depth Coverage	Accelerated Pace
• Cover pages 90–94 in class. • Discuss the revision process with students. • Help students identify the points in their stories that need strengthening.	• Assign pp. 90–94 for independent student review. • Have students brainstorm for possible reader criticism of their stories. • Have students work independently to revise their stories.

Revising Your Paragraphs

Develop Characters Fully

Look for places where you can add more details to flesh out your characters. You want them to seem like real, multifaceted people—not just stick figures with names.

REVISION STRATEGY
Fleshing Out Reactions

Review your draft, circling situations and events to which a character would have a strong reaction. In the margin, jot down a note about the character's reactions. Then, ask yourself: What gestures, words, facial expressions, thoughts, memories, or actions will reflect this reaction? Note these "fleshed-out" reactions in the margin. When you have finished marking up your draft, review these marginal notes and decide which details to include.

Writers in ACTION

"The easiest things to write about are emotions. For a writer, those are what you start with . . . because you start from the inside. You can't start with how people look and speak and behave and come to know how they feel. You must know exactly what's in their hearts and minds before they ever set visible foot on the stage. You must know all, then not tell it all, or not tell too much at once. . . ."

—Eudora Welty

Student Work IN PROGRESS

Name: Robin Myers
Maplewood Middle School
Maplewood, NJ

Fleshing Out Reactions

Robin found a few places to flesh out her narrator's reactions to her adventure—exploring an attic.

Narrator: why does the attic please her?

She likes a mystery.

She likes secrets and Nancy Drew-type mysteries.

At the top, I see that the attic is exactly as I had hoped —the kind of attic in a Nancy Drew mystery, only better, and real.

Step-by-Step Teaching Guide

Revising Develop Characters Fully

Teaching Resource: Writing Support Transparency 5-F

1. A writer has several ways to develop story characters, including showing how characters look, what they do, what they say and think, and what other characters say and think about them.
2. Display the transparency to show students how Robin fleshed out reactions in her draft.
3. Ask students to find examples of characterization of Emily in "New Clothes for School." (Appearance: young, school-age. Action: wears knickers to school. Speech: Says to her sister, "Don't let them scare you." Thought: at first, thinks her teacher wants knickers, too. Actions and thoughts of other character: principal calls assembly to criticize knickers; says that the school's reputation has suffered because of the girls' choice of clothing.)

Step-by-Step Teaching Guide

Revising: Combine Sentences to Show Connections

Teaching Resource: Writing Support Transparency 5-G

1. Display the transparency. After you explain the process of "coding clusters," ask students to identify the changes Robin made to show connections between ideas.
2. Have students scan their stories for likely places to combine sentences.
3. Then have students examine their revisions to see if they have overused any combining words. They can substitute other combining words for variety.

Integrating Speaking and Listening Skills

Suggest that students read their drafts aloud to a friend. Can the friend follow the events, or does the story need clarification?

TIME SAVERS!

Writing Support Transparencies

Use the transparencies for Chapter 5 to teach these strategies.

5.4

Revising Your Sentences

Combine Sentences to Show Connections

To show connections between ideas, combine related sentences using words telling *when, why, how,* or *which one:*

CHOPPY:	I got home. I ran to my computer to see if I had any e-mail.
COMBINED:	**As soon as** I got home, I ran to my computer to see if I had any e-mail.
CHOPPY:	I got the dog to stop growling at me. I sang softly to him in my sweetest voice.
COMBINED:	I got the dog to stop growling at me **by** singing softly to him in my sweetest voice.
CHOPPY:	I gave the package to a man. The man was wearing a gray hooded sweatshirt.
COMBINED:	I gave the package to a man **who** was wearing a gray hooded sweatshirt.

Technology Tip

If your computer's word-processing program includes a "track changes" function, turn it on during your revision process. This tool will highlight the inserts and cuts you've made. You can decide later whether you want to "accept" or "reject" these revisions.

REVISION STRATEGY
Coding Clusters

Circle clusters of short sentences. Then, draw a square around any sentence in a cluster that explains *when, why, how,* or *which one.* Combine such sentences with the sentences they explain.

Student Work IN PROGRESS

Name: Robin Myers
Maplewood Middle School
Maplewood, NJ

Showing Connections

To show connections between ideas, Robin combined sentences explaining when, why, how, *or* which one *with the sentences they explain.*

This boxed sentence explains how the painting is standing.

This boxed sentence explains why the narrator peers around the back.

Grandie had said that I could touch anything as long as I was careful. The painting is not hung up. [How?] It is propped against the wall with an old iron in front of it to prevent it from sliding. Painstakingly, I ease the painting up higher so that it is vertical. [Then, because] I want to know every inch of it. [Why?] I peer around to the back, still holding it gently by the frame.

Revising Your Word Choice

Use Vivid Verbs

Energize your writing by replacing stale, overused verbs like *said, was, had,* and *went* with colorful, expressive verbs that capture your precise meaning, as in these examples:

OVERUSED:	VIVID:
said	snickered hinted
was	exploded with exuded
went	zigzagged trudged

REVISION STRATEGY
Highlighting Verbs

Highlight all the verbs in the last three paragraphs of your story. Use one color for action verbs and another for linking verbs. Then, circle any verbs that sound weak or that you've overused. Consider replacing linking verbs with action verbs. Replace weak verbs with more inventive ones.

Technology Tip

Use your word-processing program's "search" or "find" function to locate specific verbs that you've used too often or too many times in a row.

Grammar in Your Writing
Identifying Action and Linking Verbs

A **verb** is a word that expresses an action or a state of being. An **action verb** tells what action the subject of the sentence is doing. A **linking verb** connects the subject to a noun, pronoun, or adjective that identifies or describes it later in the sentence. The most common linking verb is *be* in all its forms. Other linking verbs are *feel, look, appear, become, grow, remain, seem, smell, sound, taste, stay, turn,* and *prove.* Notice that some linking verbs can also function as action verbs.

I **looked** at her face carefully. [Subject performs **action.**]
Sucheta *was* the youngest **child** in the family. [**Noun** identifies subject.]
She *looked* **upset** about something. [**Adjective** describes subject.]

Find It in Your Reading Underline three action verbs and circle three linking verbs in "New Clothes for School" by Emily Hahn on page 78.

Find It in Your Writing Underline five action verbs and circle five linking verbs in your story. If you can't find five different action verbs, consider replacing some of your repeated verbs with more vivid or unusual choices.

To learn more about verbs, see Chapter 15.

Step-by-Step Teaching Guide

Revising: Use Vivid Verbs

1. Suggest that students brainstorm additional vivid verbs they might use in their stories. For example, here are some more vivid synonyms for *said: murmured, roared, whined, exclaimed.*
2. Students may want to consult a thesaurus for other vivid verbs.

Step-by-Step Teaching Guide

Grammar in Your Writing: Identifying Action and Linking Verbs

1. Remind students of the present and past forms of the linking verb *be: am, are, is, was,* and *were.*
2. Suggest that students write a synopsis of their stories by using and labeling both action verbs and linking verbs.
3. Point out that writers often overuse forms of *be.* Write these sentences on the board.

   The hyena was in the post office.

   The hyena lurked in the post office.

   Discuss which sentence presents a more vivid picture.

Find It in Your Reading

Possible answers: action verbs: *saw, realize, attend, go, created;* linking verbs: *was, were, seemed*

Find It in Your Writing

Suggest that students locate action verbs and linking verbs in Robin's story. They may want to jot down some of these verbs and consider using them in their own stories.

ONGOING ASSESSMENT: Monitor and Reinforce

If students are having a hard time identifying words and passages in their drafts that need revising, use the following strategy.

As a variation of the "read-aloud" strategy described on page 92, suggest that students listen as their partner reads their draft aloud. As they listen, they should write down words that sound weak or repetitive or that do not convey the meaning or mood they intended.

Step-by-Step Teaching Guide

Revising: Peer Review

1. Before students begin this activity, you may want to have them photocopy their stories and distribute copies to group members.
2. Remind reviewers to suggest specific strategies to improve the story. Students should apply strategies used in this lesson.
3. Encourage reviewers to make constructive comments and to try to include at least one positive remark in their critiques.

Critical Viewing

Analyze Students may say that the background photo is dramatic because it contains details suggesting a shipwreck. Details include the aged and weathered look of the boat and the scattered pieces of the hull. They may mention that the boat in the foreground is just for play.

5.4

Peer Review

After you've finished making major revisions to your story, you've probably read it through a few times. Every word is familiar to you, and you can probably play back the action in your imagination.

It is for this reason—your "closeness" to your own work—that you may benefit by hearing the reactions of your peers. Because they are unfamiliar with the story, their reactions will let you know how your work comes across. They can let you know whether that moment in your story when the ship goes down is as vivid on the page as it is in your imagination. Use the strategy of "say back" to get peer responses.

"Say Back"

Read your revised draft aloud twice to a small group of classmates. After your second reading, ask the group what they liked most about your story and what they wanted to know more about. Think about their comments as you revise.

▼ **Critical Viewing** Compare these two scenes. Which is the more dramatic of the two? Explain which details from the photograph in the background a writer might use to create an exciting description of a ship. **[Analyze]**

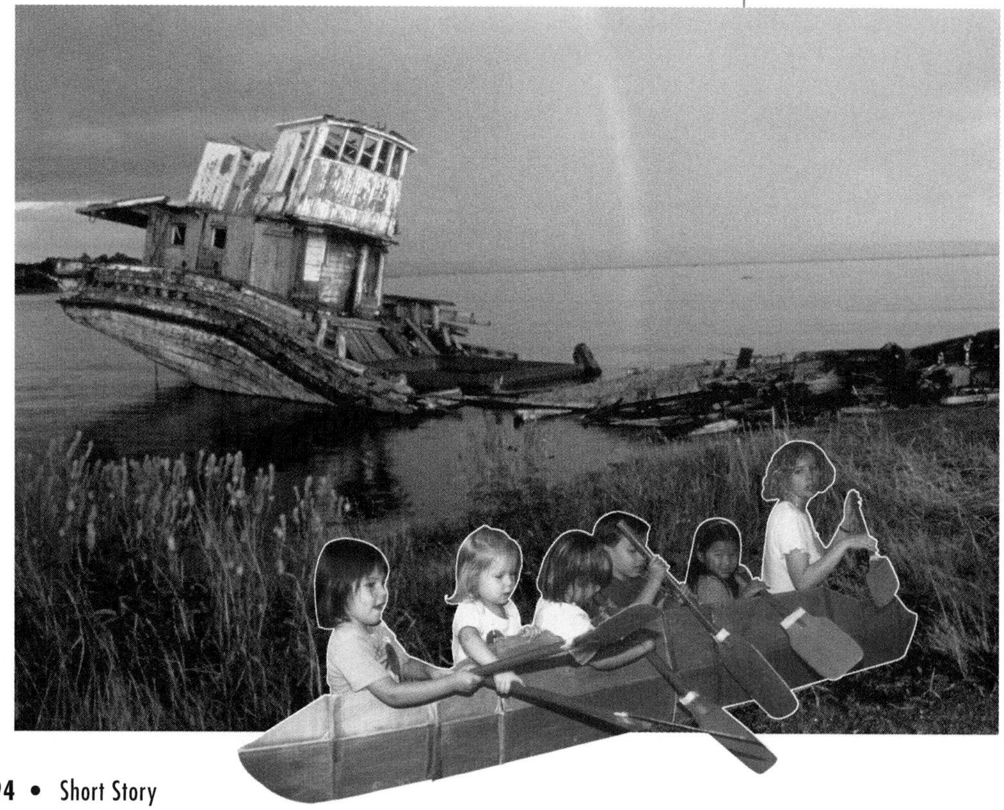

5.5 Editing and Proofreading

Proofread your story carefully to catch errors in spelling, punctuation, grammar, and usage. Unless they depict a character's way of speaking, such errors will distract your readers.

Focusing on Dialogue

As you proofread your story, pay close attention to the correct punctuation of dialogue—speech or conversation that you've written as though the character had uttered it.

Grammar in Your Writing
Punctuating and Formatting Dialogue

Dialogue is speech that is presented as though a character had uttered it. Follow these rules for punctuating dialogue:

1. Enclose dialogue in quotation marks:
   "We're never going to get there on time," Elena insisted.
2. Don't use quotation marks to simply report what a character said:
   Elena insisted that they were never going to get there on time.
3. If the dialogue comes after the words announcing speech, use a comma before the quote:
   Brian announced, "I'm going to the park to play basketball."
4. If the dialogue comes before the words announcing speech, use a comma, question mark, or exclamation point (but not a period) before the final quotation mark:
   "I'm going to the park to play basketball," announced Brian.
   "Can I come too?" pleaded his little sister, Rebecca.
   "No, you're not coming with me!" Brian barked at her.
5. Words announcing speech that interrupt the quote should be set off by punctuation marks and go outside the quotation marks:
   "Brian," wailed Rebecca, "you are just the meanest brother!"

Find It in Your Reading Skim "New Clothes for School" by Emily Hahn on page 78, and find three examples of dialogue. For each, explain why it is punctuated as it is.

Find It in Your Writing Highlight three instances of "words announcing speech" in your story. Review their punctuation, and correct any errors.

For more on punctuating with quotation marks, see Chapter 26.

TIME AND RESOURCE MANAGER

Resources
Print: Scoring Rubrics on Transparency, Chapter 5; Writing Assessment: Scoring Rubric and Scoring Models for Short Story
Technology: Writing and Grammar iText, Sections 5.5–6

In-Depth Coverage	Accelerated Pace
• Cover p. 95 in class. • Review the Rubric for Self-Assessment on p. 96. • Have students edit and proofread their stories in class. **Option** Students can work on their own with the editing and evaluation sections of Writing and Grammar iText.	• Assign pp. 95–99 for students to review independently. • Have students independently edit and proofread • Respond to individual editing issues.

Step-by-Step Teaching Guide

Editing and Proofreading

1. Point out that when the text is free of errors, readers can concentrate on the story itself.
2. Have students check their work for errors in punctuating dialogue.

Step-by-Step Teaching Guide

Grammar in Your Writing: Punctuating and Formatting Dialogue

1. Using the fourth example in the grammar box, remind students to begin a new paragraph when the speaker changes.
2. Point out the "words of saying" in the examples. *(insisted, announced, pleaded, barked, wailed)* Explain that the choice of such precise words adds color to a story.

Find It in Your Reading

Fourth paragraph: "Do you think maybe there's a law against it?" whispered Dauphine.

Sixth paragraph: "Don't let them scare you," I counselled Dauphine.

Fifth paragraph from end: "Well," I said, "what?"

Find It in Your Writing

Have students share examples from their drafts with the class.

Customize for *Bodily/Kinesthetic Learners*

Suggest that students listen to a recording by the late pianist/comedian Victor Borge, who had an entertaining routine in which he indicated punctuation with distinctive sounds.

PRENTICE HALL
Everyday Spelling

If you have taught the spelling skills in *Prentice Hall Everyday Spelling*, Grade 8, Chapter 5, in conjunction with this *Writing and Grammar* chapter, review and assess students' mastery of the skills before concluding the chapter. Remind students to apply the spelling skills as they edit and proofread their short stories.

Step-by-Step Teaching Guide

Publishing and Presenting

1. Ask students to remember the audience they wish to reach. Encourage them to explore ways to reach their intended readers. For example, they may want to illustrate their stories, laminate the pages, and bind them in an anthology for the school or classroom library.
2. Students may want to make their audiotape recordings available in the school library.

ASSESS

Step-by-Step Teaching Guide

Assessment

Teaching Resources: Scoring Rubrics on Transparency, 5; Formal Assessment, Chapter 5

1. Display the Scoring Rubric transparency and review the criteria in class.
2. Before students proceed with self-assessment, you may wish to review the Final Draft of the Student Work in Progress on pages 97–99. Have students score the Final Draft in one or more of the rubric categories. For example, how would students score the story in terms of use of language?
3. In addition to student self-assessment, you may wish to use the following assessment options:
   - Score student essays yourself, using the rubric and scoring models from Writing Assessment.
   - Review the Standardized Test Preparation Workshop on pages 104–105 and have students respond to a short story prompt within a time limit.
   - Administer the Chapter 5 Test from Formal Assessment in Teaching Resources to assess students' grasp of concepts presented.

5.6 Publishing and Presenting

Building Your Portfolio

Consider these suggestions for sharing your story:

1. **Submit Your Story** Submit your short story to your school's literary magazine, or post it on your school's Web site. Also, consider submitting your story to a national magazine, on-line journal, or contest that publishes student writing. (Ask your teacher or librarian for suggestions.)
2. **Produce an Audiotape** Make a recording of you and several classmates reading your stories aloud. If possible, include background music or sound effects to enhance your performances.

Reflecting on Your Writing

Write down a few thoughts about your experiences writing a short story. You might start off by answering these questions:

- Did you enjoy the writing process? Which part of the process did you like best? Least? Why?
- The next time you write a story, either for school or on your own, what do you think you'll do differently? Why?

Internet Tip

To see short stories scored with this rubric, go on-line: PHSchool.com

Enter Web Code: eck-8001

Rubric for Self-Assessment

Evaluate your short story using the following criteria:

	Score 4	Score 3	Score 2	Score 1
Audience and Purpose	Contains an engaging introduction; successfully entertains or presents a theme	Contains a somewhat engaging introduction; entertains or presents a theme	Contains an introduction; attempts to entertain or to present a theme	Begins abruptly or confusingly; leaves purpose unclear
Organization	Creates an interesting, clear narrative; told from a consistent point of view	Presents a clear sequence of events; told from a specific point of view	Presents a mostly clear sequence of events; contains inconsistent points of view	Presents events without logical order; lacks a consistent point of view
Elaboration	Provides insight into character; develops plot; contains dialogue	Contains details and dialogue that develop character and plot	Contains details that develop plot; contains some dialogue	Contains few or no details to develop characters or plot
Use of Language	Uses word choice and tone to reveal story's theme; contains no errors in grammar, punctuation, or spelling	Uses interesting and fresh word choices; contains few errors in grammar, punctuation, and spelling	Uses some clichés and trite expressions; contains some errors in grammar, punctuation, and spelling	Uses uninspired word choices; has many errors in grammar, punctuation, and spelling

ONGOING ASSESSMENT: Assess Mastery

Use one of the following options to assess students' final drafts.

Self-Assessment Ask students to score their short story using the rubric provided.

Teacher Assessment Use the rubric and scoring models provided in Writing Assessment, Short Story, to score students' work.

5.7 Student Work IN PROGRESS

FINAL DRAFT

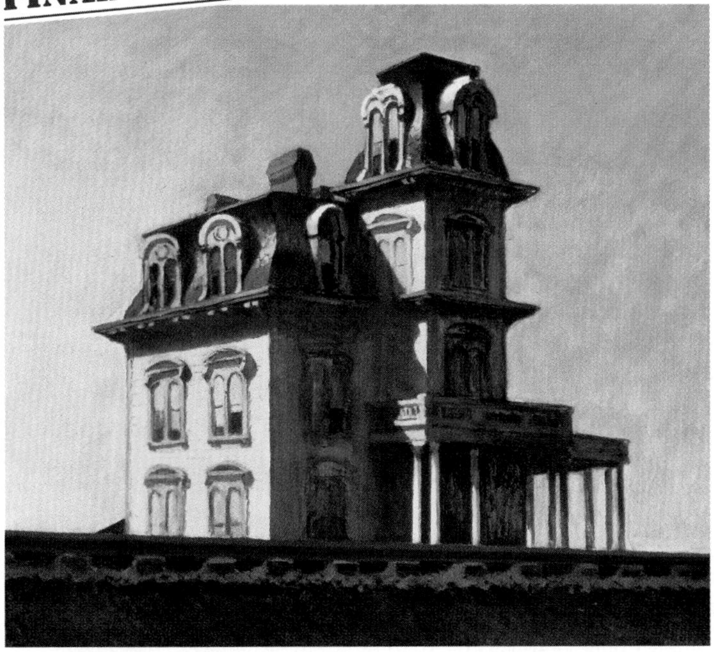

House by the Railroad, Edward Hopper, AKG Berlin

◀ Critical Viewing Compare the mood of this house with the feelings the narrator associates with her grandmother's house. **[Compare and Contrast]**

A Tear and a Smile

Robin Myers
Maplewood Middle School
Maplewood, New Jersey

The moment I open the attic door and feel the chill whoosh of dusty air, my knees begin to shake and my mouth goes dry. I can't explain why. "Grandie," I had asked my white-haired grandmother just minutes before, "can we go into your attic today?"

I had seen my grandmother infrequently since my mother died and my father and I moved to California ("to get away from sad memories," he'd always told me). But I had longed to visit the dark upstairs room of Grandie's turreted Victorian house ever since I had known what an attic was. I knew there would be something about *her* attic that was special, just like she was. It

In this engaging introduction, Robin draws readers into the story with her use of the present tense, her dramatic description of a "whoosh" of air, and details suggesting her narrator's excitement or fear.

Step-by-Step Teaching Guide

Teaching From the Final Draft

1. Explain to students how Robin's "A Tear and a Smile" contains the elements of a good story: exposition, conflict, rising action, climax, resolution. Ask students to cite these elements in Robin's story.

   Exposition. First paragraph: Grandmother has an attic that intrigues Isabella.

   Conflict. Sixth paragraph: Tension between Isabella's curiosity and her hesitation.

   Rising action. Middle of first paragraph on page 99: When Isabella spies the envelope.

   Climax. Middle of page 99: When Isabella realizes the letter is addressed to her from her mother.

   Resolution. Last sentence.
2. Lead students in a discussion of Robin's ending to her short story. Point out that while not all stories have a happy ending, all resolve the conflict the writer describes. Have students check their own stories to make sure that they too have presented a strong resolution to the conflict.

Critical Viewing

Compare and Contrast Students may say that the mood created by the house matches the narrator's feelings about her grandmother's house.

Critical Viewing

Infer Students may suggest that they create a mood of pensiveness and curiosity about the past.

5.7

would be dark and dusty and musky, with wonderful ancient things, family things, maybe even secret things, hidden in faded cardboard boxes and trunks. But every time I had asked to go up there, she had simply grinned mysteriously at me and answered, "Not just yet. When you're ready."

The grandmother's mysterious response creates suspense. It also foreshadows the narrator's discovery of something important in the attic.

"Ready for what?" I had always wondered, but I had never had the nerve to ask.

But *this* time, Grandie had pursed her lips, given me a probing, green-eyed stare, and said, "Today I think you are ready, Isabella. I'm a bit tired out, though, so why don't you take a look around while I rest awhile." This was even more thrilling than I had hoped—a chance to explore all by myself! Not that I wouldn't have welcomed Grandie's company and even her wistful memories . . . but sometimes I just prefer being alone with my own thoughts. I thanked her and eagerly ran to the attic door.

The narrator's reaction here reveals something about her character: She enjoys solitude and reflection.

"You can touch anything as long as you're careful!" Grandie had instructed in her slightly tremulous voice. "Some things are quite breakable and very precious." I had nodded solemnly and watched her disappear down the long hallway.

So here I am now, poised at the door of what could be an incredible adventure. I take a deep breath, step onto the landing, shut the heavy oak door with a creak, and ascend the attic stairs, armed with a flashlight and curiosity.

Conflict is created between the narrator's hope that she will make a discovery and the fact that she has no idea what the attic holds.

At the top, I see that the attic is exactly as I had hoped—the kind of attic in a Nancy Drew mystery, only better, and real. I poke around for awhile, finding a beautiful china tea set with delicate roses on it and a box of crinkled photographs ranging in time from when Grandie was three and smiling toothily in a frilly, old-fashioned dress to when she was middle-aged, wearing an elegant business suit and hugging my pony-tailed, bell-bottomed father at his high-school graduation. I find some toy boats, wooden blocks, patchwork quilts, a book of bird pictures, and an antique phonograph. But nothing compares to the painting.

It is taller than my father and wider than I am tall. The background is woods, thick and dark and beautiful, and in front of the woods is a meadow, a velvet green carpet embroidered with thousands of delicate wildflowers. Sitting in the meadow is a red-headed toddler, the center of the painting, playing with a butterfly and laughing. I feel instantly attached to the painting, as if I know the setting, the painter, the child, or all three. I am strangely drawn to it. I pause and think.

Grandie had said that I could touch anything as long as I was careful. The painting is not hung up; it is propped against the

▲ **Critical Viewing** What mood does a group of mementos such as these create? **[Infer]**

wall with an old iron in front of it to prevent it from sliding. Painstakingly, I ease the painting up higher so that it is vertical. Then, because I want to know every inch of it, I peer around to the back, still holding it gently by the frame. I notice immediately that there is a rip in the lining of the painting, and somewhere in the ragged folds of brown I see a square of white. I reach my hand carefully into the tear and pull out a yellowed envelope. With cautious fingers, I open it and pull out a letter on a single sheet of paper.

My dear daughter, the letter reads. I smile. Maybe this letter was from a parent who is giving the painting to a child. I check the date on the letter, and it is ten years ago tomorrow. I run my hands through my short auburn hair and read on.

I should start by saying how much I'm going to miss you. Oh, I think, maybe one of them is going on a trip or the daughter's off to college or summer camp. Or maybe the painting has nothing to do with the letter at all.

Please help Daddy, help him get through this . . . This? *. . . and help him raise you into a girl and later a woman we can both be proud of. I know you will. Also, I'd like to tell you how much I love you, which is hard because that's more than I can put into words (I've never been very good with words). And lastly, I'd like to give you this painting of you, which I completed yesterday, my final earthly gift to you.* She's dying, I realize sadly, and think of my own mother, who died . . . ten years ago tomorrow . . . It can't be. I push the thought out of my head and continue reading.

It is to help you remember me, remember us, and to remind you that there is always a part of me you can keep—that I am not leaving you, and won't, I promise, ever. This picture is purely from me to you, and I hope it shows you, better than words could, how much I love you, Bella.

I jerk my thoughts from the letter, from the swirly script that I realize I know. Bella! That's me—my childhood nickname! The letter is from my mother, a painter, who died when I was nearly three! I begin to tremble and cry.

So much love,

Your mother

P. S. Here are a tear and a smile. I experienced both as I wrote you this letter.

I stare, sobbing, at the two tiny drawings at the end of the letter. Folding the letter carefully with fumbling fingers, I place it back inside the envelope and ease the envelope back into the lining of the painting. I lie down on the dusty attic floor, crying like a three-year-old. But then, through the haze of streaming tears, I begin to smile. I feel as if my mother is here.

By alternating between passages from the letter and the narrator's thoughts, Robin builds toward her climax—the narrator's realization that the letter is from her mother to her. (Refer to the second paragraph of the story to find Robin's "setup" for this "payoff.")

The conflict—between hope and the unknown—is resolved. By venturing into the unknown, the narrator discovers something of deep significance to herself.

Real-World Connection

The fashions of bell bottoms and ponytails for men date the photograph of Isabella's father to the 1960's, just as bloomers and knickers establish a setting in the early 1900's for "New Clothes for School." Invite students to suggest fashions that could give clues to the time in which their stories are set.

Lesson Objectives

1. To write a dramatic monologue appropriate to audience and purpose.
2. To use literary devices effectively such as dialogue, suspense, and conflict.
3. To use writing processes to develop and revise drafts.
4. To present a dramatic monologue to an audience.

Step-by-Step Teaching Guide

Dramatic Monologue

Teaching Resources: Writing Support Transparency 5-H; Writing Support Activity Book 5-2

1. Bring in videotapes of plays, movie adaptations of plays, or movies in which characters deliver dramatic monologues (in particular, consider bringing in a film version of *Julius Caesar*). Show the monologue segments to students without giving them any background about the characters' situations or personality traits.
2. Ask them to guess what is happening to each of the characters when they deliver their monologues. Have students refer to particular words and moments in the monologues that reveal situation and character. Point out that writers of dramatic monologues plot out what each character will reveal about himself or herself to the audience or to other characters.
3. Model the elements that go into writing a dramatic monologue by inventing a situation with the class and writing a setting, providing stage directions, and creating the first few sentences of a monologue on the board.
4. As they prepare to write their own monologues, encourage students to think about challenges and dramatic situations they have faced in their own lives or that they have seen affect others. Explain that writers often use their own experiences or the experiences of people close to them as a source for plot and character.
5. Display the transparency to show students the kinds of information they can gather to help them develop details about their characters. Give them copies of the blank organizer for them use to use as they gather details.
6. Have students videotape themselves delivering the monologues or organize a presentation day in which they act them out for the class.

Connected Assignment

Dramatic Monologue

A play can be as simple as two characters talking on a bare stage or as complicated as a musical with hundreds of performers, motorized scenery, and computerized effects. Like a short story, a **play** is the presentation of a narrative—a series of events centered around a conflict. While a short story provides all the materials you need to stage the story in your imagination, the script of a play is actually a set of directions for a dramatic presentation of a story by actors. Elements found in most plays include

- **dialogue** (the speech of characters), which carries along the action of the plot.
- **stage directions**, such as
  - an indication of where the characters are in each scene of the play, what they look like, and how they are dressed
  - directions, when needed, for how the characters speak, and what actions they perform.

Use the following suggestions to help you write a **dramatic monologue**—a speech spoken by a single character, revealing his or her situation and character.

Prewriting Create a character facing a difficult situation. Start small—imagine a gesture the character makes, an object

MODEL

from **Julius Caesar**

Act II, Scene i

William Shakespeare

In this monologue, the nobleman Brutus is considering joining a plot against the ruler of Rome, Julius Caesar.

BRUTUS. Since Cassius first did whet me against Caesar,
I have not slept.
Between the acting of a dreadful thing
And the first motion, all the interim is
Like a phantasma, or a hideous dream.
The genius and the mortal instruments
Are then in council, and the state of a man,
Like to a little kingdom, suffers then
The nature of an insurrection.

he or she owns, a word he or she says. Build up further details about this character. Then, ask yourself: What difficult situation does this character face? It might be a tough decision the character has to make, or a conflict the character needs to resolve. Take notes on your character and his or her conflict, using a chart like the one shown. Review your notes, and circle those that are of central importance.

Character's Name: ____________________

Background	Style of Speaking	Situation	Effect of Background on Situation	Attitude Toward Situation

Drafting Hold a picture of your character in your mind's eye. Imagine the character thinking over the problem he or she faces. Jot down his or her thoughts as you overhear them. Remember, your character is reflecting on a situation he or she knows well, not explaining it to another person. Next, add the following details:

- In places where an audience will need help understanding the character's background or situation, add more information. Instead, show the character thinking over his or her situation. Take care not to make the character sound like he or she is trying to explain something.
- Add stage directions and dialogue indicating where your character is, how he or she moves, how he or she says lines, and in what activity he or she might be involved.
- Add stage directions to specify the scenery, lighting, music, sound effects, and costumes.

Revising and Editing Read your draft out loud. "Listen" to what your character is saying. Mark and revise

- sentences that are unclear.
- sentences containing details that do not apply directly to the situation.
- sentences that do not sound like what a person of the background, age, and occupation of your character would utter.

Next, read your monologue to a friend. Ask your friend to note any places where he or she grows unclear about a character's motives or situation. Consider rewriting or adding more information to these passages to help you readers understand.

Check your stage directions to make sure you have clearly shown how lines are to be spoken, what actions or gestures the character performs, what the scene looks like, and so on.

Publishing and Presenting Act out your monologue on videotape, and present it to the class.

Customize for *Less Advanced Students*

Students who are struggling with reading and writing may find it difficult to plan a dramatic monologue in writing. Tell these students that they can use a tape recorder to record thoughts, words, and reflections in the voice of the character that will deliver the monologue. Explain that they can then listen to the tape and write down the sentences or sections they want to include in their dramatic monologue. For many struggling readers, this emphasis on developing language orally first will be extremely helpful.

Lesson Objectives

1. To analyze the process that leads to the creation of works of art.
2. To make connections between a variety of artistic works and sources of information.
3. To adapt the elements of one artistic form in the creation of a new work of art.

Spotlight on the Humanities

Examining Themes Across the Arts

Focus on Film: *Frankenstein*

▲ **Critical Viewing** Explain how this photo of Boris Karloff in the role of Frankenstein's monster suggests that the monster is more than an evil creature. **[Interpret]**

Sometimes, a work of fiction takes on a life of its own—and the effect can be quite spooky! In 1816, English novelist Mary Shelley (1797-1851) was challenged to a ghost story writing contest. Her entry became a novel, *Frankenstein, or, The Modern Prometheus*. The work tells of a Dr. Frankenstein's attempt to make a living being out of corpses and of the way in which his creature comes to haunt him.

Frankenstein's monster soon came to haunt modern culture. Director James Whale (1896–1957) brought the horror film *Frankenstein* to audiences in 1931. Actor Boris Karloff (1887–1969), who starred as the monster, left a deep impression on the popular imagination. The creature that was invented for fun has come to stay, appearing in horror movies, cartoons, comedy shows, masks—even cereal boxes!

Literature Connection Shelley and Whale were working in a genre known as "Gothic." An eerie atmosphere, supernatural forces, mysteries, and grotesque events characterize this style. The earliest English Gothic novel, *The Castle of Otranto*, was written by historian and author Horace Walpole (1717–1797). Set in the Middle Ages, the book is filled with mysterious murders, dire prophecies, and evil princes. The Gothic novel prepared the way for the horror films of the twentieth century.

Theater Connection Shelley subtitled her novel after Prometheus, the character in Greek mythology who braved the wrath of the gods to bring fire to humanity and was doomed to eternal punishment. Shelley found an analogy to Prometheus in the bold ambitions of scientists such as her Dr. Frankenstein.

Prometheus is the subject of *Prometheus Bound*, a play by the Greek playwright Aeschylus (525?–456 B.C.). Aeschylus, known as "the father of Greek tragedy," introduced a second actor onto the stage, thus creating the possibility for dramatic dialogue.

Narrative Writing Activity: Film Adaptation of a Scene

Select a short horror story. Choose one of the scary episodes, and write a script adapting the scene to film. Include descriptions of the setting, instructions to the actors, and camera directions.

Step-by-Step Teaching Guide

Examining Themes Across the Arts

1. Choose one of the Spotlight elements for class discussion, or have students work individually or in groups on the element of their choice. Give students the initiative to find the necessary books, videotapes, or pictures.
2. Explain to students that finding connections among the arts is a way to expand their knowledge and explore how artists of different eras wrestle with basic human themes.
3. Ask students why Mary Shelley and James Whale might have been fascinated with the story of a man who builds and gives life to a human-like creature? Help students explore the idea, through their own responses or through additional questions, that humans have always been fascinated with how human life begins. What spark makes us live? Suggest that religion and a belief in a divine being is one answer to this question. Point out that Dr. Frankenstein is punished for trying to become a god himself.
4. Explain that Gothic writers frequently developed stories in which elements of nature and setting mirror the unnatural desires of human characters. For example, Dr. Frankenstein wants to have the power of creating new beings. The dark, dramatic settings of Mary Shelley's book create an ominous world in which his over-reaching pride will lead to death and destruction. Encourage students to explore the work of other Gothic writers.
5. Point out that Aeschylus, Mary Shelley, and James Whale explored related themes in vastly different artistic forms: a play, a novel, and film. Explain that artists borrow ideas and themes from each other across cultures and times, creating a kind of conversation about being human that is at the heart of what draws us to the arts.

Viewing and Representing

Activity Encourage students to identify the theme of the horror story they choose to adapt into a scene for a film. Remind them that horror stories, no matter how strange, are often based in some real human fear or issue. For example, *Nightmare on Elm Street*, explores the terror that we create in our own dreams. As they create their adaptations, help them build scenes that illustrate aspects of real human questions and fears.

Critical Viewing

Interpret Students may note that Frankenstein, as shown in the photograph above, doesn't seem violent or aggressive as much as imploring. Show students a scene from James Whale's movie adaptation in which Frankenstein shows his frightened or tender side. Explain that artists frequently create more complex characters by giving them conflicting characters traits and needs.

Media and Technology Skills

Analyzing Elements of a Cartoon

Every cartoon, however brief, shares the elements of a short story: character, theme, plot, pacing, and so on. To better appreciate cartoons, learn about their special use of these elements.

Think About It The central storytelling elements of a cartoon include the following:

Character Short-story writers may carefully assemble a character out of a number of specific details. Cartoonists, by contrast, make an identifiable character with one stroke of the pen. A big nose, a fancy hat, a funny way of talking—through exaggeration and a distinctive drawing style, a cartoonist creates an easily recognizable character. Viewers quickly learn to recognize these characters and to know what to expect from them.

Conflict In action cartoons, the conflict is often between a hero or group of heroes and a villain. The plot of these cartoons centers around the hero's attempt to stop the villain. In humorous cartoons, the conflict may be between a zany trickster and his or her easily frustrated hunter. The plot centers around the hunter's attempts to catch the trickster.

Theme The word *theme* (a question or message about life) may sound too fancy to apply to a cartoon. Yet cartoons have themes, such as the following:

- By pitting a scheming hunter against a zany trickster, many cartoons suggest that even the best plans can be foolishness, and that there is an element of mischief in the world.
- With the elaborate tricks and deceptions that the hunter uses—for instance, setting up a fake restaurant to trap his prey—cartoons suggest another theme: Beneath the social rules that people follow there lurk raw truths of life, such as the competition for survival.
- By showing a character falling off a cliff, then bouncing back up again, good as new, cartoonists suggest yet another theme: The imagination is powerful enough to bend the rules of reality.

Other Story Elements in Cartoons

Plot The "plot" of a comic cartoon is often no more than a series of scenes, each of which plays out the conflict between the two main characters in a different way. No permanent resolution or change in the characters occurs.

Comic Pacing To make up for their simple stories, comic cartoons often use a rapidly increasing pace for the action. Each scene "tops" the previous one, adding an exciting rhythm to the story.

Evaluate It As you watch a cartoon, complete a chart like the one shown. Using your notes, write an essay analyzing the characters, conflicts, and themes in the cartoon. Evaluate the effectiveness of each.

Character: Distinctive Physical/Personality Characteristics	Conflict	Events to Which Conflict Leads	Theme Expressed by Conflict and Events

Lesson Objectives

1. To use knowledge of literary elements to analyze contemporary, non-literary works such as cartoons.
2. To appreciate the cartoonist's craft while describing the elements used to convey meaning.
3. To write an essay that explores the effectiveness of a cartoon's use of literary elements.

Step-by-Step Teaching Guide

Analyzing Elements of a Cartoon

Teaching Resources: Writing Support Transparency 5-H; Writing Support Activity Book 5-3

1. Explain that cartoons, like movies, books, and plays, tell stories to an audience. Bring or have students bring in videos of several different kinds of cartoons.
2. Ask students to explain how they think each of the cartoonists uses elements of drawing or dialogue to develop character, conflict, and theme. For example, when Charlie Brown exclaims, "Good grief!" in one of the Peanuts movies, what is Charles Schultz revealing about his personality and outlook on life?
3. Help students describe the physical appearance of cartoon characters, and use these descriptions to further explore the themes of each of the cartoons. For example, if the cartoon character is a hero, which physical attributes has the cartoonist drawn that highlight his or her unique capabilities?
4. Using the transparency, walk students through an evaluation of a cartoon. Talk about how they can turn their observations and evaluation into an essay that analyzes the cartoon's effectiveness.
5. Give students copies of the blank organizer and have students use it while planning their own cartoon evaluations.

Lesson Objectives

1. To write a short essay response about a short story.
2. To use prewriting strategies to generate ideas.
3. To develop writing by categorizing ideas and using effective transitions.
4. To demonstrate control over grammatical elements.

Step-by-Step Teaching Guide

Responding to Questions About Short Stories

1. Explain to students that standardized test questions which ask them to write short responses to short stories require them first and foremost to have a clear, well-articulated topic sentence. Tell them that short response questions can be more difficult than essay questions because they have fewer words with which to support their topic sentence.
2. Tell students that they can put appropriate headings above their prewriting lists so that they remind themselves what kind of details to find in the story. For example, if they were collecting details for the prompt, they might want to write *Details of the Story's Conflict* at the top of their list. Ask students what heading they might put at the top of a second list of details.
3. Encourage them to develop topic sentences for which they will be able to find ample evidence in the short story.

continued

Standardized Test Preparation Workshop

Responding to Questions About Short Stories

Some standardized tests require you to write a short response about a story you have read. Before responding to a test prompt on a short story, think about how the following narrative elements shape the story:

- **Plot** is the sequence of events that catches your interest and takes you through the story.
- **Characters** are the people, animals, or other beings that take part in the story's action.
- **Setting** is the time and place in which the story takes place.
- **Theme** is the message about life that the story conveys.

As you read the story, think about how the writer uses each narrative device to present an effective short story. In your response, create a unified answer supported by details from the story.

Some prompts ask you to write a short response. Others call for an extended response. You need not so through separate prewriting, drafting, and revising stages for a short response. An extended response requires more attention. Practice for extended responses using the suggestions on the following page to help you respond to the following prompt. The clocks show the recommended portion of your test-taking time to devote to each stage.

Test Tip

If time permits, read the story or passage to which you will respond twice. The first time, read to get the general plot of the story. Then read the prompts, and reread the story with a directed purpose: to gather details for writing.

Sample Prompt

Read the story, and then respond to the following prompt.

> The story "New Clothes for School" on page 78 describes a conflict in which two students defy public opinion and dare to be different. Compare the conflict in the story and the reaction of those involved to an experience in which you or someone you know dared to be different. Support your answer with details from the story and from your experience.

TEST-TAKING TIP

Encourage students to write down important information from the writing prompt before they begin reading the story. This will help them focus their attention and give them a purpose for reading.

Prewriting

Allow about one fourth of your time for prewriting.

Create a List To generate details for your response, create two lists of details. On one, list details from the story that you can use for support; on the other, list details from your own experience.

Organize Details Before you draft, look over your lists, and decide on how to organize details. You may want to alternate details between the story and your personal experience, or deal first with the story and then your own experiences.

Drafting

Allow approximately half of your time for drafting.

Write an Introduction In your introduction, include a sentence in which you clearly state what you will cover in your response. Include the name of the piece of literature as well as a brief reference to your own experiences. You might begin with an attention-grabber, such as a provocative statement about being different.

Connect Ideas Using details and the method of organization you chose in prewriting, draft the body of your response. Because you are moving between ideas from the story and your experience, make sure you signal transitions clearly. Use words such as *by contrast, similarly, however,* and so on. You can make sure a transition is clear by writing a sentence to announce a change of topic—for instance, "My experience shows this idea to be true."

Revising, Editing, and Proofreading

Allow about one fourth of your time to revise, edit, and proofread your paper.

Check for Accuracy When using direct quotations from a piece of literature, it is important to be accurate. Double-check all quotations to make sure they have been copied from the story word for word. Make sure that each quotation is enclosed in quotation marks.

Clean It Up When you are satisfied with your answer, read the draft one last time for accuracy. If you are unsure about a grammar or mechanics problems, consider rewriting a sentence to eliminate the need to correct it. Make all corrections neatly so that the test reviewer can read your work.

Step-by-Step Teaching Guide continued

4. Reassure students that while neatness counts, examiners understand that time constraints prevent most standardized tests of this kind from being perfect finished products. Emphasize, however, that following the rules of grammar, punctuation, and spelling will make their responses clearer for their audience.

Customize for *Less Advanced Students*

Less advanced students may feel that they don't understand the main points of the short story or that writing prompts are confusing. Encourage students to look for key words and phrases in the prompts, such as *conflict, dared to be different,* or *public opinion.* Point out that these words and phrases give clues about what to look for in the story as well as what is being asked for in the test response. Tell them that they can underline or circle key words and phrases in the story as they read. Explain that this will help them remember where they found story details that they can include in their answers.

Chapter 6 Time and Resource Manager

In-Depth Lesson Plan

	LESSON FOCUS	PRINT AND MEDIA RESOURCES
DAY 1	**Introduction to Descriptive Writing** Students learn key elements of descriptive writing and analyze the Model From Literature (pp. 106–111).	***Writers at Work* Videotape**, Description ***Writing and Grammar iText* (Interactive Text)**, Ch. 6, Introduction
DAY 2	**Prewriting** Students choose and narrow a topic, consider their audience and purpose, and gather information (pp. 112–115).	**Teaching Resources** *Writing Support Transparencies,* 6-A–C ***Writing and Grammar iText* (Interactive Text)**, Section 6.2
DAY 3	**Drafting** Students organize their ideas and write their first drafts (pp. 116–117).	**Teaching Resources** *Writing Support Transparencies,* 6-D ***Writing and Grammar iText* (Interactive Text)**, Section 6.3
DAY 4	**Revising** Students revise their drafts in terms of overall structure, paragraphs, sentences, and word choice (pp. 118–123).	**Teaching Resources** *Writing Support Transparencies,* 6-E–H; *Writing Support Activity Book,* 6-1 ***Writing and Grammar iText* (Interactive Text)**, Section 6.4
DAY 5	**Editing and Proofreading; Publishing and Presenting** Students check their work for accuracy and correctness and present their final drafts (pp. 124–125).	**Teaching Resources** *Scoring Rubrics on Transparency,* Ch. 6; *Formal Assessment,* Ch. 6 ***Writing and Grammar iText* (Interactive Text)**, Sections 6.5–6

Accelerated Lesson Plan

	LESSON FOCUS	PRINT AND MEDIA RESOURCES
DAY 1	**Introduction Through Drafting** Students review the characteristics of descriptive writing, select topics, and write drafts (pp. 106–117).	**Teaching Resources** *Writing Support Transparencies,* 6-A–D ***Writing and Grammar iText* (Interactive Text)**, Ch. 6, Introduction through Section 6.3
DAY 2	**Revising Through Presenting** Students work individually or with peers to revise, edit, and proofread their work for presentation (pp. 118–125).	**Teaching Resources** *Writing Support Transparencies,* 6-E–H; *Writing Support Activity Book,* 6-1; *Scoring Rubrics on Transparency,* Ch. 6; *Formal Assessment,* Ch. 6 ***Writing and Grammar iText* (Interactive Text)**, Sections 6.4–6

Options for Adapting Lesson Plans

HOMEWORK

Have students complete any stage of the lesson for homework.

SPELLING

To teach spelling skills in conjunction with writing skills, work through *Prentice Hall Everyday Spelling,* Grade 8, Chapter 7, as you cover this *Writing and Grammar* chapter. At the Editing and Proofreading stage, remind students to apply the spelling skills to their descriptive essays.

FEATURES

Extend coverage with Connected Assignment (p. 128), Spotlight on the Humanities (p. 102), Media and Technology Skills (p. 131), and Standardized Test Preparation Workshop (p. 132).

TECHNOLOGY

Students can complete any stage of the lesson on the computer, using *Writing and Grammar iText* or a word-processing program. Have them print out their completed work.

INTEGRATED SKILLS COVERAGE

Integrating Grammar
Adjectives and Adverbs, SE p. 123
Commas in Series, SE p. 124

Reading/Writing Connection
Reading Strategy, SE p. 108
Writing Application, SE p. 111

Viewing and Representing
Critical Viewing, SE pp. 106, 108, 111, 117, 118, 126, 130
Describing a Painting, SE p. 130

Technology
ATE p. 122

ASSESSMENT SUPPORT

Standardized Test Preparation Workshop SE pp. 132–133; ATE p. 121

Standardized Test Preparation Workbook, pp. 11–12

Scoring Rubrics on Transparency, Ch. 6

Formal Assessment, Ch. 6

Writing Assessment and Portfolio Management

MEETING INDIVIDUAL NEEDS

Less Advanced Students ATE pp. 116, 133. See also Ongoing Assessments ATE pp. 109, 113, 117.

ESL Students ATE pp. 113, 122, 129

More Advanced Students ATE p. 133

Gifted/Talented Students ATE pp. 129, 131

Visual/Spatial Learners ATE p. 116

Verbal/Linguistic Learners ATE p. 118

BLOCK SCHEDULING

Pacing Suggestions
For 90-minute Blocks
- Have students complete the Prewriting and Drafting stages in a single period.
- Focus one class period on Revising and Editing and Publishing and Presenting. Allow at least 30 minutes for peer revision.

Resources for Varying Instruction
- ***Writing and Grammar iText* (Interactive Text)** A 90-minute block provides an ideal opportunity for students to work on computer.
- ***Writers at Work* Videotape** Show the Description segment in class.

Professional Development Support
- ***How to Manage Instruction in the Block*** This teaching resource provides management and activity suggestions.

MEDIA AND TECHNOLOGY

For the Student
- ***Writing and Grammar iText* (Interactive Text),** Ch. 6

For the Teacher
- ***Writers at Work* Videotape,** Description
- ***Resource Pro* CD-ROM**

WRITING AND GRAMMAR ON-LINE

iText Interactive Text (On-line or on CD-ROM)
- Easily navigable instruction with interactive Revision Checkers
- Full use of e-rater™, the essay-scoring system (on-line only)

Companion Web Site PHSchool.com
- Scoring rubrics with models (use Web Code eck-8001)

See the Go On-line! feature, SE p. iii.

LITERATURE CONNECTIONS

Related selections from *Prentice Hall Literature: Timeless Voices, Timeless Themes,* Silver:

Professional Model "Up the Slide," Jack F, SE p. 110

Topic Bank Option from *Woodsong,* Gary Paulsen, SE p. 113

CHAPTER 6
DESCRIPTION

Lesson Objectives

1. To define descriptive writing.
2. To identify four types of descriptive writing.
3. To read and interpret a descriptive excerpt from a novel.
4. To utilize strategies for choosing a topic.
5. To review strategies in the Topic Bank for choosing a topic.
6. To consider audience and purpose.
7. To use senses to gather details.
8. To use an organizational plan to clarify ideas.
9. To use sensory details to elaborate.
10. To publish and present a descriptive essay.
11. To reflect on the experience of writing.

Critical Viewing

Apply Students may suggest words describing the horse, the landscape, and the colors. The unnatural colors may suggest that the scene is a fantasy or dream.

Chapter 6

Description

Little Blue Horse, 1912, Franz Marc, Giraudon

▲ Critical Viewing
List five words that would create an image of this painting for a reader. Why do you think the painter "described" this scene using such unnatural colors? **[Apply]**

Description in Everyday Life

Description plays a big part in everyday life. What happened at the end of the football game? Is that new CD any good? How's the food at that new restaurant? The best answers to questions like these are **descriptions**—words that give the listener some idea of how something looks, sounds, smells, tastes, or feels.

If your description is successful, your listener will see, in his or her imagination, what you have experienced in life. By sharing your experience, you show that its value stretches beyond your own life—a powerful reason for writing descriptions. To transform your individual experiences into ones experienced by many, develop your descriptive writing skills.

TIME AND RESOURCE MANAGER

Resources
Technology: Writers at Work Videotape; Writing and Grammar iText, Ch. 6

In-Depth Coverage	Accelerated Pace
• Cover pp. 106–107 in class. • Show the Description section of the Writers at Work Videotape. • Discuss different types of descriptive writing. • Read the literature excerpt (pp. 108–111) and use it to brainstorm for descriptive writing topic ideas with students.	• Discuss definitions and types of descriptive writing. • Assign the Model From Literature for independent reading.

What Is Descriptive Writing?

Descriptive writing creates a picture of a person, place, thing, or event. A good description works with all of the senses: Passing through hot clouds of steam heavy with cologne and sweat, a description takes you from the locker room to the sudden chill of the court, where sneakers squeak and thump until—swish—the ball flicks through the net! Good descriptive writing includes

- vivid sensory details—details appealing to one or more of the five senses.
- a clear, consistent organization.
- links between sensory details and the feelings or thoughts they inspire.
- a main impression to which each detail adds.

To learn the criteria on which your description will be assessed, see the Rubric for Self-Assessment on page 125.

Writers in ACTION

In her restaurant reviews, Rosie McNulty, a food and restaurant critic, uses strong descriptive writing. She believes her job is to allow a reader to share her experiences as though the reader were at the table with her. "It's your job as a writer to write something that is so vivid and so detailed and so specific . . . that without ever budging from his armchair the reader will feel as if he . . . has had the same wonderful experience without ever tasting a thing."

Types of Descriptive Writing

Your descriptive writing may be one of several types:

- **Descriptions of people or places** portray the physical appearance of a person or place and show readers why the subject is important or special.
- **Remembrances** capture a memorable experience in the writer's life, either a specific moment or a longer period.
- **Observations** describe an event the writer has witnessed.
- **Vignettes** capture a single moment in the writer's life, painting a picture with words.

PREVIEW Student Work IN PROGRESS

Victoria Kilinskis, a student at St. Francis Xavier School in La Grange, Illinois, used a unique point of view to describe her backyard pond. In this chapter, you'll see how she used featured strategies to choose her topic, to gather details, to elaborate, and to revise her work. At the end of the chapter, you can read her finished description.

PREPARE and ENGAGE

Interest GRABBER Describe something to the students, such as a horse, without naming it. Use vivid words that describe physical details. You may also want to use similes and metaphors. Then ask students what you have described.

Activate Prior Knowledge

Remind students that they hear and read descriptions every day. What kinds of words do people use when they are describing something? To what senses do the words appeal? What kinds of descriptions do they find the most memorable? What is the purpose of description?

ONGOING ASSESSMENT: Diagnose

Use one of the following options to diagnose students' current level of proficiency in descriptive writing.

Option 1 Ask each student to select the strongest example of his or her descriptive writing from last year. Hold conferences to review each student's sample. Use the conferences to determine which students will need extra support in developing a descriptive essay.

Option 2 Ask students to write a few sentences describing an object, a person or animal, an experience, or a memory. Students who have difficulty completing this exercise might have difficulty in the elaboration phase of the writing process.

TEACH

Reading\Writing Connection

Reading Strategy: Infer

Writers do not always state exactly what they mean. Instead, they give hints. Readers use their imagination to infer, or "translate" those hints in ways that are meaningful to them. Ask students to think about what can be inferred from the story about a frightening experience in the woods.

Teaching From the Model

After students read the first paragraph, ask them to describe the mood of the story. They will probably say that it is creepy and suspenseful. Ask students what effect the mood has on them. Does it make them want to read more?

Step-by-Step Teaching Guide

Engage Students Through Literature

1. Read the story aloud, or ask students to take turns reading it.
2. Lead students in a discussion by asking questions such as:
   - Did the author succeed in totally engaging you in the story? How did he accomplish this?
   - Do you think Annixter's feelings and emotions were caught up in the event he describes? Why, or why not?

continued

Critical Viewing

Analyze Students may describe cold air, a piney smell, the sound of wind in the trees, the glare of sun on snow, the taste of snow.

6.1 Model From Literature

▲ Critical Viewing
Describe this scene, listing five details each appealing to a different one of the senses. **[Analyze]**

In this excerpt from a short story, Paul Annixter (pseudonym of Howard Sturtzel; 1894–1985) uses sensory language to portray a winter woodland and its inhabitants.

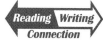

Reading Writing Connection

Reading Strategy: **Infer** A writer normally does not hand you all the information you need to know about a character or setting. To understand a description fully, you should **make inferences**, or draw conclusions, based on the details the writer provides. For instance, knowing that Paul has a lot of experience in the woods, you might infer there is a real threat behind his fear.

from Accounts Settled

Paul Annixter

There it was again, that sinister feeling in the pine shadows and a sense of something watching, waiting among the dense trees up ahead. This spruce valley was a dark, forbidding place even in summer; now the winter silence under the blue-black trees was more than silence—it was like a spell. Queer, they had had to choose this place to lay their trapline, just a week before

Annixter establishes a mood of suspense in his description, with vivid adjectives such as sinister *and* blue-black *and sensory details such as* pine shadows.

his father had come down with flu-pneumonia, leaving Gordon to cover the long line during the worst weeks of winter. He wouldn't have minded tending the old line along the lake shore, but this haunted place—

Gordon Bent was sixteen, turning seventeen, already six feet tall and scantling thin. The first fuzz of beard showed like a faint gray lichen along his lean cheek. Timber-bred, he knew the woods and creatures as well as his father, and never before had he feared any of them. But something about this valley had filled him with dread from the first. . . .

The comparison of Gordon's growth of beard to a lichen helps readers vividly visualize his face.

Almost too much to bear, it had been at first—the deathly diamond stillness of the night, the tremendous onslaught of the cold, the emptiness and the loneliness. And then he began to see and feel all the things he had longed to know: the deep woods showing him their dark and secret face, their winter side, which few men ever had the need or hardihood to learn. Only because he had been raised to like the lonely places had he grown accustomed to it. Then, in the past week or so, had come this other thing—the growing sense that he was not alone, that inimical eyes were watching him from some unguessed vantage. The feeling was so strong that he would stop often to look behind him and sometimes go back over his trail, but he saw nothing; the silence of the winter woods remained enigmatic and complete. . . .

Annixter focuses his descriptions by looking at the woods from Gordon's point of view—a mixture of familiarity, awe, respect, and (lately) fear.

[During his travels, Gordon encounters a porcupine. He lets it pass unharmed, remembering an unwritten rule among woodsmen against killing porcupines. When he returns from checking his traps, he discovers that the porcupine has stolen food from him. Later that night, Gordon wakes with a deep sense of foreboding.]

A segment of waning moon shone through the branches overhead and into the open-ended lean-to. In the faint light, Gordon half doubted the testimony of his eyes, though at the same time something within him did not. Something about the outline of the hemlock branch directly above him drew and fixed his attention. And all at once he knew that a great cougar was crouching up there; that it had been the grim fixity of the beast's regard that had jerked him out of sleep.

Annixter uses spatial order to describe Gordon's predicament. Phrases such as crouching up there *and* nine feet above him *establish the exact position of the cougar in relation to Gordon.*

The limb was nine feet above him, and Gordon knew in a flash how the cougar had reached it—by climbing a tree some hundreds of feet away and picking his way among the overlapping branches. The big cat was stretched out along the branch, its powerful foreclaws unsheathed and gripping the bark in tense but silent savagery. Its yellow-notch eyes glowed lambently in the flat,

Annixter uses precise words to describe the cougar's eerie eyes. You might tell from context that lambently *means "with a soft light."*

Step-by-Step Teaching Guide continued

3. Encourage students to brainstorm topics of descriptive writing. Here are some possibilities:
   - a person who means a lot to me
   - a funny, embarrassing, or scary event
   - a beautiful scene or landscape
4. Students may add these ideas to their own bank of topics for descriptive writing. Remind them that their descriptive writing is more likely to be successful if they choose a topic that engages their feelings.

ONGOING ASSESSMENT: Monitor and Reinforce

Students may find many unfamiliar words in the story. Try these strategies to increase reading comprehension and vocabulary.

Have students make a list of unfamiliar words. Then have them read the surrounding sentences and look for context clues, definitions, explanations, or synonyms.

Responding to Literature

Both Annixter and Jack London write about a world they have firsthand knowledge of. Their stories show how one can write about a place one knows well. Students might read one of London's stories and then write a description of a place to which they have returned again and again, perhaps in a camping trip.

Customize for *Less Advanced Students*

Discuss the continued contrast of exterior descriptions with Gordon's internal state. Point out some examples of the vivid words that Annixter favors, such as *taxed, numb, aches, frozen, prickling, pumping, tormented.* When the author introduces the rifle, he sets in motion a resolution for the plot that creates its own tension.

6.1

down-thrust head. By the savage hunger of those eyes and by every contour of the crouching form, Gordon knew that had he made a single abrupt movement on awakening, the cat would have sprung. . . .

Instinct dictated his actions in the grim moments that followed. He kept his eyes almost closed, that the beast might not catch their gleam: and his whole body remained still, in a semblance of sleep. He knew that if he so much as stirred a hand the cat would spring. But if he remained utterly still there was a slim chance that the animal might go away.

Annixter has shifted to a chronological description of events.

Then began an ordeal which taxed every atom of Gordon's physical and mental control. His body was numb and full of aches from sleeping in one position. Already his muscles cried out to be eased and stretched. Yet he dared not move an inch.

Moments passed, horrible heart-thudding moments, during which neither man nor animal stirred. The cougar remained frozen in his attitude of vigilance, head sunk on paws, every muscle set except for the slow, unconscious twitching of his rounded tail tip. His eyes held the boy unwinkingly as he waited in the fiendish way of cats for the moment when the man must stir, or make an attempt to escape, the moment when his ingrained fear of man would be swallowed up by the rising tide of his blood-lust.

The description of the cougar, frozen *except for his* twitching tail, *reinforces the air of mysterious threat.*

Gordon began to feel that he was going mad. Sweat stood out on his body now, prickling sensations ran along his cramped limbs, and he could hear the pumping of blood in his temples like the beating of a great drum. He knew that he could not hold out much longer, that soon his tormented nerves and muscles must assert an involuntary rebellion of their own, even though his will stood out against it.

Annixter uses descriptions of concrete physical sensations to strengthen his description of Gordon's unbearable feeling of suspense.

He had located the exact position of his rifle, propped against the side of the lean-to, but he knew that a single move to reach it would precipitate a lightning spring. An almost overwhelming impulse to risk all on a desperate grab for the gun obsessed him; but his cooler faculties told him he would never live to fire a shot. The cougar would be on him in a flash, his great claws like steel hooks, ripping, tearing. Yet the torture was too great for calm judgment now. He must move, in another minute, another second—.

And then, even as he was on the verge of desperate action, came interruption.

A sound smote upon his overstretched nerves—slight, yet magnified a hundred times in the breathless stillness of the forest night. It was exactly timed to upset the dramatic situation at the moment of crisis, for it electrified the cougar on his high perch.

LITERATURE

To read another example of descriptive writing about the wilderness, see "Up the Slide" by Jack London. You can find this story in *Prentice Hall Literature: Timeless Voices, Timeless Themes,* Silver.

Gordon saw a tremor pass over the lithe form of the killer. For a taut instant he held his breath. The slightest thing now, he knew, might draw a swift attack. Then he gasped in silent relief, for he had located the sound. So had the cougar. The flat head lifted in attention; then the eyes glared downward on the other side of the branch.

Quills, the porcupine, had recalled his stolen meal of bacon in Gordon's cache, and was returning in search of more. He had approached from behind the lean-to and was investigating the hole he had gnawed, giving vent to short grunts and faint rodent-like chatterings of anticipation. Fearless and one-pointed in his quest, he was oblivious to both man and cougar.

Annixter gives vivid descriptions of incidental sounds, such as Quills's short grunts and faint rodent-like chatterings.

Above him, Gordon saw the cougar quivering slightly, lashing his tail softly. For a moment or two, he knew, the cat would not leap; for its shallow brain could focus upon but one thing at a time, and the porcupine now held the stage.

Stealthily Gordon lifted the blankets and reached for his rifle, his eyes never leaving the crouched form above. His hand closed on the weapon and with a single follow-through movement he dropped to his back again and fired.

Almost in the same instant the cougar launched himself frenziedly downward. Gordon fired again from his prone position, and in mid-air the lithe outstretched body buckled and crumpled, the leap falling just short of the boy, who had flung himself aside. Again the rifle blazed death at the writhing body in the snow, and that shot took vengeance for the ordeal Gordon had undergone, and the weeks of fear that had gone before.

In the concluding paragraph, Annixter captures the excitement of the climactic action using precise verbs such as buckled *and precise adjectives such as* outstretched *in rapid order.*

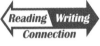

Reading Writing Connection

Writing Application: **Help Your Readers Make Inferences** Include details in your descriptive writing from which readers can infer your feelings about the person, place, or object you describe.

▶ Critical Viewing Compare the perspective of this picture with Gordon's as he confronts the cougar. **[Compare and Contrast]**

Reading\Writing Connection

Writing Application: Help Readers Make Inferences

Have students find a sentence or two in Annixter's story that gives them clues from which they can make an inference. Ask students what details they might provide to help a reader infer that the experience of walking through a graveyard at night was very frightening.

Critical Viewing

Compare and Contrast Students may say that the perspective of the photograph, looking upward through the trees, is similar to Gordon's.

Step-by-Step Teaching Guide

Prewriting: Freewriting

1. The freewriting activity depends on students allowing themselves to be relaxed enough to suspend judgment.
2. Before doing the activity, suggest that students spend a minute with their eyes closed, thinking of a beautiful, relaxing place.

Step-by-Step Teaching Guide

Prewriting: Blueprinting

Teaching Resources: Writing Support Transparency 6-A

1. Display the transparency to show students how Victoria used a blueprint to tap into recollections and impressions of a familiar place.
2. Ask students to share some of the ideas on their blueprints. Students who have blueprints with elements in common may want to discuss them in order to refine their ideas.

Customize for *Visual/Spatial Learners*

Suggest that students use their visual and spatial memories in conjunction with the blueprinting activity. Have them close their eyes and, in their imaginations, walk through the chosen space, noting any outstanding memories or events that come up.

6.2 Prewriting

Choosing Your Topic

The following strategies will help you tap into your own experiences to find a good topic for your description:

Strategies for Generating a Topic

1. **Freewriting** Set a timer for five minutes. Then, write about whatever comes to mind. During freewriting, focus more on the flow of ideas than on spelling or punctuation. After five minutes, review your writing and choose something you discussed as the topic for your description.
2. **Blueprinting** Choose a place where you spend time—your home, the park, or a friend's house. Draw a floorplan or diagram of the place you have chosen. List things you associate with each area of the plan. Circle the most interesting items, and choose your topic from among them.

iText

Try it out! Use the interactive Blueprinting activity in **Section 6.2**, on-line or on CD-ROM.

Student Work IN PROGRESS

Name: Victoria Kilinskis
St. Francis Xavier School
La Grange, IL

Blueprinting

After Victoria studied her blueprint of her home, she chose the goldfish pond as the subject of her description.

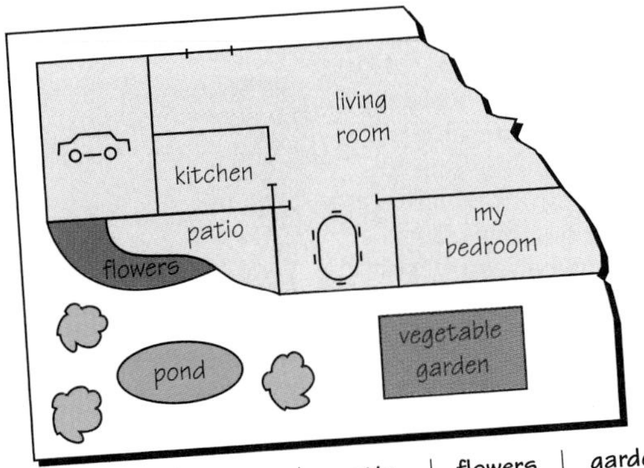

kitchen	living room	bedroom	patio	flowers	garden	pond
baking pies family dinner	television hide-and-go-seek	doll collection favorite poster	barbecues	tulips I helped plant last year	tomatoes I staked—they're huge	fish tadpoles statue of fish

TIME AND RESOURCE MANAGER

Resources
Print: Writing Support Transparencies, 6-A–C; Writing Support Activity Book, 6-1
Technology: Writing and Grammar iText, Section 6.2

In-Depth Coverage	Accelerated Pace
• Cover pp. 112–114 in class. • Guide students through the strategies for generating topics. • Have students use the "perspective" method for narrowing their topics. • Have students begin to gather their impressions. **Option** Students having difficulties may wish to select a topic from the Topic Bank.	• Discuss strategies for generating topics. • Have students work independently to choose and narrow their topics. • Have students work with partners to focus on audience, purpose, and gathering details. • Ask students to submit proposed topics for your review.

TIME SAVERS!

Writing Support Transparencies
Use the transparencies for Chapter 6 to teach these strategies.

TOPIC BANK

If you're having trouble finding a topic, consider these possibilities:

1. **Description of a Trip** Think of a memorable trip you have taken somewhere, such as to the beach, a relative's home, a big city—or even to the supermarket. Write a description of the trip and the place you visited.
2. **Remembrance of a Person** Think of the most remarkable person you know. Write a description of him or her. Describe details that show this person's special character, and include your own experiences with him or her.

Responding to Fine Art

3. Jot down notes describing the night scene depicted in this painting. Review your notes, and think of your own experiences viewing a city by night. Write a description of one of these experiences, concentrating on the "feel" of a city at night.

Van Nuys, Peter Alexander. Courtesy of the artist.

Responding to Literature

4. In his book *Woodsong,* Gary Paulsen describes a strange, glowing sight that he comes upon in the woods. It takes him a while to realize what the glow is. Read this description, or another one in the book. Then, write your own description of an experience in the woods. You can find a selection from *Woodsong* in *Prentice Hall Literature: Timeless Voices, Timeless Themes,* Silver.

Cooperative Writing Opportunity

5. **Restaurant Review** Take your cue from Rosie McNulty and review a food experience. With a group of your classmates, decide on three places to review, such as your school cafeteria and two local restaurants. At each dining place, members should each order a different meal, take notes on it, and then write a review. Reviews should describe the service and the atmosphere as well as the food. Compile the reviews in a mini-guide to area eateries.

Step-by-Step Teaching Guide

Responding to Fine Art

Van Nuys by Peter Alexander

Teaching Resource: Writing Support Transparency 6-B

1. Display the transparency and engage students in a discussion about it. The following questions may be used to prompt discussion.
   - What mood does the photograph create—loneliness, awe, pensiveness?
   - If you were to describe the photograph, what senses would your words appeal to?
2. Encourage students to brainstorm topics that the photo brings to mind. Here are some possibilities:
   - The view from a mountaintop
   - A walk through the city at night
   - Getting lost
3. Students may include these topics in their data banks and add ideas of their own.

Customize for *ESL Students*

Students may want to select a topic based on a person, place, or experience in the country they were born in.

Spotlight on the Humanities

For additional topic suggestions, refer students to the Spotlight on Humanities on page 130.

ONGOING ASSESSMENT: Monitor and Reinforce

Students may need to review the elements of good descriptive writing. Use the following strategy to help them remember the characteristics of good descriptive writing.

Encourage students to imagine that they are describing a very exciting basketball game that their favorite team won by one point. Their description would contain many of the elements of good descriptive writing.

1. vivid sensory details that appeal to one or more of the five senses
2. a clear, consistent organization
3. links between the sensory details and the feelings they inspire
4. a main impression to which each detail adds

Step-by-Step Teaching Guide

Prewriting: Narrowing Your Topic

1. Draw students' attention to the graphic organizer. Review how different the mountain is from each person's perspective.
2. Introduce an additional perspective—that of the observer. Suppose students' bedroom window looked out on a mountain. What significance would the mountain have in their life? How would it differ from the perspectives of the rock collector, artist, and hiker?
3. Ask volunteers to share their topics. You and the class can help each volunteer determine her or his perspective.
4. Remind students that keeping audience and purpose in mind will help them narrow their topic.

Step-by-Step Teaching Guide

Prewriting: Considering Your Audience and Purpose

Encourage students to think about their intended audience and discuss why this is important. For example, a description of a ski trip for skiers requires less background information than the same description for a general audience.

6.2

Narrowing Your Topic

Focus the topic you have chosen so that you can write about it effectively. Consider your perspective on it.

Select a Perspective to Narrow a Topic

A painter looks at a mountain and sees green and gray hues. A climber sees nasty overhangs and handy outcroppings. Each perspective focuses on different details. To find a perspective on your topic, answer these questions:

- What is your strongest impression of your topic?
- Are you interested in a close-up view or in the big picture?
- What interests do you have in your subject? What choices do you have to make related to it?

As you gather details about your topic, focus on those that fit your interests and perspective.

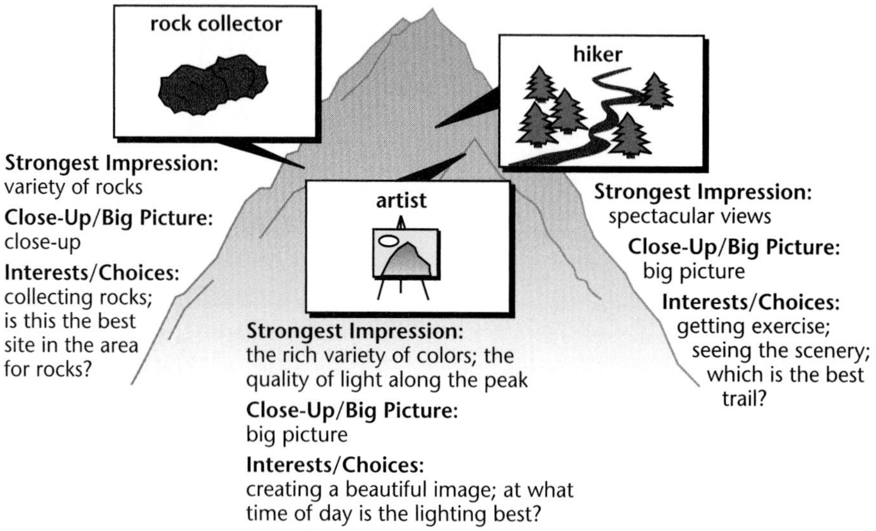

Considering Your Audience and Purpose

Before you draft, think about how familiar your topic is to your **audience**—your readers. If your audience is unfamiliar with your topic, include the most basic details about it. If they are very familiar with your topic, focus on its unique qualities.

Your **purpose** in writing a description is to create a main impression of your subject. The impression may be one of exhilaration, frantic activity, sentimentality—the possibilities are endless. As you gather details, choose those that support this impression.

Gathering Details

To help readers re-create your experiences in their imaginations, use **sensory details**—words capturing the look, smell, sound, feel, or taste of things. Sensory details aren't limited to bare appearances. For instance, you might best capture Uncle Ed's sneeze by comparing it to a volcanic eruption.

Keeping your perspective and your readers' imaginations in mind, "cube" your subject to gather details.

Cubing

To "cube" your subject, follow these steps:

1. **Describe it.** Explain how it looks, sounds, feels, tastes, or smells.
2. **Associate it.** List feelings or stories it calls to mind.
3. **Apply it.** Show how it can be used or what it does.
4. **Analyze it.** Divide it into parts.
5. **Compare or contrast it.** Compare it with a related subject.
6. **Argue for or against it.** Show its good and bad points.

Technology Tip

If you have access to a video camera or a still camera, use it to take pictures of your subject. Try to shoot your pictures from different angles to gain more information that will provide details for your writing.

Student Work IN PROGRESS

Name: Victoria Kilinskis
St. Francis Xavier School
La Grange, IL

Using Cubing

Having decided to describe the pond in her yard from the perspective of a fish, Victoria used cubing to gather details from this perspective.

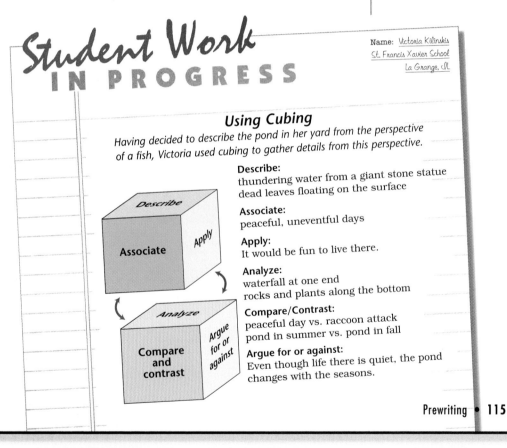

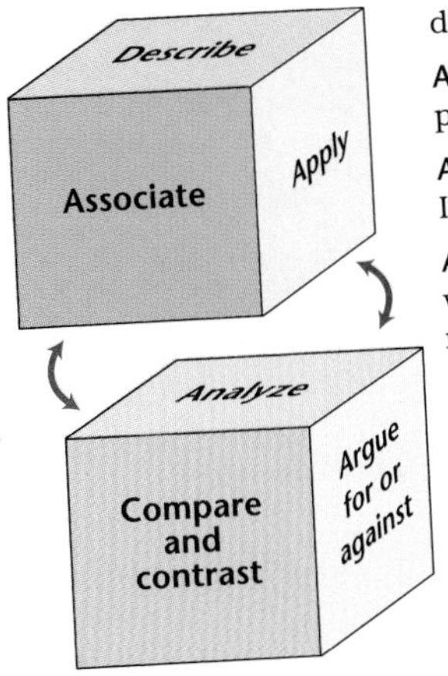

Describe:
thundering water from a giant stone statue
dead leaves floating on the surface

Associate:
peaceful, uneventful days

Apply:
It would be fun to live there.

Analyze:
waterfall at one end
rocks and plants along the bottom

Compare/Contrast:
peaceful day vs. raccoon attack
pond in summer vs. pond in fall

Argue for or against:
Even though life there is quiet, the pond changes with the seasons.

Step-by-Step Teaching Guide

Prewriting: Using Cubing to Gather Details

Teaching Resources: Writing Support Transparency 6-C; Writing Support Activity Book 6-1

1. Demonstrate the difference between general details and sensory details by writing the following examples on the board.

   The mountain was two miles high.

   The mountain looked like a giant shoulder in the sky—massive, menacing, and majestic.

2. Use the transparency to show how Victoria used cubing to gather details. Point out that cubing is a useful method for organizing a piece of descriptive writing.
3. Give students copies of the blank organizer to help them gather details for their descriptive essays.

TIME SAVERS!

Writing Support Transparencies
Use the transparencies for Chapter 6 to teach these strategies.

Writing Support Activity Book
Use the graphic organizers for Chapter 6 to facilitate these strategies.

Step-by-Step Teaching Guide

Drafting: Organize Effectively

1. Review the three organizational patterns. In a descriptive essay, any of the three could apply, although it is more likely that spatial order or order of importance would be used than chronological order.
2. Help students organize their details according to the chart. Point out that they may want to work backwards—that is, decide what point they want to build to and then figure out which details and organization will get them there.

Customize for *Visual/Spatial Learners*

Before they begin to write, have students use self-stick notes to arrange the details of their description in an organizational pattern.

Customize for *Less Advanced Students*

Help students find an organizational pattern best suited to their topic. If they are describing an event, chronological order might work best. If they are describing a place, spatial order is a good bet. If they are describing different sensory details for a memory or an experience, suggest order of importance.

Drafting Tip

One way for students to determine the pace and momentum of a descriptive essay is to try it out first as a story they are telling someone. Have them narrate it silently, or quietly out loud to themselves, paying attention to the length of the sentences and the general level of excitement they are using. Then have them try to capture that tone in their writing.

6.3 Drafting

Shaping Your Writing

Once you have gathered details for your description, begin drafting. Your first step is to organize details clearly, so that readers will be able to fit them together into a picture.

Organize Effectively

Following a Basic Organization Choose from the following methods of organization:

Spatial Order

- describes details from front to back, left to right, near to far, and so on.

Chronological Order

- describes what happened first, next, and so on; describes the causes of an event, then the event, and so on.

Order of Importance

- describes the least important details, then the most important details (or vice versa).

Building to a Point Your description should not just "sit there." To make sure it moves in a definite direction, organize details to build to a point. Consider these examples:

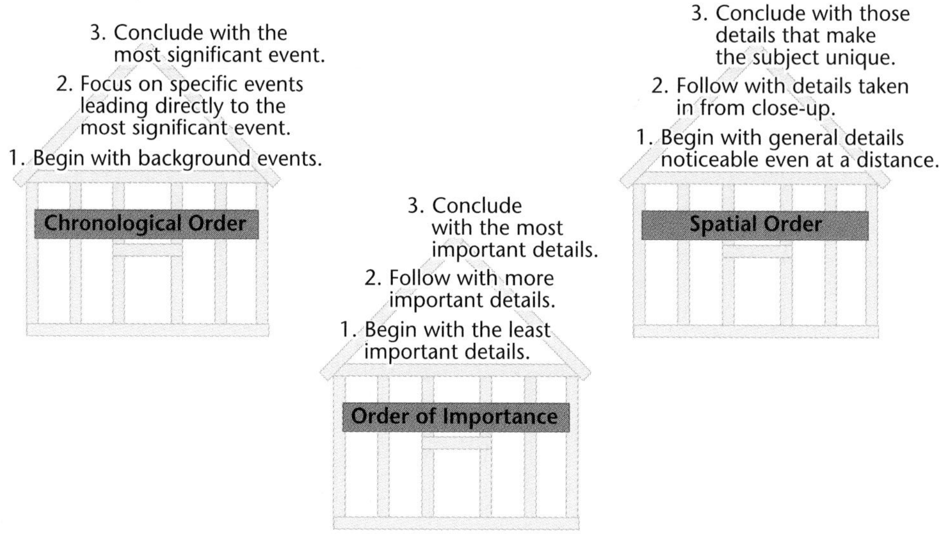

TIME AND RESOURCE MANAGER

Resources
Print: Writing Support Transparencies, 6-D
Technology: Writing and Grammar iText, Section 6.3

In-Depth Coverage	Accelerated Pace
• Cover pp. 116–117 in class. • Discuss effective organization of details with students.	• Help students organize their details into a description. • Ask students to submit their description for peer editing or for your review.

Providing Elaboration

Present a Perspective

As you draft, make sure you include details reflecting your particular perspective on your topic. For instance, if you are describing your gymnastics coach from your perspective as her student, include details about how your coach has helped your performance. You might use the following strategy to help you focus your perspective as you draft.

Focusing Your Perspective As you draft, pause occasionally. Review what you have written. Circle any items that are important, given your perspective. For instance, you might circle a detail with which you associate strong feelings or one that influenced a decision you made. Draw arrows from circled items to new lines on the page. For each, write a new sentence reflecting your memories, feelings, or concerns. Then, decide which sentences to include in your final draft.

▶ **Critical Viewing** Describe the perspective of this young woman on the scene in which she is involved. **[Interpret]**

Student Work IN PROGRESS

Name: Victoria Kilinskis
St. Francis Xavier School
La Grange, IL

Focusing Perspective

Victoria wrote her description from the perspective of a fish named Butter. To focus Butter's perspective, she revised the sentence shown below.

Around twilight, just as the muffled chirp and buzz of insects begins, a shadow may fall across the waters. The world grows quiet. Then, with lightning speed, ~~a raccoon shoots his paw into the water and tries to grab me.~~ I swim away from it at top speed, shimmying under the rocks. After a time, the raccoon leaves, and I know it is safe to come out again.

a paw shoots through the water inches in front of me, churning the water into a froth of bubbles.

Step-by-Step Teaching Guide

Drafting: Focusing Your Perspective

Teaching Resource: Writing Support Transparency 6-D

1. Display the transparency. Discuss how all of Victoria's sentences focus on Butter's perspective.
2. Ask students to contribute other details that reflect a fish's point of view.

Critical Viewing

Interpret Students may say that the woman's perspective is that of a competitor and that she is focused on doing her routine perfectly—or at least better than anyone else in the competition.

ONGOING ASSESSMENT: Monitor and Reinforce

If some students are having difficulty focusing their point of view, use one of the following options.

Option 1 Have students make a list of four or five descriptive details and add a sentence that provides emphasis or focus to the details.	**Option 2** Have students work in pairs, offering each other suggestions on details they might use.

TIME SAVERS!

Writing Support Transparencies
Use the transparencies for Chapter 6 to teach these strategies.

Step-by-Step Teaching Guide

Revising Your Overall Structure

1. An essay without an organizational plan will confuse readers. An organization plan gives the essay structure and also acts as a guide for the reader.
2. Discuss how in the drafting process writers sometimes scramble ideas and details. The good material is all there, but it is just out of order. The virtue of cutting and pasting is that it allows a writer to move around details, phrases, and even entire paragraphs to improve coherence, impact, and narrative flow. Of course, this technique is much easier on a computer, but it can also be done with paper and pencil.
3. Review the text example of cutting and pasting, pointing out the improvements.
4. Have students do the exercise in class with a photocopy of their draft. Some changes will not be improvements, so they need to have the original to go back to as a restarting point.

Customize for *Verbal/Linguistic Learners*

Encourage students to try different revisions verbally as well as visually. Tell them to listen closely to the sound of the words to get extra input as to the best order for their essay.

6.4 Revising

Revising Your Overall Structure

After your first draft is done, it's time to build on the strengths of your description and eliminate weaknesses. Begin by revising your structure.

Analyze Your Organization Plan

Review your draft to make sure you were consistent in using your chosen method of organization. Group related details near each other. Make sure your draft builds to a point, such as an insight or a description of what makes your subject unique. Use cutting and pasting to regroup details as needed.

REVISION STRATEGY

Cutting and Pasting for Order

Make an extra printout or a photocopy of your draft. Reread your work, noting details that concern the same person, place, thing, or idea. If you find related details far apart in your draft, consider putting them together. Cut each misplaced detail out of your photocopied draft and tape it next to the related details with which it belongs.

CUTTING AND PASTING

I remember the first time I met my gymnastics coach. She stood there by the rings, perfectly straight. As the team gathered around her, she said nothing. She waited until we had settled in and grown quiet.

~~At that first meeting~~ Then, she ~~spoke~~ began to speak in tones just low enough that we had to listen carefully to hear what she was saying.

At meets, the coach shows few of her reactions. She offers a smile and encouraging words to each gymnast before she performs. She speaks quietly, just like the first time we met her. ~~At that first meeting, she spoke in tones just low enough that we had to listen carefully to hear what she was saying.~~

▲ Critical Viewing Write a sentence that this young woman might write in describing her coach. **[Interpret]**

TIME AND RESOURCE MANAGER

Resources
Print: Writing Support Transparencies, 6-E–H; Writing Support Activity Book, 6-1
Technology: Writing and Grammar iText, Section 6.4

In-Depth Coverage	Accelerated Pace
• Cover pages 118–123 in class. • Discuss the cut-and-paste method of revising. Review the idea that descriptive writing needs a consistent point of view. • Encourage students to put themselves in their readers' shoes in order to gauge reader response. • Help students decide which parts of their descriptions need revising.	• Have students revise their descriptive essays independently. • Have students work in pairs to critique each other in writing.

Analyze Perspective

Part of what makes a description effective is a lively, believable perspective. After you have revised the order of details, make sure that you have focused your perspective effectively.

REVISION STRATEGY
Coding Details to Focus Perspective

Follow these steps to focus perspective:

1. On a note card, write your topic.
2. Underneath, briefly describe your perspective.
3. Underneath this description, write the three most important aspects of your topic from your perspective.
4. Run your note card down your draft, stopping at each line.
5. Circle in green details that relate to one of the aspects of your perspective that you have identified.
6. Circle in red details not related to one of those aspects.

If a paragraph has no green circles, consider adding details from your perspective. If many details are circled in red, consider eliminating some or rewriting them to make their connection to your perspective clear.

Student Work IN PROGRESS

Name: Victoria Kilinskis
St. Francis Xavier School
La Grange, IL

Coding Details for Perspective

Victoria coded her draft to focus her perspective.

2 I spend the day drifting in a dream ~~or~~ exploring among the weeds, or searching for food. ~~The people who own the pond make sure the water stays fresh and clean.~~

Topic: my pond at home

Perspective: pond described by a fish who lives there

Three Most Important Aspects of Topic:
1. fish is smaller and more vulnerable than human being
2. water is its home—it eats there, swims there; never leaves
3. fish sees events at surface from below

The sentence circled in green reflected the watery life of a fish. Victoria decided to build on it by adding a few more details about this life. She deleted the sentence in red, which had little to do with the perspective of a fish.

Step-by-Step Teaching Guide

Revising: Coding to Focus Perspective

Teaching Resource: Writing Support Transparency 6-E

1. Remind students that although description is the primary focus of a descriptive essay, point of view is a close second.
2. Point out that no matter how detailed, colorful, or lovely the descriptive writing, the author needs to give the reader some guidance on what this means to him or her. Some questions that need to be answered are: Why are you writing this? What does this object, place, or event mean to you?
3. Display the transparency. Review Victoria's work in progress and use the transparency to demonstrate the technique of coding details to focus point of view. Encourage students to use the Writing Support Activity to help them focus the perspective of their own work-in-progress.

TIME SAVERS!

Writing Support Transparencies
Use the transparencies for Chapter 6 to teach these strategies.

Step-by-Step Teaching Guide

Revising: Using Functional Paragraphs

1. Discuss with students the various kinds of functional paragraphs and the jobs they do.
2. Have students review their drafts and decide whether they can use any of the types of functional paragraphs to improve their writings.

6.4

Revising Your Paragraphs

Use Functional Paragraphs

A **topical paragraph** develops a main idea, explaining, illustrating, or defending it. A **functional paragraph** emphasizes a point, makes a transition, or adds a special effect, such as dialogue. A functional paragraph may be one sentence or a series of sentences. You can add functional paragraphs to your writing to do various jobs. Here are some examples:

FUNCTIONAL PARAGRAPHS

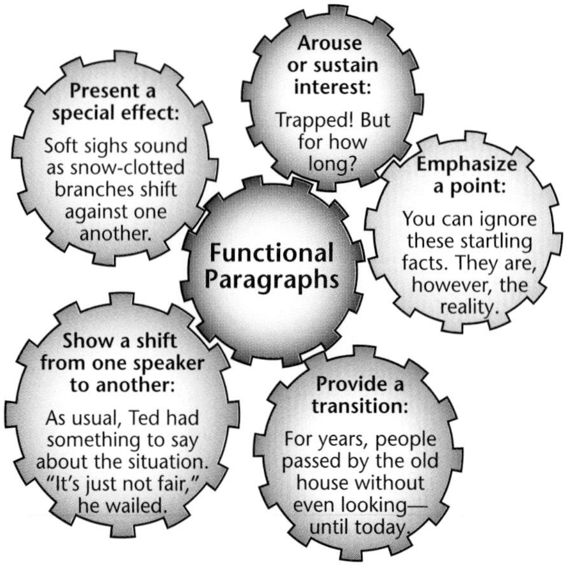
Functional Paragraphs
Present a special effect:
Soft sighs sound as snow-clotted branches shift against one another.
Arouse or sustain interest:
Trapped! But for how long?
Emphasize a point:
You can ignore these startling facts. They are, however, the reality.
Show a shift from one speaker to another:
As usual, Ted had something to say about the situation. "It's just not fair," he wailed.
Provide a transition:
For years, people passed by the old house without even looking— until today.

REVISION STRATEGY
Adding Functional Paragraphs

As you reread your draft, look for details of special interest from your chosen perspective. Consider emphasizing your perspective by adding a functional paragraph that comments on, or presents your reaction to, the detail.

Revising Your Sentences

Eliminate Awkward Parallels

It is a mark of a mature writing style to use a coordinating conjunction to link only sentence elements of the same kind —nouns with nouns, phrases with phrases, and clauses with clauses. This sentence style is called **parallelism.**

FAULTY PARALLEL:	The colors included **brown**, **patches where it was green**, and **yellow**.
PARALLEL:	The colors included **brown spots**, **green patches**, and **yellow streaks**.
FAULTY PARALLEL:	I was looking for a cup **with two handles** and **that matched my other cups**.
PARALLEL:	I was looking for a cup **that had two handles** and **that matched my other cups**.

Underline coordinating conjunctions (*and, but, for, nor, or, so*, and *yet*) to check parallelism in your draft.

REVISION STRATEGY

Underlining Conjunctions to Find Parallels

Underline the first ten coordinating conjunctions in your draft. Circle the sentence elements each conjunction joins. Balance nouns with nouns, prepositional phrases with prepositional phrases, main clauses with main clauses, and so on.

Student Work IN PROGRESS

Name: Victoria Kilinskis
St. Francis Xavier School
La Grange, IL

Finding Parallels

Notice how Victoria fixed an awkward parallel in her essay.

We would dodge the raccoon together, play hide and seek, and ~~we had~~ have bubble-blowing contests.

Step-by-Step Teaching Guide

Revising: Eliminating Awkward Parallels

***Teaching Resource:** Writing Support Transparency 6-F*

1. Review parallelism and coordinating conjunctions.
2. Display the transparency. Examine Victoria's resolution of an awkward parallel in her essay.
3. Write the following sentences on the board and ask students to change them to parallel construction:

   The paper said prices are up and people's wages have gone down. (. . . prices are up and wages are down)

   To change my mind, they tried both persuasion and to threaten me. (. . . they tried persuasion and threats)

STANDARDIZED TEST PREPARATION WORKSHOP

Parallel Construction Standardized test questions may require students to identify parallel construction. Ask students which of the following sentences uses parallel construction.

A My New Year's resolutions are to get more sleep, lose weight, and I will exercise.

B My New Year's resolutions are to get more sleep, go on a diet, and I will exercise.

C My New Year's resolutions are to get more sleep, lose weight, and exercise.

D My New Year's resolutions are to sleep more, lose weight, and I will exercise.

Item **C** is the sentence with parallel construction.

TIME SAVERS!

Writing Support Transparencies

Use the transparencies for Chapter 6 to teach these strategies.

Step-by-Step Teaching Guide

Revising: Highlighting Adjectives and Adverbs

Teaching Resource: Writing Support Transparency 6-G

1. Display the transparency. Discuss how Victoria's changes made her writing more vivid and exciting.
2. After students highlight their adjectives and adverbs, you may want to suggest that they use a thesaurus for ideas on how to improve them.

Customize for *ESL Students*

Students learning English may have trouble finding vivid adjectives. Students can work in groups to brainstorm synonyms. Suggest that they use a dictionary or thesaurus to come up with alternative wordings.

Integrating Technology Skills

See that all students know how to use the electronic thesaurus on the computer.

TIME SAVERS!

Writing Support Transparencies
Use the transparencies for Chapter 6 to teach these strategies.

6.4

Revising Your Word Choice

Replace Vague Modifiers

Check the adjectives and adverbs in your draft to ensure that they are precise. Replace vague modifiers such as *good*, *big*, and *slowly* with modifers carrying a specific meaning, such as *entertaining*, *gigantic*, and *cautiously*.

REVISION STRATEGY

Highlighting Adjectives and Adverbs

Highlight the first ten adjectives and the first five adverbs in your draft. For each, ask yourself: "What makes this word apply to what I am describing?" For instance, you might have called your dog "nice" because he is *friendly* or because he is *cuddly*. In the margin, write these modifiers "explaining" your original word choice. If they are more precise than your original modifiers, use the new words in place of your original choices.

Student Work IN PROGRESS

Name: Victoria Kilinskis
St. Francis Xavier School
La Grange, IL

Highlighting Adjectives and Adverbs

Victoria replaced a few vague modifiers in her draft with more precise ones.

	One day, though, as I was nibbling at a
tasty, delicious, nutritious	~~nice~~ tasty weed growing by a rock, a little
brown, mud-colored	~~dark~~ muddy brown creature scooted by. Its head was
big/skinny, flat	huge compared to its slender, leaflike
quickly, frantically	tail. The creature swam ~~fast,~~ frantically darting
	under rocks and lily pads as it went. I
handily, quickly	swam after it and caught up easily.

Grammar in Your Writing
Adjectives and Adverbs

Adjectives add information to the noun and pronoun they modify. They answer the questions *what kind? which one? how many?* or *how much?* **Adverbs** add information to the verb, adjective, or other adverb they modify. They answer the questions *how? where? when?* or *to what extent?*

ADJECTIVES:	yellow flower	many weeds	this rock	large meadows
ADVERBS:	flows swiftly	runs underneath	swims now	very frothily

Find It in Your Reading Identify two adjectives and two adverbs in "Accounts Settled" by Paul Annixter on page 108.

Find It in Your Writing Identify seven nouns and seven verbs in your draft. For each, evaluate whether you should add adjectives or adverbs to clarify its meaning.

For more on adjectives and adverbs, see Chapter 16.

Peer Review
Double Dyad

Exchange descriptions with a partner. Read each other's papers carefully, filling out a sheet like the one below. When you have finished, discuss your papers. Repeat these steps with a new partner. Consider the feedback you received from your partners as you make final revisions to your description.

	Very Well	Okay	Not Very Well
How well does the introduction capture your attention?			
How well does the writer use sensory details and comparisons to create a picture of the subject?			
Does the essay flow?			
Does the writer create a main impression of the subject?			
Does the conclusion leave a memorable impression?			
What is the strongest part of the paper? ______			
What is the weakest part of the paper? ______			

ONGOING ASSESSMENT: Prerequisite Skills

If students have difficulty with adjectives and adverbs, refer them to the following to ensure coverage of prerequisite skills.

In the Textbook	Print Resources	Technology
Adjectives and Adverbs, pp. 346–369	Grammar Exercise Workbook, pp. 23–38	Writing and Grammar iText, Sections 16.1–2; On-Line Exercise Bank, Sections 16.1–2

Step-by-Step Teaching Guide

Grammar in Your Writing: Adjectives and Adverbs

1. Write the following phrases on the board and have students identify which question the adjective is answering.

   slight dusting (how much?)
   elegant tracings (what kind?)
   a dozen shovels (how many?)
   that storm (which one?)

2. Write the following phrases on the board and have students identify which question the adverb is answering.

   walk slowly (how?)
   walk there (where?)
   walk now (when?)
   walk two miles (to what extent?)

Find It in Your Reading

Possible responses: adjectives—sinister, waning; adverbs—lambently, unwinkingly

Find It in Your Writing

Have students list three possible adjectives or adverbs that they can use for each noun or verb. Then have them choose the most specific one for each.

Step-by-Step Teaching Guide

Revising: Peer Review

Teaching Resources: Writing Support Transparency 6-H; Writing Support Activity Book 6-2

1. Set up the peer review activity with some ground rules about giving feedback. Remind students to treat everyone's efforts with respect and to pay attention to the language they use to offer suggestions. Tell them to think of their role as offering suggestions, not passing critical judgment. Saying "You might want to" is more effective than saying "You should."
2. Also remind students that the purpose of the peer review activity is to check essays for content. Grammar, spelling, and other issues will be handled in the next step—editing and proofreading.
3. Display the transparency and review the information students will use to evaluate each other's work. Give students copies of the blank organizer for them to use during the peer review.

Step-by-Step Teaching Guide

Editing and Proofreading: Focusing on Commas

1. Point out that after working so hard on their essays, students probably want readers to enjoy them, not be confused by careless errors. Note that commas are a frequent source of errors.
2. Encourage students to put aside their work for a short time so they can review it with a fresh eye.

Step-by-Step Teaching Guide

Grammar in Your Writing: Using Commas With Two or More Adjectives

1. Suggest that students read their essays aloud to themselves to find natural pauses that may give clues about where commas belong.
2. Write the following additional examples on the board and ask students to make any corrections needed.

   A few large trees lay across the road.

   Magnificent tall oak trees did not survive the storm. (add comma after magnificent*)*

Find It in Your Reading

Possible response: flat, down-thrust head (A comma is used because the adjectives are of equal rank.)

Find It in Your Writing

Have partners read each other's drafts aloud. Explain to students that a confused delivery may result from incorrect punctuation and that they should review passages in which the reader stumbles, looking for possible errors.

PRENTICE HALL

Everyday Spelling

If you have taught the spelling skills in *Prentice Hall Everyday Spelling,* Grade 8, Chapter 7, in conjunction with this *Writing and Grammar* chapter, review and assess students' mastery of the skills before concluding the chapter. Remind students to apply the spelling skills as they edit and proofread their descriptive essays.

6.5 Editing and Proofreading

Errors in your descriptive writing, such as misplaced or missing commas, may confuse or distract your readers.

Focusing on Commas

Commas signal readers to pause slightly. They are also used to prevent confusion. Color-code your draft to find places where you may need to add commas.

Color-Coding Clues for Commas

Using a colored pencil, draw a box around adjectives wherever you use two or more of them in a row. Read the information below, and then review what you have circled. Add any commas you need.

Grammar in Your Writing

Using Commas With Two or More Adjectives

When two or more adjectives appear in front of the noun they modify, you may need to add a comma between them.

Adjectives of equal rank Adjectives are of equal rank when you can write them in any order before a noun without changing your meaning. Use a comma between adjectives of equal rank.

The energetic, determined fish pushed its way upstream.

The **determined, energetic** fish pushed its way upstream.

Adjectives that must stay in a specific order When adjectives must stay in a specific order, do not put a comma between them.

Many small (never **Small many**) tadpoles turn into large frogs.

Large yellow (rarely **Yellow large**) fish swim in my pool.

Find It in Your Reading Find two or more adjectives used before a noun in "Accounts Settled" by Paul Annixter on page 108. Explain why a comma should or should not be used between them.

Find It in Your Writing Find places in your draft where you use two or more adjectives before a noun. Make sure you have used commas correctly.

To learn more about commas, see Chapter 26.

TIME AND RESOURCE MANAGER

Resources
Print: Scoring Rubrics in Transparency, Chapter 6; Scoring Rubric and Scoring Models for Descriptive Essay
Technology: Writing and Grammar iText, Sections 6.5–6

In-Depth Coverage	Accelerated Pace
• Review p. 124 in class. • Review the Rubric for Self-Assessment on page 125. • Have students edit and proofread their essays in class. **Option** Students can work independently with the editing and evaluation sections of Writing and Grammar iText.	• Assign pp. 124–125 for independent review. • Have students independently edit and proofread their essays. • Respond to individual editing issues as needed.

6.6 Publishing and Presenting

Building Your Portfolio

Consider these ideas for sharing your description:

1. **Submit Your Description** Find an appropriate publication for your description: a local newspaper, the school magazine, or a travel magazine. Submit your description for publication.
2. **Videotape Your Description** If you have described a subject accessible to you, videotape it as you read your description. Plan shots so that viewers will see what you are describing as they listen to you read about it. Rehearse with your assistants before the final taping, and show your final video to the class.

Reflecting on Your Writing

Jot down a few notes on your experience writing a description. To begin, answer these questions:

- As you wrote, what new insights or impressions did you gain about the subject of your description?
- Which strategy for prewriting, drafting, revising, or editing might you use again or recommend to a friend?

Internet Tip

To see descriptive essays scored with this rubric, go on-line:
PHSchool.com
Enter Web Code:
eck-8001

Rubric for Self-Assessment

Use the following criteria to evaluate your description:

	Score 4	Score 3	Score 2	Score 1
Audience and Purpose	Creates a memorable main impression through effective use of details	Creates a main impression through use of details	Contains details that distract from a main impression	Contains details that are unfocused and create no main impression
Organization	Is organized consistently, logically, and effectively	Is organized consistently	Is organized, but not consistently	Is disorganized and confusing
Elaboration	Contains rich sensory language that appeals to the five senses	Contains some rich sensory language	Contains some rich sensory language, but it appeals to only one or two of the senses	Contains only flat language
Use of Language	Uses vivid and precise adjectives; contains no errors in grammar, punctuation, or spelling	Uses some vivid and precise adjectives; contains few errors in grammar, punctuation, and spelling	Uses few vivid and precise adjectives; contains some errors in grammar, punctuation, and spelling	Uses no vivid adjectives; contains many errors in grammar, punctuation, and spelling

ONGOING ASSESSMENT: Assess Mastery

Use one of the following options to assess final drafts of students' descriptive essays.

Self-Assessment Ask students to score their essay using the rubric provided. Then have students write a paragraph reflecting on the most valuable strategy they learned in completing this essay.

Teacher Assessment Use the rubric and the scoring models provided in Writing Assessment, Descriptive Essay, to score students' work.

Step-by-Step Teaching Guide

Publishing and Presenting

1. If students described someone they know, they may want to send the description to that person.
2. If students described an experience when they were a child, it might be appropriate to read the essay to a class of younger students.
3. Ask students to remember the audience they wished to reach. Encourage them to explore ways to reach their intended readers. For example, a class-produced anthology or a school publication may be good vehicles. They may also want to show their descriptions to friends and family members.

ASSESS

Step-by-Step Teaching Guide

Assessment

Teaching Resources: Scoring Rubrics on Transparency 6; Formal Assessment, Chapter 6

1. Display the Scoring Rubric transparency and review the criteria in class.
2. Before students proceed with self-assessment, you may wish to review the Final Draft of the Student Work in Progress on pages 126–127. Have students score the Final Draft in one or more of the rubric categories. For example, how would students score the story in terms of elaboration?
3. In addition to student self-assessment, you may wish to use the following assessment options.
   - Score student essays yourself, using the rubric and scoring models from Writing Assessment.
   - Review the Standardized Test Preparation Workshop on pages 132–133.
   - Administer the Chapter Test from Formal Assessment in Teaching Resources to assess students' grasp of concepts presented.

CLOSE

Step-by-Step Teaching Guide

Teaching from the Final Draft

1. Point out the vivid language Victoria employs to give sensory details in the first two paragraphs. Words such as *cascade, fantail, sparkling, drifting,* and *exploring* give readers a vivid picture.
2. Have students list, in categories, some of the impressions Victoria describes. Which senses do they appeal to?
3. Encourage students to paraphrase Victoria's main point. Did she make the point effectively? Have them check to be sure that their essay too builds to a strong point.

continued

Critical Viewing

Analyze Students may say that the photo was taken by someone who was under water.

6.7 Student Work IN PROGRESS

FINAL DRAFT

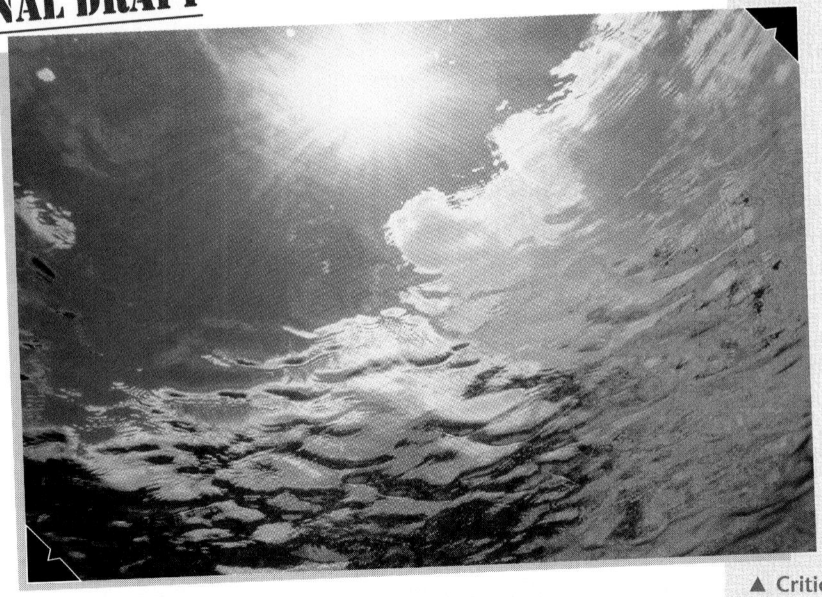

▲ **Critical Viewing** Define the perspective from which this photograph was taken. **[Analyze]**

My Home Sweet Wet Home

Victoria Kilinskis
St. Francis Xavier School
La Grange, Illinois

I live where the waters cascade down the rocks in a mighty torrent. They pour from the giant stone statue of a fish at the head of the pool where I live. My name is Butter, and I am a pale yellow goldfish with a fantail. I spend my days gliding through the sparkling waters of a pond.

Few events disturb my quiet days. In the morning, as the waters turn from black to a green-blue, one bird claw after another plunges into the waters near the top of the waterfall. Sparrows and mourning doves twitter and tweet as they splash about. After

Vivid sensory details that use specific modifiers introduce Victoria's topic—a pond fed by a fountain. She also establishes the perspective for her description—that of a goldfish in the pond.

a time, they fly off with a great rush of wings. I spend the day drifting in a dream, exploring among the weeds, or searching for food. Occasionally, I hear a low buzz as a dragonfly nears the water, dips in for prey, then darts away again. Later in the day as the water grows cooler and darker, a gentle rain of food peppers the surface. Sometimes I catch sight of the blurry form of the young girl who brings these meals.

Victoria uses chronological order throughout her draft. This order helps establish the quiet rhythm of days in the pond.

Few exciting things happen to disrupt the days. At times, a pebble gallops along above my head, making bulges in the water as it skips by. When it finally breaks through into my murky world, I watch the ripples spread and make delicate patterns of colors in the sunlight. Sometimes, I catch sight of the boy who throws the stones.

Victoria uses vivid sensory details to describe the skipping rocks and the attack of the raccoon.

He is not as dangerous, though, as another visitor. Around twilight, just as the muffled chirp and buzz of insects begins, a shadow may fall across the waters. The world grows quiet. Then, with lightning speed, a paw shoots through the water inches in front of me, churning the water into a froth of bubbles. I swim away from it at top speed, shimmying under the rocks. After a time, the raccoon leaves, and I know it is safe to come out again.

One day, though, as I was nibbling at a tasty weed growing by a rock, a little muddy brown creature scooted by. Its head was huge compared to its slender, leaflike tail. The creature swam frantically, darting under rocks and lily pads as it went. I swam after it and caught up easily. I peered into his large, friendly eyes and knew that it was harmless. From that moment on, Specky, a tadpole, and I were inseparable friends. I showed Specky around the pond. I pointed out the most mysterious hiding spots, and calm places to swim or just hang around and float. We would dodge the raccoon together, play hide and seek, and have bubble-blowing contests.

Much time has passed since Specky's arrival. Autumn has arrived, and it is my favorite season. Brilliant, glorious red and orange leaves tumble down and float above me. I push them and play games with them. Birds take baths less frequently, claws knife through the water less often, and the dragonflies have gone away. Specky's legs are already quite big. Soon, he will become a frog. I am preparing myself for a long sleep through the winter.

Victoria's description builds to a point —an insight into the presence of change everywhere in the world, even in a sleepy little pond.

As rain drizzles into our pond, making a patter of little explosions above me, I think about life in the pond. Some would say that little changes here. I think of the arrival of Specky, his current transformation, and the changing seasons.

"Life in the pond," I conclude, "is quite eventful." The rain stops. I look up to see blurry stars dotting an inky sky.

The conclusion of Victoria's descriptive essay identifies the point to which she has been building.

Step-by-Step Teaching Guide continued

4. Ask students to identify the organizational pattern Victoria used in her essay. (The essay is organized in a loose chronological order.)
5. Discuss how Victoria built her essay around the contrast of an appearance of everyday repetition and subtle change. In light of this focus, ask how the introduction of the tadpole helps her make her point. (The change of the tadpole into a frog helps underscore the central focus of the essay.)

Lesson Objectives

1. To read to appreciate the poet's craft.
2. To write a poem.
3. To choose an appropriate topic for a poem.
4. To draft, revise, and edit a poem.

Step-by-Step Teaching Guide

Poetry

Teaching Resources: Writing Support Transparency 6-I; Writing Support Activity Book 6-3

1. Read the poem on this page of the textbook, "The Freedom of the Moon," to your students as they listen intently with their eyes closed. Encourage students to respond freely to the poem. Ask them to describe some of the images "The Freedom of the Moon" brings to their minds.

2. Mention that although "The Freedom of the Moon" is about a very traditional subject for a poem—the moon—just about any topic can make a wonderful subject for a poem. Challenge students to write poems about things that have made vivid impressions and ideas that have lingered in their minds.

3. Display the transparency to demonstrate how to use a topic web to gather details and shape a perspective.

4. Suggest that students review writing strategies from Chapter 4.

5. Give students copies of the blank organizer. Ask them to use the organizer to refine their poem topics.

6. Encourage students to memorize their own or classmates' poems and recite them to the class.

Connected Assignment
Poem

As you wrote your descriptive essay, you may have found that the words you chose counted as much as the facts you described. Poetry is the place where descriptive words unleash their full power. A **poem** fuses the music of words—those that clatter and those that hum, those that soar and those that drum—with the dance of the senses, calling up strong images and feelings. Poems may include one or more of these features:

- words arranged for a rhythmical, visual, or musical effect
- figures of speech such as
 - ▸ **similes** (comparisons of unlike things using *like* or *as*)
 - ▸ **metaphors** (comparisons of unlike things without using *like* or *as*)
- sound devices such as
 - ▸ **alliteration** (the use of words beginning with the same consonant sound)
 - ▸ **onomatopoeia** (the use of words that sound like what they name)
- a repeated pattern of lines and stanzas (groups of lines)

Write your own poem, using the following strategies.

Prewriting Choose a topic by taking a new perspective on things. For instance, you might write about something

MODEL

The Freedom of the Moon
Robert Frost

I've tried the new moon tilted in the air
Above a hazy tree-and-farmhouse cluster
As you might try a jewel in your hair.
I've tried it fine with little breadth of luster,
5 Alone, or in one ornament combining
With one first-water star almost as shining.

I put it shining anywhere I please.
By walking slowly on some evening later,
I've pulled it from a crate of crooked trees
10 And brought it over glossy water, greater,
And dropped it in, and seen the image wallow,
The color run, all sorts of wonder follow.

ordinary, such as breakfast, which does not usually have attention called to it. Or, you might write on something extraordinary, such as a space launch, from an unusual perspective, such as that of a bird flying by.

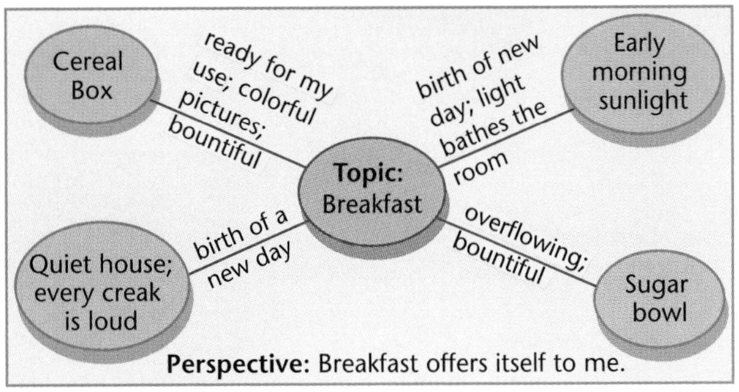

Focus your topic and gather details After selecting your topic, make a list of details about it. Review your list, and focus on aspects of your subject that will help create a unified perspective for your poem. For instance, you might focus on the idea that items on the breakfast table—cereal box, sugar bowl, milk container—are all at your service. To gather details and shape a perspective, use a graphic organizer like the one shown.

Drafting

Once you have gathered details, choose a form in which you will present them. Here are some common forms:

- **Metered poems** follow a regular pattern. Each line has a designated number of accented syllables (beats). Often, designated lines rhyme. For instance, in "The Freedom of the Moon" (opposite), Robert Frost uses alternating rhymes for the first four lines of each stanza, then rhymes the last two. Each line has five strong beats.
- **Free verse poems** do not rhyme and do not follow a regular pattern of beats. Instead, they use repetition, similar and contrasting sounds, and various rhythms to create form.
- **Haiku** are three-line poems in a traditional Japanese form. The first line contains five syllables, the second contains seven syllables, and the third has five syllables.

After you have chosen a form, begin drafting. Use the details you have gathered to convey your perspective. Create strong images using figurative language and sound devices.

Revising and Editing

Review your draft, line by line.

Focus your poem Check the contribution of each line to your poem's perspective. For instance, "the cereal box is on the table" does little to create a perspective. "The cereal box stands at crisp attention" might.

Check your form Read your poem out loud. Count the number of beats in each line. Mark, then revise, lines that do not follow the proper scheme of beats, syllables, or rhymes.

Publishing and Presenting

Read your poem at a class poetry reading. Save a copy of the poem in your portfolio.

Customize for *Gifted/Talented Students*

Students may enjoy interpreting poetry by combining art, dance, and music. Let students work in small groups to choose classmates' poems to interpret and put together multimedia performances for the rest of the class to enjoy.

Customize for *ESL Students*

Appreciating poetry in English can be difficult for students whose first language is not English. Read as many poems as time permits to these students and give them an opportunity to enjoy the sound of the poems—the rhyme scheme and meter—before you begin very limited discussions of figurative language and poetic vocabulary.

Lesson Objectives

1. To interpret and evaluate the various ways visual image makers represent meanings.
2. To evaluate the effects of varying media.
3. To write a poem based on a painting.

Critical Viewing

Interpret Most students will believe that the woman in the painting seems alienated from nature and frightened of the forest.

Step-by-Step Teaching Guide

Connecting Themes Across Cultures

1. Choose a Spotlight element for class discussion, or have students work independently or in groups on the element of their choice. Give students the initiative to find the necessary books and recordings.
2. You may want to divide the class into three groups depending on their interests and ask them to find out more about painter Elizabeth Adela Stanhope Forbes and her painting *Will o' the Wisp,* composer Claude Debussy and *Prelude to the Afternoon of a Faun,* or ballet dancer Vaslav Nijinsky and his choreography of Debussy's tone poem. Students should take turns acting as resources when the class discussion turns to the subjects they have researched.
3. Make available several CDs of performances of *Afternoon of a Faun,* books that include reproductions of Forbes's paintings, and biographies of Nijinsky for your students to use.

Spotlight on the Humanities

Connecting Themes Across Cultures

Focus on Visual Arts: *Will O' the Wisp*

Will O' the Wisp, ca. 1900, Elizabeth Adela Armstrong Forbes, The National Museum of Women in the Arts

Describing an ordinary object is hard enough. Describing a phantasm—half illusion, half reality—is even harder. Rising out of a marsh, a "will o' the wisp" is a cloud of phosphorescent gas. Flitting about the marshland, it deceives weary travelers, who may mistake its movements for a person's. As the will o' the wisp wanders, it reminds us that even the best descriptions can go astray. It also shows our readiness to perceive human activity even in the hushed darkness of the wild. In her painting *Will O' the Wisp,* Elizabeth Adela Armstrong Forbes (1859–1912) extends this trick of perception and gives the mysterious quality of nature a human shape.

▲ **Critical Viewing** What does the woman's pose suggest about her relationship to the forest? **[Interpret]**

Music Connection Composers have also personified nature. French composer Claude Debussy (1862–1918) wrote his famous musical tone poem *Prelude to the Afternoon of a Faun* in 1894. The musical piece, inspired by a poem written by Stéphane Mallarmé, portrays the thoughts of a wandering faun on a sleepy summer afternoon. (In Greek mythology, a *faun* is a wood spirit that is half man, half goat.)

▼ **Critical Viewing** What patterns in nature does this scene suggest? **[Connect]**

Ballet Connection In 1912, *Prelude to the Afternoon of a Faun* was choreographed and danced by the famous Russian ballet dancer, Vaslav Nijinsky (1890–1950). Many consider Nijinsky to be the greatest male dancer in the history of ballet. Both of Nijinsky's parents were celebrated dancers and performed throughout Russia. Nijinsky himself began dancing at a young age. He danced with the renowned Ballets Russes from 1911–1913 and again from 1916–1917.

Descriptive Writing Activity: Poem

Study the Forbes painting *Will O' the Wisp.* Then, write a poem that captures the mood of the painting.

Viewing and Representing

Activity Ask volunteers to read their poems aloud. Then discuss as a class the benefits and challenges of using one medium (writing) to describe another (painting).

Critical Viewing

Connect Students may suggest that the poses of the dancers suggest tree or branch patterns.

Media and Technology Skills

▶ *Lesson Objectives*

1. To evaluate the effects of various film techniques.
2. To assess how the medium contributes to the message.

Analyzing Visual Meanings

Activity: Analyze Visual Techniques in Film

Just as a writer's words shape your understanding of what the writer is describing, a movie uses a special "language" to shape your understanding. Learn how movie-making techniques shape your understanding of events.

Think About It Important aspects of movie "language" include:

Editing A movie may cut from one place and time or part of a scene to another. Cutting creates meaning, as in these examples:

- A cut from one person to another in a conversation helps us follow the conversation from an objective, "outside" point of view.
- A cut from the outside of a building to a room helps us know where the room is located.
- A sudden cut from the hero walking down an alley to a masked figure in a doorway creates shock and increases suspense.

Camera Movement Filmmakers may move the camera while filming. When the camera follows the action, it seems to just "show what happens." When camera movement draws attention to itself, though, as in a long, slow panning shot, the camera becomes like a narrator in a story: a voice mixed in with that of the characters.

Camera Angle When the camera films from the height of a person's head, the viewer feels like a participant in the scene. If the camera is tilted up from below or down from above, the viewer is invited to feel awe, superiority, and so on.

Framing Typically, the center of interest is at the center of the screen. When the camera focuses on one character's face while another speaks off-screen, it emphasizes the first character's reactions. When parts of an image are cut off, viewers may wonder if they are getting "the full picture."

Watch It Watch a movie. Take notes on the narrative techniques it uses in a graphic organizer like the one shown. Write a paragraph describing these techniques and their effect on the story. Consider what role they create for a viewer: all-seeing observer, invisible participant, or confused eyewitness.

Other Camera Techniques

"Zoom In" Shots In a zoom in shot, the image of a person or thing moves closer and closer, emphasizing the importance of what is shown.

"Zoom Out" Shots In a zoom out shot, the image of a person or thing moves farther and farther away, as the camera emphasizes the "big picture."

Close-up Shot The subject filmed takes up most of the screen. A sudden cut from a smooth panning shot to a close-up can create an effect of horror or suspense.

Movie: ____________________

Action	Technique Used	Effect of Technique	Role of Viewer (Follows Action/ Is Above Action/ Misses Part of Action/Shocked by Action, etc.)

Step-by-Step Teaching Guide

Analyzing Visual Meanings

Teaching Resources: Writing Support Transparency 6-J; Writing Support Activity Book 6-4

1. Show a movie on videotape to your students. As the shots mentioned on this page of the textbook occur in the movie, stop the tape and discuss the purpose and effect of the various types of shots and film techniques. If you have a video camera available, you and your students can try some of the techniques described in the textbook.
2. Display the transparency and review the information students will identify as they view their chosen films.
3. Give students copies of the blank organizer for them to use as they view their movies.
4. You may want to photocopy and make available for students several reviews of films in which the reviewer discusses visual techniques used by the filmmaker. Then ask the students to complete the writing assignment.
5. Consider assigning small groups of students to write about the same movie. When they have finished their essays, they can read them to the group and compare their reactions to the film.

Customize for *Gifted/Talented Students*

Have students work together in groups of four or five to make short films that use some of the camera techniques discussed in this lesson.

Lesson Objectives

1. To use firsthand knowledge and experience to comprehend.
2. To answer different types and levels of test questions.

Step-by-Step Teaching Guide

Strategy, Organization, and Style

Teaching Resources: Standardized Test Preparation Workbook, pp. 11–12

1. Emphasize the importance of understanding test directions to students. Have a volunteer explain what the sample test items on this page of the textbook direct them to do.
2. Go through the choices for the first sample test item. Have students attempt to answer before reading the explanation. Does their answer agree with the answer in the textbook? If not, go over the answer step by step.
3. Follow this procedure with sample test item 2.
4. Have students complete the test practice activity on page 133. Give students ten or fifteen minutes to complete the test.
5. Read students the answers. If they missed any questions, have them reread the corresponding passages.

Standardized Test Preparation Workshop

Strategy, Organization, and Style

On standardized tests, some questions require you to read a passage and then choose improvements for it.

- *Strategy* questions ask whether a certain change fits the purpose of the passage.
- *Organization* questions ask you to choose the most logical sequence of ideas or sentences.
- *Style* questions ask you to find the most appropriate and effective language for the intended audience.

Practice for such questions with the following sample items:

Test Tip

As you read the passage, note the sequence of events described. Do they follow a logical order? To understand the author's purpose, try to determine how the author wanted information presented.

Sample Test Items	Answers and Explanations
Read the passage, and then answer the questions that follow. (1) He mixed the paint and poured it in the tray. (2) Doug covered the furniture with sheets. (3) He dipped in his roller and applied it to the wall. (4) Then, he covered the floor with newspaper.	
1 Choose the most logical sentence sequence. A 2, 4, 1, 3 B 1, 3, 2, 4 C 2, 1, 3, 4 D Correct as is	The correct answer is *A*. Part (2) and Part (4) indicate events that are part of the preparation for painting, so they must come first. The transition word in (4) shows that (2) should appear before (4). Doug must complete part (1) before he completes part (3), so part (1) should come first.
2 Which is the best way to write parts (2) and (4)? F First, Doug covered the furniture with sheets; then, afterward, he covered the floor with newspaper. G Doug covered the furniture first with sheets, then with newspapers. H Doug covered the furniture with sheets, and then he covered the floor with newspaper. J Correct as is	The correct answer is *H*. This sentence combines ideas without changing the meaning of the two sentences. It also eliminates unnecessary words.

TEST-TAKING TIP

When test items describe steps in a process, students should attempt to picture the steps clearly. One way they can do this is by imagining themselves completing each step. They may even want to do quick sketches of the steps if they have time. Then students should ask themselves whether the order makes sense. They should figure out which step must come first in order to accomplish the other steps and which step describes the final outcome of the process. Then they should reorder the other steps in the process so they make the most logical sequence.

Practice 1 **Directions:** Read the passage, and then answer the questions that follow. Choose the letter of the best answer.

(1) Gather together some old magazines, scissors, white glue, and posterboard. (2) You might choose fruits, <u>sports</u>, kids, movie stars—any subject that interests you. (3) Decide on a theme for your collage. (4) Locate photographs in magazines that relate to your theme. (5) Carefully cut out the photographs that relate to your theme and set them aside. (6) You may want to add glitter or paint. (7) When you feel you have <u>enough</u>, begin arranging them on the posterboard. (8) When you are happy with the look, carefully glue the photos in place.

(9) Looking for an <u>inexpensive</u> way to express yourself? (10) Making a collage can be a fun activity—perfect for a rainy day or a party activity. (11) If you'd like to try your hand at doing this fun activity, read on for instructions.

(12) Look over your completed collage. (13) What does it tell about your theme? (14) This can also be a great record of what was going on at a certain <u>time</u> in your life. (15) Every year, a friend of mine creates one in which she includes news items, as well as personal photos and letters. (16) Give it a try; I really find it to be a lot of fun. (17) While many use collage as a personal expression, others use it to experiment with color and proportion.

1 Which of the following would be the best way, if any, to rewrite parts 4 and 5?

A Locate photographs in magazines that relate to your theme; carefully cut out the photographs and set them aside.

B Locate photographs in magazines that relate to your theme, and carefully cut out the photographs that relate to the theme and set them aside.

C Locate magazine photographs relating to your theme, carefully cut them out, and set them aside.

D Correct as is

2 In part 11, which of the following should be removed from the sentence?

F If you'd like to

G to try your hand

H at doing this fun activity

J read on for instructions

3 Which of the following is the best order for the paragraphs?

A 1, 2, 3

B 3, 2, 1

C 1, 3, 2

D 2, 1, 3

4 In which part should the underlined word be replaced by a more precise word?

F Part 2

G Part 7

H Part 9

J Part 14

5 Choose the most logical sentence sequence for paragraph 1.

A 1, 2, 3, 5, 4, 6, 8, 7

B 1, 3, 2, 4, 5, 7, 8, 6

C 1, 3, 2, 4, 7, 6, 8, 5

D 8, 7, 6, 1, 2, 4, 3, 5

Answer Key

Practice 1

1. C
2. H
3. D
4. G
5. B

Customize for *Less Advanced Students*

Students may find answering questions about passages this long quite intimidating, so you may want to have students practice without timing them. Have students choose partners and read the passage together paragraph by paragraph. After they finish a paragraph, they should describe the steps in their own words. Caution students that the steps in paragraph one are out of order. Let pairs of students answer the questions together and compare their answers with other students' answers.

Customize for *More Advanced Students*

Have students discuss multiple choice tests. Have they ever had a test item marked incorrect that they were sure was right? What did they do about it? Ask students to work together to list tips for taking multiple choice tests. Post the tips in the classroom.

Chapter 7

Time and Resource Manager

In-Depth Lesson Plan

	LESSON FOCUS	PRINT AND MEDIA RESOURCES
DAY 1	**Introduction to Persuasive Essays** Students learn key elements of persuasive writing and analyze the Model From Literature (pp. 134–139).	***Writers at Work* Videotape,** Persuasion ***Writing and Grammar iText* (Interactive Text),** Ch. 7, Introduction
DAY 2	**Prewriting** Students choose and narrow a topic, consider their audience and purpose, and gather information (pp. 140–143).	**Teaching Resources** *Writing Support Transparencies,* 7-A–C; *Topic Bank for Heterogeneous Classes,* Ch. 7 ***Writing and Grammar iText* (Interactive Text),** Section 7.2
DAY 3	**Drafting** Students organize their ideas and write their first drafts (pp. 144–145).	**Teaching Resources** *Writing Support Transparencies,* 7-D ***Writing and Grammar iText* (Interactive Text),** Section 7.3
DAY 4	**Revising** Students revise their drafts in terms of overall structure, paragraphs, sentences, and word choice (pp. 146–150).	**Teaching Resources** *Writing Support Transparencies,* 7-E–G; *Writing Support Activity Book,* 7-2 ***Writing and Grammar iText* (Interactive Text),** Section 7.4
DAY 5	**Editing and Proofreading; Publishing and Presenting** Students check their work for accuracy and correctness and present their final drafts (pp. 151–152).	**Teaching Resources** *Scoring Rubrics on Transparency,* Ch. 7; *Formal Assessment,* Ch. 7 ***Writing and Grammar iText* (Interactive Text),** Sections 7.5–6

Accelerated Lesson Plan

	LESSON FOCUS	PRINT AND MEDIA RESOURCES
DAY 1	**Introduction Through Drafting** Students review the characteristics of persuasive writing, select topics, and write drafts (pp. 134–145).	**Teaching Resources** *Writing Support Transparencies,* 7-A–D ***Writing and Grammar iText* (Interactive Text),** Ch. 7, Introduction through Section 7.3
DAY 2	**Revising Through Presenting** Students work individually or with peers to revise, edit, and proofread their work for presentation (pp. 146–152).	**Teaching Resources** *Writing Support Transparencies,* 7-E–G; *Writing Support Activity Book,* 7-2; *Scoring Rubrics on Transparency,* Ch. 7; *Formal Assessment,* Ch. 7 ***Writing and Grammar iText* (Interactive Text),** Sections 7.4–6

Options for Adapting Lesson Plans

HOMEWORK

Have students complete any stage of the lesson for homework.

SPELLING

To teach spelling skills in conjunction with writing skills, work through *Prentice Hall Everyday Spelling,* Grade 8, Chapter 8, as you cover this *Writing and Grammar* chapter. At the Editing and Proofreading stage, remind students to apply the spelling skills to their persuasive essays.

FEATURES

Extend coverage with Connected Assignment (p. 156), Spotlight on the Humanities (p. 158), Media and Technology Skills (p. 159), and Standardized Test Preparation Workshop (p. 160).

TECHNOLOGY

Students can complete any stage of the lesson on the computer, using *Writing and Grammar iText* or a word-processing program. Have them print out their completed work.

INTEGRATED SKILLS COVERAGE

Integrating Grammar
SE pp. 149, 151

Viewing and Representing
Critical Viewing, SE pp. 134, 136, 138, 139, 142, 149, 153, 155, 158
ATE pp. 139, 158

Technology
Using the Internet, ATE p. 140

Real-World Connection
ATE, pp. 138, 142

BLOCK SCHEDULING

Pacing Suggestions
For 90-minute Blocks
- Have students complete the Prewriting and Drafting stages in a single period.
- Focus one class period on Revising and Editing and Publishing and Presenting. Allow at least 30 minutes for peer revision.

Resources for Varying Instruction
- ***Writing and Grammar iText* (Interactive Text)** A 90-minute block provides an ideal opportunity for students to work on computer.
- ***Writers at Work* Videotape** Show the Persuasive Writing segment in class.

Professional Development Support
- ***How to Manage Instruction in the Block*** This teaching resource provides management and activity suggestions.

ASSESSMENT SUPPORT

Standardized Test Preparation Workshop SE pp. 160–161; ATE p. 149
Standardized Test Preparation Workbook, pp. 13–14
Scoring Rubrics on Transparency, Ch. 7
Formal Assessment, Ch. 7
Writing Assessment and Portfolio Management

MEDIA AND TECHNOLOGY

For the Student
- ***Writing and Grammar iText* (Interactive Text)**, Ch. 7

For the Teacher
- ***Writers at Work* Videotape**, Persuasion
- ***Resource Pro* CD-ROM**

MEETING INDIVIDUAL NEEDS

Less Advanced Students ATE pp. 143, 146, 157, 161. See also Ongoing Assessments ATE pp. 135, 141, 145, 148.
More Advanced Students ATE pp. 138, 161
Gifted/Talented Students ATE p. 157
Verbal/Linguistic Learners ATE p. 148
Logical/Mathematical Learners ATE p. 159

WRITING AND GRAMMAR ON-LINE

iText Interactive Text (On-line or on CD-ROM)
- Easily navigable instruction with interactive Revision Checkers
- Full use of e-rater™, the essay-scoring system (on-line only)

Companion Web Site PHSchool.com
- Scoring rubrics with models (use Web Code eck-8001)

See the Go On-line! feature, SE p. iii.

LITERATURE CONNECTIONS

Related selections from *Prentice Hall Literature: Timeless Voices, Timeless Themes,* Silver:

Professional Model "The Trouble with Television," Robert MacNeil, SE p. 139
Topic Bank Option "Achieving the American Dream," Mario Cuomo, SE p. 141

CHAPTER 7
PERSUASIVE ESSAY

Lesson Objectives

1. To identify and define a persuasive essay.
2. To read and interpret a persuasive essay.
3. To utilize strategies for choosing a topic.
4. To identify and practice strategies for narrowing a topic.
5. To identify audience and purpose.
6. To research ideas to gather support.
7. To learn to shape writing by developing a thesis statement and organizational structure.
8. To learn to use a variety of persuasive techniques.
9. To learn strategies for revising structure.
10. To use parallel structures to revise sentences.
11. To learn to repeat key words for effect.
12. To check for proper use of colons and dashes.
13. To present a persuasive essay.
14. Read and evaluate the Student Work in Progress.

Critical Viewing

Infer Students may say that the expressions on the men's faces and their body language suggests an emotionally charged atmosphere in which persuasive words would play an important role in convincing delegates what was best for the country.

Chapter 7 Persuasion
Persuasive Essay

Signing of the Constitution, Howard Chandler Christy

▲ Critical Viewing
At the Constitutional Convention of 1787, delegates from each state forged the United States Constitution. As this painting of the convention suggests, persuasive words were a major force in building the nation. Explain. **[Infer]**

Persuasion in Everyday Life

Once a word leaves your lips, its journey through the world has just begun. "Please" might end up getting your older brother to drive you to a movie. "Aw, c'mon" might bring your friends to a meeting of the chess club. "Awesome" might send fans in an on-line chat room out to buy a new CD. When you send out words to change people's thinking or to influence their actions, you are using **persuasion**.

Persuasion travels by many roads. Persuasive words roar by in an advertisement on a bus or whisk across your television screen during a commercial break. Along the way, they may unite people in a common action, viewpoint, or lifestyle. By developing your persuasive writing skills, you can have a say in which road people choose.

TIME AND RESOURCE MANAGER

Resources
Technology: Writers at Work Videotape; Writing and Grammar iText, Ch. 7

In-Depth Coverage	Accelerated Pace
• Cover pp. 134–140 in class. • Show the Writing a Persuasive Essay section of the Writers at Work Videotape. • Read the Model From Literature (pp. 136–138) in class and use it to demonstrate key techniques of persuasion.	• Assign pp. 134–140 for independent student review. • Discuss definitions and types of persuasive essays.

What Is a Persuasive Essay?

A **persuasive essay** is a written work in which a writer presents a case for or against a particular position. Each logical argument, powerful image, or striking phrase in the essay is like a step on a staircase leading to a window. As readers ascend, they come closer to looking out this "window"—to seeing things from the writer's point of view. A persuasive essay has

- an issue with more than one side.
- a clear organization that builds toward a conclusion.
- a clear statement of the writer's position.
- evidence supporting the writer's position, including arguments, statistics, expert opinions, and personal observations.
- powerful images and language.

To learn the criteria on which your persuasive essay may be assessed, see the Rubric for Self-Assessment on page 152.

Writers in ACTION

Kate Mitchell, a fundraiser, has used persuasion to raise money for an educational program on New York's Hudson River.

"To persuade somebody with your writing is one of the most empowering things that you can do."

Types of Persuasive Writing

Here are a few of the common types of persuasive writing:

- **Editorials** are brief persuasive essays, intended for publication in a newspaper, magazine, or other medium, that state and defend an opinion on a current issue.
- **Political speeches** are persuasive speeches intended to win support for a policy, law, or reform.
- **Public-service announcements** are radio or television commercials written to persuade and educate the public.

PREVIEW Student Work IN PROGRESS

In this chapter, you'll follow the work of Ryan Caparella, a student at Chain of Lakes Middle School, Orlando, Florida. You'll see how Ryan used featured prewriting, drafting, and revising strategies to write a persuasive essay on the dangers of drugs. At the end of the chapter, you can read Ryan's completed essay, "I Will Be Drug Free."

PREPARE and ENGAGE

Interest GRABBER Announce that you will consider assigning no homework tonight. Ask students for reasons why you should make this change. Point out the different types of arguments students made and how effective they were.

Activate Prior Knowledge

Ask students to describe some advertisements they like in print or on radio or television. Discuss why they like the ads and if the ads persuaded them to buy the product.

ONGOING ASSESSMENT: Prerequisite Skills

Use one of the following options to diagnose students' current level of proficiency in persuasive writing.

Option 1 Ask each student to select the strongest example of his or her persuasive writing from last year. Hold conferences in which you review each student's sample. Use the conferences to determine which students will need extra support in developing a persuasive essay.

Option 2 Ask students to write a sentence persuading a friend or family member to help them with their chores. Have students list three details that they might use to support their sentences. If students have difficulty with this exercise, you will need to devote more time to the elaboration phase of the process.

TEACH

Reading\Writing Connection

Reading: Understand a Writer's Purpose

A writer's purpose in a persuasive essay is obviously to persuade. As students read the model, they should pay attention to the strategies Krents uses to persuade his readers. Students should ask themselves if Krents is successful.

Critical Viewing

Analyze Students may mention touch (dribbling the ball), sight (looking at opponent), and sound (listening for opponent).

Step-by-Step Teaching Guide

Engage Students Through Literature

1. Have volunteers read aloud the story. Tell students that *cum laude* (pronounced KUM LAO-DAY) is Latin for "with honors."
2. Use the margin notes to guide discussion of the story. Ask students for their reactions. Point out how the author uses an ironic, even sarcastic sense of humor to make his point.
3. Ask students to describe their own reactions to disabled people they know or have encountered. Ask how the story changed their feelings.
4. If you have a differently abled student in the class, he or she might want to be the expert moderator for this discussion.

7.1 Model From Literature

In his autobiography, To Race the Wind, *lawyer, activist, and writer Harold Krents (1944–1987) attributes some of his self-confidence to the confidence his family had in him, despite his blindness. He recalls racing ahead of his mother at the age of three and learning to catch a football with his brother at the age of nine. His life story inspired the 1969 Broadway play* Butterflies Are Free *by Leonard Gershe.*

▲ Critical Viewing
What senses other than sight are these people using as they play? Give examples. **[Analyze]**

Reading Writing Connection

Reading Strategy: Understand a Writer's Purpose A writer's **purpose**—to inform, to entertain, to shape a viewpoint, to argue for or against a position—determines what facts, arguments, and images he or she uses. While reading, formulate an idea of the writer's purpose. Test whether it is effectively achieved as you read.

Darkness at Noon

Harold Krents

Blind from birth, I have never had the opportunity to see myself and have been completely dependent on the image I create in the eye of the observer. To date, it has not been narcissistic.

There are those who assume that since I can't see, I obviously also cannot hear. Very often people will converse with me at the top of their lungs, enunciating each word very carefully. Conversely, people will also often whisper, assuming that since my eyes don't work, my ears don't either.

For example, when I go to the airport and ask the ticket agent

The opening states the issue addressed by the essay—overcoming the negative perceptions some sighted people have of the blind. Krents effectively expresses his hurt and his humor about the issue with sarcastic, understated comments.

for assistance to the plane, he or she will invariably pick up the phone, call a ground hostess, and whisper: "Hi, Jane, we've got a 76 here." I have concluded that the word *blind* is not used, for one of two reasons: Either they fear that if the dread word is spoken, the ticket agent's retina will immediately detach, or they are reluctant to inform me of my condition, of which I may not have been previously aware.

On the other hand, others know that of course I can hear, but believe that I can't talk. Often, therefore, when my wife and I go out to dinner, a waiter or waitress will ask Kit if "he would like a drink" to which I respond that "indeed he would."

This point was graphically driven home to me while we were in England. I had been given a year's leave of absence from my Washington law firm to study for a diploma in law at Oxford University. During the year I became ill and was hospitalized. Immediately after admission, I was wheeled down to the X-ray room. Just at the door sat an elderly woman—elderly I would judge from the sound of her voice. "What is his name?" the woman asked the orderly who had been wheeling me.

Examples from the author's own life serve as evidence for his argument. Such evidence helps readers side with the author because it is vivid and personal.

"What's your name?" the orderly repeated to me.

"Harold Krents," I replied.

"Harold Krents," he repeated.

"When was he born?"

"When were you born?"

"November 5, 1944," I responded.

"November 5, 1944," the orderly intoned.

The repetition in the exchange is memorable and even amusing.

This procedure continued for approximately five minutes, at which point even my saintlike disposition deserted me.

"Look," I finally blurted out, "this is absolutely ridiculous. Okay, granted I can't see, but it's got to have become pretty clear to both of you that I don't need an interpreter."

"He says he doesn't need an interpreter," the orderly reported to the woman.

The toughest misconception of all is the view that because I can't see, I can't work. I was turned down by over forty law firms because of my blindness, even though my qualifications included a cum laude degree from Harvard College and a good ranking in my Harvard Law School class.

The author gives factual support for his points.

The attempt to find employment, the continuous frustration of being told that it was impossible for a blind person to practice law, the rejection letters, based not on my lack of ability but rather on my disability, will always remain one of the most disillusioning experiences of my life.

Teaching From the Model

You can use this model to help students see the uses of a light touch in persuasive writing. Rather than pounding away at the reader with logical arguments, the writer uses anecdotes and humor, a well-developed "show, don't tell" technique to make his point that the disabled, while seen too often as being "unabled," are better seen as differently abled.

More About the Author

Harold Krents's inspirational story was also adapted for television. The 1980 drama *To Race The Wind* starred Steve Guttenberg as Harold Krents.

Real-World Connection

Ask students what accommodations their school building has made for differently-abled students and teachers. For example, there may be a ramp into the building, special restrooms, and so on. Ask students where else in their town they have seen these adaptations to enable all people to participate fully.

Language Highlight

Anecdote An *anecdote* is a short account of an interesting event, usually biographical. It comes from a Greek word meaning "unpublished," because anecdotes were originally shared in conversation.

Customize for *More Advanced Students*

Have students discuss why an anecdote might be used in a persuasive essay. Encourage them to use anecdotes in the essays they write in this chapter.

Critical Viewing

Hypothesize Students may say the fighter would use his senses of touch and hearing.

7.1

Fortunately, this view of limitation and exclusion is beginning to change. On April 16, [1978,] the Department of Labor issued regulations that mandate equal-employment opportunities for the handicapped. By and large, the business community's response to offering employment to the disabled has been enthusiastic.

I therefore look forward to the day, with the expectation that it is certain to come, when employers will view their handicapped workers as a little child did me years ago when my family still lived in Scarsdale.

I was playing basketball with my father in our back yard according to procedures we had developed. My father would stand beneath the hoop, shout, and I would shoot over his head at the basket attached to our garage. Our next-door neighbor, aged five, wandered over into our yard with a playmate. "He's blind," our neighbor whispered to her friend in a voice that could be heard distinctly by Dad and me. Dad shot and missed; I did the same. Dad hit the rim; I missed entirely; Dad shot and missed the garage entirely. "Which one is blind?" whispered back the little friend.

The author has "warmed up" the reader with absurd anecdotes and his mildly sarcastic tone. These persuasive devices build toward his central argument: The disabled deserve fair treatment by employers.

This final anecdote gives readers a simple, powerful image of the future for which Krents hopes.

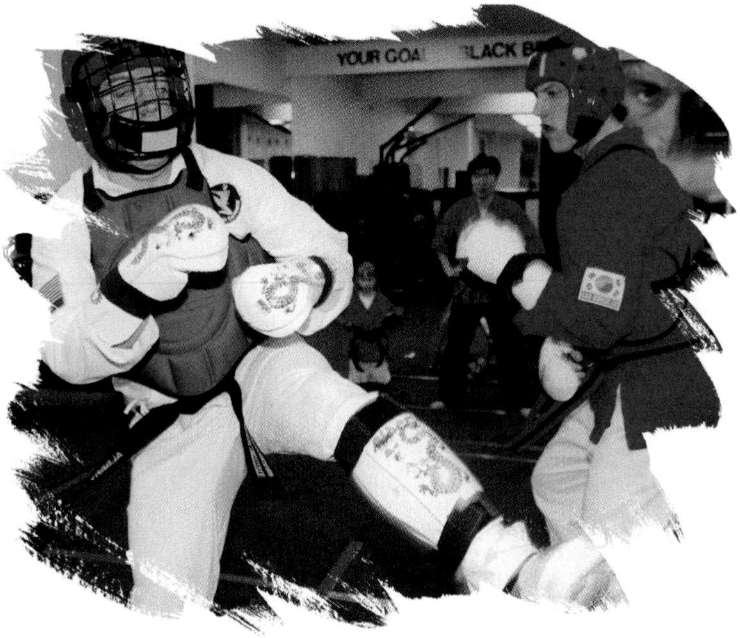

◄ **Critical Viewing** What senses might this blind martial-arts fighter use in his sport? **[Hypothesize]**

◀ **Critical Viewing** What features of this man's office building might make working there easier for him? **[Connect]**

I would hope that in the near future, when a plant manager is touring the factory with the foreman and comes upon a handicapped and a nonhandicapped person working together, his comment after watching them work will be, "Which one is disabled?"

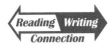

Krents concludes with another memorable image.

Reading Writing Connection

Writing Application: Make Your Purpose Clear To help your readers better understand the points in your essay, make your purpose clear in the introduction. In the body of your essay, explain the connection of each main point to your purpose.

LITERATURE

For another example of persuasive writing on a social theme, see "The Trouble with Television," by Robert McNeil. You can find this essay in *Prentice Hall Literature: Timeless Voices, Timeless Themes,* Silver.

Step-by-Step Teaching Guide

Engage Students Through Literature

1. Engage students in a discussion of why they think Krents had trouble finding a job. Ask why they think employers were reluctant to hire a blind man. Point out the erroneous assumptions made about people's abilities.
2. Continue the discussion about erroneous assumptions into the idea of the tyranny of the majority. Tell students that because a majority of people do things one way, or appear a certain way, they make the (erroneous) assumption that their way is the right or only way. The great majority of people are not sight impaired and are able to use their vision to do tasks a certain way. But that doesn't mean that visually-impaired people cannot make some adaptations and still do those same tasks competently. Nor does it make their way a wrong way.

Reading\Writing Connection

Writing: Make Your Purpose Clear

Encourage students to keep their purpose for writing in mind as they draft their essays. Readers will be better able to follow students' arguments if they understand the purpose.

Critical Viewing

Connect Students may mention automatic doors, wide hallways, and shelves placed at a low level.

Responding to Literature

Have students read Robert MacNeil's "The Trouble with Television"—but not the biographical blurb about him. After students finish, tell them that MacNeil spent many years producing and hosting a TV news program. Ask if MacNeil's essay is any more persuasive now that they know he is an expert on television.

Integrating Viewing Skills

Robert MacNeil is no longer associated with the *NewsHour,* but the show is still on public television and the format has not changed. Have students watch the *NewsHour* tonight and think about whether it is typical. Does it sell "instant gratification"? Does it merely "divert" viewers? Does it "appeal to the short attention span"? Is it "decivilizing"?

Step-by-Step Teaching Guide

Prewriting: Choosing Your Topic

Teaching, Resources: Writing Support Transparency 7-A

1. Students often have difficulty choosing a topic. The purpose of the techniques here is to guide them to a topic that interests them, has at least two differing points of view, and can be readily researched.
2. Display the transparency. Review the techniques in the text and Ryan's example of a media flip-through.
3. If there have been pressing school or local issues, see that students identify those issues in their round-table discussions.
4. Pay some attention to the groupings in the round-table exercise, assigning students of complementary strengths. You might want to sit in on any discussions that need a jump-start.
5. Encourage students to generate lots of ideas, but in the selection process try to steer them away from large, complex issues that will take a lot of research. The point is to practice writing a persuasive essay, not to suggest how to change the entire world.

Integrating Technology Skills

If the resources are available, direct students to a news site on the Internet. Some good sites include: www.msnbc.com, www.cnn.com, www.nytimes.com, www.cbs.com. For sports, suggest that students start at www.espn.com or www.foxsports.com. Always preview a site for unsuitable content before recommending it to students.

7.2 Prewriting

Choosing Your Topic

Typically, you will do your best job writing a persuasive essay if you choose a topic that is important to you. The following strategies will help you find such a topic:

Strategies for Generating a Topic

1. **Self-Interview** Pretend you're a reporter interviewing yourself. Answer the following questions: (1) What people, groups, places, and things are important in your life? Why? (2) What issues affect these people and things? Review your answers, and choose a topic from among them.
2. **Round Table** With a group of classmates, hold a discussion of issues in your school and community. What problems need solving? What perceptions need changing? Raise as many specific issues as possible. Jot down any that interest you. Select a topic for your essay from your notes.
3. **Media Flip-Through** Every day, the media bring controversies and debates into our living rooms. Over the course of a day or two, read through newspapers or watch the local and national news. Jot down topics that spark your interest, and choose one as a topic for your essay.

iText

Get instant help! Write your Self-Interview questions using the Essay Builder, accessible from the menu bar, on-line or on CD-ROM.

Student Work IN PROGRESS

Name: Ryan Caparella
Chain of Lakes Middle School
Orlando, FL

Using a Media Flip-Through

Over a few days, Ryan flipped through newspapers and watched news programs to find a topic. He jotted down the following ideas and chose one—drug abuse.

Newspapers	TV News
flooding in the Midwest (Small City News)	overexposure to sun increasing, can cause skin cancer (The Nightly News)
city council closes down a park used for youth soccer league (My Town Newspaper)	voter registration declines (The Local Eye)
young people today—dangers and dilemmas—drug abuse (Young Americans Weekly)	baseball teams spend millions to recruit high-school players (The Sports Show)

TIME AND RESOURCE MANAGER

Resources
Print: Writing Support Transparencies, 7-A–C; Writing Support Activity Book, 7-1
Technology: Writing and Grammar iText, Section 7.2

In-Depth Coverage	Accelerated Pace
• Cover pp. 140–143. • Guide students through the Strategies for Generating a Topic.	• Discuss the strategies for generating topics. • Have students work independently to choose and narrow their topics. • Have students work with partners to focus on audience, purpose, and gathering details.

TOPIC BANK

If you're having trouble finding a topic, consider these possibilities:

1. **Position Paper on Food Science** Giant ears of corn, cows that grow up in no time—these are the results of scientific advances. Some people are concerned, though, about the use of new technologies to produce food. Do research, and write a paper taking a position on a new technology.
2. **Editorial on Freedom** Some argue that freedom of expression ends at the school entrance. Choose an issue involving self-expression, such as school uniforms or the rights of school newspapers. Write an editorial expressing your position on the issue.

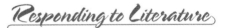

Responding to Fine Art

3. This image creates an idea of what happens when people hear the words of others—of leaders, of television commercials, and so on. Write a few notes discussing this idea. Then, choose an issue concerning communication, the media, or authority that could be illustrated by this image. Write a persuasive essay on this topic.

Untitled (Heard), Barbara Kruger, National Museum of American Art, Washington, D.C.

Responding to Literature

4. Read Mario Cuomo's essay "Achieving the American Dream." Write an essay about your own version of the American Dream. You can find the essay in *Prentice Hall Literature: Timeless Voices, Timeless Themes*, Silver.

Cooperative Writing Opportunity

5. **Fitness Advertising Campaign** With a group, investigate teen fitness. Each member can research one aspect of fitness, such as exercise techniques, proper diet, and local exercise programs. Using your research, put together a teen-fitness advertising campaign. One student might create posters, another might write a brochure, and others might illustrate the brochure with photographs and diagrams.

Step-by-Step Teaching Guide

Responding to Fine Art

Untitled (Heard) by Barbara Kruger

Teaching Resources: Writing Support Transparency 7-B

1. Display the transparency and ask students what the painting suggests to them.
2. Barbara Kruger's art has been said to take a "confrontational approach." Ask students if they think this approach is good in a persuasive essay. Why or why not?

Responding to Literature

Make sure students understand that their argument should be intended for a diverse audience. They will want a logical argument with convincing support for their main points.

Spotlight on the Humanities

For additional topic suggestions, refer students to the Spotlight on the Humanities on page 158.

ONGOING ASSESSMENT: Monitor and Reinforce

If some students are having difficulty coming up with a topic, use one of the following options.

Option 1 Suggest that students choose an idea from the Topic Bank. If many students have difficulty, work with them around one topic, modeling the process for them.

Option 2 If the Topic Bank ideas seem too complex, suggest that students try one of the assignments from the Topic Bank for Heterogeneous Classes in the teaching resources.

TIME SAVERS!

Writing Support Transparencies

Use the transparencies for Chapter 7 to teach these strategies.

Step-by-Step Teaching Guide

Prewriting: Narrowing Your Topic; Considering Audience and Purpose

1. Narrowing the topic needs to work with the student's opinion on the topic. In the example of television news, if the student has an opinion that TV news is biased or sensational, it would be wrong to narrow the topic to the audience reached by TV news. See that students align their topic with their opinion.
2. Encourage students to examine their opinion in terms of the reporter's questions. For example, if they think that TV news is sensationalized, they need to establish *what* is sensational, *why* it is that way, *how* it got that way, and *how* it affects the audience.
3. Audience and purpose are crucial. Students want to avoid taking easy positions where they are "preaching to the choir." Steer them to topics where their audience is likely to hold differing opinions. At the same time, remind them that if they choose a very technical or arcane topic, they will first need to explain the topic to the audience.

Real-World Connection

Direct students to the letters to the editor on the newspaper editorial page and to write a brief outline of differing views on a controversial topic.

Critical Viewing

Analyze Students should mention *Who? What? Where? How?* and possibly *When?*

7.2

Narrowing Your Topic

Choosing a topic shouldn't mean signing up to write a book! Narrow your topic to make sure you can cover it thoroughly in an essay. For example, your topic might concern fairness in the media. "The media" covers everything from sitcoms to newspaper editorials—it is a topic broad enough for a book. You might narrow your topic to the television news coverage of a particular international situation.

To narrow your topic, use the "reporter's questions"—*Who? What? Where? When? Why?* and *How?*

Use the "Reporter's Questions"

Follow these steps to narrow a topic with the "reporter's questions":

1. Choose a partner, and construct questions about each other's topics using the "reporter's questions."
2. Answer each question as specifically as possible. For instance, your topic might be "television news." Your partner might ask, "What news does television cover?" You may answer, "National, local, and, to a lesser extent, international news."
3. Your partner should jot down your answers.

After answering each other's questions, trade notes. Circle the most interesting issues your answers raise, and choose a narrowed topic from among them.

▲ **Critical Viewing** Which of the "reporter's questions" might a newspaper photograph answer? **[Analyze]**

Considering Your Audience and Purpose

Your **purpose** in writing a persuasive essay is to convince readers of your opinion. Knowing your **audience**—your readers—will help you find the evidence and language to best achieve this purpose. For example, if you were writing on your school's attendance policy, the arguments you would offer students might differ from those you would use with administrators.

To analyze your audience, answer the following questions:

- What do my readers know about the topic?
- What are their likely opinions or prejudices on the topic?
- About which aspects of the issue might they be most concerned?

Use your answers to help you choose the support for your position that has the best chance of convincing your readers.

Gathering Support

Before you draft, do research in reference books, magazines, and other sources to gather evidence on both sides of your issue.

Provide Support

Types of support include the following:

- **Logical arguments:** *Television news sensationalizes stories. Therefore, viewers get a distorted view of the world.*
- **Statistics:** *Eighty percent of viewers did not know the reasons behind the war.*
- **Expert opinions:** *Psychologist Joseph Lacan argues that the format of the news diminishes viewers' attention span.*
- **Personal observations:** *I watched battle footage on television for a week. I understood what the fighting was about only after I read a magazine article on the war.*

As you do research, complete a T-chart to gather evidence.

Completing a T-Chart Write your issue on a sheet of paper. Divide the sheet into two columns; label one "Pro" and the other "Con." Note support for one side of the issue under "Pro." Note opposing evidence and arguments under "Con."

Research Tip

You can often find the latest evidence about controversial issues in magazines and newspapers. Ask your librarian about on-line and print guides to periodicals.

Student Work IN PROGRESS

Name: Ryan Caparella
Chain of Lakes Middle School
Orlando, FL

Completing a T-Chart

Ryan realized that there was not a "Pro" side to the issue of drug abuse. He adapted a T-chart by labeling one side "Excuses" and the other "Realities."

Drugs Among Young People

Excuses	Realities
Keeping your friends is more important than anything.	Drugs are dangerous and bad for your health.
You have to look "cool."	What you do today will stay with you always.
You should live for today, not tomorrow.	Being responsible for yourself is more important than following your friends.

Step-by-Step Teaching Guide

Prewriting: Gathering Support

Teaching Resources: Writing Support, Transparency 7-C; Writing Support Activity Book 7-1

1. Discuss the difference between reasoned argument that is backed up with facts and assertions that amount to little more than "because I said so . . ."
2. Write the following sentences on the chalkboard and ask students to identify which is reasoned argument and which is assertion:

   I think TV news is inaccurate. A recent survey found that 73% of the news was about issues involving crime and violence. (reasoned argument)

   I think TV news is inaccurate. All they ever show is crime and violence. (assertion)
3. Point out that the opinion expressed in both comments is the same, but in the first example the opinion is based on facts that are included.
4. Display the transparency to show how Ryan's T-Chart helped him clarify both sides of the issue. Discuss how a successful persuasive essay does not ignore opposing arguments. Instead, it brings them up and attempts to prove them wrong. A T-Chart helps writers set up their own arguments and those they need to overcome.
5. Give students copies of the blank organizer for them to use to gather support.

Customize for *Less Advanced Students*

Help students set up the T-Chart by asking them to consider an opposing opinion for every argument they come up with.

TIME SAVERS!

Writing Support Transparencies
Use the transparencies for Chapter 7 to teach these strategies.

Writing Support Activity Book
Use the graphic organizers for Chapter 7 to facilitate these strategies.

Step-by-Step Teaching Guide

Drafting: Nestorian Order

1. A successful persuasive essay's first requirement is a strong thesis statement. Write the following two examples on the chalkboard.

   The First Amendment gives all Americans the right of freedom of speech. "All Americans," however, does not include anyone under the age of 18.

   Freedom of speech is a basic American right. It is part of the U.S. Constitution. Every day, people enjoy their rights. It just doesn't seem fair that kids do not have the same rights as grown-ups.

2. Point out how in the second example, the thesis is stated less clearly.
3. After examining the presentation on Nestorian Order, ask students to consider the strengths of this organizational strategy. It is effective in first establishing the thesis, establishing the opposition, then triumphing over the opposition. By giving opposing arguments such a featured place, the writer gives the appearance of fairness. When Nestorian Order is done with strong factual support, it works from reasoned argument instead of simple assertions.
4. Review with students the importance of acknowledging opposing arguments and treating them seriously. Dismissing opposing arguments out of hand, or using mockery, reflects badly on the writer's own arguments.

Language Highlight

Nestor Nestor was renowned for his wisdom and justice. His advice and authority were considered equal to those of the gods.

7.3 Drafting

Shaping Your Writing

Develop a Thesis Statement

The evidence you have gathered should support your position on your topic. Review your notes, and develop a **thesis statement**—a sentence summing up your argument. Include this statement in your introduction, and organize your essay around it.

Organize to Create Drama

The places in which persuasive argument rings loudest—the courtroom, the pulpit, the Senate floor—are all **dramatic** situations. They set up a contest between two opposing sides. A well-organized persuasive essay can also create a drama. Consider using the following types of organization:

Saving the Best for Last To use **Nestorian Order**, arrange points according to their relative strength. Begin with your second-strongest point. Present other arguments, and end with your strongest point—a dramatic way to conclude.

Facing Your Opponents Challenge yourself to add even more drama to Nestorian Order. State and then knock down an argument against your position.

This form of organization is especially dramatic: The curtain rises to show one of your best arguments. The argument builds and grows—only to meet with a strong opposing argument! After a struggle, the opposing argument is defeated. Finally, your strongest argument arrives, leaving your audience with the impression that your position is invulnerable!

Technology Tip

Use the cut-and-paste feature of your word-processing program to help organize your ideas as you draft.

NESTORIAN ORDER WITH AN ANSWER TO THE OPPOSITION

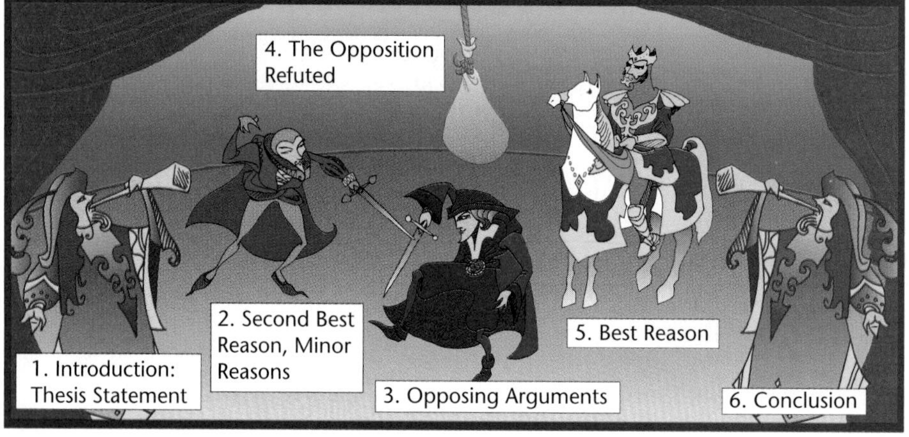

TIME AND RESOURCE MANAGER

Resources
Print: Writing Support Transparencies, 7-D
Technology: Writing and Grammar iText, Section 7.3

In-Depth Coverage	Accelerated Pace
• Cover pp. 144–145. • Work through the exercise on Nestorian Order with the entire class. • Have students write their own persuasive essay drafts in class.	• Have students review pp. 144–145 independently, then write their own persuasive essay drafts. • Respond to individual drafting issues as needed.

Providing Elaboration

Use a Variety of Persuasive Techniques

As you draft, use these techniques to sway readers:

- **Logical arguments** appeal to most readers. Take your readers step-by-step through your argument, and present accurate evidence to earn their trust.
- **Appeals to basic values** call on ideas that all readers support, but that may be applied in different ways. If you are arguing in favor of a policy, for instance, you might call it *just* (justice is a basic value). If you argue against the policy, you might call it *wasteful* (thrift is also a basic value).
- **Appeals to emotions** may take the form of a brief story or a vivid image. For instance, you might move readers to pity—and win their support—with the story of a young child who suffered because of a certain policy.
- **Repetition and parallelism** (the use of sentences with identical forms) strengthen your presentation. When words fall into a rhythm, it may feel as though each one "had" to be there—and thus, what they *say* is so must *be* so.
- **Charged words** have strong positive or negative connotations. They pack entire arguments into a few syllables. Call a plan *irresponsible*, and you create a scene: The plan is wrong; those who made it were careless, even childish; you (and your reader) are mature enough to see the fault.

Learn More

Charged words are part of a mature vocabulary. To improve your vocabulary-building skills, see Chapter 29.

Student Work IN PROGRESS

Name: Ryan Caparella
Chain of Lakes Middle School
Orlando, FL

Using a Variety of Techniques

As he drafted his introduction, Ryan included appeals to basic values and to emotions. He also used repetition.

No one wants to be thought of as a criminal. No one wants to go to jail. No one wants to die at a young age, or to lose all of his or her family. Yet a survey shows that in 1996 more than 50 percent of seniors in high school had taken the first step on a road leading to these consequences. They had used an illegal drug.

Ryan's appeals to basic values, such as the desire for respect and for a long life, are shown in red. His use of repetition is shown in green.

Step-by-Step Teaching Guide

Drafting: Elaborating with Persuasive Techniques

Teaching Resources: Writing Support Transparency 7-D

1. All five techniques are valuable. A well written persuasive essay employs a number of techniques, not just one, to form a balanced and convincing essay.
2. Display the transparency and review the techniques Ryan used in his introduction.
3. Point out that advertisers use appeals to emotion and charged words to sway their audience.
4. Help students make a list of some basic values they could refer to in their essays. Justice, fairness, efficiency, thrift, respect, consideration, caution, responsibility, and experience are all basic values they can use to support their positions.
5. Remind students of the importance of consistency and aligning their persuasive techniques. Ask students to evaluate the following: *It is unfair that kids are denied First Amendment rights. Kids are more responsible than adults.* The first sentence is a good appeal to the value of fairness, but the second has no logical support.
6. Review what kinds of charged words can help an essay and which have no place there. Words such as *irresponsible, unfair, inexperienced, failed, bankrupt* are all useful as long as they are based on logical arguments.

ONGOING ASSESSMENT: Monitor and Reinforce

If some students are having difficulty, use one of the following options.

Option 1 Have students research newspaper editorials and circle the persuasive techniques they can identify, then use these as a model for their essay.	**Option 2** Have partners share ideas about how to apply persuasive techniques to their essays.

TIME SAVERS!

Writing Support Transparencies
Use the transparencies for Chapter 7 to teach these strategies.

Step-by-Step Teaching Guide

Revising: Revising Your Overall Structure

1. Discuss the importance of arranging the main points of an argument in a sequence that builds strength. A disorganized essay will not be persuasive.
2. Once again, remind students that the main points of an argument should have some support beyond appeals to emotion.
3. The challenge in revision is stepping back from the writing to look at it with a critical eye. Ask students for ideas showing how they can accomplish this task. Putting themselves in the place of the reader is a good way to establish the necessary distance.
4. To help students distinguish main points from supporting points, tell them that supporting points work as examples of the main point. Use the following example:

   Main point: Global warming has changed the weather.

   Supporting point: Six of the 10 warmest years have taken place in the last 10 to 15 years.

Customizing for *Less Advanced Students*

Students can work with partners to code main points and supporting points.

7.4 Revising

Revision is the process of shaping and polishing your work to make sure that your ideas are expressed clearly and convincingly. Once you've finished the first draft of your essay, the cast of your persuasive drama—your arguments, examples, and creative phrases—are assembled. To get them ready for their performance, first improve your essay's overall structure. Then, revise paragraphs, sentences, and word choice.

Revising Your Overall Structure

Analyze Main Points and Support

As you reread your draft, look at the way your main points are organized. Are they presented in a logical order? Do they build toward your conclusion?

Your main points are the stars of your argument. To persuade the reader, however, you must present sufficient support and use persuasive devices, such as charged language, to back up each main point.

Code main points and support to help you present your argument effectively.

Technology Tip

Use the highlight and bold features of your word-processing program to make your main ideas stand out.

REVISION STRATEGY
Coding Main Points and Support

Highlight the main points in your essay. Then, rank each point in order according to its relative strength (1 = strongest, 2 = next strongest, and so on). For each of your main points, identify supporting points and devices, using the following symbols:

- ▲ Specific example
- ● Logical argument
- ▬ Measurable fact, such as a statistic
- ■ Expert opinion
- ▼ Personal observation
- ★ Charged language
- ✱ Striking image

Review your main points. Consider rearranging paragraphs to begin with a strong point and end with the strongest. Then, review your support for each main point. If you find places that have just a few symbols for supporting details, consider adding more support.

TIME AND RESOURCE MANAGER

Resources
Print: Writing Support Transparencies, 7-E–G; Writing Support Activity Book, 7-2
Technology: Writing and Grammar iText, Section 7.4

In-Depth Coverage	Accelerated Pace
• Cover pp. 145–150. • Work through the Revision Strategy with the entire class. • Guide students through each of the revision strategies. • Review the Grammar in Your Writing feature.	• Assign students to review pp. 146–150 independently. • Have students revise their persuasive essays independently.

Enhance Appeals to Your Audience

Reading a list of evidence can have about as much appeal as reading a phone book. Give your readers more than facts and logic. Using the strategy of "image shots," find places to add compelling images and stories to enhance your arguments.

REVISION STRATEGY
Using "Image Shots"

Review your support for each main point. For points that are supported only with logical arguments, statistics, or expert opinions, consider adding a colorful comparison, striking image, or dramatic anecdote. Flag these points with sticky notes on which you jot down a few key reminder words. Afterward, review your notes, and add the appropriate comparison, image, or anecdote. For instance, you might introduce an argument about honesty by telling the story of a child caught telling a lie.

Student Work IN PROGRESS

Name: Ryan Caparella
Chain of Lakes Middle School
Orlando, FL

Using "Image Shots"

After highlighting his main points and identifying the kind of support for each, Ryan saw that he had used a few logical arguments in a row. He used an "image shot" to add interest.

● Yet, when you think about it, peer pressure is never a good reason to use drugs. Your friends should want to be your friends because of your personality, not because you ~~imitate~~ reflect everything they do. Being someone's friend doesn't mean turning yourself into a mirror. After all, when people leave the room, a mirror has nothing of its own to show. If anything, a friend sees you for you and tells you straight what he or she sees—the good and, sometimes, the bad.

friendship isn't imitating your friends; you're a person, not somebody's mirror – use image of mirror.

Step-by-Step Teaching Guide

Revising: Enhancing Appeals to Your Audience; Using Image Shots

Teaching Resources: Writing Support Transparency 7-E

1. Tell students a good persuasive essay is both logical and interesting to read. Refer back to the Model From Literature, reminding students how Krents uses humor and anecdotes to make his points. It's really about balance: too much logical argument results in a dry unappealing essay; too much appeal to emotion and assertion may entertain but can fail to make the case for the writer's point of view.
2. Display the transparency. Discuss how adding image shots can help achieve the balance needed. Examine how Ryan added support and color to his main points.
3. Write the following example on the chalkboard:

   Main point: Global warming has changed the weather.

   Supporting point: Six of the 10 warmest years have taken place in the last 10 to 15 years.

   Image Shot: My parents talk about lots of days off because of snow when they were kids. We haven't had a snow day in the last three years.

TIME SAVERS!

Writing Support Transparencies
Use the transparencies for Chapter 7 to teach these strategies.

Step-by-Step Teaching Guide

Revising: Revising Your Paragraphs; Finding the "Glue" Between Paragraphs

Teaching Resources: Writing Support Transparency 7-F

1. Display the transparency. Examine Ryan's efforts to find the glue between paragraphs. Review the list of sequence, transitional words, and phrases that provide the glue to keep the reader interested, pointing out the different categories of words.
2. Point out that when we tell stories, we use transitional expressions, but many of those expressions *(you know what I mean . . . , as I was saying . . . ,)* have no place in a formal essay.

Customize for *Verbal/Linguistic Learners*

A good essay, like a piece of music, has its own rhythm. A persuasive essay needs to have forward momentum but not be too rushed. The reader should be able to pause over the main points to allow them to sink in. Similarly, the essay needs to pick up speed when covering weaker arguments. Encourage students to examine the transition words carefully and use them judiciously both to establish rhythm and also to vary the tempo of their persuasive essays.

7.4

Revising Your Paragraphs

Check Unity

Readers will grow confused unless each of your paragraphs connects logically with the one before it. Think of a play. If actors entered the stage at any point, shouted their lines, and left, the play would make no sense. Instead, actors time their entrances to connect logically with what happened before. Use "Finding the Glue" to check connections between paragraphs.

REVISION STRATEGY
"Finding the Glue" Between Paragraphs

Read the last sentence of each paragraph followed by the opening sentence of the next paragraph. If neither sentence shows the connection between the paragraphs, highlight the space between those paragraphs.

Next, review each place you have highlighted. Add a word, phrase, or sentence to "glue" the two paragraphs together. If you have difficulty finding a good transition, consider moving or deleting one of the paragraphs.

iText

Try it out! Use the "Finding the Glue" activity in **Section 7.4,** on-line or on CD-ROM.

Student Work IN PROGRESS

Name: Ryan Caparella
Chain of Lakes Middle School
Orlando, FL

Adding Transitions by "Finding the Glue"

When Ryan looked for the "glue" between paragraphs, he found that he needed to add a transition sentence to make the connection between these two paragraphs clear.

There is the risk of addiction, which means that you will begin to focus your entire life around getting the drugs you need to keep yourself feeling okay. These dangers of drug use are all scary, but there is one risk that might be even more dangerous: the risk to your personal integrity.

Once you say, "Yes, I will try drugs, because that is what my friends are doing," you are saying, "Yes, I will stop taking responsibility for my own future." In that event, you are less of a person.

By adding this transition sentence, Ryan shows that the second paragraph discusses a different, even scarier danger than those discussed in the first paragraph.

ONGOING ASSESSMENT: Monitor and Reinforce

If some students are having difficulty adding transitions by finding the "glue," use one of the following options.

Option 1 Have partners help each other identify places needing transitions and select good transitional words and phrases.

Option 2 Have students identify first which category of transition they need, coding the essay by category, then return to find an appropriate word or phrase from the list.

Revising Your Sentences

Construct Parallel Sentences

To make a series of parallel ideas clear, use parallel sentence structures.

PARALLEL IDEAS: After the radio was invented, ham radio enthusiasts flooded the airwaves with news. Citizens today enjoy the freedom of "broadcasting" information over the Internet.

PARALLEL IDEAS IN PARALLEL STRUCTURES: When the radio was invented, ham radio enthusiasts flooded the airwaves with news. When the Internet was created, citizens rediscovered the freedom to "broadcast" information.

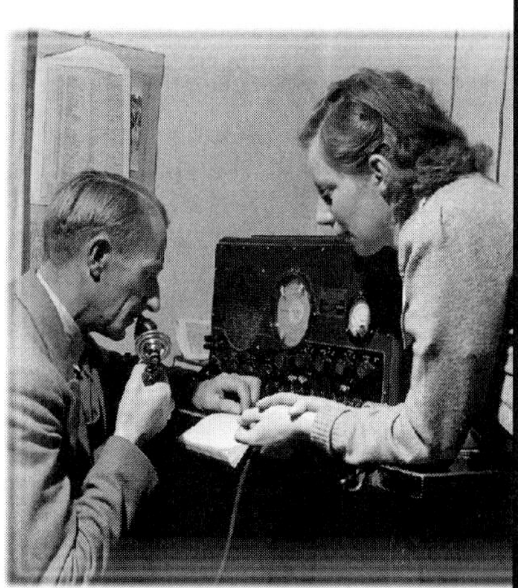

▲ Critical Viewing
Write two parallel sentences describing this scene. **[Apply]**

REVISION STRATEGY
Coding Parallel Ideas

Circle in red pairs of sentences that express parallel ideas. Then, consider revising these related sentences so that their structures are parallel.

Grammar in Your Writing
Using Complex Sentences

Two complex sentences can make an effective parallel. A **complex sentence** includes one independent clause (often called the main clause) and one or more subordinate clauses. A **subordinate clause** contains a subject and a verb but cannot stand on its own as a sentence.

[sub. clause: Whenever the news is bad,] [ind. clause: we tend to blame the messenger.]

[sub. clause: Whenever the news is good,] [ind. clause: we tend to forget who brought it.]

Find It in Your Reading Identify two complex sentences in "Darkness at Noon" by Harold Krents on page 136.

Find It in Your Writing Review your draft to identify three complex sentences. For each, be sure you have placed a comma after the subordinate clause if it appears at the beginning of the sentence. If you cannot find three examples, consider changing sentences into complex sentences for variety.

For more on complex sentences, see Chapter 20.

STANDARDIZED TEST PREPARATION WORKSHOP

Complex Sentences Standardized test questions may require students to identify different types of sentences. Write the following sentences on the chalkboard and ask students to select the complex one:

A When there is snow on the road, drivers should use caution.
B It was snowing, and it was very cold.
C Drive slowly and use caution.
D Began to snow.

Item **A** is the complex sentence. Item B is a compound sentence. Item C is a simple sentence. Item D is a fragment.

Step-by-Step Teaching Guide

Revising: Construct Parallel Sentences

1. Read aloud the example of parallel writing and discuss why it is good to use in a persuasive essay. The repetition reinforces the ideas and makes them seem more believable, as if they naturally fit together. At the same time, warn students not to overuse parallel structure. It is most effective when used sparingly. Otherwise, it becomes repetitious and tedious.
2. Students may benefit from working in pairs to identify parallel ideas.

Critical Viewing

Apply Students' responses will vary. Check to see that they have used parallel sentences.

Step-by-Step Teaching Guide

Grammar in Your Writing: Using Complex Sentences

See that students understand how complex sentences can function as parallel structure. Write the following example on the chalkboard and ask students to rewrite the second sentence into a complex sentence that parallels the first one:

Although he knew the chances of success were slim, the mayor went ahead with the plan. The governor knew the plan was doomed but preferred to remain silent. (Although the governor knew the plan was doomed, he preferred to remain silent.)

Find It in Your Reading

Possible sentences:

There are those who assume that since I can't see, I obviously also cannot hear.

This point was graphically driven home to me while we were in England.

Find It in Your Writing

If students cannot find any complex sentences, suggest that they add some to their drafts.

Step-by-Step Teaching Guide

Revising: Revising Your Word Choice

1. Read the example aloud and discuss how the repetition of the key word reinforces it, in much the same manner as parallel structure does.
2. Have students work in pairs to help each other code focus words.

Step-by-Step Teaching Guide

Peer Review

Teaching Resources: Writing Support Transparency 7-G; Writing Support Activity Book 7-2

1. Preface the exercise with a brief review of polite, constructive criticism.
2. Review the transparency. Review the Double Dyad checklist. Give students copies of the blank organizer to use in their peer review.
3. Direct students to focus on content in their feedback. Punctuation, spelling, and other mechanics will be dealt with later in the editing and proofreading phase.

7.4

Revising Your Word Choice

Repeat Key Words

Although unnecessary repetition can mar your style, repetition of key words will create emphasis and provide transitions, as in this example:

> Television promised to be a great public resource, like a **park.** The **park** has been stripped, fenced off, and overbuilt. It has been turned into a **wasteland:** a **wasteland** of silly commercials, inane sitcoms, and sensational talk shows.

REVISION STRATEGY
Coding Focus Words

Circle in blue any words that sum up your perspective. Then, circle in green the sentences in which you can repeat one of these words for emphasis. Consider adding the words in blue to these sentences.

Peer Review

"Double Dyad"

For help with revising, use the strategy of the "Double Dyad."

1. Exchange papers with a partner.
2. Use the following grid to rate your partner's paper.
3. Discuss the responses with your partner.
4. Repeat the process with another partner.

	Very Well	Okay	Not Well
How well does the introduction create interest?			
How well does the writer present the main argument?			
Does the essay flow?			
Does the writer prove his or her argument?			
Does the conclusion wrap up the argument?			
What is the strongest part of the paper?			
What is the weakest part of the paper?			

ONGOING ASSESSMENT: Monitor and Reinforce

Consider the following options in doing the peer review exercise.

Option1 Pair students carefully according to ability and compatibility. Avoid pairing students who, for a variety of reasons, may not offer good feedback to each other.

Option 2 Allow students to select their own partners, but tell them they will be evaluated on the quality of the feedback they give their peers.

7.5 Editing and Proofreading

Proofread your essay to discover and eliminate errors in spelling, punctuation, grammar, or usage in your essay.

Focusing on Colons and Dashes

As you proofread your persuasive essay, check to make sure that you have used colons and dashes where they are needed.

Grammar in Your Writing
Using Colons and Dashes in Sentences

Colons can be used to separate one part of a sentence from a list of items or from a second independent clause summarizing or illustrating the first. (Notice that if an independent clause follows the colon, the first letter in the clause is capitalized.)

List: Bicycles often come with the following accessories: rear reflector, mudguard, headlight, and handpump. [list]

Illustration: The accessories that come with bicycles are often necessities: You wouldn't want to be stuck cycling at night without a headlight. [ind. clause]

Dashes have several uses. Like a colon, they can be used to separate an independent clause from a list or from an independent clause summarizing or illustrating the first clause. Unlike a colon, a dash suggests an abrupt change of thought or other dramatic shift in focus.

His bicycle has a few accessories—the mudguard he borrowed from me, the reflector he took from Mike, and the headlight he found on the road.

Her bicycle had no accessories—is it any wonder she was stranded?

Find It in Your Reading Find one use each of a colon and a dash in "Darkness at Noon" by Harold Krents on page 136, and explain why it is used.

Find It in Your Writing Circle any colons or dashes in your draft. Correct any errors in your use of these marks. If you have not used any colons or dashes in your draft, find places where you could. Consider using them to combine sentences.

For more on using colons and dashes, see Chapter 26.

Step-by-Step Teaching Guide

Editing and Proofreading

1. Students may want to proofread for one element at a time: spelling, punctuation, grammar.
2. Suggest that they use a highlighter to mark any passages in which they have listed items or in which they change focus abruptly. They should then review highlighted passages to determine whether colons or dashes are needed for proper pronunciation.

Step-by-Step Teaching Guide

Grammar in Your Writing: Using Colons and Dashes in Sentences

1. Review the two uses of the colon presented in the text. Point out that using colons for lists is the more common.
2. Explain that although they have some similar uses, a dash, unlike a colon, indicates an abrupt change of thought or focus.

Find It in Your Reading

Colon: *For example, when I go to the airport and ask the ticket agent for assistance to the plane, he or she will invariably pick up the phone, call a ground hostess, and whisper: "Hi, Jane, we've got a 76 here."* (before dialogue)

Dash: *Just at the door sat an elderly woman—elderly I would judge from the sound of her voice.* (abrupt change)

Find It in Your Writing

Have students try to add or combine sentences using a colon and/or dash.

PRENTICE HALL
Everyday Spelling

If you have taught the spelling skills in *Prentice Hall Everyday Spelling*, Grade 8, Chapter 8, in conjunction with this *Writing and Grammar* chapter, review and assess students' mastery of the skills before concluding the chapter. Remind students to apply the spelling skills as they edit and proofread their persuasive essays.

TIME AND RESOURCE MANAGER

Resources
Print: Scoring Rubrics on Transparency, Chapter 7; Writing Assessment: Scoring Rubric and Scoring Models for Persuasive Essay
Technology: Writing and Grammar iText, Sections 7.5–6

In-Depth Coverage	Accelerated Pace
• Cover pp. 151–155 in class. • Have students edit and proofread their essays in class. • Review the Rubric for Self-Assessment in class. • Have students present their final drafts.	• Assign pp. 151–155 for independent review. • Have students independently edit and proofread their essays. • Respond to individual editing issues as needed.

Step-by-Step Teaching Guide

Publishing and Presenting

1. Students may want to present their forum to a large audience, such as other classes and family members, in the school auditorium.
2. If students submit their essays to a newspaper, they should word-process them neatly. They should also note the length of newspaper editorials. They probably will have to abridge their essays.
3. Encourage interested students to publish their essays on Web sites.
4. Make a bulletin board display of student essays.

ASSESS

Step-by-Step Teaching Guide

Assessment

Teaching Resources: Scoring Rubrics on Transparency 7; Formal Assessment, Chapter 7

1. Display the Scoring Rubric transparency and review the criteria in class.
2. Before students proceed with self-assessment, you may wish to review the Final Draft of the Student Work in Progress on pages 153–155. Have students score the Final Draft in one or more of the rubric categories. For example, how would students score the piece in terms of audience and purpose?
3. In addition to student self-assessment, you may wish to use the following assessment options.
   - Score student essays yourself, using the rubric and scoring models from Writing Assessment
   - Review the Standardized Test Preparation Workshop on pages 160–161 and have students respond to a persuasive writing prompt within a time limit
   - Administer the Chapter 7 Test from Formal Assessment in Teaching Resources to assess students' grasp of concepts presented

7.6 Publishing and Presenting

Building Your Portfolio

Consider these ideas for sharing your persuasive essay:

1. **Organize a Forum** Assemble a panel of classmates who have written essays on related topics. Have each student read his or her essay to the class. After each essay, have the class ask questions of the panel members, and ask them to vote on whether they agree or disagree with each paper.
2. **Publish in a Newspaper** Send your persuasive essay, with a cover letter, to a local newspaper. Briefly summarize your essay in the letter, and explain that you wish it to be considered for publication on the editorial page. Share your essay and any response—including a clipping of your published essay—with the class.

Reflecting on Your Writing

Write a few notes describing your experience writing a persuasive essay. Begin by answering the following questions:

- What did you learn about the issue you chose? Did you find your opinions changing as you learned more? Explain.
- What part of the writing process seemed hardest for you? Easiest?

Internet Tip

To see model essays scored with this rubric, go on-line: PHSchool.com
Enter Web Code: eck-8001

Rubric for Self-Assessment

Use the following criteria to evaluate your persuasive essay:

	Score 4	Score 3	Score 2	Score 1
Audience and Purpose	Provides arguments, illustrations, and words that forcefully appeal to the audience and effectively serve the persuasive purpose	Provides arguments, illustrations, and words that appeal to the audience and serve the persuasive purpose	Provides some support that appeals to the audience and serves the persuasive purpose	Shows little attention to the audience or persuasive purpose
Organization	Uses a clear, consistent organizational strategy	Uses a clear organizational strategy with occasional inconsistencies	Uses an inconsistent organizational strategy	Shows a lack of organizational strategy; writing is confusing
Elaboration	Provides specific, well-elaborated support for the writer's position	Provides some elaborated support for the writer's position	Provides some support, but with little elaboration	Lacks support
Use of Language	Uses transitions to connect ideas smoothly; shows few mechanical errors	Uses some transitions; shows few mechanical errors	Uses few transitions; shows some mechanical errors	Shows little connection between ideas; shows many mechanical errors

ONGOING ASSESSMENT: Assess Mastery

Use one of the following options to assess final drafts of students' persuasive essays.

Self-Assessment Ask students to score their essay using the rubric provided. Then have students write a single paragraph reflecting on the most valuable thing they learned in completing this essay.

Teacher Assessment You may want to use the rubric and scoring models provided in the Writing Assessment, Silver Level, to score the persuasive essays.

7.7 Student Work IN PROGRESS

FINAL DRAFT

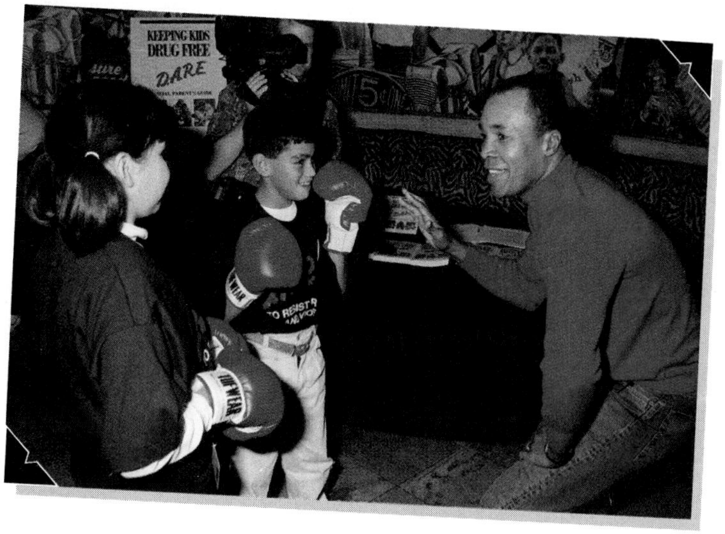

◀ **Critical Viewing** As part of educational efforts against drugs, boxing champion Sugar Ray Leonard meets with kids, as in this picture. Why might the example of a boxing star like Leonard have great persuasive force among young people? **[Draw Conclusions]**

I Will Be Drug Free

Ryan Caparella
Chain of Lakes Middle School
Orlando, Florida

Ryan begins his essay with a strong contrast between common-sense ideas and the reality of people's behavior. His effective use of repetition and parallel structure heightens the force of his argument.

No one wants to be thought of as a criminal. No one wants to go to jail. No one wants to die at a young age, or to lose all of his or her family. Yet a survey shows that in 1996 more than 50 percent of seniors in high school had taken the first step on a road leading to these consequences. They had used an illegal drug.

Using an illegal drug probably won't ruin your life instantly (although, if used in the wrong amount or combination, many can kill you right away). Using an illegal drug does expose you to risks, though. There is the risk of having a careless accident while you are under the influence and your judgment is impaired. There is the risk of disease from the way some drugs are taken. There is

Step-by-Step Teaching Guide

Teaching From the Final Draft

1. Have students read "I Will Be Drug Free," using the margin notes to guide their reading.
2. Point out the use of repetition and parallel structure in the second and third paragraphs *(There is the risk . . .).* Ask students to comment on its effectiveness.

continued

Critical Viewing

Draw Conclusions Students may say that most children want to emulate their heroes.

Step-by-Step Teaching Guide continued

3. Point out Ryan's use of logical argument supported by facts (increase from 40.7% to 50.8% in kids using drugs) with personal examples about peer pressure.
4. Good writing makes its points effectively. At the bottom of page 154, point out Ryan's deft writing:

   "Who cares about tomorrow?" This is a delusion. Even if you think you can avoid tomorrow, it's going to come.
5. In the next-to-last paragraph on page 154, call attention to Ryan's correct use of a dash.

continued

the risk of getting caught in the middle of violence from the dangerous people who sell drugs.

Drug users also take long-term risks. There is the risk that you will grow casual about drug use, so that you don't notice later on when you get into more serious problems. There is the risk of addiction, which means that you will begin to focus your entire life around getting the drugs you need to keep yourself feeling okay.

Ryan begins to make his case against drug abuse by listing facts about its consequences. Then, he makes a transition to the issue of personal integrity.

These dangers of drug use are all scary, but there is one risk that might be even more dangerous: the risk to your personal integrity. Once you say, "Yes, I will try drugs, because that is what my friends are doing," you are saying, "Yes, I will stop taking responsibility for my own future." In that event, you are less of a person.

My own position on these risks is clear: I say no to drugs. In some ways, it's an easy position to take. It's easy to remember. There are no gray areas. And it boosts my self-respect, because I know I am looking out for myself and my future.

None of these ideas that I have presented is original or hard to understand. Everybody knows about these risks. We hear about them all the time in school and in the news. Despite this widespread knowledge, a new generation of young people starts abusing drugs every year. Some even die. The trend seems to be increasing. In 1992, only 40.7 percent of kids had tried drugs by the time they were seniors. Four years later, the percentage had risen to 50.8 percent. Why?

Ryan backs up his argument with statistics.

Kids will give you a couple of reasons. Many kids say they cannot withstand peer pressure. And it's true. Often kids use drugs because they are encouraged to by their friends. After all, it's hard to say no to a friend. And what if people start to think that you're not "cool"? Hey, you might even get a reputation for being out of it!

Ryan shows that he's considered his audience—his classmates—by identifying "reasons" they might have to ignore common sense.

Yet, when you think about it, peer pressure is never a good reason to use drugs. Your friends should want to be your friends because of your personality, not because you reflect everything they do. Being someone's friend doesn't mean turning yourself into a mirror. After all, when people leave the room, a mirror has nothing of its own to show. If anything, a friend sees you for you and tells you straight what he or she sees—the good and, sometimes, the bad.

Ryan uses the transition word yet *to connect two paragraphs.*

He uses the image of a mirror with nothing to reflect as an effective persuasive device.

When faced with a choice about drugs, some kids will say, "Who cares about tomorrow?" This is a delusion. Even if you think you can avoid tomorrow, it's going to come. And when it gets here, whether you are happy or not depends on what you did today.

Some kids might even say, "Addiction and other drug-related problems may happen to some people, but not to me." Even if you are a clean, alert, attractive person today, if you get strung out on drugs, you can end up on the streets. Just think about this: Nobody whose life was ruined by drugs started out thinking, "I am going to ruin my life." Chances are, they said just what you might say: "That will never happen to me." That didn't protect them from the consequences of drug abuse. It won't protect you either if you start using drugs.

Here, Ryan refutes the opposition.

When I'm an adult, and I have a family of my own, I will want the best for my children. I won't want them to get into trouble, so I will teach them how to avoid drugs. I will be their role model. If they ask me whether I ever did drugs when I was their age, I want to be able to answer that question proudly—no. Each year, thousands of kids choose to begin using drugs. I am not going to make that number one bit higher. I am going to stay drug-free. I say no!

Ryan concludes with his strongest argument—a vision of the kind of parent he can become if he says no to drugs.

Ryan's last sentence is a ringing call to action.

◀ Critical Viewing Describe the connections between these family members, using details from the photo. Do you think the children look to their father as a role model? Explain. **[Interpret]**

Step-by-Step Teaching Guide continued

6. Point out the Nestorian Order Ryan utilizes. He sets up and refutes two counterarguments and then brings out his strongest argument—his desire to be a role model for his children and tell them he never tried drugs.

7. While Ryan's essay exhibits many of the items students have studied, there remains the issue of whether he has persuaded readers that his point of view is correct. Admittedly, this is a loaded issue, one for which students may not feel free to express contrary views. Nevertheless, engage students in a discussion of whether Ryan has succeeded in persuading them of the rightness of his views. Establish that it is possible to read a persuasive essay, admire its structure and writing, and still come away with a different point of view.

Critical Viewing

Interpret Students may say they look like a close, loving family, and that the children most likely look to their father as a role model.

Lesson Objectives

1. To write an effective advertisement
2. To choose a product and medium
3. To draft, revise, and edit an advertisement
4. To publish an advertisement for an audience

Step-by-Step Teaching Guide

Advertisement

Teaching Resources: Writing Support Transparency 7-H; Writing Support Activity Book 7-3

1. Display some magazine advertisements that you find particularly effective in the classroom and show your students a few prize-winning commercials from a videotape collection. Have students discuss which ads best catch their attention and analyze the techniques they employ.
2. Suggest that students review writing strategies from Chapter 7.
3. To help students choose subjects for their advertisements, suggest a product you have looked for and been unable to find. Have students brainstorm for product ideas. Remind students that they can also "sell" a concept such as the benefits of reading, the example in the textbook.
4. Use the transparency to demonstrate developing ideas for an advertisement.
5. Give each student a copy of the blank organizer. Ask students to record their ideas and the elements they intend to include in their advertisement.
6. Encourage students to publish their ads in the classroom or school newspaper.

Connected Assignment

Advertisement

Perhaps you've caught yourself humming a tune from a television commercial or using a product slogan to make a joke. Advertisements, one widespread form of persuasive writing, affect our daily lives in more ways than we suspect.

An **advertisement** is a persuasive message in print or broadcast form, sponsored by an individual or group to achieve a particular end, such as selling a product or persuading people to adopt an opinion. Advertisements may include

- the use of visual, musical, or dramatic elements, such as pictures, jingles, and skits.
- a **concept,** or central theme. (A commercial for a health club, for instance, might focus on *health-consciousness* by showing trim people dutifully working out, or it might focus on *glamour* by showing attractive people in nice outfits having a good time inside and outside the gym.)
- a memorable **"hook,"** such as a catchy jingle, a slogan, or an attention-grabbing image.
- appeals to people's concern with their image—for example, their desire to appear glamorous or responsible.
- use of **charged language**—words that imply a certain view of a product or issue without actually arguing for that view.
- repetition of key elements, such as words or music, to make the advertisement memorable.

To create your own advertisement, use the strategies on the next page.

MODEL

The **concept** *of this ad is* independence *—kids don't want to stay with their parents forever. One* **"hook"** *is the image of a kid stuck with his boring parents (the lighting suggests a horror-movie poster). The other is the sophisticated slogan. Instead of saying what viewers expect—"Reading is good"— the slogan "encourages" not* reading, *then shows one of its least appealing results.*

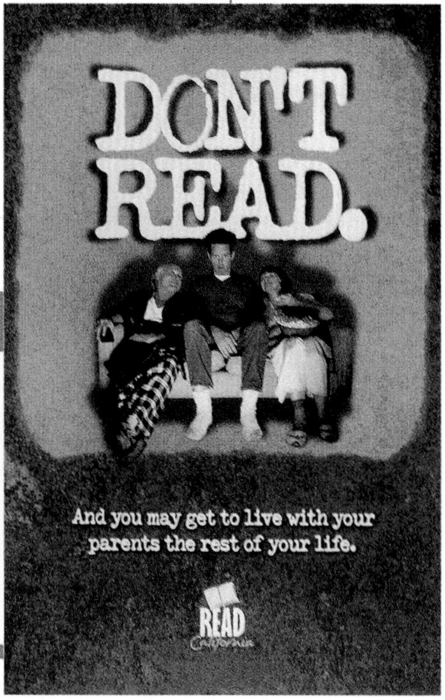

DON'T READ.
And you may get to live with your parents the rest of your life.
READ

Prewriting Invent a product or service to sell, or choose a position to promote. Next, choose the medium for your advertisement: print or broadcast. Then, invent a concept for your campaign. For instance, you might decide that your new snack food, edible notebook paper, should appeal to students' self-image as organized people who would like the efficiency of storing a snack in their notebooks.

Next, create a "hook" that will quickly convey your concept. Then, list the other elements your advertisement will incorporate, such as dramatic scenes, images, and sound effects or music. Record your ideas in a chart like the one shown.

Television Commercial for Eddy's Edible Notebook Paper

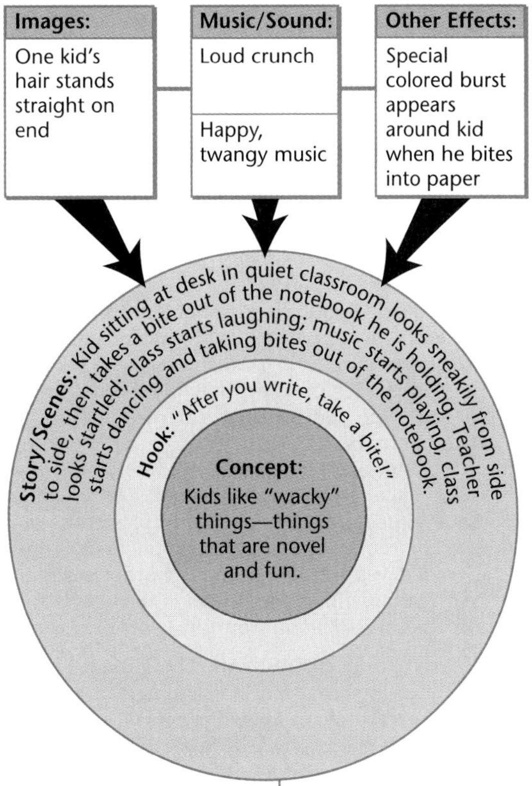

Images:
One kid's hair stands straight on end
Music/Sound:
Loud crunch
Happy, twangy music
Other Effects:
Special colored burst appears around kid when he bites into paper
Story/Scenes: Kid sitting at desk in quiet classroom looks sneakily from side to side, then takes a bite out of the notebook he is holding. Teacher looks startled; class starts laughing; music starts playing, class starts dancing and taking bites out of the notebook.
Hook: "After you write, take a bite!"
Concept:
Kids like "wacky" things—things that are novel and fun.

Drafting Assume that the audience for your advertisement is not prepared to spend much time with it. Your ad must grab their attention and convey your message quickly. As you draft, present your concept clearly with easily interpreted images (for example, a rock-and-roll guitarist), situations (for example, a supermarket aisle), and phrases. Use these strategies:

Television Commercial Create a storyboard—drawings laid out frame-by-frame to show the sequence of visuals. Follow your storyboard as you draft your script, indicating visuals, dialogue, music, and special effects.

Print Ad Lay out your ad as an attractive, attention-grabbing display. Place pictures and text and choose typestyles for the best effect. Use heads (words in large type) to catch the reader's eye and to separate sections of text. One or more of these heads should present your "hook."

Revising and Editing Review your draft to make sure that events or ideas flow in a logical sequence. Rewrite text or replace visuals as needed to convey your concept as clearly as possible.

Publishing and Presenting Consider recording your broadcast commercial or creating a poster of your print ad and presenting it to the class.

Customize for *Gifted/Talented Students*

Students may enjoy working together to create an advertising campaign, complete with print ads and television and radio commercials. If possible, have students consult with mentors who work for advertising agencies. The rest of the class can play the part of the clients to whom the gifted and talented students present their ad campaign in its most positive light.

Customize for *Less Advanced Students*

You may wish to assign small groups of students the same product to sell. Discuss each stage of the process—brainstorming, drafting, revising, editing, and proofreading—before students begin that stage. Pay particular attention in your discussion to concept development—the ideas that will make students' advertisements stand out. Make sure each student in the group can articulate his or her group's concept before students begin planning.

Lesson Objectives

1. To interpret and evaluate the various ways visual image makers represent meanings
2. To write a film review that persuades and influences

Step-by-Step Teaching Guide

Evaluating Performances

1. Choose one of the Spotlight elements for class discussion, or have students work individually or in small groups on the element of their choice. Have students take the initiative to find the necessary books and videotapes.
2. If possible, show the class a filmed performance of *Death of a Salesman* and discuss its emotional effect on students. Can they understand the overwhelming impact the play had on audiences two generations ago?
3. Ask interested students to research tragic heroes in other Greek tragedies and compare them with King Creon in *Antigone.*
4. Ask students who view and discuss *It's a Wonderful Life* to see other of director Capra's films to answer the following question: Is Capra's feel-good ending in *It's a Wonderful Life* typical or atypical of his films?
5. After students write reviews of *It's a Wonderful Life*, have them hold a debate on the merits of the film drawn from the positions they took in their reviews.

Critical Viewing

Interpret Most students will state that the need for many salespeople to travel and put in long hours is vividly expressed in the art. Many students may remark on the man's exhausted, weighed-down posture, his walking away from the viewer, and his isolation.

Spotlight on the Humanities

Evaluating Performances

Focus on Theater: *Death of a Salesman*

Persuasion is the key to a salesperson's success—but is this kind of success worth pursuing? What price does a person pay for measuring success in dollars and popularity? Considered by many to be the greatest American play ever written, *Death of a Salesman* by Arthur Miller (1915–) asks these questions with uncompromising force. Premiering in 1949, the play stunned early audiences, leaving some in tears.

Written by Miller in only six weeks, the play tells the story of a traveling salesman, Willy Loman, who finds himself trapped between his dreams of success and the reality of his ordinary life. Willy Loman is an example of the tragic hero, a character who must confront the truth about himself and who is destroyed in the confrontation. *Death of a Salesman* won the 1949 Pulitzer Prize in Drama.

Literature Connection The idea of tragedy and of the tragic hero that inspired Miller originated in ancient Greece. One famous example of ancient Greek tragedy is the play *Antigone*, written by the playwright Sophocles (496?–406? B.C.). In the play, King Creon must confront the fact that his stern rule is really self-righteousness, and that it has destroyed his family.

Film Connection The film *It's a Wonderful Life* (1946) also presents a confrontation between a character and the meaning of his life—but with a happy ending! Made by famous Hollywood director Frank Capra (1897–1991), the movie tells the story of a good man for whom everything is going wrong. In the course of the movie, he learns that the good he has done has made an important difference for others. This realization saves him from despair. The movie, starring Jimmy Stewart (1908–1997), has become a cult favorite. Because the film's climax takes place at Christmas, it is often shown on television during the holidays.

Persuasive Writing Activity: Drama Review

Watch the movie *It's a Wonderful Life.* Then, write a review of it, persuading readers to share your opinion of it. Explain what message the movie sends about success, and evaluate how effectively it conveys that message. Pay special attention to the job the actors do in winning your sympathy or making the story plausible.

THE GREATEST PLAY OF OUR GENERATION!
PULITZER PRIZE
N. Y. CRITICS' AWARD
death of a Salesman

▲ **Critical Viewing** What image of the salesman's existence does this illustration convey? **[Interpret]**

Viewing and Representing

Activity Remind students that they should support their opinions with details from the film in order to persuade readers to share their opinions. Students can present their reviews to the class when they finish the activity.

Media and Technology Skills

Analyzing How the Media Shape Perceptions

Activity: Recognizing Messages About Values in Television Commercials

Some television commercials seem to scream their persuasive messages—"Buy!" "Save!" "Call now!" Others send more complex messages. Instead of shouting, they may whisper. Learn to recognize the variety of persuasive messages in television advertising.

Think About It A commercial may last for only thirty seconds, but in that time it conveys a set of values, as in these examples:

What Is Normal? The woman shopping in the commercial looks like somebody's mom, perhaps a little prettier than average. She seems genuinely worried about what brand of cereal to buy for her family. By using "ordinary" looking actors, the commercial seems to show "normal" life—the life the viewer should expect to lead. The viewer may think, "'Normal' moms take care to buy the right brands."

What Is Happiness? While a band pumps out a driving beat, a group of laughing people play volleyball on the beach. They leap and dive in slow motion with the sun glinting behind them. These people are clearly having a good time. Nothing seems to exist for them outside of this summer moment. Viewers may come to think that such moments show what it means to be happy. Further, they may link this idea of happiness with the soda that the players drink during their break.

How Important Is Power? In a tough-guy voice, a narrator reels off facts about the car that is racing up the mountain on-screen. The commercial encourages viewers to judge cars in terms of how powerful they are. It also creates the impression that having power—in this case, the power to drive fast—should be an important concern.

How Commercials Convey Values

Identification
By choosing actors who are exceptionally handsome or pretty, commercials can create an ideal for viewers—the viewer wants to "be like" the people in the commercial. "Being like" these people includes buying the products they use.

Focus on Consumption
Commercials focus on tiny segments of people's lives—washing the floor, driving a car. In this way, commercials indicate that decisions about these activities are very important. Viewers may come to believe that the car or the detergent they buy says something important about who they are.

Analyze It Watch an hour of television, and choose three commercials to evaluate. Use a chart like this one to take notes on the persuasive messages they send about values. Then, write a brief essay comparing and contrasting these messages.

Commercial For: ____________________

Summary of Action	Description of Actors/ Speakers	General Theme ("Fun," "Power," and so on)	Specific Message	Techniques Used to Create Message

▶ Lesson Objectives

1. To interpret ideas gathered from video segments
2. To interpret and evaluate the ways visual image makers represent meanings
3. To assess how the medium and presentation contribute to the message
4. To write to record and reflect on ideas

Step-by-Step Teaching Guide

Analyzing How the Media Shape Perceptions

Teaching Resources: Writing Support Transparency 7-I; Writing Support Activity Book 7-4

1. Discuss the ways commercials convey values that are described in the textbook. See how many examples of these methods students can recall.
2. Display the transparency. Use the chart to model how to take notes on persuasive techniques while watching television commercials. If possible show a commercial on videotape as you take notes.
3. Give students copies of the blank organizer. Have students use the charts to record their impressions of the three commercials they choose to compare.
4. After they finish their essays, discuss the assignment with students. Were any particular messages or techniques most effective? Least effective? See whether any students wrote about the same commercials. Compare and contrast their analyses.

Customize for *Logical/Mathematical Learners*

Have students poll their classmates to find out which television commercials are their favorites. They should represent their findings on a pie chart or a bar graph.

Lesson Objectives

1. To write to persuade
2. To use correct grammar, spelling, and punctuation
3. To develop, draft, revise, and proofread an essay

Step-by-Step Teaching Guide

Responding to Persuasive Writing Prompts

Teaching Resources: Standardized Test Preparation Workbook, pp. 13–14

1. Have volunteers restate in their own words the four criteria for judging persuasive writing that are listed on this page of the textbook.
2. Discuss persuasive writing. Emphasize that successful persuasion depends on appeals to both logic and emotion.
3. Have students describe how writing directed to the two audiences described in the writing prompt should differ.
4. Urge students to read the scenario for the writing sample very carefully. Remind them to select one of the two prompts—not both of them. Then tell them the length of time they will have to write (no less than 15 minutes) and ask them to begin their speech or letter.

Standardized Test Preparation Workshop

Responding to Persuasive Writing Prompts

The writing prompts on standardized tests often judge your ability to write persuasively about an issue. Your writing will be evaluated on your ability to

- use language and arguments that are appropriate to the purpose and audience named in the prompt.
- use a consistent method of organization suited to the topic, such as pro-and-con organization.
- support arguments with descriptions, facts, and other details.
- use correct grammar, spelling, and punctuation.

You can practice for such tests by responding to the sample persuasive writing prompt below. Use the suggestions on the next page to help you respond. The clocks suggest the portion of your test-taking time that you should devote to each stage of the writing process.

Test Tip

When responding to a persuasive essay prompt, visualize your audience. Use this mental picture to help you choose appropriate language and support for your argument.

Sample Writing Situation

The board of directors of your local library want to install five television-viewing stations in the children's section of the library. To make room for the televisions, several bookshelves would have to be removed. At a town meeting, residents will vote on the issue. They are divided. Some believe that televisions do not belong in a library, especially if they are replacing books. Others believe that a library should provide access to all kinds of information, including televised broadcasts.

Select one of the following writing prompts:

- State your position on televisions in the library in a speech that will be read at the town meeting.
- State your position on televisions in the library in a letter that you will read at a peer discussion group.

TEST-TAKING TIP

Students will find it helpful to list both the arguments supporting the position they are taking and the arguments against it. They should then rank both sets of arguments in order of importance by using check marks or numbers in the margins. They may want to delete arguments for or against that they deem unimportant. They should then address the arguments in their speech or letter in ascending or descending order of importance.

Prewriting

One fourth of your time should be used for prewriting.

Consider Your Audience Keep your audience in mind as you gather details and draft.

The people at the town meeting are there to cast their vote. They may have already formed strong opinions on the issue. If you choose to address this audience, be sure to acknowledge the arguments of those who oppose your view. To persuade members of a peer group, use support to which they can relate. For instance, you might remind them of a televised special that was a good source of information for a school project.

Use a T-Chart Use a T-chart to gather logical arguments, facts, and examples on both sides of the issue. Review it, and identify the strongest arguments for your position. Also, note any opposing arguments that are weak. You can prove them wrong in your response. (For an example of a T-chart, see page 143.)

Drafting

Use nearly half of your time for drafting.

Introduce and Develop Your Position In your introduction, grab your audience's interest with a strong image or story. Include a sentence that clearly states your opinion on the issue. Develop support for your position in the body of your response, referring to your T-chart for details. Then, refute opposing arguments. In your conclusion, summarize your main points and restate your position.

Elaborate to Appeal to Your Audience Choose illustrations and descriptive words and phrases that will appeal to your audience. For example, residents at the town meeting may be influenced by arguments that mention *community strength* or *civic duty*. Your peers, instead, may perk up at the mention of *the latest technology*.

Revising, Editing, and Proofreading

Use almost one fourth of your time to revise, edit, and proofread.

Strengthen Support As you revise, cross out details that do not help to make your point. Change language that is inappropriate for your audience. Also, note sentences in your paper where you have used neutral words like *may*, *possibly*, or *might*. Using words like *is*, *should*, and *must*, reword these sentences to make decisive statements.

Making Corrections When you have finished revising, check your work for errors in grammar, spelling, or punctuation. When making changes, place one line through the text that you want to delete. Use a caret (^) to indicate where new text should be inserted.

Customize for *Less Advanced Students*

Help less advanced students succeed at persuasive writing by going through the first steps of the process using a different writing sample situation—perhaps a letter to the school board stating that students should (or should not) be required to wear uniforms to school. Spend some time helping students picture the intended audience and the types of arguments that would appeal to them. Summarize suggested arguments on the board and then let students begin writing their letters. Circulate among the students to make sure they understand what to do. Remind students to leave time to proofread and correct their work.

Customize for *More Advanced Students*

Ask students to write speeches or letters for the sample writing situation that go against what they actually believe. When they are finished, they can discuss how much difficulty this task presented to them.

Chapter 8

Time and Resource Manager

In-Depth Lesson Plan

	LESSON FOCUS	PRINT AND MEDIA RESOURCES
DAY 1	**Introduction to Comparison-and-Contrast Essays** Students learn key elements of comparison and contrast and analyze the Model From Literature (pp. 162–165).	***Writers at Work* Videotape,** Exposition: Making Connections ***Writing and Grammar iText* (Interactive Text),** Ch. 8, Introduction
DAY 2	**Prewriting** Students choose and narrow a topic, consider their audience and purpose, and gather information (pp. 166–169).	**Teaching Resources** *Writing Support Transparencies,* 8-A–D; *Writing Support Activity Book,* 8-1 ***Writing and Grammar iText* (Interactive Text),** Section 8.2
DAY 3	**Drafting** Students organize their ideas and write their first drafts (pp. 170–171).	**Teaching Resources** *Writing Support Transparencies,* 8-E ***Writing and Grammar iText* (Interactive Text),** Section 8.3
DAY 4	**Revising** Students revise their drafts in terms of overall structure, paragraphs, sentences, and word choice (pp. 172–175).	**Teaching Resources** *Writing Support Transparencies,* 8-F–G ***Writing and Grammar iText* (Interactive Text),** Section 8.4
DAY 5	**Editing and Proofreading; Publishing and Presenting** Students check their work for accuracy and correctness and present their final drafts (pp. 176–177).	**Teaching Resources** *Scoring Rubrics on Transparency,* Ch. 8; *Formal Assessment,* Ch. 8 ***Writing and Grammar iText* (Interactive Text),** Sections 8.5–6

Accelerated Lesson Plan

	LESSON FOCUS	PRINT AND MEDIA RESOURCES
DAY 1	**Introduction Through Drafting** Students review the characteristics of comparison-and-contrast writing, select topics, and write drafts (pp. 162–171).	**Teaching Resources** *Writing Support Transparencies,* 8-A–E; *Writing Support Activity Book,* 8–1 ***Writing and Grammar iText* (Interactive Text),** Ch. 8, Introduction through Section 8.3
DAY 2	**Revising Through Presenting** Students work individually or with peers to revise, edit, and proofread their work for presentation (pp. 172–177).	**Teaching Resources** *Writing Support Transparencies,* 8-F–G; *Scoring Rubrics on Transparency,* Ch. 8; *Formal Assessment,* Ch. 8 ***Writing and Grammar iText* (Interactive Text),** Sections 8.4–6

Options for Adapting Lesson Plans

HOMEWORK

Have students complete any stage of the lesson for homework.

SPELLING

To teach spelling skills in conjunction with writing skills, work through *Prentice Hall Everyday Spelling,* Grade 8, Chapter 9, as you cover this *Writing and Grammar* chapter. At the Editing and Proofreading stage, remind students to apply the spelling skills to their comparison-and-contrast essays.

FEATURES

Extend coverage with Connected Assignment (p. 180), Spotlight on the Humanities (p. 182), Media and Technology Skills (p. 183), and Standardized Test Preparation Workshop (p. 184)

TECHNOLOGY

Students can complete any stage of the lesson on the computer, using *Writing and Grammar iText* or a word-processing program. Have them print out their completed work.

INTEGRATED SKILLS COVERAGE

Integrating Grammar
Subject-Verb Agreement; Indefinite Pronouns, SE p. 175
Pronoun-Antecedent Agreement, SE p. 176

Reading/Writing Connection
Reading Strategy, SE p. 164
Writing Application, SE p. 165

Viewing and Representing
Critical Viewing, SE pp. 162, 164, 165, 168, 170, 178, 180, 182
Comparing Music and Art, SE p. 182

Technology
ATE p. 175

BLOCK SCHEDULING

Pacing Suggestions
For 90-minute Blocks
- Have students complete the Prewriting and Drafting stages in a single period.
- Focus one class period on Revising and Editing and Publishing and Presenting. Allow at least 30 minutes for peer revision.

Resources for Varying Instruction
- ***Writing and Grammar iText* (Interactive Text)** A 90-minute block provides an ideal opportunity for students to work on computer.
- ***Writers at Work* Videotape** Show the Exposition: Making Connections segment in class.

Professional Development Support
- ***How to Manage Instruction in the Block*** This teaching resource provides management and activity suggestions.

ASSESSMENT SUPPORT

Standardized Test Preparation Workshop SE pp. 184–185
Standardized Test Preparation Workbook, pp. 15–16
Scoring Rubrics on Transparency, Ch. 8
Formal Assessment, Ch. 8
Writing Assessment and Portfolio Management

MEDIA AND TECHNOLOGY

For the Student
- ***Writing and Grammar iText* (Interactive Text),** Ch. 8

For the Teacher
- ***Writers at Work* Videotape,** Exposition: Making Connections
- ***Resource Pro* CD-ROM**

MEETING INDIVIDUAL NEEDS

Less Advanced Students ATE pp. 168, 172, 185. See also Ongoing Assessments ATE pp. 167–169, 171, 173
More Advanced Students ATE p. 170
Visual/Spatial Learners ATE p. 166
Verbal/Linguistic Learners ATE p. 174
Bodily/Kinesthetic Learners ATE p. 166
Logical/Mathematical Learners ATE p. 181

WRITING AND GRAMMAR ON-LINE

iText Interactive Text (On-line or on CD-ROM)
- Easily navigable instruction with interactive Revision Checkers
- Full use of e-rater™, the essay-scoring system (on-line only)

Companion Web Site PHSchool.com
- Scoring rubrics with models (use Web Code eck-8001)

See the Go On-line! feature, SE p. iii.

LITERATURE CONNECTIONS

Related selections from *Prentice Hall Literature: Timeless Voices, Timeless Themes,* Silver:

Professional Model "Flowers for Algernon," Daniel Keyes, SE p. 165

Topic Bank Options "Western Wagons," Stephen Vincent Benét, SE p. 167; "The Other Pioneers," Roberto Félix Salazar, SE p. 167

CHAPTER 8
EXPOSITION: COMPARISON-AND-CONTRAST ESSAY

Lesson Objectives

1. To define a comparison-and-contrast essay.
2. To identify three types of comparison-and-contrast essays.
3. To read and interpret a comparison-and-contrast essay.
4. To utilize strategies for choosing a topic.
5. To review strategies in the Topic Bank.
6. To consider audience and purpose.
7. To use a Venn diagram to gather details.
8. To shape writing with effective organization.
9. To identify a theme.
10. To layer ideas to elaborate.
11. To check organization and balance.
12. To sharpen the theme by identifying unfocused details.
13. To check paragraph structure.
14. To combine sentences with indefinite pronouns.
15. To highlight repeated words.
16. To focus on pronoun-antecedent agreement.
17. To publish and present an essay.
18. To reflect on the experience of writing.

Chapter 8 Exposition
Comparison-and-Contrast Essay

The Empire of Light, II, René Magritte, The Museum of Modern Art, New York

▲ **Critical Viewing** Compare and contrast the upper and lower halves of this painting. What feelings do their similarities or differences create? **[Compare and Contrast]**

Comparison and Contrast in Everyday Life

If you travel away from home, you might start noticing the things that are different. Look out the window, for instance, and, instead of heaps of snow, you might see flowers. At the same time, you might be surprised by how much the diner down the street reminds you of the diner back home.

Whenever you notice something different, or whenever you are reminded of one thing by another, you have caught yourself in the act of **comparing and contrasting**—the act of noting the similarities and differences between two things.

Comparing and contrasting is a technique for learning more about the world. Comparing your home with a faraway place can show you what is special about your home. If you learn to write an effective comparison-and-contrast essay, you will sharpen your ability to discover things about your world.

Critical Viewing

Compare and Contrast Students may choose to share their ideas in a paragraph or a chart.

TIME AND RESOURCE MANAGER

Resources
Technology: Writers at Work Videotape; Writing and Grammar iText, Ch. 8

In-Depth Coverage	Accelerated Pace
• Cover pp. 162–163 in class. • Show the Exposition: Making Connections section of the Writers at Work Videotape. • Discuss different types of comparison-and-contrast essays. • Read the Model From Literature (pp. 164–165) and use it to brainstorm for comparison-and-contrast writing topic ideas with students.	• Assign pp. 162–165 for independent student review. • Discuss definitions and types of comparison-and-contrast essays.

What Is a Comparison-and-Contrast Essay?

A **comparison-and-contrast essay** uses factual details to analyze the similarities and differences between two or more persons, places, or things. Comparison-and-contrast essays can help readers look at the things being compared in a new way. Comparison-and-contrast essays include

- a topic involving two or more things that are in some ways similar and in other ways different.
- an introduction that presents the main point of the essay and body paragraphs that include details showing similarities and differences.
- an organization that highlights the points of comparison.

To learn the criteria on which your comparison-and-contrast essay may be assessed, see the Rubric for Self-Assessment on page 177.

Writers in ACTION

Bruce Brooks uses comparisons and contrasts in both his fiction and his nonfiction. His writing is rooted in simple curiosity: "I think curiosity is a writer's greatest tool. . . . I've been very curious all my life, [and] I allow that curiosity to turn into ideas."

Types of Comparison-and-Contrast Essays

There are a variety of specialized comparison-and-contrast essays. These include the following:

- **Product comparisons** compare two or more products and discuss the advantages and disadvantages of each.
- **Comparative reviews** compare books, movies, plays, or television programs and make a recommendation.
- **Comparisons of literary works** analyze similarities and differences between two or more literary works.

PREVIEW Student Work IN PROGRESS

In this chapter, you will follow the progress of Mindy Glasco from Los Alamos Middle School in Los Alamos, New Mexico. As you'll see, Mindy used prewriting, drafting, and revising techniques to develop her comparison-and-contrast essay, "Small Town, Big City."

PREPARE and ENGAGE

Interest GRABBER Ask students to think about dogs and cats. Have volunteers offer ways the two species are alike and how they are different.

Activate Prior Knowledge

Ask students to name two things that are both closely alike and, at the same time, very different. Some suggestions: boys and girls, children and adults, soccer and football, movies and TV shows, friends and siblings.

More About the Writer

Bruce Brooks is one of today's most acclaimed writers of young adult fiction. He has also written extensively for adults.

ONGOING ASSESSMENT: Diagnose

Use one of the following options to diagnose students' level of proficiency in comparison-and-contrast essays.

Option 1 Ask each student to select the strongest example of his or her comparison-and-contrast essay from last year. Hold conferences to review each student's sample. Use the conferences to determine which students will need extra support in developing a comparison-and-contrast essay.

Option 2 Ask students briefly to compare and contrast a topic of their choice. If students have difficulty with this exercise, you will need to devote more time to the prewriting phase of the writing process.

TEACH

Reading\Writing Connection

Reading Strategy: Identify Main Points

The main points of an essay should be reducible to one or two sentences. The rest of the essay provides examples and details to support the main ideas. Ask students to identify the main idea of Bruce Brooks' essay. (Animals have intelligence but cannot improvise as humans can.)

Teaching From the Model

You can use the essay as an example of a concise comparison-and-contrast essay. The author has organized a tight structure that supplies comparative and contrasting examples on the topic of the relative intelligence of humans and animals.

Step-by-Step Teaching Guide

Engage Students Through Literature

1. Read the essay aloud or have volunteers read it.
2. Point out how the author introduces his main theme in the first paragraph. He talks about it rather than stating it directly in one sentence.

continued

Critical Viewing

Compare and Contrast Students may say that some animals provide a great deal of care for their young, as do humans. However, other animals provide no care for their young at all.

8.1 Model From Literature

Bruce Brooks (1950–) was born in Washington, D.C., and grew up in North Carolina. Brooks worked at many jobs—from printing to newspaper reporting—before he published his first book. In this essay, Brooks compares animal and human behavior.

Reading Writing Connection

Reading Strategy: Identify Main Points The **main points** are the key ideas that the author wants readers to remember. As you read, identify the main points by paying careful attention to the key ideas in the first paragraph and to any sentences that sum up the ideas in paragraphs that follow.

▲ **Critical Viewing** How does the care humans give their offspring differ from the care other animals give their young? How is it similar? **[Compare and Contrast]**

Are Animals Smart?

Bruce Brooks

Even when we are careful to see an animal's actions in terms of its own life, we still notice that many animal qualities are obvious as correlates to our own experiences. We are not mistaken in giving these qualities the same names. We can tell when a cat is suspicious, a bird afraid, a dog lonesome. Why not say so? The mistake may be that we presume in the first place that these are *human* traits crudely mimicked by lesser creatures, and that by sharing our words we are elevating animal behavior above its lowly place. Who is to say humans invented suspiciousness or fear, and that we therefore own its copyright?

Animal structures allow us the same kind of correlation. We can see that a snail shell is like armor, a spiderweb like a fishnet, an ovenbird's nest like a house. But the comparison of things that are *designed* and *made* strikes deeper than does a comparison of feelings. These artifacts lead us to consider whether animals possess the most controversial quality of all, the one we imagine sets us furthest apart from the less-refined, more elemental life of creatures: intelligence.

In the introduction, Brooks identifies the two items he is comparing: animals and humans. The reader immediately senses Brooks's main theme: Animals and humans are more alike than most people choose to believe.

Most of us would say: People are smart. Animals are . . . well, something else. When a two-year-old human child uses a yard-stick to scoop a cookie off a high kitchen counter, we praise the child's native brightness but accept it as a mere step in the development of intellect. But when a bolas spider swings a strand of silk with a sticky globule on the end at a passing insect and hauls the bug in to eat, we treat it more as a bit of luck, an accidental discovery the spider managed, improbably, to repeat and pass on by instinct—a naïve sort of act, far from intellectual. . . .

Here, Brooks compares instances in which humans and animals solve a problem (getting food) in inventive ways.

It is true that human intelligence goes far beyond that of insects and birds and amphibians and reptiles and fishes and crustaceans and mollusks and our fellow mammals. We have the freedom of improvisation where the animal has the boundary of instinct. We can improvise structures when we need them; with a few exceptions, animals cannot. The ability to improvise to create new solutions to immediate problems and to plan innovative strategies without reference to others is a profoundly individual talent: Each one of us can do it because we can think alone. The restrictiveness of instinct is the opposite: It shows that each wasp or panda or octopus is essentially a member of a species that behaves *as a group* in a certain way.

LITERATURE

For an example of a comparison of a man's intelligence before and after a tragic experiment, read "Flowers for Algernon" by Daniel Keyes. You can find this short story in *Prentice Hall Literature: Timeless Voices, Timeless Themes,* Silver.

Reading Writing Connection

Writing Application: Help Readers Identify Main Points As you develop your comparison-and-contrast essay, help readers identify your main points by stating them clearly in the topic sentence of the paragraph in which you introduce them. Also, use transitions like *first, second, in addition,* and so on to introduce each main point.

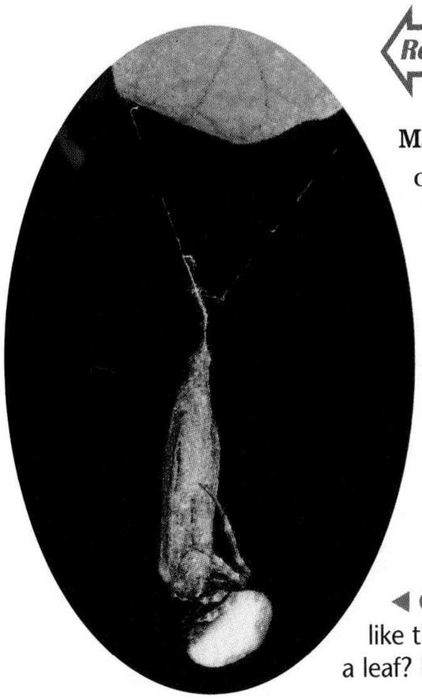

◀ Critical Viewing Does a bolas spider like this one need to learn how to hang from a leaf? Explain your answer. **[Hypothesize]**

Step-by-Step Teaching Guide continued

3. Ask students to identify the similar and differing points of the author's presentation. Be sure they understand how the author considers animal behavior and human behavior linked.
4. Discuss how the author sees humans differing from animals in their ability to improvise and come up with creative solutions to problems.
5. Ask students to tell if they have ever seen a pet or other animal exhibit creative problem solving.

Responding to Literature

"Flowers for Algernon" has also been adapted for stage and screen. Have students write a brief paragraph that compares and contrasts the character's intelligence. The story may give them ideas for a topic for a comparison-and-contrast essay.

Critical Viewing

Hypothesize Students' responses will vary, but most will say that a bolas spider may have to learn how to hang from a leaf.

Reading\Writing Connection

Writing Application: Help Readers Identify Main Points

Suggest that students identify the points they want to make first, in an outline or on note cards. Point out that each main point should relate to the topic of the essay, and should be supported by evidence. Explain that transitions in a comparison-and-contrast essay would probably include such words and phrases as *but, however, on the other hand, similarly,* or *likewise.*

Step-by-Step Teaching Guide

Prewriting: Blueprinting; Personal-Experience Timeline

Teacher Resources: Writing Support Transparency 8-A

1. The blueprinting activity should work best for more visually and spatially oriented students. Others may not be able to generate enough detail to make it useful for generating possible topics.
2. Before doing the timeline activity, talk with students about personal and physical growth. Point out its potential for comparison-and-contrast: It's still you, yet you've changed.
3. Display the transparency and examine Mindy's personal experience timeline. Use the transparency to work though the activity.
4. Treat both activities as tools, means to the end of generating possible topics. If the activities do not seem to be working for some students who are making genuine efforts, move them along to different activities.
5. Simple brainstorming is a useful activity for generating topics. Have students first select a few categories and write them at the top of a column on a piece of paper. Then have them brainstorm for items in each column. This could be done individually, in small groups, or as a whole-class activity. Some suggested brainstorming topics:

   food
   animals
   places (specific and general)
   sports
   video games
   entertainers

Customize for *Visual/Spatial and Bodily/Kinesthetic Learners*

These students may do well with the brainstorming activity, as well as the personal-experience timeline. Encourage students to develop the "dual vision" needed to compare and contrast.

8.2 Prewriting

Choosing Your Topic

An effective comparison-and-contrast essay begins with a suitable topic. Your topic should

- interest you and your potential readers.
- be something you know about or about which you'd like to learn more.
- involve two or more items that are neither completely alike nor completely different.

Use the following strategies to help you choose your topic.

Strategies for Generating a Topic

1. **Blueprinting** Think of a place you know well, such as a park or your bedroom. Draw a blueprint or map of this place. Include key details such as trees or furniture. Then, write words or phrases on the blueprint that describe objects or activities you associate with this place. Review your blueprint, and choose an item to compare to another, related item.
2. **Personal-Experience Timeline** Every time you outgrow your clothes, you can see how you are changing. These physical changes are fascinating to compare and contrast. So are your changes in attitude. Use a timeline to chart ways you've changed over time. Choose two entries as the basis for a comparison-and-contrast essay.

iText

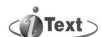

Try it out! Use the interactive Personal-Experience Timeline in **Section 8.2**, on-line or on CD-ROM.

Student Work IN PROGRESS

Name: Mindy Glasco
Los Alamos Middle School
Los Alamos, NM

Using a Personal-Experience Timeline

Mindy jotted a few events from her life on a personal-experience timeline to help her come up with a topic: a comparison of different places to live.

1997: live in big city; have many friends → 1999: move to small town; feel all alone → 2000: join team and after-school clubs; meet lots of kids → 2001: voted class president

Topic: living in a big city vs. living in a small town

TIME AND RESOURCE MANAGER

Resources
Print: Writing Support Transparencies, 8-A–D; Writing Support Activity Book, 8-1
Technology: Writing and Grammar iText, Section 8.2

In-Depth Coverage	Accelerated Pace
• Cover pp.166–169 in class. • Work through the Blueprinting and Personal-Experience Timeline strategies with the class. • Use the Responding to Fine Arts Transparency to generate additional topics. **Option** Have students work independently or in small groups with Writing and Grammar iText.	• Assign pp. 166–169 for independent student review. • Have students work independently to choose and narrow their topics. • Have students work with partners to focus on audience, purpose, and gathering details.

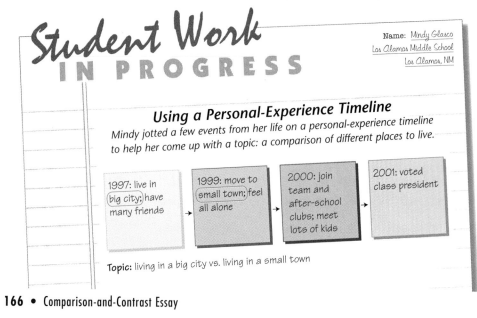

TOPIC BANK

If you're having trouble finding a topic, consider one of the following suggestions:

1. **Comparing Careers** Think about your future. What might your life be like if you became an architect? How would your life differ if you became a landscaper? Choose two professions to compare and contrast.
2. **The Same Song** Compare and contrast two songs on the same subject. Compare styles, rhythms, lyrics, mood, and so on.

Mexican Men With Burro Carrying Sticks, Joan Marron LaRue

Responding to Fine Art

3. These two paintings differ in the scenes depicted and in the types of colors and lines used. Write an essay comparing and contrasting the subject and style of each.

Empire State, Tom Christopher, Vicki Morgan Associates

Responding to Literature

4. Compare and contrast "Western Wagons" by Stephen Vincent Benét with "The Other Pioneers" by Roberto Félix Salazar. Analyze the similarities and differences in form, word choice, subject, and viewpoint. Explain how the two poems present different views of a similar subject. You can find these poems in *Prentice Hall Literature: Timeless Voices, Timeless Themes,* Silver.

Cooperative Writing Opportunity

5. **Rating Your Town** Studies are done each year to rate the quality of life in different cities, comparing culture, education, transportation, air quality, safety, and so on. Work with classmates to create a brochure citing the benefits of living in your town or city. Each of you should focus on a single feature. When you have finished your individual assignments, work together to assemble the finished product.

Step-by-Step Teaching Guide

Responding to Fine Art

Mexican Men with Burro Carrying Sticks by Joan Marron LaRue

Empire State by Tom Christopher

Teaching Resources: Writing Support Transparencies 8-B–C

1. Display the transparencies so that students can compare and contrasts the works of art.
2. The paintings have obvious contrasts of style and topic. Another contrast is "tone." Christopher's work shows a cramped and noisy and hectic city street. LaRue's work conveys a quiet, leisurely feeling. Similarities may include that both have people and buildings, both show people at work.

Responding to Literature

Benét's singsong rhythm makes the poem feel happy. The poem is optimistic—despite setbacks, good fortune is just around the corner or in the next town. Salazar's poem is written like a story. Its tone is serious and almost unbearably sad. Mexican Americans did not find fortune. They found death.

Spotlight on the Humanities

For additional topic suggestions, refer students to the Spotlight on the Humanities on page 182.

ONGOING ASSESSMENT: Monitor and Reinforce

If some students are having difficulty choosing a topic, use one of the following options.

Option 1 Suggest that student choose an idea from the Topic Bank. If many students have difficulty, work with them around one topic, modeling the process for them.

Option 2 If Topic Bank ideas seem too complex, suggest that students try one of the assignments from the Topic Bank for Heterogeneous Classes in the Teaching Resources.

TIME SAVERS!

Writing Support Transparencies
Use the transparencies for Chapter 8 to teach these strategies.

Step-by-Step Teaching Guide

Prewriting: Narrowing Your Topic, Considering Your Audience and Purpose

1. Discuss with students the necessity of narrowing or focusing a topic. As students subdivide their topic, see that they focus not only on what interests them but also on the part of the topic that is well suited to a comparison-and-contrast treatment.
2. Review the chart for audience and purpose. Examine the span of details it includes.
3. Have students write a brief description of their audience and purpose to help them narrow their topics.

Customize for *Less Advanced Students*

Comparison-and-contrast is a specialized logical skill that some students may have trouble with. Suggest that they limit their topic to one in which they compare only two items. This will simplify their use of the Venn diagram on page 169. They can use the point-by-point organizational method on page 170.

Critical Viewing

Apply Students may say that you would not have to go into great detail explaining the shots because the audience is composed of basketball players.

8.2

Narrowing Your Topic

Some topics are very broad and are better suited for a long essay—even a whole book. The topic "The Most Exciting Sport," for example, is much too broad to be discussed effectively in a brief essay. You might narrow it to "Football Versus Basketball—Which Is More Exciting?" Divide your topic into separate parts, aspects, or subtopics. Choose one of them as your narrowed topic.

Considering Your Audience and Purpose

Before you begin writing, identify your **audience**—the readers of your essay—and your **purpose**—what you hope to accomplish. Both your audience and your purpose will affect your use of language, your choice of details, and the length of your composition. Note the examples in the chart below. Create a similar chart that indicates your audience and purpose and how they will affect your writing.

▲ Critical Viewing What sorts of details should you include in a comparison of different basketball shots for this audience? **[Apply]**

Audience	Topic	Style	Important Details
teachers	compare history of two cities	formal	dates of founding
parents	compare different places to visit on vacation	formal/informal	places to stay and costs
fellow students	compare what I did on vacation with what I can do at home	informal	the joke we played at my cousin's house
Purpose	**Topic**	**Style**	**Important Details**
instruct	compare businesses in two places	formal	statistics on employees
instruct, persuade	compare museums in two places	formal/informal	school subjects that relate to the museum exhibits
entertain	compare two different amusement park rides	informal	how sick I felt after getting off each ride

ONGOING ASSESSMENT: Monitor and Reinforce

If students are having difficulty filling in the audience and purpose chart, use one of the following options.

Option 1 Students need not rigidly follow the pairings on the chart. They could seek to instruct fellow students or entertain parents.	**Option 2** Have students select an audience and purpose first, and then fill in the chart.

Gathering Details

Next, gather details you can use to develop your comparison. Write down as many descriptive details, facts, statistics, and other examples as possible. You don't have to use every detail you think of, but it's better to have too much to work with than not enough to fully develop your essay.

If you don't have a thorough knowledge of your topic, you may find it necessary to conduct research on it. Consider the following sources:

- Reference books
- Newspapers
- Magazines
- Internet sites
- Television documentaries.

Make a note about the source of each piece of outside information you write down. When you write your essay, credit outside sources you have used. See the section on Citing Sources and Preparing Manuscript on page 762 for information on citing sources.

As you gather details, consider using a Venn diagram like the one below to help you organize your information.

Use a Venn Diagram

Draw two overlapping circles, as shown below. Jot down similarities in the center section. Then, note differences in the outside parts of the circles. When you've finished your diagram, study it. Circle the items that seem most vivid and that best show comparisons and contrasts.

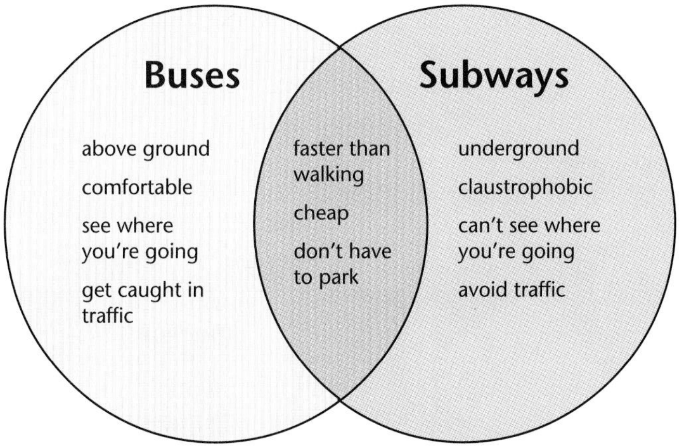

Research Tip

If you are looking for useful data to elaborate your topic, check an almanac. Use the index to see whether there is information about your topic.

Step-by Step Teaching Guide

Prewriting: Using a Venn Diagram

Teaching Resources: Writing Support Transparency 8-D; Writing Support Activity Book 8-1

1. As students research their essays and gather details, tell them to keep in mind the comparison-and-contrast goal of the essay.
2. Display the transparency. Examine the Venn diagram, which is uniquely suited to comparisons and contrasts.
3. Give students copies of the blank organizer. Have them organize their details. They need at least four points of comparison and contrast. If they are missing some, refer them back to their research to find additional points.

ONGOING ASSESSMENT: Monitor and Reinforce

If students are having difficulty filling in the Venn diagram, use one of the following options.

Option 1 Make sure that students have generated a sufficient number of comparison and contrast points. If they haven't, they need to reexamine both their topic and research to make sure those are attainable goals.

Option 2 Remind students that they are looking for ways that the topic has internal similarities and differences. Encourage them to take a step back from the topic to gain a wider perspective.

TIME SAVERS!

Writing Support Transparencies
Use the transparencies for Chapter 8 to teach these strategies.

Writing Support Activity Book
Use the graphic organizers for Chapter 8 to facilitate these strategies.

Step-by-Step Teaching Guide

Drafting: Shaping Your Writing

1. Examine both the block and point-by-point methods of organization. The block method is suited to more complex comparisons, or ones in which more than two items are being compared. The point-by-point method is better for comparisons of only two items.
2. Have students look over the details they listed on their Venn diagrams to identify a theme for their comparisons
3. Suggest that students identify their theme and sketch brief outlines using each method to decide which better serves their purposes.

Customize for *More Advanced Students*

Suggest that students extend their topics to more than two items so they can use the more complex block method of organization.

Critical Viewing

Analyze Possible response: Stores and shopping have changed dramatically in the last 100 years.

8.3 Drafting

Shaping Your Writing

Once you've gathered enough details to include in your first draft, decide how you will organize them.

Select an Effective Organization

There are several ways to organize a comparison-and-contrast essay. Your audience, purpose, and topic will influence the method you choose.

- **Block Method** To use this method, present all of the details about one subject first; then, present details about the second subject, and so on. The block method works well if you are writing about more than two things or if your topic tends to be complicated.
- **Point-by-Point Method** To use this method, discuss one aspect of both subjects, then another aspect, and so on. For example, if you are comparing buses and subways, first discuss the cost of each, then accessibility, and so on.

Find a Theme

A clear organization should not be the only structure guiding your writing. Review your notes for a **theme**—an extended comparison or a lesson involving the overall relationship between the items you are comparing.

For instance, if you were comparing a big supermarket to a tiny Mom-and-Pop grocery, many of your points of comparison might involve size. Yet, you might think the smaller store is the more valuable. You could focus your essay by comparing the grocery to a diamond—small but valuable.

▼ Critical Viewing Write a sentence stating a possible theme for a comparison between these two scenes. [Analyze]

TIME AND RESOURCE MANAGER

Resources
Print: Writing Support Transparencies, 8-E
Technology: Writing and Grammar iText, Section 8.3

In-Depth Coverage	Accelerated Pace
• Cover pp. 170–171 in class. • Work through organization and elaboration with the entire class. • Have students write their own comparison-and-contrast essay drafts in class. • Use the transparency to demonstrate layering ideas. **Option** Have students work independently or in small groups with Writing and Grammar iText.	• Have students review pp. 170–171 independently, then write their own comparison-and-contrast essay drafts. • Respond to individual drafting issues as needed.

Providing Elaboration

A house starts out as a frame. To complete it, you must add layers of wood and siding. Writing an essay is like building a house: You start with an overall structure and layer on details to develop your key points.

As you draft your paper, use the strategy that follows to develop a thorough, detailed comparison.

Layer Ideas Using SEE

To develop the main point of a paragraph, follow these steps:

State the topic of the paragraph.

Extend the idea. Restate it with new emphasis, apply it to a particular case, or contrast it with another point.

Elaborate on your main idea in one or more sentences, giving examples, explanations, supporting facts, or other details about it.

As you elaborate, look for opportunities to connect your main points to the theme of your essay.

Student Work IN PROGRESS

Name: Mindy Glasco
Los Alamos Middle School
Los Alamos, NM

Layering Ideas

Mindy used layering as she drafted this paragraph.

Statement: A small town also has a lot to offer. **Extension:** However, like a shy person, what it has to offer may not be obvious at first. **Elaboration:** After having lived in my town for a while, I can tell you about the great trails right out my back door for hiking, mountain biking, and cross-country skiing in the winter. Our town also has its own downhill ski area, just twenty minutes away.

In the first sentence of her paragraph, Mindy states a new main point.

In extending her main point, Mindy connects it to her theme.

Mindy elaborates on her main idea, listing all that a small town has to offer.

Step-by-Step Teaching Guide

Drafting: Layer Ideas Using SEE

Teaching Resources: Writing Support Transparency 8-E

1. Review the SEE method.
2. Display the transparency. Examine Mindy's work in progress to see how she uses SEE to structure her paragraphs.
3. Point out that SEE is just another way of writing a main idea sentence and then providing supporting and contrasting details. Examine how the extension statements both reinforce the main idea and present it in a slightly different way.

ONGOING ASSESSMENT: Monitor and Reinforce

If students are having difficulty layering ideas with SEE, use one of the following options.

Option 1 Help students make direct main idea statements for each comparison point and then restate the idea from a slightly different point of view.

Option 2 Have students make an outline in which the Roman numeral stands for the main idea, the capital letter for the extension, and the Arabic number for the supporting details.

TIME SAVERS!

Writing Support Transparencies
Use the transparencies for Chapter 8 to teach these strategies.

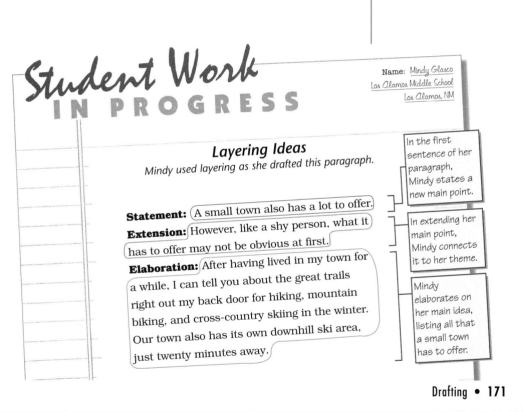

Step-by-Step Teaching Guide

Revising: Color-Coding to Check Organization and Balance

Teaching Resources: Writing Support Transparency 8-F

1. Display the transparency and examine Mindy's use of color-coding to analyze organization and balance.
2. For purposes of illustration, read students the following exaggerated example of imbalance:

   Madison is the capital city of Wisconsin. It is a beautiful city that is often cited as one of the best places to live in the country. It is the home of the University of Wisconsin.

   Milwaukee is the largest city in the state. It is located on Lake Michigan.

Customizing for *Less Advanced Students*

Students who have trouble coding the items can work with partners to help them keep track of their comparative sentences.

8.4 Revising

Not even the best writers expect a first draft to be perfect. Start revising your draft by reviewing your overall structure.

Revising Your Overall Structure

Check the Organization and Balance

Your essay should follow a consistent organization—either block or point-by-point—and should give a balanced comparison. Use color-coding to check your organization and balance.

REVISION STRATEGY

Color-Coding to Check Organization and Balance

Reread your essay. Use one color to highlight details concerning one of the items you are comparing. Highlight details about the other item in a second color. If you have many more highlights in one color than in the other, add more details on the subject about which you have written less.

Then, note whether your highlighting shows consistent organization. If you see both masses of a single color and places where colors alternate, reorganize your paper—either group together all details on a subject (block method) or alternate details concerning each topic (point-by-point method).

Student Work IN PROGRESS

Name: Mindy Glasco
Los Alamos Middle School
Los Alamos, NM

Checking Organization and Balance

When Mindy color-coded, she found a paragraph highlighted in only one color. She revised it to carry through her point-by-point organization consistently.

A good thing about our small town is that the crime rate is low. There are always people all around who know me and are willing to help.

Most big cities have more than their share of violence. In the city in which my friend lives, it is dangerous to stay out past dark, but in this town it would probably be more dangerous for the criminals than for the kids.

Mindy realized that she had no details about big cities in this paragraph. For balance, and to maintain her point-by-point organization, she added the sentence shown.

TIME AND RESOURCE MANAGER

Resources
Print: Writing Support Transparencies, 8-F–G
Technology: Writing and Grammar iText, Section 8.4

In-Depth Coverage	Accelerated Pace
• Cover pp. 172–175 in class. • Work through Revising with the entire class. • Use the transparencies for Checking Organization and Balance and Circling Unfocused Details. • Work through the Grammar in Your Writing activity on p. 175. **Option** Have students work independently or in small groups with Writing and Grammar iText.	• Assign students to review pp. 172–175 independently. • Have students revise their comparison-and-contrast essays independently.

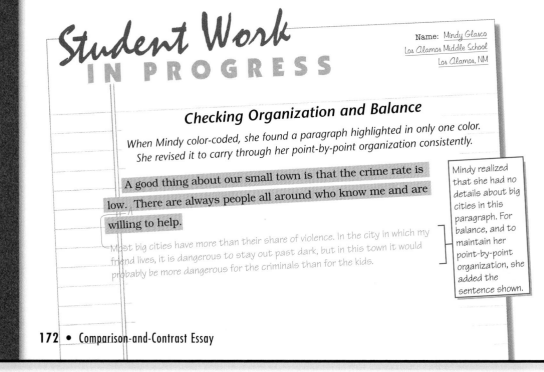

Sharpen Your Theme

An effective comparison-and-contrast essay does not simply list similarities and differences. It has a clear theme—a main idea that unifies all of the details and grows stronger from paragraph to paragraph. For example, an essay comparing buses and subways might drive home the writer's opinion that subways are a more efficient way to travel.

As you revise, eliminate details that do not contribute to your theme, and add details that help strengthen your theme. Use the strategy of circling unfocused details.

Writers in ACTION

Like all professional writers, Bruce Brooks knows that revising is a key step in the writing process: "Revising is something that I regard, really, as a privilege. I think that revision should be regarded as the chance to fix mistakes before they really happen."

REVISION STRATEGY
Circling Unfocused Details

Copy the sentence that most effectively conveys your main theme onto an index card. Run the card down your draft as you read, one line at a time. Circle details that are not clearly related to your main focus. Consider deleting these details or rewriting them to support and develop your main idea. Also, consider adding new details to strengthen the connection of the paragraph to your focus.

Student Work IN PROGRESS

Name: Mindy Glasco
Los Alamos Middle School
Los Alamos, NM

Sharpening the Focus

Notice the changes Mindy made to sharpen the focus of this paragraph.

When I was nine, my three-year-old sister was attacked by a hungry coyote. She would have been dragged off if I hadn't been holding her hand. ~~An event like this would never happen in a big city. Big city people don't realize how predictable and safe their lives actually are.~~ A coyote is as tough as any mugger—maybe tougher.

Mindy's theme is that no place is perfect. The circled sentences shift focus to a criticism of people's perceptions. To emphasize her theme, Mindy replaced them with a new sentence.

Theme:
Towns are like friends: None of them is perfect, but if you concentrate on their good sides, you will be much happier in the end.

Step-by-Step Teaching Guide

Revising: Circling Unfocused Details

Teaching Resources: Writing Support Transparency 8-G

1. A theme sharpens the focus of a comparison-and-contrast essay. For example, if the theme of the essay is the skills necessary for excelling at baseball versus soccer, a discussion of the tradition of eating hot dogs at a baseball game, although a detail of baseball, has no place in the essay.
2. Display the transparency. Examine how Mindy circled unfocused details for elimination. Encourage students to focus on their themes. Tell them that as they begin the comparison and contrast process, new details will emerge if they stay focused on the theme.

ONGOING ASSESSMENT: Monitor and Reinforce

If students are having difficulty circling unfocused details, use one of the following options.

Option 1 Have students write their theme on an index card. Tell them to hold the index card next to each sentence as they read their draft. Each time, have them look at the detail in the sentence and write down how it fits into the theme. If it doesn't fit, have them circle the detail.

Option 2 Have students write down the details in outline form under the theme. Then have them underline each focused detail in blue. Finally, go back and circle the remaining details in red.

TIME SAVERS!

Writing Support Transparencies
Use the transparencies for Chapter 8 to teach these strategies.

Step-by-Step Teaching Guide

Revising: Check Paragraph Structure; Combine Sentences With Indefinite Pronouns

1. Have students check paragraph structure by labeling sentences T, R, or I. Not every paragraph must have all three.
2. Review the problem of singsong rhythm and the solution of using indefinite pronouns. Write the following additional example on the chalkboard:

   Brenda bakes wonderful apple pies. Victor is also a great baker.

   Both Brenda and Victor are great bakers. Neither is at a loss in the kitchen.

Customize for *Verbal/Linguistic Learners*

Encourage students to find other solutions to the monotony that can result from point-by-point comparison. Suggest that they use subordinate clauses, compound sentences connected either by coordinating conjunctions or by semicolons, and varied sentence length to produce an essay that is interesting to read, yet clearly compares and contrasts the topic.

8.4

Revising Your Paragraphs

Check Paragraph Structure

Next, focus on each of the paragraphs in your essay. In a comparison-and-contrast essay, nearly every paragraph should contain these elements:

Topic sentence—a sentence that sums up the main idea

Restatement—an expanded version of the idea found in the topic sentence

Illustration—one or more specific facts, statistics, or descriptive details supporting the main idea.

Although all of your body paragraphs should contain these elements, they do not have to appear in the order listed above. Sometimes, you might want to lead with the sentence that provides an illustration, in order to hook your readers. This makes your pattern **ITR**. Or, you might again restate your topic as the final sentence, making your pattern **TRIR**.

REVISION STRATEGY
Marking Paragraph Patterns

Choose four paragraphs in your draft. Mark each sentence in these paragraphs with a *T*, an *R*, or an *I*. If you discover elements missing in any of the paragraphs, add these elements. In addition, if you notice that all four paragraphs follow the same pattern, consider revising one or more to vary the pattern.

Revising Your Sentences

Combine Sentences With Indefinite Pronouns

When comparing and contrasting two things, you may find yourself falling into a "singsong" rhythm, listing one similarity or difference after another. To eliminate this droning rhythm, combine sentences. You can combine some sentences using indefinite pronouns such as *any*, *both*, *each*, *either*, and *neither*.

REPETITIVE:	Subways are fast. Buses are also fast.
POSSIBLE IMPROVEMENTS:	Each of these types of transportation is fast. Neither one of them is slow.

Use the following strategy to eliminate a singsong rhythm.

REVISION STRATEGY
Coding Repetitive Sentences

Read your work aloud slowly and clearly. When you come across two or more sentences that make a singsong rhythm, circle them. Then, review the circled sentences and consider combining them by using indefinite pronouns.

Collaborative Writing Tip

Form a group, and read one another's work. One member should circle the subject of each sentence. Another member should underline all the verbs. Other members should take turns analyzing each sentence, checking for subject-verb agreement.

Grammar in Your Writing
Subject-Verb Agreement With Indefinite Pronouns

Indefinite pronouns refer to persons, places, and things. Some take only one form of a verb, singular or plural; a few can take either singular or plural, as shown below:

SINGULAR:	each	either	much	neither	
PLURAL:	both	few	many	others	several
SINGULAR OR PLURAL:	all	any	more	most	none

To determine which form of the verb to use with an indefinite pronoun that can be either singular or plural, consider whether its **antecedent** (the word it stands for) is singular or plural:

PLURAL: **None** of them [**buses and trains**] are fast.
SINGULAR: **None** of it [**the schedule**] makes sense.

Find It in Your Reading Find an indefinite pronoun used as a subject in the Student Work in Progress on page 178. Explain why it agrees with its verb.

Find It in Your Writing Circle each indefinite pronoun used as a subject in your draft. Check for subject-verb agreement, and correct any errors.

For more on subject-verb agreement, see Chapter 24.

Revising Your Word Choice
Avoid Unnecessary Repetition

Finally, check to see that you haven't overused any words.

REVISION STRATEGY
Highlighting Repeated Words

Draw rectangles around words you have used more than once. Evaluate whether the repetition is intentional and creates a desirable effect. If not, replace words you've repeated.

Peer Review
"Say Back"

After you have finished revising on your own, form a group with four classmates. Read your work aloud, pause briefly, and read it again. During the second reading, listeners should jot down (1) what they liked and (2) what they want to know more about. The listeners should then "say back" their comments to you. Use these comments to strengthen your essay.

Step-by-Step Teaching Guide

Grammar in Your Writing: Subject-Verb Agreement With Indefinite Pronouns

1. Review the chart of indefinite pronouns.
2. Write the following examples on the chalkboard:

   Each of the states makes its own laws. (singular)

   All are subject to federal law. (plural)

   Most of the book was exciting. (singular)

   Many of the books were too long. (plural)

Find It in Your Reading

In the third paragraph on page 179, *(Most big cities have. . . .) have* agrees with *Most.* In the fourth paragraph on page 179, *(Most people here don't lock their houses . . . .) don't* agrees with *Most.*

Find It in Your Writing

Have students work with a partner so that they can check each other's use of indefinite pronouns.

Step-by-Step Teaching Guide

Peer Review

1. Be sure that students are familiar with using a thesaurus to find synonyms for vague or overused words.
2. Discuss the strategy of repeating key words for emphasis.
3. In the peer review activity, students should not hesitate to point out weaknesses in classmates' essays. They just need to remember to be considerate and helpful, not insulting.
4. Remind students the purpose of the peer review activity is to check essays for content. Grammatical, mechanical, and other issues will be handled when they edit and proofread.

Integrating Technology Skills

Have students use the thesaurus on the word processor. You can use peer tutoring for students who are unfamiliar with accessing the thesaurus from the toolbar.

Step-by-Step Teaching Guide

Grammar in Your Writing: Pronoun-Antecedent Agreement

1. Editing and proofreading are important steps in the writing process. Discuss with students the importance of eliminating errors from their writing.
2. Tell students that a pronoun's antecedent may appear in a previous sentence. Use these sentences as an example.

   Gregory is revising his essay. He added a funny story about G. K. Chesterton.

Find It in Your Reading

Have students present their examples to the class.

Find It in Your Writing

If students do not find three pronouns, have them revise their drafts to include more.

PRENTICE HALL

Everyday Spelling

If you have taught the spelling skills in *Prentice Hall Everyday Spelling,* Grade 8, Chapter 9, in conjunction with this *Writing and Grammar* chapter, review and assess students' mastery of the skills before concluding the chapter. Remind students to apply the spelling skills as they edit and proofread their comparison-and-contrast essays.

8.5 Editing and Proofreading

Once you've finished revising, check your essay for errors in spelling, grammar, punctuation, and usage.

Focusing on Pronouns

When pronouns are separated from their antecedents, there may be problems in pronoun-antecedent agreement. Use the chart below to help you check agreement in your writing.

SINGULAR

PERSONAL	POSSESSIVE
I me	my, mine
you	your, yours
he, she, it him, her	his, hers, its

PLURAL

PERSONAL	POSSESSIVE
we us	our, ours
you	your, yours
they them	their, theirs

Grammar in Your Writing

Pronoun-Antecedent Agreement

A pronoun must agree with its antecedent in both person and number. **Person** indicates whether a pronoun refers to the person speaking (**first person**), the person spoken to (**second person**), or the person, place, or thing spoken about (**third person**). **Number** indicates whether a pronoun is singular (referring to one) or plural (referring to more than one).

INCORRECT: A *person* living in a small town should visit a big city. Seeing different lifestyles will broaden **your** perspective. [third person/second person]

INCORRECT: A *person* living in a small town should visit a big city. Seeing different lifestyles will broaden **their** perspective. [singular/plural]

CORRECT: A *person* living in a small town should visit a big city. Seeing different lifestyles will broaden **his or her** perspective. [third person singular/third person singular]

Find It in Your Reading Review "Are Animals Smart?" by Bruce Brooks on page 164. Find two pronouns, and identify the antecedents of each.

Find It in Your Writing Circle in blue three pronouns in your draft. Then, circle the antecedent of each in green. Revise any pronouns that do not agree with their antecedents.

For more on pronouns and their antecedents, see Chapter 24.

TIME AND RESOURCE MANAGER

Resources
Print: Scoring Rubrics on Transparency, Chapter 8; Writing Assessment; Scoring Rubrics and Scoring Models for Comparison-and-Contrast
Technology: Writing and Grammar iText, Sections 8.5–6

In-Depth Coverage	Accelerated Pace
• Cover pp. 176–179 in class. • Review p. 176 in class, including Grammar in Your Writing. • Have students edit and proofread their essays in class. • Give step-by-step coverage to Publishing and Presenting, p. 177.	• Assign pp. 176–179 for independent review. • Have students independently edit and proofread their essays. • Respond to individual editing issues as needed.

8.6 Publishing and Presenting

Building Your Portfolio

Consider the following ideas for sharing your work with a larger audience:

1. **Publish a Local Column** If you compared and contrasted subjects of local interest, such as two restaurants, submit your essay to a local newsletter or newspaper.
2. **Start a Family Tradition** If your essay contains family history, present it at the next family gathering. In the future, you can extend the essay, serving as the family historian.

Reflecting on Your Writing

Now that you have completed your essay, write a few notes about the experience of writing it. Begin by answering these questions:

- What did you enjoy most about writing your comparison-and-contrast essay? What did you like the least? Why?
- If you could begin again, what would you do differently? Explain your answers.

Internet Tip

To read comparison-and-contrast essays scored with this rubric, go on-line: PHSchool.com
Enter Web Code: eck-8001

Rubric for Self-Assessment

Evaluate your comparison-and-contrast essay using the following criteria:

	Score 4	Score 3	Score 2	Score 1
Audience and Purpose	Clearly attracts audience interest in the comparison and contrast	Adequately attracts audience interest in the comparison and contrast	Provides a reason for the comparison and contrast	Does not provide a reason for a comparison and contrast
Organization	Clearly presents information in a consistent organization best suited to the topic	Presents information using an organization suited to the topic	Chooses an organization not suited to comparison and contrast	Shows a lack of organizational strategy
Elaboration	Elaborates ideas with facts, details, or examples; links all information to comparison and contrast	Elaborates most ideas with facts, details, or examples; links most information to comparison and contrast	Does not elaborate all ideas; does not link some details to comparison and contrast	Does not provide facts or examples to support a comparison and contrast
Use of Language	Demonstrates excellent sentence and vocabulary variety; includes very few mechanical errors	Demonstrates adequate sentence and vocabulary variety; includes few mechanical errors	Demonstrates repetitive use of sentence structure and vocabulary; includes many mechanical errors	Demonstrates poor use of language; generates confusion; includes many mechanical errors

ONGOING ASSESSMENT: Assess Mastery

Use one of the following options to assess final drafts of students' comparison-and-contrast essays.

Self-Assessment Ask students to score their essay using the rubric provided. Then have students write a paragraph reflecting on the most valuable thing they learned in completing this essay.

Teacher Assessment Use the rubric and scoring models provided in the Writing Assessment, Comparison-and-Contrast Essay, to score students' work.

Step-by-Step Teaching Guide

Publishing and Presenting: Start a Family Tradition

1. Students may want to include snapshots of people and places mentioned in their essays.
2. Students can make copies of their essay to send to family members who live elsewhere.
3. Have students complete the Reflecting on Your Writing exercise and encourage volunteers to share their reflections with the class.
4. Have students use the rubric to self-assess their comparison-and-contrast essay.

ASSESS

Step-by-Step Teaching Guide

Assessment

Teaching Resources: Scoring Rubrics on Transparency 8; Formal Assessment, Chapter 8

1. Display the Scoring Rubric transparency and review the criteria in class.
2. Before students proceed with self-assessment, you may wish to review the Final Draft of the Student Work in Progress on pages 178–179. Have students score the Final Draft in one or more of the rubric categories. For example, how would students score the essay in terms of audience and purpose?
3. In addition to students' self-assessment, you may wish to use the following assessment options.
   - Score student essays yourself, using the rubric and scoring models from Writing Assessment.
   - Review the Standardized Test Preparation Workshop on pages 184–185 and have students respond to a writing prompt within a time limit.
   - Administer the Chapter 8 Test from Formal Assessment in Teaching Resources to assess students' grasp of concepts presented.

Step-by-Step Teaching Guide

Teaching From the Final Draft

1. Read aloud Mindy's final draft or have volunteers read it.
2. Use the margin notes to guide the discussion of Mindy's essay.
3. Point out how Mindy extends her main idea in the second sentence of the second paragraph.

continued

Critical Viewing

Compare and Contrast Students' responses will vary, but they may focus on the different animals and the different environments in each photograph.

8.7 Student Work IN PROGRESS

FINAL DRAFT

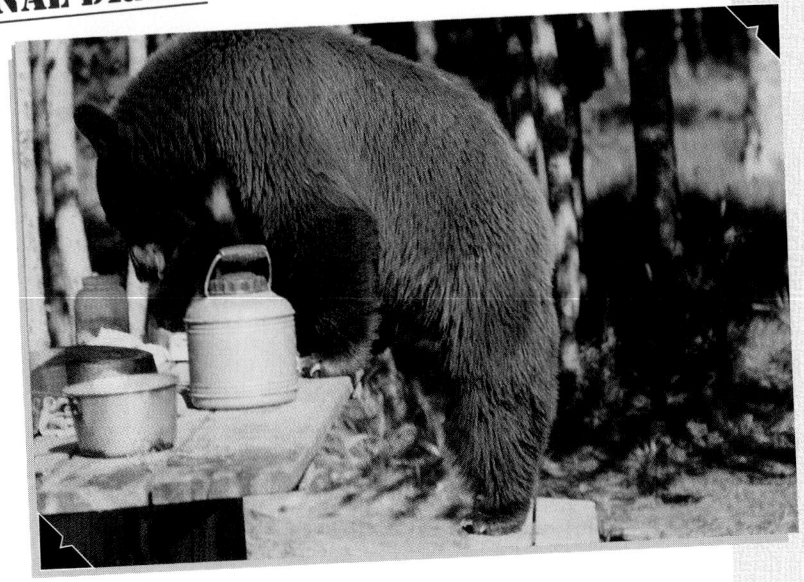

◀ **Critical Viewing** Compare this scene with the one shown on the next page. **[Compare and Contrast]**

Small Town, Big City

Mindy Glasco
Los Alamos Middle School
Los Alamos, New Mexico

I was born in a large city with a population of over 2,000,000 people. I now live in a small, friendly town in the Jemez Mountains with a population of under 15,000 people. I never had much of a choice where I lived, mainly because I'm only thirteen. But, someday I'm going to have to decide where I will spend the rest of my life. As I think about this decision, I compare the different places I have lived and wonder, which is the better place to live, a small town or a big city?

In her introduction, Mindy offers a purpose for her essay and explains her topic.

When people think about the differences between cities and small towns, they think of all the obvious advantages a city offers. A city provides convenient entertainment and shopping. Like a lively, generous friend, it lets you know right away what it has to give.

A small town also has a lot to offer. However, like a shy person, what it has to offer may not be obvious at first. After having lived in my town for a while, I can tell you about the great trails right out my back door for hiking, mountain biking, and cross-country skiing in the winter. Our town also has its own downhill ski area, just twenty minutes away. We have a nice outdoor ice-skating rink, a golf course, and a place for just about any sport imaginable.

Mindy's focus—comparing cities and towns to different kinds of friends—is strengthened in this paragraph.

This is really nice for people who love sports, but it can get boring. Then, go to the mall, right? Not here. There isn't a mall or even a chain store. In most big towns, people can practically walk out their front door and find a mall. We have to drive at least an hour for a simple thing like a birthday present. We have only a few stores, so we aren't surprised if we see three people wearing the same outfit. We have a few local restaurants, but going to some fast-food restaurants is still a special treat we get only in the "big city." In fact, the one local fast-food restaurant made the front page of our only newspaper when it built a play area.

By contrasting shopping experiences, Mindy illustrates an important difference between big cities and small towns.

A good thing about our small town is that the crime rate is low. Most big cities have more than their share of violence. In the city in which my friend lives, it is dangerous to stay out past dark, but in this town it would probably be more dangerous for the criminals than for the kids. There are always people all around who know me and are willing to help. I can't even walk across town after my violin lesson without three people offering to drive me home.

It's strange when we go to the city, because I am not used to cars being locked. Most people here don't lock their houses or their vehicles. The last theft in the area occurred when my neighbors threw some burnt cookies out the back door. Some bears came along and stole them!

That's one good thing about big cities: You don't have to worry about wildlife as much. It's scary when you're out hiking and see a bear or a mountain lion or a coyote. When I was nine, my three-year-old sister was attacked by a hungry coyote. She would have been dragged off if I hadn't been holding her hand. A coyote is as tough as any mugger—maybe tougher. If I choose to remain in a small town in the future, that is one thing I hope I never experience again. It does show, though, that like a shy person, even a quiet little town can have an unexpectedly tough side.

This effective moment highlights the dangers of small-town living for the reader.

Both small towns and big cities have their good sides and bad sides, but the most important thing is to be content wherever you are. Towns are like friends: None of them is perfect, but if you concentrate on their good sides, you will be much happier in the end.

Mindy's conclusion restates her focus: Places to live are like different kinds of friends. That leaves the reader with a provocative thought.

Step-by-Step Teaching Guide continued

4. Ask students whether the essay contains more comparisons or contrasts. (Mindy finds many more opposing points between her small town and big cities.)
5. Ask students to identify the organizational plan Mindy uses. (point-by-point)
6. Ask students to evaluate Mindy's essay on two levels: how effectively she compares and contrasts her subjects, and its interest level.

> **Lesson Objectives**
> 1. To write a consumer report appropriate to audience and purpose.
> 2. To use prewriting strategies to choose and narrow a topic.
> 3. To gather and organize details.
> 4. To draft, revise, edit, and publish a consumer report.
> 5. To use correct grammar, spelling, and mechanics.

Step-by-Step Teaching Guide

Consumer Report

Teaching Resources: Writing Support Transparency 8-H; Writing Support Activity Book 8-2

1. Ask whether students know what a consumer report is. List elements of correct responses on the chalkboard, and amplify students' definitions as needed. You may want to bring a few issue of *Consumer Report* magazine to class so that students can leaf through them and get ideas for topics for their own reports.
2. Point out that the genre of this writing assignment lends itself very well to a particular text structure: comparison and contrast. The purpose of a consumer report is to rate competing products, discussing their similarities and differences. Students may want to discuss each product in turn, or they may prefer to begin each new section of the report with a category (such as price, efficiency, or style) and describe how each product rates in this category.
3. As students look at models in *Consumer Report* or other magazines, they will notice numerous graphic organizers. Encourage them to include graphic organizers in their own reports. Point out that these graphics help readers sum up a good deal of text at a glance.

Connected Assignment
Consumer Report

If you are a smart shopper, you probably make comparisons and contrasts among several products before deciding which one to buy. Comparing and contrasting is a good way to find a bargain. It also helps you find the product that fits your needs exactly. By writing your own consumer report on the products you are comparing, you are sure to make the best buy.

A **consumer report** is a comparison of the strengths and weaknesses of different products. It draws conclusions about the advantages of using one over another. Useful consumer reports feature

- a detailed comparison of two or more similar products.
- a rating of the products, backed by facts.

Write your own consumer report, using the strategies that follow.

▲ Critical Viewing How might a consumer report on clothing help these shoppers? **[Draw Conclusions]**

Prewriting To choose a topic, consider writing about an item you or your family has recently purchased, or about an item that you are planning to purchase.

Narrow Your Topic After choosing your topic, make sure that it is focused. Browse through advertisements, catalogs, and brochures to find products comparable to the one you purchased or plan to purchase. Look for products that perform the same basic functions but between which there are a few key differences. For instance, if your topic is skateboards, you might choose a basic model and one with premium fittings.

Consider Your Audience Next, think about the audience for whom you are writing your report. Your audience consists of those who are interested in buying the products you are comparing. Determine the needs of your audience. For instance, if purchasers of your product are young people about your own age, then they are probably concerned with the affordability of the product. In evaluating the needs of your readers, consider these factors:

- How long do they want the product to last?
- Will they use it out of necessity, just for fun, for style, or to develop some skill?
- How much money do they have to spend?

4. Display the transparency to show students how they can organize information for their reports. Give them copies of the blank organizer for them to use as they gather details. You may want to allow students to work together on their consumer reports, especially if students want to do a good deal of research or include numerous graphic organizers.

Critical Viewing

Draw Conclusions Possible answers: It can compare sizes, styles, colors, and prices. It can describe working conditions in clothing factories, so that customers can boycott brands made in sweatshops. It can tell readers in which countries the garments were made.

On an index card, jot down notes on your audience and its needs. Refer to this card as you gather details and draft.

Gather Details Do some research to gather details on the items you are comparing. Visit the manufacturers' Web sites, pick up brochures at a store, and consult magazines for consumers. As you gather information, record it in a chart like the one shown.

Consumer Report On: Bicycles
Audience: Kids my age

Audience Need		Bicycle 1	Bicycle 2
• affordable	→	• cheaper • replacement parts are also cheap	• expensive for a kid • foreign-made: replacement parts are expensive
• durable (might use every day and on long trips)	→	• might last only a few years • needs repairs more often	• lasts a lifetime • needs repairs infrequently
• on- and off-road	→	• can be used for both	• can be used for both

Drafting

After you've gathered information, organize details by category. If you are comparing two bicycles, for example, you might examine each of the following categories: price, durability, cost of replacement parts, materials, weight, recommended use (city or trail), and so on.

Start off your draft with an introduction that

- clearly states your topic.
- defines the audience for whom you are writing.
- defines the categories of your product evaluation.
- summarizes your final evaluation.

In the body of your report, compare products in each of the categories you have defined. Support each point with details about the product.

Then, conclude with your recommendations. You do not have to tell readers to buy one product or the other. Instead, you might recommend one product for readers with special interests, and the other for readers with basic needs.

Revising and Editing

After completing your first draft, rearrange sentences to make sure that you have created a clear, logical order for details. To make your organization clear, add transitions, such as *in contrast*, where needed.

Then, review your report with your audience description in mind. Consider whether your audience needs some information that you have not provided. If so, add the missing details. Underline sentences containing information that your audience probably doesn't need. Unless these sentences add color or amusement to your report, consider deleting them.

Publishing and Presenting

Submit your consumer report to a magazine that reviews products of the sort you have evaluated.

Customize for *Logical/Mathematical Learners*

Have students graph some of the information in their reports. For example, students can draw graphs that show comparative prices. Students should explain what each graph shows and why this information is best presented in a graph rather than in the text. Challenge students to include at least two different types of graphs in their reports.

Lesson Objectives

1. To compare and contrast themes in the arts.
2. To compare and contrast modern jazz and modern art.

Step-by-Step Teaching Guide

Comparing Themes in the Arts

1. Choose a Spotlight element for class discussion, or have students work independently or in groups on the element of their choice. Give students the initiative to find the necessary books and recordings.
2. Bring a copy of Williams's poem to class and read it aloud to students. Have them discuss their reactions to the painting and the poem. Which elements in the poem are reflected in the painting? What do the two have in common in terms of style and tone? Which do students prefer, and why?
3. Give students some background on Parker and Gillespie. They developed bebop in rebellion against the strict rhythms and lack of improvisation of the big-band swing of the 1940's. Because swing was dance music, it had a strict rhythm, and since dancers like to hear familiar songs, swing improvisations stuck fairly closely to the tunes. Bebop harked back to the classic jazz era of the 1920's with its emphasis on solo improvisation and rhythmic inventiveness. Instead of ornamenting a tune, a bebop player would invent whole new melodies on that tune's chord progressions. This took great skill.
4. Explain to students that jazz tunes are in a four-beat meter. Most Parker and Gillespie tunes students might listen to will have an introduction, followed by several choruses. Blues choruses have twelve measures; pop song choruses have thirty-two measures. In bebop, one soloist usually improvises a melody for a full chorus, and another soloist will take over for the next chorus.

Spotlight on the Humanities

Comparing Themes in the Arts

Focus on Art: *I Saw the Figure 5 in Gold*

A successful comparison and contrast usually involves two items that are of the same kind. Yet the world is made out of dramatically different things. The sky and a stone, the word *hair* and a strand of hair in a comb—all belong in the same world, but they are also worlds apart.

In the painting *I Saw the Figure 5 in Gold*, American painter Charles Demuth (1883–1935) makes a comparison between unlike things. Inspired by William Carlos Williams's poem "The Great Figure," Demuth creates a striking contrast between dynamic diagonal lines and the simple, flat calm of the numeral 5. Like Williams's poem, the painting provides an abstract impression of a fire engine marked "5" moving through the night, suggested by the blacks, reds, and golds in the painting. The repetition of the number suggests that the engine is drawing closer. Yet in some sense, the number remains still amid the bustle of the world, simply meaning what it means, however fast or slowly it moves.

I Saw the Figure 5 in Gold, Charles Demuth

▼▲ Critical Viewing List details in the painting and in the photos of Dizzy Gillespie that go against traditions in art or music. **[Analyze]**

Music Connection In the 1950's and 1960's, the poetry of Williams was well received by jazz musicians like Charlie Parker (1920–1955) and Dizzy Gillespie (1917–1993). Pioneers of the style called bebop, they are remembered as two of the greatest jazz musicians ever.

Comparison-and-Contrast Writing Activity: Poem Comparing Painting With Music

Patterns and repetition are important in music as well as in painting. Listen to a few tunes featuring Parker and Gillespie. Then, write a poem comparing the energy and movement of their music with the energy and movement in the painting *I Saw the Figure 5 in Gold.* Consider how both the music and the painting use repetition, and think of ways you might reflect that repetition in your poem. Share your poem with your classmates.

Viewing and Representing

Activity Remind students that their poems need not rhyme. Students may want to write free verse. Alternatively, they may welcome the challenge of writing in a particular rhyme scheme and meter. Urge students to think about poetic qualities suggested by the painting and the jazz recordings.

Critical Viewing

Analyze Students may say that the painting is not representational. Gillespie's trumpet is literally bent out of shape.

Media and Technology Skills

Comparing Stories in Different Media

Activity: Comparing Book and Movie Versions

Movie makers often make movies based on works of literature, whether classics from centuries ago or today's bestsellers. Between the page and the screen, a story can undergo major changes. Learn to compare and contrast book and film versions of the same story.

Learn About It Consider the following differences between books and movies:

- **Rhythm** A well-written dialogue between two characters can hold your attention for many pages. Movies, though, speak the "language" of action. A long conversation may be too static for the pacing of a movie.
- **Duration** Books can take days or weeks to read. The reader is not inconvenienced, however, because he or she can put the book down and pick it up again. Most movies are designed to be viewed at one sitting. To keep audiences from growing uncomfortable, most do not run for more than two hours.
- **Expressive Elements** Movie makers tell a story in visual images and sound. To add to the mood, suspense, or humor of a story, movies use lighting, color, camera angles, the timing of cuts from one scene to another, music, and other expressive elements. By contrast, writers create a whole atmosphere with words. A carefully crafted description can create a scene in a reader's imagination as real as any picture that flickers across the movie screen.

Movies made from books sometimes make the mistake of trying to copy the book too faithfully. If a movie maker forgets that he or she is making a movie, as well as telling a story from a book, then the result may not succeed as a movie.

Other Differences to Consider

Economics
Books may appeal only to a limited audience and still make enough money for those who produce them. Movies cost a great deal to make. To make money, most movie makers must appeal to the greatest number of people possible.

Watch It Take notes on a movie version of a story you have read, using a chart like the one shown. Then, write a brief comparison of the two versions. Evaluate each difference between the two that you discuss. Are changes to the story necessary to making a good movie, or do the changes destroy something essential to the story?

	Written Version	Movie Version	Possible Reason for Difference	Does Difference Improve Movie?
Events				
Characters				
Special Effects (Written Descriptions and Figurative Language vs. Lighting, Color, Music, Camerawork)				

Lesson Objectives

1. To watch a movie version of a familiar book.
2. To compare two media versions of the same story.

Step-by-Step Teaching Guide

Comparing Stories in Different Media

Teaching Resources: Writing Support Transparency 8-I; Writing Support Activity Book 8-3

1. Ask students to list a few stories they have both read and seen dramatic presentations of. Have them list a few similarities and differences. Ask which version students preferred and why.
2. Point out that many films write new endings for books and stories they dramatize. At the conclusion of Bernard Malamud's novel *The Natural,* for example, baseball player Roy Hobbs fails to get a crucial hit at the end of an important game. In Barry Levinson's film of the novel, Hobbs hits a home run to win his team the pennant. Ask students why they think filmmakers tend to prefer "happy" endings.
3. You may want to have a video screening for the whole class of a story or book they have all read. Before they begin writing, students can share their reactions to the differences between the film and the book in a whole-class discussion.
4. Use the transparency to demonstrate comparing and contrasting the two versions of the story. Then give students copies of the blank organizer so that students can complete the writing activity.

Lesson Objectives

1. To write a comparison-contrast essay appropriate to audience and purpose.
2. To draft, revise, and edit a comparison-contrast essay.
3. To use correct grammar, spelling, and mechanics.

Step-by-Step Teaching Guide

Comparing and Contrasting in Response to Writing Prompts

Teaching Resources: Standardized Test Preparation Workbook, pp. 15–16

1. Review the terms *comparison* and *contrast.* Point out that this type of answer naturally falls into a two-part structure; one section discussing similarities and the other discussing differences. Students should find it very easy to organize their answers to this type of writing prompt.
2. Remind students of the importance of including specific details in their answers. Students should not only contrast the intelligence of animals and humans, for example, but should support their statements with examples of human and animal behavior.
3. Remind students to vary their transitional words. Many of these words mean the same thing, but it is best not to use the same word over and over again. A reader will be irritated by too much repetition.

Standardized Test Preparation Workshop

Comparing and Contrasting in Response to Writing Prompts

Some writing prompts on standardized tests measure your ability to write an expository essay in which you compare and contrast things. Your purpose in responding to such a prompt is to

- show the similarities and differences between items, following the requirements of the prompt exactly.
- use examples to support each point.
- use a consistent method of organization suited to the topic.
- unify your essay through the use of transitions.

Although on some tests you will not lose points for errors in spelling and grammar, always try to use correct English.

Some prompts ask you to write a short response. Others require a long response. If you are given a short-response prompt, do not go through the prewriting and revising stages. Your drafting skills will be sufficient. However, a long-response prompt needs more attention. You can practice for such tests by responding to the sample expository writing prompt below. Use the suggestions on the next page to help you respond. The clocks represent the portion of your allotted time that you should devote to each stage of your writing.

Test Tip

When choosing a method of organization for your response, consider how complicated the subject matter is. If you must explain a great deal about each item being compared, consider using the block method. Otherwise, point-by-point organization will probably lead to a more interesting essay.

Sample Writing Situation

Read "Are Animals Smart?" by Bruce Brooks on page 164, and then answer the prompt below.

> In "Are Animals Smart?" the writer evaluates animal intelligence by comparing animal behavior to that of humans. How are animals and humans SIMILAR and DIFFERENT in behavior and intelligence? Use details and information from the selection to support your answer.

TEST-TAKING TIP

If students have difficulty with Venn diagrams, suggest a two-column chart headed *Similarities* on the left and *Differences* on the right. Because a standardized test limits their time, students may not want to bother with drawing circles of the right size and trying to squeeze all relevant details inside them. Two-column charts are much easier to keep neat and organized when a student has one eye on the clock.

Prewriting

Use nearly one fourth of your time for prewriting.

Consider Your Purpose Before you start to gather details for your essay, make sure that you are clear on your purpose in writing. This is already decided by the prompt. For instance, in responding to the sample prompt, you should focus on the similarities and differences between animal and human behavior with regard to intelligence. Avoid discussing similarities and differences in areas that do not involve such behavior.

Gather Details Use a Venn diagram to gather details. As you read Brooks's essay, list similarities in the section where the circles overlap. List differences in the outer section of the appropriate circle. (For an example of a Venn diagram, see page 169.)

Drafting

Use almost half of your time for drafting.

Organize Details Choose a method of organization. You may want to use the point-by-point method used in "Are Animals Smart?" To use this method, discuss each aspect of both subjects in turn. After you have chosen a method, follow it in sketching an outline for your response.

Provide an Introduction After organizing details, write an introductory paragraph in which you make a general statement comparing animal and human behavior and explaining what the comparison suggests about animal intelligence.

Elaborate Follow your outline in presenting details that show how animal and human behavior is alike and different. To satisfy the prompt, you must explain what each point of comparison indicates about the intelligence of animals. Use transitional words like *yet*, *too*, *similarly*, and *however* to show connections between sentences or between paragraphs. Conclude by summarizing your main idea.

Revising, Editing, and Proofreading

Use about one fourth of your time for revising and editing. Use the last few minutes for proofreading.

Review Organization and Balance Check the organization of your essay against your outline. If you have not followed your outline, make sure that the departure is an improvement. If not, reorganize details to create a more logical order. Then, check to make sure that your comparison is balanced—you have discussed the same number of details for each subject. For example, if you give more details about animal behavior than about human behavior, add details about human behavior.

Make Corrections Check for spelling, grammar, and punctuation errors. When making changes, put one line through text you are deleting. Use a caret (^) to indicate the places where you are adding words.

Customize for
Less Advanced Students

Students may find it difficult to articulate similarities and differences. Have each students find a topic in which he or she is interested, such as baseball, and have the students devise five comparison-contrast writing prompts relating to this topic (for example, *Compare and contrast Ty Cobb's and Babe Ruth's contributions to baseball)*. Go over students' lists to be sure that their writing prompts are appropriate for test practice. Then have each student complete an answer to one prompt every night for five nights. Students should soon show improvement in their ability to organize a comparison-contrast essay.

Chapter 9 Time and Resource Manager

In-Depth Lesson Plan

	LESSON FOCUS	PRINT AND MEDIA RESOURCES
DAY 1	**Introduction to Cause-and-Effect Essays** Students learn key elements of a cause-and-effect essay and analyze the Model From Literature (pp. 186–189).	***Writers at Work* Videotape,** Exposition: Giving Information ***Writing and Grammar iText* (Interactive Text),** Ch. 9, Introduction
DAY 2	**Prewriting** Students choose and narrow a topic, consider their audience and purpose, and gather information (pp. 190–193).	**Teaching Resources** *Writing Support Transparencies,* 9-A–D; *Writing Support Activity Book,* 9-1 ***Writing and Grammar iText* (Interactive Text),** Section 9.2
DAY 3	**Drafting** Students organize their ideas and write their first drafts (pp. 194–195).	**Teaching Resources** *Writing Support Transparencies,* 9-E ***Writing and Grammar iText* (Interactive Text),** Section 9.3
DAY 4	**Revising** Students revise their drafts in terms of overall structure, paragraphs, sentences, and word choice (pp. 196–200).	**Teaching Resources** *Writing Support Transparencies,* 9-F–G ***Writing and Grammar iText* (Interactive Text),** Section 9.4
DAY 5	**Editing and Proofreading; Publishing and Presenting** Students check their work for accuracy and correctness and present their final drafts (pp. 201–202).	**Teaching Resources** *Scoring Rubrics on Transparency,* Ch. 9; *Formal Assessment,* Ch. 9 ***Writing and Grammar iText* (Interactive Text),** Sections 9.5–6

Accelerated Lesson Plan

	LESSON FOCUS	PRINT AND MEDIA RESOURCES
DAY 1	**Introduction Through Drafting** Students review the characteristics of autobiographical writing, select topics, and write drafts (pp. 186–195).	**Teaching Resources** *Writing Support Transparencies,* 9-A–E; *Writing Support Activity Book,* 9-1 ***Writing and Grammar iText* (Interactive Text),** Ch. 9, Introduction through Section 9.3
DAY 2	**Revising Through Presenting** Students work individually or with peers to revise, edit, and proofread their work for presentation (pp. 196–202).	**Teaching Resources** *Writing Support Transparencies,* 9-F–G; *Scoring Rubrics on Transparency,* Ch. 9; *Formal Assessment,* Ch. 9 ***Writing and Grammar iText* (Interactive Text),** Sections 9.4–6

Options for Adapting Lesson Plans

HOMEWORK

Have students complete any stage of the lesson for homework.

SPELLING

To teach spelling skills in conjunction with writing skills, work through *Prentice Hall Everyday Spelling,* Grade 8, Chapter 10, as you cover this *Writing and Grammar* chapter. At the Editing and Proofreading stage, remind students to apply the spelling skills to their cause-and-effect essays.

FEATURES

Extend coverage with Connected Assignment (p. 205), Spotlight on the Humanities (p. 206), Media and Technology Skills (p. 207), and Standardized Test Preparation Workshop (p. 208).

TECHNOLOGY

Students can complete any stage of the lesson on the computer, using *Writing and Grammar iText* or a word-processing program. Have them print out their completed work.

INTEGRATED SKILLS COVERAGE

Integrating Grammar
SE pp. 199, 201

Viewing and Representing
Critical Viewing, SE pp. 186, 188, 189, 195, 196, 200, 203-207
SE pp. 206, 207

Speaking and Listening
Presenting an Outline, ATE p. 194

Real-World Connection
ATE p. 193

Workplace Skills
Writing Daily Reports, ATE p. 199

Technology
ATE p. 190

BLOCK SCHEDULING

Pacing Suggestions
For 90-minute Blocks
- Have students complete the Prewriting and Drafting stages in a single period.
- Focus one class period on Revising and Editing and Publishing and Presenting. Allow at least 30 minutes for peer revision.

Resources for Varying Instruction
- ***Writing and Grammar iText* (Interactive Text)** A 90-minute block provides an ideal opportunity for students to work on computer.
- ***Writers at Work* Videotape** Show the Exposition: Giving Information segment in class.

Professional Development Support
- ***How to Manage Instruction in the Block*** This teaching resource provides management and activity suggestions.

ASSESSMENT SUPPORT

Standardized Test Preparation Workshop SE pp. 208–209; ATE p. 198
Standardized Test Preparation Workbook, pp. 17–18
Scoring Rubrics on Transparency, Ch. 9
Formal Assessment, Ch. 9
Writing Assessment and Portfolio Management

MEDIA AND TECHNOLOGY

For the Student
- ***Writing and Grammar iText* (Interactive Text),** Ch. 9

For the Teacher
- ***Writers at Work* Videotape,** Exposition: Giving Information
- ***Resource Pro* CD-ROM**

MEETING INDIVIDUAL NEEDS

Less Advanced Students ATE pp. 194, 209. See also Ongoing Assessments ATE pp. 189, 191, 195, 200.
ESL Students ATE pp. 188, 190, 204
More Advanced Students ATE p. 195
Verbal/Linguistic Learners ATE pp. 188, 204
Logical/Mathematical Learners ATE pp. 196, 198

WRITING AND GRAMMAR ON-LINE

iText Interactive Text (On-line or on CD-ROM)
- Easily navigable instruction with interactive Revision Checkers
- Full use of e-rater™, the essay-scoring system (on-line only)

Companion Web Site PHSchool.com
- Scoring rubrics with models (use Web Code eck-8001)

See the Go On-line! feature, SE p. iii.

LITERATURE CONNECTIONS

Related selections from *Prentice Hall Literature: Timeless Voices, Timeless Themes,* Silver:

Professional Model "Why Leaves Turn Color in Fall," Diane Ackerman, SE p. 189
Topic Bank Option "Cub Pilot on the Mississippi," Mark Twain, SE p. 191

CHAPTER 9
EXPOSITION: CAUSE-AND-EFFECT ESSAY

Lesson Objectives

1. To recognize various types of cause-and-effect essays.
2. To learn the topic-generating strategies of browsing and self-interview.
3. To narrow an essay topic by using classical invention.
4. To identify ways to appeal to an audience through an essay's structure and style.
5. To use a KWL chart to gather details.
6. To outline a cause-and-effect essay.
7. To "explode the moment" to provide elaboration.
8. To analyze the organization of an essay.
9. To add specific details that support the explanation of causes and effects.
10. To check for correct verb tenses in an essay.
11. To underline and revise vague verbs.
12. To practice the "say-back" technique of peer review.
13. To identify and correct the improper use of prepositions and prepositional phrases.
14. To publish a cause-and-effect essay.

Critical Viewing

Hypothesize Students may say that if he hits the ball a certain way, the effect may be a better run.

Chapter 9

Exposition

Cause-and-Effect Essay

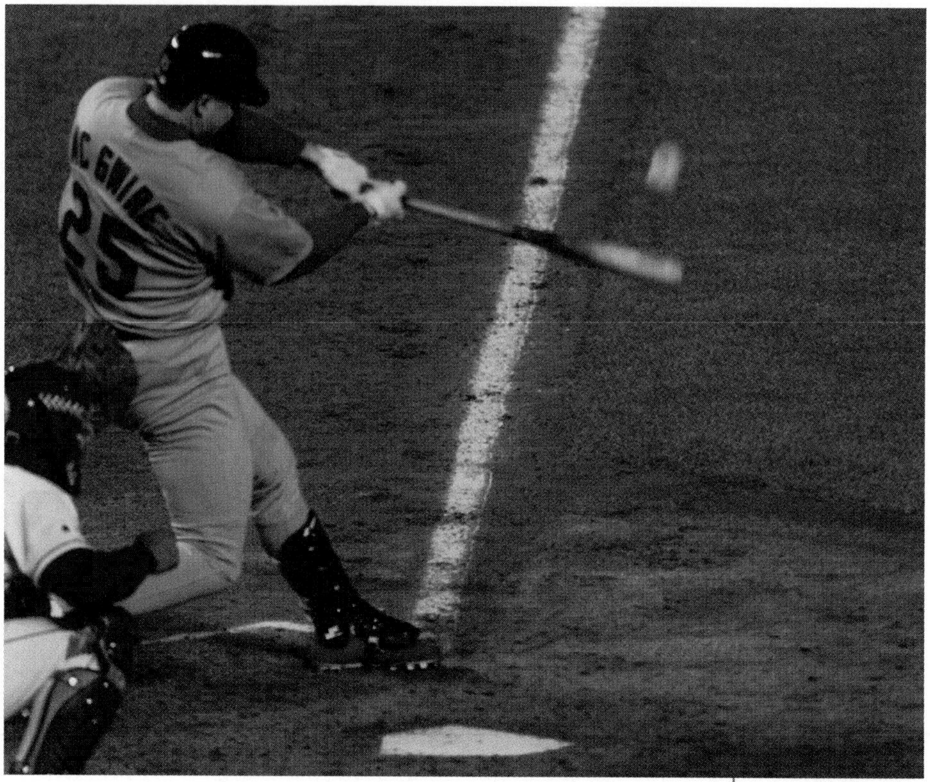

▲ **Critical Viewing** How might this batter use knowledge of cause-and-effect relationships to help him hit better? **[Hypothesize]**

Cause-and-Effect Explanations in Everyday Life

A baseball player with a powerful swing hits the ball in just the right spot, launching it over the left-field fence. A teacher announces that there will be a test the next day, leading students to spend their evening studying their textbooks. These stories capture **causes** and **effects**—specific actions and the events or situations that they produce.

Almost anything that happens—from simple daily events to those that affect people all over the world—involve causes and effects. For this reason, analyzing causes and effects helps us better understand our lives and our world.

TIME AND RESOURCE MANAGER

Resources
Technology: Writers at Work Videotape; Writing and Grammar iText, Ch. 9

In-Depth Coverage	Accelerated Pace
• Cover pp. 186–187 in class. • Show the Exposition: Giving Information section of the Writers at Work Videotape. • Read the Model From Literature (pp. 188–189).	• Have students review pp. 186–189 independently.

What Is a Cause-and-Effect Essay?

Expository writing is writing that informs or explains. A **cause-and-effect essay** is a specific type of expository writing that explains the reasons something happened or its results. Effective cause-and-effect essays include

- a clear explanation of how one or more events or situations resulted in another event or situation.
- a thorough presentation of facts, statistics, and other details that support the explanation presented.
- a clear and consistent organization that makes it easy to follow the connections among events and details.

To learn the criteria on which your cause-and-effect essay may be assessed, see the Rubric for Self-Assessment on page 202.

Writers in ACTION

Dutch philosopher Benedict Spinoza (1632–1677) wrote:

"Nothing exists from whose nature some effect does not follow."

However big or small, he thought, everything in the world is linked to other things by causes and effects.

Types of Cause-and-Effect Essays

Following are some of the specific types of writing that explain causes and effects:

- **Historical essays** explain the impact of key events and developments in the past.
- **Scientific reports** explain the results of an experiment or analyze the causes and effects of a natural event.
- **News reports** explain the causes and effects of current events or developments.

PREVIEW Student Work IN PROGRESS

Emily Meade is a student at Ingersoll Middle School in Canton, Illinois. She chose to write about the causes and effects of the Dust Bowl. In this chapter, you will see her work in progress, including her use of featured activities and strategies to develop her topic while writing. At the end of the chapter, you can read Emily's completed essay.

PREPARE and ENGAGE

Interest GRABBER Write a student's name on the board. Ask the class to guess why you wrote this name. (Possible answers: you want to see the student after class, the student didn't turn in homework) Point out that students have given possible *causes* for writing the name on the board. Now explain your real reason for writing the name (Give a positive reason, "I wrote Sean's name as a reminder to thank him for working hard in class yesterday.") Now that you've explained the cause, have students look at Sean to see the *results*. (Possible answers: Sean is happy, embarrassed, proud.)

Activate Prior Knowledge

Ask students to tell a positive event that occurred in their lives within the past week. Examples might include taking a trip to the beach or getting a good grade. Next, ask students to identify the cause or result of these events. The result of a trip to the beach might be learning to surf. Or the cause of getting a good grade might be studying the night before.

More About the Writer

Spinoza valued independence and the freedom of thought to such a great extent that he supported himself with menial work rather than accept financial aid from the schools he attended.

TEACH

Reading\Writing Connection

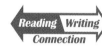

Reading Strategy: Identify Connections Among Causes and Effects

As students read the essay, have them note cause-and-effect clue words. *(because, that is why, if, account, when, that is why, affects, gives, cause, cause)*

Teaching From the Model

Ask students to discuss the likely audience for this essay. (Answers might include students or other people who are interested in science, or people who are interested in learning about the ocean.)

Step-by-Step Teaching Guide

Engage Students Through Literature

1. Read aloud "Why Is the Sea Blue?" Ask students to discuss what the article says in answer to the question in its title.
2. Point out that these answers are causes that have the effect of making the sea look blue.

(continued)

Critical Viewing

Analyze Students might name the following relationships: the causes of a rainbow, the effects of a rainbow on a viewers mood, the causes of waves, the causes of the color of the sea, and so on.

Customize for *Verbal/Linguistic Learners*

Invite students to take turns reading aloud the article instead of reading it aloud yourself.

Customize for *ESL Students*

Students may be unfamiliar with some scientific vocabulary in the article: *spectrum, wavelengths, suspended, algae, runoff, light-sensitive cells, retina.* Ask students to note these terms, then work in pairs or groups to find the meanings.

9.1 Model From Literature

This essay explores the reasons that the sea appears blue. Note that the author presents three causes of this one effect.

▲ Critical Viewing
Name three different cause-and-effect relationships you might illustrate with this photograph. **[Analyze]**

Reading Writing Connection **Reading Strategy: Identify Connections Among Causes and Effects** The key to understanding a cause-and-effect essay is paying close attention to the relationships among the details it presents. Look for words that indicate causes and effects. These may include verbs—for example, *causes, produces,* and *affects*—and transitions—*because of, as a result,* or *for this reason.*

Why Is the Sea Blue?

Denis Wallis, et al.

All color in the world comes from light. Without light, we would see no color in the greenest grass, a peacock's feather, a bunch of flowers, or a brilliant rainbow. Three factors determine the colors we see: the light itself, the material it falls on, and the ability of the human eye to distinguish colors.

In the introduction, the writer clearly states the three factors, or causes, that make the sea appear blue.

A beam of light appears to us to have no color. Shine it through a prism, and it breaks down into a spread of colors resembling those in a rainbow. Indeed, that is why rainbows appear in the sky: a shower of raindrops acts to open up the full spectrum of light into all its different and wonderful wavelengths.

We see a ripe tomato as being bright red because its skin reflects the red light in the spectrum, and absorbs all other colors. Grass isn't in itself colored green, nor are other objects in our world a myriad variety of colors. Their surface texture reflects light of a particular wavelength. That is why some objects appear to change color if they are tilted towards or away from the light. A shiny fabric, for example, may look green from one angle and blue from another.

The writer provides examples to help the reader understand the connection between a cause and an effect.

If the light source is changed, an object's color may alter. A woman buying some curtains is wise to take them into the daylight: Fluorescent store lights have more blue light; sunshine increases the amount of red in a fabric.

Travelers know that the seas appear to be dark green in some places and turquoise blue in others. The Mediterranean is renowned for its dark-blue color. The sky and its reflection in the water account partly for the sea's color. On gray and stormy days of heavy cloud, the water looks leaden.

When light strikes water, much is reflected, possibly causing glare. Of the light that penetrates the surface, some is absorbed; the rest is broken up and scattered back towards the surface. It is this scattering of light from beneath the surface that gives the sea its color.

Different wavelengths of light penetrate to different depths. If the water is clear, the red and yellow wavelengths of light are soon absorbed, leaving only blue-green light to be scattered back. That is why clear seas appear bluer.

▼▲ Critical Viewing Compare the color of the water in these pictures. According to the essay, what might account for the difference? **[Analyze]**

The time of year also affects the ocean's color. If the water is rich in nutrients, as it may become through chemicals carried down by rivers, it may encourage spring and summer weed growths. Fine particles suspended in the water will alter its color. Blooms of algae, for example, can suddenly turn seas red.

A combination of red-brown seaweed and blue sky sometimes gives seas such as the Mediterranean a magenta or purple hue. Runoff from coastal rivers, bringing a range of different vegetable and mineral particles, may cause the sea to look red-brown on one day and almost yellow on another. And close to shore any light-colored sand will make the water look blue-green rather than blue.

If you don't agree with a companion that the sea is a brilliant blue, the cause undoubtedly lies in your eyes. Our perception of color varies according to how light-sensitive cells are distributed in the retina. What looks like dark blue to one person may be gray-blue to another.

LITERATURE

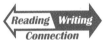

To read another example of cause-and-effect writing, see Diane Ackerman's book, *A Natural History of the Senses.* You can find an excerpt from this work in *Prentice Hall Literature: Timeless Voices, Timeless Themes,* Silver.

Reading Writing Connection

Writing Application: **Linking Causes and Effects** When you write your essay, use appropriate verbs and transitions to help readers see the connections among causes and effects.

Step-by-Step Teaching Guide continued

3. After students have read the article, lead a discussion based on these questions.
   - What different colors of water have you seen in rivers, lakes, or the ocean? What do you think caused these colors?
   - Have you ever bought an article of clothing that you thought was one color but turned out to be a different color when you got it home? Why do you think this happened?
4. Ask students if reading or discussing the color of the sea has given them any ideas for a cause-and-effect essay topic.

Critical Viewing

Analyze Students should mention that nutrients and blooms of algae can affect the waters' colors.

Responding to Literature

Have students note the causes and effects that Ackerman relates as they read the excerpt.

Reading\Writing Connection

Writing: Linking Causes and Effects

Have students keep a list of cause-and-effect words they can use as they draft their essays. Explain that these transitional words make the connections between causes and effects easier for the reader to comprehend.

ONGOING ASSESSMENT: Monitor and Reinforce

The following strategies might help students who need further explanation to understand cause and effect.

Option 1 To identify a cause, ask yourself, "What made this happen?"	**Option 2** To identify an effect, ask yourself, "What happened?"

Step-by-Step Teaching Guide

Prewriting: Browsing; Self-Interview

Teaching Resources: Writing Support Transparency 9-A

1. Play "Topic Association." Have students write down the first topic that comes to mind when you read the following list of topic ideas. For instance, if you say *snake,* students might write *python, cobra, venom* as topics that come to mind. After you read the entire list, ask students to share the topics they thought of. Topic List: planet, shark, World War II, heart transplant, lightning, colorblindness, football, opera, redwood tree.
2. Encourage students to browse through books, magazines, and newspapers to come up with more topics.
3. Display the transparency. Point out Emily's self-interview questions. Have students answer the questions for themselves, circling any answers that would make interesting cause-and-effect topics.

Customize for *ESL Students*

Encourage students to focus on photos, graphics, and other visuals as they browse for essay topics. When they see a visual that interests them, they can read the caption or nearby text to look for a cause-and-effect topic.

Integrating Technology Skills

Encourage students to visit Web sites designed just for kids. These sites often focus on especially interesting topics that serve as "grabbers" to catch readers' attention. The grabbers might give students ideas for cause-and-effect topics.

TIME SAVERS!

Writing Support Transparencies
Use the transparencies for Chapter 9 to teach these strategies.

9.2 Prewriting

Choosing Your Topic

To begin, choose a topic by thinking of historical or current events, occurrences in nature, and other situations that might have interesting explanations. Use these strategies to help you:

Strategies for Generating a Topic

1. **Browsing** Browse through newspapers and magazines, focusing on headlines and story titles. Jot down headlines and story titles that catch your interest. Review your notes to find an interesting topic that involves causes and effects.
2. **Self-Interview** Ask yourself questions such as those in the example below. Write down your answers. Review your answers to identify those that involve causes and effects. Then, circle the most interesting one and choose it as your topic.

iText
Try it out! Use the interactive Conducting a Self-Interview activity in **Section 9.2,** on-line or on CD-ROM.

Student Work IN PROGRESS

Name: Emily Meade
Ingersoll Middle School
Canton, IL

Conducting a Self-Interview

After looking at her self-interview, Emily decided she wanted to learn more about the causes of the plight of farmers during the Depression.

What is my favorite book?	"Of Mice and Men" by John Steinbeck
What natural or historical events are crucial to the story?	• the Depression • the migration of farmers to the West after their land was destroyed
What interesting facts have I learned in science class?	• Earth's core is made of molten lava. • Redwood trees can live from 500 to 700 years
What political leader do I admire most?	Franklin D. Roosevelt
What was happening in the world at the time of his or her term?	America was in the middle of its worst economic depression.
What invention am I most grateful for?	the Internet

TIME AND RESOURCE MANAGER

Resources
Print: Writing Support Transparencies, 9-A–D; Writing Support Activity Book, 9-1
Technology: Writing and Grammar iText, Section 9.2

In-Depth Coverage	Accelerated Pace
• Cover pp. 190–193 in class. • Have students use the topic-generating strategies on p. 190 to choose a topic for their cause-and-effect essays. • Tell students who are having difficulties to choose topics from the Topic Bank.	• Have students read pp. 190–193 independently. • Have students submit their topics for a cause-and-effect essay for your approval.

TOPIC BANK

If you're having trouble finding a topic, consider the following possibilities:

1. **Cause-and-Effect Essay About a Historical Event** Think about events you have been studying in your social studies class. Which ones interest you the most? What caused these events? Write a cause-and-effect essay about an event that you find interesting.
2. **Cause-and-Effect Essay About the Weather** What causes snow? What produces hurricanes and tornadoes? Think about various weather conditions. Choose one that especially interests you. Then, write an essay in which you analyze its causes and effects.

Responding to Fine Art

3. Jot down a few notes on what this painting suggests about the effects of industry. Write an essay in which you explore some aspect of the topic of industry—the causes of its growth, for instance, or its economic or social effects on a geographic area.

Pittsburgh, 1927, Elsie Driggs, ©1996: Whitney Museum of American Art, NYC

Responding to Literature

4. In *Life on the Mississippi,* Mark Twain tells us about his experiences learning to become a riverboat pilot. Read an excerpt from *Life on the Mississippi.* Think about a time when you were an apprentice, learning how to do a particular job. What effects did your experience have on you? You can find an excerpt from Twain's work in *Prentice Hall Literature: Timeless Voices, Timeless Themes,* Silver.

Cooperative Writing Opportunity

5. **Success Manual** With a group, brainstorm a list of people in your community whom you would call "successful." Then, brainstorm a list of interview questions on success. Have each member interview your subjects, taking careful notes. Each member should then write an essay on the causes of success based on his or her interview. Assemble the interviews and essays into a "success manual."

Step-by-Step Teaching Guide

Responding to Fine Art

Pittsburgh, 1927, by Elsie Driggs

Teaching Resources: Writing Support Transparency 9-B

1. Display the transparency.
2. The painting might inspire students to investigate the causes of air pollution, the effects of recycling and other conservation efforts on air cleanliness, or the effect of environmental regulations on air quality.

Responding to Literature

As students read excerpts from *Life on the Mississippi,* ask them to recall situations in which they have learned new skills. What caused them finally to "get the hang of it"?

More About the Author

Mark Twain's experiences as an apprentice riverboat pilot were not always pleasant. Apprentices were often treated cruelly by their masters. Perhaps this cruel treatment influenced Twain to choose a literary career over the life of a river man.

Spotlight on the Humanities

For additional topic suggestions, refer students to the Spotlight on the Humanities on page 206.

ONGOING ASSESSMENT: Monitor and Reinforce

The following strategies might be helpful for students who have difficulty choosing a topic for their cause-and-effect essays.

Option 1 As you're browsing for topics, let your eyes be your guide. When a word or visual grabs your attention, you've got a possible topic.

Option 2 Ask other students for ideas. Students who have already found a topic may be willing to share some of their leftover topic ideas with you.

Step-by-Step Teaching Guide

Prewriting: Use the "Classical Invention" Questions

Teaching Resources: Writing Support Transparency 9-C

1. Invite students to imagine that they are in the company of Plato or Aristotle as you read aloud the description of classical invention.
2. Display the transparency. Direct students' attention to Emily's completed classical invention chart. Point out how Emily used this strategy to narrow her topic.
3. Have students complete a classical invention chart to narrow the topics they have chosen for a cause-and-effect essay.

Language Highlight

When people see the word *invention,* they usually think of gizmos and gadgets—the inventions of creative thinkers. But the original meaning of the word *invent* was "to find or to find out." That is why classical invention is a strategy for "finding out" specific thoughts, ideas, and details about a subject.

9.2

Narrowing Your Topic

Even the most interesting topic can lead to an unsuccessful essay if it is too broad. For example, you couldn't effectively examine all of the causes of poverty in a brief essay. You could, however, explain the impact of a drought on the fortunes of people in a specific country. Use the following strategy to help you narrow your topic.

Use the "Classical Invention" Questions

"Classical Invention" is the name of a questioning strategy used to analyze and refine a topic. To use the strategy, answer the questions that appear below, substituting your topic for Emily's. Review your responses, and circle a series of related events that catch your interest. Come up with one statement that summarizes them, and use this as your narrowed topic.

Student Work IN PROGRESS

Name: Emily Meade
Ingersoll Middle School
Canton, IL

Using "Classical Invention" Questions

Emily answered the "Classical Invention" questions about her topic, circled ideas she intended to use, and summarized them to create a narrowed topic.

General Topic: Farmers During the Depression

- In what group or general category does your topic belong?
  agriculture; historical events
- How is your topic similar to or different from other topics in this category?
  agriculture: the farmers had really bad luck; not only was the economy bad, there was a series of huge storms lasting for years
  historical events: the Depression was totally unexpected; the Depression lasted a long time—almost ten years
- What causes are involved with this topic?
  stock market crash; drought
- What effects are involved in this topic?
  farmers migrated to the West; the government helped farmers; the Great Plains was nicknamed the Dust Bowl
- What came before this event?
  the 1920's, a time of prosperity
- What might come (or came) after this event?
  protection against dust storms

Narrowed Topic: The causes and effects of the Dust Bowl.

TIME SAVERS!

Writing Support Transparencies
Use the transparencies for Chapter 9 to teach these strategies.

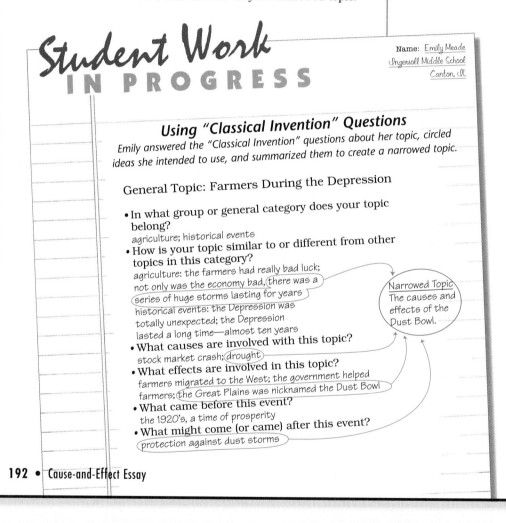

Considering Your Audience and Purpose

Appeal to Your Audience

As a writer, you need to think about your **audience**—the people who will read your writing. Unless you plan to send your essay to a specific audience (the school paper, for example), assume that your essay will be shared with your classmates. List two or three ideas for making your thoughts clear and interesting to them.

Define Your Purpose

Before drafting, consider your **purpose**—the goal of your writing. Ask yourself, "What do I want my readers to think or do when they finish reading my essay?" Jot down your answer to this question as a handy reminder while you write.

Gathering Details

Conduct Research

Unless you're already an expert on your topic, you will need to conduct research to gather the facts, examples, and other details you will need to thoroughly illustrate cause-and-effect relationships. Use the Internet or nonfiction sources, such as books and magazines from the library.

Using a K-W-L Chart A K-W-L chart is an excellent tool for planning and guiding your research. In one column, list what you already know about your topic. In a second column, list questions you would like to answer. Fill in a third column with what you learn as you conduct your research.

K-W-L CHART

What I Know	What I Want to Know	What I Learned
Air pollution is increasing.	How can it be reduced?	
Air pollution is dangerous.	What causes it besides cars & factories?	
Polluted air smells bad.	Which countries or cities are the worst?	
Cars & factories cause it.	How can we stop it?	
It hurts people and animals.	What does it do to people? To animals?	

Research Tip

Encyclopedias on CD-ROM make browsing and research especially easy. Many allow you to begin by identifying an area of interest, such as performing arts, science, hobbies, sports, or pets.

Step-by-Step Teaching Guide

Prewriting: Considering Your Audience and Purpose; Gathering Details

Teaching Resources: Writing Support Transparency 9-D; Writing Support Activity Book 9-1

1. The topic of a cause-and-effect essay can help define the audience. For instance, an essay about how factory emissions affect air quality would be appropriate for an audience of the ages 13 and above, but not for younger children.
2. When students are defining the purpose of their essays, have them imagine their audience sitting before them. This visual image may help students answer the question, "What do I want my readers to think or do as a result of my essay?"
3. Research is especially important in cause-and-effect essays, since they often cover historical, technical, or scientific topics.
4. Display the transparency and lead students through the K-W-L chart. Give students copies of the blank organizer. Have students complete the chart before they begin their research.

Real-World Connection

Ask students to imagine being a private or police detective. Have them discuss how using a K-W-L chart would help in the investigation of a crime.

Integrating Vocabulary Skills

Have students look up the meaning of the word *acronym.* (a word formed from the initial letters of words in a set phrase or series) Ask students to provide examples of acronyms, such as MADD (Mothers Against Drunk Driving). Challenge students to modify KWL to make it an acronym. (Possible answer: KnoWaLl)

Step-by-Step Teaching Guide

Drafting: Shaping Your Writing

1. Divide the class into small groups and ask group members to help each other select the best type of organization for their topics.
2. Ask volunteers to represent each of the three types of organization. Have these students put their cause-and-effect outlines on the board. Review them with the class.

Integrating Speaking Skills

Ask the students who wrote their cause-and-effect outlines on the board to present the information informally in front of the class. As an option, offer to interview each student in front of the class, rather than have the student present the information on his or her own.

Customize for *Less Advanced Learners*

The single cause/single effect outline will be most manageable. Check that they've chosen a topic that fits this format.

9.3 Drafting

Shaping Your Writing

Focus and Organize Your Ideas

Review your information, and circle the main causes and effects. Identify which description below best fits your topic. Then, organize your information accordingly. You may find it helpful to create an outline in which you list the main causes and effects with supporting details.

Many Causes/Single Effect or Single Cause/Many Effects If your topic has several causes of a single event, develop a paragraph to discuss each cause. Weave its contribution to the overall effect into the paragraph. For one cause with several effects, devote a paragraph to each effect.

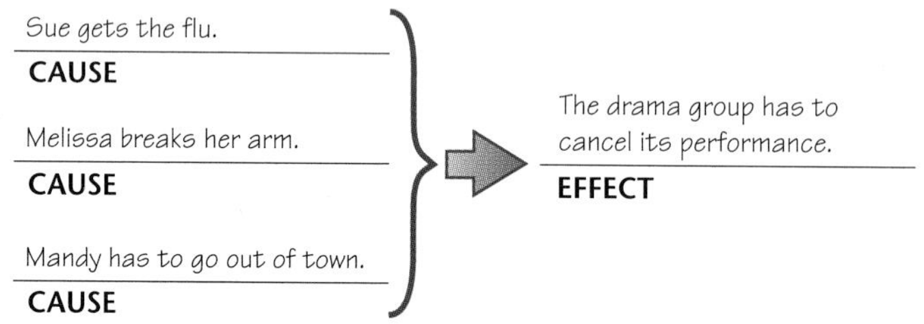

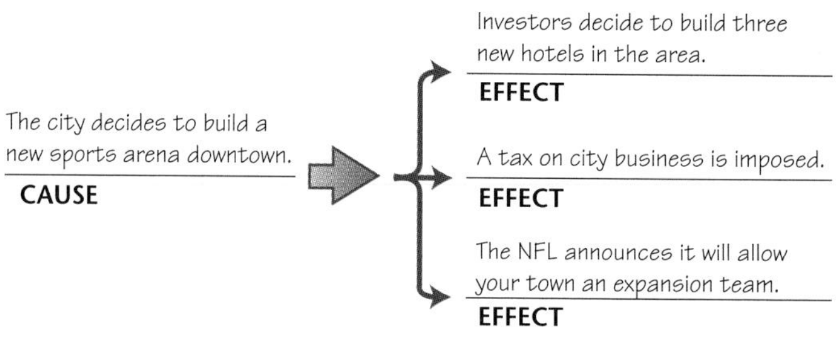

Chain of Causes and Effects If you are presenting a chain of causes and effects, present them in chronological order with transitions to show the connections.

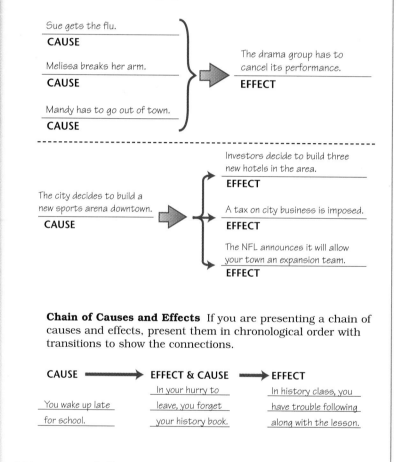

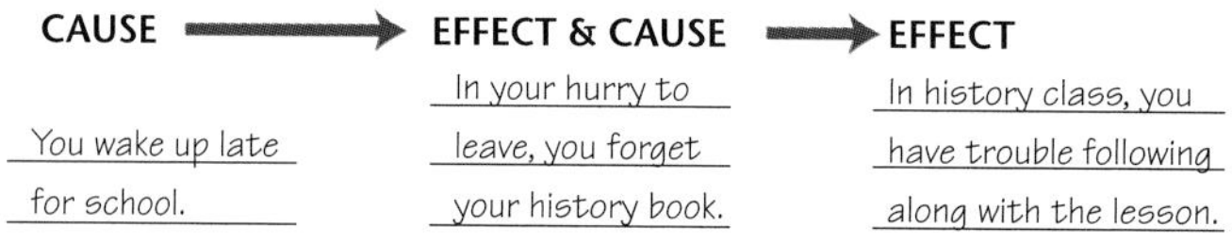

CAUSE
You wake up late for school.
EFFECT & CAUSE
In your hurry to leave, you forget your history book.
EFFECT
In history class, you have trouble following along with the lesson.

Learn More

To learn more about making an outline, see Chapter 31.

TIME AND RESOURCE MANAGER

Resources
Print: Writing Support Transparencies, 9-E
Technology: Writing and Grammar iText, Section 9.3

In-Depth Coverage	Accelerated Pace
• Go over pp. 194–195 in class. • Have students draft their essays in class.	• Have students review pp. 194–195 independently. • Assign students the task of creating cause-and-effect outlines for their topics. • Have students apply the elaboration strategies on p. 195 as they draft.

Providing Elaboration

Elaborate on Causal Connections

As you draft, add details that explain the connections between the causes and effects you are discussing. Ties between causes and effects include the following:

Natural Laws Some causes are linked to their effects by natural laws or principles.

EVENTS: Meteors burn up when they enter Earth's atmosphere.

LOGIC: The resistance of the atmosphere creates friction, which produces heat. *(Natural Law: Friction)*

Physical Processes Some cause-and-effect relationships take the form of a regular series of physical events.

EVENTS: Nitrogen-fixing bacteria help plants grow.

LOGIC: Plants need nitrogen to grow, but they can only use it in the form of nitrates. Bacteria produce the nitrates plants need. *(Process: Nitrogen Cycle)*

Motives and Habits Usually, the way people or groups of people behave is explained in terms of motives, habits, or social laws reflecting those motives and habits.

EVENTS: As skilled labor grew more scarce, wages went up.

LOGIC: Employers will pay more if they have trouble finding employees. *(Law: Supply and Demand)*

▲ Critical Viewing What natural phenomenon do you know of that might cause this effect? How might it cause this girl's hair to rise? **[Hypothesize]**

Student Work IN PROGRESS

Name: Emily Meade
Ingersoll Middle School
Canton, IL

Explaining the Logic

As she wrote her essay on the Dust Bowl, Emily explained the logic connecting two events: the destruction of grass and the looseness of the soil. She corrected errors in her draft later.

Plowing by farmers also killed much of the tall prairie grass that covered the Plains. Tall grass had an extremely complex root system, so it held the soil in place very well. With this natural protection gone, the soil was at further risk of being blown away.

By adding this sentence, Emily explains the natural process that links tall grass with the preservation of the soil.

Step-by-Step Teaching Guide

Drafting: Providing Elaboration

Teaching Resources: Writing Support Transparency 9-E

1. Review the types of causal connections that students can include in their essays.
2. Display the transparency. Ask students how Emily's changes improve her essay.
3. Have students apply this strategy as they draft their essays.

Customize for *More Advanced Learners*

Encourage students to choose a topic that fits the chain of causes and effects outline format. At the least, they should work with either the many causes/single effect or the single cause/many effects format.

Critical Viewing

Hypothesize Students may say static electricity; negatively charged particles cause the hair to rise.

ONGOING ASSESSMENT: Monitor and Reinforce

If students have difficulty elaborating on causal connections, have them try the following strategy.

Have students write their drafts and then read through them to identify the causes and effects in their writing. For each cause and effect, have students determine if they need to elaborate the causal connection.

TIME SAVERS!

Writing Support Transparencies
Use the transparencies for Chapter 9 to teach these strategies.

Step-by-Step Teaching Guide

Revising: Analyze Your Organization

1. Select a student's draft of the cause-and-effect essay and make a copy of one page. Display this page on an overhead projector.
2. Ask volunteers to circle all the causes they see on the page. Ask other students to underline all the effects.
3. Have the class analyze the page to see if:
   - all effects appear after their cause or causes.
   - the paragraph organization fits the type of cause-and-effect relationship featured in this essay.
   - the paragraphs match the original outline (have the student writer provide the outline).
4. Point out that the student writer who (bravely) provided the draft now has some direction for revising. Have the other students go through the same process with their drafts.

Customizing for *Logical/Mathematical Learners*

Encourage students to recopy their essay outlines onto graph paper before they follow the revision strategy above. The lines on the graph paper will enable students to create neat, orderly outlines that will help them locate main and subordinate points in their essays.

Critical Viewing

Interpret Students may say that it demonstrates the chain of cause and effect—by knocking over the first domino, a chain reaction is set in motion in which all the dominoes are knocked over.

9.4 Revising

Once you've finished your first draft, put your work aside for a day, if time allows. Then, review it carefully with a fresh eye.

Revising Your Overall Structure

Analyze Your Organization

Start your revision process by checking to see whether you have used a consistent organization that suits your topic. You might use the following strategy.

REVISION STRATEGY
Marking Main Causes and Effects

Follow these steps to check your organization.

1. Go through your entire draft, and circle each description of a main cause in one color and each description of a main effect in another. Write the letter *C* above causes and the letter *E* above effects.
2. Look at the order of the portions you have circled.
3. Make sure that all the effects appear *after* the correspon-ding cause(s). If not, you may need to reorganize sentences or paragraphs.
4. Check that you have used an order that fits the type of cause-and-effect relationship you're explaining. For help, review the discussion of the types of relationships on page 194.

▼ **Critical Viewing** Why does this picture make a good model for a sequence of causes and effects? **[Interpret]**

TIME AND RESOURCE MANAGER

Resources
Print: Writing Support Transparencies, 9-F–G
Technology: Writing and Grammar iText, Section 9.4

In-Depth Coverage	Accelerated Pace
• Go over pp. 196–200 in class. • Have the class complete the Grammar in Your Writing activity on p. 199. • Help students revise their essays.	• Have students read pp. 196–200 independently. • Have students revise their essays.

Revising Your Paragraphs

Use Topical Paragraphs

In a cause-and-effect essay, most of your body paragraphs should be topical paragraphs. **Topical paragraphs** develop a single main idea. Typically, a topical paragraph includes a sentence stating this main idea, called the **topic sentence.** The other sentences support or illustrate the topic sentence.

Review your draft to make sure each paragraph has a clear topic sentence. Check to see that each of the other sentences relates to the topic sentence. Eliminate or rewrite any that do not. Then, make sure you have illustrated the topic sentence with sufficient details, using the following strategy.

Learn More

For more on the different types of paragraphs, see Chapter 3.

REVISION STRATEGY
Adding Specific Illustrations

Use a highlighter to mark the topic sentence in each paragraph. Then, check off each sentence in the paragraph that illustrates the topic with facts, statistics, or descriptions to support each explanation. Review paragraphs with few or no checkmarks. Add appropriate illustrations.

Student Work IN PROGRESS

Name: Emily Meade
Ingersoll Middle School
Canton, IL

Adding Specific Illustrations

After coding her essay on the Dust Bowl, Emily realized that this paragraph needed more illustrations.

As a result, when high winds started to blow across the Plains, the dried-up topsoil did not stand a chance. It filled the air ~~as dust~~ in great, black choking clouds and covered farms, fields, and houses in huge drifts. The winds blew on and off for ten years. In 1935, one storm carried twice as much soil as was removed in digging the Panama Canal. Some claim that the wind came through so strongly that dust was blown all the way from Kansas to Albany, New York. In an average year, fifty storms would blow across the Plains, justifying the nickname of the Dust Bowl.

Emily added colorful descriptive language, an impressive fact, and a speculation to illustrate the topic of this paragraph—the effects of the winds on the topsoil of the region.

Step-by-Step Teaching Guide

Revising: Use Topical Paragraphs: Adding Specific Illustrations

Teaching Resources: Writing Support Transparency 9-F

1. Each body paragraph in a cause-and-effect essay should be a topical paragraph. Have students check this aspect of their drafts by underlining the topic sentence in each body paragraph.
2. Next, have students highlight the facts, statistics, quotations, or descriptions that illustrate the topic sentence in each paragraph.
3. Display the transparency. Point out that Emily added a comparison, a specific fact, and a speculation to further illustrate a topic sentence.
4. Have students revise their essays as needed to provide adequate illustration.

Revision Tip

As students are adding illustrations to their drafts, remind them that the new details must relate closely to the topic sentence in the paragraph. If students can't find relevant details, they should ask themselves if the paragraph is really necessary.

TIME SAVERS!

Writing Support Transparencies

Use the transparencies for Chapter 9 to teach these strategies.

Step-by-Step Teaching Guide

Revising: Clarify Time Relationships

Teaching Resources: Writing Support Transparency 9-G

1. Display the transparency. Point out how Emily reviewed the chronological order of events in her paragraph. She then checked and corrected verb tenses so the chronological order would also be clear to the reader.
2. Have students check their essays to make sure they have used the correct verb tenses to reflect the time frames of the events in their essays.

Customize for *Logical/Mathematical Learners*

As students review their drafts for correct use of verb tenses, have them number the events within a paragraph chronologically. For example, have students write a 1 by the event that occurred first, a 2 by the event that occurred next, and so on. The numbers will help students match verb tenses to the chronological order.

9.4

Revising Your Sentences

Clarify Time Relationships

After strengthening your paragraphs, be sure that you have used verb tenses correctly to indicate the time relationship among events.

REVISION STRATEGY

Circling Events to Analyze Order

Determine the time frame for the events in your paper—the past, the present, or the future. Then, review your paper, circling any events occurring before or after the group of events you're explaining. Also, circle continuing events or conditions, such as natural processes and general truths. Use the information on the next page to choose the correct verb tense to use in these cases.

Student Work IN PROGRESS

Name: Emily Meade
Ingersoll Middle School
Canton, IL

Clarifying Time of Events

Emily circled not only events that happened before other events she discussed but also continuing processes and general truths. She then checked and corrected the tenses that she used to describe these events and truths.

Plowing by farmers also killed much of the tall prairie grass that ^had^ once covered the Plains. Tall grass ~~had~~ ^has^ an extremely complex root system, so it held the soil in place very well. With this natural protection gone, the soil was at further risk of being blown away.

This condition came before and ended before a past event (the farmers plowing). It should be expressed in the past perfect "had covered."

The first part of this sentence expresses a general truth about grass, so Emily changed it to the present tense.

STANDARDIZED TEST PREPARATION WORKSHOP

Prepositions Standardized test questions may ask students to identify prepositions in sentences. Ask which of the underlined words in the following sentence is not a preposition.

We spend the Fourth <u>of</u> July <u>at</u> the Show of Lights <u>in</u> <u>our</u> city's downtown park.

A of
B at
C in
D our

Item **D** is the correct answer. *Our* is a pronoun.

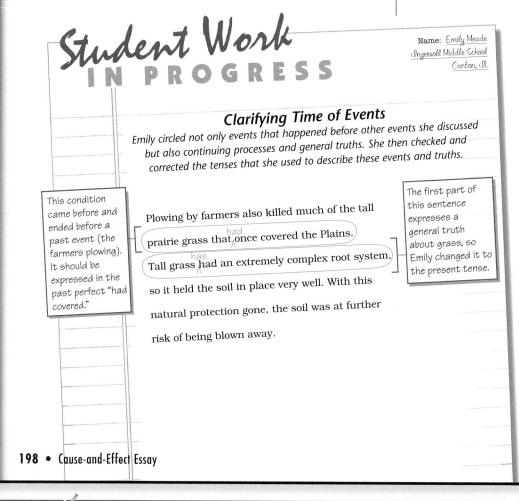

Grammar in Your Writing
Using Perfect Verb Tenses

Using correct verb tense is essential to showing the order of events in a cause-and-effect essay. **Verb tense** refers to changes in the form of a verb to show when the action the verb expresses occurred (or when the condition it expresses was the case).

The **perfect tenses** are used to indicate an action that occurs before another action. The perfect tenses are formed by adding the appropriate tense of *have* to the past participle of the verb:

Use the perfect tense in combination with other tenses to express the sequence of events, as shown below:

Perfect Tenses

Tense	Example	Past Participle +
Present perfect	"I have spoken."	Present form of *have*
Past perfect	"I had spoken."	Past form of *have*
Future perfect	"I will have spoken."	Future form of *have*

One Event Takes Place Before a Present Event = Present Perfect + Present
I have spoken to Sarah and Hunter about the meeting, and they plan to attend.

One Past Event Takes Place Before Another = Past Perfect + Past
I had spoken to Autumn and Greg about the meeting, but they were busy on Monday.

One Future Event Takes Place Before Another = Future Perfect + Present
I will have spoken to all the club members before they arrive to see what they think about our fund-raising ideas.

Find It in Your Reading Review "Why Is the Sea Blue?" by Denis Wallis on page 188. On a sheet of paper, list each verb that is used in a paragraph, and identify its tense.

Find It in Your Writing Review your draft, examining any verb in a different tense from the others. If the change in tense is not justified, make the tense consistent with the rest of your draft.

To learn more about verb tenses, see Chapter 22.

Step-by-Step Teaching Guide

Grammar in Your Writing: Using Perfect Verb Tenses

1. Divide the class into small groups. Assign each group a few paragraphs from "Why Is the Sea Blue?" Have the group members write a list of all the verbs that occur in their paragraphs.
2. While the students are writing the verbs, copy the verb tense chart onto the chalkboard.
3. When the students have completed their lists, ask them to check the chart on the board for any verb tenses that aren't represented in the paragraphs they reviewed. Have the group create a sentence for each missing verb tense.
4. Have members of one group take turns reading the verbs from their list to the class. Ask the members of the group to figure out the tense of each verb as it is read (refer students to the chart on the board). Have group members read the sentences they created and ask the rest of the class to identify the verb tenses.
5. Repeat step 4 with the other groups.

Find It in Your Reading

Students will have found all verbs from the Model From Literature.

Find It in Your Writing

Have students explain why they changed the verb tenses as they did.

Integrating Workplace Skills

Many careers require that individuals write daily reports that accurately show events that occur over time. Have students discuss how using correct verb tense is important in these jobs:

- night watchman
- intensive care nurse
- zoo nursery attendant
- factory supervisor

Step-by-Step Teaching Guide

Revising: Underlining Vague Verbs; Peer Review

1. Write the following sentences on the chalkboard:

   The soldiers ran onto the battlefield.

   The cannons were loud.

   Gun smoke filled the air.

   Ask students to suggest more vivid replacements for the verbs in the sentences. (Possible answers: *ran: dashed, charged; were loud: boomed, roared; filled: blackened, singed*)
2. Have students review their drafts, replacing vague verbs with more vivid verbs.
3. Have students practice the "say back" strategy in small groups.
4. Direct students to make final revisions on their cause-and-effect essays.

Critical Viewing

Apply Students may say that the storm is ferociously battering the trees.

9.4

Revising Your Word Choice

Replace Vague Verbs

In addition to presenting time relationships correctly, the verbs you use in a cause-and-effect essay should capture events as precisely as possible. Use the following strategy to strengthen your use of verbs.

▲ Critical Viewing
Use vivid verbs to describe the event pictured here.
[Apply]

REVISION STRATEGY
Underlining Vague Verbs

Read through your draft again. Underline vague verbs—ones that do not create vivid pictures of actions in a reader's mind. Then, go back and replace each verb you've underlined with one that more vividly captures the action. Look at this example:

DRAFT SENTENCE:	During the hurricane, the rain fell on houses throughout the village.
REVISED SENTENCE:	During the hurricane, the rain **pelted** the houses throughout the village.

Peer Review

Your classmates can help you put the finishing touches on your essay by identifying problems you may have missed. You can get their help using the strategy of "Say Back."

"Say Back"

Read your essay to a group of classmates while they listen. Then, read your essay a second time. Pause for about one minute. During the pause, your classmates should begin making quick notes of things that stood out for them in your essay. Ask reviewers to respond to the following questions:

1. What were the main causes?
2. What were the main effects?
3. Where can I add details to more clearly illustrate causes or effects?

What your classmates tell you about your main causes and effects should match with what you intended to say. If they don't mention an important cause or effect that your essay discusses, consider adding more information about the cause or effect, or even reorganizing your draft to make the connections between events clear.

ONGOING ASSESSMENT: Monitor and Reinforce

Some students may need to review the two main types of verbs.

Option 1 An action verb describes something that a person or object does. For example:

A kite *flies.*

The girl *skated.*

Sometimes the action is invisible. For example:

The student *thinks.*

I *imagine* the future.

Option 2 A state-of-being verb describes the state, or situation, of something. For example:

A kite *is* light.

The girl *was* a skater.

9.5 Editing and Proofreading

Proofread your essay for errors in spelling, punctuation, and grammar. Take an especially close look at your use of prepositions.

Focusing on Prepositions

Prepositions include words such as *after, before, in, on, of,* and *up*. Whenever possible, try to avoid ending sentences with a preposition. (If you find that revising a sentence to avoid having it end with a preposition makes it sound awkward, consult with your teacher.)

DRAFT SENTENCE: Which credit card are you paying **with**?
REVISED SENTENCE: **With** which credit card are you paying?

Grammar in Your Writing

Prepositions and Prepositional Phrases

A **preposition** is a word that relates the noun or pronoun following it to another word in a sentence. Prepositions indicate relations such as these:

SEQUENCE	LOCATION	DIRECTION	(OTHER)
after	in	around	about
before	near	down	for
during	under	up	of

A **prepositional phrase** consists of a preposition, its object, and any words modifying the object. The object of a preposition is the noun or pronoun following the preposition.

Example:
preposition object
under the kitchen **table**

preposition object
against the thick **wall**

Find It in Your Reading Find three prepositional phrases in "Why Is the Sea Blue?" by Denis Wallis on page 188. For each, identify the object.

Find It in Your Writing Find five prepositional phrases in your essay. Add modifiers where needed to make the objects vivid and specific.

To learn more about prepositional phrases, see Chapter 20.

Step-by-Step Teaching Guide

Editing and Proofreading: Prepositions and Prepositional Phrases

1. As a reminder for students, write the following list of prepositions on the board: *by, as, about, for, on, to, in, into, among, between, at, with, beside, behind, of, above, after, before, below, from off, out, under.*
2. Point out that prepositions are connecting words that show the relationship of a noun or pronoun to another word in the sentence.
3. Have students check their essays for proper construction in sentences that have prepositions.

Find It in Your Reading

Prepositional phrases in the essay include the following: *in the world, from light, without light, in the greenest grass, of the human eye, of light, through a prism, of colors, in a rainbow, in the sky, of raindrops, of light, in the spectrum, in our world, of colors, from light, into the daylight, of red, in some places, in others, in the water, towards the surface, from beneath the surface, of light, through chemicals, by rivers, in the water, from coastal rivers, in your eyes,* and *in the retina.*

Find It in Your Writing

Have students share examples from their essays with the class.

PRENTICE HALL
Everyday Spelling

If you have taught the spelling skills in *Prentice Hall Everyday Spelling*, Grade 8, Chapter 10, in conjunction with this *Writing and Grammar* chapter, review and assess students' mastery of the skills before concluding the chapter. Remind students to apply the spelling skills as they edit and proofread their cause-and-effect essays.

TIME AND RESOURCE MANAGER

Resources
Print: Scoring Rubrics on Transparency, Chapter 9; Writing Assessment: Scoring Rubric and Scoring Models for Cause-and-Effect Essay
Technology: Writing and Grammar iText, Sections 9.5–6

In-Depth Coverage	Accelerated Pace
• Cover pp. 201–204 in class. • Have students edit and proofread their essays in class. • Review the Rubric for Self-Assessment in class. • Have students present their final drafts.	• Assign pp. 201–204 for independent student review. • Have students edit and proofread their essays as homework. • Have students present their final drafts.

Step-by-Step Teaching Guide

Publishing and Presenting: Building Your Portfolio

1. Ask students who would like to publish their cause-and-effect essays on the Internet to identify possible Web sites.
2. Before students submit their essays to Web sites, have them print out examples of articles or other works from the sites. Ask students to evaluate how their essays fit the format and style of the Web site. Have students revise if necessary, then submit their essays.

ASSESS

Step-by-Step Teaching Guide

Assessment

Teaching Resources: Scoring Rubrics on Transparency, 9; Formal Assessment, Chapter 9

1. Display the Scoring Rubric transparency and review the criteria in class.
2. Before students proceed with self-assessment, you may wish to review the Final Draft of the Student Work in Progress on pages 203–204. Have students score the Final Draft in one or more of the rubric categories. For example, how would students score the essay in terms of audience and purpose?
3. In addition to student self-assessment, you may wish to use the following assessment options.
   - Score student essays yourself, using the rubric and scoring models from Writing Assessment.
   - Review the Standardized Test Preparation Workshop on pages 208–209 and have students respond to a writing prompt within a time limit.
   - Administer the Chapter 9 Test from Formal Assessment in Teaching Resources to assess students' grasp of concepts presented.

9.6 Publishing and Presenting

Building Your Portfolio

Consider the following suggestions for publishing and presenting your work:

1. **Post Your Work on the Internet** Search the Internet for Web sites related to your topic, and find out whether the site would be interested in posting your essay.
2. **Organize a Group Reading** Hold a group reading with your classmates in which you take turns reading your essays. Allow time for discussion.

Reflecting on Your Writing

Write a few notes on your experience writing a cause-and-effect essay. Begin by answering the following questions:

- What did you enjoy about analyzing the cause(s) and effect(s) of your topic? What did you learn?
- What was the biggest problem you encountered while writing your essay? How did you resolve it? What did you learn as a result?

Include a copy of these reflections, along with your cause-and-effect essay, in your portfolio.

Internet Tip

To see cause-and-effect essays scored with this rubric, go on-line: PHSchool.com Enter Web Code: eck-8001

Rubric for Self-Assessment

Evaluate your cause-and-effect essay using the following criteria:

	Score 4	Score 3	Score 2	Score 1
Audience and Purpose	Consistently targets an audience through word choice and details; clearly identifies purpose in introduction	Targets an audience through most word choice and details; identifies purpose in introduction	Misses a target audience by including a wide range of word choice and details; presents no clear purpose	Addresses no specific audience or purpose
Organization	Presents a clear, consistent organizational strategy to show cause and effect	Presents a clear organizational strategy with occasional inconsistencies to show cause and effect	Presents an inconsistent organizational strategy; creates illogical presentation of causes and effects	Demonstrates a lack of organizational strategy; creates a confusing presentation
Elaboration	Successfully links causes with effects; fully elaborates connections among ideas	Links causes with effects; elaborates connections among most ideas	Links some causes with some effects; elaborates connections among some ideas	Develops and elaborates no links between causes and effects
Use of Language	Chooses clear transitions to convey ideas; presents very few mechanical errors	Chooses transitions to convey ideas; presents few mechanical errors	Misses some opportunities for transitions to convey ideas; presents many mechanical errors	Demonstrates poor use of language; presents many mechanical errors

ONGOING ASSESSMENT: Assess Mastery

Use one of the following options to assess final drafts of students' cause-and-effect essays.

Self-Assessment Ask students to score their essay using the rubric provided. Then have students write a paragraph reflecting on the most valuable strategy they learned in completing this essay.

Teacher Assessment Use the rubric and the scoring models provided in Writing Assessment, Cause-and-Effect Essay, to score students' work.

9.7 Student Work IN PROGRESS

FINAL DRAFT

▲ Critical Viewing
What might have caused this scene? **[Hypothesize]**

The Dust Bowl

Emily Meade
Ingersoll Middle School
Canton, Illinois

The Dust Bowl is the name that was given to the Great Plains area during the 1930's. The name refers to the great drifts of soil that covered the region because of constant dust storms. These storms rained on an area about 1350 miles long and 600 miles wide, covering thirteen states. They lasted anywhere from one hour to three days. The main reason was a climate of high winds. Winds alone would not have caused the Dust Bowl, though. The dryness of the soil allowed the winds to blow the soil around easily. There were three contributing causes that led to the dried-up soil: the use of a new plow that was, perhaps, too efficient; poor land management by farmers; and a severe drought during much of the 1930's.

Emily's essay is clearly organized with an introduction, a body, and a conclusion.

CLOSE

Step-by-Step Teaching Guide

Teaching From the Final Draft

1. Read "The Dust Bowl" aloud to the class.
2. Ask students to analyze how well the essay included these features of an effective cause-and-effect essay:
   - a clear explanation of how one or more events or situations resulted in another event or situation
   - a thorough presentation of details that support the causes and effects in the essay
   - a clear and consistent organization
   - effective use of verb tenses to show the order of events
   - effective use of vivid verbs and precise prepositional phrases

Critical Viewing

Hypothesize Students may say that a dust storm might have caused this scene.

Customize for *Verbal/Linguistic Learners*

Have students take turns reading "The Dust Bowl" aloud to the class.

Customize for *ESL Students*

The historical events surrounding the dust bowl phenomenon may be unfamiliar to students. You may want to familiarize students with the history and geography of the Midwest to enhance their understanding of the essay.

Critical Viewing

Connect Students may say that by knowing the causes of storms, the farmer may have been able to avoid some of the terrible effects, such as drought.

9.7

First, the use of a new plow helped cause the dust storms because the plow dug deeper into the ground, exposing the ground to the sun. The soil dried out more quickly than before. It became light enough for the wind to carry off easily. Plowing by farmers also killed much of the tall prairie grass that had once covered the Plains. Tall grass has an extremely complex root system, so it held the soil in place very well. With this natural protection gone, the soil was at further risk of being blown away.

Notice that Emily is describing several causes of a single event. This paragraph focuses on the first cause.

Second, farmers did not manage their land wisely. They replaced the prairie grass with crops that had shallow root systems. The simple root systems allowed lots of dirt to break loose, and when the wind came, it was blown around. In addition, any beneficial prairie grass that remained after plowing was used to feed cattle.

Notice that Emily uses the transitions second *and* third *to introduce each new cause.*

Third, the weather played a big role in the dust storms. There was an irregular weather pattern in the 1930's. Beginning in 1931, a severe drought affected the Plains. This drought lasted about eight years.

As a result, when high winds started to blow across the Plains, the dried-up topsoil did not stand a chance. It filled the air in great, black choking clouds and covered farms, fields, and houses in huge drifts. The winds blew on and off for ten years. In 1935, one storm carried twice as much soil as was removed in digging the Panama Canal. Some claim that the wind came through so strongly that dust was blown all the way from Kansas to Albany, New York. In an average year, fifty storms would blow across the Plains, justifying the nickname of the Dust Bowl.

The phrase as a result *indicates that Emily is now describing the effects of the causes that she has laid out.*

When the drought started in the early 1930's, it was hard enough to get food and water, but when the dust storms began, it was even harder. People had to eat through handkerchiefs and still got a mouthful of dust. The storms caused thousands of families in the Dust Bowl to move away.

In 1936, the restoration of the Dust Bowl area was underway. The U.S. government planted over 18,500 miles of trees to break the wind in that region. The government also sent out people to teach the farmers to conserve and protect the soil. They encouraged farmers to plant tall grasses and to cut back on cattle grazing. In this way, they protected themselves against a few of the major causes of the dust storms that swept through the Dust Bowl region.

▼ **Critical Viewing** How might a better knowledge of causes and effects have helped this Dust Bowl farmer? **[Connect]**

Connected Assignment

Documentary Video Script

Cause-and-effect explanations make the news every day in news reports and documentaries. These shows analyze how one event or situation leads to another. A **documentary video script** sets down the words that are spoken on a documentary. These words include recorded interviews, as well as narration. A video script also includes directions to the camera operators, sound and lighting engineers, and the editor who will put the video together.

Write a documentary video script. Use the suggestions that follow to guide you.

▲ Critical Viewing What narration and sounds might a documentary use with the footage this cameraman is gathering? **[Speculate]**

Prewriting Watch a television newsmagazine show to see how documentary segments are organized. Note how interviews, scenes of events or places, and the reporter's explanations are woven together.

Choose a Topic After taking notes on the structure of documentaries, choose an event or issue that interests you. For instance, you might choose a recent event in your community, such as the opening of a new store.

Gather Details Next, list cause-and-effect questions about your topic. Then, do research in a variety of sources to answer your questions. If possible, conduct interviews with experts, participants, and eyewitnesses. Tape the interviews, using a video recorder if one is available.

Drafting Before you begin writing, organize the facts you have gathered, using an organizer like the one shown. As you draft, follow your organizer. Present the narration of the documentary, including interviews and commentary, indicating in each case who is speaking. For each scene, give directions for camera movements and angles and for sound effects and music.

Title of Documentary: <u>*Opening of Hopper's General Store*</u>

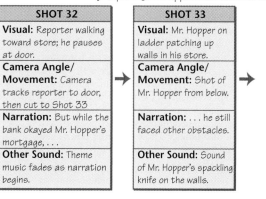

SHOT 32		SHOT 33	
Visual: *Reporter walking toward store; he pauses at door.*		**Visual:** *Mr. Hopper on ladder patching up walls in his store.*	
Camera Angle/ Movement: *Camera tracks reporter to door, then cut to Shot 33*	→	**Camera Angle/ Movement:** *Shot of Mr. Hopper from below.*	→
Narration: *But while the bank okayed Mr. Hopper's mortgage, . . .*		**Narration:** *. . . he still faced other obstacles.*	
Other Sound: *Theme music fades as narration begins.*		**Other Sound:** *Sound of Mr. Hopper's spackling knife on the walls.*	

Revising and Editing Read your script aloud. Mark places where the order of ideas or images grows confused. Add transitions or rearrange elements to improve the flow.

Publishing and Presenting If you have access to video equipment, produce your segment and show it to the class.

▶ Lesson Objectives

1. To write a documentary video script appropriate to audience and purpose.
2. To use prewriting strategies to choose and narrow a topic.
3. To gather and organize details.
4. To draft, revise, edit, and produce a documentary video.

Step-by-Step Teaching Guide

Documentary Video Script

Teaching Resources: Writing Support Transparencies 9-H; Writing Support Activity Book 9-2

1. Ask students to explain what a documentary film is. How does it differ from other kinds of films? Make sure all students understand that a documentary is nonfiction.
2. Point out that films discussing historical events are documentaries. Challenge students to choose interesting topics from history, such as the construction of the Panama Canal, the fall of the Berlin Wall, or the bombing of Pearl Harbor. You may want to allow students to work with partners, depending on the amount of research required and the time available.
3. Display the transparency to show students how they can organize the facts they gather. Give students copies of the blank organizer for them to complete before they start writing their drafts.
4. Remind students that most documentary films do not just present information, they interpret it. The filmmaker usually has an idea about the topic, and writes the script in such a way that the film will support this interpretation. Tell students that they must support their opinions and analyses with facts.

Critical Viewing

Speculate Students may mention a description of who is marching in the parade and sounds of the cheering crowds.

Lesson Objectives

1. To write a cause-and-effect essay.
2. To research and analyze influences on a dancer or composer.

Step-by-Step Teaching Guide

Presenting Information Visually

1. Choose one of the Spotlight elements for class discussion, or have students work individually or in groups on the element of their choice. Give students the initiative to find the necessary book, tapes, or recordings.
2. Tell students that the Parthenon sculptures now housed in the British Museum were a major inspiration for Isadora Duncan's choreography. Encourage students to locate photographs of the Parthenon friezes and compare and contrast the poses and costumes of the figures with the illustration of Duncan on this page.
3. In her turn, Isadora Duncan influenced others. One was Martha Graham, who saw Duncan dance at the end of her career. Young dancer Graham was greatly impressed and resolved to follow in Duncan's footsteps. By the time of her own death, Martha Graham had done more than any other person to revolutionize theatrical dance in America.
4. Tell students that Beethoven influenced every composer who came after him, particularly those who wrote symphonies. Beethoven revolutionized the symphony as a form. He was the first to add a chorus to a symphony, and he expanded the number and types of instruments used in the orchestra. Throughout the nineteenth and well into the twentieth century, most composers regarded Beethoven as the greatest composer who ever lived.

Spotlight on the Humanities

Presenting Information Visually

Focus on Dance: Isadora Duncan

One important cause of the success of modern dance was dancer Isadora Duncan (1878–1927). She was the first American dancer to develop a concept of natural breathing while dancing, as well as the first to compare the art of dance to other arts. Her implementation of simple settings and costumes—as opposed to lofty scenery and elaborate dress—revolutionized dance in America and abroad. She established a lasting reputation in Europe as well as in the United States.

Music Connection One of Duncan's greatest ballets was constructed around Ludwig van Beethoven's Ninth Symphony. A German composer, Beethoven (1770–1827) took the musical precision of the eighteenth century and added to it the romantic yearnings and furies of the nineteenth century. Beethoven wrote a total of nine symphonies in his lifetime. In the Ninth Symphony (1824), his most famous, a chorus sings the words to "The Ode to Joy," a poem by Friedrich Schiller. Beethoven also wrote concertos, chamber music, and sonatas.

▼▲ Critical Viewing Explain how notations like those below can "cause" movements like Duncan's, above. **[Analyze]**

Theater Connection In 1905, Isadora Duncan became friends with one of the theater's great actresses, Eleonora Duse (1859–1924). Duse took Duncan to her homeland of Italy to assist in the production of a Henrik Ibsen drama. There, Duncan danced in the hills of Rome.

Duse's portrayal of Ibsen's heroines was highly regarded. At age 14, she had her first success on the stage playing Juliet in Shakespeare's *Romeo and Juliet.* Years later, in 1895, she appeared on the Paris stage with another of the theater's foremost actresses, Sarah Bernhardt. Most noted for her simplicity in acting and lack of pretentiousness, Duse remains one of the great actresses of world theater.

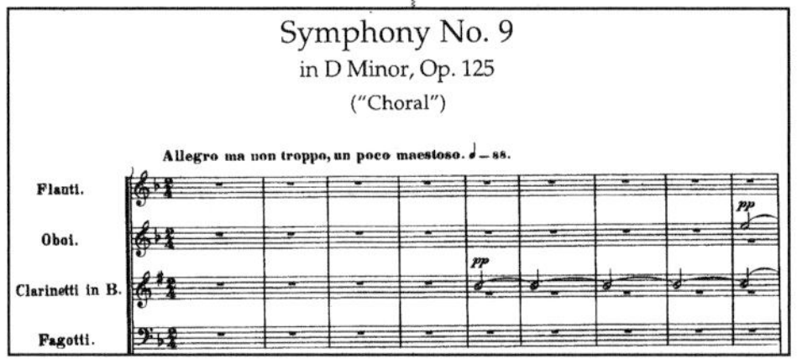

Cause-and-Effect Writing Activity: "Family Tree" for an Artist

Write a cause-and-effect essay tracing the influences on a dancer or a composer. Include other artists who influenced your subject, as well as trends and events that shaped his or her vision. Then, create a "family-tree"–style chart, including graphics and explanations, mapping these influences.

Viewing and Representing

Activity Students will need to do some research for this activity. *Grove's Dictionary of Music and Musicians*, a multivolume encyclopedia that covers the history of music, would be an excellent place for them to start. Encourage students to research figures from jazz, musical theater, or any other area that interests them.

Critical Viewing

Analyze Have students who read music explain the notations on the score: tempo markings, key signature, clefs, dynamic markings, and names of the instruments. Students should see that the long, sustained, soft notes on horn and clarinet might inspire the dancer to move slowly.

Media and Technology Skills

Analyzing Media Images

Activity: Evaluating Effective Photographs

A photograph records an actual event or scene. It also makes a statement about the person, place, or event it depicts. Learn about the elements photographers use to create such statements.

Think About It An effective photograph makes a strong statement, using these key elements:

- **a central point of interest—**The central point of interest is the actions, objects, or people that a photograph focuses on. In this photograph by French photographer Henri Cartier-Bresson (1908–), the person carrying a tray is an important focus. The child in light clothes, half-hidden by the railing and contrasting with the black-clad figures, adds a kind of "secret" point of interest.
- **composition—**Composition involves the placement of objects and the use of space and of light and dark. For instance, the photograph shown is divided into several spaces by the lamp and the three different stretches of fencing. The fences lead the eye deeper into the picture. Their strong black lines contrast with the light textured walkways and the rounded forms of the people. Another "line" of interest runs from the figure with the tray through the boy at the lamp to the doorway of the building on the right.
- **emotional impact—**The complex geometrical composition and the quiet activity of the scene create a sense of calm. Yet the tilt of the left side of the photograph and the mysterious figure looking through the railing seem to question this calm. The figure behind the railing seems to challenge its strong lines, since he can "see through it."
- **choice of subject—**The photographer has chosen a street scene as his subject. His choice of subject shows the beauties and small mysteries to be found even in ordinary daily life.

Evaluate It Choose two photographs in a weekly newsmagazine. Write a paragraph for each image in which you explain why it is or is not effective, using the categories listed above.

Types of Photographs
- **Documentary—**records an event
- **Commercial—**features posed subjects or objects used to sell products
- **Abstract—**focuses on form and pattern

▼ Critical Viewing What makes this picture different from a typical newspaper photograph? **[Distinguish]**

Critical Viewing

Distinguish Possible answers: The photograph does not show an important event. It does not show celebrities or important people. Little action is taking place.

▶ Lesson Objectives

1. To interpret and evaluate photographs.
2. To explain what makes a photograph effective.

Step-by-Step Teaching Guide

Analyzing Media Images

1. Discuss the differences between paintings and photographs. Use the photograph on the page to demonstrate that, just like a painter, a photographer must compose design elements within a frame. A photograph consists of masses of light and dark, lines and angles, and the illusion of three dimensions. Photographers consider all of these elements before they take a picture.
2. Go through the bulleted list of elements on the page. Ask questions like *Where is this photograph's central point of interest? Why do you think so? What is the emotional impact of the photograph? Which elements in the picture cause this impact?*
3. Point out that although a photograph is a record of what is actually present, it is still composed by the photographer. The photographer decides on the angle, the point of view, and the central focus of the photograph. Therefore, the photographer interprets the scene; he or she does not simply record it.
4. Explain that Cartier-Bresson was not a newspaper photographer, but an artistic photographer. The purpose of his photographs was to create works of art, not to provide images to illustrate a newspaper article. Students should begin the writing activity with this difference in mind. If you wish, you may allow them to evaluate artistic photographs such as those of Ansel Adams or Dorothea Lange instead of contemporary magazine photographs.

Lesson Objectives

1. To write a cause-and-effect essay.
2. To draft, revise, and edit a cause-and-effect essay.
3. To use correct grammar, spelling, and mechanics.

Step-by-Step Teaching Guide

Using Cause-and-Effect Writing in Response to Writing Prompts

Teaching Resources: Standardized Test Preparation Workbook, pp. 17–18

1. Review the terms *cause* and *effect.* Remind students that effects have multiple causes and causes have multiple effects. Students should also remember that a chain of events links these causes and effects.
2. Have a volunteer read the writing prompt aloud. Write the phrase *explain the causes* on the chalkboard. Point out that this is the clue that tells students how to organize their essays.
3. Remind students to stick to answering the question asked in the prompt. They should write about the reasons for the different colors of the sea.

Standardized Test Preparation Workshop

Using Cause-and-Effect Writing in Response to Writing Prompts

Some writing prompts on standardized tests measure your ability to show the relationships between causes and their effects. The following are the criteria on which your writing will be evaluated:

- Did you respond directly to the prompt?
- Have you made your writing thoughtful and interesting?
- Have you organized ideas so they are clear and easy to follow?
- Did you develop your ideas thoroughly by using appropriate details and precise language?
- Did you stay focused on your purpose for writing, so that each sentence contributes to your composition as a whole?
- Did you communicate effectively by using correct spelling, capitalization, punctuation, grammar, usage, and sentence structure?

Following is an example of one type of writing prompt you might find on a standardized test. Use the suggestions on the following page to help you respond.

When writing for a timed test, plan to devote a specified amount of time to prewriting, drafting, revising, and proofreading. The clocks next to each stage show a suggested percentage of time to devote to each stage.

Test Tip

When writing about a short story, be careful not to retell the story. Instead, follow key words in the prompt, such as *compare* or *explain.* These words show what you must accomplish in your answer.

Sample Writing Situation

Read "Why Is the Sea Blue?" on page 188. Then, respond to the following prompt.

> The sea may be any one of a number of different shades of blue, or even a different color entirely. Using details from "Why Is the Sea Blue?", explain the causes of the different colors of the sea.

TEST-TAKING TIP

Go over the Test Tip on the page. Ask students why they should not retell or summarize the text of "Why Is the Sea Blue?" Emphasize that students must always read a writing prompt carefully and be sure they answer only the question that is being asked. For practice, you might give students a few sample writing prompts. Have students paraphrase the questions being asked and describe the information their answers should include.

Prewriting

Allow about one fourth of your time for prewriting.

Use a Cause-and-Effect Organizer To gather details for your response, use a cause-and-effect organizer. See page 194 for examples of how to visually represent several causes for a single event or condition. Use one organizer for each color you explain.

Keep a Consistent and Clear Purpose As you gather details, make sure you include only those details that directly relate to the prompt. Go through your organizer and eliminate any irrelevant details.

Drafting

Allow about half of your time for drafting.

Organize Details Organize the details you will use in your response. Develop an outline listing each effect you discuss in order of importance. For instance, the most general effect you might discuss is the fact that objects have color. Mention this effect first. Under each main effect, list causes in order of importance or in order of sequence.

Elaborate Follow your outline as you draft. Since your cause-and-effect essay will discuss many effects, start by devoting a paragraph to each effect, or each group of similar effects. Elaborate on your ideas by providing specific illustrations from "Why Is the Sea Blue?"

Revising, Editing, and Proofreading

Allow about one fourth of your time for revising, editing, and proofreading.

Connect Ideas Look for places in your paper where the connections between causes and effects are not clear. Then, use transitional words, such as *as a result* or *consequently*, to show relationships between causes and effects.

Explain the Logic Check for places where you have linked a cause and effect without explaining why the cause leads to that effect. Add any details available to explain the connection.

Make Corrections Correct any errors in spelling, grammar, and punctuation. Draw a single line through text you are deleting. Use a caret (^) to indicate places where you are adding words.

Customize for *Less Advanced Students*

If students have difficulty identifying causes and effects, give them extra practice. Find five articles or short stories in which cause-and-effect is a central element of the structure. Have students read one item each night and write a paragraph analyzing the writer's use of cause and effect. Go over students' paragraphs, or assign them student tutors from among the best writers in the class. By the end of the week, students should benefit from the extra practice.

Chapter 10

Time and Resource Manager

In-Depth Lesson Plan

	LESSON FOCUS	PRINT AND MEDIA RESOURCES
DAY 1	**Introduction to How-to Essays** Students learn key elements of a how-to essay and analyze the Model From Literature (pp. 210–213).	***Writers at Work* Videotape,** Exposition ***Writing and Grammar iText* (Interactive Text),** Ch.10, Introduction
DAY 2	**Prewriting** Students choose and narrow a topic, consider their audience and purpose, and gather information (pp. 214–217).	**Teaching Resources** *Writing Support Transparencies,* 10-A–B ***Writing and Grammar iText* (Interactive Text),** Section 10.2
DAY 3	**Drafting** Students organize their ideas and write their first drafts (pp. 218–219).	**Teaching Resources** *Writing Support Transparencies,* 10-C ***Writing and Grammar iText* (Interactive Text),** Section 10.3
DAY 4	**Revising** Students revise their drafts in terms of overall structure, paragraphs, sentences, and word choice (pp. 220–224).	**Teaching Resources** *Writing Support Transparencies,* 10-D–E ***Writing and Grammar iText* (Interactive Text),** Section 10.4
DAY 5	**Editing and Proofreading; Publishing and Presenting** Students check their work for accuracy and correctness and present their final drafts (pp. 225–226).	**Teaching Resources** *Scoring Rubrics on Transparency,* Ch. 10; *Formal Assessment,* Ch. 10 ***Writing and Grammar iText* (Interactive Text),** Sections 10.5–6

Accelerated Lesson Plan

	LESSON FOCUS	PRINT AND MEDIA RESOURCES
DAY 1	**Introduction Through Drafting** Students review the characteristics of a how-to essay, select topics, and write drafts (pp. 210–219).	**Teaching Resources** *Writing Support Transparencies,* 10-A–C ***Writing and Grammar iText* (Interactive Text),** Ch. 10, Introduction through Section 10.3
DAY 2	**Revising Through Presenting** Students work individually or with peers to revise, edit, and proofread their work for presentation (pp. 220–226).	**Teaching Resources** *Writing Support Transparencies,* 10-D–E; *Scoring Rubrics on Transparency,* Ch. 10; *Formal Assessment,* Ch. 10 ***Writing and Grammar iText* (Interactive Text),** Sections 10.4–6

Options for Adapting Lesson Plans

HOMEWORK

Have students complete any stage of the lesson for homework.

SPELLING

To teach spelling skills in conjunction with writing skills, work through *Prentice Hall Everyday Spelling,* Grade 8, Chapter 11, as you cover this *Writing and Grammar* chapter. At the Editing and Proofreading stage, remind students to apply the spelling skills to their how-to essays.

FEATURES

Extend coverage with Connected Assignment (p. 229), Spotlight on the Humanities (p. 230), Media and Technology Skills (p. 231), and Standardized Test Preparation Workshop (p. 232).

TECHNOLOGY

Students can complete any stage of the lesson on the computer, using *Writing and Grammar iText* or a word-processing program. Have them print out their completed work.

INTEGRATED SKILLS COVERAGE

Integrating Grammar
Adverb Clauses and Phrases, SE p. 222
Commas and Semicolons in Series, SE p. 225

Reading/Writing Connection
Reading Strategy, SE p. 212
Writing Application, SE p. 213

Viewing and Representing
Critical Viewing, SE pp. 210, 212, 213, 217, 221, 224, 227, 229, 230

Speaking and Listening
Considering Audience, ATE p. 216

Real-World Connection
Adverb Clauses and Phrases in Journalism, ATE p. 222

ASSESSMENT SUPPORT

Standardized Test Preparation Workshop SE pp. 232–233, ATE p. 223
Standardized Test Preparation Workbook, pp. 19–20
Scoring Rubrics on Transparency, Ch. 10
Formal Assessment, Ch. 10
Writing Assessment and Portfolio Management

MEETING INDIVIDUAL NEEDS

Less Advanced Students ATE pp. 220, 233. See also Ongoing Assessments ATE pp. 215, 219, 222.
ESL Students ATE pp. 214, 223
More Advanced Students ATE pp. 219, 233
Gifted/Talented Students ATE p. 233
Visual/Spatial Learners ATE pp. 217, 218
Verbal/Linguistic Learners ATE p. 218
Bodily/Kinesthetic Learners ATE p. 217
Logical/Mathematical Learners ATE p. 231

BLOCK SCHEDULING

Pacing Suggestions
For 90-minute Blocks
- Have students complete the Prewriting and Drafting stages in a single period.
- Focus one class period on Revising and Editing and Publishing and Presenting. Allow at least 30 minutes for peer revision.

Resources for Varying Instruction
- ***Writing and Grammar iText* (Interactive Text)** A 90-minute block provides an ideal opportunity for students to work on computer.
- ***Writers at Work* Videotape** Show the Exposition: Giving Information segment in class.

Professional Development Support
- ***How to Manage Instruction in the Block*** This teaching resource provides management and activity suggestions.

MEDIA AND TECHNOLOGY

For the Student
- ***Writing and Grammar iText* (Interactive Text),** Ch. 10

For the Teacher
- ***Writers at Work* Videotape,** Exposition: Giving Information
- ***Resource Pro* CD-ROM**

WRITING AND GRAMMAR ON-LINE

iText Interactive Text (On-line or on CD-ROM)
- Easily navigable instruction with interactive Revision Checkers
- Full use of e-rater™, the essay-scoring system (on-line only)

Companion Web Site PHSchool.com
- Scoring rubrics with models (use Web Code eck-8001)

See the Go On-line! feature, SE p. iii.

LITERATURE CONNECTIONS

Related selections from *Prentice Hall Literature: Timeless Voices, Timeless Themes,* Silver:

Professional Model "The Adventure of the Speckled Band," Sir Arthur Conan Doyle, SE p. 213

Topic Bank Option "Baseball," Lionel G. García, SE p. 215

CHAPTER 10
EXPOSITION: HOW-TO ESSAY

Lesson Objectives

1. To write to inform, such as to explain.
2. To select and use voice and style appropriate to the audience and purpose.
3. To punctuate correctly to clarify and enhance meaning.
4. To generate ideas and plans for writing by using prewriting strategies.
5. To revise drafts for coherence, progression, and logical support of ideas.
6. To edit drafts for specific errors in grammar, spelling, and punctuation.
7. To analyze published examples as models for writing.

Critical Viewing

Speculate Students may mention that the first step includes checking the kite's structural integrity and its parts, the amount of available wind and space to fly it, and so on.

Chapter 10 Exposition
How-to Essay

▲ **Critical Viewing** What do you think was the first step in getting this kite off the ground? Where might you find more information on the subject? **[Speculate]**

How-to Essays in Everyday Life

If you purchase a new computer or CD player, you probably use the how-to instructions in the manual to help you set up your new equipment. Similarly, you might look carefully at the washing instructions on the label of a new outfit you just bought.

How-to instructions are one of the most important types of writing that you encounter in your daily life. They help make it easier to use a wide range of items—from foods to power tools to recreational items such as kites and musical instruments. Learn how to write your own how-to, and share your knowledge with others.

TIME AND RESOURCE MANAGER

Resources:
Technology: Writers at Work Videotape; Writing and Grammar iText, Ch. 10

In-Depth Coverage	Accelerated Pace
• Cover pp. 210–211 in class. • Show the Exposition: Giving Information section of the Writers at Work Videotape. • Discuss different types of how-to essays. • Read the Model From Literature (pp. 212–213) with students.	• Assign pp. 210–213 for independent student review. • Discuss definitions and types of how-to essays.

What Is a How-to Essay?

Exposition is writing that informs or explains. A **how-to essay** is a short, focused piece of expository writing that explains how to do or make something. The writer breaks the process down into a series of logical steps and explains them in the order in which the reader should do them. The key features of an effective how-to essay include

- a focused topic that can be fully explained in the length of an essay.
- clear explanations of any terms or materials that may be unfamiliar to readers.
- a series of logical steps explained in chronological, or time, order.
- charts, illustrations, and diagrams as necessary to make complicated procedures understandable.

To learn the criteria on which your essay may be assessed, see the Rubric for Self-Assessment on page 226.

Writers in ACTION

As a television news correspondent, Gary Matsumoto uses expository writing techniques to research, write, and revise the stories that he presents on camera. His writing must be clear and to the point, so he must select only essential facts:

"The only way to make intelligent choices about what facts to include is to think and ask yourself questions. What is important? And why? You can't include every single fact."

Types of How-to Essays

Following are some of the types of how-to essays you might write:

- How to do something ("How to Fly a Kite")
- How to make something ("How to Make a Kite")
- How to improve a skill ("How to Steer and Maneuver a Kite")
- How to achieve a desired effect ("How to 'Paint the Sky' With Kites")

PREVIEW Student Work IN PROGRESS

Katherine Ann Roshani Stewart, a student at Villa Duchesne School in St. Louis, Missouri, wrote an essay explaining how to groom a sheepdog. In this chapter, you will see the strategies she used to choose a topic, to gather details, to elaborate, and to revise her overall structure and word choice. At the end of the chapter, you can read the final draft of Katherine's how-to essay.

PREPARE and ENGAGE

Interest GRABBER Write the following steps on the chalkboard. Tell students that they need to arrange these steps in the proper order to explain to a Martian commander how Earthlings brush their teeth.

a. Rinse toothbrush
b. Remove toothbrush from holder
c. Wet toothbrush
d. Rinse mouth
e. Brush teeth
f. Put toothpaste on toothbrush
g. Put toothbrush in holder

(b, c, f, e, d, a, g)

Activate Prior Knowledge

Ask students to explain how to do something: play their favorite video game, get from home to a friend's house, do a dance. Have them discuss how they determined what information to provide.

More About the Writer

Gary Matsumoto has been a foreign correspondent with NBC Television News since July 1990. He played an important role in NBC's coverage of the Gulf War, reporting from Iraq, and throughout the Middle East. Matsumoto began at NBC as a radio correspondent in 1984.

TEACH

Reading\Writing Connection

Reading: Follow Steps in a Sequence

Keeping things in the correct order is always helpful, but in how-to essays it is crucial. Whether baking a cake or programming a VCR, doing things out of order can result in failure. In a how-to essay, the use of transition words provides cues for the reader as to the sequence of steps.

Teaching From the Model

You can use this Model From Literature to show students what a formal how-to essay looks like. Clear directions can be given in an expository structure that both explains materials needed and steps for assembly.

Step-by-Step Teaching Guide

Engage Students Through Literature

1. Have volunteers read aloud the essay.
2. Use the margin notes to guide the reading.
3. Point out the clear list of materials and the numbered steps. Tell students that steps can also be explained in paragraph format using transition words such as *next, then, after.*
4. Ask students if they think that this is a successful how-to essay. Do students think they could make a shadow puppet following the instructions in the essay?

Critical Viewing

Infer Students may mention a marker, scissors, paper, and cardboard.

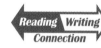

10.1 Model From Literature

David Currell has been making puppets since he was fourteen. He gave his first public performance at age sixteen. In this how-to essay, he explains how to make a shadow puppet, a type of paper cutout figure.

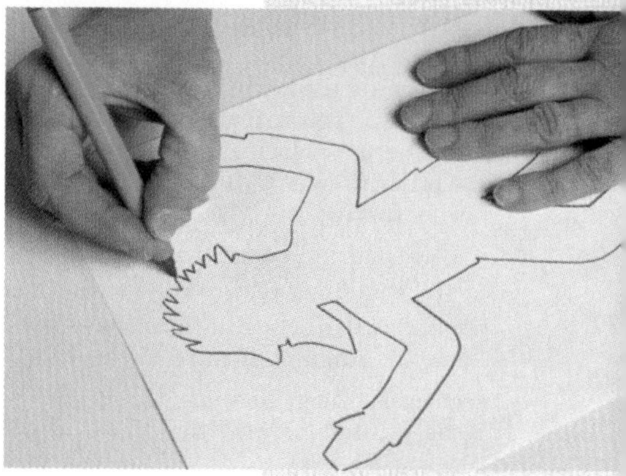

▼▲ **Critical Viewing** Judging from these two photos, what are four items you would need to make a shadow puppet? **[Infer]**

Reading Writing Connection

Reading Strategy: Follow Steps in a Sequence As you read a how-to essay like this one, pay close attention to transitional words, such as *next* and *then*, and numbers assigned to steps to indicate time sequence.

A Simple Shadow Puppet

David Currell

Shadow puppets are normally flat, cutout figures held by a rod or wire and illuminated against a translucent screen, hence their name. Traditionally made of parchment or hide, now they are usually made from cardboard.

The introduction gives an overview of shadow puppets—what they are and how they are used.

For a simple silhouette, black cardboard is ideal, but not essential. Any fairly strong board, such as that from a cereal box, will make a good puppet. Think about the size of your puppets in relation to the size of the screen, leaving space for all planned actions.

MATERIALS
- Black cardboard
- Scissors
- Craft glue
- Glue brush
- 12-inch length of 3/8-inch diameter softwood dowel
- Thumbtack

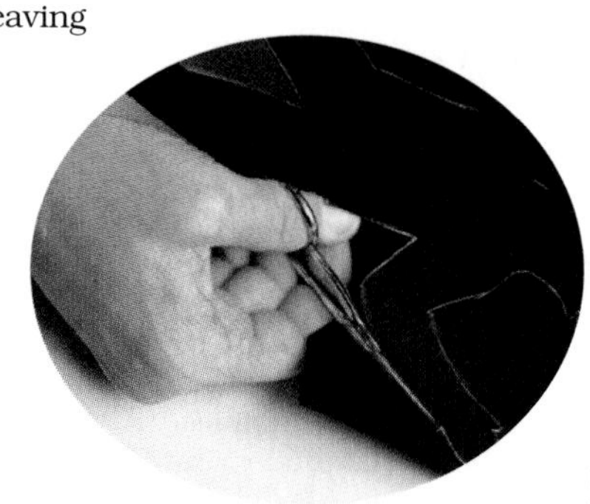

Numbered steps and illustrations, presented in chronological order, detail each step of the process of creating a shadow puppet.

ONGOING ASSESSMENT: Diagnose

Use one of the following options to diagnose students' current level of proficiency in expository how-to writing.

Option 1 Ask each student to select the strongest example of his or her how-to writing from last year. Hold conferences to review each student's sample. Use the conferences to determine which students will need extra support in developing a how-to essay.

Option 2 Ask students to write a four-step sequence—how to get from the classroom to the cafeteria, for instance. If they have trouble separating the steps and relating them in the proper sequence, you will need to devote more time to ordering and sequence.

1. Transfer the design from paper onto cardboard. For a screen that is 28 inches high, make puppets up to 12 inches high.
2. Cut out the shape with sharp scissors for a clean outline. If you wish, you can stiffen the cardboard by coating it with white glue.
3. Hold the puppet gently between your thumb and index finger, adjusting the position to find the point of balance. Attach the dowel control rod slightly above this point, so that there is just a little more weight below the control rod than above. This is to make sure that the puppet remains naturally upright, rather than tending to somersault as you operate it.
4. Secure the rod to the puppet with the thumbtack, just above the point of balance. You will need to tap the thumbtack in securely to make sure that the puppet turns with the rod and does not swing uncontrolled. With this type of control rod, the puppet cannot turn around, but it is very easy to make a duplicate facing in the opposite direction.

The author explains the control rod so readers understand the reason for this step.

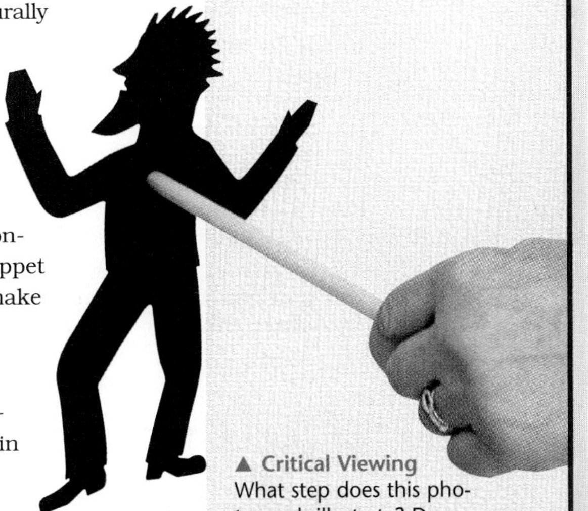

▲ **Critical Viewing** What step does this photograph illustrate? Does it make the step easier to follow? **[Evaluate]**

DECORATION

You can add to the design of your shadow puppets by cutting out decorative or key shapes within the outline using a sharp craft knife or small, pointed scissors or by punching holes. You will find it helpful to study Javanese *wayang kulit* shadow puppets and Chinese figures, as they use cutout decoration to superb effect. Remember that these figures are made of leather that can hold its shape even when much of it has been removed, but do not cut away too much of your cardboard figures or they will be too weak to withstand a performance!

As an alternative to cutting out intricate decorations, you can cut away larger areas and cover the exposed sections with suitably textured materials that allow light to show through the design—for example, nets, lace, or paper doilies.

Reading Writing Connection

Writing Application: **Present a Clear Sequence** In your how-to essay, present a clear sequence of steps and use transitions or numbers to help readers follow this sequence.

LITERATURE

For a "how-to" on solving mysteries, read a Sherlock Holmes story. You can find "The Adventure of the Speckled Band" by Sir Arthur Conan Doyle in *Prentice Hall Literature: Timeless Voices, Timeless Themes,* Silver.

Critical Viewing

Evaluate Students may say the photograph illustrates how to secure the rod to the puppet.

Responding to Literature

How-to essays need not be limited to how to do physical activities. Sir Arthur Conan Doyle's story is a good example of a "how-to" on a very different subject.

Integrating Technology Skills

Have students go on-line to find newspaper editorial pages and read editorials, letters to the editor, and columns that contain how-to content about such issues as government, education, and the environment.

Reading\Writing Connection

Writing: Present a Clear Sequence

Have students discuss how Currell's essay provides a clear sequence of steps to help readers follow the process. Remind students to apply the same strategy when writing their essays.

Step-by-Step Teaching Guide

Prewriting: Invisible Ink

1. Give students carbon paper, instructing them to place the carbon (shiny) side down between two blank sheets of paper. If students are doing the exercise on the computer, have them turn off or darken the monitor so the print cannot be seen.
2. The point of the activity is for students to generate ideas without stopping to look at them. In this form of freewriting, the goal is to brainstorm without censoring or judging the ideas.

Step-by-Step Teaching Guide

Prewriting: Listing

Teaching Resources: Writing Support Transparency 10-A

1. Have students fold a piece of paper in four columns and label the columns *people, places, things, events.*
2. Encourage students to list ideas freely without thinking about whether they are appropriate. Be sure that they understand that the selection process is a separate step.
3. When students have finished the list, have them go back over it and look for connections. Have them circle related items and draw lines connecting them.
4. Display the transparency. Draw students' attention to the student model to show how Katherine identified and connected items.
5. Encourage students to seek out topics in the links they have made on their lists.

Customize for *ESL Students*

Students learning English could have difficulties with the freewriting nature of the two activities here. One option is for them to do the activities in their native language, if they are comfortable doing so. A better option might be for you to work with them individually or in small groups to help them select topics.

10.2 Prewriting

Choosing Your Topic

To write an effective how-to essay, you need to know your topic well. Choose a process or a type of product with which you are familiar. Make sure it is simple enough for readers to be able to learn how to do it from a brief essay. Following are some strategies you can use to help you settle on a topic:

Strategies for Generating a Topic

1. **Invisible Ink** Put carbon paper between two blank sheets of paper, and "write" on the blank top sheet with a pen that has run dry. Write freely about items you use and activities you enjoy. (As an alternative to using carbon paper, you can write on a computer with the monitor shut off.) Review what has been recorded on the carbon copy, and choose a topic from among the ideas you have jotted down.
2. **Listing** Make a list of people, places, things, and activities that you associate with your home or school. Circle words and draw lines to show connections between items on the lists. These links may suggest a topic.

iText

Get instant help! Create your list using the Essay Builder, accessible from the menu bar, on-line or on CD-ROM.

Student Work IN PROGRESS

Name: Katherine Ann Roshani Stewart
Villa Duchesne School
St. Louis, MO

Listing to Discover a Topic

Katherine used listing to find her topic. As she studied her lists, she found links that brought to mind the process of grooming her dog, Biscuit.

Things	Activities	Places
my bicycle	chores	my bedroom
rollerblades	watching TV	the backyard
Biscuit's leash	practicing piano	kitchen
favorite chair	helping Mom with dinner	Biscuit's doghouse
CD collection	walking Biscuit	

Topic: grooming Biscuit

TIME AND RESOURCE MANAGER

Resources
Print: Writing Support Transparencies, 10-A–B
Technology: Writing and Grammar iText, Section 10.2

In-Depth Coverage	Accelerated Pace
• Cover pp. 214–217 in class. • Work through the Invisible Ink and Listing strategies with the class (p. 214). • Use the Responding to Fine Arts transparency to generate additional topics. • Do the Audience Profile activity in class. **Option** Have students work independently or in small groups with Writing and Grammar iText.	• Assign pp. 214–217 for independent student review. • Have students work independently to choose and narrow their topics. • Have students work with partners to focus on audience, purpose, and gathering details.

TOPIC BANK

If you're having trouble finding a topic, consider the following possibilities:

1. **How to Make Your Favorite Food** Mmmm . . . It might be brownies, or it might be scrambled eggs. Choose a favorite food, and explain how to prepare it.
2. **How to Make a Craft** You might have a knack for making jewelry, clothing, model cars, or paper airplanes. Or, you might have always wanted to learn how to make something. Choose a craft item, and write a how-to explaining how to make it.

Responding to Fine Art

3. The gentleman in this sculpture appears to be having difficulty—or a very successful game. Write a brief note giving your opinion. Then, think of a pastime in which you have improved. Write a how-to essay giving others tips on improving in the activity.

Strike, 1992, Red Grooms, Marlborough Gallery

Responding to Literature

4. Read "Baseball" by Lionel G. García. Use his explanation to write a how-to essay in which you explain the steps of playing his special version of baseball. You can find "Baseball" in *Prentice Hall Literature: Timeless Voices, Timeless Themes*, Silver.

Cooperative Writing Opportunity

5. **Holiday Celebration Manual** Get together with a group of classmates. Choose a holiday that all of you celebrate. Brainstorm for all the holiday activities. Then, categorize the activities under headings such as food preparation, decorating, and entertainment. Each person should choose a different category and develop a set of how-to instructions related to it. Work together to assemble your completed instructions into a comprehensive manual.

Step-by-Step Teaching Guide

Responding to Fine Art

Strike, 1992, by Red Grooms

Teaching Resources: Writing Support Transparency 10-B

1. Display the transparency. Have students describe their reactions to the sculpture.
2. In addition to topics related to favorite pastimes and other physical activities, students may also want to write a how-to essay about an artistic process, such as sculpting.

Responding to Literature

Tell students that Garcia's story is not a how-to essay. Students may want to write each step in the process on a separate index card, then put the cards in a sensible order.

Spotlight on Humanities

For additional topic suggestions, refer students to the Spotlight on Humanities on page 230.

ONGOING ASSESSMENT: Monitor and Reinforce

If some students are having difficulty coming up with a topic, use one of the following options.

Option 1 Suggest that students choose an idea from the Topic Bank. If many students have difficulty, work with them around one topic, modeling the process for them.	**Option 2** If the Topic Bank ideas seem too complex, suggest that students try one of the assignments from the Topic Bank for Heterogeneous Classes in the teaching resources.

TIME SAVERS!

Writing Support Transparencies

Use the transparencies for Chapter 10 to teach these strategies.

Step-by-Step Teaching Guide

Prewriting: Narrowing Your Topic; Considering Your Audience and Purpose

1. Help students narrow their topic by modeling the process with the following examples:

   Too broad: How to cook

   Narrow enough: How to make great hamburgers

   Too broad: How to Play Basketball

   Narrow enough: How to improve your rebounding

2. Have students work in small groups, or in a whole-class activity, to provide feedback on narrowing topics.
3. Ask students whose topics are too broad to consider some of the major points in their topic and evaluate whether one of the major points would be a more appropriate topic.
4. Have students complete the audience profile and evaluate how the audience might affect the selection of their topic.

Integrating Speaking and Listening Skills

The topic of an essay or a talk needs to be geared to the audience and the time or space available. Tell students that we all would share information differently on a long car ride than on a long-distance phone call.

10.2

Narrowing Your Topic

Once you've chosen a topic, evaluate whether you can cover it thoroughly in an essay. Some topics require a great deal of steps or explanation. If this is the case, you will need to narrow your topic. For example, the topic "How to Play Baseball" is probably too broad for a short essay. However, in a short paper you could easily cover a more narrow topic, such as "How to Swing a Bat," "How to Play Shortstop," or "How to Improve Your Fielding."

Divide Your Topic Into Subtopics

To help you evaluate and narrow your topic, divide it into as many subtopics as you can identify. Then, review your list of subtopics. If each one looks as if it will take about a paragraph to explain, your topic is probably narrow enough. If there are several steps or processes within each subtopic, you will probably want to write about a single subtopic.

Considering Your Audience and Purpose

How-to essays have a clearly defined **purpose**—to explain the steps of a process or provide help in using a product. However, they can have many different **audiences**, or potential readers. Identify your audience and consider how it will affect your use of language and choice of details.

Complete an Audience Profile

To help you identify and address the needs of your audience, create an *audience profile*, a note card with information about your audience that you can refer back to as you write. Following are questions to consider in creating your audience profile:

- **Knowledge Level—How much does my audience know about the topic?** Do they need a little or a lot of information? What terms will I need to define?
- **Age—What is the age of my audience?** If you are writing for younger children, use simple vocabulary. If you are writing for adult readers, use more sophisticated terms.
- **Skill Set—What skills do my readers have?** Does my audience understand the basic skills required for the process I am explaining? Should I review those skills as well as cover the specific steps of the procedure?

iText

Get instant help! Create your Audience Profile using the Essay Builder, accessible from the menu bar, on-line or on CD-ROM.

ONGOING ASSESSMENT: Monitor and Reinforce

Some students fall into the habit of considering you, the teacher, their audience. Use one of the following options to alter this pattern.

Option 1 Have students select a specific person as their audience, someone other than you. This will get them focused away from you and will also affect the level of detail, language, and formality that they put into the essay.

Option 2 Have students identify a purpose in writing, telling them that appealing to or impressing the teacher is not a good primary purpose.

Gathering Details

Use Research

To write an effective how-to essay, you need to be an expert on your topic. If you are not already extremely knowledgeable about your topic, conduct research in the library or on the Internet to make yourself an expert. Follow this strategy:

Creating a K-W-L Chart Use a three-column K-W-L (*K*now–*W*ant to Know–*L*earned) Chart to assess your knowledge of your topic and to guide your research. Fill in the first column with what you know about your topic. List what you want to learn in the second column. Use the information in the second column to guide your research, and fill in the third column with what you learn.

Gather Visual Aids

Remember that your readers may never have attempted the process you are explaining. For this reason, you may want to create or gather visual aids such as the following to help your readers picture the process you're describing:

- photos or illustrations with explanatory captions
- diagrams, charts, or maps.

Research Tip

If you are writing a how-to on cooking or home improvement, watch a television program on the subject for ideas about how to present information.

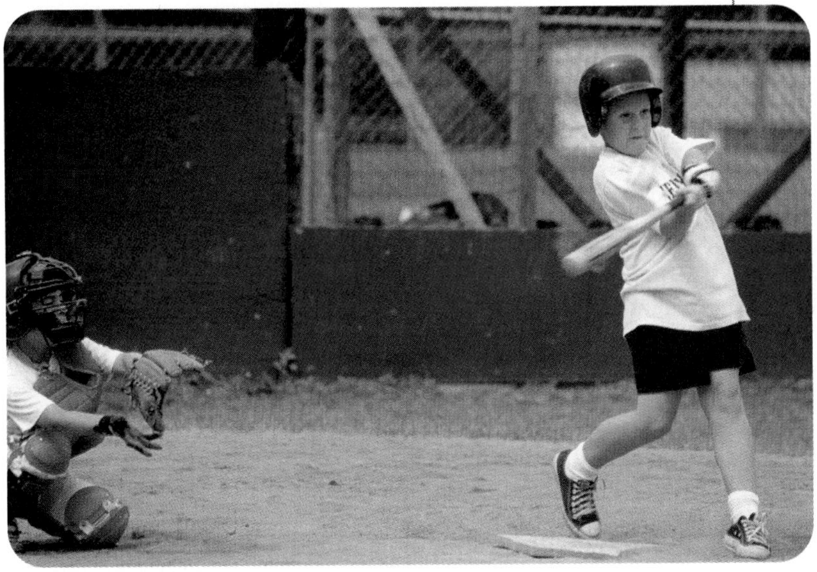

▲ **Critical Viewing** What more might each of these boys need to know about baseball? What kind of visual aid could help them? **[Apply]**

Step-by-Step Teaching Guide

Prewriting: Research to Gather Details

1. The K-W-L chart will tell students what they know and what they need to know. Have them fill out the chart and then identify what sources they are going to use to find out the information they need to know.
2. Have students make plans for gathering visual aids that they can include in their essays.

Customize for *Bodily/Kinesthetic Learners*

Tell students that sometimes they can remember steps in a sequence by acting them out. Have them "walk" through the process by miming the action of each step.

Customize for *Visual/Spatial Learners*

Suggest that students draw sketches of the steps of the process as they write them down.

Critical Viewing

Apply Students may mention the rules of the game or tips on how to hit the ball better. A diagram or chart might help them.

Step-by-Step Teaching Guide

Drafting: Organize Details in Chronological Order

1. Most how-to essays feature steps arranged in chronological order. Even personal how-to essays still will have steps that need to be listed in chronological order.
2. To be absolutely sure their steps are in the correct order, have students write them on sticky notes and arrange them in what they believe is the correct order. Then have students double-check the order.
3. Have students consider what format will work for them. Refer them back to the Model From Literature to see how a numbered list can be used in an essay.

Customize for *Verbal/Linguistic Learners*

Talking about their topic may help some students. Have partners take turns narrating and copying down the steps in the process of the how-to essay.

Customize for *Visual/Spatial Learners*

Students may be helped in the process by sketching a storyboard of the process. They could use sticky notes to sketch each frame of the storyboard and then arrange the notes into the proper order.

10.3 Drafting

Shaping Your Writing

Before you begin writing, organize your details. Because most how-to essays describe a process that takes place over time, chronological order is often the most effective organization.

Organize Details in Chronological Order

To help you organize your details in chronological order, you may want to write each detail on a sticky note or note card.

Using Sticky Notes to Organize Details Write each step on an individual sticky note. Arrange the steps in order, and then add or rearrange steps as needed.

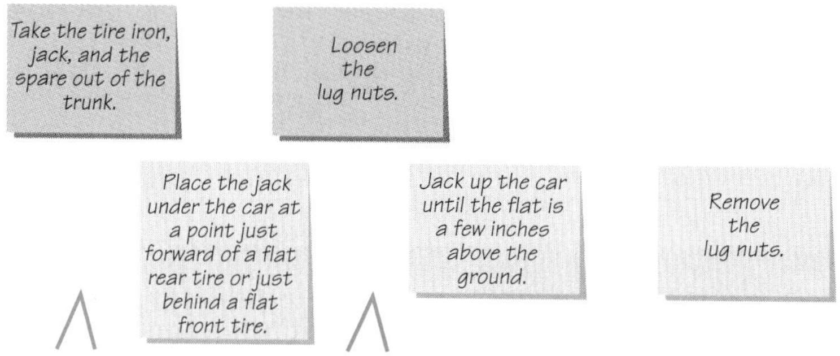

Choose the Best Format

In how-to essays, paragraphs are not always the best way to present information. Different readers will have different needs at different times:

- A reader who is considering doing the activity outlined in your how-to essay will want a quick overview of materials and steps.
- A reader who is in the middle of performing your instructions will need to locate a step quickly.
- A reader who is looking for special tips or background information will want additional information.

To meet the needs of each of these readers, consider the following formatting possibilities as you draft:

- Present essential steps as a series of numbered points or in a bulleted list.
- Provide additional information in separate sections, such as boxes inset alongside your main instructions.

TIME AND RESOURCE MANAGER

Resources
Print: Writing Support Transparencies, 10-C
Technology: Writing and Grammar iText, Section 10.3

In-Depth Coverage	Accelerated Pace
• Cover pp. 218–219 in class. • Have students draft their essays in class. • Use the transparency to demonstrate the strategy of Exploding the Moment. **Option** Have students work independently or in small groups with Writing and Grammar iText.	• Have students review pp. 218–219 independently and then draft their own how-to essays. • Respond to individual drafting issues as needed.

Providing Elaboration

As your writing takes shape, you may find that your explanations need more details before your readers will understand exactly what is required. Use the following strategies to make your instructions clear.

Use Graphic Devices

Graphics—photos, diagrams, and drawings—are a great way to help readers follow an explanation. Create or obtain graphics to reinforce your instructions, and place them at the appropriate points in your essay. Follow these guidelines:

- Each graphic must be clear and complete.
- Each graphic must clearly illustrate a step in your essay.
- Each graphic should be accompanied by a label clearly describing it and linking it to your essay.

Add Details by "Exploding the Moment"

Pause after you write each paragraph. Circle any important detail about which readers will need to know: *what kind, how much, how long,* or *to what degree.* Answer these questions on sticky notes and attach them to your draft. Consider adding these details to give readers precise explanations.

iText

Try it out! Use the Exploding the Moment activity in **Section 10.3,** on-line or on CD-ROM.

Student Work IN PROGRESS

Name: Katherine Ann Roshani Stewart
Villa Duchesne School
St. Louis, MO

"Exploding the Moment"

Katherine added details answering the question "what kind?" to make her essay more useful.

Assemble the proper materials to give the dog a bath. When you are buying shampoo, get the right shampoo for your dog and the right brushes. The towels I gather are thick so they will soak up water quickly.

different types for dogs with long hair and for dogs with short hair

brushes with metal bristles get the tougher tangles

Step-by-Step Teaching Guide

Drafting: Add Details by Exploding the Moment

Teaching Resources: Writing Support Transparency 10-C

1. Demonstrate Exploding the Moment by using the transparency of the student work in progress. Point out how the details Katherine adds provide more specific examples.
2. Exploding the Moment can add vivid detail. That detail makes both the writing more interesting and gives the reader more information for completing the task.
3. Have students create construction paper "explosions" to attach to their papers.

Customize for *More Advanced Students*

Have students use a spreadsheet to organize and draft their how-to essay. Spreadsheet software is useful for visualizing, organizing, and recording a sequence of actions.

ONGOING ASSESSMENT: Monitor and Reinforce

If students are having difficulty elaborating by Exploding the Moment, use one of the following options.

Option 1 Have students add visual details to each of their sticky notes.	**Option 2** Have partners tell each other details of the process as the partner writes them down.

TIME SAVERS!

Writing Support Transparencies

Use the transparencies for Chapter 10 to teach these strategies.

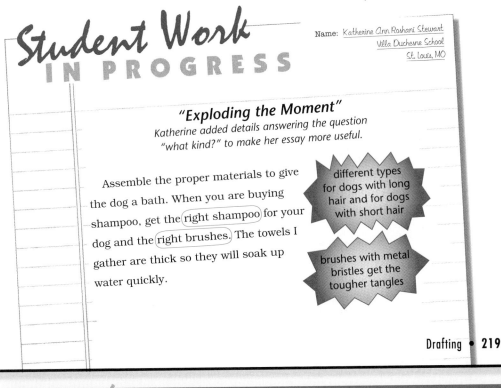

Step-by-Step Teaching Guide

Revising: Revising Your Overall Structure

Teacher Resources: Writing Support Transparency 10-D

1. Good structure lets readers know what the main idea is and then provides details that support the main idea.
2. Demonstrate the power of main steps and substeps. Write the following example on the chalkboard:

   Good preparation is the key to successful baking. Before you begin, check to see that you have all the necessary ingredients.
3. Point out how the main step, preparation, is supported by the example of having the necessary ingredients.
4. Display the transparency to examine how Katherine used main steps and substeps to make the steps in her essay clearer.

Customizing for *Less Advanced Students*

Students might have difficulty coding their main point and supporting points. They can work in pairs, or you can work with them yourself to help them see the relationship between main and supporting points.

10.4 Revising

Revising Your Overall Structure

After completing a first draft, review your work to find ways to improve it. Begin by looking at the structure of your how-to essay.

Distinguish Main Steps From Substeps

One of the most important parts of a clear how-to is a streamlined set of instructions. Consider how to best organize the steps and substeps in your process, using the following strategy:

REVISION STRATEGY
Highlighting Main Steps and Substeps

Use one color highlighter to mark the main, or most important, steps. Use another color highlighter to mark the substeps within each main step. Review your highlighting and decide whether you should set off any of the substeps in numbered or bulleted lists.

Student Work IN PROGRESS

Name: Katherine Ann Roshani Stewart
Villa Duchesne School
St. Louis, MO

Highlighting Main Steps and Substeps

Katherine highlighted main steps and substeps in her essay in different colors. Then, she made decisions about how to present them in her final draft.

When you groom your dog, the steps include bathing, brushing, and clipping its nails. You will need: shampoo, conditioner, one brush with long metal teeth and one brush with short bristles, towels, a nail clipper, and a restraint.

main step 1

substep 1A
I will make this part of the main step into a bulleted list to help readers.

Before you start, assemble the proper materials to give the dog a bath and brushing. When you are buying shampoo, get the right shampoo for your dog's type of fur. For instance, for a long-haired dog like Biscuit, I buy shampoo for dogs with long hair.

main step 2
I will move this part of the main step before the list of materials.

substep 2A
This substep will just get in the way of the main steps. I will move it to a sidebar box.

TIME SAVERS!

Writing Support Transparencies
Use the transparencies for Chapter 10 to teach these strategies.

TIME AND RESOURCE MANAGER

Resources
Print: Writing Support Transparencies, 10-D–E
Technology: Writing and Grammar iText, Section 10.4

In-Depth Coverage	Accelerated Pace
• Cover pp. 220–224 in class. • Work through the revision strategy with the entire class. **Option** Have students work independently or in small groups with Writing and Grammar iText, focusing on revision activities and tools.	• Assign students to review pages 220–224 independently. • Have students revise their how-to essays independently.

◀ **Critical Viewing**
Give some advice to this goalie in three sentences. Use transition words in two of them. **[Apply]**

Revising Your Paragraphs

Identify Paragraph Purpose

Once you're comfortable with the general structure of your paper, carefully focus on each individual paragraph. The purpose of each paragraph will determine which words or phrases you may need to add in order to make your meaning clearer.

REVISION STRATEGY
Using Steps, Stacks, Chains, and Balances

As you analyze each paragraph, decide which of the following descriptions most closely fits its purpose:

- **Steps** If the paragraph explains a step or several related steps for which time order is important, the sequence should be indicated. Use words such as *first, next,* and *finally.*
- **Stacks** If the paragraph explains how one part of a process adds to or contributes to another, point out the connection with words such as *and, furthermore,* and *for instance.*
- **Chains** If the paragraph shows the cause-and-effect relationship between steps, use words such as *so, because,* and *consequently.*
- **Balances** If the paragraph shows choice or contrast, use words or phrases such as *but, however, on the other hand,* and *rather.*

Collaborative Writing Tip

Exchange drafts with a peer. Mark places where the transition from one step to another seems abrupt. Consider your peer's marks when looking for places to add transitions.

Step-by-Step Teaching Guide

Revising: Using Steps, Stacks, Chains, and Balances

1. Students shouldn't try to explain too many steps in one paragraph. Suggest that students limit the number of steps to no more than two in each paragraph. Have them record how many steps are in each paragraph.
2. Suggest that students note in the margin next to each paragraph what kind of information it contains. Have them note whether it is time order, connected elements of the process, cause and effect relationships, choice, or contrast. Have them use this information to guide their revision of each paragraph.
3. Have students break up paragraphs that have too many steps.
4. Tell students to check each topic sentence to see that it states the paragraph's main idea.

Critical Viewing

Apply Students may say that the goalie should keep her eyes on the ball. Then she should place her body between the ball and the goal. Finally, she should use her hands to block the kick.

Step-by-Step Teaching Guide

Revising: Vary Sentence Beginnings

1. Before you begin the activity, ask students to quickly scan their drafts, looking just at the sentence openers. Are there any noticeable patterns?
2. Have students highlight their sentence beginnings and note sentences that can be opened differently.

Step-by-Step Teaching Guide

Grammar in Your Writing: Adverb Clauses and Adverb Phrases

1. Examine the kind of information provided by adverb phrases and clauses. Point out that *where, why, when, in what manner,* and *to what extent* are the kinds of information that would naturally occur in a how-to essay, since it is dealing with a process.
2. Suggest that students add adverb clauses and phrases to their essays to vary sentence beginnings.

Find It in Your Reading

adverb phrase: . . . using a sharp craft knife or small, pointed scissors or by punching holes. (explains how)
adverb clause: . . . so that there is just a little more weight below the control rod than above. (gives a reason)

Find It in Your Writing

Students may want to work with partners to identify where more detail would be helpful to readers.

Real-World Connection

The type of information conveyed by adverb clauses and phrases occurs often in journalism. Have students read newspaper articles and highlight the adverb clauses and phrases. Then have them reread the article, omitting the highlighted items, to see how important they are to the sense of article.

10.4

Revising Your Sentences

Vary Sentence Beginnings

After you've revised your paragraphs, look carefully at your sentences. Make sure that you've used a variety of sentence beginnings so your writing flows smoothly.

REVISION STRATEGY
Underlining Sentence Beginnings

Follow these steps to help make sure your sentence beginnings are varied:

1. Choose three paragraphs in your draft. Underline the first few words of each sentence in them.
2. Review underlined words and determine whether most of your sentences begin with the subject of the sentence.
3. If so, look for ways to rewrite or combine sentences to begin with a different word.
4. Also, notice whether you've used transitions at the beginnings of sentences. If not, you may want to use words such as *next, then,* or *now* to help readers follow the progression of steps.

Grammar and Style Tip

One way to vary sentences and clearly show the connections between steps in a process is to use complex sentences. For help combining sentences into complex sentences, see Chapter 21.

Grammar in Your Writing
Adverb Clauses and Adverb Phrases

In many places in your essay, you will want to use words and groups of words that give more information about a step. Adverb phrases and clauses add details that point out *where, why, when, in what manner,* or *to what extent* something is being done.

Where? With the dog facing you, brush its chest.

Why? The towels are thick so they will soak up water quickly.

When? After the shampoo is lathered up, begin rinsing.

In what manner? Dispense the shampoo and lather, rubbing vigorously.

To what extent? Except for its head, immerse the dog completely in water.

Find It in Your Reading Find two adverb phrases or clauses in "A Simple Shadow Puppet" by David Currell on page 212. Explain what information each one adds.

Find It in Your Writing Find three adverb clauses or phrases that you have used in your how-to essay. If you can't find three of each, consider combining sentences by changing one sentence to an adverb phrase or adverb clause and adding it to another.

To learn more about adverb clauses and adverb phrases, see Chapter 20.

ONGOING ASSESSMENT: Prerequisite Skills

If students have difficulty with adverb phrases and clauses, you may find it necessary to review the following to assure coverage for prerequisite knowledge.

In the Textbook	Print Resources	Technology
Phrases and Clauses, pp. 432–459	Grammar Exercise Workbook, pp. 73–74, 89–92	On-Line Exercise Bank, Sections 20.1–2

Revising Your Word Choice

Evaluate Repeated Words

For a mature, sophisticated style, varying your word choice is as important as varying your sentence beginnings. Go back through your essay and look for overused words. One way to evaluate whether you have overused any words is to circle those that are repeated.

REVISION STRATEGY
Circling Repeated Words

Go through your essay and circle any nouns, verbs, or adjectives that you have used more than once. After circling repeated words, evaluate each use to determine whether you should replace the word with a synonym or even rephrase the sentence.

Writers in ACTION

Gary Matsumoto values peer review. "It helps to have someone else look at your [writing] because it's another pair of eyes; it's another set of sensibilities. And they can see something that perhaps you didn't see or think of something that you didn't think of. And they can make a contribution. So, never be defensive when someone criticizes [your writing] or makes suggestions, because very often that person can make it better."

Student Work IN PROGRESS

Name: Katherine Ann Roshani Stewart
Villa Duchesne School
St. Louis, MO

Circling Repeated Words

In these steps, Katherine found she had repeated a few words—dog, dry, fur, and towel. She decided that only her repetition of dry was intrusive, and made the changes shown.

1. Little by little, working from the tail up, (dry) each part of your (dog) by squeezing [the water from] the (fur) ~~(dry)~~ with (towels).

2. When the (dog) is [barely damp] ~~mostly (dry)~~, have it sit on a [fresh] ~~(dry)~~ (towel) till its (fur) completely (dries).

Step-by-Step Teaching Guide

Revising: Circling Repeated Words

Teaching Resources: Writing Support Transparency 10-E

1. Explain to students how repeated words can result in monotony and make the writing seem flat.
2. Display the transparency. Have students explain how Katherine's revisions improved her essay.
3. Have students review their drafts and circle repeated words that are used too frequently.
4. Have students use a thesaurus to find synonyms for words that are used too frequently and rewrite those sentences or paragraphs that need rewriting.

Customize for *ESL Students*

Students learning English may use certain words repetitively because of a limited English vocabulary. Have students work in groups to brainstorm for synonyms. Suggest that they use a dictionary or thesaurus to come up with alternative wordings.

Integrating Technology Skills

Suggest that students use the thesaurus on their word processor, if available, to come up with synonyms for repeated words.

STANDARDIZED TEST PREPARATION WORKSHOP

Vocabulary Standardized test questions may require students to recognize multiple meanings of words. Write the following sentences and word choices on the chalkboard and ask students to find the word that fits in both sentences:

Linda learned how to use a power ___.

I ___ your mom's new truck yesterday.

A drill
B tool
C saw
D see

Item **C** fits both sentences, as a noun and a verb.

TIME SAVERS!

Writing Support Transparencies
Use the transparencies for Chapter 10 to teach these strategies.

Step-by-Step Teaching Guide

Revising: Peer Review

1. Explain to students that the best way to see if their essays are clear and understandable is to have another person read them.
2. Divide the class into small groups. Review the bulleted list of questions that reviewers should keep in mind as they listen to each student's essay.
3. Remind students that a peer review is an opportunity to provide *constructive* criticism.

Critical Viewing

Relate Students' responses will vary depending on their level of comfort reading in front of a group.

10.4

Peer Review

Feedback is a useful tool when revising a how-to essay. The purpose of a how-to essay is to explain something to another person. Peer reviewers will be able to help assess how clear your explanation is and whether additional information is needed.

Ask a Group to Try It Out

Read your essay aloud to a small group. Then, read it aloud again, guiding the group through the process you are explaining. The group should go through the motions of each step, taking notes on where they are confused or unsure. After you have finished the second reading, ask reviewers to respond to the following questions:

- Which step or steps could have been explained more clearly?
- What was confusing about those steps?
- In which sections was more or less information needed?
- What other questions or comments do you have?

Use your peers' responses to guide your final revision.

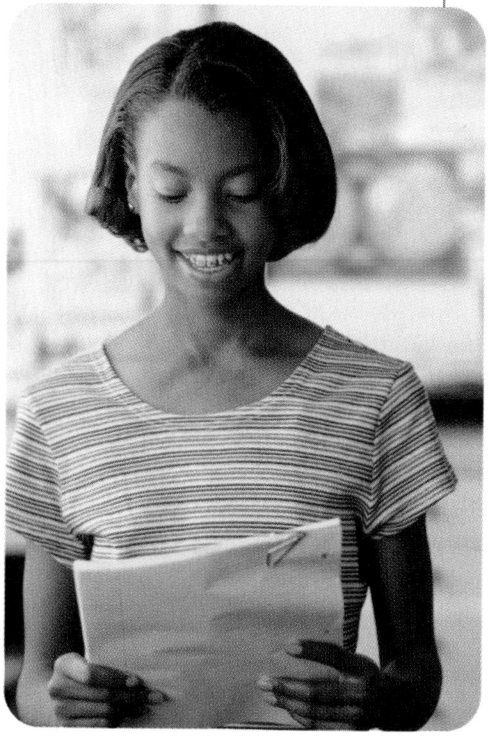

▶ Critical Viewing
How might you feel if, like this girl, you had to read your draft to a group of peers? **[Relate]**

10.5 Editing and Proofreading

Errors in spelling, punctuation, grammar, or usage can create confusion. Proofread your how-to essay to discover and eliminate errors that might mislead a reader.

Be especially attentive to your use of commas and semicolons. The correct use of these punctuation marks can make your how-to easier to understand. Incorrect use of these marks, though, can lead to confusion—even to your reader's failure to perform your how-to correctly!

Focusing on Commas and Semicolons

Commas and semicolons help you separate steps in a series or materials in a list. By separating descriptions or names of items, commas and semicolons help readers distinguish one description from the next. As you proofread, use the examples below to guide you.

Grammar in Your Writing
Using Commas and Semicolons to Separate Items in a Series

When three or more similar items are listed in a series, punctuation is needed to separate them. Generally, you will use commas to separate words, phrases, or clauses that you list in a series. However, in order to avoid confusion, semicolons are used when some items already contain commas.

The steps of dog grooming include shampooing, rinsing, and using conditioner; drying; brushing; and nail clipping.

Find It in Your Reading In "A Simple Shadow Puppet" by David Currell on page 212, find an example of a series of three or more items. Explain how the author punctuates it to aid the reader's understanding.

Find It in Your Writing Look for series of three or more items in your essay. Make sure you have punctuated them correctly with commas or with semicolons, if the items already contain commas.

For more on commas and semicolons, see Chapter 26.

Step-by-Step Teaching Guide

Editing and Proofreading

1. Editing and proofreading are important steps in the writing process. If Katherine's unproofread essay talked about how to wash a "dig," "log," or "dot" instead of a dog, readers would have trouble following it!
2. Have students be sure that a paragraph explaining a sequence of actions in time has the necessary commas after the words *first, next,* or *finally.*

Step-by-Step Teaching Guide

Grammar in Your Writing: Using Commas and Semicolons to Separate Items in a Series

1. Remind students that a series consists of three or more items of the same kind. These items can be single words, phrases, or clauses.
2. Write the following example on the chalkboard:

   I have groomed small dogs, medium-sized dogs, and huge dogs; some breeds are St. Bernards, Newfoundlands, and Great Danes.
3. Point out the use of commas to punctuate the items in a series.

Find It in Your Reading

Responses will vary, but students should see that Currell uses commas or semicolons to help make each item in the series stand out.

Find It in Your Writing

Have students share examples from their essays and explain why they punctuated each one as they did.

TIME AND RESOURCE MANAGER

Resources
Print: Scoring Rubrics on Transparency, Chapter 10; Writing Assessment: Scoring Rubric and Scoring Models for How-to Essay
Technology: Writing and Grammar iText, Sections 10.5–6

In-Depth Coverage	Accelerated Pace
• Cover pp. 225–228 in class. • Have students edit and proofread their essays in class. • Review the Rubric for Self-Assessment in class. • Have students present their final drafts.	• Assign pp. 225–228 for independent student review. • Have students edit and proofread their essays as homework. • Have students present their final drafts.

PRENTICE HALL
Everyday Spelling

If you have taught the spelling skills in *Prentice Hall Everyday Spelling,* Grade 8, Chapter 11, in conjunction with this *Writing and Grammar* chapter, review and assess students' mastery of the skills before concluding the chapter. Remind students to apply the spelling skills as they edit and proofread their how-to essays.

Step-by-Step Teaching Guide

Publishing and Presenting

1. Have students rehearse before giving a demonstration. If resources are available, you can have them make overheads and use an overhead projector to display them. In any case, encourage students to add visual displays to enhance their presentations.
2. Students will need to work in pairs for the video activity. If necessary, hold a workshop in how to use the video camera, so students will know what they are doing. Be careful not to let students lose their focus on the essay as the primary means of information in this exercise.
3. Have students complete the Reflecting on Your Writing exercise and share their reflections with the class.
4. Have students use the rubric to evaluate their own writing.

ASSESS

Step-by-Step Teaching Guide

Assessment

Teaching Resources: Scoring Rubrics on Transparency, 10; Formal Assessment, Chapter 10

1. Display the Scoring Rubric transparency and review the criteria in class.
2. Before students proceed with self-assessment, you may wish to review the Final Draft of the Student Work in Progress on pages 227–228. Have students score the Final Draft in one or more of the rubric categories. For example, how would students score the essay in terms of audience and purpose?
3. In addition to student self-assessment, you may wish to use the following assessment options.
   - Score student essays yourself, using the rubric and scoring models from Writing Assessment.
   - Review the Standardized Test Preparation Workshop on pages 232–233 and have students respond to a writing prompt within a time limit.
   - Administer the Chapter 10 Test from Formal Assessment in Teaching Resources to assess students' grasp of concepts presented.

10.6 Publishing and Presenting

Building Your Portfolio

Consider these ideas for sharing your how-to essay:

1. **Give a Demonstration** How-to explanations lend themselves to oral presentation. Demonstrate the steps of your explanation as you present it to the class. Incorporate diagrams you have created listing or illustrating steps.
2. **Make a Video** Tape your how-to explanation with a video camera. Plan out shots. While taping, have a classmate read your essay while you demonstrate the steps that are being explained. Change camera position as necessary to capture the visual details of each step. Show your video to the class.

Reflecting on Your Writing

After you've finished writing, jot down a few notes on your experience. Use these questions to guide you:

- Having written a how-to essay, will you find it easier to follow instructions in the future? Explain.
- As a result of writing a how-to essay, what more did you learn about the activity or skill about which you wrote?

Internet Tip

To see how-to essays scored with this rubric, go on-line: PHSchool.com
Enter Web Code: eck-8001

Rubric for Self-Assessment

Use the following criteria to assess your how-to essay:

	Score 4	Score 3	Score 2	Score 1
Audience and Purpose	Clearly focuses on procedures leading to a well-defined end	Focuses on procedures leading to a well-defined end	Includes procedures related to an end, but presents some vaguely	Includes only vague descriptions of procedures and results
Organization	Gives instructions in logical order; subdivides complex actions into steps	Gives instructions in logical order; subdivides some complex actions into steps	For the most part, gives instructions in logical order	Gives instructions in a scattered, disorganized manner
Elaboration	Provides appropriate amount of detail; gives needed explanations	Provides appropriate amount of detail; gives some explanations	Provides some detail; gives few explanations	Provides few details; gives few or no explanations
Use of Language	Shows overall clarity and fluency; uses transitions effectively; contains few mechanical errors	Shows some sentence variety; uses some transitions; includes few mechanical errors	Uses awkward or overly simple sentence structures; contains many mechanical errors	Contains incomplete thoughts and confusing mechanical errors

ONGOING ASSESSMENT: Assess Mastery

Use one of the following options to assess final drafts of students' persuasive essays.

Self-Assessment Ask students to score their essay using the rubric provided. Then have students write a single paragraph reflecting on the most valuable thing they learned in completing this essay.

Teacher Assessment You may want to use the rubric and scoring models provided in the Writing Assessment, How-to Essay, to score students' work.

10.7 Student Work IN PROGRESS

FINAL DRAFT

◀ **Critical Viewing** What step in Katherine's how-to essay does this photograph illustrate? What formatting devices made it easy for you to find this step? **[Connect]**

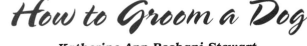

How to Groom a Dog

Katherine Ann Roshani Stewart
Villa Duchesne School
St. Louis, Missouri

Grooming your dog can be easy and fun if you have the right materials. I have a sheepdog with long hair. Her name is Biscuit. Biscuit is medium height with golden brown and white hair. My dog is now six years old, but in dog years she would be 42. When you groom your dog, the steps include bathing, brushing, and clipping its nails. Before you start, assemble the proper materials to give the dog a bath and brushing.

Materials

- shampoo
- one brush with short bristles
- one brush with long metal teeth
- conditioner
- restraint attachment
- nail clipper
- thick towels

TIPS

- When you are buying shampoo, get the right shampoo for your dog's type of fur. For instance, for a long-haired dog like Biscuit, I buy shampoo for dogs with long hair.
- When you get your brushes, ones with metal bristles are better than the nylon ones because the metal bristles get the tougher tangles.
- The towels I gather are thick so they will soak up water quickly.

CLOSE

Step-by-Step Teaching Guide

Teaching From the Final Draft

1. Review the key elements that make Katherine's work a successful how-to essay.
   - The topic is manageable and is useful and interesting.
   - The essay addresses a general audience, and the purpose is clear—explaining a useful skill.
   - A good introduction describes Biscuit.
   - Lists and steps are used well. Katherine lists materials and the steps in bathing, drying, and brushing. The body of the essay provides good examples for the points she makes.
   - She ends with a short but conclusive sentence.

continued

Critical Viewing

Connect Students should say the photograph illustrates step 1 in "Drying and Brushing." The boldfaced heads and numbered steps make it easy to find this information.

2. Discuss how Katherine's essay passes a credibility test. Her writing sounds believable. Readers trust that she is giving accurate information. Review that credibility comes from a thoughtful essay, one that is well researched, structured, and well written.
3. Ask students who have dogs if they would use this essay as a guide for grooming their dog.

10.7

Bathing

1. Fill the tub with tepid water. Make sure the water is not too hot or cold!
2. Immerse the dog, except for its head, in water.
3. Brush all the mats out with the brush that has long bristles.
4. Evenly dispense the shampoo and lather by rubbing vigorously. After the shampoo is lathered up, begin rinsing while using a gentle scrubbing motion with the same brush.
5. If you want your dog's coat to be soft and manageable, use conditioner. But be careful! Do not use too much, otherwise the dog's coat will become too oily. Make sure to completely wash out ALL the conditioner so no residue remains.
6. Take the dog out of the tub or shower.

TIPS
- I give Biscuit a bath before I brush her. The reason is that when the dog's hair is wet, it is easier to comb out all the mats and tangles.
- Depending on how big your dog is, make sure to use a bathtub or shower stall because it is hard to soak and rinse the dog by pouring water on it. Some dogs enjoy baths, while others despise them. Biscuit hates having a bath.
- If you decide to use a restraint attachment, attach it to the tub or shower with a suction cup.

To help readers with different needs, Katherine uses numbered steps for quick reference to essential information. She presents additional explanations and tips in boxed sidenotes.

Drying and Brushing

1. Little by little, working from the tail up, dry each part of your dog by squeezing the water from the fur with towels.
2. When the dog is barely damp, have it sit on a fresh towel till its fur completely dries.
3. Have the dog sit facing you so you can brush its chest. Then, work down its legs to its lower tummy, making sure all the tangles are out.
4. Use the brush with short bristles to make your dog's coat soft.

Using transitions such as when the dog is barely damp, *Katherine answers readers' questions about exactly how to carry out steps.*

Nail Clipping

If your dog's nails are too long, you can cut them, using a special nail clipper for dogs. The clipper should have a big head for large nails. Make sure not to cut over the quick, which is the red part of the nail. If you do, you can always dip the nail in baby powder or flour to stop the bleeding.

Once you have completed all these steps of grooming your dog, you can be proud of your well-groomed dog.

Clipping a dog's nails is not as involved or complicated as bathing and brushing, so Katherine returns to a paragraph format to explain the process.

Katherine's concludes her essay with a statement that lets readers know why she grooms her own dog.

Connected Assignment Problem-and-Solution Essay

For just about any problem in the world—a park filled with litter, a school schedule that could be more productive, a war that must be ended—people have proposed a solution. These proposals may take the form of a problem-and-solution essay. A **problem-and-solution essay** describes a problem and offers one or more solutions to it. Like a how-to essay, a problem-and-solution essay sets out the steps for achieving an end. An effective problem-and-solution essay

- clearly explains the problem and the proposed solutions.
- defends the solutions using facts and examples.

Prewriting To find a topic, list people, groups, places, and issues that are important to you. For each, list an associated problem. Choose a topic from your list.

Next, do research into the problem and possible solutions. Gather facts, expert opinions, and other evidence to support your solutions. Note the connections between the problem and its solutions in a cause-and-effect diagram like the one shown.

Problem: Homelessness

Causes of Problem →	Solution →	Effect on Problem
not enough affordable housing • little profit for builders; no new housing being built	City should give tax break to builders of affordable housing.	Tax break will encourage builders to build new affordable housing.

Drafting After gathering facts, write an introduction in which you clearly state the problem you will address. Include an overview of the solutions you will propose. In the body of your essay, lay out the background information your readers need to understand the problem. Then, explain your solutions. For each, show specifically how it will solve the problem. Support each with facts, expert opinions, and other evidence.

Revising and Editing Once you have finished your first draft, review it. Focus on these two types of revision:

- Test each solution by considering possible objections. Consider answering these objections.
- Check the support you provide for each main point. If you have not spelled out the reasons for a claim, add sentences to support it.

Finally, proofread your essay to eliminate grammatical and mechanical errors.

Publishing and Presenting Consider sending a version of your essay as a letter to the editor of a local newspaper.

▼ Critical Viewing
What problem might these teenagers be helping to solve? **[Hypothesize]**

▶ *Lesson Objectives*

1. To write a problem-solution essay.
2. To choose an appropriate topic for a problem-solution essay.
3. To draft, revise, and edit a problem-solution essay.
4. To publish a problem-solution essay.

Step-by-Step Teaching Guide

Problem-and-Solution Essay

Teaching Resources: Writing Support Transparency 10-F; Writing Support Activity Book 10-1

1. Mention to students a minor problem you have noticed in the classroom. Have students suggest ways to solve the problem. Explain that the writing assignment on this page will call on students to think of problems that are important to them and come up with solutions.
2. Suggest that students review writing strategies from Chapter 10.
3. Display the transparency to serve as a model for students' prewriting activity.
4. Give students copies of the blank organizer. Ask them to follow your example to develop a list of potential topics, and then to choose one to write about.
5. Encourage students to use their essays to actually try to solve the problems they wrote about. They may have to present their arguments on the phone, in letters to the editor of a newspaper, in e-mails, or in person.

Critical Viewing

Hypothesize Most students will believe that the teenagers are beautifying the neighborhood by painting a fence or wall. They may also say that the teenagers may be covering up graffiti or other damage to the wall.

Lesson Objectives

1. To interpret and evaluate the various ways visual image makers represent meanings.
2. To evaluate the effects of different media.
3. To select visuals to complement meanings.
4. To explain how to do a dance.

Critical Viewing

Interpret Students are likely to say that Baker's performances were probably dramatic and fun to watch.

Step-by-Step Teaching Guide

Making Connections Across Cultures

1. Choose a Spotlight element for class discussion, or have students work independently or in groups on the element of their choice. Give students the initiative to find the necessary books and recordings.
2. Play selected cuts from Duke Ellington CDs for your students. Be sure to include "Take the 'A' Train." Ask students whether this music is new to them and whether they like it.
3. Show the class photographs from a biography of Josephine Baker and read selected passages. You may want to locate and play video clips of Baker dancing. (Since Baker's dances were somewhat risqué, be sure to review the video before you show it to the class.)
4. Students may want to research other African American artists who found homes in Paris in the 1920's. What did these artists say about their experiences?

Spotlight on the Humanities

Making Connections Across Cultures

Focus on Dance: Josephine Baker

A how-to on baking a cake may be easy to follow, but the best how-to for learning to dance is a teacher. Josephine Baker (1906–1975), an American dancer and singer, taught France how to swing. In the 1920's, Baker introduced the Charleston, a new, jazz-based dance, to Parisians. Under her guidance, they learned to love jazz and to adore her.

Born in St. Louis, Missouri, Baker danced at New York City's famous Cotton Club. In 1925, Baker traveled to Paris with the first African American stage show to arrive in France from the United States. Her show opened at the prestigious Théâtre des Champs-Élysées.

Baker spent a great portion of her life in Paris. She did undercover work against the Germans in World War II and aided many refugees who flooded into France.

▲ Critical Viewing Judging from this photograph, what qualities might a performance by Baker have had? **[Interpret]**

Music Connection In the 1920's, Duke Ellington and his band played nightly at the Cotton Club in Harlem, where Josephine Baker had danced. During the 1930's and 1940's, Ellington introduced many classic jazz tunes, such as "Take the 'A' Train."

Visual Arts Connection Under Baker's spell, Parisians in the 1920's became fascinated with African American culture. In 1929, artist Paul Colin (1892–1985), inspired by jazz, published a book of stunning color lithographs (prints made from an artist's drawings) entitled *Le Tumulte Noir (The Black Commotion)*. Baker wrote the dedication to the book. Colin's images combine modern European influences, including Cubism and Art Deco, with styles drawn from African sculpture. The work confirmed the new, fruitful friendship between African American and French cultures.

Expository Writing Activity: Dance Lesson
Prepare a presentation on how to learn the Charleston for your class. Include diagrams and samples of music. Give a brief history of the dance. You might even perform a few steps!

***Male Dancer with Blue* from *Le Tumulte Noir*,** Paul Colin, National Portrait Gallery, Smithsonian Institution

▶ Critical Viewing Point out details in this Colin print that represent different traditions. **[Analyze]**

Viewing and Representing

Activity Ask students to post their diagrams showing the steps of the Charleston in the class. Ask an adult volunteer to bring in music and teach the class how to do the Charleston.

Critical Viewing

Analyze Students may say that the print is highly stylized and shows the lines and curves of Art Deco and the simple forms of African sculpture.

Media and Technology Skills

Using Computer Technology

Activity: Getting Help On-line

Any computer program you use probably comes with its own "how-to"—on-line help the user can access while using the program. By mastering Help, you can quickly solve problems or answer questions that come up while you are using the program.

Learn About It On-line help comes in various forms, each suited to different situations:

- **Balloon Help** brings up a balloon describing the function of each feature of the interface (buttons, dialog boxes, and so on) as you roll your mouse over it.
- **On-line manuals** offer detailed help, often indexed both by category and alphabetically. You can typically call up the manual by selecting Help from the program's menu bar.
- **Manufacturers' Web sites** provide the latest information on a program, typically in the form of FAQ (Frequently Asked Questions) sheets. They also provide software updates.
- **Other Forms of Help** Printed manuals offer detailed information on operating the program. Read Me Files, installed with the program, contain tips about specific problems in running the program.

You will learn to use a program best if you try your own solutions to minor problems before consulting Help. Use Help only when you are first starting out, when you run out of possible solutions, or when you face a major problem

Tips for Using Help

Index

- If a feature or command with which you need help has a standard name, use the Index feature of the on-line manual to find out more about it. Typically, typing in the first few letters of the name will scroll down a list to your topic.

Contents

- If a standard name does not cover your topic, browse the Contents of the manual.

Apply It Choose an application, such as a word-processing program, to which you have access. Consult two forms of on-line help to answer three questions about program features or problems you have encountered. Record your results in a graphic organizer like the one shown. Then, write a brief essay evaluating the helpfulness of each form of on-line help.

Program: ____________________

My Question	Form of Help	Found Answer?	How Easy/Hard to Find? Explain

Lesson Objectives

1. To evaluate on-line help.
2. To write to inform.

Step-by-Step Teaching Guide

Using Computer Technology

Teaching Resources: Writing Support Transparency 10-G; Writing Support Activity Book 10-2

1. Have a student expert or experts demonstrate how to use the help functions for a software program your students use by choosing three questions about the program's features and looking up the answers. Explain that students will be asked to write an evaluation of an application of their choice.
2. Display the transparency. Use the graphic organizer to record the information students learned from the demonstration.
3. Give students copies of the blank organizer. Have students use the organizer to record the answers to the questions they devise about software program features and problems.
4. After students finish their written evaluations, they should discuss which forms of on-line help they found most useful and why.

Customize for *Logical/Mathematical Learners*

Students may want to devise a numerical rating system for the various features of the different help modes and present their findings in chart form.

Lesson Objectives

1. To write to explain.
2. To use correct grammar, spelling, and punctuation.
3. To develop, draft, revise, and proofread an essay.

Step-by-Step Teaching Guide

Giving Instructions in Response to Expository Writing Prompts

Teaching Resources: Standardized Test Preparation Workbook, pp. 19–20

1. Read the sample writing situation to your class and make sure students understand what to do.
2. Urge students to choose a simple appliance to write about.
3. They should choose a topic quickly and jot down words or phrases that describe the steps. Then they should reorder, eliminate, or add steps.
4. After that, students should draft and revise their how-to essays, allotting their time approximately as suggested in the textbook.
5. Remind students that the most important element of a how-to essay is the clarity of the instructions. The first sentence should describe what the essay will teach the reader to do, the following sentences tell the reader how to do or make the item, and the last sentences describe the benefits of learning how to do or make the item.

Standardized Test Preparation Workshop

Giving Instructions in Response to Expository Writing Prompts

The writing prompts on standardized tests often judge your ability to write a "how-to" essay (sometimes called an "informative narrative"). For this type of writing, you will need to present clear instructions and explanations. The following are the criteria on which your writing will be evaluated:

- logical, consistent organization
- elaboration of your explanations using details appropriate to your specific audience and purpose
- use of complete sentences and proper grammar
- correct spelling and punctuation.

The writing process, even when it is used for a test, can be broken down into stages. Plan to use a specific amount of time for prewriting, drafting, revising, and proofreading.

The sample expository writing prompt below is an example of one type of question you may find on a standardized test. On the following page are suggestions to help you respond. The clocks represent the amount of your allotted time that you should devote to each stage.

Test Tip

When writing a how-to for a test, visualize yourself performing the steps. This will help you to describe the steps and to present them in the correct order.

Sample Writing Situation

A friend of yours has asked you to show him or her how to operate an electronic appliance. However, you will not have time to stop by his or her house. Choose an electronic appliance with which you are familiar. Write directions to your friend in which you explain an important procedure in the use of the appliance.

TEST-TAKING TIP

When students write how-to essays on standardized tests, they may find it helpful to organize their writing by grouping the various stages involved in the instructions. For example, if they were teaching someone how to make a hand puppet, they might group some steps under "Gathering Materials," some under "Cutting and Gluing," and some under "Adding Finishing Touches."

Prewriting

Allow close to one fourth of your time for prewriting.

Consider Your Audience As you start gathering details about operating the appliance, keep your audience in mind. Your friend probably has some basic knowledge of how such appliances work. Also, he or she may have a model that is different from yours. For both of these reasons, do not clutter your instructions. For example, if you were writing about a videocassette recorder, you might write "press the 'Record' button," instead of "press the red 'Record' button on the bottom left." Further, because you are writing to a friend, you can use contractions and less formal language.

Drafting

Allow almost half of your time for drafting.

Use Chronological Order Organize your details logically—present them in the order in which they are done. To help you place your steps in the right order, use a timeline. For an example of one type of timeline, see the sticky note graphic organizer on page 218.

Provide Support Review the steps you have listed on your timeline. Add any substeps or definitions that will make your explanation clearer. Look for places where you can add details, like those describing what your friend should look for to make sure he or she is performing a step correctly.

Use Transitional Words Make it easier for your friend to follow your instructions by connecting steps using transitional words. Use words like *first, then, next,* and *finally* to indicate the order in which things should be done. To show the cause-and-effect relationships between steps, use words such as *so, because,* and *consequently.*

Revising, Editing, and Proofreading

Allow almost one fourth of your time for revising. Allow several minutes to check for spelling and punctuation errors.

Run Through Your Instructions As you read over your work, visualize each step in succession. Look for steps that are out of order or missing. Also, look for information your reader will need to fully understand a step. If you need to add a step or provide further explanation, neatly insert the new material.

Eliminate Errors At this stage, if you find an error, you will not have time to copy your work over. Put a single line through any misspelled word or incorrect sentence and neatly write the replacement above it. For any list of steps or items, check to make sure you have used commas and semicolons correctly.

Customize for *Less Advanced Students*

Give students a choice of two simple topics for their how-to essays rather than having them select topics on their own so that they can concentrate on conceptualizing the various steps and writing them in the proper order rather than worrying about selecting a topic.

Customize for *Gifted/Talented Students*

Students will find that steps that are out of order or neglected in their essays will become readily apparent if they do thumbnail sketches of the various steps. These students may want to invent fanciful appliances for their how-to essays rather than describing actual ones.

Chapter 11 Time and Resource Manager

In-Depth Lesson Plan

	LESSON FOCUS	PRINT AND MEDIA RESOURCES
DAY 1	**Introduction to Research Reports** Students learn key elements of research reports and analyze the Model From Literature (pp. 234–237).	***Writers at Work* Videotape,** Reports ***Writing and Grammar iText* (Interactive Text),** Ch.11, Introduction
DAY 2	**Prewriting** Students choose and narrow a topic, consider their audience and purpose, and gather information (pp. 238–241).	**Teaching Resources** *Writing Support Transparencies,* 11-A–C; *Writing Support Activity Book,* 11-1 ***Writing and Grammar iText* (Interactive Text),** Section 11.2
DAY 3	**Drafting** Students organize their ideas and write their first drafts (pp. 242–243).	**Teaching Resources** *Writing Support Transparencies,* 11-D ***Writing and Grammar iText* (Interactive Text),** Section 11.3
DAY 4	**Revising** Students revise their drafts in terms of overall structure, paragraphs, sentences, and word choice (pp. 244–248).	**Teaching Resources** *Writing Support Transparencies,* 11-E–F ***Writing and Grammar iText* (Interactive Text),** Section 11.4
DAY 5	**Editing and Proofreading; Publishing and Presenting** Students check their work for accuracy and correctness and present their final drafts (pp. 249–251).	**Teaching Resources** *Scoring Rubrics on Transparency,* Ch. 11; *Formal Assessment,* Ch. 11 ***Writing and Grammar iText* (Interactive Text),** Sections 11.5–6

Accelerated Lesson Plan

	LESSON FOCUS	PRINT AND MEDIA RESOURCES
DAY 1	**Introduction Through Drafting** Students review the characteristics of research reports, select topics, and write drafts (pp. 234–243).	**Teaching Resources** *Writing Support Transparencies,* 11-A–D; *Writing Support Activity Book,* 11-1 ***Writing and Grammar iText* (Interactive Text),** Ch. 11, Introduction through Section 11.3
DAY 2	**Revising Through Presenting** Students work individually or with peers to revise, edit, and proofread their work for presentation (pp. 244–251).	**Teaching Resources** *Writing Support Transparencies,* 11-E–F; *Scoring Rubrics on Transparency,* Ch. 11; *Formal Assessment,* Ch. 11 ***Writing and Grammar iText* (Interactive Text),** Sections 11.4–6

Options for Adapting Lesson Plans

HOMEWORK

Have students complete any stage of the lesson for homework.

SPELLING

To teach spelling skills in conjunction with writing skills, work through *Prentice Hall Everyday Spelling,* Grade 8, Chapter 13, as you cover this *Writing and Grammar* chapter. At the Editing and Proofreading stage, remind students to apply the spelling skills to their research report.

FEATURES

Extend coverage with Connected Assignment (p. 255), Spotlight on the Humanities (p. 256), Media and Technology Skills (p. 257), and Standardized Test Preparation Workshop (p. 258).

TECHNOLOGY

Students can complete any stage of the lesson on the computer, using *Writing and Grammar iText* or a word-processing program. Have them print out their completed work.

INTEGRATED SKILLS COVERAGE

Integrating Grammar
Participial Phrases, SE p. 247
Punctuating Titles of Works, SE p. 250

Reading/Writing Connection
Reading Strategy, SE p. 236
Writing Application, SE p. 237

Viewing and Representing
Critical Viewing, SE pp. 234, 236, 237, 242, 244, 249, 252, 253, 255, 256
Framing Research Questions, SE p. 256

Spelling
Integrating Spelling Skills ATE p. 249

BLOCK SCHEDULING

Pacing Suggestions
For 90-minute Blocks
- Have students complete the Prewriting and Drafting stages in a single period.
- Focus one class period on Revising and Editing and Publishing and Presenting. Allow at least 30 minutes for peer revision.

Resources for Varying Instruction
- ***Writing and Grammar iText* (Interactive Text)** A 90-minute block provides an ideal opportunity for students to work on computer.
- ***Writers at Work* Videotape** Show the Reports segment in class.

Professional Development Support
- ***How to Manage Instruction in the Block*** This teaching resource provides management and activity suggestions.

ASSESSMENT SUPPORT

Standardized Test Preparation Workshop SE pp. 258–259, ATE p. 250

Standardized Test Preparation Workbook, pp. 21–22

Scoring Rubrics on Transparency, Ch. 11

Formal Assessment, Ch. 11

Writing Assessment and Portfolio Management

MEDIA AND TECHNOLOGY

For the Student
- ***Writing and Grammar iText* (Interactive Text)**, Ch. 11

For the Teacher
- ***Writers at Work* Videotape**, Reports
- ***Resource Pro* CD-ROM**

MEETING INDIVIDUAL NEEDS

Less Advanced Students ATE pp. 237, 245, 259. See also Ongoing Assessments ATE pp. 239, 243, 246, 247.

ESL Students ATE p. 238

More Advanced Students ATE p. 240

Visual/Spatial Learners ATE p. 239

Verbal/Linguistic Learners ATE p. 243

WRITING AND GRAMMAR ON-LINE

iText Interactive Text (On-line or on CD-ROM)
- Easily navigable instruction with interactive Revision Checkers
- Full use of e-rater™, the essay-scoring system (on-line only)

Companion Web Site PHSchool.com
- Scoring rubrics with models (use Web Code eck-8001)

See the Go On-line! feature, SE p. iii.

LITERATURE CONNECTIONS

Related selections from *Prentice Hall Literature: Timeless Voices, Timeless Themes,* Silver:

Professional Model from "Harriet Tubman: Guide to Freedom," Ann Petry, SE p. 236

Topic Bank Option "The Drummer Boy of Shiloh," Ray Bradbury, SE p. 239

CHAPTER 11
RESEARCH REPORT

Lesson Objectives

1. To write to inform, such as to explain, describe, report, and narrate.
2. To select and use voice and style appropriate to audience and purpose.
3. To capitalize and punctuate correctly to clarify and enhance meaning.
4. To generate ideas and plans for writing by using prewriting strategies.
5. To revise drafts for coherence, progression, and logical support of ideas.
6. To select and use reference materials and resources.
7. To evaluate how well one's writing achieves its purposes.
8. To frame questions to direct research.

Chapter 11 Research
Research Report

▲ **Critical Viewing** Cite two questions for research suggested by this Civil War photo. **[Question]**

Research in Everyday Life

Where does your world end? It doesn't stop with your nose. It doesn't even stop with the walls of your room. Your world stretches on and on into places you can't even see. Every fact that you know, from the fact that China lies on the other side of the world to the fact that tomorrow is your aunt's birthday, expands the limits of your world.

To stretch your world even further, all you need is to learn new facts. You might ask a relative for facts about your early childhood, or an elderly neighbor for facts about your street. Asking questions like these is a form of **research**. The answers help define your world. When you do research on general topics for a report, you stretch your world even further. Improve your research writing skills, and broaden your horizons.

Critical Viewing

Question Students may say *How did soldiers live during the war?* and *How well was the war documented by photographers?*

TIME AND RESOURCE MANAGER

Resources
Technology: Writers at Work Videotape; Writing and Grammar iText, Ch. 11

In-Depth Coverage	Accelerated Pace
• Cover pp. 234–235 in class. • Show Writing a Research Report section of the Writers at Work Videotape. • Discuss different types of persuasive essays. • Read the Model From Literature (pp. 236–237) with students.	• Assign pp. 234–237 for independent student review. • Discuss definitions and types of research reports.

What Is a Research Report?

A **research report** presents information gathered from reference books, observations, interviews, or other sources. By citing these sources, a research writer lets others check the facts for themselves. A good research report also helps readers form an overall picture of the subject. The elements of an effective research report include

- an overall focus or main idea expressed in a thesis statement.
- information gathered from a variety of sources.
- clear organization and smooth transitions.
- facts and details to support each main point.
- accurate, complete citations identifying sources.

To preview the criteria on which your report may be evaluated, see the Rubric for Self-Assessment on page 251.

Writers in ACTION

Virginia Hamilton grew up in Ohio, where her grandfather settled after escaping slavery. In her novels and nonfiction, she relies on research:

"I use primary sources, which are actual events that are written down by the participants. . . . I work on something that I'm reporting until the very last minute, until they literally yank it out of my hands, because I want to get everything right. So I look at the facts over and over again."

Types of Research Reports

In addition to a traditional research report, the following are some other types of reports you might write.

- **Biographical sketches**, which report high points in the life of a notable person.
- **Reports of scientific experiments**, which present the materials, procedures, and results of experiments.
- **Documented essays**, which use research to support a point or examine a trend.

PREVIEW Student Work IN PROGRESS

Joseph Hochberger, a student at Gotha Middle School in Windermere, Florida, wrote a research report about Benjamin Franklin. In this chapter, you will see how Joseph used featured strategies to choose a topic, to gather information, to elaborate, and to analyze patterns between and within paragraphs. At the end of the chapter, you can read Joseph's completed report.

PREPARE and ENGAGE

Interest GRABBER Scoops "R" Us is offering a year of free ice cream to the person who learns the most about ice cream. Ask students how they would go about learning everything there is to know about this important food. Explain to them that they will learn more about researching in this chapter.

Activate Prior Knowledge

Ask students to recall a time when they read a book or article about something new. What did they learn? Where do they think the author of the article got the information?

More About the Writer

Virginia Hamilton is the author of more than 34 books. One of the most honored writers for children, her titles include, *Bluish, The Justice Cycle Trilogy: Justice and Her Brothers, Dustland,* and *The Gathering.* Hamilton is an enthusiastic user of the Internet who uses her home page (www.virginiahamilton.com) to communicate with readers. On the page she writes her reason for writing: "I write for myself and strangers who read my books and become my friends."

ONGOING ASSESSMENT: Diagnose

Use one of the following options to diagnose students' current level of proficiency in writing a research report.

Option 1 Ask each student to select the strongest example of his or her research report writing from last year. Hold conferences to review each student's sample. Use the conferences to determine which students will need extra support in developing a research report.

Option 2 Ask students to write a list of questions they would ask before writing a research report. Review their list of questions for its completeness and be sure that students understand the need to find information in sources that answer these questions.

TEACH

Reading\Writing Connection

Reading: Question

Discuss how much we learn when we are active readers. Asking questions is important for guiding our reading and keeping focused. Tell students to start with the title. Ask: *What was the Underground Railroad? Was it really underground? Was it really a railroad? If not, why were these terms used to describe it? How did it work?*

Teaching From the Model

You can use this Model From Literature to show students what a research report looks like, how it is structured, how a thesis statement is used, and how the author cites sources for facts.

Step-by-Step Teaching Guide

Engage Students Through Literature

1. Read this report aloud or have volunteers read it to the class.
2. Ask students what they learned. As they recite facts about the Underground Railroad, guide the discussion back to the effectiveness of the report.
3. Point out that the author's thesis statement, the clear organization, the citation of sources, and the way he answers the questions *where? when? how did it work? how many slaves escaped?* Tell students that effective research reports do not call attention to themselves, but we come away having learned something.

Critical Viewing

Interpret Students may say that the man is focusing on the journey ahead, while the woman is looking back to see if anyone is after them. Because he is looking ahead and by holding a child, the man represents the future the family is seeking. Because she is looking behind, the woman indicates the past the family is fleeing.

11.1 Model From Literature

Robert W. Peterson (1925–) has written four history books and numerous magazine articles.

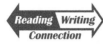

A Ride for Liberty—The Fugitive Slaves, Eastman Johnson, The Brooklyn Museum

▲ Critical Viewing In this painting of a family escaping slavery, the woman looks behind while the man holds the child and looks ahead. Explain the significance of these poses. **[Interpret]**

Reading Writing Connection — Reading Strategy: Question

To get the most out of reading research reports, **ask questions.** For instance, Peterson explains that the Underground Railroad was an organization that helped slaves escape to freedom. You might ask, "Where did escaped slaves go?" As you read the excerpt below, you will learn the answer.

The Underground Railroad

Robert W. Peterson

Before the Civil War, thousands of slaves escaped on this invisible train to freedom. The Underground Railroad wasn't underground and it wasn't a railroad. But it was real just the same. And it was one of the brightest chapters in American history.

Peterson's introduction includes a thesis statement giving his topic.

The Underground Railroad was a secret network of people who helped slaves flee to freedom before the Civil War (1861–1865). The slaves were black people from families who had been brought from Africa in chains. They were owned by their white masters and forced to work without pay.

The first slaves arrived in Jamestown, Virginia, in 1619—the year before the Pilgrims landed at Plymouth, Massachusetts (Buckmaster 11). Two hundred years later, there were nearly four million slaves in the United States (Siebert 378). Most worked on large plantations in the South. By then, slavery had been outlawed in most northern states.

LITERATURE

To read more research on this topic, see *Harriet Tubman: Conductor on the Underground Railroad* by Ann Petry. You can find an excerpt from this book in *Prentice Hall Literature: Timeless Voices, Timeless Themes,* Silver.

Responding to Literature

Tell students that the Model above is a documented essay. Ann Petry's book on Harriet Tubman is a biographical sketch. Ask students why you gave the essays these descriptions.

Thousands of slaves ran away each year. Some fled to get away from harsh masters. Others wanted to enjoy liberty. The Underground Railroad was started to help them.

Its "stations" were homes, shops, and churches where runaway slaves were hidden and fed. The "agents" or "station-masters" were people—both black and white—who hated slavery. They wanted to help slaves get free.

Its "conductors" led or transported fugitives from station to station on their way to free states. They had to watch for slave catchers, who were paid to capture runaways and return them. Some conductors guided slaves all the way to Canada (Siebert 187). . . .

The Underground Railroad network covered all of the Northeast and went as far west as Kansas and Nebraska. Ohio had more stations than any other state. Thousands of runaway slaves crossed over the Ohio River into Ohio from Kentucky and what is now West Virginia (Siebert 134–135).

Not all fugitive slaves headed north to find freedom. A few went to Mexico. Some fled to Florida and were given refuge by Seminole Indians. Indians in other parts of the continent also sheltered runaway slaves. In Ohio, the Ottawa tribe took them in (Buckmaster 12, 35, 186, 187). In Ontario, Canada, Mohawk Chief Joseph Brant welcomed escaped slaves (Siebert 203). . . .

We can only guess how many slaves used the Underground Railroad. Historians estimate the total at between 40,000 and 100,000 by the time the Civil War began in 1861 ("Underground Railroad" 126). The war was fought in large part over the slavery issue.

In 1863, President Abraham Lincoln declared slaves free. That was the end of the Underground Railroad. There were no ceremonies and no celebrations. The invisible railroad ended as it began—quietly and without fanfare.

Works Cited

Buckmaster, Henrietta. *Let My People Go.* Boston: Beacon Press, 1941.

Siebert, Wilbur H. *The Underground Railroad from Slavery to Freedom.* New York: Macmillan, 1898, reprinted 1992.

"Underground Railroad." *Encyclopedia Britannica,* vol. 12. 15th ed., 1998.

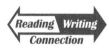

Reading Writing Connection Writing Application: **Help Readers Answer Questions** As you draft your report, answer questions readers would be likely to have.

▼ Critical Viewing
Explain why this secret hiding space was needed by people escaping slavery. **[Hypothesize]**

Peterson organizes his points logically: First, he gives background on slavery. Then, he describes the operations of the Railroad. Then, he gives its history.

Throughout the report, Peterson provides specific facts to create a picture of the scope of the Railroad. He documents specific facts with internal citations.

Peterson provides a "Works Cited" list that gives his sources in a standard format.

Critical Viewing

Hypothesize Students may say that escaped slaves needed safe places to rest and eat during their long journeys.

More About the Author

Robert W. Peterson has written history books on a wide range of subjects, from apartheid in South Africa to space exploration.

Customize for *Less Advanced Students*

Students may be disturbed by the source citations in parentheses. Instruct them to skip over the source citations and not let them interrupt the narrative flow. They can return to them later if they need to know where to check facts.

Reading\Writing Connection

Writing: Help Readers Answer Questions

Explain to students that a research report provides information on a subject in order to teach readers. Therefore, writers need to make sure that readers are not left with unanswered questions. Ask students if they have any questions they feel were left unanswered by Peterson.

Step-by-Step Teaching Guide

Prewriting: Browsing; Newswatch

1. These activities are best done out of class, unless you can bring in newsmagazines and other research sources.
2. The purpose of the activity is twofold: to acquaint students with research sources and to stimulate them to select a topic.

Step-by-Step Teaching Guide

Prewriting: Self-Interview

Teaching Resources: Writing Support Transparency 11-A; Writing Support Activity Book 11-1

1. Use the transparency to examine Joseph's work in progress. Point out how he connected items in his list.
2. Give students copies of the blank organizer. Encourage them to use their memories and imaginations in doing this activity.
3. Have students examine their connections to come up with a topic for the research report.

Customize for *ESL Students*

Suggest that students think about people, places, and events in their home cultures. Any of these could be a good topic for a research report.

11.2 Prewriting

Choosing Your Topic

Use the following strategies to choose a research topic that interests you and on which enough information is available:

Strategies for Generating a Topic

1. **Browsing** Scan reference books at the library: a volume from an encyclopedia set, a biographical dictionary, an almanac, an atlas, and so on. You might also surf on the Internet. Jot down each interesting subject that you find. Review your notes, and choose your topic.
2. **Newswatch** Flip through recent magazines or newspapers. Tune in to television or radio broadcasts. List people, places, events, or current issues that you want to investigate. Choose one of these issues as a topic for research.
3. **Self-Interview** Create a chart like the one below, and answer the questions shown. Circle words and draw lines to show connections between items on your list. Choose a topic from among these linked items.

iText

Try it out! Use the interactive Conducting a Self-Interview activity in **Section 11.2,** on-line or on CD-ROM.

Student Work IN PROGRESS

Name: Joseph Hochberger
Gotha Middle School
Windermere, FL

Conducting a Self-Interview

Joseph used a self-interview to identify people, places, and things in which he was interested. He remembered that his science teacher, Mr. Sanchez, had mentioned Benjamin Franklin's experiments with electricity.

People	Places	Things	Events
What interesting people do I know or know about?	What interesting places have I been to or heard about?	What interesting things do I know about?	What interesting events have happened to me or have I heard about?
Jan Ben Franklin Michael Jordan Melissa	hospital hockey rink library Philadelphia zoo	baseball compact disk hat newspaper kite	hockey game homecoming crafts fair July Fourth parade

TIME AND RESOURCE MANAGER

Resources
Print: Writing Support Transparencies, 11-A–C; Writing Support Activity Book, 11-1
Technology: Writing and Grammar iText, Section 11.2

In-Depth Coverage	Accelerated Pace
• Cover pp. 238–241 in class. • Work through the Browsing and Newswatch strategies with the class. Use the Responding to Fine Arts transparency to generate additional topics. • Do the Self-Interview activity in class. **Option** Have students work independently or in small groups with Writing and Grammar iText.	• Assign pp. 238–241 for independent student review. • Have students work independently to choose and narrow their topics. • Have partners focus on audience, purpose, and gathering details.

TOPIC BANK

If you're having trouble finding a topic, consider the following possibilities:

1. **Biographical Report** Choose someone who had a major impact on a specific period in American history—for example, the American Revolution, World War II, or the civil rights movement of the 1960's. Write a biographical report explaining his or her decision to become involved in important affairs.
2. **Research Report on a Planet** Choose a planet in our solar system. Research its atmosphere, composition, orbit, and so on. Have any probes landed there? What information have they gathered? Write a report of your findings, and include photographs if possible.

Responding to Fine Art

3. Jot down a few notes about this painting. Review your notes for suggestions about research topics on American life during the nineteenth century. Choose one of these topics for your research paper.

Miners in the Sierras, Charles Christian Nahl, National Museum of American Art, Washington, DC

Responding to Literature

4. Read "The Drummer Boy of Shiloh," a short story by Ray Bradbury. List topics related to the Civil War suggested by the story, such as soldiers' daily lives. Choose one of these topics for your report. You can find "The Drummer Boy of Shiloh" in *Prentice Hall Literature: Timeless Voices, Timeless Themes*, Silver.

Cooperative Writing Opportunity

5. **Teenagers of the Past** With a small group, investigate the life of teenagers in nineteenth-century America. Divide the following tasks: researching life on the frontier using primary sources, such as letters and journals; researching life in the big cities; and creating charts, drawings, and other graphics to illustrate the report. Compile your research in a report and present it to the class.

Step-by-Step Teaching Guide

Responding to Fine Art

Miners in the Sierras **by Charles Christian Nahl**

Teaching Resources: Writing Support Transparency 11-B

1. Display the transparency.
2. Encourage students to put their imaginations into the picture. Ask the following questions:

Who are these men?

How did it feel to be there?

How did they endure the hardships?

What dreams did they have?

How many struck it rich?

Customize for *Visual/Spatial Learners*

Encourage students to use their visual/spatial gifts to put themselves into the picture and try to note the feel of the mountain air, the sound of the water, the brilliance of the light.

Responding to Literature

Bradbury's story may get some students interested in what it feels like to be in a battle. Their reports could include firsthand accounts by local people who fought in Vietnam or the Gulf War.

Spotlight on the Humanities

For additional topic suggestions, refer students to the Spotlight on the Humanities on page 256.

ONGOING ASSESSMENT: Monitor and Reinforce

If some students are having difficulty coming up with a topic, use one of the following options.

Option 1 Suggest that students choose an idea from the Topic Bank. If many students have difficulty, work with them on one topic, modeling the process for them.	**Option 2** If Topic Bank ideas seem too complex, suggest that students try one of the assignments from the Topic Bank for Heterogeneous Classes in the Teaching Resources.

TIME SAVERS!

Writing Support Transparencies

Use the transparencies for Chapter 11 to teach these strategies.

Prewriting: Use "Classical Invention" Questions

Teaching Resources: Writing Support Transparency 11-C

1. Discuss the importance of choosing a topic that is suitable for a short research report. "Important Leaders of the American Revolution" is much too broad for a short report. Even a report on a single leader such as George Washington could be too broad, considering the extent of Washington's accomplishments and influence on events of the time. A report on one leader that focuses on some of his or her accomplishments might be just right.

2. Display the transparency. Examine how Joseph used classical invention to come up with a topic that is both interesting and narrow enough for a short research report.

Customize for
More Advanced Students

Encourage students to seek out a challenging topic, one that they have some curiosity about. Steer them toward library research sources and the Internet to find information they can use first to identify and then to narrow the topic.

11.2

Narrowing Your Topic

Once you have chosen a topic, you may still need to modify it. Make sure that your topic is narrow enough to cover fully in a short report. One strategy for narrowing a topic is a questioning strategy called "Classical Invention."

Use "Classical Invention" Questions

To help you narrow your topic, answer questions about your topic like the ones shown in the feature below. Simply replace "Benjamin Franklin" with a phrase summarizing your own topic.

Review your answers to the Classical Invention questions. Circle interesting details, and look for links among them. Then, summarize the narrowed topic to which these linked details belong. Use this topic as the focus of your research paper.

Try it out! Use the interactive Classical Invention activity in **Section 11.2**, on-line or on CD-ROM.

Student Work
IN PROGRESS

Name: Joseph Hochberger
Gotha Middle School
Windermere, FL

Using "Classical Invention" to Group Details

Joseph used Classical Invention to narrow his topic: the life of Benjamin Franklin.

General Topic: Benjamin Franklin

- In what general category does your topic belong?
 (Inventor,) (Founding Father)

- How is your topic similar to or different from other topics in this category?
 (People still know Franklin's sayings,) unlike words of other Founding Fathers; Jefferson was also an inventor.

- Into what other topics can your topic be divided?
 Franklin's (role in American politics;) Franklin's (writings;) (Franklin's inventions)

- What causes and effects does your topic involve?
 Franklin helped invent the postal system; Franklin (persuaded others) to approve the Constitution.

Franklin's (contribution) to American politics.

Franklin's (contribution) to American literature.

(Narrowed Topic)
The variety of Franklin's accomplishments.

Franklin's (contribution to) science.

**Narrowed Topic:
Franklin's
Contribution to
Science**

240 • Research Report

⏱ TIME SAVERS!

Writing Support Transparencies
Use the transparencies for Chapter 11 to teach these strategies.

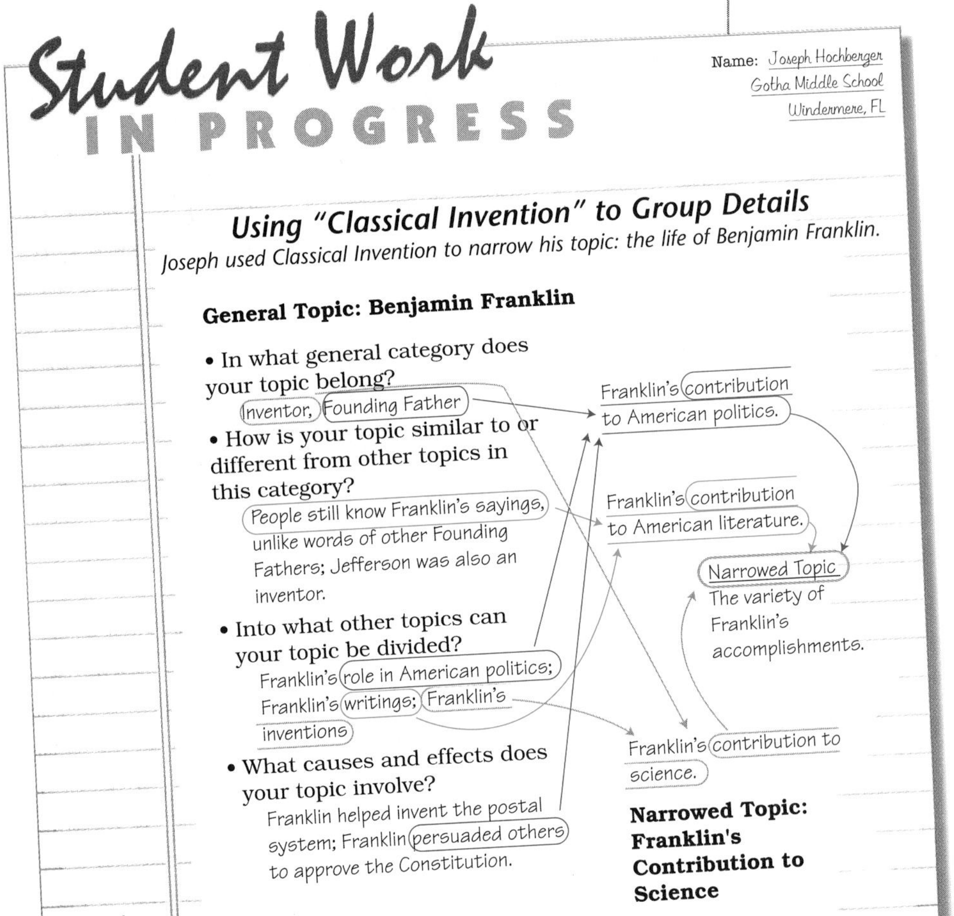

Considering Your Audience and Purpose

The **purpose** of any research report is to present facts on the topic clearly. A report may be written, though, for different groups of readers, or **audiences.** Your audience's background and interest in your topic will determine how much you say about each detail.

For instance, you would explain the most basic facts about pollution to a group of young children. For readers of the local newspaper, you might focus just on the aspects of the topic affecting them directly, such as the results of a recent water test in the area. For a science class, though, you would want to explain the complexities of pollution in detail.

Gathering Details

Use a Variety of Sources

By using several different sources, you can ensure that your information is current, accurate, and balanced. Follow these guidelines for improving accuracy:

- Check to see when printed sources were published to make sure that the information in them is up-to-date.
- If you note discrepancies in the information given by two sources, check the facts in a third source. If three or more sources disagree, mention the disagreement in your paper.
- Whenever possible, cross-check information from the Internet or from an interview by consulting other sources.

Take Notes

Use Note Cards When you find information related to your topic, take detailed notes on index cards.

- Write one note on each card.
- Double-check the spelling of names and technical terms.
- Use quotation marks whenever you copy words exactly.
- On each card, record the title of the book or article and the page number, or the name of the Web site or interviewee.
- Create a source card for each book, article, Web site, or interviewee. For print sources, list the author, title, publisher, and place and date of publication. For Internet sources, list the sponsor, page name, date of last revision, the date you visited it, and the address. For an interview, give the date and the person's name, address, and phone number.

Use Technology You can also make photocopies of source material or print out pages from the Internet. Highlight the information you will use on your copy.

Research Tip

For more sources on your topic, check the bibliographies of reference books you use.

Step-by-Step Teaching Guide

Prewriting: Considering Your Audience and Purpose

1. Discuss the importance of knowing your audience. In a short essay, writers need to decide how much background information to include.
2. If they are writing for people with little knowledge of their topic, they need to include considerable background information. For a report to eighth graders on Benjamin Franklin, they would need to recount the circumstances of his youth and rise to prominence in Philadelphia. For an audience of historians, a brief reminder of that information would suffice.

Step-by-Step Teaching Guide

Prewriting: Gathering Details

1. Review the importance of noting sources and taking notes so students can be sure they have recorded the information accurately.
2. Remind students that not everything on the Internet is equal. The American Historical Association is a respected group of teachers and writers of history. The American Historical Society (if there is one) might be two people who are interested in history. Anyone can create a Web site. Students must double-check every source they use from the Internet to make sure it is legitimate.
3. Review the rules of paraphrasing information and using direct quotations. Encourage students to put information in their own words. They should quote only when there is a good reason to do so.

Step-by-Step Teaching Guide

Drafting: Shaping Your Writing

1. Discuss choosing a perspective. Remind students that in a short report, they can cover only so much ground. A perspective is closely related to a thesis statement but comes before it. For a biographical study, here are four possible perspectives.

   A person's most important accomplishments

   A person's personal history and characteristics

   A person's influence on others and history

   A person's reputation throughout history

2. A thesis statement is the main idea in a nutshell: one sentence. Share the following examples with students.

   Alexander Hamilton was a great leader because he assured the financial security of the United States.

   George Washington was called the father of this country because without him, the colonists would have lost the Revolution and the new republic would have torn itself apart with political rivalries.

3. Use the transparency to help students make a formal outline for their research reports. Show them how the structure of Roman numerals and capital letters organizes main ideas, subideas, and supportive details for their report. Be sure to tell them that every writer, amateur and professional, uses some kind of outline for structuring his or her work in advance.

Critical Viewing

Apply Students' responses will vary. Most students will mention that Roosevelt had polio.

11.3 Drafting

Shaping Your Writing

After you have gathered your information, decide how to organize and present it. Drafting your report is the process of bringing your details together and making sense of them.

▲ Critical Viewing Cite a fact you know about Franklin D. Roosevelt. Then, write a thesis statement for a report that might include this fact. **[Apply]**

Choose a Perspective

Review your notes, and choose a perspective for your report. A **perspective** is a point of view on your subject—the "spin" or "take" you offer on your subject. For example, one biographical report might use facts from a person's life to illustrate one or two personal characteristics such as cleverness or bravery. Another report might use those same facts to explain the significance of the person's contribution to a field.

Develop a Thesis Statement

Once you know your perspective, sum up the point of your paper in a sentence, called a **thesis statement**. For example, in a report on Franklin D. Roosevelt, your thesis statement might read: "In fighting for the New Deal, Roosevelt showed the same characteristic he showed in fighting his disability—determination." Include your thesis statement in the introduction to your report.

Make an Outline

Using a Formal Outline For your outline, use Roman numerals (I, II, III) for your most important points. Under each Roman numeral, use capital letters (A, B, C) for the details that support each main point.

Title of Your Report

I. Introduction
II. First main point
  A. Supporting detail #1
  B. Supporting detail #2
  C. Supporting detail #3
III. Second main point . . .

TIME AND RESOURCE MANAGER

Resources
Print: Writing Support Transparencies, 11-D
Technology: Writing and Grammar iText, Section 11.3

In-Depth Coverage	Accelerated Pace
• Cover pp. 242–243 in class. **Option** Have students work independently or in small groups with Writing and Grammar iText.	• Have students review pp. 242–243 independently and then write their own research report drafts. • Respond to individual drafting issues as needed.

Providing Elaboration

Be Your Own Reader

After you write each paragraph, pause. Pretend you are a typical reader from your selected audience. What statements or details might confuse or surprise such a reader? Add clarifying details, such as definitions and explanations, where needed to help your reader. (For help defining your audience, see page 241.)

Bring Out Your Perspective

If you have done a good job researching your topic, you will have gathered more details than you can use. As you draft, make sure that you include the details that are most relevant to your perspective. Consider the following example:

TOPIC:	California Gold Rush
PERSPECTIVE:	The lives led by miners were often harsh.
APPROPRIATE DETAIL:	facts about miners' housing
UNNECESSARY DETAIL:	facts about routes to California

After you write a paragraph, pause and review the details you have included. Eliminate or revise those that do not contribute to your perspective. Build on those details that do.

Student Work IN PROGRESS

Name: Joseph Hochberger
Gotha Middle School
Windermere, FL

Sharpening Perspective

Joseph's perspective in his report on Franklin was that Franklin's talents were diverse. He changed this paragraph to bring out that perspective more. He also added explanations to help readers with little background in his subject.

Writer, community planner, and inventor—but Ben didn't stop there. He became drawn into politics as well. His ~~Franklin's~~ involvement in public service began with his appointments as clerk of the Pennsylvania Legislature in 1736 and as postmaster of Philadelphia in 1737. He served in both these positions for over fifteen years. In 1753, he became Deputy Postmaster General, in charge of all mail for the northern colonies.

Joseph added the first sentence here to tie this paragraph to his perspective.

By adding this phrase, Joseph clarifies the significance of Franklin's new job.

ONGOING ASSESSMENT: Monitor and Reinforce

If some students are having difficulty elaborating by bringing out perspective, use one of the following options.

Option 1 Have students review their outline, checking facts and details against their perspective and thesis statement.	**Option 2** Have partners check facts and details from the outline.

Step-by-Step Teaching Guide

Drafting: Bring Out Your Perspective

Teaching Resources: Writing Support Transparency 11-D

1. Discuss the importance of considering the audience in all phases of the writing process. Remind students of the tendency we have to think that everyone knows what we know. In the research process, students are gaining information that their audience may not know. They need to consider what needs explaining, what needs including, and also what needs to be left out.
2. Writers can get a little lost in the drafting process. Some information was hard to find, and it is very interesting—but it doesn't fit neatly into the report. There is no choice but to leave it out. See that students understand the value of focus and brevity.
3. Have students write their thesis statement on a sticky note and paste it to their writing paper. Remind them to consult it at all times while they are writing.
4. Display the transparency to show students how Joseph sharpened his perspective. Remind them of the importance of staying focused and reinforcing the thesis statement. Tell them to evaluate every fact and example they are going to include in terms of the thesis statement. Some deviation is allowed, but mostly they should be guided by the statement. If the facts are leading them away from the statement, rewrite the thesis statement to fit the facts.

Customize for *Verbal/Linguistic Learners*

Students might benefit from talking through their main ideas and supporting details. Have students work in pairs, with one partner working as scribe, copying down the other's ideas as they are spoken.

Step-by-Step Teaching Guide

Revising: Revising Your Overall Structure

1. Have students compare their drafts to their outlines. Discuss the importance of a close correspondence between the two. Also tell students that a short transitional paragraph or two that were not included on the outline are all right.
2. Talk about the use of the outline as a guide but not a straightjacket. It is natural to get new ideas as the drafting process proceeds. What is important in revising is to be sure that there is still organizational coherence with main ideas and supporting ideas and facts.
3. Have students check their drafts against their perspective. Again, have them use the perspective as a guide only. One or two stray details, if interesting enough to warrant inclusion, are not likely to confuse the reader and can add to the report.

Critical Viewing

Interpret Students may say that the poster presents the Gold Rush as an opportunity not to be missed.

11.4 Revising

Revising Your Overall Structure

Analyze Organization

After you have completed a first draft, analyze the organization of your report to make sure it works well.

REVISION STRATEGY

Matching Your Draft to Your Outline

Mark each paragraph with a Roman numeral and a capital letter showing where the paragraph fits on your outline. For example, if topic I.A. on your outline concerns opinion surveys, mark any paragraph discussing them "I.A." When you have finished labeling each paragraph, review your labels.

- Are all of the paragraphs tagged with the same Roman numeral placed next to each other in the draft?
- Are all of the paragraphs with the same Roman numeral–capital letter combination next to each other?
- Does the sequence of Roman numerals and capital letters in the report match your outline? If not, is the change an improvement? Why or why not?

Consider reordering paragraphs so that those with the same label are next to each other, and so that the order of paragraphs matches your outline.

▼ **Critical Viewing** What perspective on the Gold Rush does this poster present? **[Interpret]**

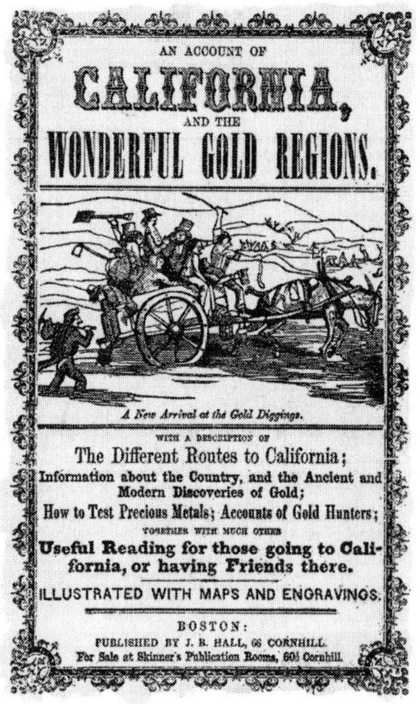

Analyze Perspective

Next, check your draft to make sure it effectively presents your perspective. Use the following strategy:

REVISION STRATEGY

Coding Details for Perspective

To check your perspective, follow these steps:

1. On an index card, write a sentence or phrase summarizing the perspective of your report.
2. Run the card down your draft, holding it under each line in turn.
3. When you find a detail related to your overall perspective, draw a rectangle around it. Circle details that are unrelated to your perspective and that do not provide needed background information.

Review your draft. Consider eliminating circled details. If you find a paragraph without any details connected to your perspective, consider revising it.

TIME AND RESOURCE MANAGER

Resources
Print: Writing Support Transparencies, 11-E–F
Technology: Writing and Grammar iText, Section 11.4

In-Depth Coverage	Accelerated Pace
• Cover pp. 244–248 in class. • Work through the revising strategy with the entire class. • Do the Grammar in Your Writing activity on p. 247.	• Assign students to review pp. 244–248 independently. • Have students revise their research reports independently.

Revising Your Paragraphs

Develop Paragraph Blocks

Sometimes you will need more than one paragraph to discuss one of the main points in your report. You may need to create a series, or "block," of paragraphs.

A **paragraph block** is a group of paragraphs concerning a single topic. The topic sentence of the first paragraph gives the topic of the entire block. Subsequent paragraphs are linked back to the first paragraph with transitional phrases and clauses, such as "The problem grew worse when . . . ".

REVISION STRATEGY
Coding Paragraph Blocks

Review your draft. When you find two or more paragraphs in a row discussing different aspects of the same topic, mark them with brackets: [ ]. Then, review the first sentence of each paragraph in the block. Circle first sentences that simply state a new fact without connecting it back to the previous paragraph. Then, to every paragraph with a circled first sentence, add a transition sentence showing its connection to the block.

Learn More

To learn more about paragraph blocks, see Chapter 3.

Student Work IN PROGRESS

Name: Joseph Hochberger
Gotha Middle School
Windermere, FL

Unifying Paragraph Blocks

Joseph found a paragraph block about Franklin's public service. He circled the first sentence of the second paragraph because it did not clearly link the paragraphs in a block. Then, he added a transition sentence.

[His involvement in public service began with his appointments as clerk of the Pennsylvania Legislature in 1736 and as postmaster of Philadelphia in 1737. He served in both these positions for over fifteen years. . . .

Franklin's public service was not limited to the United States.
~~Four years later, in~~ In 1757, ~~Franklin~~ he traveled to England to negotiate between the family of William Penn, the founder of Pennsylvania, and the state government over tax matters. . . .]

To make a paragraph block about Franklin's public service, Joseph added transitions connecting these two paragraphs.

Step-by-Step Teaching Guide

Revising: Coding Paragraph Blocks

Teaching Resources: Writing Support Transparency 11-E

1. Use the transparency to demonstrate the strategy of forming paragraph blocks. Remind students to use their outlines as guides. If they have a main idea that is too long for a single paragraph, they should use transitional phrases in the following paragraphs to refer back to the first paragraph with the main idea. For blocks of three or more paragraphs, students can restate the main idea in the third or fourth paragraph.
2. Have students code first sentences looking for links between paragraphs in the same section. Paragraphs between different sections (Roman numerals on the outline) do not need to link.

Customize for *Less Advanced Students*

Students may have difficulty with this important part of the revising process. Show them how each capital letter on their outline should be a paragraph block, walking them through transitions that will link the paragraphs in the block.

Step-by-Step Teaching Guide

Revising: Coding the Main Action

Teaching Resources: Writing Support Transparency 11-F

1. Write the following sentences on the chalkboard:

   Washington was a good general. He knew the value of preserving his fighting force. He waited for the right moment to strike.

2. Ask students to evaluate the sentences. Elicit that the repeated pattern creates monotony and is boring to read or listen to.
3. Ask students to help rewrite the sentences into one sentence, using phrases to combine ideas.

   Knowing the value of preserving his fighting force, Washington was a good general and waited for the right moment to strike.

4. Display the transparency. Examine how Joseph identified a cluster of short sentences and combined them.

11.4

Revising Your Sentences

Use Sentence Structure to Create Emphasis

Using the right sentence structure, you can show connections between ideas. One way to show connections is to combine sentences by rewriting some as phrases, as in this example:

SEPARATE: He dreamed of fame. He asked the queen for funds. This money would make his voyage possible.

COMBINED: *Dreaming of fame,* he asked the queen *to fund his voyage.*

The second example expresses in phrases the ideas supporting the main action. Use the following strategy for combining sentences to show connections between ideas.

REVISION STRATEGY
Coding the Main Action

Circle clusters of short sentences. In each cluster, draw a triangle next to sentences expressing a main action. Rewrite other sentences in the cluster as phrases, and add them to the sentence expressing the main action.

iText

Get instant help! Apply the combining Sentences by Coding the Main Action strategy by using the Essay Builder, accessible from the menu bar, on-line or on CD-ROM.

Student Work IN PROGRESS

Name: Joseph Hochberger
Gotha Middle School
Windermere, FL

Combining Sentences by Coding the Main Action

When Joseph found this cluster of short sentences, he decided to combine them.

Born in Boston, Massachusetts, the tenth son of seventeen children, he

~~Franklin was born in Boston, Massachusetts. He was the tenth son of seventeen children.~~ ▲ ~~He~~ was raised by parents who had immigrated from England.

Having attended school for two years and worked for his father in the soap trade,

~~Franklin attended school for only two years. He also worked for his father in the soap trade.~~ ▲ ~~Then,~~ Franklin next became an apprentice in his older brother James's printing shop.

Joseph first coded sentences expressing a main action. Then, he rewrote other supporting sentences as phrases and added them to the sentence expressing the main action. Notice his use of participial phrases.

ONGOING ASSESSMENT: Monitor and Reinforce

If students are having difficulty identifying short sentences and combining them into longer sentences, use one of the following options:

Option 1 Have partners read aloud each other's draft. Instruct students to listen for repeated sentence patterns.	**Option 2** Have students use their visual skills and circle any sentences of five words or fewer, then analyze if their pattern is repetitive.

Grammar in Your Writing
Participial Phrases

To show the relationship between ideas in a sentence, you may need to use participial phrases. A **present participle** is the *-ing* form of a verb. A **past participle** is the past form of a verb, typically ending in *-ed* or *-d.*

Present Participles:	voting	exploring	hiding
Past Participles:	voted	explored	hidden

A **participial phrase** combines a participle with another group of words. It acts as an adjective, answering the question *What kind? Which one? How much?* or *How many?* about another word in the sentence. To avoid confusing your reader, always place a participial phrase near the word it modifies.

participial phrase → word modified

Gliding swiftly, the **canoe** approached the rapids.

In a participial phrase, a present or past participle may be joined with an adverb or adverb phrase modifying (telling more about) the participle. A participial phrase may also include a **complement,** a word or group of words naming the thing that receives the action of the participle.

With Modifiers: Gliding **swiftly,** the canoe approached the rapids. (participle ← adverb)

The canoe, tossed **by the current,** nearly overturned. (participle ← adverb phrase)

With Complements: Seeing **the danger,** he steered away from the rocks. (participle → complement)

He nearly hit a boat crossing **his path.** (participle → complement)

Find It in Your Reading Find two participial phrases in the Student Work in Progress on pages 252–254. Explain what information each phrase adds to the sentence.

Find It in Your Writing Identify two participial phrases in your research report. If you can't find two examples, challenge yourself to use at least two participial phrases in your report.

To learn more about participial phrases, see Chapter 20.

Step-by-Step Teaching Guide

Grammar in Your Writing: Participial Phrases

1. Review the text examples. The role of participial phrases is to tell *how, when, where,* or *why.* Discuss how participial and infinitive phrases are excellent tools for altering sentence patterns and combining ideas.
2. Write the following example on the chalkboard:

   The canoe was gliding swiftly. It approached the rapids.
3. The first sentence is in the passive voice—the canoe isn't doing anything; it is receiving the action. The other problem is two short sentences. Ask students to suggest a use of a participial phrase that would create more action and combine the two sentences.

   Gliding swiftly, the canoe approached the rapids.
4. This example both creates a sense of action and is a combined, graceful sentence.

Find It in Your Reading

Born in Boston, Having attended school; these give information about where these events happened.

Find It in Your Writing

Encourage students to use the techniques they have just studied and examined in the student work in progress to combine sentences in their drafts using participial phrases.

ONGOING ASSESSMENT: Prerequisite Skills

If students have difficulty with participial phrases, you may find it necessary to review the following to assure coverage for prerequisite knowledge.

In the Textbook	Print	Technology
Phrases and Clauses, pp. 432–447	Grammar Exercise Workbook, pp. 75–78	On-Line Exercise Bank, Section 20.1

Step-by-Step Teaching Guide

Revising: Check Specialized Words

1. Use examples on the transparency to point out specialized words.
2. If students are dealing with a historical topic, they will probably come across words that were used differently long ago or are no longer used. Any technical topic may have words that are special to it.
3. Write *grenadier* on the board and ask students to use a dictionary to find its meaning (military units armed with grenades). Point out how this is both a specialized word and an archaic one, no longer in use.
4. Students should not use specialized or difficult words just to show off. The Model From Literature is an excellent essay that uses only familiar vocabulary. The only term some readers might not know, *slave catchers,* is explained.
5. Ask students to consider Virginia Hamilton's advice to "revise, revise, revise." Every writer goes through this process. Professional writers like Hamilton—she has written 34 books!—still need to go over and over their drafts, looking for ways to improve.

Step-by-Step Teaching Guide

Revising: Peer Review

1. Discuss ground rules in setting up the peer review exercise. Remind students of the importance of phrasing suggestions in a helpful rather than a critical or insulting manner. Suggest they find items to praise before offering feedback, which could be phrased as "suggestions for improving your report."
2. On the other hand, a peer's suggestions, even (or especially) negative ones, are valuable tools for improving their reports.

11.4

Revising Your Word Choice

Check Specialized Words

In doing research, you will learn more about an interesting topic. You may come across new words, and you may also encounter words that look familiar but are used with specialized meanings. For example, in sources about Revolutionary America, the word *mechanic* might mean a manual laborer or small manufacturer, rather than a person who does repairs. Dictionaries identify older or obsolete meanings for words with the label *Archaic.* Make sure you have defined archaic or specialized words in your report.

Writers in ACTION

Virginia Hamilton comments as follows on the importance of revision: "It's like being at the bottom of a lake and rising to the top. You want to make things clearer and clearer, and the way to do that is revise, revise, revise."

REVISION STRATEGY

Highlighting Technical Words

Review your prewriting notes and highlight archaic or specialized words. Check each word in a dictionary and in the source where you found it to make sure you understand its use. Then, reread your report to see whether you have used these terms. Add a definition for each term the first time it appears in your draft.

Peer Review

Analytic Talk

Once you have finished revising your report on your own, you can still benefit from the suggestions of your classmates. Analytic talk allows you to polish specific parts of your writing.

Join a group of four other classmates. Read your entire report to the group, pause briefly, then read it a second time. Listeners should take notes during the second reading. Then, ask your peers to answer the following questions:

- Was the opening clear and interesting?
- Would I continue reading if I read the opening in a magazine?
- Did I ever get lost or confused during the reading? If so, where?
- Was I left hanging at the end? If so, what extra information did I need?

Consider your classmates' comments as you prepare the final revision of your draft.

11.5 Editing and Proofreading

Your report may contain complete and accurate information, but you have not finished work on it until you have proofread it for errors in grammar, spelling, and mechanics. To ensure that readers can check the sources you have used, make sure that you have followed one of the standard forms for citation.

Focusing on Citations

In a research report, you should cite the sources for quotations, facts that are not common knowledge, and ideas that are not your own. One widely used form of citation is the Modern Library Association style for internal citations.

Internal Citations An internal citation appears in parentheses. It includes the author's last name and the page number on which the information appears. The citation directly follows the information from the source cited. If several sentences in a row contain information from the same source, the citation need only appear at the end of the last sentence.

"The duke of Lancaster in 1888 . . . controlled more than 163,000 acres of British countryside" (Pool 163).

◀ Critical Viewing Using the section on Citing Sources and Preparing Manuscript on page 762, explain how this student should cite the information she gains from this interview. **[Apply]**

Step-by-Step Teaching Guide

Editing and Proofreading: Focusing on Citations

1. Point out that obvious errors in a report undermine the author's credibility: If the author has been so careless with the rules of grammar, spelling, and punctuation, how can readers trust his or her claims about the facts?
2. Review the rules for internal citations and for the Works Cited list.
3. See that students understand when to cite sources using internal citations. For example, it is not necessary to cite a source for a fact like the following: *Benjamin Franklin was born in Boston in 1706*. Explain that for well-known, undisputed facts, no citation is necessary.
4. Internal citations are needed for less widely known facts and for the opinions of experts.
5. Write the following names on the board and ask students to alphabetize them, last name first.
   Alan Bullock
   Charles Beard
   Jean Blashfield
   Stephen Ambrose
   (Ambrose, Beard, Blashfield, Bullock)

Integrating Spelling Skills

Explain the importance of taking care in compiling a Works Cited list to double- and even triple-check spelling. Students will be using author and publisher names that may not be commonly known, and the only way to avoid spelling errors is to recheck for errors.

PRENTICE HALL
Everyday Spelling

If you have taught the spelling skills in *Prentice Hall Everyday Spelling*, Grade 8, Chapter 13, in conjunction with this *Writing and Grammar* chapter, review and assess students' mastery of the skills before concluding the chapter. Remind students to apply the spelling skills as they edit and proofread their research reports.

TIME AND RESOURCE MANAGER

Resources
Print: Scoring Rubrics on Transparency, Chapter 11; Writing Assessment: Scoring Rubric and Scoring Models for Research Report
Technology: Writing and Grammar iText, Sections 11.5–6

In-Depth Coverage	Accelerated Pace
• Cover pp. 249–254 in class. • Have students edit and proofread their essays in class. • Review the Rubric for Self-Assessment in class. • Have students present their final drafts.	• Assign pp. 249–254 for independent student review. • Have students edit and proofread their essays as homework. • Have students present their final drafts.

Step-by-Step Teaching Guide

Grammar in Your Writing: Quotation Marks and Underlining With Titles of Works

1. The basic rule: Longer works get underlined; shorter works take quotation marks. If entered on a word processor, longer works appear in italics instead of underlining.
2. Review the distinctions between longer and shorter works. A chapter in a book is shorter, the book is longer; an episode of a TV series is shorter, the TV series title is longer.
3. Write the following examples on the board, omitting the punctuation, and ask students to provide the correct punctuation.

   The Life of George Washington (book)

   The Father of Our Country (TV miniseries)

   Dark Days at Valley Forge (book chapter)

   I Cannot Tell a Lie (short story)

   Remembering George Washington Today (newspaper article)

11.5

"Works Cited" List Provide full information about your sources in an alphabetical "Works Cited" list at the end of your report. The following is an example of the correct form:

Pool, Daniel. *What Jane Austen Ate and Charles Dickens Knew: From Fox Hunting to Whist—the Facts of Daily Life in Nineteenth-Century England.* New York: Simon and Schuster, 1993.

For each work cited, follow these guidelines:

- Give the author's last name first. If no author is credited, list the work by its title.
- If there are two or more authors, list the authors in the order in which they are credited in the work. Only the name of the first author is listed last name first.
- If an organization, rather than an individual, is credited with the work, use the name of the organization.
- Use a period after the author's name, after the title of the work, and at the end of the citation. Use a colon between the place of publication and the publisher. Use a comma between the publisher and the year of publication.
- Give the place of publication listed that is closest to you. To avoid confusion, add necessary information. For instance, you would write "Cambridge, MA" to distinguish this city from Cambridge, England.

Grammar in Your Writing

Quotation Marks and Underlining With Titles of Works

Underline (or style in italics) the titles of long written works and the titles of magazines and other periodicals. Also, underline or italicize the titles of movies, television series, and works of music and art.

Sounder (book) — the Pastorale (symphony)
Birth of a Nation (film) — Guernica (painting)

Use quotation marks around the titles of short written works, such as short stories, poems, and newspaper articles. Also, use quotation marks for song titles and Internet sites.

"The Tell-Tale Heart" (short story) — "Dog Bites Man" (newspaper article)
"Ring Out, Wild Bells" (poem) — "Greensleeves" (song)

Find It in Your Reading Read the Works Cited list on page 237. Notice how italics and quotation marks are used for the titles of works.

Find It in Your Writing Review your essay to see whether you have used underlining and quotation marks correctly for the titles of works.

To learn more about the form for titles, see Chapters 26 and 27.

STANDARDIZED TEST PREPARATION WORKSHOP

Mechanics Standardized test questions may require students to use correct mechanics when citing longer and shorter works of literature, art, or music. Ask students to choose the correct way of citing the following works:

1. Charlotte's Web (a novel)
   A "Charlotte's Web"
   B "Charlotte's Web"
   C Charlotte's Web
   D CHARLOTTE'S WEB
2. Victory at Yorktown (chapter in a book)
   A Victory at Yorktown
   B "Victory at Yorktown"
   C VICTORY AT YORKTOWN
   D **Victory at Yorktown**

The correct answers are Items **C** and **B.**

11.6 Publishing and Presenting

Building Your Portfolio

Consider the following ideas for publishing and presenting your report:

1. **Sharing With a Large Audience** Do research to determine which organizations (historical societies, fan clubs, and so on) might be interested in the topic of your report. Submit a copy of your report to such a group for publication in its newsletter or on its Web site.
2. **Panel Discussion** Join with classmates who have written on a similar subject, and organize a panel discussion. Each student should present his or her report and respond to questions and comments from other panel members.

Reflecting on Your Writing

Jot down a few notes about your experience writing a research report. You might begin by answering these questions:

- What was the most interesting thing you learned about your topic? Why?
- Which strategy for prewriting, drafting, revising, or editing might you recommend to a friend? Why?

Internet Tip

To see research reports scored with this rubric, go on-line: PHSchool.com
Enter Web Code: eck-8001

Rubric for Self-Assessment

Use these criteria to evaluate your research report:

	Score 4	Score 3	Score 2	Score 1
Audience and Purpose	Focuses on a clearly stated thesis, starting from a well-framed question; gives complete citations	Focuses on a clearly stated thesis; gives citations	Focuses mainly on the chosen topic; gives some citations	Presents information without a clear focus; few or no citations
Organization	Presents information in logical order, emphasizing details of central importance	Presents information in logical order	Presents information logically, but organization is poor in places	Presents information in a scattered, disorganized manner
Elaboration	Draws clear conclusions from information gathered from multiple sources	Draws conclusions from information gathered from multiple sources	Explains and interprets some information	Presents information with little or no interpretation or synthesis
Use of Language	Shows overall clarity and fluency; contains few mechanical errors	Shows good sentence variety; contains some errors in spelling, punctuation, or usage	Uses awkward or overly simple sentence structures; contains many mechanical errors	Contains incomplete thoughts and mechanical errors that make the writing confusing

ONGOING ASSESSMENT: Assess Mastery

Use one of the following options to assess final drafts of students' research reports.

Self Assessment Ask students to score their essay using the rubric provided. Then have students write a paragraph reflecting on the most valuable strategy they learned in completing this essay.

Teacher Assessment Use the rubric and the scoring models provided in Writing Assessment, Research Report, to score students' work.

Step-by-Step Teaching Guide

Publishing and Presenting

1. Before submitting their essays to organizations, students should find out the requirements, such as maximum length, format, and so on.
2. Students can also add visuals to their reports and create a bulletin board display.
3. Have students complete the Reflecting on Your Writing exercise and share their reflections with the class.
4. Have students use the rubric to evaluate their own writing.

ASSESS

Step-by-Step Teaching Guide

Assessment

Teaching Resources: Scoring Rubrics on Transparency, 11; Formal Assessment, Chapter 11

1. Display the Scoring Rubric transparency and review the criteria in class.
2. Before students proceed with self-assessment, you may wish to review the Final Draft of the Student Work in Progress on pages 252–254. Have students score the Final Draft in one or more of the rubric categories. For example, how would students score the essay in terms of audience and purpose?
3. In addition to student self-assessment, you may wish to use the following assessment options:
   - Score student essays yourself, using the rubric and scoring models from Writing Assessment.
   - Review the Standardized Test Preparation Workshop on pages 258–259.
   - Administer the Chapter 11 Test from Formal Assessment in Teaching Resources to assess students' grasp of concepts presented.

Step-by-Step Teaching Guide

Teaching From the Final Draft

1. Examine Joseph's opening paragraph and point out the thesis: Franklin's greatness is in the diversity of his achievements. Ask students what questions this first paragraph should generate for readers. (What did Franklin achieve as a writer, scientist and statesman? How did Franklin influence the historical events of his time? Where did Franklin live?)
2. Ask students to consider the title and first paragraph together. Discuss how the author has already explained his title in the first paragraph.

continued

Critical Viewing

Draw Conclusions Most students will recognize the man as Benjamin Franklin, which is a testament to his fame.

11.7 Student Work IN PROGRESS

FINAL DRAFT

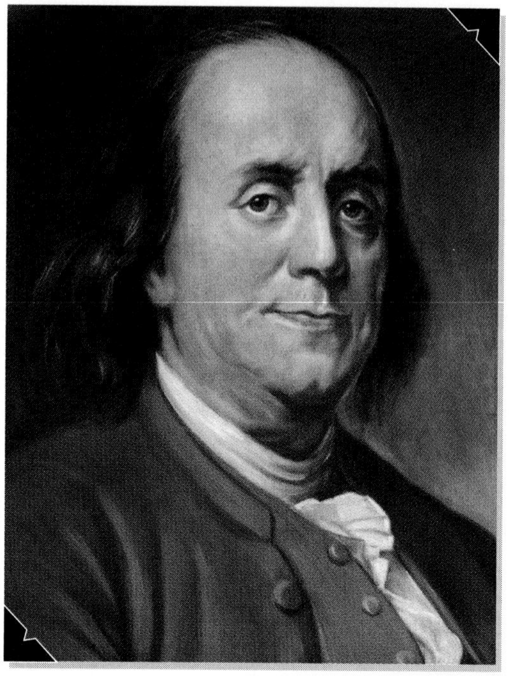

◀ Critical Viewing Do you recognize the man in this portrait as Benjamin Franklin? What does your answer suggest about his fame? **[Draw Conclusions]**

Ben Franklin: Man of Many Talents

Joseph Hochberger
Gotha Middle School
Windermere, Florida

Benjamin Franklin (1706–1790) is recognized today as one of the greatest figures in American history. Any one of his many careers would have earned him this reputation. As a writer, scientist, and statesman, he made outstanding contributions to the life of his time. The true measure of his greatness, though, is the diversity of his achievements. We expect today's leaders to excel at one thing.

In his first paragraph, Joseph explains his topic (the diversity of Franklin's achievements) and his perspective: "The true measure of his greatness, though, is the diversity of his achievements."

When we compare them to Franklin, Franklin seems like a giant simply because he excelled in many fields (Foster 112–113).

Franklin's beginnings did not show much promise of his destiny. Born in Boston, Massachusetts, the tenth son of seventeen children, he was raised by parents who had immigrated from England. Having attended school for two years and worked for his father in the soap trade, Franklin next became an apprentice in his older brother James's printing shop (Adler 8–13). There, his career as a writer began. He contributed articles to his brother's paper, slipping them under the door in a different handwriting to hide his authorship. When his brother discovered the real author's identity, the two brothers quarreled and Ben lost his job (Cousins 25–29).

▲ Critical Viewing What does this picture suggest about Franklin's motive for designing bifocals? **[Infer]**

Despite the quarrel, it seemed that Ben's future lay in printing. At the age of seventeen, he found another printing job in Philadelphia. The governor of Pennsylvania offered to set him up on his own, and he persuaded Ben to travel to England to buy presses and type. The governor failed to keep his word, though, Ben was left stranded and penniless in London (Foster 27–37).

With skill and luck, however, Ben found work in a printing house and remained in England for nearly two years. Then, he returned to Philadelphia.

From printing, Ben turned to journalism. He purchased the *Pennsylvania Gazette* in 1729. Franklin turned a dull newspaper with few readers into a lively, popular paper (Adler 23–24). In addition to producing the best newspaper in the colonies, Franklin wrote and printed *Poor Richard's Almanack* from 1732 to 1757. This publication was full of wit and wisdom, and it made Franklin a lot of money. The proverbs in the almanac were especially popular—for example, "Early to bed and early to rise, makes a man healthy, wealthy, and wise" (Lemay 1474–1480).

Joseph organizes his details by type to discuss Franklin's different careers, but he always shows the sequence of events using chronological order.

Franklin's literary successes were enough to earn him a place in history. At the same time, though, he was busying himself with other projects. He started a subscription library, a fire service, a street-cleaning department, and a college that was later to become the University of Pennsylvania (Cousins 59–68).

The first sentence of this paragraph helps to relate this part of the report to the writer's overall perspective: Franklin excelled in many fields.

Franklin also had a deep interest in science. His scientific inventions and experiments were especially remarkable. In 1752, he performed his kite experiment, which proved that lightning consists of an electrical charge, and he also invented the lightning rod. Franklin's other inventions included the stove that is named after him, as well as bifocal lenses, or eyeglasses that enable a person to see both near and far (Adler 30–33).

Step-by-Step Teaching Guide continued

3. Examine Joseph's organizational structure: how he tracks both chronology and different careers.
4. Point out the paragraph blocking in the second and third paragraphs on this page and the linking phrase, "With skill and luck."
5. Ask students to explain why *Pennsylvania Gazette* appears in italics. (It was a newspaper.)
6. Also have students note the author's use of citations. Why doesn't he provide a citation for Franklin's dates? (They are generally known.) But he does cite facts less well known.

continued

Critical Viewing

Infer Students may say that the picture suggests Franklin designed bifocals to help his own eyesight.

Step-by-Step Teaching Guide continued

7. Discuss how well Joseph dealt with all the dates. Note the number of sentences that begin *In [year]*.
8. Review the Works Cited list. Be sure that students understand the basic rules of underlining and quotation marks.

11.7

Writer, community planner, and inventor—but Ben didn't stop there. He became drawn into politics as well. His involvement in public service began with his appointments as clerk of the Pennsylvania Legislature in 1736 and as postmaster of Philadelphia in 1737. He served in both these positions for over fifteen years. In 1753, he became Deputy Postmaster General in charge of all mail for the northern colonies (Lemay 1475–1479).

Joseph uses internal citations throughout his report to show where he got his information.

Franklin's public service was not limited to the United States. In 1757, he traveled to England to negotiate between the family of William Penn, the founder of Pennsylvania, and the state government over tax matters. Once he had helped the parties reach a compromise, Franklin returned to Philadelphia in 1762 (Adler 34–36).

Franklin is well remembered for the next part of his political career. During the later 1760's, Franklin served as a Pennsylvania agent in London. The colonists were fed up with British taxes, and after a while Franklin realized that the American Revolution could not be avoided. In early 1775, he sailed home to Philadelphia to join the other colonists. The day after he arrived in Philadelphia, he attended the Second Continental Congress as a delegate. (The Congress was the group of American leaders that drafted the Declaration of Independence.) (Foster 81–91)

Joseph realizes that his readers might not know the significance of the Second Continental Congress in American history, so he explains it.

In July 1776, Benjamin Franklin signed the Declaration of Independence. Late that year, he traveled to France to ask the French for money and supplies for the Revolutionary War. When the war was over, six years later, Franklin took part in the peace-treaty negotiations. In 1787, he became a member of the Constitutional Convention, which wrote the Constitution of the United States (Adler 40–44).

After this life of diverse achievements, Franklin died in April 1790. He was given the grandest funeral that had ever been held in the city of Philadelphia (Foster 111). Someone of the time said that "he snatched the lightning from the skies and the scepter from tyrants" (Wright 269). This sentence helps sum up the breadth of Franklin's accomplishments. He was great, not just in one field, but in several. Few people today can match that achievement.

Works Cited

Adler, David. *Benjamin Franklin: Printer, Inventor, Statesman.* New York: Holiday House, 1992.

Cousins, Margaret. *Ben Franklin of Old Philadelphia.* New York: Random House, 1952, 1980.

Foster, Leila Merrell. *Benjamin Franklin: Founding Father and Inventor.* Springfield, NJ: Enslow Publishers Inc., 1997.

Lemay, J.A. Leo, ed. *Franklin: Writings.* New York: Literary Classics of America, 1987.

Wright, Esmond. *Franklin of Philadelphia.* Cambridge, MA: Harvard University Press, 1986.

Joseph provides a complete list of works cited using standard form.

Connected Assignment I-Search Report

In an **I-search report,** you present the results of your investigation into a topic that especially interests you. Unlike a research report, an I-search report includes the story of your experience researching your topic. It includes these elements:

- a topic you want or need to know more about
- an account of your interest in the topic
- an account of how you researched the topic
- a report of what you learned
- the use of the pronoun *I* to tell your story.

Write an I-search report using these suggestions:

Topic: The History of My House

Know	Want to Know	Learned
It was built during the Revolutionary War.	When was the passageway built? (source: I can look in the phone book for the local Historical Society. I can also check with the town department of records.)	
There is a secret passageway in one of the walls.	Was the passageway used by revolutionaries in the War of Independence? (source: same.)	

Prewriting Choose a topic in which you have a real interest. For instance, you might want to learn the history of your house or find out how one becomes a nurse. Focus your topic by selecting the aspect that most directly concerns you.

After focusing your topic, list questions to which you want answers in the "W" column of a K-W-L chart like the one shown. For each question, list a possible source of information, such as a book or a government agency.

Take notes on note cards as you do research. Enter brief notes in the "Learned" column of your chart, indicating questions you have answered. Record your research experiences on a separate set of note cards or in a notebook.

Drafting Organize your details using an outline. Your outline should integrate the story of your research with the facts you learned. For instance, you might begin by explaining your interest in the topic. Next, you might tell about your research. Then, you might sum up what you learned. Follow your outline as you draft.

Revising and Editing Review your draft. Check that you have presented events and ideas in a clear sequence. Use transition sentences to move from paragraphs about your research experience to paragraphs about what you learned.

Publishing and Presenting After revising your I-search report, collect the reports of the class, bind them, and ask the school librarian to keep a copy for other students' reference.

▼ Critical Viewing
Name three types of sources this student might find using the reference tool pictured. **[Analyze]**

▶ *Lesson Objectives*

1. To write an I-search report appropriate to audience and purpose.
2. To use prewriting strategies to choose and narrow a topic.
3. To gather and organize details.
4. To draft, revise, edit, and publish a report.

Step-by-Step Teaching Guide

I-Search Report

Teaching Resources: Writing Support Transparency 11-G; Writing Support Activity Book 11-2

1. Make sure students understand the term *I-search.* You might use the introduction to a nonfiction book as a model. A writer usually addresses such an introduction directly to a reader. An introduction often describes how the writer became interested in the topic, how he or she researched it, and what the results were.
2. Ask students to discuss the value of an I-search report. Point out that this report serves the same purpose as a scholarly introduction. It acquaints the reader with the writer and gives the reader clues about the writer's background and his or her bias. These reports are very helpful to readers.
3. Display the transparency and review how to record information in a K-W-L chart. Then give students copies of the blank organizer for them to use to help them focus their topics.
4. Remind students to write in the first person. Since they are addressing their readers directly, the first person is appropriate. Students should feel free to allow their personalities and their opinions to color their writing.

Critical Viewing

Analyze Students may mention a book, a journal, or a videotape recording.

Lesson Objectives

- To write a research report.

Critical Viewing

Interpret Students may suggest that Amanda protects and takes care of Laura; they may suggest that Laura tries to keep her feelings private but that Amanda wants her to share them.

Step-by-Step Teaching Guide

Framing Questions for Research

1. Choose a Spotlight element for class discussion, or have students work independently or in groups on the element of their choice. Give students the initiative to find the necessary books and recordings.
2. Give students some additional background on *The Glass Menagerie.* Explain that Laura is shy and introverted, in part because of a physical disability that makes her walk with a limp. Amanda, a former Southern belle, cherishes the illusion that "gentleman callers" will come to the house to see Laura. When Tom does bring a young man to dinner, Laura begins to come out of her shell, only to discover that he is already engaged. This is the play's major crisis.
3. Explain that glass is made from sand that has been melted at extremely high temperatures. This liquid glass is either blown through long pipes into various shapes, or it is pressed in a mold. Students may be interested to know that all glass is naturally green; if they see window glass stacked in a hardware store, they will see that it is green at the edges. Clear glass, like that in most drinking glasses, has a chemical added to it that makes it clear.

Spotlight on the Humanities

Framing Questions for Research

Focus on Theater: *The Glass Menagerie*

▲ Critical Viewing Using details from this scene from *The Glass Menagerie,* describe the relationship between Laura and her mother. **[Interpret]**

By doing research into the past, people can make connections between the present and the past. Historical research can explain, for instance, why a certain building is located where it is, or why a certain law was written.

Research is only one of the many complicated ways that people have of connecting the past to the present, though. In his famous play *The Glass Menagerie,* American playwright Tennessee Williams (1911–1983) portrays a family trying to escape from the present.

Amanda Wingfield and her two children, Laura and Tom, struggle to survive on Tom's income. Laura, isolated and innocent, lives each day immersed in her glass animal collection or playing the family's old record player. Through these objects from the past, Laura retreats into childlike innocence. When one of the animals breaks, it marks the end of the past's hold over the family.

Williams was one of the most significant American playwrights. He changed the voice of American theater, bringing a new poetic style to the stage. *The Glass Menagerie* was an instant success after premiering in New York on March 31, 1945.

Art Connection Glass figurines such as those treasured by Laura are a good symbol of the past: For centuries, people have collected them as works of art. Venice, Italy, has been a central site for the art of glass blowing, and Venetian glass is highly prized.

The manufacture of glassware in Venice goes back to the thirteenth century. By the sixteenth and seventeenth centuries, the Venetian glass blowers were creating drinking glasses decorated with animals or masks. The art of creating glass figurines remains a part of Venetian culture today.

▲ Critical Viewing What qualities of a figurine such as this one might a collector prize? **[Analyze]**

Research Writing Activity: Research Report on Glass

Come up with a question about the changing uses and value of glass from the past to the present. Do research to answer this question, and write up your results in a report.

Viewing and Representing

Activity Encourage a variety of questions. Students may want to ask very specific questions, such as *What was life like for a glassblower in thirteenth-century Venice?* or *What was glass first used for?* or *How was glass manufactured in ancient Rome?* Suggest that students begin their research by looking up key terms in the Encyclopedia Britannica.

Critical Viewing

Analyze Students may suggest that a figurine is prized for its beauty, delicacy, rarity, colors, or shape; because it was made by a certain glass blower; or because it was made in a certain place and time.

Media and Technology Skills

Using Technology for Research

Activity: Evaluating On-line Sources

One advantage of the Internet over print references is the easy access it offers to information. Not every on-line source is reliable, though. Learn how to evaluate Internet sources.

Learn About It Always evaluate the sources of information you find on the Internet. Use these guidelines:

Check Time of Last Update A sponsor can put up a Web site and then lose interest, leaving only outdated information on it. Check the last time the site was updated to make sure information is current (this information may appear on the home page or in the listing for the site provided by a search engine).

Identify the Sponsor Identify the individual or group that sponsored the page. Sources to look at carefully include

- personal home pages. The person putting up the page may have little incentive to provide accurate information.
- sites sponsored by businesses or political activists. Such sites may present mainly information favorable to the sponsor's interests.

Reliable sources include sites

- sponsored by the government (addresses ending in ".gov"), by educational institutions (addresses ending in ".edu"), and by nonprofit organizations (addresses ending in ".org").
- sponsored by publishers of reference materials, producers of educational television programs, news organizations, and so on.
- that acknowledge and cite sources of information and that present both sides of any controversial subject.

Confirm Information in Other Sources When doing research, you should always consult a variety of sources on your subject. Do not rely exclusively on information you find on a Web page. Confirm the information using another source.

Evaluate It Do research using the Internet to answer three questions on a topic. Record your evaluation of each source in a chart like the one shown. Then, write a report on your Internet experience.

Research Question: ____________________

Name and Address of Web Site	Last Updated?	Sponsor	How Credible Is the Sponsor? Why?	Sources Cited?	Does a Print Source Confirm the Information?

Tips for Using a Search Engine

Evaluate Search Results Quickly
A search engine lists sites with the closest matches to your search term first. If you do not find the information among the the first forty sites listed, consider trying another search term.

Use Quotation Marks
If you are searching for information on a person, place, or brand name, place quotation marks around your search term. The search engine will focus on pages including exactly that name.

▶ *Lesson Objectives*

1. To use technology for research.
2. To evaluate on-line sources.

Step-by-Step Teaching Guide

Using Technology for Research

Teaching Resources: Writing Support Transparency 11-H; Writing Support Activity Book 11-3

1. The day before you teach this lesson, have each student go on-line and print out a source of information to bring to class the next day. Each student should pose a research question and bring in the on-line source that answers it. In class, have students share their sources and discuss their reliability. What are some clues that help students evaluate whether or not an on-line source can be trusted?
2. Explain to students that book publishers require source documentation and accountability. The author of a nonfiction book must document all of his or her sources. The Internet has no such standards; anyone can post anything he or she wishes on the Internet. This is the reason researchers need to beware of Internet sources.
3. Go through the bulleted list of sponsors on the page. Give examples of each, and have students contribute examples. Ask students to evaluate Web sites they have visited. Did they seem reliable? Why or why not?
4. Use the transparency to demonstrate evaluating Web sites. Then give students copies of the blank organizer so that they can complete the writing activity.

Lesson Objectives

1. To read a passage critically.
2. To revise and edit a passage.

Step-by-Step Teaching Guide

Revising and Editing

Teaching Resources: Standardized Test Preparation Workbook, pp. 21–22

1. Remind students that revising and editing is the next step after finishing a first draft. Revising and editing ensure that the passage says exactly what the writer intends to say. Once his or her ideas are all down on paper, a writer needs to go back over them, making sure that they are presented in the appropriate order, that they are supported by details or examples, and that nothing important has been left out.
2. Remind students that on a multiple-choice test, two options for each question can usually be eliminated as obviously wrong. Students will then have to choose between the other two answers. Remind them that their job is to choose the best answer of the ones on the page, even if students think none of the options is a perfect answer. Encourage students to stick with their first instinct about which answer is correct. This will usually help them.
3. You may want to treat the test on the following page as a sample, working through each question with the whole class. Discuss and resolve any differences of opinion about the correct answers. As an alternative, you may wish to give students a set amount of time to complete the test on their own. Since this is a practice test, have them give a brief explanation of each answer they choose. This will help them be sure they have chosen the correct answer.

Standardized Test Preparation Workshop

Revising and Editing

A crucial step in research is revising and editing your draft to make sure the information is presented in the clearest way possible. On a standardized test, you may be asked questions that measure your ability to revise and edit a passage. Below is a sample test item that shows one format for such questions.

Test Tip

When asked to choose the best topic sentence for a paragraph, be suspicious of any choice that makes a sweeping statement—it may not be focused enough.

Sample Test Item	Answer and Explanation
Read the following passage from a science textbook. Then, answer the multiple-choice question that follows. Some black holes have a companion star. When the gases from the companion star are pulled into the black hole, the gases are heated. Before the gases are sucked into the black hole and lost forever, they may give off a burst of X-rays. So scientists can detect black holes by the X-rays given off when matter falls into the black hole.	
1 Which of these sentences would make the **BEST** topic sentence for this paragraph? **A** Black holes are hard to detect. **B** Black holes can be detected indirectly through their effect on matter. **C** Black holes are known as the "vacuum cleaners" of the cosmos. **D** Black holes should have a companion star.	The correct answer is *B*. All the other sentences present details that develop, support, or explain the idea expressed in *B*.

TEST-TAKING TIP

Remind students that they need not spend time reading an entire passage. They should only read the entire passage if the question requires it. For example, the question in the sample on this page means that students will have to read the whole passage. However, the questions on page 259 only refer to specific sections of the passage. By looking at the questions before they read the passage, students will have a better idea how to budget their time.

Practice **Directions:** Read the following passage. Then, answer the questions below, choosing the letter of the best answer.

The most abundant gas in the atmosphere is nitrogen. Living things needed nitrogen to make proteins. Proteins are complex compounds that contain nitrogen. These compounds are required for the growth and repair of body parts. The muscles of your body are made mostly of protein, as are parts of the skin and internal organs. Likewise, plants and animals are not able to use nitrogen in the air directly to make proteins. Certain kinds of bacteria that live in the soil are able to combine the nitrogen from the atmosphere with other chemicals to make compounds called *nitrates.* These bacteria are nitrogen-fixing bacteria. Plants are able to use the nitrates formed by the nitrogen/fixing bacteria to make plant proteins. In turn, animals get the proteins they need by eating plants.

1 What is the **BEST** change, if any, to make to the sentence in lines 2–3 ("*Living . . . proteins.*")?
- **A** Change ***Living things*** to **Humans**
- **B** Change ***nitrogen*** to **it**
- **C** Change ***needed*** to **need**
- **D** Make no change.

2 Which of the following sentences would **BEST** fit after the sentence in lines 7–9 ("*The . . . organs.*")?
- **F** Plants and animals get proteins in the same way that we do.
- **G** Protein is also found in blood, where its job is to carry oxygen from your lungs to your cells.
- **H** After protein, oxygen is the next most abundant gas in the atmosphere.
- **J** Without muscles, your body would collapse.

3 What is the **BEST** change, if any, to make to the sentence in lines 10–12 ("*Likewise, . . . proteins.*")?
- **A** Change ***Likewise,*** to **However,**
- **B** Change ***Likewise,*** to **In contrast,**
- **C** Delete ***Likewise,***
- **D** Make no change.

4 Which of these sentences **BEST** fits the ideas in lines 18–22 ("*Plants . . . plants.*")?
- **F** Healthy muscles require protein.
- **G** Nitrogen is readily available in the atmosphere.
- **H** Nitrates are formed when nitrogen is combined with other chemicals.
- **J** Without nitrogen-fixing bacteria, animals could not survive.

5 What is the **BEST** change, if any, to make to the sentence in lines 18–20 ("*Plants . . . proteins.*")?
- **A** Delete ***formed by the nitrogen/fixing bacteria***
- **B** Change ***nitrogen/fixing*** to **nitrogen:fixing**
- **C** Change ***nitrogen/fixing*** to **nitrogen-fixing**
- **D** Make no change.

6 Which is the **BEST** way to combine the two sentences in lines 18–22 ("*Plants . . . plants.*")?
- **F** Plants use nitrates from nitrogen-fixing bacteria to make proteins, and animals get the protein they need by eating plants.
- **G** Plants use nitrates to make plant proteins, consequently providing animals with their source of protein —plant proteins.
- **H** Plants and animals get the proteins they need by eating plants.
- **J** Plants make plant proteins, but animals do not.

7 Which of the following sentences would **BEST** conclude the passage?
- **A** Bacteria help us use the nitrogen that is so plentiful in the air.
- **B** Not all bacteria are dangerous.
- **C** Nitrogen is the most abundant gas.
- **D** Nitrates have a variety of uses.

Answer Key

Practice 1

1. C
2. G
3. C
4. J
5. C
6. G
7. A

Customize for *Less Advanced Students*

Challenge students to revise and edit the sample test item on page 258. Have them include the topic sentence from the test question. Students should consider whether the sentences in the passage are in the most logical order possible, whether they are all relevant to the topic sentence, whether the grammar and mechanics of the passage are correct, and whether any important information is missing. Go over students' revisions with them, asking them to explain all the changes they made. If students felt that no changes needed to be made, have them defend this opinion.

Chapter 12 Time and Resource Manager

In-Depth Lesson Plan

	LESSON FOCUS	PRINT AND MEDIA RESOURCES
DAY 1	**Introduction to Responses to Literature** Students learn key elements of a response to literature and analyze the Model From Literature (pp. 260–263).	***Writers at Work* Videotape,** Responding to Literature ***Writing and Grammar iText* (Interactive Text),** Ch.12, Introduction
DAY 2	**Prewriting** Students choose and narrow a topic, consider their audience and purpose, and gather information (pp. 264–269).	**Teaching Resources** *Writing Support Transparencies,* 12-A–D; *Writing Support Activity Book,* 12-1–3; *Topic Bank for Heterogeneous Classes,* Ch. 12 ***Writing and Grammar iText* (Interactive Text),** Section 12.2
DAY 3	**Drafting** Students organize their ideas and write their first drafts (pp. 270–271).	**Teaching Resources** *Writing Support Transparencies,* 12-E ***Writing and Grammar iText* (Interactive Text),** Section 12.3
DAY 4	**Revising** Students revise their drafts in terms of overall structure, paragraphs, sentences, and word choice (pp. 272–277).	**Teaching Resources** *Writing Support Transparencies,* 12-F–H ***Writing and Grammar iText* (Interactive Text),** Section 12.4
DAY 5	**Editing and Proofreading; Publishing and Presenting** Students check their work for accuracy and correctness and present their final drafts (pp. 278–279).	**Teaching Resources** *Scoring Rubrics on Transparency,* Ch. 12; *Formal Assessment,* Ch. 12 ***Writing and Grammar iText* (Interactive Text),** Sections 12.5–6

Accelerated Lesson Plan

	LESSON FOCUS	PRINT AND MEDIA RESOURCES
DAY 1	**Introduction Through Drafting** Students review the characteristics of research reports, select topics, and write drafts (pp. 260–271).	**Teaching Resources** *Writing Support Transparencies,* 12-A–E; *Writing Support Activity Book,* 12-1–3 ***Writing and Grammar iText* (Interactive Text),** Ch. 12, Introduction through Section 12.3
DAY 2	**Revising Through Presenting** Students work individually or with peers to revise, edit, and proofread their work for presentation (pp. 272–279).	**Teaching Resources** *Writing Support Transparencies,* 12-F–H; *Scoring Rubrics on Transparency,* Ch. 12; *Formal Assessment,* Ch. 12 ***Writing and Grammar iText* (Interactive Text),** Sections 12.4–6

Options for Adapting Lesson Plans

HOMEWORK

Have students complete any stage of the lesson for homework.

SPELLING

To teach spelling skills in conjunction with writing skills, work through *Prentice Hall Everyday Spelling,* Grade 8, Chapter 14, as you cover this *Writing and Grammar* chapter. At the Editing and Proofreading stage, remind students to apply the spelling skills to their responses to literature.

FEATURES

Extend coverage with Connected Assignment (p. 282), Spotlight on the Humanities (p. 284), Media and Technology Skills (p. 285), and Standardized Test Preparation Workshop (p. 286).

TECHNOLOGY

Students can complete any stage of the lesson on the computer, using *Writing and Grammar iText* or a word-processing program. Have them print out their completed work.

INTEGRATED SKILLS COVERAGE

Integrating Grammar
Compound and Complex Sentences, SE p. 275
Punctuating and Formatting Quotations, SE p. 278

Reading/Writing Connection
Reading Strategy, SE p. 262
Writing Application, SE p. 263

Viewing and Representing
Critical Viewing, SE pp. 260, 262, 267, 269, 271, 272, 277, 280, 282, 284
Making a Collage, SE p. 284

BLOCK SCHEDULING

Pacing Suggestions
For 90-minute Blocks
- Have students complete the Prewriting and Drafting stages in a single period.
- Focus one class period on Revising and Editing and Publishing and Presenting. Allow at least 30 minutes for peer revision.

Resources for Varying Instruction
- ***Writing and Grammar iText* (Interactive Text)** A 90-minute block provides an ideal opportunity for students to work on computer.
- ***Writers at Work* Videotape** Show the Responding to Literature segment in class.

Professional Development Support
- ***How to Manage Instruction in the Block*** This teaching resource provides management and activity suggestions.

ASSESSMENT SUPPORT

Standardized Test Preparation Workshop SE pp. 286–287, ATE p. 274
Standardized Test Preparation Workbook, pp. 23–24
Scoring Rubrics on Transparency, Ch. 12
Formal Assessment, Ch. 12
Writing Assessment and Portfolio Management

MEDIA AND TECHNOLOGY

For the Student
- ***Writing and Grammar iText* (Interactive Text),** Ch. 12

For the Teacher
- ***Writers at Work* Videotape,** Responding to Literature
- ***Resource Pro* CD-ROM**

MEETING INDIVIDUAL NEEDS

Less Advanced Students ATE p. 269. See also Ongoing Assessments ATE pp. 265, 267, 273, 275.
ESL Students ATE p. 268
More Advanced Students ATE p. 287

WRITING AND GRAMMAR ON-LINE

iText Interactive Text (On-line or on CD-ROM)
- Easily navigable instruction with interactive Revision Checkers
- Full use of e-rater™, the essay-scoring system (on-line only)

Companion Web Site PHSchool.com
- Scoring rubrics with models (use Web Code eck-8001)

See the Go On-line! feature, SE p. iii.

LITERATURE CONNECTIONS

Related selections from *Prentice Hall Literature: Timeless Voices, Timeless Themes,* Silver:

Professional Model from *I Know Why the Caged Bird Sings*, Maya Angelou, SE p. 263

Topic Bank Options "Poets to Come," Walt Whitman, SE p. 265; "love is a place," E. E. Cummings, SE p. 265

CHAPTER 12
RESPONSE TO LITERATURE

Lesson Objectives

1. To define a response to literature.
2. To identify three types of responses to literature.
3. To utilize strategies for choosing a topic.
4. To use a pentad to focus a response.
5. To shape writing with details and defined focus.
6. To revise paragraphs by adding support, highlighting related and contrasting points.
8. To revise word choice with key terms.
9. To publish and present an essay.
10. To reflect on the experience of writing.

Critical Viewing

Interpret Students' responses will vary. Make sure they support their responses with details from the image.

Chapter 12 Response to Literature

Mask Maker, Venice, Joanna Calabro, Courtesy of the artist

▲ Critical Viewing Describe the characters that two of these masks suggest to you. **[Interpret]**

Responding to Literature in Everyday Life

Some things you can't do on your own. It takes two to have a conversation or to play a game of catch. Reading, though, is an activity just for one. No one but you can read the words on a page and weave them into a picture in your mind. Yet, the first thing that might occur to you after finishing a book is, "I've got to tell someone else about this!"

By telling others about a book, you turn what you experienced by yourself into something others can also appreciate. Responding to a work in conversation or in writing will also prompt you to understand the work better. Reading may start out as a solitary activity—but a response to literature quickly gets others involved.

TIME AND RESOURCE MANAGER

Resources
Technology: Writers at Work Videotape; Writing and Grammar iText, Ch. 12

In-Depth Coverage	Accelerated Pace
• Cover pp. 260–261 in class. • Show the Responding to Literature section of Writers at Work Videotape. • Discuss different types of responses to literature. • Read the Model From Literature (pp. 262–263) and use it to brainstorm for topic ideas with students.	• Assign pp. 260–263 for independent student review. • Discuss definitions and types of responses to literature.

What Is a Response to Literature?

A **response to literature** is an essay or other form of writing that discusses what is of value in a book, short story, essay, article, or poem. A response might show why a story is moving, point out the beauties of a poem, or analyze the shortcomings of a play. A response to literature includes

- a strong, interesting focus on some aspect of the work.
- a clear organization.
- a summary of the important features of the work.
- supporting details for each main idea.
- a judgment about the success or value of the work.

To learn the criteria on which your response will be assessed, see the Rubric for Self-Assessment on page 279.

Writers in ACTION

Marilyn Stasio is a reviewer of mystery novels for a newspaper. This is what she said about responding to literature in the course of her critical work:

"Too often people think that the critic is someone who is always criticizing, but that's not what I do at all. What I do is I love the books and I respond to the books. And it's sort of passing on your enthusiasm to the reader."

Types of Responses to Literature

These are some of the responses to literature that you might write:

- **Book reviews** sum up the reviewer's experience of a book, often comparing it with other works, then encourage readers either to read it or to avoid reading it.
- **Letters to an author** let a writer know what a reader found enjoyable or disappointing in a work. It may include suggestions for future work and questions about past work.
- **Comparisons of works** highlight aspects of two or more works by comparing them.

PREVIEW Student Work IN PROGRESS

Stacy Osborn, a student in the Gilmer Independent School District in Gilmer, Texas, wrote a response to a short story by Pearl S. Buck. In this chapter, you will see how Stacy applied featured strategies to choose a topic and revise her work. The final draft of her work appears at the end of the chapter.

PREPARE and ENGAGE

Interest GRABBER Tell students how you responded to a story that they know—the main character was a lot like you, or the plot reminded you of something in your own life, or it made you feel happy or sad, or it taught you something interesting.

Activate Prior Knowledge

Encourage students to discuss stories they liked, and to tell why they liked them. Ask them to describe the story, characters, and setting, and tell whether or not they would recommend the work to others.

ONGOING ASSESSMENT: Diagnose

Use one of the following options to diagnose students' current level of proficiency in responding to literature.

Option 1 Ask each student to select the strongest example of his or her written responses to literature from last year. Hold conferences to review each students' sample. Use the conferences to determine which students will need extra support in developing a response to literature.

Option 2 Ask students to write two or three paragraphs describing a story they read recently and explaining their response to it. Students' paragraphs should address how the writing fits the story's theme.

TEACH

Reading\Writing Connection

Reading: Identify Evidence

Identifying evidence is finding factual details that support the general points or main ideas of an essay. Ask students what evidence Russell supplies to support her claim that *Frightful's Mountain* is a good book.

Teaching From the Model

You can use this model as an example of a well-written book review. The author organized the review in a way the reader can easily follow, provided details to support her claims about the book, and also communicated a genuine enthusiasm about the book.

Step-by-Step Teaching Guide

Engage Students Through Literature

1. Point out the organization of the essay, particularly in the first two paragraphs. The author provides background on the book and distinguishes it from its predecessors.

continued

Critical Viewing

Connect Students may mention the book's focus on the falcon and facts it presents about falcon nutrition and behavior.

12.1 Model From Literature

◄ Critical Viewing What qualities of this scene illustrate points Russell makes about *Frightful's Mountain*? **[Connect]**

Mary Harris Russell has written book reviews for The New York Times Book Review *and other periodicals. Her subject here is Jean Craighead George, a noted writer for young adults.*

Reading Writing Connection

Reading Strategy: Identify Evidence Nonfiction writers should provide evidence to support each main point. Identify the evidence as you read for better understanding.

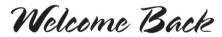

Welcome Back

Mary Harris Russell

FRIGHTFUL'S MOUNTAIN Written and illustrated by Jean Craighead George. 258 pp. New York: Dutton Children's Books.

[Jean Craighead] George's books place her young protagonists outside the family, finally achieving a fiercely won harmony with the natural world. In *My Side of the Mountain*, Sam Gribley, with his parents' tacit consent, leaves his crowded New York apartment to live wild in the Catskills. The fascinating details have attracted generations of young readers, with an appeal part *Walden*, part *Swiss Family Robinson*. . . .

In her opening paragraphs, Russell gives background information on the books in the series. She notes one important improvement she finds in the latest one.

Frightful's Mountain continues the story of Sam Gribley and the wilderness, but with a formal difference that I think strengthens its appeal. Both *My Side of the Mountain* and *On the Far Side of the Mountain* are first-person narratives, and the narrator, Sam, speaks with a tone more measured than that of most teenagers. That tone grates on some readers. In *Frightful's Mountain,* however, he's replaced by an omniscient narrator, necessitated by the plot focus on the peregrine falcon that in the first book Sam had captured from her nest, given the name Frightful, and trained as his hunting partner.

Russell organizes her review logically. First, she discusses the central role of the falcons in the book. Next, she notes the wealth of details on falcons. Finally, she draws a conclusion about the effect of this information on a reader.

George rigorously refuses to anthropomorphize the falcons, and at times—for example, when Frightful does not know how to brood or nurture her nestlings—the effect is shocking. Frightful departs from falcon norms because she was not taught them. The central question for Sam and the reader is whether or not Frightful can truly live wild and unlearn the behaviors she learned from him.

George shares detailed information on falcon nutrition, development and behavior, and about the breathtaking intricacies of migration and flight. The first few pages of the novel are slow, as George quickly retells Frightful's story from the earlier two books. It's not very long, however, before the amazing wealth of details about falcon ways has lured you in.

With precise words such as breathtaking, slow, amazing, *and* lured, *Russell clearly expresses her response to the book.*

Frightful's Mountain is a novel that will change the way you look at the world, even if you are among the majority of us who don't see falcons every day, because of the education it gives about what birds, especially predators, need to live and what they can contribute to the environment. After watching Frightful's need for food and her introduction of food to her brood, you'll never again think "eats like a bird" means dieting.

There is a plot involving human beings and civic ecological issues, based partly on real-life events concerning a bridge over the Hudson. On the whole, however, the human beings and their conversations are much less interesting than the aerial world. You've probably not read anything else quite like this. The parental struggles of Frightful and a bird named 426 (for a Fish and Wildlife Service band he carries) become a genuine page turner. Sam and his sister Alice and many other human and animal characters recur from the earlier books, but to my mind Frightful steals the show.

LITERATURE

To read about a writer's childhood responses to literature, see Maya Angelou's *I Know Why the Caged Bird Sings.* An excerpt from this work can be found in *Prentice Hall Literature: Timeless Voices, Timeless Themes,* Silver.

Reading Writing Connection

Writing Application: Provide Evidence
As you draft your own response to literature, provide evidence for each of your points.

Step-by-Step Teaching Guide continued

2. Point out the use of topic sentences in organizing each paragraph and how the author supplies details to support each main idea.
3. Ask students if they think they would like *Frightful's Mountain.* Ask them to identify details in the review that made them think this is a book they would or would not like to read.

Responding to Literature

Maya Angelou would not want a life without books to read. They open up the entire world to her. She thinks that giving someone a book and helping that person enjoy literature is the gift of love.

Reading\Writing Connection

Writing: Provide Evidence

Tell students that every writer should support his or her main points with evidence. Otherwise, readers will have a hard time accepting what they are reading. Have students keep in mind the importance of providing evidence as they draft their essays.

Step-by-Step Teaching Guide

Prewriting: Reader's Response Journal; Self-Interview

1. Have students review their reader's response journal if they keep one. If not, encourage them to search their memories for something they read recently that moved them. Remind students that they shouldn't restrict themselves to pieces they liked. Something that disturbed them or that they disliked can also make a good topic.
2. The self-interview activity also requires students to search their memories. Again, remind them that tackling something they didn't like can be a good topic. Encourage students who have preferences to indulge them. For instance, if a student has exhibited dislike for upbeat, "preachy" material or, conversely, for cool, cynical writing, this is an opportunity to give vent to those feelings about this kind of writing.

Step-by-Step Teaching Guide

Prewriting: Browsing

Teaching Resources: Writing Support Transparency 12-A; Writing Support Activity Book 12-1

1. Have students draw four columns on a sheet of paper and label the columns *Story, Author, Subject, Characters.*
2. Ask students to recall stories they have read recently and fill in information on the chart.
3. Tell students to spend a few minutes thinking about each selection on their lists, focusing on their memories of the story, what they liked, what they didn't, and on what they might say in a review.
4. Display the transparency. Draw students' attention to Stacy's model and the details she recorded. Give students copies of the blank organizer for them to use to help choose a topic.

12.2 Prewriting

Choosing Your Topic

Your liveliest responses to literature will probably involve a work to which you have a strong reaction—positive or negative. Use the strategies that follow to choose such a work.

Strategies for Generating a Topic

1. **Reader's Response Journal** If you have recorded your thoughts about your reading in a reader's response journal, look through your journal for works to which you had a strong reaction. Select one of these works as your topic.
2. **Interview Yourself** Ask yourself questions about your favorite kind of reading, your favorite books, the character you would most like to be, and the fictional place you would most like to visit. Write down your answers, and review them. Choose your topic from the works you mention.
3. **Browsing** Browse the literature sections of a library or bookstore. Flip through works you have already read or new short works by familiar authors. Take notes on each, and choose the most interesting one as your topic.

iText

Try it out! Take notes using the interactive Browsing chart in **Section 12.2**, on-line or on CD-ROM.

Student Work IN PROGRESS

Name: Stacy Osborn
Gilmer Independent School District
Gilmer, TX

Browsing

Stacy looked through several anthologies of short stories. She listed features of the stories in a chart and chose "Christmas Day in the Morning" as her subject.

STORY	AUTHOR	SUBJECT	CHARACTERS
"Christmas Day in the Morning"	Pearl S. Buck	How people express love for each other	Rob, his wife, his father
"Charles"	Shirley Jackson	How parents don't see their kids as they really are	Laurie, his parents, his teacher
"The Necklace"	Guy de Maupassant	A couple work for 10 years to replace a cheap necklace	Mathilde, her husband, Mme. Forestier

TIME AND RESOURCE MANAGER

Resources
Print: Writing Support Transparencies, 12-A–D; Writing Support Activity Book, 12-1–3
Technology: Writing and Grammar iText, Section 12.2

In-Depth Coverage	Accelerated Pace
• Cover pp. 264–269 in class. • Work through the Reader's Response Journal, Self-Interview, and Browsing strategies with the class. • Use the Responding to Fine Arts Transparency to generate additional topics. • Do the Pentad and Hexagonal Writing activities in class.	• Assign pp. 264–269 for independent student review. • Discuss strategies for generating topics. • Have students work independently to choose and narrow their topics. • Have students work with partners to focus on audience, purpose, and gathering details.

TOPIC BANK

If you're having trouble finding a topic, consider the following possibilities:

1. **Analyze a Theme** Think of a novel, short story, essay, or poem that sends a message to readers. Write an essay showing how the author uses plot, characters, images, language, and other techniques to convey the message. Then, give your own opinion of the theme.
2. **Essay About an Author** Write about two or more works by the same author. Detail what is similar and what is different about the works. Draw conclusions about the writer's subject matter and style.

Responding to Fine Art

3. Jot down notes on this painting. Who is the woman? What is she doing? What do formal elements of the painting—colors, her pose and position—suggest about her mood? Review your notes, and then list characters from stories and novels of which the painting reminds you. Select a work to write about from your list.

The Girl I Left Behind Me, Eastman Johnson, National Museum of American Art, Washington, D.C.

Responding to Literature

4. Read and take notes on Walt Whitman's poem, "Poets to Come." Think about what he means when he asks poets of the future to "justify" him. Then, read a poem by E. E. Cummings such as "love is a place." Explain whether you think Cummings's experiments with punctuation and line shape "justify" Whitman. You can find both poems in *Prentice Hall Literature: Timeless Voices, Timeless Themes,* Silver.

Cooperative Writing Opportunity

5. **Festival for a Work** With a group of students, choose a poem, short story, or novel. Plan a festival to celebrate it. Divide the following tasks: acting out scenes from the work; inventing games based on the work for other students to play; and designing posters or creating commercials to advertise the work. As part of the day's events, hold a panel discussion about the work.

Step-by-Step Teaching Guide

Responding to Fine Art

Teaching Resources: Writing Support Transparency 12-B

1. Display the transparency.
2. Ask students what kind of books the girl might be carrying.

Responding to Literature

Students may say that Whitman may have hoped that future poets would use his work (and the works of other poets) as inspiration to write even better poetry. He may have felt that if he could influence others, his efforts would have been worthwhile. They may feel that Cummings's experiments with language and mechanics broke new ground, just as Whitman's innovations did in his century. They may also point out similarities in both poets' exhilarating and exuberant viewpoints, which opened the mind to seeing new possibilities.

Spotlight on the Humanities

For additional topic suggestions, refer students to the Spotlight on the Humanities on page 284.

ONGOING ASSESSMENT: Monitor and Reinforce

If some students have difficulty finding a topic, use one of the following options.

Option 1 Suggest that students choose an idea from the Topic Bank. If many students have difficulty, work with them around a single topic, modeling the process for them.	**Option 2** If Topic Bank ideas seem too complex, suggest that students try one of the assignments from the Topic Bank for Heterogeneous Classes in the Teaching Resources.

TIME SAVERS!

Writing Support Transparencies
Use the transparencies for Chapter 12 to teach these strategies.

Writing Support Activity Book
Use the graphic organizers for Chapter 12 to facilitate these strategies.

Prewriting: Use a Pentad

Teaching Resources: Writing Support Transparency 12-C; Writing Support Activity Book 12-2

1. Discuss the necessity of narrowing or focusing a topic. What approach will students take to their topics? How will they find evidence to back up their general statements about the story?

2. Display the transparency to show students how Stacy used a pentad to focus her response.

3. Give students copies of the blank organizer to help them highlight points they want to cover in their essays.

12.2

Focusing Your Response

After you have chosen a work to which to respond, read or review it carefully. Then, use a pentad to focus your topic.

Use a Pentad

Draw a large five-pointed star as a graphic organizer. Label each point as follows:

- **Actors** Who performed the action?
- **Acts** What was done?
- **Scenes** When or where was it done?
- **Agencies** How was it done?
- **Purposes** Why was it done?

Fill in the star with details matching each label. Highlight details that interest you, and sum them up to create a focus.

Student Work IN PROGRESS

Name: Stacy Osborn
Gilmer Independent School District
Gilmer, TX

Using a Pentad

Once Stacy decided on "Christmas Day in the Morning" as her topic, she filled out a pentad and highlighted the points she wanted to cover in her paper.

Rob in the present; Rob in the past; Rob's wife; Rob's children; Rob's father; Rob's mother

Actors

Purposes **Acts**

to awaken love by giving love; to create happiness by sharing love

Agencies **Scenes**

love; gifts; memories; Christmas spirit

Rob's children won't share Christmas with him; young Rob discovers his father's love for him and in return milks the cows; old Rob decides to write his wife a love letter.

old Rob wakes up early in the morning (present); he remembers his wife's unhappiness about Christmas (recent past); flashback: young Rob in the past (distant past); old Rob on Christmas morning

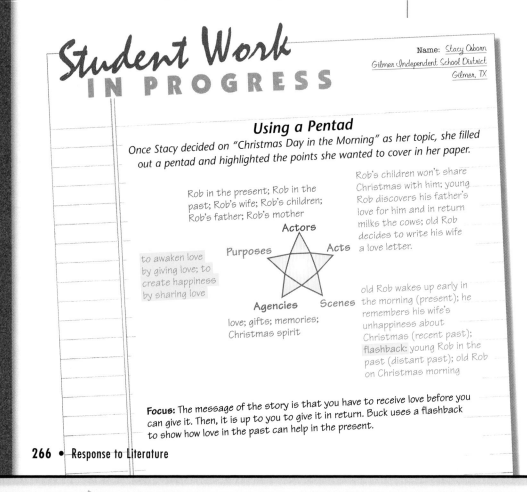

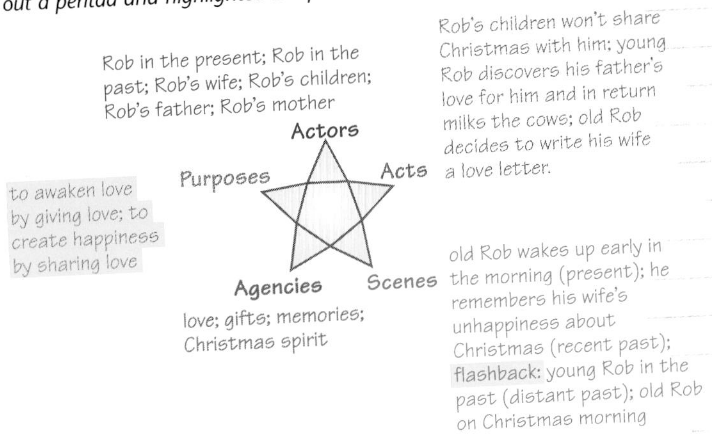

Focus: The message of the story is that you have to receive love before you can give it. Then, it is up to you to give it in return. Buck uses a flashback to show how love in the past can help in the present.

266 • Response to Literature

⏱ TIME SAVERS!

📄 Writing Support Transparencies
Use the transparencies for Chapter 12 to teach these strategies.

📖 Writing Support Activity Book
Use the graphic organizers for Chapter 12 to facilitate these strategies.

☑ ONGOING ASSESSMENT: Monitor and Reinforce

Graphic organizers are useful teaching tools, but they tend to work better for more visually-oriented students. Use the following options for students who are experiencing difficulty using the graphic organizer.

Option 1 Have students simply list each heading on a piece of paper and fill in the information below the heading.	**Option 2** Some students may benefit from peer assistance when organizing their material.

Considering Your Audience and Purpose

After focusing your topic, think about your audience and your purpose for writing. Use your answers to the following questions to guide you as you gather details and draft:

My Audience

- **Are my readers practiced, older readers?** If so, you need not explain every detail of the work. For instance, you might sum up the pacing and setting of a book as follows: "From desolate moors to high-class hotels, the book rushes headlong from one exotic location to the next."
- **Am I writing for less sophisticated readers?** Spell out each point, with specific references to the work. For instance, you might give these readers a feel for the rhythm of a book by writing: "The heroine of the book must travel to many exotic places in her search for her lost brother. Each chapter is set in a different place, so the reader may feel as if he or she is rushing around the globe."

My Purpose

- **Am I trying to persuade readers?** If your purpose is to persuade readers to read (or to avoid reading) the work, concentrate on examples supporting your evaluation.
- **Am I trying to enhance readers' appreciation of the work?** Concentrate on qualities and patterns in the work that a reader might not otherwise see.

◀ Critical Viewing
What details about this scene from *Oliver Twist* might you need to spell out for less sophisticated readers? What details might you highlight to enhance a reader's appreciation of the scene? **[Apply]**

Step-by-Step Teaching Guide

Prewriting: Considering Your Audience and Purpose

1. Even if students are responding to a work the whole class has read, the essay should be addressed to people who do not know the work.
2. The Model From Literature is written for readers who don't know George's book but might be interested in it.
3. Discuss how the two purposes listed are not necessarily mutually exclusive. Students can both try to persuade people to read a work and help them appreciate it.

Critical Viewing

Apply Students may say that you might need to explain who the characters are and why they are there. They may highlight the boys' pinched, hungry faces and ill-fitting clothes or the plumpness of the man.

ONGOING ASSESSMENT: Monitor and Reinforce

Some students consider the teacher their audience. Use the following option to modify this pattern.

Have students select one specific person, such as a family member or friend, as their audience. This will encourage them to write for another audience and will also affect the level of detail, language, and formality that they put into the essay.

Step-by-Step Teaching Guide

Prewriting: Use Hexagonal Writing

Teaching Resources: Writing Support Transparency 12-D; Writing Support Activity Book 12-3

1. Tell students that the drafting process will be much easier if they first gather the necessary details about their topics.
2. Display the transparency. Have a volunteer read each of the categories in the hexagon.
3. Give students copies of the blank organizer and have them gather details for their essays.

Customize for *ESL Students*

Students who are still acquiring English vocabulary may want to choose a shorter work or one at a lower grade level. Help students focus on crafting a good response rather than choosing an unnecessarily demanding topic.

12.2

Gathering Details

Before you can write a response to a literary work, you must gather details from the work—examples of what makes the work unique. Use the following strategies to help.

Use Hexagonal Writing

Cut out six triangles of equal size, three each from two different-colored sheets of construction paper. Arrange the triangles and label them, as shown below. Then, fill in each triangle with details from the work for that category. If you need more room, make another hexagon or use note cards labeled with the categories shown.

Student Work IN PROGRESS

Name: *Stacy Osborn*
Gilmer Independent School District
Gilmer, TX

Using a Hexagon

Stacy used a hexagon to gather details on the short story to which she was responding.

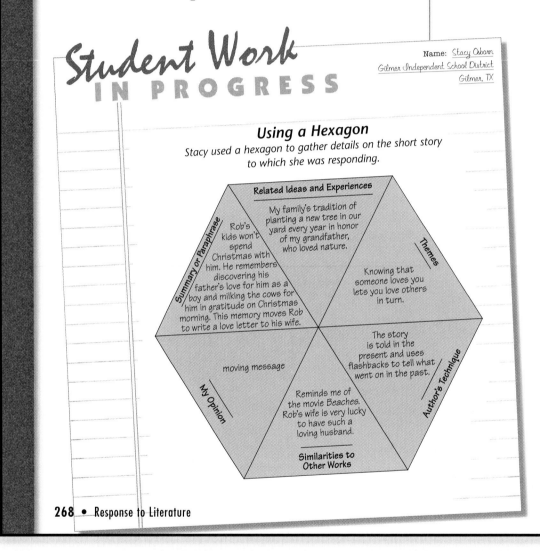

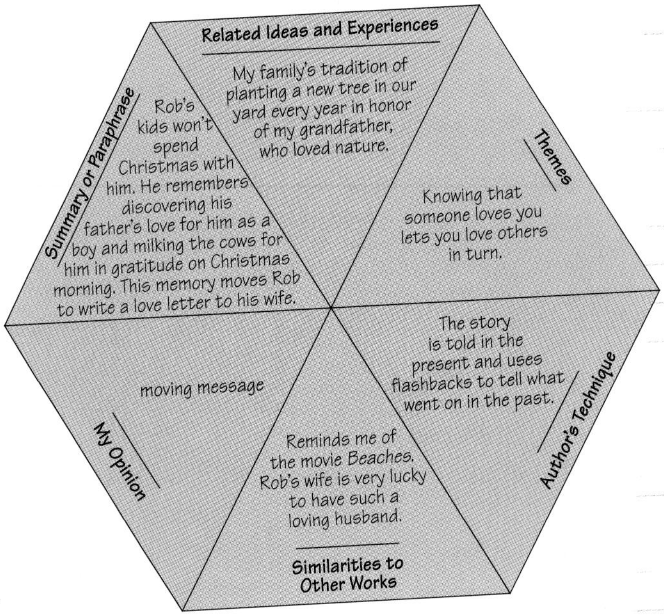

Related Ideas and Experiences
My family's tradition of planting a new tree in our yard every year in honor of my grandfather, who loved nature.
Themes
Knowing that someone loves you lets you love others in turn.
Author's Technique
The story is told in the present and uses flashbacks to tell what went on in the past.
Similarities to Other Works
Reminds me of the movie Beaches. Rob's wife is very lucky to have such a loving husband.
My Opinion
moving message
Summary or Paraphrase
Rob's kids won't spend Christmas with him. He remembers discovering his father's love for him as a boy and milking the cows for him in gratitude on Christmas morning. This memory moves Rob to write a love letter to his wife.

TIME SAVERS!

Writing Support Transparencies
Use the transparencies for Chapter 12 to teach these strategies.

Writing Support Activity Book
Use the graphic organizers for Chapter 12 to facilitate these strategies.

Look for Patterns

As you fill out a "hexagonal" on literature to which you are responding, look for patterns in the details you are gathering. Works of literature use patterns such as repetitions, contrasts, and resemblances to create or convey meaning. Often, writers use patterns to suggest **themes** (lessons or questions about life).

Here are some examples of the way patterns may create themes:

CHARACTERS:	The main characters are brothers. One is a success in business, the other a failure.
THEME:	This contrast may cause readers to ask questions about the nature or value of success. "Success" is a theme of the story.
IMAGES:	A poem uses images of stray kittens and abandoned cars.
THEME:	These images resemble each other in one way: They suggest the idea of neglect or abandonment. "Abandonment" is a theme of the poem.
WORDS:	The poet uses words such as *looping, slothful,* and *sprawling* to describe a river.
THEME:	The sounds of these words, as well as the meanings, suggest slow, lazy speeds. "Ease" or "inactivity" may be themes of the poem.

Finding Patterns To find patterns in the work, go through your notes a few times. Each time, think of different ways to describe the events, characters, images, and ideas you have noted. For instance, you might describe two main characters as "two young men" or "one a failure, one a success." Note when your descriptions fit together in interesting ways.

▼ **Critical Viewing** What theme does this photograph suggest? **[Analyze]**

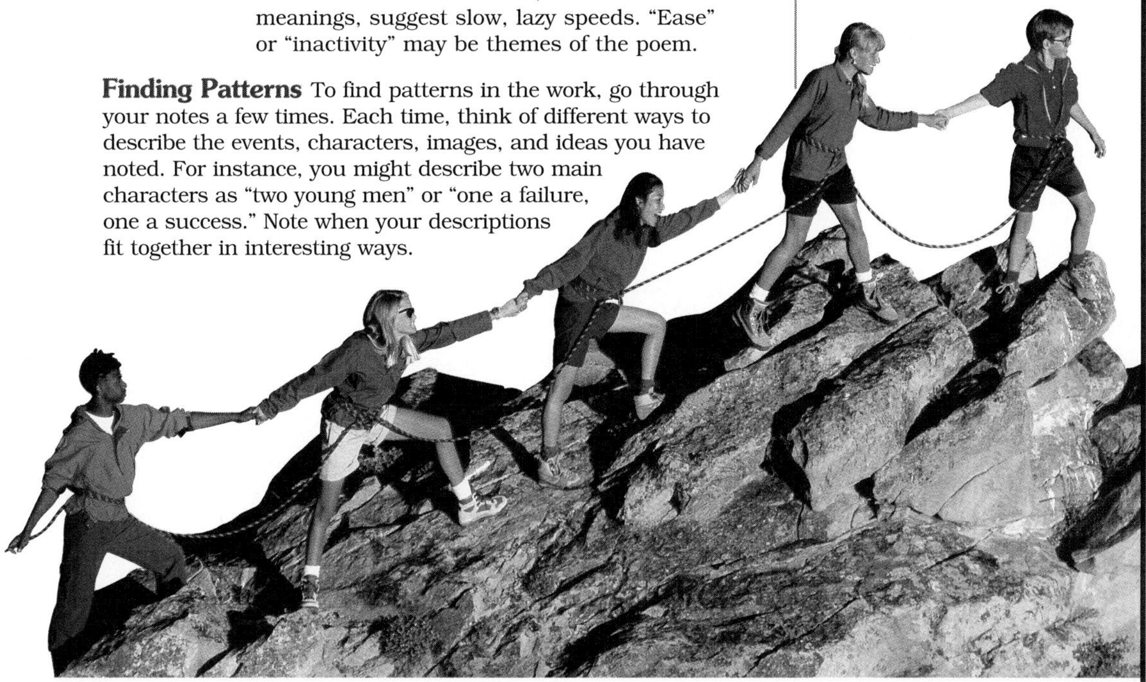

Step-by-Step Teaching Guide

Prewriting: Look for Patterns

Discuss patterns. Often we learn by constructing relationships among words, ideas, facts, and feelings. Encourage students to look for patterns among the different entries on the hexagonal. These patterns can serve as the main ideas of their book review.

Customize for *Less Advanced Students*

Students may need assistance filling in the hexagonal. See that they have gathered sufficient details in the previous activity. If necessary, small groups can select the same topic and work together on this project.

Critical Viewing

Analyze Students may suggest teamwork and cooperation or working toward a goal as themes.

Step-by-Step Teaching Guide

Drafting: Develop and Define Your Focus; Conclude With an Insight

1. Students at the drafting stage usually follow one of two courses of action: the procrastinators dawdle, and the hasty start writing before they have organized their notes and given sufficient thought to the topic and the writing process.
2. Encourage the hasty to spend some time first organizing their information, then thinking about it. Help them see the importance of sitting and pondering to the creative process.
3. A focus is the main idea for the essay. To get there, have students review their notes and try to focus on the entire topic. Remind them that a focus statement should be one or at most two sentences that summarize what they want to say about the topic.
4. An insight is the "how-to" part of the focus statement. In the insight, students need to act as the reader's guide and tell how the author accomplished whatever is in the focus statement.

Drafting Tip

Talk with students about the importance of a strong focus. If they don't know what they're saying, it will show in the essay. If students have gathered details properly, urge them to be patient and make different attempts at getting a focus statement together. Have them analyze each attempt and try to combine pieces of each effort to put together a good focus.

12.3 Drafting

Shaping Your Writing

Once you have gathered details from the work, you must organize them. As you draft, create a center of interest—a focus—to which each detail connects. You should also build to a main point—an insight into the work.

Define and Develop Your Focus

You have already narrowed your topic, but you must still find a focus for your response. A **focus** is a statement of your reaction to a specific aspect of the work.

To define a focus for your response, review your notes. Then, write out your response to the work in a single sentence, explaining which aspect of the work led to your response.

FOCUS: In "The Tell-Tale Heart," Edgar Allan Poe creates a nightmare experience by telling of a murder from the murderer's point of view.

Elaborate on your focus statement as you draft.

Conclude With an Insight

A good response to literature gives insight into a work. An insight might include an evaluation of the work, an interpretation of the theme, or an analysis of how the parts of the piece work together.

To achieve an insight into the work, consider your focus statement. Ask yourself the following questions:

- What details of the work contributed to my reaction? How?
- How do they fit with other details in the work?

For instance, in the case of "The Tell-Tale Heart," your insight might concern Poe's use of the first-person perspective to add to the horror of the tale.

INSIGHT: A first-person perspective makes the tale even more like a nightmare from which you can't wake up.

The narrator "collars" the reader and offers no break in the story until the end.

Because the narrator is the reader's only source of information, the reader feels stuck inside the narrator's delusion.

TIME AND RESOURCE MANAGER

Resources
Print: Writing Support Transparencies, 12-E
Technology: Writing and Grammar iText, Section 12.3

In-Depth Coverage	Accelerated Pace
• Cover pp. 270–271 in class. • Work through the activities on defining and developing a focus, concluding with an insight and turning your perspective upside-down with the entire class. • Have students write their own book review drafts in class.	• Have students review pp. 270–271 independently, and then write their own book review drafts. • Respond to individual drafting issues as needed.

Providing Elaboration

As you draft your response, consider the different perspectives the work includes. Literary works have complex meanings. A poem doesn't simply say "black" or "white." It might say "either black or white" or "both black and white." As you draft, draw on these varied perspectives.

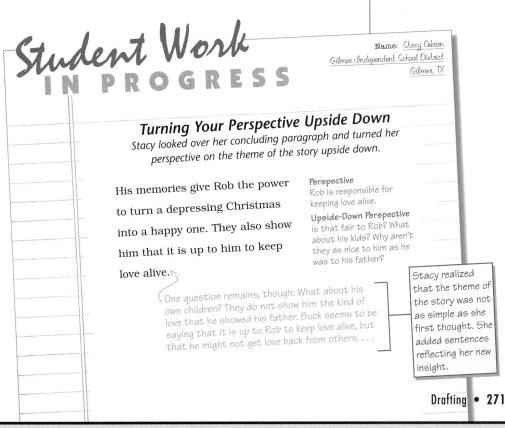

▲ **Critical Viewing** Explain how the artist has made one scene out of two. **[Analyze]**

Turn Your Perspective Upside Down

After you write a paragraph on an important point, look it over. In the margin, jot down the perspective of the paragraph. For instance, you might write, "Dr. Morbid is a selfish, evil villain."

Then, turn your perspective upside down. Look for the negative in the positive or the positive in the negative. You might write, for example, "In a way, Dr. Morbid is enviable, because he does whatever he pleases."

Student Work IN PROGRESS

Name: Stacy Osborn
Gilmer Independent School District
Gilmer, TX

Turning Your Perspective Upside Down

Stacy looked over her concluding paragraph and turned her perspective on the theme of the story upside down.

His memories give Rob the power to turn a depressing Christmas into a happy one. They also show him that it is up to him to keep love alive.

Perspective
Rob is responsible for keeping love alive.

Upside-Down Perspective
Is that fair to Rob? What about his kids? Why aren't they as nice to him as he was to his father?

One question remains, though: What about his own children? They do not show him the kind of love that he showed his father. Buck seems to be saying that it is up to Rob to keep love alive, but that he might not get love back from others. . . .

Stacy realized that the theme of the story was not as simple as she first thought. She added sentences reflecting her new insight.

Step-by-Step Teaching Guide

Drafting: Your Perspective Upside-Down

Teaching Resources: Writing Support Transparency 12-E

1. Point out that perspective does not follow the exact path of opinion, but it is close enough to use as a model. Emphasize that there is usually a different or contrary perspective to any point of view. To see it, we need to look at the topic differently. If Dr. Morbid is greedy, how did he that way? Does he see his own greed? If a character is generous and altruistic, ask whether he or she has low self-esteem and needs the approval of others.
2. Display the transparency. Draw students' attention to Stacy's concluding paragraph and her differing perspectives. Have students discuss how Stacy's elaboration adds to the power of her conclusion.

Critical Viewing

Analyze Students may say that the picture shows white birds flying at night and black birds flying during the day. Escher is able to achieve this effect by representing the birds and parts of the terrain below using shapes that fit together like jigsaw puzzle pieces.

TIME SAVERS!

Writing Support Transparencies
Use the transparencies for Chapter 12 to teach these strategies.

Step-by-Step Teaching Guide

Revising: Analyze for Focus

1. Students may have a tendency to regard drafting as the major part of the writing process and not give sufficient attention to the revision stage. Tell them that professional writers regard the revision stage as the real workshop where a finished product is made; revision, rather than drafting, is where the real work begins.
2. Ask students to recall a conversation with a friend or relative in which they weren't quite sure what the point was, one that took a great deal of explaining and questioning to understand the point. Students have patience with friends, but they can't expect that same patience from readers. They need to make their points in an organized, compelling way that readers can understand and that gives them a reason to keep reading.
3. Read through the text directions. See that students understand the importance of carefully identifying and structuring their points to provide support for their focus.

Revising Tip

Tell students that revising is equal parts inspiration and "perspiration." They need to step back from their draft and regard it critically, examining both large structures and small details. And they need to filter the details through their creative minds to figure out how to fashion a rough draft into a finished essay.

Critical Viewing

Speculate Students may say that Poe might have been fascinated by disturbing and morbid subjects.

12.4 Revising

Revising Your Overall Structure

Now that you have finished your first draft, review it to build on its strengths and eliminate its weaknesses. Start by looking at your overall structure—the organization of your main points and support. Then, analyze your paragraphs, sentences, and word choice.

Analyze for Focus

Your focus should be a central organizing force in your response. Check to make sure that you have included a statement of your focus in your introduction. Then, code points related to your focus to determine how your organization can be improved.

REVISION STRATEGY
Coding Points Related to Focus

Jot down your focus statement on an index card. Run the card down your draft, one line at a time. Underline sentences that relate to your focus. When you have finished coding, review your draft. If you find a paragraph with few or no underlined sentences in it, consider eliminating the paragraph or adding details related to your focus.

Build to a Point

An effective response does not just have a logical order—it should also have a dramatic order, building to a point. Use the following strategy to help you build to a point:

REVISION STRATEGY
Building to Your Best Point

Read your paper over quickly. Circle the strongest point you made. It could be a statement that sums up your other ideas. It might be your most interesting insight.

Consider moving this point to the end of your paper. If you do move this point to the end, review your draft for places where you can add ideas preparing for this point. For instance, after each of your less important points in a paper on "The Tell-Tale Heart," you might add a sentence such as this: "While this technique is important, it does not fully explain the way Poe increases the terror of his tale." Your best point would, in fact, explain how Poe achieves his results.

▼ Critical Viewing
Why might Edgar Allan Poe have been drawn to write tales of horror? **[Speculate]**

TIME AND RESOURCE MANAGER

Resources
Print: Writing Support Transparencies, 12-F–H
Technology: Writing and Grammar iText, Section 12.4

In-Depth Coverage	Accelerated Pace
• Cover pp. 272–277 in class. • Work through Grammar in Your Writing on p. 275.	• Assign students to review pp. 272–277 independently. • Have students independently revise their responses to literature.

Revising Your Paragraphs

Add Support

In a response to a literary work, you should support every point you make with details from the work. Use the following strategy to ensure that you have provided necessary support.

REVISION STRATEGY
Adding Support by Using Points to Illuminate

Follow these steps to "illuminate" your work:

1. Circle each general statement you make about the work.
2. Cut out a few five-pointed stars from construction paper, one for each main point in your draft. Label the points of each star with the following terms: *quotation, character, event, figure of speech,* and *theme.*
3. Glue a star near each circled sentence.
4. Inside each star, check off supporting details for your general point. For instance, if you illustrate a point with two quotations, place two check marks under "quotations."
5. Next, review your stars. If, overall, there are few check marks for a certain kind of support, consider adding details of that kind. If there are no check marks in a star, consider adding more support for the corresponding point.

Student Work IN PROGRESS

Name: Stacy Osborn
Gilmer Independent School District
Gilmer, TX

Using Points to Illuminate

This is an example of how Stacy used the strategy of illuminating.

To show that he returns this love, Rob wakes up extra early on Christmas morning and milks the cows all by himself. This is his surprise gift to his father. Once the father realizes what Rob has done, he ~~is very happy.~~

kneels down and gives Rob a big hug. " 'Nobody ever did a nicer thing—' " he tells Rob.

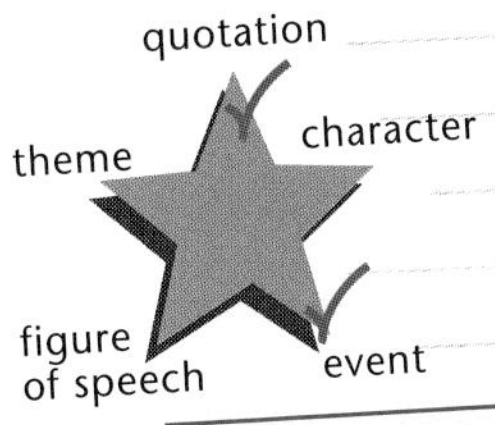

Stacy realized that she needed more details to illustrate the father's reaction. She added a summary of an action and a quotation of dialogue.

Step-by-Step Teaching Guide

Revising Paragraphs: Using Points to Illuminate

Teaching Resources: Writing Support Transparency 12-F

1. A good response to literature contains support for all the statements made. The support will usually be an example from the work students are discussing.
2. Display the transparency. Have students discuss how Stacy clarified each highlighted point.
3. Have students construct stars to help them and support to their essays.

ONGOING ASSESSMENT: Monitor and Reinforce

This activity favors students with good visual skills. For students who have difficulty with the exercise, use one of the following options.

Option 1 Have students highlight sentences that do not offer support and then rewrite the sentences with one of the five points included in it.	**Option 2** Have students work in peer groups to help them identify sentences needing supporting details.

TIME SAVERS!

Writing Support Transparencies
Use the transparencies for Chapter 12 to teach these strategies.

Step-by-Step Teaching Guide

Revising: Highlighting Related and Contrasting Points

Teaching Resources: Writing Support Transparency 12-G

1. Remind students that although they know what they are thinking and what they want to write, readers are dependent on what is on the page. Encourage students to try to write compact prose with related sentences.
2. Display the transparency. Ask students to explain why Stacy made the revision she did.

12.4

Revising Your Sentences

Use Sentence Structure to Link Ideas

Variety in the structure of your sentences can make your writing more interesting to read. In addition, you can show the relationships between ideas by using the right structure.

REVISION STRATEGY
Highlighting Related and Contrasting Points

In one color, highlight pairs of sentences in your draft that make related points. In another color, highlight sentences that make contrasting points. Consider combining these pairs of sentences into compound or complex sentences.

RELATED POINTS:	The three sisters keep talking about a trip they hope to take. They are dreamers.
COMBINED:	The three sisters, who are dreamers, keep talking about a trip they hope to take.
CONTRASTING POINTS:	His triumph is celebrated by the town. His private life, however, is as bad as ever.
COMBINED:	His triumph is celebrated by the town; his private life, however, is as bad as ever.

Grammar and Style Tip

A complex sentence can suggest specific links between ideas: The idea in the independent clause is the focus of the sentence, to which the subordinate clauses contribute.

Student Work IN PROGRESS

Name: Stacy Osborn
Gilmer Independent School District
Gilmer, TX

Highlighting Related and Contrasting Points

After highlighting related points, Stacy decided to combine sentences.

Rob is fifteen years old. He overhears his father tell his mother that he hates to wake Rob for the chores~~.~~, because ~~He~~ he thinks Rob needs his sleep. When Rob hears ~~this. He~~ this, he realizes that his father loves him.

STANDARDIZED TEST PREPARATION WORKSHOP

Compound and Complex Sentences
Standardized test questions may require students to identify compound and complex sentences. Write the following examples on the board, and ask students to identify both the compound and the complex sentence.

A I urge you to read this book, and I promise you will be well rewarded for your efforts.

B When you finish this book, you will feel that you have lost a best friend.

C This book will go on my list of all-time favorites.

D This book made me laugh and cry at the same time.

A is a compound sentence because it contains two independent clauses. **B** is a complex sentence; it contains a subordinate clause followed by an independent clause. **C** and **D** are simple sentences.

TIME SAVERS!

Writing Support Transparencies
Use the transparencies for Chapter 12 to teach these strategies.

Grammar in Your Writing
Compound and Complex Sentences

To join two ideas, you can create a compound sentence or a complex sentence.

Compound Sentences

A **compound sentence** is made up of two or more independent clauses. (A clause is a group of words with its own subject and verb. An **independent clause** is a clause that can stand on its own as a sentence.) In a compound sentence, the clauses are either joined with a comma and one of the coordinating conjunctions—*and, but, for, nor, or, so,* or *yet*—or with a semicolon.

Comma and Coordinating Conjunction: [We were sorry for the delay,] (independent clause) **but** [it couldn't be avoided.] (independent clause)

Semicolon: [My brother promised to do better] (independent clause); [we were doubtful.] (independent clause)

Complex Sentences

A **complex sentence** consists of one independent clause—called the main clause—and one or more subordinate clauses. A **subordinate clause** has a subject and verb, but it cannot stand on its own as a sentence. Subordinate clauses begin with one of the relative pronouns—*who, whom, whose, which,* or *that*—or with a subordinating conjunction, such as *after, although, as, because, before, if, since, when, where, while, until,* or *unless.* If the subordinate clause comes before the main clause, it is followed by a comma.

In the following examples, the relative pronoun and subordinating conjunction are in boldface.

Relative Pronoun: [I'm the only one] (main clause) [**who** understands the situation.] (subordinate clause)

Subordinating Conjunction: [**Unless** we hear otherwise,] (subordinate clause) [we'll meet the bus at 3:00 P.M.] (main clause)

Find It in Your Reading Find one compound sentence and one complex sentence in "Welcome Back" by Mary Harris Russell on page 262. Identify the independent clauses in each.

Find It in Your Writing Find one compound sentence and one complex sentence in your response to literature. Identify the independent clauses in each See whether there are other places where using compound and complex sentences will make your writing smoother or clearer.

To learn more about compound and complex sentences, see Chapter 20.

ONGOING ASSESSMENT: Prerequisite Skills

If students have difficulty with compound and complex sentences, you may want to refer them to the following to assure coverage of prerequisite skills.

In the Textbook	Print	Technology
Phrases and Clauses, pp. 448–459	Grammar Exercise Workbook, pp. 93–96	On-Line Exercise Bank, Section 20.2

Step-by-Step Teaching Guide

Grammar in Your Writing: Compound and Complex Sentences

1. Write the following examples on the chalkboard. Demonstrate that when ideas are combined in a single sentence, it is easier for the reader to see the connection between them.

   The time-out call seemed insignificant at the time. In the closing seconds, the lack of a time-out changed the outcome.

   The time-out call seemed insignificant at the time, but in the closing seconds, the lack of a time-out changed the outcome.

2. Write the following sentences on the chalkboard for additional practice and ask students to combine them into compound or complex sentences.

   The plot of this book is clever. The characters are much less interesting. (The plot of this book is clever, but the characters are much less interesting.)

   The main character does not engage the reader. She has only one emotion. (The main character does not engage the reader because she has only one emotion.)

Find It in Your Reading

Complex: <u>*Frightful's Mountain* continues the story of Sam Gribley and the wilderness, but with a formal difference</u> that I think strengthens its appeal.

Compound: <u>Sam and his sister Alice and many other human and animal characters recur from the earlier books</u>, but <u>to my mind Frightful steals the show</u>.

Find It in Your Writing

If students cannot find examples, challenge them to revise their sentences to include at least one example of each.

Step-by-Step Teaching Guide

Revising: Coding Key Terms

Teaching Resources: Writing Support Transparency 12-H

1. Let students know that repetition is something writers are often urged to avoid, although repeating a key term can be an effective strategy to reinforce a point.
2. Read the following passage to students as an example of the unifying effects of repeating a key term:

   Freedom. The word popped into Julio's mind as he glanced out the window at the flock of migrating geese. Freedom. It was more than an idea. It was another way of being, almost another country from the dull routine of the job in which his lack of education trapped him. Freedom. That's what was lacking. And finishing his education was the only way to achieve that freedom.
3. Display the transparency to show students how Stacy coded key terms to strengthen her writing. Prompt students to combine related points in their own work.

TIME SAVERS!

Writing Support Transparencies
Use the transparencies for Chapter 12 to teach these strategies.

12.4

Revising Your Word Choice

Choose and Reuse Key Terms

To unify a piece of writing about a literary work, you can reuse a phrase that refers to one of the features on which you are focusing. For instance, in a response to Poe's "The Tell-Tale Heart," you might refer to the "claustrophobia" of the tale—the reader's feeling of being stuck in a nightmare. You might use this word whenever you refer to details that add to that feeling. By reusing your word or phrase, you can join the parts of your paper into a unified whole.

REVISION STRATEGY
Coding Key Terms

Circle each of the main points you make in your paper. Review them, and underline any phrase or term you use that could apply to more than one of your points. For example, you might use the term *brotherhood* when discussing a theme or the phrase *surprising metaphors* when describing a poet's style.

Then, mark with a red triangle places in your draft where you discuss ideas related to this term or phrase. Consider reusing the word or phrase in the places you have marked.

Student Work IN PROGRESS

Name: Stacy Osborn
Gilmer Independent School District
Gilmer, TX

Coding Key Terms

Stacy found a key term in Buck's story that she decided to repeat for effect.

▲ In the story "Christmas Day in the Morning," Pearl S. Buck shows the way one person's love can ~~help another person love.~~ awaken another's.

Stirred by the memory of his gift to his father, he realizes that he is able to love his wife so much because he learned long ago that his father loved him. Here, Buck states the central message of her story: "love alone could waken love." Rob then decides to write his wife a letter telling her how much he loves her.

Stacy discovered Buck's memorable statement in one paragraph and underlined it. She realized she could repeat it effectively in her introductory paragraph as well.

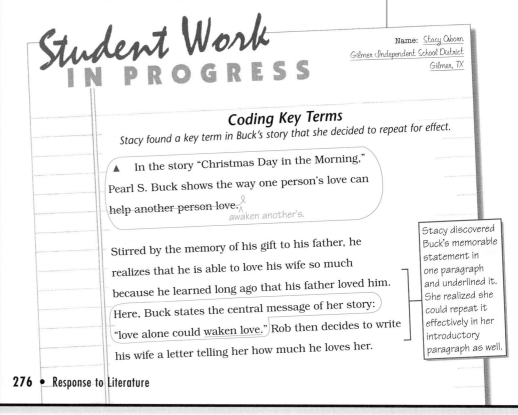

Peer Review

You have finished revising on your own, but you can still get extra help polishing your draft. For suggestions, share your writing process—what goals you set and what steps you took toward them—with peers. Use the following strategy.

Conduct a "Process Share"

In a small group, describe what you planned to achieve in your writing and what stage you have reached in the writing process. Then, read your draft to the group. To start a discussion about your draft, the others should ask these questions:

- Do you think you succeeded in doing what you intended?
- What problems have you encountered?
- What changes have you made already? Why did you make them?
- About what aspects of your writing do you have doubts?
- On what aspects of your response do you want suggestions from the group?

As you answer these questions, group members should make suggestions to you about your work. Take notes on what they tell you. Use what you learn in preparing the final version of your writing.

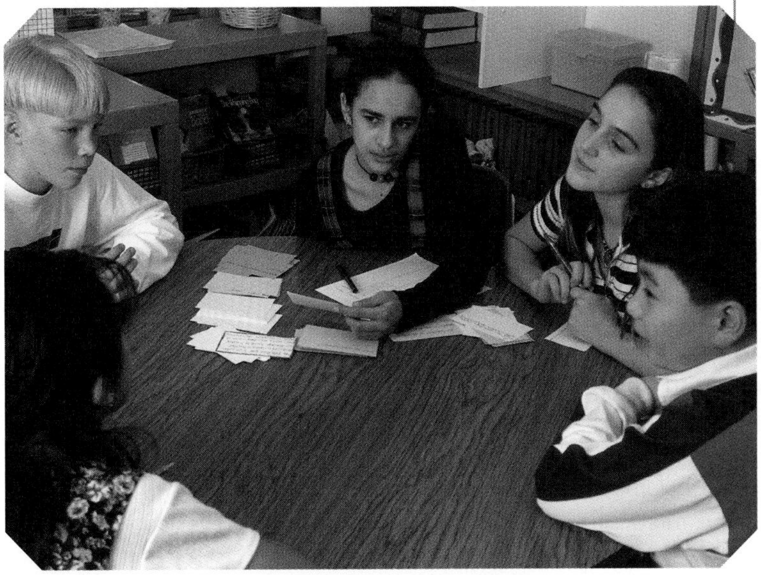

◀ **Critical Viewing** Explain how well prepared this writer appears for her peer review session. **[Evaluate]**

Step-by-Step Teaching Guide

Revising: Peer Review

1. The point of peer review is both to reinforce what writers do well and to offer suggestions for improvement. Reviewers should mention pluses first, then discuss minuses.
2. Remind students that the purpose of the peer review activity is to check essays for clarity and content. Grammatical, mechanical, and other issues will be handled in the next step, editing and proofreading.
3. Encourage students to spot opportunities for sentence-combining to improve the text's clarity.
4. Suggest that students record the questions on this page in their journals, and apply them to their own writing assignments in the future.

Critical Viewing

Evaluate Students may say she seems well prepared because she looks alert and has her writing in front of her.

Step-by-Step Teaching Guide

Editing and Proofreading

1. Discuss the necessity of eliminating errors from writing: Even the best idea can be misunderstood if there are errors in spelling and punctuation.
2. Review the difference between direct quotations and indirect quotes or paraphrases.

Step-by-Step Teaching Guide

Grammar in Your Writing: Punctuating and Formatting Quotations

1. Explain that quotations four or more lines in length must be indented (MLA style).
2. Write the following on the chalkboard and ask students to supply the missing punctuation marks.

   A typical example is the following passage: Jerry pulls up to the drive-in window and asks, How do you spell Mississippi? *(A typical example is the following passage: "Jerry pulls up to the drive-in window and asks, 'How do you spell* Mississippi?'")

Find It in Your Reading

There are several examples of quotations in the Student Work in Progress. Students should note that each quotation uses quotation marks and one uses a dash to separate it from the rest of the sentence.

Find It in Your Writing

You may want to have students exchange papers with a partner to make sure that they have punctuated and formatted their quotations correctly.

PRENTICE HALL

Everyday Spelling

If you have taught the spelling skills in *Prentice Hall Everyday Spelling*, Grade 8, Chapter 14, in conjunction with this *Writing and Grammar* chapter, review and assess students' mastery of the skills before concluding the chapter. Remind students to apply the spelling skills as they edit and proofread their responses to literature.

12.5 Editing and Proofreading

Whenever you write, proofread carefully to catch errors in spelling, punctuation, or grammar. In a response to literature, pay close attention to the indenting, capitalization, and punctuation of quotations you use to support your points.

Focusing on Quotations

Long quotations from a literary work should be indented in your writing. Shorter quotations are treated exactly like the quotations in the dialogue of a story. Be sure that, when you quote, you copy the words exactly as they appear in the work.

Grammar in Your Writing

Punctuating and Formatting Quotations

Following are two ways to present quotations from a literary work:

Long quotations Introduce the quotation with a colon; indent the entire quotation on the left.

The writer uses several unusual similes to describe Terry's feelings:

> When the concert began, Terry felt as excited as a puppy in a roomful of kittens. She couldn't wait for her turn. As she walked onto the stage, her knees felt like rubber bands. "If I can only get to the piano," she said to herself, "I'll be calm as a robot."

Brief quotations Use quotation marks and commas to separate the quotation from the rest of a sentence. Use single quotation marks for a quotation within another quotation:

> Terry's excitement is clear when she gets offstage and says to her brother, "Did you hear me? I made three mistakes, but no one noticed. The emcee told me, 'Good work, kid.'"

Find It in Your Reading Find an example of a quotation in the Student Work in Progress on page 280, and note how it is punctuated.

Find It in Your Writing Read over your response to literature, and check each quotation to be sure that it is set off or punctuated correctly.

To learn more about punctuating quotations, see Chapter 26.

TIME AND RESOURCE MANAGER

Resources
Print: Scoring Rubrics on Transparency, Chapter 12; Writing Assessment: Scoring Rubric and Scoring Models for Response to Literature
Technology: Writing and Grammar iText, Sections 12.5–6

In-Depth Coverage	Accelerated Pace
• Cover pp. 278–281 in class. • Have students edit and proofread their essays in class. • Review the Rubric for Self-Assessment in class. • Have students present their final drafts.	• Assign pp. 278–281 for independent student review. • Have students edit and proofread their essays as homework. • Have students present their final drafts.

12.6 Publishing and Presenting

Building Your Portfolio

Consider the following ideas for publishing and presenting your response to literature.

1. **"Good Reading for Teens" Booklet** Working with other students, assemble your responses to literature into a book-review booklet for your school or public library. Include your ratings of the works.
2. **Electronic Recommendations** With classmates, create a literary list or page on a Web site on the school server. Post your responses to literature, and invite visitors to share their own opinions and reactions.

Reflecting on Your Writing

Jot down some notes on your experience of writing a response to literature. Begin by answering the following questions:

- Did writing about a work of literature help you to understand it more completely or in a deeper way? Did your feelings about the work change as you thought and wrote about it?
- What advice would you give another student about writing a response to literature? Did you encounter problems that could have been avoided?

Internet Tip

To see responses to literature scored with this rubric, go on-line: PHSchool.com
Enter Web Code: eck-8001

Rubric for Self-Assessment

Evaluate your response to literature using the following criteria:

	Score 4	Score 3	Score 2	Score 1
Audience and Purpose	Presents sufficient background on the work(s); presents the writer's reactions forcefully	Presents background on the work(s); presents the writer's reactions clearly	Presents some background on the work(s); presents the writer's reactions at points	Presents little or no background on the work(s); presents few of the writer's reactions
Organization	Presents points in logical order, smoothly connecting them to the overall focus	Presents points in logical order and connects many to the overall focus	Organizes points poorly in places; connects some points to an overall focus	Presents information in a scattered, disorganized manner
Elaboration	Supports reactions and evaluations with elaborated reasons and well-chosen examples	Supports reactions and evaluations with specific reasons and examples	Supports some reactions and evaluations with reasons and examples	Offers little support for reactions and evaluations
Use of Language	Shows overall clarity and fluency; uses precise, evaluative words; makes few mechanical errors	Shows good sentence variety; uses some precise evaluative terms; makes some mechanical errors	Uses awkward or overly simple sentence structures and vague evaluative terms; makes many mechanical errors	Presents incomplete thoughts; makes mechanical errors that create confusion

ONGOING ASSESSMENT: Assess Mastery

Use one of the following options to assess final drafts of students' responses to literature.

Self-Assessment Ask students to score their essay using the rubric provided. Then have students write a paragraph reflecting on the most valuable thing they learned in completing this essay.

Teacher Assessment You may wish to use the rubric and scoring models provided in the Writing Assessment, Response to Literature, to score students' work.

Step-by-Step Teaching Guide

Publishing and Presenting

1. Students from several classes might combine their finished work in a loose-leaf binder and put it in the school library for other students to consult.
2. Have students complete the Reflecting on Your Writing activity and encourage volunteers to share their reflections with the class.
3. Have students use the rubric to assess their responses to literature.

ASSESS

Step-by Step Teaching Guide

Assessment

Teaching Resources: Scoring Rubrics on Transparency 12; Formal Assessment, Chapter 12

1. Display the Scoring Rubric transparency and review the criteria in class.
2. Before students proceed with self-assessment, you may wish to review the Final Draft of the Student Work in Progress on pages 280–281. Have students score the Final Draft in one or more of the rubric categories. For example, how would students score the essay in terms of audience and purpose?
3. In addition to student self-assessment, you may wish to use the following assessment options.
   - Score student essays yourself, using the rubric and scoring models from Writing Assessment.
   - Review the Standardized Test Preparation Workshop on pages 286–287 and have students respond to a writing prompt within a time limit.
   - Administer the Chapter 12 Test from Formal Assessment in Teaching Resources to assess students' grasp of concepts presented.

CLOSE

Step-by-Step Teaching Guide

Teaching From the Final Draft

1. Draw students' attention to how "A Response to 'Christmas Day in the Morning' by Pearl S. Buck" incorporates the elements of a well-written response to literature.
2. Analyze Stacy's opening paragraph, pointing out the concise way she states her topic and focus. In reading the essay aloud, pause here and ask students to consider how the author has oriented readers and told them what to expect and look for as they read on.

continued

Critical Viewing

Distinguish Students may mention the love that someone has for a loved one, the solemnity of observing an important event, or the joy of celebrating an achievement or milestone.

12.7 Student Work IN PROGRESS

FINAL DRAFT

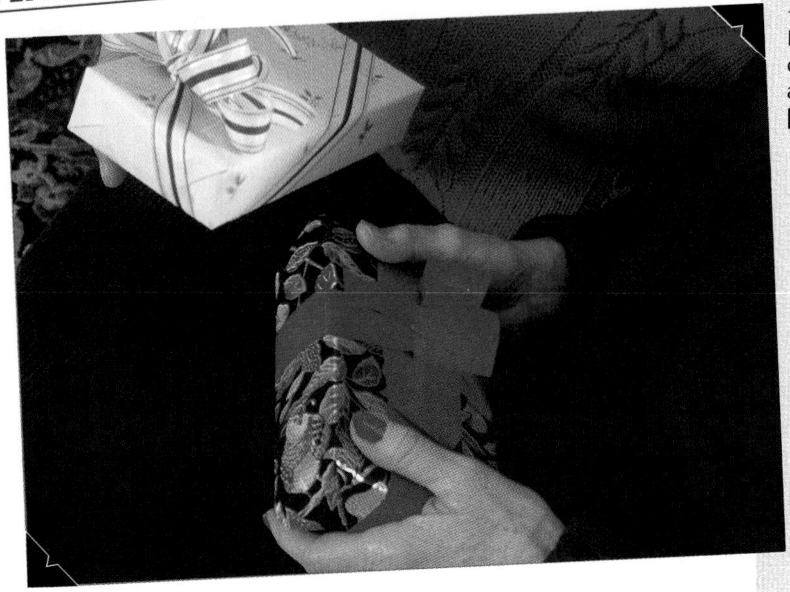

◄ **Critical Viewing** List two or three different feelings a gift can express. **[Distinguish]**

A Response to

"Christmas Day in the Morning" by Pearl S. Buck

Stacy Osborn
Gilmer Independent School District
Gilmer, Texas

In the story "Christmas Day in the Morning," Pearl S. Buck shows the way one person's love can awaken another's. She also suggests that individuals have to remember this fact and act on it. The story is enjoyable because of this moving message. The use of a flashback definitely adds to its effectiveness.

In her introduction, Stacy presents her topic and her focus.

Step-by-Step Teaching Guide continued

The story begins when the main character, Rob, and his wife are facing a Christmas day on their own. Their grown children want "their children to build Christmas memories about *their* houses, not his." This is a depressing scene. Yet on Christmas morning, Rob wakes up early and remembers what happened on that long-ago Christmas when he discovered that his father loved him dearly. Buck uses a flashback to bring us back to that time.

Stacy discusses a special technique used in the work—flashback.

Rob is fifteen years old. He overhears his father tell his mother that he hates to wake Rob for the chores, since he thinks Rob needs his sleep. When Rob hears this, he realizes that his father loves him. To show that he returns this love, Rob wakes up extra early on Christmas morning and milks the cows all by himself. This is his surprise gift to his father. Once the father realizes what Rob has done, he kneels down and gives Rob a big hug. "'Nobody ever did a nicer thing—'" he tells Rob.

Now, back in the present-day, depressing Christmas, Rob decides to show his wife his love for her. He gets up early and sets up the tree. Stirred by the memory of his gift to his father, he realizes that he is able to love his wife so much because he learned long ago that his father loved him. Here, Buck states the central message of her story: "love alone could waken love." Rob then decides to write his wife a letter telling her how much he loves her.

Stacy supports her idea of the theme of the work with a quotation. She repeats Buck's metaphor of "love wakening love" a few times in her response. It is a key term for her.

Though the story began with a depressing holiday scene, it ends with the phrase "Such a happy, happy Christmas!" The message seems to be that it is only by giving love that you can awaken love in others and make yourself happy.

This story uses a flashback, starting in the present Christmas and explaining what happened on the past Christmas, then telling about the present again. The flashback works especially well in this story because the story shows how a past lesson can affect the present. Rob's letter to his wife is a special gift, like the gift he gave his father. In a way, one gift leads to another.

Here, Stacy shares an insight into Buck's use of flashback.

His memories give Rob the power to turn a depressing Christmas into a happy one. They also show him that it is up to him to keep love alive. One question remains, though: What about his own children? They do not show him the kind of love that he showed his father. Buck seems to be saying that it is up to Rob to keep love alive, but that he might not get love back from others. In this way, the story doesn't say all loneliness can be ended just by showing your love. It does say, though, that people can use the memory of love to find strength. This moving message makes the story very special.

In her conclusion, Stacy looks at another perspective presented by the work. She ends with a strong restatement of her response to the story.

3. Note the emphasis Stacy puts on the use of a flashback in the second paragraph. According to Stacy, the flashback is more than a structural device. It is also a symbol of how the past is connected to the present. Ask students whether they think Stacy makes this last point clearly enough.
4. Ask students to respond to Stacy's response on two levels: its effectiveness as a response to literature and whether the story she describes is something in which they would be interested.

Lesson Objectives

1. To write a movie review appropriate to audience purpose.
2. To use prewriting strategies to choose and narrow a topic.
3. To gather and organize details.
4. To draft, revise, edit, and publish a movie review.

Step-by Step Teaching Guide

Movie Review

Teaching Resources: Writing Support Transparency 12-I; Writing Support Activity Book 12-4

1. Ask for a show of hands of those students who discuss films with friends or family members. Point out that such a discussion is a review. After seeing a movie together, most people talk over their reactions, pointing out performances and scenes in the film that they strongly liked or disliked. Students already have many of the critical skills they need to write movie reviews.
2. Ask students whether they ever read movie reviews. Make a class list of their reasons for reading reviews (they want more information about an intriguing title, they are interested in a particular critic's opinion, etc.). This list will indicate the kinds of information and opinions students should include when they write their reviews.
3. Remind students that personal opinion is an important aspect of a movie review. Everyone who sees a movie will have a personal reaction to it, and this personal reaction will often be the focus of the review. However, students must defend their personal reactions with specific details from the film.

continued

Connected Assignment
Movie Review

Like a response to literature, a movie review starts with a response to a basic question—did you enjoy the work?—and then explains the reasons for the response. A movie review features

- reactions to and an evaluation of the movie.
- details from the movie used to support your opinions.
- descriptions of and facts about the movie.
- a recommendation to viewers.

▲ **Critical Viewing** Name a movie that you would recommend to these moviegoers. Explain your choice. **[Apply]**

Prewriting Choose a movie that impressed or disappointed you, and view it again. Record your opinion of the movie in a graphic organizer like the one shown on page 283. Then, use the organizer to collect details explaining your reaction. Include notes on the story, as well as on acting, pacing, music, use of camera techniques, and special effects.

MODEL

Review of
Just One Day Until Tomorrow

Has anyone told Dirk Broccoli lately that there's more to acting than turning up the smile? In most of his movies, poor Dirk seems stuck with two expressions: the wide winning grin and the even wider winning grin. At least in his latest movie, science-fiction thriller *Just One Day Until Tomorrow*, he has a scene in which he must actually—careful not to hurt yourself there, Dirk—*cry!* . . .

> The reviewer gets the attention of the reader with wisecracks about the star of the film.

. . . Amid all the howling bad dialogue and bogus special effects, Julie Druse still wins my heart with her fresh, quirky acting. Too bad she's only on screen for a total of fifteen minutes. . . . I have just one piece of advice to movie goers: If there's just one day until tomorrow, don't waste it seeing this film.

> Precise words such as howling, bogus, fresh, and quirky give color to the review.

> The review concludes with a recommendation.

Critical Viewing

Apply Students should recommend films that would appeal to a wide variety of people of their own age.

Drafting Before drafting, familiarize yourself with the style of movie reviews by reading a few in newspapers or magazines. (Avoid reviews of the movie you are reviewing.) Notice which aspects of a film they focus on, their language, and the support they offer for the opinions they express.

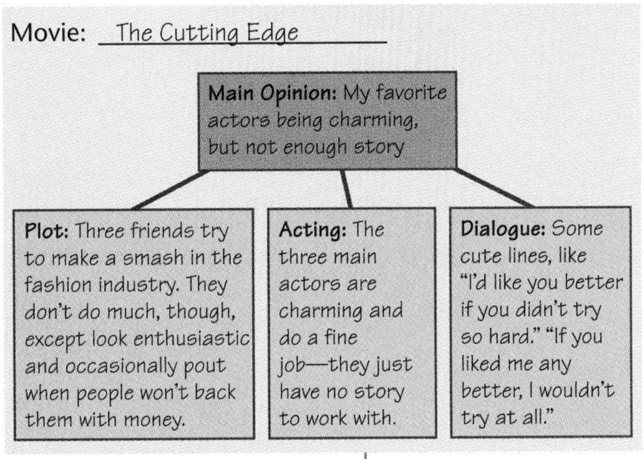

Movie: The Cutting Edge
Main Opinion: My favorite actors being charming, but not enough story
Plot: Three friends try to make a smash in the fashion industry. They don't do much, though, except look enthusiastic and occasionally pout when people won't back them with money.
Acting: The three main actors are charming and do a fine job—they just have no story to work with.
Dialogue: Some cute lines, like "I'd like you better if you didn't try so hard." "If you liked me any better, I wouldn't try at all."

Introduction Begin by writing an introduction that will grab your readers' attention and give them an idea of your opinion of the film. As you draft your introduction, keep in mind your audience: readers who probably have some knowledge of recent movies and current movie stars. In your introduction, you might include

- a funny or insightful observation or interesting fact.
- a sentence explaining your opinion of the film.

Body In the body of your review, familiarize readers with the basics of the movie—the type of movie it is (action, science fiction, romance, mystery, and so on), its plot, characters, setting, and cast. The body of your review should

- give a brief summary of the story.
- explain your reaction to the movie.
- provide examples illustrating your descriptions and evaluations of the movie.

Conclusion Your conclusion should end in a vein similar to that of your introduction—engaging and possibly humorous. It should give a recommendation about the movie to viewers.

Revising and Editing After you have finished your first draft, review it. Underline spots where a reader might need more information about the story or the characters to follow what you have written. Go back and add the necessary clarifications to these passages. Make sure that you have expressed reactions in vivid language. Replace vague words, such as *entertaining* or *bad*, with forceful ones, such as *action-packed* or *implausible*.

Publishing and Presenting After revising your movie review, submit it to a school or local newspaper. Then, compare your review with professionally written reviews of the same movie.

Step-by Step Teaching Guide continued

4. Have students clear their movie choices with you before they begin writing. Remind students reviewing adaptations of plays, novels, or stories that they should discuss whether the movie made important changes to its source, and whether these changes were successful.
5. Display the transparency to show students how they collect details to support their opinions of the movies they have chosen. Then give them copies of the blank organizer for them to use as they collect details.
6. Have students read the model review on page 282 and discuss it as a class. Go over the marginal notes and have students give their reactions to these aspects of the model. Ask questions like *What do you think of the tone of this review? Why? Which details support the recommendation in the final sentence?*
7. Remind students that critics often refer to previous films by particular writers, directors, and actors. These references may remind readers of where they have seen certain actors before. Readers may also be warned to avoid films made by writers or directors whose earlier films they saw and disliked.
8. Remind students to adopt a tone appropriate to the film being reviewed. A flippant tone like that in the model would be inappropriate for a serious, substantial film such as *The Bridge Over the River Kwai.* A serious tone would not be appropriate for a science-fiction parody such as *Galaxy Quest.*
9. Encourage each student to share his or her draft review with a person who has *not* seen the film it discusses. This reader should be able to point out unclear references to the story or themes of the film; a reader who had seen the film might not notice such problems because this reader can fill in blanks with his or her knowledge of the film.

Lesson Objectives

- To examine how media shape perceptions.

Step-by-Step Teaching Guide

Examining How Media Shape Perceptions

1. Choose a Spotlight element for class discussion, or have students work independently or in groups on the element of their choice. Give students the initiative to find the necessary books and recordings.
2. Give students some background on *Casablanca's* story and characters, and on the historical period in which it is set. Students may be interested to know that most of the film's minor characters, European refugees from the Nazis, were played by real European refugees, many of whom had been star performers in Germany, Austria, and Hungary before Hitler came to power. Many critics feel that this gave the film an edge and a realism it might have lacked otherwise.
3. Tell students that Max Steiner composed the score for *Casablanca.* Although Steiner did not want to use the song "As Time Goes By," he agreed to the producer's demands, and his featuring of this forgotten popular song earned it a lasting popularity. Ask students to name some songs they associate with movies, and to discuss the connection between music and drama. Have students try to imagine their favorite movie without its music. What would movies lose if they had no musical scores?
4. You may wish to show *Casablanca* in class, or have students view it as a homework assignment. After they have seen the film, have students discuss the theme of heroism. Is Rick the film's only hero? Which other characters do students find heroic? Why are they heroic? Students should also discuss the effect of the song "As Time Goes By" on the film.

Spotlight on the Humanities

Examining How Media Shape Perceptions

Focus on Film: *Casablanca*

▲ **Critical Viewing** What feelings and situations does this poster for *Casablanca* suggest? **[Interpret]**

One person may write a response to a work of literature. When an entire culture falls in love with a work, though, it writes a response on people's hearts and imaginations. Generations of moviegoers have been captivated by the film *Casablanca* since its release in 1943. Images and lines from the film, such as "Here's looking at you, kid," are familiar to millions.

Rick, played by Humphrey Bogart, is a secretly honorable man living in dishonorable times, a man who calls himself a realist but who cannot help acting on principle. Tough yet inwardly tender, Rick stands for an idea of manliness that still lives in the popular imagination. And Rick's self-sacrificing gesture at the end of the movie can still hit a viewer right in the heart.

Set during World War II and filled with romance, intrigue, and suspense, the film was named the second greatest film of all time by the American Film Institute. It won three Academy Awards for Best Adapted Screenplay, Best Director, and Best Film.

Music Connection The memorable theme song of the movie, "As Time Goes By," is also familiar to millions. Written by Herman Hupfeld for the film, the song is played in the movie by Sam, the piano player in Rick's Café Americain. Rick requests the song with the famous line "Play it, Sam" (often remembered as "Play it again, Sam"). The movie made this song, along with "It Had to Be You," famous, illustrating the way in which movies and music can work together to create memories shared by many.

Response to Literature Writing Activity: Collage of Cultural Ideals

Leaf through magazines featuring celebrity profiles. Choose several actors and actresses—older stars, such as Bogart, as well as contemporary celebrities—who have served as heroes to moviegoers. Assemble a collage of images of these actors. Then, write an essay commenting on your choices. What qualities does each represent? How do they compare with one another?

Viewing and Representing

Activity Have students do some reading about the actors they choose. You might limit them to four actors or actresses, to keep the research manageable. Remind students that some performers were heroes off-screen as well as on. Humphrey Bogart, for example, publicly protested the rampant McCarthyism of the postwar era.

Critical Viewing

Interpret Students should say that the poster suggests love and closeness between Bergman and Bogart's characters, because they are embracing. However, they look troubled and they are not looking at one another; this suggests that they are facing some kind of external crisis or conflict.

Media and Technology Skills

Interpreting Literature in a Variety of Media

Activity: Creating a Multimedia Interpretation

When you read a literary work to others, your tone of voice, the speed at which you read, and your pauses, all create an interpretation of the work. You can add to a presentation of a work by combining a variety of media with your reading.

Tips for Presenting Literature With Multimedia

- Practice your full presentation—reading while your images and sounds play—several times through.
- Pace your reading to allow your audience to take in changing images and sounds. Do not read so slowly, though, that the audience loses track of the connection between one line and the next.

Learn About It

List Equipment As you plan a multimedia presentation, list the equipment you will need—tape recorders, slide projectors, software, and so on. Then, familiarize yourself with the equipment. Consult manuals, and ask experienced users for help.

Use Audio Elements First, hone your reading of the work you have chosen. Read it aloud slowly and with expression several times. Then, add other audio effects to your reading, such as appropriate music and sound effects. To coordinate narration and other sound, work with a partner or use a tape recorder that allows overdubbing. You may tape your reading and your "soundtrack" on a single tape, or you may practice synchronizing your "soundtrack" with your live reading.

Use Visual Elements Enhance your reading with visual elements. You might display drawings, show slides, or play a videotape of significant scenes as you read. Prepare the necessary materials in advance, and practice your reading with them. Develop a way to synchronize changes in image with your reading.

Apply It Choose a work of literature to present. Use a storyboard organizer like this one to plan your presentation. Present your finished work to the class.

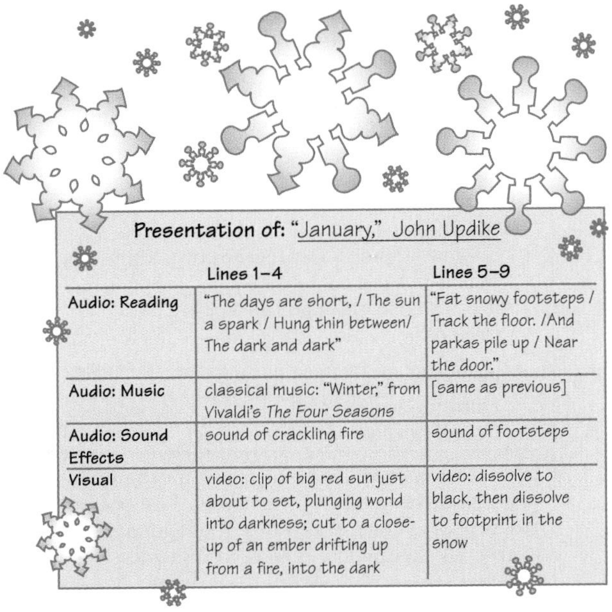

Presentation of: "January," John Updike

	Lines 1–4	Lines 5–9
Audio: Reading	"The days are short, / The sun a spark / Hung thin between/ The dark and dark"	"Fat snowy footsteps / Track the floor. /And parkas pile up / Near the door."
Audio: Music	classical music: "Winter," from Vivaldi's *The Four Seasons*	[same as previous]
Audio: Sound Effects	sound of crackling fire	sound of footsteps
Visual	video: clip of big red sun just about to set, plunging world into darkness; cut to a close-up of an ember drifting up from a fire, into the dark	video: dissolve to black, then dissolve to footprint in the snow

▶ Lesson Objectives

1. To interpret literary work.
2. To create a multimedia presentation of a literary work.

Step-by Step Teaching Guide

Interpreting Literature in a Variety of Media

Teaching Resources: Writing Support Transparency 12-J; Writing Support Activity Book, 12-5

1. Have students clear their literary choices with you before they begin working on their presentations. Have them give you the name of the work and the amount of time it takes to read it aloud. Limit them to five minutes. Allow students interested in dramatic readings from plays to work in pairs or small groups, one student per character.
2. Have students discuss the contribution that sound effects and music make to movies and plays. Thinking about the purpose of these sound effects will help students choose music and devise sound effects appropriate to their purposes.
3. Encourage students to rehearse their readings and to perform them for audiences before they present them in class. An audience preview can help students correct technical errors and identify weak spots.
4. Caution students against cluttering up their readings with too many effects. Some students may find that only visual and sound effects are appropriate for their readings; others may find that they want to use music, but no other sound effects. You may want to meet with individuals and groups in the planning stages, giving them any necessary guidance about shaping their presentations.
5. Use the transparency to demonstrate organizing a multimedia presentation. Pass out blank copies of the organizer so that students can complete the writing activity.

Lesson Objectives

1. To write a response to literature.
2. To use correct grammar, spelling, and mechanics.

Step-by-Step Teaching Guide

Responding to Literature-Based Prompts

Teaching Resources: Standardized Test Preparation Workbook, pp.23–24

1. Remind students that a question asking for a personal response to literature has no right or wrong answers. Students need not worry about trying to recall information. They need only read the literary work and articulate their reactions to it.
2. Point out that, like most writing prompts, this prompt gives clues that should help students organize their answers. It reminds students to support their responses with specific details from the poem as well as from their lives and other artistic media.
3. Point out that the first questions students should ask themselves after reading a literary-response prompt is *Did I like this poem/story/passage? Why or why not?* The answer to the second question will provide the supporting details the prompt requires.

Standardized Test Preparation Workshop

Responding to Literature-Based Prompts

Some standardized test questions evaluate the way you respond to literature. These questions measure your ability to respond to a writing prompt in an essay that

- responds directly to the prompt.
- is thoughtful and interesting.
- organizes ideas so that they are clear and easy to follow.
- develops ideas thoroughly, using appropriate details and precise language.
- stays focused on your purpose for writing, so each sentence contributes to your composition as a whole.
- uses correct spelling, capitalization, punctuation, grammar, and sentence structure to communicate effectively.

The writing process for a test can be divided into stages. Plan to use a specific amount of time for prewriting, drafting, revising, and proofreading. The clocks on the next page suggest the portion of your time to spend on each stage.

Use the suggestions on the following page to help you respond to the following sample prompt.

Test Tip

When writing a literary response for a test, place quotation marks around quotations—words, phrases, and sentences you take directly from the text.

Sample Writing Situation

Read the following poem. Then, respond to the prompt below.

If I can stop one Heart from breaking
Emily Dickinson.

If I can stop one Heart from breaking
I shall not live in vain
If I can ease one Life the Aching
Or cool one Pain

Or help one fainting Robin
Unto his Nest again
I shall not live in Vain.

In an essay, explain how you think the poet's message applies to the lives of you and your friends. Use specific details from the poem to support your interpretation of the message. Use examples from personal experience, books, and movies to support your response.

TEST-TAKING TIP

Remind students to punctuate titles correctly. When they write a response to a literary work, they will probably want to refer to it by title. Give students the following titles and have them punctuate them correctly.

- Three Blind Mice (song) ("Three Blind Mice")
- The Cask of Amontillado (short story) ("The Cask of Amontillado")
- The Grapes of Wrath (novel) (*The Grapes of Wrath*)
- The Raven (poem) ("The Raven")

Prewriting

Allow close to one fourth of your time for prewriting.

Use a Hexagon To gather details for your response to literature, use the hexagonal writing strategy. (Follow the model on page 268.) Then, review the prompt. Circle details in your hexagon that match what is requested in the prompt.

Analyze the Prompt The prompt instructs you to support your interpretation of the poet's message with specific details from the poem. Therefore, you should include direct quotations and paraphrases to illustrate the message. Then, use the types of examples identified in the prompt to show how the message applies to the lives of contemporary students.

Drafting

Allow almost half of your time for drafting.

Develop a Focus Statement Referring to the prompt, write a focus statement that states what you will discuss in your essay. Include this statement in your introduction.

Make an Outline Referring to the details you gathered in your hexagon, make an outline for your essay. Group related ideas and supporting details under main headings. Your essay should fall into two main parts: an explanation of the message and an application of that message to the lives of you and your friends. Under each main heading, jot down the specific examples you will use to support your ideas.

Conclude With an Insight End your essay with a memorable quotation or image. Tie an image from the poem to an image from one of your contemporary examples.

Revising, Editing, and Proofreading

Allow a little more than one quarter of your time for revising, editing, and proofreading.

Focus on Details Review your response for details that do not relate directly to the prompt, and remove them. Look for places where interesting details could be expanded upon, and elaborate on them. Eliminate slang or clichés and, instead, use formal, precise language.

Clean It Up Check for errors in spelling, grammar, and punctuation. When making changes, place a line through text that you are eliminating. Use a caret (^) to indicate where you are adding words.

Customize for *More Advanced Students*

Encourage students to keep reading journals. Every time they read a literary work, either as an assignment or for pleasure, students should write their responses to it in a special notebook kept for this purpose. Responses should include author and title, whether the student liked the work, and why or why not. Students can write long responses or brief ones. Challenge them to keep their responses focused and to support all their opinions with specific details from the texts. Keeping a reading journal will help students hone and sharpen their writing skills and will force them to read more critically and thoughtfully.

Chapter 13 Time and Resource Manager

In-Depth Lesson Plan

	LESSON FOCUS	PRINT AND MEDIA RESOURCES
DAY 1	**Introduction to Writing for Assessment** Students learn key elements of writing for assessment (pp. 288–289).	***Writers at Work* Videotape** ***Writing and Grammar iText* (Interactive Text)**, Ch.13, Introduction
DAY 2	**Prewriting** Students choose and narrow a topic, consider their audience and purpose, and gather information (pp. 290–291).	**Teaching Resources** *Writing Support Transparencies*, 13-A; ***Writing and Grammar iText* (Interactive Text)**, Section 13.1
DAY 3	**Drafting** Students organize their ideas and write their first drafts (pp. 292–293).	**Teaching Resources** *Writing Support Transparencies*, 13-B–C; *Writing Support Activity Book*, 13-1 ***Writing and Grammar iText* (Interactive Text)**, Section 13.2
DAY 4	**Revising** Students revise their drafts in terms of overall structure, paragraphs, sentences, and word choice (pp. 294–295).	***Writing and Grammar iText* (Interactive Text)**, Section 13.3
DAY 5	**Editing and Proofreading; Publishing and Presenting** Students check their work for accuracy and correctness and present their final drafts (pp. 296–297).	**Teaching Resources** *Scoring Rubrics on Transparency*, Ch. 13; *Formal Assessment*, Ch. 13 ***Writing and Grammar iText* (Interactive Text)**, Sections 13.4–5

Accelerated Lesson Plan

	LESSON FOCUS	PRINT AND MEDIA RESOURCES
DAY 1	**Introduction Through Drafting** Students review the characteristics of writing for assessment, select topics, and write drafts (pp. 288–293).	**Teaching Resources** *Writing Support Transparencies*, 13-A–C; *Writing Support Activity Book*, 13-1 ***Writing and Grammar iText* (Interactive Text)**, Ch. 13, Introduction through Section 13.2
DAY 2	**Revising Through Presenting** Students work individually or with peers to revise, edit, and proofread their work for presentation (pp. 294–297).	**Teaching Resources** *Scoring Rubrics on Transparency*, Ch. 13; *Formal Assessment*, Ch. 13 ***Writing and Grammar iText* (Interactive Text)**, Sections 13.3–5

Options for Adapting Lesson Plans

HOMEWORK

Have students complete any stage of the lesson for homework.

SPELLING

To teach spelling skills in conjunction with writing skills, work through *Prentice Hall Everyday Spelling*, Grade 8, Chapter 15, as you cover this *Writing and Grammar* chapter. At the Editing and Proofreading stage, remind students to apply the spelling skills to their essays for assessment.

FEATURES

Extend coverage with Connected Assignment (p. 300), Spotlight on the Humanities (p. 302), Media and Technology Skills (p. 303), and Standardized Test Preparation Workshop (p. 304).

TECHNOLOGY

Students can complete any stage of the lesson on the computer, using *Writing and Grammar iText* or a word-processing program. Have them print out their completed work.

INTEGRATED SKILLS COVERAGE

Integrating Grammar
Avoiding Comma Splices, SE p. 296

Viewing and Representing
Critical Viewing, SE pp. 288, 289, 295, 298, 300, 302

Speaking and Listening
Reading Aloud, ATE p. 299

Real-World Connection
ATE p. 291

Workplace Skills
Direct Mail, ATE p. 292

BLOCK SCHEDULING

Pacing Suggestions
For 90-minute Blocks
- Have students complete the Prewriting and Drafting stages in a single period.
- Focus one class period on Revising and Editing and Publishing and Presenting. Allow at least 30 minutes for peer revision.

Professional Development Support
- ***How to Manage Instruction in the Block*** This teaching resource provides management and activity suggestions.

ASSESSMENT SUPPORT

Standardized Test Preparation Workshop SE pp. 304–305; ATE p. 293

Standardized Test Preparation Workbook, pp. 25–26

Scoring Rubrics on Transparency, Ch. 13

Formal Assessment, Ch. 13

Writing Assessment and Portfolio Management

MEDIA AND TECHNOLOGY

For the Student
- ***Writing and Grammar iText*** **(Interactive Text),** Ch. 13

For the Teacher
- ***Resource Pro*** **CD-ROM**

MEETING INDIVIDUAL NEEDS

Less Advanced Students See Ongoing Assessment ATE p. 296.

ESL Students ATE pp. 290, 299, 301

More Advanced Students ATE pp. 301, 303

Gifted/Talented Students ATE p. 299

Verbal/Linguistic Learners ATE p. 290

WRITING AND GRAMMAR ON-LINE

*i*Text Interactive Text (On-line or on CD-ROM)
- Easily navigable instruction with interactive Revision Checkers
- Full use of e-rater™, the essay-scoring system (on-line only)

Companion Web Site PHSchool.com
- Scoring rubrics with models (use Web Code eck-8001)

See the Go On-line! feature, SE p. iii.

CHAPTER 13
WRITING FOR ASSESSMENT

Lesson Objectives

1. To recognize the characteristics of effectively written responses to assessment.
2. To recognize various types of writing for assessment, including essay tests, short-answer tests, and personal essays.
3. To learn the topic-generating strategies of scanning topic choices, examining the format of the questions, and mentally gathering details.
4. To organize details in Nestorian order and chronological order.
5. To give details through definitions, explanations, elaboration, and illustrations.
6. To check the introduction against the writing prompt.
7. To analyze the conclusion for effectiveness.
8. To circle topic sentences and check for unity.
9. To eliminate fragments and run-ons.
10. To revise to include more vivid word "pictures."
11. To identify and avoid comma splices.

Critical Viewing

Compare and Contrast Students may say that the room they usually study in is similar or different, and so on.

Chapter 13 Writing for Assessment

Girl Writing, 1908, Pierre Bonnard, Barnes Foundation, Merion, Pennsylvania

▲ Critical Viewing This girl might be studying for a test. Compare her study habits with your own. **[Compare and Contrast]**

Assessment in Everyday Life

You make assessments every day. They range from the informal—"That's a great jacket!" or "Learning to inline skate was fun but grueling."—to the formal, such as writing an evaluation of a poem for your English class.

In school, some testing situations are called "writing for assessment." To do well on these tests, you must call on all the writing techniques you've learned in the past. You also must learn some special tips and practice certain skills that will help you succeed in testing situations. This chapter will prepare you for writing for assessment.

TIME AND RESOURCE MANAGER

Resources
Technology: Writing and Grammar iText, Ch. 13

In-Depth Coverage	Accelerated Pace
• Go over pp. 288–289 in class. • Invite students to share their responses to the Critical Viewing prompt. • Ask students to give examples of titles for the different types of writing discussed on p. 289.	• Have students review the information on pp. 288–289 independently.

What Is Writing for Assessment?

When you give a written answer on a test to present your ideas or show what you have learned, you are producing **writing for assessment.** Although the length of your written response may vary from test to test or from question to question, most successful writing for assessment contains

- responses that match the question or questions asked.
- main points that are supported by various types of details.
- a clear and logical organization of details.
- correct grammar, spelling, and punctuation.

To learn the criteria on which your essay may be evaluated, see the Rubric for Self-Assessment on page 297.

Types of Writing for Assessment

A writing prompt on a test may call for a full-length essay or for a short response of ten to fifteen lines. Prompts may call for writing of the following kinds:

- **Persuasive writing** requires you to support an opinion on an issue, using persuasive language.
- **Expository writing** requires you to give information in a clear and well-organized fashion. It includes:
  - **Comparison-and-contrast writing,** requiring you to compare in an organized form the similarities and differences between two subjects.
  - **Cause-and-effect writing,** requiring you to explain a process or series of events.

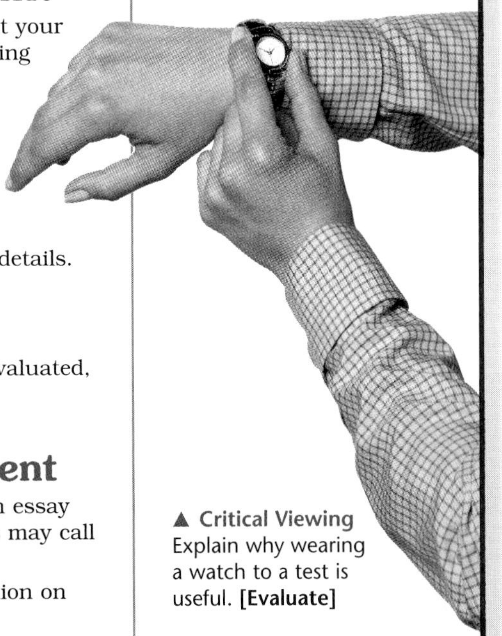

▲ Critical Viewing Explain why wearing a watch to a test is useful. **[Evaluate]**

PREVIEW Student Work IN PROGRESS

In this chapter, you'll follow the work of Paul Keller, a student at Roosevelt Middle School in Oceanside, California, as he responds to a writing prompt on an essay test. You will see how Paul used featured strategies to prewrite and draft his essay. A completed version of Paul's essay appears at the end of this chapter.

PREPARE and ENGAGE

Interest GRABBER Invite students to complete the following sentences.

I really like . . .

I can't stand . . .

It's fun to . . .

If I had a choice, I would . . .

Point out that students have just made assessments. In this case, the assessments, or evaluations, were based on their personal experiences.

Activate Prior Knowledge

Ask students to share the most difficult essay- or short-answer-test question they ever had to respond to. Discuss what made these questions especially difficult. (The questions might have called for facts that had to be remembered, or the students may not have been sure what to include in their answers, and so on.) Explain that this chapter will teach students strategies that will help them respond more effectively to writing assessments.

Critical Viewing

Evaluate Students may say that being aware of the time helps them gauge how long they should spend on various parts of a test.

ONGOING ASSESSMENT: Diagnose

Use one of the following options to diagnose students' current level of proficiency in writing for assessment.

Option 1 Ask each student to select the strongest example of his or her writing assessment from last year. Review the samples to determine which students will need extra support in writing for assessment.

Option 2 Ask students to write a paragraph about tests. Have them list three reasons or items of evidence describing why they do or do not like them. Students who have difficulty completing this exercise might need extra support in learning how to write for assessment.

Step-by-Step Teaching Guide

Prewriting: Choosing Your Topic

1. After you review the material under Choosing Your Topic, have students read the three choices in the Topic Bank and choose one to write about.
2. Have volunteers state the topic they have chosen and the related details they plan to include in their writing.
3. If students are having difficulty choosing a topic, assign one to them.

Customize for *ESL Students*

Read aloud the topic list on the board and the Topic Bank questions as you go through the Step-by-Step Teaching Guide above.

Customize for *Verbal/Linguistic Learners*

Ask students to share aloud the five details they thought of in response to the topic list you wrote on the chalkboard.

13.1 Prewriting

Choosing Your Topic

Finding a topic is not a problem when you're writing for assessment. Someone else, a teacher, has already chosen the topic for you. In some cases, though, you may choose your topic from among two or three different options.

If you do have a choice, carefully consider the topic alternatives, the types of writing required, and the target audiences. Use the following strategies to help you decide on a topic:

Strategies for Choosing an Assessment Topic

- **Scan all the topic choices.** Eliminate questions for which your knowledge is limited or incomplete. Then, from the remaining choices, choose the topic you find most interesting.
- **Examine the purpose and the type of writing specified.** A prompt will always specify a purpose for and type of writing. It may ask you, for instance, to identify, examine, analyze, or evaluate a certain topic. Make sure you are comfortable with the purpose for writing specified for the question you choose.
- **Examine the format required.** Sometimes, a question tells what form the answer should take. For example, a question may ask you to write a letter. Consider the format with which you are most comfortable as you decide which question to answer.
- **Mentally gather details.** Choose to answer the question for which you can immediately think of at least five related facts, arguments, or other details.

TOPIC BANK

Following are some sample essay-test questions. If you plan to practice writing for assessment, choose one of these, or ask your teacher to provide you with one.

1. **Effects of a Historical Event** In an essay, examine how the Great Depression affected the day-to-day life of most Americans.
2. **Comparison of Presidents** Evaluate the presidencies of Abraham Lincoln and John F. Kennedy. Then, support your ideas in an essay about who was the "greater" president.
3. **Analysis of Insect Societies** Choose a social insect, and analyze the workings of its society, including the different roles of the insects, their means of obtaining food, the care they give their young, and the type of home they use.

TIME AND RESOURCE MANAGER

Resources
Print: Writing Support Transparencies, 13-A
Technology: Writing and Grammar iText, Section 13.1

In-Depth Coverage	Accelerated Pace
• Cover pp. 290–291 in class. • Guide students through the strategies for choosing topics. • Guide students through the strategy for narrowing a topic.	• Have students read through pp. 290–291 independently.

Narrowing Your Topic

Before you start writing, narrow your topic by clarifying what the question is asking, what the main point of your response will be, and which details will help you make your case. Use the following strategy to help you narrow your topic:

Analyze the Prompt

1. **Identify the question.** Copy the essay question. Underline the specific subject it concerns and what it asks you to do—for instance, *explain.*
2. **Circle the format.** Circle the format the response is to take, if it is specified in the question.
3. **Box the audience.** If an audience is specified, draw a box around the phrase that identifies it. Decide what effect the audience should have on your choice of details and words.
4. **Write a thesis statement.** Below the essay question, jot down your thesis statement—the main point you plan to make in your response.

Student Work IN PROGRESS

Name: *Paul Keller*
Roosevelt Middle School
Oceanside, CA

Narrowing a Topic

Paul copied down the essay question he was to answer. Then, he made the following notations to be sure that his topic was narrow and focused.

Assignment: Assume the role of a colonist living in America in 1776. Write a letter to King George explaining what problems you are experiencing. Use detailed, historical examples to support your point of view. Propose at least one solution to these problems, and convince King George that your solutions are viable.

Thesis: Colonists want to settle western lands. If they do, they will help England.

I need to follow letter format.

I need to write in a respectful tone, since I'm writing to a king.

I need to explain a problem and propose a solution in a persuasive way.

Step-by-Step Teaching Guide

Prewriting: Analyze the Prompt

Teaching Resources: Writing Support Transparency 13-A

1. Lead students through the four steps for narrowing a topic. Display the transparency and discuss notations Paul made to help him narrow his topic.
2. After students copy down the essay question they have chosen to answer, have them use the strategy on this page to narrow the topic.

Real-World Connection

On timed tests, students may not have time to copy the entire question. In these cases, they can simply write:

- what the question is asking them to answer
- the format their response should take
- the audience, if specified
- their thesis statement

TIME SAVERS!

Writing Support Transparencies
Use the transparencies for Chapter 13 to teach these strategies.

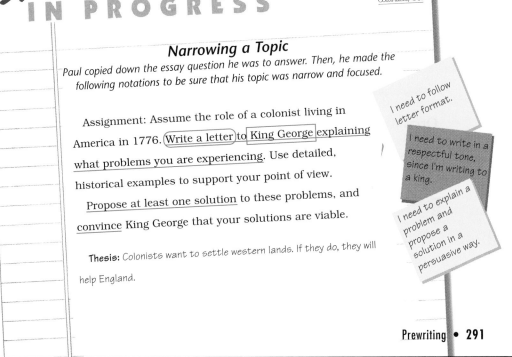

Step-by-Step Teaching Guide

Drafting: Organize Details

Teaching Resources: Writing Support Transparency 13-B, Writing Support Activity Book 13-1

1. Lead students in a discussion of Nestorian and chronological order. Ask volunteers which organization best applies to their topic.
2. Display the transparency for chronological order. Give students copies of the blank organizer. You may want to help students who choose this organization fill in their timelines.
3. Have students organize their outlines.

Integrating Workplace Skills

Direct-mail solicitations often use the P.S. to communicate their best offer. Ask students why the P.S. is an effective location for a convincing argument. (The P.S. stands out; it is short and easy to read; it is personal.) Have students compare this advertising strategy with Nestorian order.

13.2 Drafting

Shaping Your Writing

One of your most important goals in writing for assessment is to organize your ideas in a clear, logical way. Your final score on a writing test depends to a large degree on how well you have organized your writing. Keep in mind, though, that your time is limited, so choose a clear, simple organization.

Organize Details in Order of Importance

When you want to persuade someone or to emphasize certain key points, organize your ideas according to **Nestorian order.** When you choose this method of organization:

- Label or number your main ideas, from most important to least important.
- Then, create an outline. Save your most important point for the end, so you can conclude with a "bang." Lead off the body of your essay with your second-most important point. Then, present your remaining points, except your most important one, in decreasing order of importance. End with your most convincing point.

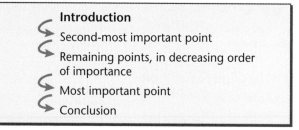

Introduction
→ Second-most important point
→ Remaining points, in decreasing order of importance
→ Most important point
→ Conclusion

Organize Details in Chronological Order

If you are writing a summary, an explanation, or a narrative, you'll probably organize your details in **chronological order** (the order in which events happen). Make a timeline like the one below to help you organize your ideas.

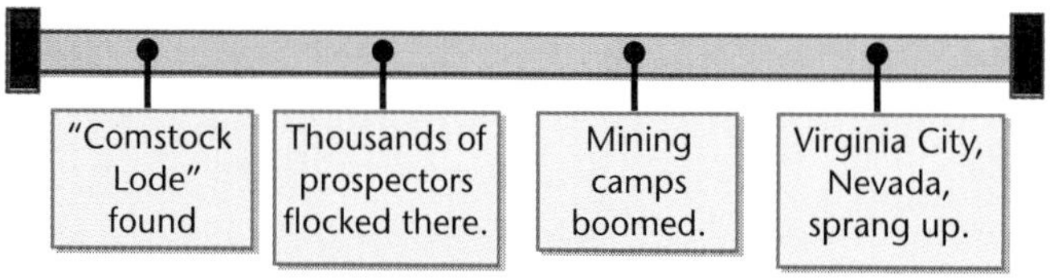
"Comstock Lode" found
Thousands of prospectors flocked there.
Mining camps boomed.
Virginia City, Nevada, sprang up.

iText

Try it out! Use the interactive Timeline in **Section 13.2,** on-line or on CD-ROM.

TIME SAVERS!

Writing Support Transparencies
Use the transparencies for Chapter 13 to teach these strategies.

Writing Support Activity Book
Use the graphic organizers for Chapter 13 to facilitate these strategies.

TIME AND RESOURCE MANAGER

Resources
Print: Writing Support Transparencies, 13-B–C; Writing Support Activity Book, 13-1
Technology: Writing and Grammar iText, Section 13.2

In-Depth Coverage	Accelerated Pace
• Go over pp. 292–293 in class. • Discuss Nestorian and chronological order and elaboration. • Help students shape their writing by organizing details and providing elaboration.	• Have students review the information on pp. 292–293 independently. • Ask students to submit their drafts for peer editing or for your review.

Providing Elaboration

Give Details

Once you've organized your ideas, look in your notes for places where you can add explanation or support. Next to each main idea on your outline, add details you can use to support the idea. As you draft, draw on your notes. Follow these guidelines for incorporating details in your writing:

- **Define.** Provide definitions to show that you fully understand your subject.
- **Explain.** Give reasons for your statements. Reasons may be scientific or historical, or they may be drawn from personal experience.
- **Support.** Cite statistics, expert testimony, and examples from your life to make your arguments convincing.
- **Illustrate.** Give examples from history, science, your own experience, or everyday life to illustrate your points.

Student Work IN PROGRESS

Name: Paul Keller
Roosevelt Middle School
Oceanside, CA

Giving Details

As he drafted, Paul included several types of details to make his writing effective and convincing.

Sire, my name is Lieutenant Colonel Paul Keller of the 23rd Infantry Brigade, Boston, Massachusetts. I feel very honored and privileged to wake up and salute the British flag. But, Your Majesty, I write to you to protest a grave injustice. For did I not fight against the French and did we not win? As part of their surrender, they had to give the land west of the Appalachians to England. Now, as I write, British troops stand constant vigil over the land for which so many of us died. I plead with you, let us settle the land west of the Appalachians, for the greater glory of England!

As required by the prompt, Paul assumes the identity of a colonist.

Paul explains the exact historical situation he is addressing.

In ringing tones, he presents a summary of the support he will provide for his argument.

Step-by-Step Teaching Guide

Drafting: Give Details

Teaching Resource: Writing Support Transparency 13-C

1. Review the guidelines for adding details that support the main idea.
2. Display the transparency. Discuss the methods Paul used to add details to his writing.
3. You may want to have students who have chosen the same topic to work in pairs or small groups to discuss possible details they can add to their drafts.

STANDARDIZED TEST PREPARATION WORKSHOP

Chronological Order Standardized tests may require students to place events in chronological order. Ask students to choose the correct order for the following events.

A A light is hung in Old North Church.
B The Revolutionary War begins.
C Paul Revere rides to Lexington.

1. A, B, C
2. A, C, B
3. C, B, A
4. C, A, B

Choice 2 is the correct order.

Step-by-Step Teaching Guide

Revising: Checking Your Introduction and Conclusion

1. Read through the bulleted points. Explain that the initial activity of identifying the test question (see page 291, "Narrowing Your Topic") helps students check their introduction and conclusion to make sure they provide the required responses.
2. Ask students why they think the conclusion should leave the reader with a final thought, summary, or call to action.
3. Have partners discuss their introductions and conclusions.

Step-by-Step Teaching Guide

Revising: Checking for Unity

1. Choose a student example from the Step-by-Step Guide above and display it on an overhead projector.
2. Have a student circle each main idea sentence. Point out any paragraphs that are missing topic sentences.
3. Ask a student to analyze the details in one of the paragraphs, crossing out any sentences that do not support the main idea or topic sentence.

13.3 Revising

When writing for assessment, always make time, even if it is only a few minutes, to revise your work.

Revising Your Overall Structure

One way to show evaluators that your writing is well-organized is to include a strong introduction and conclusion.

REVISION STRATEGY

Checking Your Introduction and Conclusion

Reread the writing prompt to make sure that you have interpreted it correctly. Then, read your introduction. Ask yourself the following questions as you revise:

- Does my introduction accurately reflect the instructions in the writing prompt?
- Does it clearly state what I will explain, argue, summarize, or narrate in the rest of my paragraphs?

Now, read your conclusion, and ask yourself the following questions as you revise:

- Does my conclusion accurately restate what I have explained, summarized, narrated, or argued in the essay?
- Does it leave the reader with a final thought on the subject or with a call to action?

Revising Your Paragraphs

Paragraphs are the basic blocks from which a good essay is built. Check to be sure that they are effective and unified.

REVISION STRATEGY

Checking for Unity

Identify the main idea in each paragraph. Then, study the details the paragraph includes. Does each sentence support, illustrate, or add to the paragraph's topic or main idea? If not, neatly cross out the sentence. If necessary, replace the crossed-out sentence with one that effectively supports the main idea.

TIME AND RESOURCE MANAGER

Resources
Technology: Writing and Grammar iText, Section 13.3

In-Depth Coverage	Accelerated Pace
• Go over pp. 294–295 in class. • Discuss the revision process and discuss the idea that an essay must be organized and unified. • Encourage students to revise their essays to eliminate run-ons and to replace flat words with vivid and precise words.	• Have students read the information on pp. 294–295 independently. • Have students work independently to revise their essays.

Revising Your Sentences

Teachers will evaluate your writing for assessment to see how well your sentences are constructed.

REVISION STRATEGY
Eliminating Fragments and Run-Ons

Read through your sentences, and check to be sure that each expresses a complete thought. If not, you have a fragment that should be rewritten to make it a full sentence. Next, reread to find sentences that have more than one subject. Check each of them to be sure that the sentence is correctly punctuated and is not a run-on sentence.

Revising Your Word Choice

Choose Precise and Vivid Words

A good writer works hard to select words that convey ideas vividly and precisely. To get a good score on a writing test, make sure that you choose words that say exactly what you mean. If you are describing a person, place, or thing, use words that will help readers picture the subject in their minds. If you are writing to persuade, use words with strong emotional associations that will help convince your readers.

REVISION STRATEGY
Replacing Flat Word Choices

As you revise your writing for assessment, look for places to improve your word choices. In a descriptive passage, look for places where you can substitute a more vivid word or phrase. In a persuasive passage, look for places where you can substitute a word that conveys a strong favorable or unfavorable impression. The sentences below illustrate how much more effective a sentence that uses precise, vivid words is than one that does not.

FLAT: I pulled in the fish, and it landed in our boat.

VIVID: I reeled in a huge, rainbow trout, and it slapped into the bottom of our little rowboat.

▼ **Critical Viewing**
Write a sentence using precise, vivid words to describe how this boy feels. **[Apply]**

Step-by-Step Teaching Guide

Revising: Eliminating Fragments and Run-ons; Choosing Precise and Vivid Words

1. Review the revising strategy of eliminating fragments and run-ons. Give examples of sentence fragments ("the girl with the basketball") and run-ons (She shot a basket the crowd roared"). Ask students to correct each example.
2. Review the strategy of revising word choice. Remind students that the dictionary and the thesaurus are good places to look for alternative word choices.

Language Highlight

The word *vivid* came from the Latin word *vividus,* meaning "full of life," "lively." Today, the meanings of *vivid* include "realistic," "lifelike," "true to life," "striking," and "dramatic." When choosing vivid words in their writing, students should think in pictures, then use words to depict what they see.

Critical Viewing

Apply Students may say that the boy feels proud, triumphant, jubilant.

Step-by-Step Teaching Guide

Editing and Proofreading: Punctuation

1. You may want to encourage students to pair off and proofread each other's essays. Remind them that it's easier to see typographical and other kinds of proofreading errors in someone else's writing than in one's own.
2. Have students lightly mark corrections in their partners' essays. They should then discuss changes with their partners.

Step-by-Step Teaching Guide

Grammar in Your Writing: Avoiding Comma Splices

1. Point out that the clauses joined by a comma in the examples are independent clauses—that is, they can stand on their own as sentences.
2. Ask students to name other conjunctions that can be used to join independent clauses. (*but, so, yet, or, for, nor*)

PRENTICE HALL
Everyday Spelling

If you have taught the spelling skills in *Prentice Hall Everyday Spelling,* Grade 8, Chapter 15, in conjunction with this *Writing and Grammar* chapter, review and assess students' mastery of the skills before concluding the chapter. Remind students to apply the spelling skills as they edit and proofread their essays for assessment.

13.4 Editing and Proofreading

Before turning in your writing for assessment, check it carefully to be sure that you have eliminated all errors in grammar, spelling, and punctuation.

Focusing on Punctuation

Check the punctuation of sentences within your essay to be sure that your punctuation of compound sentences is correct.

Grammar in Your Writing
Avoiding Comma Splices

One of the most common sentence errors students make involves joining two clauses with just a comma. This error is called a **comma splice.** Look for comma splices in your writing, and use the following techniques to correct them.

INCORRECT

Comma Splice:	Responsible teenagers deserve to have the right to drive, we ask you to help us keep this right.

CORRECT

Comma With Conjunction:	Responsible teenagers deserve to have the right to drive, and we ask you to help us keep this right.
Semicolon:	Responsible teenagers deserve to have the right to drive; we ask you to help us keep this right.
Two Sentences:	Responsible teenagers deserve to have the right to drive. We ask you to help us keep this right.

To learn more about avoiding comma splices, see Chapter 21.

ONGOING ASSESSMENT: Prerequisite Skills

If students have difficulty identifying comma splices, refer them to the following to ensure coverage of prerequisite skills.

In the Textbook	Print	Technology
Effective Sentences, pp. 476–497	Grammar Exercise Workbook, pp. 111–112	Writing and Grammar iText, Section 21.4 On-Line Exercise Bank, Section 21.4

13.5 Publishing and Presenting

Building Your Portfolio

Consider these possibilities for sharing your work:

1. **Group Discussion** Share your thoughts about the test—the choices offered, the difficulties encountered—in a group. Then, exchange drafts, and comment on the choices others made in responding on the test.
2. **Create a Review Folder** Create a folder for old tests, and place a copy of your writing for assessment in it. When studying for future tests, leaf through your review folder for reminders about strategies that did or did not work for you.

Reflecting on Your Writing

Take a few moments to think about writing for assessment. Then, answer the following questions, and save your responses in your portfolio.

- Were you satisfied with your choice of a question to answer? Why or why not?
- Which stage of the writing process did you find most useful as you wrote for assessment? Why?

Internet Tip

To see essays scored with this rubric, go on-line: PHSchool.com
Enter Web Code: eck-8001

Rubric for Self-Assessment

Evaluate your writing for assessment essay using these criteria:

	Score 4	Score 3	Score 2	Score 1
Audience and Purpose	Uses word choices and supporting details appropriate to the specified audience; clearly addresses writing prompt	Mostly uses word choices and supporting details appropriate to the specified audience; adequately addresses prompt	Uses some inappropriate word choices and details; addresses writing prompt	Uses inappropriate word choices and details; does not address writing prompt
Organization	Presents a clear, consistent organizational strategy	Presents a clear organizational strategy with few inconsistencies	Presents an inconsistent organizational strategy	Shows a lack of organizational strategy
Elaboration	Adequately supports the thesis; elaborates on each idea; links all details to the thesis	Supports the thesis; elaborates on most ideas; links most information to the thesis	Partially supports the thesis; does not elaborate on some ideas	Provides no thesis; does not elaborate on ideas
Use of Language	Uses excellent sentence variety and vocabulary; includes very few mechanical errors	Uses adequate sentence variety and vocabulary; includes few mechanical errors	Uses repetitive sentence structure and vocabulary; includes some mechanical errors	Demonstrates poor use of language; includes many mechanical errors

ONGOING ASSESSMENT: Assess Mastery

Use one of the following options to assess students' final drafts.

Self-Assessment Ask students to score their essays using the rubric provided.

Teacher Assessment Use the rubric and scoring models provided in Writing Assessment, Writing for Assessment, to score students' work.

Step-by-Step Teaching Guide

Publishing and Presenting

1. Ask volunteers to read their essays to the class. After reading, they should point out why they think their essays successfully fulfill the assignment.
2. Encourage students to work in pairs or small groups to discuss each other's essays, pointing out good aspects of the essays and working on areas that need improvement.

ASSESS

Step-by-Step Teaching Guide

Assessment

Teaching Resources: Scoring Rubrics on Transparency, 13; Formal Assessment, Chapter 13

1. Display the Scoring Rubric transparency and review the criteria in class.
2. Before students proceed with self-assessment, you may wish to review the Final Draft of the Student Work in Progress on pages 298–299. Have students score the Final Draft in one or more of the rubric categories. For example, how would students score the essay in terms of organization?
3. In addition to student self-assessment, you may wish to use the following assessment options.
   - Score student essays yourself, using the rubric and scoring models from Writing Assessment.
   - Review the Standardized Test Preparation Workshop on pages 304–305 and have students complete the proofreading practice items.
   - Administer the Chapter Test from Formal Assessment in Teaching Resources to assess students' grasp of concepts presented.

CLOSE

Step-by-Step Teaching Guide

Teaching From the Final Draft

1. Read aloud the first paragraph of "A Letter to His Majesty, King George III."
2. Ask students to identify words and phrases that show how Paul "painted a word picture" of the setting in which the letter was written ("to wake up and salute the British flag," "Now as I write," and so on)

continued

Critical Viewing

Distinguish Students may say that King George's clothing, hair style, and surroundings distinguished him from the colonist.

13.5 Student Work IN PROGRESS

FINAL DRAFT

King George III of England, c. 1767, Allan Ramsay, Scottish
National Portrait Gallery

▲▶ **Critical Viewing** What details in this image distinguish King George III from the American colonist on the next page? **[Distinguish]**

Assignment:

Assume the role of a colonist living in America in 1776. Write a letter to King George explaining what problems you are experiencing. Use detailed, historical examples to support your point of view.

Propose at least one solution to these problems, and convince King George that your solutions are viable.

A Letter to His Majesty, King George III

Paul Keller
Roosevelt Middle School
Oceanside, California

Sire, my name is Lieutenant Colonel Paul Keller of the 23rd Infantry Brigade, Boston, Massachusetts. I feel very honored and privileged to wake up and salute the British flag. But, Your Majesty, I write to you to protest a grave injustice. For did I not fight against the French and did we not win? As part of their surrender, they had to give the land west of the Appalachians to England. Now, as I write, British troops stand constant vigil over the land for which so many of us died. I plead with you, let us settle the land west of the Appalachians, for the greater glory of England!

Paul's introduction addresses the audience specified in the assignment: King George III of England. He uses formal, respectful language suited to this audience.

Your Majesty, when I proudly fought for you against the French, many of my comrades fell, and I thought it was not in vain. But the land they died for I cannot go to, and it angers me.

Here, Paul presents one of his strongest reasons for opening the West to colonists—they fought on behalf of the King to keep it.

After the war, I received news that my children and wife died in a fire. I decided to go to the new land and build a new family, but this idea was cut short by the Proclamation you made. I see my troops talk about treason every day and it sickens me. Sire, the taxes and punishments you have put on us have been unfair. Many people wish for war. If you take no action, it will come. But, if you give something back to us, I am sure they will give to you.

I know that the British troops are there for our protection, but I, like many of us, am well skilled with muskets. My plan is that your troops could train and outfit a group with muskets. These men would leave soon after completing their training. Their destination would be about five hundred kilometers west of the Appalachians. These men would establish a fort and start building homes and a town. These houses would be fortified for better protection. Then, we would repeat this process, sending soldiers about fifteen kilometers away from the original fort.

Paul outlines his plan in detail, organizing its parts in consistent chronological order.

The next stage would be moving colonists back and forth throughout the dangerous plains and woods. While in the war, I noticed the tactics of the Indians native to this land. They wore leaves and painted their bodies like their surroundings, then shot with pinpoint accuracy. If we dressed up in the same manner as they do, we could hide in the woods and ambush the enemy. With some luck, we could have a thriving colony in a few years. The furs alone could provide the treasury with towers upon towers of money.

The phrase the next stage *makes a transition from one paragraph to the next.*

The land west of the Appalachians is a mine of riches, waiting to be discovered. I would like to remind you that one time the Atlantic Ocean was thought of as impassable; now in this modern age we cross it freely. The west could prove a formidable defense against Spain. Last, I fear that if we do not find some way to relieve the constant pressure on the colonies, war will break out.

Paul supports his plan with predictions of its effects.

As always, Your Majesty, I wish you good health and hope you can heed my warning.

Respectfully, your loyal servant,

Lieutenant Colonel Paul Keller
23rd Infantry Brigade
Boston, Massachusetts
February 7, 1776

He uses letter format, which was given in the assignment, consistently.

Step-by-Step Teaching Guide continued

3. Ask students to point out details Paul uses that:
   - come from his imagination.
   - come from historical events.
4. Point out that Paul uses strong arguments to persuade King George to let the colonists settle the lands west of the Appalachian Mountains. Have students rate the arguments from weakest to strongest. Do they agree with the order in which Paul arranged his arguments in his essay. Why or why not?

Customize for *Gifted/Talented Students*

Have students research King George's actual response to the colonists' protests, then write a decree that conveys his response.

Customize for *ESL Students*

Have students write down unfamiliar words as they read and listen to the Final Draft. Encourage the students to look up these words and learn their meanings.

Integrating Speaking Skills

Invite students to play the role of Lieutenant Colonel Paul Keller reading his final draft aloud before sending it to King George III.

▶ Lesson Objectives

1. To write an open-book test essay appropriate to audience and purpose.
2. To choose among essay questions on an open-book test.
3. To draft, revise, and edit an open-book test essay.

Step-by-Step Teaching Guide

Open-Book Test

Teaching Resources: Writing Support Transparency 13-D; Writing Support Activity Book 13-2

1. Go over the suggestions for taking open-book tests listed in the textbook. Emphasize the importance of understanding exactly what type of essay is asked for on an essay test. The textbook should be used as a source of information that supports the main point or thesis statement.
2. Suggest that students review writing strategies from Chapter 13.
3. Use the transparency to model using a timeline to record a series of events to write about in an open-book test essay.
4. Give students copies of the blank organizer. Ask students to use the timeline to record significant events to write about on an open-book essay test.
5. Have students develop self-assessment rubrics for their open-book essay test questions. They can complete their evaluations of their essays, clip the evaluation sheets to the essays, and include them in their portfolios.

Critical Viewing

Apply Most students will stress the importance of developing a point of view and outlining one's essay before consulting reference materials.

Connected Assignment
Open-Book Test

▲ Critical Viewing What advice might you give this student for the best use of reference materials when taking a take-home test? **[Apply]**

The emphasis of an open-book test is not on your ability to remember information. Instead, you will be assessed on your ability to find information and present it in an organized form for some purpose, such as explaining or persuading. It is particularly important on such a test that you take care in the written expression of your ideas.

An open-book test essay may be graded according to these criteria:

- It should include relevant facts, such as specific names, dates, events, or formulas, available in your reference material.
- It should use those facts for the purpose specified in the test question—to draw conclusions, to explain, to persuade, and so on.
- It should sum up your main idea in a thesis statement that clearly addresses the test question.
- It should show a clear and logical organization.
- It should be free of errors in spelling, grammar, and punctuation.

Use the following strategies to do your best on open-book tests.

Prewriting Organize your time well. Use a little more than a fourth of your time for prewriting.

Prepare and Organize When preparing for a test on which you can use your notes, highlight, underline, or color-code main ideas in your notebook so that you will be able to refer to them easily.

When taking the test, you may first have to make a choice among questions. Avoid questions about which you know little. Select the one about which you can think of a few related details, such as examples, facts, or arguments, without referring to your materials.

Even though you may feel that all of the answers lie in the textbook or notes in front of you, do not refer to them at first. Instead, begin by outlining your answer to the question you have chosen. For questions involving a series of events, you might use a timeline like the one on page 301.

Use Textbook Features When you have finished your rough outline, briefly research each specific point of your outline in your reference materials. Use the index of a book to locate specific information quickly. If you must browse the text, scan the large heads on a page, stopping only at those that concern the information for which you are searching. Use the coding in your notebook to help you find information readily.

As you gather details about each point, add them to your outline. Revise your outline if you discover any errors in it.

CIVIL WAR TIMELINE

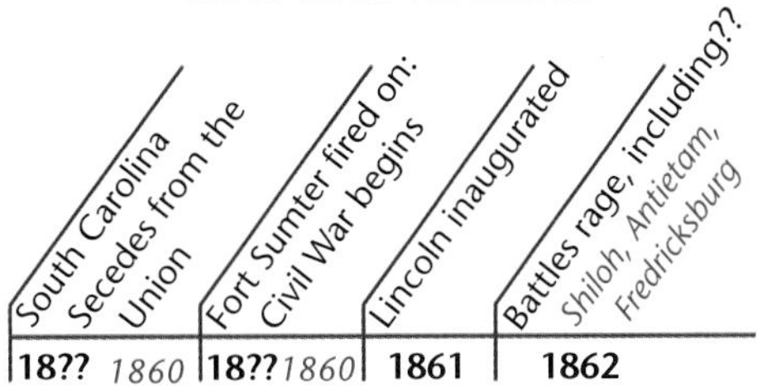

Drafting

Use roughly half the available time for drafting.

As you draft, focus on the question you are answering. Follow these strategies:

- **Indicate your main focus.** In your introduction, include a one-sentence statement that indicates the main focus of your answer to the question. This statement should closely follow the wording of the question, repeating words or phrases.
- **Provide details.** As you draft the body of your paper, discuss each main point of your outline in a paragraph or two. Use quotations, exact statistics, and other specific details you have gathered from your reference materials to support or explain each main point. Because you are permitted to use your reference materials, your answer should be more detailed than it might be on a closed-book test.
- **Go beyond the facts.** The questions on the test may ask you to develop conclusions or make arguments based on the facts. As you draft, make sure that you are using facts toward the purpose specified in the question—analyzing them, explaining them, or commenting on them.
- **Come to a conclusion.** In your final paragraph, sum up your answer to the question and your supporting reasons.

Revising and Editing

Allow a fourth of your time for revising.

Reread your essay As you read, underline points that need more support. Circle sections in which you recite facts without showing their connection to your purpose. Then, review coded text. Add support where needed, and draw out the implications of facts to better address your purpose. In the last few minutes of the test, proofread your draft.

Publishing and Presenting

After your open-book test has been graded, you can add it to your portfolio.

Customize for *More Advanced Students*

Have students work together to develop the standards that will be used to evaluate their open-book test essays. Expect these students to write longer and more detailed open-book test essays than other students. Their arguments should be sophisticated, and each point should be supported by evidence of various kinds.

Customize for *ESL Students*

You may want to direct students to the appropriate sections of the textbook as they write open-book test essays. Proofreading errors should be overlooked for testing purposes and can serve as discussion points and learning opportunities at some later date.

Lesson Objectives

1. To interpret and evaluate the various ways visual image makers represent meanings.
2. To compare the same theme across various media.
3. To write a report card on the ages of man.

Step-by-Step Teaching Guide

Connecting Themes Across the Arts

1. Choose one of the Spotlight items for class study or divide the class into groups and have each group research the topic they prefer from these: Titian's *The Three Ages of Man*, Shakespeare's *As You Like It*, or Thornton Wilder's plays on the ages of man. Gather biographies of Titian, Shakespeare, and Wilder as well as the above plays for your students to use.
2. Students researching Shakespeare may enjoy viewing a video of *As You Like It*. Videotaped performances of Wilder's *Our Town* may also be available.
3. All students should be expected to draw on their research as they complete the assessment writing activity. You may want to discuss categories for the report card as a class before students begin writing. Categories might include eating, playing, working, and so on.

Critical Viewing

Analyze Students may mention the subject's dress, her pose, and the platter of food she is carrying.

Spotlight on the Humanities

Connecting Themes Across the Arts

Focus on Art: Titian

The value of an artwork is often assessed by how well it stands the test of time. Will people still listen to that hit song ten years later? Will they still sigh in wonder when they first glimpse that mural? The work of Titian, born Tiziano Vecellio (ca. 1488–1576), the foremost artist in the Italian Venetian school of painters, has passed the test of time with high marks. Centuries after his death, painters still study his brilliant use of color.

Influenced by the painter Giorgione, Titian worked with frescoes (paintings done on plaster walls) in his early years. Later, he moved into portraiture, producing rich works like the portrait shown. Titian remained active as an artist until his death at about age 88.

Girl with a Basket of Fruits, Tiziano Vecellio

▲ Critical Viewing Through what details in this portrait does Titian suggest the personality of his subject? **[Analyze]**

Literature Connection In one famous painting, *The Three Ages of Man*, Titian depicted infancy, youth, and old age. This theme of man's "ages," or the stages of life, was popular during the Renaissance period (beginning in Italy in the fourteenth century and ending in the seventeenth century).

In England, playwright William Shakespeare (1564–1616) wrote on this theme in his comedy *As You Like It* (ca. 1600). Seven ages of man are described in the famous monologue that begins "All the world's a stage. . . ." (The number of ages may vary from one source to another.) This lyrical play contrasts the manners of the Elizabethan court with those of the English countryside. It is considered one of Shakespeare's most mature comedies.

Theater Connection Pulitzer Prize-winning author Thornton Wilder (1897–1975) was composing a series of plays on the ages of man before his death. Four of the plays are finished enough for performance: *Infancy, Childhood, Youth,* and *The Rivers Under the Earth.* Wilder is best known in the theatrical world for his 1938 play *Our Town,* which earned him the Pulitzer Prize.

Assessment Writing Activity: Report Card on the Ages of Man

Write a report card on each of the five stages of life: infancy, childhood, adolescence, adulthood, and old age. Come up with categories for comparison, and give a grade to each stage in each category.

Media and Technology Skills

Mastering Available Technology to Support Learning

Activity: Taking Computer-Based Tests

When you take tests on computers—academic standardized tests, for instance, or school entrance exams—you must use many of the same test-taking skills you use on print tests. There are a few additional strategies you should follow, however, when taking a computer-based test.

Tips on Computer Test Taking

- Read directions carefully. Pay special attention to instructions about navigating the test (moving from one screen to the next).
- If you are having trouble with your computer, ask for help immediately.

Learn About It

Review instructions. Read all instructions and information carefully before taking the test. Make sure that you understand how to enter answer choices and how your work will be graded. Then, decide on a strategy for answering questions on the test. For instance:

- Should you answer the easy questions first, and then return to the hard ones, or are you required to answer each question in turn?
- Will incorrect guesses count against you, or is it worth making a guess, if you can eliminate two answer choices?

Take on-line practice tests. You can find practice tests on CD-ROM and over the Internet. Take a few of these tests. By practicing with them, you will become more comfortable with computer test taking. In addition, the feedback for each answer on computer-based tests can help you to improve your test-taking skills and to learn more about the subject covered.

Analyze It Take a computer-based test a few times. As you proceed, take notes on any special instructions necessary for taking the test. Also, note any difficulties you encounter because of the test format, or any features that make the test easy to navigate or complete. Review your notes, and write a brief how-to guide, with tips on taking the test, for other students who may also have to take it.

Name of Test: ____________________

How to Answer a Question	How to Move Between Screens	Special Instructions/ Features	Special Problems

▶ *Lesson Objectives*

1. To take computer-based tests.
2. To analyze the instructions on computer-based tests.

Step-by-Step Teaching Guide

Mastering Available Technology to Support Learning

Teaching Resources: Writing Support Transparency 13-E; Writing Support Activity Book 13-3

1. Locate on-line tests and ask all your students to take the same tests, either in the classroom or in your school's computer lab. Emphasize that the purpose of taking the test is to become familiar with the types of instructions and procedures computer-based tests require, not to concentrate on the content of the tests. Students should rely on each other for advice when they don't understand the instructions and come to you or to your computer lab's monitor only as a last resort.
2. Display the transparency and review the information students should record about the particular test.
3. Give students copies of the blank organizer for them to complete as they take the test.
4. Display students' test-taking tips in the classroom or assemble them into a test-taking booklet for the school library.

Customize for *More Advanced Students*

Have students use screen shots of the various pages of a computer-based test to make a poster or bulletin-board display that shows as well as explains how to take tests on the computer.

Lesson Objectives

- To proofread passages to correct errors.

Step-by-Step Teaching Guide

Proofreading

Teaching Resources: Standardized Test Preparation Workbook, pp. 25–26

1. Carefully review the strategies students can use when answering questions that require them to proofread.
2. Draw students' attention to the Test Tip. Encourage students to read the questions before re-reading the passage a second time. This will help focus their attention on the possible errors in the passage.
3. Students may benefit from planning a strategy of attack for questions that require them to look for a wide variety of errors. For example, they may want to scan the passage first for errors in mechanics, then grammar, and then usage. This strategy may help them feel less overwhelmed in test-taking situations.

Standardized Test Preparation Workshop

Proofreading

Standardized tests often measure your ability to recognize mechanical errors. In multiple-choice items like those you'll see in this workshop, tests ask you to evaluate specific words, phrases, or sentences for errors. When addressing these types of questions, consider the following points to help you in your decision-making process.

- Pay close attention to spelling, capitalization, and punctuation errors in the passage, rather than focusing on its factual accuracy.
- Be aware that some items will not contain mistakes.

The following sample test items will give you practice with correcting mechanical errors in writing on standardized tests.

Test Tips

- Pay careful attention to homophones, words that sound the same but are spelled differently and have different meanings.
- Make sure that all proper nouns are capitalized.

Sample Test Items	Answers and Explanations
Read the following passages, and decide which type of error, if any, appears in the underlined sections. Choose the letter for your answer. I knew that I would <u>have plenty of ajustments to make once I moved to a new town.</u> **1 A** Spelling error **B** Capitalization error **C** Punctuation error **D** No error	The correct answer is *A. Adjustments* is spelled incorrectly.
<u>I have been attending woodland high school</u> since my freshman year. **2 F** Spelling error **G** Capitalization error **H** Punctuation error **J** No error	The correct answer is *G. Woodland High School* should be capitalized in the passage.

TEST-TAKING TIP

Explain to students that punctuation errors are often overlooked in test-taking situations. Have students pay careful attention to all punctuation used in a given passage to make sure that small errors do not go unnoticed.

Practice 1 **Directions:** Read the passage and decide which type of error, if any, appears in each underlined section. Mark the letter for your answer.

Since the meteorologists forecasted a snow-storm arriving wednesday, (1) our school took measures to make sure everyone was prepared. Teachers handed out relay phone lists so that students could notify one another of late openings and delays. (2) Students were also given an extra homework assignment and were instructed to complete it only if the school was closed, on Wednesday. (3)

1 A Spelling error
B Capitalization error
C Punctuation error
D No error

2 F Spelling error
G Capitalization error
H Punctuation error
J No error

3 A Spelling error
B Capitalization error
C Punctuation error
D No error

Practice 2 **Directions:** Read the passage and decide which type of error, if any, appears in each underlined section. Mark the letter for your answer.

To our surprise, there was no snow on the ground on Wensday morning. (1) After all of that planning the meteorologist said the direction of the storm had changed (2) and just missed this area. At least our school will be prepared if their's another storm in the future. (3)

1 A Spelling error
B Capitalization error
C Punctuation error
D No error

2 F Spelling error
G Capitalization error
H Punctuation error
J No error

3 A Spelling error
B Capitalization error
C Punctuation error
D No error

Answer Key

Practice 1

1. B
2. J
3. C

Practice 2

1. A
2. H
3. A

Objectives

1. To understand parts of speech and basic sentence patterns and to apply relevant concepts to their own writing
2. To learn and apply key concepts governing usage of verbs
3. To understand concepts of agreement relating to subjects and verbs and pronouns and antecedents, and to apply this understanding to their own writing
4. To compose sentences of increasing sophistication and appropriateness
5. To analyze works of literature as models of appropriate and effective English usage
6. To recognize appropriate English usage in their own reading and writing
7. To use "hands-on" strategies to reinforce understanding of grammar and usage concepts
8. To master the conventions of capitalization, punctuation, and spelling, and to apply them accurately to their own writing

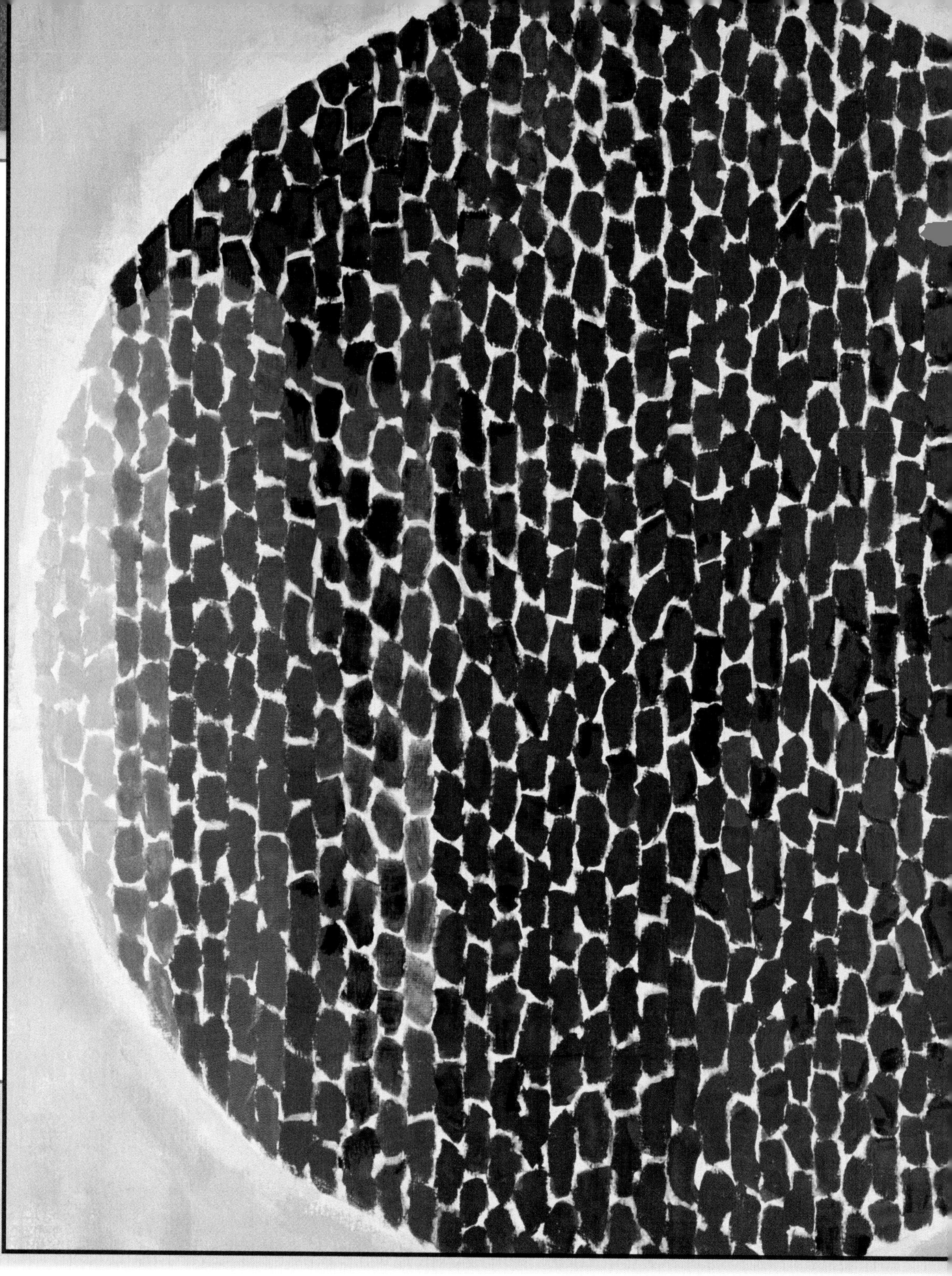

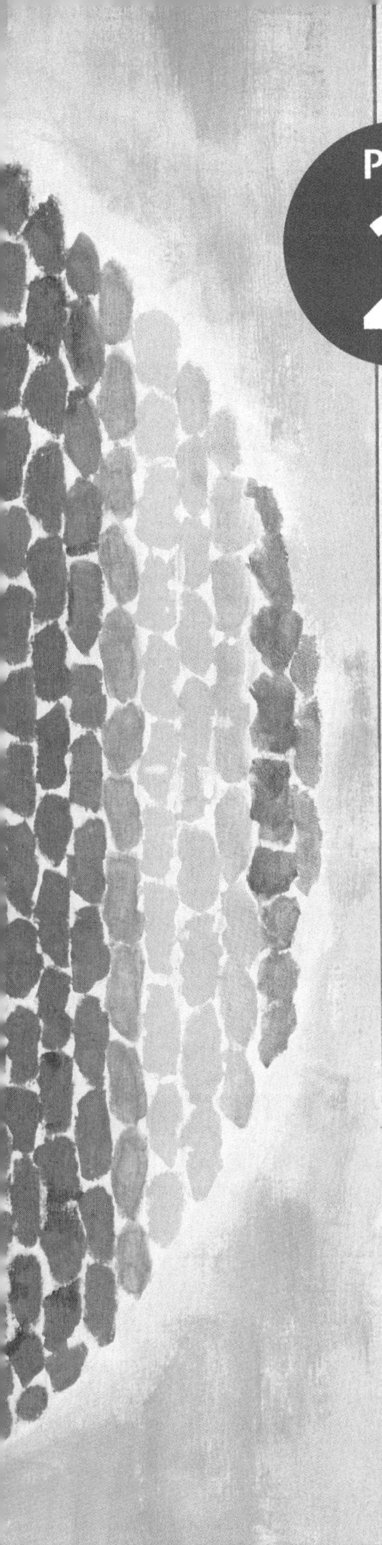

Snoopy-Early Sun Display on Earth, 1970, Alma Woodsey Thomas, National Museum of Art, Washington, D.C.

PART 2

Grammar, Usage, and Mechanics

Step-by-Step Teaching Guide

Responding to Fine Art

Snoopy-Early Sun Display on Earth
by Alma Woodsey Thomas

Use this work of art to start a discussion about the functions of grammar, usage, and mechanics.

1. Have students examine the painting on pages 306–307. You might use the following questions to prompt discussion:

   If you did not know the title of this painting, what would you say it represents?

   How do the colors make you feel?

2. Point out to students that the artist uses repeating shapes to create a larger object in the painting. Ask students if they see any connections between this artistic pattern and language. Lead students to see that our language is made up of smaller units (words), which when put together, create meaningful sentences.

Chapter 14 Time and Resource Manager

In-Depth Lesson Plan

	LESSON FOCUS	PRINT AND MEDIA RESOURCES
DAY 1	**Nouns** Students identify nouns. They work with collective and compound nouns. They distinguish between common and proper nouns. They complete a Hands-on Grammar activity (pp. 308–315).	**Teaching Resources** *Grammar Exercise Workbook,* pp. 1–7; *Grammar Exercises Answers on Transparencies,* Ch. 14; *Hands-on Grammar Activity Book,* Ch. 14 ***Writing and Grammar iText* (Interactive Text),** Section 14.1
DAY 2	**Pronouns** Students identify pronouns and their antecedents. They work with the common personal pronouns (pp. 316–318).	**Teaching Resources** *Grammar Exercise Workbook,* pp. 8–10; *Grammar Exercises Answers on Transparencies,* Ch. 14 ***Writing and Grammar iText* (Interactive Text),** Section 14.2
DAY 3	**Pronouns** *(continued)* Students identify and distinguish among demonstrative, relative, interrogative, and indefinite pronouns (pp. 319–323).	**Teaching Resources** *Grammar Exercise Workbook,* pp. 8–10; *Grammar Exercises Answers on Transparencies,* Ch. 14 ***Writing and Grammar iText* (Interactive Text),** Section 14.2
DAY 4	**Review and Assess** Students review the chapter and demonstrate mastery of nouns and pronouns (pp. 324–327).	**Teaching Resources** *Formal Assessment,* Ch. 14; *Grammar Exercises Answers on Transparencies,* Ch. 14 ***Writing and Grammar iText* (Interactive Text),** Ch. 14, Chapter Review; ***On-Line Exercise Bank,*** Sections 14.1–2

Accelerated Lesson Plan

	LESSON FOCUS	PRINT AND MEDIA RESOURCES
DAY 1	**Nouns** Students review collective, compound, common, and proper nouns (pp. 308–315).	**Teaching Resources** *Grammar Exercise Workbook,* pp. 1–7; *Grammar Exercises Answers on Transparencies,* Ch. 14; *Hands-on Grammar Activity Book,* Ch. 14 ***Writing and Grammar iText* (Interactive Text),** Section 14.1
DAY 2	**Pronouns** Students review personal, demonstrative, relative, interrogative, and indefinite pronouns. They identify antecedents (pp. 316–323).	**Teaching Resources** *Grammar Exercise Workbook,* pp. 8–10; *Grammar Exercises Answers on Transparencies,* Ch. 14 ***Writing and Grammar iText* (Interactive Text),** Section 14.2
DAY 3	**Review and Assess** Students review the chapter and demonstrate mastery of nouns and pronouns (pp. 324–327).	**Teaching Resources** *Formal Assessment,* Ch. 14; *Grammar Exercises Answers on Transparencies,* Ch. 14 ***Writing and Grammar iText* (Interactive Text),** Ch. 14, Chapter Review; ***On-Line Exercise Bank,*** Sections 14.1–2

Options for Adapting Lesson Plans

FEATURES

Extend coverage with the Grammar in Literature features (pp. 311, 321) and the Standardized Test Preparation Workshop (pp. 326–327).

SPELLING

To teach spelling skills in conjunction with grammar, mechanics, and usage, work through *Prentice Hall Everyday Spelling,* Grade 8, Chapter 16, as you cover this *Writing and Grammar* chapter.

TECHNOLOGY

Students can use *Writing and Grammar iText* to complete the exercises interactively on computer. They can complete additional exercises in the *On-line Exercise Bank:* The Auto Check feature will grade their work. Go online: PHSchool.com Use Web code: eck-8002

INTEGRATED SKILLS COVERAGE

Grammar in Literature
SE pp. 311, 321

Reading
Find It in Your Reading, SE pp. 314, 315, 323

Writing
Find It in Your Writing, SE pp. 314, 315, 323
Writing Application, SE pp. 315, 323, 325

Viewing and Representing
Critical Viewing, SE pp. 308, 310, 312, 316, 319

Vocabulary
Irregular Plurals, ATE p. 311

Real-World Connection
Pronouns in Radio Broadcasting, ATE p. 317

Workplace Skills
Using Correct Pronouns, ATE p. 317

ASSESSMENT SUPPORT

Standardized Test Preparation Workshop SE pp. 326–327, ATE p. 314

Standardized Test Preparation Workbook, pp. 27–28

Formal Assessment, Ch. 14

MEETING INDIVIDUAL NEEDS

Less Advanced Students See Ongoing Assessments ATE pp. 313, 319, 321.

ESL Students ATE p. 313

BLOCK SCHEDULING

Pacing Suggestions
For 90-minute Blocks
- Administer the Diagnostic Test to students to determine instructional coverage.
- Have students complete the necessary exercises in class. Use the Hands-on Grammar Activity to provide a change of pace.

Resources for Varying Instruction
- ***Writing and Grammar iText*** **(Interactive Text)** A 90-minute block provides an ideal opportunity for students to work on computer.

Professional Development Support
- ***How to Manage Instruction in the Block*** This teaching resource provides management and activity suggestions.

MEDIA AND TECHNOLOGY

For the Student
- ***Writing and Grammar iText*** **(Interactive Text),** Ch. 14
- ***On-line Exercise Bank,*** Sections 14.1–2

For the Teacher
- ***Resource Pro*** **CD-ROM**

WRITING AND GRAMMAR ON-LINE

iText **Interactive Text (On-line or on CD-ROM)**
- Easily navigable instruction with on-line supporting resources
- Self-scoring exercises and diagnostic tests

Companion Web Site **PHSchool.com**
- On-line Exercise Bank (use Web Code eck-8002)

See the Go On-line! feature, SE p. iii.

LITERATURE CONNECTIONS

Grammar in Literature selection from *Prentice Hall Literature: Timeless Voices, Timeless Themes,* Silver:

from "E-Mail From Bill Gates," John Seabrook, SE pp. 311, 321

CHAPTER 14
NOUNS AND PRONOUNS

Lesson Objectives

1. To identify nouns.
2. To distinguish among collective, compound, common, and proper nouns.
3. To recognize the antecedent of a pronoun.
4. To distinguish among personal, demonstrative, relative, interrogative, and indefinite pronouns.

Critical Viewing

Infer Students may use such nouns as *workman, engineer,* or *electrician.*

Answer Key

Diagnostic Test

Each item in the Diagnostic Test corresponds to a specific concept in the chapter on nouns and pronouns. This will enable you to tailor instruction to the particular needs of your students. See "Ongoing Assessment: Diagnose" below for further details.

Chapter 14 Nouns and Pronouns

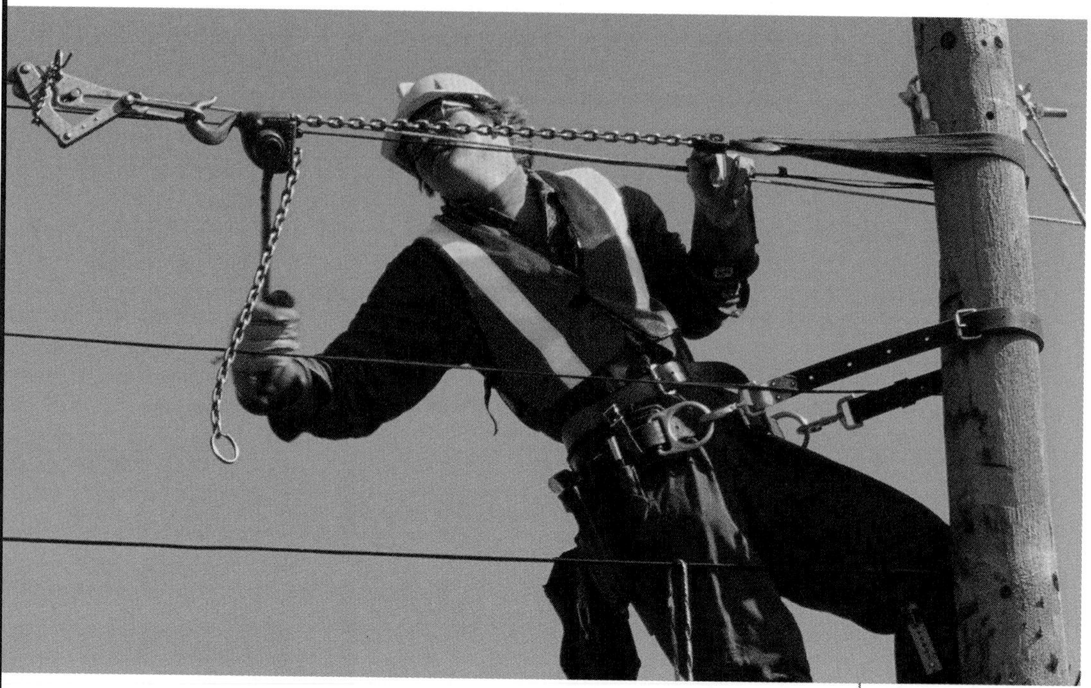

▲ **Critical Viewing** Power lines such as these keep communications moving. Use two or three nouns in a sentence to describe who this worker is. **[Infer]**

Words are the building blocks of communication. You assemble words to deliver your ideas to other people. Communication technology—including computers—has grown rapidly over the last five decades. Because words are the tools of communication, it makes sense to study them in detail.

The English language has eight kinds of words, or parts of speech: nouns, pronouns, verbs, adjectives, adverbs, prepositions, conjunctions, and interjections. This chapter will help you learn more about two important parts of speech: nouns and pronouns.

ONGOING ASSESSMENT: Diagnose

If students miss more than one item in each category, direct them to the relevant pages of the text and assign exercises for practice and review.

Nouns and Pronouns	Diagnostic Test Items	Teach	Practice	Section Review	Chapter Review
Skill Check A					
Nouns	A 1–10	p. 310	Ex. 1	Ex. 6	Ex. 26
Skill Check B					
Kinds of Nouns	B 11–15	pp. 311–313	Ex. 2–5	Ex. 7–9	Ex. 26–27, 31–33

Diagnostic Test

Directions: Write all answers on a separate sheet of paper.

Skill Check A. List the nouns from the following sentences. Label each one *person*, *place*, or *thing*.

1. Communication is the way we connect with one another.
2. People have communicated in one form or another since the beginning of human history.
3. Writing and speaking are two methods of communication.
4. Communication can also be accomplished by other means.
5. We can also communicate how we feel or what we need through body language and gestures.
6. Another type of communication that is growing rapidly is electronic communication.
7. This includes such things as computers, radio, and television.
8. Many people around the world use electronic communication several times every day.
9. The technology of electronic communication keeps growing and is becoming faster and easier to use in today's world.
10. These developments are a big part of everyone's life and are used in both business and education.

Skill Check B. Copy the following phrases, and underline the nouns. Label each noun *common* or *proper*. If the noun is collective or compound, label it so.

11. a family of computers
12. in the United States or Canada
13. to call a trouble-shooter for help
14. a team of specialists
15. Alexander Graham Bell and other inventors

Skill Check C. Identify the pronouns in the following sentences, and label each pronoun *personal*, *demonstrative*, *relative*, *interrogative*, or *indefinite*.

16. Who took her class on computer technology?
17. Someone told me about it, but that was only yesterday.
18. Did she teach her class on the computers of today?
19. These are some good questions about computers: How did they begin, and what will they be like in the future?
20. I can't believe the many improvements that have been made to computers since the first ones were introduced.
21. The first computer was invented by Herman Hollerith; he invented it in the 1890's.
22. My teacher also described how companies began building calculators, which were the first forms of computers.
23. Did your teacher tell you what year they built these calculators?
24. Does anyone know if it was in the 1930's?
25. We have much to learn about the growth of technology in communication. I need to take another class!

Skill Check A

1. Communication—thing; way—thing
2. People—person; form—thing; beginning—thing, history—thing
3. Writing—thing; speaking—thing; methods—thing; communication—thing
4. Communication—thing; means—thing
5. language—thing; gestures—thing
6. type—thing; communication—thing (twice)
7. things—thing; computers, radio, television—things
8. people—person; world—place; communication—thing; times—thing; day—thing
9. technology—thing; communication—thing; world—place
10. developments, part, life, businesses, education—things

Skill Check B

11. a family of computers—common collective, common
12. in the United States or Canada—proper compound, proper
13. to call a trouble-shooter for help—common compound, common
14. a team of specialists—common collective, common
15. Alexander Graham Bell and other inventors—proper compound, common

Skill Check C

16. Who—interrogative; her—personal
17. Someone—indefinite; me—personal; it—personal; that—demonstrative
18. she—personal; her—personal
19. These—demonstrative; some—indefinite; they—personal; what—interrogative; they—personal
20. I—personal; many—indefinite; ones—indefinite
21. he—personal; it—personal
22. My—personal; which—relative
23. your—personal; you—personal; they—personal; these—demonstrative
24. anyone—indefinite; it—personal
25. We—personal; I—personal; another—indefinite

ONGOING ASSESSMENT: Diagnose *continued*

Nouns and Pronouns	Diagnostic Test Items	Teach	Practice	Section Review	Chapter Review
Skill Check C					
Pronouns	C 16–25	pp. 316–322	Ex. 13–18	Ex. 19–22	Ex. 28–32
Cumulative Reviews and Applications				Ex. 9–12, 23–25	Ex. 32–34

PREPARE and ENGAGE

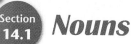

Interest GRABBER Write the headings *Person, Place,* and *Thing* on the chalkboard. Have students tell in which category the following words belong and write them under the headings: octopus, backpack, George Washington Carver, Grand Canyon, intelligence, acrobat, dachshund, Main Street, Queen Elizabeth, Egypt, doctor, happiness, idea.

Activate Prior Knowledge

Ask why some of the nouns on the board are capitalized. (They name specific people or places; they are proper nouns.)

TEACH

Step-by-Step Teaching Guide

Nouns

1. Go over the nouns in the chart with the class. Point out that nouns can refer to specific people and places or to a general category of person or place. *Africa* is a specific place; *continent* is a general category.
2. Ask students to suggest more intangible things that are nouns.

Critical Viewing

Describe Possible answer: Using wireless technology, a cell phone allows a man to communicate in the woods.

Answer Key

Exercise 1

1. medium—thing; means—thing; communication—thing; word—thing; *medius*—thing; middle—place
2. Media—thing; forms—thing; communication—thing or idea
3. media, messages—things; way, distance, time—ideas
4. computer, medium, messages—things; communicators—person
5. radios, books, telephones, media—things

Section 14.1

Nouns

Nouns are naming words. Nouns help people identify what they are talking or thinking about.

KEY CONCEPT A **noun** is the name of a person, place, thing, or idea. ■

Study the list of nouns in the chart. (You may be surprised that some of these are, in fact, nouns.)

People	
farmer	Alexander Graham Bell
Bostonians	pilot
Places	
Chicago	waiting room
theater	Madison Square Garden
Things	
Living and Nonliving Things That You Can See	
flowers	ballpoint pen
goldfish	modem
elephant	poem
Ideas and Things That You Cannot Usually See	
success	revolution
happiness	fairness
anger	health

Exercise 1 **Identifying Nouns** Identify the nouns in each of the following sentences. Explain why each word you have identified functions as a noun.

1. A *medium* is defined as a means of communication, and comes from the Latin word *medius*, meaning "the middle" or "between."
2. *Media* is plural, describing all the various forms of communication.
3. The media provide a way for messages to travel over distance and time.
4. A computer, for instance, is a medium for sending messages between communicators.
5. Radios, books, and telephones are media used by almost everyone.

Theme: Communication

In this section, you will learn how nouns are classified. The examples and exercises are about the ways in which we communicate.

Cross-Curricular Connection: Science and Social Studies

▼ **Critical Viewing** This man is able to communicate while biking in the woods. Explain how he does this, using nouns for things you can and cannot see in your sentences. **[Describe]**

TIME AND RESOURCE MANAGER

Resources
Print: Grammar Exercise Workbook, pp. 1–6; Hands-on Grammar Activity Book, Chapter 14
Technology: Writing and Grammar iText, Section 14.1; On-Line Exercise Bank, Section 14.1

In-Depth Coverage	Accelerated Pace
• Cover pp. 310–313 in class. • Assign and review Exercises 1–5. • Complete Hands-on Grammar activity, p. 314.	• Assign pp. 310–313 for independent student review. • Assign Section Review Exercises 6–7.

Recognizing Collective Nouns

Certain nouns name groups of people or things. For example, a jury is a group of people; a herd is a group of animals. These nouns are called *collective nouns*.

KEY CONCEPT A **collective noun** is a noun that names a group of individual people or things. ■

Following are some examples of collective nouns:

EXAMPLES: team, class, committee, crowd, group, audience

Exercise 2 **Recognizing Collective Nouns** On your paper, list the nouns in the following sentences. Underline the five that are collective nouns.

1. It was common for a group to use drums, signals, or lanterns to send messages.
2. These messages could only be seen or heard by a crowd a short distance away.
3. During World War I, messages were tied to the legs of pigeons and sent to distant troops.
4. Flags or lights were used by a team to send a message over hilltops or between ships at sea.
5. These codes were called *semaphore systems* by their audience.

More Practice

Grammar Exercise Workbook
- pp. 1–4

On-line Exercise Bank
- Section 14.1

Go on-line:
PHSchool.com
Enter Web Code:
eck-8002

iText

Get instant feedback! Exercise 2 is available on-line or on CD-ROM.

GRAMMAR IN LITERATURE

from E-Mail From Bill Gates
John Seabrook

The nouns in this excerpt are highlighted in blue italics. The noun in red is a collective noun.

At the *moment*, the best *way* to communicate with another *person* on the *information highway* is to exchange electronic *mail*: to write a *message* on a *computer* and send it through the *telephone lines* into someone else's *computer*.

Step-by-Step Teaching Guide

Recognizing Collective Nouns

1. Give students other examples of collective nouns: *orchestra, jury, faculty, couple, family, pack, squad,* and most animal groups (*litter, pride,* and so on).
2. Collective nouns are considered one unit, so they take singular verbs when they refer to the group as a whole.

   The audience showed its appreciation by clapping.

   The jury returned its verdict.

Answer Key

Exercise 2

1. group, drums, signals, lanterns, messages
2. messages, crowd, distance
3. World War I, messages, legs, pigeons, troops
4. Flags, lights, team, message, hilltops, ships, sea
5. codes, *semaphore systems,* audience

Step-by-Step Teaching Guide

Grammar in Literature

1. Have a volunteer read aloud the sentence from "E-Mail From Bill Gates."
2. Ask students whether the compound noun *information superhighway* is a thing or a place. A good case can be made for either answer. Encourage students to justify their opinions.

Integrating Vocabulary Skills

Irregular Plurals In addition to *medium,* other English words that come from Latin form plurals with *a* rather than *s*. Examples: *datum/data, curriculum/curricula, auditorium/auditoria, atrium/atria, podium/podia, paramecium/paramecia*

Step-by-Step Teaching Guide

Recognizing Compound Nouns

1. Let students know that the only way to know if a compound noun is one word, two words, or hyphenated is to use the dictionary. Similar words do not all follow the same pattern: *lunch box, lunch counter, lunchroom, lunchtime.*
2. Point out that nouns with prefixes, whether hyphenated *(ex-president)* or one word *(audiocassette),* are not compounds. A compound noun must have two or more *words.*

Answer Key

Exercise 3

The U.S. Postal Service was established by the government. The position of postmaster general was created to supervise the mail service. The first postmaster general was Benjamin Franklin. The pony express was started by the United States Post Office. The riders carried mail on horseback and were known for their prompt delivery. Mail was also carried on stagecoaches. Today, the United States Postal Service is self-supporting and is exploring many new technologies.

Critical Viewing

Support Possible compound nouns associated with Franklin: eyeglasses, printing press, lightning rod, Franklin stove, Continental Congress, Declaration of Independence

TIME SAVERS!

Answers on Transparency Use the Grammar Exercises Answers on Transparencies for Chapter 14 to have students correct their own or one another's exercises.

On-Line Exercise Bank Have students complete the exercises on computer. The Auto Check feature will grade their work for you!

14.1

Recognizing Compound Nouns

You have probably used the words *soft* and *drink* separately many times. When both words are used together, however, they form a single noun that has a special meaning, as in "She had a soft drink with her pizza."

KEY CONCEPT A **compound noun** is a noun made up of two or more words. ■

Compound nouns are usually written in one of three ways:

TYPES OF COMPOUND NOUNS		
Separate Words	Hyphenated Words	Combined Words
hard drive chief justice Empire State Building	cure-all cha-cha mother-in-law	congresswoman network classroom

Check a dictionary for the spelling of unfamiliar compound nouns. If a word is not listed, write it as two separate words.

Exercise 3 **Recognizing Compound Nouns** The following paragraph has a total of ten compound nouns. Copy the paragraph onto your paper, and underline each compound noun.

EXAMPLE: A special mail service was established in the United States in 1789.

ANSWER: A special mail service was established in the United States in 1789.

The U.S. Postal Service was established by the government. The position of postmaster general was created to supervise the mail service. The first postmaster general was Benjamin Franklin. The pony express was started by the United States Post Office. The riders carried mail on horseback and were known for their prompt delivery. Mail was also carried on stagecoaches. Today, the United States Postal Service is self-supporting and is exploring many new technologies.

▼ Critical Viewing The first postmaster general of the United States was Benjamin Franklin. Tell what else you know about him, using compound nouns in your sentences. **[Support]**

Using Common and Proper Nouns

All nouns can be divided into two large groups: *common nouns* and *proper nouns.*

KEY CONCEPT A **common noun** names any one of a class of people, places, or things. A **proper noun** names a specific person, place, or thing. ■

Common nouns are not capitalized. Proper nouns are always capitalized.

Common Nouns	Proper Nouns
inventor	Alexander Graham Bell
village	Tarrytown
story	"Rikki-tikki-tavi"

Exercise 4 **Identifying Common and Proper Nouns** Copy the following nouns. Place a *C* after each common noun and a *P* after each proper noun. Write a proper noun that gives an example of each common noun. Then, write a common noun that gives an example of a class to which each proper noun belongs.

1. government
2. pony express
3. postmaster general
4. United States
5. city
6. president
7. postal service
8. Benjamin Franklin
9. century
10. history

Exercise 5 **Using Common and Proper Nouns** Copy the following paragraph. Replace each underlined common noun (and its article) with one of the proper nouns supplied. You will use one of the proper nouns twice. Make other minor changes as needed.

Samuel F. B. Morse | New York
Morse Code | United States

The telegraph was the first electronic medium. It sent and received electrical signals over long-distance wires. One of the first inventors of the telegraph was <u>a man</u>. He was an artist and inventor who lived in <u>a country</u>. In 1837, <u>the man</u> demonstrated the system in <u>a city/state</u>. <u>The code</u> later evolved from his invention.

Grammar and Style Tip

Adding proper nouns will help make your writing more informative. Instead of writing "The telephone was invented in the 1800's," you might write, "The telephone was invented by Alexander Graham Bell in the 1800's."

More Practice

Grammar Exercise Workbook
- pp. 5–6

On-line Exercise Bank
- Section 14.1

Go on-line: PHSchool.com *Enter Web Code:* eck-8002

Spelling Tip

If you're not sure whether or not a noun is proper and should be capitalized, always check in a dictionary.

Answer Key

Exercise 4

Answers will vary. Samples are given.

1. government, C; Congress
2. pony express, C; Wells Fargo
3. postmaster general, C; Benjamin Franklin
4. United States, P; country
5. city, C; Santa Fe
6. president, C; Theodore Roosevelt
7. postal service, C: U.S. Postal Service
8. Benjamin Franklin, P; inventor
9. century, C; Victorian Era
10. history, C; *The Decline and Fall of the Roman Empire*

Exercise 5

The telegraph was the first electronic medium. It sent and received electrical signals over long-distance wires. One of the first inventors of the telegraph was Samuel F. B. Morse. He was an artist and inventor who lived in the United States. In 1837, Samuel F. B. Morse demonstrated the system in New York. Morse Code later evolved from his invention.

Customize for *ESL Students*

In Spanish and many other languages, nouns have gender; they are masculine or feminine. In this respect, English is easier: English nouns have no gender.

ONGOING ASSESSMENT: Monitor and Reinforce

If students miss more than two items in Exercises 3–5, refer them to the following for additional practice.

In the Textbook	Print Resources	Technology
Section Review, Ex. 7–8, p. 315	Grammar Exercise Workbook, pp. 5–6	On-Line Exercise Bank, Section 14.1

Step-by-Step Teaching Guide

Collecting Compound Nouns Hallway

Teaching Resources: Hands-on Grammar Activity Book, Chapter 14

1. Have students refer to their Hands-on Grammar activity books or give them copies of the relevant pages for this activity.
2. As an alternative to this activity, students may find it more convenient to make a simple three-column chart in their notebooks.

Find It in Your Reading

Literature written in the long past may contain hyphenated compounds that are spelled as one word today. English literature may sometimes have different spellings from American. Encourage students to share and discuss compound words they have found in their reading.

Find It in Your Writing

Encourage students to share their lists, and check each other's compound nouns to see if they are spelled correctly.

14.1

Hands-on Grammar

Collecting Compound Nouns Hallway

In this exercise, you will collect and display compound nouns that are formed in different ways. Follow the directions given and look at the illustration.

1. Take a piece of 5-1/4" x 6-1/2" paper and fold it in half the long way. Make a fold about 2" from the end so the paper will stand up.
2. Cut three doors in one half of your paper. Make each door approximately 1-1/4" wide and deep. On the first door, write *Separate Words*. On the second door, write *Hyphenated Words*; on the third, *Combined Words*.
3. Cut three strips of paper, 1" wide x 4" long. Tape a strip of paper inside each of the three doors. You can fold them up like steps so that you can close the doors.
4. Write appropriate compound nouns on the strips of paper behind each door. For example, for *Separate Words*, you can use *hard drive, chief justice, high school;* for *Hyphenated Words*, use *mother-in-law, maid-of-honor;* and for *Combined Words*, use *network, classroom, football.*
5. Keep this hallway in your notebook and add compound nouns to the list when you come across them in your reading and writing. If you are unsure how to form the compound noun, look it up in a dictionary.

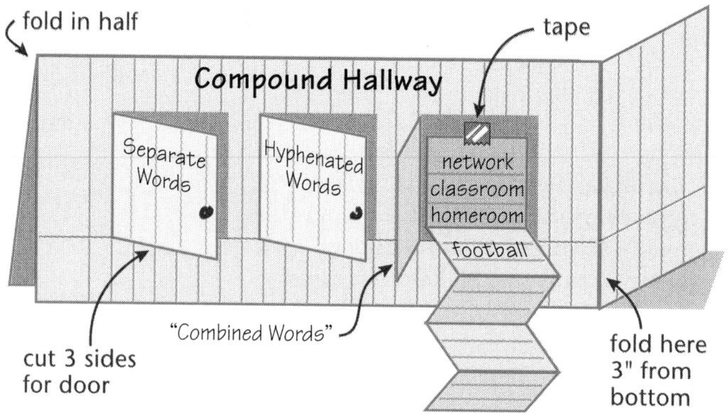

Find It in Your Reading As you read your assignments in your textbooks, look for and jot down compound nouns. Then, put them behind the appropriate door in your hallway.

Find It in Your Writing Look through some essays in your portfolio for examples of compound nouns. Make sure that you have spelled them correctly. Add them to your lists.

TIME SAVERS!

Hands-on Grammar Book Use the Hands-on Grammar activity sheet for Chapter 14 to facilitate this activity.

STANDARDIZED TEST PREPARATION WORKSHOP

Spelling Standardized tests often ask students to find the spelling mistake in a passage or a series of sentences. Ask students which of the following sentences contains a spelling error. Remind students that writing a one-word compound as two words, or omitting a necessary hyphen, is a spelling error.

A Benjamin Franklin was one of the most respected members of the Constitutional Convention.

B Franklin had represented the United States in discussions with European governments.

C While still in his teens, Franklin had left home to start his own print shop in Philadelphia.

D Franklin invented eye-glasses, the Franklin stove, and the lightning rod.

The correct answer is **D.** *Eyeglasses* is not hyphenated.

Section 14.1 **Section Review**

GRAMMAR EXERCISES 6–12

Exercise 6 **Identifying Nouns** Identify the nouns in each of the following sentences. Explain why each word that you identified functions as a noun.

1. Alexander Graham Bell invented the telephone.
2. His invention was patented in 1876.
3. This invention was able to transmit a voice over wires.
4. Before the telephone, people could only transmit clicks, using the telegraph.
5. Bell then founded the Bell Telephone Company.

Exercise 7 **Classifying Nouns** Write the *collective, compound,* or *proper* noun in each of the following sentences. Label each type of noun.

1. In 1895, a system was built that enabled a group to send and receive signals through the air.
2. This system of sending electrical signals was called *radio* by its audience.
3. A crowd in New York heard the first broadcast in 1906.
4. Philo T. Farnsworth was the first American inventor to use television technology.
5. The first regularly scheduled program was broadcast on July 1, 1941, in New York City.
6. Eventually, department stores began to carry these new appliances.
7. Thanks to teams of experts, radio technology improved rapidly.
8. Today, radio stations offer communities many choices.
9. How would Americans follow football without radio and television?
10. In the United States, about one of every 250 Americans had a telephone by the year 1894.

Exercise 8 **Supplying Nouns** In the following sentences, fill in the missing word with the kind of noun requested.

1. (Proper noun) invented the (common noun).
2. A television transmission is called a (compound noun).
3. Because we have (compound noun), we are able to watch more than 60 channels.
4. Before the (common noun), people had to listen to the radio for news.
5. My favorite baseball (collective noun) is the (proper noun).

Exercise 9 **Writing Sentences With Nouns** Use each of the following kinds of nouns in a sentence.

1. common noun that names a place
2. proper noun that names a person
3. collective noun
4. hyphenated compound noun
5. noun that names an idea

Exercise 10 **Find It in Your Reading** Examine a newspaper or magazine article to find examples of common and proper nouns.

Exercise 11 **Find It in Your Writing** Review a piece of your own writing to find at least two examples of collective and compound nouns.

Exercise 12 **Writing Application** Write ten sentences of your own to describe your use of a type of technology. Include at least ten common nouns and four proper nouns in your description.

ASSESS and CLOSE

Section Review

Each of these exercises correlates to a concept in the section on nouns, pages 310–314. The exercises may be used for more practice, for reteaching, or for review of the Key Concepts presented. Answers for all chapter exercises are available in *Grammar Exercises Answers on Transparencies* in your Teaching Resources.

Answer Key

Exercise 6

1. Alexander Graham Bell—person; telephone—thing
2. invention—thing; 1876—thing
3. invention—thing; voice—thing; wires—thing
4. telephone—thing; people—person; clicks—thing; telegraph—thing
5. Bell—person; Bell Telephone Company—thing

Exercise 7

1. group—collective
2. audience—collective
3. crowd—collective; broadcast—compound
4. Philo T. Farnsworth—compound and proper
5. New York City—compound and proper
6. department stores—compound
7. teams—collective
8. radio stations—compound
9. Americans—proper; football—compound
10. United States—compound and proper; American—proper

Exercise 8

Answers will vary. Samples are given.

1. Benjamin Franklin invented the lightning rod.
2. broadcast
3. cable television
4. television
5. My favorite baseball team is the Chicago Cubs.

continued

Answer Key continued

Exercise 9

Answers will vary. Samples are given.

1. We live in a very large city.
2. Mark Twain was a great writer.
3. The orchestra played a symphony by Mozart.
4. I just met my future mother-in-law.
5. I wish you the best of success.

Exercise 10

Find It in Your Reading
Have students bring in their articles for class discussion.

Exercise 11

Find It in Your Writing
Ask students to be sure that they correctly used singular verbs and pronouns with collective nouns.

Exercise 12

Writing Application
Students who wrote about the same technology can compare their sentences to see how many of the same nouns they used.

PREPARE and ENGAGE

Interest GRABBER Ask students to change some of the words in the following sentences so they sound better.

A spider has eight legs on a spider's (its) body.

Spiders trap spiders' (their) prey in webs.

The female black widow spider may eat the black widow's (her) mate.

Tarantulas can be 10 inches long, but tarantulas (they) are not as dangerous as black widows.

Activate Prior Knowledge

Ask students why they replaced nouns with pronouns in the Interest Grabber. (The sentences were repetitive; they sounded awkward.)

Critical Viewing

Classify Possible answers: girl = *she, her, hers;* computers = *they;* keyboard = *it*

Section 14.2

Pronouns

Pronouns are words that take the place of nouns. They are generally used when it would not make sense to repeat a noun over and over again. Imagine, for example, that you are writing about Aunt Jenny. If you were using only nouns, you might write the following sentence:

WITH NOUNS: Aunt Jenny was late because *Aunt Jenny* had waited for *Aunt Jenny's* computer technician.

WITH PRONOUNS: Aunt Jenny was late because *she* had waited for *her* computer technician.

KEY CONCEPT A **pronoun** is a word that takes the place of a noun or of a group of words acting as a noun.

Sometimes a pronoun takes the place of a noun in the same sentence.

EXAMPLE: My father opened *his* files first.

A pronoun can also take the place of a noun used in an earlier sentence.

EXAMPLE: My father opened his e-mail first. *He* couldn't wait any longer.

A pronoun may take the place of an entire group of words.

EXAMPLE: Trying to make the team is hard work. *It* takes hours of practice every day.

Theme: Computers

In this section, you will learn about pronouns. The examples and exercises are about the history and uses of computers.

Cross-Curricular Connection: Science and Social Studies

▼ Critical Viewing
What pronouns would you use to take the place of nouns in describing this photograph? **[Classify]**

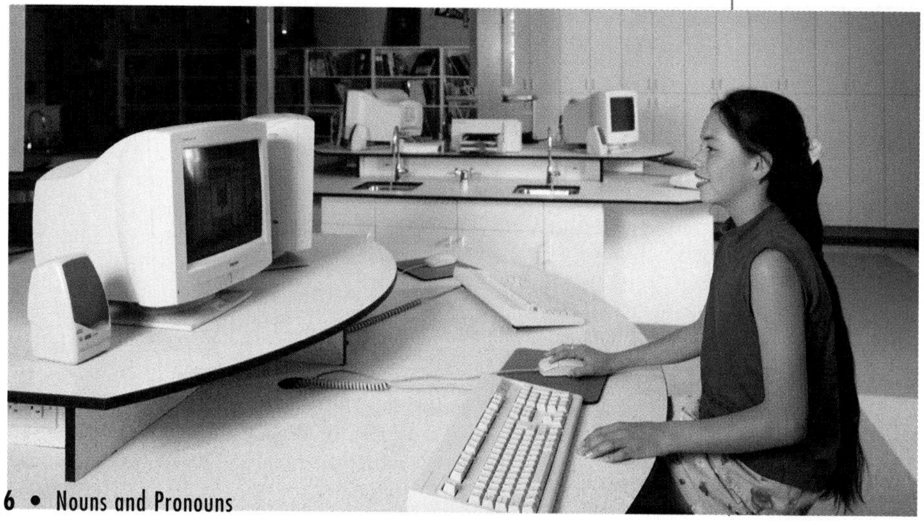

TIME AND RESOURCE MANAGER

Resources
Print: Grammar Exercise Workbook, pp. 7–12
Technology: Writing and Grammar iText, Section 14.2; On-Line Exercise Bank, Section 14.2

In-Depth Coverage	Accelerated Pace
• Work through all key concepts, pp. 316–322. • Assign and review Exercises 13–18. • Read and discuss Grammar in Literature, p. 321.	• Assign pp. 316–322 for independent student review. • Assign Section Review Exercises 20–22.

Recognizing Antecedents of Pronouns

A pronoun is closely related to the noun it replaces. The noun that the pronoun replaces has a special name. It is called the *antecedent.*

KEY CONCEPT An **antecedent** is the noun (or group of words acting as a noun) for which a pronoun stands. ■

The Latin prefix *ante-* means "before," and most antecedents do come before the pronouns that take their place. In the following examples, *father* and *Trying to make the team* are the antecedents of the pronouns *his* and *It.*

EXAMPLES: My *father* opened *his* mail first. He couldn't wait any longer.
Trying to make the team is hard work. *It* takes hours of practice every day.

Sometimes an antecedent will come after the pronoun.

EXAMPLE: Although *he* was known as an expert software developer, *Darryl* enjoyed selling computers.

Occasionally, a pronoun will have no definite antecedent.

EXAMPLES: *Who* will represent the class?
Everything was lost in the flood.

In these examples, the pronouns *who* and *everything* do not stand for any specific person or thing.

Exercise 13 **Recognizing Antecedents** In each of the numbered items below, a pronoun is underlined. Write the antecedent for each pronoun on your paper.

EXAMPLE: People use their computers for all kinds of work.
ANSWER: People

1. The earliest computers were used to calculate numbers. They were used in the 1890's to total the U.S. Census.
2. International Business Machines Company (IBM) was founded in 1924. The electromechanical calculator was its invention.
3. The first general-purpose computer in America was called the Electrical Numerical Integrator and Computer (ENIAC). It was completed in 1945.
4. One of its inventors was John P. Eckert. He and John W. Mauchly later built the first computer for commercial use.
5. The explosion of word-processing technology occurred in the 1970's. It gave us the ability to compose documents on computers.

iText

Get instant feedback! Exercise 13 is available on-line or on CD-ROM.

More Practice

Grammar Exercise Workbook
- pp. 8–10

On-line Exercise Bank
- Section 14.2

Go on-line:
PHSchool.com
Enter Web Code:
eck-8002

TEACH

Step-by-Step Teaching Guide

Recognizing Antecedents of Pronouns

Remind students of the collective nouns they learned about earlier. They are generally singular, so pronouns that refer to them must also be singular.

The team won its (not their) last three games.

The class scheduled its trip to the museum for Friday.

Answer Key

Exercise 13

1. computers
2. IBM
3. ENIAC
4. ENIAC
5. explosion

Real-World Connection

Radio broadcasters of sporting events must be sure to establish antecedents for their pronouns. Since listeners cannot see what is happening, they would never know to whom the pronouns *he, him, they, it, them,* and so on referred unless the broadcasters made it clear.

Integrating Workplace Skills

Correct pronouns are important at work. When an employee writes a progress report for the boss, there is a big difference among "My/his/our/your idea resulted in record profits for the company."

TIME SAVERS!

Answers on Transparency
Use the Grammar Exercises Answers on Transparencies for Chapter 14 to have students correct their own or one another's exercises.

On-Line Exercise Bank
Have students complete the exercises on computer. The Auto Check feature will grade their work for you!

Step-by-Step Teaching Guide

Using Personal Pronouns

1. Usually it is obvious whether a pronoun refers to a male or female.

   Luisa lost her umbrella.

   Luis lost his umbrella.

   When it could have been either a man or woman who lost the umbrella, the pronoun(s) must reflect the uncertainty.

   The student lost his or her umbrella.

2. *He or she* and *his or her* can become awkward and annoying if they occur often. This can be avoided by using a plural antecedent.

   Each student raised his or her hand. → The students raised their hands.

Answer Key

Exercise 14

Pronouns may vary.

1. Most computer users have accessed the Internet through their service providers. Antecedent: users
2. Karen, my (or your) service provider is one of many. Antecedent: None (or Karen)
3. Mark got his service through AmeriServe; it also provides Internet access. Antecedents: Mark, AmeriServe
4. I (or He) used Local Serve Network at one time. It was another Internet provider. Antecedents: none (or Mark), Local Serve Network
5. Jan just installed a Local Area Network (LAN) on her computer system. Antecedent: Jan

TIME SAVERS!

Answers on Transparency
Use the Grammar Exercises Answers on Transparencies for Chapter 14 to have students correct their own or one another's exercises.

On-Line Exercise Bank
Have students complete the exercises on computer. The Auto Check feature will grade their work for you!

14.2

Using Personal Pronouns

The pronouns used most often are *personal pronouns.*

KEY CONCEPT **Personal pronouns** refer to (1) the person speaking, (2) the person spoken to, or (3) the person, place, or thing spoken about. ■

PERSONAL PRONOUNS	
I, me, my, mine	we, us, our, ours
you, your, yours	you, your, yours
he, him, his she, her, hers it, its	they, them, their, theirs

First-person pronouns, such as *I, my, we,* and *our,* are used by the person or people speaking to refer to himself, herself, or themselves.

EXAMPLE: *I* waited for *my* computer to boot up.

Second-person pronouns, such as *you* and *your,* are used to speak directly to another person or to other people.

EXAMPLE: Sheila, *you* left *your* computer on.

Third-person pronouns have many forms. There are separate masculine pronouns *(he, him, his)* and feminine pronouns *(she, her, hers)* for people and neuter pronouns *(it, its)* for things. Third-person pronouns refer to someone or something that may not even be present.

EXAMPLE: I haven't seen my grandfather in a year. *He* will arrive from Florida tomorrow.

Exercise 14 **Supplying Personal Pronouns** Copy the sentences below, filling the blanks with an appropriate pronoun. Then, identify each pronoun's antecedent. If a pronoun has no antecedent, write *none.*

1. Most computer users have accessed the Internet through ___?___ service providers.
2. Karen, ___?___ service provider is one of many.
3. Mark got ___?___ service through AmeriServe; ___?___ also provides Internet access.
4. ___?___ used Local Serve Network at one time. ___?___ was another Internet provider.
5. Jan just installed a Local Area Network (LAN) on ___?___ computer system.

More Practice

Grammar Exercise Workbook
• pp. 7–8
On-line Exercise Bank
• Section 14.2
Go on-line:
PHSchool.com
Enter Web Code:
eck-8002

Using Demonstrative Pronouns

Demonstrative pronouns are pointers.

KEY CONCEPT A **demonstrative pronoun** points out a specific person, place, or thing. ■

There are four demonstrative pronouns:

DEMONSTRATIVE PRONOUNS			
Singular		Plural	
this	that	these	those

A demonstrative pronoun can come before or after its antecedent.

EXAMPLES: *This* is the book I chose.
Those are my new friends.
Of all my stamps, *these* are the most valuable.
We stopped in Bad Neustadt and Salz. *These* are the towns where our ancestors lived.

Exercise 15 **Recognizing Demonstrative Pronouns** For the numbered items below, write each demonstrative pronoun, and give its antecedent.

EXAMPLE: That is not the network I would have chosen.
ANSWER: That (network)

1. Our home computer has a large memory. This helps it operate faster.
2. Today's computers have developed rapidly since the 1970's. These represent the latest technology.
3. We can use computers for graphic design. That is some people's favorite use of the computer.
4. One can also send electronic mail; most people call this *e-mail.*
5. My mom made her airline reservations on our computer. That is something my grandmother could never do.

▼ Critical Viewing
Use two demonstrative pronouns in a sentence to describe what the man in the photograph is doing. **[Infer]**

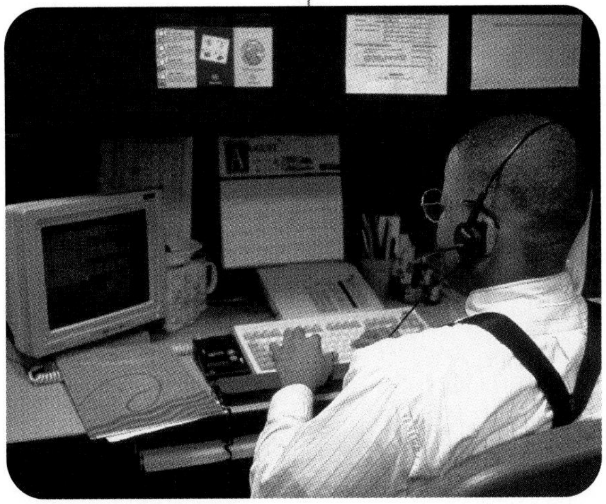

Step-by-Step Teaching Guide

Using Demonstrative Pronouns

1. *These* is the plural of *this,* and *those* is the plural of *that.* Make sure students understand the difference between *this/these* and *that/those. This* connotes a closeness in space between the speaker and the person or thing referred to. *That* suggests a physical distance.

   I'll take this side of the room where we are standing; you look on that side over there.

   The speaker refers to the physically nearer side as *this* and the distant one as *that.*
2. Have students think of *this* as meaning "here" and *that* as meaning "there." Explain that the expressions *this here* and *that there* are redundant because each pronoun already carries the suggestion of here or there.

Answer Key

Exercise 15

1. This—memory
2. These—computers
3. That—graphic design
4. this—electronic mail
5. That—made her airline reservations on our computer

Critical Viewing

Infer Possible answers: This man is typing on a keyboard. Those are headphones on his head.

ONGOING ASSESSMENT: Monitor and Reinforce

If students miss more than two items in Exercises 13–14, refer them to the following for additional practice.

In the Textbook	Print	Technology
Section Review, Ex. 19–20, p. 323	Grammar Exercise Workbook, pp. 7–8	On-Line Exercise Bank, Section 14.2

Step-by-Step Teaching Guide

Using Relative Pronouns

1. Explain the difference in meaning among the relative pronouns. *Who, whom,* and *whose* are used only to refer to people. *That* and *which* can refer to people, places, or things.
2. *Whom* is an object pronoun, whereas *who* is a subject pronoun. *Whom* is always used to replace a direct or indirect object; *who* is used to replace a subject. Use the examples in the chart on this page to demonstrate this.

Answer Key

Exercise 16

1. that
2. who
3. who
4. which
5. whose

14.2

Using Relative Pronouns

Relative pronouns are connecting words.

KEY CONCEPT A **relative pronoun** begins a subordinate clause and connects it to another idea in the same sentence. ■

There are five relative pronouns:

RELATIVE PRONOUNS				
that	which	who	whom	whose

The following chart gives examples of relative pronouns connecting subordinate clauses to independent clauses. (See Section 20.2 for more information about relative pronouns and clauses.)

Independent Clauses	Subordinate Clauses
Here is the book	that Betsy lost.
Dino bought our old house,	which needs many repairs.
She is a singer	who has an unusual range.
Is this the man	whom you saw earlier today?
She is the one	whose house has a fire alarm.

Exercise 16 **Supplying Relative Pronouns** On your paper, write the appropriate relative pronoun for each sentence below.

EXAMPLE: Anyone __?__ can type can use a computer.
ANSWER: who

1. Communication technology is one thing __?__ is continually changing.
2. It has influenced everyone __?__ needs to communicate with someone else.
3. All societies have had people __?__ tried to improve communication.
4. Writing, __?__ was one of the first forms of communication technology, paved the way for many other developments.
5. The last century saw many people __?__ lives changed after the invention of radio and television.

More Practice

Grammar Exercise Workbook
- pp. 9–10

On-line Exercise Bank
- Section 14.2

Go on-line:
PHSchool.com
Enter Web Code:
eck-8002

iText

Get instant feedback! Exercise 16 is available on-line or on CD-ROM.

TIME SAVERS!

Answers on Transparency Use the Grammar Exercises Answers on Transparencies for Chapter 14 to have students correct their own or one another's exercises.

On-Line Exercise Bank Have students complete the exercises on computer. The Auto Check feature will grade their work for you!

Using Interrogative Pronouns

Some relative pronouns can also be used as *interrogative pronouns.*

KEY CONCEPT An **interrogative pronoun** is used to begin a question. ■

INTERROGATIVE PRONOUNS				
what	which	who	whom	whose

GRAMMAR IN LITERATURE

from E-Mail From Bill Gates

John Seabrook

In this excerpt from a letter to Bill Gates, John Seabrook has used two relative pronouns (blue italics). He has also used one interrogative pronoun (red italics).

Dear Bill,

I am the guy *who* is writing the article about you for the New Yorker. It occurs to me that we ought to be able to do some of the work through e-mail. *Which* raises this fascinating question—*What* kind of understanding of another person can e-mail give you? . . .

Exercise 17 **Recognizing Interrogative Pronouns** Write the interrogative pronoun in each of the following sentences.

1. What did the first computer look like?
2. Do you know which of these software programs you use most often?
3. He asked, "Who is the computer expert here?"
4. To whom did you speak about your computer?
5. Who knows the best kind of computer for word processing?
6. Who can help me purchase a computer?
7. One computer is making a strange sound. Whose is it?
8. What happened? Which one is making the noise?
9. Of these keys, which one will make it stop?
10. What did I do wrong?

Step-by-Step Teaching Guide

Using Interrogative Pronouns

1. *Which* is used to select one or more items from a specific set of items.

   Which is the shortest route to the library—Elm Avenue, Main Street, or Park Drive?

   Sentence 9 in Exercise 17 is a good example of this type of sentence.
2. *What* is used when there are an infinite number or answers, or the possible answers are unknown. Sentence 10 below is an example.

Step-by-Step Teaching Guide

Grammar in Literature

1. Have a volunteer read aloud the excerpt from "E-Mail From Bill Gates."
2. Ask students to identify the other pronouns in the paragraph and tell the antecedents. (I—John Seabrook; *you*—Bill Gates; it—none; *me*—John; *we*—Bill and John; some—work; this—question; another—person; *you*—anyone, someone, people who use e-mail)

Answer Key

Exercise 17

1. What
2. which
3. Who
4. whom
5. Who
6. Who
7. Whose
8. What, Which
9. which
10. What

ONGOING ASSESSMENT: Monitor and Reinforce

If students miss more than two items in Exercises 15–18, refer them to the following for additional practice.

In the Textbook	Print Resources	Technology
Section Review, Ex. 21–22, p. 323	Grammar Exercise Workbook, pp. 9–12	On-Line Exercise Bank, Section 14.2

Step-by-Step Teaching Guide

Using Indefinite Pronouns

1. Indefinite pronouns are so called because they do not refer to specific numbers of people.
2. Point out the pronoun *one* and the compound pronouns that end in *-one* or *-body.* These pronouns, even when they stand for a group of people, always take singular verbs. This is because by themselves, the words *one* and *body* are singular.

Answer Key

Exercise 18

1. Everyone
2. Many
3. Some
4. everyone
5. Others

PRENTICE HALL
Everyday Spelling

If you have taught the spelling skills in *Prentice Hall Everyday Spelling,* Grade 8, Chapter 16, in conjunction with this *Writing and Grammar* chapter, review and assess students' mastery of the skills before concluding the chapter.

14.2

Using Indefinite Pronouns

You should learn to recognize one other kind of pronoun—the *indefinite pronoun.*

KEY CONCEPT **Indefinite pronouns** refer to people, places, or things, often without specifying which ones. ■

Notice that a few indefinite pronouns can be either singular or plural, depending upon their use in the sentence.

INDEFINITE PRONOUNS

Singular		Plural	Singular or Plural
another	much	both	all
anybody	neither	few	any
anyone	nobody	many	more
anything	no one	others	most
each	nothing	several	none
either	one		some
everybody	other		
everyone	somebody		
everything	someone		
little	something		

WITHOUT ANTECEDENTS: *Anyone* can learn to operate a computer.

WITH ANTECEDENTS: *All* of the students learned to operate a computer.

Exercise 18 **Recognizing Indefinite Pronouns** Write the indefinite pronoun(s) in the sentences below.

EXAMPLE: Only a few of my relatives have ever used a computer.
ANSWER: few

1. Everyone agrees that new technologies provide new opportunities.
2. Many do their banking, shopping, and research at home on their computers.
3. Some believe this is a much more convenient way to conduct their business.
4. Almost everyone uses a credit card made available through technology.
5. Others go to the grocery store, where technology—a scanner—will tally their purchases.

iText

Get instant feedback! Exercise 18 is available on-line or on CD-ROM.

More Practice

Grammar Exercise Workbook
• pp. 11–12
On-line Exercise Bank
• Section 14.2
Go on-line:
PHSchool.com
Enter Web Code:
eck-8002

TIME SAVERS!

Answers on Transparency Use the Grammar Exercises Answers on Transparencies for Chapter 14 to have students correct their own or one another's exercises.

On-Line Exercise Bank Have students complete the exercises on computer. The Auto Check feature will grade their work for you!

ONGOING ASSESSMENT: Assess Mastery

Use the following resources to assess student mastery of nouns and pronouns.

In the Textbook	Print Resources	Technology
Chapter Review, Ex. 26–34, pp. 324–325 Standardized Test Preparation Workshop, pp. 326–327	Formal Assessment, Ch. 14	Writing and Grammar iText, Ch. 14, Chapter Review; On-Line Exercise Bank, Sections 14.1–2

Section 14.2 **Section Review**

GRAMMAR EXERCISES 19–25

Exercise 19 Recognizing Antecedents On your paper, write the antecedent for each underlined pronoun.

1. Electronic communication is continually expanding. We use it daily.
2. Humans have a complex system of language. It is sometimes confusing.
3. We use language every day because it conveys our ideas and emotions.
4. Individuals as well as entire cultures have their own unique languages.
5. The Latin language, for instance, is no longer spoken, but it is still written.

Exercise 20 Identifying Personal Pronouns Identify the personal pronoun(s) in each of the following sentences.

1. Not only do languages have a spoken form, they also have a written form.
2. Our teacher told us that the oldest written languages are more than 5,000 years old.
3. She also said that they began in the form of drawings.
4. The earliest pictures, she told us, were found in France.
5. I know the drawings represented the lives of people and what was happening to them at that time.

Exercise 21 Recognizing Personal, Demonstrative, Relative, Indefinite, and Interrogative Pronouns Write the personal, demonstrative, relative, indefinite, and interrogative pronouns in the following sentences. Label each type.

1. Those paintings in France are more than 30,000 years old.
2. These are the symbols representing words.
3. The person to whom you are speaking may be a good listener.
4. He or she is the one who is on the other side of this conversation.
5. There were two people. To which one were you speaking?

Exercise 22 Supplying Indefinite Pronouns On your paper, write an appropriate indefinite pronoun to fill in each blank.

1. Were it not for __?__ discovering electricity, much of today's communication might never have taken place.
2. __?__ of the most revolutionary devices was the telegraph.
3. Before 1861, __?__ expected to send signals of any kind across the country.
4. After 1861, __?__ saw telegraph lines constructed along railway lines.
5. Not __?__ thinks about the telegraph anymore, but at one time it seemed like a miracle to __?__.

Exercise 23 Find It in Your Reading Reread a favorite short story or poem. Identify at least five personal or indefinite pronouns.

Exercise 24 Find It in Your Writing Look through your portfolio. Find an example of a demonstrative, relative, or interrogative pronoun.

Exercise 25 Writing Application Write a dialogue in which two people discuss their friends. Use pronouns in the conversation, and underline each one.

ASSESS and CLOSE

Section Review

Each of these exercises correlates to a concept in the section on pronouns, pages 316–322. The exercises may be used for more practice, for reteaching, or for review of the Key Concepts presented. Answers for all chapter exercisers are available in *Grammar Exercises Answers on Transparencies* in your Teaching Resources.

Answer Key

Exercise 19

1. communication
2. system
3. language
4. Individuals
5. language

Exercise 20

1. they
2. Our; us
3. She, they
4. she, us
5. I, them

Exercise 21

1. Those—demonstrative
2. These—demonstrative
3. Whom—relative; you—personal
4. He, she—personal; one—indefinite; who—relative; this—demonstrative
5. which—interrogative; one—indefinite; you—personal

Exercise 22

Answers will vary. Samples are given.

1. someone
2. One
3. no one
4. everyone
5. everybody, all

Exercise 23

Find It in Your Reading
Have students read some of their examples aloud. Listeners can identify each pronoun by type.

Exercise 24

Find It in Your Writing
Have students find at least one example of each type of pronoun.

Exercise 25

Writing Application
Students may want to work with partners to write their dialogues.

CHAPTER REVIEW

Each of these exercises correlates to a concept in the chapter on nouns and pronouns, pages 308–322. The exercises may be used for more practice, for reteaching, or for review of the Key Concepts presented. Answers for all chapter exercises are available in *Grammar Exercises Answers on Transparencies* in your Teaching Resources.

Answer Key

Exercise 26

1. World Wide Web, P; network, C; popularity, C; 1990's, C
2. information, C; Web, P; computers, C; world, C
3. capabilities, C; people, C; information, C; products, C; research, C; services, C
4. world, C; access, C; Web, P; information, C
5. subscriber, C; information, C; way, C

Exercise 27

The (World Wide Web) is a link between two types of computers. The computer-based (network) uses codes for communications between the computers. A <u>group</u> may place its informational material on the Web so others can use it. A <u>class</u> of students can use the Web to connect to a library or museum. A (football) <u>team</u> can find new plays on the Web.

Exercise 28

1. When John wants to access the Web, <u>he</u> uses <u>his</u> browser. (arrow from *he* to *John;* arrow from *his* to *John*)
2. Sometimes, connecting can be difficult for <u>him</u>; <u>it</u> may take a few attempts. (arrow from *him* to *John* in sentence 1; arrow from *it* to *connecting*)
3. Susan has dial-up access on <u>her</u> computer, so <u>she</u> connects through a modem. (arrow from *her* to *Susan;* arrow from *she* to *Susan*)
4. A modem is simple hardware; <u>it</u> sends information over telephone lines. (arrow from *it* to *modem*)
5. John said that almost any computer of <u>his</u> can connect to the Web. (arrow from *his* to *John*)

Chapter 14 Chapter Review

GRAMMAR EXERCISES 26–34

Exercise 26 Distinguishing Between Common and Proper Nouns Identify the nouns in each of the following sentences. Place a *C* after each common noun and a *P* after each proper noun.

1. The World Wide Web is an electronic communication network that first gained popularity in the 1990's.
2. The information found on the Web is spread among computers all around the world.
3. Due to its capabilities, people can give information about their products, research, or services.
4. Anyone in the world with access to the Web can view most of the information available.
5. Are you a subscriber who receives information in this way?

Exercise 27 Recognizing Collective and Compound Nouns Copy the paragraph below onto your paper. Underline each collective noun, and circle each compound noun.

The World Wide Web is a link between two types of computers. The computer-based network uses codes for communications between the computers. A group may place its informational material on the Web so others can use it. A class of students can use the Web to connect to a library or museum. A football team can find new plays on the Web.

Exercise 28 Recognizing Personal Pronouns and Their Antecedents Copy these sentences onto your paper. Draw a line under each personal pronoun, and draw an arrow to its antecedent.

1. When John wants to access the Web, he uses his browser.
2. Sometimes, connecting can be difficult for him; it may take a few attempts.
3. Susan has dial-up access on her computer, so she connects through a modem.
4. A modem is simple hardware; it sends information over telephone lines.
5. John said that almost any computer of his can connect to the Web.

Exercise 29 Supplying Personal Pronouns On your paper, write the personal pronoun that best completes the sentence.

1. I was delighted when __?__ best friend finally got on-line.
2. For months after we moved, she would write __?__ letters and __?__ wouldn't respond.
3. Then, __?__ decided to join the computer age.
4. Now, when __?__ writes me, __?__ respond immediately.
5. The computer age has saved __?__ relationship!

Exercise 30 Distinguishing Between Demonstrative and Relative Pronouns On your paper, write the demonstrative or relative pronoun in each sentence. Write *D* after each demonstrative pronoun and *R* after each relative pronoun.

Exercise 29

1. my
2. me, I
3. she
4. she, I
5. our

Exercise 30

1. that, R
2. that, D
3. that, R
4. who, R
5. whose, R

1. Interest in the Web concept has led historians to observe that it was developed by Timothy Berners-Lee, a British physicist.
2. He began working on it in the 1980's, but that was well before he gained recognition in 1989.
3. The technology of the World Wide Web is something that is continually being improved.
4. The scientists who have worked on the Web foresee continual change in several areas.
5. Developments will continue to help users of the Web, whose desire for access to libraries will grow.

Exercise 31 **Identifying Nouns and Pronouns** Read the paragraph below and make lists of the following: *common nouns, proper nouns, collective nouns, compound nouns, interrogative pronouns, indefinite pronouns, personal pronouns, demonstrative pronouns*, and *relative pronouns.*

Decades ago, no one could have imagined how communication technology would grow. Every day someone is envisioning possibilities for faster, more efficient communications. Who are these experts who are transforming our lives? Actually, many so-called experts are people who developed their skills on their own. Anyone can improve his or her computer knowledge through practice. Many wonder what technologies will emerge, but who can accurately foresee new developments?

Exercise 32 **Writing Sentences With Nouns and Pronouns** Write a sentence for each of the numbered items below, using the specified word in the manner indicated.

1. Use *that* as a relative pronoun.
2. Use *what* as an interrogative pronoun.
3. Use *few* as an indefinite pronoun.
4. Use *which* as an interrogative pronoun.
5. Use *anybody* as an indefinite pronoun.
6. a proper noun that names a person
7. a separate compound noun
8. a collective proper noun
9. a noun that names an idea
10. a hyphenated compound noun

Exercise 33 **Revision Practice: Replacing Nouns** Rewrite the following sentences, replacing the underlined words with proper nouns. If a noun is repeated in a sentence, replace it with a pronoun. You may have to make other adjustments to the sentences.

1. Martha makes telephone calls from Martha's desk in Martha's office.
2. A city is the home of a famous museum.
3. Ralph and I worked on Ralph and my report on a famous inventor.
4. The baseball team from the largest city in the United States won the World Series in 1999.
5. Were there telephones and computers at the time that the author wrote the author's famous book *The Adventures of Tom Sawyer?*

Exercise 34 **Writing Application** Write ten sentences about a form of communication you use frequently. Include at least ten nouns, four of which are proper nouns. In addition, use at least five pronouns. Underline all of the nouns in your sentences, and circle all of the pronouns.

EXAMPLE: (I) love to talk on the phone with (my) friend Stephanie. (We) can talk for hours.

Exercise 31

Common nouns: Decades, technology, day, possibilities, communications, experts, lives, experts, people, skills, knowledge, practice, technologies, developments

Proper nouns: none

Collective nouns: none

Compound nouns: none

Demonstrative pronouns: these

Interrogative pronouns: Who, who

Indefinite pronouns: no one, someone, many, Anyone, Many

Personal pronouns: our, their, their, his, her

Relative pronouns: who, who, what

Exercise 32

Answers will vary.

Exercise 33

Answers may vary.

1. Martha makes telephone calls from her desk in her office.
2. Chicago is the home of the Chicago Art Institute.
3. Ralph and I worked on our report on Thomas Alva Edison.
4. The New York Yankees won the World Series in 1999.
5. Were there telephones and computers at the time that Mark Twain wrote his famous book *The Adventures of Tom Sawyer*?

Exercise 34

Writing Application
Encourage students to read their sentences aloud to the class.

TIME SAVERS!

Answers on Transparency Use the Grammar Exercises Answers on Transparencies for Chapter 14 to have students correct their own or one another's exercises.

On-Line Exercise Bank Have students complete the exercises on computer. The Auto Check feature will grade their work for you!

Lesson Objectives
- To complete analogies.

Step-by-Step Teaching Guide

Completing Analogies

Teaching Resources: Standardized Test Preparation Workbook, pp. 27–28

1. Go over the sample problems with the whole class. You might have students cover up the answers and solve the analogies. If several students choose the same wrong answers, spend more time on this concept.
2. If one of the words in an analogy is new to students, they can try to decide its meaning by looking at the word's roots, prefix, and/or suffix, or by thinking about other words they know that look like the new word. For instance, *technique* looks like the words *technical* and *technology.*
3. Give students five minutes to complete the practice exercises. In real test situations, it is unwise for students to spend many minutes on a question they cannot answer. They need to answer the questions they know, then go back to the questions that puzzled them in whatever time is left.

Standardized Test Preparation Workshop

Completing Analogies

An analogy expresses a comparison between two pairs of words. The relationship between the words in the first pair is similar to the relationship between the words in the second pair. Analogy questions can test the relationships of synonyms, words with the same meaning. For example, *energy is to power as calmness is to tranquillity.* Or they may express a definitional relationship, in which one noun defines a characteristic of the other noun. For example, *storm is to violence as wedding is to happiness.*

Most standardized tests set up analogies in similar ways. The following two test items will give you practice in responding to analogies. Two different formats are used to show you the two most common ways these items appear on tests.

Test Tips

- Determine whether the original pair are synonyms or have a definitional relationship. Then, choose a pair with the closest relationship to the original.
- Use the parts of speech as a clue. If the original pair consists of two nouns, make sure your answer choice does also.

Sample Test Items	Answers and Explanations
Complete each item by choosing the word that best completes the sentence. Technique is to method as (A) problem is to cause. (B) power is to ruler. (C) puzzle is to mystery. (D) question is to answer. (E) solution is to answer.	The correct answer is E. The nouns *technique* and *method* are synonyms that name ways of solving a problem. The nouns *solution* and *answer* are also synonyms, both naming the result of problem-solving.
Each question below consists of a related pair of words, followed by five pairs of words labeled A through E. Select the pair that best expresses a relationship similar to that expressed in the original pair. ADVENTURE : EXCITEMENT :: (A) accomplishment : feat (B) foot : shoe (C) achievement : challenge (D) confusion : calmness (E) disaster : mishap	The correct answer is C. The noun *excitement* defines a characteristic of the noun *adventure,* just as the noun *challenge* defines a characteristic of the noun *achievement.* The words in answer choices *A* and *E* express relationships of synonyms, or words that share the same meanings. Answer choices *B* and *D* express other types of relationships.

TEST-TAKING TIP

If students are not sure of the relation of the first pair of words, they can begin by eliminating answer choices that they know are wrong. If the first words are similar in some unknown way, answer choices that are antonyms are obviously incorrect. Cross them out and examine the choices that remain.

Practice 1 **Directions:** Each question below consists of a related pair of words or phrases, followed by five pairs of words or phrases labeled A through E. Select the pair that best expresses a relationship similar to that expressed in the original pair.

1 GIFT : PRESENT ::
(A) children : playfulness
(B) guitar : instrument
(C) celebration : party
(D) winner : contest
(E) tree : growth

2 TOY : FUN ::
(A) storm : hurricane
(B) phone : communication
(C) movie : viewer
(D) computer : screen
(E) house : building

3 HURRICANE : WIND ::
(A) jungle : denseness
(B) forest : trees
(C) dryness : dampness
(D) beach : ocean
(E) house : windows

4 SKYSCRAPER : HEIGHT ::
(A) car : gas
(B) office : privacy
(C) library : books
(D) bullet train : speed
(E) team : winners

5 EXPLANATION : DEFINITION ::
(A) example : meaning
(B) wealth : poverty
(C) popularity : loneliness
(D) confusion : chaos
(E) confidence : courage

Practice 2 **Directions:** Complete each item by choosing the word that best completes the sentence.

6 Winner is to luck as
(A) astronaut is to space.
(B) teacher is to learning.
(C) player is to games.
(D) celebrity is to media.
(E) athlete is to skill.

7 Proclamation is to declaration as
(A) sorrow is to happiness.
(B) a yell is to a whisper.
(C) privacy is to publicity.
(D) announcement is to invitation.
(E) conflict is to problem.

8 Hoax is to trick as
(A) automobile is to car.
(B) angry is to annoyance.
(C) deceit is to honesty.
(D) refusal is to acceptance.
(E) road is to sidewalk.

9 Transportation is to motion as
(A) store is to purchases.
(B) speech is to words.
(C) airplane is to sky.
(D) garage is to car.
(E) lumber is to wood.

10 Exhaustion is to tiredness as
(A) sickness is to health.
(B) eagerness is to laziness.
(C) illness is to disease.
(D) adventure is to fun.
(E) laughter is to clown.

Answer Key

Practice 1

1. C—synonyms
2. B—the first word names a means to achieving the result named by the second.
3. B—The first word names a part of the thing named by the second.
4. D—the second word describes a quality of the thing named by the first
5. D—Synonyms

Practice 2

6. E—The second word names the quality that defines the first word.
7. E—the words are synonyms
8. A—the words are synonyms
9. B—the first word names something that utilizes the thing named by the second
10. C—the words are synonyms

Chapter 15

Time and Resource Manager

In-Depth Lesson Plan

	LESSON FOCUS	PRINT AND MEDIA RESOURCES
DAY 1	**Action Verbs** Students learn to identify action verbs and to distinguish between transitive and intransitive verbs (pp. 330–333).	**Teaching Resources** *Grammar Exercise Workbook,* pp. 13–16; *Grammar Exercises Answers on Transparencies,* Ch. 15 **_Writing and Grammar iText_ (Interactive Text),** Section 15.1; ***On-line Exercise Bank,*** Section 15.1
DAY 2	**Linking Verbs** Students learn to identify linking verbs, including forms of the irregular linking verb *be*, and to distinguish between linking verbs and action verbs (pp. 334–337).	**Teaching Resources** *Grammar Exercise Workbook,* pp. 17–20; *Grammar Exercises Answers on Transparencies,* Ch. 15 **_Writing and Grammar iText_ (Interactive Text),** Section 15.2; ***On-line Exercise Bank,*** Section 15.2
DAY 3	**Helping Verbs and Verb Phrases** Students learn to identify and use helping verbs and verb phrases, and they complete the Hands-on Grammar activity (pp. 338–341).	**Teaching Resources** *Grammar Exercise Workbook,* pp. 21–22; *Grammar Exercises Answers on Transparencies,* Ch. 15; *Hands-on Grammar Activity Book,* Ch. 15 **_Writing and Grammar iText_ (Interactive Text),** Section 15.3; ***On-line Exercise Bank,*** Section 15.3
DAY 4	**Review and Assess** Students review the chapter and demonstrate mastery of verbs (pp. 342–345).	**Teaching Resources** *Formal Assessment,* Ch. 15; *Grammar Exercises Answers on Transparencies,* Ch. 15 **_Writing and Grammar iText_ (Interactive Text),** Ch. 15, Chapter Review

Accelerated Lesson Plan

	LESSON FOCUS	PRINT AND MEDIA RESOURCES
DAY 1	**Action Verbs and Linking Verbs** Students learn to distinguish between action verbs and linking verbs (pp. 330–337).	**Teaching Resources** *Grammar Exercise Workbook,* pp. 13–20; *Grammar Exercises Answers on Transparencies,* Ch. 15 **_Writing and Grammar iText_ (Interactive Text),** Section 15.1–2; ***On-line Exercise Bank,*** Sections 15.1–2
DAY 2	**Helping Verbs and Verb Phrases** Students learn to identify and use helping verbs and verb phrases (pp. 338–341).	**Teaching Resources** *Grammar Exercise Workbook,* pp. 21–22; *Grammar Exercises Answers on Transparencies,* Ch. 15; *Hands-on Grammar Activity Book,* Ch. 15 **_Writing and Grammar iText_ (Interactive Text),** Section 15.3; ***On-line Exercise Bank,*** Section 15.3
DAY 3	**Review and Assess** Students review the chapter and demonstrate mastery of verbs (pp. 342–345).	**Teaching Resources** *Formal Assessment,* Ch. 15; *Grammar Exercises Answers on Transparencies,* Ch. 15 **_Writing and Grammar iText_ (Interactive Text),** Ch. 15, Chapter Review

Options for Adapting Lesson Plans

HOMEWORK

Have students complete any stage of the lesson for homework.

SPELLING

To teach spelling skills in conjunction with grammar, mechanics, and usage, work through *Prentice Hall Everyday Spelling,* Grade 8, Chapter 17, as you cover this *Writing and Grammar* chapter.

TECHNOLOGY

Students can use *Writing and Grammar iText* to complete the exercises interactively on computer. They can complete additional exercises in the *On-line Exercise Bank:* The Auto Check feature will grade their work. Go online: PHSchool.com Use Web code: eck-8002

FEATURES

Extend coverage with the Grammar in Literature feature (p. 336) and the Standardized Test Preparation Workshop (p. 344).

INTEGRATED SKILLS COVERAGE

Grammar in Literature
SE p. 336

Reading
Find It in Your Reading, SE pp. 333, 337, 340, 341

Writing
Find It in Your Writing, SE pp. 333, 337, 340, 341
Writing Application, SE pp. 333, 337, 341, 343

Viewing and Representing
Critical Viewing, SE pp. 328, 331, 332, 336

Workplace Skills
Action Verbs, ATE p. 331

BLOCK SCHEDULING

Pacing Suggestions
For 90-minute Blocks
- Administer the Diagnostic Test to students to determine instructional coverage.
- Have students complete the necessary exercises in class. Use the Hands-on Grammar Activity to provide a change of pace.

Resources for Varying Instruction
- ***Writing and Grammar iText* (Interactive Text)** A 90-minute block provides an ideal opportunity for students to work on computer.

Professional Development Support
- ***How to Manage Instruction in the Block*** This teaching resource provides management and activity suggestions.

ASSESSMENT SUPPORT

Standardized Test Preparation Workshop SE pp. 344–345; ATE pp. 335, 339

Standardized Test Preparation Workbook, pp. 29–30

Formal Assessment, Ch. 15

MEDIA AND TECHNOLOGY

For the Student
- ***Writing and Grammar iText* (Interactive Text),** Ch. 15
- ***On-line Exercise Bank,*** Sections 15.1–3

For the Teacher
- ***Resource Pro* CD-ROM**

MEETING INDIVIDUAL NEEDS

ESL Students ATE p. 339

WRITING AND GRAMMAR ON-LINE

iText Interactive Text (On-line or on CD-ROM)
- Easily navigable instruction with on-line supporting resources
- Self-scoring exercises and diagnostic tests

Companion Web Site PHSchool.com
- On-line Exercise Bank (use Web Code eck-8002)

See the Go On-line! feature, SE p. iii.

LITERATURE CONNECTIONS

Grammar in Literature selection from *Prentice Hall Literature: Timeless Voices, Timeless Themes,* Silver: from *Harriet Tubman: Conductor of the Underground Railroad,* Ann Petry, p. 336

CHAPTER 15
VERBS

Lesson Objectives

1. To identify action verbs.
2. To identify transitive and intransitive verbs.
3. To identify forms of the verb be as linking verbs and other linking verbs.
4. To distinguish between action verbs and linking verbs.
5. To identify helping verbs as part of a verb phrase.
6. To recognize forms of the verb *be* and other helping verbs.
7. To recognize verb phrases.
8. To employ standard English usage in writing.

Critical Viewing

Analyze Students may say *wait, march, organize, stand,* and *talk.*

Chapter 15 Verbs

▲ **Critical Viewing** This illustration shows a group of newly freed slaves, along with Union soldiers, during the Civil War. What verbs would you use to describe the action in this image? **[Analyze]**

Verbs are a necessary part of every sentence—they indicate whether events are taking place in the present, past, or future. Verbs do more than just tell time, however. Some verbs express action. Actions can be dramatic, or they can be subtle. Other verbs provide a link between two parts of a sentence. Still others simply point out that something exists.

This chapter will describe the two main kinds of verbs—*action verbs* and *linking verbs*—and will show you how these verbs can be used with another kind of verb—*helping verbs.*

ONGOING ASSESSMENT: Diagnose

If students miss more than one item in each category, direct them to the relevant pages of the text and assign exercises for practice and review.

Verbs	Diagnostic Test Items	Teach	Practice	Section Review	Chapter Review
Skill Check A					
Transitive and Intransitive Verbs	A 1–5	pp. 331–332	Ex. 3–4, 8	Ex. 6–8	Ex. 32, 37
Skill Check B					
Linking Verbs	B 6–10	pp. 334–335	Ex. 12–15	Ex. 16–17	Ex. 33–34

Diagnostic Test

Directions: Write all answers on a separate sheet of paper.

Skill Check A. Write the verb or verb phrase that appears in each sentence below, and label it *transitive* or *intransitive.*

1. In 1861, the Northern states (the Union) and the Southern states (the Confederacy) prepared themselves for a civil war.
2. This "War for Southern Independence" lasted more than four years.
3. The Civil War left devastating effects on America.
4. The war took more than 600,000 lives.
5. The war eliminated the possibility of secession from the Union by the Southern states.

Skill Check B. Write the following sentences. Underline the linking verb in each, and draw a double-headed arrow connecting the words linked by the verb.

6. Slavery was a major issue leading to the Civil War.
7. Slavery had been illegal in the North.
8. However, in the South, slave labor was an important part of the economy.
9. Slavery in newly acquired western lands also became an issue between the North and South.
10. It would be a bloody four-year war.

Skill Check C. Write the verb(s) or verb phrase(s) from each sentence below, and label each one *action* or *linking.*

11. Each side—North and South—grew increasingly hostile.
12. Disagreement over the various issues grew into full-fledged war.
13. To the South, the election of Abraham Lincoln in 1860 seemed a threat.
14. To many in the South, President-elect Lincoln appeared unsympathetic to their interests.
15. As war seemed likely, both the North and the South looked for ways to win.

Skill Check D. Write the complete verb phrase in each sentence below, and underline the helping verbs within each phrase.

16. Before 1862, the Civil War might have been considered only a series of minor skirmishes.
17. However, battles were becoming bloodier and more frequent.
18. By the height of the war, military actions had been occurring almost daily.
19. For instance, on October 3 and 4 of 1862, the South was fighting in Corinth, Mississippi.
20. The next day, a thirty-minute battle was fought at La Vergen, Tennessee.

Answer Key

Diagnostic Test

Each item in the Diagnostic Test corresponds to a specific concept in the chapter on verbs. This will enable you to tailor instruction to the particular needs of your students. See "Ongoing Assessment: Diagnose" below for further details.

Skill Check A

1. prepared—transitive
2. lasted—intransitive
3. left—transitive
4. took—transitive
5. eliminated—transitive

Skill Check B

6. Slavery <u>was</u> a major issue leading to the Civil War. (arrow between *Slavery* and *issue*)
7. Slavery <u>had been</u> illegal in the North. (arrow between *Slavery* and *illegal*)
8. However, in the South, slave labor <u>was</u> an important part of the economy. (arrow between *labor* and *part*)
9. Slavery in newly acquired western lands also <u>became</u> an issue between the North and South. (arrow between *Slavery* and *issue*)
10. It <u>would be</u> a bloody four-year war. (arrow between *It* and *war*)

Skill Check C

11. grew—linking
12. grew—action
13. seemed—linking
14. appeared—linking
15. seemed—linking; looked—action

Skill Check D

16. <u>might</u> <u>have</u> <u>been</u> considered
17. <u>were</u> becoming
18. <u>had</u> <u>been</u> occurring
19. <u>was</u> fighting
20. <u>was</u> fought

ONGOING ASSESSMENT: Diagnose *continued*

Verbs	Diagnostic Test Items	Teach	Practice	Section Review	Chapter Review
Skill Check C					
Action and Linking Verbs	C 11–15	pp. 330, 336	Ex. 1–2, 15	Ex. 5, 18–19	Ex. 31, 36
Skill Check D					
Helping Verbs and Verb Phrases	D 16–20	pp. 338–340	Ex. 23–24	Ex. 25–27	Ex. 35
Cumulative Reviews and Applications				Ex. 9–11 Ex. 20–22 Ex. 28–30	Ex. 37–39

TIME SAVERS!

Answers on Transparency Use the Grammar Exercise Answers on Transparencies for Chapter 15 to have students correct their own or one another's exercises.

On-Line Exercise Bank Have students complete the exercises on computer. The Auto Check feature will grade their work for you!

PREPARE and ENGAGE

Interest GRABBER Write this sentence on the chalkboard:

The man moved across the field.

Ask students to brainstorm for more descriptive words that could replace *moved.* Point out that *moved* and each word that replaces it are action verbs.

Activate Prior Knowledge

Write the following sentences on the chalkboard and ask students to identify the verbs in each one:

I carried her suitcase. (carried)

We baked cookies last night. (baked)

Lead students to see that these verbs express actions.

TEACH

Step-by-Step Teaching Guide

Action Verbs

1. Review with students the idea that not all action is visible. Ask them if being bored, in itself, is a visible action. While some actions that show boredom—gazing into space, squirming in your seat—are visible, the fact of being bored is a mental, invisible action, just as is thinking or dreaming.
2. Have students work in pairs or small groups to create their own lists of visible and nonvisible actions. Have each group share its list with the class and compile a master list on the board or for a bulletin board display.

Answer Key

Exercise 1

1. study
2. call
3. split
4. thought
5. concerned
6. used
7. believed
8. opposed
9. disagreed
10. debated

Section 15.1

Action Verbs

The following verbs—*see, plan, run, eat, shout, tell,* and *sit*—are used frequently and have one thing in common: They all express *action.*

KEY CONCEPT An **action verb** tells what action someone or something is performing. ■

In the sentence "My father *waited* at the station for the train," the verb *waited* tells what the father did. In the sentence "The swans *float* gracefully on the water," the verb *float* tells what swans do. The performers of the action *(father, swans)* are the subjects of the verbs. You may think of action as something you can see someone or something *do.* Some verbs, such as *hear* and *hope,* express mental actions—actions that cannot be seen.

Theme: The Civil War

In this section, you will learn about action verbs and the difference between transitive and intransitive action verbs. The examples and exercises are about the United States Civil War.

Cross-Curricular Connection: Social Studies

Exercise 1 **Identifying Action Verbs** Identify the action verb in each of the following sentences.

EXAMPLE: Most people consider slavery the chief cause of the Civil War.

ANSWER: consider

1. We study the Civil War in history class.
2. Many call it the War Between the States.
3. Indeed, the war split our nation apart.
4. Some people thought the issues unresolvable.
5. The main issues concerned slavery and the economy.
6. The Southern states used slaves to support their economy.
7. Most Northerners believed slavery to be immoral.
8. Few Northerners, however, strongly opposed slavery.
9. Most of them just disagreed with it.
10. The North and South debated the slavery issue before the war.

More Practice

Grammar Exercise Workbook
- pp. 13–14

On-line Exercise Bank
- Section 15.1

Go on-line: PHSchool.com
Enter Web Code: eck-8002

iText

Get instant feedback! Exercise 1 is available on-line or on CD-ROM.

Exercise 2 **Writing Sentences Using Action Verbs** Write a sentence for each of the following action verbs.

1. examine
2. sprint
3. exploded
4. regretted
5. involve
6. listened
7. convinced
8. charged
9. argue
10. divided

TIME AND RESOURCE MANAGER

Resources
Print: Grammar Exercise Workbook, pp. 13–16
Technology: Writing and Grammar iText, Section 15.1; On-Line Exercise Bank, Section 15.1

In-Depth Coverage	Accelerated Pace
• Work through all key concepts, pp. 330–332. • Assign and review Exercises 1–4.	• Assign pp. 330–332 for independent student review. • Assign Section Review Exercises 5–8, p. 333.

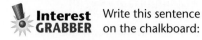

Using Transitive Verbs

Some action verbs are *transitive.*

KEY CONCEPTS An action verb is **transitive** if the receiver of the action is named in the sentence. The receiver of the action is called the **object** of the verb. ■

EXAMPLES: Sandy opened the window with great difficulty.

The truck suddenly hit the pedestrian.

In the first example, *window* receives the action of the verb *opened. Opened* is transitive because the object of the verb—*window*—tells what Sandy opened. In the second example, *hit* is transitive because the object of the verb—*pedestrian*—tells whom the truck hit.

Exercise 3 **Recognizing Transitive Action Verbs** Copy the following sentences. Underline each transitive action verb, and draw an arrow from the verb to its object.

EXAMPLE: The North and the South fought a war.

1. Differing opinions drove the North and South apart.
2. Southerners used slaves to work their extensive cotton plantations.
3. The North developed an industrialized economy that was not dependent on slavery.
4. The South imported most manufactured goods.
5. The South, therefore, opposed high tariffs.
6. The North demanded high tariffs to protect its products from competition.
7. The election of Abraham Lincoln angered the South.
8. Southerners rejected Lincoln's position on slavery.
9. The North supported Lincoln in his fight to end slavery.
10. Such differences finally ignited the Civil War.

▶ **Critical Viewing**
This painting shows escaping enslaved Africans receiving help from abolitionists. Write a brief caption for the painting, using transitive verbs in your sentences. **[Speculate]**

iText

Get instant feedback! Exercise 3 is available on-line or on CD-ROM.

More Practice

Grammar Exercise Workbook
- pp. 15–16

On-line Exercise Bank
- Section 15.1

Go on-line:
PHSchool.com
Enter Web Code:
eck-8002

Step-by-Step Teaching Guide

Using Transitive Verbs

1. A transitive verb directs action toward someone or something named in the same sentence. The word that receives the action is called the *object.*
2. Tell students that they can ask *What?* or *Whom?* of the verb to identify the object of the verb.
3. Write examples on the chalkboard for additional practice:

   All of the kids do chores at home. (Chores answers the question *Do what?*)

   Leo washes the dishes. (Dishes answers *Washes what?*)

Integrating Workplace Skills

Many jobs require communication skills, not only in presenting your ideas but also in persuading fellow workers to act on your ideas. Precise action verbs can be effective in these situations.

Critical Viewing

Speculate Students may say that the abolitionists help the slaves or the slaves risk their lives.

Answer Key

Exercise 2 *(page 330)*

Answers will vary. Samples are given.

1. I should examine the text.
2. She sprints the 400-yard dash.
3. The rocket exploded.
4. The student regretted her decision.
5. The game involves a ball.
6. The student listened to the lectures.
7. I am convinced that I saw him.
8. He charged the dinner on his credit card.
9. They argue over everything.
10. The earth divided where the earthquake hit.

Exercise 3

1. Differing opinions drove the North and South apart. (arrow from *drove* to *North and South*)
2. Southerners used slaves to work their extensive cotton plantations. (arrow from *used* to *slaves*)

continued

Answer Key continued

3. The North developed an industrialized economy that was not dependent on slavery. (arrow from *developed* to *economy*)
4. The South imported most manufactured goods. (arrow from *imported* to *goods*)
5. The South, therefore, opposed high tariffs. (arrow from *opposed* to *tariffs*)
6. The North demanded high tariffs to protect its products from competition. (arrow from *demanded* to *tariffs*)
7. The election of Abraham Lincoln angered the South. (arrow from *angered* to *South*)
8. Southerners rejected Lincoln's position on slavery. (arrow from *rejected* to *position*)
9. The North supported Lincoln in his fight to end slavery. (arrow from *supported* to *Lincoln*)
10. Such differences finally ignited the Civil War. (arrow from *ignited* to *Civil War*)

Step-by-Step Teaching Guide

Using Intransitive Verbs

1. An intransitive verb has no receiver of the action named in the sentence. The best way to determine if a verb is transitive or intransitive is to try to identify an object of the verb.

   Annie slept late. (intransitive)

   Annie ate the cake. (transitive— cake *is the object of the verb* ate*)*

2. Remind students that certain shortcuts can backfire. For instance, students may think that in a short sentence, the verb is intransitive. Yet in *Lou grabbed the hammer,* the four-word sentence has an object *(hammer),* making the verb transitive.

3. Show students the usefulness of being able to identify other parts of speech. In *The bus raced through the traffic light,* it is helpful to recognize that *through the traffic light* is a prepositional phrase and thus cannot be the receiver of the action.

Critical Viewing

Infer Students' responses will vary. Make sure that students have used intransitive verbs.

Answer Key

Exercise 4

The verbs are intransitive because there are no objects in the sentences to receive the action of the verbs.

1. grew
2. fought
3. believed
4. benefited
5. would interfere
6. hoped
7. dominated
8. grew
9. struggled
10. prepared

Using Intransitive Verbs

Some action verbs are *intransitive.*

KEY CONCEPT An action verb is **intransitive** if no receiver of the action is named in the sentence. An intransitive verb does not have an object. ■

EXAMPLES: The war began.
The bus raced through the traffic light.

Exercise 4 **Recognizing Intransitive Action Verbs** On your paper, write the intransitive action verb in each sentence below. Be prepared to explain why the verb is intransitive.

EXAMPLE: Political disagreements mounted between the North and the South.
ANSWER: mounted

1. The North and South grew further apart.
2. The North fought continually for a central government.
3. Northerners believed in government help for citizens.
4. The North's trading and financial interests benefited from a strong central government.
5. A strong central government would also interfere with slavery.
6. Many people hoped for a country built on compromise.
7. Neither the North nor the South dominated in the Senate.
8. The Senate grew with the addition of Alabama in 1819.
9. Other territories struggled over the question of being "free" or "slave."
10. The North and South prepared for war.

More Practice

Grammar Exercise Workbook
- pp. 15–16

On-line Exercise Bank
- Section 15.1

Go on-line: PHSchool.com
Enter Web Code: eck-8002

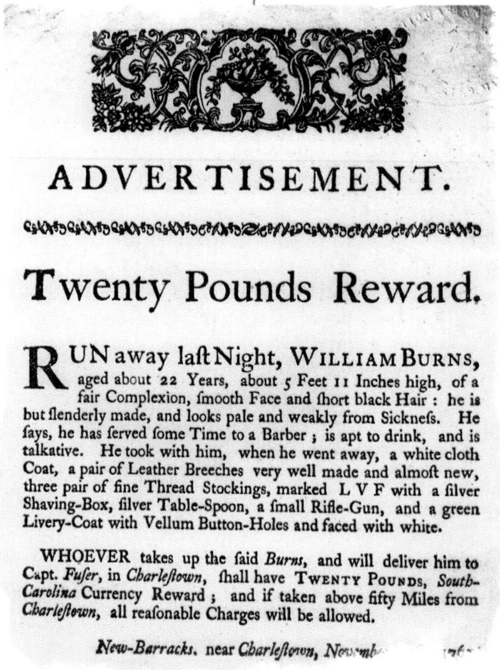

ADVERTISEMENT.

Twenty Pounds Reward.

RUN away laſt Night, WILLIAM BURNS, aged about 22 Years, about 5 Feet 11 Inches high, of a fair Complexion, ſmooth Face and ſhort black Hair : he is but ſlenderly made, and looks pale and weakly from Sickneſs. He ſays, he has ſerved ſome Time to a Barber ; is apt to drink, and is talkative. He took with him, when he went away, a white cloth Coat, a pair of Leather Breeches very well made and almoſt new, three pair of fine Thread Stockings, marked L V F with a ſilver Shaving-Box, ſilver Table-Spoon, a ſmall Rifle-Gun, and a green Livery-Coat with Vellum Button-Holes and faced with white.

WHOEVER takes up the ſaid *Burns,* and will deliver him to Capt. *Fuſer,* in *Charleſtown,* ſhall have TWENTY POUNDS, *South-Carolina* Currency Reward ; and if taken above fifty Miles from *Charleſtown,* all reaſonable Charges will be allowed.

New-Barracks, near *Charleſtown,*

▶ Critical Viewing This "advertisement" offers a reward for the return of a runaway slave. Write your own advertisement, offering a reward for helping the slave to escape. Use sentences with intransitive verbs. **[Infer]**

ONGOING ASSESSMENT: Assess Mastery

Use the following resources to assess student mastery of action verbs.

In the Textbook	Technology
Chapter Review, Ex. 31–32, p. 342 Standardized Test Preparation Workshop, p. 344	On-Line Exercise Bank, Section 15.1

Section 15.1 Section Review

GRAMMAR EXERCISES 5–11

Exercise 5 Identifying Action Verbs On your paper, write the action verb in each sentence below.

1. On July 1, 1863, Union and Confederate armies stumbled onto each other near Gettysburg, Pennsylvania.
2. The forces quickly began a fierce battle.
3. Union troops held a position on Cemetery Hill for two days.
4. Dramatic action occurred on the third day of battle.
5. General Pickett of the Confederate Army charged the Union forces.

Exercise 6 Recognizing Transitive Action Verbs Rewrite the following sentences. Underline each transitive verb, and draw an arrow from the verb to its object.

1. During the Civil War, armies used the railroads for the first time in a large conflict.
2. Railroads quickly transported thousands of soldiers and tons of supplies.
3. The North had almost twice as many railroad lines as the South.
4. The telegraph also brought many advantages to the combatants.
5. Generals could coordinate military movements on the battle fronts.

Exercise 7 Recognizing Intransitive Action Verbs Write the intransitive action verb used in each sentence below. Be prepared to explain why the verb is intransitive.

1. In the Civil War, almost all exchanges of prisoners stopped in 1864.
2. People argued in the North and South about the treatment of prisoners.
3. Union prisoners suffered in Confederate camps such as the one at Andersonville.
4. Confederates suffered in Union camps such as Camp Douglas.
5. Enormous death rates resulted from ill treatment, sanitation problems, and malnutrition.

Exercise 8 Revising Sentences With Transitive Verbs Revise the following sentences by adding an object to each sentence, making the intransitive verbs transitive.

1. The soldier fired.
2. Both armies suffered.
3. The officer shouted.
4. The cannonball destroyed.
5. After the war, people rebuilt.

Exercise 9 Find It in Your Reading Write down the verbs that are used in these lines from Ray Bradbury's "The Drummer Boy of Shiloh." Then, label each one *transitive* or *intransitive.*

> . . . He swallowed. He wiped his eyes. He cleared his throat. He settled himself.

Exercise 10 Find It in Your Writing Choose a paper from your portfolio, and identify the action verbs. If you find many forms of the verb *be (am, is, are, was, were)*, try to revise by using action verbs.

Exercise 11 Writing Application Write a paragraph about what it might feel like to be a soldier on the first day of battle. Include at least three transitive verbs and three intransitive verbs.

ASSESS and CLOSE

Section Review

Each of these exercises correlates to a concept in the section on action verbs, pages 330–332. These exercises may be used for more practice, for reteaching, or for review of the Key Concepts presented.

Answer Key

Exercise 5

1. stumbled
2. began
3. held
4. occurred
5. charged

Exercise 6

1. During the Civil War armies used the railroads for the first time in a large conflict. (arrow from *used* to *railroads*)
2. Railroads quickly transported thousands of soldiers and tons of supplies. (arrow from *transported* to *thousands;* arrow from *transported* to *tons*)
3. The North had almost twice as many railroad lines as the South. (arrow from *had* to *lines*)
4. The telegraph also brought many advantages to the combatants. (arrow from *brought* to *advantages*)
5. Generals could coordinate military movements on the battle fronts. (arrow from *coordinate* to *movements*)

Exercise 7

All verbs are intransitive because there are no objects to receive the action of the verbs.

1. stopped
2. argued
3. suffered
4. suffered
5. resulted

continued

Answer Key continued

Exercise 8

1. The soldier fired his gun.
2. Both armies suffered many casualties.
3. The officer shouted his orders.
4. The cannonball destroyed the fort.
5. After the war, people rebuilt their towns.

Exercise 9

Find It in Your Reading
swallowed—intransitive; wiped—transitive; cleared—transitive; settled—transitive

Exercise 10

Find It in Your Writing
Students can discuss their answers with partners to be sure the verbs really do show action.

Exercise 11

Writing Application
Have students label each verb transitive or intransitive.

TIME SAVERS!

Answers on Transparency Use the Grammar Exercises Answers on Transparencies for Chapter 15 to have students correct their own or one another's exercises.

On-Line Exercise Bank Have students complete the exercises on computer. The Auto Check feature will grade their work for you!

PREPARE and ENGAGE

Interest GRABBER Write the following sentences on the chalkboard and ask students to identify the missing part of speech and provide a word to complete the sentence:

Gettysburg a pivotal battle.

Tell students that the sentence needs a linking verb, such as *Gettysburg was* to link the subject to the rest of the sentence.

Activate Prior Knowledge

Ask students to provide the correct form of the verb *to be:*

I (am)

we (are)

you (are)

he/she/ it (is)

they (are)

Remind students that the verb *to be* is an important linking verb.

TEACH

Step-by-Step Teaching Guide

Linking Verbs

1. Students know linking verbs better from use than from the concept and function. Explain that a linking verb links the subject of a sentence with a word that describes or identifies it.
2. Discuss how linking verbs differ from action verbs. Action verbs describe action; linking verbs mostly describe states of being.
3. Review the different forms of the verb *to be* with students. Have them use each form in a sentence.

Answer Key

Exercise 12

1. Many events were responsible for the Civil War.
2. The Missouri Compromise was not enough to prevent slavery.
3. It was a solution to keep balance in the Senate.
4. Later, the Compromise of 1850 was an agreement making California a free state.
5. The other states were "slave" or "free" by choice.

Section 15.2

Linking Verbs

Some widely used verbs do not show action. These are called *linking verbs.*

KEY CONCEPT A **linking verb** is a verb that connects a subject with a word that describes or identifies it. ■

EXAMPLES: He is a general for the North.
The winners were Tony and I.
He looks tired from all the fighting.

Recognizing Forms of *Be*

The verb *be* is the most commonly used linking verb.

THE FORMS OF *BE*

am	can be	have been
are	could be	has been
is	may be	had been
was	might be	could have been
were	must be	may have been
am being	shall be	might have been
are being	should be	must have been
is being	will be	shall have been
was being	would be	should have been
were being		will have been
		would have been

Exercise 12 **Recognizing Forms of *Be* as Linking Verbs** Copy each of the following sentences onto your paper. Underline the form of *be*, and draw a double-headed arrow connecting the words that are linked by the verb.

EXAMPLE: The Civil War was a long campaign.

ANSWER: The Civil War was a long campaign.

1. Many events were responsible for the Civil War.
2. The Missouri Compromise was not enough to prevent slavery.
3. It was a solution to keep balance in the Senate.
4. Later, the Compromise of 1850 was an agreement making California a free state.
5. The other states were "slave" or "free" by choice.

Theme: The Civil War

In this section, you will learn about linking verbs and the difference between linking verbs and action verbs. The examples and exercises are about the United States Civil War.

Cross-Curricular Connection: Social Studies

More Practice

Grammar Exercise Workbook
• pp. 17–18

On-line Exercise Bank
• Section 15.2

Go on-line: PHSchool.com
Enter Web Code: eck-8002

iText

Get instant feedback! Exercise 12 is available on-line or on CD-ROM.

TIME AND RESOURCE MANAGER

Resources
Print: Grammar Exercise Workbook, pp. 17–20
Technology: Writing and Grammar iText, Section 15.2; On-Line Exercise Bank, Section 15.2

In-Depth Coverage	Accelerated Pace
• Work through all key concepts, pp. 334–336. • Assign and review Exercises 12–15. • Read and discuss Grammar in Literature, p. 336.	• Assign pp. 334–336 for independent student review. • Assign Section Review Exercises 16–18.

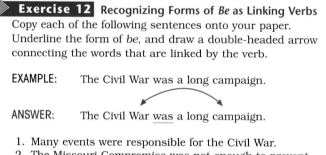

Using Other Linking Verbs

In addition to the verb *be*, a number of other verbs can be used as linking verbs.

OTHER LINKING VERBS					
appear	feel	look	seem	sound	taste
become	grow	remain	smell	stay	turn

These verbs often set up the same relationship between words as the linking verb *be* does. The words that follow the verbs identify or describe the words that precede the verbs.

EXAMPLES: He *became* a general in the Northern army.
Everything *smells* damp and musty.
He *looks* very dirty from all the fighting.

Exercise 13 **Identifying Other Linking Verbs** Copy each of the following sentences onto your paper. Underline the linking verb in each. Then, draw a double-headed arrow connecting the words that are linked by the verb.

1. At the outset, both sides felt confident of a victory.
2. However, their goals remained different.
3. The Confederacy stayed focused on its goal of independence.
4. The goal of the North looked impossible.
5. The North appeared stronger at the beginning.

Exercise 14 **Supplying the Correct Form of Linking Verbs** On a separate sheet of paper, supply an appropriate linking verb for each of the following sentences.

1. Northerners __?__ hopeful of getting Southerners to submit by weakening their ability to fight.
2. The South __?__ very determined, however.
3. Lincoln __?__ unrelenting in pursuing his goal of keeping the Union together.
4. Winfield Scott __?__ a prominent figure in Lincoln's plan.
5. Scott's plan for winning the war __?__ foolproof.
6. After several early Union defeats, however, the war __?__ bloody and drawn out.
7. The Union plan __?__ to seize the Confederate capital, Richmond.
8. The South's leaders __?__ that fighting a defensive battle __?__ enough to win.
9. Instituting a draft meant that Union armies __?__ larger.
10. Many believed that the North's advantage in resources __?__ enough to defeat the South.

More Practice

Grammar Exercise Workbook
- pp. 17–18

On-line Exercise Bank
- Section 15.2

Go on-line:
PHSchool.com
Enter Web Code:
eck-8002

iText

Get instant feedback! Exercise 13 is available on-line or on CD-ROM.

STANDARDIZED TEST PREPARATION WORKSHOP

Grammar and Usage Many standardized tests require students to identify verbs. Ask students to read the following sentences and tell which contains a linking verb:

A The dog smelled the bush.

B The dog smelled bad.

C The dog smelled around the hole.

D The dog smelled for the scent of the rabbit.

Students should recognize that *smelled* is a linking verb in item B. The dog's nose is not doing any smelling. In item A, the dog is sniffing the bush, so *smelled* is an action verb. Items C and D have only prepositional phrases after the verbs, so they have intransitive action verbs.

Step-by-Step Teaching Guide

Using Other Linking Verbs

1. Review with students the other linking verbs. Point out that, in contrast to action verbs, linking verbs routinely describe states of being rather than actions.
2. Tell students that linking verbs do not take objects. If there is no action, then there is nothing to be acted on:

   Luis is the teacher.

   Gloria looks silly.

Answer Key

Exercise 13

1. At the outset, both sides felt confident of a victory. (arrow between *sides* and *confident*)
2. However, their goals remained different. (arrow between *goals* and *different*)
3. The Confederacy stayed focused on its goal of independence. (arrow between *Confederacy* and *focused*)
4. The goal of the North looked impossible. (arrow between *goal* and *impossible*)
5. The North appeared stronger at the beginning. (arrow between *North* and *stronger*)

Exercise 14

Answers may vary. Sample answers are given.

1. Northerners felt hopeful of getting Southerners to submit by weakening their ability to fight.
2. The South remained very determined, however.
3. Lincoln seemed unrelenting in pursuing his goal of keeping the Union together.
4. Winfield Scott became a prominent figure in Lincoln's plan.
5. Scott's plan for winning the war appeared foolproof.
6. After several early Union defeats, however, the war turned bloody and drawn out.
7. The Union plan was to seize the Confederate capital, Richmond.
8. The South's leaders felt that fighting a defensive battle was enough to win.
9. Instituting a draft meant that Union armies grew larger.
10. Many believed that the North's advantage in resources remained enough to defeat the South.

Step-by-Step Teaching Guide

Distinguishing Between Action Verbs and Linking Verbs

1. Explain to students that the way in which verbs are used in sentences determines what kinds of verbs they are.
2. In the example of *feel,* the difference is between General Lee's state of being and the actions of the doctor actively touching the patient.
3. Explain to students that substituting a form of the verb *be* for the verb in the sentence helps them see whether the verb describes a state of being. If the sentence still makes sense with the substitution, the original verb is a linking verb.

   George felt sick.

   George is sick. (linking)

   George felt my forehead.

   George ~~is~~ my forehead. (action)

Step-by-Step Teaching Guide

Grammar in Literature

1. Have a volunteer read aloud the passage from *Harriet Tubman: Conductor of the Underground Railroad*
2. Point out that the verb *fell* functions as a linking verb because the words that follow it describe the subject.

More About the Author

Harriet Tubman was an ex-slave who was the most famous "conductor" on the Underground Railroad, leading nineteen dangerous missions from the South to freedom.

Critical Viewing

Infer Students may say that the photograph seems to show that Harriet Tubman was serious. She stares intently at the camera.

Answer Key

Exercise 15

1. became—LV
2. became—LV
3. grew—LV
4. turned—LV
5. looked—AV

15.2

Distinguishing Between Action Verbs and Linking Verbs

Most of the twelve verbs in the chart on page 335 can be used as either linking verbs or action verbs.

LINKING:	General Lee felt confident.
ACTION:	The doctor felt my pulse.
LINKING:	The meal tasted cold to the soldiers.
ACTION:	The chef tasted the cake.

To see whether a verb is a linking verb or an action verb, substitute *am, is,* or *are* for the verb. If the sentence still makes sense and if the new verb links a word before it to a word after it, then the original verb is a linking verb.

EXAMPLE:	The soldiers *look* tired.
SUBSTITUTION:	The soldiers *are* tired. (LV)

▲ **Critical Viewing** Write several sentences describing what you infer from this photograph about Harriet Tubman's personality and character. Be sure to use at least one action verb and one linking verb in your sentences. **[Infer]**

GRAMMAR IN LITERATURE

from Harriet Tubman: Conductor on the Underground Railroad

Ann Petry

In this excerpt, the linking verb in blue italics is one that often acts as an action verb.

. . . For a while, as they walked, they seemed to carry in them a measure of contentment; some of the serenity and the cleanliness of that big warm kitchen lingered on inside them. But as they walked farther and farther away from the warmth and the light, the cold and the darkness entered into them. They *fell* silent, sullen, suspicious.

Exercise 15 **Distinguishing Between Action Verbs and Linking Verbs** On your paper, write the verb from each of the following sentences. After each action verb, write *AV,* and after each linking verb, write *LV.*

1. The drafting of civilians during wartime became a serious issue.
2. In 1863, the draft became effective in New York City.
3. The laboring class grew fearful of being drafted.
4. They turned against police, firemen, and local militia.
5. New York City looked to the federal army for control.

More Practice

Grammar Exercise Workbook
- pp. 19–20

On-line Exercise Bank
- Section 15.2

Go on-line: PHSchool.com *Enter Web Code:* eck-8002

ONGOING ASSESSMENT: Assess Mastery

Use the following resources to assess student mastery of linking verbs.

In the Textbook	Technology
Chapter Review, Ex. 33–34, 36, pp. 342, 343 Standardized Test Preparation Workshop, p. 344	On-Line Exercise Bank, Section 15.2

Section 15.2 **Section Review**

GRAMMAR EXERCISES 16–22

Exercise 16 **Recognizing Forms of *Be* as Linking Verbs** Copy the sentences below, then underline the form of *be* in each. Draw a double-headed arrow connecting the words linked by the verb.

1. Antietam was the most devastating one-day battle of the Civil War.
2. A victory for the South could have been the turning point of the war.
3. Antietam would be a one-day battle.
4. Neither of the armies would be victorious in this battle.
5. However, Antietam would be a major success for the Union.

Exercise 17 **Identifying Other Linking Verbs** Copy the sentences below, then underline the linking verb in each. Draw a double-headed arrow connecting the words linked by the verb.

1. Lee grew apprehensive about invading the North.
2. The battle at Antietam appeared to change Union policy.
3. Lincoln remained consistent in his dream of an undivided Union.
4. After Antietam, Lincoln's views seemed changed.
5. In Lincoln's mind, the abolition of slavery became crucial.

Exercise 18 **Distinguishing Between Action Verbs and Linking Verbs** Write the verb from each sentence below. Label each action verb *AV,* and each linking verb *LV.*

1. Nearly every American became involved in the Civil War in some way.
2. Women's roles grew in the workplace.
3. Business looked to women to fill jobs in factories and hospitals.
4. Many Southern women remained dutiful and courageous.
5. Southern women stayed on their family farms and tended them.

Exercise 19 **Writing Sentences Using Action Verbs and Linking Verbs** Write two sentences for each word below. In the first sentence, use the verb as an action verb; in the second sentence, use it as a linking verb.

1. feel
2. taste
3. look
4. appear
5. sound
6. become
7. grow
8. smell
9. turn
10. remain

Exercise 20 **Find It in Your Reading** In this excerpt from *Harriet Tubman: Conductor on the Underground Railroad,* identify the two linking verbs.

> There were eleven in this party, including one of her brothers and his wife. It was the largest group that she had ever conducted.

Exercise 21 **Find It in Your Writing** Review a draft of a paper you are currently working on, and identify the linking verbs. To make your writing more lively, try to replace some of the linking verbs with action verbs.

Exercise 22 **Writing Application** Write an account of an event from which you have learned something important. It might be a historical event, the results of a science experiment, or an event from your life. Underline the verb(s) in each sentence, and label them *AV* or *LV.*

ASSESS and CLOSE

Section Review

Each of these exercises correlates to a concept in the section on linking verbs, pages 334–336. These exercises may be used for more practice, for reteaching, or for review of the Key Concepts presented.

Answer Key

Exercise 16

1. Antietam <u>was</u> the most devastating one-day battle of the Civil War. (arrow between *Antietam* and *battle*)
2. A victory for the South <u>could have been</u> the turning point in the war. (arrow between *victory* and *turning point*)
3. Antietam <u>would be</u> a one-day battle. (arrow between *Antietam* and *battle*)
4. Neither of the armies <u>would be</u> victorious in this battle. (arrow between *Neither* and *victorious*)
5. However, Antietam <u>would be</u> a major success for the Union. (arrow between *Antietam* and *success*)

Exercise 17

1. Lee <u>grew</u> apprehensive about invading the North. (arrow between *Lee* and *apprehensive*)
2. The battle at Antietam <u>appeared</u> to change Union policy. (arrow between *battle* and *to change*)
3. Lincoln <u>remained</u> consistent in his dream of an undivided Union. (arrow between *Lincoln* and *consistent*)
4. After Antietam, Lincoln's views <u>seemed</u> changed. (arrow between *views* and *changed*)
5. In Lincoln's mind the abolition of slavery <u>became</u> crucial. (arrow between *abolition* and *crucial*)

Exercise 18

1. became—LV
2. grew—AV
3. looked—AV
4. remained—LV
5. stayed, tended—AV

Exercise 19

Answers will vary.

Exercise 20

Find It in Your Reading
There *were* eleven. . .; It *was* the largest group. . .

continued

Answer Key continued

Exercise 21

Find It in Your Writing
Students can try to act out their verbs to be sure they are action verbs.

Exercise 22

Writing Application
Have students trade papers with a partner for checking.

PREPARE and ENGAGE

Interest GRABBER Ask students to describe something they wish they had done recently but failed to do or something they hope to do in the future. Write their words on the board, underlining the helping verbs in the verb phrases. Tell students they are going to learn more about these helping verbs in verb phrases.

Activate Prior Knowledge

Have volunteers define action and linking verbs. Ask if the helping verbs from the charts on page 338 can be used with both action and linking verbs. Students should give example sentences to illustrate their answers. (Yes. *The dog is smelling the bush. The dog will smell bad if it jumps in the mud puddle.*)

TEACH

Step-by-Step Teaching Guide

Helping Verbs

1. Tell students that a verb phrase is made up of a main verb and one or more helping verbs. Helping verbs are so named because they help the main verb describe action or a kind of idea to the subject.
2. Review the list of helping verbs. Ask students to form verb phrases using helping verbs and other verbs.

   is playing

   might have written

   had been opened

   should have been trained

   might have been seen
3. Without getting too technical, you can tell students that helping verbs are used to indicate whether an action takes place in the past or future or whether an action is continuing or completed. We also use helping verbs to describe conditional or "maybe" situations using *might, should,* or *would.*

Section 15.3

Helping Verbs

The following verbs—*be, do, have, will,* and *can*—are also used often and have one thing in common: They all *help other verbs* to create verb phrases.

KEY CONCEPT Helping verbs are placed before other verbs to form verb phrases. ■

In the following examples, the helping verbs are italicized. Notice how they help to change the meaning of *opened.*

EXAMPLES: *has* opened
will have opened
could have been opened
is being opened

Forms of the verb *be* are often used as helping verbs.

SOME FORMS OF *BE* USED AS HELPING VERBS

Helping Verbs	Verbs
is	opening
was being	trained
should be	written
had been	sent
might have been	played

Some other verbs can also be used as helping verbs.

OTHER HELPING VERBS

do	have	shall	can
does	has	should	could
did	had	will	may
		would	might
			must

Many different verb phrases can be formed using one or more of these helping verbs. The chart below shows just a few.

VERB PHRASES

Helping Verbs	Verbs
does	find
had	gone
should	see
will have	talked
might have	told

Theme: The History of Human Flight

In this section, you will learn about helping verbs and how they are used in verb phrases. The examples and exercises are about the history of flight by humans.

Cross-Curricular Connection: Social Studies

TIME AND RESOURCE MANAGER

Resources
Print: Grammar Exercise Workbook, pp. 21–22, Hands-on Grammar Activity Book, Chapter 15
Technology: Writing and Grammar iText, 15.3; On-Line Exercise Bank, Section 15.3

In-Depth Coverage	Accelerated Pace
• Work through all key concepts, pp. 338–340. • Assign and review Exercises 23–24. • Complete the Hands-on Grammar activity, p. 340.	• Assign pp. 338–340 for independent student review. • Assign Section Review Exercises 25–26.

Exercise 23 **Identifying Helping Verbs** For each sentence below, identify the helping verb(s) and the main verb.

EXAMPLE: More people should have been encouraged to study flight.
ANSWER: should have been (helping verbs) encouraged (main verb)

1. During the eighteenth century, few people had applied themselves to the study of flight.
2. Flapping-wing machines had been studied by Leonardo da Vinci during the fifteenth century.
3. Three important aviation devices were being invented in Europe.
4. These early inventions might have been an inspiration to Leonardo.
5. By 1809, Sir George Cayley had begun to develop the concept of the modern airplane.

Sometimes the words in a verb phrase are separated by other words, such as *not* or *certainly*. The parts of the verb phrase in certain questions are also usually separated. In the following examples, the parts of each verb phrase are italicized.

WORDS SEPARATED: She *could* certainly *have been reached* by phone earlier.
This *has* not *happened* before.
Did you ever *expect* to see such a heavy machine floating in the air?

Exercise 24 **Recognizing Verb Phrases** On your paper, write the complete verb phrase from each sentence below.

EXAMPLE: Patty did not leave the airport until after four.
ANSWER: did leave

1. The airplane, like many other life-changing inventions throughout history, was not immediately recognized for its potential.
2. Prior to World War I, the airplane had occasionally been presented at county fairs.
3. Daredevil pilots would often draw large crowds and a few investors.
4. The United States War Department had quickly expressed interest in the heavier-than-air craft.
5. The Wright brothers did not demonstrate their airplane until 1908.

More Practice

Grammar Exercise Workbook
- pp. 21–22

On-line Exercise Bank
- Section 15.3

Go on-line: PHSchool.com
Enter Web Code: eck-8002

iText

Get instant feedback! Exercises 23 and 24 are available on-line or on CD-ROM.

Grammar and Style Tip

Some words within verb phrases may not be verbs themselves. They may be adverbs that describe the main verb.

Answer Key

Exercise 23

1. helping verb: had; main verb: applied
2. helping verbs: had been; main verb: studied
3. helping verbs: were being; main verb: invented
4. helping verbs: might have; main verb: been
5. helping verb: had; main verb: begun

Step-by-Step Teaching Guide

Helping Verbs

1. It is important that students do not form or latch on to shortcuts that don't work. Verb phrases are frequently separated by other words, so it is a mistake to expect them always to be uninterrupted.
2. Write the following examples on the chalkboard for additional practice:

   The dog had quickly stolen the hamburger.

   She was not troubled by her theft.

Customize for *ESL Students*

Using the examples of perfect and conditional tenses may help English learners understand the basic concepts involved. See that they understand the irregular conjugations of *be* and *do*.

Answer Key

Exercise 24

1. was recognized
2. had been presented
3. would draw
4. had expressed
5. did demonstrate

STANDARDIZED TEST PREPARATION WORKSHOP

Standard Usage: Verbs Standardized tests often measure students' ability to use the correct form of a verb.

Choose the letter of the word or group of words that best completes the sentence.

Jayce and I ___ to the mall tomorrow to find a birthday gift for my mother.

A went
B go
C goes
D are going

The correct choice is item **D**. The other choices have verbs whose tense is inconsistent with the time frame of the sentence.

PRENTICE HALL Everyday Spelling

If you have taught the spelling skills in *Prentice Hall Everyday Spelling*, Grade 8, Chapter 17, in conjunction with this *Writing and Grammar* chapter, review and assess students' mastery of the skills before concluding the chapter.

Step-by-Step Teaching Guide

Helping-Verb Ring Toss

Teaching Resources: Hands-on Grammar Activity Book, Chapter 15

1. Have students refer to their Hands-on Grammar Activity Books or give them copies of the relevant pages.
2. Carefully review the directions for constructing the stakes and rings. You may want to make these ahead of time.
3. To make judging easier, you may want to have the class divide into two teams.

Find It in Your Reading

Have students underline the helping verbs once and the main verbs twice.

Find It in Your Writing

Have students underline the verbs as above. If students cannot find ten examples, have them write new sentences.

15.3

Hands-on Grammar

Helping-Verb Ring Toss

To help you understand the way helping verbs function in sentences, create a helping-verb ring toss game, and play it with your classmates. Cut the center out of about ten paper plates to use as rings. Around the rim of each ring, write a different helping verb. See the examples below.

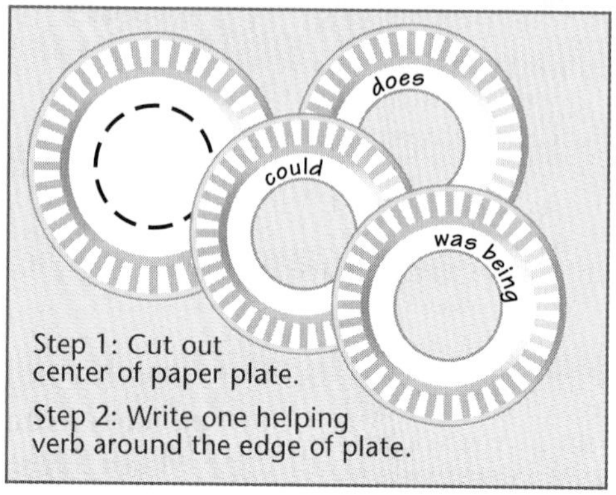

Follow these steps to create the stakes onto which the rings will be tossed: (1) Cut out five cardboard T's. The stem of each T should be 1" wide by 7" long; the top of each T should be 1" wide by 5" long. In the center of the top, cut a 1" slot, as shown below. Turn the T upside down, so that the top is now on the bottom. (2) Cut out five more pieces, approximately 1" wide by 5" long. Each of these pieces, when inserted in the slot of each of the five T's, creates a base. On each stake, write a verb in the present tense that is not a helping verb.

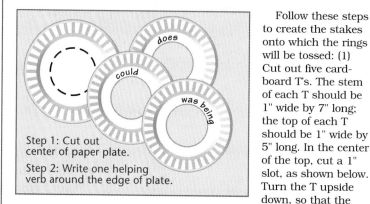

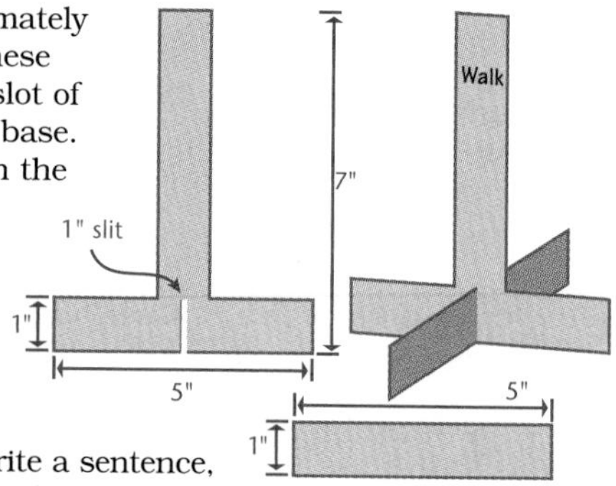

Take turns tossing different rings onto different stakes. Once a player succeeds in getting a ring onto a stake, the other team must write a sentence, using both the helping verb on the plate and the verb on the stake correctly. Award points for correct sentences. Your teacher can judge whether a sentence is correct. Continue playing until both sides have had an opportunity to write sentences using each helping verb and each verb on a stake.

Find It in Your Reading In your language arts and social studies textbooks, find five to ten sentences that use helping verbs. For each of the sentences, identify the helping verb(s) and the main verb.

Find It in Your Writing Review your writing portfolio to find ten sentences that include helping verbs. For each sentence, identify the helping verbs and the main verb.

ONGOING ASSESSMENT SYSTEM

Use the following resources to assess student mastery of verbs.

In the Text	Print Resources	Technology
Chapter Review, Ex. 35, p. 343 Standardized Test Preparation Workshop, pp. 344–345	Formal Assessment, Chapter 15	On-Line Exercise Bank, Section 15.3

Section 15.3 **Section Review**

GRAMMAR EXERCISES 25–30

Exercise 25 Identifying Helping Verbs For each of the following sentences, identify the helping verb(s) and the main verb.

1. The year 1913 has been called the "glorious year of flying."
2. Airplanes would be flown with acrobatic maneuverability.
3. Long-distance flights had been made from France to Egypt.
4. A plane might fly across the Mediterranean Sea without any stops.
5. Commercial aviation would begin in January of 1914.
6. This accomplishment might have been credited to the pioneering of the Wright brothers.
7. Commercial aviation would develop slowly during the 1920's and 1930's.
8. In the 1920's, the air-cooled engine had been perfected.
9. This invention would soon influence the airline industry.
10. After World War II, the airline industry would become prosperous.

Exercise 26 Identifying Verb Phrases Write the complete verb phrase from each sentence below, and label its helping and main verbs.

1. Commercial aviation was being used as early as 1914.
2. The first passenger line was being operated between St. Petersburg, Florida, and Tampa, Florida.
3. Improvements in airplane technology were encouraged by World War I.
4. Many pilots had been hired to accommodate the rapid growth of the airlines.
5. Pilots were put through extensive training and were given rigorous written examinations.

Exercise 27 Writing Sentences With Verb Phrases Use the following verb phrases in original sentences.

1. had long been using
2. did not recognize
3. would soon create
4. should be opened
5. have not been tested
6. might have been lost
7. must not disobey
8. can run
9. is climbing
10. could not be heard

Exercise 28 Find It in Your Reading On your paper, write the verb phrases that appear in the following lines from Mark Twain's "Cub Pilot on the Mississippi." Underline the helping verbs.

> . . . An hour later Henry entered the pilothouse, unaware of what had been going on. He was a thoroughly inoffensive boy, and I was sorry to see him come, for I knew Brown would have no pity on him.

Exercise 29 Find It in Your Writing Look over the draft of one of your recent papers, and identify five sentences using verb phrases. On a separate sheet of paper, revise each verb or verb phrase to express your thoughts more precisely.

Exercise 30 Writing Application Write a brief narrative telling what happened on a trip you took in an airplane, a train, a boat, a bus, or a car. Choose verbs that make the event clear. Then, underline each of your verb phrases.

ASSESS and CLOSE

Section Review

Each of these exercises correlates to a concept in the section on helping verbs, pages 338–339. These exercises may be used for more practice, for reteaching, or for review of the Key Concepts presented.

Answer Key

Exercise 25

1. helping verbs: has been; main verb: called
2. helping verbs: would be; main verb: flown
3. helping verbs: had been; main verb: made
4. helping verb: might; main verb: fly
5. helping verb: would; main verb: begin
6. helping verbs: might have been; main verb: credited
7. helping verb: would; main verb: develop
8. helping verbs: had been; main verb: perfected
9. helping verb: would; main verb: influence
10. helping verb: would; main verb: become

Exercise 26

Helping verbs are underlined once. Main verbs are underlined twice.

1. <u>was being</u> <u>used</u>
2. <u>was being</u> <u>operated</u>
3. <u>were</u> <u>encouraged</u>
4. <u>had been</u> <u>hired</u>
5. <u>were</u> <u>put</u>; <u>were</u> <u>given</u>

Exercise 27

Answers will vary. Samples are given.

1. She had long been using a computer.
2. The computer did not recognize that command.

continued

Answer Key continued

3. Our society would soon create a need for computers.
4. Files should be opened correctly.
5. The samples have not been tested.
6. Your data might have been lost.
7. Children must not disobey.
8. The computer can run all day.
9. My tech stock is climbing rapidly.
10. The teacher could not be heard.

Exercise 28

Find It in Your Reading
<u>had been</u> going, <u>would</u> have

Exercise 29

Find It in Your Writing
Students can label the action and linking verbs in their papers.

Exercise 30

Writing Application
Have students label the helping and main verbs in their narratives.

TIME SAVERS!

Answers on Transparency Use the Grammar Exercises Answers on Transparencies for Chapter 15 to have students correct their own or one another's exercises.

On-Line Exercise Bank Have students complete the exercises on computer. The Auto Check feature will grade their work for you!

CHAPTER REVIEW

Each of these exercises correlates to a concept in the chapter on verbs, pages 328–340. These exercises may be used for more practice, for reteaching, or for review of the Key Concepts presented. Answers for all chapter exercises are available in *Grammar Exercises Answers on Transparencies* in your Teaching Resources.

Answer Key

Exercise 31

1. studied
2. thought
3. studied
4. discovered
5. inspired

Exercise 32

1. developed—transitive
2. abandoned—transitive
3. provided—transitive
4. thought—intransitive
5. stood—intransitive
6. built—transitive
7. made—transitive
8. was built—intransitive
9. did succeed—intransitive
   got—intransitive
10. continued—transitive

Exercise 33

1. My uncle was a pilot for Fly Right, an airline in his hometown. (arrow between *uncle* and *pilot*)
2. My uncle's example is the reason for my enrollment in air flight school. (arrow between *example* and *reason*)
3. I will be a certified pilot only after completing the full program. (arrow between *I* and *pilot*)
4. I will be ready to fly in most weather conditions. (arrow between *I* and *ready*)
5. A job for a new pilot may be hard to find. (arrow between *job* and *hard*)

Exercise 34

1. A bus may seem easy to drive. (arrow between *bus* and *easy*)
2. However, bus drivers feel enormously responsible for their passengers. (arrow between *drivers* and *responsible*)
3. Drivers must always appear calm and courteous. (arrow between *Drivers* and *calm;* arrow between *Drivers* and *courteous*)
4. They can never become distracted or inattentive. (arrow between *They* and *distracted;* arrow between *They* and *inattentive*)
5. On the contrary, the driver must stay alert. (arrow between *driver* and *alert*)
6. In addition, the driver's record must remain clean. (arrow between *record* and *clean*)
7. Surely, an experienced driver grows familiar with his route. (arrow between *driver* and *familiar*)
8. To some, a ride across the country on a bus sounds romantic. (arrow between *ride* and *romantic*)
9. To others, a ride to school or work on a bus feels routine. (arrow between *ride* and *routine*)
10. My little brothers always appear excited when their bus appears in the morning. (arrow between *brothers* and *excited*)

Chapter 15

Chapter Review

GRAMMAR EXERCISES 31–39

Exercise 31 Identifying Action Verbs Identify the action verb in each sentence below.

1. Before the eighteenth century, few people studied flight.
2. Leonardo da Vinci, however, thought about air flight during the fifteenth century.
3. Da Vinci studied mainly the flight of birds.
4. Engineers discovered da Vinci's work in the late nineteenth century.
5. Da Vinci's accomplishments eventually inspired would-be engineers.

Exercise 32 Distinguishing Between Transitive and Intransitive Action Verbs Write the action verb(s) in the sentences below, and label each one *transitive* or *intransitive*.

1. Between 1799 and 1809, Sir George Cayley developed the idea of a model airplane.
2. Cayley abandoned the idea of using the wings for both lift and thrust.
3. In the models, the wing provided lift alone.
4. In 1843, William Henson thought about an aerial steam carriage.
5. A fixed-wing monoplane with propellers, a fuselage, and landing gear with wheels stood out as the main features of his design.
6. Clement Ader built a steam-powered airplane.
7. Ader's "heavier-than-air" craft made the first piloted flight.
8. His craft was built in 1890.
9. Ader did not succeed in flying the craft far; it barely got off the ground.
10. Afterward, inventors continued their dream of flying a craft.

Exercise 33 Recognizing Forms of *Be* as Linking Verbs Copy each of the following sentences onto your paper. Underline the form of *be* in each. Then, draw an arrow connecting the words linked by the verb.

1. My uncle was a pilot for Fly Right, an airline in his hometown.
2. My uncle's example is the reason for my enrollment in flight school.
3. I will be a certified pilot only after completing the full program.
4. I will be ready to fly in most weather conditions.
5. A job for a new pilot may be hard to find.

Exercise 34 Identifying Other Linking Verbs Copy each of the following sentences onto your paper. Underline the linking verb or verb phrase in each sentence, and draw an arrow connecting the words linked by the verb.

1. A bus may seem easy to drive.
2. However, bus drivers feel enormously responsible for their passengers.
3. Drivers must always appear calm and courteous.
4. They can never become distracted or inattentive.
5. On the contrary, the driver must stay alert.
6. In addition, the driver's record must remain clean.
7. Surely, an experienced driver grows familiar with his route.
8. To some, a ride across the country on a bus sounds romantic.
9. To others, a ride to school or work on a bus feels routine.
10. My little brothers always appear excited when their bus arrives in the morning.

Exercise 35 **Identifying Helping Verbs** For each of the following sentences, identify the helping verb(s) and the main verb.

1. You can ride on two types of monorails.
2. On one type of monorail, you will travel on top of a single beam.
3. On another type, the suspended monorail, you will be hanging from a beam.
4. A monorail in Germany has been running for more than a hundred years.
5. Still another type of monorail was developed in France; each car was designed to hang by four wheels along two beams.

Exercise 36 **Distinguishing Between Action and Linking Verbs** Write the complete verb or verb phrase in each sentence below. Then, label it *action* or *linking*. If it is an action verb or phrase, label it *transitive* or *intransitive*.

1. The first passenger cars on trains looked very different from today's cars.
2. For one thing, they resembled horse-drawn carriages.
3. Larger passenger cars were developed before the American Civil War.
4. Each of these cars held more than fifty passengers.
5. Before the 1900's, all passenger cars were made entirely of wood.

Exercise 37 **Revising Sentences to Change Intransitive Verbs to Transitive Verbs** Rewrite the following sentences, adding objects or replacing verbs so that each sentence contains a transitive verb.

1. Orville and Wilbur Wright experimented with flying.
2. The Wright brothers first test-flew on December 17, 1903.
3. At Kitty Hawk, North Carolina, Orville piloted while Wibur watched.
4. Their airplane flew!
5. The test flight succeeded.

Exercise 38 **Writing Application** Write an advertisement about your favorite form of travel. In your advertisement, try to persuade your reader about the benefits of this type of travel. Underline your verbs and verb phrases, and label each one *action* or *linking*.

Exercise 39 **CUMULATIVE REVIEW Nouns and Pronouns** List all the nouns from the following paragraph in one column and all the pronouns in another column. Label each noun *singular* or *plural*, *common* or *proper*. Then, label any collective nouns. In the second column, label each pronoun *personal*, *demonstrative*, *relative*, *interrogative*, or *indefinite*.

What would be your dream car? Almost everyone has an idea of the kind of car he or she would like. While one person might like a sleek sports car, another might prefer a bulky 4 x 4 model. When a family of four take a vacation, they may be happy and comfortable in a spacious minivan, which seems to be made for families with children. A person who drives long distances to work will probably want a smaller car, to save money on gas. Anyone who is shopping for a car these days, however, will see many amazing new features. The salesperson at a dealership will be sure to point those out. Since the days of Henry Ford and his Model T, automobile technology has certainly made tremendous advances.

Answer Key

Exercise 35

1. helping verb: can; main verb: ride
2. helping verb: will; main verb: travel
3. helping verbs: will be; main verb: hanging
4. helping verbs: has been; main verb: running
5. helping verb: was; main verb: developed; helping verb: was; main verb: designed

Exercise 36

1. looked—linking
2. resembled—linking
3. were developed—action, intransitive
4. held—action, transitive
5. were made—action, intransitive

Exercise 37

Answers will vary. Samples are given.

1. Orville and Wilbur Wright performed experiments with airplanes.
2. The Wright brothers first tested their airplane on December 17, 1903.
3. At Kitty Hawk, North Carolina, Orville piloted the airplane while Wilbur watched him.
4. Their airplane carried Orville through the air.
5. The test flight made them famous.

Exercise 38

Writing Application
Volunteers can read their paragraphs aloud. Ask the audience to tell—politely—if they were persuaded.

Exercise 39

Cumulative Review
Nouns:
car—singular, common; idea—singular, common; kind—singular, common; car—singular, common; person—singular, common; car—singular, common; model—singular, common; family—singular, collective, common; four—singular, common; vacation—singular, common; minivan—singular, common; families—plural, collective, common; children—plural, common; person—singular, common; distances—plural, common; work—singular, common; car—singular, common; money—singular, common; gas—

continued

Answer Key continued

singular, common; car—singular, common; days—plural, common; features—plural, common; salesperson—singular, common; dealership—singular, common; days—plural, common; Henry Ford—singular, proper; Model T—singular, proper; technology—singular, common; advances—plural, common
Pronouns:
What—interrogative
your—personal
everyone—indefinite
he—personal
she—personal
another—indefinite
they—personal
which—relative
Anyone—indefinite
who—relative
these—demonstrative
those—demonstrative
his—personal

Lesson Objectives

- To use the correct form of verbs.

Step-by-Step Teaching Guide

Standard English Usage: Verbs

Teaching Resources: Standardized Test Preparation Workbook, pp. 29–30

1. Review the steps for answering questions that involve standard usage of verbs.
2. Point out to students the importance of using context clues to determine the time frame of the action, as well as the type of verb needed to best complete the sentence.
3. Have students cover the "Answer and Explanation" column in their textbooks.
4. Have a volunteer read the passage. Ask students to identify the context clues they can use to help them make their choice.

Standardized Test Preparation Workshop

Standard English Usage: Verbs

The ability to use verbs correctly is essential in effective speaking and writing. Standardized tests often measure your ability to use the correct form of a verb to complete a sentence. These types of questions are composed of a written passage with numbered blanks. You will be asked to read the passage and select one of four word choices to complete the sentence correctly.

When you are tested on verbs in standardized tests, read the passage carefully. Decide whether an action verb or a linking verb is needed. Use context clues to help you decide whether the passage concerns the past, the present, or the future. Then, select the form of the verb that best completes the sentence. The following examples will help you practice verb questions.

Test Tip

Verb tenses should remain consistent in a given passage, except when referring to different periods of time or when showing a cause-and-effect relationship.

Sample Test Item	Answer and Explanation
Read the passage, and choose the letter of the word or group of words that belongs in each space. Frederick Douglass did not limit himself to fighting for African Americans' civil rights. He also __(1)__ the suffragists in their battle to win the vote.	
1 A helps B will be helping C helped D did help	The sentence calls for an action verb that shows something happening in the past. Therefore, choice C, *helped*, best completes the passage.

TEST-TAKING TIP

Remind students that the last step in answering each question should involve reading the entire passage with their choices in place. This will help them avoid errors in judgment.

Practice 1 **Directions:** Read the passage, and choose the letter of the word or group of words that belongs in each space.

"I ___(1)___ to have time to look for my children and ___(2)___ how many I can find. Maybe I shall find them among the dead. ___(3)___ me, my chiefs. I am tired; my heart ___(4)___ sick and sad. From where the sun now stands I ___(5)___ no more forever." Chief Joseph

1 **A** did want
B wanted
C will want
D want

2 **F** saw
G see
H sees
J seen

3 **A** Hear
B Heard
C Hears
D Did hear

4 **F** was
G will be
H were
J is

5 **A** was fighting
B did fight
C will fight
D fought

Practice 2 **Directions:** Read the passage, and choose the letter of the word or group of words that belongs in each space.

To this day, two framed silhouettes ___(1)___ on the parlor wall in Grandmother's house. My sister and I ___(2)___ them to her for her eighty-third birthday. Tanya Larrabee, the silhouette artist downtown, ___(3)___ them, and her husband, Frank, ___(4)___ them. Grandmother always ___(5)___ people that they are her most precious possessions, from her most precious girls.

1 **A** hang
B hangs
C hung
D hanged

2 **F** give
G gives
H gave
J had given

3 **A** cut
B will cut
C cuts
D did cut

4 **F** framed
G frames
H will frame
J did frame

5 **A** told
B telling
C did tell
D tells

Answer Key

Practice 1

1. D
2. G
3. A
4. J
5. C

Practice 2

1. A
2. H
3. A
4. F
5. D

Chapter 16 Time and Resource Manager

In-Depth Lesson Plan

	LESSON FOCUS	PRINT AND MEDIA RESOURCES
DAY 1	**Adjectives** Students learn to use adjectives and articles. They learn to recognize various other parts of speech used as adjectives. They complete the Hands-on Grammar activity (pp. 346–359).	**Teaching Resources** *Grammar Exercise Workbook,* pp. 23–32; *Grammar Exercises Answers on Transparencies,* Ch. 16; *Hands-on Grammar Activity Book,* Ch. 16 ***Writing and Grammar iText* (Interactive Text),** Section 16.1; ***On-line Exercise Bank,*** Section 16.1
DAY 2	**Adverbs** Students learn to recognize and use adverbs and to distinguish between adjectives and adverbs (pp. 360–366).	**Teaching Resources** *Grammar Exercise Workbook,* pp. 33–38; *Grammar Exercises Answers on Transparencies,* Ch. 16 ***Writing and Grammar iText* (Interactive Text),** Section 16.2; ***On-line Exercise Bank,*** Section 16.2
DAY 3	**Review and Assess** Students review the chapter and demonstrate mastery of adjectives and adverbs (pp. 367–369).	**Teaching Resources** *Formal Assessment,* Ch. 16; *Grammar Exercises Answers on Transparencies,* Ch. 16 ***Writing and Grammar iText* (Interactive Text),** Ch. 16, Chapter Review

Accelerated Lesson Plan

	LESSON FOCUS	PRINT AND MEDIA RESOURCES
DAY 1	**Adjectives** Students learn to recognize and use adjectives and other parts of speech used as adjectives (346–359).	**Teaching Resources** *Grammar Exercise Workbook,* pp. 16–20; *Hands-on Grammar Activity Book,* Ch. 16; *Grammar Exercises Answers on Transparencies,* Ch. 16 ***Writing and Grammar iText* (Interactive Text),** Section 16.1; ***On-line Exercise Bank,*** Section 16.1
DAY 2	**Adverbs; Review and Assess** Students learn to recognize and use adverbs. They review the chapter and demonstrate mastery of adjectives and adverbs. (360–369).	**Teaching Resources** *Formal Assessment,* Ch. 16; *Grammar Exercise Workbook,* pp. 21–23; *Grammar Exercises Answers on Transparencies,* Ch. 16 ***Writing and Grammar iText* (Interactive Text),** Ch. 16, Section 16.2 through Chapter Review; ***On-line Exercise Bank,*** Section 16.2

Options for Adapting Lesson Plans

HOMEWORK

Have students complete any stage of the lesson for homework.

SPELLING

To teach spelling skills in conjunction with grammar, mechanics, and usage, work through *Prentice Hall Everyday Spelling,* Grade 8, Chapter 19, as you cover this *Writing and Grammar* chapter.

TECHNOLOGY

Students can use *Writing and Grammar iText* to complete the exercises interactively on computer. They can complete additional exercises in the *On-line Exercise Bank:* The Auto Check feature will grade their work. Go online: PHSchool.com Use Web code: eck-8002

FEATURES

Extend coverage with the Grammar in Literature features (pp. 349, 356, 365) and the Standardized Test Preparation Workshop (p. 369).

INTEGRATED SKILLS COVERAGE

Grammar in Literature
SE pp. 349, 356, 365

Writing
Find It in Your Writing, SE pp. 358, 359, 366
Writing Application, SE pp. 359, 366, 368

Viewing and Representing
Critical Viewing, SE pp. 346, 348, 350, 353, 354, 361, 363–365

BLOCK SCHEDULING

Pacing Suggestions
For 90-minute Blocks
- Administer the Diagnostic Test to students to determine instructional coverage.
- Have students complete the necessary exercises in class. Use the Hands-on Grammar Activity to provide a change of pace.

Resources for Varying Instruction
- ***Writing and Grammar iText* (Interactive Text)** A 90-minute block provides an ideal opportunity for students to work on computer.

Professional Development Support
- ***How to Manage Instruction in the Block*** This teaching resource provides management and activity suggestions.

ASSESSMENT SUPPORT

Standardized Test Preparation Workshop SE p. 369; ATE pp. 351, 364

Standardized Test Preparation Workbook, pp. 31–32

Formal Assessment, Ch. 16

MEDIA AND TECHNOLOGY

For the Student
- ***Writing and Grammar iText* (Interactive Text),** Ch. 16
- ***On-Line Exercise Bank,*** Sections 16.1–2

For the Teacher
- ***Resource Pro* CD-ROM**

MEETING INDIVIDUAL NEEDS

Less Advanced Students ATE p. 361. See also Ongoing Assessments ATE pp. 350, 352, 355, 356, 361, 363.

ESL Students ATE pp. 355, 364

Gifted/Talented Students ATE p. 353

WRITING AND GRAMMAR ON-LINE

iText Interactive Text (On-line or on CD-ROM)
- Easily navigable instruction with on-line supporting resources
- Self-scoring exercises and diagnostic tests

Companion Web Site PHSchool.com
- On-line Exercise Bank (use Web Code eck-8002)

See the Go On-line! feature, SE p. iii.

LITERATURE CONNECTIONS

Grammar in Literature selections from *Prentice Hall Literature: Timeless Voices, Timeless Themes,* Silver:
from "*Brown* vs. *Board of Education,*" Walter Dean Myers, SE pp. 349, 356
from "Saving the Wetlands," Barbara A. Lewis, SE p. 365

CHAPTER 16
ADJECTIVES AND ADVERBS

Lesson Objectives

1. To understand how adjectives modify nouns and pronouns.
2. To distinguish between definite and indefinite articles.
3. To identify nouns used as adjectives.
4. To recognize proper and compound adjectives.
5. To recognize pronouns used as possessive, demonstrative, interrogative, and indefinite adjectives.
6. To understand how adverbs modify verbs.
7. To understand how adverbs modify adjectives and adverbs.
8. To distinguish between adjectives and adverbs.
9. To use adjectives and adverbs appropriately.

Critical Viewing

Analyze Students may use these adjectives: *grand, awe-inspiring, classical, stone, columned, Greek*

Chapter 16 Adjectives and Adverbs

The stately U.S. Supreme Court building stands majestically in Washington, D.C.

Sometimes a noun cannot communicate all that you want to express. For example, what if you wanted to describe your local courthouse? What words would you use—*large, gray, marble, imposing?* These descriptive words are called adjectives, and they add information about the noun *courthouse.*

Adverbs also help to clarify the meaning of a sentence. They make the meaning of verbs, adjectives, or other adverbs more precise.

There are many uses for adjectives and adverbs. This chapter will cover some of the most common of these uses.

▲ Critical Viewing
Write three additional adjectives to describe this famous courthouse.
[Analyze]

ONGOING ASSESSMENT: Diagnose

If students miss more than one item in each category, direct them to the relevant pages of the text and assign exercises for practice and review.

Adjectives and Adverbs	Diagnostic Test Items	Teach	Practice	Section Review	Chapter Review
Skill Check A					
Adjectives	A 1–5	pp. 348–354	Ex. 1, 3–6	Ex. 11	Ex. 31
Skill Check B					
Articles	B 6–10	pp. 350	Ex. 2	Ex. 12	Ex. 31

Diagnostic Test

Directions: Write all answers on a separate sheet of paper.

Skill Check A. Write the underlined adjective on your paper, and then label each one *adjective, proper adjective, noun used as an adjective,* or *compound adjective.* Next to each adjective, write the noun it modifies.

1. The Supreme Court is an important American institution.
2. Article III of the United States Constitution sets definite provisions for the establishment of the Supreme Court.
3. The United States Supreme Court is composed of a Chief Justice and eight associate justices.
4. The nine-member bench has been constant in size since 1869.
5. The bench began with six justices in 1789.

Skill Check B. On your paper, write the article that will correctly complete each of the following sentences.

6. (definite) United States government is controlled by a written constitution with rules that guide government leaders.
7. (definite) judicial system makes sure those rules are interpreted and followed correctly.
8. The courts are (indefinite) part of the judicial system used to interpret the laws.
9. Cases generally reach the Supreme Court either from (indefinite) lower federal court or from a state supreme court.
10. The Supreme Court usually takes cases from (indefinite) appeal of a lower court.

Skill Check C. Write each underlined word, and label it *possessive adjective, demonstrative adjective, interrogative adjective,* or *indefinite adjective.* Then, write the noun each adjective modifies. If the word is not used as an adjective, write *pronoun.*

11. When can the defendant appeal this court case to a higher court?
12. Whose court case needs to be appealed?
13. We count on our courts to interpret the law.
14. How many court cases are like that?
15. Few court cases are involved with these proceedings.

Skill Check D. Write the adverbs in each sentence. After each adverb, write the verb, adjective, or adverb it modifies.

16. The sessions of the Supreme Court open in October of each year and almost always adjourn toward the end of June.
17. The Supreme Court rarely ever calls a special session outside that time period.
18. Only four special sessions were called in the last century.
19. A session normally lasts approximately 38 weeks.
20. Justices too often find themselves working between sessions.

ONGOING ASSESSMENT: Diagnose *continued*

Adjectives and Adverbs	Diagnostic Test Items	Teach	Practice	Section Review	Chapter Review
Skill Check C					
Types of Adjectives	C 11–15	pp. 355–357	Ex. 7–10	Ex. 13	Ex. 32, 33
Skill Check D					
Adverbs	D 16–20	pp. 360–365	Ex. 17–23	Ex. 24–27	Ex. 34–37
Cumulative Reviews and Applications				Ex. 14–16, 28–30	Ex. 38–39

Answer Key

Diagnostic Test

Each item in the diagnostic test corresponds to a specific concept in the chapter on adjectives and adverbs. This will enable you to tailor instruction to the particular needs of your students. See "Ongoing Assessment: Diagnose" below for further details.

Skill Check A

1. important—adjective, American—proper adjective; both modify *institution*
2. definite—adjective; modifies *provisions*
3. United States—proper adjective, compound adjective, and noun used as adjective; modifies *Supreme Court*; associate—adjective; modifies *justices*
4. nine-member—compound adjective; modifies *bench*
5. six—adjective; modifies *justices*

Skill Check B

6. The
7. The
8. a
9. a
10. an

Skill Check C

11. this—demonstrative adjective; modifies *case*
12. Whose—interrogative adjective; modifies *case*
13. our—possessive adjective; modifies *courts*
14. that—pronoun
15. Few—indefinite adjective; modifies *cases*

Skill Check D

16. *almost* modifies *always ;always* modifies *adjourn*
17. *rarely* and *ever* modify *calls*
18. *Only* modifies *four*
19. *normally* modifies *lasts; approximately* modifies *38*
20. *too* modifies *often; often* modifies *find*

PREPARE and ENGAGE

Interest GRABBER Write the following quotation from Dickens's *A Christmas Carol* on the chalkboard:

Oh, but he was a tight-fisted hand at the grindstone, Scrooge! a squeezing, wrenching, grasping, scraping, clutching, covetous old sinner!

Call on a volunteer to underline the words that describe Scrooge. (*squeezing, wrenching, grasping, scraping, clutching, covetous, old*) If students underline *tight-fisted,* tell them the term really describes *hand.* Explain that these words are called adjectives. They describe the noun *Scrooge.*

Activate Prior Knowledge

Ask students what questions the adjectives in the Dickens quotation answer about Scrooge. (What kind of person is he?) Adjectives always answer one of four questions: *What kind? Which one? How much?* or *How many?*

TEACH

Step-by-Step Teaching Guide

Adjectives With Nouns and Pronouns

1. Point out the word *modify* on the page. Explain that an adjective acts like the focusing adjustment on a camera. Write the sentence *Scrooge was a miserly old man* on the chalkboard beside the Dickens quotation. Have students discuss how Dickens uses a series of adjectives to bring the image of Scrooge into focus for the reader.
2. Review predicate adjectives. Predicate adjectives are linked to the nouns and pronouns they modify by linking verbs such as *seemed* or *was.*

Critical Viewing

Compare and Contrast Students may suggest these possible answers for both buildings: monumental, Greek, neoclassical and for Capitol: domed, round

Section 16.1

Adjectives

Adjectives add description and other kinds of information to two other parts of speech.

KEY CONCEPT An **adjective** is used to describe a noun or a pronoun. ■

Here are some examples of adjectives used with nouns: *serious* judges, *sleek* jets, *violet* eyes, *tall, majestic* oaks.

Adjectives With Nouns and Pronouns To *modify* means to "change slightly." Adjectives are modifiers because they slightly change the meaning of nouns and pronouns. Adjectives modify meaning by adding information that answers one of four questions: *What kind? Which one? How many?* or *How much?* In the following chart, notice how adjectives answer these questions.

What Kind?	
brick house	*white* paper
Which One?	
that judge	*each* answer
How Many?	
one daffodil	*several* roses
How Much?	
no time	*enough* raisins

An adjective usually comes before the noun it modifies, as do all the adjectives in the chart. Sometimes, however, adjectives come after the nouns they modify.

EXAMPLE: The legal system, *serious* and *complex*, fascinated her.

Predicate adjectives and adjectives that modify pronouns usually come after linking verbs. Sometimes, however, adjectives may come before pronouns.

EXAMPLE: The judge seemed *kind* and *understanding.*
She was *quiet* and *thoughtful.*
Tall and *elegant*, she walked into the room.

Theme: Justice System

In this section, you will learn how adjectives modify the meaning of nouns and pronouns. The examples and exercises in this section are about courts and the American justice system.

Cross-Curricular Connection: Social Studies

▼ **Critical Viewing** Compare the Capitol building with the Supreme Court building on page 346. Use four adjectives in your comparison. **[Compare and Contrast]**

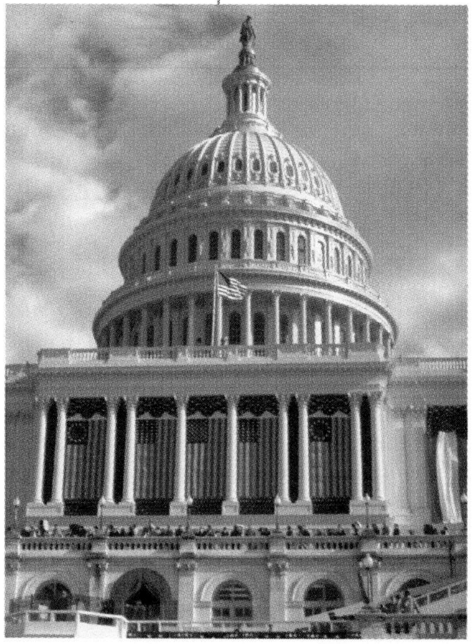

TIME AND RESOURCE MANAGER

Resources
Print: Grammar Exercise Workbook, pp. 23–32
Technology: Writing and Grammar iText, Section 16.1; On-Line Exercise Bank, Section 16.1

In-Depth Coverage	Accelerated Pace
• Work through all key concepts, pp. 348–357. • Assign and review Exercises 1–10. • Read and discuss Grammar in Literature, pp. 349, 356. • Do the Hands-on Grammar Activity, p. 358.	• Assign pp. 348–357 for independent student review. • Assign Section Review Exercises 11–13.

GRAMMAR IN LITERATURE

from Brown vs. Board of Education

Walter Dean Myers

In this passage, the adjectives segregated, 1896, *and* legal *come before the nouns they modify.* Separate, equal, *and* legal *are predicate adjectives—they follow a linking verb and describe the subject.*

The states with *segregated* schools relied upon the ruling of the Supreme Court in the *1896* *Plessy* vs. *Ferguson* case for *legal* justification: Facilities that were "*separate* but *equal*" were *legal*.

Exercise 1 Recognizing Adjectives and the Words They Modify Copy the following sentences onto your paper. Draw an arrow from each underlined adjective to the noun or pronoun it modifies.

EXAMPLE: Originally, legal aid was financed almost exclusively by private donations.

1. Providing legal counsel for poor people is called legal aid.
2. It is available in civil and criminal cases.
3. The government assumes responsibility for the legal aid of criminal defendants.
4. In some jurisdictions, the judge appoints private lawyers to represent poor people.
5. In 1963, the U.S. Supreme Court declared that every poor defendant charged with a felony is entitled to free counsel as a matter of constitutional right.
6. As a result, the number of public defenders multiplied, as did governmental budgets for legal aid.
7. In 1965, civil legal aid to poor people increased substantially.
8. Free counsel for poor people in civil cases does not yet exist, although some see a slight tendency in that direction.
9. Certain civil cases have been found to be a constitutional right in some state supreme courts.
10. Different types of legal aid in civil cases exist in other countries.

More Practice

Grammar Exercise Workbook
- pp. 16–18

On-line Exercise Bank
- Section 16.1

Go on-line: PHSchool.com
Enter Web Code: eck-8002

iText

Get instant feedback! Exercise 1 is available on-line or on CD-ROM.

Step-by-Step Teaching Guide

Grammar in Literature

1. Have a volunteer read aloud the excerpt from "*Brown* vs. *Board of Education.*" Ask students if they can find any adjectives in this excerpt that are not highlighted. If students are stumped, point out *the* and *that.* Tell students that these are special categories of adjectives that they will study in the next few pages of this chapter.
2. Explain that although *1896* is a noun—the name of a specific year—it is used here as an adjective to modify *Plessy* vs. *Ferguson.* Remind students that Dickens used verb forms such as *squeezing* and *wrenching* as adjectives in his description of Scrooge. Any word used to describe, or modify, a noun or pronoun becomes an adjective.

More About the Writer

Walter Dean Myers grew up in New York City's Harlem. This colorful, lively neighborhood is the setting for several of his novels, including *The Young Landlords* and *Fallen Angels.* Most of Myers's stories deal with the problems of contemporary youngsters in poor urban settings. He has also written some historical fiction.

Answer Key

Exercise 1

1. arrow from *poor* to *people;* arrow from *legal* to *aid*
2. arrow from *available* to *It;* arrow from *civil* to *cases;* arrow from *criminal* to *cases*
3. arrow from *legal* to *aid;* arrow from *criminal* to *defendants*
4. arrow from *private* to *lawyers;* arrow from *poor* to *people*
5. arrow from *poor* to *defendant;* arrow from *free* to *counsel;* arrow from *constitutional* to *right*
6. arrow from *public* to *defenders;* arrow from *governmental* to *budgets;* arrow from *legal* to *aid*
7. arrow from *civil* to *aid;* arrow from *legal* to *aid;* arrow from *poor* to *people*

continued

Answer Key continued

8. arrow from *Free* to *counsel;* arrow from *poor* to *people;* arrow from *civil* to *cases;* arrow from *slight* to *tendency*
9. arrow from *Certain* to *civil cases;* arrow from *civil* to *cases;* arrow from *constitutional* to *right;* arrow from *state* to *courts;* arrow from *supreme* to *courts*
10. arrow from *Different* to *types;* arrow from *legal* to *aid;* arrow from *civil* to *cases*

Language Highlight

Legal Terms Point out the abbreviation *vs.* in the literature excerpt. Explain that it stands for *versus. Versus* is a Latin word meaning "against." "*Plessy* vs. *Ferguson*" means that Plessy and Ferguson are arguing opposite sides of a case. Many other legal terms are Latin—*habeas corpus, sine die, pro bono,* and so on.

Step-by-Step Teaching Guide

Articles

1. Use the literature excerpt on the previous page to demonstrate how *the* functions as an adjective. In the excerpt, it answers the questions *Which states? Which ruling? Which court? Which case?* Explain that the indefinite articles *a* and *an* function in the same way.
2. Have students read aloud the examples in the middle of the page so that everyone can hear the difference between the sounds at the beginning of words. Words beginning with *o* that have a *w* sound, like *one,* take the article *a.* So do words beginning with *u* that sound as though they begin with *y,* like *university.* Encourage students to pronounce words aloud if they are unsure about the indefinite article.

Answer Key

Exercise 2

1. the
2. An, the
3. A, a
4. The
5. a, the

Critical Viewing

Identify Students may suggest the Capitol dome, the flag, a dome, an acute angle, a state.

16.1

Articles

Three commonly used adjectives are called *articles—the, a,* and *an.* These three words are adjectives because they come before nouns and answer the question *Which one?* Because of the way it modifies nouns, *the* is called the *definite* article.

KEY CONCEPT *The,* the **definite article,** refers to a specific person, place, or thing.

EXAMPLES: *the* court *the* attorney *the* broken law

The other two articles, *a* and *an,* are not as specific as *the.*

KEY CONCEPT *A* and *an,* the **indefinite articles,** refer to any one of a class of people, places, or things. ■

EXAMPLES: *a* court *an* attorney *a* broken law

A is used before consonant sounds. *An* is used before vowel sounds. Notice that you choose between *a* and *an* according to *sound.* The letter *h,* a consonant, may sound like either a consonant or a vowel. *O* and *u* are vowels, but they may sometimes sound like consonants.

EXAMPLES: *a* hero
an honor
a university
an understanding
a one-act play
an open door

▼ **Critical Viewing** Identify three objects in the picture—one that can be introduced by *the,* one by *a,* and one by *an.* **[Identify]**

Exercise 2 **Distinguishing Between Definite and Indefinite Articles** On your paper, write the article that will correctly complete each of the following sentences. The word in parentheses tells you *what kind* of article.

1. The right to legal representation is (definite) basis of our legal tradition.
2. (indefinite) honest lawyer does not profit from (definite) outcome of a case if it is contrary to the client's interests.
3. (Indefinite) lawyer's primary responsibility toward (indefinite) client may conflict with certain ethical principles.
4. (definite) majority of lawyers believe the conflict must be resolved in favor of the client in most cases.
5. In (indefinite) criminal case, for example, a lawyer may have to choose between losing (definite) case or knowingly allowing the client to commit perjury in testifying.

More Practice

Grammar Exercise Workbook
- pp. 16–18

On-line Exercise Bank
- Section 16.1

Go on-line:
PHSchool.com
Enter Web Code:
eck-8002

ONGOING ASSESSMENT: Monitor and Reinforce

If students miss more than two items in Exercises 2–3, refer them to the following for additional practice.

In the Textbook	Print Resources	Technology
Section Review, Ex. 11–12, p. 359	Grammar Exercise Workbook, pp. 23–26	On-Line Exercise Bank, Section 16.1

Nouns Used as Adjectives

Nouns are sometimes used as adjectives. When a noun is used as an adjective, it comes before another noun and answers the question *What kind?* or *Which one?*

NOUNS: court, morning
ADJECTIVES: a court date, a morning appointment

Exercise 3 **Identifying Nouns Used as Adjectives** Each of the following sentences contains one noun used as an adjective. Write the modifying noun on your paper, and next to it write the noun it modifies.

EXAMPLE: The states, not Congress, make state laws.
ANSWER: state (laws)

1. Congress makes public laws.
2. Congress is made up of two government houses, the House of Representatives and the Senate.
3. When the President of the United States signs a bill, it becomes not just state law, but the law of the land.
4. Congress is also responsible for determining whether public policies are being administered according to the law.
5. Both houses of Congress are concerned with protecting citizen rights.
6. House members and senators are expected to represent the people in their districts and states.
7. Although the two houses of Congress meet separately, they sometimes meet in joint sessions.
8. Often, business begins after a roll call of all members.
9. House members must have been citizens of the United States for at least seven years before running for office.
10. Sometimes, government business in Congress may be broadcast to the public on radio or television.

Proper Adjectives Some proper adjectives are simply proper nouns used as adjectives. Others are adjectives made from proper nouns.

KEY CONCEPTS A **proper adjective** is (1) a proper noun used as an adjective or (2) an adjective formed from a proper noun.

When a proper noun is used as an adjective, its form does not change.

Step-by-Step Teaching Guide

Nouns Used as Adjectives

1. Write a few examples of nouns used as adjectives on the chalkboard, such as *pencil sharpener, paper cutter, garbage can,* and *computer screen.* Ask what purpose the first noun in each pair serves. (It describes the second noun.) Explain that even though these words are usually nouns, they become adjectives when they answer one of the four questions listed on page 348 of this chapter.
2. Use sentence 3 in Exercise 3 to demonstrate that a prepositional phrase can be substituted for a noun used as an adjective.

   state law: state *is a noun used as an adjective*

   law of the state: of the state *is a prepositional phrase describing what kind of law*

   Suggest that students may want to mix prepositional phrases and nouns used as adjectives to vary their writing.

Answer Key

Exercise 3

1. public (laws)
2. government (houses)
3. state (law)
4. public (policies)
5. citizen (rights)
6. House (members)
7. joint (sessions)
8. roll (call)
9. House (members)
10. government (business)

STANDARDIZED TEST PREPARATION WORKSHOP

Grammar and Usage Standardized tests often ask students to choose the correct form of a particular word in a sentence. Ask students to choose the correct word to complete the following sentence:

The passengers on the ___ ship Titanic were excited about the maiden voyage.

A England
B English
C Britain
D None of the above

The correct answer is item B. The correct choice must be an proper adjective that modifies the noun *ship.* Items A and C are proper nouns and are not the correct form.

TIME SAVERS!

Answers on Transparency Use the Grammar Exercises Answers on Transparencies for Chapter 16 to have students correct their own or one another's exercises.

On-Line Exercise Bank Have students complete the exercises on computer. The Auto Check feature will grade their work for you!

Step-by-Step Teaching Guide

Proper Adjectives

1. Briefly review proper nouns. Personal names of people (George Washington) and places (the White House), months of the year (January), days of the week (Tuesday), brand names (Sony), and certain periods in history (Renaissance) are proper nouns. Explain that the adjectival forms of these nouns are called proper adjectives.
2. Go over the examples of proper adjectives in the chart at the top of the page. Tell students that although many proper adjectives end in *-an* or *-ian,* many others do not. Challenge students to suggest some proper adjectives that have different endings. (Possible answers: *French, Jewish, Portuguese*)
3. Remind students that like proper nouns, proper adjectives should be capitalized. Give students some sample sentences in which none of the proper adjectives are capitalized and ask them to correct these sentences.

   Why are you putting french dressing on french fries?

   This is my german shepherd's favorite snack.

   My irish setter prefers danish pastry.

Answer Key

Exercise 4

1. United States (citizens)
2. Senate (seats)
3. Oregon (initiative)
4. Kansas (senator)
5. Civil War (era)
6. Senate (leaders)
7. House (leaders)
8. United States (Constitution)
9. President's (appointments); Supreme Court (justices)
10. Senate (approval); House (approval)

16.1

Proper Nouns	Used as Proper Adjectives
Arizona	*Arizona* desert (*What kind* of desert?)
Tuesday	*Tuesday* morning (*Which* morning?)
Churchill	*Churchill* memorial (*Which* memorial?)

Proper Nouns	Proper Adjectives Formed From Proper Nouns
Elizabeth	*Elizabethan* literature (*What kind* of literature?)
Boston	*Bostonian* architecture (*What* kind of architecture?)

Exercise 4 **Recognizing Proper Adjectives** Find the proper adjective(s) in each sentence, and write them on your paper. Next to each proper adjective, write the noun it modifies.

EXAMPLE: The United States senators serve in the upper house of the Congress.

ANSWER: United States (senators)

1. United States citizens elect senators every six years.
2. Until the 1900's, however, Senate seats were filled by members elected by individual state legislatures.
3. Then, an Oregon initiative began direct election of senators by the citizens of the state.
4. In 1911, a Kansas senator offered a resolution proposing a constitutional amendment for the election of all senators by the people.
5. The oath taken by each senator to uphold the Constitution dates back to the Civil War era.
6. The Senate floor leaders are elected by the members of their party.
7. Party leaders in the Senate often meet with House party leaders.
8. The United States Constitution gives the Senate certain unique powers.
9. For example, the Senate has the power to accept or reject the President's appointments of Supreme Court justices.
10. However, both Senate and House approval are needed to send a bill to the President for signing.

More Practice

Grammar Exercise Workbook
- pp. 16–18

On-line Exercise Bank
- Section 16.1

Go on-line: PHSchool.com *Enter Web Code:* eck-8002

iText

Get instant feedback! Exercise 4 is available on-line or on CD-ROM.

ONGOING ASSESSMENT: Prerequisite Skills

If students have difficulty with proper adjectives, you may find it necessary to review the following to ensure coverage of prerequisite knowledge.

In the Textbook	Print Resources	Technology
Nouns and Pronouns, pp. 294–299	Grammar Exercise Workbook, pp. 5–6	Writing and Grammar iText, Section 14.1; On-Line Exercise Bank, Section 14.1

Exercise 5 **Revising Sentences With Proper Adjectives**
Revise each sentence, replacing the underlined phrase with a proper adjective.

EXAMPLE: Our court system is based on the common law of England.

ANSWER: Our court system is based on English common law.

1. Law in Asia developed differently from our own.
2. Between 403 B.C. and 221 B.C., legalists in China believed that every aspect of life should be ruled by a set of strict and impersonal laws.
3. The beginnings of our legal system came from laws of ancient Greece.
4. Democracy in Athens included a jury system to decide court cases.
5. Later, in courts of ancient Rome, juries composed of senators and knights ruled on crimes such as corruption, treason, and poisoning.
6. Most legal systems of Europe grew out of the laws of these ancient cultures.
7. Both the court system of America and the court system of Britain share the same historic roots.
8. In the sixteenth and seventeenth centuries, it was determined that the monarch of England would be subject to the law, and the courts would be independent of the monarch.
9. Now, many countries in North America, South America, Asia, Africa, and Europe have independent court systems.
10. Some other legal systems are tied to a national religion; for example, law in Iran is based on the beliefs of Islam.

▼ Critical Viewing
Lawyers in England wear white wigs such as this. What proper adjective would you use to describe a lawyer from England? **[Connect]**

Answer Key

Exercise 5

1. Asian law developed differently from our own.
2. Between 403 B.C. and 221 B.C., Chinese legalists believed that every aspect of life should be ruled by a set of strict and impersonal laws.
3. The beginnings of our legal system came from ancient Greek laws.
4. Athenian democracy included a jury system to decide court cases.
5. Later, in ancient Roman courts, juries composed of senators and knights ruled on crimes such as corruption, treason, and poisoning.
6. Most European legal systems grew out of the laws of these ancient cultures.
7. Both the American court system and the British court system share the same historic roots.
8. In the sixteenth and seventeenth centuries, it was determined that the English monarch would be subject to the law, and the courts would be independent of the monarch.
9. Now, many North American, South American, Asian, African, and European countries have independent court systems.
10. Some other legal systems are tied to a national religion; for example, Iranian law is based on Islamic beliefs.

Critical Viewing

Connect Students might suggest English or British.

Customize for *Gifted/Talented Students*

Give students the names of the following writers. Have them find the "authorial adjective" to describe each one: Aristotle, Balzac, Brontë, Byron, Chaucer, Chekhov, Dickens, Dryden, Eliot, Faulkner, Gibbon, Hemingway, James, Joyce, Kafka, Milton, Petrarch, Shaw, Thoreau, Thurber, and Trollope.

TIME SAVERS!

Answers on Transparency
Use the Grammar Exercises Answers on Transparencies for Chapter 16 to have students correct their own or one another's exercises.

On-Line Exercise Bank
Have students complete the exercises on computer. The Auto Check feature will grade their work for you!

Step-by-Step Teaching Guide

Compound Adjectives

1. Ask students to define the word *compound* (having more than one part). Explain that compound adjectives, like other compound words students have studied, include more than one word.
2. Explain that the hyphen in a compound adjective shows a reader that the two adjectives are linked and that, together, they modify the noun that comes after them.
3. In every compound adjective, the two words together modify the noun or pronoun. Each compound adjective describes the noun that follows it.

Answer Key

Exercise 6

1. two-chambered (Congress)
2. two-year (terms)
3. Population-based (seats)
4. day-to-day (activities)
5. outspoken (representatives)

Critical Viewing

Analyze Students may suggest these possible answers: awe-inspiring dome, three-tiered dome, twenty-foot-tall columns, even-spaced columns.

16.1

◀ **Critical Viewing** Here is one compound adjective and noun pairing to describe the Capitol building: *backbreaking steps.* Can you name three others? **[Analyze]**

Compound Adjectives

Just as there are compound nouns, there are also *compound adjectives.* A compound adjective is made up of more than one word.

Most compound adjectives are written as hyphenated words. Sometimes, however, they are written as combined words. If you are uncertain about which way to write a compound adjective, consult a dictionary for the correct spelling.

HYPHENATED: one-sided opinion
so-called expert

COMBINED: heartbreaking news
nearsighted witness

Exercise 6 **Recognizing Compound Adjectives** Find the compound adjective in each sentence and write it on your paper. Next to the compound adjective, write the noun it modifies.

EXAMPLE: A member of Congress should be well qualified for his or her job.
ANSWER: well qualified (member)

1. The House of Representatives is the larger governmental body in our two-chambered Congress.
2. Members of the House of Representatives serve two-year terms, and the entire membership stands for reelection every second year.
3. Population-based seats in the House are used to assure fair representation for all citizens.
4. The day-to-day activities of the House of Representatives can be seen on cable television.
5. You may notice outspoken representatives arguing about some issues.

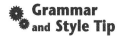

Grammar and Style Tip

Sometimes two or more adjectives of equal importance are used to describe a noun. These should be separated with commas. A compound adjective, however, is not written with commas and may sometimes require a hyphen.

Pronouns Used as Adjectives

Pronouns, like nouns, can sometimes be used as adjectives.

KEY CONCEPT A pronoun is used as an adjective if it modifies a noun. ■

Four kinds of pronouns are sometimes used as adjectives. They are *personal, demonstrative, interrogative,* and *indefinite* pronouns.

Possessive Adjectives The following personal pronouns are often called *possessive adjectives: my, your, his, her, its, our,* and *their.* Because they have antecedents, they are considered to be pronouns. They are also adjectives, because they answer the question *Which one?*

EXAMPLE: The President is preparing *his* state-of-the-union message.

This example shows that *his* is an adjective modifying the noun *message. His* is also a pronoun because it has an antecedent, *President.*

Exercise 7 **Identifying Possessive Adjectives** On your paper, make three columns as shown in the example. Write the underlined word in the first column. Then, find the noun it modifies and its antecedent, and put them in the second and third columns.

EXAMPLE: The President exerts a unifying influence through <u>his</u> position as head of state.

ANSWER:

Possessive Adjective	Noun Modified	Antecedent
his	position	President

1. The President of the United States performs <u>his</u> many duties as head of state, head of government, and Commander in Chief of the armed forces.
2. Presidential candidates are nominated by <u>their</u> political parties.
3. The President is officially elected only after the Electoral College announces <u>its</u> vote tally.
4. We as a nation count on <u>our</u> President to uphold the Constitution.
5. As First Lady, the President's wife also has a responsibility to <u>her</u> country.

More Practice

Grammar Exercise Workbook
• pp. 19–20
On-line Exercise Bank
• Section 16.1
Go on-line:
PHSchool.com
Enter Web Code:
eck-8002

iText

Get instant feedback! Exercise 7 is available on-line or on CD-ROM.

Step-by-Step Teaching Guide

Pronouns Used as Adjectives

1. Explain that pronouns used as adjectives come in special categories. On the chalkboard, list the four categories named at the top of the page. Ask students to share any ideas they have about how to define these four categories.
2. Ask students to define the word *possessive.* (showing ownership) Possessive pronouns, therefore, show whom or what a noun belongs to. Have students list possessive pronouns, such as *his, my,* and *our.* Make sure students understand why these words are both pronouns (because they have antecedents) and adjectives (because they modify nouns or pronouns).

Customize for *ESL Students*

Spanish-speaking students have memorized the rule that English possessives (unlike Spanish ones) add *'s.* They may now mistakenly apply this rule to pronouns used as adjectives, creating *their's house* and *it's height.* Tell them that a pronoun is a special possessive that does not change no matter how it is used.

Answer Key

Exercise 7

1. *his* modifies *duties;* its antecedent is *President*
2. *their* modifies *parties;* its antecedent is *candidates*
3. *its* modifies *tally;* its antecedent is *Electoral College*
4. *our* modifies *President;* its antecedent is *We*
5. *her* modifies *country;* its antecedent is *wife*

ONGOING ASSESSMENT: Monitor and Reinforce

Use the following resources to assess students' mastery of articles, compound and proper adjectives, and nouns used as adjectives.

In the Textbook	Print Resources	Technology
Section Review, Ex. 11, 12, p. 359	Grammar Exercise Workbook, pp. 25–28	Writing and Grammar iText, Section 16.1, Section Review; On-Line Exercise Bank, Section 16.1

TIME SAVERS!

Answers on Transparency Use the Grammar Exercises Answers on Transparencies for Chapter 16 to have students correct their own or one another's exercises.

On-Line Exercise Bank Have students complete the exercises on computer. The Auto Check feature will grade their work for you!

Step-by-Step Teaching Guide

Demonstrative Adjectives

When students are in doubt about whether a demonstrative pronoun is being used as an adjective, have them look for a word it modifies. If it describes a noun or pronoun, then they know it is being used as an adjective.

Answer Key

Exercise 8

1. This (pronoun)
2. This (office)
3. These (pronoun)
4. those (judgeships)
5. that (ambassador)

Step-by-Step Teaching Guide

Grammar in Literature

Ask students to identify other adjectives in the passage, identify their types, and point out the word or words they modify. (*N.A.A.C.P.* is a noun used as an adjective; it modifies *attorneys. African* is a proper adjective modifying *Americans. Their* is a possessive adjective modifying *battles.*)

16.1

Demonstrative Adjectives The four demonstrative pronouns—*this, that, these,* and *those*—can be used as demonstrative adjectives.

PRONOUN: I saw *this.*
ADJECTIVE: I'll vote on *this* issue.

PRONOUN: I want *those.*
ADJECTIVE: Count *those* ballots.

Exercise 8 **Recognizing Demonstrative Adjectives** Find the word *this, that, these,* or *those* in each of the sentences below and copy it. If it is used as a pronoun, write *pronoun* after it. If it is used as an adjective, write the noun it modifies.

EXAMPLE: That is the United States President.
ANSWER: That (pronoun)

1. Chief Executive: This is the one title of the President.
2. This office has powers as well as limitations.
3. These are the cabinet members appointed by the President.
4. The Senate now must approve those judgeships recommended by the President.
5. The President appointed that ambassador.

More Practice

Grammar Exercise Workbook
- pp. 19–20

On-line Exercise Bank
- Section 16.1

Go on-line:
PHSchool.com
Enter Web Code:
eck-8002

iText

Get instant feedback! Exercise 8 is available on-line or on CD-ROM.

GRAMMAR IN LITERATURE

from **Brown vs. Board of Education**

Walter Dean Myers

In this passage, the demonstrative adjective these *modifies the nouns* men *and* women.

It was Thurgood Marshall and a battery of N.A.A.C.P. attorneys who began to challenge segregation throughout the country. *These* men and women were warriors in the cause of freedom for African Americans, taking their battles into courtrooms across the country.

Interrogative Adjectives Three interrogative pronouns—*which, what,* and *whose*—can be used as *interrogative adjectives.*

PRONOUN: *What* did he want?
ADJECTIVE: *What* sentence did he give?

PRONOUN: *Whose* is that?
ADJECTIVE: *Whose* courtroom is that?

Exercise 9 **Recognizing Interrogative Adjectives** Find the word *which, what,* or *whose* in each of the sentences below and copy it. If it is used as a pronoun, write *pronoun* after it. If it is used as an adjective, write the noun it modifies.

EXAMPLE: What verdict is the jury going to reach?
ANSWER: What (verdict)

1. What would cause the impeachment of a judge?
2. Which law states that a judge must have good behavior?
3. Whose salary cannot be reduced while he or she holds office?
4. What are the powers of the Supreme Court justices?
5. Which court has the authority to hear a case without its being heard elsewhere first?

Indefinite Adjectives A number of indefinite pronouns—*both, few, many, each, most,* and *all,* among others—can also be used as *indefinite adjectives.*

PRONOUN: I bought one of *each.*
ADJECTIVE: *Each* judge writes an opinion.

PRONOUN: I don't want *any.*
ADJECTIVES: I don't want *any* help.

Exercise 10 **Recognizing Indefinite Adjectives** Write the indefinite pronoun or adjective in each of the sentences below onto your paper. If it is used as a pronoun, write *pronoun* after it. If it is used as an adjective, write the noun it modifies.

EXAMPLE: Few cases are thrown out of court.
ANSWER: Few (cases)

1. Each Supreme Court justice may serve for life.
2. All Supreme Court justices are appointed by the President.
3. Very few judicial questions are not resolved.
4. Many are the basis of new laws.
5. The Supreme Court acts as both referee and overseer.

Spelling Tip

The interrogative pronoun *whose* is one word. The word *who's* is a contraction formed from the two words *who* and *is.*

Step-by-Step Teaching Guide

Interrogative and Indefinite Adjectives

1. Remind students that interrogative sentences ask questions. Interrogative adjectives also ask questions. They are familiar question words: *which, what,* and *whose.*
2. When in doubt about how an interrogative pronoun is being used, students can rewrite the question in which it appears as a statement and then look for a noun or pronoun that *which, what,* or *whose* modifies. If they can find such a word, then they know the pronoun is being used as an adjective.
3. Have a volunteer read aloud the paragraph about indefinite adjectives. Ask students to define *indefinite.* (not specific; not exact; vague) Have students look at the indefinite pronouns listed on the page and explain why they are called *indefinite.* (They do not name specific numbers or quantities.)
4. Ask students if they can think of other indefinite adjectives besides those listed here. (Possible answers: *several, some*)

Answer Key

Exercise 9

1. What (pronoun)
2. Which (law)
3. Whose (salary)
4. What (pronoun)
5. Which (court)

Exercise 10

1. Each (justice)
2. All (justices)
3. few (questions)
4. Many (pronoun)
5. both (referee and overseer)

ONGOING ASSESSMENT: Monitor and Reinforce

If students miss more than two items in Exercises 7–10, refer them to the following for additional practice.

In the Textbook	Print Resources	Technology
Section Review, Ex. 13, p. 359	Grammar Exercise Workbook, pp. 29–32	On-Line Exercise Bank, Section 16.1

TIME SAVERS!

Answers on Transparency Use the Grammar Exercises Answers on Transparencies for Chapter 16 to have students correct their own or one another's exercises.

On-Line Exercise Bank Have students complete the exercises on computer. The Auto Check feature will grade their work for you!

Step-by-Step Teaching Guide

Demonstrative, Interrogative, and Indefinite Adjectives Pop-up

Teaching Resources: Hands-on Grammar Activity Book, Chapter 16

1. Have students refer to their Hands-on Grammar Activity Books or give them copies of the relevant pages for this activity.
2. You may want to have students work in pairs so that they can check the accuracy of each others' work.
3. Have students close their papers. Ask what the interrogative words are now. (pronouns)

Find It in Your Reading

You may want to assign the same story for all students to use.

Find It in Your Writing

Have students keep a list of the errors in agreement they find. This way they will know the areas in which they need extra practice.

16.1

Hands-on Grammar

Demonstrative, Interrogative, and Indefinite Adjectives Pop-up

1. Fold a piece of 6-1/2" X 8-1/2" paper so that it has a pocket as shown.
2. On the left side of the fold, list all the demonstrative, interrogative, and indefinite pronouns, such as *this, that, these, those, each, few, what,* and *whose.*
3. On the right side of the fold, complete the sentence, and making sure that the verb agrees in number with the pronoun: *This is the best. Those are the best.*
4. Now, make a list of nouns in the pocket, so that when you open the paper fully, you get a complete sentence in which adjective, noun, and verb all agree in number.
5. When you open the paper, the pronouns become adjectives.

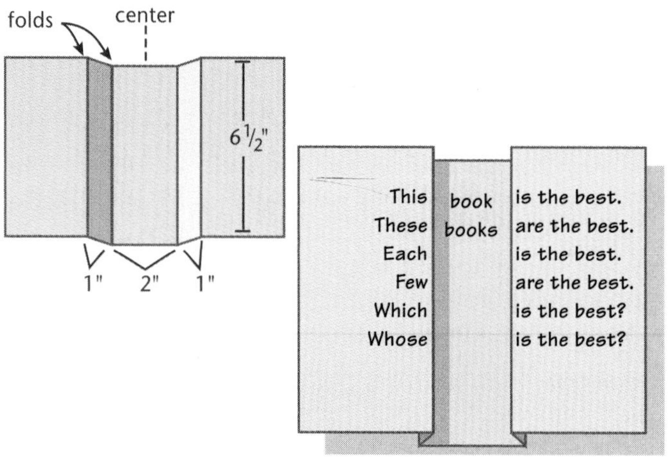

Find It in Your Reading In a short story or in a textbook, pick out examples of demonstrative, interrogative, and indefinite adjectives. Rewrite the examples, using the adjectives as pronouns.

Find It in Your Writing Look through your portfolio to find examples of demonstrative, interrogative, and indefinite adjectives. Make sure that they agree in number with the nouns they modify and with the verbs.

TIME SAVERS!

Hands-on Grammar Use the Hands-On Grammar sheet for Chapter 16 to facilitate this chapter.

ONGOING ASSESSMENT: Assess Mastery

Use the following resources to assess students' mastery of adjectives.

In the Textbook	Technology
Chapter Review, Ex. 31–32, pp. 367–368 Standardized Test Preparation Workshop, pp. 369–370	Writing and Grammar iText, Section 16.1, Section Review; On-Line Exercise Bank, Section 16.1

Section 16.1 Section Review

GRAMMAR EXERCISES 11–16

Exercise 11 **Recognizing and Classifying Adjectives and the Words They Modify** Copy each sentence onto your paper. Draw an arrow pointing from each underlined adjective to the noun it modifies. Indicate whether each underlined word is (a) an *adjective,* (b) a *proper adjective,* (c) a *compound adjective,* (d) a *possessive adjective,* or (e) a *noun used as an adjective.*

1. A court is a government agency.
2. It makes decisions in legal disputes.
3. The disputes are often serious.
4. Courts also provide much-needed protection from illegal actions.
5. Sometimes courts resolve disputes of great political and social significance.
6. Our court system is based on English common law.
7. Defense attorneys offer legal advice.
8. American, Canadian, and English governments abide by common law.
9. In 1848, David Dudley Field worked on the New York code of civil procedure.
10. His work influenced the development of our modern judicial system.

Exercise 12 **Using Definite and Indefinite Articles** On your paper, write the article or articles that correctly complete each of the following sentences.

1. A dispute before a court may be called (indefinite) action.
2. (Indefinite) civil case involves possible violation of (indefinite) person's rights.
3. (Indefinite) broken contract suit is (indefinite) example of a civil case.
4. (Indefinite) criminal case involves alleged violations of (definite) public laws.
5. Crimes are seen as (indefinite) threat to (definite) whole society.

Exercise 13 **Revising Sentences With Demonstrative, Interrogative, and Indefinite Adjectives and Pronouns** Identify whether each underlined word in the following sentences is being used as a *pronoun* or an *adjective.*

1. The Supreme Court made that decision.
2. Whose case was in court today?
3. The defendant denied he took those.
4. All felt he was guilty.
5. Any defendant can waive the right to a jury trial.
6. What did the jury decide in the case?
7. That is a lie, the plaintiff argued.
8. Which juror was the foreperson?
9. Is either eligible for jury service?
10. The judge will use these facts to decide.

Exercise 14 **Find It in Your Reading** In this passage from "Brown *vs.* Board of Education," find a proper adjective and two nouns used as adjectives

At Howard there was a law professor, Charles Hamilton Houston, who would affect the lives of many African-American lawyers and who would influence the legal aspects of the civil rights movement.

Exercise 15 **Find It in Your Writing** Look in your portfolio for a paragraph that describes something or someone. Circle the adjectives you used.

Exercise 16 **Writing Application** Imagine that you are a court reporter covering a civil or criminal trial. Write a brief description of events or people that you notice in the courtroom.

ASSESS and CLOSE

Section Review

Each of these exercises correlates to a concept in the section on adjectives, pages 348–357. The exercises may be used for more practice, for reteaching, or for review of the Key Concepts presented.

Answer Key

Exercise 11

1. arrow from *government* to *agency* (noun used as an adjective)
2. arrow from *legal* to *disputes* (adjective)
3. arrow from *serious* to *disputes* (adjective)
4. arrow from *much-needed* to *protection*; arrow from *illegal* to *actions* (compound adjective; adjective)
5. arrow from *great* to *significance*; arrow from *political* to *significance*; arrow from *social* to *significance* (adjectives)
6. arrow from *our* to *court*, arrow from *English* to *law* (possessive adjective; proper adjective)
7. arrow from *defense* to *attorneys*, arrow from *legal* to *advice* (noun used as adjective; adjective)
8. arrows from *American*, *Canadian*, *English* to *governments* (proper adjectives)
9. arrow from *New York* to *code* (proper adjective)
10. arrows from *his* to *work*, *our* to *system*, *judicial* to *system* (possessive adjective; possessive adjective; adjective)

Exercise 12

1. an
2. A, a
3. A, an
4. A, the
5. a, the

continued

Answer Key continued

Exercise 13

1. adjective
2. adjective
3. pronoun
4. pronoun
5. adjective
6. pronoun
7. pronoun
8. adjective
9. pronoun
10. adjective

Exercise 14

Find It in Your Reading
Proper adjective: African-American
Nouns used as adjectives: law, civil rights

Exercise 15

Find It in Your Writing
Have students identify each adjective's type—possessive, compound, or proper.

Exercise 16

Writing Application
Have students choose partners, exchange papers, and identify the types of adjectives in each other's paragraphs.

TIME SAVERS!

Answers on Transparency Use the Grammar Exercises Answers on Transparencies for Chapter 16 to have students correct their own or one another's exercises.

On-Line Exercise Bank Have students complete the exercises on computer. The Auto Check feature will grade their work for you!

PREPARE and ENGAGE

Interest GRABBER Write the following sentences on the board.

He hit the ball firmly.

The ball landed on the green and rolled slowly to the hole.

The golfer was very excited afterward.

Ask students to tell what is the function of the underlined word in each sentence. (They add detail.) Ask whether these words are adjectives. (No; they don't modify nouns or pronouns.) Explain that these words are adverbs. They modify verbs, adjectives, and adverbs.

Activate Prior Knowledge

Go back to the sample sentences from the Interest Grabber and ask students what questions the adverbs answer. (They answer the questions *In what manner? To what extent?* and *When?*) Explain that adverbs can also answer the question *Where?*

TEACH

Step-by-Step Teaching Guide

Adverbs Modifying Verbs

1. Go over the examples in the chart with the class. Demonstrate how each of the italicized adverbs answers the question.
2. Point out that adverbs almost always modify action verbs, not linking verbs. Have students try writing sentences or phrases in which an adverb answers one of the four questions from the chart about a verb, such as *am, are, is, was, were.* (Students may come up with a sentence such as *I am here.*)

Answer Key

Exercise 17

1. primarily (are caused; To what extent?)
2. Often (result; When?)
3. slowly (moves; In what way?)
4. then (will rise; When?)
5. there (develop; Where?)

Section 16.2

Adverbs

Adverbs modify three different parts of speech.

KEY CONCEPT An **adverb** modifies a verb, an adjective, or another adverb. ■

To recognize adverbs, you need to know how they modify each of these three parts of speech.

Adverbs Modifying Verbs

An adverb modifying a verb will answer one of four questions about the verb: *Where? When? In what way?* or *To what extent?*

ADVERBS MODIFYING VERBS

Where?	
drove *down* is *here*	stay *nearby* jump *away*
When?	
report *later* will leave *soon*	come *tomorrow* appeared *suddenly*
In What Way?	
cautiously approached smiled *happily*	walk *quietly* tell *unwillingly*
To What Extent?	
nearly won *hardly* counted	had *almost* left *scarcely* escaped

Exercise 17 **Recognizing How Adverbs Modify Verbs** Write the underlined adverb and the verb it modifies on your paper. Then, identify the question the adverb answers about the verb.

EXAMPLE: Animals in the wetlands interact somewhat.
ANSWER: somewhat (interact; *To what extent?*)

1. Wetlands primarily are caused by water saturating an area.
2. Often, these wetlands result from ground water coming to the surface.
3. Ground water moves slowly through the soil and accumulates near the surface.
4. The water table will then rise.
5. If the water table in an area reaches the surface, wetlands develop there.

Theme: Life in the Wetlands

In this section, you will learn how adverbs modify the meaning of verbs, adjectives, and other adverbs. The examples and exercises in this section are about plant and animal life in wetlands.

Cross-Curricular Connection: Science

More Practice

Grammar Exercise Workbook
- pp. 21–23

On-line Exercise Bank
- Section 16.2

Go on-line: PHSchool.com *Enter Web Code:* eck-8002

TIME AND RESOURCE MANAGER

Resources
Print: Grammar Exercise Workbook, pp. 33–38
Technology: Writing and Grammar iText, Section 16.2; On-Line Exercise Bank, Section 16.2

In-Depth Coverage	Accelerated Pace
• Work through all key concepts, pp. 360–365. • Assign and review Exercises 17–23. • Read and discuss Grammar in Literature, p. 365.	• Assign pp. 360–365 for independent student review. • Assign Section Review Exercises 24–27.

Exercise 18 Revising Sentences by Adding Adverbs
Rewrite each sentence below, adding an adverb that answers the question in parentheses.

EXAMPLE: Wetland vegetation (to what extent?) includes woody plants, such as trees.

ANSWER: Wetland vegetation mostly includes woody plants, such as trees.

1. Wetlands (to what extent?) form in places where water is trapped.
2. Wetlands (to what extent?) look mossy, grassy, shrubby, or wooded.
3. In a marshy wetland, tall grassy plants sway (in what way?) above the water.
4. Cypress trees grow (in what way?) in swampy areas of the South.
5. Because rain falls (when?) in these areas, plant life thrives.
6. Swamps (to what extent?) have a distinct odor of decay.
7. Tannic acid, derived from decaying vegetation, (in what way?) changes the color of the swamp water.
8. The water (where?) becomes dark brown or tea-colored.
9. Wetlands along Florida's coasts are (to what extent) dominated by mangrove forests.
10. The thick roots of mangrove trees anchor them (in what way?) against tropical winds and storms.

▼ Critical Viewing
Use adverbs in sentences to describe how the wind is blowing, how the grasses are swaying, and how the clouds are moving in the Everglades National Park in Florida. **[Analyze]**

Answer Key

Exercise 18

Possible answers:

1. generally (form)
2. typically (look)
3. gently (sway)
4. abundantly (grow)
5. frequently (falls)
6. usually (have)
7. slowly (changes)
8. below (becomes)
9. partly (dominated)
10. protectively (anchor)

Critical Viewing

Analyze Students may suggest: The wind is blowing lustily. The grasses are swaying gracefully. The clouds are moving briskly.

Customize for *Less Advanced Students*

Give students extra practice by having them identify the question each adverb in Exercise 17 answers about the verb it modifies.

ONGOING ASSESSMENT: Monitor and Reinforce

If students miss more than two items in Exercise 17 or 18, refer them to the following for additional practice.

In the Textbook	Print Resources	Technology
Section Review, Ex. 24, 26, p. 366	Grammar Exercise Workbook, pp. 33–34	On-Line Exercise Bank, Section 16.2

TIME SAVERS!

Answers on Transparency Use the Grammar Exercises Answers on Transparencies for Chapter 16 to have students correct their own or one another's exercises.

On-Line Exercise Bank Have students complete the exercises on computer. The Auto Check feature will grade their work for you!

Step-by-Step Teaching Guide

Adverbs Modifying Adjectives and Other Adverbs

1. Explain that since only certain adverbs can answer the question *To what extent?* only certain adverbs can modify adjectives and adverbs. For example, *happily* cannot answer this question, but *almost* can. Have students suggest other examples of adverbs that can and cannot answer this question. (not, nearly, unusually, mildly, seriously)
2. Go over the answers to Exercise 21 on page 363 after students have completed it. List these common adverbs that modify other adverbs, such as *too, very, nearly, most,* and so on on the chalkboard. Have students copy the list and keep it for reference.

Answer Key

Exercise 19

1. somewhat (similar)
2. mostly (grassy)
3. usually (treeless and shrubless)
4. mostly (soft-stemmed)
5. nearly (still)
6. partly (submerged)
7. rather (wide)
8. relatively (open)
9. Completely (submerged)
10. quite (marshlike)

Exercise 20

Possible answers:

1. a very deep
2. It usually forms
3. Rather thick
4. sand usually loses
5. support very heavy
6. be completely trapped
7. stay relatively calm
8. swim frantically with
9. arms completely stretched
10. Then, quickly roll

16.2

Adverbs Modifying Adjectives

When an adverb modifies an adjective, it answers the question *To what extent?*

ADVERBS MODIFYING ADJECTIVES		
almost right	*not* sad	*unusually* rich

Exercise 19 Recognizing Adverbs That Modify Adjectives On your paper, write the adverb from each sentence. After each adverb, write the adjective it modifies.

EXAMPLE: Marshes can be very peaceful.
ANSWER: very (peaceful)

1. A marsh is somewhat similar to a swamp.
2. A marsh has meadow plants and mostly grassy vegetation.
3. Marshes are usually treeless and shrubless.
4. They tend to have mostly soft-stemmed plants.
5. In a marsh, plants are surrounded by nearly still water.
6. Cattails, rushes, arrowheads, and pickerel weed grow with partly submerged stems and leaves.
7. Waterlilies root in the bottom of a marsh, and their rather wide leaves float on the water's surface.
8. Tiny duckweed, water lettuce, and water hyacinth sprout in the relatively open waters of southern marshes and swamps.
9. Completely submerged aquatic plants, such as pondweeds and waterweeds, grow in the deepwater marshes.
10. Pondweeds and waterweeds can grow near the shore of shallow ponds, which can be quite marshlike.

Exercise 20 Revising Sentences With Adverbs On your paper, write each sentence given below and add at least one adverb to modify the adjective or the verb.

1. Quicksand is a deep mass of fine sand.
2. It forms on stream bottoms and along seacoasts.
3. Thick layers of quicksand are dangerous.
4. The sand loses its firmness.
5. It cannot support heavy weight.
6. Unwary people and animals can be trapped.
7. If you fall into quicksand, it is important that you stay calm.
8. Do not try to swim with your arms and legs.
9. Fall on your back with your arms stretched out.
10. Then, roll off the sand to firm ground.

More Practice

Grammar Exercise Workbook
- pp. 21–23

On-line Exercise Bank
- Section 16.2

Go on-line: PHSchool.com
Enter Web Code: eck-8002

iText

Get instant feedback! Exercise 19 is available on-line or on CD-ROM.

Adverbs Modifying Other Adverbs

When adverbs modify other adverbs, they again answer the question *To what extent?*

ADVERBS MODIFYING ADVERBS	
traveled *less* slowly	move *very* cautiously
lost *too* easily	lived *almost* happily

Exercise 21 **Recognizing Adverbs That Modify Other Adverbs** In each sentence, find an adverb that modifies another adverb by answering the question *To what extent?* Write this adverb, followed by the adverb it modifies.

1. Wetland animal life is rather highly diverse and includes many aquatic insects.
2. Some aquatic insects spend only their very early stages of life in the water.
3. Other aquatic insects are nearly permanently bound to the water.
4. The anhinga, or snakebird, is most often seen spearing its fish as it dives beneath the open-water areas of marshes.
5. Muskrats quite voluntarily frequent cattail marshes, where they feed on the roots of cattail plants.
6. Large groups of muskrats can almost completely clear an entire area of cattails.
7. Many species of amphibians most certainly live in wetlands.
8. Alligators are quite often found in Florida swamp areas during the dry season.
9. Many of the animals that inhabit swamps almost always live in marshes, too.
10. The raccoon and beaver are hardly ever seen in dry areas of the forest.

Exercise 22 **Writing Sentences With Adverbs That Modify Other Adverbs** Write sentences using the following adverbs.

1. unusually slowly
2. most often
3. quite easily
4. very quickly
5. hardly ever

▼ **Critical Viewing** Use at least four adverbs in sentences describing how this alligator moves, looks, or feeds. **[Infer]**

Answer Key

Exercise 21

1. rather (highly)
2. very (early)
3. nearly (permanently)
4. most (often)
5. quite (voluntarily)
6. almost (completely)
7. most (certainly)
8. quite (often)
9. almost (always)
10. hardly (ever)

Exercise 22

Possible answers:

1. Turtles move unusually slowly.
2. I see them most often in the early morning.
3. I could catch one quite easily.
4. I wouldn't even need to move very quickly.
5. My brother hardly ever sees them.

Critical Viewing

Infer Students may suggest: The alligator suns itself *very lazily* on an *unusually* large log that floats *slowly* down the stream.

ONGOING ASSESSMENT: Monitor and Reinforce

If students miss more than two items in Exercise 20 or 21, refer them to the following for additional practice.

In the Textbook	Print Resources	Technology
Section Review, Ex. 25–26, p. 366	Grammar Exercise Workbook, pp. 35–38	On-Line Exercise Bank, Section 16.2

Step-by-Step Teaching Guide

Adverb or Adjective?

1. Have a volunteer read the sample sentences. Point out that *fast* and *much* are examples of words that keep the same spelling whether they are used as adverbs or adjectives. Challenge students to suggest other words that follow this pattern. (Possible answers: *early, far, high, low*)
2. The adjectives in the chart are not the only *-ly* adjectives. Provide these additional examples.

   an only child

   the lonely girl

   early riser

   Ask students to suggest others.

Customizing for *ESL Students*

Explain to students that adjectives usually appear next to or near the words they modify. Adverbs, however, often are placed far away from the words they modify. This is not always incorrect, but it sometimes creates awkward sentences. *Jorge carefully drew a right triangle* is preferable to *Jorge drew a right triangle carefully. Yin threw away all the broken crayons* is better than *Yin threw all the broken crayons away.*

Critical Viewing

Speculate Students may suggest: The great blue herons often live in large marshlands because they can obtain delicious food easily.

16.2

Adverb or Adjective?

Some words can be either adverbs or adjectives. An adverb always modifies a verb, an adjective, or another adverb. An adjective modifies a noun or a pronoun.

ADVERB MODIFYING VERB:	He drove *fast.*
ADJECTIVE MODIFYING NOUN:	He is a *fast* driver.
ADVERB MODIFYING ADJECTIVE:	She is *much* happier now.
ADJECTIVE MODIFYING NOUN:	I ate too *much* food.

Although many adverbs end in *-ly*, not all words ending in *-ly* are adverbs. Some adjectives are formed by adding *-ly* to nouns.

Nouns	Adjectives With *-ly* Endings
a beautiful *home*	a *homely* animal
an *elder* in the church	an *elderly* man
his true *love*	*lovely* flowers

▼ **Critical Viewing** These great blue herons live in a marshland. Use adjectives and adverbs to write a brief description of the advantages for these birds of living in a marshland. **[Speculate]**

STANDARDIZED TEST PREPARATION WORKSHOP

Using Adjectives and Adverbs Standardized tests often measure students' abilities to recognize and correctly use adjectives and adverbs. Share the following sample test item with students.

Choose the letter of the word that best completes the sentences.

We had ___ been on the road for an hour before our car got a flat tire.

A long
B lately
C barely
D easy

The correct choice is item **C**. An adverb is needed to complete the sentence, and only *barely* completes the sentence correctly.

GRAMMAR IN LITERATURE

from Saving the Wetlands

Barbara A. Lewis

The adverb highlighted in blue italics describes how he *was carried. It modifies the verb* carried.

Then he carried him *upside-down* for a quarter of a mile—all the way to his house. He knew that skunks can't spray when held by the tail.

Exercise 23 **Distinguishing Between Adverbs and Adjectives** On your paper, indicate whether the underlined word in each of the following sentences is an adverb or an adjective.

EXAMPLE: Some might consider a salt marsh ugly.
ANSWER: adjective

1. Many lively animals inhabit Florida's Everglades.
2. Some species of snakes live only in the Everglades.
3. The Florida panther is not the only endangered animal living there.
4. Naturalists hope they have not begun too late to save the Florida panther.
5. It is a truly beautiful animal.
6. Suzette was a late arrival to our touring group.
7. The animal I enjoyed most was the flamingo.
8. The best time to view many swamp animals is early in the morning.
9. Most swamp birds have long, thin legs.
10. The herons flew straight to their homes in the wetland marsh.

More Practice

Grammar Exercise Workbook
- pp. 21–23

On-line Exercise Bank
- Section 16.2

Go on-line:
PHSchool.com
Enter Web Code:
eck-8002

iText

Get instant feedback! Exercise 23 is available on-line or on CD-ROM.

◀ **Critical Viewing** Imagine that you are walking down this nature trail in the Big Cypress Swamp in Florida. Briefly describe what you might see and hear. Use adjectives and adverbs in your sentences. **[Infer]**

Step-by-Step Teaching Guide

Grammar in Literature

1. Ask a student to give an example of *upside-down* as an adjective. (Possible answer: pineapple upside-down cake)
2. Have students identify all the other adverbs and adjectives in the excerpt as well as the words they modify. (Adverbs: *Then* modifies *carried, not (n't)* modifies *can spray, when* modifies *held.* Adjectives: *a* modifies *quarter, a* modifies *mile, all* modifies *way, the* modifies *way, his* modifies *house, the* modifies *tail.*)

Answer Key

Exercise 23

1. adjective
2. adverb
3. adjective
4. adverb
5. adverb
6. adjective
7. adverb
8. adjective
9. adjective
10. adverb

Critical Viewing

Infer Students might suggest: The nature trail goes peacefully along the very swampy areas where many interesting plants and animals live.

PRENTICE HALL
Everyday Spelling

If you have taught the spelling skills in *Prentice Hall Everyday Spelling,* Grade 8, Chapter 19, in conjunction with this *Writing and Grammar* chapter, review and assess students' mastery of the skills before concluding the chapter.

ONGOING ASSESSMENT: Assess Mastery

Use the following resources to assess students' mastery of adjectives and adverbs.

In the Textbook	Print Resources	Technology
Chapter Review, Ex. 34–37, pp. 367–368 Standardized Test Preparation Workshop, pp. 369–370	Formal Assessment, Chapter 16	Writing and Grammar iText, Ch. 16, Chapter Review; On-Line Exercise Bank, Sections 16.1–2

TIME SAVERS!

Answers on Transparency Use the Grammar Exercises Answers on Transparencies for Chapter 16 to have students correct their own or one another's exercises.

On-Line Exercise Bank Have students complete the exercises on computer. The Auto Check feature will grade their work for you!

ASSESS and CLOSE

Section Review

Each of these exercises correlates to a concept in the section on adverbs, pages 360–365. The exercises may be used for more practice, for reteaching, or for review of the Key Concepts presented.

Answer Key

Exercise 24

1. mostly—To what extent?, filled
2. there—Where?, make
3. commonly—To what extent?, found
4. nearly—To what extent?, circular
5. normally—In what manner?, known
6. rather—To what extent? bright
7. pleasantly—To what extent?, fragrant
8. jointly—In what manner?, created
9. often—When? hide
10. nearly—To what extent?, always, always—When?, search

Exercise 25

1. adjective
2. adverb
3. adjective
4. adverb
5. adverb

Exercise 26

Answers will vary.

Exercise 27

Answers will vary.

1. very; adjective
2. extremely; adjective
3. often; verb
4. usually; verb
5. very; adverb

Exercise 28

Find It in Your Reading
finally—came
away—throw

Exercise 29

Find It in Your Writing
Students can decide whether the adverbs should be moved closer to the words they modify.

Exercise 30

Writing Application
You may want to bring in, or have students bring in, magazines with photos students can use for this activity.

Section 16.2

Section Review

GRAMMAR EXERCISES 24–30

Exercise 24 **Recognizing Adverbs and the Words They Modify** On your paper, write the adverbs in the sentences below. Then, identify the question each answers and the word each modifies.

1. This marsh is mostly filled with plants.
2. Many snails make their homes there.
3. The waterlily is very commonly found in the wetlands.
4. It is characterized by large, nearly circular leaves.
5. Its wide, floating leaves are normally known as lily pads.
6. Its rather bright flowers can be white, yellow, pink, scarlet, blue, or purple.
7. The pleasantly fragrant flowers attract insects.
8. Clams, shrimp, and worms jointly created a burrow system in this swamp.
9. The small creatures often hide within these muddy tunnels.
10. Fishermen nearly always search for these areas.

Exercise 25 **Distinguishing Between Adverbs and Adjectives** On your paper, label the underlined word in each sentence *adverb* or *adjective.*

1. Raccoons take nightly trips for food.
2. They can move very fast.
3. They are not the only night prowlers.
4. Raccoons come out in the daytime only if they are not feeling well.
5. The raccoon came too late to find food.

Exercise 26 **Revising With Adverbs** On your paper, revise the following paragraph by adding adverbs.

The eastern diamondback rattlesnake is the largest poisonous snake in the United States. Eastern diamondbacks can grow as long as eight feet, with the average length being two to six feet. Like other rattlesnakes, they make a buzzing sound with the rattles on their tails when they feel threatened. They live in the southeastern United States and eat rabbits, rodents, and birds.

Exercise 27 **Revising Sentences by Adding Adverbs** Add an adverb to modify the underlined word. Identify the part of speech of the underlined word.

1. Coral snakes are beautiful.
2. Coral snakes are also poisonous.
3. They live in the southern United States.
4. They can be identified by their bands of color.
5. If you see one, move cautiously.

Exercise 28 **Find It in Your Reading** Identify two adverbs in this sentence from "Saving the Wetlands." Tell what words they modify.

I finally came clean, but we had to throw my sneakers away.

Exercise 29 **Find It in Your Writing** Look through your portfolio for sentences that describe how someone did something. Circle any adverbs you used.

Exercise 30 **Writing Application** Imagine that you have put together a photo essay from your visit to a swamp. Write captions for several photos, making sure to include adverbs.

Chapter 16 Chapter Review

GRAMMAR EXERCISES 31–39

Exercise 31 **Recognizing Adjectives and the Words They Modify** Each of the following sentences contains at least one underlined adjective. Write the adjectives on your paper, and label each one *adjective, proper adjective, compound adjective, noun used as adjective, definite article* or *indefinite article.*

1. The American bittern is a typical bird of the wetlands.
2. Many bitterns have brownish bodies with dark, longitudinal stripes.
3. The stripes help them blend in with the tall grasses in their habitats.
4. They feed on small aquatic animals.
5. The American bittern builds its small nest on the ground.
6. A well-known Floridian attraction is the marshland areas of the Everglades.
7. This became the home region of the Seminole Indians.
8. Its mangrove swamps are fascinating to explore.
9. Visitors can often spot alligator nests.
10. The American government is trying to protect endangered animals there.
11. Gallinules are birds that have cone-shaped bills.
12. They live in weed-filled Florida marshes and swamps.
13. One common gallinule is sooty-colored with a red, shieldlike forehead.
14. The more colorful purple gallinule is quite attractive.
15. Their widespread toes permit them to walk on lily pads or aquatic plants.

Exercise 32 **Recognizing Demonstrative, Interrogative, and Indefinite Adjectives** Label each underlined word in the following sentences *pronoun* or *adjective.*

1. Is that a green tree frog?
2. What place does it call home?
3. That one lives in a swamp in Georgia.
4. Those feet allow the tree frog to cling to tree trunks.
5. This coloration helps him blend into the background.
6. Which are its favorite foods?
7. Insects like these are what he eats.
8. What is that threadlike green stuff?
9. Few people in our group had ever seen it before.
10. Did you see which tree had Spanish moss on it?

Exercise 33 **Writing Sentences With Demonstrative, Interrogative, and Indefinite Adjectives** Use each of the words below in a sentence.

1. which (pronoun)
2. what (adjective)
3. each (pronoun)
4. few (adjective)
5. this (pronoun)
6. that (adjective)
7. his (adjective)
8 any (adjective)
9. whose (pronoun)
10. those (pronoun)

Exercise 34 **Identifying Adverbs and the Words They Modify** In each of the following sentences, identify the adverb and the word it modifies. Also, identify the part of speech of the modified word.

1. The red-winged blackbird commonly inhabits wetland marshes.
2. It generally flies in the marshes and upland fields of North America.
3. The male red-winged blackbird clearly bears flashing-red shoulder patches.
4. Many blackbirds nest sociably in colonies.

CHAPTER REVIEW

Each of these exercises correlates to a concept in the chapter on adjectives and adverbs, pages 346–365. The exercises may be used for more practice, for reteaching, or for review of the Key Concepts presented.

Answer Key

Exercise 31

1. proper; adjective
2. adjective; adjective; adjective; adjective
3. definite article; adjective
4. adjective; adjective
5. proper; adjective; definite
6. indefinite article; compound; proper; compound; noun used as adjective
7. noun used as adjective, proper
8. noun used as adjective, adjective
9. noun used as adjective
10. proper; adjective
11. compound
12. compound; noun used as adjective, proper
13. indefinite; adjective; compound; indefinite, compound
14. adjective
15. compound; adjective

Exercise 32

1. pronoun
2. adjective
3. adjective
4. adjective
5. adjective
6. pronoun
7. pronoun
8. pronoun
9. adjective
10. adjective

continued

Answer Key continued

Exercise 33

Possible answers:

1. Which are your shoes?
2. What color are they?
3. Each needs cleaning.
4. Few shoes are leather today.
5. This is torn.
6. That shoe needs a lace.
7. His sneakers wore out.
8. Any slippers will do.
9. Whose are in the brown box?
10. Those belong to me.

Exercise 34

1. commonly inhabits, verb
2. generally flies, verb
3. clearly bears, verb
4. sociably, nest, verb

continued

TIME SAVERS!

Answers on Transparency Use the Grammar Exercises Answers on Transparencies for Chapter 16 to have students correct their own or one another's exercises.

On-Line Exercise Bank Have students complete the exercises on computer. The Auto Check feature will grade their work for you!

Exercise 34 continued

5. strictly, feed, verb
6. exclusively aquatic, adjective
7. nearly oval, adjective
8. surprisingly long, adjective
9. noticeably showy, adjective
10. terribly troublesome, adjective

Exercise 35

1. adverb
2. adjective
3. adverb
4. adjective
5. adverb, adjective

Exercise 36

Sample answers

1. Only I jog slowly.
2. The young boy works hard on his science report.
3. My English teacher is a young woman.
4. The science project was finished early.
5. The pretty bird flew away quickly.
6. Whose snapping turtle is that?
7. The Florida marshlands are very interesting.
8. Have you been on the new nature trail alone?
9. Did you alone really see that huge bird?
10. The green snake moved quickly through the cold water.

Exercise 37

1. My hands are very dirty.
2. The star was so far away we could hardly see it.
3. Which flowers are more beautiful?
4. That is quite an accomplishment.
5. I go away once each year.
6. Both children looked unhappy.
7. I will discard my worn-out socks tomorrow.
8. We were almost home when the rain suddenly began.
9. These dogs live nearby.
10. I usually run slowly, but today I ran unusually fast.

Chapter Review Exercises cont'd.

5. These birds feed strictly on insects, seeds, and grain.
6. Water hyacinth is an exclusively aquatic plant found in wetland areas.
7. The plants have nearly oval leaves with large shoots that aid in flotation.
8. A surprisingly long, feathery root dangles below the water's surface.
9. These large, noticeably showy violet flowers have bright markings.
10. The water hyacinth has become a terribly troublesome weed.

Exercise 35 **Distinguishing Between Adverbs and Adjectives** On your paper, label the underlined word in each of the following sentences *adverb* or *adjective*.

1. Some turtles live <u>only</u> in swamps.
2. Turtles are the <u>only</u> reptiles with shells.
3. Because of their <u>short</u> legs and heavy shells, turtles cannot run <u>fast</u>.
4. Compared to other turtles, snapping turtles are <u>fast</u>.
5. An African pancake tortoise lays <u>only</u> one egg at a time; it is the <u>only</u> turtle to do that.

Exercise 36 **Revising Sentences With Adjectives and Adverbs** Revise the following sentences by adding adjectives to modify the nouns or pronouns and adverbs to modify the adjectives, verbs, and adverbs.

1. I jog.
2. The boy works on his report.
3. My teacher is a woman.
4. The project was finished.
5. The bird flew away.
6. Whose turtle is that?
7. The marshlands are interesting.
8. Have you been on the nature trail?
9. Did you see that bird?
10. The snake moved through the water.

Exercise 37 **Writing Sentences With Adjectives and Adverbs** Write sentences using the following adjectives or adverbs or both.

1. very / dirty
2. hardly / far
3. which / beautiful
4. that / quite
5. away / each
6. both / unhappy
7. worn-out / tomorrow
8. almost / suddenly
9. these / nearby
10. slowly / unusually / fast

Exercise 38 **Writing Application** Imagine that you are an animal in a wetland area. Identify the kind of animal you are, and describe the events of a typical day. Use adverbs and adjectives to make your descriptions vivid.

Exercise 39 **CUMULATIVE REVIEW Nouns, Pronouns, and Verbs** On your paper, make a chart with these headings: *Common Nouns, Proper Nouns, Action Verbs, Linking Verbs,* and *Pronouns.* Put each underlined word below under its appropriate heading.

<u>Scientists</u> are working on a <u>plan</u> to preserve the <u>Everglades</u> in <u>Florida</u>. Plants and animals <u>are</u> in danger there. One plan <u>involves</u> building a system of pipes and canals to refill drained areas with fresh <u>water</u>. <u>This</u> will <u>restore</u> homes for many animals. <u>We</u> hope this plan <u>works</u>. There is a need to preserve animal life. <u>Everyone</u> in the <u>United States</u> should support the plan.

TIME SAVERS!

Answers on Transparency Use the Grammar Exercises Answers on Transparencies for Chapter 16 to have students correct their own or one another's exercises.

On-Line Exercise Bank Have students complete the exercises on computer. The Auto Check feature will grade their work for you!

Exercise 38

Writing Application

Ask some volunteers to read their paragraphs aloud. Challenge the listeners to identify the adverbs and adjectives.

Exercise 39

Cumulative Review

Common Nouns: scientists, plan, water
Proper Nouns: Everglades, Florida, United States
Action Verbs: involves, restore, works
Linking Verb: are
Pronouns: This, We, Everyone

Standardized Test Preparation Workshop

Using Adjectives and Adverbs

A knowledge of how adjectives and adverbs function will help you answer several types of standardized test questions. The following test item will give you practice with items that measure your ability to use adjectives and adverbs.

Test Tip

Read through answer choices, and eliminate choices that would change the meaning of the sentence.

Sample Test Item

Directions Read the passage, and choose the letter of the word or group of words that belongs in each space.

Yesterday, the class took a __1__ bus ride to the museum.

1 A slowly
B very
C hardly
D long

Answer and Explanation

The correct answer is *D*. Because the word in the blank space is meant to modify bus ride, a noun, the only correct choice is an adjective.

Practice 1 **Directions** Read the passage, and choose the letter of the word or group of words that belongs in each space.

All my relatives gather __(1)__ to celebrate the Fourth of July. We choose a spot that is __(2)__ for everyone, so that each person can get there __(3)__. __(4)__ we meet in a park. When we get together as a group, my family can be __(5)__.

1 **A** year
B yearly
C some
D silly

2 **F** nearly
G outside
H conveniently
J convenient

3 **A** fair
B fairly
C easy
D easily

4 **F** Some
G Never
H Frequently
J Rare

5 **A** lately
B soon
C loud
D loudly

▶ *Lesson Objectives*

- To correctly use adjectives and adverbs in sentences.

Step-by-Step Teaching Guide

Using Adjectives and Adverbs

Teaching Resources: Standardized Test Preparation Workbook, pp.31–32

1. Have students find the word or words the answer will modify first.
2. Explain to students that although only one adjective was given in the sample answers, they will sometimes need to choose between or among adjectives, also.

Answer Key

Practice 1

1. B
2. J
3. D
4. H
5. C

TEST-TAKING TIP

In order to tell whether a word is an adverb or adjective, identify the word it modifies first. For example, in the sample test item, the correct word must modify the noun *bus ride*, so only an adjective is correct.

Chapter 17
Time and Resource Manager

In-Depth Lesson Plan

	LESSON FOCUS	PRINT AND MEDIA RESOURCES
DAY 1	**Prepositions** Students learn to recognize and use prepositions (pp. 370–373).	**Teaching Resources** *Grammar Exercise Workbook,* pp. 39–40; *Grammar Exercises Answers on Transparencies,* Ch. 17; *Hands-on Grammar Activity Book,* Ch. 17 ***Writing and Grammar iText* (Interactive Text),** Ch. 17; ***On-line Exercise Bank,*** Ch. 17
DAY 2	**Prepositional Phrases; Prepositions and Adverbs** Students learn to recognize and use prepositional phrases and to distinguish between prepositions and adverbs. They also complete a Hands-on Grammar activity (pp. 374–377).	**Teaching Resources** *Grammar Exercise Workbook,* pp. 39–42; *Grammar Exercises Answers on Transparencies,* Ch. 17 ***Writing and Grammar iText* (Interactive Text),** Ch. 17; ***On-line Exercise Bank,*** Ch. 17
DAY 3	**Review and Assess** Students review the chapter and demonstrate mastery of prepositions (pp. 378–379).	**Teaching Resources** *Formal Assessment,* Ch. 17; *Grammar Exercises Answers on Transparencies,* Ch. 17 ***Writing and Grammar iText* (Interactive Text),** Ch. 17, Chapter Review

Accelerated Lesson Plan

	LESSON FOCUS	PRINT AND MEDIA RESOURCES
DAY 1	**Prepositions; Prepositional Phrases; Prepositions and Adverbs** Students learn to recognize and use prepositions and prepositional phrases, as well as to distinguish between prepositions and adverbs (370–377).	**Teaching Resources** *Grammar Exercise Workbook,* pp. 39–42; *Grammar Exercises Answers on Transparencies,* Ch. 17; *Hands-on Grammar Activity Book,* Ch. 17 ***Writing and Grammar iText* (Interactive Text),** Ch. 17; ***On-line Exercise Bank,*** Ch. 17
DAY 2	**Review and Assess** Students review the chapter and demonstrate mastery of prepositions (378–379).	**Teaching Resources** *Formal Assessment,* Ch. 17; *Grammar Exercises Answers on Transparencies,* Ch. 17 ***Writing and Grammar iText* (Interactive Text),** Ch. 17, Chapter Review

Options for Adapting Lesson Plans

HOMEWORK

Have students complete any stage of the lesson for homework.

SPELLING

To teach spelling skills in conjunction with grammar, mechanics, and usage, work through *Prentice Hall Everyday Spelling,* Grade 8, Chapter 20, as you cover this *Writing and Grammar* chapter.

TECHNOLOGY

Students can use *Writing and Grammar iText* to complete the exercises interactively on computer. They can complete additional exercises in the *On-line Exercise Bank:* The Auto Check feature will grade their work. Go online: PHSchool.com Use Web code: eck-8002

FEATURES

Extend coverage with the Grammar in Literature feature (p. 376) and the Standardized Test Preparation Workshop (p. 379).

INTEGRATED SKILLS COVERAGE

Grammar in Literature
SE p. 376

Writing
Find It in Your Writing, SE p. 377
Writing Application, SE p. 378

Viewing and Representing
Critical Viewing, SE pp. 370, 373, 375, 376

BLOCK SCHEDULING

Pacing Suggestions
For 90-minute Blocks
- Administer the Diagnostic Test to students to determine instructional coverage.
- Have students complete the necessary exercises in class. Use the Hands-on Grammar Activity to provide a change of pace.

Resources for Varying Instruction
- ***Writing and Grammar iText*** **(Interactive Text)** A 90-minute block provides an ideal opportunity for students to work on computer.

Professional Development Support
- ***How to Manage Instruction in the Block*** This teaching resource provides management and activity suggestions.

ASSESSMENT SUPPORT

Standardized Test Preparation Workshop SE p. 379; ATE p. 374
Standardized Test Preparation Workbook, pp. 33–34
Formal Assessment, Ch. 17

MEDIA AND TECHNOLOGY

For the Student
- ***Writing and Grammar iText*** **(Interactive Text),** Ch. 17
- ***On-line Exercise Bank,*** Ch. 17

For the Teacher
- ***Resource Pro*** **CD-ROM**

WRITING AND GRAMMAR ON-LINE

iText Interactive Text (On-line or on CD-ROM)
- Easily navigable instruction with on-line supporting resources
- Self-scoring exercises and diagnostic tests

Companion Web Site PHSchool.com
- On-line Exercise Bank (use Web Code eck-8002)

See the Go On-line! feature, SE p. iii.

MEETING INDIVIDUAL NEEDS

Less Advanced Students ATE p. 372
ESL Students ATE p. 375

LITERATURE CONNECTIONS

Grammar in Literature selection from *Prentice Hall Literature: Timeless Voices, Timeless Themes,* Silver:
from "Raymond's Run," Toni Cade Bambara, SE p. 376

CHAPTER 17
PREPOSITIONS

Lesson Objectives

1. To recognize prepositions in sentences.
2. To recognize compound prepositions in sentences.
3. To identify prepositional phrases in sentences.
4. To recognize a preposition used as an adverb.

Critical Viewing

Analyze Students may suggest such prepositions as *over* or *across*.

Chapter

17 Prepositions

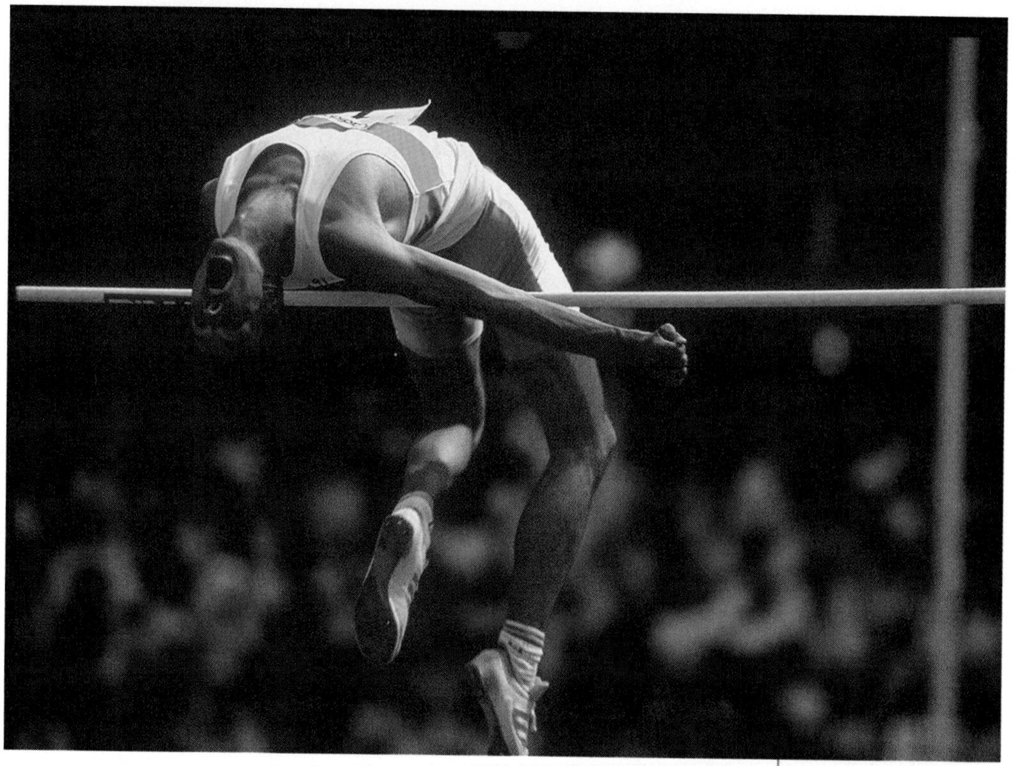

▲ **Critical Viewing** What prepositions can you use to tell the location of the high jumper in relation to the bar? **[Analyze]**

Prepositions show how some words in your sentences relate to others. They can make important differences in your ideas. For instance, in writing about track-and-field events, it might be important to identify the distance *between* two competitors, the leaders *in* a race, the runner who sprinted first *across* the finish line. As you see, prepositions help to identify location.

In this chapter, you will learn to recognize prepositions and to use them effectively in your sentences.

ONGOING ASSESSMENT: Diagnose

If students miss more than one item in any category, direct them to the relevant pages of the text and assign exercises for practice and review.

Prepositions	Diagnostic Test Items	Teach	Practice	Chapter Review
Skill Check A				
Identify Prepositions	A 1–5	p. 372	Ex. 1	Ex. 6
Skill Check B				
Compound Prepositions	B 6–10	p. 373	Ex. 2	Ex. 6
Skill Check C				
Prepositional Phrases	C 11–15	p. 374	Ex. 3	Ex. 7

Diagnostic Test

Directions: Write all answers on a separate sheet of paper.

Skill Check A. Identify the prepositions in the following sentences.

1. You can think about a sport as an athletic game or a test of skill.
2. Sports can be a source of diversion for those who play or observe them.
3. Sports have existed for various purposes since the times of the ancient Egyptians and Greeks.
4. The ancient Egyptians swam, raced, wrestled, and played games with sticks and round objects.
5. At first, the ancient Greeks held athletic contests in honor of the gods or in thanksgiving to them.

Skill Check B. Identify the compound preposition in each sentence.

6. The games provided entertainment, in addition to having religious significance.
7. According to historians, the games were a vital part of ancient Greek civilization.
8. Eventually, professional athletes played in place of volunteer citizens.
9. Because of the importance of the games, winners were treated as heroes.
10. Warring city-states sometimes called a truce due to the games.

Skill Check C. Write the prepositional phrase(s) you find in each sentence below. Circle the object of each preposition.

11. In Rome, games took place at the beginning of each year.
12. At first, the public treasury provided funds for the events.
13. Corrupt politicians later tried winning the support of the people by lavishly spending excessive amounts of money on the games.
14. These politicians held games on the slightest pretext so that they could compete for the favor of the public.
15. Over time, athletic events lost their original religious meaning and purpose among the people.

Skill Check D. Write *prep* if the underlined word in each sentence below is used as a preposition. Write *adv* if it is used as an adverb.

16. We have learned a lot <u>about</u> the games.
17. They were celebrated <u>over</u> the summer every four years.
18. Each city-state brought <u>along</u> its best athletes.
19. The athletes walked <u>about</u>, waiting to be called.
20. Some stood in lines <u>along</u> the edge of the arena.

Answer Key

Diagnostic Test

- Each item in the Diagnostic Test corresponds to a specific concept in the chapter on prepositions. This will enable you to tailor instruction to the particular needs of your students. See "Ongoing Assessment" below for further details.
- Answers for the Diagnostic Test and all chapter exercises are available in *Grammar Exercises Answers on Transparencies* in your teaching resources.

Skill Check A

1. about, of
2. of, for
3. for, since, of
4. with
5. At, in, of, in, to

Skill Check B

6. in addition to
7. According to
8. in place of
9. Because of
10. due to

Skill Check C

11. In (Rome), at the (beginning), of each (year)
12. At (first), for the (events)
13. of the (people), of (money), on the (games)
14. on the slightest (pretext), for the (favor), of the (public)
15. Over (time), among the (people)

Skill Check D

16. prep
17. prep
18. adv
19. adv
20. prep

ONGOING ASSESSMENT: Diagnose *continued*

Prepositions	Diagnostic Test Items	Teach	Practice	Chapter Review
Skill Check D				
Preposition or Adverb?	D 16–20	p. 375	Ex. 4–5	Ex. 8
Cumulative Reviews and Applications				Ex. 9–10

TIME SAVERS!

Answers on Transparency Use the Grammar Exercises Answers on Transparencies for Chapter 17 to facilitate corrections by students.

On-Line Exercise Bank Have students complete the exercises on computer. The Auto Check feature will grade their work for you!

PREPARE and ENGAGE

Interest GRABBER Show students two small objects, such as a stapler and a paperweight. Place the two items in various positions relative to each other and have students describe the positions. Write their answers (such as *below, against, behind,* and *near*) on the chalkboard. Tell them that these words are called prepositions.

Activate Prior Knowledge

Have students choose partners for a treasure hunt. One student hides a small object. The partner follows verbal directions to find it. Students should be using such phrases as *behind the books, in the top drawer,* or *on the third shelf down.* Point out how necessary prepositions are for giving directions.

TEACH

Step-by-Step Teaching Guide

Recognizing Prepositions

1. Have a volunteer read aloud the key concept. Explain that a preposition relates two nouns or pronouns in terms of space (words such as *near, behind,* and *inside*) or time (words such as *before, during,* and *after*).
2. Another way to look at prepositions is that they answer the questions *Where?* or *When?*

   The monkey is in the tree. (Where is the monkey?)

   The cheerleaders performed during halftime. (When do the cheerleaders perform?)

Customize for *Less Advanced Students*

Write the word *preposition* on the chalkboard, underlined as shown. Remind students that the word *position* means "where something is." This will help them remember that many prepositions show where nouns are relative to other nouns.

17

Recognizing Prepositions

Prepositions are words such as *against, among, at, beyond, during, of,* and *on.*

KEY CONCEPT A **preposition** relates the noun or pronoun following it to another word in the sentence. ■

The chart below lists fifty of the most commonly used prepositions.

FREQUENTLY USED PREPOSITIONS

about	behind	during	off	to
above	below	except	on	toward
across	beneath	for	onto	under
after	beside	from	opposite	underneath
against	besides	in	out	until
along	between	inside	outside	up
among	beyond	into	over	upon
around	but	like	past	with
at	by	near	since	within
before	down	of	through	without

Exercise 1 **Recognizing and Revising Prepositions** Write the preposition in each of the following sentences. Then, revise the sentence, using a different preposition.

EXAMPLE: The boys played basketball at noon.
ANSWER: at—The boys played basketball before noon.

1. Basketball is a game played between two opposing five-person teams.
2. The basketball court features a large circle at the center.
3. A basketball hoop is suspended above each end.
4. Each player has a position to play in the game.
5. The center often stands beneath the basket to catch rebounds.
6. There are also two guards, who are leaders within the team, as well as two forwards.
7. In the beginning, a jump ball gets the game started.
8. Shooting the ball into the hoop can give a team either one, two, or three points.
9. A team must also defend its basket from its opponents' attacks.
10. The team that has the most points by the end wins.

Theme: Sports

In this chapter, you will learn about prepositions and prepositional phrases. The examples and exercises are about sports.

Cross-Curricular Connection: Physical Education

More Practice

Grammar Exercise Workbook
- pp. 39–40

On-line Exercise Bank
- Chapter 17

Go on-line: PHSchool.com
Enter Web Code: eck-8002

TIME AND RESOURCE MANAGER

Resources
Print: Grammar Exercise Workbook, pp. 39–42
Technology: Writing and Grammar iText, Ch. 17; On-Line Exercise Bank, Ch. 17

In-Depth Coverage	Accelerated Pace
• Work through all key concepts, pp. 372–376. • Assign and review Exercises 1–2. • Do the Hands-on Grammar activity on p. 377.	• Assign pp. 372–376 for independent student review.

KEY CONCEPT Prepositions consisting of two or three words are called *compound prepositions.* ■

Some compound prepositions are listed in this chart.

COMPOUND PREPOSITIONS		
according to	by means of	instead of
ahead of	in addition to	in view of
apart from	in back of	next to
aside from	in front of	on account of
as of	in place of	on top of
because of	in spite of	out of

The choice of preposition affects the way the other words in a sentence relate to each other. In the following example, read the sentence using each preposition in turn. Notice how each preposition changes the relationship between *played* and *gym.*

EXAMPLE: The girls played {near / opposite / in back of} the gym.

Exercise 2 **Recognizing Compound Prepositions** Identify the compound preposition in each of the following sentences.

EXAMPLE: In spite of its limited popularity in the United States, soccer is one of the most popular sports in the world.
ANSWER: in spite of

1. According to archaeologists, kicking games were played in many ancient societies.
2. However, the modern game of soccer was developed in England in the nineteenth century, in addition to other kicking games developed there.
3. In 1863, out of the many different varieties of kicking games, the London Football Association recognized two: rugby football and association football ("soccer" in the United States).
4. In rugby football, the athlete controls the ball by means of handling and carrying; however, association football forbids the use of hands.
5. Later, because of the rules established by the London Football Association, soccer became widely popular among people of the working classes.

▼ Critical Viewing
How many different prepositions can you use to describe the positions of the players in relation to one another and in relation to the ball? **[Analyze]**

Step-by-Step Teaching Guide

Compound Prepositions

1. Review compound words: two or more words that are put together to function as one, such as *applesauce* and *sister-in-law.* A compound preposition is two or more words that are put together to function as one preposition. Point out that many of the words in compound prepositions are prepositions: *in* addition *to, on* account *of.*
2. In the example, the phrase *in back of* functions as one part of speech, even though it is three words long. Challenge students to substitute a one-word preposition for this phrase without changing the meaning of the sentence. (Possible response: *behind*) Try the same challenge with other compound prepositions on the chart. (Students might change *next to* to *near, ahead of* to *before,* and so on.)

Critical Viewing

Analyze Students may suggest such prepositions as *next to, in back of, in front of, near,* or *around.*

Answer Key

Exercise 1 *(page 372)*

Answers may vary. Samples are given.

1. between—Basketball is a game played with two opposing five-person teams.
2. at—The basketball court features a large circle in the center.
3. above—A basketball hoop is suspended over each end.
4. in—Each player has a position to play throughout the game.
5. beneath—The center often stands under the basket to catch rebounds.
6. within—There are also two guards who are leaders on the team, as well as two forwards.
7. In—At the beginning, a jump ball gets the game started.
8. into—Shooting the ball through the hoop can give a team either one, two, or three points.
9. from—A team must also defend its basket against its opponents' attacks.
10. by—The team that has the most points at the end wins.

Answer Key continued

Exercise 2

1. According to
2. in addition to
3. out of
4. by means of
5. because of

continued

Step-by-Step Teaching Guide

Prepositional Phrases

1. Use the sentences in Exercise 2 on page 373 to demonstrate objects of prepositions. Ask students to identify the word to which each compound prepositions refers. For example, the phrase *according to* in Sentence 1 refers to *archaeologists.* Explain that the word the preposition refers to is its object.
2. Point out the phrases *to play* (sentence 4) and *to catch* (sentence 5) in Exercise 1 on page 372. In these phrases, *to* is not a preposition. When *to* appears immediately before a verb, the phrase is an infinitive. Remind students that the object of a preposition has to be a noun or pronoun. This will help them remember the difference between prepositional phrases and infinitives.
3. Read aloud the first sentence at the top of the page. Point out the implied rule that a sentence should never end with a preposition. A preposition must always be part of a phrase; it must have an object, and the object always follows it in a correctly written sentence. The one exception to this rule is prepositions used as adverbs, which students will learn about on page 375 of this chapter.

Answer Key

Exercise 3

1. in <u>1871</u>
2. at <u>Wembley Stadium</u>, in <u>London</u>, with the annual <u>Cup Final</u>
3. After its <u>organization</u>, through <u>England</u>
4. Around <u>1888</u>, in many <u>areas</u>, of the <u>country</u>
5. in <u>1871</u>, at <u>Glasgow</u>, between all-star <u>teams</u>, from <u>England</u> and <u>Scotland</u>
6. About the <u>end</u> of the nineteenth <u>century</u>, across the <u>globe</u>
7. with <u>them</u>, around the <u>world</u>
8. in <u>Europe</u>, to the <u>sport</u>
9. In <u>South America</u>, to <u>it</u>, with the <u>game</u>
10. as the <u>World Cup</u>, in <u>1933</u>, around the <u>world</u>

17

Recognizing Prepositional Phrases

A preposition must always be followed by a noun or a pronoun. The group of words beginning with the preposition and ending with the noun or pronoun is called a *prepositional phrase.* The noun or pronoun that follows the preposition is called the *object of the preposition.* Notice that when identifying the object of a preposition, you do not include any modifiers of the noun or pronoun.

EXAMPLES:
- (PREP) with (OBJ of PREP) <u>us</u>
- (PREP) according to the new (OBJ of PREP) <u>coach</u>
- (PREP) inside the large, modern (OBJ of PREP) <u>stadium</u>

Exercise 3 **Recognizing Prepositional Phrases** Write the prepositional phrase or phrases in each sentence, and underline the object of each preposition.

EXAMPLE: Professional football players were recognized for the first time in 1885.

ANSWER: for the first <u>time</u>; in <u>1885</u>

1. The Football Association Cup, a soccer tournament, was first organized in 1871.
2. The tournament, which is still played today, finishes at Wembley Stadium in London with the annual Cup Final.
3. After its organization, soccer spread rapidly through England.
4. Around 1888, regular league play was begun in many areas of the country.
5. In 1872, the first international game took place at Glasgow between all-star teams from England and Scotland.
6. About the end of the nineteenth century, soccer spread across the globe.
7. British sailors, traders, and workers carried the game with them around the world.
8. In Europe, Germans, Austrians, and Italians quickly took to the sport.
9. In South America, Brazilians, Argentines, and Uruguayans adapted to it quickly and enjoyed the challenges that came with the game.
10. Finally, the first World Championship, now known as the World Cup, was organized in 1930, and it is now wildly popular all around the world.

Grammar and Style Tip

The object of a preposition may be more than one word, such as a compound proper noun *(in the <u>Grand Canyon</u>)* or two objects linked by a conjunction *(between the <u>defenders</u> and the <u>goal</u>).*

STANDARDIZED TEST PREPARATION WORKSHOP

Grammar and Usage Standardized tests often ask students to identify certain grammatical elements in sentences. Ask students to identify the underlined words in the following sentence:

Tinker threw the ball <u>to Evers</u>, who tagged the spikes <u>of the sliding runner</u>, leaped <u>over him</u>, and hurled the ball <u>through the air</u> to smack into Chance's glove <u>at first base</u>.

A prepositional phrases
B compound prepositions
C adverbs
D A, B, and C

The correct choice is item **A.** There are no prepositions more than one word long, so item **B** is incorrect. None of the prepositions stands alone and modifies a verb, so item **C** is incorrect.

Distinguishing Between Prepositions and Adverbs

Some words can be either prepositions or adverbs, depending on how they are used in a sentence. To be a *preposition*, a word must have an object and be part of a prepositional phrase. An *adverb* modifies a verb and has no object.

PREPOSITION:	The ball flew *past* third base.
ADVERB:	The umpire ran *past* quickly.
PREPOSITION:	They sat *inside* the dugout.
ADVERB:	Please come *inside* soon.

Exercise 4 Distinguishing Between Prepositions and Adverbs In each of the following pairs of sentences, one sentence contains a word used as a preposition, and the other contains the same word used as an adverb. Find the words that appear in both sentences. If the word acts as a preposition, write *preposition* on your paper. If the word acts as an adverb, write *adverb*.

EXAMPLE: Umpires stand along the baselines. We waited for the hot dog vendor to come along.

ANSWER: along the baselines (preposition)
along (adverb)

1. In modern baseball, an umpire stands behind home plate. A single strikeout can cause one team to win a game or to fall behind.
2. At a night game, the lights are turned on. The pitcher stands on the mound.
3. The players warm up before the game. They've practiced the skills many times before.
4. Through popular legend, Abner Doubleday invented baseball. However, those doubting the claim find it quite easy to see through.
5. Most scholars believe that a variety of similar games over time eventually gave rise to baseball. They believe these games carried over from other cultures.
6. By April, the season has begun. By November, it has gone by.
7. Eager fans are in line for tickets. All want to get in on time.
8. The pitcher threw the ball across the plate. The catcher ran across to the pitcher.
9. The ball was pitched low and outside. Nevertheless, the batter hit it outside the park.
10. Fans don't like to sit around waiting for hits. They like to see players running around the bases.

▲ **Critical Viewing** Where might the ball have gone? Use one or more prepositions in your answer. Then, see if you can use the same word as an adverb. **[Speculate]**

More Practice

Grammar Exercise Workbook
- pp. 41–42

On-line Exercise Bank
- Chapter 17

Go on-line:
PHSchool.com
Enter Web Code:
eck-8002

ONGOING ASSESSMENT: Prerequisite Skills

If students have difficulty with prepositions used as adverbs, you may find it necessary to review the following to ensure coverage of prerequisite knowledge.

In the Textbook	Print Resources	Technology
Adverbs, pp. 360–366	Grammar Exercise Workbook, pp. 33–38	Writing and Grammar iText, Section 16.2; On-Line Exercise Bank, Section 16.2

Step-by-Step Teaching Guide

Preposition or Adverb?

1. Remind students that an adverb answers the question *Where? When? In what way?* or *To what extent?*
2. Ask students to identify the question that *past* and *inside* answer in the sentences on page 375 labeled *adverb*, and then identify the words these adverbs modify. (Both answer the question *Where?* about the verbs *ran* and *come*.)
3. To distinguish between a preposition and an adverb, students can try rewriting the sentence so that the preposition is part of a prepositional phrase. If they can do this, the preposition is not an adverb:

   I am the one the baseball belongs to.

   The baseball belongs to me.

Customizing for *ESL Students*

Help students understand that the absence of a prepositional phrase indicates that the preposition is used as an adverb.

Critical Viewing

Speculate Students might suggest sentences such as, *He hit the ball out of the park. He struck out.*

Answer Key

Exercise 4

1. behind—preposition, adverb
2. on—adverb, preposition
3. before—preposition, adverb
4. through—preposition, adverb
5. over—preposition, adverb
6. by—preposition, preposition, adverb
7. in—preposition, adverb
8. across—preposition, adverb
9. outside—adverb, preposition
10. around—adverb, preposition

PRENTICE HALL
Everyday Spelling

If you have taught the spelling skills in *Prentice Hall Everyday Spelling,* Grade 8, Chapter 20, in conjunction with this *Writing and Grammar* chapter, review and assess students' mastery of the skills before concluding the chapter.

Step-by-Step Teaching Guide

Grammar in Literature

1. Highlight the phrases *to win* and *to run* in this passage. Ask whether these are prepositional phrases and have students explain their answers. (No. The word after *to* is a verb in both cases, so these are infinitives.)
2. Have students identify the objects of the highlighted prepositions. *(feet, kindergarten, myself, neighborhood)* If students make mistakes, remind them that the object does not include any modifiers in the prepositional phrase.

More About the Writer

Toni Cade Bambara (1939–1995) used her African American heritage as a vehicle for her writing. Her stories also often revolved around the emerging identify of black women. She hoped that her writing "might lift someone's spirits, or enable someone to see more clearly."

Critical Viewing

Analyze Students might write sentences with prepositional phrases, such as *Her teammate took the baton in her hand and ran as hard as she could.*

Answer Key

Exercise 5

Answers will vary. Samples are given.

1. Wilma Rudolph crossed the finish line in first place.
2. Crossing the flag behind the others, Aubrey collapsed in exhaustion and disappointment.
3. By noon, the contestants in the marathon had been running for a long time.
4. Jesse Owens was so fast that he defeated all the other sprinters with ease.
5. The speed with which Willie Mays ran to the center field wall to make the catch was beyond belief.
6. After a while, I realized that I could not hope to break the school 800-meter record.
7. Eric Liddell was far behind, but he won the race in spite of the distance he had to make up.
8. Harold Abrahams dashed past the others to win the gold medal in the 100-meter race.
9. We knew we could do well in the track meet against the competition from the other schools.
10. The marathon is the greatest test of endurance in all sports.
11. The fans watched the track as the runner sped around again.
12. The team came in second in the relay.
13. Though she trained indoors, she would race outside.
14. He raced along as though he were going to win.
15. She reached the finish line and sailed across.

17

GRAMMAR IN LITERATURE

from Raymond's Run

Toni Cade Bambara

In the following passage from "Raymond's Run," the prepositional phrases appear in blue. The prepositions are underlined.

. . . I'm the fastest thing *on two feet.*

There is no track meet that I don't win the first place medal. I used to win the twenty-yard dash when I was a little kid *in kindergarten.* Nowadays, it's the fifty-yard dash. And tomorrow I'm subject to run the quarter-meter relay all *by myself* and come in first, second, and third. The big kids call me Mercury cause I'm the swiftest thing *in the neighborhood.*

Exercise 5 **Writing Sentences With Prepositional Phrases and Adverbs** Using the following prepositional phrases, write ten sentences about running or a runner. Then, write five more sentences, using words 11–15 as adverbs.

1. in first place
2. behind the others
3. for a long time
4. with ease
5. beyond belief
6. after a while
7. in spite of the distance
8. past the others
9. against the competition
10. of endurance
11. around
12. in
13. outside
14. along
15. across

▼ **Critical Viewing** What will happen when this relay runner hands off her baton? Answer using at least one prepositional phrase. **[Analyze]**

Hands-on Grammar

Bridge and Tunnel Preposition Practice

With a partner, build and use a bridge and tunnel to help you practice your prepositions and prepositional phrases.

Begin with two sheets of paper. One sheet will be your base. Fold another sheet in half the short way, and roll it into a cylinder with the edges overlapping about two inches. Tape the edges together; then, tape down the cylinder the long way in the middle of your base sheet. Using a ruler as a guide, draw a two-lane road entering and leaving the "tunnel." Next, cut out a strip that is 8 1/2" long and 1 1/2" wide. Draw a two-lane road down the middle of the strip. Position the "bridge" horizontally on your base, over the tunnel, and tape it to the edges of the paper. Finally, from another piece of paper, cut out two small, simple cars, one for you and one for your partner. (See illustration.)

Now, with your partner, take turns "driving" your cars. See how many prepositional phrases you can use to describe where each car is and where it is going in relation to the bridge, the tunnel, and the other car. You should be able to think of at least fifteen prepositions.

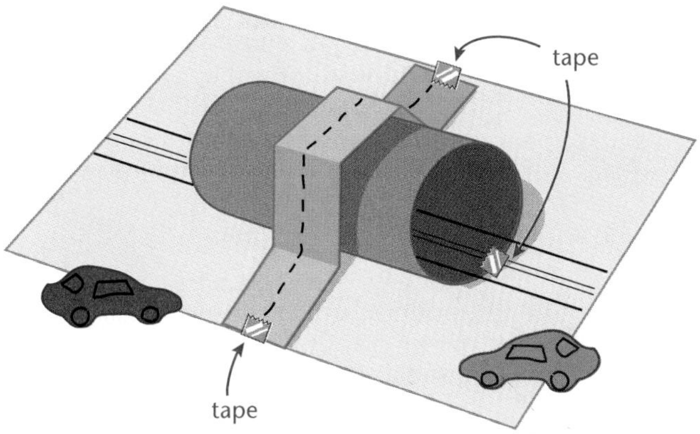

Find It in Your Reading Read several paragraphs of a sports article. See how many prepositional phrases you can identify. Can you find any adverbs that are commonly used as prepositions?

Find It in Your Writing Review a piece of your writing, and identify the prepositonal phrases. See if you can find places where you can add a prepositional phrase to expand or clarify information.

Step-by-Step Teaching Guide

Bridge and Tunnel Preposition Practice

Teaching Resources: Hands-on Grammar Activity Book, Chapter 17

1. Have students refer to their Hands-on Grammar activity books or give them copies of the relevant pages for this activity.
2. Review the instructions for making the bridge and tunnel.
3. Have students write down each of the prepositional phrases they use and identify the object of each preposition.

Find It in Your Reading

Have students underline each prepositional phrase they find. If they find prepositions used as adverbs, have them explain how they know it is an adverb.

Find It in Your Writing

Have students exchange papers with a partner once they are done to check each other's work.

ONGOING ASSESSMENT SYSTEM: Assess Mastery

Use the following resources to assess student mastery of prepositions.

In the Text	Print Resources	Technology
Chapter Review, Ex. 6–8, p. 378 Standardized Test Preparation Workshop, p. 379	Formal Assessment, Chapter 17	On-Line Exercise Bank, Section 17

TIME SAVERS!

Hands-on Grammar Book Use the Hands-on Grammar activity sheet for Chapter 17 to facilitate this activity.

ASSESS and CLOSE

Chapter Review

Each of these exercises correlates to a concept in the chapter on prepositions, pages 2–9. The exercises may be used for more practice, for reteaching, or for review of the Key Concepts presented. Answers for all chapter exercises are available in *Grammar Exercises on Transparencies* in your teaching resources.

Answer Key

Exercise 6

1. for, to
2. about
3. at, in, in
4. into
5. between

Exercise 7

Answers will vary. Samples are given.

1. According to my coach, a good attitude improves a player's performance.
2. By focusing on the game, rather than on myself, I find I can play better.
3. Each of the players on my team contributes to the team's success.
4. Soccer, which is played throughout the world, is practically a nonstop game.
5. Both teams attempt to move the ball toward a goal net.

Exercise 8

1. preposition
2. adverb
3. adverb
4. preposition
5. preposition

Exercise 9

Writing Application
Have students trade papers before underlining. Partners can identify and underline the prepositional phrases in each other's paragraphs. Have partners discuss and resolve any disagreements.

Chapter 17 Chapter Review

GRAMMAR EXERCISES 6–10

Exercise 6 Identifying Prepositions On your paper, write the preposition(s) in each sentence. Some sentences contain a compound preposition.

1. Pierre de Coubertin is remembered for his contribution to the Olympics.
2. What do you know about the early Olympic games?
3. The first games at Olympia in ancient Greece were held in 776 B.C.
4. The 776 B.C. games were the first ones organized into festivals.
5. The marathon commemorated a run between Marathon and Athens.

Exercise 7 Supplying Prepositions and Prepositional Phrases Supply a preposition or a prepositional phrase for each of the following sentences.

1. __?__ my coach, a good attitude improves a player's performance.
2. By focusing __?__ the game, rather than on myself, I find I can play better.
3. Each __?__ the players on my team contributes to the team's success.
4. Soccer, which is played __?__, is practically a nonstop game.
5. Both teams attempt to move the ball __?__ a goal net.

Exercise 8 Distinguishing Between Prepositions and Adverbs Indicate whether each underlined word is used as a preposition or an adverb.

1. The 1896 Olympic games included events in cycling, gymnastics, swimming, tennis, and track and field.
2. Athletes were everywhere, running, jumping, and walking around.
3. The American athletes, several of whom had gone over from Princeton University, dominated the games.
4. Athletes' performances have improved on those of the past, as shown by Burke's record for the 100-meter dash.
5. This American athlete's record was below the world record of the time by more than a full second.

Exercise 9 Writing Application Write a brief narrative about an event during a game that you enjoy. Use at least five prepositions. Underline each prepositional phrase you form.

Exercise 10 CUMULATIVE REVIEW Nouns, Pronouns, Verbs, Adjectives, and Adverbs Write the underlined words in the following passage. Label each one a *common noun*, a *proper noun*, a *pronoun*, an *action verb*, a *linking verb*, a *verb phrase*, an *adjective*, or an *adverb*. Be specific.

The ancient Greeks are famous for much more than athletics. The achievements of the Greeks in science, math, and government have greatly influenced modern thinking. The Archimedes Principle, named after the ancient Greek scientist, explains why things float. We use Greek letters as mathematical symbols. The concept of democracy comes to us from the Greeks.

The arts also owe a debt to the ancient Greeks. One of the most famous works in Western literature, the *Iliad* is believed to have been written by Homer, a Greek. This epic poem tells the story of the final stages of the Trojan War.

Exercise 10

1. are—linking verb
2. achievements—common noun
3. Greeks—proper noun
4. have greatly influenced—verb phrase with adverb
5. float—action verb
6. Greek—adjective
7. ancient—adjective
8. Western—adjective

Standardized Test Preparation Workshop

Prepositions

One way standardized test questions evaluate your knowledge of standard grammar and usage is to test your ability to connect ideas using prepositional phrases. Before you answer this type of question, first read the entire passage. Then, choose the answer that best uses prepositional phrases to connect similar ideas and eliminate unnecessary words.

The following sample test item will give you practice with questions that measure your ability to use prepositional phrases.

Test Tip

Identify repeated ideas and words in the passages chosen. Combining those ideas with a prepositional phrase and eliminating unnecessary words will provide the best rewrite.

Directions Read the passage, and choose the letter of the best way to write the underlined sentences.

The eighteenth century was a time when there were shoemakers. Every town had a shoemaker.

1 A The eighteenth century was a time of shoemakers in every town.

B During the eighteenth century, there were shoemakers, and every town had one.

C During the eighteenth century, every town had a shoemaker.

D The eighteenth century was a time for every town to have a shoemaker.

The best answer is C. By turning the first sentence into a prepositional phrase, the meaning is kept, and extra words and the repetition of *shoemaker* are eliminated. Choices *A* and *B* are awkward sentences, and choice *D* changes the meaning of the original.

Practice 1 **Directions:** Read the passage, and choose the letter of the best way to write the underlined sentences.

In 1773, a man could go to George Wilson's (1) shop and select shoes. The shop was in Williamsburg. Wilson had a stock of "sale shoes." The shoes were ready-made. (2) They were popular styles, just like today's.

1 **A** It was within George Wilson's shop in 1773 in Williamsburg, and a man could go in and select shoes.

B In George Wilson's shop in Williamsburg, a man could go and select shoes in 1773.

C In 1773 in Williamsburg, a man could go into George Wilson's shop and select shoes.

D In 1773, a man could go into George Wilson's shop in Williamsburg and select shoes.

2 **F** The shoes were ready-made, and they were popular styles, just like today's.

G Just like today's, the shoes were ready-made with popular styles,

H The shoes were ready-made in the popular styles of today.

J The shoes were ready-made in popular styles, just like today's.

Lesson Objectives

- To connect ideas in sentences using prepositonal phrases.

Step-by-Step Teaching Guide

Prepositions

Teaching Resources: Standardized Test Preparation Workbook, pp.33–34

1. Call students' attention to the test tip in their textbooks. Encourage them to highlight any repeated information in the passages they read.
2. Students can then use their notes when reading the choices to see the best way to combine this information.

Answer Key

Practice 1

1. D
2. J

TEST-TAKING TIP

Remind students to carefully read each choice. Two choices may combine related ideas into a phrase using the same preposition. Students will then have to determine which prepositional phrase is placed correctly.

Chapter 18
Time and Resource Manager

In-Depth Lesson Plan

	LESSON FOCUS	PRINT AND MEDIA RESOURCES
DAY 1	**Coordinating and Correlative Conjunctions** Students learn to recognize and use coordinating and correlative conjunctions (pp. 380–384).	**Teaching Resources** *Grammar Exercise Workbook,* pp. 43–44; *Grammar Exercises Answers on Transparencies,* Ch. 18 ***Writing and Grammar iText*** **(Interactive Text),** Section 18.1
DAY 2	**Subordinating Conjunctions** Students learn to recognize and use subordinating conjunctions. They will also complete the Hands-on Grammar activity (pp. 384–387).	**Teaching Resources** *Grammar Exercise Workbook,* pp. 45–46; *Grammar Exercises Answers on Transparencies,* Ch. 18; *Hands-on Grammar Activity Book,* Ch. 18 ***Writing and Grammar iText*** **(Interactive Text),** Section 18.1
DAY 3	**Interjections** Students learn to recognize and use interjections (pp. 388–390).	**Teaching Resources** *Grammar Exercise Workbook,* pp. 47–48; *Grammar Exercises Answers on Transparencies,* Ch. 18 ***Writing and Grammar iText*** **(Interactive Text),** Section 18.2
DAY 4	**Review and Assess** Students review the chapter and demonstrate mastery of conjunctions and interjections. They will also complete a cumulative review (pp. 391–395).	**Teaching Resources** *Formal Assessment,* Ch. 18; *Grammar Exercises Answers on Transparencies,* Ch. 18 ***Writing and Grammar iText*** **(Interactive Text),** Ch. 18, Chapter Review

Accelerated Lesson Plan

	LESSON FOCUS	PRINT AND MEDIA RESOURCES
DAY 1	**Conjunctions** Students learn to recognize and use coordinating, correlative, and subordinating conjunctions (pp.380–387).	**Teaching Resources** *Grammar Exercise Workbook,* pp. 43–46; *Grammar Exercises Answers on Transparencies,* Ch. 18; *Hands-on Grammar Activity Book,* Ch. 18 ***Writing and Grammar iText*** **(Interactive Text),** Section 18.1
DAY 2	**Interjections** Students learn to identify and use interjections (pp. 388–390).	**Teaching Resources** *Grammar Exercise Workbook,* pp. 47–48; *Grammar Exercises Answers on Transparencies,* Ch. 18 ***Writing and Grammar iText*** **(Interactive Text),** Section 18.2
DAY 3	**Review and Assess** Students review the chapter and demonstrate mastery of conjunctions and interjections. They will also complete a cumulative review (pp. 391–395).	**Teaching Resources** *Formal Assessment,* Ch. 18; *Grammar Exercises Answers on Transparencies,* Ch. 18 ***Writing and Grammar iText*** **(Interactive Text),** Ch. 18, Chapter Review

Options for Adapting Lesson Plans

HOMEWORK
Have students complete any stage of the lesson for homework.

SPELLING
To teach spelling skills in conjunction with grammar, mechanics, and usage, work through *Prentice Hall Everyday Spelling,* Grade 8, Chapter 21, as you cover this *Writing and Grammar* chapter.

TECHNOLOGY
Students can use *Writing and Grammar iText* to complete the exercises interactively on computer. They can complete additional exercises in the *On-line Exercise Bank:* The Auto Check feature will grade their work. Go online: PHSchool.com Use Web code: eck-8002

FEATURES
Extend coverage with the Grammar in Literature feature (p. 385) and the Standardized Test Preparation Workshop (p. 393).

INTEGRATED SKILLS COVERAGE

Grammar in Literature
SE p. 385

Writing
Find It in Your Writing, SE pp. 386, 387, 390
Writing Application, SE pp. 387, 390, 392, 395

Viewing and Representing
Critical Viewing, SE pp. 380, 382, 385, 388, 389

Workplace Skills
Using Correct Conjunctions, ATE p. 384

ASSESSMENT SUPPORT

Standardized Test Preparation Workshop SE p. 393; ATE p. 384

Standardized Test Preparation Workbook, pp. 35–36

Formal Assessment, Ch. 18

MEETING INDIVIDUAL NEEDS

Less Advanced Students See Ongoing Assessments ATE pp. 385, 389.

ESL Students ATE p. 389

BLOCK SCHEDULING

Pacing Suggestions
For 90-minute Blocks

- Administer the Diagnostic Test to students to determine instructional coverage.
- Have students complete the necessary exercises in class. Use the Hands-on Grammar Activity to provide a change of pace.

Resources for Varying Instruction
- ***Writing and Grammar* (Interactive Text)** A 90-minute block provides an ideal opportunity for students to work on computer.

Professional Development Support
- ***How to Manage Instruction in the Block*** This teaching resource provides management and activity suggestions.

MEDIA AND TECHNOLOGY

For the Student
- ***Writing and Grammar* (Interactive Text),** Ch. 18
- ***On-Line Exercise Bank,*** Sections 18.1–2

For the Teacher
- ***Resource Pro* CD-ROM**

WRITING AND GRAMMAR ON-LINE

iText Interactive Text (On-line or on CD-ROM)
- Easily navigable instruction with on-line supporting resources
- Self-scoring exercises and diagnostic tests

Companion Web Site PHSchool.com
- On-line Exercise Bank (use Web Code eck-8002)

See the Go On-line! feature, SE p. iii.

LITERATURE CONNECTIONS

Grammar in Literature selection from *Prentice Hall Literature: Timeless Voices, Timeless Themes,* Silver: from *Travels with Charley,* John Steinbeck, SE p. 385

CHAPTER 18
CONJUNCTIONS AND INTERJECTIONS

Lesson Objectives

1. To understand, recognize, and use coordinating conjunctions.
2. To understand, recognize, and use correlative conjunctions.
3. To understand, recognize, and use subordinating conjunctions.
4. To understand, recognize, and use interjections.

Critical Viewing

Connect Students may suggest such conjunctions as *and*, *but*, and *or*.

Chapter 18

Conjunctions and Interjections

The Vietnam Veterans Memorial in Washington, D.C., honors soldiers who fought in the Vietnam War.

▲ **Critical Viewing** What are some elements that link the soldiers in this picture? What are some words that link ideas in sentences? **[Connect]**

Conjunctions and interjections play special roles in sentences. Conjunctions connect ideas, and interjections help to clarify a writer's feelings.

Whatever you write, you will undoubtedly use conjunctions. In an essay about famous landmarks, for instance, you would need conjunctions to add one fact or detail to another or to clarify relationships among your ideas. You will use conjunctions both in your formal writing and in your informal writing.

Interjections, on the other hand, are usually single-word additions to sentences that express a writer's personal feelings. Most often, you will use interjections in your informal writing.

ONGOING ASSESSMENT: Diagnose

If students miss more than one item in any category, direct them to the relevant pages of the text and assign exercises for practice and review.

Conjunctions and Interjections	Diagnostic Test Items	Teach	Practice	Section Review	Chapter Review
Skill Check A					
Coordinating Conjunctions	A 1–5	p. 382	Ex. 1	Ex. 5–9	Ex. 18–21
Skill Check B					
Correlative Conjunctions	B 6–10	p. 383	Ex. 2	Ex. 5–9	Ex. 18–21

Diagnostic Test

Directions: Write all answers on a separate sheet of paper.

Skill Check A. Copy the following sentences, and circle the coordinating conjunction in each. Then, underline the words or groups of words connected by the conjunction.

1. The Arlington National Cemetery is a historic burial place, and it is reserved for soldiers.
2. There are more than 240,000 graves, yet there is room for more.
3. The land previously belonged to Robert E. Lee and his family.
4. During the Civil War, the Union army took over the property, so the residents had to leave.
5. Many recipients of the Medal of Honor or the Distinguished Flying Cross are buried there.

Skill Check B. Copy the following sentences, and circle both parts of the correlative conjunction in each. Then, underline the two words or the two groups of words connected by the conjunction.

6. Both soldiers and war heroes are buried in Arlington.
7. Not only men are buried there, but also many brave women.
8. Many graves are of soldiers who died in either the Vietnam War or the Civil War.
9. Neither the cemetery nor its inspiring memorials existed before the Civil War.
10. People buried in the cemetery today must either have died in war or spent twenty years in the military.

Skill Check C. Copy the following sentences, and circle the subordinating conjunction in each. Then, underline the dependent idea following the conjunction.

11. Wherever important events have occurred, there are landmarks.
12. Monuments and other landmarks are constructed so that important people and events can be remembered.
13. Many are built after the people themselves have died.
14. Some landmarks were constructed because they mark an important historic spot.
15. Whenever people visit, they are reminded of the person or event.
16. Even though many landmarks are old, they remain popular.
17. As long as important events occur, landmarks will be built.
18. If you want to see monuments honoring American heroes, you should visit Washington, D.C.
19. Although the landmarks are crowded, they are worth visiting.
20. Because many landmarks are free, your visit will not be costly.

Skill Check D. List the interjections in the following sentences.

21. Wow! This park is amazing!
22. Yeah, but I am sure that it gets cold here in the winter.
23. Oh, I would hate to be stuck outside in the cold.
24. Ouch! I knew this bench would be freezing cold!
25. I, uh, would much rather be at home in my warm house.

ONGOING ASSESSMENT: Diagnose *continued*

Conjunctions and Interjections	Diagnostic Test Items	Teach	Practice	Section Review	Chapter Review
Skill Check C					
Subordinating Conjunctions and Dependent Ideas	C 11–20	p. 384	Ex. 3–4	Ex. 5–9	Ex. 18–21
Skill Check D					
Interjections	D 21–25	p. 388	Ex. 10	Ex. 11–17	Ex. 22–23
Cumulative Reviews and Applications				Ex. 7–9 Ex. 15–17	Ex. 24–26

Answer Key

Diagnostic Test

Each item in the diagnostic test corresponds to a specific concept in the conjunctions and interjections chapter. This will enable you to tailor instruction to the particular needs of your students. See "Ongoing Assessment: Diagnose" below for further details.

Skill Check A

1. is a historical burial place (and) it is reserved for soldiers.
2. There are more than 240,000 graves, (yet) there is room for more.
3. Robert E. Lee (and) his family.
4. During the Civil War, the Union Army took over the property, (so) the residents had to leave.
5. Medal of Honor (or) the Distinguished Flying Cross

Skill Check B

6. (Both) soldiers (and) war heroes
7. (Not only) men, (but also) women
8. (either) the Vietnam War (or) the Civil War
9. (Neither) the cemetery (nor) memorials
10. (either) died in war (or) spent twenty years in the military

Skill Check C

11. (Wherever) important events have occurred
12. (so that) important people and events can be remembered.
13. (after) the people themselves have died.
14. (because) they mark an important historical spot.
15. (Whenever) people visit
16. (Even though) many landmarks are old
17. (As long as) important events occur
18. (If) you want to see monuments honoring American heroes
19. (Although) the landmarks are crowded
20. (Because) many landmarks are free

Skill Check D

21. Wow
22. Yeah
23. Oh
24. Ouch
25. uh

PREPARE and ENGAGE

Interest GRABBER Ask students to think about their favorite foods, music groups, or professional athletes. Then have them write a single sentence that tells what their top two favorites are for any one of the categories. Ask students how they combined their two separate choices in one sentence. Point out that they combined their choices with the word *and*, probably the most common conjunction.

Activate Prior Knowledge

Have students alter the Interest Grabber sentences by substituting any other conjunctions they can think of, such as *but*, *both. . . and*, and *although*. The following are a few examples.

Ken Griffey, Jr., is my favorite professional athlete, but Derek Jeter is a close second. Both Ken Griffey, Jr., and Derek Jeter are my favorite professional athletes. Although Ken Griffey, Jr., is my favorite professional athlete, Derek Jeter is a close second.

TEACH

Step-by-Step Teaching Guide

Conjunctions

1. Point out that in each example, similar kinds or groups of words are joined by the coordinating conjunction.
2. Have students look over the list of conjunctions. Tell them that *then* is an adverb, but they will often see it misused as a conjunction. A sample misuse is shown in the following sentence:

   We visited the Capitol Building, then the White House.

   Correctly written, the sentence would have the comma replaced with the conjunction *and:*

   We visited the Capitol Building and then the White House.

Critical Viewing

Analyze Students may suggest responses such as *remakable and exciting; expensive but worthwhile.*

Section 18.1

Conjunctions

Conjunctions act like the cement between bricks. Words such as *and*, *as*, and *when* connect individual words or groups of words. They are the "cement" of sentences.

KEY CONCEPT A **conjunction** connects words or groups of words. ■

Conjunctions fall into three groups: *coordinating conjunctions*, *correlative conjunctions*, and *subordinating conjunctions*.

Coordinating Conjunctions

KEY CONCEPT **Coordinating conjunctions** connect words of the same kind, such as two or more nouns or verbs. They can also connect larger groups of words, such as prepositional phrases or even entire sentences. ■

COORDINATING CONJUNCTIONS			
and	for	or	yet
but	nor	so	

In the following examples, the coordinating conjunctions are circled. The words they connect are italicized.

CONNECTING NOUNS: My *cousin* (and) his *wife* left yesterday for a trip to Washington, D.C.

CONNECTING VERBS: They *printed* out directions (but) *forgot* to bring them.

CONNECTING PREPOSITIONAL PHRASES: Put the luggage *on the doorstep* (or) *in the garage.*

CONNECTING TWO SENTENCES: *Our family wanted to go to the White House,* (but) *we decided to go to the Capitol first.*

Theme: U.S. Landmarks

In this section, you will learn how conjunctions link words and ideas. The examples and exercises are about historic landmarks in the United States.

Cross-Curricular Connection: Social Studies

▶ **Critical Viewing** What thoughts come to mind when you view this photograph of Mount Rushmore? Link two thoughts with *and* and two others with *but*. **[Analyze]**

TIME AND RESOURCE MANAGER

Resources
Print: Grammar Exercise Workbook, pp. 43–46; Hands-on Grammar Actvity Book, Chapter 18
Technology: Writing and Grammar iText, Section 18.1, On-Line Exercise Bank, Section 18.1

In-Depth Coverage	Accelerated Pace
• Work through all key concepts, pp. 382–385. • Assign and review Exercises 1–4. • Read and discuss Grammar in Literature, p. 385. • Do the Hands-on Grammar Activity on p. 386.	• Assign pp. 382–385 for independent student review. • Assign Section Review Exercises 5–9, p. 387.

Exercise 1 **Recognizing Coordinating Conjunctions** Copy the following sentences onto your paper, and circle the coordinating conjunction in each. Then, underline the words or groups of words connected by the conjunction.

EXAMPLE: South Dakota is an exciting (and) interesting vacation spot.

1. Are you going to visit Mount Rushmore or the Black Hills?
2. At Mount Rushmore, the faces of Washington, Jefferson, Lincoln, and Roosevelt are carved out of a mountain.
3. Gutzon Borglum and his workers carved the monument.
4. Visitors hike near the monument but cannot climb on it.
5. The mountain is rugged, yet the carved faces look smooth.
6. Borglum began work in 1927 and finished in 1939.
7. His original plan called for the sculptures to be formed from the waist up, but that would have been very costly.
8. The stone was hard, so only the faces were sculpted.
9. The project was expensive but clearly worth it.
10. The sculpture was carved into Mt. Rushmore 152 meters, or approximately 500 feet, above the valley floor.

Correlative Conjunctions

KEY CONCEPT **Correlative conjunctions** connect the same kinds of words or groups of words as do coordinating conjunctions, but correlative conjunctions are used in pairs. ■

CORRELATIVE CONJUNCTIONS		
both . . . and	**neither . . . nor**	**whether . . . or**
either . . . or	**not only . . . but also**	

CONNECTING NOUNS:	We have seen both the *Hoover Dam* and the *Grand Canyon Dam.*
CONNECTING PRONOUNS:	Either *you* or *I* will be the leader on the trail.
CONNECTING VERBS:	The sick hiker would neither *eat* nor *drink.*
CONNECTING PREPOSITIONAL PHRASES:	We hiked slowly, whether *in a large group* or *by ourselves.*
CONNECTING TWO SENTENCES:	Not only *are the Sierra Mountains rugged,* but *they are* also *beautiful.*

More Practice

Grammar Exercise Workbook
- pp. 43–46

On-line Exercise Bank
- Section 18.1

Go on-line:
PHSchool.com
Enter Web Code:
eck-8002

iText

Get instant feedback! Exercise 1 is available on-line or on CD-ROM.

Answer Key

Exercise 1

1. Are you going to visit Mount Rushmore (or) the Black Hills?
2. At Mount Rushmore, the faces of Washington, Jefferson, Lincoln, (and) Roosevelt are carved out of a mountain.
3. Gutzon Borglum (and) his workers carved the monument.
4. Visitors hike near the monument (but) cannot climb on it.
5. The mountain is rugged, (yet) the carved faces look smooth.
6. Borglum began work in 1927 (and) finished in 1939.
7. His original plan called for the sculptures to be formed from the waist up, (but) that would have been very costly.
8. The stone was hard, (so) only the faces were sculpted.
9. The project was expensive (but) clearly worth it.
10. The sculpture was carved into Mt. Rushmore 152 meters, (or) approximately 500 feet, above the valley floor.

Step-by-Step Teaching Guide

Correlative Conjunctions

1. Point out how in each example similar groups of words are joined by the pairs of correlative conjunctions.
2. Write the following additional examples on the board:

   We went to both the Empire State Building and the World Trade Center.

   Either he or you has the subway map.

   Tom will neither take a cab nor ride the bus.

   We couldn't decide whether to walk around Times Square or Central Park.

   New York is not only exciting but also very beautiful.

Answer Key

Exercise 2

1. Pearl Harbor is both majestic and awe inspiring.
2. Visitors can see either the Pearl Harbor monument or the memorial to the USS *Arizona*, a ship that was partly sunk.
3. The Japanese air attack shocked the United States not only because it was a surprise attack, but also because it was the first attack on American soil.
4. Before the attack, the United States had been uncertain about whether to join the war or to let European countries fight by themselves.
5. Neither the Japanese nor the Germans believed the United States would recover from the attack.

Step-by-Step Teaching Guide

Subordinating Conjunctions

1. Tell students that the function of subordinating conjunctions is in the name: they subordinate. Subordinating conjunctions make one idea unable to stand alone; the idea is dependent on (subordinate to) the sentence's main idea.
2. Tell students the subordinate idea always reads like a sentence fragment: *after he made reservations.* The subordinate conjunction introduces the subordinate idea.

Integrating Workplace Skills

Workplaces often post signs for employees and customers. If the signs use incorrect conjunctions, there can be serious consequences. Ask students to compare the effects of using each conjunction on the following workplace signs.

Employees must wear a hairnet (and/or) gloves at all times.

(Neither/Not only) stopping (nor/but also) parking is allowed in front of this loading dock.

Exercise 2 **Recognizing Correlative Conjunctions** Copy the following sentences onto your paper, and circle the correlative conjunction in each. Then, underline the two words or groups of words connected by the conjunction.

EXAMPLE: The attack on Pearl Harbor was not only unexpected but also devastating.

1. Pearl Harbor is both majestic and awe inspiring.
2. Visitors can see either the Pearl Harbor monument or the memorial to the USS *Arizona*, a ship that was partly sunk.
3. The Japanese air attack shocked the United States not only because it was a surprise attack, but also because it was the first attack on American soil.
4. Before the attack, the United States had been uncertain about whether to join the war or to let European countries fight by themselves.
5. Neither the Japanese nor the Germans believed the United States would recover from the attack.

Subordinating Conjunctions

KEY CONCEPT **Subordinating conjunctions** connect two ideas by making one idea dependent on the other. ■

FREQUENTLY USED SUBORDINATING CONJUNCTIONS			
after	as though	since	until
although	because	so that	when
as	before	than	whenever
as if	even though	though	where
as long as	if	till	wherever
as soon as	in order that	unless	while

You will find that the subordinating conjunction always comes before the dependent idea. The subordinating conjunction connects the dependent idea to the main idea.

EXAMPLES: I did the planning after *he made reservations.*
When *he phoned this morning*, he was unable to reach the senator.

The examples show that the main idea can come at the beginning or at the end of the sentence. Notice the important difference in punctuating the two examples. When the dependent idea comes first, it must be separated from the main idea with a comma.

More Practice

Grammar Exercise Workbook
- pp. 43–46

On-line Exercise Bank
- Section 18.1

Go on-line:
PHSchool.com
Enter Web Code:
eck-8002

iText

Get instant feedback! Exercise 2 is available on-line or on CD-ROM.

STANDARDIZED TEST PREPARATION WORKSHOP

Grammar and Usage Many standardized tests require students to identify conjunctions in sentences. Ask students to identify the underlined words in the following sentence.

Mr. Walters wants to see you as soon as you get to school.

A coordinating conjunction
B correlative conjunction
C subordinating conjunction
D none of the above

The correct choice is item **C** because *as soon as* begins a dependent idea. Only a subordinating conjunction can be used in this instance.

Exercise 3 **Recognizing Subordinating Conjunctions** Copy the following sentences onto your paper, and circle the subordinating conjunction in each. Then, underline the dependent idea following the conjunction.

EXAMPLE: (Because) we were in Washington, we decided to visit the Washington Monument.

1. Although George Washington was much admired, the government would not finance a memorial honoring him.
2. When no action was taken, a group of citizens formed the Washington National Monument Society in 1833.
3. The monument was not dedicated until 1885 even though it had been started almost fifty years earlier.
4. The monument includes two different colors of bricks since there was a shortage of the original brick.
5. Because the base is a 55-foot square, the monument is ten times taller than it is wide.

Exercise 4 **Writing Sentences With Subordinating Conjunctions** Write a sentence using each of the following subordinating conjunctions.

1. after
2. while
3. as long as
4. because
5. until

The Washington Monument stands 555 feet high.

▲ **Critical Viewing** In a sentence, explain how or why this monument is a good symbol for George Washington. Try to use a subordinating conjunction in your sentence. **[Interpret]**

GRAMMAR IN LITERATURE

from Travels with Charley

John Steinbeck

The author uses coordinating, correlative, and subordinating conjunctions to link ideas in the passage: And *is a coordinating conjunction,* not . . . but *is a correlative conjunction, and* because *is a subordinating conjunction.*

. . . The grieving sky turned the little water to a dangerous metal *and* then the wind got up—*not* the gusty, rabbity wind of the seacoasts I know *but* a great bursting sweep of wind with nothing to inhibit it for a thousand miles in any direction. *Because* it was a wind strange to me, . . . it set up mysterious responses in me.

ONGOING ASSESSMENT: Monitor and Reinforce

If students miss more than two items in Exercises 1–3, refer them to the following for additional practice.

In the Textbook	Print Resources	Technology
Section Review, Ex. 5–9, p. 387	Grammar Exercise Workbook, pp. 43–46	On-Line Exercise Bank, Section 18.1

Critical Viewing

Interpret Possible response: Because the monument is powerful and dignified, it is a good symbol.

Answer Key

Exercise 3

1. (Although) George Washington was much admired, the government would not finance a memorial honoring him.
2. (When) no action was taken, a group of citizens formed the Washington National Monument Society in 1833.
3. The monument was not dedicated until 1885 (even though) it was started almost fifty years earlier.
4. The monument includes two different colors of bricks (since) there was a shortage of the original brick.
5. (Because) the base is a 55-foot square, the monument is ten times taller than it is wide.

Exercise 4

Students' responses will vary.

Step-by-Step Teaching Guide

Grammar in Literature

1. Have a volunteer read aloud the excerpt from *Travels with Charley.*
2. Ask volunteers to name the words or ideas that are connected by the conjunctions.

More About the Author

John Steinbeck (1902–1968) was one of the greatest American novelists of the twentieth century. His novel about the Great Depression, *The Grapes of Wrath* (1939), won the Pulitzer Prize and endures as a work that summed up an era. His memoir, *Travels with Charley* (1962), from which this excerpt is taken, is about a cross-country automobile trip the author made with Charley, his pet poodle.

Step-by-Step Teaching Guide

Conjunction Chains

Teaching Resources: Hands-on Grammar Activity Book, Chapter 18

1. Have students refer to their Hands-on Grammar activity books or give them copies of the relevant pages.
2. Encourage students to experiment with the different conjunctions in order to make the best choice.
3. Point out that the conjunction *but* is used twice.

Find It In Your Reading

Have students compare the original sentences with the rewritten sentence. Discuss which version they prefer and why.

Find It In Your Writing

It may be helpful to have pairs of student proofread each other's work to make sure conjunctions are used correctly.

18.1

Hands-on Grammar

Conjunction Chains

In this exercise, you will illustrate how conjunctions are the links that hold sentences together.

1. Cut ten strips of paper approximately 1/2" x 6 1/2" long. Cut five strips of paper 1/2" x 4 1/2" long.
2. On each of the ten longer strips of paper, write one of the following sentences:
   We went to the zoo.
   We saw the gorillas.
   We wanted to see the lions.
   They were hiding.
   Should we go to the beach?
   Should we go to the mountains?
   We want to go surfing.
   We should go to the beach.
   Mom doesn't want to surf.
   Dad does.
3. On each of the five shorter strips of paper, write the coordinating conjunctions *and, or, but, so,* and *yet.*
4. Combine each pair of sentences with a coordinating conjunction by forming the longer strips of paper into circles and joining them with the conjunction to form a paper chain.

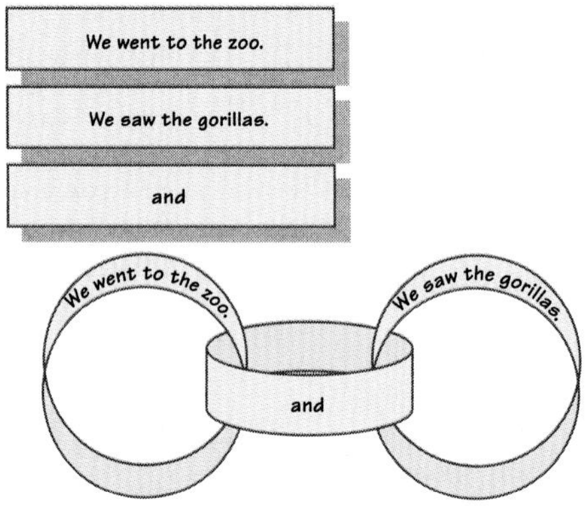

Find It in Your Reading In your textbook or in a story you are reading, find sentences that can be joined together with a conjunction. Alternatively, find sentences that are already joined together and use them to create a chain.

Find It in Your Writing Look through your writing portfolio for sentences that can be combined. Rewrite the sentences, joining them with a coordinating conjunction.

TIME SAVERS!

Hands-on Grammar Book Use the Hands-on Grammar activity sheet for Chapter 18 to facilitate this activity.

ONGOING ASSESSMENT: Assess Mastery

Use the following resources to assess mastery of conjunctions.

In the Textbook	Technology
Chapter Review, Ex. 17–21, pp. 391–392	Writing and Grammar iText, Section 18.1, Section Review; On-Line Exercise Bank, Section 18.1

Section 18.1 Section Review

GRAMMAR EXERCISES 5–9

Exercise 5 Recognizing Conjunctions Copy the following sentences onto your paper. Then, circle each conjunction and label it *coordinating*, *correlative*, or *subordinating*. Underline the words or groups of words connected by the conjunction.

1. The Lincoln Memorial is constructed of marble, granite, and limestone.
2. Even though construction was begun in 1914, it was not completed until 1922.
3. The architect Henry Bacon wanted the memorial to reflect the greatness of Lincoln's life, so he followed the style of classical Greek architecture.
4. The building itself is impressive, but the Lincoln statue inside is the memorial's highlight.
5. Gettysburg, Pennsylvania, contains both a Civil War memorial and a historic site dedicated to President Eisenhower.
6. Visiting Gettysburg, you can tour either a battlefield or a cemetery.
7. Not only was the Battle of Gettysburg a fierce confrontation, but it was also a major turning point in the Civil War.
8. The Statue of Liberty greets travelers as soon as they enter New York Harbor.
9. Since the statue's dedication in 1886, it has been a symbol of freedom to all.
10. Learn about the statue's symbolism so that you can fully appreciate it.

Exercise 6 Combining Sentences With Conjunctions Combine each of the following pairs of sentences with a coordinating, correlative, or subordinating conjunction.

1. Henry Bacon, the architect, wanted the Lincoln Memorial to reflect the greatness of Lincoln's life. He followed the style of classical Greek architecture.
2. The building itself is impressive. The Lincoln statue inside is the monument's highlight.
3. You might visit St. Louis, Missouri. You will see the city's famous Gateway Arch.
4. It has become a symbol for St. Louis. It dramatizes that St. Louis is the "Gateway to the West."
5. The Alamo is a great tourist attraction in San Antonio. The River Walk is also a great tourist attraction there.

Exercise 7 Find It in Your Reading Identify the conjunctions in this passage from *Travels With Charley:*

> I waited for him to ask something or to say something so we could go on, but he didn't. And as the silence continued, it became more and more impossible to think of something to say.

Exercise 8 Find It in Your Writing Look through examples of your own writing to find conjunctions. Challenge yourself to use conjunctions to combine ideas and sentences.

Exercise 9 Writing Application Imagine that you are leading a tour of a famous monument. Write a description of the monument, linking ideas with different types of conjunctions.

ASSESS and CLOSE

Section Review

Each of these exercises correlates to a concept in the section on conjunctions, pages 382–386. These exercises may be used for more practice, for reteaching, or for review of the Key Concepts presented.

Answer Key

Exercise 5

1. The Lincoln Memorial is constructed out of marble, granite, and limestone. coordinating
2. Even though construction was begun in 1914, it was not completed until 1922. subordinating
3. The architect Henry Bacon wanted the memorial to reflect the greatness of Lincoln's life, so he followed the style of classic Greek architecture. coordinating
4. The building itself is impressive, but the Lincoln statue inside is the memorial's highlight. coordinating
5. Gettysburg, Pennsylvania, contains both a Civil War Memorial and a historic site dedicated to President Eisenhower. correlative
6. Visiting Gettysburg, you can tour either a battlefield or a cemetery. correlative
7. Not only was the Battle of Gettysburg a fierce confrontation, but it was also a major turning point in the Civil War. correlative
8. The Statue of Liberty greets travelers as soon as they enter New York Harbor. subordinating
9. Since the statue's dedication in 1886, it has been a symbol of freedom for all. subordinating
10. Learn about the statue's symbolism so that you can fully appreciate it. subordinating

Exercise 6

1. Henry Bacon, the architect, wanted the Lincoln Memorial to reflect the greatness of Lincoln's life, so he followed the style of classical Greek architecture.
2. The building itself is impressive, and the Lincoln statue inside is the monument's highlight.

continued

Answer Key continued

3. You might visit St. Louis, Missouri, where you will see the city's famous Gateway Arch.
4. It has become a symbol for St. Louis because it dramatizes that St. Louis is the "Gateway to the West."
5. Both the Alamo and the River Walk are great tourist attractions in San Antonio.

Exercise 7

Find It In Your Reading
or, so, but, and

Exercise 8

Find It In Your Writing
When students combine sentences, they may also need to change verbs to agree with new compound subjects.

Exercise 9

Writing Application
Suggest that students read their descriptions aloud, without mentioning the monument. Can the class guess what is being described?

PREPARE and ENGAGE

Interest GRABBER Ask students to think of ways of expressing the different emotions that follow—using only one word:

joy	*surprise*
anger	*disbelief*
boredom	*pain*

Explain to students that the words they have come up with are *interjections*—words that express strong emotions. To emphasize the arbitrariness of some interjections, have students use *Oh* in sentences expressing sadness, pain, joy, and surprise.

Activate Prior Knowledge

Write the following sentences on the chalkboard and ask volunteers to add an appropriate interjection to each sentence. Have volunteers explain their thinking when they are done.

Your dog bit me. (Ouch! Hey! Oh!)

We won the game! (Hurray! Yay!)

TEACH

Step-by-Step Teaching Guide

Interjections

1. Review the list of interjections with students. Point out that often a person adopts a few favorite interjections and uses them to the point that his or her quick, immediate response to emotional situations becomes predictable to family and friends.
2. Go over the list of emotions and the list of interjections. Acknowledge that many interjections can be used sarcastically. A word such as *Great!* can be used to express not only joy but also impatience or disgust, depending on tone of voice alone.

Critical Viewing

Connect Students may suggest awe (*wow*) or surprise (*ah*).

Section 18.2 Interjections

The *interjection* is the part of speech that is used the least. Its only use is to express feelings or emotions.

KEY CONCEPT An **interjection** expresses feeling or emotion and functions independently from the rest of a sentence. ■

An interjection has no grammatical relationship to any other word in a sentence. It is, therefore, set off from the rest of the sentence with a comma or an exclamation mark.

Interjections can express different feelings or emotions:

JOY:	*Wow!* I can't believe the size of this statue.
SURPRISE:	*Oh,* I didn't expect to hear from you.
PAIN:	*Ouch!* That hurts.
IMPATIENCE:	*Tsk!* How long do they expect me to wait?
HESITATION:	I, *uh,* think we should leave now.

Some other common interjections include *ah, alas, gee, golly, hah, help, hey, hooray, no way, oh my, oh no, oh, oops, psst, so, ugh, uh-oh, well, whew, whoa,* and *yeah.*

The statue of Abraham Lincoln dominates the Lincoln Memorial.

Theme: U.S. Landmarks

In this section, you will learn how interjections add emotions and feelings to your writing. The examples and exercises are about additional historic landmarks in the United States.

Cross-Curricular Connection: Social Studies

◀ **Critical Viewing** What emotions do you feel when you see this statue? What are some words you might use to express those emotions? **[Connect]**

Grammar and Style Tip

Use interjections to express feelings in your informal writing, but don't use them in formal writing except as part of a quotation or other special reference.

TIME AND RESOURCE MANAGER

Resources
Print: Grammar Exercise Workbook, pp. 47–48
Technology: Writing and Grammar iText, Section 18.2; On-Line Exercise Bank, Section 18.2

In-Depth Coverage	Accelerated Pace
• Work through the key concept on pp 388–389. • Assign and review Exercise 10.	• Assign pp. 388–389 for independent student review. • Assign Section Review Exercise 11–17, p. 390.

The Alamo still reminds Texans of their war to win independence from Mexico.

Exercise 10 **Supplying Interjections** Rewrite each of the following sentences using an appropriate interjection in place of the feeling shown in parentheses.

EXAMPLE: (sadness) I missed the tour of the Alamo.
ANSWER: Gee, I missed the tour of the Alamo.

1. (surprise) The Alamo is neat.
2. (impatience) Can we go inside now?
3. (impatience) How long do we have to wait for the tour to begin?
4. (fear) I heard the Alamo was haunted.
5. I (uncertainty) think maybe we should leave.
6. (anger) It's not haunted.
7. (amazement) I can't believe you guys were so scared.
8. (fear) I hear something.
9. (pain) Something poked me in the arm.
10. (impatience) Please watch where you are going!

▲ Critical Viewing
What emotions do you think some Texans feel when they see the Alamo? Can you express those emotions in additional sentences for Exercise 10? **[Connect]**

More Practice
Grammar Exercise Workbook
• pp. 47–48
On-line Exercise Bank
• Section 18.2
Go on-line:
PHSchool.com
Enter Web Code:
eck-8002

Customize for *ESL Students*

Have the class work together to list all the interjections they know in various languages. Then have them explain the meanings that they know.

Critical Viewing

Connect Possible response: pride or sadness; *Gee! I want to visit the Alamo; Oh! There were so many brave people who lost their lives at the Alamo.*

Answer Key

Exercise 10

Answers will vary. Samples are given.

1. Aha! The Alamo is neat.
2. Hey! Can we go inside now?
3. Tsk! How long do we have to wait for the tour to begin?
4. Oh-oh, I heard the Alamo was haunted.
5. I, uh, think maybe we should leave.
6. No way! It's not haunted.
7. Wow! I can't believe you guys were so scared.
8. Oh, my. I hear something.
9. Ouch! Something poked me in the arm.
10. Hey! Please watch where you are going!

PRENTICE HALL
Everyday Spelling

If you have taught the spelling skills in *Prentice Hall Everyday Spelling,* Grade 8, Chapter 21, in conjunction with this *Writing and Grammar* chapter, review and assess students' mastery of the skills before concluding the chapter.

ONGOING ASSESSMENT: Monitor and Reinforce

If students miss more than one item in Exercise 10, refer them to the following for additional practice.

In the Textbook	Print Resources	Technology
Chapter Review, Ex. 11–17, p. 390	Grammar Exercises Workbook, pp. 47–48	On-Line Exercise Bank, Section 18.2

TIME SAVERS!

Answers on Transparency Use the Grammar Exercises Answers on Transparencies for Chapter 18 to facilitate corrections by students.

On-Line Exercise Bank Have students complete the exercises on computer. The Auto Check feature will grade their work for you!

ASSESS and CLOSE

Section Review

Each of these exercises correlates to a concept in the section on interjections, pages 388–389. These exercises may be used for more practice, for reteaching, or for review of the Key Concepts presented. Answers for all chapter exercises are available in *Grammar Exercises Answers on Transparencies* in your teaching resources.

Answer Key

Exercise 11

1. Wow
2. Man
3. Oh, no
4. Ouch
5. Stop

Exercise 12

Answers and punctuation will vary. Samples are given.

1. Hey! Devil's Tower sure is tall.
2. Wow! I can't believe it was formed by lava.
3. Ow! I bet it would hurt to fall from up there.
4. Whoa! I don't think I want to find out.
5. Tsk! Let's get hiking.
6. Aha! Did you know this was a landmark for Native Americans?
7. I, uh, think they believed it was formed by the claws of a giant bear!
8. Gee! It would have to have been a very large bear.
9. Alas, we can't climb that.
10. Yeah, you're right. Let's go.

Exercise 13

Answers and punctuation will vary. Samples are given.

JOE: Alas, Custer's battlefield sure is a sad place.

TOM: Wow! A lot of people died there.

JOE: Oh my, is it true that you can sometimes still find slugs from bullets?

TOM: Aha! I think I see one!

JOE: Oh, it's only a rock.

Exercise 14

Sentences will vary.

Exercise 15

Find It in Your Reading
Point out that the interjection, *huh*, is found at the end of the sentence. Invite students to look for other examples of interjections at the end of sentences.

Exercise 16

Find It in Your Writing
Students can trade papers with partners to check for correct punctuation.

Exercise 17

Writing Application
Students may want to e-mail their letters to their friends.

Section 18.2 Section Review

GRAMMAR EXERCISES 11–17

Exercise 11 Identifying Interjections On your paper, list the interjections in the following sentences.

1. Wow, the Oregon Trail sure is long!
2. Man, I can't believe we decided to follow it on mountain bikes.
3. Oh, no! This trip is going to take us months.
4. Ouch! My feet hurt!
5. Stop! I can't go any farther.

Exercise 12 Supplying Interjections Rewrite each of the following sentences using an appropriate interjection in place of the feeling shown in parentheses.

1. (amazement) Devil's Tower sure is tall.
2. (amazement) I can't believe it was formed by lava.
3. (pain) I bet it would hurt to fall from up there.
4. (uncertainty) I don't think I want to find out.
5. (impatience) Let's get hiking.
6. (surprise) Did you know this was a landmark for Native Americans?
7. I (uncertainty) think they believed it was formed by the claws of a giant bear.
8. (amazement) It would have to have been a very large bear!
9. (disappointment) We can't climb that.
10. (agreement) You're right. Let's go.

Exercise 13 Supplying Interjections Rewrite the following dialogue. Replace the words in parentheses with appropriate interjections.

JOE: (sadness) Custer's battlefield sure is a sad place.
TOM: (amazement) A lot of people died there.
JOE: (wonder) Is it true that you can sometimes still find slugs from bullets?
TOM: (excitement) I think I see one!
JOE: (disappointment) It's only a rock.

Exercise 14 Writing Sentences With Interjections Use each of the following interjections in a sentence.

1. Oops!
2. Uh-oh!
3. Oh, no!
4. Tsk!
5. uh

Exercise 15 Find It in Your Reading Identify the interjection in this dialogue from *Travels With Charley*. What other interjections might be used in a dialogue such as this?

LOCAL MAN: "New York, huh?"
ME: "Yep."
LOCAL MAN: "I was there in nineteen thirty-eight—or was it thirty-nine . . .?"
ALICE: "It was thirty-six . . . ."

Exercise 16 Find It in Your Writing Revise a piece of dialogue from your own writing by adding interjections to show the speakers' emotions.

Exercise 17 Writing Application Write a brief letter to a friend describing an interesting landmark you have visited. Use at least two interjections in your letter.

Chapter 18 Chapter Review

GRAMMAR EXERCISES 18–26

Exercise 18 **Recognizing Conjunctions** Copy the following sentences, and circle the conjunction in each. Label each conjunction *coordinating, correlative,* or *subordinating,* and underline the words or groups of words being connected.

1. Yellowstone Park was formed when volcanoes exploded and violent earthquakes shook the land.
2. Neither Yosemite nor Yellowstone Park was visited by explorers before 1800.
3. Not only do many tourists visit these parks today, but tourists also visited them in the 1850's.
4. It is difficult to visit the park unless you go during the summer.
5. Whenever you visit a park, you should be prepared for weather changes.
6. In 1959, an earthquake with a magnitude of 7.5 or more on the Richter scale caused major damage.
7. In August 1988, fires broke out in Yellowstone, so emergency efforts were begun to protect park landmarks.
8. The fire was a catastrophe for many officials and rangers.
9. Firefighters tried to control the fires, but they finally had to rely on snow to extinguish the blaze.
10. The firefighters worked valiantly, yet 35 percent of the park burned.
11. Luckily, there were very few casualties among birds or forest animals.
12. The fire disturbed them, but they were more upset by firefighters' helicopters.
13. Tourists enjoyed observing both natural wonders and abundant wildlife.
14. Rock climbers often visit Yosemite to climb either El Capitán or Half Dome.
15. While you are sightseeing in the park, be sure to take your camera.

Exercise 19 **Classifying Conjunctions** Identify the conjunctions you find in the following paragraph. Then, label each one *coordinating* or *correlative.*

(1) Thousands of California residents and tourists travel across the Golden Gate Bridge every day. (2) They are traveling south toward San Francisco or north toward Marin County. (3) Not only is the bridge dramatically beautiful, but it is also a technological wonder. (4) The bridge has been rocked by several earthquakes, but it has not been damaged. (5) Both painters and ironworkers provide constant maintenance. (6) The workers must fear neither heights nor wind. (7) Although most bridges are painted either gray or silver, the Golden Gate is a bright orange color. (8) Its architect felt that orange fit better with the bridge's surroundings and design. (9) Whether you are visiting San Francisco or traveling nearby, you should go to the Golden Gate Bridge. (10) The view is magnificent, so you will enjoy the side trip.

Exercise 20 **Revising With Conjunctions** Rewrite the following paragraph, adding conjunctions to connect and relate ideas clearly. Underline the conjunctions you use.

You visit St. Louis, Missouri. You must see the city's famous Gateway Arch. It is a stainless-steel structure. It glistens in the light. It stands more than 600 feet high. It forms a graceful curve, arching above the ground. The Gateway Arch was completed in 1965. It has become a part of St. Louis history. The arch is dramatic. The arch is symbolic. It shows that St. Louis is the "Gateway to the West." Residents appreciate its beauty. Tourists appreciate its

CHAPTER REVIEW

Each of these exercises correlates to a concept in the chapter on conjunctions and interjections, pages 380–389. These exercises may be used for more practice, for reteaching, or for review of the Key Concepts presented. Exercises 20, 21, 23, 24, and 25 have questions where student answers will vary.

Answer Key

Exercise 18

1. Yellowstone Park was formed when volcanoes exploded (and) violent earthquakes shook the land. coordinating
2. (Neither) Yosemite (nor) Yellowstone Park was visited by explorers before 1800. correlative
3. (Not only) do many tourists visit these parks today, (but) tourists (also) visited them in the 1850s. correlative
4. It is difficult to visit the park (unless) you go during the summer. subordinating
5. (Whenever) you visit a park, you should be prepared for weather changes. subordinating
6. In 1959, an earthquake with a magnitude of 7.5 (or) more on the Richter scale caused major damage. coordinating
7. In August 1988, fires broke out in Yellowstone, (so) emergency efforts were begun to protect park landmarks. coordinating
8. The fire was a catastrophe for many officials (and) rangers. coordinating
9. Firefighters tried to control the fires, (but) they finally had to rely on snow to extinguish the blaze. coordinating
10. The firefighters worked valiantly, (yet) 35 percent of the park burned. coordinating
11. Luckily, there were very few casualties among birds (or) forest animals. coordinating
12. The fire disturbed them, (but) they were more upset by firefighters' helicopters. coordinating
13. (both) natural wonders (and) wildlife. correlative
14. (either) El Capitán (or) Half Dome. correlative
15. (While) you are sightseeing in the park, be sure to take your camera. subordinating

continued

Answer Key continued

Exercise 19

1. and—coordinating
2. or—coordinating
3. Not only . . . but also—correlative
4. but—coordinating
5. Both . . . and—correlative
6. neither . . . nor—correlative
7. or—coordinating
8. and—coordinating
9. Whether . . . or—correlative
10. so—coordinating

Exercise 20

Answers will vary. Samples are given.

If you visit St. Louis, Missouri, you must see the city's famous Gateway Arch. It is a stainless-steel structure *and* glistens in the light. It stands more than 600 feet high and forms a graceful curve, arching above the ground. The Gateway Arch was completed in 1965 and has become a part of St. Louis history. Because the Arch is dramatic and symbolic, it shows that St. Louis is the "gateway to the West." Both residents and tourists appreciate its beauty. When you visit it, don't forget to go up to its observation desk. You will see not only a fantastic view of several rivers but also a view of downtown St. Louis and surrounding areas in Missouri and Illinois.

Exercise 21

1. George and Dave went camping and canoeing in New Hampshire.
2. They wanted to have a campfire because it was cold the first night.
3. On Saturday, they could have either hot dogs or stew for dinner.
4. George had not been camping since he was eight years old.
5. They were going to make pancakes for breakfast, but it was raining when they got up.

Exercise 22

1. Wow
2. Gee
3. Oh, no
4. Whew
5. Whoa

Exercise 23

Sentences will vary.

Exercise 24

1. because
2. Wow
3. Whew
4. when
5. Goodness! ... as

Exercise 25

Answers will vary. Samples are given.

Stan: *Hey! Do you remember when we visited the Golden Gate Bridge?*

Belinda: *Yeah. Because the sun was just beginning to set, it was beautiful.*

Stan: *The fog began to come in, and things changed quickly. Within a few minutes we couldn't see the bay or the hillsides.*

Belinda: *It was pretty eerie but exciting.*

Exercise 26

Writing Application

Partners may want to act out their narratives.

Chapter Review Exercises cont'd.

beauty. You visit it. Don't forget to go up to its observation deck. You will see a fantastic view of several rivers. You will see downtown St. Louis. You will see surrounding areas in Missouri and Illinois.

Exercise 21 **Combining Sentences With Conjunctions** Use the type of conjunction specified to join the following pairs of sentences.

1. George and Dave went camping in New Hampshire. They went canoeing there, too. (coordinating conjunction)
2. They wanted to have a campfire. It was cold the first night. (subordinating conjunction)
3. On Saturday, they could have hot dogs for dinner. They could also have stew. (correlative conjunction)
4. George had not been camping for a long time. The last time he had been camping, he was eight years old. (subordinating conjunction)
5. They were going to make pancakes for breakfast. It was raining when they got up. (coordinating conjunction)

Exercise 22 **Identifying Interjections** On your paper, list the interjections in the following sentences.

1. Wow, Yellowstone Park is beautiful!
2. Gee, I think we are too late to see Old Faithful erupt.
3. Oh, no! I think we're lost and won't ever find Old Faithful.
4. Whew! There it is at last.
5. Whoa! I think I see a buffalo over there.

Exercise 23 **Writing Sentences With Interjections** On your paper, write a sentence for each of the following interjections.

1. Ouch!
2. Wow!
3. Quick!
4. Help!
5. Hey!

Exercise 24 **Supplying Conjunctions and Interjections** Supply a conjunction or interjection to complete each sentence.

1. Sarita took many pictures on our trip __?__ she is the best photographer.
2. __?__ this shot is really terrific!
3. __?__ You captured the bear just as he was breaking into our food supply.
4. We forgot to protect our food __?__ we set up our campsite.
5. __?__ A bear looks huge __?__ he is walking near your tent at night.

Exercise 25 **Revising to Include Conjunctions and Interjections** Rewrite the following dialogue, adding conjunctions and interjections to help connect ideas and show emotion.

STAN: Do you remember when we visited the Golden Gate Bridge?

BELINDA: The sun was just beginning to set. It was beautiful.

STAN: The fog began to come in. Things changed quickly. Within a few minutes, we couldn't see the bay. We couldn't see the hillsides.

BELINDA: It was pretty eerie. It was exciting.

Exercise 26 **Writing Application** Write a brief narrative about two friends visiting a famous landmark or park. Identify the place they are visiting, and include words and sentences they say to each other. Use conjunctions and interjections in your narrative, and underline them.

Standardized Test Preparation Workshop

Revising and Editing

Standardized test questions measure your knowledge of standard grammar and usage, such as when to use conjunctions. Conjunctions, such as *and, but, or,* and *for,* join closely related ideas together. When answering these types of questions, read the entire passage first. Then, note how using a conjunction could connect like ideas. Finally, choose the letter of the best rewrite of the underlined sentences.

Test Tip

When choosing the best rewrite of a sentence, make sure that a comma is used before a conjunction connecting two independent clauses. If not, this choice is a run-on sentence and thus incorrect.

Read the passage, and choose the letter of the best way to write the underlined sentences. If the underlined section needs no change, mark the choice "Correct as is."

(1) The Sioux lived on the Northern Plains of North America. The Sioux were famous for their bravery.

1 A The Sioux lived on the Northern Plains of North America and the Sioux were famous for their bravery.

B The Sioux lived on the Northern Plains of North America but they were famous for their bravery.

C The Sioux lived on the Northern Plains of North America, and they were famous for their bravery.

D Correct as is.

The best answer is C. The conjunction *and* joins two independent clauses that contain similar ideas—information about the Sioux—without changing the sentence's meaning.

Practice **Directions:** Read the passage, and choose the letter of the best way to write the underlined sentences. If the underlined section needs no change, mark the choice "Correct as is."

(1) Tension developed between the Sioux and the United States. It increased during the 1800's. (2) The Sioux had a valid reason for outrage. Settlers were slaughtering buffalo.

1 **A** Tension developed between the Sioux and the United States, and it increased during the 1800's.

B Tension developed between the Sioux and the United States, but it increased during the 1800's.

C Tension developed and increased between the Sioux and the United States during the 1800's.

D Correct as is

2 **F** The Sioux had a valid reason for outrage, but settlers were slaughtering buffalo.

G The Sioux had a valid reason for outrage, for settlers were slaughtering buffalo.

H The Sioux had a valid reason for outrage and settlers were slaughtering buffalo.

J Correct as is

▶ Lesson Objectives

- To use conjunctions correctly and appropriately.

Step-by-Step Teaching Guide

Revising and Editing

Teaching Resources: Standardized Test Preparation Workbook, pp.35–36

1. Encourage students to find the conjunction in each sentence. Then have them focus on the words or ideas that are linked.
2. Some students may benefit from reading the answer choices aloud.
3. Have volunteers explain their answer choices.

Answer Key

Practice 1

1. A
2. G

TEST-TAKING TIP

Students may benefit from creating simple charts that list each type of conjunction along with the relationship each conjunction expresses between ideas.

Answer Key

Exercise A

1. Great Lakes—plural, proper, compound noun; group—singular, common noun; lakes—plural, common noun; North America—singular, proper, compound noun
2. They—personal pronoun; part—singular, common noun; border—singular, common noun; United States—singular, compound, proper noun; Canada—singular, proper noun; one—indefinite pronoun; United States— singular, compound, proper noun
3. This—demonstrative pronoun; province—singular, common noun; Ontario—singular, proper noun; lakes—plural, common noun
4. Their—personal pronoun; outlet—singular, common noun; St. Lawrence River—singular, compound, proper noun; which—relative pronoun; Atlantic Ocean—singular, compound, proper noun
5. system—singular, common noun; percent—singular, common noun; world's—singular, common noun; water—singular, common noun
6. resources—plural, common noun; cities— plural, common noun; Chicago—singular, proper noun; Toronto— singular, proper noun; North America's—singular, compound, proper noun; heartland—singular, common noun
7. shoreline—singular, common noun; Great Lakes—plural, compound, proper noun; areas—plural, common noun; people—plural, collective noun; United States—singular, proper noun; Canada—singular, proper noun
8. Which—interrogative pronoun; Great Lake—singular, compund, proper noun
9. Lake Superior—singular, compound, proper noun; which—relative pronoun; lake—singular, common noun; world—singular, common noun; surface area—singular, compound, common noun
10. It—personal pronoun; sea level—singular, compound, common noun

Cumulative Review

PARTS OF SPEECH

Exercise A **Identifying Nouns and Pronouns** Identify the nouns and pronouns in the following sentences. Label each noun *collective, compound, common,* or *proper,* as well as *singular* or *plural.* Label each pronoun *personal, demonstrative, relative, interrogative,* or *indefinite.*

1. The Great Lakes form a group of five freshwater lakes in North America.
2. They form part of the border between the United States and Canada, while one lies fully within the United States.
3. This means that the Canadian province of Ontario borders four lakes.
4. Their primary outlet is the St. Lawrence River, which flows to the Atlantic Ocean.
5. The lake system holds twenty percent of the world's fresh water.
6. The resources help cities, such as Chicago and Toronto, in North America's heartland.
7. The shoreline of the Great Lakes provides many recreational areas for people of the United States and Canada.
8. Which is the largest Great Lake?
9. Lake Superior, which is the largest freshwater lake in the world, is the largest in surface area.
10. It is also the highest above sea level.

Exercise B **Recognizing Verbs** Write the verbs in the following sentences and label each one *action* or *linking* and *transitive* or *intransitive.* Include and underline all helping verbs.

1. Lake Superior has an irregular coastline with several large bays.
2. Rocky cliffs, some up to one thousand feet high, line the northern shore.
3. The Pictured Rocks, near Munising, Michigan, are colorful sandstone cliffs.
4. Large forests containing streams and rivers border the lake in some places.
5. The Nipigon River flows into Lake Superior from the north.
6. The lake also receives the St. Louis River from the west.
7. The St. Marys River connects Lake Superior to Lake Huron.
8. This river is navigable through the Sault Sainte Marie Canals.
9. Lake Superior rarely freezes over, but ice closes many ports during the winter.
10. Étienne Brûlé, a French explorer, probably had discovered the lake in 1610.

Exercise C **Recognizing Adjectives and Adverbs** Label the underlined words in the following sentences *adjective* or *adverb.* Then, write the word each one modifies.

1. Lake Huron is the <u>second</u> largest of the five Great Lakes.
2. The <u>maximum</u> length of Lake Huron is <u>nearly</u> 200 miles.
3. It receives water from Lake Michigan <u>only</u> through the Straits of Mackinac.
4. The population of <u>several</u> fish species was <u>seriously</u> reduced in the mid-twentieth century.
5. <u>Government</u> programs have since helped the <u>fishing</u> industry recover.
6. Lake Huron is <u>heavily</u> used by shipping vessels, especially those carrying <u>iron</u> ore.
7. In <u>early</u> April the ice melts, reopening the <u>main</u> ports to navigation.
8. The Huron confederacy of the <u>Iroquois</u> family <u>historically</u> inhabited the area east of Lake Huron.
9. Their population declined <u>quickly</u> after <u>European</u> explorers arrived.
10. <u>Jesuit</u> missionaries <u>initially</u> settled the shoreline in 1638.

Exercise B

1. has—linking
2. line—action, transitive
3. are—linking
4. border—action, transitive
5. flows—action, intransitive
6. receives—action, transitive
7. connects—action, transitive
8. is—linking
9. freezes—action, intransitive; closes—action, transitive
10. <u>had</u> discovered—action, transitive

Exercise C

1. adverb—largest
2. adjective—length; adverb—200
3. adverb—receives; adjective—Straits of Mackinac
4. adjective—species; adverb—was reduced
5. adjective—programs; adjective—industry
6. adverb—is used; adjective—ore
7. adjective—April; adjective—ports
8. adjective—family; adverb—inhabited
9. adverb—declined; adjective—explorers
10. adjective—missionaries; adverb—settled

Exercise D **Recognizing Prepositions** Identify the prepositions in the following sentences. Write the object of each preposition.

1. Lake Erie, with an area of 9,910 square miles, is the fourth largest of the Great Lakes.
2. It has an average depth of only 62 feet.
3. Because it is so shallow, the lake is quickly stirred by storms.
4. Lake Erie was polluted by the dumping of industrial waste by industries, cities, and farms.
5. Since the United States and Canada agreed to clean up the lake in 1972, the quality of the water has improved greatly and the supply of fish has increased.

Exercise E **Recognizing Conjunctions and Interjections** Identify the conjunctions and interjections in the following sentences. Label the conjunctions *coordinating, correlative,* or *subordinating.*

1. Hey, who discovered Lake Erie before the French built fur-trading posts?
2. During the French and Indian War, Great Britain won control of the lake.
3. Not only did Jay's Treaty divide control of the lake, but also Lake Erie was the scene of a battle in the War of 1812.
4. Wow! The Americans triumphed over the British.
5. Now, Lake Erie sees a great deal of freight shipping even though navigation can be hazardous.
6. Yes, both the St. Lawrence Seaway and the Erie Canal service the lake.
7. Products including iron ore, steel, and coal travel from various ports.
8. Several states are involved in this trade, but ice closes the lake for the winter.
9. The Niagara River and the Welland Canal feed into Lake Ontario.
10. Neither Cattaraugus Creek nor the Raisin River feeds large amounts of water into Lake Erie.

Exercise F **Identifying All the Parts of Speech** Write the part of speech of each underlined word in the following paragraph. Be specific.

Lake Michigan is the only Great Lake that lies entirely within the United States. Oh, it touches Michigan, Wisconsin, and Illinois. The Chicago Sanitary and Ship Canal connects the lake to the Mississippi River. Green Bay is located on the western shore, and Grand Traverse Bay is on the eastern shore. These form the main indentations in the lake.

Exercise G **Revising Sentences** Rewrite the following sentences, adding the part of speech indicated.

1. Buffalo, New York, (verb) on Lake Erie.
2. (pronoun) was founded (preposition) the Dutch in 1803.
3. The site was chosen (conjunction) it lay at the western end of an important Indian trail.
4. Buffalo is the (noun) of two United States presidents—Millard Fillmore and Grover Cleveland.
5. The Erie Canal (verb) from Lake Erie at Buffalo (preposition) the Hudson River at Troy, New York.

Exercise H **Writing Application** Write a short narrative about a body of water with which you are familiar. Include nouns, pronouns, verbs, adjectives, adverbs, prepositions, conjunctions, and interjections, and underline at least one example of each. Then, label each word's part of speech as specifically as possible.

Exercise D

1. with—area; of—miles; of—Great Lakes
2. of—feet
3. by—storms
4. by—dumping; of—waste; by—industries, cities, farms
5. in—1972; of—water; of—fish

Exercise E

1. Hey—interjection; before—subordinating conjunction
2. and—coordinating conjunction
3. Not only ... but also—correlative conjunction
4. Wow—interjection
5. even though—subordinating conjunction
6. Yes—interjection; both ... and—correlative conjunction
7. and— coordinating conjunction
8. but— coordinating conjunction
9. and— coordinating conjunction
10. Neither ... nor—correlative conjunction

Exercise F

entirely—adverb modifies *lies*; Oh—interjection; touches—transitive, action verb; Green Bay—singular, proper compound noun; is located—intransitive, action verb with helping verb; western—adjective modifies *shore;* These—demonstrative pronoun; indentations—plural, common noun; in—preposition

Exercise G

1. lies
2. It; by
3. because
4. hometown
5. flows; into

Exercise H

Writing Application
As an extension, you may want to have students write another narrative in which they do not identify any parts of speech. Students can exchange papers with partners and then identify the different parts of speech.

Chapter 19 Time and Resource Manager

In-Depth Lesson Plan

	LESSON FOCUS	PRINT AND MEDIA RESOURCES
DAY 1	**The Basic Sentence** Students learn what a sentence is. They put subjects and verbs together to form complete sentences (pp. 396–401).	**Teaching Resources** *Grammar Exercise Workbook,* pp. 49–50; *Grammar Exercises Answers on Transparencies,* Ch. 19 ***Writing and Grammar iText* (Interactive Text),** Section 19.1
DAY 2	**Subjects and Predicates** Students identify complete subjects and complete predicates, as well as compound subjects and verbs. They also complete the Hands-on Grammar activity (pp. 402–409).	**Teaching Resources** *Grammar Exercise Workbook,* pp. 51–54; *Grammar Exercises Answers on Transparencies,* Ch. 19; *Hands-on Grammar Activity Book,* Ch. 19 ***Writing and Grammar iText* (Interactive Text),** Sections 19.2–3
DAY 3	**Hard-to-Find Subjects** Students identify subjects in sentences that do not follow subject-verb order (pp. 410–415).	**Teaching Resources** *Grammar Exercise Workbook,* pp. 55–58; *Grammar Exercises Answers on Transparencies,* Ch. 19 ***Writing and Grammar iText* (Interactive Text),** Section 19.4
DAY 4	**Complements** Students identify complements in sentences, including direct objects, indirect objects, objects of prepositions, and predicate adjectives (pp. 416–425).	**Teaching Resources** *Grammar Exercise Workbook,* pp. 59–72; *Grammar Exercises Answers on Transparencies,* Ch. 19 ***Writing and Grammar iText* (Interactive Text),** Section 19.5
DAY 5	**Review and Assess** Students review the chapter and demonstrate mastery of basic sentence parts (pp. 426–429).	**Teaching Resources** *Formal Assessment,* Ch. 19; *Grammar Exercises Answers on Transparencies,* Ch. 19 ***Writing and Grammar iText* (Interactive Text),** Ch. 19, Chapter Review; On-line Exercise Bank, Sections 19.1–5

Accelerated Lesson Plan

	LESSON FOCUS	PRINT AND MEDIA RESOURCES
DAY 1	**Basic Sentence Parts** Students work with basic sentence parts (pp. 396–409).	**Teaching Resources** *Grammar Exercise Workbook,* pp. 49–54; *Grammar Exercises Answers on Transparencies,* Ch. 19 ***Writing and Grammar iText* (Interactive Text),** Sections 19.1–3
DAY 2	**Hard-to-Find Subjects** Students identify hard-to-find subjects in sentences that do not follow standard subject-verb order (pp. 410–415).	**Teaching Resources** *Grammar Exercise Workbook,* pp. 55–58; *Grammar Exercises Answers on Transparencies,* Ch. 19 ***Writing and Grammar iText* (Interactive Text),** Section 19.4
DAY 3	**Complements** Students work with complements, including direct objects, indirect objects, objects of prepositions, and predicate adjectives (pp. 416–425).	**Teaching Resources** *Grammar Exercise Workbook,* pp. 59–72; *Grammar Exercises Answers on Transparencies,* Ch. 19 ***Writing and Grammar iText* (Interactive Text),** Section 19.5
DAY 4	**Review and Assess** Students review the chapter and demonstrate mastery of basic sentence parts (pp. 426–429).	**Teaching Resources** *Formal Assessment,* Ch. 19; *Grammar Exercises Answers on Transparencies,* Ch. 19 ***Writing and Grammar iText* (Interactive Text),** Ch. 19, Chapter Review; On-line Exercise Bank, Sections 19.1–5

Options for Adapting Lesson Plans

HOMEWORK

Have students complete any stage of the lesson for homework.

SPELLING

To teach spelling skills in conjunction with grammar, mechanics, and usage, work through *Prentice Hall Everyday Spelling,* Grade 8, Chapter 22, as you cover this *Writing and Grammar* chapter.

TECHNOLOGY

Students can use *Writing and Grammar iText* to complete the exercises interactively on computer. They can complete additional exercises in the *On-line Exercise Bank:* The Auto Check feature will grade their work. Go online: PHSchool.com Use Web code: eck-8002

INTEGRATED SKILLS COVERAGE

Grammar in Literature
SE pp. 403, 408, 417

Writing
Find It in Your Writing, SE pp. 401, 404, 405, 409, 415, 425
Writing Application, SE pp. 401, 405, 409, 415, 425, 427

Viewing and Representing
Critical Viewing, SE pp. 396, 399, 400, 402, 407, 411, 412, 416, 421

Integrating Grammar Skills
Understood Subjects in Imperatives, ATE p. 410

BLOCK SCHEDULING

Pacing Suggestions
For 90-minute Blocks
- Administer the Diagnostic Test to students to determine instructional coverage.
- Have students complete the necessary exercises in class. Use the Hands-on Grammar Activity to provide a change of pace.

Resources for Varying Instruction
- ***Writing and Grammar* (Interactive Text)** A 90-minute block provides an ideal opportunity for students to work on computer.

Professional Development Support
- ***How to Manage Instruction in the Block*** This teaching resource provides management and activity suggestions.

ASSESSMENT SUPPORT

Standardized Test Preparation Workshop SE pp. 428–429, ATE p. 412

Standardized Test Preparation Workbook, pp. 37–38

Formal Assessment, Ch. 19

MEDIA AND TECHNOLOGY

For the Student
- ***Writing and Grammar iText* (Interactive Text),** Ch. 19
- ***On-line Exercise Bank,*** Sections 19.1–5

For the Teacher
- ***Resource Pro* CD-ROM**

MEETING INDIVIDUAL NEEDS

Less Advanced Students ATE pp. 399, 414, 419, 422. See also Ongoing Assessments ATE pp. 400, 403, 408, 411, 413, 419, 420, 423.

ESL Students ATE p. 411

More Advanced Students ATE p. 403

Gifted/Talented Students ATE p. 418

Bodily/Kinesthetic Learners ATE p. 398

Verbal/Linguistic Learners ATE pp. 422, 423

WRITING AND GRAMMAR ON-LINE

iText Interactive Text (On-line or on CD-ROM)
- Easily navigable instruction with on-line supporting resources
- Self-scoring exercises and diagnostic tests

Companion Web Site PHSchool.com
- On-line Exercise Bank (use Web Code eck-8002)

See the Go On-line! feature, SE p. iii.

LITERATURE CONNECTIONS

Grammar in Literature selections from *Prentice Hall Literature: Timeless Voices, Timeless Themes,* Silver:
from "The White Umbrella," Gish Jen, SE p. 408
from *An American Childhood,* Annie Dillard, SE p. 417

Lesson Objectives

1. To recognize and use subjects and verbs to express complete thoughts.
2. To recognize and identify complements in subjects and predicates.

Critical Viewing

Speculate Possible response: Cowhands played an important part in the history of the West. They tended to the cattle on large ranches.

Answer Key

Diagnostic Test

Each item in the diagnostic test corresponds to a specific concept in the chapter on Basic Sentence Parts. This will enable you to tailor instruction to the particular needs of your students. See "Ongoing Assessment: Diagnose" on the bottom for further details.

Skill Check A (p. 397)

1. We | hear stories of the Wild West and the cowboys.
2. Pecos Bill | is a legendary cowboy of the Southwest.
3. Ingenuity | was one of his characteristics.
4. This legendary cowboy | was born in Texas in the 1830's.
5. Stories of his early escapades | entertain readers.

Chapter 19

Basic Sentence Parts

The Coming and Going of the Pony Express, Frederic Remington

The western frontier of the United States during the 1800's is sometimes referred to as the Wild West. The Wild West and the cowhands who lived there are an exciting part of history. To learn and share information about the Wild West, you need more than just words. You must put words together in patterns that express ideas.

By assembling the eight parts of speech in various patterns, you can express your ideas and communicate them to others. Patterns of words that communicate ideas are called **sentences**. All sentences must have certain basic parts. In this chapter, you will learn about the basic parts of a sentence and how you can use them to express your thoughts clearly.

▲ **Critical Viewing** Write several sentences describing this scene. Be sure to use basic sentence parts correctly. **[Speculate]**

ONGOING ASSESSMENT: Diagnose

If students miss more than one item in each category, direct them to the relevant pages of the text and assign exercises for practice and review.

Basic Sentence Parts	Diagnostic Test Items	Teach	Practice	Section Review	Chapter Review
Skill Check A				Ex. 3–4	
Subjects and Predicates	A 1–5	pp. 398–404	Ex. 1–2, 8	Ex. 9–10	Ex. 46
Skill Check B					
Compound Subjects and Predicates	B 6–10	pp. 406–409	Ex. 14–16	Ex. 17–18	Ex. 47
Skill Check C					
Hard-to-Find Subjects	C 11–15	pp. 410–414	Ex. 22–25	Ex. 26–28	Ex. 48

Diagnostic Test

Directions: Write all answers on a separate sheet of paper.

Skill Check A. Copy the following sentences onto your paper. Draw a vertical line between the complete subject and the complete predicate. Underline each subject once and each verb twice.

1. We hear stories about cowboys and life in the old West.
2. Pecos Bill is a legendary cowboy of the Southwest.
3. Ingenuity was one of his characteristics.
4. This legendary cowboy was born in Texas in the 1830's.
5. Stories of his early escapades entertain readers.

Skill Check B. In the sentences below, label each compound subject and compound verb.

6. Strength, courage, and humor also characterized Pecos Bill.
7. According to legend, roping and branding were his inventions.
8. He teethed on a bowie knife and played with bears.
9. Young Bill became lost and was raised by coyotes.
10. Paul Bunyan and other fictional heroes were the models for this character.

Skill Check C. Identify the subject in each sentence below.

11. Have you heard the legend of Pecos Bill?
12. Listen carefully!
13. There are many exaggerations in the legend.
14. Long ago in the West lived this hero of American folklore.
15. Are the myths about Pecos Bill true?

Skill Check D. Copy the following sentences, underlining each direct object once and each indirect object twice. Circle each object of a preposition. (Not every sentence has all three.)

16. William Cody showed his fans and audiences an entertaining perspective of the "Wild West."
17. The name "Buffalo Bill" gave Cody a character for his shows.
18. Wild West shows brought entertainment to crowds across the country.
19. However, they gave their audience incorrect ideas about what life was like in the West.
20. William Cody also founded the town of Cody, Wyoming.

Skill Check E. Copy the following sentences, labeling each *predicate noun, predicate pronoun,* and *predicate adjective.*

21. Pecos Bill and Paul Bunyan are only two of the numerous legends of the Wild West.
22. My favorite legendary heroes are those two.
23. Cowboys were part of the foundation of the Wild West.
24. The stories about these characters are always humorous.
25. The settlement of the West was exciting and entertaining.

Skill Check B

6. Strength, courage, humor—compound subject
7. roping, branding—compound verb
8. teethed, played—compound verb
9. became, was raised—compound verb
10. Paul Bunyan, heroes—compound subject

Skill Check C

11. you
12. you
13. exaggerations
14. hero
15. myths

Skill Check D

16. William Cody showed his <u>fans and audiences</u> an entertaining <u>perspective</u> of the ("Wild West").
17. The name "Buffalo Bill" gave <u>Cody</u> a <u>character</u> for his (shows).
18. Wild West shows brought <u>entertainment</u> to (crowds) across the (country).
19. However, they gave their <u>audience</u> incorrect <u>ideas</u> about what life was like in the (West).
20. William Cody also founded the <u>town</u> of (Cody), Wyoming.

Skill Check E

21. Pecos Bill and William Cody are only two [PN] of the numerous legends of the Wild West.
22. My favorite legendary heroes are those two [PN].
23. Cowboys were part [PN] of the foundation of the Wild West.
24. The stories about these characters are always humorous [PA].
25. The settlement of the West was exciting [PA] and entertaining [PA].

ONGOING ASSESSMENT: Diagnose *continued*

Punctuation	Diagnostic Test Items	Teach	Practice	Section Review	Chapter Review
Skill Check D					
Direct Objects, Indirect Objects, Objects of Prepositions	D 16–20	pp. 416–421	Ex. 32–36	Ex. 40–41	Ex. 49–50
Skill Check E					
Subject Complements	E 21–25	pp. 422–424	Ex. 37–39	Ex. 42	Ex. 51–52
Cumulative Review and Applications				Ex. 5–7, 11–13, 19–21, 29–31, 43–45	Ex. 53–55

TIME SAVERS!

Answers on Transparency
Use the Grammar Exercises Answers on Transparencies for Chapter 19 to have students correct their own or one another's exercises.

On-Line Exercise Bank
Have students complete the exercises on computer. The Auto Check feature will grade their work for you!

PREPARE and ENGAGE

Interest GRABBER Write the following nouns and verbs on the board. Ask students to combine one of each to make grammatically correct—but ridiculous—sentences with subjects and predicates.

Nouns	*Verbs*
lizard	*tiptoe*
piglet	*slither*
senator	*dog-paddle*
eighth	*grader climb*
mime	*slurp*

Activate Prior Knowledge

Have students copy five sentences from a newspaper and identify the subject and verb of each sentence.

TEACH

Step-by-Step Teaching Guide

The Basic Sentence

1. Write the following sentences on the chalkboard and ask students to identify the subject.

    Sara delivers the newspaper. (Sara)

    Her customers like getting the paper delivered. (customers)

    The newspaper is important to them. (newspaper)

2. Write the following sentences on the chalkboard and ask students to identify the verb.

    The paper prints three editions. (prints)

    Sara delivers 68 papers every day. (delivers)

    She gets paid once a week. (gets paid)

    It has been a good job for Sara. (has been)

Customize for *Bodily/Kinesthetic Learners*

Students can act out some of the sentences, using gestures, expressions, and motion to identify subjects and, especially, verbs.

Section 19.1 The Basic Sentence

A sentence is a group of words that expresses a complete thought. A sentence has two basic parts—a subject and a verb.

KEY CONCEPT A **complete sentence** has a subject and a verb and expresses a complete thought. ■

KEY CONCEPT The **subject** of a sentence is the word or group of words that answers the question *Who?* or *What?* before the verb. ■

EXAMPLES: Cowboys herd cattle for a living. (V: herd)

Our ranch was in Texas. (V: was)

In the first example, the noun *Cowboys* is the subject that tells us *who* herd cattle. The noun *ranch* in the second example is the subject that tells *what* was in Texas.

Not all subjects are this easy to find. (See Section 19.4 for more information about finding subjects in sentences.)

KEY CONCEPT The **verb** in a sentence tells *what the subject does, what is done to the subject,* or *what the condition of the subject is.* ■

EXAMPLES: Bobby gave an unforgettable show. (S: Bobby)

Their prize horse was stolen. (S: horse)

She has been blue all day. (S: She)

Gave is the verb in the first example. It tells what the subject, *Bobby,* did. In the second example, *was stolen* tells what was done to the subject *horse. Has been* in the third example is a linking verb. It tells something about the condition of the subject by linking *she* to the word *blue.*

Theme: The Western Frontier

In this section, you will learn about the two basic elements of a sentence. The examples and exercises are about life on the western frontier of the United States during the 1800's.

Cross-Curricular Connection: Social Studies

TIME AND RESOURCE MANAGER

Resources
Print: Grammar Exercise Workbook, pp. 49–50
Technology: Writing and Grammar iText, Section 19.1; On-Line Exercise Bank, Section 19.1

In-Depth Coverage	Accelerated Pace
• Work through all key concepts, pp. 398–400. • Assign and review Exercises 1–2.	• Assign pp. 398–400 for independent student review.

Exercise 1 **Recognizing Subjects and Verbs** Copy each of the following sentences onto your paper. Underline each subject once and each verb twice.

EXAMPLE: Sometimes, cowboys searched for their cattle for hours.

1. Cowboys are described as "mounted herders" in the United States.
2. The term simply describes these cowboys on a horse.
3. They have many responsibilities to their herds of cattle.
4. The cattle must be kept together in a group.
5. The herd may be driven to the pasture for grazing.
6. While on a drive, the cattle must be protected from rustlers, or thieves.
7. Other herds might mix with the cattle.
8. All cattle are branded by the cattle owner's unique symbol.
9. The brand distinguishes one herd from another.
10. In the United States, people admire these heroes of the West.

More Practice

Grammar Exercise Workbook
- pp. 49–50

On-line Exercise Bank
- Section 19.1

Go on-line:
PHSchool.com
Enter Web Code:
eck-8002

iText

Get instant feedback! Exercise 1 is available on-line or on CD-ROM.

KEY CONCEPT A group of words expresses a **complete thought** if it can stand by itself and still make sense. ■

Making sure that your words express complete thoughts is especially important when you write. *Incomplete thoughts* will leave readers with questions in their minds. Consider the group of words in the following example:

INCOMPLETE THOUGHT: The man in the cowboy hat.

"What about the man in the cowboy hat?" a reader might ask. Standing by itself, this group of words makes no sense. An important element is missing—the verb. Using *man* as a subject, you can turn this incomplete thought into a sentence by adding any number of different verbs.

▶ Critical Viewing Write a brief monologue in which the man pictured below is talking to his horse. Be sure that your sentences express complete thoughts. **[Speculate]**

Partners, Charles M. Russell

Answer Key

Exercise 1

1. Cowboys are described as "mounted herders" in the United States.
2. The term simply describes these cowboys on a horse.
3. They have many responsibilities to their herds of cattle.
4. The cattle must be kept together in a group.
5. The herd may be driven to the pasture for grazing.
6. While on a drive, the cattle must be protected from rustlers, or thieves.
7. Other herds might mix with the cattle.
8. All cattle are branded by the cattle owner's unique symbol.
9. The brand distinguishes one herd from another.
10. In the United States, people admire these heroes of the West.

Critical Viewing

Speculate Possible response: "I know you're awfully hungry. But this is my dinner!"

Customize for *Less Advanced Students*

Work with students individually or in a small group to review the key concepts about subjects and verbs. Make sure that students understand that both elements must be present in a sentence.

Step-by-Step Teaching Guide

The Need to Express a Complete Thought

1. Review the importance of finding the subject and verb to be sure that a group of words is a complete thought.
2. Write the following examples on the chalkboard and ask students to identify what is missing in the fragment and supply a word or group of words that will make the fragment a complete sentence.

   ran down the hill (subject)

   Walter in the garden (verb)

   in the house at the end of the road (subject and verb)

   (Possible responses: The dog ran down the hill. Walter planted corn in the garden. My friend Zack lives in the house at the end of the road.)

Critical Viewing

Analyze Students may say the cowboy is herding cattle.

Answer Key

Exercise 2

Sentences will vary. Samples are given.

1. sentence
2. The hats on their heads are made of cowhide.
3. He wore a handkerchief around his neck.
4. sentence
5. Leather chaps protect them from grass and brush.
6. sentence
7. I put the saddle on the horse.
8. sentence
9. sentence
10. They use the lasso in order to rope steer.

TIME SAVERS!

Answers on Transparency Use the Grammar Exercises Answers on Transparencies for Chapter 19 to have students correct their own or one another's exercises.

On-Line Exercise Bank Have students complete the exercises on computer. The Auto Check feature will grade their work for you!

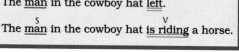

19.1

COMPLETE THOUGHTS

The man (S) in the cowboy hat rides (V) gracefully.

The man (S) in the cowboy hat left (V).

The man (S) in the cowboy hat is riding (V) a horse.

Notice that each of the examples in the chart has all of the ingredients necessary for a sentence: Each has a *subject* and a *verb*, and each expresses a *complete thought.*

Sometimes, an incomplete thought may be a group of words with no word in it that can be used as a subject.

INCOMPLETE THOUGHT: Near the stream by the roadside.

This incomplete thought is merely two prepositional phrases. Both a subject and a verb are needed.

COMPLETE: Wild irises (S) are growing (V) near the stream by the roadside.

In grammar, incomplete thoughts are often called *fragments.*

Exercise 2 **Revising to Create Complete Sentences** Five of the following items are sentences. The rest are incomplete thoughts. If a group of words is a sentence, write *sentence.* If a group of words expresses an incomplete thought, add words to make it a sentence. Underline the subject once and the verb twice in each new sentence.

EXAMPLE: The cowboy's attire.

ANSWER: The cowboy's attire serves practical purposes.

1. Cowboys dress according to their environment.
2. The hats on their heads.
3. Wore a handkerchief.
4. Cowboys wear leather chaps to protect their legs.
5. Protect them from grass and brush.
6. Boots are worn to keep their feet in the stirrups.
7. The saddle on the horse.
8. The lasso is coiled around the saddle horn.
9. Sometimes, cowboys must use a lasso or lariat on their cattle.
10. They use the lasso in order to.

▼ **Critical Viewing** Use complete sentences to describe the skills being exhibited by the cowboy pictured below. **[Analyze]**

More Practice

Grammar Exercise Workbook
- pp. 49–50

On-line Exercise Bank
- Section 19.1

Go on-line: PHSchool.com *Enter Web Code:* eck-8002

ONGOING ASSESSMENT: Monitor and Reinforce

If students miss more than two items in Exercises 1–2, refer them to the following for additional practice.

In the Textbook	Print Resources	Technology
Section Review, Ex. 3–4, p. 401	Grammar Exercise Workbook, pp. 49–50	On-Line Exercise Bank, Section 19.1

Section 19.1 Section Review

GRAMMAR EXERCISES 3–7

Exercise 3 Recognizing Subjects and Verbs Copy each of the following sentences. Underline each subject once and each verb or verb phrase twice.

1. After the Civil War, cowboys often drove their cattle to the nearest railroad.
2. Then, the cattle were shipped to the East in response to a demand for beef.
3. The cowboy performed his job from sunup to sundown.
4. The cattle drive may have earned him about one dollar each day.
5. The cook was a very important member of the drive.
6. He prepared three meals a day for many hungry cowboys.
7. The meals might have included beans, biscuits, coffee, beef stew, and sometimes a sweet dessert.
8. In his spare time, the cook served as a doctor, dentist, barber, and mediator.
9. Eventually, the need for cattle drives diminished.
10. However, cowboys remained in the public eye through competition in rodeos.
11. Rodeos began in the mid-nineteenth century on cattle drives.
12. They started as informal competitions between cowhands.
13. The cowhands displayed their roping skills and horsemanship.
14. The first formal rodeo was held in Cheyenne, Wyoming, in 1872.
15. Americans have continued to be fascinated with the lives of cowboys.

Exercise 4 Revising to Create Complete Sentences Five of the following items are sentences. The rest are incomplete thoughts. If a group of words is a sentence, write *sentence*. If a group of words expresses an incomplete thought, add words to make it a sentence.

1. The western United States during the 1800's had many colorful characters.
2. During the second half of the nineteenth century.
3. We read about many of the men and women of the West.
4. Calamity Jane was among them.
5. She was an American frontierswoman who grew up in the West.
6. A sharpshooter and horsewoman.
7. Always created contention.
8. Calamity Jane said that she was equal to any man.
9. Wore men's clothing.
10. A scout in the United States Cavalry.

Exercise 5 Find It in Your Reading Identify the two subjects and the two verbs in these lines from the poem "The Closing of the Rodeo" by William Jay Smith. Underline the subject of each sentence once and the verb twice.

The lariat snaps; the cowboy rolls
His pack . . .

Exercise 6 Find It in Your Writing Review a paragraph from a piece of your writing to make sure that every sentence expresses a complete thought. Underline the subject of each sentence once and the verb twice.

Exercise 7 Writing Application Write a brief narrative of an event that might have occurred in the frontier West. Write at least five complete sentences. In each sentence, underline each subject once and each verb twice.

ASSESS and CLOSE

Section Review

Each of these exercises correlates to a concept in the section on the basic sentence, pages 398–400. These exercises may be used for more practice, for reteaching, or for review of the Key Concepts presented. Answers for all chapter exercises are available in *Grammar Exercises Answers on Transparencies* in your teaching resources.

Answer Key

Exercise 3

1. After the Civil War, cowboys often drove their cattle to the nearest railroad.
2. Then the cattle were shipped to the East in response to a demand for beef.
3. The cowboy performed his job from sunup to sundown.
4. The cattle drive may have earned him about one dollar each day.
5. The cook was a very important member of the drive.
6. He prepared three meals a day for many hungry cowboys.
7. The meals might have included beans, biscuits, coffee, beef stew, and sometimes a sweet dessert.
8. In his spare time, the cook served as a doctor, dentist, barber, and mediator.
9. Eventually, the need for cattle drives diminished.
10. However, cowboys remained in the public eye through competition in rodeos.
11. Rodeos began in the mid-nineteenth century on cattle drives.
12. They started as informal competitions between cowhands.
13. The cowhands displayed their roping skills and horsemanship.
14. The first formal rodeo was held in Cheyenne, Wyoming, in 1872.
15. Americans have continued to be fascinated with the lives of cowboys.

Exercise 4

Answers will vary. Samples are given.

1. sentence
2. Many well-known figures lived during the second half of the nineteenth century.
3. sentence

continued

Answer Key continued

4. sentence
5. sentence
6. She was a sharpshooter and a horsewoman.
7. Jane always created contention.
8. sentence
9. She wore men's clothing.
10. She became a scout in the United States Calvary.

Exercise 5

Find It in Your Reading
subjects: lariat, cowboy
verbs: snaps, rolls

Exercise 6

Find It in Your Writing
If students find incomplete sentences, they should rewrite them to express a complete thought.

Exercise 7

Writing Application
Students can trade narratives with partners to check.

PREPARE and ENGAGE

Interest GRABBER Write the following sentence on the chalkboard and ask students to identify the complete subject and predicate.

The fearless bank robber grabbed the money and galloped at full speed out of town.

Activate Prior Knowledge

Ask students to write two long sentences about cowboys or cowgirls and identify the complete subject and predicate in each sentence.

TEACH

Step-by-Step Teaching Guide

Complete Subjects and Predicates

1. The simple subject is always a noun or pronoun. The simple predicate is always a verb. The complete subject and the complete predicate include all modifiers, articles, and prepositions relating to each.
2. Review the examples given and see that students understand the components of the complete subject and complete predicate.
3. Write the following sentences on the chalkboard and ask volunteers to come up and draw a line between the complete subject and complete predicate.

   The confused pinto pony | ran in circles around the corral.

   One of the young cowboys | looked on in a state of wonder.

   A black and brown shepherd dog | ran around barking.

Critical Viewing

Compare and Contrast Possible Response: Travel by covered wagon is much slower than travel by car.

Section 19.2

Complete Subjects and Predicates

Every sentence is built around its two essential elements, the subject and the verb. The subject and verb together support the many details that a sentence may include to express a complete thought.

DIFFERENT SENTENCES BUILT AROUND THE SAME SUBJECT AND VERB

Cowboys	ride.
Many cowboys	ride daily.
Many cowboys in our town	ride daily at the ranch.

Notice the line that divides the parts of each sentence. The words to the left of the line include the subject *cowboys* and any other words that add details to it. In each sentence, the words to the left of the line make up the *complete subject.* (In this case, the subject *cowboys* is often called, in contrast, the *simple subject.*)

KEY CONCEPT The **complete subject** of a sentence consists of the subject and any words related to it. ■

As you can see in the examples above, a complete subject may be just one word—the subject itself—or it may be several words.

In the preceding examples, the words to the right of the line include the verb *ride* and any words that add details to it. This part of the sentence is called the *complete predicate.* (The verb itself, a word such as *ride* or a phrase such as *has ridden,* is often called the *simple predicate.*)

KEY CONCEPT The **complete predicate** of a sentence consists of the verb and any words related to it. ■

As you can see in the examples, a complete predicate may be just one word—a verb—or it may be several words.

Theme: The Western Frontier

In this section, you will learn about complete subjects and complete predicates. The examples and exercises are about life on the western frontier of the United States during the 1800's.

Cross-Curricular Connection: Social Studies

▼ **Critical Viewing** Use complete subjects and complete predicates in sentences comparing this mode of transportation with traveling by automobile. **[Compare and Contrast]**

TIME AND RESOURCE MANAGER

Resources

Print: Grammar Exercise Workbook, pp. 51–52; Hands-on Grammar Activity Book, Chapter 19

Technology: Writing and Grammar iText, Section 19.2; On-Line Exercise Bank, Section 19.2

In-Depth Coverage	Accelerated Pace
• Work through all key concepts, pp. 402–403. • Assign and review Exercise 8. • Do the Hands-on Grammar Activity, p. 404.	• Assign pp. 402–404 for independent student review. • Assign Section Review Exercises 9–13.

GRAMMAR IN LITERATURE

from The Closing of the Rodeo

William Jay Smith

In the following excerpt, the complete subjects are shown in red and the complete predicates in blue.

Plumes of smoke from the factory sway
In the setting sun. The curtain falls,
A train in the darkness pulls away.

Exercise 8 Recognizing Complete Subjects and Predicates

Copy each of the following sentences onto your paper. Underline the subject once and the verb twice. Then, draw a vertical line between the complete subject and the complete predicate, as shown in the example.

EXAMPLE: Some famous outlaws | played a big part in the Wild West.

1. Jesse James was an American outlaw.
2. He was known throughout the country for bank and train robberies.
3. The young man joined a band of pro-Confederate raiders at the age of fifteen.
4. The group was led by William Clarke Quantrill.
5. Jesse James later organized his own group of robbers.
6. The members of the group included his older brother, Frank, and Robert Younger.
7. One infamous bank robbery occurred at the First National Bank of Northfield in Minnesota.
8. The clerk would not open the safe.
9. The gang shot him before they escaped.
10. Jesse, along with his brother Frank, was able to avoid capture.

More Practice

Grammar Exercise Workbook
- pp. 51–52

On-line Exercise Bank
- Section 19.2

Go on-line: PHSchool.com
Enter Web Code: eck-8002

iText

Get instant feedback! Exercise 8 is available on-line or on CD-ROM.

ONGOING ASSESSMENT: Monitor and Reinforce

If students miss more than two items in Exercise 8, refer them to the following for additional practice.

In the Textbook	Print Resources	Technology
Section Review, Ex. 9–13, p. 405	Grammar Exercise Workbook, pp. 51–52	On-Line Exercise Bank, Section 19.2

Step-by-Step Teaching Guide

Grammar in Literature

1. Have a volunteer read aloud the passage from "The Closing of the Rodeo."
2. Ask students why they think it is important to be able to identify subjects and predicates in sentences. (Knowing the subject and predicate can help you better understand the meaning of a sentence.)

Customize for *More Advanced Students*

Give students a copy of a brief article from a newspaper or magazine. Ask them to identify simple and complete subjects and predicates in the sentences.

Answer Key

Exercise 8

1. Jesse James | was an American outlaw.
2. He | was known throughout the country for bank and train robberies.
3. The young man | joined a band of pro-Confederate raiders at the age of fifteen.
4. The group | was led by William Clarke Quantrill.
5. Jesse James later | organized his own group of robbers.
6. The members of the group | included his older brother, Frank, and Robert Younger.
7. One infamous bank robbery | occurred at the First National Bank of Northfield in Minnesota.
8. The clerk | would not open the safe.
9. The gang | shot him before they escaped.
10. Jesse, along with his brother Frank, | was able to avoid capture.

Step-by-Step Teaching Guide

Sentence-Part Grab Bag

Teaching Resource: Hands-on Grammar Activity Book, Chapter 19

1. Have students refer to their *Hands-on Grammar activity books* or give them copies of the relevant pages for this activity.
2. Point out that students can use action and linking verbs in the complete predicates. You may wish to suggest topics for students to write about.

Find It in Your Reading

Students may also wish to find sentences from books in you classroom library.

Find It in Your Writing

Encourage students to look for interesting sentences that make sense out of context.

19.2

Hands-on Grammar

Sentence-Part Grab Bag

Create a sentence-part grab bag to help you understand the way subjects and predicates function. Create two sets of index cards. On the first set, write the part of a sentence that tells the person, place, or thing that does the action, including all the adjectives, adverbs, phrases, and clauses that rename or describe the noun.

EXAMPLE: Movies about cowboys and the Old West

On the second set of cards, write actions or conditions.

EXAMPLE: are fun to watch.

Create eight to ten cards for each set. Try to use a wide variety of nouns, verbs, and modifiers. Then, take two envelopes, and label one "Complete Subjects" and the other "Complete Predicates."

Place each set of cards in its labeled envelope. Working with a partner, randomly select complete subjects and complete predicates and put them together to create different sentences. Chances are, some of your sentences will be very humorous. Next, try selecting just one card—a complete predicate or a complete subject. Write it on your paper along with an original subject or predicate to complete the sentence. Another activity to try is blindly selecting a sentence part from one envelope or the other and trying to identify whether it is a complete subject or a complete predicate. Then, use it in an original complete sentence.

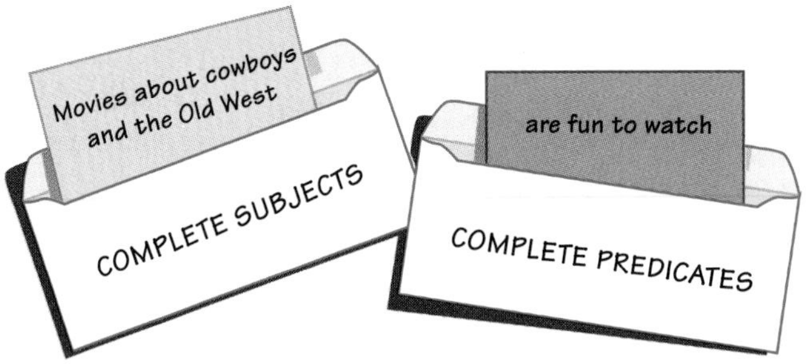

Find It in Your Reading Choose several sentences from your social studies or language arts textbooks to add to your grab bag. You may have to reorder some words to get all the words of the complete predicate on one card.

Find It in Your Writing Review your writing portfolio for appropriate sentences to add to your grab bag. Choose several sentences and write their complete subjects and complete predicates on index cards. If necessary, reorder the words to get all the words of the complete predicate on one card. Add the sentences to their appropriate envelopes.

TIME SAVERS!

Hands-on Grammar Book
Use the Hands-on Grammar activity sheet for Chapter 19 to facilitate this activity.

Section 19.2 Section Review

GRAMMAR EXERCISES 9–13

Exercise 9 **Recognizing Complete Subjects and Predicates** Make two columns labeled *Complete Subject* and *Complete Predicate*. Write each complete subject in the first column and each complete predicate in the second column.

1. Jesse James was living with his family in Saint Joseph, Missouri, in 1882.
2. The outlaw was using the name Thomas Howard at that time.
3. Governor Thomas Crittenden issued a reward of $10,000 for the capture of Jesse and his brother Frank.
4. They were wanted dead or alive.
5. A member of James's own gang wanted the reward money.
6. He shot Jesse James from behind.
7. Jesse was mortally wounded and died later that day, on April 3, 1882.
8. After his brother's death, the American public treated Frank like a hero.
9. Juries acquitted him twice.
10. The James brothers have gained worldwide notoriety for both real and legendary actions.
11. Billy the Kid was another well-known outlaw of the West.
12. He was born in New York City in 1859.
13. His given name was William H. Bonney.
14. He moved to Silver City, New Mexico, in 1873 after his father's death.
15. He soon became known for robbery and murder.

Exercise 10 **Writing Sentences By Combining Complete Subjects and Predicates** Write a complete sentence for each item below by following the directions in parentheses.

1. In the old western movie, a rancher (Add a complete predicate.)
2. herded the cattle to a town on the line. (Add a complete subject.)
3. stampeded during a lightning storm and many were lost. (Add a complete subject.)
4. Once in town, the cowboys (Add a complete predicate.)
5. The town's sheriff (Add a complete predicate.)
6. led to holding pens near the railroad station. (Add a complete subject.)
7. Next, the cattle herd (Add a complete predicate.)
8. After the train left, the cowboys (Add a complete predicate.)
9. were relieved that the cowboys had finally left. (Add a complete subject.)
10. Back at the ranch, the rancher and his wife (Add a complete predicate.)

Exercise 11 **Find It in Your Reading** Reread the excerpt from "The Closing of the Rodeo" on page 403. In the excerpt, the complete subjects are red and the complete predicates are blue. Identify each simple subject and simple verb.

Exercise 12 **Find It in Your Writing** Choose a paragraph from your writing. Identify the complete subject and complete predicate in each sentence. Revise any sentences that do not have a complete subject or a complete predicate.

Exercise 13 **Writing Application** Write a short essay telling why you would or would not have wanted to live during the days of the frontier West. Choose five sentences, and underline the complete subject once and the complete predicate twice.

ASSESS and CLOSE

Section Review

Each of these exercises correlates to a concept in the section on complete subjects and predicates, pages 402–404. These exercises may be used for more practice, for reteaching, or for review of the Key Concepts presented. Answers for all chapter exercises are available in *Grammar Exercises Answers on Transparencies* in your teaching resources.

Answer Key

Exercise 9

Complete Subjects	Complete Predicates
1. Jesse James	was living with his family in Saint Joseph, Missouri, in 1882
2. The outlaw	was using the name Thomas Howard at that time
3. Governor Thomas Crittenden	issued a reward of $10,000 for the capture of Jesse and his brother Frank
4. They	were wanted dead or alive
5. A member of James's own gang	wanted the reward money
6. He	shot Jesse James from behind
7. Jesse	was mortally wounded and died later that day, on April 3, 1882.
8. the American public	treated Frank like a hero [After his brother's death]
9. Juries	acquitted him twice
10. The James brothers	have gained worldwide notoriety for both real and legendary actions
11. Billy the Kid	was another well-known outlaw of the West.
12. He	was born in New York City in 1859.
13. His given name	was William H. Bonney.
14. He	moved to Silver City, New Mexico in 1873 after his father's death.
15. He	soon became known for robbery and murder.

continued

Answer Key continued

Exercise 10

Sentences will vary.

Exercise 11

Find It in Your Reading
subject: plumes; predicate; sway
subject: curtain; predicate; falls
subject: train; predicate; pulls

Exercise 12

Find It in Your Writing
Have students underline the nouns and verbs in each sentence.

Exercise 13

Writing Application
Pairs of students, one pro and one con, can read their essays aloud to the class.

PREPARE and ENGAGE

Interest GRABBER Have partners make a list of subjects and verbs. Then ask them to combine their lists into sentences, one with two subjects, one with two verbs, and a third with two subjects and two verbs.

Activate Prior Knowledge

Ask students to write a sentence about themselves and a friend. Then have them write another in which they and the friend do two different activities.

TEACH

Step-by-Step Teaching Guide

Recognizing Compound Subjects

1. Remind students it can be misleading simply to look for the conjunction to identify compound subjects. Conjunctions can join objects of introductory prepositional phrases, as in *In Denver and Dallas, football is the most popular sport.* Here the subject is *football.*
2. The best way to identify the subject in a sentence is to ask the question *Who?* or *What?* of the verb. In *Louisa and Steve jumped for joy,* identify the verb *(jumped)* and ask *Who jumped?*

Answer Key

Exercise 14

1. Music, rhythm
2. styles, types
3. feelings, ideas
4. region, era
5. culture, society
6. cultures, people
7. classical, popular
8. Jazz, rap, rhythm and blues, rock
9. Opera, ballet, motion pictures
10. Singing, banging

Section 19.3 Compound Subjects and Compound Verbs

Many sentences have a single subject and a single verb. Some sentences, however, have more than one subject. Others have more than one verb.

Recognizing Compound Subjects

A sentence with more than one subject is said to have a *compound subject.*

KEY CONCEPT A **compound subject** is two or more subjects that have the same verb and are joined by a conjunction such as *and* or *or.* ■

The parts of the compound subjects in the following examples are underlined once. Each verb is underlined twice.

EXAMPLES: Ted and Louise are both musicians.
My sister or she will represent our music club.
Pianos, flutes, and saxophones are sold at that store.

Exercise 14 **Recognizing Compound Subjects** Identify the subjects that make up each compound subject in the following sentences.

EXAMPLE: Sound and time are two important components of music.
ANSWER: Sound, time

1. Music or rhythm plays a role in all societies throughout the world.
2. Many styles or types of music exist in different societies.
3. Feelings and ideas are both expressed in music.
4. Geographical region and historical era will influence the type of music in a society.
5. Each culture or society has its own unique style of music.
6. Western cultures and people define music as an art form.
7. Classical and popular are two of the principal forms of music in western culture.
8. Jazz, rap, rhythm and blues, and rock are some of the forms of popular music.
9. Opera, ballet, and motion pictures use many music styles.
10. Singing and banging tools or rocks together may have created the earliest music forms.

Theme: Musical Instruments

In this section, you will learn how to recognize and form compound subjects and compound verbs. The examples and exercises are about musical instruments.

Cross-Curricular Connection: Music

More Practice

Grammar Exercise Workbook
- pp. 53–54

On-line Exercise Bank
- Section 19.3

Go on-line: PHSchool.com
Enter Web Code: eck-8002

iText

Get instant feedback! Exercise 14 is available on-line or on CD-ROM.

TIME AND RESOURCE MANAGER

Resources
Print: Grammar Exercise Workbook, pp. 53–54
Technology: Writing and Grammar iText, Section 19.3; On-Line Exercise Bank, Exercise 19.3

In-Depth Coverage	Accelerated Pace
• Work through all key concepts, pp. 406–408. • Assign and review Exercises 14–16.	• Assign pp. 406–408 for independent student review. • Assign Section Review Exercises 17–18.

Recognizing Compound Verbs

A sentence with two or more verbs is said to have a *compound verb.*

KEY CONCEPT A **compound verb** is two or more verbs that have the same subject and are joined by a conjunction such as *and* or *or.* ■

EXAMPLES: He reads music and plays the piano.
The composition will succeed or fail within a year.
She composes, plays, and often directs her own pieces.

Sometimes, a sentence will have both a compound subject and a compound verb.

EXAMPLE: Jane and Sharon both sing and dance.

Exercise 15 **Recognizing Compound Verbs** Identify the verbs that make up each compound verb in the following sentences.

EXAMPLE: Musical instruments provide and expand musical sound.
ANSWER: provide, expand

1. Instruments are played and enjoyed around the world.
2. Different instruments are played in various ways and make distinctive sounds.
3. Stringed instruments may be plucked or strummed.
4. Musicians blow into or strike other instruments.
5. While listening to instruments, people often clap, stamp, whistle, hum, and sing, simply for fun.

iText

Get instant feedback! Exercise 15 is available on-line or on CD-ROM.

More Practice

Grammar Exercise Workbook
- pp. 53–54

On-line Exercise Bank
- Section 19.3

Go on-line: PHSchool.com
Enter Web Code: eck-8002

◀ **Critical Viewing** Use compound subjects and compound verbs in sentences describing your favorite muscial instrument. **[Compare]**

Step-by-Step Teaching Guide

Recognizing Compound Verbs

Write the following sentences on the chalkboard and ask students to identify the compound verbs:

Shelly directed and produced the play. (directed, produced)

The audience applauded and cheered. (applauded, cheered)

Shelly bowed and waved to the audience. (bowed, waved)

Answer Key

Exercise 15

1. are played, enjoyed
2. are played, make
3. may be plucked, strummed
4. blow, strike
5. clap, stamp, whistle, hum, sing

Critical Viewing

Compare Possible response: Guitar and piano are my favorite instruments. I compose and play piano music.

TIME SAVERS!

Answers on Transparency Use the Grammar Exercises Answers on Transparencies for Chapter 19 to have students correct their own or one another's exercises.

On-Line Exercise Bank Have students complete the exercises on computer. The Auto Check feature will grade their work for you!

Step-by-Step Teaching Guide

Grammar in Literature

1. Have a volunteer read aloud the passage from "The White Umbrella."
2. Review the use of the compound subject *(Mona and I)* and compound verb *(was* and *had).*
3. Be sure students realize that neither Miss Crosman nor her couch is the subject, even though these nouns appear first.

More About the Author

Gish Jen (born 1956) grew up in Scarsdale, New York. The daughter of Chinese immigrant parents, Jen has mined her multicultural experience. She says that by growing up in Scarsdale, with its significant Jewish population, she has been influenced both by the experience of Jewish culture and Jewish American writers.

Answer Key

Exercise 16

Sentences will vary. Samples are given.

1. Sarah is going to the next music recital and performing in it.
2. She is singing with the choir and dancing in a solo performance.
3. Rhonda will play and then Emily will perform.
4. We will arrive early and be sure to find good seats.
5. The students and their teacher prefer singing to dance.
6. Rap and rock are the music of choice for many students.
7. Sarah and Emily have large collections of compact discs.
8. Serena enjoys buying new compact discs and selling her old ones.
9. Jazz and blues are unfamiliar styles of music for the girls.
10. They don't realize that jazz and blues inspired and have been played by modern musicians.

19.3

GRAMMAR IN LITERATURE

from The White Umbrella

Gish Jen

The compound verb in the following excerpt is highlighted in blue italics.

Huddling at the end of Miss Crosman's nine-foot leatherette couch, Mona and I watched Eugenie play. She *was* a grade ahead of me and, according to school rumor, *had* a boyfriend in high school.

Exercise 16 **Combining Sentences With Compound Subjects and Compound Verbs** Combine each pair of sentences below by using compound subjects or compound verbs.

EXAMPLE: Violins are stringed instruments.
Cellos are stringed instruments.

ANSWER: Violins and cellos are stringed instruments.

1. Sarah is going to the next music recital.
Sarah is performing in the next music recital.
2. She is singing with the choir.
She is also dancing in a solo performance.
3. First Rhonda will play.
After Rhonda, Emily will perform.
4. We will arrive early at the recital.
We will be sure to find good seats.
5. The students prefer singing to dance.
Their teacher prefers singing, too.
6. Rap music is the music of choice for many students.
Rock music is also preferred by the students.
7. Sarah has a large collection of compact discs.
Emily has many compact discs in her collection.
8. Serena enjoys buying new music on compact discs.
She enjoys selling her oldest compact discs.
9. Jazz is a type of music with which the girls aren't familiar.
Blues is another style of music that they have never heard.
10. They don't realize that jazz and blues have inspired modern musicians.
They don't realize that jazz and blues have been played by modern musicians.

More Practice

Grammar Exercise Workbook
- pp. 53–54

On-line Exercise Bank
- Section 19.3

Go on-line:
PHSchool.com
Enter Web Code:
eck-8002

ONGOING ASSESSMENT: Monitor and Reinforce

If students miss more than two items in Exercises 14–16, refer them to the following for additional practice.

In the Textbook	Print Resources	Technology
Section Review, Ex. 17–18, p. 409	Grammar Exercise Workbook, pp. 53–54	On-line Exercise Bank, Section 19.3

Section 19.3

Section Review

GRAMMAR EXERCISES 17–21

Exercise 17 **Recognizing Compound Subjects and Compound Verbs** Identify the compound subject or compound verb in each sentence. If there are none, write *none*.

1. Beethoven, Bach, Mozart, and Haydn were all famous composers.
2. They coordinated and synthesized music in a very special way.
3. Many musicians admire Bach's music.
4. In the 1800's, there was an interest in and revival of Bach's music.
5. Felix Mendelssohn arranged and performed one of Bach's compositions.
6. Other composers and musicians may have been greater.
7. His expressiveness and touch inspire listeners everywhere.
8. String quartets, chamber music, songs, an opera, and nine symphonies were among Beethoven's compositions.
9. Mozart and Haydn influenced the musical compositions of Beethoven.
10. His forceful style and dreamy melodies have made Beethoven's music timeless.

Exercise 18 **Revising to Combine Sentences With Compound Subjects and Verbs** Combine each pair of sentences below by using compound subjects, compound verbs, or both.

1. The history of Western music has been influenced by Johann Sebastian Bach. The development of Western music has been influenced by Johann Sebastian Bach.
2. Musicians consider him one of the most talented composers of all time. Other admirers also consider him one of the most talented composers ever.
3. Bach was a self-taught musician. Bach followed in the musical traditions of his family.
4. In seven generations of his family, fifty-three members studied music. They also became prominent musicians.
5. Bach composed during the 1700's. During the 1700's, Bach conducted.
6. He combined different rhythmic patterns in one composition. He expanded rhymic patterns in the same composition.
7. Bach composed 295 cantatas. Bach also produced the cantatas.
8. Casual listeners still play many of these pieces today. Many music critics greatly enjoy them, too.
9. Bach's music was forgotten and neglected for 80 years after his death. His musical theories were also forgotten and neglected.
10. Bach's style was unique. His method was one-of-a-kind.

Exercise 19 **Find It in Your Reading** In the excerpt from "The White Umbrella" on page 408, identify the compound subject.

Exercise 20 **Find It in Your Writing** Look through your writing portfolio. In your writing, find at least one example of a compound subject and one example of a compound verb. If you cannot find any, add at least one.

Exercise 21 **Writing Application** Write a description of a musical instrument that you play or enjoy hearing. Include at least one sentence with a compound subject and one sentence with a compound verb.

ASSESS and CLOSE

Section Review

Each of these exercises correlates to a concept in the section on compound subjects and compound verbs, pages 406–408 These exercises may be used for more practice, for reteaching, or for review of the Key Concepts presented. Answers for all chapter exercises are available in *Grammar Exercises Answers on Transparencies* in your teaching resources.

Answer Key

Exercise 17

1. Beethoven, Bach, Mozart, Haydn
2. coordinated, synthesized
3. none
4. interest, revival
5. arranged, performed
6. composers, musicians
7. expressiveness, touch
8. quartets, chamber music, songs, opera, symphonies
9. Mozart, Haydn
10. style, melodies

Exercise 18

Sentences will vary. Samples are given.

1. The history and development of Western music have been influenced by Johann Sebastian Bach.
2. Musicians and admirers consider him one of the most talented composers ever.
3. Bach was a self-taught musician and followed in the musical traditions of his family.
4. In seven generations of his family, fifty-three members studied music and became prominent musicians.
5. Bach composed and conducted during the 1700's.
6. He combined and expanded rhythmic patterns in the same composition.
7. Bach composed and produced 295 cantatas.
8. Casual listeners and music critics still listen to and greatly enjoy many of these pieces.
9. Bach's music and musical theories were forgotten and neglected for 80 years after his death.
10. Bach's style and method were unique.

continued

Answer Key continued

Exercise 19

Find It in Your Reading
Mona and I

Exercise 20

Find It in Your Writing
If the compound subject uses *and,* have students rewrite the sentence to use *or.* If it uses *or,* rewrite to use *and.*

Exercise 21

Writing Application
Challenge students also to include a sentence that has a compound subject and compound verb.

PREPARE and ENGAGE

Interest GRABBER Write the following sentence on the chalkboard and ask students to identify the subject.

There may be a prize of a free computer for you if you can identify the subject in this sentence.

If students identify *prize* as the subject, tell them about the conditional tense.

Activate Prior Knowledge

Ask students to write a sentence beginning with *There* or *Here* and then identify the subject of the sentence.

TEACH

Step-by-Step Teaching Guide

Hard-to-Find Subjects

1. Review normal word order in declarative sentences and discuss the importance of being able to identify the subject even when it does not appear before the verb.
2. In sentences that give orders or directions, the implied or understood subject is *you.*
3. Write the following sentences on the chalkboard for additional practice. Review with students to be sure that they understand the understood *you.*

   Wait here! (You wait here!)

   Play it again, slowly this time. (You play it again, slowly this time.)

   Go to the end of the hall and turn right. (You go to the end of the hall and turn right.)

Integrating Grammar Skills

Any form of directions is usually written in the imperative without a stated subject. If possible, give students a set of directions for assembling something and have them read through it to see the absence of a stated subject.

Section 19.4

Hard-to-Find Subjects

Theme: Musical Instruments

In this section, you will learn how to recognize sentences that do not follow normal word order. The examples and exercises are about musical instruments.

Cross-Curricular Connection: Music

In the first three sections of this chapter, each subject that you were asked to find appeared somewhere early in the sentence—with the verb following immediately or soon after. This pattern—a subject followed by a verb—is the pattern most often used in English.

SUBJECT-VERB WORD ORDER:

The song (S) raced (V) up the charts.

Yesterday morning after breakfast, Uncle George (S) left (V) on a concert tour.

Delayed by bad weather and traffic, he (S) finally arrived (V).

In several kinds of sentences, however, the subject and verb do not follow normal word order. In some sentences, the subject may seem to be missing entirely. In others, the subject may follow the verb or come between the parts of a verb phrase. This section will give you practice in recognizing sentences that do not follow normal word order. It will also help you find the subjects in these sentences.

Finding the Subject in Orders and Directions

Some sentences give orders or directions. In most of these sentences, the subject does not appear before the verb.

KEY CONCEPT In sentences that give orders or directions, the subject is understood to be *you.* ■

On the left side of the following chart are three examples of sentences that give orders or directions. The verbs are underlined twice. On the right side, the same sentences appear with the understood subjects shown in parentheses.

Order or Direction	With Understood *You* Added
Drive carefully!	(You) Drive carefully!
After waiting a moment, sing the song again.	After waiting a moment, (you) sing the song again
Lucy, leave the room.	Lucy, (you) leave the room.

TIME AND RESOURCE MANAGER

Resources
Print: Grammar Exercise Workbook, pp. 55–58
Technology: Writing and Grammar iText, Section 19.4; On-Line Exercise Bank, Exercise 19.4

In-Depth Coverage	Accelerated Pace
• Work through all key concepts, pp. 410–414. • Assign and review Exercises 22–25.	• Assign pp. 410–414 for independent student review. • Assign Section Review Exercises 26–31.

Exercise 22 **Recognizing Subjects That Give Orders or Directions** Write the subject of each of the following sentences. (Three of the sentences give orders or directions. The other two are ordinary sentences in normal word order.)

EXAMPLE: David, listen!
ANSWER: (you)

1. Popular music is produced for a broad audience.
2. Learn about jazz, country-and-western music, soul music, and rock music.
3. After listening to various artists, choose your favorite music.
4. A person's musical tastes may change over time.
5. David, try listening to some operatic music.

Finding the Subject in Questions

A sentence that is not in normal word order is usually in *inverted word order*. The subject in such a sentence comes after its verb. This order is seen most often in questions.

KEY CONCEPT In questions, the subject often follows the verb. ■

Many questions begin with a verb or a helping verb. Others begin with such questioning words as *what, which, whose, who, when, why, where,* and *how*. In the following examples, notice that the subject sometimes comes between the parts of a verb phrase.

VERB FIRST:	Are the songs very long?
HELPING VERB FIRST:	Have you opened your compact disc?
QUESTIONING WORD FIRST:	Where are the compact discs? When will they begin the concert?

If you have trouble finding the subject in a question, you can use a trick: Simply reword the question as a statement. The subject will then appear before the verb.

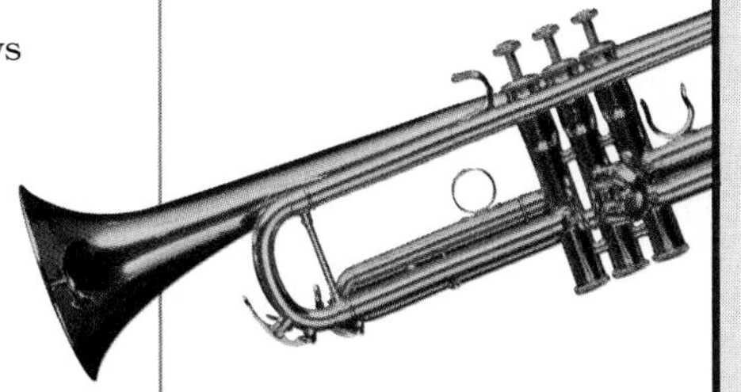

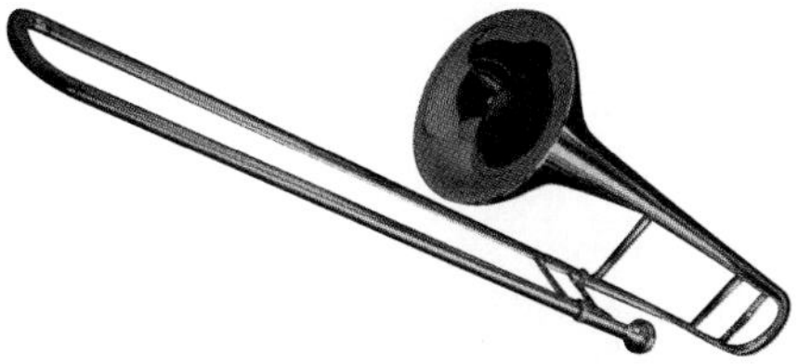

More Practice

Grammar Exercise Workbook
• pp. 55–56
On-line Exercise Bank
• Section 19.4
Go on-line:
PHSchool.com
Enter Web Code:
eck-8002

▲▼ **Critical Viewing** Write three questions, one for each of the instruments pictured on this page. **[Analyze]**

Answer Key

Exercise 22

1. Popular music
2. you
3. you
4. tastes
5. you

Critical Viewing

Analyze Possible responses: Do you play the sax? Is the trombone a brass instrument? Where is the trumpet?

TEACH

Step-by-Step Teaching Guide

Subjects in Questions

1. In the inverted word order of questions, the subject usually follows the verb. Point out that a helping verb usually is the first word in the sentence.
2. Review other interrogative pronouns that also begin sentences. Write the following words on the chalkboard and ask students to use each in a question: *how, when, why, what, which, who, whom, whose.*
3. Point out that some questions are not in inverted word order.

Customize for *ESL Students*

Work with students in identifying the subject in the inverted word order of questions. Some languages, like Spanish, do not have helping verbs. See that they all understand the use of helping verbs and interrogative pronouns to begin sentences.

ONGOING ASSESSMENT: Monitor and Reinforce

If students miss more than one item in Exercise 23, refer them to the following for additional practice.

In the Textbook	Print Resources	Technology
Section Review, Ex. 27, p. 415	Grammar Exercise Workbook, pp. 55–56	On-Line Exercise Bank, Section 19.4

TIME SAVERS!

Answers on Transparency Use the Grammar Exercises Answers on Transparencies for Chapter 19 to have students correct their own or one another's exercises.

On-Line Exercise Bank Have students complete the exercises on computer. The Auto Check feature will grade their work for you!

Critical Viewing

Analyze Possible responses: When do you practice? What instrument will I play?

Answer Key

Exercise 23

1. melody
2. you
3. stars
4. tickets
5. groups

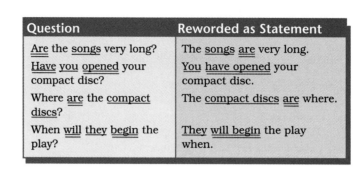

Question	Reworded as Statement
Are the songs very long?	The songs are very long.
Have you opened your compact disc?	You have opened your compact disc.
Where are the compact discs?	The compact discs are where.
When will they begin the play?	They will begin the play when.

Many questions use inverted word order, but some do not.

EXAMPLES: Which songs were selected by the band?
Who has taken my compact disc player?

Exercise 23 **Finding the Subject in Questions** Write the subject of each sentence below.

EXAMPLE: Which type of popular music do you like best?
ANSWER: you

1. Is melody important in popular music?
2. Have you listened to any jazz music?
3. Where are those country music stars performing?
4. When will the tickets for their concert go on sale?
5. Which groups are most popular today?

iText

Get instant feedback! Exercise 23 is available on-line or on CD-ROM.

More Practice

Grammar Exercise Workbook
- pp. 55–56

On-line Exercise Bank
- Section 19.4

Go on-line: PHSchool.com
Enter Web Code: eck-8002

◀ **Critical Viewing** Imagine that you want to join this music group. Write several questions you would ask before joining. **[Analyze]**

TIME SAVERS!

Answers on Transparency Use the Grammar Exercises Answers on Transparencies for Chapter 19 to have students correct their own or one another's exercises.

On-Line Exercise Bank Have students complete the exercises on computer. The Auto Check feature will grade their work for you!

STANDARDIZED TEST PREPARATION WORKSHOP

Grammar and Usage Many standardized tests require students to identify the subject in sentences in inverted word order. Ask students to find the subject in the following sentence.

There are the people who set up the meeting.

A there **C** who
B people **D** meeting

If students reorder the sentence as *The people who set up the meeting are there,* they will see that **B** (people) is the subject of the sentence.

Finding the Subject in Sentences Beginning With *There* or *Here*

Sentences beginning with *there* or *here* are usually in inverted word order.

KEY CONCEPT *There* or *here* is never the subject of a sentence. ■

There can be used in two ways at the beginning of sentences. First, it can be used to start the sentence.

SENTENCE STARTER: There are (V) two musicians (S) from Tennessee in the office.

There can also be used as an adverb at the beginning of sentences, as can the word *here*. As adverbs, these two words point out *where* and modify the verbs.

ADVERBS: There goes (V) the rock star (S).

Here are (V) the invitations (S) to the party.

Be alert to sentences beginning with *there* and *here*. They are probably in inverted word order. If you cannot find the subject, reword the sentence in normal word order. If *there* is just a sentence starter, it can be dropped from the sentence.

Sentence Beginning With *There* or *Here*	Reworded With Subject Before Verb
There is a mistake on your paper.	A mistake is on your paper.
Here comes the star of the show.	The star of the show comes here.

Exercise 24 **Finding the Subject in Sentences Beginning With *There* or *Here*** Write the subject of each sentence below.

1. There were many pioneers of rock-and-roll music, including Elvis Presley, Chuck Berry, and Bill Haley.
2. Here are some memorable songs from the rock-and-roll period.
3. There were many singing groups in the early 1960's.
4. There, in the cabinet, are some old records by the Beatles.
5. There was an expansion of the music in the late 1960's.

Grammar and Style Tip

Try to use sentences with inverted word order, including some beginning with *here* or *there*, in your own writing. Such sentences add variety to your writing, making it more pleasing to read.

iText

Get instant feedback! Exercise 24 is available on-line or on CD-ROM.

More Practice

Grammar Exercise Workbook
- pp. 57–58

On-line Exercise Bank
- Section 19.4

Go on-line: PHSchool.com
Enter Web Code: eck-8002

Step-by-Step Teaching Guide

Finding Subjects in Sentences Beginning With *There* or *Here*

1. The key concept is very direct: *There* or *here* is never the subject of a sentence. Point out that these sentences are in inverted word order.
2. Write the following sentences on the chalkboard and ask students to identify the subject:

   There is a test tomorrow. (test)

   Here are the tickets we ordered. (tickets)

   There is a full moon tonight. (moon)
3. Show students how *there* and *here* can function as adverbs modifying the verb. Write the following examples on the chalkboard:

   Here is the TV remote.

   There goes another day.
4. Review the process of putting sentences beginning with *There* or *Here* into normal word order for easier identification of the subject.

Answer Key

Exercise 24

1. pioneers
2. songs
3. groups
4. records
5. expansion

ONGOING ASSESSMENT: Monitor and Reinforce

If students miss more than one item in Exercise 24, refer them to the following for additional practice.

In the Textbook	Print Resources	Technology
Section Review, Ex. 28, p. 415	Grammar Exercise Workbook, pp. 57–58	On-Line Exercise Bank, Section 19.4

Step-by-Step Teaching Guide

Finding Subjects in Sentences Inverted for Emphasis

1. Inverted word order can be used for emphasis. The subject, withheld at first, is emphasized by the introductory clause(s).
2. Write the following sentences on the chalkboard and ask students to rewrite them in normal word order and identify the subject.

   In the back of the closet huddled the shivering puppy. (puppy. The shivering puppy huddled in the back of the closet.)

   Across the meadow ran the mare with her foal at her side. (mare. The mare, with her foal at her side, ran across the meadow.)

Customize for *Less Advanced Students*

Review the trick of rewriting inverted word order sentences into normal word order. One technique is first to find the verb, which should be the most obvious part of the sentence. Tell students that in inverted word order, the subject will come after the verb. Have them identify the subject, then write it first followed by the predicate to create normal word order.

Answer Key

Exercise 25

1. development
2. elements
3. singers
4. Nashville
5. albums

TIME SAVERS!

Answers on Transparency Use the Grammar Exercises Answers on Transparencies for Chapter 19 to have students correct their own or one another's exercises.

On-Line Exercise Bank Have students complete the exercises on computer. The Auto Check feature will grade their work for you!

19.4

Finding the Subject in Sentences Inverted for Emphasis

Sometimes a subject is intentionally put after its verb to draw attention to the subject.

KEY CONCEPT In some sentences, the subject follows the verb in order to receive greater emphasis. ■

In the following example, notice how the order of the words builds suspense by leading up to the subject.

EXAMPLE: In the midst of the crowd outside the theater stood (V) Buddy Holly (S).

Sentences such as this one can be reworded in normal word order to make it easier to find the subject.

Inverted Word Order	Reworded With Subject Before Verb
In the midst of the crowd outside the theater stood Buddy Holly.	Buddy Holly stood in the midst of the crowd outside the theater.

Exercise 25 **Finding the Subject in Inverted Sentences** Write the subject of each sentence below.

EXAMPLE: With the increased popularity of the guitar came the growth of country-and-western music.

ANSWER: growth

1. Important in this history of music is the development of rock-and-roll.
2. Combined with rock-and-roll were the elements of country-and-western music.
3. Out of this combination came country singers such as Johnny Cash, Waylon Jennings, and Dolly Parton.
4. Now known as the home of country music is Nashville, Tennessee.
5. High on the weekly sales charts sit country-and-western albums.

More Practice

Grammar Exercise Workbook
• pp. 57–58

On-line Exercise Bank
• Section 19.4

Go on-line: PHSchool.com *Enter Web Code:* eck-8002

iText

Get instant feedback! Exercise 25 is available on-line or on CD-ROM.

Section 19.4 Section Review

GRAMMAR EXERCISES 26–31

Exercise 26 Recognizing Subjects That Give Orders and Directions Write the subject of each of the following sentences. (Some sentences give orders or directions; others are in normal word order.)

1. Zachary, come here!
2. Listen to this music from the 1970's.
3. Disco, punk rock, reggae, and funk were introduced during this time.
4. These styles were less individualized than previous styles.
5. After comparing these styles, watch this music video.

Exercise 27 Finding the Subject in Questions Write the subject in each sentence below.

1. Which compact disc did you buy?
2. Are the compact discs very expensive?
3. Have you bought the latest single yet?
4. Where can we find the compact discs?
5. Which artist sold the most records?
6. When was *Thriller*, by Michael Jackson, released?
7. Are you sure of that date?
8. Who recorded the most albums during the 1980's?
9. Have you heard of Bruce Springsteen or the artist formerly known as Prince?
10. Did you watch the Grammy Awards?

Exercise 28 Revising Sentences by Reversing the Order of Subjects and Verbs Some of the sentences that follow are in normal word order; others are not. Rewrite each sentence, reversing the subject-verb order. When you have finished, underline the subject of each sentence.

1. There have been many changes in popular music over time.
2. Los Angeles, Nashville, and New York City are among the cities associated with popular music.
3. The musicians work and write their songs here.
4. In Los Angeles and New York are many sophisticated recording studios.
5. Many would-be country music stars live in the city of Nashville.
6. Among the hot spots for country music is the Grand Ole Opry.
7. Here can be seen the biggest names in country music.
8. Country legend Dolly Parton stood in the midst of the crowd outside the theater.
9. High above the audience on the stage were the enormous speakers.
10. In concert halls all over the world sit fans of popular music.

Exercise 29 Find It in Your Reading Look through newspaper articles for sentences with hard-to-find subjects. Write down examples of the following: a sentence giving an order, a sentence asking a question, a sentence beginning with *there* or *here*, and a sentence whose subject-verb order is changed for emphasis.

Exercise 30 Find It in Your Writing Look through your writing portfolio. Find two questions and two sentences beginning with *here* or *there*. Identify the subject in each sentence.

Exercise 31 Writing Application Write a description of a concert you have attended or a music video you have seen. Include one sentence beginning with *here* or *there*, one that asks a question, and one sentence inverted for emphasis.

ASSESS and CLOSE

Section Review

Each of these exercises correlates to a concept in the section on hard-to-find subjects, pages 410–414. These exercises may be used for more practice, for reteaching, or for review of the Key Concepts presented. Answers for all chapter exercises are available in *Grammar Exercises Answers on Transparencies* in your teaching resources.

Answer Key

Exercise 26

1. you
2. you
3. Disco, punk rock, reggae, and funk
4. styles
5. you

Exercise 27

1. you
2. discs
3. you
4. we
5. artist
6. *Thriller*
7. you
8. Who
9. you
10. you

Exercise 28

1. Many <u>changes</u> in popular music have taken place over time.
2. Among the cities associated with popular music are <u>Los Angeles</u>, <u>Nashville</u>, and <u>New York City</u>.
3. Here <u>musicians</u> work and write their songs.
4. Many sophisticated recording <u>studios</u> are in Los Angeles and New York.
5. In the city of Nashville live many would-be country music <u>stars</u>.
6. The <u>Grand Ole Opry</u> is among the hot spots for country music.
7. The biggest <u>names</u> in country music can be seen here.
8. In the midst of the crowd outside the theater stood country legend <u>Dolly Parton</u>.
9. The enormous <u>speakers</u> were high above the audience on the stage.
10. <u>Fans</u> of popular music sit in concert halls all over the world.

continued

Answer Key continued

Exercise 29

Find It in Your Reading
Responses will vary.

Exercise 30

Find It in Your Writing
Students may want to work with partners or in small groups to find these hard-to-find subjects.

Exercise 31

Writing Application
Students can trade sentences with partners to underline the subjects.

PREPARE and ENGAGE

Interest GRABBER Give students this scenario: You go to the store and buy all sorts of ingredients. You come home and prepare, mix, cook, bake. You set the table with a tablecloth, nice china and silverware, glasses, maybe some candles. Then ask students what is still needed to complete the picture. Elicit that people are needed to enjoy the meal. Discuss how, while a subject and verb are the basic requirements for a sentence, most of the time, additional *complements* are needed for a complete thought.

Activate Prior Knowledge

Write the following sentence on the chalkboard: *I baked cookies.* Ask students to identify the function of each word in the sentence. (who did what)

TEACH

Step-by-Step Teaching Guide

Complements

1. With the exception of two-word sentences such as *Dogs bark,* every sentence contains complements.
2. Write the following additional sentences on the chalkboard to familiarize students with the idea of complements. Ask them to identify the complement in each sentence.

   Terry made pizza. (pizza)

   She served me a slice. (me, slice)

   The pizza was good. (good)

   Terry is a great chef. (great, chef)

Critical Viewing

Interpret Possible responses: The mechanic worked quickly. The engine needed many repairs. He said the repairs would be expensive.

Section 19.5

Complements

Often, a subject and verb alone can express a complete thought. For example, "Birds fly" can stand by itself as a sentence, even though it contains only a subject and a verb. In other sentences, however, the thought begun by a subject and its verb must be completed with other words. For example, the sentences "Toni bought," "The eyewitness told," "Our mechanic is," and "Richard feels" all contain a subject and verb, but none expresses a complete thought. All these ideas need *complements.*

KEY CONCEPT A **complement** is a word or group of words that completes the meaning of a subject and verb. ■

Complements are usually nouns, pronouns, or adjectives. They are located right after or very close to the verb. In the chart that follows, the subjects are underlined once and the verbs twice, and the complements are boxed.

DIFFERENT KINDS OF COMPLEMENTS

Toni bought [cars].

The eyewitness told [us] the [story].

Our mechanic is a [poet].

Richard feels [sad].

This section will describe three types of complements: *direct objects, indirect objects,* and *subject complements.*

Theme: Automobiles

In this section, you will learn about complements, such as direct objects, indirect objects, and subject complements. The examples and exercises are about the history of the automobile.

Cross-Curricular Connection: Social Studies

◄ Critical Viewing
Add complements to the following subject-verb pairs to complete the thoughts about this photograph:
1. mechanic worked
2. engine needed
3. he said
[Interpret]

TIME AND RESOURCE MANAGER

Resources
Print: Grammar Exercise Workbook, pp. 59–72
Technology: Writing and Grammar iText, Section 19.5; On-Line Exercise Bank, Exercise 19.5

In-Depth Coverage	Accelerated Pace
• Work through all key concepts, pp. 416–426. • Assign and review Exercises 32–39. • Read and discuss Grammar in Literature, p. 417.	• Assign pp. 416–426 for independent student review. • Assign Section Review Exercises 40–45.

Recognizing Direct Objects

Direct objects are complements that are used after action verbs.

KEY CONCEPT A **direct object** is a noun or pronoun that receives the action of a transitive verb. ■

A direct object can be found by asking *Whom?* or *What?* after an action verb.

EXAMPLE: The message reached the [lawyer] (DO).
Reached *whom? Answer:* lawyer

Direct objects, like subjects and verbs, can be compound.

EXAMPLE: Mother invited [Uncle Bill] (DO) and [Aunt Clara] (DO).
Invited *whom? Answer:* Uncle Bill, Aunt Clara

GRAMMAR IN LITERATURE

from An American Childhood

Annie Dillard

The direct objects in the following excerpt are highlighted in blue italics.

It was a swift spirit; it was an awareness. It made *noise.* It had two joined *parts,* a head and a tail, like a Chinese dragon. It found the *door, wall,* and *headboard;* and it swiped *them,* charging them with its luminous glance.

iText

Get instant feedback! Exercise 32 is available on-line or on CD-ROM.

Exercise 32 **Recognizing Direct Objects** Copy each sentence below, and underline each direct object. (Some of the sentences have compound direct objects.)

1. In the fourteenth century, Martini, an Italian painter, designed a human-propelled carriage on four wheels.
2. However, the Greeks used wheels and carts as far back as the eighth century B.C.
3. Henry Ford introduced his first automobile as the "Quadricycle."
4. The name *automobile* gained acceptance in 1897.
5. Some of the first powered cars employed windmills and clockwork motors.

More Practice

Grammar Exercise Workbook
- pp. 59–60

On-line Exercise Bank
- Section 19.5

Go on-line:
PHSchool.com
Enter Web Code:
eck-8002

Step-by-Step Teaching Guide

Recognizing Direct Objects

1. Write the following sentences on the chalkboard. Ask students to identify the direct object and tell whether it answers *Whom?* or *What?*

I remember him well. (him, Whom?)

The bus driver closed the door. (door, What?)

We made a videotape. (videotape, What?)

He fed the dog. (dog, Whom?)

Step-by-Step Teaching Guide

Grammar in Literature

1. Have a volunteer read aloud the passage from *An American Childhood*
2. Point out the use of direct objects. Ask what parts of speech they are. (nouns, pronoun). This would have to be the case because only a person or thing can receive the action of a verb.

More About the Author

Annie Dillard (born 1945) is an American writer known for her meditations on nature and God. Her best-known book, *Pilgrim at Tinker Creek* (1974), won the Pulitzer Prize for nonfiction. The selection is taken from *An American Childhood* (1987), Dillard's autobiographical memoir. She has also written several volumes of essays, poetry, and a novel.

Answer Key

Exercise 32

1. In the fourteenth century, Martini, an Italian painter, designed a human-propelled carriage on four wheels.
2. However, the Greeks used wheels and carts as far back as the eighth century B.C.
3. Henry Ford introduced his first automobile as the "Quadricycle."
4. The name *automobile* gained acceptance in 1897.
5. Some of the first powered cars employed windmills and clockwork motors.

TIME SAVERS!

Answers on Transparency
Use the Grammar Exercises Answers on Transparencies for Chapter 19 to have students correct their own or one another's exercises.

On-Line Exercise Bank
Have students complete the exercises on computer. The Auto Check feature will grade their work for you!

Step-by-Step Teaching Guide

Direct Object, Adverb, or Object of a Preposition?

1. The point of the key concept is that words following verbs are not automatically direct objects. They can be adverbs modifying the verb or objects of prepositions. In other words, students should never assume a word is a direct object. For it to be a direct object, it must answer the question *Whom?* or *What?*
2. Review the example sentence in the middle of the page. Point out that the direct object *car* answers the question *What?* The adverb *quickly* modifies the verb *drove* by describing how Joanne drove. The prepositional phrase *through the park* describes where she drove.

Customize for *Gifted/Talented Students*

Have students work together to write a short sketch in which every sentence contains at least one of the following elements: direct object, adverb, object of a preposition, and at least one sentence per paragraph that contains all three.

Answer Key

Exercise 33

1. A British inventor built a steam automobile (in 1801).
2. This automobile moved rather (quickly) (at twelve miles per hour).
3. People complained (immediately) (about the automobiles' noise).
4. The speed limit restricted drivers (to four miles per hour).
5. Many countries developed automobiles (during this time).

19.5

Distinguishing Between Direct Objects, Adverbs, and Objects of Prepositions

Not all action verbs have direct objects. Be careful not to confuse a direct object with an adverb or with the object of a preposition.

KEY CONCEPT A direct object is never an adverb or the noun or pronoun at the end of a prepositional phrase. ■

Compare the following examples. Notice that the action verb *drove* has a direct object only in the first sentence.

EXAMPLES: Joanne drove her car. (DO: car)
Joanne drove quickly.
Joanne drove through the town.

Each example shows a very common sentence type. The first consists of a subject, a verb, and a direct object. The noun *car* is the direct object of the verb *drove*. The second example consists of a subject, a verb, and an adverb. Nothing answers the question *What?*, so there is no direct object. *Quickly* modifies the verb. The third example consists of a subject, a verb, and a prepositional phrase. Again, no noun or pronoun answers the question *What?* The prepositional phrase tells *where* Joanne drove.

Notice also that a single sentence can contain more than one of these three.

EXAMPLE: Joanne drove her car quickly through the town. (DO: car; ADV: quickly; PREP PHRASE: through the town)

Exercise 33 Distinguishing Between Direct Objects, Adverbs, and Objects of Prepositions Copy each of the following sentences onto your paper. Underline each direct object. Circle any adverbs or prepositional phrases. (Not every sentence has all three.)

EXAMPLE: The first steam-driven automobile moved (slowly) (at two miles per hour.)

1. A British inventor built a steam automobile in 1801.
2. This automobile moved rather quickly at twelve miles per hour.
3. People complained immediately about the automobiles' noise.
4. The speed limit restricted drivers to four miles per hour.
5. Many countries developed automobiles during this time.

iText

Get instant feedback! Exercise 33 is available on-line or on CD-ROM.

More Practice

Grammar Exercise Workbook
- pp. 61–62

On-line Exercise Bank
- Section 19.5

Go on-line: PHSchool.com
Enter Web Code: eck-8002

Finding Direct Objects in Questions

A direct object in a sentence in normal word order is located after the verb. In questions, which are often in inverted order, the position of a direct object in the sentence may change.

KEY CONCEPT A direct object in a question is sometimes near the beginning of the sentence, before the verb. ■

In the chart below, compare the positions of the direct objects in the sentences. The sentences in the first column are questions. In the second column, the questions have been reworded as statements in normal word order.

Questions	Normal Word Order
DO: Whom — Whom did you ask for help?	DO: whom — You did ask whom for help.
DO: What — What does he want from us?	DO: what — He does want what from us.
DO: car — Which car does he want from the dealership?	DO: car — He does want which car from the dealership.

If you have trouble finding the direct object in a question, rephrase the sentence in normal word order, as shown in the examples.

Exercise 34 **Finding Direct Objects in Questions** Copy each of the following sentences onto your paper, and underline each direct object. (Note that in two of the sentences, the direct objects follow the verbs.)

EXAMPLE: What have you heard about the early electric-powered vehicle?

1. Which articles did she read about this experimental vehicle?
2. What disadvantages did the electric automobile have?
3. What does he know about the size and reliability of its batteries?
4. Whom did you see in the automobile museum?
5. When did manufacturers begin production of the electric automobile?

iText

Get instant feedback! Exercise 34 is available on-line or on CD-ROM.

More Practice

Grammar Exercise Workbook
- pp. 63–64

On-line Exercise Bank
- Section 19.5

Go on-line: PHSchool.com
Enter Web Code: eck-8002

Step-by Step Teaching Guide

Finding Direct Objects in Questions

1. The inverted word order of questions puts the direct object before the verb instead of after the verb as in normal word order.
2. A good way to identify the direct object is to rewrite the question into normal word order so that the direct object follows the verb.

Customize for *Less Advanced Students*

Rewriting questions into "normal" word order can be challenging. Tell them to start by finding the subject. Here's a helpful hint for finding the subject of questions: Since most questions are usually addressed to and about people, the subject is likely to be a pronoun or proper noun. Once students have found the subject, follow it with the verb and other complements.

Answer Key

Exercise 34

1. Which articles did she read about this experimental vehicle?
2. What disadvantages did the electric automobile have?
3. What does he know about the size and reliability of its batteries?
4. Whom did you see in the automobile museum?
5. When did manufacturers begin production of the electric automobile?

ONGOING ASSESSMENT: Monitor and Reinforce

If students miss more than one item in Exercises 34, refer them to the following for additional practice.

In the Textbook	Print Resources	Technology
Chapter Review, Ex. 40, p. 425	Grammar Exercise Workbook, pp. 63–64	On-Line Exercise Bank, Section 19.5

TIME SAVERS!

Answers on Transparency Use the Grammar Exercises Answers on Transparencies for Chapter 19 to have students correct their own or one another's exercises.

On-Line Exercise Bank Have students complete the exercises on computer. The Auto Check feature will grade their work for you!

Step-by-Step Teaching Guide

Recognizing Indirect Objects

1. There are several clues to use in identifying an indirect object.

   A sentence must have a direct object for there to be an indirect object.

   It follows the verb and precedes the direct object.

   It is always a noun or pronoun.

   It answers the question To or for whom? or To or for what?

2. See that students understand first the key concept and then the examples. Go over each clue, reminding them again of the perils of shortcuts or jumping to conclusions.

Answer Key

Exercise 35

1. customers
2. cars
3. makers
4. neighbors, friends
5. driver, passengers
6. owners, drivers
7. car, passengers
8. automobile, engine
9. Americans
10. drivers

19.5

Recognizing Indirect Objects

Sentences with a direct object may also contain another kind of complement, called an *indirect object.* A sentence cannot have an indirect object unless it has a direct object.

KEY CONCEPT An **indirect object** is a noun or pronoun that comes after an action verb and before a direct object. It names the person or thing to which something is given or for which something is done. ■

An indirect object answers the questions *To or for whom?* or *To or for what?* after an action verb. To find an indirect object, find the direct object first. Then, ask the appropriate question.

EXAMPLE: I told them (IO) the story (DO).
Told *to whom? Answer:* them

Keep in mind the following pattern: Subject + Verb + Indirect Object + Direct Object. An indirect object will almost always come between the verb and the direct object in a sentence.

Like a subject, verb, or direct object, an indirect object can be compound.

EXAMPLE: Dave gave each car (IO) and truck (IO) a new color (DO).
Gave *to what? Answer:* car, truck

Exercise 35 **Recognizing Indirect Objects** Copy the sentences below, and underline the simple or compound indirect objects.

1. In 1912, twenty companies offered customers electric cars.
2. The internal-combustion engine gave the electric cars new competition.
3. Engineers had given automobile makers plans for internal-combustion automobiles.
4. Owners showed neighbors and friends their automobile.
5. However, the automobile often taught the driver and passengers humility.
6. Automobile engines often gave owners and drivers problems.
7. Ever-dependable horses would then give the car and stranded passengers a tow.
8. The ability of a horse to pull gave the automobile and its engine a new name for its power: "horsepower"!
9. However, cars driven by steam gave Americans a dependable method of travel.
10. Stanley Steamers gave drivers the thrill of quick, noisy travel.

iText

Get instant feedback! Exercise 35 is available on-line or on CD-ROM.

More Practice

Grammar Exercise Workbook
• pp. 65–66
On-line Exercise Bank
• Section 19.5
Go on-line: PHSchool.com
Enter Web Code: eck-8002

TIME SAVERS!

Answers on Transparency Use the Grammar Exercises Answers on Transparencies for Chapter 19 to have students correct their own or one another's exercises.

On-Line Exercise Bank Have students complete the exercises on computer. The Auto Check feature will grade their work for you!

ONGOING ASSESSMENT: Monitor and Reinforce

If students miss more than one item in Exercise 35, refer them to the following for additional practice.

In the Textbook	Print Resources	Technology
Section Review, Ex. 4, p. 425	Grammar Exercise Workbook, pp. 65–66	On-Line Exercise Bank, Section 19.5

Distinguishing Between Indirect Objects and Objects of Prepositions

Do not confuse an indirect object with the object of a preposition.

KEY CONCEPT An indirect object never follows the preposition *to* or *for* in a sentence. ■

Compare the following examples:

EXAMPLES: Father bought him (IO) a car (DO).

Father bought a car (DO) for him.

In the first example, *him* is an indirect object. It comes after the verb and before the direct object. In the second, *him* is the object of the preposition *for* and follows the direct object.

Exercise 36 **Distinguishing Between Indirect Objects and Objects of Prepositions** Copy each sentence below. Underline each indirect object. Circle each object of a preposition.

EXAMPLE: Automobiles brought people other problems.

1. The automobile brought danger for drivers.
2. Accidents caused town officials great concern.
3. Towns quickly set low speed limits for motorists.
4. They soon gave speeders fines.
5. All motorists have a responsibility to their passengers and other drivers.

iText

Get instant feedback! Exercise 36 is available on-line or on CD-ROM.

More Practice

Grammar Exercise Workbook
- pp. 67–68

On-line Exercise Bank
- Section 19.5

Go on-line:
PHSchool.com
Enter Web Code:
eck-8002

◀ Critical Viewing
Compare and contrast the automobile pictured here with one you know well. When you have finished, go back and identify any complements you have used. **[Compare and Contrast]**

Step-by-Step Teaching Guide

Distinguishing Between Indirect Objects and Objects of Prepositions

1. Indirect objects are easily confused with objects of prepositions. Objects of preposition are nouns and pronouns, as are indirect objects. But they do not come after the verb; they come at the end of a prepositional phrase.
2. Write the following sentences on the chalkboard and ask students to identify the indirect object:

   Susan sang Julie a lullaby. (Julie)

   The crowd gave the referee a mock cheer for his bad calls. (referee)
3. Ask which sentence contains an object of a preposition. (second sentence—for his bad calls)

Answer Key

Exercise 36

1. The automobile brought danger for (drivers).
2. Accidents caused town officials great concern.
3. Towns quickly set low speed limits for (motorists).
4. They soon gave speeders fines.
5. All motorists have a responsibility to their (passengers) and other (drivers).

Critical Viewing

Compare and Contrast Point out that students can focus on appearance, performance, and features of the two cars.

Step-by-Step Teaching Guide

Using Subject Complements

1. Review the chart with students, reinforcing the point of a predicate noun renaming the subject.
2. Students may confuse predicate nouns or pronouns with direct objects because both answer the question *What?* in different forms. A predicate noun essentially renames the subject, whereas a direct object receives the action of the verb.

   Allison is a student. (linking verb: is, predicate noun: student)

   Allison scored a goal. (action verb: scored, direct object: goal)

Customize for *Less Advanced Students*

Review linking verbs to be sure that students understand the difference between linking verbs and action verbs and how the verb determines the type of complement.

Customize for *Verbal/Linguistic Learners*

Have students continue the idea of predicate nouns renaming the subject. Ask them to make a list of nouns to finish the sentence *I am a/an* ___.

19.5

Using Subject Complements

Both direct objects and indirect objects are complements used with action verbs. Linking verbs, however, have a different kind of complement, called a *subject complement.*

KEY CONCEPT A **subject complement** is a noun, a pronoun, or an adjective that follows a linking verb and tells something about the subject. ■

Predicate Nouns and Pronouns

Both nouns and pronouns are sometimes used as subject complements after linking verbs.

KEY CONCEPT A **predicate noun** or **predicate pronoun** follows a linking verb and renames or identifies the subject of the sentence. ■

It is easy to recognize *predicate nouns* and *predicate pronouns.* The linking verb acts much like an equal sign between the subject and the noun or pronoun that follows the verb. Both the subject and the predicate noun or pronoun refer to the same person or thing.

PREDICATE NOUNS AND PRONOUNS

Examples	Relationships
Ronnie will be the captain (PN) of our team.	The predicate noun *captain* renames the subject *Ronnie.*
Ford's first car was the Model A (PN).	The predicate noun *Model A* identifies the subject *car.*
The two winners are they (PRED PRON).	The predicate pronoun *they* identifies the subject *winners.*

Learn More

The verbs in these examples are all forms of the linking verb *be.* See Chapter 15, Verbs, for a complete list of the forms of *be* and other linking verbs.

Exercise 37 **Recognizing Predicate Nouns and Pronouns** Identify the predicate noun or predicate pronoun in each sentence below.

EXAMPLE: The automobile is an American institution.
ANSWER: institution

1. Europe was the home of some early automobiles.
2. Americans quickly became fans of the automobile.
3. Hartford and Cleveland were the cities in which the American auto industry began.
4. The first successful American car was the Duryea brothers' invention.
5. Many car models were poor designs.
6. Henry Ford was the man who had financial backing for his invention.
7. He was the inventor of the Model A.
8. Ford was also the inventor of the Model T, his most popular automobile.
9. He was the creator of the world's first auto assembly line.
10. The assembly line was a method of constructing cars on a conveyor belt.

Predicate Adjectives

A linking verb can also be followed by a *predicate adjective.*

KEY CONCEPT A **predicate adjective** follows a linking verb and describes the subject of the sentence. ■

A predicate adjective is considered part of the complete predicate of a sentence because it comes after a linking verb. In spite of this, a predicate adjective does not modify the words in the predicate. Instead, it describes the noun or pronoun that serves as the subject of the linking verb.

PREDICATE ADJECTIVES

Examples	Relationship of Words
The flight to Houston was swift (PA).	The predicate adjective *swift* describes the subject *flight.*
The saleswoman seems very sensitive (PA) to the needs of her customers.	The predicate adjective *sensitive* describes subject *saleswoman.*

More Practice

Grammar Exercise Workbook
- pp. 69–70

On-line Exercise Bank
- Section 19.5

Go on-line: PHSchool.com
Enter Web Code: eck-8002

iText

Get instant feedback! Exercise 37 is available on-line or on CD-ROM.

Answer Key

Exercise 37

1. home
2. fans
3. cities
4. invention
5. designs
6. man
7. inventor
8. inventor
9. creator
10. method

Step-by-Step Teaching Guide

Predicate Adjectives

Write the following examples of sentences with predicate adjectives on the chalkboard for additional practice. Ask students to identify the predicate adjective.

She is smart. (smart)

We will be happy after the test. (happy)

The weather was miserable. (miserable)

You are forgetful. (forgetful)

Customize for *Verbal/Linguistic Learners*

Have students continue the predicate noun renaming activity. This time ask them to complete the sentence *I am ___,* listing as many adjectives as they can that they feel are applicable.

ONGOING ASSESSMENT: Monitor and Reinforce

If students miss more than one item in Exercises 37, refer them to the following for additional practice.

In the Textbook	Print Resources	Technology
Section Review, Ex. 44, p. 425	Grammar Exercise Workbook, pp. 69–70	On-Line Exercise Bank, Section 19.5

TIME SAVERS!

Answers on Transparency Use the Grammar Exercises Answers on Transparencies for Chapter 19 to have students correct their own or one another's exercises.

On-Line Exercise Bank Have students complete the exercises on computer. The Auto Check feature will grade their work for you!

Answer Key

Exercise 38

1. efficient
2. unpleasant
3. tired
4. inescapable
5. smart

Step-by-Step Teaching Guide

Compound Subject Complements

Write the following sentences on the chalkboard. Ask students to identify the compound subject complements by underlining the compound predicate nouns and circling the compound predicate adjectives.

The two guards are Zack and Kevin.

Zack is fast and agile.

Answer Key

Exercise 39

1. The Museum of Automobile History in Syracuse, New York, is exciting and interesting to people of all ages. (arrow from *exciting* to *Museum;* arrow from *interesting* to *Museum*)
2. Information on thousands of cars is available and accessible to all visitors. (arrow from *available* to *Information;* arrow from *accessible* to *Information*)
3. The display of collector's items is sleek and huge. (arrow from *sleek* to *display;* arrow from *huge* to *display*)
4. The museum has become both a historic site and a showroom for classic cars.
5. It will be a popular attraction and tourist site for years to come.

PRENTICE HALL
Everyday Spelling

If you have taught the spelling skills in *Prentice Hall Everyday Spelling,* Grade 8, Chapter 22, in conjunction with this *Writing and Grammar* chapter, review and assess students' mastery of the skills before concluding the chapter.

Exercise 38 **Recognizing Predicate Adjectives** Write the predicate adjective in each sentence below.

EXAMPLE: The Model T was popular with early drivers.
ANSWER: popular

1. The assembly line was extremely efficient, constructing one car in 93 minutes.
2. However, assembly line work was unpleasant.
3. Workers grew tired of the daily monotony and pressure of production quotas.
4. A monthly labor turnover of 40 to 60 percent was inescapable.
5. Ford's plan for doubling the daily wage was smart.

Compound Subject Complements

Like other sentence parts, subject complements can be compound.

KEY CONCEPT A **compound subject complement** consists of two or more predicate nouns, pronouns, or adjectives. ■

EXAMPLES: My two best friends are Phil (PN) and Mark (PN).

The highway seems slick (PA) and icy (PA).

Exercise 39 **Recognizing Compound Subject Complements** Copy the following sentences onto your paper, and underline the parts of each compound subject complement. If a compound subject complement is made up of predicate adjectives, draw arrows pointing from each adjective to the subject.

EXAMPLE: In America, the automobile became a fixture as well as a necessity in everyday life.

1. The Museum of Automobile History in Syracuse, New York, is exciting and interesting to people of all ages.
2. Information on thousands of cars is available and accessible to all visitors.
3. The display of collector's items is sleek and huge.
4. The museum has become both a historic site and a showroom for classic cars.
5. It will be a popular attraction and tourist site for years to come.

More Practice

Grammar Exercise Workbook
- pp. 69–72

On-line Exercise Bank
- Section 19.5

Go on-line:
PHSchool.com
Enter Web Code:
eck-8002

iText

Get instant feedback! Exercises 38 and 39 are available on-line or on CD-ROM.

ONGOING ASSESSMENT: Assess Mastery

Use the following resources to assess student mastery of complements.

In the Textbook	Technology
Chapter Review, Ex. 49–52, pp. 426–427 Standardized Test Preparation Workshop, pp. 428–429	On-Line Exercise Bank, Section 19.5

Section 19.5 Section Review

GRAMMAR EXERCISES 40–45

Exercise 40 **Distinguishing Between Direct Objects, Adverbs, and Objects of Prepositions** Copy each of the following sentences onto your paper. Underline each direct object. Circle any adverbs or prepositional phrases. (Not every sentence has all three.)

1. More automobiles created more traffic and traffic jams.
2. Soon, drivers needed traffic lights for safety.
3. The automobile has created conveniences for drivers.
4. Banks and restaurants provide service quickly to drive-through customers.
5. What effects has the automobile had on your life?

Exercise 41 **Distinguishing Between Indirect Objects and Objects of Prepositions** Copy the sentences below onto your paper, and underline each indirect object or compound indirect object. Circle each object of a preposition. (Not every sentence has both.)

1. Connecticut gave drivers the first license plates for their vehicles.
2. The state also provided a leather strap for the license plate.
3. The state assigned each driver and vehicle an identification number.
4. In 1903, Massachusetts offered each owner state-made license plates.
5. States soon required a license for each driver.

Exercise 42 **Revision Practice: Sentence Combining** Combine sentences in the following paragraph by using compound complements.

License plates are now more attractive than in the past. They are also more personal. The buyer of that personalized license plate is she. The owner is she, too. Such plates are common now. They are inexpensive to purchase. In today's busy world, cars are an essential means of transportation. They are a popular means of transportation. Fortunately, they have also become safer. Cars have also become more efficient. Cars have become a hobby for many. They are a pastime for others. Some old cars are restored for car shows. Other old cars are stripped for their parts. One winner at the car show was that couple. Another winner was that woman. The Model T was the oldest car. It was also the most well preserved.

Exercise 43 **Find It in Your Reading** Reread the excerpt from *An American Childhood* on page 417. Identify two predicate nouns.

Exercise 44 **Find It in Your Writing** Look through your writing portfolio. Find a piece of writing that contains two direct objects, two indirect objects, one predicate noun, and one predicate adjective. Copy the appropriate sentences onto another piece of paper and identify each complement.

Exercise 45 **Writing Application** Write an advertisement for your dream car. Underline all the complements in your sentences. Include at least one example of each of the following: direct object, indirect object, predicate noun, predicate adjective.

ASSESS and CLOSE

Section Review

Each of these exercises correlates to a concept in the section on complements, pages 416-424. These exercises may be used for more practice, for reteaching, or for review of the Key Concepts presented. Answers for all chapter exercises are available in *Grammar Exercises Answers on Transparencies* in your teaching resources.

Answer Key

Exercise 40

1. More automobiles created more traffic and traffic jams.
2. (Soon) drivers needed traffic lights (for safety).
3. The automobile has created conveniences (for drivers).
4. Banks and restaurants provide service (quickly) (to drive-through) (customers).
5. What effects has the automobile had (on your life)?

Exercise 41

1. Connecticut gave drivers the first license plates for their (vehicles).
2. The state also provided a leather strap for the license (plate).
3. The state assigned each driver and vehicle an identification number.
4. In 1903, Massachusetts offered each owner state-made license plates.
5. States soon required a license for each (driver).

Exercise 42

License plates are now more attractive and personal than in the past.

The buyer and owner of that personalized plate is she.

Such plates are common and inexpensive to purchase.

In today's busy world, cars are an essential and popular means of transportation.

Fortunately, they have also become safer and more efficient.

Cars have become a hobby and pastime for many.

Some old cars are restored for car shows or stripped for their parts.

Winners at the car show were that couple and that woman. The Model T was the oldest and most well-preserved car.

continued

Answer Key continued

Exercise 43

Find It in Your Reading
spirit, awareness

Exercise 44

Find It in Your Writing
Ask students to tell what words the predicate noun and predicate adjective rename.

Exercise 45

Writing Application
Students can combine the best features of individual advertisements into one advertisement for a super-duper dream car.

CHAPTER REVIEW

Each of these exercises correlates to a concept in the chapter on basic sentence parts, pages 398–425. These exercises may be used for more practice, for reteaching, or for review of the Key Concepts presented. Answers for all exercises are available in *Grammar Exercises Answers on Transparencies* in your teaching resources.

Answer Key

Exercise 46

1. Some drivers | enjoy automobile racing.
2. The sport | tests the skills.
3. The drivers | race over tracks or courses.
4. Each course | has a different length, design, and construction.
5. incomplete
6. This activity | is a year-round sport.
7. Racing cars | have two categories.
8. incomplete
9. The wheels | are not under the fenders in open-wheeled vehicles.
10. incomplete

Exercise 47

Sentences may vary. Samples are given.

1. Motorcycles and cars are two types of vehicles used in racing.
2. Dirt and asphalt make up the tracks on which the vehicles race.
3. Many automobile racing teams own and drive several cars.
4. The support crew changes tires and fills the gas tank during pit stops.
5. The crew and the crew chief communicate by radio as the driver speeds around the track.

Exercise 48

1. courses
2. you
3. driver
4. race
5. crew

Chapter 19

Chapter Review

GRAMMAR EXERCISES 46–55

Exercise 46 Recognizing Complete Subjects and Predicates Copy the following items onto your paper. For each complete sentence, underline the subject once and the verb twice. Then, draw a vertical line between the complete subject and the complete predicate. If a group of words expresses an incomplete thought, write *incomplete.*

1. Some drivers enjoy automobile racing.
2. The sport tests the skills.
3. The drivers race over tracks or courses.
4. Each course has a different length, design, and construction.
5. It has become one of the most popular.
6. This activity is a year-round sport.
7. Racing cars have two categories.
8. Open-wheeled vehicles and closed-wheeled vehicles.
9. The wheels are not under the fenders in open-wheeled vehicles.
10. In closed-wheeled vehicles.

Exercise 47 Completing Sentences With Compound Subjects and Compound Verbs On your paper, rewrite the sentences below, filling in each blank with another noun or verb that would create a logical compound.

1. Motorcycles and __?__ are two types of vehicles used in racing.
2. Dirt and __?__ make up the tracks on which the vehicles race.
3. Many automobile racing teams own and __?__ several cars.
4. The support crew changes tires and __?__ the gas tank during pit stops.
5. The __?__ and the crew chief communicate by radio as the driver speeds around the track.

Exercise 48 Recognizing Hard-to-Find Subjects Write the subject of each of the following sentences. (Some sentences give orders, some ask questions, and some are in inverted order.)

1. Are the courses very long?
2. Have you looked at the race car?
3. Which driver will win?
4. When will the race begin?
5. There in the pit is the crew.

Exercise 49 Distinguishing Between Direct Objects, Adverbs, and Objects of Prepositions Copy each of the following sentences onto your paper. Underline each simple and compound direct object. Circle any adverbs or prepositional phrases. (Not every sentence has all three.)

1. The Indy 500 attracts both old and young on Memorial Day weekend.
2. The first race at the Indianapolis Motor Speedway covered exactly 500 miles.
3. Ray Harroun won the race with his car, the "Marmon Wasp."
4. The "Marmon Wasp" contained the first single seat in a race car.
5. It also included the first rearview mirror.
6. Whom did you invite to the race?
7. Which car did he drive in the race?
8. The TV station will broadcast the Indianapolis 500 early in the day.
9. What racecourse does the driver prefer?
10. Racing provides thrills for fans.

Exercise 50 Recognizing Direct and Indirect Objects Copy the following sentences. Underline each direct object once and each indirect object twice. Circle each object of a preposition.

1. Preston's dad bought him several tiny cars for his birthday.
2. He told Preston and his friends stories about the "matchbox" cars.
3. In 1952, one of their creators gave his daughter a small "Road Roller" in a matchbox-sized container.
4. Two toy-store owners gave the "matchbox" name to the cars.
5. Initially, stores sold children and adults four different models of these cars.

Exercise 51 **Recognizing Subject Complements** Copy the following sentences onto your paper. Label each predicate noun, predicate pronoun, and predicate adjective.

1. Over the next few years, one brand of toy cars became very popular.
2. Sales were successful, gaining the toy-car maker a world record in sales.
3. By 1973, forty models were available.
4. The most accurate models of today's vehicles were those cars.
5. However, other toy cars would soon become competitors in the market.

Exercise 52 **Completing Sentences With Complements** Complete each sentence below by adding a complement. You may add other words as needed to make sense. Label each complement you add a *direct object*, a *predicate noun*, or a *predicate adjective*.

1. I saw __?__.
2. They brought __?__.
3. Which driver was __?__?
4. That car appears __?__.
5. My favorite racing team won __?__.
6. They gathered __?__.
7. A news reporter asked __?__.
8. We told __?__.
9. I am __?__.
10. He felt __?__.

Exercise 53 **Revision Practice: Sentence Combining** Combine some sentences in the following paragraph by using compound complements. You may make other minor changes as necessary.

It was Henry Ford who made the auto a part of everyday American life. He also made the assembly line a part of American life. In this method of production, workers are stationed in one place. They are required to perform single tasks. As a car frame edged along on a moving belt, one group of workers would bolt seats onto it. The next would add the roof. The assembly line greatly reduced the time needed to build a car. It greatly reduced the cost, as well. The assembly line allowed for the mass production of cars. Later, it allowed for the mass production of other products.

Exercise 54 **Writing Application** Write a description of your favorite car for someone who has never seen it. Underline each of your subjects once and your verbs twice. Label each subject complement a *direct object*, a *predicate noun*, or a *predicate adjective*.

Exercise 55 **CUMULATIVE REVIEW** **Parts of Speech** Identify the part of speech of each underlined word.

(1) Millions <u>of</u> racing fans watch the Indianapolis 500 every <u>Memorial Day</u> weekend. (2) <u>This</u> event <u>is</u> the oldest race in America. (3) <u>Since</u> 1911, the Indy 500 has taken place every year, except during world wars. (4) The Indianapolis Motor Speedway <u>covers</u> 2.5 miles. (5) Many automobile manufacturers test their vehicles <u>there</u>.

Exercise 49 (p. 426)

1. The Indy 500 attracts both <u>old</u> and <u>young</u> (on Memorial Day) (weekend).
2. The first race (at the Indianapolis) (Motor Speedway) covered (exactly) 500 <u>miles</u>.
3. Ray Harroun won the <u>race</u> (with) (his car), the "Marmon Wasp."
4. The "Marmon Wasp" contained the first single <u>seat</u> (in a race car).
5. It (also) included the first <u>rearview mirror</u>.
6. <u>Whom</u> did you invite (to the) (race)?
7. Which <u>car</u> did he drive (in the) (race)?
8. The TV station will broadcast the <u>Indianapolis 500</u> (early) (in the) (day).
9. What <u>racecourse</u> does the driver prefer?
10. Racing provides <u>thrills</u> (for fans).

Exercise 50

1. Preston's dad bought <u>him</u> several matchbox <u>cars</u> for his (birthday).
2. He told <u>Preston and his friends</u> <u>stories</u> about the "matchbox" (cars).
3. In 1952, one of their creators gave his <u>daughter</u> a small <u>"Road Roller"</u> in a matchbox-sized (container).
4. Two toy-store owners gave the "matchbox" <u>name</u> to the (cars).
5. Initially, stores sold <u>children and adults</u> four different <u>models</u> of (cars).

Exercise 51

1. Over the next few years, one brand of toy cars became very popular [PA].
2. Sales were successful [PA], gaining the toy-car maker a world record in sales.
3. By 1973, forty models were available [PA].
4. The most accurate models of today's vehicles were those cars [PN].
5. However, other toy cars would soon become competitors [PN] in the market.

Exercise 52

Sentences will vary.

continued

Answer Key continued

Exercise 53

Sentences will vary. Samples are given.

It was Henry Ford who made the auto and the assembly line a part of everyday American life. In this method of production, workers are stationed in one place and perform single tasks. As a car frame edged along on a moving belt, one group of workers would bolt seats onto it, and the next would add the roof. The assembly line greatly reduced the time and cost needed to build a car. The assembly line allowed for the mass production of cars and other products.

Exercise 54

Writing Application

Suggest that students trade descriptions with partners, who try to draw the car as it is described.

Exercise 55

Cumulative Review

1. preposition, proper noun
2. adjective, verb
3. preposition
4. verb
5. adverb

Lesson Objectives

- To recognize appropriate sentence construction.

Step-by-Step Teaching Guide

Recognizing Appropriate Sentence Construction

Teaching Resources: Standardized Test Preparation Workbook, pp.37–38

1. Remind students to look for fragments and the correct use of complements.
2. Invite volunteers to explain their thinking for their choices in the Practice exercises.

Standardized Test Preparation Workshop

Recognizing Appropriate Sentence Construction

Knowing how to use the basic parts of a sentence correctly is the foundation for good writing. Every sentence must contain a subject—the who or what that performs the action—and a verb—the action the subject is performing—and express a complete thought. If one of these parts is missing, you have an incomplete sentence, or a fragment.

Standardized tests measure your ability to identify complete sentences. When answering these test questions, check each group of words for a subject and a verb, and then determine whether it expresses a complete thought. Finally, choose the group of words that contains all of the elements of a complete sentence to replace any sentence fragments.

The following question will give you practice with the format used for testing your knowledge of basic sentence parts.

Test Tip

Remember that a verb can either follow or come before its subject. Also, a form of *be* can act as the main verb of a sentence, but it does not express action; instead, it links words together.

Sample Test Item	Answer and Explanation
Choose the letter of the best way to write each underlined section. If the underlined section needs no change, choose "Correct as is." (1) <u>The movie was better. Others I've seen on the same subject were not as good.</u>	
1 A I've seen better movies on the same subject. **B** The movie was better than others I've seen on the same subject. **C** The movie I've seen was better than others. Even if they were on the same subject. **D** Correct as is	The correct answer is *B*. The sentence fragment *The movie was better* contains a subject—*movie*—and a verb—*was*—but it does not express a complete idea. To complete the comparison, answer *B* combines the fragment and the next sentence, using the conjunction *than*.

TEST-TAKING TIP

Encourage students to highlight the subjects and verbs they find in order to determine if the sentence is complete. Students can also write down any errors they find in sentence construction to help them determine the best way to reunite a given passage.

Practice 1 **Directions:** Choose the letter of the best way to write each underlined section. If the underlined section needs no change, choose "Correct as is."

<u>Hector pulled the jeep over. To the side of the road.</u> (1) <u>Rosa gazed toward the abandoned mining town. Which was at the end of the dusty path.</u> (2) <u>They approached the town cautiously. They walked hand in hand.</u> (3)

1 **A** Hector pulled over. To the side.
B Hector pulled the jeep over to the side of the road.
C The jeep was pulled over by Hector to the side of the road.
D Correct as is

2 **F** Rosa gazed toward the abandoned mining town. It was at the end of the dusty path.
G Rosa gazed toward town at the end of the dusty path.
H Rosa gazed toward the abandoned mining town at the end of the dusty path.
J Correct as is

3 **A** They approached the town cautiously when they walked hand in hand.
B Approaching the town cautiously. They walked hand in hand.
C Walking hand in hand, they approached the town cautiously.
D Correct as is

Practice 2 **Directions:** Choose the letter of the best way to write each underlined section. If the underlined section needs no change, choose "Correct as is."

<u>It was an old town that had been abandoned a long time ago. They walked a bit closer, then stopped.</u> (1) <u>A tear rolled down her face. Rosa imagined the hardship of a life lived there.</u> (2) <u>It was a town of many stories. They would always be kept secret.</u> (3)

1 **A** It was an old town that had been abandoned until they walked a bit closer, then stopped.
B Abandoned a long time ago, it was an old town. They walked a bit closer, then stopped.
C It was an old town. It had been abandoned a long time ago. They walked a bit closer, then stopped.
D Correct as is

2 **F** A tear rolled down Rosa's face as she imagined the hardship of a life lived there.
G She cried tears when Rosa imagined the hardship of a life lived there.
H A tear rolled down Rosa's face because it must have been hard for her to live there.
J Correct as is

3 **A** It was a town of many stories, these secret stories.
B It was a town of many stories that would always be kept secret.
C The town was of many secret stories.
D Correct as is

Answer Key

Practice 1

1. B
2. H
3. C

Practice 2

1. D
2. F
3. B

Chapter 20 Time and Resource Manager

In-Depth Lesson Plan

	LESSON FOCUS	PRINT AND MEDIA RESOURCES
DAY 1	**Prepositional Phrases** Students learn to identify and use prepositional phrases (pp. 430–434).	**Teaching Resources** *Grammar Exercise Workbook,* pp. 72–84; *Grammar Exercises Answers on Transparencies,* Ch. 20 ***Writing and Grammar iText* (Interactive Text),** Section 20.1
DAY 2	**Other Types of Phrases** Students work with appositive, gerund, participial, and infinitive phrases. They also complete the Hands-on Grammar activity (pp. 435–447).	**Teaching Resources** *Grammar Exercise Workbook,* pp. 72–84; *Grammar Exercises Answers on Transparencies,* Ch. 20; *Hands-on Grammar Activity Book,* Ch. 20 ***Writing and Grammar iText* (Interactive Text),** Section 20.1
DAY 3	**Clauses** Students learn to identify and distinguish between independent and subordinate clauses (pp. 448–453).	**Teaching Resources** Grammar Exercise Workbook, pp. 85–92; *Grammar Exercises Answers on Transparencies,* Ch. 20 ***Writing and Grammar iText* (Interactive Text),** Section 20.2
DAY 4	**Classifying Sentences** Students learn to identify and distinguish among simple, compound, complex, and compound-complex sentences (pp. 454–459).	**Teaching Resources** *Grammar Exercise Workbook,* pp. 93–94; *Grammar Exercises Answers on Transparencies,* Ch. 20 ***Writing and Grammar iText* (Interactive Text),** Section 20.2
DAY 5	**Review and Assess** Students review the chapter and demonstrate mastery of phrases and clauses (pp. 460–463).	**Teaching Resources** *Formal Assessment,* Ch. 20; *Grammar Exercises Answers on Transparencies,* Ch. 20 ***Writing and Grammar iText* (Interactive Text),** Ch. 20, Chapter Review; ***On-Line Exercise Bank,*** Sections 20.1–2

Accelerated Lesson Plan

	LESSON FOCUS	PRINT AND MEDIA RESOURCES
DAY 1	**Phrases** Students learn to identify and use various types of phrases (pp. 430–447).	**Teaching Resources** *Grammar Exercise Workbook,* pp. 72–84; *Grammar Exercises Answers on Transparencies,* Ch. 20; *Hands-on Grammar Activity Book,* Ch. 20 ***Writing and Grammar iText* (Interactive Text),** Section 20.1
DAY 2	**Clauses; Classifying Sentences** Students learn to identify and distinguish between independent and subordinate clauses. They learn to distinguish among four types of sentences (pp. 448–459).	**Teaching Resources** *Grammar Exercise Workbook,* pp. 85–94; *Grammar Exercises Answers on Transparencies,* Ch. 20 ***Writing and Grammar iText* (Interactive Text),** Section 20.2
DAY 3	**Review and Assess** Students review the chapter and demonstrate mastery of phrases and clauses (pp. 460–463).	**Teaching Resources** *Formal Assessment,* Ch. 20; *Grammar Exercises Answers on Transparencies,* Ch. 20 ***Writing and Grammar iText* (Interactive Text),** Ch. 20, Chapter Review; ***On-Line Exercise Bank,*** Sections 20.1–2

Options for Adapting Lesson Plans

FEATURES

Extend coverage with the Grammar in Literature features (pp. 439, 458) and the Standardized Test Preparation Workshop (pp. 462–463).

SPELLING

To teach spelling skills in conjunction with grammar, mechanics, and usage, work through *Prentice Hall Everyday Spelling,* Grade 8, Chapter 23, as you cover this *Writing and Grammar* chapter.

TECHNOLOGY

Students can use *Writing and Grammar iText* to complete the exercises interactively on computer. They can complete additional exercises in the *On-line Exercise Bank:* The Auto Check feature will grade their work. Go online: PHSchool.com Use Web code: eck-8002

INTEGRATED SKILLS COVERAGE

Grammar in Literature
SE pp. 439, 458

Writing
Find It in Your Writing, SE pp. 446, 447, 459
Writing Application, SE pp. 446, 447, 459, 461

Viewing and Representing
Critical Viewing, SE pp. 430, 436, 440, 444, 445, 449, 451, 454, 456

Speaking and Listening
Reading Aloud, ATE pp. 439, 458

Workplace Skills
Variety in Sentence Construction, ATE p. 455

ASSESSMENT SUPPORT

Standardized Test Preparation Workshop SE pp. 462–463
Standardized Test Preparation Workbook, pp. 39–40
Formal Assessment, Ch. 20

MEETING INDIVIDUAL NEEDS

Less Advanced Students ATE p. 438. See Ongoing Assessments ATE pp. 433, 434, 453, 455.
ESL Students ATE pp. 433, 449
More Advanced Students ATE p. 457

BLOCK SCHEDULING

Pacing Suggestions
For 90-minute Blocks
- Administer the Diagnostic Test to students to determine instructional coverage.
- Have students complete the necessary exercises in class. Use the Hands-on Grammar Activity to provide a change of pace.

Professional Development Support
- ***How to Manage Instruction in the Block*** This teaching resource provides management and activity suggestions.

MEDIA AND TECHNOLOGY

For the Student
- ***Writing and Grammar iText*** **(Interactive Text),** Ch. 20
- ***On-line Exercise Bank,*** Sections 20.1–2

For the Teacher
- ***Resource Pro*** **CD-ROM**

WRITING AND GRAMMAR ON-LINE

iText Interactive Text (On-line or on CD-ROM)
- Easily navigable instruction with on-line supporting resources
- Self-scoring exercises and diagnostic tests

Companion Web Site PHSchool.com
- On-line Exercise Bank (use Web Code eck-8002)

See the Go On-line! feature, SE p. iii.

LITERATURE CONNECTIONS

Grammar in Literature selection from *Prentice Hall Literature: Timeless Voices, Timeless Themes,* Silver:
from "Hamadi," Naomi Shihab Nye, SE p. 458

CHAPTER 20
PHRASES AND CLAUSES

Lesson Objectives

1. To identify and use prepositional phrases.
2. To identify and use appositive phrases.
3. To identify and use verbal phrases.
4. To recognize and use subordinate and independent clauses, including adjective and adverb clauses.
5. To classify sentence structure as simple, compound, complex, or compound-complex.

Critical Viewing

Analyze Students may mention rock formations, sand, and plants. Encourage student to note hills and other features of the landscape.

Chapter 20 Phrases and Clauses

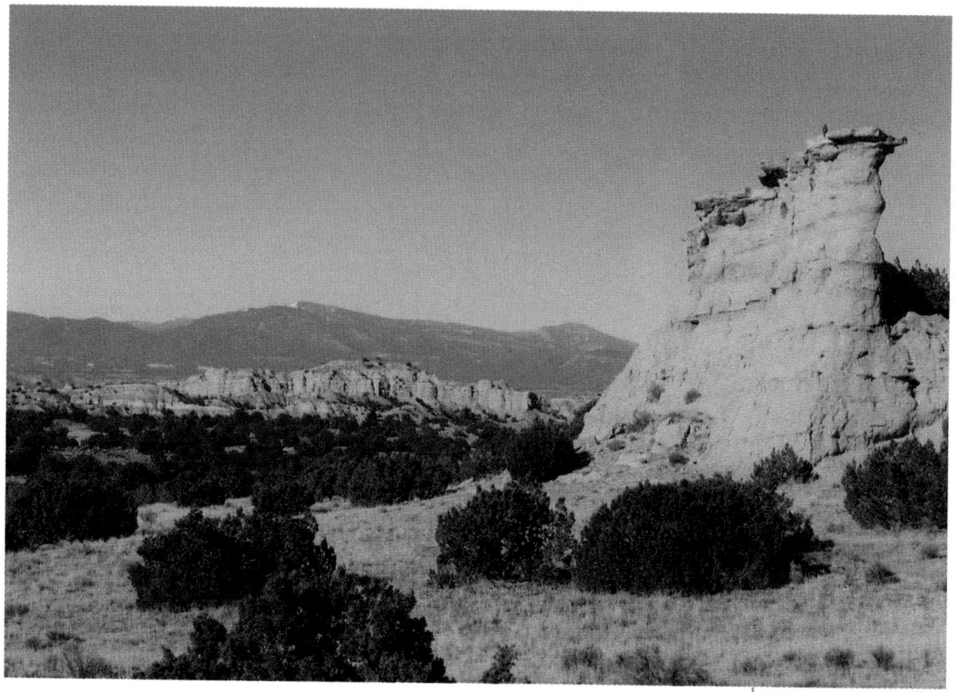

The formation of a culture occurs at the beginning of its history. Everything, even small things, that happens has an influence on what that culture will become. Sentences, like cultures, are made up of little things. What a sentence is, or what a sentence means, depends on its parts. In this chapter, you will learn the sentence parts—phrases and clauses—and their different variations.

▲ Critical Viewing
What are the different parts, or features, that make up this landscape? **[Analyze]**

ONGOING ASSESSMENT: Diagnose

If students miss more than one item in each category, direct them to the relevant pages of the text and assign exercises for practice and review.

Agreement	Diagnostic Test Items	Teach	Practice	Section Review	Chapter Review
Skill Check A					
Adjective and Adverb Phrases	A 1–5	pp. 432–434	Ex. 1–6	Ex. 22	Ex. 47
Skill Check B					
Appositives and Participles	B 6–10	pp. 435–440	Ex. 7–12	Ex. 22	Ex. 46, 47

Diagnostic Test

Directions: Write all answers on a separate sheet of paper.

Skill Check A. Label each underlined phrase below an *adjective phrase* or an *adverb phrase.*

1. A huge silver deposit was discovered during the year 1546.
2. The soldiers thought the mountains of New Mexico looked like the mountains in Mexico where the silver had been discovered.
3. This led them to expand their exploration into New Mexico.
4. A merchant decided to sponsor an expedition to New Mexico.
5. He was personally interested in the area.

Skill Check B. Identify appositives, appositive phrases, participles, and participial phrases in the following sentences. Label each item you identify.

6. Gaspar Castano de Sosa, a lieutenant-governor from Spain, thought that exploring New Mexico would win him riches.
7. The people of the area, the Native Americans, told him legends of wealth in the unexplored areas.
8. De Sosa, the governor, threw a silver cup into the ore sample.
9. The sample showed the desired results, a high silver content.
10. Thus, he was able to convince many people that the desired destination, New Mexico, was indeed a worthy goal.

Skill Check C. Identify gerunds, gerund phrases, and infinitives in the following sentences. Label each item you identify.

11. In 1590, 170 people left from Almaden to seek their fortunes.
12. Searching for wealth proved fruitless in the New Mexico desert.
13. Two months later, soldiers set out to arrest de Sosa.
14. The soldiers returned him to New Spain to be thrown into prison.
15. However, de Sosa's traveling was important because his was the first expedition to New Mexico to be supported by a private party.

Skill Check D. Label each underlined word below *gerund, verb,* or *participle.* If it is a participle, tell whether it is *present* or *past.* Then, label each sentence *simple, complex, compound,* or *compound-complex.*

16. Establishing San Gabriel, Juan de Onate led a group to New Mexico at the end of the sixteenth century.
17. When they arrived, the Native Americans shared their homes with the settlers, and they helped them to find urgently needed food.
18. At this time, the Spanish were planning to build a town next to the Indian pueblo, but Onate ordered them to build San Gabriel next to the west bank of the Rio Grande.
19. While Onate was settling the area, he claimed that his purpose was establishing peace with the Indians.
20. However, it seems that becoming rich was his desire; in addition to his packing the ordinary supplies, Onate had also brought mining tools.

Answer Key

Diagnostic Test

Each item in the diagnostic test corresponds to a specific concept in the chapter on phrases and clauses. This will enable you to tailor instruction to the particular needs of your students.

Skill Check A

1. adverb phrase
2. adjective phrase; adjective phrase
3. adverb phrase
4. adjective phrase
5. adverb phrase

Skill Check B

6. a lieutenant-governor from Spain—appositive phrase exploring—participle
7. the Native Americans; appositive; unexplored—participle
8. the governor—appositive
9. desired—participle; a high silver content—appositive
10. desired—participle; New Mexico—appositive

Skill Check C

11. to seek—infinitive
12. Searching for wealth—gerund phrase
13. to arrest—infinitive
14. to be thrown—infinitive
15. traveling—gerund, to be—infinitive

Skill Check D

16. gerund, simple
17. past participle, compound-complex
18. present participle, compound
19. verb, gerund, complex
20. gerund, gerund, present participle, compound-complex

ONGOING ASSESSMENT: Diagnose *continued*

Agreement	Diagnostic Test Items	Teach	Practice	Section Review	Chapter Review
Skill Check C					
Gerunds and Infinitives	C 11–15	pp. 441–445	Ex. 13–18	Ex. 20–21	Ex. 46, 47
Skill Check D					
Sentence Structure	D 16–20	pp. 454–458	Ex. 32–39	Ex. 41–42	Ex. 50–52

TIME SAVERS!

Answers on Transparency Use the Grammar Exercises Answers on Transparencies for Chapter 20 to have students correct their own or one another's exercises.

On-Line Exercise Bank Have students complete the exercises on computer. The Auto Check feature will grade their work for you!

PREPARE and ENGAGE

Interest GRABBER Have students imagine what it would be like if people could speak only in the simplest sentences. Put some examples on the board: *I walked. I ate. I arrived.* Ask how we convey additional meaning in the sentences we speak and write.

Activate Prior Knowledge

Students' knowledge of the basic parts of speech is essential to their success with this chapter. In order to learn the uses and characteristics of phrases and clauses that act as prepositions, adjectives, verbs, and adverbs, students should begin with a firm grasp of how these parts of speech function as individual words.

TEACH

Step-by-Step Teaching Guide

Prepositional Phrases

1. There are several kinds of phrases, and each of them has a different use in sentences. A phrase is a group of words that function in a sentence as a single part of speech. Write an example on the board.

   He walked to the school.

2. *To the school* is a phrase that gives information about where he walked.
3. The prepositional phrase is one of the most common phrases, and it is easy to spot because it always begins with a preposition, such as *in, on, to, from, after, with, above, under,* and so on.

Answer Key

Exercise 1

1. to the north, of New Mexico
2. of this beautiful state
3. By the sixteenth century, in Mexico
4. about rich treasures, in the land, to the north, of Mexico
5. with the land

Exercise 2

Answers will vary.

Section 20.1

Phrases

Theme: New Mexico

In this section, you will learn about phrases. The examples and exercises are about New Mexico.

Cross-Curricular Connection: Social Studies

Sentences are built with more than just a subject and a predicate. *Phrases* of all kinds play an important role by adding information to a sentence.

KEY CONCEPT A **phrase** is a group of words that functions in a sentence as a single part of speech. Phrases do not contain a subject and verb. ■

There are several kinds of phrases: *prepositional, appositive, participial, gerund,* and *infinitive.* They get their names from the word that begins the phrase or from the most important word in it. You are probably most familiar with the prepositional phrase.

Using Prepositional Phrases

A *prepositional phrase* begins with a preposition and ends with a noun or pronoun called the *object of the preposition.*

EXAMPLES: under (PREP) the window (OBJ)   near (PREP) them (OBJ)   at (PREP) the store (OBJ)

Prepositional phrases may also have compound objects.

EXAMPLE: near (PREP) the flowers (OBJ) and the trees (OBJ)

In a sentence, a prepositional phrase can act as an adjective and modify a noun or pronoun. It can also act as an adverb and modify a verb, an adjective, or an adverb.

Exercise 1 **Identifying Prepositional Phrases** Identify the prepositional phrase(s) in each of the following sentences.

1. Colorado lies to the north of New Mexico.
2. The southern border of this beautiful state is Mexico.
3. By the sixteenth century, Spanish explorers had arrived in Mexico.
4. They heard grand tales about rich treasures in the land to the north of Mexico.
5. They called this land "new" Mexico. They did not find gold when they arrived, but the name has remained with the land ever since.

Exercise 2 **Writing With Prepositional Phrases** Write a description of the photograph on page 430. Use at least five prepositional phrases. Circle each one.

TIME AND RESOURCE MANAGER

Resources
Print: Grammar Exercise Workbook, pp. 72–84; Hands-on Grammar Activity Book, Chapter 20
Technology: Writing and Grammar iText, Section 20.1; On-Line Exercise Bank, Section 20.1

In-Depth Coverage	Accelerated Pace
• Work through all key concepts, pp. 432–445. • Assign and review Exercises 1–18. • Do the Hands-on Grammar Activity, p. 446.	• Assign pp. 432–445, for independent student review. • Assign Section Review Exercises 19–22.

Using Prepositional Phrases That Act as Adjectives

A prepositional phrase that acts as an adjective is called an *adjective phrase.*

KEY CONCEPT An **adjective phrase** is a prepositional phrase that modifies a noun or pronoun by telling *what kind* or *which one.* ■

The following chart compares adjective phrases to one-word adjectives. Notice that an adjective phrase usually follows its noun or pronoun.

Adjectives	Adjective Phrases
The *New Mexican* climate is warm.	The climate *of New Mexico* is warm.
The *blue-eyed* acrobat slipped and fell.	The acrobat *with the blue eyes* slipped and fell.

The adjective phrases answer the same questions as the one-word adjectives. *Which* climate is warm? The climate *of New Mexico* is warm. *Which one* of the acrobats slipped and fell? The acrobat *with the blue eyes* did.

Exercise 3 **Identifying Adjective Phrases** Copy the following sentences onto your paper. Underline each adjective phrase, and draw an arrow pointing from it to the word it modifies.

1. Scientists believe that the first humans in this area were the Sandia People.
2. Caves in the central mountains were their homes.
3. Bones and fossils of these people are 25,000 years old.
4. Ruins around this area can still be seen today.
5. Now, the Native Americans from the area are the Pueblo, the Navajo, and the Apache Indians.

Exercise 4 **Writing With Adjective Phrases** Write a series of sentences in which you use each of the following nouns as part of an adjective phrase or in which you use an adjective phrase to describe the noun.

1. desert
2. Santa Fe
3. weavings
4. attractions
5. mountains

More Practice

Grammar Exercise Workbook
- pp. 73–74

On-line Exercise Bank
- Section 20.1

Go on-line:
PHSchool.com
Enter Web Code:
eck-8002

iText

Get instant feedback! Exercise 3 is available on-line or on CD-ROM.

ONGOING ASSESSMENT: Prerequisite Skills

If students have difficulty with prepositional phrases, refer them to the following to ensure coverage of prerequisite skills.

In the Textbook	Print Resources	Technology
Prepositions, pp. 370–379	Grammar Exercise Workbook, pp. 39–42	On-Line Exercise Bank, Ch. 17

Step-by-Step Teaching Guide

Prepositional Phrases That Act as Adjectives

1. Start by having students tell what an adjective does. (Adjectives make nouns and pronouns more vivid and precise.)
2. Write the following examples on the board.

   apple *red apples*

   two apples *that apple*

   The adjectives all give information about or modify the noun *apples*.
3. Prepositional phrases can be used in the same way, with the entire phrase acting like an adjective. Write the following sentence on the board as an example.

   Apples in the basket were red.

Customize for *ESL Students*

Students learning English may have difficulty making subtle distinctions between different parts of speech. Start each set of key concepts with a careful review of basic concepts such as the difference between adjectives and adverbs, nouns and pronouns, and conjunctions and prepositions.

Answer Key

Exercise 3

1. in this area—humans (arrow to *humans*)
2. in the central mountains—Caves (arrow to *Caves*)
3. of these people—Bones and fossils (arrow to *Bones and fossils*)
4. around this area—ruins (arrow to *ruins*)
5. from the area—*Native Americans* (arrow to *Native Americans*)

Exercise 4

1. plants of the desert
   desert of white sand
2. sights of Santa Fe
   Santa Fe of my dreams
3. pictures of the weavings
   weavings of colored threads
4. tickets for the attractions
   attractions for children
5. history of the mountains
   mountains of pine trees

Step-by-Step Teaching Guide

Using Prepositional Phrases as Adverbs

1. Ask students what an adverb does. (Adverbs answer the questions *how? when? where?* and *to what extent?*)
2. One helpful way to differentiate between adverbs and adjectives is to remember that adverbs modify the words that adjectives don't: verbs, adjectives, and other adverbs.
3. Write the following sentences on the board.

   She ate the apple quickly.

   She ate the very red apple.

   The word *quickly* modifies the verb *ate,* and *very* modifies the adjective *red.*
4. Explain that prepositional phrases can be used in the same way, with the entire phrase acting like an adverb.

   She lifted the apples out of the basket one by one.

Answer Key

Exercise 5

1. from a shipwreck—escaped
2. through the Mexican desert—walked
3. for eight years—journeyed
4. During their journey—covered
5. to an area—traveled; to the Spaniards—known

Exercise 6

Answers will vary.

1. through the warm desert
2. down the mountain
3. after ten minutes
4. in the morning
5. to the horizon

20.1

Using Prepositional Phrases as Adverbs

Prepositional phrases can also be used as adverbs.

KEY CONCEPT An **adverb phrase** is a prepositional phrase that modifies a verb, an adjective, or an adverb. Adverb phrases point out *where, when, in what way,* or *to what extent.* ■

The examples in the following chart show that adverb phrases serve the same function as one-word adverbs.

Adverb	Adverb Phrases
The bus left *late.*	The bus left *after a two-hour delay.*
Put the package *there.*	Put the package *in the closet.*

In the first pair of examples, both *late* and *after a two-hour delay* answer the question *Left when?* In the second pair, *there* and *in the closet* answer the question *Put where?*

Like one-word adverbs, adverb phrases can modify verbs, adjectives, or adverbs. Unlike adjective phrases, adverb phrases do not always appear close to the words they modify. They can appear in almost any position in a sentence.

Exercise 5 **Identifying Adverb Phrases** Copy the following sentences onto your paper. Underline each adverb phrase, and draw an arrow pointing from it to the word it modifies.

1. Cabeza de Vaca escaped from a shipwreck in 1528.
2. He and his men then walked through the Mexican desert.
3. They journeyed for eight years.
4. During their journey, they covered about 10,000 miles.
5. Eventually, they traveled to an area that would later be known to the Spaniards as New Mexico.

Exercise 6 **Writing With Adverb Phrases** Rewrite each item below as a complete sentence by adding an adjective phrase.

1. The tourists journeyed . . .
2. At Taos ski resort, expert skiers plunge . . .
3. The heat subsided . . .
4. The sun rose . . .
5. The desert extended . . .

More Practice

Grammar Exercise Workbook
- pp. 73–74

On-line Exercise Bank
- Section 20.1

Go on-line: PHSchool.com *Enter Web Code:* eck-8002

iText

Get instant feedback! Exercise 5 is available on-line or on CD-ROM.

ONGOING ASSESSMENT: Monitor and Reinforce

If students miss more than two items in Exercises 5–6, refer them to the following additional practice.

In the Textbook	Print Resources	Technology
Section Review, Ex. 22, p. 447	Grammar Exercise Workbook, pp. 73–74	On-Line Exercise Bank, Section 20.1

Using Appositives in Phrases

Appositives, like adjective phrases, give information about nouns or pronouns.

KEY CONCEPT An **appositive** is a noun or pronoun placed after another noun or pronoun to identify, rename, or explain the preceding word. ■

Appositives are very useful in writing because they give additional information without using many words.

EXAMPLES: The poet *Robert Frost* is much admired.

This antique car, a *Studebaker*, is worth thousands of dollars.

The conquistador *Francisco de Coronado* led a group of 1,100 people looking for gold.

An appositive with its own modifiers creates an *appositive phrase*.

KEY CONCEPT An **appositive phrase** is a noun or pronoun with modifiers. It is placed next to a noun or pronoun and adds information or details. ■

The modifiers in the phrase can be adjectives or adjective phrases.

EXAMPLES: San Juan de los Caballeros, *the Spanish capital of the New Mexico territory*, was moved to a new site in 1610.

The painting, *a mural in many bright colors*, highlights the entrance.

Appositives and appositive phrases can also be compound.

EXAMPLES: Volunteers, *boys* or *girls*, are wanted.

These poems, "The Sea Gypsy" and "Before the Squall," are about a love for the sea.

Grammar and Style Tip

Appositives provide an excellent way to combine certain types of sentences. Look at the following pair of sentences: "This antique car is a Studebaker. It is worth thousands of dollars." These sentences can be combined using an appositive, as in the example.

Step-by-Step Teaching Guide

Using Appositives in Phrases

1. Remind students that they can look for certain clues to identify different kinds of phrases. For example, prepositional phrases always begin with prepositions.
2. The appositive phrase can be identified because it always begins with an article, a noun, or a pronoun.The noun or pronoun in an appositive phrase always follows the noun or pronoun that the phrase modifies.
3. Write the following sentences on the board to help explain the role of appositives and appositive phrases.

   The student, a girl in the eighth grade, ran onto the field.

   The words *student* and *girl* are nouns in this sentence. Both words refer to the same person, and *girl* simply gives more information about *student.*
4. Appositive phrases contain additional modifiers that give more information about the main noun or pronoun being modified.

Answer Key

Exercise 7

1. The capital, Santa Fe, was the place from which the Spaniards ran their territorial government. (arrow to *capital*)
2. El Palacio, the Palace of the Governors, was the building where government business was carried out. (arrow to *El Palacio*)
3. Pope, a Native American leader, led a revolt against the Spanish in 1680. (arrow to *Pope*)
4. This revolt drove their enemies, the Spanish, out of the area. (arrow to *their enemies*)
5. Twelve years later, the Spanish general Diego de Vargas returned to conquer the area for the Spaniards again. (arrow to *general*)

Exercise 8

1. After Mexico won its independence in 1821, the New Mexico Territory, present-day Arizona, New Mexico, Nevada, and Utah, was open to settlement by Americans. (arrow to *the New Mexico Territory*)
2. When trade began with the United States, the Santa Fe Trail, a route from Santa Fe to Missouri, became popular. (arrow to *the Santa Fe Trail*)
3. In 1846, the United States declared war on Mexico, and the capture of northern Mexico, New Mexico, became one of its first objectives. (arrow to *northern Mexico*)
4. A United States officer, General Stephen Watts Kearny, entered and captured Santa Fe. (arrow to *officer*)
5. Today, New Mexico, a state filled with rich cultural traditions, has a diverse population. (arrow to *New Mexico*)

Critical Viewing

Connect Students may suggest that New Mexico had a Native American history.

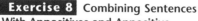

Exercise 7 **Identifying Appositives and Appositive Phrases** Copy the following sentences onto your paper. Underline each appositive or appositive phrase, and draw an arrow pointing from it to the noun or pronoun it renames.

1. The capital, Santa Fe, was the place from which the Spaniards ran their territorial government.
2. El Palacio, the Palace of the Governors, was the building where government business was carried out.
3. Pope, a Native American leader, led a revolt against the Spanish in 1680.
4. This revolt drove their enemies, the Spanish, out of the area.
5. Twelve years later, the Spanish general Diego de Vargas returned to conquer the area for the Spaniards again.

▼ **Critical Viewing** What can you learn about New Mexico from this photograph alone? **[Connect]**

Exercise 8 **Combining Sentences With Appositives and Appositive Phrases** Combine each pair of sentences below by using an appositive or appositive phrase.

EXAMPLE: New Mexico is a popular tourist destination. The state is known for its beauty.

ANSWER: New Mexico, a popular tourist destination, is known for its beauty.

1. After Mexico won its independence in 1821, the New Mexico Territory was open to settlement by Americans. The territory consisted of present-day Arizona, New Mexico, Nevada, and Utah.
2. When trade began with the United States, the Santa Fe Trail became popular. It was a route from Santa Fe to Missouri.
3. In 1846, the United States declared war on Mexico, and the capture of northern Mexico became one of its first objectives. The area is now known as New Mexico.
4. A United States officer entered and captured Santa Fe. His name was General Stephen Watts Kearny.
5. Today, New Mexico has a diverse population. It is a state filled with rich cultural traditions.

Using Verbals and Verbal Phrases

Verbals are verb forms that are used as another part of speech. There are three kinds of verbals: *participles, gerunds,* and *infinitives.* Participles are used as adjectives, gerunds as nouns, and infinitives as nouns, adjectives, or adverbs.

Verbals have two important characteristics of verbs: (1) They can be followed by a complement, and (2) they can be modified by adverbs and adverb phrases. A verbal with a complement or a modifier is called a *verbal phrase.*

Participles

Many of the adjectives you use are actually *participles.*

KEY CONCEPT A **participle** is a form of a verb that acts as an adjective. ■

There are two kinds of participles: *present participles* and *past participles.* Present participles end in *-ing.*

PRESENT PARTICIPLES: going, playing, growing, telling, reading

Past participles usually end in *-ed,* although those formed from irregular verbs will have different endings, such as *-t* or *-en.* (See Section 22.1 for a list of irregular verb endings.)

PAST PARTICIPLES: marked, jumped, moved, hurt, chosen

Present Participles	Past Participles
A *growing* baby sleeps much of the day.	The *conquered* territory was under Spanish control.
Many people in New Mexico live in *farming* communities.	*Troubled,* she asked for advice.

Exercise 9 **Identifying Present and Past Participles** Write the participle from each sentence below, and label it *past* or *present.*

1. New Mexico's tiring distances made it difficult to commute.
2. Until 1847, there was only one completed schoolhouse.
3. Only a selected few were given education at this time.
4. The sons of the educated wealthy were sent east to school.
5. In 1847, a Catholic bishop, John B. Lamy, started a free school where his students were taught in English.

More Practice

Grammar Exercise Workbook
- pp. 75–80

On-line Exercise Bank
- Section 20.1

Go on-line:
PHSchool.com
Enter Web Code:
eck-8002

iText

Get instant feedback! Exercise 9 is available on-line or on CD-ROM.

Step-by-Step Teaching Guide

Using Verbals and Verbal Phrases

1. When verbs are used as other parts of speech, they are called verbals. The first kind of verbal is called a participle, which is the name for a verb that acts as an adjective.
2. Write the following sentences on the board.

   He had chosen the restaurant.

   He arrived at the chosen restaurant.

   Chosen is a verb in the first sentence. The verb in the second sentence is *arrived; chosen* has become an adjective that modifies *restaurant.*
3. All present participles end in *-ing* and most past participles end in *-ed.* Put the following lists of present and past participles and the words they modify on the board to reinforce students' understanding of participle use.

   Examples of Present Participles
   the inspiring leader
   the running soccer player
   the frightening movie

   Examples of Past Participles
   the tired players
   the idolized rock star
   the burnt toast
   the frozen pond
4. Ask students why they think the last two past participles above do not end in *-ed.* (*Burn* and *freeze* are irregular verbs.)

Answer Key

Exercise 9

1. tiring—present
2. completed—past
3. selected—past
4. educated—past
5. no participles

Step-by-Step Teaching Guide

Participle or Verb?

1. Ask students to look at the list of present and past participles you put on the board, as well as the ones provided in their textbooks. There is one other important rule to remember about participles: They always stand alone, and they always modify a noun or a pronoun.
2. Write the following sentences on the board to illustrate this rule.

   The running players reached the ball at the same time.

   The players were running toward the soccer ball.

   Ask students how they can tell that the word *running* in the first sentence is a participle. (It is a verb acting like an adjective by giving more information about and modifying the noun *players.*)
3. Point out that in the second sentence the word *running* is next to a helping verb, *were,* and acts as a verb describing the players' actions.

Customize for *Less Advanced Students*

Students may find it difficult to differentiate between verbs and participles. Spend some time helping them identify helping verbs, then work with them to create new sentences using the helping verbs. Then ask students to create new sentences in which verbs are used as participles.

Answer Key

Exercise 10

1. verb
2. participle—legislature
3. verb
4. participle—population
5. participle—schools
6. verb
7. verb, verb
8. participle—land
9. participle—fences
10. verb, verb

20.1

Participle or Verb?

Sometimes, verb phrases (verbs with helping verbs) are confused with participles. In the chart, however, note that a verb phrase always begins with a helping verb. A participle used as an adjective stands by itself and modifies a noun or pronoun.

Verb Phrases	Participles
The car *was racing* around the curve.	The *racing* car crashed into the wall.
Cabeza de Vaca and his group *may have walked* through New Mexico.	The *walked* trail may have gone through New Mexico.

Exercise 10 **Distinguishing Between Verbs and Participles** Label each underlined word a *verb* or a *participle.* If the word is a participle, also write the word it modifies.

EXAMPLE: Preaching missionaries taught religion and also set up schools.

ANSWER: participle (missionaries)

1. By 1856, the government was taking steps to create a public-school system.
2. Progressing, the legislature passed the first public-school law in 1860.
3. This encouraged other districts that were building schools in other parts of the territory.
4. The University of New Mexico was built for the increasing population of Albuquerque in 1889.
5. Established schools became more numerous in some areas by the early 1900's.
6. Also rising in popularity were cattle ranches.
7. These, however, declined when sheep were brought in.
8. Homesteaders needed fenced land to farm.
9. Consequently, ranchers would run into newly built fences where they used to graze their cattle.
10. With competition that was coming from two directions, many cattle owners were giving up cattle ranching.

More Practice

Grammar Exercise Workbook
- pp. 75–80

On-line Exercise Bank
- Section 20.1

Go on-line: PHSchool.com *Enter Web Code:* eck-8002

iText

Get instant feedback! Exercise 10 is available on-line or on CD-ROM.

Participial Phrases

A participle can be expanded into a phrase by adding one or more modifiers or complements to it.

KEY CONCEPT A **participial phrase** is a present or past participle that is modified by an adverb or adverb phrase or that has a complement. The entire phrase acts as an adjective in a sentence. ■

The following examples show a few of the ways that participles can be expanded into phrases.

EXAMPLES: The diner, *chewing rapidly*, called for a waiter.

The waiter, *eating his lunch*, did not respond.

The first participial phrase is formed by adding the adverb *rapidly*, the second by adding the direct object *lunch*.

In these examples, notice that each participial phrase appears right after the noun it modifies. Both sentences could be reworded to move the phrases before the modified words.

EXAMPLES: *Chewing rapidly*, the diner called for a waiter.

Eating his lunch, the waiter did not respond.

GRAMMAR IN LITERATURE

from A Horseman in the Sky

Ambrose Bierce

Notice how the writer has used participles in this passage. The present participles are red, and the past participle is blue.

. . . the left hand, holding the bridle rein, was invisible. In silhouette against the sky the profile of the horse was cut with the sharpness of a cameo; it looked across the heights of air to the confronting cliffs beyond. The face of the rider, turned slightly away, showed only an outline of temple and beard. . . .

Step-by-Step Teaching Guide

Participial Phrases

1. Participial phrases always begin with participles. Participial phrases also include an adverb or adverb phrase that modifies the participle, or they contain a participle with a complement.
2. Write the following sentences, which contain participial phrases, on the board.

   The construction worker, thinking quickly, moved to the right.

   The construction worker, entering into the building, heard a loud noise.

   The construction worker, wearing a hard hat, looked up at the sky.

   Ask students to identify the participial phrase in each sentence. *(thinking quickly, entering the building, wearing a hard hat)*
4. Elicit that all of the participial phrases follow the noun that they are modifying, which is the word *worker.* Remind students that participial phrases are always right next to, whether in front of or after, the nouns or pronouns they modify. In each of the examples, the participial phrase could be moved before *the construction worker*. You can illustrate this point with the following sentence.

   Thinking quickly, the construction worker moved to the right.
5. Participial phrases can be formed in a number of ways. Ask students to explain how each participial phrase above was formed. Help them identify the adverb *quickly,* which was added in the first sentence, the prepositional phrase *into the building* in the second sentence, and the complement *a hard hat* in the third sentence.

More About the Writer

Ambrose Bierce's (1842–1914?) writing and philosophy of life were shaped by his career as a Union officer in the Civil War. After the war, Bierce settled in San Francisco as a journalist. His column "The Prattler," which appeared from 1877 to 1896, mixed political and social satire, literary reviews, and gossip. He also published two collections of short stories, *Tales of Soldiers and Civilians* and *Can Such Things Be?* His best-known work is *The Devil's Dictionary* (1906). In 1913, at age 71, the lonely writer traveled to Mexico, a country in the midst of a bloody civil war. To this day, his fate is unknown.

Step-by-Step Teaching Guide

Grammar in Literature

1. Have a student volunteer read the passage aloud.
2. Have students tell what each participle modifies.

Answer Key

Exercise 11

1. Discovered in the northwest, petroleum reserves helped to boost the economy of New Mexico. (arrow to *petroleum reserves*)
2. More oil reserves, hiding in the southeast, were also found in the 1920's. (arrow to *more oil reserves*)
3. Twenty years later, the federal government, looking for a sparsely populated area, went to New Mexico. (arrow to *federal government*)
4. They decided that the desert, acting as a testing site, was to be used to explode atomic bombs during World War II. (arrow to *desert*)
5. Los Alamos, established as the headquarters, became busy with atomic energy research. (arrow to *Los Alamos*)

Exercise 12

1. The first atomic bomb, exploded on the White Sands Proving Grounds, was tested in 1945.
2. The production of atomic weapons, beginning at Sandia Base of Albuquerque, gave rise to many other industries.
3. Oil reserves found on the Navajo and Jicarilla reservations increased New Mexico's wealth.
4. These resources, now owned by the Navajo and Jicarilla, generate income for Native Americans there.
5. Improving living conditions, the money is also used for education.

Critical Viewing

Describe Students may suggest the following. *Rising in the east, the sun shines on this scene* or *The cliff, lit by the sun, is brighter than the rest of the picture.*

20.1

Exercise 11 **Recognizing Participial Phrases** Copy the following sentences. Underline each participial phrase and draw an arrow pointing from it to the word or words it modifies.

1. Discovered in the northwest, petroleum reserves helped to boost the economy of New Mexico.
2. More oil reserves, hiding in the southeast, were also found in the 1920's.
3. Twenty years later, the federal government, looking for a sparsely populated area, went to New Mexico.
4. They decided that the desert, acting as a testing site, was to be used to explode atomic bombs during World War II.
5. Los Alamos, established as the headquarters, became busy with atomic energy research.

Exercise 12 **Combining Sentences Using Participial Phrases** Combine each pair of sentences below into a single sentence containing a participial phrase.

EXAMPLE: A new dam was completed in 1916. It made large-scale irrigation farming possible.

ANSWER: A new dam, making large-scale irrigation farming possible, was completed in 1916.

1. The first atomic bomb was tested in 1945. It was exploded on the White Sands Proving Grounds.
2. The production of atomic weapons began at Sandia Base of Albuquerque. It gave rise to many other industries.
3. Oil reserves were found on the Navajo and Jicarilla reservations. The reserves increased New Mexico's wealth.
4. These resources are now owned by the Navajo and the Jicarilla. They generate income for Native Americans there.
5. The money has been used for areas such as education. It has improved living conditions.

More Practice

Grammar Exercise Workbook
- pp. 77–82

On-line Exercise Bank
- Section 20.1

Go on-line: PHSchool.com
Enter Web Code: eck-8002

iText

Get instant feedback! Exercises 11 and 12 are available on-line or on CD-ROM.

▼ Critical Viewing
Write two sentences to describe this picture, and include a participial phrase in each one. **[Describe]**

Gerunds

Like present participles, *gerunds* end in *-ing*. While present participles are used as adjectives, gerunds are used as nouns. Like other nouns, gerunds can be used as subjects, direct objects, predicate nouns, and objects of prepositions.

KEY CONCEPT A **gerund** is a form of verb that acts as a noun. ■

USE OF GERUNDS IN SENTENCES	
Subject	*Remodeling* the building's style was a good idea.
Direct Object	Michael enjoys *painting*.
Predicate Noun	His favorite sport is *fishing*.
Object of a Preposition	Lucille never gets tired of *singing*.

Exercise 13 **Identifying Gerunds** Write the gerund(s) from the sentences below, and label each one *subject, direct object, predicate noun,* or *object of a preposition.*

EXAMPLE: Touring New Mexico's beautiful sites is recommended.

ANSWER: Touring (subject)

1. Tourists in New Mexico may enjoy horseback riding at a dude ranch.
2. Hiking and camping are year-round activities in New Mexico.
3. Visitors may also find excitement in visiting the ancient ruins of the Native Americans who have lived here for thousands of years.
4. Native American dancing and festivals draw many visitors to New Mexico.
5. Above all, touring New Mexico is a pleasant vacation.

Exercise 14 **Writing With Gerunds** Write a series of sentences using each of the following gerunds.

1. weaving
2. skiing
3. traveling
4. ballooning
5. golfing

Step-by-Step Teaching Guide

Gerunds

1. Verbs can also become nouns in sentences.
2. Write the following sentences on the board to show how a word can be a verb in one sentence and a gerund in another.

   She bowls.

   She likes bowling as a sport.

   Bowls describes an action, while *bowling* describes a thing: the sport of bowling.
3. Write the following list of verbs on the board and assign students to work with partners to turn the verbs into gerunds, which they can then use in sentences.

   see *start*
   hold *watch*
   clean
4. Remind students that gerunds are simply verbs acting as nouns and that nouns are used many different ways in sentences. They can be subjects, direct objects, predicate nouns, or objects of a preposition.
5. Use the sentences students created from the words listed above to help them practice identifying the different ways gerunds are used. Have several students read aloud their sentences and then copy them onto the board. Make sure their gerund use is correct; then help them identify how the gerund is being used in each sentence.

Answer Key

Exercise 13

1. riding—direct object
2. Hiking, camping—subject
3. visiting—object of preposition
4. dancing—subject
5. touring—subject

Exercise 14

1. Jenny likes weaving rugs.
2. Mike goes skiing often.
3. Traveling is my favorite hobby.
4. I like to go ballooning.
5. George goes golfing on Tuesdays.

Step-by-Step Teaching Guide

Gerund Phrases

1. Gerunds can also be expanded into phrases. Unlike participles introducing participial phrases, however, gerunds don't always introduce gerund phrases. Write the following sentence on the board as an example.

   The frantic, worried whispering continued for several minutes.

   The gerund whispering, a noun form of the verb whisper, acts as part of phrase that includes the adjectives that modify it.

2. Explain that the best way to identify gerund phrases is to identify the gerund first, decide how that gerund is being used in the sentence, and then find the other words that expand the meaning of the gerund. In addition to appearing with adjectives, gerunds form phrases with direct objects, with prepositional phrases, and with adverbs and prepositional phrases.

Answer Key

Exercise 15

1. Setting turquoise stones in silver—subject
2. shaping pottery—object of a preposition
3. baking a piece of pottery—object of a preposition; painting it—predicate noun
4. pottery making—direct object
5. pottery making—object of a preposition
6. Camping, fishing—subject
7. attracting tourists—object of a preposition
8. video recording—subject
9. making a living—object of a preposition; raising livestock—object of preposition
10. farming—direct object

20.1

Gerund Phrases

A gerund can also be part of a phrase.

KEY CONCEPT A **gerund phrase** is a gerund with modifiers or a complement, all acting together as a noun. ■

The chart shows how gerunds are expanded.

GERUND PHRASES	
Gerund With Adjectives	*The loud, shrill howling* continued all morning.
Gerund With Direct Object	*Using trees as lumber* is an important part of the New Mexican economy.
Gerund With Prepositional Phrase	He helped the police by *telling about his experience.*
Gerund With Adverb and Prepositional Phrase	Pueblo tribe members astound spectators by *dancing skillfully on stage.*

Exercise 15 **Identifying Gerund Phrases** Write the gerund phrase(s) in the sentences below. Label each one *subject, direct object, predicate noun,* or *object of a preposition.*

EXAMPLE: One skill of the Pueblo people in New Mexico is making jewelry.

ANSWER: making jewelry (predicate noun)

1. Setting turquoise stones in silver is a common jewelry-making practice.
2. The Pueblo also earn their money by shaping pottery.
3. The next step after baking a piece of pottery is painting it.
4. Some Pueblo groups teach pottery making to tourists.
5. The San Ildefonso Pueblo is famous for its black-on-black pottery making.
6. Camping and fishing on the Isleta Reservation are popular tourist activities.
7. Not all Pueblo people are interested in attracting tourists.
8. During some of the ceremonial dances, video recording is not allowed.
9. Another way of making a living is by raising livestock.
10. Government reports consider farming a major source of employment in the area.

More Practice

Grammar Exercise Workbook
- pp. 81–82

On-line Exercise Bank
- Section 20.1

Go on-line:
PHSchool.com
Enter Web Code:
eck-8002

iText

Get instant feedback! Exercise 15 is available on-line or on CD-ROM.

Infinitives

Infinitives can be used as three different parts of speech: nouns, adjectives, and adverbs.

KEY CONCEPT An **infinitive** is the form of a verb that comes after the word *to* and acts as a noun, an adjective, or an adverb. ■

As a noun, an infinitive can be used as a subject, direct object, predicate noun, object of a preposition, or appositive, as shown in the chart below.

INFINITIVES USED AS NOUNS	
Subject	*To whistle* is difficult for some people.
Direct Object	As soon as she gets home, she hopes *to write.*
Predicate Noun	His dream has always been *to travel.*
Object of a Preposition	The Spaniards had no choice except *to leave.*
Appositive	Her decision, *to listen,* was a wise one.

Infinitives can also be used as adjectives and adverbs. In the chart below, infinitives answer the same questions as adjectives and adverbs.

INFINITIVES USED AS ADJECTIVES AND ADVERBS	
Adjective	In New Mexico, the first radio station *to succeed* was KOB in Albuquerque. (Which kind of station?) The person *to contact* is the dean. (Which person?)
Adverb	This is easy *to do.* (Easy in what manner?) Ready *to please,* the guides at Carlsbad Caverns work hard to provide enjoyable tours. (Ready in what manner?)

Grammar and Style Tip

Prepositional phrases beginning with the word *to* are often confused with infinitives. If the word immediately following *to* is a verb, then the phrase is an infinitive; otherwise, *to* begins a prepositional phrase.

Step-by-Step Teaching Guide

Infinitives

1. The infinitive form of any verb is created by simply putting *to* in front of the verb. Write the following examples on the board.

<u>*Verb*</u>	<u>*Infinitive*</u>
run	*to run*
see	*to see*
worry	*to worry*

2. Have students add to this list verbally so that they will feel comfortable working with verbs as infinitives.
3. Explain that infinitives can be used as nouns, adjectives, and adverbs. Have students review the descriptions of infinitives used as nouns, adjectives, and adverbs in their textbooks. Then write the following sentences on the board.

   <u>To run</u> away would be a bad idea. (noun)

   The first person <u>to run</u> was the captain. (adjective)

   Eager <u>to run</u>, they set off quickly. (adverb)

4. Ask students to use each of the other infinitives above *(to see, to worry)* in three sentences of their own, with each sentence containing a different form of infinitive usage.

TIME SAVERS!

Answers on Transparency Use the Grammar Exercises Answers on Transparencies for Chapter 20 to have students correct their own or one another's exercises.

On-Line Exercise Bank Have students complete the exercises on computer. The Auto Check feature will grade their work for you!

Answer Key

Exercise 16

1. to accommodate
2. to look
3. To use
4. to sleep
5. to have

Exercise 17

Answers will vary.

1. To sing a song is a sign of happiness.—noun
2. Teenagers think having a car to drive is happiness.—adjective
3. People went to the meeting to give thanks.—adverb
4. To walk to school takes 10 minutes.—noun
5. I promised to tell no one.—noun
6. We were asked to contribute.—noun
7. It was difficult to act.—adverb
8. I want to be alone.—noun
9. A wish to sleep is not always granted.—adjective
10. Time to dream is a luxury.—adjective

Critical Viewing

Describe Possible explanations might include *To reach the upper levels is difficult.*

Exercise 16 **Identifying Infinitives** List the infinitives in the following sentences.

EXAMPLE: The Taos were said to be the first apartment-house builders.
ANSWER: to be

1. Tall homes, some five stories high, were built to accommodate the ancient Taos population.
2. When the Europeans arrived, they thought the houses were fascinating to look at.
3. To use these same houses today is not uncommon.
4. The Navajo tribe had homes to sleep in called hogans.
5. Navajo hogans, in contrast to the homes of the Taos, were built to have only one room.

Exercise 17 **Writing Sentences With Infinitives** Use the infinitives below to write ten sentences. Label each use of an infinitive a *noun*, an *adjective*, or an *adverb*.

1. to sing
2. to drive
3. to give
4. to walk
5. to tell
6. to contribute
7. to act
8. to be
9. to sleep
10. to dream

More Practice

Grammar Exercise Workbook
- pp. 83–84

On-line Exercise Bank
- Section 20.1

Go on-line: PHSchool.com
Enter Web Code: eck-8002

▼ **Critical Viewing** The homes in which the Taos lived, called pueblos, are pictured here. How would you describe them? What infinitives might you use in your description? **[Describe]**

TIME SAVERS!

Answers on Transparency Use the Grammar Exercises Answers on Transparencies for Chapter 20 to have students correct their own or one another's exercises.

On-Line Exercise Bank Have students complete the exercises on computer. The Auto Check feature will grade their work for you!

Infinitive Phrases

Infinitives, like gerunds and participles, can be combined with other words to form phrases.

KEY CONCEPT An **infinitive phrase** is an infinitive with modifiers or a complement, all acting together as a single part of speech. ■

The following chart shows how infinitives can be expanded.

INFINITIVE PHRASES	
Infinitive With Adverb	It will be important *to listen carefully.*
Infinitive With Prepositional Phrase	*To ski in New Mexico,* you must travel high into the mountains.
Infinitive With Direct Object	In 1912, the United States Legislature decided *to admit New Mexico* to the Union.
Infinitive With Indirect and Direct Objects	I need *to give you my new telephone number.*

Exercise 18 **Identifying Infinitive Phrases** List the infinitive phrases in the following sentences.

EXAMPLE: It is an advantage for a state to have rich mineral resources.

ANSWER: to have rich mineral resources

1. New Mexico has petroleum, potash, copper, and natural gas—to name a few.
2. During the spring of 1950, a man bent down to pick up a yellow rock.
3. This rock turned out to be high-grade uranium ore.
4. New Mexico now claims to have 72 percent of the country's uranium reserves.
5. Uranium is a radioactive element that is used to create nuclear energy.

▼ Critical Viewing Judging by this photograph, what can you conclude about a miner's work? **[Analyze]**

Step-by-Step Teaching Guide

Infinitive Phrases

1. Focus on the example sentence for an infinitive phrase with a direct object.
2. Be sure students can differentiate between the infinitive *(to admit)* and the prepositional phrase *(to the Union).*
3. Have students use the chart and give their own examples of infinitives with adverbs, prepositional phrases, direct objects, and indirect objects.

Answer Key

Exercise 18

1. to name a few
2. to pick up a yellow rock
3. to be high grade uranium ore
4. to have 72 percent
5. to create nuclear energy

Critical Viewing

Analyze Students may suggest to work as a miner is boring, difficult, or dangerous.

ONGOING ASSESSMENT: Assess Mastery

Use the following resources to assess mastery of different types of phrases.

In the Textbook	Technology
Chapter Review, pp. 460–461 Standardized Test Preparation Workshop, pp. 462–463	On-Line Exercise Bank, Section 20.1

Step-by-Step Teaching Guide

Fill in the Blanks with Phrases

Teaching Resources: Hands-on Grammar Activity Book, Chapter 20

1. Have students refer to their Hands-on Grammar activity books or give them copies of the relevant pages for this activity.
2. Have students identify the phrases in the white strips as adverb phrases and those in the tinted strip as adjective phrases.
3. Ask students how the verbs (action or linking) might help with this identification.

Find It in Your Reading

Explain how their choices change the meaning of the original piece.

Find It in Your Writing

Have students work with a partner to experiment with other adjective and adverb phrases for samples of each other's writing.

20.1

Hands-on Grammar

Fill in the Blanks With Phrases

To demonstrate how adjective and adverb phrases affect the overall meaning of a sentence, complete the following activity with a small group.

Brainstorm for a list of sentences in which you leave a blank for an adjective phrase or an adverb phrase. (See the examples below.) Write these sentences with magic markers on construction paper.

Then, come up with different adverb phrases and adjective phrases you can use to complete each sentence. Have a group member record each phrase that is suggested.

When you have finished, try piecing some of the sentences together to form a paragraph. Share your paragraph with the class.

We left ______________.

We left at three in the morning.

We left after a three-hour delay.

We left before anyone else.

The singer ______________ was the first to perform.

The singer with the terrible voice was the first to perform.

The singer with the bright blue suit was the first to perform.

Find It in Your Reading Take some of your sentences from a short story or piece of nonfiction you have just read.

Find It in Your Writing Try this process with a piece of your own writing. Cut out small pieces of paper, and place them over the adjective and adverb phrases. Experiment with other adjective and adverb phrases. See if any of the replacements convey your intended meaning better than the original phrase.

TIME SAVERS!

Hands-on Grammar
Use the Hands-on Grammar activity sheet for Chapter 20 to facilitate this activity.

Section 20.1 **Section Review**

GRAMMAR EXERCISES 19–25

Exercise 19 **Identifying Verbs and Participles** Label each underlined word a *verb* or a *participle*. If it is a participle, write the word it modifies.

1. When the Spaniards arrived in New Mexico, the Pueblo population numbered between 40,000 and 50,000.
2. Many had adopted a farming lifestyle.
3. Domesticated animals included dogs and turkeys.
4. The arriving Spaniards gave the name "Pueblos," meaning "Townsmen," to the people of this area because most of them lived in organized cities.
5. Almost all of their well-built villages were eventually destroyed.

Exercise 20 **Identifying Gerunds and Gerund Phrases** Write the gerund or gerund phrase from each sentence below.

1. Living in the desert posed a problem for some early settlers.
2. Spanish power was destroyed because of internal bickering.
3. The organizing of a revolt by Native Americans was undertaken by a man named Pope.
4. The planning took about five years.
5. Most of the five years were spent uniting the various Pueblo peoples.

Exercise 21 **Identifying Infinitives and Infinitive Phrases** Write the infinitive or infinitive phrase from each sentence.

1. Pope's revolt included plans to launch a surprise attack on the Spaniards.
2. He thought the weakly guarded settlement would be easy to conquer.
3. Pope wanted to return the Native Americans to their former way of life.
4. He wanted to completely expel the Spaniards from the region.
5. Even though many supported Pope, this idea was not to be popular among all of the Pueblo people.

Exercise 22 **Classifying All Types of Phrases** Identify the adverb phrases, adjective phrases, appositives, participles, gerunds, and infinitives in the following:

Our visit to New Mexico was great. Watching the sun rise over the desert is one of the greatest memories I have from any vacation. Taos, a small town in the mountains, was my favorite place to visit. The skiing there is fantastic, and the town is filled with great restaurants and interesting shops.

Exercise 23 **Find It in Your Reading** Identify the prepositional phrases and participial phrases in this passage from a story by Ambrose Bierce.

So Carter Druse, bowing reverently to his father, who returned the salute with a stately courtesy that masked a breaking heart, left the home of his childhood to go soldiering.

Exercise 24 **Find It in Your Writing** Look through your portfolio. Find two examples of each type of phrase you've learned about in this section.

Exercise 25 **Writing Application** Write a short paper about New Mexico. Include sentences that contain prepositional phrases, participial phrases, and appositive phrases. Circle and label each example.

ASSESS and CLOSE

Section Review

Each of these exercises correlates to a concept in the section on phrases, pages 432–445. These exercises may be used for more practice, for reteaching, or for review of the Key Concepts presented. Answers for all chapter exercises are available in *Grammar Exercises Answers on Transparencies* in your teaching resources.

Answer Key

Exercise 19

1. verb
2. participle—lifestyle
3. participle—animals
4. participle—Spaniards; participle—cities
5. participle—villages; verb

Exercise 20

1. Living in the desert
2. internal bickering
3. The organizing
4. The planning
5. uniting the various Pueblo peoples

Exercise 21

1. to launch
2. to conquer
3. to return
4. to completely expel
5. to be popular

Exercise 22

1. to New Mexico—adjective phrase
2. Watching—gerund; over the desert—adverb phrase; of the greatest moments—adjective phrase, from any vacation—adverb phrase
3. a small town in the mountains—appositive, in the mountains—adjective phrase; to visit—infinitive
4. skiing—gerund, interesting—participle [Note that *with* functions as part of the verb and does not introduce a prepositional phrase.]

Exercise 23

Find It in Your Reading
prepositional phrases: to his father, with a stately courtesy, of his childhood
participial phrases: bowing reverently, breaking heart

continued

Answer Key continued

Exercise 24

Find It in Your Writing
Suggest that students work in small groups to compare their sentences.

Exercise 25

Writing Application
Encourage students to use an encyclopedia to add facts not mentioned in this book.

PREPARE and ENGAGE

Interest GRABBER Ask students if they used building blocks when they were younger. Ask what they built. Explain that clauses are like the building blocks of sentences, with several different basic kinds of clauses combining to form every type of sentence used in speech and writing.

Activate Prior Knowledge

Ask students to tell what they remember about phrases: a group of words that functions as an adjective, an adverb, a verb, or a noun; does not have a subject and verb.

TEACH

Step-by-Step Teaching Guide

Clauses

1. Clauses, like phrases, are the building blocks of sentences. Unlike phrases, however, clauses do contain a subject and verb. Independent clauses, just as their name implies, can stand independently as sentences.
2. Have students review the first set of examples in their textbooks; then put the following groups of words on the board.

   what he would see

   walking around the corner

   He guessed.

   Ask which is a sentence. (*He guessed,* because it contains a subject and a verb and expresses a complete thought, which also makes it an independent clause.)
3. Write the following subordinate clause and sentence on the board.

   if he walked around the corner

   He guessed what he would see if he walked around the corner.

   Ask students whether *if he walked around the corner* is a sentence. Point out that it does have a verb, *walked,* and a subject, *he.* The clause lacks something, however, which is a description of what would happen if he walked around the corner. Therefore, it does not express a complete thought. A clause that cannot stand alone is called a subordinate clause.

Section 20.2

Clauses

This section explains the second important sentence element, the *clause.*

KEY CONCEPT A **clause** is a group of words with its own subject and verb. ■

There are two basic types of clauses, which have an important difference between them. The first type is called an *independent clause.*

KEY CONCEPT An **independent clause** has a subject and a verb and can stand by itself as a complete sentence. ■

The length of a clause has little to do with whether it can stand alone. Each of the following examples can stand alone because it expresses a complete thought.

INDEPENDENT CLAUSES:
The reporter shouted.
Jerusalem is a relatively small city in area.
The Dome of the Rock, a Jerusalem landmark, is a holy site.

The second type of clause is called a *subordinate clause.* Like an independent clause, it contains both a subject and a verb. A subordinate clause, however, is not a sentence.

KEY CONCEPT A **subordinate clause** has a subject and a verb but cannot stand by itself as a sentence. It is only part of a sentence. ■

A subordinate clause does not express a complete thought, even though it contains a subject and a verb.

SUBORDINATE CLAUSES:
when the phone (S) rang (V)
whom I (S) often admired (V)
since the country (S) was divided (V)

Each of these clauses has a subject and a verb, but each lacks something. Examine, for example, the first clause: *when the phone rang. When the phone rang,* what happened? More information is needed to complete the thought.

Theme: Jerusalem

In this section, you will learn about clauses. The examples and exercises are about Jerusalem.

Cross-Curricular Connection: Social Studies

More Practice

Grammar Exercise Workbook
- pp. 85–86

On-line Exercise Bank
- Section 20.2

Go on-line: PHSchool.com *Enter Web Code:* eck-8002

TIME AND RESOURCE MANAGER

Resources
Print: Grammar Exercise Workbook, pp. 85–92
Technology: Writing and Grammar iText, Section 20.2; On-Line Exercise Bank, Section 20.2

In-Depth Coverage	Accelerated Pace
• Work through all key concepts, pp. 448–453. • Assign and review Exercises 26–31.	• Assign Section Review Exercises 40–41.

KEY CONCEPT Subordinate clauses begin with subordinating conjunctions or relative pronouns. ■

Why does a subordinate clause not express a complete thought? The answer can often be found in the first word of the clause. Some subordinate clauses begin with subordinating conjunctions, such as *if, since, when, although, because,* and *while.* Others begin with relative pronouns, such as *who, which,* or *that.* These words are clues that the clause may not be able to stand alone. Compare, for example, the independent clauses and the subordinate clauses in the following chart. Notice how the addition of subordinating words changes the meaning of the independent clauses.

COMPARING TWO KINDS OF CLAUSES

Independent	Subordinate
He (S) arrived (V) this morning	*if* he (S) arrived (V) this morning
The mosque (S) has (V) a golden dome.	*since* the mosque (S) has (V) a dome

In order to make sense, a subordinate clause usually must be combined with an independent clause. In the following examples, the subordinate clauses are italicized.

EXAMPLES: *Since he arrived this morning,* he has been working at top speed.
I will call the manager of the hotel tomorrow *if the room is not clean.*

Exercise 26 **Identifying Subordinate and Independent Clauses** Copy each of the following sentences. Underline the main clause twice. Underline the subordinate clause once.

1. Even though it is not large, Jerusalem has many museums and holy sites.
2. Since the city was politically divided in 1948, various religions have claimed ownership of the holy sites.
3. When the city was divided, Jerusalem became known as East and West Jerusalem.
4. East Jerusalem has most of the tourist attractions and museums because it is centered around the walled Old City.
5. Because Jerusalem has three Sabbaths, a large portion of West Jerusalem closes down on Friday, Saturday, and Sunday.

▼ **Critical Viewing** Use the subordinate clause *Because the buildings are close together* in a sentence about this picture. **[Describe]**

Critical Viewing

Describe Students may suggest: Because the buildings are close together, there isn't any more room for newer ones.

Step-by-Step Teaching Guide

Subordinate Clauses

1. Subordinate clauses often begin with words that hint at other information that is not provided in the clause. Write the following subordinate clauses on the board and ask students to place them in complete sentences that provide the missing information.

   Subordinating Conjunctions
   while I waited
   since she understood the problem

   Relative Pronouns
   who ran into the building
   which we didn't understand

2. Use students' sentences to reinforce the idea that recognizing signal words such as subordinating conjunctions and relative pronouns is a good way to identify subordinate clauses.

Customize for *ESL Students*

Students learning English may have difficulty understanding the distinctions between sentence types. Long words such as *independent, subordinate,* and *coordinating conjunctions* may be confusing and hard to pronounce. Help students remember what these words mean by pointing to parts of the words with which students may be familiar.

Answer Key

Exercise 26

1. Even though it is not large, Jerusalem has many museums and holy sites.
2. Since the city was politically divided in 1948, various religions have claimed ownership of the holy sites.
3. When the city was divided, Jerusalem became known as East and West Jerusalem.
4. East Jerusalem has most of the tourist attractions and museums because it is centered around the walled Old City.
5. Because Jerusalem has three Sabbaths, a large portion of West Jerusalem closes down on Friday, Saturday, and Sunday.

Step-by-Step Teaching Guide

Adjective Clauses

1. The basic concept students learned when studying phrases holds true for clauses: A group of words can act as a single part of speech. Remind them that subordinate clauses contain a verb and a subject, but they need to be matched with an independent clause to form a complete thought. Explain that when subordinate clauses act as adjectives, they add information to a sentence by answering the questions *What kind?* and *Which one?*
2. Illustrate how adjective clauses modify a noun or a pronoun in a sentence and add information to it with the following examples.

   I enjoyed the movie.

   that we just saw

   I enjoyed the movie that we just saw.

   Ask whether the first two examples are complete sentences. (The first one is a complete sentence, but *that we just saw* is not.) Have students explain what makes the second example an incomplete thought. (It doesn't tell us what was just seen.)
3. Ask which word the subordinate clause *that we just saw* modifies in the third example. *(movie)*

Answer Key

Exercise 27

1. East Jerusalem covers an area that is almost twice as large as West Jerusalem. modifies *area*
2. East Jerusalem includes the Old City, which lies on the site of ancient Jerusalem. modifies *Old City*
3. West Jerusalem has modern factories that produce chemicals, clothing, leather goods, and machinery. modifies *factories*
4. In ancient times, the temple, which was the heart of the city, stood on a hill in eastern Jerusalem. modifies *temple*
5. In the time since the temples were destroyed, other buildings have been constructed on the site. modifies *time*

20.2

Using Adjective Clauses

Some subordinate clauses act as adjectives.

KEY CONCEPT An **adjective clause** is a subordinate clause that modifies a noun or pronoun. ■

Adjective clauses, like one-word adjectives or adjective phrases, answer the questions *What kind?* or *Which one?*

Recognizing Adjective Clauses

Most adjective clauses begin with one of the five relative pronouns: *that, which, who, whom,* or *whose.* Sometimes, an adjective clause will begin with an adverb such as *when* or *where.*

In the following chart, the adjective clauses are italicized. The arrow in each sentence points to the word in the independent clause that the adjective clause modifies.

ADJECTIVE CLAUSES
They visited the memorial *that remembers Holocaust victims.*
That British stamp, *which depicts Queen Victoria,* will be sold at auction.
The man *who opened the door* is my brother-in-law.
Marcia is the student *whom we chose to represent us in the debate.*
The museum *whose artifacts include the Dead Sea Scrolls* is located in West Jerusalem.

Exercise 27 **Identifying Adjective Clauses** Copy the following sentences onto your paper, and underline each adjective clause. Then, identify the word each clause modifies.

1. East Jerusalem covers an area that is almost twice as large as West Jerusalem.
2. East Jerusalem includes the Old City, which lies on the site of ancient Jerusalem.
3. West Jerusalem has modern factories that produce chemicals, clothing, leather goods, and machinery.
4. In ancient times, the temple, which was the heart of the city, stood on a hill in eastern Jerusalem.
5. In the time since the temples were destroyed, other buildings have been constructed on the site.

Spelling Tip

The possessive form of the word *who* is *whose.* The word *who's* is a contraction of *who is.*

iText

Get instant feedback! Exercise 27 is available on-line or on CD-ROM.

More Practice

Grammar Exercise Workbook
• pp. 85–88
On-line Exercise Bank
• Section 20.2
Go on-line: PHSchool.com
Enter Web Code: eck-8002

Combining Sentences With Adjective Clauses

Two sentences can be combined into one sentence by changing one of them into an adjective clause. Such a combination is useful when the information in both sentences is closely related. Notice how the two sentences in the following example are changed into one sentence. The new sentence consists of an independent clause and an adjective clause.

TWO SENTENCES: My history teacher has written books on John Adams, Thomas Jefferson, and Benjamin Franklin. My teacher is considered by many scholars to be an expert on the American Revolution.

SENTENCE WITH ADJECTIVE CLAUSE: My history teacher, *who is considered by many scholars to be an expert on the American Revolution,* has written books on John Adams, Thomas Jefferson, and Benjamin Franklin.

▼ Critical Viewing
Describe the scene shown here in a single sentence that contains an adjective clause. **[Describe]**

Exercise 28 **Combining Sentences Using Adjective Clauses** Change the second sentence in each of the following pairs into an adjective clause. Then, make the adjective clause part of the first sentence. You may have to add commas before and after some of the adjective clauses.

EXAMPLE: Israel is a small country in southwestern Asia. Israel is made up of the Coastal Plain, the Judeo-Galilean Highlands, the Rift Valley, and the Negev Desert.

ANSWER: Israel, which is made up of the Coastal Plain, the Judeo-Galilean Highlands, the Rift Valley, and the Negev Desert, is a small country in southwestern Asia.

1. Most Israelis live in the Coastal Plain.
   The Coastal Plain is a strip of fertile land along the Mediterranean Sea.
2. The Dead Sea is in the Rift Valley.
   The Rift Valley is a narrow strip of land in eastern Israel.
3. The West Bank is in the Judeo-Galilean Highlands.
   Several mountain ranges run through the Judeo-Galilean Highlands.
4. Parts of the Negev Desert are being irrigated to grow crops.
   The Negev Desert is the driest part of Israel.
5. The River Jordan empties into the Dead Sea.
   The River Jordan flows through the Rift Valley.

Step-by-Step Teaching Guide

Combining Sentences with Adjective Clauses

1. Because adjective clauses answer the questions *What kind?* and *Which one?* they can often be used to combine information from separate sentences.
2. The examples in the textbook illustrate how adjective clauses can be used to make sentences less choppy or repetitive. All of the information from one of the sentences is placed into an adjective clause that begins with *who* and answers the question *What kind?*
3. Have students read the example aloud. Ask what word the adjective clause modifies. *(teacher)* Point out that adjective clauses can actually replace sentences and help sentences convey more information.

Critical Viewing

Decsribe Students may respond: The animals that are in the picture are moving slowly.

Answer Key

Exercise 28

1. Most Israelis live in the Coastal Plain, which is a strip of fertile land along the Mediterranean Sea.
2. The Dead Sea is in the Rift Valley, which is a narrow strip of land in eastern Israel.
3. The West Bank is in the Judeo-Galilean Highlands, which contain several mountain ranges.
4. Parts of the Negev Desert, which is the driest part of Israel, are being irrigated to grow crops.
5. The River Jordan, which empties into the Dead Sea, flows through the Rift Valley.

Step-by-Step Teaching Guide

Adverb Clauses

1. Adverb clauses are subordinate clauses that modify verbs, adjectives, and adverbs. Adverb clauses also contain a noun and a verb but cannot stand alone as sentences. Adverb clauses, like all subordinate clauses, are usually incomplete thoughts, but they add meaning to sentences by answering the question *Where? When? In what manner? To what extent? Under what condition?* or *Why?*
2. Have students read the list of subordinating conjunctions and discuss how these words can answer the questions listed above. For example, *so that* can answer the question *Why?* Have students pick out several other conjunctions and match them with questions that adverb clauses answer.
3. Write the following sentences and clauses on the board.

   The carpenter began working.

   even though the oak boards hadn't yet been delivered

   The carpenter began working even though the oak boards hadn't yet been delivered.

   Ask whether the first two examples are complete sentences. (The first one is a complete sentence, but *even though the oak boards hadn't yet been delivered* is not, even though it contains a subject and verb.) Have students explain what makes the second example an incomplete thought. (It doesn't tell us what happened as a result of the oak boards' not having been delivered.)

20.2

Using Adverb Clauses

Some subordinate clauses act as adverbs.

KEY CONCEPT An **adverb clause** is a subordinate clause that modifies a verb, an adjective, or an adverb. ■

Adverb clauses can answer any of the following questions about the words they modify: *Where? When? In what manner? To what extent? Under what condition?* or *Why?*

Recognizing Adverb Clauses

Adverb clauses begin with subordinating conjunctions.

SUBORDINATING CONJUNCTIONS				
after	because	in order that	though	whenever
although	before	since	unless	where
as	even though	so that	until	wherever
as if	if	than	when	while
as long as				

In the following example, the adverb clause is italicized. The arrow points to the word that the clause modifies.

EXAMPLE: Jerusalem is interesting *because it is home to several diverse religions.*

When an adverb clause begins a sentence, a comma is used.

EXAMPLE: *When she reached the station,* Marie phoned.

Exercise 29 **Identifying Adverb Clauses** Copy the sentences below onto your paper, and underline each adverb clause.

1. Because most of the region is desert, climate dictates where people live in the Middle East.
2. Unless there is enough rain, farming is not possible.
3. Wherever there have been floods, fertile soil is left behind.
4. Ancient Egyptians built irrigation systems so that they could grow crops in the desert.
5. As population grows in the Middle East, the demands for water will become greater.

Answer Key

Exercise 29

1. Because most of the region is desert, climate dictates where people live in the Middle East.
2. Unless there is enough rain, farming is not possible.
3. Wherever there have been floods, fertile soil is left behind.
4. Ancient Egyptians built irrigation systems so that they could grow crops in the desert.
5. As population grows in the Middle East, the demands for water will become greater.

Exercise 30 **Combining Sentences With Adverb Clauses** Combine each pair of sentences by changing one of them into an adverb clause. Choose an appropriate subordinating conjunction from the chart on the previous page. Compare your sentences to a classmate's, and discuss how the choice of the subordinating conjunction affects the meaning of the sentence.

1. Jerusalem is a great vacation destination. It is filled with interesting historical sites.
2. Traveling through the desert in Israel can be tiring for visitors. Temperatures often exceed 100 degrees.
3. We went to Israel. We experienced jet lag on our first day there.
4. Israel won its independence in 1948. The people celebrated.
5. Tel Aviv is the largest city in Israel. Many more tourists visit Jerusalem.

Elliptical Adverb Clauses

In certain adverb clauses, words are left out. These clauses are said to be *elliptical.*

KEY CONCEPT In an *elliptical adverb clause*, the verb or the subject and verb are understood rather than stated. ■

Many elliptical adverb clauses are introduced by one of two subordinating conjunctions: *as* or *than.* In the following examples, the understood words have been added in parentheses. The first elliptical adverb clause is missing a verb; the second is missing a subject and a verb.

EXAMPLES: My brother can eat as much *as I* (*can eat*).
I liked this book more *than* (*I liked*) that one.

Exercise 31 **Recognizing Elliptical Adverb Clauses** For each of the following sentences, write the elliptical clause. Next to it, write out the full adverb clause, adding the understood words.

1. The Dead Sea in Israel has a lower elevation than Death Valley in California.
2. I enjoyed Jerusalem more than Tel Aviv.
3. Israel's population is larger than Ireland's.
4. Israel's history is as interesting as ours.
5. I have spent more time in Israel than in Lebanon.

More Practice

Grammar Exercise Workbook
- pp. 89–92

On-line Exercise Bank
- Section 20.2

Go on-line:
PHSchool.com
Enter Web Code:
eck-8002

iText

Get instant feedback! Exercise 31 is available on-line or on CD-ROM.

Answer Key

Exercise 30

Sample answers

1. Because it is filled with interesting historical sites, Jerusalem is a great vacation destination.
2. Traveling through the desert in Israel can be tiring because temperatures often exceed 100 degrees.
3. When we went to Israel, we experienced jet lag on our first day there.
4. After Israel won its independence in 1948, the people celebrated.
5. Although Tel Aviv is the largest city in Israel, many more tourists visit Jerusalem.

Step-by-Step Teaching Guide

Elliptical Adverb Clauses

1. In certain cases, the subject or the verb of an adverb phrase can be understood rather than stated.
2. Write the following sentences on the board.

   Our high school has more students than their high school does.

   Our high school has more students than theirs does.

   The subject of the adverb clause, *high school,* is understood in the second sentence. The writer is comparing high schools. By using an elliptical adverb clause, the sentence is less repetitive.
3. Elliptical adverb clauses often begin with the subordinating conjunctions *as* and *than.*

Answer Key

Exercise 31

1. than Death Valley in California; than the elevation of Death Valley in California
2. than Tel Aviv; than I enjoyed Tel Aviv
3. than Ireland's; than Ireland's population
4. as ours; as our history
5. than in Lebanon; than I have spent in Lebanon

ONGOING ASSESSMENT: Monitor and Reinforce

If students miss more than two items in Exercises 19–24, refer them to the following additional practice.

In the Textbook	Print Resources	Technology
Section Review, Ex. 41, p. 459 Standardized Test Preparation Workshop, pp. 462–463	Grammar Exercise Workbook, pp. 85–92	On-Line Exercise Bank, Section 20.2

Step-by-Step Teaching Guide

The Simple Sentence

1. All sentences can be organized into four basic sentence structures: *simple, compound, complex,* and *compound-complex.* Sentences are classified according to the number and kind of clauses they contain.
2. A simple sentence contains only one independent clause.
3. Review the list of simple sentence types and the examples. Have students read the examples aloud and explain why each adheres to the basic definition of an independent clause.
4. Note that simple sentences can have many elements, including prepositional phrases *(in the play),* and multiple subjects and verbs, as long as the sentence contains only one clause.

Answer Key

Exercise 32

1. The Dome of the Rock was completed around 692.
2. The dome surrounds a huge rock.
3. The dome is a holy site for Muslims.
4. The walls and ceiling of this shrine are decorated in Islamic style.
5. Jews and Christians also have holy places in Jerusalem.

Exercise 33

Answers will vary.

Critical Viewing

Describe Students may write that the dome is gold.

20.2

Classifying Sentences by Structure

There are four basic sentence structures: *simple, compound, complex,* and *compound-complex.*

The Simple Sentence

KEY CONCEPT A **simple sentence** consists of a single independent clause. ■

A simple sentence can be short or long. It must contain a subject and a verb. It may also contain complements, modifiers, and phrases. Some simple sentences contain various compounds—a compound subject, a compound verb, or both. Other parts of the sentence may also be compound. A simple sentence, however, does not contain any subordinate clauses.

The following examples show a few of the many possible variations of a simple sentence. The subjects have been underlined once and the verbs twice.

ONE SUBJECT AND VERB:	The siren sounded.
COMPOUND SUBJECT:	Cats and dogs ran down the street.
COMPOUND VERB:	My sister acts and sings in the play.
COMPOUND SUBJECT AND VERB:	Art and archaeology reflect and explain Jerusalem's history.
WITH PHRASES AND COMPLEMENTS:	A written history dating back to 600 B.C. was found in a cave near Jerusalem.

Exercise 32 **Recognizing Simple Sentences** Copy each of these simple sentences onto your paper, and underline the subject once and the verb twice. (Some of the subjects and verbs may be compound.)

1. The Dome of the Rock was completed around 692.
2. The dome surrounds a huge rock.
3. The dome is a holy site for Muslims.
4. The walls and ceiling of this shrine are decorated in Islamic style.
5. Jews and Christians also have holy places in Jerusalem.

Exercise 33 **Identifying Simple Sentences in Real-World Writing** Read through an article in a newsmagazine to identify ten simple sentences. Notice whether these sentences appear together or are mixed in with other types of sentences.

Grammar and Style Tip

Following a series of longer sentences with a brief simple sentence is a good way to reinforce or emphasize a key point in your writing.

▼ Critical Viewing
Write a simple sentence describing the outside of the Dome of the Rock (shown here). **[Describe]**

TIME SAVERS!

Answers on Transparency Use the Grammar Exercises Answers on Transparencies for Chapter 20 to have students correct their own or one another's exercises.

On-Line Exercise Bank Have students complete the exercises on computer. The Auto Check feature will grade their work for you!

TIME AND RESOURCE MANAGER

Resources
Print: Grammar Exercise Workbook, pp. 93–94
Technology: Writing and Grammar iText, Section 20.2; On-Line Exercise Bank, Section 20.2

In-Depth Coverage	Accelerated Pace
• Cover pp. 454–458 in class. • Assign and review Exercises 32–39.	• Assign pp. 454–458 for independent student review. • Assign Section Review Exercises 41–42.

The Compound Sentence

Independent clauses are the key elements in a *compound sentence.*

KEY CONCEPT A **compound sentence** consists of two or more independent clauses. ■

The independent clauses in most compound sentences are joined by a comma and one of the coordinating conjunctions (*and, but, for, nor, or, so, yet*). Sometimes a semicolon (;) is used to join independent clauses in a compound sentence. Like simple sentences, compound sentences contain no subordinate clauses.

EXAMPLE: The population of Israel is approximately 4,700,000, but only 8 percent of the people live in rural areas.

Exercise 34 **Recognizing Compound Sentences** Copy the following compound sentences. Underline the subject once and the verb twice in each independent clause.

EXAMPLE: Israel is a democratic republic, and it has a parliament-cabinet form of government.

ANSWER: Israel is a democratic republic, and it has a parliament-cabinet form of government.

1. The prime minister is the head of the government, but the people also elect a president.
2. The president is elected to a five-year term, yet most of his or her duties are ceremonial.
3. The Knesset is the name of the parliament, and it is made up of 120 elected members.
4. Eighteen-year-olds can vote in Israel, but they must also serve in the armed forces.
5. Israeli men and women serve in the armed forces; men serve for three years, and women serve for two years.

Exercise 35 **Combining Simple Sentences to Form Compound Sentences** Go through a magazine article or a piece of your own writing to find five pairs of simple sentences that are related in meaning. Then, combine each pair of sentences into a compound sentence by adding a coordinating conjunction or a semicolon.

More Practice

Grammar Exercise Workbook
- pp. 93–94

On-line Exercise Bank
- Section 20.2

Go on-line:
PHSchool.com
Enter Web Code:
eck-8002

iText

Get instant feedback! Exercise 34 is available on-line or on CD-ROM.

ONGOING ASSESSMENT SYSTEM: Monitor and Reinforce

If students miss more than two items in Exercises 32 and 34, refer them to the following for additional practice.

In the Textbook	Print Resources	Technology
Ex. 42, p. 459 Ex. 51, p. 461	Grammar Exercise Workbook, pp. 93–94	On-Line Exercise Bank, Section 20.2

Step-by-Step Teaching Guide

The Compound Sentence

1. Compound sentences contain two or more independent clauses, joined in one sentence. There are no subordinate clauses in compound sentences.
2. Write the following sentences on the board.

   I liked the movie.

   I got tired near the end of it.

   Ask if both of these examples are independent clauses. Do both have a subject and a verb? Are both complete thoughts? Finally, have students suggest ways of joining the two sentences into one: *I liked the movie, but I got tired near the end of it.*
3. Review coordinating conjunctions (Chapter 18) and the use of semicolons (Chapter 26).

Integrating Workplace Skills

Being able to create fluid and interesting sentences will make students more successful in jobs in which they are required to write. Series of choppy sentences in which subjects are repeated detracts from students' ability to convey meaning and information efficiently.

Answer Key

Exercise 34

1. The prime minister is the head of the government, but the people also elect a president.
2. The president is elected to a five-year term, yet most of his or her duties are ceremonial.
3. The Knesset is the name of the parliament, and it is made up of 120 elected members.
4. Eighteen-year-olds can vote in Israel, but they must also serve in the armed forces.
5. Israeli men and women serve in the armed forces; men serve for three years, and women serve for two years.

Exercise 35

Answers will vary.

Step-by-Step Teaching Guide

The Complex Sentence

1. Complex sentences contain one independent clause and one or more subordinate clauses.
2. Independent clauses are often called main clauses in complex sentences. Students can use this information to help them remember the different roles of the clauses in complex sentences. The main or independent clause expresses the main idea of the sentence, while the subordinate clause, which acts as an adverb or an adjective, modifies other words in the sentence.

Answer Key

Exercise 36

1. (Because the city was on a hill surrounded by canyons and caverns,) its location was very safe.
2. However, David discovered, (when he came to conquer the city with his army,) (that the Jebusites got their drinking water from a spring outside the city walls.)
3. The water entered the city from tunnels (that were built under the city).
4. David's nephew, Joab, was able to unlock the city gates by night (when he swam through the tunnel).
5. (Because David's army entered the city unexpectedly,) the Jebusites were conquered.

Critical Viewing

Connect Encourage students to use complex sentences when describing whether they would like to visit Temple Mount. For example, *Because it is so large and impressive-looking, I would like to visit Temple Mount.*

The Complex Sentence

A sentence with an adjective or adverb clause is called a *complex sentence.*

KEY CONCEPT A **complex sentence** consists of one independent clause and one or more subordinate clauses. ■

The independent clause in a complex sentence is often called the *main clause* to distinguish it from the subordinate clause or clauses. The main clause and each subordinate clause have their own subjects and verbs. Those in the independent clause are called the *subject of the sentence* and the *main verb.*

EXAMPLES: When the fog lifted, (subordinate clause) we continued our trip. (main clause)

The person (main clause) who will speak last (subordinate clause) is my sister. (main clause)

In the first example, *we* is the subject of the sentence, and *continued* is the main verb. In the second example, *person* is the subject of the sentence, and *is* is the main verb.

Exercise 36 **Identifying the Parts of Complex Sentences** Copy each of the following complex sentences onto your paper. In each clause, underline the subject once and the verb twice. Then, put parentheses around each subordinate clause.

EXAMPLE: Four thousand years ago, the land where the Temple Mount now lies was in the hands of the Jebusites.

ANSWER: Four thousand years ago, the land (where the Temple Mount now lies) was in the hands of the Jebusites.

1. Because the city was on a hill surrounded by canyons and caverns, its location was very safe.
2. However, David discovered, when he came to conquer the city with his army, that the Jebusites got their drinking water from a spring outside the city walls.
3. The water entered the city from tunnels that were built under the city.
4. David's nephew, Joab, was able to unlock the city gates at night when he swam through the tunnel.
5. Because David's army entered the city unexpectedly, the Jebusites were conquered.

▼ **Critical Viewing** Judging by this picture, would you be interested in visiting Temple Mount? Why or why not? **[Connect]**

The Compound-Complex Sentence

A *compound-complex sentence*, as the name indicates, contains the elements of both a compound sentence and a complex sentence.

> **KEY CONCEPT** A **compound-complex sentence** consists of two or more independent clauses and one or more subordinate clauses. ■

EXAMPLE:
 subordinate clause *independent clause*
As <u>he was leaving</u> for school, <u>Larry</u> <u>remembered</u>

 independent clause
to take his lunch, but <u>he</u> <u>forgot</u> the report

 subordinate clause
that <u>he had finished</u> the night before.

> **Exercise 37** Identifying the Parts of Compound-Complex Sentences Copy each of the following compound-complex sentences onto your paper. In each clause, underline the subject once and the verb twice. Then, put parentheses around each subordinate clause.

EXAMPLE: The Israel Museum, which is found in West Jerusalem, has artifacts dating back to prehistoric man, and it keeps them on display for visitors.

ANSWER: <u>The Israel Museum</u>, (which is found in West Jerusalem), <u>has</u> artifacts dating back to prehistoric man, and <u>it</u> <u>keeps</u> them on display for visitors.

1. Tools and weapons that date back to before 500 B.C. show great skill, and they serve as evidence that their makers were very talented.
2. Because Israelites picked up many customs from the Egyptians, idols and extravagant jewelry are also on display; these artifacts date back to the time of Moses.
3. When we visited the museum, we also marveled at documents containing historical accounts written thousands of years ago; the accounts are recorded on clay and stone.
4. Because they have been preserved well over time, many ancient scrolls can be read by those who know Hebrew; included on these scrolls is the oldest spelling of "Jerusalem."
5. These writings have been determined to be as old as 2,600 years; because they are so old, they must be carefully protected behind glass.

> **More Practice**
>
> Grammar Exercise Workbook
> • pp. 93–94
> On-line Exercise Bank
> • Section 20.2
> *Go on-line:*
> PHSchool.com
> *Enter Web Code:*
> eck-8002
>
> **iText**
>
> Get instant feedback! Exercise 37 is available on-line or on CD-ROM.

PRENTICE HALL
Everyday Spelling

If you have taught the spelling skills in *Prentice Hall Everyday Spelling,* Grade 8, Chapter 23, in conjunction with this *Writing and Grammar* chapter, review and assess students' mastery of the skills before concluding the chapter.

> **Step-by-Step Teaching Guide**

The Compound-Complex Sentence

1. Write the following compound-complex sentence on the board:

 She was happy with her discovery, an ancient bowl, but she had to get it back to the laboratory, which was 60 miles away.

2. Ask which word signals that this sentence might contain more than one independent clause. *(but)* Ask what kind of clause might be introduced by *which.* (subordinate) Remind students that compound-complex sentences contain more than one independent clause and at least one subordinate clause. Ask if the sentence meets these criteria. (yes)

Customize for *More Advanced Students*

Ask students to work together to write the longest compound-complex sentence they can. Have them write it on the board and name each of the clauses.

Answer Key

> **Exercise 37**

1. <u>Tools</u> and <u>weapons</u> (that date back to before 500 b.c.) <u>show</u> great skill, and <u>they</u> <u>serve</u> as evidence (that their <u>makers</u> <u>were</u> very talented.)
2. (Because <u>Israelites</u> <u>picked up</u> many customs from the Egyptians,) <u>idols</u> and extravagant <u>jewelry</u> <u>are</u> also on display; these <u>artifacts</u> <u>date</u> back to the time of Moses.
3. (When <u>we</u> <u>visited</u> the museum), <u>we</u> also <u>marvelled</u> at documents containing historical accounts written thousands of years ago; the <u>accounts</u> <u>are recorded</u> on clay and stone.
4. (Because <u>they</u> <u>have been preserved</u> well over time,) many ancient <u>scrolls</u> <u>can be read</u> by those who know Hebrew; <u>included</u> on these scrolls <u>is</u> the oldest <u>spelling</u> of "Jerusalem."
5. The <u>writings</u> <u>have been determined</u> to be as old as 2,600 years; (because <u>they</u> <u>are</u> so old,) <u>they</u> <u>must be</u> carefully <u>protected</u> behind glass.

Step-by-Step Teaching Guide

Grammar in Literature

1. Have a volunteer read the passage aloud.
2. Ask students to identify the subject and verb in *That's*. (That is)
3. Have students discuss why Nye might have used complex sentences in her writing

More About the Writer

A poet, storyteller, songwriter, and teacher, Naomi Shihab Nye (born in 1952) spent her teenage years in Jerusalem. That enabled her to learn about her Arab heritage, which is reflected in much of her work.

Integrating Speaking and Listening Skills

Have students choose paragraphs from *Timeless Voices, Timeless Themes,* Silver by writers who use different kinds of sentences. Ask students to prepare and then read these paragraphs aloud, and ask the audience to listen for the way the sentences are structured.

Answer Key

Exercise 38

Answers will vary.

Exercise 39

Possible answer.

The Shrine of the Book, part of the Israel Museum, was designed and built to hold the Dead Sea Scrolls, which were discovered in 1947. This building, considered one of the finest examples of modern architecture, has enjoyed this reputation throughout its brief history. To preserve the Dead Sea Scrolls, the humidity, temperature, and light are all controlled in the museum. The scrolls are believed to be ancient religious texts, although only fragments of each exist, and the restoration of these fragments is a slow and painstaking process.

20.2

GRAMMAR IN LITERATURE

from Hamadi

Naomi Shihab Nye

In the following passage, the writer has used complex sentences. The subjects are underlined once, the verbs are underlined twice, and the subordinate clauses are in parentheses.

Sometimes Susan felt polite with them, (sorting attendance cards during her free period,) (listening to them gab about fingernail polish and television.) And other times she felt (she could run out of the building yelling.) That's when she daydreamed about Saleh Hamadi, (who had nothing to do with any of it.)

Exercise 38 **Writing Different Types of Sentences** Write a brief composition about a tourist destination that you find especially interesting. Vary the types of sentences that you use. Make sure that your paper includes at least two examples of each of the four sentence structures.

Exercise 39 **Revising to Improve Sentence Variety** Revise the following passage, combining simple sentences into compound, complex, and compound-complex sentences to improve variety.

The Shrine of the Book is part of the Israel Museum. It was designed and built to hold the Dead Sea Scrolls. The Dead Sea Scrolls were discovered in 1947. The Shrine of the Book has been considered one of the finest examples of modern architecture. The building has enjoyed this reputation throughout its brief history. The humidity, temperature, and light are controlled in the museum. This is done to preserve the Dead Sea Scrolls. The scrolls are believed to be ancient religious texts. However, only fragments of each exist. The restoration of the fragments is a slow and painstaking process.

ONGOING ASSESSMENT: Assess Mastery

Use the following resources to assess student mastery of phrases and clauses.

In the Textbook	Technology
Chapter Review, Ex. 49–52, pp. 460–461 Standardized Test Preparation Workshop, pp. 462–463	On-Line Exercise Bank, Section 20.2

Section 20.2 **Section Review**

GRAMMAR EXERCISES 40–45

Exercise 40 **Identifying Types of Clauses** Copy the paragraph below. Circle each independent clause. Underline the subject and the verb. Put two lines under each subordinate clause, and identify it as an adjective clause or an adverb clause.

Although Israel is 260 miles long, in places it is no more than twelve miles wide. Even though it is small, Israel has several different kinds of geological features. A coastal plain that lines the western side of Israel and borders the Mediterranean Sea has the country's richest farmland. East of the border between Egypt and Israel lies a range of rough hills, which are separated from the southern hills by a fertile plain. A deep, narrow valley that borders the west side of Jordan lies to the east of this range.

Exercise 41 **Combining Sentences With Adverb and Adjective Clauses** Combine each pair of sentences below by using an adjective or adverb clause.

1. The ancient Hebrews migrated into the Fertile Crescent. The Fertile Crescent supports agriculture.
2. The kingdom of Israel dates from about 1025 B.C. It started in Canaan.
3. Israel flourished under David and Solomon. They were its two greatest kings.
4. King David was a skilled general. He unified Israel.
5. Solomon was David's son. He was noted for his wisdom.

Exercise 42 **Identifying Sentence Structure** Label the following sentences *simple, complex, compound,* or *compound-complex.*

1. The area that is known as the Middle East stands at the crossroads of three continents.
2. Since ancient times, it has connected major trade routes, over land and sea.
3. Caravans from India and China brought goods to the busy markets.
4. Over thousands of years, migrating peoples spread the ideas, inventions, and achievements of many civilizations.
5. Some of these ideas we use today, and others have been lost.

Exercise 43 **Find It in Your Reading** Read this passage from "Hamadi" by Naomi Nye. Identify the subject, verb, and types of phrases.

She would picture the golden Sphinx sitting quietly in the desert with sand blowing around its face, never changing its expression.

Exercise 44 **Find It in Your Writing** Look through your writing portfolio to find examples of simple, compound, complex, and compound-complex sentences. Combine two pairs of simple sentences into compound, complex, or compound-complex sentences.

Exercise 45 **Writing Application** (1) Write a complex sentence that contains an adjective clause. (2) Write a compound-complex sentence that contains an adverb clause. (3) Make three simple sentences out of sentence 2. (4) Write a compound sentence connected by the conjunction *yet.* (5) Write a compound-complex sentence containing an elliptical adverb clause and the conjunction *but.*

ASSESS and CLOSE

Section Review

Each of these exercises correlates to a concept in the section on clauses and sentence structure, pages 448–458. These exercises may be used for more practice, for reteaching, or for review of the Key Concepts presented. Answers for all chapter exercises are available in *Grammar Exercises Answers on Transparencies* in your teaching resources.

Answer Key

Exercise 40

1. Although Israel is 260 miles long (adverb clause) in places it is not more than twelve miles wide. Even though it is small (adverb clause), Israel has several different kinds of geological features. A coastal plain that lines the western side of Israel and borders the Mediterranean Sea (adjective clause) has the country's richest farmland. East of the border between Egypt and Israel lies a range of rough hills, which are separated from the southern plains by a fertile plain (adjective clause). A deep, narrow valley that borders the west side of Jordan (adjective clause) lies to the east of this range.

Exercise 41

1. The ancient Hebrews migrated into the Fertile Crescent, which supports agriculture.
2. The kingdom of Israel dates from about 1025 B.C., when it started in Canaan.
3. Israel flourished under David and Solomon, who were its two greatest kings.

continued

Answer Key continued

4. King David was a skilled general who unified Israel.
5. Solomon, who was David's son, was noted for his wisdom.

Exercise 42

1. complex
2. simple
3. simple
4. simple
5. compound

Exercise 43

Find It in Your Reading
subject: She; verb: would picture; independent clause

Exercise 44

Find It in Your Writing
Students can explain one example of each to a partner.

Exercise 45

Writing Application
Let students work in groups to complete this exercise.

TIME SAVERS!

Answers on Transparency Use the Grammar Exercises Answers on Transparencies for Chapter 20 to have students correct their own or one another's exercises.

On-Line Exercise Bank Have students complete the exercises on computer. The Auto Check feature will grade their work for you!

CHAPTER REVIEW

Each of these exercises correlates to a concept in the chapter on phrases and clauses, pages 432–458. These exercises may be used for more practice, for reteaching, or for review of the Key Concepts presented.

Answer Key

Exercise 46

1. King of the Israelites—appositive
2. leading into the city—participial
3. crawling through the aqueduct—participial
4. to support the flow of water—infinitive; coming from the Judean Hills—participial; the land outside the city—appositive
5. Excavating the temple ruins—participial
6. none
7. to set up—infinitive
8. conquering other parts of the world—gerund
9. Researching—gerund
10. finding the correct location of ancient Jewish temples—gerund and appositive

Exercise 47

Answers will vary

Exercise 48

1. The Mount of Olives is a site that gives a perfect view of Old Jerusalem. adjective
2. The mountain was given its name because it was filled with olive trees. adverb
3. Since the eleventh century began, pilgrims have been attracted to the Mount of Olives. adverb
4. The Western Wall, which is the last remaining wall of the ancient temple, is 160 feet long. adjective
5. As long as they are between the ages of 5 and 16, children in Israel must attend school. adverb

Exercise 49

Possible answers

1. Rain and snow are expected today.
2. In January it is bitter cold, and February is not much better.
3. We eat and drink at least three times a day.
4. When the rain stopped, the sun came out.
5. When John rode his bike to school, there was no air in his tires, so his bike wobbled.

Chapter 20 Chapter Review

GRAMMAR EXERCISES 46–54

Exercise 46 Identifying Phrases

Label the phrase in each of the following sentences *appositive, participial, gerund,* or *infinitive.*

1. David, King of the Israelites, conquered Jerusalem.
2. The aqueduct leading into the city was Jerusalem's weak spot.
3. The Israelites, crawling through the aqueduct, surprised the residents of Jerusalem.
4. David built a system of canals below the city to support the flow of water coming from the Judean Hills, the land outside the city.
5. Excavating the temple ruins, archaeologists can see many parts of the canals.
6. The water from these human-built aqueducts was used in temple ceremonies.
7. Napoleon attempted to set up an empire in the Middle East.
8. However, conquering other parts of the world was easier, so he gave up.
9. Researching has been the life of Tuvia Sagiv for the past several years.
10. His project, finding the correct location of ancient Jewish temples, has cost many thousands of dollars.

Exercise 47 Supplying Phrases

Write a sentence on each topic below, using the kind of phrase specified.

1. the history of your state; infinitive phrase
2. a river in your state; present participial phrase
3. the governor of your state; gerund phrase
4. your favorite poet; adjective phrase
5. your favorite artist; appositive phrase
6. your favorite musician; prepositional phrase used as an adjective
7. a national park near you; prepositional phrase used as an adverb
8. industry in your state; past participial phrase
9. your favorite sport; infinitive phrase as the direct object
10. your future career; gerund phrase as a predicate noun

Exercise 48 Classifying Clauses

Label the clause in each of the following sentences *independent* or *subordinate.* Underline the main clause once and the subordinate clause twice. Indicate whether the subordinate clause is used as an *adjective* or as an *adverb.*

1. The Mount of Olives is a site that gives a complete view of Old Jerusalem.
2. The mountain was given its name because it was filled with olive trees.
3. Since the eleventh century began, pilgrims have been attracted to the Mount of Olives.
4. The Western Wall, which is the last remaining wall of the ancient temple, is 160 feet long.
5. As long as they are between the ages of five and sixteen, children in Israel must attend school.

Exercise 49 Supplying Clauses

Follow each of the directions given below.

1. Write a simple sentence with a compound subject using *rain* and *snow.*
2. Write a compound sentence about the weather in your state in the winter. Join your independent clauses with *and* or *but.*

3. Write a simple sentence with a compound verb using *eat* and *drink*.
4. Write a complex sentence using the phrase *when the rain stopped* as a subordinate clause.
5. Write a compound-complex sentence combining the following sentences: *John rode his bike to school. There was no air in the tires. His bike wobbled.*

Exercise 50 **Combining Sentences** Combine each pair of sentences below by making one of them a main clause and the other a subordinate clause.

1. The Old City of Jerusalem is divided into four neighborhoods. The Old City of Jerusalem is called East Jerusalem.
2. Israel is filled with historic sites that date back thousands of years. Israel is a modern country with the same conveniences we enjoy in the United States.
3. Israel's major cities are like the cities in most countries. Israel's major cities have problems with traffic and pollution.
4. Tel Aviv is Israel's second largest city. Tel Aviv is the financial and industrial center of the country.
5. Haifa is located on the Mediterranean Sea. Haifa is Israel's chief port.

Exercise 51 **Classifying Sentence Structures** Label each of the following sentences *simple, compound, complex,* or *compound-complex.*

1. Israel is also a nice place to visit.
2. Because the country lies next to the Mediterranean Sea, the climate is very temperate.
3. Precipitation, which includes mostly rain, can reach up to 42 inches per year in the north; the southern desert area may get as little as 1 inch a year.
4. Its summers are hot and dry, and its winters are cool and wet.
5. Warm beaches that all can enjoy line the western Israeli border.

Exercise 52 **Revision Practice: Varying Sentence Structure** Revise the following paragraph, combining sentences to create complex and compound sentences.

The Dead Sea is a fun place to visit. Swimmers can float without effort. The high salt content makes the water denser than the human body. Visitors are free to enjoy themselves. Visitors are warned to stay in the water for no longer than 20 minutes. By bathing in the salt water, you quickly become dehydrated. Many tourists visit Israel. They also cross the border into Egypt. They can see famous landmarks such as the Sphinx. This was built by the Egyptian pharaohs.

Exercise 53 **Writing Application** Write a series of sentences in which you use the word *cooking* in the following ways:

1. as a gerund
2. as a participle
3. as a verb
4. in an adjective clause
5. in an adverb phrase

Exercise 54 **CUMULATIVE REVIEW Basic Sentence Parts** Read the following paragraph. Label the underlined words: *subject, verb, direct object, prepositional phrase, adverb, predicate noun,* or *predicate adjective.*

<u>Israel</u> is <u>on the east side</u> of the Mediterranean Sea. The coastal plain <u>has</u> the country's richest <u>farmland</u>. The Sea of Galilee is the starting point of the Jordan <u>River</u>, <u>which</u> flows <u>south</u> to the Dead Sea. <u>Nothing</u> is able to live <u>in the Dead Sea</u> because the salt content is <u>too high</u>.

Exercise 50

1. The Old City of Jerusalem, which is called East Jerusalem, is divided into four neighborhoods.
2. Although Israel is a modern country with the same conveniences we enjoy in the United States, it is filled with historic sites that date back thousands of years.
3. Israel's major cities, which have problems of traffic and pollution, are like the cities in most countries.
4. Tel Aviv, which is the financial and industrial center of the country, is Israel's second largest city.
5. Haifa, which is Israel's chief port, is located on the Mediterranean Sea.

Exercise 51

1. simple
2. complex
3. compound-complex
4. compound
5. complex

Exercise 52

Answers will vary. A sample is given.

The Dead Sea is a fun place to visit. Swimmers can float without effort because the high salt content makes the water denser than the human body. Visitors are free to enjoy themselves but are warned to stay in the water for no longer than 20 minutes; bathing in salt water, you quickly become dehydrated. Many tourists who visit Israel also cross the border into Egypt, where they can see famous landmarks such as the

continued

Answer Key continued

Sphinx built by Egyptian pharaohs.

Exercise 53

Writing Application

Answers will vary. Samples are given.

1. Cooking is fun.
2. The cooking odors disappeared quickly.
3. I was cooking oatmeal.
4. The chef, whose cooking I like, works here.
5. He became a good chef by cooking meals for himself.

Exercise 54

Cumulative Review

Israel—subject
on the east side—prepositional phrase
has—verb
farmland—direct object
River—object of preposition
which—subject
south—adverb
Nothing—subject
in the Dead Sea—prepositional phrase
too—adverb
high—predicate adjective

TIME SAVERS!

Answers on Transparency Use the Grammar Exercises Answers on Transparencies for Chapter 20 to have students correct their own or one another's exercises.

On-Line Exercise Bank Have students complete the exercises on computer. The Auto Check feature will grade their work for you!

Lesson Objectives

- To recognize appropriate sentence construction when revising sentences.

Step-by-Step Teaching Guide

Recognizing Appropriate Sentence Constuction

Teaching Resources: Standardized Test Preparation Workbook, pp. 39–40

1. Have students carefully read each passage and identify any related ideas that can be combined into one sentence.
2. Then have students read each answer choice and identify what information (if any) is missing or in error. Students can eliminate these choices.
3. Be sure students understand that choice B on the sample test item contains the correct information but it does not combine sentences.

Standardized Test Preparation Workshop

Recognizing Appropriate Sentence Construction

Many standardized tests measure your ability to use phrases and clauses to combine sentences. For example, you may be given a written passage, part of which is underlined. You may then be asked to choose the best way to rewrite the underlined portion. The revision of such a passage often involves combining sentences in a way that will not alter the author's intended meaning.

To answer such questions, first study the underlined segment and determine the author's intent. Then, before looking at the choices, think about how you can combine sentences without altering the meaning.

Look at the following example.

Test Tip

Be careful not to choose a revision with added material not included in the original passage.

Sample Test Item	Answer and Explanation
Read the passage, and choose the letter of the best way to rewrite the underlined sentence. Ian just bought an airline ticket for his (1) upcoming vacation. The ticket is flexible, and this means that he can travel to more than one destination. 1 A Ian just bought an airline ticket, and he will travel to more than one destination. B Ian bought an airline ticket for his upcoming vacation. He can travel to more than one destination because the ticket is flexible. C Ian just bought an airline ticket for his flexible vacation, meaning that he can travel to more than one destination. D Ian just bought a flexible airline ticket for his upcoming vacation, which means that he can travel to several destinations.	The correct answer is *D*. This is the best rewrite of the two sentences because it combines related ideas without changing the meaning of the paragraph or the author's intent.

TEST-TAKING TIP

Have students make sure all of the original material is in the answers they choose. Students may be fooled by choices that are constructed appropriately but are missing key information from the original version.

Practice 1 **Directions:** Read the passage, and choose the letter of the best way to rewrite the underlined sentences.

There are several places Ian wants to visit. (1) The places are Hong Kong, Thailand, and New Zealand. The flight leaves from (2) New York. There is a stopover in Alaska. From (3) Alaska, the flight continues to Hong Kong. In Hong Kong, he will spend a week studying the architecture there.

1 **A** Ian wants to visit Hong Kong, Thailand, and New Zealand in several places.
B There are several places Ian wants to visit, and they are Hong Kong, Thailand, and New Zealand.
C There are several places, Hong Kong, Thailand, and New Zealand, that Ian wants to visit.
D Ian wants to visit Hong Kong, Thailand, and New Zealand.

2 **F** The flight leaves from New York and stops over Alaska.
G The flight leaves from New York, with a stopover in Alaska.
H The flight leaves from New York and then it is a stopover in Alaska.
J The flight leaves New York and ends up in Alaska.

3 **A** From Alaska, the flight continues to Hong Kong, where he will study architecture.
B From Alaska to Hong Kong, he will spend a week studying architecture.
C From Alaska, the flight continues to Hong Kong, where he'll spend a week studying the architecture.
D From Alaska, the flight continues on to Hong Kong. In Hong Kong, he will study architecture.

Practice 2 **Directions:** Read the passage, and choose the letter of the best way to rewrite the underlined sentences.

Ian will stay for two weeks in Bangkok. He (1) will spend another two weeks touring Thailand. Then, he'll be ready to move on. (2) New Zealand is the next stop. He is (3) interested in the culture of the Maoris. They are the first known people in New Zealand.

1 **A** Ian will stay for two weeks in Bangkok and then will spend another two weeks touring.
B Ian will stay in Bangkok for two weeks. Then, Ian will spend another two weeks on a tour in Thailand.
C Ian will stay in Bangkok for two weeks, then tour Thailand.
D Ian will stay for two weeks in Bangkok, from there he will spend two weeks touring Thailand.

2 **F** Then, he'll be ready to move on to his next stop, New Zealand.
G Then, he'll be ready to move on to his next stop at New Zealand.
H After that, he'll be ready for New Zealand to move to the next stop.
J New Zealand, the next stop, is where he'll be ready to move on to.

3 **A** He is interested in the Maoris' culture. They were the first people in New Zealand.
B He is interested in the Maoris, who were the first known people.
C He is interested in the Maoris' culture and the Maoris were the first known people in New Zealand.
D He is interested in the culture of the Maoris, the first known people in New Zealand.

Answer Key

Practice 1

1. D
2. G
3. C

Practice 2

1. A
2. F
3. D

Chapter 21 Time and Resource Manager

In-Depth Lesson Plan

	LESSON FOCUS	PRINT AND MEDIA RESOURCES
DAY 1	**The Four Functions of a Sentence** Students distinguish among the four functions of sentences (pp. 464–468).	**Teaching Resources** *Grammar Exercise Workbook*, pp. 97–98; *Grammar Exercises Answers on Transparencies*, Ch. 21 ***Writing and Grammar iText* (Interactive Text),** Section 21.1
DAY 2	**Combining Sentences** Students combine phrases, clauses, and short sentences to make longer sentences. They also complete a Hands-on Grammar activity (pp. 469–475).	**Teaching Resources** *Grammar Exercise Workbook*, pp. 99–100; *Grammar Exercises Answers on Transparencies*, Ch. 21 *Hands-on Grammar Activity Book*, Ch. 21 ***Writing and Grammar iText* (Interactive Text),** Section 21.2
DAY 3	**Varying Sentences** Students vary sentence length and sentence beginnings (pp. 476–479).	**Teaching Resources** *Grammar Exercise Workbook*, pp. 101–104; *Grammar Exercises Answers on Transparencies*, Ch. 21 ***Writing and Grammar iText* (Interactive Text),** Section 21.3
DAY 4	**Avoiding Sentence Problems** Students learn to recognize and correct sentence fragments, run-on sentences, misplaced modifiers, and double negatives (pp. 480–497).	**Teaching Resources** *Grammar Exercise Workbook*, pp. 105–120; *Grammar Exercises Answers on Transparencies*, Ch. 21 ***Writing and Grammar iText* (Interactive Text),** Section 21.4
DAY 5	**Review and Assess** Students review the chapter and demonstrate mastery of sentence construction. They will also complete a cumulative review (pp. 498–503).	**Teaching Resources** *Formal Assessment*, Ch. 21; *Grammar Exercises Answers on Transparencies*, Ch. 21 ***Writing and Grammar iText* (Interactive Text),** Ch. 21, Chapter Review; ***On-Line Exercise Bank*,** Sections 21.1–4

Accelerated Lesson Plan

	LESSON FOCUS	PRINT AND MEDIA RESOURCES
DAY 1	**Sentences** Students distinguish among the four functions of sentences. They combine phrases, clauses, and short sentences to make longer sentences. They vary sentence length and sentence beginnings (pp. 464–479).	**Teaching Resources** *Grammar Exercise Workbook*, pp. 97–104; *Grammar Exercises Answers on Transparencies*, Ch. 21 *Hands-on Grammar Activity Book*, Ch. 20 ***Writing and Grammar iText* (Interactive Text),** Sections 21.1–3
DAY 2	**Avoiding Sentence Problems** Students learn to recognize and correct sentence fragments, run-on sentences, misplaced modifiers, and double negatives (pp. 480–486).	**Teaching Resources** *Grammar Exercise Workbook*, pp. 105–120; *Grammar Exercises Answers on Transparencies*, Ch. 21 ***Writing and Grammar iText* (Interactive Text),** Section 21.4
DAY 3	**Review and Assess** Students review the chapter and demonstrate mastery of sentence construction (pp. 498–503).	**Teaching Resources** *Formal Assessment*, Ch. 21; *Grammar Exercises Answers on Transparencies*, Ch. 21 ***Writing and Grammar iText* (Interactive Text),** Ch. 21, Chapter Review; ***On-Line Exercise Bank*,** Sections 21.1–4

Options for Adapting Lesson Plans

HOMEWORK

Have students complete any stage of the lesson for homework.

SPELLING

To teach spelling skills in conjunction with grammar, mechanics, and usage, work through *Prentice Hall Everyday Spelling*, Grade 8, Chapter 25, as you cover this *Writing and Grammar* chapter.

TECHNOLOGY

Students can use *Writing and Grammar iText* to complete the exercises interactively on computer. They can complete additional exercises in the *On-line Exercise Bank:* The Auto Check feature will grade their work. Go online: PHSchool.com Use Web code: eck-8002

INTEGRATED SKILLS COVERAGE

Grammar in Literature
SE p. 493

Writing
Find It in Your Writing, SE pp. 468, 474, 475, 479, 497
Writing Application, SE pp. 468, 475, 479, 497, 499

Viewing and Representing
Critical Viewing, SE pp. 464, 467, 469, 472, 478, 482, 486, 488, 495, 496

Listening and Speaking
Integrating Speaking and Listening Skills, ATE p. 490

Real-World Connection
Effective Sentences in Journalism, ATE p. 469
Using Fragments for Literary Effect, ATE p. 483

ASSESSMENT SUPPORT

Standardized Test Preparation Workshop SE pp. 500–501, ATE p. 484

Standardized Test Preparation Workbook, pp. 41–42

Formal Assessment, Ch. 21

MEETING INDIVIDUAL NEEDS

Less Advanced Students ATE p. 489. See also Ongoing Assessments ATE pp. 471, 483, 488, 495.

ESL Students ATE p. 466

Verbal/Linguistic Learners ATE p. 480

Visual/Spatial Learners ATE p. 492

BLOCK SCHEDULING

Pacing Suggestions
For 90-minute Blocks
- Administer the Diagnostic Test to students to determine instructional coverage.
- Have students complete the necessary exercises in class. Use the Hands-on Grammar Activity to provide a change of pace.

Resources for Varying Instruction
- ***Writing and Grammar iText* (Interactive Text)** A 90-minute block provides an ideal opportunity for students to work on computer.

Professional Development Support
- ***How to Manage Instruction in the Block*** This teaching resource provides management and activity suggestions.

MEDIA AND TECHNOLOGY

For the Student
- ***Writing and Grammar iText* (Interactive Text),** Ch. 21
- ***On-Line Exercise Bank,*** Sections 21.1–4

For the Teacher
- ***Resource Pro* CD-ROM**

WRITING AND GRAMMAR ON-LINE

iText Interactive Text (On-line or on CD-ROM)
- Easily navigable instruction with on-line supporting resources
- Self-scoring exercises and diagnostic tests

Companion Web Site PHSchool.com
- On-line Exercise Bank (use Web Code eck-8002)

See the Go On-line! feature, SE p. iii.

LITERATURE CONNECTIONS

Grammar in Literature selection from *Prentice Hall Literature: Timeless Voices, Timeless Themes,* Silver:
from "The Story-Teller," Saki (H.H. Munro), SE p. 493

CHAPTER 21 EFFECTIVE SENTENCES

Lesson Objectives

1. To identify the function and end punctuation of declarative, interrogative, imperative, and exclamatory sentences.
2. To combine sentences by using a compound subject, verb, or object.
3. To combine sentences by changing one to a subordinate clause or a phrase.
4. To vary sentence length.
5. To vary sentence beginnings with different parts of speech or subject-verb order.
6. To identify sentence fragments.
7. To identify phrases as fragments.
8. To identify subordinate clauses as fragments.
9. To identify run-on sentences.
10. To correct run-ons with end marks.
11. To identify misplaced modifiers.
12. To learn to revise sentences with misplaced modifiers.
13. To identify double negatives.
14. To identify and correct common usage problems.

Critical Viewing

Connect Students may mention that most trains and sentences are composed of a string of connected elements that follow one another in a particular order.

Chapter 21 Effective Sentences

▲ Critical Viewing
How is a train like a sentence? **[Connect]**

Just as a train is one of the basic forms of transportation, a sentence is a basic unit of communication. We use sentences every day—to ask questions, make statements, express emotions, or share information. Trains must be assembled correctly in order to provide transportation. In the same way, words must be put together correctly in sentences to provide effective and clear communication.

In this chapter, you will learn about how sentences can function in different ways. You will learn how to vary sentence styles and how to combine ideas into a more efficient sentence. You will also learn how to avoid some of the problems that writers encounter when they are writing sentences.

ONGOING ASSESSMENT: Diagnose

If students miss more than one item in each category, direct them to the relevant pages of the text and assign exercises for practice and review.

Effective Sentences	Diagnostic Test Items	Teach	Practice	Section Review	Chapter Review
Skill Check A					
Identifying Sentence Type	A 1–5	pp. 466–467	Ex. 1	Ex. 2–7	Ex. 47
Skill Check B					
Combining Sentences	B 6–10	pp. 469–474	Ex. 8–12	Ex. 13–18	Ex. 48

Diagnostic Test

Directions: Write all answers on a separate sheet of paper.

Skill Check A. Indicate whether each of the following sentences is *declarative, interrogative, imperative,* or *exclamatory*. After each answer, write the appropriate end mark for that sentence.

1. In the late nineteenth century, trains run by steam power were challenged by electric locomotives
2. Why don't we use very many electric trains today
3. Imagine the high cost of overhead wire and power substations
4. Wow That would surely be expensive
5. In addition, electric trains lack the flexibility of diesel trains

Skill Check B. Combine each pair of sentences below as indicated in parentheses.

6. Electric trains are still used today. Diesel trains are still used today. (Combine the subjects.)
7. The electric locomotive has a few drawbacks. Many of the advantages of the diesel locomotive are also found in the electric locomotive. (Use the conjunction *however.*)
8. Electric trains are clean. Electric motors do not pollute the environment. (Use the conjunction *because.*)
9. Electric train operations can be profitable. They are usually profitable only in areas with large, dense populations. (Use the conjunction *but.*)
10. Large, dense populations are found in many cities. Tokyo, New York, New Delhi, and Paris are a few of them. (Use a semicolon.)

Skill Check C. On your paper, write *F* if the numbered item below is a fragment, *RO* if it is a run-on, *MM* if it has a misplaced modifier, or *DN* if it contains a double negative.

11. The invention of the diesel locomotive.
12. Which caused great increases in operating efficiency.
13. Rudolf Diesel was a German mechanical engineer, he invented the diesel engine in the 1890's.
14. People rode trains from New York to Chicago with diesel engines.
15. By the mid-1930's, the Union Pacific Railroad didn't use no steam power for its new, streamlined passenger trains.

Skill Check D. For each of the following sentences, choose the correct word or phrase from the choices in parentheses.

16. During World War II, most railroads (didn't use no, didn't use) steam- or electric-powered trains.
17. Diesel power was used (further, farther) as time went on.
18. The reason railroads converted to diesel from steam engines was (because, that) the diesel was more efficient.
19. While railroads (in, into) the United States were switching to diesel trains, a similar trend was occurring worldwide.
20. By 1957, all American trains, (except, accept) for a few, were diesel-powered.

Answer Key

Diagnostic Test

Each item in the diagnostic test corresponds to a specific concept in the chapter on effective sentences. This will enable you to tailor instruction to the particular needs of your students. See "Ongoing Assessment" on the bottom of page 2 for further details.

Skill Check A

1. declarative .
2. interrogative ?
3. imperative .
4. exclamatory !
5. declarative .

Skill Check B

6. Electric trains and diesel trains are still used today.
7. The electric locomotive has a few drawbacks; however, many of the advantages of the diesel are also found in the electric locomotive.
8. Electric trains are clean because electric motors do not pollute the environment.
9. Electric train operations can be profitable, but they are usually profitable only in areas with large, dense populations.
10. Large, dense populations are found in many cities; Tokyo, New York, New Delhi, and Paris are a few of them.

Skill Check C

11. F
12. F
13. RO
14. MM
15. DN

Skill Check D

16. didn't use
17. further
18. that
19. in
20. except

ONGOING ASSESSMENT: Diagnose *continued*

Effective Sentences	Diagnostic Test Items	Teach	Practice	Section Review	Chapter Review
Skill Check C					
Avoiding Sentence Problems	C 11–15	pp. 480–490	Ex. 28–35	Ex. 40–41, 44–45	Ex. 50
Skill Check D					
Identifying Common Usage Problems	D 16–20	pp. 491–496	Ex. 36–39	Ex. 42–43	Ex. 51–53

PREPARE and ENGAGE

Interest GRABBER Read the following passage and ask students to identify how many different types of sentences it contains.

How are you today? We are going to have a good day. Sit quietly. Wow! You're actually doing it!

Activate Prior Knowledge

Ask students to write a statement, a question, an imperative sentence, and an exclamation.

TEACH

Step-by Step Teaching Guide

Classifying the Four Functions of a Sentence

1. Review the four types of sentences. Point out the three different end marks for sentences, and confirm that students understand when to use each.
2. Write the following sentences on the board (without end marks) and ask students to identify the sentence types and supply the end marks.

   What a beautiful night (exclamatory !)

   Have you ever seen anything like this (interrogative ?)

   There are thousands of fireflies here (declarative .)

   Remember this night (imperative .)

Customize for *ESL Students*

Review the different sentence types, paying particular attention to imperative and exclamatory sentences. Be sure that students understand that the subject of imperative sentences is *you*, and that they understand the use of exclamation marks.

Section 21.1

The Four Functions of a Sentence

Sentences can be classified according to what they do. The four types of sentences in English are *declarative, interrogative, imperative,* and *exclamatory.*

Declarative sentences are the most common type. They are used to state, or "declare," facts.

KEY CONCEPT A **declarative sentence** states an idea and ends with a period. ■

DECLARATIVE: A great network of railways crisscrosses the vast Indian subcontinent.
The trains are fast and efficient.

Interrogative means "asking." An *interrogative sentence* is a question.

KEY CONCEPT An **interrogative sentence** asks a question and ends with a question mark. ■

INTERROGATIVE: Whose ticket is this?
Which countries in Europe and Asia have high-speed trains?

The word *imperative* comes from the Latin word for commanding. *Imperative sentences* are commands.

KEY CONCEPT An **imperative sentence** gives an order or a direction and ends with either a period or an exclamation mark. ■

Most imperative sentences start with a verb. In this type of sentence, the subject is understood to be *you.*

IMPERATIVE: Follow the directions carefully to get to the correct platform.
Wait for me!

Notice the punctuation at the end of these examples. In the first sentence, the period suggests that a mild command is being given, in an ordinary tone of voice. The exclamation mark at the end of the second sentence suggests a strong command, one given in a loud voice.

To exclaim means to "shout out." Exclamatory sentences are used to "shout out" emotions such as happiness, fear, delight, and anger.

Theme: Railroads

In this section, you will learn how to recognize and use four types of sentences. The examples and exercises are about railroads.

Cross-Curricular Connection: Social Studies

TIME AND RESOURCE MANAGER

Resources
Print: Grammar Exercise Workbook, pp. 97–98
Technology: Writing and Grammar iText, Section 21.1; On-Line Exercise Bank, Section 21.1

In-Depth Coverage	Accelerated Pace
• Work through all key concepts, pp. 466–467. • Assign and review Exercise 1.	• Assign pp. 466–467 for independent student review.

KEY CONCEPT An **exclamatory sentence** conveys strong emotion and ends with an exclamation mark. ■

EXCLAMATORY: She's not telling the truth!
What an outrage that is!

Exercise 1 **Identifying the Four Types of Sentences** On your paper, identify each of the following sentences as *declarative, interrogative, imperative,* or *exclamatory*. After each answer, write the appropriate end mark for that sentence.

EXAMPLE: A vehicle that runs on rails and is self-propelled is called a train

ANSWER: declarative (.)

1. A locomotive can use several forms of energy
2. Steam, electricity, and diesel power are a few forms of energy used to run a train
3. What was the first form of energy used to run a train
4. The first steam locomotive was built in 1804
5. What does a train do
6. A train pulls railroad cars carrying a variety of different things
7. That's what a train does
8. Ride one when you get a chance
9. I can't *believe* how much trains have changed
10. Hey Our train is *really* late

▲ **Critical Viewing** Some people consider steam trains part of our romantic past. What sort of emotion does this picture bring out in you? **[Relate]**

More Practice

Grammar Exercise Workbook
• pp. 97–98

On-line Exercise Bank
• Section 21.1

Go on-line:
PHSchool.com
Enter Web Code:
eck-8002

iText

Get instant feedback! Exercise 1 is available on-line or on CD-ROM.

Critical Viewing

Relate Students may mention emotions as diverse as awe, pride, loneliness, joy, sadness, and excitement.

Answer Key

Exercise 1

1. declarative [.]
2. declarative [.]
3. interrogative [?]
4. declarative [.]
5. interrogative [?]
6. declarative [.]
7. declarative [.]
8. imperative [.]
9. declarative [.]
10. exclamatory [!]

TIME SAVERS!

Answers on Transparency Use the Grammar Exercises Answers on Transparencies for Chapter 21 to have students correct their own or one another's exercises.

On-Line Exercise Bank Have students complete the exercises on computer. The Auto Check feature will grade their work for you!

ASSESS and CLOSE

Section Review

Each of these exercises correlates with a concept in the section on the four functions of a sentence, pages 466–467. These exercises may be used for more practice, for reteaching, or for review of the Key Concepts presented.

Answer Key

Exercise 2

1. declarative
2. interrogative
3. imperative
4. exclamatory
5. interrogative
6. declarative
7. interrogative
8. declarative
9. exclamatory
10. imperative

Exercise 3

1. trains.—imperative
2. history?—interrogative
3. locomotives.—declarative
4. Wow!—exclamatory
5. trains.—imperative
6. imported.—declarative
7. trains?—interrogative
8. States.—declarative
9. like?—interrogative
10. engine.—declarative

Exercises 4–7

Students' sentences will vary. Check to see that students can recognize and write sentences of all four types.

TIME SAVERS!

Answers on Transparency Use the Grammar Exercises Answers on Transparencies for Chapter 21 to have students correct their own or one another's exercises.

On-Line Exercise Bank Have students complete the exercises on computer. The Auto Check feature will grade their work for you!

Section 21.1 Section Review

GRAMMAR EXERCISES 2–7

Exercise 2 Identifying the Four Types of Sentences Read the following sentences, and identify each one as *declarative, interrogative, imperative,* or *exclamatory.*

1. The steam locomotive was first developed in 1804 in England.
2. What was the first steam locomotive like?
3. Picture a steam engine mounted on a wheeled vehicle on rails.
4. How neat!
5. How well did it work?
6. It could haul about twenty-five tons, but it was too heavy for the wooden track.
7. How long was it until there was a steam train designed to carry people?
8. The Stockton and Darlington Railway opened in 1825.
9. That was quick!
10. Look up more information on-line.

Exercise 3 Punctuating the Four Types of Sentences Copy the sentences below onto your paper. Add the appropriate end mark, and identify the type of sentence.

1. Tell me about English trains
2. How did English locomotives play a role in early American railroad history
3. The American railways imported more than 100 English locomotives
4. Wow
5. Realize that the United States could not have made its own trains
6. *The Stourbridge Lion* was one of the first trains to be imported
7. When did the U.S. start building trains
8. In 1830, the first locomotive was built for sale in the United States
9. What were American trains like
10. Henry Campbell designed an eight-wheeled engine

Exercise 4 Writing the Four Types of Sentences Write one sentence for each of the numbered directions below.

1. Write a declarative sentence about a method of travel.
2. Write an exclamatory sentence about bad weather.
3. Write an imperative sentence reminding a friend to do something.
4. Write a declarative sentence about a favorite movie or TV show.
5. Write an interrogative sentence about weekend plans.

Exercise 5 Find It in Your Reading Have a closer look at a book you are reading. Identify and write down two examples of each of the four sentence types. If you can't find all four types, give an explanation of why you think the writer has used only the types you found.

Exercise 6 Find It in Your Writing Look through your portfolio for a piece of writing containing examples of all four types of sentences. If you can't find examples of each, revise your writing to vary the sentence types.

Exercise 7 Writing Application Think of something that happened to you yesterday. Then, write four sentences about what happened, one of each type. Label and punctuate each one correctly.

Section 21.2

Combining Sentences

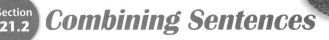

Writing should include sentences of varying lengths and complexity so that the ideas flow. One way to achieve sentence variety is by combining sentences. Look at the examples below.

EXAMPLE: We went to the railroad yard.
We saw trains.

COMBINED: We went to the railroad yard and saw trains.
We saw trains at the railroad yard.
When we went to the railroad yard, we saw trains.

Theme: Railroads

In this section, you will learn several methods for combining sentences. The examples and exercises tell more about railroads.

Cross-Curricular Connection: Social Studies

Combining Sentence Parts

KEY CONCEPT Sentences can be combined by using a compound subject, a compound verb, or a compound object. ■

EXAMPLE: Joe enjoyed seeing the trains.
Martha enjoyed seeing the trains.

COMPOUND SUBJECT: Joe and Martha enjoyed seeing the trains.

EXAMPLE: Mike bought a whistle. Mike blew on the whistle.

COMPOUND VERB: Mike bought a whistle and blew on it.

EXAMPLE: Brandon examined the steam train.
Brandon examined the diesel.

COMPOUND OBJECT: Brandon examined the steam train and the diesel.

▼ Critical Viewing
In what ways is this train similar to or different from the one in the photograph on page 464? Use at least one compound subject or compound verb in your response. **[Compare and Contrast]**

TIME AND RESOURCE MANAGER

Resources
Print: Grammar Exercise Workbook, pp. 99–100; Hands-on Grammar Activity Book, Chapter 21
Technology: Writing and Grammar iText, Section 21.2; On-Line Exercise Bank, Section 21.2

In-Depth Coverage	Accelerated Pace
• Work through all key concepts, pp. 469–474. • Assign and review Exercises 8–12. • Do the Hands-on Grammar Activity, p. 474.	• Assign pp. 469–474 for independent student review.

PREPARE and ENGAGE

Interest GRABBER Write the following sentences on the board and invite students to combine the short sentences into one longer one.

The spaceship is blue. The spaceship is round. The spaceship carries 700 passengers. The spaceship can travel 100 million miles without refueling. (The round, blue spaceship carries 700 passengers and can travel 100 million miles without refueling.)

Activate Prior Knowledge

Ask students to write three sentences: one with a compound subject, one with a compound verb, and one with a compound object.

TEACH

Step-by-Step Teaching Guide

Combining Sentences

To be sure that students understand compound subjects, verbs, and objects, write the following sentences on the board and ask students to identify the compounds.

Mozart and Beethoven wrote beautiful music and changed music history. (Mozart and Beethoven—compound subject; wrote and changed—compound verb)

Luis played Mozart and Beethoven. (Mozart and Beethoven—compound object)

Real-World Connection

Have students read newspaper or magazine articles and identify sentences with compound subjects, verbs, and objects.

Critical Viewing

Compare and Contrast Sample answer: The first train and the second train both transport things. Both trains are old and probably run on diesel.

Answer Key

Exercise 8

1. Early in the twentieth century, railroads were challenged by new modes of transportation and started to decline due to losses in employment and traffic. (compound verb)
2. Finished products and people were transported by trains for much of the century. (compound subject)
3. Trains were the principal method of transporting materials and mail. (compound object)
4. The locomotives were awesome, powerful machines and were capable of pulling many loaded freight cars. (compound verb)
5. Thousands of people ride trains from their homes to work or travel by train just for the fun of it. (compound verb)

Step-by-Step Teaching Guide

Joining Clauses

1. An independent clause can stand by itself as a sentence. It contains a subject and verb, and it expresses a complete thought.
2. Write the following related independent clauses and ask students to join them with a coordinating conjunction to form a compound sentence.

   The weather forecast said it would be cold and clear. We ended up with almost a foot of snow. (The weather forecast said it would be cold and clear, but we ended up with almost a foot of snow.)

   The snow plows cleared the roads. People shoveled out their driveways. (The snow plows cleared the roads, and people shoveled out their driveways.)

TIME SAVERS!

Answers on Transparency Use the Grammar Exercises Answers on Transparencies for Chapter 21 to have students correct their own or one another's exercises.

On-Line Exercise Bank Have students complete the exercises on computer. The Auto Check feature will grade their work for you!

Exercise 8 **Combining Sentences Using Compound Subjects, Verbs, or Objects** Combine each pair of sentences below in the most logical way, identifying each combination as *compound subject, compound verb,* or *compound object.*

EXAMPLE: Railroads appeared in the early nineteenth century.
Railroads played a major role in the Industrial Revolution.

ANSWER: Railroads appeared in the early nineteenth century and played a major role in the Industrial Revolution. (compound verb)

1. Early in the twentieth century, railroads were challenged by new modes of transportation. Railroads started to decline due to losses in employment and traffic.
2. Finished products were transported by trains for much of the century. People were transported by trains for much of the century.
3. Trains were the principal method of transporting materials. Trains were the principal method of transporting mail.
4. The locomotives were awesome, powerful machines. They were capable of pulling many loaded freight cars.
5. Thousands of people ride trains from their homes to work. Thousands travel by train just for the fun of it.

Joining Clauses

KEY CONCEPT Sentences can be combined by joining two independent clauses to create a compound sentence. ■

Use a compound sentence when combining ideas that are related but independent. Compound sentences are created by joining two independent clauses with a comma and a coordinating conjunction, such as *and, but, nor, for, so, or,* and *yet.* You can combine two sentences with a semicolon if they are closely related.

EXAMPLE: John Henry was an actual person.
His deeds were the subject of tall tales.

COMPOUND SENTENCE: John Henry was an actual person, but his heroic deeds were the subject of tall tales.

EXAMPLE: John Henry had a contest with a steam engine.
He beat the steam engine.

COMPOUND SENTENCE: John Henry had a contest with a steam engine; he beat the steam engine.

More Practice

Grammar Exercise Workbook
- pp. 99–100

On-line Exercise Bank
- Section 21.2

Go on-line:
PHSchool.com
Enter Web Code:
eck-8002

iText

Get instant feedback! Exercise 8 is available on-line or on CD-ROM.

Spelling Tip

Sometimes, compound nouns are written as two words, such as *pen pal.* However, the compound noun *railroad* is written as one word.

Exercise 9 **Combining Independent Clauses to Make Compound Sentences** Combine the following sentences, using the connector indicated in parentheses.

EXAMPLE: A railroad is a form of land transportation. The rails provide a track for cars pulled by engines. (semicolon)

ANSWER: A railroad is a form of land transportation; the rails provide a track for cars pulled by engines.

1. During the seventeenth century, horse-drawn wagons were used in European mines. Between 1797 and 1813, Richard Trevithick adapted steam locomotives for use in the mines. (comma with *but*)
2. In 1825, George Stephenson built the twenty-mile Stockton and Darlington Railway. It was the first public railway to be powered by a steam locomotive. (semicolon)
3. Railroads first appeared in England. Railroads had the most dramatic growth in the United States. (comma with *yet*)
4. More than 3,000 miles of railroad were built in the eastern states by 1840. This figure is 40 percent greater than the railroad mileage in Europe. (semicolon)
5. By the end of the Civil War, the railroad in the United States was more than 30,000 miles long. It had replaced steamboats in commercial transportation. (comma with *and*)

KEY CONCEPT Two sentences can be combined by changing one of them into a subordinate clause. ■

Use a compound sentence when you are combining sentences to show the relationship between ideas. A subordinating conjunction will help readers understand the relationship. Common subordinating conjunctions are *after, although, because, before, if, since, unless,* and *when.*

EXAMPLE: George Stephenson was a coal mine engineer. He built his first locomotive in 1814.

COMBINED WITH A SUBORDINATE CLAUSE: George Stephenson was a coal mine engineer before he built his first locomotive in 1814.

EXAMPLE: The railroads decided on a standard gauge. Tracks were different widths all over the country.

COMBINED WITH A SUBORDINATE CLAUSE: Because tracks were different widths all over the country, the railroads decided on a standard gauge.

Journal Tip

Does the history of railroads interest you? If so, jot down in your journal some facts from this section; then, review them to find a topic for an expository essay or a research report.

Learn More

To find out more about subordinating conjunctions, see Chapter 18.

Answer Key

Exercise 9

1. During the seventeenth century, horse-drawn wagons were used in European mines, but between 1797 and 1813, Richard Trevithick adapted steam locomotives for use in the mines.
2. In 1825, George Stephenson built the twenty-mile Stockton and Darlington Railway; it was the first public railway to be powered by a steam locomotive.
3. Railroads first appeared in England, yet railroads had the most dramatic growth in the United States.
4. More than 3,000 miles of railroad were built in the eastern states by 1840; this figure is 40 percent greater than the railroad mileage in Europe.
5. By the end of the Civil War, the railroad in the United States was more than 30,000 miles long, and it had replaced steamboats in commercial transportation.

Step-by-Step Teaching Guide

Combining Clauses

1. Students also can use conjunctive adverbs to form a compound sentence with a subordinate clause. Examples include *accordingly, also, besides, consequently, hence, however, moreover, nevertheless, otherwise, then, therefore, thus,* and *still.*
2. The subordinate clause can come before or after the independent clause.

ONGOING ASSESSMENT: Monitor and Reinforce

If students miss more than two items in Exercises 8–12, refer them to the following for additional practice.

In the Textbook	Print Resources	Technology
Section Review, Ex. 13–18, p. 475	Grammar Exercises Workbook, pp. 99–100	On-Line Exercise Bank, Section 21.2

Answer Key

Exercise 10

1. When George Stephenson and his son Robert worked together as engineers, they made major contributions to the first English locomotives and railroads.
2. Before he built his first locomotive, George Stephenson was a builder of engines used in coal mines.
3. When the Stockton and Darlington Railway was planned, George Stephenson was hired as the company's engineer.
4. He convinced the owners of Stockton and Darlington Railway to use steam power as he built the line's first locomotive.
5. After Stephenson transferred to the Liverpool and Manchester Railway, he and his son Robert built the *Rocket*.

Exercise 11

1. <u>After</u> the British invented the steam locomotive, the first railroads appeared in the United States during the 1820's.
2. <u>After</u> the Delaware and Hudson Canal and Railroad Company purchased a British-built locomotive in 1829, they found it to be too heavy for the track in the United States.
3. <u>When</u> the South Carolina Railroad began passenger service with the *Best Friend of Charleston,* it became the first railroad in the nation to use steam power.
4. <u>When</u> the *Best Friend of Charleston* had pulled a passenger train over the six miles of completed lines, the locomotive exploded.
5. The engine's fireman had tied down the safety valve of the boiler <u>because</u> the noise bothered him.

Critical Viewing

Analyze Students may say it is a steam train because of the smoke coming out of the smokestack. They might also notice the steam on either side of the cowcatcher.

Exercise 10 Combining Sentences With Subordinating Conjunctions Rewrite the following sentence pairs, using the subordinating conjunction indicated in parentheses.

1. George Stephenson and his son Robert worked together as engineers. They made major contributions to the first English locomotives and railroads. (when)
2. George Stephenson was a builder of engines used in coal mines. He built his first locomotive. (before)
3. The Stockton and Darlington Railway was planned. George Stephenson was hired as the company's engineer. (when)
4. He convinced the owners of Stockton and Darlington Railway to use steam power. He built the line's first locomotive. (as)
5. Stephenson transferred to the Liverpool and Manchester Railway. He and his son Robert built the *Rocket.* (after)

Exercise 11 Combining Sentences by Forming Subordinate Clauses Combine each of the following pairs of sentences with a subordinating conjunction. Underline the subordinating conjunction.

1. The first railroads appeared in the United States during the late 1820's. The British invented the steam locomotive.
2. The Delaware and Hudson Canal and Railroad Company purchased a British-built locomotive in 1829. They found it to be too heavy for the track in the United States.
3. The South Carolina Railroad began passenger service with the *Best Friend of Charleston.* It became the first railroad in the nation to use steam power.
4. The *Best Friend of Charleston* had pulled a passenger train over the six miles of completed lines. The locomotive exploded.
5. The engine's fireman had tied down the safety valve of the boiler. The noise bothered him.

▼ **Critical Viewing** Is this a steam train or a diesel? How can you tell? Include a sentence with a subordinate clause in your response. **[Analyze]**

KEY CONCEPT Two sentences can be combined by changing one of them into a phrase. ■

When you are combining a pair of sentences in which one simply adds detail, change one of the sentences into a phrase.

EXAMPLE: The Pennsylvania Railroad Museum is interesting. It is in Strasberg.

COMBINED: The Pennsylvania Railroad Museum in Strasberg is interesting.

EXAMPLE: The Pennsylvania Railroad Museum is interesting. It is the home of the *John Bull* replica.

COMBINED: The Pennsylvania Railroad Museum, home of the *John Bull* replica, is interesting.

Exercise 12 **Combining Sentences Using Phrases** Rewrite the following sentence pairs, combining them by changing one into a phrase.

EXAMPLE: Many trains have been invented over the years. English and American engineers invented them.

ANSWER: Many trains have been invented over the years by English and American engineers.

1. The *Rocket* was an early English locomotive. George and Robert Stephenson built it.
2. The *Rocket* won a competition sponsored by the Liverpool and Manchester Railway in 1829. The competition was called the Rainhill Trials.
3. The *Rocket* completed the trials. It had an average speed of fifteen mph.
4. George went on to become engineer of the Birmingham and London Railway. George was Robert's son.
5. George also built several famous bridges. He built them in addition to engineering trains.
6. The *John Bull* was a locomotive built in England. Robert Stephenson and Company built it.
7. The *John Bull* was exported to the Camden and Amboy Railroad. It was exported in 1831.
8. The *John Bull* was acquired by the Smithsonian. The Smithsonian acquired it in 1884.
9. In 1981, the *John Bull* was driven on the Old Georgetown Branch railroad tracks. It was its 150th anniversary.
10. Compare the *John Bull* with a modern-day diesel train. The *John Bull* was quite small.

More Practice

Grammar Exercise Workbook
- pp. 99–100

On-line Exercise Bank
- Section 21.2

Go on-line:
PHSchool.com
Enter Web Code:
eck-8002

iText

Get instant feedback! Exercise 12 is available on-line or on CD-ROM.

Step-by-Step Teaching Guide

Combining Sentences

Give students a list of subordinating conjunctions to choose from for Exercise 12: *after, although, because, before, since, unless, until, when, where, while.*

Answer Key

Exercise 12

1. George and Robert Stephenson built the *Rocket*, an early English locomotive.
2. The *Rocket* won Rainhill Trials, a competition sponsored by the Liverpool and Manchester Railway in 1829.
3. The *Rocket* completed the trials with an average speed of fifteen mph.
4. Robert's son George went on to become engineer of the Birmingham and London Railway.
5. In addition to engineering trains, George built several famous bridges.
6. The *John Bull* was a locomotive built in England by Robert Stephenson and Company.
7. The *John Bull* was exported in 1831 to the Camden and Amboy Railroad.
8. The *John Bull* was acquired by the Smithsonian in 1884.
9. On its 150th anniversary in 1981, the *John Bull* was driven on the old Georgetown Branch railroad tracks.
10. Compared to a modern-day diesel train, the *John Bull* was quite small.

TIME SAVERS!

Answers on Transparency Use the Grammar Exercises Answers on Transparencies for Chapter 21 to have students correct their own or one another's exercises.

On-Line Exercise Bank Have students complete the exercises on computer. The Auto Check feature will grade their work for you!

Step-by-Step-Teaching Guide

Sentence Combining Twosome

Teaching Resources: Hands-on Grammar Activity Book, Chapter 21

1. Have students refer to their Hands-on Grammar activity books or give them copies of the relevant pages for this activity.
2. Encourage students to discuss with one another the meaning of each conjunction as it is used in a sentence. Is its meaning related to time, causation, opposition, equality of ideas, or some other concept?

Find It in Your Reading

Have students circle the conjunctions they find, and see what other ways each one can be positioned.

Find It in Your Writing

Have students share examples with class.

Hands-on Grammar

Sentence Combining Twosome

With a classmate, form a twosome to practice combining sentences. First, cut out thirteen small rectangles, and print one of these conjunctions on each of them: *and, but, yet, after, although, because, before, if, since, unless, until, when,* and *while.* Put them in an envelope. Then, cut eleven strips of paper, 6" x 3/4", and on each, print one of these sentences:

THE TRAIN PULLED INTO THE STATION
AUNT LUCY HAD FORGOTTEN THE TICKETS
ALICE WAS WATCHING THE LUGGAGE
THE WHISTLE BLEW
THE PASSENGERS MOVED TOWARD THE TRAIN
DAD BROUGHT THE TICKETS
ALICE AND JASON SAW THEIR FRIEND MICHAEL
IT WAS ALMOST NOON
THE CONDUCTOR CALLED, "ALL ABOARD"
THE TRAIN WAS READY TO DEPART
MICHAEL JOINED ALICE AND JASON

To begin, one person chooses a sentence strip. The other person then pulls a conjunction randomly from the envelope. Now, the first person uses the conjunction to combine the sentence logically with another sentence strip. Lay out the combined sentence on a desk or table. (See examples.)

IT WAS ALMOST NOON	**WHEN**	THE WHISTLE BLEW
WHEN	THE WHISTLE BLEW	IT WAS ALMOST NOON
DAD BROUGHT THE TICKETS	**WHEN**	IT WAS ALMOST NOON

Continue taking turns, combining the sentences in as many different ways as you can. Try to use each of the conjunctions in the envelope and each sentence strip at least twice.

Find It in Your Reading Look through a story or essay for several examples of sentences that have been combined using conjunctions. Notice how the writer varied the position of the conjunctions.

Find It in Your Writing See if you can smooth a piece of your writing and add interest to it by combining some of the sentences.

TIME SAVERS!

Hands-on Grammar Book Use the Hands-on Grammar activity sheet for Chapter 21 to facilitate this activity.

ONGOING ASSESSMENT: Assess Mastery

Use the following resources to assess mastery of sentence combining.

In the Textbook	Technology
Chapter Review, Ex. 48, p. 498	On-Line Exercise Bank, Section 21.2

Section 21.2 **Section Review**

GRAMMAR EXERCISES 13–18

Exercise 13 **Combining Sentences** Combine each pair of sentences below in the way that makes the most sense. Identify each combination as *compound subject, compound verb,* or *compound object.*

1. The Japanese and French built high-speed trains. The British built a high-speed train.
2. The Japanese had built their famous "bullet" train by 1964. The Japanese began to operate their famous "bullet" train by 1964.
3. The famous train was called the *Shinkansen.* The *Shinkansen* ran from Tokyo to Nagoya.
4. The French completed their train in 1981. They called it the *Train à Grande Vitesse (TGV).*
5. The *TGV* uses dedicated track. *Shinkansen* uses dedicated track.

Exercise 14 **Combining Clauses** Rewrite each sentence pair below with a comma and a coordinating conjunction, a semicolon, or a subordinating conjunction.

1. Oregon and California joined the United States. Interest in a transcontinental railroad increased.
2. The transcontinental railroad became a reality on May 10, 1869. The tracks of the Union Pacific met those of the Central Pacific at Promontory, Utah.
3. The Central Pacific built eastward from Sacramento, California. The Union Pacific built westward from Omaha, Nebraska.
4. The two railroads hired about 25,000 laborers. They built the railroads.
5. The Union Pacific laid 1,086 miles of track. The Central Pacific laid only 689 miles of track.

Exercise 15 **Combining Sentences Using Phrases** Combine each sentence pair below by changing one sentence into a phrase.

1. George Westinghouse was an American. George Westinghouse was an inventor and an industrialist.
2. He invented a brake for trains. The brake was called an air brake.
3. George Westinghouse obtained patents. He obtained approximately 400 patents in his lifetime.
4. In 1865, he patented a device. The device helped return derailed freight cars to tracks.
5. He founded the Westinghouse Air Brake Company. He founded the company in 1869.

Exercise 16 **Find It in Your Reading** Read the following sentence from Adrien Stoutenburg's retelling of the tall tale "Hammerman." Identify the ideas that have been combined and state each idea as a separate sentence.

Down South, and in the North, too, people still talk about John Henry and how he beat the steam engine at the Big Bend Tunnel.

Exercise 17 **Find It in Your Writing** Look through your portfolio for a paragraph that contains several short sentences. Combine two of the short sentences to form one longer sentence.

Exercise 18 **Writing Application** Write five sentences about your hobbies. Combine ideas, using one of the ways suggested in this section.

ASSESS and CLOSE

Section Review

Each of these exercises correlates to a concept in the section on sentence combining, pages 469–474. These exercises may be used for more practice, for reteaching, or for review of the Key Concepts presented. Answers for all chapter exercises are available in *Grammar Exercises Answers on Transparencies* in your teaching resources.

Answer Key

Exercise 13

1. The Japanese, French, and British built high-speed trains. (compound subject)
2. The Japanese had built and begun to operate their famous "bullet" train by 1964. (compound verb)
3. The famous train was called the *Shinkansen* and ran from Tokyo to Nagoya. (compound verb)
4. The French completed their train in 1981 and called it the *Train à Grande Vitesse* (*TGV*). (compound verb)
5. The *TGV* and the *Shinkansen* use dedicated track. (compound subject)

Exercise 14

1. After Oregon and California joined the United States, interest in a transcontinental railroad increased.
2. The transcontinental railroad became a reality on May 10, 1869, when the tracks of the Union Pacific met those of the Central Pacific at Promontory, Utah.
3. The Central Pacific built eastward from Sacramento, California, and the Union Pacific built westward from Omaha, Nebraska.
4. The two railroads hired about 25,000 laborers, and they built the railroads.
5. The Union Pacific laid 1,086 miles of track, but the Central Pacific laid only 689 miles of track.

Exercise 15

Answers will vary. Samples are given.

1. George Westinghouse, an inventor and industrialist, was an American.

continued

Answer Key continued

2. He invented a brake for trains called an air brake.
3. George Westinghouse obtained approximately 400 patents in his lifetime.
4. In 1865 he patented a device that helped return derailed freight cars to tracks.
5. He founded the Westinghouse Air Brake Company in 1869.

Exercise 16

Down South, people still talk about John Henry and how he beat the steam engine at the Big Bend Tunnel. In the North, too, people still talk about John Henry. . . .

Exercises 17 and 18

Answers will vary according to students' sentences.

PREPARE and ENGAGE

Interest GRABBER Read the following paragraph to students and ask them how it could be improved.

The storm caused havoc. Cars went off the road. Traffic backed up for miles. Flights were canceled. Trains couldn't get into the station. People were stranded. It was a mess. (too many short sentences)

Activate Prior Knowledge

Ask students to suggest ways to make the Interest Grabber sound better. Encourage them to explain how varying sentence lengths might improve the effect of the paragraph.

TEACH

Step-by-Step Teaching Guide

Varying Sentences

1. Sentences do more than just state information. They can be crafted to show relationships such as comparison, contrast, cause and effect, and sequence.
2. In the text example, the first two sentences show contrast, as does the next-to-last sentence. The long next-to-last sentence sets up the main point in a short, direct sentence at the end.

Answer Key

Exercise 19

Answers will vary. Samples are given.

Years ago, when most of today's model railroaders were still growing up, the toy world offered a number of fantastic electric train sets. They were often purchased as Christmas gifts and were set up only during the holiday season each year. Although these trains were generally sold as toys, adults enjoyed them as much as children did. The children often stood by while their parents played engineer. These basic sets hinted at how much more could be accomplished with a little imagination and a little more money.

Section 21.3

Varying Sentences

Vary your sentences to create a rhythm, to achieve an effect, or to emphasize the connections between ideas. There are several ways you can create variety in your sentences.

Theme: Model Railroads

In this section, you will learn ways to vary sentence length, word order, and sentence beginnings. The examples and exercises are about model railroads.

Cross-Curricular Connection: Social Studies

Varying Sentence Length

You have already learned that you can combine several short, choppy sentences to create a longer, more fluid sentence. However, too many long sentences in a row is as uninteresting as too many short sentences. When you want to emphasize a point or surprise a reader, insert a short, direct sentence to interrupt the flow of long sentences.

EXAMPLE: In the 1830's, model railroading was not a hobby. However, during that decade the first true miniature railroad was built. Mathias Baldwin crafted a small model of a locomotive, several passenger cars, and an area of track. His creation was not for entertainment; it was a model for a locomotive he was planning to build. *That first model served its purpose well.*

Some sentences in the example contain only one idea and can't be broken down. It may be possible, however, to state the idea in a shorter sentence. Other sentences contain two or more ideas and might be shortened by breaking down the ideas.

Exercise 19 **Revising to Create Shorter Sentences** Revise the paragraph below to create shorter, more direct sentences.

Years ago, when most of today's model railroaders were still growing up, the toy world offered a number of fantastic electric train sets that included engines with real steam and whistles that blew, train stations with people waiting for trains, and even trees and houses for landscaping. The train sets were often purchased as Christmas gifts for children and were brought out of the closet and set up only during the holiday season each year. Although these train sets were generally sold and used as toys for children who had spent the year looking longingly through shop windows, adults seemed to enjoy them as much or more. The children would have to wait for hours while their fathers and mothers played engineer. These sets fascinated the would-be modeler, hinting at how much more could be accomplished with some imagination and a little more money.

TIME AND RESOURCE MANAGER

Resources
Print: Grammar Exercise Workbook, pp. 101–104
Technology: Writing and Grammar iText, Section 21.3; On-Line Exercise Bank, Section 21.3

In-Depth Coverage	Accelerated Pace
• Work through all key concepts, pp. 476–478. • Assign and review Exercises 19–21.	• Assign pp. 476–478 for independent student review.

Varying Sentence Beginnings

Another way to create sentence variety is to avoid starting each sentence in the same way. You can start sentences with different parts of speech.

START WITH A NOUN:	*A model boxcar* is not hard to build.
START WITH AN ADVERB:	Surprisingly, a model boxcar is not hard to build.
START WITH AN INFINITIVE:	*To build* a model boxcar is not hard.
START WITH A PREPOSITIONAL PHRASE:	*For the model railroading enthusiast,* a model boxcar is not hard to build.

Exercise 20 Revising to Vary Sentence Beginnings

Rewrite the following sentences, revising them to begin with the part of speech indicated in parentheses.

EXAMPLE:	When miniature trains were first built, they were only design models. (adverb)
ANSWER:	Originally, miniature trains were built to serve as design models.

1. Model trains were carefully detailed to resemble what the manufacturer planned to build. (participle)
2. Constructed carefully, the models were made of hand-tooled metal and hand-crafted wood. (noun)
3. Many models were made with a combination of both metal and wood. (prepositional phrase)
4. The more elaborate models were powered by miniature steam engines. (noun)
5. Train sets, carefully made to withstand heavy usage, lasted for years. (adverb)
6. Today's model railroader's hobby did not get underway until the mid 1930's, when motors and electrical systems became readily available. (adverb)
7. Just as model railroading began to be a popular new hobby, World War II interrupted it. (participle)
8. After the war, the numbers of hobbyists of model railroads again increased at an amazing rate until the competition from television began. (noun)
9. When the novelty of television wore off, people began to return to model railroading. (noun)
10. In recent years, the hobby has seen an impressive growth. (adverb)

More Practice

Grammar Exercise Workbook
- pp. 101–104

On-line Exercise Bank
- Section 21.3

Go on-line:
PHSchool.com
Enter Web Code:
eck-8002

Step-by-Step Teaching Guide

Varying Sentence Beginnings

1. Different rhythms are created by different sentence beginnings.
2. Write the following additional examples on the board and review them with students.

   Noun: Dogs are great companions.

   Adverb: Obviously, dogs make great companions.

   Participle: Having talked with many people, it is obvious that dogs make great companions.

   Prepositional phrase: For a great companion, get a dog.

Answer Key

Exercise 20

Answers will vary. Samples are given.

1. Resembling what the manufacturer planned to build, model trains were carefully detailed.
2. Models were made of carefully constructed, hand-tooled metal and hand-crafted wood.
3. For stability, many models were made with a combination of both metal and wood.
4. Power for the more elaborate models was provided by miniature steam engines.
5. Carefully made train sets, developed to withstand heavy usage, lasted for years.
6. Finally, the hobby got underway in the mid 1930's, when motors and electrical systems became readily available.
7. Beginning to be a popular new hobby, model railroading was interrupted by World War II.
8. Interest in model railroads again increased after the war at an amazing rate until the competition from television began.
9. People began to return to model railroading when the novelty of television wore off.
10. Recently, the hobby has seen an impressive growth.

Answer Key

Exercise 21

1. A great variety of trains and accessories is available at all prices.
2. Between $35 and $60 is the cost of a simple train set.
3. Costing less than the ready-made version are landscape features made at home.
4. Some elaborate locomotives and cars built from expensive kits are here.
5. To the price of the kits are added the costs of tools and other supplies.

Customize for *More Advanced Students*

Give students several paragraphs from a lower grade text and ask them to rewrite the passage into varied sentences by starting sentences with adverbs, participles, and prepositional phrases, and by inverting subject-verb word order.

Critical Viewing

Infer Sample answer: There is a need for acute observational skills and precise building skills in order to build a model locomotive like this one.

TIME SAVERS!

Answers on Transparency Use the Grammar Exercises Answers on Transparencies for Chapter 21 to have students correct their own or one another's exercises.

On-Line Exercise Bank Have students complete the exercises on computer. The Auto Check feature will grade their work for you!

▲ **Critical Viewing** Describe the attention to detail needed to build a model locomotive like this one. Use inverted word order in your response. **[Infer]**

KEY CONCEPT You can also vary sentence beginnings by reversing the traditional subject-verb order.

EXAMPLES:

S V ADV
The bus is here.

ADV V S
Here is the bus.

S V PREP PHRASE
The ship sailed into the bay.

PREP PHRASE V S
Into the bay sailed the ship.

Exercise 21 **Revising Word Order** Revise these sentences by inverting the subject-verb order. Make any other changes necessary to retain the meaning of the sentence.

EXAMPLE: Arriving every month at the hobby shop are new model railroad kits.

ANSWER: Every month, new model railroad kits arrive at the hobby shop.

1. There is a great variety of trains and accessories available at all prices.
2. The cost of a simple train set is between $35 and $60.
3. Landscape features made at home cost less than the ready-made versions.
4. Here are some elaborate locomotives and cars built from expensive kits.
5. The costs of tools and other supplies are added to the price of the kits.

More Practice

Grammar Exercise Workbook
• pp. 101–104
On-line Exercise Bank
• Section 21.3
Go on-line:
PHSchool.com
Enter Web Code:
eck-8002

Section 21.3 Section Review

GRAMMAR EXERCISES 22–27

Exercise 22 Revising to Create Simpler Sentences Revise the sentences below to be simpler and more direct.

1. Railroading modelers build locomotives with a lot of details using tools that are specially made for model building.
2. One of the most difficult parts of model building is applying the tiny decals that come with the kits and create an accurate model of a train.
3. Tweezers and a magnifying glass are helpful tools in model building, as well as a dish of water for soaking the decals until they are wet enough.
4. The quality of detail is more important than the quantity; however, it is necessary that the model have more detail than is usually expected to be considered "super detailed."
5. The term "scratch built" means that the builder has made all of the pieces of the layout by hand instead of using "store-bought" pieces, which are considered good enough for amateurs.

Exercise 23 Revising to Vary Sentence Beginnings Revise the following sentences to begin with the parts of speech indicated in parentheses.

1. Most model railroading costs come at the beginning of the hobby, when one is just getting started. (participle)
2. To begin, one usually needs a model train set containing the basics. (adverb)
3. A locomotive, some cars, several pieces of railroad track, and a relatively simple power pack are enough to get a beginning modeler started. (noun)
4. It is wise to take a good look at what is available before buying a train set. (prepositional phrase)
5. A hobby shop usually carries a selection of model railroad sets. (adverb)

Exercise 24 Inverting Sentences Invert the following sentences by reversing the subject-verb order.

1. There are three ways to power full-size locomotives.
2. Most model trains run on electricity.
3. The important aspect of full-size locomotives to the modeler is the way the trains look.
4. Most types of steam engines have been given names.
5. Diesel engines are classified with letters and numerals.

Exercise 25 Find It in Your Reading Notice the use of long and short sentences in this passage from *Baseball* by Lionel G. García.

> We loved to play baseball. We would take the old mesquite stick and the old ball across the street to the parochial school grounds to play a game. Father Zavala enjoyed watching us.

Exercise 26 Find It in Your Writing Find examples of long sentences in compositions in your portfolio. Rewrite them, forming shorter, more direct sentences.

Exercise 27 Writing Application Write a paragraph about model building. Use both short and long sentences in your paragraph. Vary sentence beginnings.

ASSESS and CLOSE

Section Review

Each of these exercises correlates to a concept in the section on varying sentences, pages 476–478. These exercises may be used for more practice, for reteaching, or for review of the Key Concepts presented. Answers for all chapter exercises are available in *Grammar Exercises Answers on Transparencies* in your teaching resources.

Answer Key

Exercise 22

Answers will vary. Samples are given.

1. Railroading modelers build detailed locomotives, using special tools.
2. It is difficult but important to apply the tiny decals to make an accurate model.
3. Tweezers, a magnifying glass, and a dish of water can make this task easier.
4. Quality is more important than quantity, but a model must have more detail than usual to be considered "super detailed."
5. For a "scratch built" model, the builder has made all the layouts and built the model entirely by himself or herself.

Exercise 23

Answers will vary. Samples are given.

1. Railroading costs come at the beginning of the hobby, when one is just getting started.
2. Usually one begins with a model train set containing the basics.
3. Sets containing a locomotive, some cars, several pieces of railroad track, and a relatively simple power pack are enough to get a beginning modeler started.
4. Before buying a train set, it is wise to take a good look at what is available.
5. Usually a hobby shop carries a selection of model railroad sets.

Exercise 24

Answers will vary. Samples are given.

1. Full-size locomotives are powered in three ways.
2. Electricity runs most model trains.
3. The way the trains look is the important aspect of full-size locomotives to the modeler.
4. Names have been given to most types of steam engines.

continued

Answer Key continued

5. With letters and numerals are diesel engines classified.

Exercise 25

Find It in Your Reading
Have students revise the passage to make all the sentences short. Ask them which version they prefer and why.

Exercise 26

Find It in Your Writing
Have students share examples of their shorter, more direct sentences with the class.

Exercise 27

Writing Application
Have students read their paragraphs to the class.

PREPARE and ENGAGE

Interest GRABBER Ask students to turn the following into sentences.

The county fair had many attractions, I liked the prize vegetables best.

a pumpkin three feet tall

after I tripped over the giant zucchini

Some children raised pigs they raised lambs too.

Activate Prior Knowledge

Ask students which of the above are run-ons and which are fragments.

TEACH

Step-by-Step Teaching Guide

Avoiding Sentence Problems

Sentence fragments lack either a complete subject or a complete verb. Also they do not express a complete thought. The reader (or listener) is wondering, "What about a three-foot-tall pumpkin?" and "What happened after you tripped over the giant zucchini?"

Customize for *Verbal/Linguistic Learners*

Explain that the subject tells who or what a sentence is about: *Tamika studied hard. She wants to pass the test.* A verb names an action (even a mental action) or expresses a state of being. *Tamika studied hard. She wants to pass the test.*

Section 21.4

Avoiding Sentence Problems

Being able to recognize the parts of sentences can help you avoid certain errors in your writing.

Avoiding Sentence Fragments

Some groups of words, even though they have a capital letter at the beginning and a period at the end, are not complete sentences. They are *fragments.*

KEY CONCEPT A **fragment** is a group of words that does not express a complete thought. A fragment is only *part of a sentence.* ■

A complete sentence always has a subject and a verb. A fragment does not. A fragment can be a group of words with no subject; a group of words that includes a possible subject but no verb; or a group of words with a possible subject and only part of a possible verb. It can even be a subordinate clause standing alone. See the examples in the first chart.

FRAGMENTS
In the early evening.
Felt happy and relaxed.
The sign in the corridor.
The train coming around the bend.
When she first smiled.

In this chart, you see the fragments turned into complete sentences.

COMPLETE SENTENCES
The flight arrived *in the early evening.*
I *felt happy and relaxed.*
The sign in the corridor is surprising.
The train was *coming around the bend.*
When she first smiled, the whole world seemed to light up.

Each of the preceding examples needed one or more new parts. The first needed both a subject and a verb. The second needed only a subject. The third became complete when a verb and an adjective were added. The fourth became complete when a helping verb was added. The final example needed a complete independent clause to go with the subordinate clause.

Theme: Transportation

In this section, you will learn about sentence fragments and run-ons, misplaced modifiers, and many common usage problems. The examples and exercises are about transportation.

Cross-Curricular Connection: Social Studies

Speaking and Listening Tip

One trick to telling whether a group of words expresses a complete thought is to read the words aloud. With a partner or alone, practice reading aloud each italicized fragment in the chart on the left; then, read the complete sentence. Can you hear the difference?

TIME AND RESOURCE MANAGER

Resources
Print: Grammar Exercise Workbook, pp. 105–120
Technology: Writing and Grammar iText, Section 21.4; On-Line Exercise Bank, Section 21.4

In-Depth Coverage	Accelerated Pace
• Work through all key concepts, pp. 480–496. • Assign and review Exercises 28–39.	• Assign pp. 480–496 for independent student review.

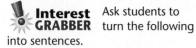

Exercise 28 **Recognizing Sentence Fragments** On your paper, write *F* for each numbered item below that is a fragment, and *S* for each one that is a sentence.

EXAMPLE: From place to place.
ANSWER: F

1. Transportation is the movement of persons and goods.
2. From one location to another.
3. From ancient times to the twentieth century.
4. Humans have tried to make their transportation facilities more efficient.
5. We want to move people and products with the least amount of time, effort, and cost.
6. Improvements in transportation have helped make.
7. Possible the progress toward better living.
8. Modern systems of manufacturing and commerce are possible because of transportation.
9. There are many types of vehicles for transportation.
10. Cars, trains, buses, airplanes, bicycles, and ships.

Avoiding Phrase Fragments

A phrase by itself is a fragment. It cannot stand alone because it does not have a subject and a verb.

KEY CONCEPT A phrase should not be capitalized and punctuated as though it were a sentence. ■

A *phrase fragment* can be corrected by adding it to a nearby sentence. The example below shows a prepositional phrase following a complete sentence.

FRAGMENT:	The explorers left for the Arctic. *On the morning of March 4.*
ADDED TO NEARBY SENTENCE:	The explorers left for the Arctic *on the morning of March 4.*

You can correct other fragments simply by attaching them to the beginning of a sentence. The participial phrase fragment in the next example can easily be corrected in this manner.

FRAGMENT:	*Arriving at the airport.* The prince and princess were greeted by cheers.
ADDED TO NEARBY SENTENCE:	*Arriving at the airport*, the prince and princess were greeted by cheers.

You may not be able to correct a phrase fragment by adding it to a nearby sentence. You might have to correct the fragment by adding to the phrase whatever is needed to make it a complete sentence, usually a subject and a verb.

More Practice

Grammar Exercise Workbook
• pp. 105–108
On-line Exercise Bank
• Section 21.4
Go on-line:
PHSchool.com
Enter Web Code:
eck-8002

iText

Get instant feedback! Exercise 28 is available on-line or on CD-ROM.

Technology Tip

If you notice that the grammar checker on your word-processing program indicates a problem that is not immediately obvious to you, check to be sure that you have typed a complete sentence and not a fragment.

Answer Key

Exercise 28

1. S
2. F
3. F
4. S
5. S
6. F
7. F
8. S
9. S
10. F

Step-by-Step Teaching Guide

Avoiding Sentence Problems

1. Review the differences among the three types of phrases.
2. A prepositional phrase begins with a preposition, such as *in, on, before, after, under, over,* and *to.*
3. A participial phrase usually begins with an *-ing* or *-ed* word. For example, *jumping over the puddle* and *stuffed full of turkey* are participial phrases.
4. An infinitive phrase begins with a *to* verb: *to swim, to dance, to sleep, to stumble.*
5. Be sure that students do not confuse infinitive phrases with prepositional phrases beginning with *to.* A prepositional phrase has an object but no verb. In *I want to fly to the moon, to fly* is an infinitive phrase; *to the moon* is a prepositional phrase, and *moon* is the object of the preposition *to.*

TIME SAVERS!

Answers on Transparency Use the Grammar Exercises Answers on Transparencies for Chapter 21 to have students correct their own or one another's exercises.

On-Line Exercise Bank Have students complete the exercises on computer. The Auto Check feature will grade their work for you!

Step-by-Step Teaching Guide

Avoiding Sentence Problems

Review the chart at the top of the page. See that students are comfortable with forming complete sentences out of phrases and that they can identify what is missing from the fragments.

Answer Key

Exercise 29

Answers will vary. Samples are given.

1. Leaving early to catch the plane, she saw Charlie delivering newspapers.
2. She stopped the car on the way because a flat tire needed to be changed.
3. Making it there late, I had trouble finding a parking space.
4. Pulling in quickly, I looked at my watch.
5. Running to catch the plane, I almost tripped on the stairs.
6. Traveling by plane is a good way to see the nation's varied landscapes.
7. Watching out the window, I saw miles of prairie.
8. She was excited thinking of the friends she would see.
9. After she arrived, she unpacked her suitcase.
10. Greeting her friends was a relief after the long trip.

CHANGING PHRASE FRAGMENTS INTO SENTENCES

Phrase Fragment	Complete Sentence
Near the old creek.	The treasure was found *near the old creek.*
Touching his hand.	*Touching his hand,* she asked for her father's advice.
To type well.	Sam learned *to type well.*

There are, of course, many ways to add words to phrase fragments in order to make them into sentences. If your teacher points out a phrase fragment in your writing, first try adding it to a nearby sentence. If that does not work, then add the necessary words to turn the fragment into a sentence.

Exercise 29 **Changing Phrase Fragments Into Sentences**
Use each of the following phrase fragments in a sentence. You may use the phrase at the beginning, at the end, or in any other position in the sentence. Check to see that each of your sentences contains a subject and a verb.

EXAMPLE: In the morning after breakfast.
ANSWER: In the morning after breakfast, we left on our trip.

1. Leaving early to catch the plane.
2. Stopped the car on the way.
3. Making it there late.
4. Pulling in quickly.
5. Running to catch the plane.
6. Traveling by plane.
7. Watching out the window.
8. Thinking of the friends she would see.
9. After she arrived.
10. Greeting her friends.

More Practice

Grammar Exercise Workbook
- pp. 105–108

On-line Exercise Bank
- Section 21.4

Go on-line:
PHSchool.com
Enter Web Code:
eck-8002

▼ **Critical Viewing** Identify several features of this plane that make it different from other types of planes. In your response, use at least one complete sentence containing a phrase. **[Distinguish]**

TIME SAVERS!

Answers on Transparency
Use the Grammar Exercises Answers on Transparencies for Chapter 21 to have students correct their own or one another's exercises.

On-Line Exercise Bank
Have students complete the exercises on computer. The Auto Check feature will grade their work for you!

Avoiding Clause Fragments

All clauses have subjects and verbs, but some cannot stand alone as sentences.

KEY CONCEPT A subordinate clause should not be capitalized and punctuated as though it were a sentence. ■

Like phrase fragments, *clause fragments* can usually be corrected in either of two ways: by attaching the fragment to a nearby sentence or by adding whatever words are needed to make the fragment into a sentence.

FRAGMENT:	The class enjoyed the poem. *That I recited to them as part of my oral report.*
ADDED TO NEARBY SENTENCE:	The class enjoyed the poem *that I recited to them as part of my oral report.*
FRAGMENT:	I'll play the game. *If you play it, too.*
ADDED TO NEARBY SENTENCE:	I'll play the game *if you play it, too.*

To change a clause fragment into a sentence by using the second method, you must add an independent clause.

CHANGING CLAUSE FRAGMENTS INTO SENTENCES

Clause Fragment	Complete Sentence
That you described.	I found the necklace *that you described.* The necklace *that you described* has been found.
When he knocked.	I opened the door *when he knocked.* *When he knocked,* I opened the door.

Exercise 30 **Changing Clause Fragments Into Sentences** Add a clause to each fragment below to create a complete sentence.

EXAMPLE: That she wanted to use.
ANSWER: I lent her the suitcase that she wanted to use.

1. Where she had planned.
2. That she got there on time.
3. That she rode.
4. When she left.
5. As long as we go together.

Grammar and Style Tip

Although you should avoid fragments in formal writing, you may find them useful when writing dialogue. However, to keep the sense of your dialogue clear, take care not to overuse fragments.

Learn More

See Chapter 20 for more information about subordinate clauses and the words that begin them.

Step-by-Step Teaching Guide

Avoiding Sentence Problems

A subordinate clause, even though it has a subject and verb, cannot stand by itself. It is a fragment. Examine the two methods shown for turning clause fragments into complete sentences.

Real-World Connection

Students may protest that they see fragments in their reading. If professional writers whose work is included in textbooks can use fragments, why can't they use them too? Explain that all professional writers learned grammar and know the difference between a sentence and a fragment. Sometimes they use a fragment for literary effect. For example, James Herriot wrote, "A feline retriever!" He could have written, "Buster was a feline retriever!" but he *chose* to use a fragment instead. Emphasize the difference between this scenario and another in which a student uses a fragment unintentionally because he or she doesn't know the difference between a sentence and a fragment.

Answer Key

Exercise 30

Answers will vary. Samples are given.

1. The exhibition did not take place where she had planned.
2. It was a great relief to everyone that she got there on time.
3. I adored the horse that she rode.
4. When she left, all of the spectators rose and applauded.
5. As long as we go together, my brother and I never have trouble finding the fairgrounds.

ONGOING ASSESSMENT: Monitor and Reinforce

It students miss more than one item in Exercises 29 and 30, refer them to the following for additional practice.

In the Textbook	Print Resources	Technology
Section Review, Ex. 40, p. 497	Grammar Exercise Workbook, pp. 105–108	On-Line Exercise Bank, Section 21.4

Step-by-Step Teaching Guide

Avoiding Sentence Problems

1. A run-on sentence has (at least) two subjects and two verbs. In the first example sentence, the subjects are *I* and *section;* the verbs are *use* and *is.*
2. A run-on sentence is different from a sentence that contains a compound subject or a compound verb or both. In addition to the fact that it is grammatical, a sentence with compounds is correct because it expresses only one thought.
3. Reading students' writing aloud is a great way for them to begin to catch run-ons; insist that they listen carefully and ask themselves if each sentence is a complete thought. Also, does it sound right?

Answer Key

Exercise 31

1. RO
2. S
3. S
4. S
5. RO

21.4

Avoiding Run-ons

A fragment is an incomplete sentence. A *run-on,* on the other hand, is an overcrowded sentence—one that has too much information.

KEY CONCEPT A **run-on** is two or more complete sentences that are not properly joined or separated. ■

Recognizing Two Kinds of Run-ons

There are two kinds of run-ons. One kind consists of two sentences run together without any punctuation between them. The other kind consists of two or more sentences separated only by a comma.

RUN-ONS	
With No Punctuation	**With Only a Comma**
I use our library often the reference section is my favorite part.	The Florida Keys are a chain of small islands, they are located off the southern tip of Florida.

Exercise 31 **Recognizing Run-ons** On your paper, write *S* if an item below is a sentence and *RO* if an item is a run-on.

EXAMPLE: Transportation has made its greatest improvements in the last two centuries it has changed the economic life of the entire world.

ANSWER: RO

1. In the 1760's, James Watt perfected the steam engine it provided power for many factories in England.
2. From there, inventors tried to apply the steam engine to navigation.
3. In 1775, Jacques Perier built an early steamboat.
4. The steamer *Savannah* crossed the Atlantic in 1819.
5. By the middle of the nineteenth century, steam navigation was replacing the sailing vessel many new ships were built of iron rather than wood.

More Practice

Grammar Exercise Workbook
- pp. 109–110

On-line Exercise Bank
- Section 21.4

Go on-line: PHSchool.com
Enter Web Code: eck-8002

iText

Get instant feedback! Exercise 31 is available on-line or on CD-ROM.

STANDARDIZED TEST PREPARATION WORKSHOP

Run-on Sentences Students may be asked on standardized tests to identify run-on sentences. Write the following sentences on the board and ask students to identify the run-on.

A The car wasn't much to look at, but it was a good value. The body was in good shape.

B The salesman was very friendly, he said we could take the car home overnight.

C We took it to Gene's garage. Gene said it was in great shape.

D I am so excited that I am actually going to have a car.

B is the run-on sentence.

Correcting Run-ons

Run-ons usually result from haste. Check your sentences carefully to see where one sentence ends and the next begins.

KEY CONCEPT Use an end mark to separate a run-on into two sentences. ■

Properly used, an end mark splits a run-on into two shorter but complete sentences. Which end mark you use depends upon the function of the sentence.

RUN-ON: In his search for a northeast passage to the Orient, Marco Polo finally reached northern China he made the name Cathay famous on his return to Italy.

CORRECTED SENTENCES: In his search for a northeast passage to the Orient, Marco Polo finally reached northern China. He made the name Cathay famous on his return to Italy.

RUN-ON: Have you heard of James Cook, he sailed his ship the *Endeavour* to the East Indies in 1768.

CORRECTED SENTENCES: Have you heard of James Cook? He sailed his ship the *Endeavour* to the East Indies in 1768.

KEY CONCEPT Form a compound sentence by using a comma and a coordinating conjunction to join two or more independent clauses. ■

The five coordinating conjunctions used most often are *and, but, or, for,* and *nor.*

RUN-ON: My mother and father go shopping on Saturdays, I stay home and clean.

CORRECTED SENTENCE: My mother and father go shopping on Saturdays, and I stay home and clean.

RUN-ON: I want to go to the circus, I haven't any money.

CORRECTED SENTENCE: I want to go to the circus, but I haven't any money.

KEY CONCEPT Form a compound sentence by using a semicolon to join two closely related independent clauses. ■

RUN-ON: The first train to the city leaves at 6:05 A.M., the express doesn't leave until an hour later.

CORRECTED SENTENCE: The first train to the city leaves at 6:05 A.M.; the express doesn't leave until an hour later.

Grammar and Style Tip

When referring to the specific name of a ship or a train, be sure to capitalize and underline it. If you are using a word-processing program, use italics instead of underlining.

Step-by-Step Teaching Guide

Avoiding Sentence Problems

1. The easiest way to correct run-ons is to create two sentences with an end mark.
2. Write the following run-on sentences on the board for additional practice. Ask students to supply end marks to correct the run-on.

   Keesha likes her job well enough, she mostly enjoys the other kids she works with. (Keesha likes her job well enough. She mostly enjoys the other kids she works with.)

   Did you see Jennifer fall on the ice she will be on crutches for six weeks. (Did you see Jennifer fall on the ice? She will be on crutches for six weeks.)
3. Although end marks are the easiest way to deal with run-on sentences, that solution can result in choppy sentences if both clauses are relatively short. Review the use of a coordinating conjunction and comma and of a semicolon as other possible solutions to run-ons.
4. Remind students that the coordinating conjunctions they can use are *and, but, or, nor, so, yet,* and *for.*
5. Write the following sentence on the board. Ask students to correct the run-on, using a comma and a coordinating conjunction.

   We are having a test today I studied hard. (We are having a test today, but [or: *and, so*] *I studied hard.)*
6. Write the following sentence on the board. Ask students to correct the run-on, using a semicolon.

   The beach is quiet in late afternoon many people have left. (The beach is quiet in late afternoon; many people have left.)

Answer Key

Exercise 32

Answers will vary. Samples are given.

1. Originally, humans domesticated animals for transportation. The first animals to be used this way were camels, goats, and oxen.
2. Another important event was the invention of the wheel. This led to the later invention of crude carts and wagons.
3. The trails used by pack animals could not be used by wheeled vehicles, so soon early roads were being built.
4. On the new roads, travelers could move at speeds of six miles per hour, a rate that was not significantly increased until the early nineteenth century.
5. Transportation was aided by other inventions as well; the horse collar, coaches with springs, and new methods of road construction are just a few of these inventions.

Critical Viewing

Support Students may say this kind of transportation has made it easier to get around. Reasons will vary.

TIME SAVERS!

Answers on Transparency Use the Grammar Exercises Answers on Transparencies for Chapter 21 to have students correct their own or one another's exercises.

On-Line Exercise Bank Have students complete the exercises on computer. The Auto Check feature will grade their work for you!

21.4

▲ **Critical Viewing** How has this kind of transportation affected life in cities over the past century? Give reasons for your answer. **[Support]**

Exercise 32 **Correcting Run-ons** Rewrite each of the following run-ons, using any of the three methods described in this section. Use each method at least once.

EXAMPLE: Forms of transportation have been around for a long time primitive humans trained animals to carry small loads.

ANSWER: Forms of transportation have been around for a long time. Primitive humans trained animals to carry small loads.

1. Originally, humans domesticated animals for transportation the first animals to be used this way were camels, goats, and oxen.
2. Another important event was the invention of the wheel, later crude carts and wagons were invented.
3. The trails used by pack animals could not be used by wheeled vehicles, soon early roads were being built.
4. On the new roads, travelers could move at speeds of six miles per hour, the rate was not significantly increased until the nineteenth century.
5. Transportation was aided by other inventions as well the horse collar, coaches with springs, and new methods of road construction are just a few of these inventions.

More Practice

Grammar Exercise Workbook
- pp. 111–112

On-line Exercise Bank
- Section 21.4

Go on-line: PHSchool.com
Enter Web Code: eck-8002

Correcting Misplaced Modifiers

A phrase or clause that acts as a modifier should be placed close to the word it modifies. Otherwise, the meaning of the sentence may be unclear. Paying close attention to the placement of modifiers will help you to avoid confusion, and sometimes unintended humor, in your writing.

KEY CONCEPT A modifier should be placed as close as possible to the word it modifies. ■

Misplaced Modifiers

When a modifier is placed too far away from the word it modifies, it is called a *misplaced modifier*. Because they are misplaced, such phrases and clauses modify the wrong word in a sentence.

MISPLACED MODIFIER: We rented a house in the mountains *with a view.*

The misplaced modifier is the phrase *with a view*. In this sentence, it sounds as though the mountains have a view. The sentence needs to be reworded to put the modifier closer to *house.*

CORRECTED SENTENCE: In the mountains, we rented a house *with a view.*

The following example is a somewhat different type of misplaced modifier.

MISPLACED MODIFIER: *Sailing into the harbor*, the Statue of Liberty was awe inspiring.

In this sentence, *Sailing into the harbor* should modify a person or a ship. Instead, it incorrectly modifies *Statue of Liberty*, making it seem as though it is the statue doing the sailing. The sentence not only needs to be reworded, but the person or ship sailing into the harbor needs to be added.

CORRECTED SENTENCE: *Sailing into the harbor*, Elizabeth found the Statue of Liberty awe inspiring.

ALTERNATE: *Sailing into the harbor*, our ship provided an awe-inspiring view of the Statue of Liberty.

Spelling Tip

Compound adjectives such as *awe inspiring* are not hyphenated if they follow the noun they modify. However, if they come before the noun, they should be hyphenated: *the awe-inspiring Statue of Liberty*.

Step-by-Step Teaching Guide

Avoiding Sentence Problems

1. Misplaced modifiers often result from an excess of enthusiasm during the drafting process. A change of thought in midsentence can create, as in the text example, mountains with a view.
2. Discuss with students the importance of carefully revising their drafts to catch misplaced modifiers as shown in the text.
3. Write the following example on the board for additional practice. Ask students to identify the misplaced modifier and rewrite the sentence so that the phrase modifies the correct noun.

   She was wearing a colorful scarf around her neck that she had bought at the mall. (misplaced modifier—that she had bought at the mall; Corrected sentence: Around her neck she was wearing a colorful scarf that she had bought at the mall.)

Answer Key

Exercise 33

1. Floating down the river (Subject needs to be added.)
2. that were made out of hollowed logs (canoes)
3. with bundles of papyrus rushes (watercrafts)
4. by sea (voyage)
5. with a single sail (ships)
6. Before the Europeans (Phoenicians)
7. When sailing at night (sailors)
8. When weather kept them from seeing the stars (Chinese)
9. that were silent, swift, and light (ships)
10. with three masts (ships)

Critical Viewing

Speculate Responses will vary.

21.4

Exercise 33 **Recognizing Misplaced Modifiers** On your paper, copy the sentences below, and underline the misplaced modifier in each one. Then, write the word that is being modified.

EXAMPLE: Transportation began early in human history over water.

ANSWER: Transportation began early in human history over water. (transportation)

1. Floating down the river, the trees looked lovely.
2. Dugout canoes were used by people that were made out of hollowed logs.
3. The Egyptians built with bundles of papyrus rushes crude watercrafts.
4. The earliest recorded voyage took place about 3200 B.C. by sea.
5. Ships were later built by the Phoenicians with a single sail.
6. Before the Europeans, the ships of the Phoenicians were the first to sail around Africa.
7. When sailing at night, the constellations kept the sailors on course.
8. When weather kept them from seeing the stars, magnetized needles were used by Chinese to navigate.
9. Around A.D. 835, strong ships were made by the Vikings that were silent, swift, and light.
10. Ships built in England, France, Portugal, and Spain were a vast improvement with three masts over earlier craft.

More Practice

Grammar Exercise Workbook
- pp. 113–114

On-line Exercise Bank
- Section 21.4

Go on-line:
PHSchool.com
Enter Web Code:
eck-8002

▶ **Critical Viewing** Imagine a trip across the ocean on a ship like this! How many people do you think this ship would hold? **[Speculate]**

TIME SAVERS!

Answers on Transparency Use the Grammar Exercises Answers on Transparencies for Chapter 21 to have students correct their own or one another's exercises.

On-Line Exercise Bank Have students complete the exercises on computer. The Auto Check feature will grade their work for you!

ONGOING ASSESSMENT: Monitor and Reinforce

If students miss more than two items in Exercise 33, refer them to the following for additional support.

In the Textbook	Print Resources	Technology
Section Review, Ex. 41, p. 497	Grammar Exercise Workbook, pp. 113–116	On-Line Exercise Bank, Section 21.4

Revising Sentences With Misplaced Modifiers

Among the most common misplaced modifiers are prepositional phrases, participial phrases, and adjective clauses. All are corrected in the same way—by placing the modifier as close as possible to the word it modifies.

First, consider a misplaced prepositional phrase. This error usually occurs in a sentence with two or more prepositional phrases in a row.

MISPLACED: Ships called dhows were sailed by ancient Arabs *with triangular sails.*

In this example, the misplaced modifier (and second prepositional phrase) should be moved closer to *dhows.*

CORRECTED: Ships called dhows *with triangular sails* were sailed by ancient Arabs.

Participial phrases are sometimes used at the beginning of sentences. When a participial phrase is used in this position, it must be followed immediately by a word that it can logically modify.

MISPLACED: *Flying over the mountains,* an electrical storm endangered our safety.

What is flying over the mountains? The sentence needs to be rewritten to insert a logical word, such as *airplane,* next to the modifier.

CORRECTED: *Flying over the mountains,* our airplane was endangered by an electrical storm.

A misplaced adjective clause should also be moved closer to the word it modifies. In the following sentence, the clause is so far away from *ring* that it seems to modify *months* or *searching.* The sentence needs to be rearranged.

MISPLACED: I found the ring after several months of searching *that my grandmother gave me.*

CORRECTED: After several months of searching, I found the ring *that my grandmother gave me.*

Internet Tip

To learn about the history of sailing ships, go to the Age of Exploration Time Line of The Mariners' Museum at this site: **http://www.mariner.org/age/menu.html**

Step-by-Step Teaching Guide

Avoiding Sentence Problems

1. The basic rule for modifiers is that they should be placed close to the word(s) they modify.
2. Write the following additional examples of a misplaced prepositional phrase, participial phrase, and adjective clause on the board. Ask students to identify the errors and rewrite the sentences correctly.

   I worked on a car at the garage with a bad alternator. (error: misplaced prepositional phrase; corrected: At the garage I worked on a car with a bad alternator.)

   Running on the track, a big dog got in the way. (error: misplaced participial phrase; corrected: When I was running on the track, a big dog got in my way.)

   I returned the gift right away that my parents gave me. (error: misplaced adjective clause; corrected: I returned the gift my parents gave me right away.)

Customize for *Less Advanced Students*

Students may need help to understand the relationship of a modifier to the word(s) being modified. Work through each sentence, showing how, for the sake of clarity, the phrase or clause needs to be placed adjacent to what is modified.

Answer Key

Exercise 34

1. Submarines with sharply pointed bows and long, slender hulls were used in the two world wars. (arrow to *Submarines*)
2. These early submarines with immature designs could remain underwater only a few hours at a time. (arrow to *submarines*)
3. During the majority of their time at sea, the submarines had to function at the water's surface. (arrow to *function*)
4. In contrast, nuclear submarines were designed with bluntly rounded bows and tapering sterns for lengthy underwater operation. (arrow to *designed*)
5. For stability, surface frames are widest above the waterline. (arrow to *widest*)
6. Underwater frames with more circular cross sections increase strength and reduce surface area friction and drag. (arrow to *frames*)
7. The submarine framework with a double steel shell is called a hull. (arrow to *framework*)
8. Ballast tanks are opened and flooded with seawater when the vessel submerges. (arrow to *flooded*)
9. For surfacing, ballast tanks are refilled with compressed air after they force out the seawater. (arrow to *refilled*)
10. When the desired depth is reached, trim tanks in the vessel keep the craft stable by adjusting the water level within the tanks. (arrow to *tanks* following *trim*)

Exercise 35

Answers will vary. Samples are given.

Ship size continued to increase with new technology in the eighteenth century. Growing trade markets around the world also contributed to increasing ship size. Sailors found the new ships difficult to control because of their greater size. Working with new technology, ship designers developed a steering wheel for ships. This new arrangement allowed a smoother, less effortful operation of the rudder.

Integrating Speaking and Listening Skills

Ask students to think of favorite phrases that they and their friends use. Have them write at least five on a piece of paper and analyze them for grammatical correctness.

Exercise 34 Revising to Correct Misplaced Modifiers

Revise the following sentences to eliminate the misplaced modifiers. In each new sentence, underline the modifier that was misplaced in the original. Then, draw an arrow pointing from the modifier to the word it modifies.

EXAMPLE: A submarine is basically a frame designed to withstand deep ocean pressures and move easily in water with an air space.

ANSWER: A submarine is basically a frame with an air space designed to withstand deep ocean pressures and move easily in water.

1. Submarines were used in the two world wars with sharply pointed bows and long, slender hulls.
2. These early submarines could remain underwater only a few hours at a time with immature designs.
3. During the majority of their time at sea, at the water's surface the submarines had to function.
4. In contrast, nuclear submarines were designed for lengthy underwater operation with bluntly rounded bows and tapering sterns.
5. Surface frames for stability are widest above the waterline.
6. Underwater frames increase strength and reduce surface area and friction drag with more circular cross sections.
7. The submarine framework is called a hull with a double steel shell.
8. Ballast tanks are opened and flooded when the vessel submerges with seawater.
9. For surfacing, ballast tanks are refilled after they force out the seawater with compressed air.
10. When the desired depth is reached, trim tanks keep the craft stable by adjusting the water level within the tanks in the vessel.

Exercise 35 Revising a Paragraph to Correct Misplaced Modifiers

Revise the following paragraph, correcting the misplaced modifiers.

Ship size continued to increase in the eighteenth century with new technology. Growing trade markets also contributed to increasing ship size around the world. The ships were found difficult to control by sailors with their greater size. Working with new technology, a steering wheel for ships was developed by ship designers. A smoother operation of the rudder resulted from this new arrangement with less effort.

More Practice

Grammar Exercise Workbook
- pp. 115–118

On-line Exercise Bank
- Section 21.4

Go on-line: PHSchool.com
Enter Web Code: eck-8002

Get instant feedback! Exercise 34 is available on-line or on CD-ROM.

Solving Special Problems

Many mistakes involve words and expressions considered wrong by today's standards, or words that are confused because they are spelled almost alike. In the following pages, note those problems that might occur in your speaking or writing.

Avoiding Double Negatives

Some people use *double negatives*—two negative words—when only one is required.

KEY CONCEPT Do not use sentences with double negatives. ■

Notice in the following chart that double negatives can be corrected in either of two ways.

Double Negatives	Corrected Sentences
Silas did*n't* invite *nobody.*	Silas did*n't* invite anybody. Silas invited *nobody.*
I have*n't* *no* time now.	I have*n't* any time now. I have *no* time now.
She *never* told us *nothing* about her party.	She *never* told us anything about her party. She told us *nothing* about her party.

Exercise 36 **Revising to Correct Double Negatives** Correct each sentence below in two ways.

EXAMPLE: There isn't no invention that has had a greater effect on the twentieth century than the airplane.

CORRECT: There isn't any invention that has had a greater effect on the twentieth century than the airplane. There is no invention that has had a greater effect on the twentieth century than the airplane.

1. A powered aircraft wasn't invented by nobody before the Wright *Flyer I.*
2. There wasn't no one who could fly it.
3. It couldn't never "fly by itself" because it had to be constantly controlled by the pilot.
4. Inventors didn't think no aircraft should be unstable.
5. They didn't know no reason the design could not be improved.

Speaking and Listening Tip

If you find that using double negatives is a habit, try practicing the correct usage aloud. Together with a classmate, take turns reading the examples and exercises on this page to accustom yourselves to using negatives correctly.

Step-by-Step Teaching Guide

Avoiding Sentence Problems

1. Double negatives, whether the result of enthusiasm, vehemence, or carelessness, are always wrong. If the word *not* is in a sentence by itself or in a contraction, there is no need for an additional negative.
2. Write the following sentences on the board and ask students to correct them.

   There is not nobody who can dance better than you. (There is nobody who can dance better than you. Or: There is not anybody who can dance better than you.)

   We haven't nothing that will do the job better. (We haven't anything that will do the job better. Or: We have nothing that will do the job better.)

Answer Key

Exercise 36

1. No powered aircraft was invented before the Wright *Flyer I.* A powered aircraft was not invented before the Wright *Flyer I.*
2. There was no one who could fly it. There wasn't anyone who could fly it.
3. It could never "fly by itself" because it had to be constantly controlled by the pilot. It could not "fly by itself" because it had to be constantly controlled by the pilot.
4. Inventors didn't think any aircraft should be unstable. Inventors thought no aircraft should be unstable.
5. They didn't know any reason the design could not be improved. They knew no reason the design could not be improved.

Step-by-Step Teaching Guide

Avoiding Sentence Problems

1. Review the usage problems presented in the text. Talk with students about these common errors. Point out the close similarity of each pair of words. Ask students to suggest ways to remember the correct usage for each.
2. There are two related methods for correct usage. One is practice. Encourage students to write a short sentence using each term a number of times, and explain that there is a connection between the kinesthetic act of writing and memory. The other route is for individuals to devise their own memory devices.
3. *Affect* and *effect* are frequently confused. See that students understand the difference between the verb meaning "to influence, or bring about a change" and the noun meaning "result."

Customize for *Visual/Spatial Learners*

Encourage students to employ their visual memory to remember the correct usage for each word. Have them try to imprint the image of each word in the sentences they read and write.

Answer Key

Exercise 37

1. that
2. you are
3. except
4. advice
5. effect

TIME SAVERS!

Answers on Transparency Use the Grammar Exercises Answers on Transparencies for Chapter 21 to have students correct their own or one another's exercises.

On-Line Exercise Bank Have students complete the exercises on computer. The Auto Check feature will grade their work for you!

21.4

Solving Common Usage Problems

Listed below are expressions that you should avoid or words that are often confused.

(1) accept, except *Accept,* a verb, means "to agree to." *Except,* a preposition, means "other than."

VERB:	She willingly *accepted* a ride on the bus.
PREPOSITION:	Everyone *except* him will be at the party.

(2) advice, advise *Advice,* a noun, means "an opinion." *Advise,* a verb, means "to give an opinion to."

NOUN:	My mother gave me *advice* on how to dress.
VERB:	My mother *advised* me to wear a skirt.

(3) affect, effect *Affect,* a verb, means "to influence" or "to cause a change in." *Effect,* usually a noun, means "result."

VERB:	The cold weather *affected* the car's engine.
NOUN:	What is the *effect* of global warming?

(4) at Do not use *at* after *where.*

INCORRECT:	Do you know *where* we're *at?*
CORRECT:	Do you know *where* we are?

(5) because Do not use *because* after *the reason.* Eliminate one or the other.

INCORRECT:	*The reason* I am late is *because* I got lost.
CORRECT:	*The reason* I am late is *that* I got lost.

Exercise 37 **Avoiding Common Usage Problems** For each of the following sentences, choose the correct form from the choices in parentheses and write it on your paper.

EXAMPLE:	Don't (accept, except) a ride in a car with a stranger.
ANSWER:	accept

1. The reason humans use automobiles is (because, that) they can transport people and small cargoes quickly.
2. An automobile can quickly take you from where (you are, you are at) to where you want to go.
3. The parts of cars and trucks are basically the same (except, accept) for the body.
4. One word of (advice, advise) is to always wear a seat belt when riding in any kind of vehicle.

More Practice

Grammar Exercise Workbook
- pp. 119–120

On-line Exercise Bank
- Section 21.4

Go on-line: PHSchool.com
Enter Web Code: eck-8002

iText

Get instant feedback! Exercise 37 is available on-line or on CD-ROM.

5. If he had not been wearing a seat belt, the accident would have had a serious (affect, effect) on him.

(6) beside, besides These two prepositions have different meanings and cannot be interchanged. *Beside* means "at the side of" or "close to." *Besides* means "in addition to."

EXAMPLES: We stood *beside* the house until the car arrived.
No one *besides* us was there.

(7) different from, different than *Different from* is generally preferred over *different than.*

EXAMPLE: The trip across country was *different from* what I had hoped.

(8) farther, further *Farther* is used to refer to distance. *Further* means "additional" or "to a greater degree or extent."

EXAMPLES: A mile is *farther* than a kilometer.
When he began raising his voice, I listened no *further.*

(9) in, into *In* refers to position. *Into* suggests motion.

POSITION: The truck is *in* the garage.
MOTION: Put the ruler *into* the top drawer.

(10) kind of, sort of Do not use *kind of* or *sort of* to mean "rather" or "somewhat."

INCORRECT: My new sweater feels *kind of* itchy.
CORRECT: My new sweater feels somewhat itchy.

GRAMMAR IN LITERATURE

from The Story-Teller

Saki

The words in blue italics demonstrate the correct use of words that sometimes cause usage problems.

An aunt belonging *to* the children occupied one corner seat, and the . . . seat on the opposite side was occupied by a bachelor *who* was a stranger to *their* party, but the small girls and the small boy emphatically occupied the compartment.

Step-by-Step Teaching Guide

Avoiding Sentence Problems

1. Use the following examples to illustrate the correct usage of *beside* and *besides.*

   The dog ran *beside* her.

   Besides running every day, she takes three dance classes a week.

2. Use the following examples to illustrate correct usage for *farther* and *further.*

   We read *further* in the book.

   We rode *farther* out than we ever had before.

Step-by-Step Teaching Guide

Grammar in Literature

1. Have a prepared student read the passage.
2. Invite students to explain why the words in blue italics are correctly used.

Step-by-Step Teaching Guide

Avoiding Sentence Problems

1. Homophone confusion is usually the result of haste.
2. Write the following examples on the board (or read them aloud) for additional practice and ask students to supply the correct answer.

   (There/They're) was little chance the kids would reach (there/their) goal. They did, and (there/they're) proud of themselves.

   The (two/too) buses took us (to/two) Maine and Vermont (too/two).

(11) like *Like*, a preposition, means "similar to" or "in the same way as." It should be followed by an object. Do not use *like* before a subject and a verb. Use *as* or *that* instead.

PREPOSITION: The rubbing alcohol felt *like* ice (Obj) on my feverish skin.

INCORRECT: This neighborhood doesn't look *like* I (S) remember (V).
CORRECT: This neighborhood doesn't look *as* I remember.

(12) that, which, who *That* and *which* refer to things. *Who* should be used to refer only to people.

THINGS: The car *that* I raced won first prize.
PEOPLE: The dancer *who* performed is my brother.

(13) their, there, they're Do not confuse the spelling of these three words. *Their*, a possessive adjective, always modifies a noun. *There* is usually used either as a sentence starter or as an adverb. *They're* is a contraction for *they are*.

POSSESSIVE ADJECTIVE: The teams won all of *their* games.
SENTENCE STARTER: *There* is a new record set each year.
ADVERB: Drive the truck over *there*.
CONTRACTION: *They're* trying to set new track records.

(14) to, too, two Do not confuse the spelling of these words. *To*, a preposition, begins a prepositional phrase or an infinitive. *Too* is an adverb and modifies adjectives and other adverbs. *Two* is a number.

PREPOSITION:	*to* the vehicle	*to* Maine
INFINITIVE:	*to* eat	*to* see
ADVERB:	*too* lonely	*too* slowly
NUMBER:	*two* buttons	*two* buses

(15) when, where, why Do not use *when, where*, or *why* directly after a linking verb such as *is*. Reword the sentence.

INCORRECT: In the evening *is when* I drive to work.
CORRECT: I drive to work in the evening.

INCORRECT: The gym *is where* our wrestling team practices.
CORRECT: Our wrestling team practices in the gym.

INCORRECT: To see Yellowstone National Park *is why* we came to Wyoming.
CORRECT: We came to Wyoming to see Yellowstone National Park.

Grammar and Style Tip

Using *there is* or *there are* as a sentence starter is grammatically correct. However, if you can revise a sentence to eliminate those words, you will make it more direct.

Example: There is a new record set each year.

Revised: A new record is set each year.

Exercise 38 **Avoiding Common Usage Problems** For each of the following sentences, choose the correct form from the choices in parentheses and write it on your paper.

EXAMPLE: Passengers usually stand (beside, besides) a bus stop sign to wait for a ride.
ANSWER: beside

1. The bus is the most common form of public transportation (into, in) the United States and throughout the world.
2. (Beside, Besides) the fact that it is relatively inexpensive to purchase and operate, a bus can also be used on existing roads and highways.
3. The bus is (kind of, somewhat) similar to a large passenger van; it is equipped with seats for passengers.
4. (Farther, Further), a bus is usually operated on a regular schedule along a fixed route.
5. A bus system is not too different (from, than) any other transit system.
6. When we traveled from Michigan to California, it was the (farthest, furthest) I'd ever gone on a bus.
7. (They're, There are) almost no words to describe the beauty of the Rocky Mountains.
8. We passed through some spectacular deserts, (to, too).
9. It was interesting and fun, just (like, as) a vacation should be.
10. The bus trip was much different (from, than) the train trip we took the next year.

More Practice

Grammar Exercise Workbook
- pp. 119–120

On-line Exercise Bank
- Section 21.4

Go on-line:
PHSchool.com
Enter Web Code:
eck-8002

▼ Critical Viewing
How does traveling by bus compare to traveling by train? Include at least two of the usage topics in your response. **[Compare and Contrast]**

Answer Key

Exercise 38

1. in
2. Besides
3. somewhat
4. Further
5. from
6. farthest
7. There are
8. too
9. as
10. from

Critical Viewing

Sample answer: Besides the cost difference, traveling by train is not much different from traveling by bus.

ONGOING ASSESSMENT: Monitor and Reinforce

If students miss more than two items in Exercises 37–39, refer them to the following for additional practice.

In the Textbook	Print Resources	Technology
Section Review, Ex. 43, p. 497	Grammar Exercises Workbook, pp. 119–120	On-Line Exercise Bank, Section 21.4

TIME SAVERS!

Answers on Transparency
Use the Grammar Exercises Answers on Transparencies for Chapter 21 to have students correct their own or one another's exercises.

On-Line Exercise Bank
Have students complete the exercises on computer. The Auto Check feature will grade their work for you!

Answer Key

Exercise 39

1. that
2. They're
3. used to travel throughout
4. correct
5. countries where
6. two
7. their
8. that
9. reason I
10. there

Critical Viewing

Infer Answers will vary. Samples are given. Bicycling is different from running, and I prefer the thrill of achieving high speeds. I rode farther into the countryside than I had planned.

PRENTICE HALL
Everyday Spelling

If you have taught the spelling skills in *Prentice Hall Everyday Spelling,* Grade 8, Chapter 25, in conjunction with this *Writing and Grammar* chapter, review and assess students' mastery of the skills before concluding the chapter.

Exercise 39 **Revising to Correct Common Usage Problems** Revise each of the following sentences, correcting the problems in usage. If a sentence contains no error, write *correct.*

EXAMPLE: The bicycle, to, is a common form of transportation.
ANSWER: The bicycle, too, is a common form of transportation.

1. A two-wheeled vehicle who is propelled by its rider is called a bicycle.
2. There the most energy-efficient form of transportation.
3. The bicycle is used throughout the world to travel.
4. In developing countries such as China, the bicycle has been the common form of local transportation for years.
5. In developing countries is where the bike is the common form of transportation, it is normal to see 300 or more bikes on the road.
6. We rode on the boardwalk on a tandem bicycle, which is a bicycle built for too.
7. The children were too short to get on they're bicycles by themselves.
8. Noon is the time when we were supposed to meet.
9. Bicycling is the reason why I came with this group to Iowa.
10. Take a picture of us over their!

More Practice

Grammar Exercise Workbook
- pp. 119–120

On-line Exercise Bank
- Section 21.4

Go on-line: PHSchool.com
Enter Web Code: eck-8002

▼ **Critical Viewing** Describe how someone might feel zooming down a hill on a bicycle. Use at least two of the usage topics in your response. **[Infer]**

TIME SAVERS!

Answers on Transparency Use the Grammar Exercises Answers on Transparencies for Chapter 21 to have students correct their own or one another's exercises.

On-Line Exercise Bank Have students complete the exercises on computer. The Auto Check feature will grade their work for you!

ONGOING ASSESSMENT: Assess Mastery

Use the following resources to assess student mastery of avoiding sentence problems.

In the Textbook	Technology
Chapter Review, Ex. 50–52, pp. 498–499 Standardized Test Preparation Workshop, pp. 500–501	Writing and Grammar iText, Section 21.4, Section Review; On-Line Exercise Bank, Section 21.4

Section 21.4 **Section Review**

GRAMMAR EXERCISES 40–46

Exercise 40 **Changing Fragments Into Sentences** Correct the fragments below by adding words to form sentences.

1. Most American bicycles.
2. Riding his bike.
3. When I went car shopping.
4. To get to the top.
5. Which are useful for pedaling.
6. That you admired.
7. Exerting all his effort.
8. Up the hill.
9. That he just bought.
10. Finally arriving.

Exercise 41 **Revising to Correct Run-ons and Misplaced Modifiers** Identify each sentence below as a run-on *(RO)* or misplaced modifier *(MM)*. Then, revise the sentences to eliminate the run-on or misplaced modifier.

1. A self-propelled vehicle is considered a motorcycle with two wheels.
2. Motorcycles have become lighter and faster they are usually specialized.
3. Four-stroke engines generally power large street bikes with two cylinders.
4. Off-road motorbikes typically have two-stroke engines, four-stroke engines are regaining popularity though.
5. Motorcycles are designed to be ridden on streets as well as off the road that meet federal requirements.

Exercise 42 **Revising to Eliminate Double Negatives** Revise the sentences below, correcting the double negatives.

1. Some sailors don't call no vessel a boat unless it can be carried on a ship.
2. Tug boats and ferryboats aren't small enough to be carried by no ships, but they are still considered boats.
3. Sailboats without no sails will move only short distances.
4. Hardly no small boats are propelled by oars or a motor.
5. A boat can't transport nobody without no water to float on.

Exercise 43 **Revising to Eliminate Usage Problems** Revise the sentences below, eliminating problems in usage.

1. Roller-skating is a sport who involves moving on special shoes.
2. The first roller skates were as ice skates with the wheels in one row.
3. The affect of roller-skating on the knees is under investigation.
4. Other people beside children, enjoy roller-skating.
5. Roller skates are different than ice skates.

Exercise 44 **Find It in Your Reading** In your reading, you have no doubt seen sentence fragments. Explain why writers might choose to use sentence fragments.

Exercise 45 **Find It in Your Writing** Look through your portfolio to see whether you have used fragments, run-ons, or misplaced modifiers. Rewrite the incorrect sentences.

Exercise 46 **Writing Application** Write a description of a trip you have taken. Use a variety of sentences to describe the kind of transportation you used. Write at least five sentences, avoiding common usage errors.

ASSESS and CLOSE

Section Review

Each of these exercises correlates to a concept in the section on avoiding sentence problems, pages 480–496. These exercises may be used for more practice, for reteaching, or for review of the Key Concepts presented. Answers for all chapter exercises are available in *Grammar Exercises Answers on Transparencies* in your teaching resources.

Answer Key

Exercise 40

Answers will vary. Samples are given.

1. Most American bicycles have more than one gear.
2. Tom was riding his bike, an American five-speed model.
3. When I went car shopping, I wished Tom were with me, but he was riding up Shaw's Ridge.
4. To get to the top, he had to pedal hard.
5. Tom wears shoes with grooved soles, which are useful for pedaling.
6. The shoes that you admired are not very practical.
7. Exerting all his effort, Tom crowned the ridge.
8. When I looked up the hill, I couldn't spot Tom.
9. He is wearing a green racing jacket that he just bought.
10. Finally arriving, he got off and rested his tired legs.

Exercise 41

1. MM. A self-propelled vehicle with two wheels is considered a motorcycle.
2. RO. Modern motorcycles have become lighter and faster. They are usually specialized.
3. MM. Four-stroke engines with two cylinders generally power large street bikes.
4. RO. Off-road motorbikes typically have two-stroke engines. Four-stroke singles are regaining popularity though.
5. MM. Motorcycles that meet federal requirements are designed to be ridden on streets as well as off the road.

Exercise 42

1. Some sailors don't call any vessel a boat unless it can be carried on a ship.

continued

Answer Key continued

2. Tug boats and ferryboats aren't small enough to be carried by most ships, but they are still considered boats.
3. Sailboats without any sails will move only short distances.
4. Few small boats are propelled by oars or a motor.
5. A boat can't transport any persons or things without water to float on.

Exercise 43

1. that
2. like
3. effect
4. Besides children, other people enjoy roller-skating.
5. from

Exercise 44

Students may mention writers' use of fragments for literary effect.

Exercise 45

Sentences will vary.

Exercise 46

Students' descriptions will vary but should contain a variety of sentences.

CHAPTER REVIEW

Each of these exercises correlates to a concept in the chapter on effective sentences, pages 464–497. These exercises may be used for more practice, for reteaching, or for review of the Key Concepts presented. Answers for all exercises are available in *Grammar Exercises Answers on Transparencies* in your teaching resources.

Answer Key

Exercise 47

1. declarative .
2. imperative .
3. interrogative ?
4. declarative .
5. interrogative ?; exclamatory !

Exercise 48

Answers will vary. Samples are given.

1–2. Ships using mechanical power have almost entirely replaced ships using a sail, but a few ships using a sail still remain.
3–4. By 1934, only forty square-rigged sailing ships remained afloat, and sixteen of these ships were used for training purposes by various countries.
5–6. Commercial use of the sailing ship is dying out; today only about twenty large sailing ships remain in service worldwide.
7. One sailing ship that did not die out with the rest is the yacht.
8. The yacht is a sailing vessel used for both travel and racing purposes.
9–10. Yachting spread worldwide, and it especially changed after World War II.

Exercise 49

Answers will vary. Samples are given.

1. Slowly came the age of the steamship.
2. Not trusting steam, shipbuilders continued to include masts and sails on their ships.
3. The *Savannah* was the first United States steamship to cross the Atlantic Ocean.
4. During the 27-day voyage, the *Savannah's* steam engine operated for only eighty hours.
5. To get across, the *Savannah* had to use her dozen sails.

Chapter 21 Chapter Review

GRAMMAR EXERCISES 47–54

Exercise 47 Identifying the Four Types of Sentences Identify each sentence below as *declarative, imperative, interrogative,* or *exclamatory*. Add the appropriate end mark.

1. Ships in the nineteenth century needed a great cargo capacity
2. Imagine the space needed to carry people and supplies
3. Were they large
4. The ships usually needed four to seven masts
5. Did you say four to seven masts They must have been *huge*

Exercise 48 Revising to Combine Sentences and Vary Sentence Length Revise the following paragraph, combining some short sentences and leaving others short for emphasis.

(1) Ships using mechanical power have almost entirely replaced ships using a sail. (2) A few ships using a sail still remain. (3) By 1934, only forty square-rigged sailing ships remained afloat. (4) Sixteen of these ships were used for training purposes by various countries. (5) Commercial use of the sailing ship is dying out. (6) Today, only about twenty large sailing ships remain in service worldwide. (7) One sailing ship that did not die out with the rest is the yacht. (8) The yacht is a sailing vessel used for both travel and racing purposes. (9) Yachting spread worldwide. (10) It especially changed after World War II.

Exercise 49 Varying Sentence Beginnings Rewrite the following sentences on your paper, starting them with the part of speech indicated in parentheses.

1. The age of the steamship came slowly. (adverb)
2. Shipbuilders did not trust steam and continued to include masts and sails on their ships. (participle)
3. The first United States steamship to cross the Atlantic Ocean was the *Savannah.* (noun)
4. The *Savannah's* steam engine operated for only eighty hours during the 27-day voyage. (prepositional phrase)
5. The *Savannah* had to use her dozen sails to get across. (infinitive)

Exercise 50 Revising to Correct Phrase Fragments, Clause Fragments, Run-ons, and Misplaced Modifiers Revise each of the following items, correcting all errors in sentence structure.

1. A local railroad that provides rapid transportation for many people.
2. A third rail gets electricity to the cars mounted parallel to the rails of the subway train.
3. Near the end of the nineteenth century, subway systems were developed in London and Berlin with electric railways.
4. That include elevated railroads and surface-level railroad tracks.
5. Surface railroads are usually used.
6. Boston built the first United States subway it had streetcars instead of trains.
7. New York City opened its first subway in 1904 they continued to improve it for the next forty years.
8. The economic depression and the loss of subway passengers slowed new subway construction to new automobiles.
9. Subway construction resumed after World War II in most parts of the world the United States was the exception.
10. Which were steam operated.

Exercise 50

1. A local railroad provides rapid transportation for many people.
2. A third rail mounted parallel to the rails gets electricity to the cars of the subway train.
3. Near the end of the nineteenth century, subway systems with electric railways were developed in London and Berlin.
4. These are systems that include elevated railroads and surface-level railroad tracks.
5. Surface railroads are usually used for short-distance travel.
6. Boston built the first United States subway. It had streetcars instead of trains.
7. New York City opened its first subway in 1904. The city continued to improve it for the next 40 years.
8. The economic depression and the loss of subway passengers to new automobiles slowed new subway construction.
9. Subway construction resumed at a rapid pace after World War II in most parts of the world. The United States was the exception.
10. Many trains were steam operated.

Exercise 51 **Correcting Double Negatives** On your paper, write *C* for each sentence below that is correct and *DN* for each sentence that contains a double negative. Then, correct the double negatives.

1. The hot-air balloon is an aircraft that never uses no wings or motors.
2. Instead, air is heated and contained in the balloon, and then the balloon won't stay on the ground no longer.
3. Without some kind of a basket, it will never carry no passengers.
4. If the balloon didn't have no hot air inside it, it wouldn't rise.
5. Neither hydrogen nor helium was used in the first balloons.

Exercise 52 **Avoiding Usage Problems** For each sentence below, write the correct form from the pair in parentheses.

1. The trucking industry is made up of persons or firms (that, who) use semi-trailers to transport products.
2. An independent truck owner (excepts, accepts) jobs to transport goods for businesses.
3. Firms or companies (in, into) the business of hiring truckers to transport goods are called carriers.
4. The three major types of carriers are different (than, from) each other.
5. Private carriers use trucks to transport only (there, their, they're) own products or materials.
6. Contract carriers sign agreements (to, too, two) transport materials.
7. Trucks will go (further, farther) from the base than cars.
8. Modern engineering advances have (affected, effected) today's semitrailers.
9. The reason semi-trailers are designed the way they are is (because, that) they need to perform specific functions.
10. (There, Their, They're) are many reasons for trucks to have differently shaped trailers.

Exercise 53 **Revising a Paragraph** Revise the following paragraph, eliminating all errors in usage and sentence structure. Create variety by combining some sentences and shortening others.

Planes, trains, and automobiles, common forms of transportation. Trains go fast. Planes go further faster. How did your first airplane ride effect you? Did the food taste like you expected it too? Can you even remember the first time you rode in a car? You were probably an infant and can't remember nothing about it. The reason many people enjoy trains is because they can relax during there trip. Traveling by train, the seats are more comfortable than in an airplane. However, if they drive they're own cars, people can go where they want when they want, nobody can tell them what to do.

Exercise 54 **Writing Application** Write a paragraph about a plane, boat, or train trip. Include some of the kinds of sentences specified below.

1. a sentence containing a compound subject
2. a sentence containing a compound verb
3. a sentence containing two independent clauses
4. a sentence containing a subordinating clause
5. a sentence combined with a phrase
6. a declarative sentence containing the word *except*
7. an imperative sentence containing the word *advice*
8. a declarative sentence containing the word *besides*
9. an interrogative sentence containing the word *further* or *farther*
10. an exclamatory sentence containing the word *too*

Exercise 51

1. DN The hot-air balloon is an aircraft that uses no wings or rotors.
2. DN Instead, air is heated and contained in the balloon, and then the balloon will no longer stay on the ground.
3. DN Without some kind of a basket hanging below the balloon, it will carry no passengers.
4. DN If the balloon didn't have hot air inside it, it wouldn't rise.
5. C

Exercise 52

1. that
2. accepts
3. in
4. from
5. their
6. to
7. farther
8. affected
9. that
10. There

Exercise 53

Answers will vary. Samples are given.

Planes, trains, and automobiles are common forms of transportation. Though trains go fast, planes go farther faster. How did your first airplane ride affect you? Did the food taste as you expected it to? Can you even remember the first time you rode in a car? Since you were probably an infant, you probably can't remember anything about it. The reason many people enjoy trains is that they can relax during their trip. People who travel by train believe that train seats are more comfortable than airplane seats. However, people who drive their own cars can go where they want when they want; nobody can tell them what to do.

Exercise 54

Writing Application
Encourage students to combine their descriptions into a class book organized by type of transportation. Have students trade their sentences with a partner to check.

Lesson Objectives

- To recognize appropriate sentence construction.

Step-by-Step Teaching Guide

Recognizing Appropriate Sentence Construction

Teaching Resources: Standardized Test Preparation Workbook, pp. 41–42

1. Review with students the bulleted list of points.
2. Encourage students to jot down any notes in the margins as they read each passage. Have them quickly identify any errors in sentence construction they find.
3. Then have students carefully read all of the choices. They can quickly eliminate any choices that clearly contain errors. This will make choosing their final answer easier.

Standardized Test Preparation Workshop

Recognizing Appropriate Sentence Construction

Using sentences correctly and effectively is necessary for logical, clear communication. Because this skill is so important, standardized tests evaluate your ability to write effectively. Questions that test this skill often ask you to choose among sentence revisions that eliminate fragments or run-on sentences, combine two or more choppy sentences, or vary sentence beginnings. When deciding on an answer choice, remember these points:

- Avoid choices that fail to correct a run-on or fragment.
- Avoid choices in which combined sentences result in a misplaced modifier.
- Look for choices that combine sentences so that errors are corrected, and the original meaning is not changed.

The following item will give you practice in questions that test your ability to write effective sentences.

Test Tip

Remember that a fragment is a group of words that does not express a complete thought. A run-on sentence contains two or more complete sentences joined without punctuation or only by a comma.

Sample Test Item	Answer and Explanation
Choose the letter of the best way to write the underlined section. If the underlined section needs no change, choose "Correct as is." The movie was better. Others I've seen (1) on the same subject were not as good.	
1 A I've seen better movies on the same subject. **B** The movie was better than others I've seen on the same subject. **C** The movie I've seen was better than others. Even if they were on the same subject. **D** Correct as is	The correct answer is *B*. This choice combines the two sentences into one complex sentence that retains the original meaning. Choice *A* changes the meaning of the original, and choice *C* adds extra words and introduces a fragment.

TEST-TAKING TIP

Tell students to carefully check their chosen answer to the original sentences in the passage. They should make sure that no important information has been deleted or that the original meaning of the sentence has not been altered.

Practice 1 **Directions:** Choose the letter of the best way to write each underlined section. If the underlined section needs no change, choose "Correct as is."

Hector pulled the small truck over to the side of the road seeing a place to stop. (1) The wind picked up. A tumbleweed rolled by. (2)

Rosa gazed toward the abandoned mining town, it was at the end of the dusty path. (3)

1 A The small truck was pulled over to the side of the road by Hector, who saw a place to stop.
B Hector pulled the small truck over to the side of the road, having seen a place to stop.
C Seeing a place to stop, Hector pulled the small truck over to the side of the road.
D Correct as is

2 F The wind picked up as a tumbleweed rolled by.
G The wind picked up, and a tumbleweed rolled by.
H A tumbleweed rolled by. Then, it got windy.
J Correct as is

3 A Rosa gazed toward the abandoned mining town. It was at the end of the dusty path.
B At the end of the dusty path, Rosa saw the abandoned mining town.
C Rosa gazed toward the abandoned mining town at the end of the dusty path.
D Correct as is

Practice 2 **Directions:** Choose the letter of the best way to write each underlined section. If the underlined section needs no change, choose "Correct as is."

It was an old town that had been abandoned a long time ago. They walked a bit closer, then stopped. (1) Hector stood a moment. Hector was silent. (2) A tear rolled down her cheek. Rosa imagined the hardship of a life lived there. (3)

1 A It was an old town that had been abandoned until they walked a bit closer, then stopped.
B Abandoned a long time ago, it was an old town. They walked a bit closer, then stopped.
C It was an old town. It had been abandoned a long time ago. They walked a bit closer, then stopped.
D Correct as is

2 F Hector was silent as he stood a moment.
G In silence stood Hector for a moment.
H Hector stood a moment in silence.
J Correct as is

3 A A tear rolled down Rosa's cheek as she imagined the hardship of a life lived there.
B A tear rolling down Rosa's cheek, Rosa imagined the hardship of a life lived there.
C A tear rolled down Rosa's cheek because it must have been hard for people who lived there.
D Correct as is

Answer Key

Practice 1

1. C
2. G
3. C

Practice 2

1. D
2. H
3. A

Answer Key

Exercise A

1. I; enjoy; sports (direct object); exclamatory
2. It; is; game (predicate noun); declarative
3. versions; have; rules, regulations (direct objects); declarative
4. rules, rules; are; used (predicate adjective); declarative
5. ball; resemble; ball (direct object); interrogative
6. you; toss; me (indirect object); ball (direct object); imperative
7. you, Sam; play; periods (direct object); interrogative
8. break; gives; us (indirect object); time (direct object); declarative
9. way; is; awesome (predicate adjective); exclamatory
10. that; was; shot (predicate noun); exclamatory

Exercise B

1. Water polo and swimming involve similar skills.
2. Swimming uses the hands and feet to move.
3. Humans take strokes in the water and don't use a walking motion, as animals do.
4. Strokes are usually quick and powerful.
5. David gave me and Mary a swimming lesson.

Exercise C

1. which is also called the freestyle (adjective clause); by an English swimmer (adverb prepositional); in the 1870's (adverb prepositional); compound-complex
2. Moving the arm (gerund); through the air and water (adverb prepositional); through the water (adverb prepositional); simple
3. to kick (infinitive); while he or she makes the arm movements (adverb clause); complex
4. Turning the head to one side (participial); of air (adjective prepositional); simple
5. an American swimmer (appositive); with an alternating arm backstroke (adverb prepositional); in 1912 (adverb prepositional); simple
6. which involves turning the back to the water (adjective clause); complex
7. Known since the seventeenth century (participial); of swimming (adjective prepositional); simple
8. who lies face down in the water (adjective clause); making a series (gerund); of horizontal movements (adjective prepositional); complex
9. over the head (adverb prepositional); through the water (adverb prepositional); compound
10. For the dolphin leg kick (adjective prepositional); which is more difficult (adjective clause); to keep the feet together (infinitive); complex

Cumulative Review

USAGE

Exercise A Recognizing Basic Sentence Parts Copy the following sentences, underlining each simple subject once and each simple predicate twice. Circle the complements, and label each *direct object, indirect object, predicate noun,* or *predicate adjective.* Then, identify the function of each sentence as *declarative, imperative, interrogative,* or *exclamatory.*

1. I really enjoy sports like water polo!
2. It is a fast-paced game in a swimming pool.
3. The two versions of water polo have slightly different rules and regulations.
4. The international rules and the collegiate rules are used at different levels of competition.
5. Does the water polo ball resemble a soccer ball?
6. Toss me the ball!
7. Will you and Sam play all four periods of the game?
8. The two-minute break gives us time to rest.
9. The way you score goals is awesome!
10. Wasn't that an amazing shot from the middle of the pool!

Exercise B Revising Basic Sentences Revise the sentences below according to the directions in parentheses. In your new sentences, underline each simple subject once and each simple predicate twice. Circle each complement.

1. Water polo involves skills similar to swimming. (Rewrite, creating a compound subject.)
2. Swimming uses body parts to move. Those body parts are the hands and feet. (Combine, creating a compound direct object.)
3. Humans take strokes in the water. They don't use a walking motion, as animals do. (Combine, creating a compound verb.)
4. Strokes are usually quick. They are powerful, too. (Combine by creating a compound predicate adjective.)
5. David gave me a swimming lesson, and he gave one to Mary. (Rewrite, creating a compound indirect object.)

Exercise C Identifying Phrases and Clauses Label the phrases in the following sentences *adjective prepositional, adverb prepositional, appositive, participial, gerund,* or *infinitive.* Label each clause *adjective* or *adverb.* Then, identify the structure of the sentence as *simple, complex, compound,* or *compound-complex.*

1. The crawl stroke, which is also called the freestyle, was developed by an English swimmer; it was first used in the 1870's.
2. Moving the arm through the air and water pulls the swimmer through the water.
3. The swimmer tries to kick continuously while he or she makes the arm movements.
4. Turning the head to one side, the swimmer takes a breath of air and exhales underwater.
5. Harry Hebner, an American swimmer, competed with an alternating arm backstroke in 1912.
6. The backstroke, which involves turning the back to the water, resembles the crawl.
7. Known since the seventeenth century, the breaststroke is the oldest style of swimming.

8. The swimmer, who lies face down in the water, moves forward after making a series of horizontal movements.
9. The butterfly stroke brings both arms over the head; then, they are pulled backward through the water.
10. For the dolphin leg kick, which is more difficult, the swimmer needs to keep the feet together.

Exercise D Revising to Combine Sentences With Phrases and Clauses

Rewrite the sentences below according to the instructions given in parentheses. Underline the newly created sentence part.

1. Waterskiing can be a recreational sport. It can be competitive. (Combine by creating an adjective clause.)
2. The sport was invented in 1939. That was the year the first tournament was held. (Combine by creating an adverb clause.)
3. Skiers are towed across the water, and they are towed by motorboats. (Rewrite, creating an adverb prepositional phrase.)
4. Fins are located on the underside of skis. They add stability. (Combine by creating a participial phrase.)
5. The skier crouches, and the boat begins acceleration. (Rewrite, creating an infinitive phrase.)
6. A skier needs strong arms. A skier also needs strong legs. (Create a compound sentence.)
7. The skier streaks across the water. He or she causes waves to form. (Begin with a participial phrase.)
8. Waterskiing is an activity I've always loved. It is a true summertime sport. (Combine using an appositive phrase.)
9. I think about our week at the lake. In May, I begin thinking about it. (Combine by replacing the object of a preposition.)
10. Get the boat powered up. I'm on my way! (Rewrite, creating an adverb clause.)

Exercise E Revising a Passage

Revise the following sentences, combining or shortening sentences to add variety, and correcting usage problems.

In synchronized swimming, a set of choreographed maneuvers. The reason this sport is appealing is because the music is used to showcase the athlete's skills. Synchronized swimming isn't a sport only about grace and beauty, but it is also about great athletic skill, which is something that is needed by those who participate in the sport. Having impressive strength, agility, and timing, most spectators enjoy watching the sport. The figures competition is when swimmers perform several combinations of movements. Judges award points. They base their judgments on the athlete's timing, height, stability, and control. The free routines last from two to five minutes, the swimmers perform their own choreography of figures and strokes. By using original movements, routines are enhanced by the swimmers. Musical interpretation and the presentation of the performance effect the judges' artistic-impression marks. Water ballet was a sport in the early twentieth century. Synchronized swimming developed from that.

Exercise F Writing Application

Write a short description of a water sport or activity that you have enjoyed doing or watching. Be sure to vary the lengths and structures of your sentences. Underline each simple subject once and each simple predicate twice. Then, circle at least three phrases and three clauses. Try to avoid fragments, run-ons, double negatives, misplaced modifiers, and the common usage problems you have studied.

Exercise D

Answers will vary. Samples are given.

1. Waterskiing, which can be a recreational sport, can also be competitive.
2. The sport was invented in 1939, when the first tournament was held.
3. Skiers are towed across the water by motorboats.
4. Located on the underside of skis, fins add stability.
5. The skier crouches, and the boat begins to accelerate.
6. A skier needs strong arms, and he or she needs strong legs.
7. Streaking across the water, the skier causes waves to form.
8. Waterskiing, a true summertime sport, is an activity I've always loved.
9. In May, I begin thinking about our week at the lake.
10. Get the boat powered up because I'm on my way!

Exercise E

Answers will vary. Sample is given.

Synchronized swimming involves a set of choreographed maneuvers. This sport is appealing because the music is used to showcase the athlete's skills. Synchronized swimming isn't only about grace and beauty, but also about the great athletic skill needed by those who participate. Most spectators enjoy watching the sport. The figures competition involves swimmers performing several combinations of movements. Judges award points based on the athlete's timing, height, stability, and control. The free routines, during which swimmers perform their own choreography of figures and strokes, last from two to five minutes. Using original movements, swimmers enhance the routines. The judges' artistic-impression marks are affected by the swimmer's musical interpretation and presentation. Synchronized swimming developed from water ballet, which was a sport in the early twentieth century.

Exercise F

Have students identify all the phrases and clauses in their descriptions.

Chapter 22 Time and Resource Manager

In-Depth Lesson Plan

	LESSON FOCUS	PRINT AND MEDIA RESOURCES
DAY 1	**The Principal Parts of Verbs** Students learn to identify and use the four principal parts of a verb (pp. 504–515).	**Teaching Resources** *Grammar Exercise Workbook,* pp. 121–124; *Grammar Exercises Answers on Transparencies,* Ch. 22 ***Writing and Grammar iText* (Interactive Text),** Section 22.1; ***On-line Exercise Bank,*** Section 22.1
DAY 2	**The Six Tenses of Verbs and Active and Passive Voice** Students conjugate regular and irregular verbs in their six tenses. Students learn to use and distinguish between the active and the passive voice. They also complete a Hands-on Grammar activity (pp. 516–527).	**Teaching Resources** *Grammar Exercise Workbook,* pp. 125–132; *Grammar Exercises Answers on Transparencies,* Ch. 22; *Hands-on Grammar Activity Book,* Ch. 22 ***Writing and Grammar iText* (Interactive Text),** Section 22.2; ***On-line Exercise Bank,*** Section 22.2
DAY 3	**Troublesome Verbs** Students work with common regular and irregular verbs that pose special problems (pp. 528–533).	**Teaching Resources** *Grammar Exercise Workbook,* pp. 133–134; *Grammar Exercises Answers on Transparencies,* Ch. 22 ***Writing and Grammar iText* (Interactive Text),** Section 22.3; ***On-line Exercise Bank,*** Section 22.3
DAY 4	**Review and Assess** Students review the chapter and demonstrate mastery of verbs (pp. 534–537).	**Teaching Resources** *Formal Assessment,* Ch. 22; *Grammar Exercises Answers on Transparencies,* Ch. 22 ***Writing and Grammar iText* (Interactive Text),** Ch. 22, Chapter Review

Accelerated Lesson Plan

	LESSON FOCUS	PRINT AND MEDIA RESOURCES
DAY 1	**The Principal Parts, the Tenses, and the Voices of Verbs** Students work with the four principal parts of regular and irregular verbs. Students work with the six tenses of regular and irregular verbs. They learn to use active and passive voice (pp. 505–527).	**Teaching Resources** *Grammar Exercise Workbook,* pp. 121–132; *Grammar Exercises Answers on Transparencies,* Ch. 22; *Hands-on Grammar Activity Book,* Ch. 22 ***Writing and Grammar iText* (Interactive Text),** Sections 22.1–2; ***On-line Exercise Bank,*** Sections 22.1–2
DAY 2	**Troublesome Verbs** Students work with common regular and irregular verbs that are easily confused or pose other special problems (pp. 528–533).	**Teaching Resources** *Grammar Exercise Workbook,* pp. 133–134; *Grammar Exercises Answers on Transparencies,* Ch. 22 ***Writing and Grammar iText* (Interactive Text),** Section 22.3; ***On-line Exercise Bank,*** Section 22.3
DAY 3	**Review and Assess** Students review the chapter and demonstrate mastery of verbs (pp. 534–537).	**Teaching Resources** *Formal Assessment,* Ch. 22; *Grammar Exercises Answers on Transparencies,* Ch. 22 ***Writing and Grammar iText* (Interactive Text),** Ch. 22, Chapter Review

Options for Adapting Lesson Plans

HOMEWORK

Have students complete any stage of the lesson for homework.

SPELLING

To teach spelling skills in conjunction with grammar, mechanics, and usage, work through *Prentice Hall Everyday Spelling,* Grade 8, Chapter 26, as you cover this *Writing and Grammar* chapter.

TECHNOLOGY

Students can use *Writing and Grammar iText* to complete the exercises interactively on computer. They can complete additional exercises in the *On-line Exercise Bank:* The Auto Check feature will grade their work. Go online: PHSchool.com Use Web code: eck-8002

INTEGRATED SKILLS COVERAGE

Grammar in Literature
SE p. 510

Writing
Find It in Your Writing, SE pp. 515, 526, 527, 533
Writing Application, SE pp. 515, 527, 533, 535

Viewing and Representing
Critical Viewing, SE pp. 504, 508, 510, 513, 514, 519, 528, 530

ASSESSMENT SUPPORT

Standardized Test Preparation Workshop SE pp. 536–537, ATE p. 519

Standardized Test Preparation Workbook, pp. 43–44

Formal Assessment, Ch. 22

MEETING INDIVIDUAL NEEDS

Less Advanced Students ATE pp. 506, 511, 521. See Ongoing Assessments ATE pp. 507, 508, 511, 513, 517, 521, 523, 526, 532.

ESL Students ATE pp. 508, 511, 518

More Advanced Students ATE p. 517

Verbal/Linguistic Learners ATE pp. 507, 531

Visual/Spatial Learners ATE p. 509

Auditory Learners ATE p. 509

Bodily/Kinesthetic Learners ATE p. 523

BLOCK SCHEDULING

Pacing Suggestions
For 90-minute Blocks
- Administer the Diagnostic Test to students to determine instructional coverage.
- Have students complete the necessary exercises in class. Use the Hands-on Grammar Activity to provide a change of pace.

Resources for Varying Instruction
- ***Writing and Grammar iText*** **(Interactive Text)** A 90-minute block provides an ideal opportunity for students to work on computer.

Professional Development Support
- ***How to Manage Instruction in the Block*** This teaching resource provides management and activity suggestions.

MEDIA AND TECHNOLOGY

For the Student
- ***Writing and Grammar iText*** **(Interactive Text),** Ch. 22
- ***On-line Exercise Bank,*** Sections 22.1–3

For the Teacher
- ***Resource Pro*** **CD-ROM**

WRITING AND GRAMMAR ON-LINE

iText Interactive Text (On-line or on CD-ROM)
- Easily navigable instruction with on-line supporting resources
- Self-scoring exercises and diagnostic tests

Companion Web Site PHSchool.com
- On-line Exercise Bank (use Web Code eck-8002)

See the Go On-line! feature, SE p. iii.

CHAPTER 22
USING VERBS

Lesson Objectives

1. To identify the four principal parts of verbs.
2. To understand how to form the past participle of regular verbs.
3. To know how to form the past participle of irregular verbs.
4. To demonstrate knowledge of past tense and past participle of irregular verbs.
5. To demonstrate understanding of basic and progressive forms of tenses.
6. To demonstrate understanding of conjugation of regular and irregular verbs in six tenses.
7. To understand progressive forms of verbs.
8. To know how to conjugate progressive forms of verbs.
9. To identify and use correctly active and passive voice.
10. To demonstrate how to form a passive verb phrase.
11. To understand the need to use the active voice whenever possible.
12. To demonstrate knowledge of how and when to use the passive voice.
13. To demonstrate knowledge of forms of troublesome verbs.

Critical Viewing

Connect Answers will vary. Samples are given. Sailors studied maps with great care. They embarked for new lands and waters with a spirit of discovery. Often they found native peoples in new lands.

Chapter 22 Using Verbs

Over the years, rules have been established that reflect the way most educated Americans use their language. The rules in this and the following chapters are those of standard English. Learning and following these rules will help you convey ideas more clearly when you are writing or speaking.

Verb usage is an area that causes many communication problems. Because verbs have many forms and uses, you may find yourself occasionally making mistakes with them. This chapter will help you learn their various forms and will guide you in using them correctly in your speaking and writing. The themes of this chapter—education, statistics, and exploration—all reflect the importance of clear and precise communication.

▲ Critical Viewing Write three sentences describing actions of people who might have used this old map. Use past-tense verbs in your sentences. **[Connect]**

ONGOING ASSESSMENT: Diagnose

If students miss more than one item in each category, direct them to the relevant pages of the text and assign exercises for practice and review.

Using Verbs	Diagnostic Test Items	Teach	Practice	Section Review
Skill Check A				
Principal Parts of Regular Verbs	A 1–5	pp. 506–508	Ex. 1–2	Ex. 9–11
Skill Check B				
Principal Parts of Irregular Verbs	B 6–10	pp. 509–514	Ex. 3–8	Ex. 9–11
Skill Check C				
Progressive Tenses	C 11–15	pp. 520–522	Ex. 18–19	Ex. 24, 27

Diagnostic Test

Directions: Write all answers on a separate sheet of paper. (The sentences that follow are not intended to maintain a consistent verb tense. Read each sentence as though it were standing alone.)

Skill Check A. Identify the principal part used to form each italicized verb or verb phrase below as *present, present participle, past,* or *past participle.* Label each verb *regular* or *irregular.*

1. My mother *teaches* at a middle school for boys.
2. She *has worked* there for nine years.
3. Ten years ago, she *sold* cars at a local dealership.
4. She *has helped* me so much.
5. We *are becoming* very close friends.

Skill Check B. Write the present participle, the past, and the past participle of the following verbs.

6. tutor
7. shut
8. find
9. lose
10. do

Skill Check C. Copy each of the following sentences onto your paper, supplying the form of the verb indicated in parentheses.

11. My math teacher (teach—past progressive) a lesson on fractions.
12. He (call—past perfect) on me to explain my answer.
13. I (speak—past) in a very shaky voice.
14. My classmates (notice—past perfect progressive) my fear.
15. I (shout—future) at them at lunch later today.

Skill Check D. Indicate whether the verb in each sentence below is in the *active* or *passive* voice.

16. My teacher gave me a good grade.
17. My sister was given a bad grade.
18. She was reprimanded by our parents.
19. Recently, I had helped her prepare for the big test.
20. By next year, we will have been challenged for a full ten months by new math standards.

Skill Check E. In the sentences below, write the correct verb from the choices in parentheses.

21. My math score (ain't, isn't) the highest in my class.
22. I think I should (have, of) studied more for the test.
23. When I got the test back, I realized that my tutor hadn't (learned, taught) me much at all about fractions.
24. I hope my teacher will (leave, let) me take it again.
25. I have no idea why I (done, did) so badly on the test.

ONGOING ASSESSMENT: Diagnose *continued*				
Using Verbs	**Diagnostic Test Items**	**Teach**	**Practice**	**Section Review**
Skill Check D				
Active and Passive Voice	D 16–20	pp. 522–526	Ex. 20–22	Ex. 26, 28
Skill Check E				
Troublesome Verbs	E 21–25	pp. 528–532	Ex. 30–31	Ex. 32–34

Answer Key

Diagnostic Test

- Each item in the diagnostic test corresponds to a specific concept in the chapter on using verbs. This will enable you to tailor instruction to the particular needs of your students. See "Ongoing Assessment: Diagnose" on the bottom of pp. 504–505 for further details.
- Answers for the Diagnostic Test and all chapter exercises are available in *Grammar Exercises Answers on Transparencies* in your teaching resources.

Skill Check A

1. present—irregular
2. past participle—regular
3. past—irregular
4. past participle—regular
5. present participle—irregular

Skill Check B

6. (am) tutoring, tutored, (have) tutored
7. (am) shutting, shut, (have) shut
8. (am) finding, found, (have) found
9. (am) losing, lost, (have) lost
10. (am) doing, did, (have) done

Skill Check C

11. My math teacher was teaching a lesson on fractions.
12. He had called on me to explain my answer.
13. I spoke in a very shaky voice.
14. My classmates had been noticing my fear.
15. I will shout at them at lunch later today.

Skill Check D

16. active
17. passive
18. passive
19. active
20. passive

Skill Check E

21. isn't
22. have
23. taught
24. let
25. did

PREPARE and ENGAGE

Interest GRABBER Have students use the verb *gargle* in as many different forms as they can think of. Encourage them to talk about gargling in the past and present, as well as their plans for future gargling.

Activate Prior Knowledge

Ask students what they will do when they get home today, and have them compare that to what they did when they got home from school yesterday. Write the verbs and verb phrases they use on the board and ask students to note the difference between past and future constructions.

TEACH

Step-by-Step Teaching Guide

The Principal Parts of Verbs

1. Verbs have two main functions: to express actions and states of being and to express time. Check to see that students understand that without verbs it would be impossible to talk about the past, present, and future.
2. Go over the four principal parts of verbs: present, present participle, past, and past participle. Discuss the helping verbs that are used with participles, reminding students that they studied helping verbs in Chapter 15.
3. Remind students that the helping verb with the verb is a verb phrase, as in *I am talking to my friend.*

Customize for *Less Advanced Students*

Review helping verbs and verb phrases with students. Use the material from Chapter 15, pointing out the use of participles with helping verbs to form verb phrases.

Section 22.1

The Principal Parts of Verbs

Theme: Teachers

In this section, you will learn about principal parts of verbs. The examples and exercises are about teachers and schools.

Cross-Curricular Connection: Social Studies

Verbs take different forms in order to indicate time. The form of the verb *talk* in the sentence "She *talks* about her plans" expresses action in the present. In "She *talked* about her plans," the verb shows that the action occurred in the past. These forms of verbs are known as *tenses.* To use the various tenses of verbs correctly, you must know how to form the *principal parts* of a verb.

KEY CONCEPT A verb has four principal parts: *present, present participle, past,* and *past participle.* ■

Following are the four principal parts of the verb *talk:*

PRINCIPAL PARTS OF *TALK*

Present	Present Participle	Past	Past Participle
talk	(am) talking	talked	(have) talked

Notice in the chart the first principal part, the present. This is the form of the verb that you would find listed in a dictionary. Notice also the second and fourth principal parts and the words before them in parentheses. When these two principal parts are used as verbs in sentences, helping verbs are always used with them. Common helping verbs include *has, have, had, am, is, are, was,* and *were.*

A principal part together with its helping verbs is called a *verb phrase.*

Each of the following four sentences uses one of the principal parts of the verb *talk.*

EXAMPLES: I sometimes *talk* too much in class. (present)
We *were talking* to the guidance counselor about courses for next year. (present participle)
They *talked* together for hours. (past)
He *has talked* about becoming a teacher for a long time. (past participle)

By looking at the third and fourth principal parts of a verb, you can learn whether the verb is *regular* or *irregular.*

TIME AND RESOURCE MANAGER

Resources
Print: Grammar Exercise Workbook, pp. 121–124
Technology: Writing and Grammar iText, Section 22.1; On-Line Exercise Bank, Section 22.1

In-Depth Coverage	Accelerated Pace
• Work through all key concepts, pp. 506–514. • Assign and review Exercises 1–8.	• Assign pp. 506–514 for independent student review. • Review irregular verbs, pp. 509–514.

Using Regular Verbs

Most verbs in English are *regular,* which means that the formation of the past and past participle follows a predictable pattern.

KEY CONCEPT The past and past participle of a regular verb are formed by adding *-ed* or *-d* to the present form. ■

The past and past participle of such regular verbs as *lift* and *contain,* which do not end in *e,* are formed by adding *-ed* to the present form. With regular verbs that end in *e,* such as *save* and *change,* you simply add *-d* to the present form.

Sometimes you will have to double the final consonant before adding *-ed* (or *-ing,* to form the present participle).

PRINCIPAL PARTS OF REGULAR VERBS

Present	Present Participle	Past	Past Participle
lift contain save change	(am) lifting (am) containing (am) saving (am) changing	lifted contained saved changed	(have) lifted (have) contained (have) saved (have) changed

Exercise 1 **Recognizing the Principal Parts of Regular Verbs** The verb or verb phrase in each of the following sentences is underlined. Identify the principal part used to form each verb.

EXAMPLE: Frank was grading papers when he heard the news.
ANSWER: present participle

1. Teachers have helped students for thousands of years.
2. In ancient Greece, Socrates worked with small groups of students.
3. He was opening their minds to new ideas.
4. In the Middle Ages, students learned from priests and other church officials.
5. Only wealthy children would have attended those schools.
6. Most other children received lessons at home.
7. Today, students usually attend formal schools.
8. Recently, our society has noted many advances in science and technology.
9. These advances are creating new opportunities for learning.
10. We will need well-prepared teachers to help children understand the world of the future.

More Practice

Grammar Exercise Workbook
- pp. 121–122

On-line Exercise Bank
- Section 22.1

Go on-line:
PHSchool.com
Enter Web Code:
eck-8002

iText

Get instant feedback! Exercise 1 is available on-line or on CD-ROM.

Step-by-Step Teaching Guide

The Principal Parts of Verbs

1. Regular verbs follow a clear pattern in English. The rule is simple: Add *-ed* to form the past and past participle. For verbs ending in *-e,* such as *wave, rave, store, create,* and *charge,* add *d.*
2. For verbs ending in *-e,* drop the *-e* before adding *-ing* to form the present participle. Write the following verbs on the board and ask students to form the present participle.

   store (storing)
   create (creating)
   flame (flaming)
   charge (charging)
3. With some verbs, the final consonant must be doubled before adding *-ed* to form the past and past participle. Write the following verbs on the board and ask students to form the past and past participle forms.

   wrap (wrapped)
   snap (snapped)
   cram (crammed)
   bag (bagged)
   bill (billed)

Customize for *Verbal/Linguistic Learners*

Challenge small groups of students to compile lists of participles for which the final consonant must be doubled before adding *-ed* or *-ing.* Have each group write its list on the board, and invite students to generalize about rules concerning doubling final consonants.

Answer Key

Exercise 1

1. past participle
2. past
3. present participle
4. past
5. past participle
6. past
7. present
8. past participle
9. present participle
10. present

ONGOING ASSESSMENT: Prerequisite Skills

If students have difficulty forming the principal parts of regular verbs, you may find it necessary to review the following to ensure coverage of prerequisite knowledge.

In the Textbook	Print Resources	Technology
Verbs, pp. 328–345	Grammar Exercise Workbook, pp. 13–22	On-Line Exercise Bank, Section 15.1

Answer Key

Exercise 2

1. My friends and I are studying the history of education in the United States.
2. Young people have attended schools since the early days of United States history.
3. Even in colonial times, people created laws about schools.
4. In 1647, a law in the colony of Massachusetts ordered towns with fifty or more families to establish a school for their children.
5. In the 1700's, secondary schools, called "academies," were opened.
6. Some of these schools were offering classes in bookkeeping and navigation.
7. Girls were allowed to attend some academies.
8. The state of Georgia established a charter for the first state university.
9. In 1874, the Michigan Supreme Court ruled that taxes could be collected to support public schools.
10. Recent laws assure that education will be available to all citizens.

Critical Viewing

Connect Sample sentences: The teacher is explaining an abstract topic. The students listened attentively.

Customize for *ESL Students*

Review the principal parts of verbs with students, making sure they understand the formation and functions of various parts. Encourage them to talk about how tenses are formed in their home language. Encourage their efforts by telling them that regular verbs follow easy rules for forming the past and the past participle.

22.1

Exercise 2 **Using the Principal Parts of Regular Verbs** Copy each of the following sentences onto your paper, writing the correct form of the word given in parentheses.

EXAMPLE: The student has (ask) for more help from his teacher.

ANSWER: The student has asked for more help from his teacher.

1. My friends and I are (study—present participle) the history of education in the United States.
2. Young people have (attend—past participle) schools since the early days of United States history.
3. Even in colonial times, people (create—past) laws about schools.
4. In 1647, a law in the colony of Massachusetts (order—past) towns with fifty or more families to establish a school for their children.
5. In the 1700's, secondary schools, called "academies," were (open—past participle).
6. Some of these schools were (offer—present participle) classes in bookkeeping and navigation.
7. Girls were (allow—past participle) to attend some academies.
8. The state of Georgia (establish—past) a charter for the first state university.
9. In 1874, the Michigan Supreme Court (rule—past) that taxes could be (collect—past participle) to support public schools.
10. Recent laws (assure—present) that education will be available to all citizens.

◀ **Critical Viewing** Write a sentence about this teacher, using the present participle form of a verb. Write a sentence about the students, using the past form of a verb. **[Connect]**

ONGOING ASSESSMENT: Monitor and Reinforce

If students miss more than two items in Exercise 1 or 2, refer them to the following for additional practice.

In the Textbook	Print Resources	Technology
Section Review, Ex. 9–14, p. 515	Grammar Exercise Workbook, Using Verbs, pp. 121–124	On-Line Exercise Bank, Section 22.1

Memorizing Irregular Verbs

While most verbs in the English language are regular, many of the most commonly used English verbs are *irregular,* which means that the formation of the past and past participle does not follow a predictable pattern. Irregular verbs can pose some special problems for writers and speakers.

KEY CONCEPT With an irregular verb, the past and past participle are *not* formed by adding *-ed* or *-d* to the present form. ■

The third and fourth principal parts of irregular verbs are formed in many different ways. You will need to memorize these principal parts. With some irregular verbs, the past and past participles are spelled the same, as shown in the chart below. With some other irregular verbs, the present, past, and past participle forms are all the same word, as shown in the chart at the top of page 510.

SOME IRREGULAR VERBS WITH THE SAME PAST AND PAST PARTICIPLE

Present	Present Participle	Past	Past Participle
bring	(am) bringing	brought	(have) brought
build	(am) building	built	(have) built
buy	(am) buying	bought	(have) bought
catch	(am) catching	caught	(have) caught
fight	(am) fighting	fought	(have) fought
find	(am) finding	found	(have) found
get	(am) getting	got	(have) got *or* (have) gotten
hold	(am) holding	held	(have) held
lay	(am) laying	laid	(have) laid
lead	(am) leading	led	(have) led
lose	(am) losing	lost	(have) lost
pay	(am) paying	paid	(have) paid
say	(am) saying	said	(have) said
sit	(am) sitting	sat	(have) sat
spin	(am) spinning	spun	(have) spun
stick	(am) sticking	stuck	(have) stuck
swing	(am) swinging	swung	(have) swung
teach	(am) teaching	taught	(have) taught

Step-by-Step Teaching Guide

The Principal Parts of Verbs

1. Irregular verbs do not follow rules. There are no shortcuts for remembering the correct principal parts. Indeed, looking for shortcuts will lead to errors. *Drink* and *think,* for example, do not conjugate similarly. Tell students that the best way to remember irregular verbs is to use them in speech and writing.
2. Review the verbs individually. Suggest that students create their own devices for remembering irregular verb parts. Have students share their memory devices with the class.

Customize for *Visual/Spatial and Auditory Learners*

Encourage students to find their own best ways to memorize irregular verbs. Visual/spatial learners might study the charts and commit the words to visual memory. Auditory learners can repeat the verb parts quietly to themselves and attempt to develop a sound memory of the parts of each verb.

TIME SAVERS!

Answers on Transparency Use the Grammar Exercises Answers on Transparencies for Chapter 22 to facilitate corrections by students.

On-Line Exercise Bank Have students complete the exercises on computer. The Auto Check feature will grade their work for you!

Answer Key

Exercise 3

1. The student burst into the room.
2. He hurried to his desk and put/set down his books.
3. "I must tell you something before I burst," he said.
4. "On-line the other day, my father bid on tickets to the playoffs, and he got them!"
5. "Playoff tickets usually cost a lot, but these cost practically nothing."

Step-by-Step Teaching Guide

Grammar in Literature

1. Have a volunteer read aloud the excerpt from "The Ninny."
2. Write the following sentences on the board and have students change the form of the irregular verb from the passage to complete each sentence:

   The waiters often drop and ___ dishes. (break)

   We ___ late for school. (were)

   He ___ up the boxes. (tears)

   She ___ working while I continue talking. (keeps)

Critical Viewing

Connect Samples: These people are getting acquainted.

SOME IRREGULAR VERBS WITH THE SAME PRESENT, PAST, AND PAST PARTICIPLE			
Present	**Present Participle**	**Past**	**Past Participle**
bid	(am) bidding	bid	(have) bid
burst	(am) bursting	burst	(have) burst
cost	(am) costing	cost	(have) cost
hurt	(am) hurting	hurt	(have) hurt
put	(am) putting	put	(have) put
set	(am) setting	set	(have) set

Exercise 3 **Supplying Irregular Verbs** Use the verbs in the chart above to complete the following sentences. You may use some verbs more than once.

1. The student __?__ into the room.
2. He hurried to his desk and __?__ down his books.
3. "I must tell you something before I __?__," he said.
4. "On-line the other day, my father __?__ on tickets to the playoffs, and he got them!"
5. "Playoff tickets usually __?__ a lot, but these __?__ practically nothing."

▲ **Critical Viewing** Use the past or past participle forms of *get* and *put* in a sentence about this picture. **[Connect]**

GRAMMAR IN LITERATURE

from The Ninny

Translated by Robert Payne

Regular verbs are printed in red italics and irregular verbs in blue italics in this passage.

"Then around New Year's Day you *broke* a cup and saucer. *Subtract* two rubles. The cup *cost* more than that—it was an heirloom, but we won't *bother* about that. We're the ones who *pay.* Another matter. Due to your carelessness Kolya *climbed* a tree and *tore* his coat. . . . You ought to have *kept* your eyes open. So we *dock* off five more."

SOME IRREGULAR VERBS THAT CHANGE IN OTHER WAYS			
Present	Present Participle	Past	Past Participle
arise	(am) arising	arose	(have) arisen
be	(am) being	was	(have) been
begin	(am) beginning	began	(have) begun
blow	(am) blowing	blew	(have) blown
break	(am) breaking	broke	(have) broken
choose	(am) choosing	chose	(have) chosen
come	(am) coming	came	(have) come
do	(am) doing	did	(have) done
draw	(am) drawing	drew	(have) drawn
drink	(am) drinking	drank	(have) drunk
drive	(am) driving	drove	(have) driven
eat	(am) eating	ate	(have) eaten
fall	(am) falling	fell	(have) fallen
fly	(am) flying	flew	(have) flown
freeze	(am) freezing	froze	(have) frozen
give	(am) giving	gave	(have) given
go	(am) going	went	(have) gone
grow	(am) growing	grew	(have) grown
know	(am) knowing	knew	(have) known
lie	(am) lying	lay	(have) lain
ride	(am) riding	rode	(have) ridden
ring	(am) ringing	rang	(have) rung
rise	(am) rising	rose	(have) risen
run	(am) running	ran	(have) run
see	(am) seeing	saw	(have) seen
shake	(am) shaking	shook	(have) shaken
sing	(am) singing	sang	(have) sung
sink	(am) sinking	sank	(have) sunk
speak	(am) speaking	spoke	(have) spoken
spring	(am) springing	sprang	(have) sprung
swear	(am) swearing	swore	(have) sworn
swim	(am) swimming	swam	(have) swum
take	(am) taking	took	(have) taken
tear	(am) tearing	tore	(have) torn
throw	(am) throwing	threw	(have) thrown
wear	(am) wearing	wore	(have) worn
write	(am) writing	wrote	(have) written

Check a dictionary whenever you are in doubt about the correct form of an irregular verb.

Internet Tip

You can use the present participle to find information on the Internet. For example, to find information about choral groups or songs, you can type "singing" on the search engine.

Customize for *ESL Students*

Students can put the pronouns *I, you, we,* or *they* in front of the present tense verbs on the chart: *I arise, you break, we know, they swim,* and so on. The one exception is *be.* Though students have heard (or perhaps said) "I be going to school" or "She be a sophomore," these forms are incorrect. *Be* always requires a helping verb, such as *I can be there by six o'clock; we might be late;* and *that would be fun.*

Customize for *Less Advanced Students*

Some students may have difficulty remembering the different forms of these irregular verbs. Distribute index cards and have students create flash cards as memory aids. Students can write the present tense on one side and the three remaining forms on the other side.

ONGOING ASSESSMENT: Monitor and Reinforce

If students have difficulty with key concepts on pp. 509–511, refer them to the following for additional practice.

In the Textbook	Print Resources	Technology
Section Review, Ex. 9–14, pp. 515	Grammar Exercise Workbook, Using Verbs, pp. 123–124	On-Line Exercise Bank, Section 22.1

TIME SAVERS!

Answers on Transparency Use the Grammar Exercises Answers on Transparencies for Chapter 22 to facilitate corrections by students.

On-Line Exercise Bank Have students complete the exercises on computer. The Auto Check feature will grade their work for you!

Answer Key

Exercise 4

1. see, saw, seen
2. letting, let, let
3. go, going, went
4. spin, spinning, spun
5. sleep, slept, slept
6. eating, ate, eaten
7. creeping, crept, crept
8. speak, speaking, spoke
9. get, getting, gotten
10. teach, taught, taught

Exercise 5

1. came—past
2. stood—past
3. put—past
4. shaking—present participle
5. spoke—past
6. told—past
7. worn—past participle
8. grew—past
9. saw—past; knew—past
10. teaching—present participle
11. sitting—present participle
12. fought—past
13. said—past; done—past participle
14. made—past participle
15. choose—present

Exercise 4 Completing the Principal Parts of Irregular Verbs

Without looking back at the charts, write the missing principal parts for the following irregular verbs on your paper.

	Present	Present Participle	Past	Past Participle
EXAMPLE:	?	writing	?	?
ANSWER:	write		wrote	written

	Present	Present Participle	Past	Past Participle
1.	?	seeing	?	?
2.	let	?	?	?
3.	?	?	?	gone
4.	?	?	spun	?
5.	?	sleeping	?	?
6.	eat	?	?	?
7.	creep	?	?	?
8.	?	?	?	spoken
9.	?	?	got	?
10.	?	teaching	?	?

Exercise 5 Identify the Principal Parts of Irregular Verbs

For each of the following sentences, identify the irregular verb(s) and the principal part(s) used.

EXAMPLE: After the principal had shaken my hand, he spoke to me.

ANSWER: shaken (past participle); spoke (past)

1. A new student teacher came to our class today.
2. She stood up after the bell rang.
3. She put her name at the top of the chalkboard.
4. She was shaking with nervousness.
5. She spoke to us in a very soft voice.
6. She told us a little bit about herself.
7. She had worn a bright yellow dress to class.
8. After a few minutes, she grew less nervous.
9. We quickly saw that she knew a lot about algebra.
10. She was teaching a small group of students.
11. They were sitting in a circle around her.
12. They all fought to answer her questions first.
13. They said that she had done a great job.
14. I have made a decision.
15. I will choose to be in her group tomorrow.

More Practice

Grammar Exercise Workbook
- pp. 121–124

On-line Exercise Bank
- Section 22.1

Go on-line: PHSchool.com
Enter Web Code: eck-8002

iText

Get instant feedback! Exercises 4 and 5 are available on-line or on CD-ROM.

TIME SAVERS!

Answers on Transparency
Use the Grammar Exercises Answers on Transparencies for Chapter 22 to facilitate corrections by students.

On-Line Exercise Bank
Have students complete the exercises on computer. The Auto Check feature will grade their work for you!

Exercise 6 **Using the Past and Past Participle of Irregular Verbs** For each sentence below, choose the correct verb from the choices in parentheses, and write it on your paper.

EXAMPLE: We (freezed, froze) the leftovers.
ANSWER: froze

1. For the final project, our science teacher had (gave, given) us a choice of topics.
2. My group (choosed, chose) to build a robot cow.
3. Unfortunately, our teacher had (set, setted) a one-week time limit for finishing the project.
4. Completing the project on time (become, became) our goal.
5. We (sticked, stuck) to a strict plan.
6. The project had (drove, driven) us to work hard.
7. Whenever a problem (arose, arised), we worked diligently to fix it.
8. We even (spoke, spoken) to science students in other schools via the Internet.
9. The robot cow was a success, and we (got, gotten) *A*'s.
10. More important, our classmates (payed, paid) us many compliments.

▼ Critical Viewing
Write a sentence about this teacher, using the past form of *hold.* Write a sentence about the children, using the past form of *stand.* **[Connect]**

Answer Key

Exercise 6

1. given
2. chose
3. set
4. became
5. stuck
6. driven
7. arose
8. spoke
9. got
10. paid

Critical Viewing

Connect Answers will vary. Samples are given. The teacher held the hand of one student. The other children stood in a long, straight line behind the first child.

ONGOING ASSESSMENT: Monitor and Reinforce

If students miss more than two items in Exercises 3–8, refer them to the following for additional practice.

In the Textbook	Print Resources	Technology
Section Review, Ex. 9–14, p. 515	Grammar Exercise Workbook, pp. 123–124	On-Line Exercise Bank, Section 22.1

Answer Key

Exercise 7

1. The world has seen many great teachers.
2. Perhaps one of the most remarkable was Anne Mansfield Sullivan.
3. Sullivan found great joy in teaching the blind.
4. In 1887, she had begun teaching Helen Keller, a young girl who was deaf and blind.
5. Slowly, Sullivan taught Keller to read the Braille writing system.
6. By age ten, Keller knew how to write using a special typewriter.
7. She had also spoken her first words.
8. Keller eventually went to Radcliffe College.
9. She wrote many books about her experiences.
10. Keller's book *The Story of My Life* has led many people to admire her.

Exercise 8

1. seen
2. risen
3. correct
4. have known
5. come
6. correct
7. chose
8. given
9. written
10. have begun; have done/did

Critical Viewing

Analyze Answers will vary. Possible verbs include *be, do, go, grow, know, see, sing, speak, take,* and *write.*

22.1

Exercise 7 Supplying the Correct Principal Part of Irregular Verbs Copy the following sentences onto your paper, writing the correct past or past participle form of the verb given in parentheses.

EXAMPLE: The substitute had (draw—past participle) up a lesson plan.
ANSWER: The substitute had drawn up a lesson plan.

1. The world has (see—past participle) many great teachers.
2. Perhaps one of the most remarkable (be—past) Anne Mansfield Sullivan.
3. Sullivan (find—past) great joy in teaching the blind.
4. In 1887, she had (begin—past participle) teaching Helen Keller, a young girl who was deaf and blind.
5. Slowly, Sullivan (teach—past) Keller to read the Braille writing system.
6. By age ten, Keller (know—past) how to write using a special typewriter.
7. She had also (speak—past participle) her first words.
8. Keller eventually (go—past) to Radcliffe College.
9. She (write—past) many books about her experiences.
10. Keller's book *The Story of My Life* has (lead—past participle) many people to admire her.

▲ Critical Viewing Name two irregular verbs you might use in sentences about this photograph of Helen Keller. **[Analyze]**

Exercise 8 Revising Sentences With Incorrect Principal Parts of Irregular Verbs Where necessary, revise each sentence below to use the correct principal part of an irregular verb. If a sentence is correct, write *correct.*

EXAMPLE: Angel has spoke to his guidance counselor.
ANSWER: Angel has spoken to his guidance counselor.

1. Education has saw many changes over the years.
2. Good teachers have rose to meet new challenges.
3. Skilled teachers have become invaluable.
4. I am sure that you known many good teachers.
5. These teachers have came from all backgrounds.
6. The profession has drawn people with many different talents.
7. Early on, they chosen to use their skills to enrich young people.
8. Over the years, they have gave their best to help their students.
9. Many grateful students have wrote about the help and encouragement of their teachers.
10. In recent years, many teachers began to receive recognition for what they had did.

TIME SAVERS!

Answers on Transparency Use the Grammar Exercises Answers on Transparencies for Chapter 22 to facilitate corrections by students.

On-Line Exercise Bank Have students complete the exercises on computer. The Auto Check feature will grade their work for you!

ONGOING ASSESSMENT: Assess Mastery

Use the following resources to assess student mastery of identifying the principal parts of irregular verbs.

In the Textbook	Technology
Chapter Review, Ex. 38, p. 534	On-Line Exercise Bank, Section 22.1

Section 22.1 **Section Review**

GRAMMAR EXERCISES 9–14

Exercise 9 **Identifying Regular and Irregular Verbs** Label the following verbs *regular* or *irregular.*

1. bring
2. impress
3. cut
4. lose
5. deliver
6. stick
7. cover
8. remove
9. shake
10. say

Exercise 10 **Recognizing the Principal Parts of Verbs** On your paper, write the verb or verb phrase in each of the following sentences. Then, identify the principal part used to form the verb.

1. Maria Montessori was an Italian educator and physician.
2. In 1907, she introduced a new method for the education of young children.
3. Her method encourages self-reliance in children.
4. The Montessori method has become popular throughout the world.
5. Today, thousands of children are attending Montessori schools.

Exercise 11 **Supplying the Correct Principal Part** Copy the following sentences onto your paper. Supply the correct principal part. If there is no helping verb in the sentence, do not add one.

1. Before writing was (develop), teachers (present) their lessons orally.
2. The invention of writing (lead) to new methods of teaching.
3. In ancient Egyptian schools, students (spend) hours writing the same passages over and over again.
4. They were (give) arithmetic lessons by copying business records.
5. Most of their teachers (be) priests, and classes were (hold) in the temples.
6. In ancient Greece, all children (receive) physical and military training.
7. Only a few children were also (teach) how to read and write.
8. The ancient Hebrews (offer) an education to boys of all economic groups.
9. Hebrew girls (spend) their time learning at home.
10. The Roman system was (pattern) after the one used in ancient Greece.
11. However, the Romans (permit) girls to attend classes.
12. Roman students (speak) both Greek and Latin in class.
13. Roman teachers were (instruct) older boys in engineering and law.
14. These students also (read) and (write) poems.
15. We are (begin) a study of the history of education in our social studies class.

Exercise 12 **Find It in Your Reading** Find two irregular verbs and one regular verb in the following passage from "The Ninny." Which principal part is used?

> I gave her the eleven rubles. With trembling fingers she took them and slipped them into her pocket.

Exercise 13 **Find It in Your Writing** Look through your writing portfolio for examples of sentences that contain regular and irregular verbs. Identify the principal parts of each verb you find.

Exercise 14 **Writing Application** Write a description of your favorite elementary-school teacher. Identify the four principal parts of any verbs you use.

ASSESS and CLOSE

Section Review

Each of these exercises correlates to a concept in the section on principal parts of verbs, pages 506–514. These exercises may be used for more practice, for reteaching, or for review of the Key Concepts presented. Answers for all chapter exercises are available in *Grammar Exercises Answers on Transparencies* in your teaching resources.

Answer Key

Exercise 9

1. irregular
2. regular
3. irregular
4. irregular
5. regular
6. irregular
7. regular
8. regular
9. irregular
10. irregular

Exercise 10

1. was—past
2. introduced—past
3. encourages—present
4. has become—past participle
5. are attending—present participle

Exercise 11

1. developed, presented
2. led
3. spent
4. given
5. were, held
6. received
7. taught
8. offered
9. spent
10. patterned
11. permitted
12. spoke
13. instructing
14. read, wrote
15. beginning

Exercise 12

Find It in Your Reading
gave, took—both irregular past
slipped—regular past

Exercise 13

Find It in Your Writing
Suggest that students label each verb *regular* or *irregular.*

continued

Answer Key continued

Exercise 14

Writing Application
Students may want to e-mail their descriptions to the teachers they wrote about.

PREPARE and ENGAGE

Interest GRABBER Write the following sentences on the board and ask students to identify the errors:

Zach and I will go to the store yesterday.

By the time you get home, I leave for vacation.

Students should see that the verb tenses are incorrect. In the first sentence, the verb should be *went*. In the second sentence, the verb should be *will have left*.

Activate Prior Knowledge

Ask students to write sentences about what they like doing after school and what they hope to do on their next vacation. Discuss how verb tenses help people communicate clearly.

TEACH

Step-by-Step Teaching Guide

The Six Tenses of Verbs

1. The present perfect tense expresses action that takes place at no particular time in the past. It is formed using the helping verb *has* or *have: We have studied verbs for two weeks* indicates that the verbs are still being studied.
2. The past perfect tense expresses action completed in the past before some other action. It is formed using the helping verb *had*.
3. The future perfect tense expresses action that will be completed in the future before some other action or event. It is formed using *shall have* or *will have*.

Answer Key

Exercise 15

1. present
2. present
3. present perfect
4. present
5. present perfect
6. past
7. past
8. past
9. future
10. future perfect

Section 22.2

The Six Tenses of Verbs

In English, verbs have six *tenses*—the *present*, the *past*, the *future*, the *present perfect*, the *past perfect*, and the *future perfect*.

KEY CONCEPT A **tense** is a form of a verb that shows time of action or state of being. ■

Every tense has both *basic* forms and *progressive* forms.

Theme: Statistics
In this section, you will learn about the six tenses of verbs in their basic and progressive forms. The examples and exercises are about collecting data and using statistics.

Cross-Curricular Connection: Mathematics

Identifying the Basic Forms of the Six Tenses

The following chart shows the *basic* forms of the six tenses, using the verb *speak* as an example. As you can see in the third column, the six basic forms make use of just three of the principal parts: the present, the past, and the past participle.

BASIC FORMS OF THE SIX TENSES OF *SPEAK*

Tense	Basic Form	Principal Part Used
Present	I speak	Present
Past	I spoke	Past
Future	I will speak	Present
Present Perfect	I have spoken	Past Participle
Past Perfect	I had spoken	Past Participle
Future Perfect	I will have spoken	Past Participle

Exercise 15 **Identifying the Basic Forms of Verbs** Identify the tense of the underlined verb in each sentence below.

EXAMPLE: We have collected data on recycling savings.
ANSWER: present perfect

1. Statistics is a branch of mathematics.
2. It deals with the study of numerical data.
3. Many people have studied statistics for work or fun.
4. Batting averages and scoring averages represent statistics.
5. People have compiled statistics for thousands of years.
6. Ancient Egyptians kept records of their livestock and crops.
7. Ancient Hebrews took a census after they left Egypt.
8. Later, the Romans conducted a census of their own.
9. People will gather statistics for many years to come.
10. By the next century, people will have benefited from statistics for nearly four thousand years.

More Practice

Grammar Exercise Workbook
• pp. 125–126
On-line Exercise Bank
• Section 22.2
Go on-line:
PHSchool.com
Enter Web Code:
eck-8002

iText
Get instant feedback! Exercise 15 is available on-line or on CD-ROM.

TIME AND RESOURCE MANAGER

Resources
Print: Grammar Exercise Workbook, pp. 125–132; Hands-on Grammar Activity Book, Chapter 22
Technology: Writing and Grammar iText, Section 22.2; On-Line Exercise Bank, Section 22.2

In-Depth Coverage	Accelerated Pace
• Work through all key concepts, pp. 516–525. • Assign and review Exercises 15–22.	• Assign pp. 516–525 for independent student review. • Review forming tenses of passive verbs, pp. 524–525.

Conjugating the Basic Forms of Verbs

A helpful way to become familiar with all the forms of a verb is by *conjugating* it.

KEY CONCEPT A **conjugation** is a list of the singular and plural forms of a verb in a particular tense. ■

Each tense in a conjugation has six forms that correspond to the first-, second-, and third-person forms of the personal pronouns. (See Chapter 14 for a review of personal pronouns.)

To conjugate any verb, begin by listing its principal parts.

PRINCIPAL PARTS OF *GO*

Present	Present Participle	Past	Past Participle
go	going	went	gone

The following chart shows the conjugation of all the basic forms of *go* in all six tenses.

CONJUGATION OF THE BASIC FORMS OF *GO*

	Singular	Plural
Present	I go you go he, she, it goes	we go you go they go
Past	I went you went he, she, it went	we went you went they went
Future	I will go you will go he, she, it will go	we will go you will go they will go
Present Perfect	I have gone you have gone he, she, it has gone	we have gone you have gone they have gone
Past Perfect	I had gone you had gone he, she, it had gone	we had gone you had gone they had gone
Future Perfect	I will have gone you will have gone he, she, it will have gone	we will have gone you will have gone they will have gone

Step-by-Step Teaching Guide

The Six Tenses of Verbs

1. Conjugating verbs is the best way to be sure that students know the correct forms of verbs to use with all tenses. Begin by reviewing the four principal parts of *go*.
2. Review the conjugation chart of *go*. You might work your way around the room and have students in sequence use one form of the verb in a sentence. This will reinforce both the conjugation of the verb and the proper use of all six tenses.
3. Also you could divide the class into small groups and have each group construct a similar chart, using either a verb they choose or one you assign them.

Customize for *More Advanced Students*

Have students work together to write a short sketch in which they use as many forms of verbs in as many tenses as they can. Ask them to color-code each verb they use to help keep track of how many forms and tenses they use.

ONGOING ASSESSMENT: Monitor and Reinforce

If students have difficulty with Key Concepts pp. 516–517, refer them to the following for additional practice.

In the Textbook	Print Resources	Technology
Section Review, Ex. 23, p. 527	Grammar Exercise Workbook, Exercises, pp. 125–126	On-Line Exercise Bank, Section 22.2

Answer Key

Exercise 16

1. I collected, I will collect, I have collected, I had collected, I will have collected
2. you split, you will split, you have split, you had split, you will have split
3. they taught, they will teach, they have taught, they had taught, they will have taught
4. we gave, we will give, we have given, we had given, we will have given
5. it remained, it will remain, it has remained, it had remained, it will have remained

Step-by-Step Teaching Guide

The Six Tenses of Verbs

1. The verb *be* is the most irregular in the English language. Because of its frequent use, it is essential for students to know all of its forms and tenses.
2. Review the conjugation chart. You might go around the room and have each student read a form of the verb and then use it in a sentence.

Customize for *ESL Students*

Learning the verb *be* or its equivalent is one of the hurdles in learning any language. Work carefully through the conjugation chart with students either individually or in a group, taking care to answer all questions.

If you have some students in your classroom who speak Spanish, remind them that *be* is the equivalent of *ser* and *estar*. Ask them to give some examples of when to use either *ser* or *estar*.

Exercise 16 **Conjugating the Basic Forms of Verbs** The following sentences are written in the present tense. Rewrite each sentence in each of the other five tenses. Refer to the chart on the previous page if you need help.

1. I collect.
2. You split.
3. They teach.
4. We give.
5. It remains.

An important verb to know how to conjugate is the verb *be*. It is both the most common and the most irregular verb in English. You will use the basic forms of *be* when you conjugate the progressive forms of verbs later in this section.

PRINCIPAL PARTS OF *BE*

Present	Present Participle	Past	Past Participle
be	being	was	been

CONJUGATION OF THE BASIC FORMS OF *BE*

	Singular	Plural
Present	I am you are he, she, it is	we are you are they are
Past	I was you were he, she, it was	we were you were they were
Future	I will be you will be he, she, it will be	we will be you will be they will be
Present Perfect	I have been you have been he, she, it has been	we have been you have been they have been
Past Perfect	I had been you had been he, she, it had been	we had been you had been they had been
Future Perfect	I will have been you will have been he, she, it will have been	we will have been you will have been they will have been

Exercise 17 **Supplying the Correct Tense** On your paper, write the basic form of the verb indicated in parentheses.

EXAMPLE: Selena (calculate—past) the average score in her head.

ANSWER: Selena calculated the average score in her head.

1. Over the years, people (collect—present perfect) statistics to study a wide range of subjects.
2. A sociologist routinely (apply—present) statistics to study how people live and work together.
3. Demographics (be—present) the study of population patterns and movement.
4. Researchers (study—present perfect) such factors as age, income, and education among different groups of people.
5. Demographics, as a field of study, (begin—past) many centuries ago.
6. Before the telephone was invented, researchers (conduct—past perfect) most polls in person.
7. Today, researchers routinely (collect—present) data by using the telephone.
8. Some researchers also (take—present perfect) advantage of e-mail to collect data.
9. In the future, it is likely that researchers (develop—future) even more sophisticated ways to gather information about people.
10. By the year 2040, an infant born in 1990 (live—future perfect) for fifty years.

▼ **Critical Viewing** What finding have the students made from their survey? Write two sentences using verbs in present perfect or past perfect tense. **[Speculate]**

Answer Key

Exercise 17

1. have collected
2. applies
3. is
4. have studied
5. began
6. had conducted
7. collect
8. have taken
9. will develop
10. will have lived

Critical Viewing

Speculate Answers will vary. Samples are given. Students have learned their peers' views on diet and nutrition. Students had been curious about these views before they conducted the survey.

STANDARDIZED TEST PREPARATION WORKSHOP

Grammar and Usage Many standardized tests require students to identify tense errors in sentences. Ask students to choose the correct form of the underlined verb in the following sentence.

Barney has lived in Denver since last year.

A lives **C** will have lived

B lived **D** correct as written

The correct choice is item **D**. The action began in the past and is continuing, so it requires the present perfect tense. Item A is in the present tense, item B in the past tense, and item C in the future perfect tense.

TIME SAVERS!

Answers on Transparency Use the Grammar Exercises Answers on Transparencies for Chapter 22 to facilitate corrections by students.

On-Line Exercise Bank Have students complete the exercises on computer. The Auto Check feature will grade their work for you!

Step-by-Step Teaching Guide

The Six Tenses of Verbs

1. The progressive forms of the six tenses are used to express ongoing or continuing action. Progressive tenses are formed by combining linking and/or helping verbs with the present participle form of the main verb.
2. Review the chart with students, going over each progressive tense of the verb *analyze.* Point out the use of helping and linking verbs in forming the verb phrase that makes up the progressive form of the particular tense.
3. Write the following sentences on the board for additional practice, asking students to identify the tenses.

   I am running home. (present progressive)

   I was running home. (past progressive)

   I will be running home. (future progressive)

   I have been running home (present perfect progressive)

   I had been running home. (past perfect progressive)

   I will have been running home. (future perfect progressive)

Answer Key

Exercise 18

1. present progressive
2. past progressive
3. present perfect progressive
4. future progressive
5. past perfect progressive
6. past progressive
7. present progressive
8. present perfect progressive
9. future progressive
10. past progressive
11. future perfect progressive
12. past perfect progressive
13. future progressive
14. past progressive
15. past perfect progressive
16. present perfect progressive
17. future progressive
18. future perfect progressive
19. past perfect progressive
20. present perfect progressive

22.2

Recognizing the Progressive Forms of Verbs

The charts on pages 517 and 518 showed the six tenses of *go* and *be* in their basic forms. Each of these tenses also has a *progressive* form. All six of the progressive forms of a verb are made using just one principal part: the present participle. This is the principal part that ends in *-ing*.

The chart below shows the progressive form for all six tenses of the verb *analyze*.

PROGRESSIVE FORMS OF THE SIX TENSES OF *ANALYZE*

Tense	Progressive Form	Principal Part Used
Present	I am analyzing	Present Participle
Past	I was analyzing	
Future	I will be analyzing	
Present Perfect	I have been analyzing	
Past Perfect	I had been analyzing	
Future Perfect	I will have been analyzing	

Exercise 18 **Identifying the Tense of Progressive Forms of Verbs** Study the preceding chart, which shows the progressive form for the six tenses of a verb. Then, identify the tense of each of the following verb phrases.

EXAMPLE: was counting
ANSWER: past progressive

1. am measuring
2. was comparing
3. have been checking
4. will be demanding
5. had been noticing
6. were outlining
7. are verifying
8. have been joining
9. will be ordering
10. were requesting
11. will have been digging
12. had been migrating
13. will be entering
14. were exiting
15. had been handling
16. has been delaying
17. will be renting
18. will have been questioning
19. had been rating
20. have been changing

Conjugating Progressive Forms

Conjugating the progressive forms of any verb is easy if you know how to conjugate the basic forms of the verb *be*.

KEY CONCEPT To conjugate the progressive forms of a verb, add the present participle of the verb to a conjugation of the basic forms of *be*. ■

A complete conjugation of the basic forms of *be* is shown on page 518. Compare that conjugation with the following conjugation of the progressive forms of *go*. To form the progressive forms of a verb, you must know the basic forms of *be*.

CONJUGATION OF THE PROGRESSIVE FORMS OF *GO*

	Singular	Plural
Present Progressive	I am going you are going he, she, it is going	we are going you are going they are going
Past Progressive	I was going you were going he, she, it was going	we were going you were going they were going
Future Progressive	I will be going you will be going he, she, it will be going	we will be going you will be going they will be going
Present Perfect Progressive	I have been going you have been going he, she, it has been going	we have been going you have been going they have been going
Past Perfect Progressive	I had been going you had been going he, she, it had been going	we had been going you had been going they had been going
Future Perfect Progressive	I will have been going you will have been going he, she, it will have been going	we will have been going you will have been going they will have been going

Step-by-Step Teaching Guide

The Six Tenses of Verbs

1. Conjugating the progressive forms of the six tenses is the best way to assure students' knowledge of and comfort with the tenses.
2. Correct use of the progressive tenses relies on knowing and being comfortable with the conjugation of *be*. If necessary, briefly review that conjugation.
3. Review the conjugation chart with students. Go around the room and have each student read a form of the verb and then use it in a sentence.
4. Students may find the conjugation chart tedious. Point out that they already routinely use the progressive forms of tenses in conversation.

Customize for *Less Advanced Students*

Review the conjugation chart with students individually or in a small group. Help students make up a sentence for each form in every tense. If necessary, help them act out the action so that they understand the concept of ongoing action in the progressive tenses.

Integrating Workplace Skills

A cover letter for a résumé often requires the progressive forms of tenses, as in this example: *For the last few months, I have been working in . . . Before that I had been studying . . .* Guide students through writing a cover letter for a résumé that describes what they have been, had been, and will be doing.

ONGOING ASSESSMENT: Monitor and Reinforce

If students miss more than two items in Exercise 18 or 19, refer them to the following for additional practice.

In the Textbook	Print Resources	Technology
Section Review, Ex. 23–24, p. 527	Grammar Exercise Workbook, Using Verbs, pp. 125–128	On-Line Exercise Bank, Section 22.2

Answer Key

Exercise 19

1. Many scholars are studying the effect of modern inventions on people's lifestyles.
2. The impact of technology on people's lives has been intriguing social scientists for many years.
3. People are living today in a way that is very different from the way their parents and grandparents once lived.
4. Until about sixty years ago, many families had been functioning without refrigerators and telephones.
5. Without the convenience of refrigerators, most people were shopping for only small quantities of food.
6. Other changes have been affecting people's spending patterns and lifestyles.
7. Before credit cards became popular, few people had been buying things with borrowed money.
8. Today, the average American is borrowing more money than ever before.
9. It is likely that most Americans will be using even more credit in the future.
10. By the year 2020, people probably will have been spending their money using advanced electronic methods for many years.

TIME SAVERS!

Answers on Transparency Use the Grammar Exercises Answers on Transparencies for Chapter 22 to facilitate corrections by students.

On-Line Exercise Bank Have students complete the exercises on computer. The Auto Check feature will grade their work for you!

Exercise 19 **Supplying the Correct Tense** Copy each of the following sentences onto your paper, supplying the progressive form of the verb as directed in parentheses.

EXAMPLE: He (study—past perfect progressive) the birthrate of Canadians.

ANSWER: He had been studying the birthrate of Canadians.

1. Many scholars (study—present progressive) the effect of modern inventions on people's lifestyles.
2. The impact of technology on people's lives (intrigue—present perfect progressive) social scientists for many years.
3. People (live—present progressive) today in a way that is very different from the way their parents and grandparents once lived.
4. Until about sixty years ago, many families (function—past perfect progressive) without refrigerators and telephones.
5. Without the convenience of refrigerators, most people (shop—past progressive) for only small quantities of food.
6. Other changes (affect—present perfect progressive) people's spending patterns and lifestyles.
7. Before credit cards became popular, few people (buy—past perfect progressive) things with borrowed money.
8. Today, the average American (borrow—present progressive) more money than ever before.
9. It is likely that most Americans (use—future progressive) even more credit in the future.
10. By the year 2020, people probably (spend—future perfect progressive) their money using advanced electronic methods for many years.

More Practice

Grammar Exercise Workbook
- pp. 127–128

On-line Exercise Bank
- Section 22.2

Go on-line: PHSchool.com *Enter Web Code:* eck-8002

iText

Get instant feedback! Exercise 19 is available on-line or on CD-ROM.

Identifying Active and Passive Voice

Just as verbs change tense to show time, they may also change form to show whether or not the subject of the verb is performing an action.

KEY CONCEPT **Voice** is a verb form that shows whether or not the subject is performing the action. ■

In English, most verbs have two *voices—active,* to show that the subject is performing an action, and *passive,* to show that the subject is having an action performed upon it.

KEY CONCEPT A verb is in the **active voice** when its subject performs the action. ■

ACTIVE VOICE: Sharon (S) *is conducting* (V) a survey (DO).

Bob (S) *responded* (V) to the questionnaire.

In each example, the subject performs the action. Sharon did the conducting; Bob did the responding. Notice also that an active verb may or may not have a direct object.

KEY CONCEPT A verb is in the **passive voice** when its subject does not perform the action. ■

PASSIVE VOICE: The survey (S) *is being conducted* (V) by Sharon.

Bob (S) *was asked* (V) to respond.

In each example, the subject is the receiver rather than the performer of the action. In the first sentence, the performer is Sharon. *Sharon*, however, is the object of the preposition *by* and is no longer the subject. In the second sentence, the performer of the action is not named. The sentence does not tell who asked Bob to respond.

Exercise 20 **Distinguishing Between Active and Passive Voice** On your paper, write the verb or verb phrase from each sentence below, and label its voice *active* or *passive*.

EXAMPLE: Those flowers were sent without a card.
ANSWER: were sent (passive)

1. The researchers conducted the poll.
2. The poll was conducted by volunteers.
3. Volunteers used the phone to conduct interviews.
4. Random people were selected for the poll by volunteers.
5. Some people were visited by pollsters.
6. The poll was designed by a famous scholar from Holland.
7. The statistics were collected by the researcher.
8. A philanthropist supplied the funding for the research.
9. The conclusion was supported by his data.
10. The conclusion will be issued by a publisher in Ohio.

Step-by-Step Teaching Guide

The Six Tenses of Verbs

1. Tell students that one way to describe the difference between active and passive voice is the difference between interesting, engaging writing and poor, boring writing.
2. Students may not immediately see or "hear" the difference between the voices. In all of the example sentences, there is a verb and action is occurring. *Passive* may imply to them that no one is doing anything.
3. Ask students to define the subject of a sentence. (the part about which something is being said)
4. To find the subject, students need to decide whether a given sentence element is acting or being acted *upon*.

Customize for *Bodily/Kinesthetic Learners*

Have students pantomime acting and receiving action with verbs such as *glance, speak,* and *greet.* Ask them if they can distinguish between active and passive in their pantomiming.

Answer Key

Exercise 20

1. conducted (active)
2. was conducted (passive)
3. used (active)
4. were selected (passive)
5. were visited (passive)
6. was designed (passive)
7. were collected (passive)
8. supplied (active)
9. was supported (passive)
10. will be published (passive)

ONGOING ASSESSMENT: Monitor and Reinforce

If students miss more than two items in Exercise 20, refer them to the following for additional practice.

In the Textbook	Print Resources	Technology
Section Review, Ex. 26, p. 527 Chapter Review, Ex. 43, p. 535	Grammar Exercise Workbook, Using Verbs, pp. 129–132	On-Line Exercise Bank, Section 22.2

Step-by-Step Teaching Guide

The Six Tenses of Verbs

1. Passive constructions are wordier than active ones. They always involve a verb phrase using a form of *be* and the past participle.
2. Review the conjugation of passive forms of *report*. Use each form in a sentence, such as *It is reported that students are learning about passive verbs.*
3. Using the active voice in writing and speaking cannot be stressed enough. Discuss with students the effect of writing in the active voice versus writing in the passive voice.
4. Read a selection of a sports article from a newspaper that features the active voice. Ask students to raise their hands when they *hear* it.
5. Then reread the article, substituting the passive voice for some of the verbs. Ask students how this substitution changes the effect of the writing.

Answer Key

Exercise 21

1. it is demonstrated, it was demonstrated, it will be demonstrated, it has been demonstrated, it had been demonstrated, it will have been demonstrated
2. they are restored, they were restored, they will be restored, they have been restored, they had been restored, they will have been restored

Forming the Tenses of Passive Verbs

A passive verb always has two parts:

KEY CONCEPT A **passive verb** is always a verb phrase made from a form of *be* plus a past participle. ■

Here is a short conjugation of the passive forms of the verb *report* with the pronoun *it:*

CONJUGATION OF THE PASSIVE FORMS OF *REPORT*

Tense	Passive Form
Present	it is reported
Past	it was reported
Future	it will be reported
Present Perfect	it has been reported
Past Perfect	it had been reported
Future Perfect	it will have been reported

Exercise 21 **Conjugating Verbs in the Passive Voice**

Using the chart above as your model, conjugate the following two verbs in the passive voice. Use the pronoun in parentheses.

1. demonstrate (it)
2. restore (they)

Using Active and Passive Voices

Each of the two voices has its proper use in English.

KEY CONCEPT Use the active voice whenever possible. ■

Sentences with active verbs are less wordy and more forceful than those with passive verbs. Compare, for example, the following sentences. Notice the different number of words each sentence needs to report the same information.

ACTIVE: Students *conducted* a taste test.

PASSIVE: A taste test *was conducted* by students.

Although you should aim to use the active voice in most of your writing, there will be times when you will need to use the passive voice.

KEY CONCEPT Use the passive voice to emphasize the receiver of an action rather than the performer of the action. ■

In the following example, the receiver of the action is the subject *candidate.*

EMPHASIS ON RECEIVER:	The candidate *was supported* by the voters.

The passive voice should also be used when there is no performer of the action.

KEY CONCEPT Use the passive voice to point out the receiver of an action when the performer is unknown or unimportant and is not named in the sentence. ■

PERFORMER UNKNOWN:	The secret research *was ordered* sometime last year.
PERFORMER UNIMPORTANT:	The crime scene *was* quickly *closed* while the police searched for clues.

Exercise 22 **Revising Sentences to Use the Active Voice** Revise the following sentences, changing the verb from the passive voice to the active voice whenever possible. If you choose to leave a sentence in the passive voice, explain why.

EXAMPLE:	This old watch was found by me in my grandmother's bureau.
ANSWER:	I found this old watch in my grandmother's bureau.

1. Research on people's habits has often been conducted by scientists.
2. A study on television-viewing habits was initiated by a team of researchers from the local university.
3. Two hundred people were selected to participate in the study.
4. By the time the study began, dozens of questions had been prepared by the team.
5. These questions were answered by participants.
6. The number of hours of television each participant watched daily was recorded by researchers.
7. The participants have been visited by field workers on a weekly basis since the beginning of the research.
8. The data have been carefully examined to determine trends.
9. All findings will soon be published by the university.
10. The findings will certainly be valued by television executives.

More Practice

Grammar Exercise Workbook
- pp. 129–132

On-line Exercise Bank
- Section 22.2

Go on-line:
PHSchool.com
Enter Web Code:
eck-8002

Step-by-Step Teaching Guide

The Six Tenses of Verbs

1. Let students know that the passive voice does have its uses. It provides emphasis on a subject as the receiver of the action. It is required when the performer or doer of the action is unknown or unimportant.
2. Model the use of the passive voice to place the emphasis on the receiver. Point out that in the sentence *The candidate was supported by the voters,* it is the candidate who is important. The sentence written in the active voice *(The voters supported the candidate)* emphasizes the voters, not the candidate.
3. Write the following additional examples on the board.

   Emphasis on receiver: The dog was unhappy on the leash.

   Performer unknown: The car was stolen last night.

   Performer unimportant: School was closed until the flooding went down.

Answer Key

Exercise 22

Answers will vary. Samples are given.

1. Scientists have often conducted research on people's habits.
2. A team of researchers from the local university initiated a study on television viewing habits.
3. The research team selected two hundred people to participate in the study.
4. By the time the study began, the team had prepared dozens of questions.
5. These questions were answered by participants. (The focus of the sentence should be on the questions.)
6. Researchers recorded the number of hours of television each participant watched daily.
7. Field workers have visited the participants on a daily basis since the beginning of the research.
8. The research team has examined the data carefully to determine trends.
9. The university will soon publish all findings.
10. Television executives will certainly value the findings.

Step-by-Step Teaching Guide

Turning to Active Verbs

Teaching Resource: Hands-on Grammar Activity Book, Chapter 22

1. Have students refer to their Hands-on Grammar activity books or give them copies of the relevant pages for this activity.
2. Carefully review the instructions for creating the flip cards.
3. Encourage students also to *hear* the relative strength of the active voice and the relative weakness of the passive voice as they listen to a peer reading pairs of sentences.

Find It in Your Reading

Have students change each example from the active to the passive voice, and vice versa. Have them explain the effects of these changes.

Find It in Your Writing

Have students explain why they chose the voice they did for each example.

22.2

Hands-on Grammar

Turning to Active Verbs

You should use active voice verbs in most of your sentences. Use the passive voice only when you want to emphasize the receiver of an action or when you are not naming the performer. In those two cases, passive voice verbs are proper. To practice revising sentences from passive to active voice, try the following activity.

Take several index cards and cut out an opening in each to create a box with two arms, as in the model below. In the box on one side of the card, write a verb phrase consisting of *was* or *were* and a past participle form of a verb. Examples: *was given, were selected, was taught, were found.* Flip the card over and write a subject and the past form of the verb. Examples: *Sandra gave, they selected, Henry taught, I found.*

Tape the edges of the wings of a card onto a piece of paper. In the opening, write an article or a possessive adjective and a noun. On the paper to the right of the card, write an article and a direct object. You should now be able to see a sentence such as *My brother was given a tangerine.* Now, fold the card over on its wings and you will see *Sandra gave my brother a tangerine.* The new active voice sentence is more direct and provides more information than the passive voice sentence. (An active voice sentence is also shorter; to include the performer of the action, *Sandra,* in your passive voice sentence, you would have needed to add *by Sandra* at the end of the passive sentence.) Note that if you did not know the performer of the action, your sentence would stay in passive voice.

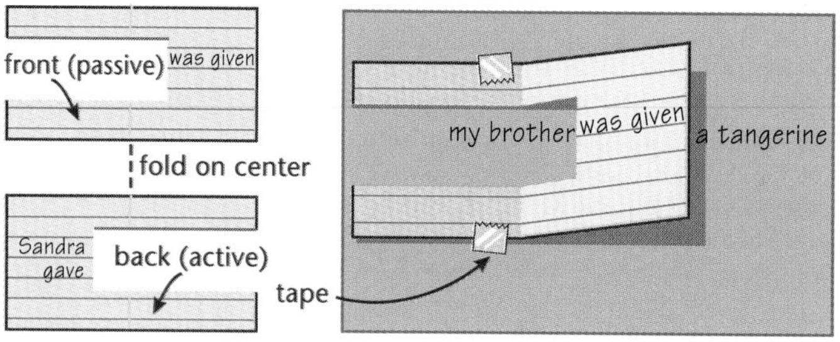

Find It in Your Reading Select a paragraph from a story in your literature book that contains sentences with both active and passive voice verbs. Discuss with a partner why the writer chose each voice.

Find It in Your Writing Use this activity to determine whether some of the sentences in your own compositions should be changed from passive to active voice. If you discover some passive voice sentences, consider whether to revise them to be in active voice.

TIME SAVERS!

Hands-on Grammar Book Use the Hands-on Grammar activity sheet for Chapter 22 to facilitate this activity.

ONGOING ASSESSMENT: Assess Mastery

Use the following resources to assess mastery of the six tenses of verbs and active and passive voice.

In the Textbook	Technology
Chapter Review, Ex. 41–43, pp. 534–535 Standardized Test Preparation Workshop, pp. 536–537	On-Line Exercise Bank, Section 22.2

Section 22.2

Section Review

GRAMMAR EXERCISES 23–29

Exercise 23 **Identifying the Tense and Form of Verbs** Write the tense and form of the underlined verbs.

1. The arithmetic mean has been used frequently in statistics.
2. You probably know it by another name.
3. People often call it the average.
4. What was your average score in math?
5. Your teacher will determine your average score at the end of the semester.
6. You are working to improve your grade.
7. People routinely have been determining averages in sports.
8. Until recently, statisticians had computed averages with pencil and paper.
9. People had been doing that for years.
10. Baseball fans will be compiling batting averages as long as baseball is played.

Exercise 24 **Forming Progressive Tenses of Verbs** Write the tense indicated for each verb below.

1. present perfect progressive of *decide*
2. future progressive of *permit*
3. past perfect progressive of *tear*
4. present progressive of *determine*
5. past progressive of *break*.

Exercise 25 **Revising to Eliminate Problems With Verb Forms** Revise the following sentences by writing the correct form of the underlined verb.

(1) Electronics experts have develop calculators for many industries. (2) You may have saw an electrician carrying a calculator to measure code requirements. (3) Another calculator has be build for real estate agents to figure mortgage rates. (4) Carpet installers are now determine room size with an electronic tape measure. (5) Undoubtedly, plans for new calculators be draw up in the future.

Exercise 26 **Revising Sentences to Use the Active Voice** Revise the following sentences, changing the verb from the passive voice to the active voice whenever possible. If you choose to leave a sentence in the passive voice, explain why.

1. Opinion polls are relied on by politicians.
2. Around election time, many surveys are conducted by pollsters.
3. These polls are used by politicians to determine how voters feel about issues.
4. Opinion polls have been transformed into vital political tools by analysts.
5. The results of polls are often published in newspapers.

Exercise 27 **Find It in Your Reading** Identify the basic and progressive forms of the verbs used in this passage from "Flowers for Algernon" by Daniel Keyes.

> . . . They're all pretending that Algernon's behavior is not . . . significant for me. But it's hard to hide the fact that some of the other animals who were used in this experiment are showing strange behavior.

Exercise 28 **Find It in Your Writing** Look through your writing portfolio for sentences that contain active and passive verbs. Rewrite the sentences with passive verbs, changing them to active verbs.

Exercise 29 **Writing Application** Write several questions for an opinion poll to gauge your classmates' radio-listening habits. Use both basic and progressive verb forms in your questions.

Section Review

Each of these exercises correlates to a concept in the section on the six tenses of verbs, pages 516–526. These exercises may be used for more practice, for reteaching, or for review of the Key Concepts presented. Answers for all chapter exercises are available in *Grammar Exercises Answers on Transparencies* in your teaching resources.

Answer Key

Exercise 23

1. present perfect
2. present
3. present
4. past
5. future
6. present progressive
7. present perfect progressive
8. past perfect
9. past perfect progressive
10. future progressive

Exercise 24

1. have been deciding
2. will be permitting
3. had been tearing
4. am determining
5. was breaking

Exercise 25

(1) have developed (2) may have seen (3) has been built (4) are determining (5) will be drawn up

Exercise 26

1. Politicians rely on opinion polls.
2. Around election time, pollsters conduct many polls.
3. Politicians use these polls to determine how voters feel about issues.
4. Analysts have transformed opinion polls into vital political tools.
5. Passive voice is appropriate because it puts focus on "results."

Exercise 27

Find It in Your Reading
are pretending—present progressive
is—present
is—present, were used—past
are showing—present progressive

continued

Answer Key continued

Exercise 28

Find It in Your Writing
If students think they were right to use the passive voice, they should explain why.

Exercise 29

Writing Application
Students should combine their questions and conduct the poll. They can show their results in a graph.

PREPARE and ENGAGE

Interest GRABBER Have partners role-play a brief, normal conversation about any topic they choose. Then ask them to pretend that one of them is the school principal and conduct another conversation the same topic. Keep the role-plays brief, no more than a couple of minutes each. Ask students if they noted any difference in the conversations. Discuss how we talk and use language differently, depending on whom we are talking to and the situation. Point out that informal, colloquial speech often includes grammatical errors.

Activate Prior Knowledge

Write the following sentences on the board and ask students to choose the correct word in parentheses.

The Saint Bernard (dragged/drug) Marco down the street.

It was the biggest dog he had ever (saw/seen).

Afterward, Marco (set/sat) down on the grass to rest.

Marco's advice: Owning a pet stronger than you (isn't/ain't) a good idea.

TEACH

Step-by-Step Teaching Guide

Glossary of Troublesome Verbs

1. Students probably made the correct choices in Activate Prior Knowledge. When they see the choices side by side, they know which word to choose.
2. Students use the wrong word when they are working quickly or choose the first word that pops into their mind.
3. Review the four examples. Urge students to remember the words, so that when they find them in their own writing, they will know to stop and reconsider.

Critical Viewing

Analyze Students' responses will vary.

Section 22.3

Troublesome Verbs

The following verbs cause problems for many speakers and writers. Some of the problems involve using the principal parts of certain verbs. Other problems involve learning to distinguish between the meanings of certain confusing pairs of verbs. As you read through the following list, note those verbs that have caused you difficulty in the past and concentrate on them. Use the exercises to test your understanding. When you are writing and revising your compositions, refer to this section to check your work.

(1) *ain't* *Ain't* is not considered correct English. Avoid using it in speaking and in writing.

INCORRECT: He *ain't* the first person to explore this island.
CORRECT: He *isn't* the first person to explore this island.

(2) *did, done* Remember that *done* is a past participle and can be used as a verb only with a helping verb such as *have* or *has*. Instead of using *done* without a helping verb, use *did*. Otherwise, you can add the helping verb before *done*.

INCORRECT: I already *done* my history project.
CORRECT: I already *did* my history project.
I *have* already *done* my history project.

(3) *dragged, drug* *Drag* is a regular verb. Its principal parts are *drag, dragging, dragged,* and *dragged. Drug* is never correct as the past or past participle of *drag.*

INCORRECT: The sailor *drug* the heavy box up the gangplank. You *should have drug* the sack of potatoes below deck.
CORRECT: The sailor *dragged* the heavy box up the gangplank. You *should have dragged* the sack of potatoes below deck.

(4) *gone, went* *Gone* is the past participle of *go* and can be used as a verb only with a helping verb such as *have* or *has. Went* is the past of *go* and is never used with a helping verb.

INCORRECT: Jean and Frank *gone* to the museum.
We *should have went* along with them.
CORRECT: Jean and Frank *have gone* to the museum.
Jean and Frank *went* to the museum.
We *should have gone* along with them.

Theme: Explorers of the Americas
In this section, you will learn about twelve verbs that often cause problems for speakers and writers. The examples and exercises are about explorers of North and South America.
Cross-Curricular Connection: Social Studies

▲ Critical Viewing
Find direct objects in this picture to go with each of these verbs: *set, raised, laid.* **[Analyze]**

TIME AND RESOURCE MANAGER

Resources
Print: Grammar Exercise Workbook, pp. 133–134
Technology: Writing and Grammar iText, Section 22.3; On-Line Exercise Bank, Section 22.3

In-Depth Coverage	Accelerated Pace
• Work through all examples. • Assign and review Exercises 30–31.	• Assign pp. 528–532 for independent student review.

(5) *have, of* In conversation, the words *have* and *of* often sound very similar. Be careful not to write *of* when you really mean the helping verb *have* or its contraction *'ve.*

INCORRECT: Columbus should *of* continued until he reached India.

CORRECT: Columbus should *have* continued until he reached India.
Columbus *should've* continued until he reached India.

(6) *lay, lie* These verbs are troublesome to many people because they look and sound almost alike and have similar meanings. The first step in learning to distinguish between *lay* and *lie* is to become thoroughly familiar with their principal parts. Memorize the principal parts of both verbs.

PRINCIPAL PARTS:				
	lay	laying	laid	laid
	lie	lying	lay	lain

The next step is to compare the meaning and use of the two verbs. *Lay* usually means "to put (something) down" or "to place (something)." This verb is almost always followed by a direct object.

EXAMPLES: The captain *lays* his map (DO) and glasses (DO) on the desk.

The workers *will be laying* new flooring (DO) in the ship's galley tomorrow.

Lie usually means "to rest in a reclining position." It also can mean "to be situated." This verb is used to show the position of a person, place, or thing. *Lie* is never followed by a direct object.

EXAMPLES: The sailors must *lie* down in narrow bunks.
Pieces of the shattered ship *are lying* in the water.

Pay special attention to one particular area of confusion between *lay* and *lie*. *Lay* is the present tense of *lay*. *Lay* is also the past tense of *lie*. The past tense of *lay* is *laid.*

PRESENT TENSE OF LAY: I *lay* the treasure map on the dining room table.

PAST TENSE OF LIE: The sailor *lay* down on his narrow bunk.

PAST TENSE OF LAY: The sailors *laid* their uniforms on their bunks.

Step-by-Step Teaching Guide

Troublesome Verbs

1. Point out the verb origin of the common error of using *of* for *have.* Have students note how in writing it makes no sense at all.
2. Work carefully through the principal parts of *lay* and *lie.* This pair is often confused and needs careful consideration. Tell students to ask themselves the following question each time they are faced with a *lay/lie* choice:

   What meaning am I looking for—to put something down (lay) or to recline (lie)?

   This will not always lead them to the correct choice, as *lay* is also the past tense of *lie,* adding an extra element of confusion. There is a foolproof solution to the problem: use a dictionary.
3. Write the following sentences on the board and ask students to chose the correct word.

   The dog likes to (lie/lay) in front of the fire. (lie)

   The governor (laid/lied) a wreath at the monument. (laid)

Step-by-Step Teaching Guide

Troublesome Verbs

1. The confusion of *learn* and *teach* has its origins in colloquial speech. Discuss with students how learning is (one hopes) the result of teaching.
2. Write the following additional sentences on the board.

   Dan taught his little sister, Martina, how to tie her shoes.

   Martina learned how to tie her shoes.
3. Review the meanings of *leave* and *let.* Use the following sentence.

   I will leave the book for you if you let me use your skateboard.
4. See that students know the principal parts of both *raise* and *rise*. Write the following on the chalkboard: *raise, raised, raising; rise, rose, risen, rising.*

Critical Viewing

Connect One would raise the flag, and the flag would rise when pulled.

22.3

◀ **Critical Viewing** Would you *rise* or *raise* the flag above this ship? Would the flag *rise* up or *raise* up when pulled? **[Connect]**

(7) *learn, teach* *Learn* means "to receive knowledge." *Teach* means "to give knowledge." Do not use *learn* in place of *teach.*

INCORRECT: Dan *learned* me how to use a compass.
CORRECT: Dan *taught* me how to use a compass.

(8) *leave, let* *Leave* means "to allow to remain." *Let* means "to permit." Do not reverse the meanings.

INCORRECT: *Leave* me think in peace!
Let the poor dog alone!
CORRECT: *Let* me think in peace!
Leave the poor dog alone!

(9) *raise, rise* *Raise* has several common meanings: "to lift (something) upward," to build (something)," "to grow (something)," "to increase (something)." The verb is usually followed by a direct object.

EXAMPLES: *Raise* the anchor (DO) so we can cast off.
The captain *raised* $3,000 (DO) to finance the voyage.

Rise, on the other hand, is not usually followed by a direct object. This verb means "to get up," "to go up," or "to be increased."

EXAMPLES: The sailors must *rise* before five in the morning.
The waves *rose* and fell, rocking the ship.

(10) *saw, seen* *Seen* is a past participle and can be used as a verb only with a helping verb such as *have* or *has*. Instead of using *seen* without a helping verb, use *saw*. Otherwise, you can add the helping verb before *seen*.

INCORRECT: I *seen* that exhibit on sixteenth-century ships when it was in town last year.

CORRECT: I *saw* that exhibit on sixteenth-century ships when it was in town last year.

(11) *says, said* A common mistake in reporting what someone said is to use *says* (present tense) rather than *said* (past tense).

INCORRECT: The captain turned ghostly white, and then he *says*, "I need to sit down."

CORRECT: The captain turned ghostly white, and then he *said*, "I need to sit down."

(12) *set, sit* The first step in learning to distinguish between *set* and *sit* is to become thoroughly familiar with their principal parts.

PRINCIPAL PARTS:	set	setting	set	set
	sit	sitting	sat	sat

To avoid confusing these two verbs, understand the difference in their meanings. *Set* commonly means "to put (something) in a certain place or position." It is usually followed by a direct object.

EXAMPLES: He *set* (not *sat*) the cup (DO) on the coaster.

They *are setting* the sails (DO) into proper position.

We have *set* the spice plants (DO) safely in the cargo bay.

Sit usually means "to be seated" or "to rest." It is usually not followed by a direct object.

EXAMPLES: The house where the famous explorer was born *sits* (not *sets*) atop that hill.
The mutineers *have been sitting* in a tiny cell for six months.
Mona *sat* on the captain's chair.
The parrot *has sat* on the perch since it learned to speak last year.

Step-by-Step Teaching Guide

Troublesome Verbs

1. The basic confusion with *saw* and *seen* occurs because of the common error of using the past participle alone as a verb. This is an instance where teaching students the grammatical reasons for usage should help correct errors.
2. See that students understand that *says* is the present tense and should not be used when *said* is called for.
3. Review the meanings and principal parts of *set* and *sit.* These verbs are commonly confused. As with *lay* and *lie,* students need to ask themselves this question:

   What meaning am I looking for—to put something (set) or to rest or be seated (sit)?

Customize for *Verbal/Linguistic Learners*

Multiple-Meaning Words Some of these troublesome words have more meanings than are described in the text. Challenge students to find the meanings of the following words and use them in sentences that make these meanings clear.

done—adjective
drug—noun and verb
gone—adjective
lie—noun
leave—noun
raise—noun
rise—noun
saw—two different nouns
set—noun and adjective

Answer Key

Exercise 30

1. isn't
2. did
3. said
4. let
5. went
6. dragged
7. set
8. rose, saw
9. lay
10. have, taught

Exercise 31

(1) History books have taught us many facts about Sir Francis Drake. (2) Much of Drake's fame lies in his having sailed around the world. (3) What he did was amazing. (4) In 1577, sailing from England, Drake went around the world. (5) After traveling through the Straits of Magellan, which lie off the southern tip of South America, he traveled up the western coast of South America. (6) During that leg of his journey, he saw the Pacific Ocean. (7) When Magellan saw that body of water, he said that it was pacific, or peaceful, so he gave the ocean that name. (8) Drake eventually reached the area near what is now San Francisco and set his anchor in the water there. (9) Drake rose early one morning and began sailing even farther west. (10) By the time Drake finally reached England again in 1580, he had dragged his crew on an epic voyage for almost three years.

PRENTICE HALL
Everyday Spelling

If you have taught the spelling skills in *Prentice Hall Everyday Spelling,* Grade 8, Chapter 26, in conjunction with this *Writing and Grammar* chapter, review and assess students' mastery of the skills before concluding the chapter.

Exercise 30 Avoiding Problems With Troublesome Verbs

For each of the following sentences, choose the word in parentheses that supplies the correct verb and write it on your paper.

EXAMPLE: They (did, done) what they wanted to do.
ANSWER: did

1. It (ain't, isn't) often that a person changes our understanding of the world.
2. Christopher Columbus (done, did) just that.
3. Columbus (says, said) to the king and queen of Spain, "I believe the world is round."
4. He begged them to (let, leave) him lead an expedition to find a westward route to Asia.
5. Sailing from Palos, Spain, he (gone, went) west.
6. Before sailing, Columbus's crew (drug, dragged) supplies onto their three ships.
7. They (set, sat) these supplies in the ships' cargo decks.
8. After more than two months at sea, the sailors' hopes (raised, rose) when the lookout (saw, seen) land.
9. Columbus and his crew landed on an island that (lay, laid) in the Caribbean Sea.
10. Although Columbus was thousands of miles away from Asia, where he should (of, have) been, his voyage (learned, taught) other Europeans much about the Western Hemisphere.

Exercise 31 Revising Usage of Troublesome Verbs

Rewrite the paragraph below, correcting errors in verb usage.

(1) History books have learned us many facts about Sir Francis Drake. (2) Much of Drake's fame lays in his having sailed around the world. (3) What he done was amazing. (4) In 1577, sailing from England, Drake had went around the world. (5) After traveling through the Straits of Magellan, which laid off the southern tip of South America, he traveled up the western coast of South America. (6) During that leg of his journey, he seen the Pacific Ocean. (7) When Magellan saw that body of water, he says that it was pacific, or peaceful, so he gave the ocean that name. (8) Drake eventually reached the area near what is now San Francisco and sat his anchor in the water there. (9) Drake raised up early one morning and began sailing even farther west. (10) By the time Drake finally reached England again in 1580, he had drug his crew on an epic voyage for almost three years.

More Practice

Grammar Exercise Workbook
- pp. 133–134

On-line Exercise Bank
- Section 22.3

Go on-line: PHSchool.com
Enter Web Code: eck-8002

iText

Get instant feedback! Exercises 30 and 31 are available on-line or on CD-ROM.

TIME SAVERS!

Answers on Transparency
Use the Grammar Exercises Answers on Transparencies for Chapter 22 to facilitate corrections by students.

On-Line Exercise Bank
Have students complete the exercises on computer. The Auto Check feature will grade their work for you!

ONGOING ASSESSMENT: Monitor and Reinforce

If students miss more than two items in Exercises 30–31, refer them to the following for additional practice.

In the Textbook	Print Resources	Technology
Section Review, Ex. 32–34, p. 533	Grammar Exercise Workbook, Using Verbs, pp.133–134	On-Line Exercise Bank, Section 22.3

Section 22.3 **Section Review**

GRAMMAR EXERCISES 32–37

Exercise 32 **Recognizing Verbs That Use Direct Objects** Write each verb below on your paper. Write *yes* next to each verb that is usually followed by a direct object and *no* next to each one that is *not* usually followed by a direct object.

1. raised
2. laid
3. sat
4. rose
5. lain
6. set
7. lay (past tense)
8. sits
9. lay (present tense)
10. raises

Exercise 33 **Revising to Eliminate Verb Usage Errors** Revise the sentences below, correcting verb usage errors. Write *correct* if the sentence contains no errors.

1. She done a project on explorers.
2. Her interests laid in John Cabot.
3. He was raised in Italy in the mid-1400's.
4. In school, he was learned about mapmaking.
5. In the 1480's, he had went to England to live.
6. Cabot seen reports about Christopher Columbus.
7. He wished he could of sailed along with Columbus.
8. Cabot asked several kings to leave him have a ship.
9. He believed a route to the Indies lay north of where Columbus had sailed.
10. He met with the king of Portugal and says, "I plan to find that route."

Exercise 34 **Supplying Correct Verb Forms** Choose the correct verb in parentheses, and write it on your paper.

1. Cabot (sat, set) his idea before the kings of Portugal and Spain.
2. He (said, says), "I know I can find the Indies and make you rich."
3. Neither king would help him (raise, rise) the funds for the voyage.
4. Somewhat depressed, Cabot (dragged, drug) himself to the king of England.
5. Henry VII said, "(Let, Leave) me think about your plan."
6. Henry (saw, seen) the positive side of Cabot's plan.
7. A few months later, Cabot's English ship (lay, laid) just off the coast of Canada.
8. He became the first European to (sit, set) foot in that part of the world.
9. Although he never reached the Indies, Cabot (did, done) what he said.
10. The wealth of England (raised, rose) as a result of his discoveries.

Exercise 35 **Find It in Your Reading** Look through newspapers and magazines to find sentences in which the troublesome verbs in this section are used correctly.

Exercise 36 **Find It in Your Writing** Look through your writing portfolio. Find examples of sentences in which you have used some of the troublesome verbs in this section. Make certain that you used them correctly.

Exercise 37 **Writing Application** Imagine that you are leading an expedition to an uncharted island in the middle of the Pacific Ocean. Write an entry in your captain's log, describing part of your journey. Try to use some of the troublesome verbs described in this section in your journal entry.

ASSESS and CLOSE

Section Review

Each of these exercises correlates to a concept in the section on troublesome verbs, pages 528–532. These exercises may be used for more practice, for reteaching, or for review of the Key Concepts presented. Answers for all chapter exercises are available in *Grammar Exercises Answers on Transparencies* in your teaching resources.

Answer Key

Exercise 32

1. yes
2. yes
3. no
4. no
5. no
6. yes
7. no
8. no
9. yes
10. yes

Exercise 33

1. She did a project on explorers.
2. Her interests lay in John Cabot.
3. correct
4. In school, he was taught about mapmaking.
5. In the 1480s, he had gone to England to live.
6. Cabot saw reports about Christopher Columbus.
7. He wished he could have sailed along with Columbus.
8. Cabot asked several kings to let him have a ship.
9. correct.
10. He met with the King of Portugal and said, "I plan to find that route."

Exercise 34

1. set
2. said
3. raise
4. dragged
5. Let
6. saw
7. lay
8. set
9. did
10. rose

Exercise 35

Find It in Your Reading
Students may want to copy some of these sentences to reinforce their learning.

Exercise 36

Find It in Your Writing
If students are not sure that some of the words are used correctly, they can check with a partner or use a dictionary.

continued

Answer Key continued

Exercise 37

Writing Application
Students can compile their entries into one long log titled "The Perils of Exploration."

CHAPTER REVIEW

Each of these exercises correlates with a section of the chapter on using verbs, pages 504–533. These exercises may be used for more practice, for reteaching, or for review of the Key Concepts presented. Sample answers are given. Answers for all exercises are available in *Grammar Exercises Answers on Transparencies* in your teaching resources.

Answer Key

Exercise 38

1. present; present, basic
2. present participle; present progressive
3. past participle; present perfect, basic
4. past; past, basic
5. present participle; past progressive

Exercise 39

1. bind, bound, bound
2. catch, caught, caught
3. begin, began, begun
4. take, took, taken
5. know, knew, known

Exercise 40

Sentences will vary.

1. present perfect, progressive
2. present perfect, basic
3. future, basic
4. present, progressive
5. past perfect, progressive
6. future perfect, progressive
7. past perfect, basic
8. present perfect, basic
9. past, progressive
10. future perfect, basic

Exercise 41

1. present perfect; basic
2. present; basic
3. present perfect progressive
4. future; basic
5. present progressive
6. future progressive
7. present; basic
8. past perfect; basic
9. present perfect; basic
10. past; basic
11. past perfect progressive
12. present perfect progressive
13. future; basic
14. future perfect; basic
15. future perfect progressive

Chapter 22 Chapter Review

GRAMMAR EXERCISES 38–46

Exercise 38 **Recognizing Principal Parts and Verb Tense** On your paper, identify the principal part used to form each underlined verb in the following sentences. Then identify the tense and form of the verb.

1. Exploration happens almost every day.
2. At this very moment, people are exploring new and interesting places.
3. In the past fifty years, explorers have ventured below the sea and into the sky.
4. In 1953, Sir Edmund Hillary climbed higher on Earth than anyone from the Western Hemisphere had ever gone.
5. He was standing on the summit of Mount Everest.

Exercise 39 **Supplying Principal Parts** On your paper, write the present, the past, and the past participle of the following verbs.

1. binding
2. catching
3. beginning
4. taking
5. knowing

Exercise 40 **Identifying and Using Verb Tenses and Forms** Identify the tense of each verb below, and indicate whether it is in basic or progressive form. Then, write sentences with five of the verbs.

1. have been sailing
2. have explored
3. will seek
4. am striving
5. had been traveling
6. will have been arriving
7. had wandered
8. have realized
9. was entering
10. will have ventured

Exercise 41 **Recognizing Verb Tenses and Forms** Write the tense and form of the italicized verb in each sentence.

1. Many people *have longed* to explore.
2. People often *fantasize* about exploring new lands.
3. Not all exploration *has been occurring* in exotic locations.
4. People *will discover* unusual things in local parks and backyards.
5. Others *are mapping* historic locations in their towns or cities.
6. Advanced methods of transportation *will be assisting* modern explorers.
7. Oceanographers and undersea explorers *dive* below the ocean's surface.
8. They are reaching depths that people *had* once *thought* were inaccessible.
9. Other explorers *have set* foot on untouched polar regions.
10. Naomi Uemura from Japan *reached* the North Pole by dogsled in 1978.
11. Many people *had been doubting* that such a trip was possible.
12. Some explorers *have been focusing* their efforts on outer space.
13. In the twenty-first century, it is likely that space explorers *will chart* new worlds.
14. During the next century, explorers *will have added* much to our knowledge.
15. By then, space explorers *will have been traveling* across vast stretches of outer space for many years.

Exercise 42 **Supplying the Correct Verb Tense and Form** On your paper, revise each sentence below, writing the correct form of the verb in parentheses.

1. Marco Polo has long (be) recognized as a daring explorer.
2. In 1271, he (venture) from Italy to China.

3. Sometimes, he (creep) through the rugged terrain.
4. At last, he (set) his feet on Chinese soil.
5. By 1295, he had (take) numerous excursions throughout Asia.
6. He (spend) time in India, China, and Tibet.
7. He (seek) to build trade between Asia and Europe.
8. He (bring) spices, silk, and other Asian wonders back to Europe.
9. After he returned home, he (wind) up in an Italian prison, where he wrote about his adventures.
10. By the time he died, Marco Polo had (write) a moving account of his travels in Asia.

Exercise 43 **Revising Sentences to Use the Active Voice** Revise the following sentences, changing the verb from the passive voice to the active voice whenever possible. If you choose to leave a sentence in the passive voice, explain why.

1. New routes to popular destinations have often been discovered by explorers.
2. In the late 1400's, a westward route to Asia was sought by many explorers.
3. In 1497, a great feat was accomplished by Vasco da Gama of Portugal.
4. A sea route around Africa to reach India was found by him.
5. A boost to trade between Asia and Europe was provided by his efforts.
6. Indian spices were sought by many Europeans.
7. Asian silk also was valued by wealthy Europeans.
8. At the time, great fortunes were being made by European ship captains and enterprising explorers.
9. Vasco da Gama's route to Asia was carefully guarded by Portugal.
10. Vasco da Gama's voyage has been celebrated in Portugal for over 500 years.

Exercise 44 **Revising Sentences With Troublesome Verbs** Rewrite the sentences below, correcting errors in verb usage. If a sentence is correct, write *correct.*

1. Samuel de Champlain raised to fame as an early explorer of Canada.
2. You might of heard a lot about him.
3. Champlain's father learned him how to navigate a ship.
4. As a young man, he had went to Spanish colonies in the Americas.
5. He wrote a book about the riches that laid in America.
6. He set a goal to find a northern route through North America to Asia.
7. He says to the king of France, "Leave me try to find the northern route."
8. The king helped him rise the money.
9. In 1603, Champlain began exploring the area that lay near Niagara Falls.
10. He done a lot of exploring in Canada over the next twenty years.

Exercise 45 **Revising a Passage to Eliminate Errors in Verb Usage** Rewrite the paragraph below, correcting any errors in verb usage.

(1) Juan Ponce de Leon lead the first Spanish expedition to Florida. (2) He had first came to America with Christopher Columbus. (3) On the later voyage, he seeked the Fountain of Youth in Florida. (4) Hope raised in him when he heard that its waters could make old people young again. (5) By the time he left, he had gave the land the name "Florida" because of the many flowers he finded there.

Exercise 46 **Writing Application**

On your paper, write a paragraph about any place in the world or in outer space that you would like to explore someday. Circle all the verbs. Try to use at least three different verb tenses and forms in your paragraph.

Exercise 42

1. been
2. ventured
3. crept
4. set
5. taken
6. spent
7. sought
8. brought
9. wound
10. written

Exercise 43

1. Explorers have often discovered new routes to popular destinations.
2. In the late 1400's, many explorers sought a westward route to Asia.
3. In 1497, Vasco da Gama of Portugal accomplished a great feat.
4. He found a sea route around Africa to reach India.
5. His efforts provided a boost to trade between Africa and Europe.
6. Many Europeans sought Indian spices.
7. Wealthy Europeans also valued Asian silk.
8. At the time, European ship captains and enterprising explorers made great fortunes.
9. Leave as is—gives emphasis to the route
10. For over 500 years, Portugal has celebrated Vasco da Gama's voyage.

Exercise 44

1. rose
2. have
3. taught
4. gone
5. lay
6. correct
7. said, Let
8. raise
9. correct
10. did

Exercise 45

1. led
2. come
3. sought
4. rose
5. given, found

Exercise 46

Writing Application
Have students identify the tenses and forms of each of the verbs they circled.

Lesson Objectives

- To use the tenses and forms of verb correctly.

Step-by-Step Teaching Guide

Using Verbs

Teaching Resources: Standardized Test Preparation Workbook, pp. 43–44

1. Tell students that they will have to use context clues to determine the tense of the verb needed to complete each passage.
2. Once students have determined the time frame of the passage in question, they should eliminate all choices that do not fit within the time of the passage. Eliminating incorrect choices will help them avoid making careless mistakes.

Standardized Test Preparation Workshop

Standard English Usage: Using Verbs

Standardized tests are often used to evaluate your ability to correctly use parts of speech, including verbs. These types of questions will ask you to choose the best verb to complete a sentence. You will be given several word choices that could be placed in the blank to complete the passage. Before you begin, read the entire passage. Decide whether the passage concerns the past, present, or future, and then determine whether a verb that shows action or connection is needed. Choose the verb that best completes the sentence. The following examples will help you answer questions about verb usage.

Test Tip

Choose verbs that fit the right tense and also agree with their subjects in number.

Sample Test Item	Answer and Explanation
Read the passage, and choose the letter of the word or group of words that belongs in each space. Artist Marc Chagall, known for his fantastic paintings, __(1)__ the first living painter to have his work displayed at the Louvre.	
1 **A** will be **B** were **C** will have been **D** was	The correct answer is *D, was*. The sentence calls for a connecting verb, and is written about events that took place in the past.

TEST-TAKING TIP

Make sure students read the passage with their choice in place before making any final decisions. This way they can double-check their answers to make sure it reads correctly.

Practice 1 **Directions:** Read the passage, and choose the letter of the word or group of words that belongs in each space.

Martin Luther King, Jr., __(1)__ on January 15, 1929, in Atlanta, Georgia. His parents, the Reverend and Mrs. M. L. King, __(2)__ three children. Dr. King __(3)__ the teachings of Gandhi, and __(4)__ in nonviolent civil disobedience. Today, we __(5)__ the memory of the late Dr. King each year in January.

1 **A** were born
B is born
C was born
D borned

2 **F** raised
G raises
H will raise
J does raise

3 **A** studying
B studied
C studies
D will study

4 **F** has believed
G believes
H will believe
J believed

5 **A** honor
B honors
C honored
D will be honoring

Practice 2 **Directions:** Read the passage, and choose the letter of the word or group of words that belongs in each space.

The winter __(1)__ deceptively warm that year. Much to everyone's surprise, a howling February blizzard __(2)__ the entire county. A storm that weather forecasters couldn't have predicted __(3)__ us all. Schools __(4)__ and businesses were unable to open. Children __(5)__ bags, lids, and even plastic pools into sleds.

1 **A** is
B was
C were
D had been

2 **F** halted
G halt
H halts
J did not halt

3 **A** will have been surprised
B surprise
C surprised
D surprises

4 **F** will be closed
G was closed
H were closed
J closed

5 **A** transformed
B transform
C will transform
D are transforming

Answer Key

Practice 1

1. C
2. F
3. B
4. J
5. A

Practice 2

1. D
2. F
3. C
4. H
5. A

Chapter 23 Time and Resource Manager

In-Depth Lesson Plan

	LESSON FOCUS	PRINT AND MEDIA RESOURCES
DAY 1	**Cases of Personal Pronouns** Students learn to identify and distinguish between nominative-case and objective-case pronouns (pp. 538–542).	**Teaching Resources** *Grammar Exercise Workbook,* pp. 137–141; *Grammar Exercises Answers on Transparencies,* Ch. 23 ***Writing and Grammar iText* (Interactive Text),** Ch. 23; ***On-line Exercise Bank,*** Ch. 23
DAY 2	**Cases of Personal Pronouns** *(continued)* Students work with pronouns in the possessive case. They also complete the Hands-on Grammar activity (pp. 543–547).	**Teaching Resources** *Grammar Exercise Workbook,* pp. 137–141; *Grammar Exercises Answers on Transparencies,* Ch. 23; *Hands-on Grammar Activity Book,* Ch. 23 ***Writing and Grammar iText* (Interactive Text),** Ch. 23; ***On-line Exercise Bank,*** Ch. 23
DAY 3	**Review and Assess** Students review the chapter and demonstrate mastery of pronouns (pp. 548–551).	**Teaching Resources** *Formal Assessment,* Ch. 23; *Grammar Exercises Answers on Transparencies,* Ch. 23 ***Writing and Grammar iText* (Interactive Text),** Ch. 23, Chapter Review

Accelerated Lesson Plan

	LESSON FOCUS	PRINT AND MEDIA RESOURCES
DAY 1	**Using Pronouns** Students identify and distinguish among nominative-case, objective-case, and possessive-case pronouns (pp. 538–546).	**Teaching Resources** *Grammar Exercise Workbook,* pp. 137–141; *Grammar Exercises Answers on Transparencies,* Ch. 23; *Hands-on Grammar Activity Book,* Ch. 23 ***Writing and Grammar iText* (Interactive Text),** Ch. 23; ***On-line Exercise Bank,*** Ch. 23
DAY 2	**Review and Assess** Students review the chapter and demonstrate mastery of pronouns (pp. 548–551).	**Teaching Resources** *Formal Assessment,* Ch. 23; *Grammar Exercises Answers on Transparencies,* Ch. 23 ***Writing and Grammar iText* (Interactive Text),** Ch. 23, Chapter Review

Options for Adapting Lesson Plans

HOMEWORK

Have students complete any stage of the lesson for homework.

SPELLING

To teach spelling skills in conjunction with grammar, mechanics, and usage, work through *Prentice Hall Everyday Spelling,* Grade 8, Chapter 27, as you cover this *Writing and Grammar* chapter.

TECHNOLOGY

Students can use *Writing and Grammar iText* to complete the exercises interactively on computer. They can complete additional exercises in the *On-line Exercise Bank:* The Auto Check feature will grade their work. Go online: PHSchool.com Use Web code: eck-8002

FEATURES

Extend coverage with the Grammar in Literature feature (p. 544) and the Standardized Test Preparation Workshop (pp. 550–551).

INTEGRATED SKILLS COVERAGE

Grammar in Literature
SE p. 544

Writing
Find It in Your Writing, SE p. 547
Writing Application, SE p. 549

Viewing and Representing
Critical Viewing, SE pp. 538, 541, 544, 546

BLOCK SCHEDULING

Pacing Suggestions
For 90-minute Blocks
- Administer the Diagnostic Test to students to determine instructional coverage.
- Have students complete the necessary exercises in class. Use the Hands-on Grammar Activity to provide a change of pace.

Resources for Varying Instruction
- ***Writing and Grammar iText* (Interactive Text)** A 90-minute block provides an ideal opportunity for students to work on computer.

Professional Development Support
- ***How to Manage Instruction in the Block*** This teaching resource provides management and activity suggestions.

ASSESSMENT SUPPORT

Standardized Test Preparation Workshop SE pp. 550–551, ATE p. 544

Standardized Test Preparation Workbook, pp. 45–46

Formal Assessment, Ch. 23

MEDIA AND TECHNOLOGY

For the Student
- ***Writing and Grammar iText* (Interactive Text)**, Ch. 23
- **On-line Exercise Bank**, Ch. 23

For the Teacher
- ***Resource Pro* CD-ROM**

MEETING INDIVIDUAL NEEDS

Less Advanced Students ATE p. 541. See also Ongoing Assessment ATE p. 543.

ESL Students ATE p. 542

Verbal/Linguistic Learners ATE p. 543

WRITING AND GRAMMAR ON-LINE

iText Interactive Text (On-line or on CD-ROM)
- Easily navigable instruction with on-line supporting resources
- Self-scoring exercises and diagnostic tests

Companion Web Site PHSchool.com
- On-line Exercise Bank (use Web Code eck-8002)

See the Go On-line! feature, SE p. iii.

LITERATURE CONNECTIONS

Grammar in Literature selection from *Prentice Hall Literature: Timeless Voices, Timeless Themes,* Silver:
from "Baseball," Lionel G. García, SE p. 544

CHAPTER 23
USING PRONOUNS

Lesson Objectives

1. To understand and recognize the nominative, objective, and possessive cases.
2. To correctly use the nominative case for the subject of a verb and a predicate pronoun.
3. To correctly use the objective case for a direct object, indirect object, and an object of a preposition.
4. To correctly use the possessive case for pronouns that show ownership.
5. To correctly use *who* and *whom.*
6. To write with increasing accuracy when using pronoun case.

Critical Viewing

Analyze Students may state that the little boy playing stickball is holding *his* bat behind *him* as *he* prepares to swing.

Chapter 23 Using Pronouns

▲ Critical Viewing
Using the personal pronouns *he, him,* and *his,* describe the stickball action in this photograph. **[Analyze]**

Some pronouns change form according to how they are used. For example, in the sentence "I hit the ball," the pronoun *I* is a subject. However, in "The ball hit me," *I* changes to *me* to show that the pronoun is now a direct object. In "The ball was hit by my stick," the possessive form *my* is used to show ownership. The relation between a pronoun's form and its use is known as its *case.*

This chapter will show you how to use pronouns correctly by making sure that their case fits the way you use them in your sentences.

ONGOING ASSESSMENT: Diagnose

If students miss more than one item in each category, direct them to the relevant pages of the text and assign exercises for practice and review.

Using Pronouns	Diagnostic Test Items	Teach	Practice	Section Review	Chapter Review
Skill Check A					
Pronoun Case	A 1–5	p. 540	Ex. 1, 5		Ex. 8
Skill Check B					
Nominative Case	B 6–10	p. 541	Ex. 2, 5		Ex. 9–10, 12, 15
Skill Check C					
Objective Case	C 11–15	p. 542	Ex. 3, 5		Ex. 9

Diagnostic Test

Directions: Write all answers on a separate sheet of paper.

Skill Check A. Write *nominative*, *objective*, or *possessive* to identify the case of the underlined personal pronoun in each sentence.

1. Many of our children's games are based on rules and routines that are as old as organized society.
2. Some of them have been adapted from ancient ceremonies.
3. Today, we may play games that originated in folk customs.
4. The running, jumping, throwing, and tagging of outdoor games provide us with a form of exercise.
5. Children invent their own versions of such old favorites as hopscotch and hide-and-seek.

Skill Check B. Identify the nominative pronoun(s) in each sentence. Then, tell how each pronoun is used in the sentence.

6. I read that the game of marbles originated long ago.
7. It is played all over the world in many different forms.
8. In one version, a player will shoot a marble, called a shooter, at other marbles in a circle marked on the ground; he or she will win any marbles that are driven out of the circle.
9. It is she who won the most marble games.
10. However, it was he who won the marble tournament.

Skill Check C. Write an objective pronoun to complete each sentence. Then, tell how each pronoun is used in the sentence.

11. Jacks requires special equipment—a small rubber ball and ten or twelve jacks—without __?__ you cannot play the game.
12. After snatching up jacks and catching a bouncing ball, a player must keep __?__ all in his hand in order to win.
13. Jessica and I played jacks at recess. I let __?__ go first.
14. I threw __?__ the ball so that she could begin.
15. The ball fell out of my hand when I fumbled __?__.

Skill Check D. Choose the correct word in parentheses.

16. My friend Josh brought (his, his') ball so we could play stickball.
17. The stick we used for a bat was (ours, our's).
18. (It's, Its) weight and balance are perfect for big hits.
19. (It's, Its) a great game if you have a big group of players.
20. Stella said that pitcher is a favorite position of (her's, hers).

Skill Check E. Use *who* and *whom* correctly to complete each of the following sentences.

21. __?__ wants to play jacks?
22. Josh was the one __?__ she had defeated earlier.
23. Emily was the one __?__ asked to play next.
24. By __?__ was she taught the game?
25. Emily thanked Susan, from __?__ she had learned to play.

Answer Key

Diagnostic Test

Each item in the diagnostic test corresponds to a specific concept in the chapter on pronouns. This will enable you to tailor instruction to the particular needs of your students. See "Ongoing Assessment: Diagnose" for further details.

Skill Check A

1. our—possessive
2. them—objective
3. we—nominative
4. us—objective
5. their—possessive

Skill Check B

6. I—subject
7. It—subject
8. he, she—subject
9. It—subject, she—predicate pronoun
10. it—subject, he—predicate pronoun

Skill Check C

11. them—object of preposition
12. them—direct object
13. her—direct object
14. her—indirect object
15. it—direct object

Skill Check D

16. his
17. ours
18. Its
19. It's
20. hers

Skill Check E

21. Who
22. whom
23. who
24. whom
25. whom

ONGOING ASSESSMENT: Diagnose *continued*

Using Pronouns	Diagnostic Test Items	Teach	Practice	Section Review	Chapter Review
Skill Check D					
Possessive Case	D 16–20	pp. 543–544	Ex. 4–5		Ex. 11–12, 14
Skill Check E					
Who and *Whom*	E 21–25	pp. 545–546	Ex. 6–7		Ex. 13–14
Cumulative Reviews and Applications					Ex. 15–16

TIME SAVERS!

Answers on Transparency Use the Grammar Exercise Answers on Transparencies for Chapter 23 to facilitate correction by students.

On-Line Exercise Bank Have students complete the Diagnostic Test on computer. The Auto Check feature will grade their work for you!

PREPARE and ENGAGE

Interest GRABBER Ask students to listen for pronouns as you read the following paragraph:

Saturday I spent the afternoon with Archie, Lulu, Floyd, and Mitzi. We all had lunch at his house and then went to the movies. Floyd wanted to sit in the front row, but she said that was too close. Mitzi bought popcorn and shared it with her. They spilled their sodas. I liked the movie. So did they, but he disagreed.

Then, ask students if they have *any* idea who did what. Explain that pronouns are a convenience so that we don't have to repeat, but if not used correctly, they can confuse.

Activate Prior Knowledge

Have students work in pairs or small groups to improvise a sketch in which they refer only to people or things that are visible. They cannot use any proper names or nouns. Have them point and use gestures along with pronouns.

TEACH

Step-by-Step Teaching Guide

Cases of Personal Pronouns

1. Quickly review person of pronouns and introduce case. Help students identify the pronouns of each case.
2. Introduce nominative pronouns.

   She plays soccer. He studies math.

   We will be there. They are lost.
3. Present objective pronouns.

   Give me the ball.

   The magician fooled you.

   The test results made us happy.
4. Introduce possessive pronouns.

   How is your dog?

   Their team is doing well.

Answer Key

Exercise 1

1. nominative
2. possessive
3. possessive
4. objective
5. possessive
6. nominative
7. nominative
8. objective
9. possessive
10. objective

Recognizing Cases of Personal Pronouns

In Chapter 14, you learned that personal pronouns can be arranged in three groups: first person, second person, and third person. Pronouns can also be grouped by their *cases.*

KEY CONCEPT English has three cases: *nominative, objective,* and *possessive.* ■

The chart below shows the personal pronouns grouped according to the three cases.

THE THREE CASES OF PERSONAL PRONOUNS

Nominative Case	Use in a Sentence
I, we you he, she, it, they	subject of a verb predicate pronoun
Objective Case	**Use in a Sentence**
me, us you him, her, it, them	direct object indirect object object of a preposition
Possessive Case	**Use in a Sentence**
my, mine, our, ours your, yours his, her, hers, its, their, theirs	to show ownership

Exercise 1 **Identifying Case** Identify the case of each underlined personal pronoun below.

EXAMPLE: Melvin left the marbles for us.
ANSWER: objective

1. John, Ashley, and I played marbles on the playground.
2. We took turns trying to hit our opponents' marbles.
3. John hit my marble on the first try.
4. I gave him my marble because he hit it.
5. Ashley hit her own marble by accident.
6. She didn't win any of our marbles during that round.
7. We decided to play longer so that we could have an extra turn.
8. Everyone wanted to play with us.
9. I let some friends use my marbles.
10. I hope they don't lose them.

Theme: Street and Stoop Games

In this chapter, you will learn about the different cases of pronouns and how to use them correctly in sentences. The examples and exercises are about games you play outdoors.

Cross-Curricular Connection: Physical Education

More Practice

Grammar Exercise Workbook
- pp. 135–138

On-line Exercise Bank
- Chapter 23

Go on-line:
PHSchool.com
Enter Web Code:
eck-8002

TIME AND RESOURCE MANAGER

Resources
Print: Grammar Exercise Workbook, pp. 137–141
Technology: Writing and Grammar iText, Ch. 23; On-Line Exercise Bank, Ch. 23

In-Depth Coverage	Accelerated Pace
• Work through all key concepts, pp. 540–546. • Assign and review Exercises 1–7. • Read and discuss Grammar in Literature, p. 544. • Do the Hands-on Grammar Activity, p. 547.	• Assign pp. 540–546 for independent student review. • Assign Section Review Exercises 8–14.

The Nominative Case

Personal pronouns in the nominative case have two uses:

KEY CONCEPT Use the nominative case (1) for the subject of a verb and (2) for a predicate pronoun. ■

Note that predicate pronouns follow linking verbs. Pronouns that follow linking verbs should normally be in the nominative case.

SUBJECTS: *She* hopes to be on our team.
With excitement, *they* prepared for the game.

PREDICATE PRONOUNS: It was (LV) *I* who suggested a picnic.
The best players are (LV) *she* and Mark.

People seldom forget to use the nominative case for a pronoun that is used by itself as a subject. Problems sometimes arise, however, when the pronoun is part of a compound subject.

INCORRECT: John and *me* played jacks.

To make sure you are using the correct case of the pronoun in a compound subject, use just the pronoun with the verb in the sentence. *Me played* is obviously wrong, so the nominative case *I* should be used instead.

CORRECT: John and *I* played jacks.

Exercise 2 **Supplying Pronouns in the Nominative Case** Complete each sentence, using a nominative pronoun. Identify how the pronoun is used in the sentence.

EXAMPLE: Gordon and __?__ played hopscotch.
ANSWER: she (subject)

1. Yesterday, my little sister Jessica and __?__ played hopscotch on the sidewalk.
2. It was __?__ who drew the hopscotch board with chalk.
3. __?__ collected rocks to mark our places on the hopscotch board.
4. __?__ kept getting stuck on number six.
5. It was __?__ who finally won the game.

▼ **Critical Viewing**
Using the nominative case pronouns *she* and *it*, tell one possible outcome of this game. **[Speculate]**

Step-by-Step Teaching Guide

The Nominative Case

1. Using the nominative case with subjects is the easy part. Predicate nominatives and compound subjects can present students with problems. The source of incorrect usage is often informal speech patterns. Review with students that they don't (you hope!) talk the same way in every situation. In more formal situations, they need to use correct grammar in speech and their writing.
2. Review linking verbs with students as a key to recognizing predicate nominatives. Linking verbs do not show action. They link, or connect, words in a sentence.
   Fifi was late for school today.
   Fifi felt embarrassed to interrupt the class.
   Fifi will be prompt tomorrow.
3. Tell students to use the pronoun verb test for predicate nominatives. In the example, *It was I who suggested a picnic,* a test of correct usage is to shift the pronoun before the verb. *I was* sounds right.
4. The pronoun followed by verb test will also prevent mistakes with compound subjects. Remind students that if a pronoun is part of the subject, it has to be a nominative pronoun. Identifying and remembering the correct cases of *I* and *me* will eliminate many common mistakes.

Customize for *Less Advanced Students*

The definition most students memorize is, "Verbs show action." The fact that there is a whole group of verbs that do not show action is confusing. Use the charts in Chapter 15 to review linking verbs, especially forms of *be.*

Critical Viewing

Speculate Encourage students to suggest sentences such as: *She* looks as if she will win *it* by herself.

Answer Key

Exercise 2

1. I—subject
2. I (or she)—predicate pronoun
3. We (or I or She)—subject
4. I (or We or She)—subject
5. I (or she)—predicate pronoun

Step-by-Step Teaching Guide

The Objective Case

1. When pronouns are receivers of action, they must be used in the objective case.
2. Review how to find direct and indirect objects in sentences. The direct object and indirect object answer the question *What?* or *Whom?* about the verb.

   Roy gave the dog a bone.

   Gave what? Bone.

   Roy gave the dog a bone.

   Gave to what/whom? Dog.
3. Objects of prepositions are easy. Just find the prepositional phrase: *on the desk, around us, under the bed, after school, in it, beside him, beyond the Milky Way.* The object is the noun or pronoun.
4. Offer examples for extra practice with compound subjects and objects:

   Jeff and I played ball.

   Sid played ball with Jeff and me.
5. An easy way to use the correct pronoun in compounds is to rephrase the sentence in the singular. *I* (not *me*) *played ball. Sid played ball with me* (not *I*). The pronoun does not change just because Jeff joined the ball game. This strategy works every time.
6. Review the common errors made in compound objects. The test of simply using the pronoun as the object is useful. But rather than relying purely on sound, remind students that if they correctly identify the pronoun as a receiver of action and know the objective pronouns, they will be less likely to make a mistake.

Customize for *ESL Students*

The different word order in English (*Margo bought it)* and Spanish *(Margo it bought)* need not cause confusion. The answer to *Bought what?* is "it," no matter which language you are using. Prepositional phrases have the same structure in both languages. But students learning English may need extra practice. Working with a grammar buddy on the exercises may help.

23

The Objective Case

Personal pronouns in the objective case have three uses:

KEY CONCEPT Use the objective case (1) for a direct object, (2) for an indirect object, and (3) for the object of a preposition. ■

DIRECT OBJECT:	Frank's comment on the game upset *me.*
INDIRECT OBJECT:	Tell *her* the good news.
OBJECT OF PREPOSITION:	The players swarmed around *me.*

As with the nominative case, people seldom forget to use the objective case for a pronoun that is used by itself as a direct object, indirect object, or object of a preposition. Problems may arise, however, when the pronoun is part of a compound object.

INCORRECT: The players swarmed around Lucy and *I.*

To make sure you are using the correct case of the pronoun in a compound object, use just the pronoun with the rest of the sentence. *The players swarmed around I* is obviously wrong, so the objective case *me* should be used instead.

CORRECT: The players swarmed around Lucy and *me.*

Exercise 3 **Supplying Pronouns in the Objective Case** Complete each sentence below, using an objective pronoun. Then, tell how each pronoun is used in the sentence.

EXAMPLE: His grandmother's old jump rope gave __?__ a clue about her childhood.

ANSWER: him (indirect object)

1. Skipping rope is a good form of exercise. Some athletes use __?__ in their training.
2. My sister loves to jump rope. It gives __?__ a chance to exercise and have fun.
3. My mother gave my friends and __?__ a long jump rope to use for our game.
4. I taught __?__ a rhyme to sing while we jumped.
5. It was hard for some of __?__ to jump and sing at the same time.

Learn More

For a review of direct and indirect objects and objects of prepositions, you can turn to Chapter 17.

More Practice

Grammar Exercise Workbook
- pp. 137–138

On-line Exercise Bank
- Chapter 23

Go on-line: PHSchool.com
Enter Web Code: eck-8002

Answer Key

Exercise 3

1. it—direct object
2. her—indirect object
3. her—indirect object
4. them—indirect object
5. them (or us)—object of preposition

The Possessive Case

Personal pronouns in the possessive case show ownership of one sort or another.

KEY CONCEPT Use the possessive case of personal pronouns before nouns to show possession. In addition, certain personal pronouns may also be used by themselves to indicate possession. ■

BEFORE NOUNS: The team won *its* game.
Chris held *my* baseball glove.

BY THEMSELVES: Is this marble *yours* or *mine*?
Hers was the best score.

Personal pronouns in the possessive case are never written with an apostrophe. Keep this in mind, especially with possessive pronouns that end in *s*.

INCORRECT: These seats are *our's*, not *their's*.
CORRECT: These seats are *ours*, not *theirs*.

When the pronoun *it* is followed by an apostrophe and an *s*, it becomes a contraction of *it is*. The possessive pronoun *its* does not have an apostrophe.

CONTRACTION: *It's* going to rain.
POSSESSIVE PRONOUN: The team loved *its* uniforms.

Exercise 4 **Using Pronouns in the Possessive Case** Choose the correct word from the pair in parentheses to complete each sentence.

EXAMPLE: Fortunately, the lost ball was not (our's, ours).
ANSWER: ours

1. Jake and I love playing box ball with our friends after school. Yesterday, it was (his, his') turn to host the game.
2. Jake's family has a great concrete surface in (their, theirs) backyard on which we can play.
3. (Its, It's) surface is very smooth.
4. The chalk we used to draw the box for the game is (my, mine).
5. The ball we played with is (our's, ours).

Spelling Tip

Keep in mind the two homonyms of the word *their*: *Their* is used to show possession. *There* normally refers to a place. *They're* is a contraction of *they are*.

More Practice

Grammar Exercise Workbook
- pp. 139–140

On-line Exercise Bank
- Chapter 23

Go on-line: PHSchool.com
Enter Web Code: eck-8002

iText

Get instant feedback! Exercise 4 is available on-line or on CD-ROM.

Step-by-Step Teaching Guide

The Possessive Case

1. Possessive pronouns show possession when used with a noun. They can also be used by themselves.

   I like my bat.

   Can I use your glove?

   That house is theirs.

2. Ask students to use possessive pronouns to answer the following questions (point when necessary):

   Whose class is this? (ours)

   Whose desk is this [teacher's desk]? (yours)

   Whose book is that? (his or hers)

3. Review the common error of adding *'s* to possessive pronouns. Remind students that *it's* is a contraction for *it is*. Possessive pronouns do not contain apostrophes.

Customize for *Verbal/Linguistic Learners*

Define *homophones:* words that are pronounced alike but have different spellings and meanings—*to, two, too.* Also define *homonyms:* words pronounced and spelled alike but with different meanings—*clog* (a shoe) and *clog* (to obstruct). Challenge students to list homophones and/or homonyms for these pronouns: *its (it's); theirs (there's); mine* (a gold mine or to dig for something); *ours (hours).*

Answer Key

Exercise 4

1. his
2. their
3. Its
4. mine
5. ours

ONGOING ASSESSMENT: Monitor and Reinforce

If students miss more than two items in Exercise 1 to 4, refer them to the following for additional practice.

In the Textbook	Print Resources	Technology
Chapter Review, Ex. 8–12, pp. 548–549	Grammar Exercise Workbook, pp. 137–140	On-Line Exercise Bank, Section 23

TIME SAVERS!

Answers on Transparency Use the Grammar Exercise Answers on Transparencies for Chapter 23 to facilitate correction by students.

On-Line Exercise Bank Have students complete the Diagnostic Test on computer. The Auto Check feature will grade their work for you!

Step-by-Step Teaching Guide

Grammar in Literature

1. Have a volunteer read aloud the passage by Lionel G. García.
2. Help students to identify the case of each italicized pronoun: *my* (possessive), *us* (objective), *he* (nominative), *he* (nominative), *us* (objective), *us* (objective), *we* (nominative).
3. Ask students to write a sentence that uses pronouns in all three cases. For example: *I* [N] *gave my* [P] *glove to them* [O].

More About the Author

Lionel García was born in San Diego, Texas, in 1935. As a boy, he lived with his grandfather, who was a goat herder. This may be one reason why he grew up to be a veterinarian. His work chronicles the lives of people of Mexican ancestry throughout the United States.

Answer Key

Exercise 5

1. me
2. I
3. Its
4. correct
5. They; I
6. me; correct
7. correct; she
8. correct
9. correct
10. correct; he

Critical Viewing

Analyze Students may say that *it* has red stitching and *its* color is white.

GRAMMAR IN LITERATURE

from Baseball

Lionel G. García

Notice how the author has used pronouns in all three cases in this passage.

My uncle Adolfo, who had pitched for the Yankees and the Cardinals in the majors, had given *us* the ball several years before. Once when *he* returned for a visit, *he* saw *us* playing from across the street and walked over to ask *us* what *we* were doing.

▼ Critical Viewing Use *it* and *its* in a sentence describing the distinctive features of a baseball. **[Analyze]**

Exercise 5 **Revising to Correct the Case of Personal Pronouns** Some of the underlined pronouns in the following sentences are incorrect. On your paper, revise each sentence that contains an error. If the pronoun is used correctly, write *correct*.

EXAMPLE: We played HORSE with Jeremy and he.
ANSWER: We played HORSE with Jeremy and him.

1. HORSE is a game that is often played by my friend and I on the basketball court.
2. Jesse, Tara, and me like to play the game.
3. It's rules are not difficult.
4. A player who misses a difficult shot that someone else has already made is given a letter in the word *HORSE*. After a player has five misses, he or she is eliminated.
5. Them and me try to get each other out by setting up shots that are difficult to make.
6. Tara gave Jesse and I an "H" when we couldn't make over-the-shoulder shots.
7. It was her who spelled HORSE first and had to sit out.
8. Jesse and I both had "H-O-R-S."
9. He shot over his head and made it.
10. When I missed the shot and got an "E," the winner was him.

More Practice

Grammar Exercise Workbook
- pp. 135–140

On-line Exercise Bank
- Chapter 23

Go on-line: PHSchool.com *Enter Web Code:* eck-8002

iText

Get instant feedback! Exercise 5 is available on-line or on CD-ROM.

TIME SAVERS!

Answers on Transparency Use the Grammar Exercise Answers on Transparencies for Chapter 23 to facilitate correction by students.

On-Line Exercise Bank Have students complete the Diagnostic Test on computer. The Auto Check feature will grade their work for you!

STANDARDIZED TEST PREPARATION WORKSHOP

Grammar and Usage Many standardized tests require students to identify the pronoun and case to use in sentences. Ask students to choose the answer to complete the following sentence.

Frank gave the uniforms to Liz and ___.

A we **C** us
B they **D** I

Items A, B, and D are all in the nominative case, while the blank in the sentence is an object of the preposition *to*.

Item **C** is the only choice that makes a grammatically correct sentence.

Cases of *Who* and *Whom* The pronouns *who* and *whom* are often confused. *Who* is a nominative case pronoun, and *whom* is an objective case pronoun. *Who* and *whom* have two common uses in sentences: They can be used in questions or to begin subordinate clauses in complex sentences.

Learn More

To learn more about subordinate clauses, turn to Chapter 20.

KEY CONCEPTS Use *who* for the subject of a verb. Use *whom* (1) for the direct object of a verb and (2) for the object of a preposition. ■

You will often find *who* used as the subject of a question.

SUBJECT IN A QUESTION: *Who* hit the most home runs?

Who may also be used as the subject of a subordinate clause in a complex sentence.

SUBJECT IN A SUBORDINATE CLAUSE: I admire the player *who* hit the most home runs.

In the example above, *who* is part of an adjective clause—*who hit the most home runs.* Within the clause itself, *who* is the subject of the verb *hit.*

The following examples show *whom* used in questions.

DIRECT OBJECT: *Whom* did he see at the game?

OBJECT OF PREPOSITION: From *whom* is she getting the new softball?

Questions that include *whom* will generally be in inverted word order. If you reword the first example in normal word order, you will see that *whom* is the direct object of the verb *did see: He did see whom at the game.* In the second example, it is easy to see that *whom* is the object of the preposition *from.* Again, rewording may help: *She is getting the new softball from whom.*

Rewording is also useful when *whom* is part of a subordinate clause. A subordinate clause that should begin with *whom* will always be in inverted word order. To check whether you have used the correct case of the pronoun, isolate the clause and put it into normal word order.

INVERTED ORDER: I know the person *whom* he met at the game.

REWORDED ORDER: He met *whom* at the game.

INVERTED ORDER: Janet thanked her aunt, from *whom* she had received a ball.

REWORDED ORDER: She had received a ball from *whom.*

Step-by-Step Teaching Guide

Cases of *Who* and *Whom*

1. *Who* and *whom* are the source of frequent errors. See that students understand that *who* is a nominative case pronoun and *whom* is an objective case pronoun. It follows that *who* is used for the subject, and *whom* for an object.
2. Review the use of *who* and *whom* in questions and subordinate clauses.

   Who is up next?

   Whom did the manager pick?

   From whom did you hear the news?

   Who knows how to hit this guy's pitches?

   The manager likes players who never stop trying to win.
3. Review inverted word order with *whom.* Point out that rewording the order of sentences will help students use *whom* correctly.

Answer Key

Exercise 6

1. Who
2. who
3. Whom
4. Whom
5. who
6. Who
7. whom
8. whom
9. Who
10. whom

Exercise 7

1. who will be counting—subject
2. who is counting—subject
3. whom we caught hiding behind the car—direct object
4. from whom he was running—object of preposition
5. who will count next time—subject
6. who was hiding behind the tree—subject
7. whom did he chase—direct object
8. whom he called out—object of preposition
9. who was chosen to be the counter—subject
10. who goes next—subject

Critical Viewing

Question Students may suggest: Who is playing in the street? Whom did they invite to play the game?

23

◀ Critical Viewing
Using *who* and *whom*, ask two questions about what is happening in this photograph.
[Question]

Exercise 6 **Using *Who* and *Whom* in Questions** For each of the following sentences, choose the correct pronoun from the pair given in parentheses.

EXAMPLE: (Who, Whom) did you invite to play stickball?
ANSWER: Whom

1. We are going to play stickball in the street. (Who, Whom) would like to play first base?
2. The best pitcher would be (who, whom)?
3. (Who, Whom) would you like to be catcher?
4. (Who, Whom) were you thinking about as shortstop?
5. Of those remaining, (who, whom) will be playing outfield?
6. (Who, Whom) is setting up the batting order?
7. The stick and the ball are being brought by (who, whom)?
8. Our parents asked, "With (who, whom) are you playing?"
9. (Who, Whom) made the first out?
10. The first run was scored by (who, whom)?

Grammar and Style Tip

One way to know when to use *who* or *whom* is to substitute the pronoun *him.* If the sentence is correct using *him*, you can safely use *whom;* if not, use *who.*

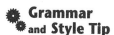

Exercise 7 **Revising to Correct *Who* and *Whom* in Subordinate Clauses** Revise the sentences below in which *who* or *whom* is used incorrectly. Then, indicate how *who* or *whom* is used in each sentence.

EXAMPLE: Let's decide whom will start the game.
ANSWER: Let's decide who will start the game. (subject)

1. To play Kick the Can, the group must make a decision about whom will be counting.
2. Everyone else must hide from the person who is counting.
3. It was Tom who we caught hiding behind the car.
4. Tara was the one from whom he was running.
5. We know whom will count next time.
6. The boy who was hiding behind the tree kicked the can.
7. Who did he chase?
8. I wasn't the one to whom he called out.
9. Is Helen the one whom was chosen to be the counter?
10. Now we've lost track of whom goes next.

More Practice

Grammar Exercise Workbook
• pp. 140–141
On-line Exercise Bank
• Chapter 23
Go on-line:
PHSchool.com
Enter Web Code:
eck-8002

TIME SAVERS!

Answers on Transparency
Use the Grammar Exercise Answers on Transparencies for Chapter 23 to facilitate correction by students.

On-Line Exercise Bank
Have students complete the Diagnostic Test on computer. The Auto Check feature will grade their work for you!

Hands-on Grammar

Nominative Case Pronouns Two-Way Reader

Make a two-way reader to help you practice using pronouns in the nominative case correctly. Cut a sheet of 6 1/2" x 8 1/2" paper to make a strip that is 6 1/2" x 5". Fold in each side edge 1 3/4", leaving a space of about 1 1/2" wide in the middle. Next, use a ruler to draw eight lines across the paper at 3/4" intervals and a vertical line along each folded edge. Then, open the folds, finish drawing the lines on the inside from crease to crease, and refold the edges. On the lines down the middle section, print eight of the following pronouns: *I, he, it, they, he and she, he and I, you, she, we, you and I, we,* and *they.*

Next, on the outside of the left fold, write a question on each line that might be answered by the pronoun facing it in the middle. Examples: *Who is the boss? I. Who were my friends?* Then, cut the lines as far as the fold on each side, creating a double "fringe." Inside the fold on the left, write each answer so that the pronoun becomes a predicate pronoun; on the right, write the answer so that the pronoun is the subject. Examples: *The boss is I am the boss. My friends were* he and she *were my friends.* The illustration below shows the you part of a reader.

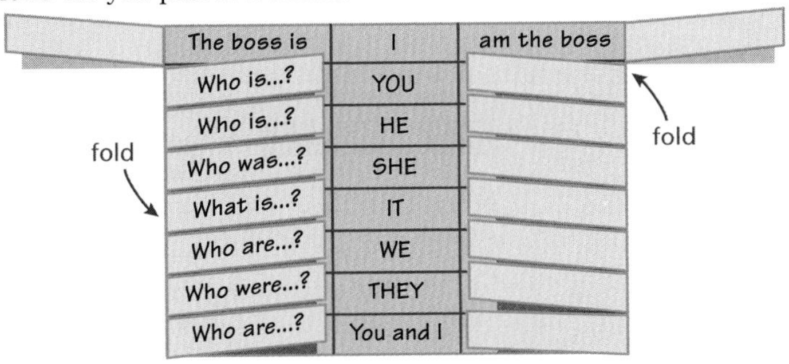

Finally, with a partner, practice answering the questions on the other person's two-way reader. Check under each piece of "fringe" to see if you are correct. Practice reading aloud in order to accustom yourselves to hearing the correct usage of nominative pronouns, especially when they are compound subjects or predicate nouns.

Find It in Your Reading Read a biographical sketch in your literature book or a magazine. Note the number of pronouns in the three cases.

Find It in Your Writing Review a piece of your autobiographical writing, and check to see that you have used all personal pronouns correctly. Correct those that are in the wrong case.

Step-by-Step Teaching Guide

Nominative Case Pronouns Two-Way Reader

Teaching Resources: Hands-on Grammar Activity Book, Chapter 23

1. Have students refer to their Hands-on Grammar activity books or give them copies of the relevant pages for this activity.
2. You may want to have students work in pairs so that they can answer each others' questions.
3. Ask students if the two-way reader would work with action verbs. Have students try one like *call.*

Find It in Your Reading

You may want to assign the same story for all students to use. Compare the numbers of pronouns they find.

Find It in Your Writing

Have students keep a list of the errors they find. This way they will know the cases they need to review.

PRENTICE HALL
Everyday Spelling

If you have taught the spelling skills in *Prentice Hall Everyday Spelling,* Grade 8, Chapter 27, in conjunction with this *Writing and Grammar* chapter, review and assess students' mastery of the skills before concluding the chapter.

ONGOING ASSESSMENT: Assess Mastery

Use the following resources to assess student mastery of using pronouns.

In the Textbook	Technology
Chapter Review, Ex. 8–14, pp. 548–549	Writing and Grammar iText, Ch. 23, Chapter Review; On-Line Exercise Bank, Ch. 23

TIME SAVERS!

Hands-on Grammar
Use the Hands-on Grammar activity sheet for Chapter 23 to facilitate this activity.

ASSESS and CLOSE

Chapter Review

Each of these exercises correlates to a concept in the chapter on pronouns, pages 540–546. These exercises may be used for more practice, for reteaching, or for review of the Key Concepts presented. Answers for all exercises are available in *Grammar Exercises Answers on Transparencies* in your teaching resources.

Answer Key

Exercise 8

1. nominative
2. possessive
3. objective
4. nominative
5. possessive
6. possessive
7. nominative
8. objective
9. possessive
10. objective

Exercise 9

1. We are going to play Little League baseball again this year. subject
2. My mom coached us last year, and we asked her to do it again. direct object
3. Actually, it was she who volunteered for the job. predicate pronoun
4. She was great at it! subject
5. She gave us positions to play. indirect object
6. I got to play first base. subject
7. Ellen is fast, so Mom put her in the outfield. direct object
8. We had a good time. subject
9. We played twelve games and won most of them. object of preposition
10. After the season, it was I who asked my mom to be coach next year. predicate pronoun

Exercise 10

1. me
2. He; I
3. he; I
4. him
5. him; her
6. me
7. She; he
8. her
9. she
10. me

Exercise 11

1. ours
2. my
3. her
4. hers
5. It's
6. their
7. yours
8. theirs
9. our
10. its

Chapter 23

Chapter Review

GRAMMAR EXERCISES 8–16

Exercise 8 Identifying Case Identify the case of the personal pronouns that are underlined in the following sentences.

1. We are going to the soccer game.
2. My mother is bringing her friend.
3. They will drive me to the game.
4. I hope I can make a goal today.
5. Our team name is the Robins.
6. We have a tough opponent; their name is the Condors.
7. They have played five games so far this season.
8. At the end of the season, the league will give us trophies.
9. The coach blows his whistle.
10. We all work hard for him.

Exercise 9 Supplying Pronouns in the Nominative or Objective Case Complete each of the following sentences by writing a nominative or objective case pronoun. Then, tell how the pronoun is used in the sentence.

1. __?__ are going to play Little League baseball again this year.
2. My mom coached us last year, and we asked __?__ to do it again.
3. Actually, it was __?__ who volunteered for the job.
4. __?__ was great at it!
5. She gave __?__ positions to play.
6. __?__ got to play first base.
7. Ellen is fast, so Mom put __?__ in the outfield.
8. __?__ had a good time.
9. We played twelve games and won most of __?__.
10. After the season, it was __?__ who asked my mom to be coach next year.

Exercise 10 Using Compound Subjects and Objects That Include Pronouns To complete each sentence, select the correct pronoun from the choices in parentheses.

1. The coach gave John and (I, me) our uniforms early.
2. (He, Him) and (I, me) have played flag football together for two years.
3. Flag football is a game that (he, him), and (I, me) really enjoy.
4. I have been best friends with Tami and (he, him) for a long time.
5. I seldom go anywhere without (he, him) or (she, her).
6. Tami joined John and (I, me) on the team.
7. (She, Her) and (he, him) catch passes.
8. I threw each pass to either John or (she, her).
9. John and (she, her) scored touchdowns.
10. John gave Tami and (I, me) a "high five."

Exercise 11 Using Pronouns in the Possessive Case Choose the pronoun in parentheses that completes each sentence correctly.

1. The first game was (ours, our's).
2. I put (my, mine) marbles in the circle.
3. She put (her, hers) marbles in next.
4. The first shot was (hers, her's).
5. (It's, Its) my turn next.
6. Others waited for (their, theirs) turn.
7. You can win by keeping the marbles that are (yours, your's) inside the circle.
8. Kelly and Adam are waiting to play. The next game is (their's, theirs).
9. Once they have finished, we get (our, ours) chance to play.
10. My marble is nicked on (its, it's) surface.

Exercise 12 **Correcting the Case of Personal Pronouns** Rewrite these sentences, correcting pronoun errors. If a sentence has no errors, write *correct.*

1. Him and me went to the playground.
2. We wanted to play kickball with them.
3. They allowed us into theirs game.
4. Kickball is the perfect game for Steve and I.
5. Its lots of fun to kick the ball and run.
6. The pitcher rolled the ball toward me.
7. I kicked it over his' head.
8. The first run scored was our's.
9. The highest scorers were Steve and me.
10. My dad was proud of him and I.

Exercise 13 **Using *Who* and *Whom* in Questions** Choose the correct pronoun from the choices given to complete each sentence.

1. (Who, Whom) knows how to play handball?
2. Is he the one (who, whom) will choose sides?
3. To (who, whom) did she hit the ball?
4. (Who, Whom) did she choose first?
5. (Who, Whom) was chosen after Bob?
6. (Who, Whom) hit Janine with the ball?
7. Did she forgive Bob, by (who, whom) she had been hit?
8. To (who, whom) does this jersey belong?
9. (Who, Whom) will be the next captain?
10. (Who, Whom) will serve the ball?

Exercise 14 **Revising Sentences for Correct Pronoun Usage** Rewrite these sentences, correcting errors in pronoun usage. For sentences without errors, write *correct.*

1. On rainy days, Sally and me play indoor games.
2. Its more fun to play outdoors with she.
3. Little children like to play some indoor games at their birthday parties.
4. Her and me played "Button, Button, Who's Got the Button?" at my sister's party.
5. A player must guess who has the button.
6. Players sit in a circle with one of them in it's center.
7. A button is passed quickly along a string among those whom are in the circle.
8. They keep theirs hands in motion constantly as if receiving or passing the button.
9. If the center player can guess to who the button has been passed, he wins the round.
10. By whom was this game invented?

Exercise 15 **Writing Application** Imagine that you are a sportscaster announcing a game of your favorite outdoor sport. Write a play-by-play account of part of the action. Make sure you include pronouns in all three cases in your play-by-play account. Underline each pronoun, and identify its case.

Exercise 16 **CUMULATIVE REVIEW Verb Usage** The following paragraph contains errors in verb usage. Rewrite the paragraph, correcting the errors.

Sherry and I gone to day camp one summer. During the final week, we take part in a sports competition. The highlight of the event be a tug-of-war contest. Two captains choose the people for their sides. I seen that the other team had bigger contestants, but our team members were stronger. I knowed that we going to win. The teams standed on opposite sides of a mud puddle. I told Sherry, "Hold on tight, and don't leave go of the rope." Slowly, we were pull the other team toward the puddle. After their first player had fall into the puddle, we were declared the winners.

Exercise 12

1. He and I went to the playground.
2. correct
3. They allowed us into their game.
4. Kickball is the perfect game for Steve and me.
5. It's lots of fun to kick the ball and run.
6. correct
7. I kicked it over his head.
8. The first run scored was ours.
9. The highest scorers were Steve and I.
10. My dad was proud of him and me.

Exercise 13

1. Who
2. who
3. whom
4. Whom
5. Who
6. Who
7. whom
8. whom
9. Who
10. Who

Exercise 14

1. On rainy days, Sally and I play indoor games.
2. It's more fun to play outdoors with her.
3. correct
4. She and I played Button, Button, Who's Got the Button? at my sister's party.
5. correct
6. Players sit in a circle with one of them in its center.
7. A button is passed quickly along a string among those who are in the circle.
8. They keep their hands in motion constantly as if receiving or passing the button.
9. If the center player can guess to whom the button has been passed, he wins the round.
10. correct

Exercise 15

Writing Application
Students may want to present their accounts with partners. The writer can read the account as the partner acts it out.

continued

Answer Key continued

Exercise 16

Cumulative Review
(1) Sherry and I went to day camp one summer. (2) During the final week, we took part in a sports competition. (3) The highlight of the event was a tug-of-war contest. (4) Two captains chose the people for their sides. (5) I saw that the other team had bigger contestants, but our team members were stronger. (6) I knew that we were going to win. (7) The teams stood on opposite sides of a mud puddle. (8) I told Sherry, "Hold on tight, and don't let go of the rope." (9) Slowly we pulled the other team toward the puddle. (10) After their first player had fallen into the puddle, we were declared the winners.

Lesson Objectives

- To use pronouns correctly.

Step-by-Step Teaching Guide

Standard English Usage: Pronouns

Teaching Resources: Standardized Test Preparation Workbook, pp. 45–46

1. If students recognize that the pronoun for (1) in the first sample must be in the possessive case, the rest becomes easy.
2. In the second sample, they need to decide if the answer should be singular or plural, too.

Standardized Test Preparation Workshop

Standard English Usage: Pronouns

Standardized tests measure your knowledge of the rules of standard grammar, such as correct pronoun usage. Questions test your ability to use the three cases of personal pronouns correctly. When answering these questions, determine what type of pronoun is needed in the sentence—nominative case pronouns are used as subjects or predicate pronouns; objective case pronouns are used as direct objects, indirect objects, or objects of prepositions; and possessive case pronouns are used to show ownership.

The following test items will give you practice with the format of questions that test your knowledge of pronoun usage.

Test Tip

When an object or subject is compound, check to see if the case is correct by using only the pronoun in the compound construction—for example, *She invited Kate and I/me.* Correct: *She invited me.* Incorrect: *She invited I.*

Sample Test Item	Answers and Explanations
Read the passage, and choose the letter of the word or group of words that belongs in each space. Yesterday, our team and __(1)__ played the first soccer match of the season. Although we tied, I felt the better game was played by __(2)__ .	
1 **A** them **B** they **C** theirs **D** they're	The correct answer is **C**. The sentence calls for a possessive pronoun, to be consistent with the possessive form in *our team.* Choice *A* is in the objective case, choice *B* is in the nominative case, and choice *D* is a contraction of *they are.*
2 **A** us **B** our **C** we **D** me	The correct answer is **A**. The sentence calls for a word that can function as the object of the preposition *by*. Therefore, the objective case pronoun *us* best completes the sentence. Choice *B* is in the possessive case, and choice *C* is in the nominative case, so they do not work. Choice *D* is in the right case but does not make sense in the context of the sentence.

TEST-TAKING TIP

Tell students that, if they identify the case and whether the pronoun should be singular or plural, they will be able to eliminate some choices and make it easier to find the correct answer.

Practice 1 **Directions:** Read the passage, and choose the letter of the word or group of words that belongs in each space.

The referee blew __(1)__ whistle and the game started. Kelly kicked the ball to me, and I ran between __(2)__ and Marci. An opposing midfielder caught up with __(3)__. __(4)__ struggled for the ball. I won __(5)__ from her and continued down the field.

1 **A** his
B his'
C him
D their

2 **F** hers
G she
H her's
J her

3 **A** my
B me
C I
D mine

4 **F** Her and I
G Her and me
H She and me
J She and I

5 **A** them
B it
C its
D it's

Practice 2 **Directions:** Read the passage, and choose the letter of the word or group of words that belongs in each space.

I heard the midfielder shout, "__(1)__ going to be sorry!" Then, I saw Becky out of the corner of __(2)__ eye. She was heading for the goal, and I passed __(3)__ the ball. No defensive players were near __(4)__. __(5)__ goal unprotected, Becky blasted the ball into the net.

1 **A** Your
B Yours
C You're
D You

2 **F** my
G mine
H me
J her

3 **A** her
B hers
C her's
D she

4 **F** we
G us
H our
J ours

5 **A** There
B They're
C Their
D Theirs

Answer Key

Practice 1

1. A
2. J
3. B
4. J
5. B

Practice 2

1. C
2. F
3. A
4. G
5. C

Chapter 24 Time and Resource Manager

In-Depth Lesson Plan

	LESSON FOCUS	PRINT AND MEDIA RESOURCES
DAY 1	**Subject-Verb Agreement** Students review singular and plural nouns and verbs and subject-verb agreement (pp. 552–556).	**Teaching Resources** *Grammar Exercise Workbook,* pp. 143–144; *Grammar Exercises Answers on Transparencies,* Ch. 24 ***Writing and Grammar iText*** **(Interactive Text),** Section 24.1
DAY 2	**Subject-Verb Agreement** *(continued)* Students review agreement with compound subjects and work with indefinite pronouns (pp. 557–561).	**Teaching Resources** *Grammar Exercise Workbook,* pp. 143–144; *Grammar Exercises Answers on Transparencies,* Ch. 24 ***Writing and Grammar iText*** **(Interactive Text),** Section 24.1
DAY 3	**Pronoun-Antecedent Agreement** Students work on pronoun-antecedent agreement and agreement between personal and indefinite pronouns. They also complete a Hands-on Grammar activity (pp. 562–567).	**Teaching Resources** *Grammar Exercise Workbook,* pp. 143–144; *Grammar Exercises Answers on Transparencies,* Ch. 24; *Hands-on Grammar Activity Book,* Ch. 24 ***Writing and Grammar iText*** **(Interactive Text),** Section 24.2
DAY 4	**Review and Assess** Students review the chapter and demonstrate mastery of agreement (pp. 568–571).	**Teaching Resources** *Formal Assessment,* Ch. 24; *Grammar Exercises Answers on Transparencies,* Ch. 24 ***Writing and Grammar iText*** **(Interactive Text),** Ch. 24, Chapter Review

Accelerated Lesson Plan

	LESSON FOCUS	PRINT AND MEDIA RESOURCES
DAY 1	**Subject-Verb Agreement** Students review subject-verb agreement with both simple and compound subjects (pp. 552–561).	**Teaching Resources** *Grammar Exercise Workbook,* pp. 143–144; *Grammar Exercises Answers on Transparencies,* Ch. 24 ***Writing and Grammar iText*** **(Interactive Text),** Section 24.1
DAY 2	**Pronoun-Antecedent Agreement** Students review pronoun-antecedent agreement and agreement between personal and indefinite pronouns (pp. 562–567).	**Teaching Resources** *Grammar Exercise Workbook,* pp. 151–152; *Grammar Exercises Answers on Transparencies,* Ch. 24; *Hands-on Grammar Activity Book,* Ch. 24 ***Writing and Grammar iText*** **(Interactive Text),** Section 24.2
DAY 3	**Review and Assess** Students review the chapter and demonstrate mastery of agreement (pp. 568–571).	**Teaching Resources** *Formal Assessment,* Ch. 24; *Grammar Exercises Answers on Transparencies,* Ch. 24 ***Writing and Grammar iText*** **(Interactive Text),** Ch. 24, Chapter Review

Options for Adapting Lesson Plans

HOMEWORK

Have students complete any stage of the lesson for homework.

SPELLING

To teach spelling skills in conjunction with grammar, mechanics, and usage, work through *Prentice Hall Everyday Spelling,* Grade 8, Chapter 28, as you cover this *Writing and Grammar* chapter.

TECHNOLOGY

Students can use *Writing and Grammar iText* to complete the exercises interactively on computer. They can complete additional exercises in the *On-line Exercise Bank:* The Auto Check feature will grade their work. Go online: PHSchool.com Use Web code: eck-8002

FEATURES

Extend coverage with the Standardized Test Preparation Workshop (pp. 570–571).

INTEGRATED SKILLS COVERAGE

Writing
Find It in Your Writing, SE pp. 561, 566, 567
Writing Application, SE pp. 561, 567, 569

Viewing and Representing
Critical Viewing, SE pp. 552, 554, 557, 559, 562, 563, 565

Vocabulary
Definitions, ATE p. 556

Speaking and Listening
Words From Other Languages, ATE pp. 558, 560

ASSESSMENT SUPPORT

Standardized Test Preparation Workshop SE pp. 570–571, ATE p. 557

Standardized Test Preparation Workbook, pp. 47–48

Formal Assessment, Ch. 24

MEETING INDIVIDUAL NEEDS

Less Advanced Students See also Ongoing Assessments ATE pp. 555, 558, 559, 563.

ESL Students ATE p. 565

Gifted/Talented Students ATE p. 558

Verbal/Linguistic Learners ATE p. 563

BLOCK SCHEDULING

Pacing Suggestions
For 90-minute Blocks
- Administer the Diagnostic Test to students to determine instructional coverage.
- Have students complete the necessary exercises in class. Use the Hands-on Grammar Activity to provide a change of pace.

Resources for Varying Instruction
- ***Writing and Grammar iText*** **(Interactive Text)** A 90-minute block provides an ideal opportunity for students to work on computer.

Professional Development Support
- ***How to Manage Instruction in the Block*** This teaching resource provides management and activity suggestions.

MEDIA AND TECHNOLOGY

For the Student
- ***Writing and Grammar iText*** **(Interactive Text),** Ch. 24
- ***On-line Exercise Bank,*** Sections 24.1–2

For the Teacher
- ***Resource Pro*** **CD-ROM**

WRITING AND GRAMMAR ON-LINE

iText Interactive Text (On-line or on CD-ROM)
- Easily navigable instruction with on-line supporting resources
- Self-scoring exercises and diagnostic tests

Companion Web Site PHSchool.com
- On-line Exercise Bank (use Web Code eck-8002)

See the Go On-line! feature, SE p. iii.

CHAPTER 24
MAKING WORDS AGREE

Lesson Objectives

1. To recognize the number of nouns and pronouns.
2. To recognize the number of verbs.
3. To determine agreement with singular and plural subjects.
4. To determine agreement with compound subjects.
5. To determine agreement in sentences with unusual word order and with indefinite pronouns.
6. To determine agreement between personal pronouns and antecedents.
7. To avoid shifts in person and number.
8. To determine agreement between personal and indefinite pronouns.

Critical Viewing

Analyze Students' sentences should reflect an understanding of the difference between singular and plural (*plane flies, planes fly*).

Chapter

24 Making Words Agree

B17 Mustangs fly in formation during a World War II mission.

Subjects and verbs work together in sentences. For example, you would never say, *"I are going* to write a report about World War II," or *"Am you going* to class today?" You would hear that something is wrong with these sentences. The problem is that the subjects and verbs do not *agree.*

In most of the sentences you speak and write, you automatically make subjects and verbs agree. In some sentences, however, the mind can be tricked into making the verb agree with a word that is not the subject of the sentence. In such a case, check to find the real subject and make sure it agrees with its verb.

Pronouns, too, must agree with the words they replace, their *antecedents.* This chapter will explain the importance of agreement and will give you practice making the parts of sentences work together.

▲ Critical Viewing Think of two sentences about this picture—one that describes what all of the planes are doing and one that describes what only one of the planes is doing. How do your verbs change when the number of the subject changes? **[Analyze]**

ONGOING ASSESSMENT: Diagnose

If students miss more than one item in any category, direct them to the relevant pages of the text and assign exercises for practice and review.

Agreement	Diagnostic Test Items	Teach	Practice	Section Review	Chapter Review
Skill Check A					
Subject-Verb Agreement	A 1–15	pp. 554–560	Ex. 1–8	Ex. 9–11	Ex. 25–27
Skill Check B					
Pronoun-Antecedent Agreement	B 16–25	pp. 562–565	Ex. 15–18	Ex. 19–21	Ex. 28–30
Cumulative Reviews and Applications				Ex. 12–14, 22–24	Ex. 31–32

Diagnostic Test

Directions: Write all answers on a separate sheet of paper.

Skill Check A. Choose the verb in parentheses that agrees with the subject of each sentence.

1. World War II (was, were) a conflict that took place from 1939 to 1945.
2. The leader of Allied forces during World War II (was, were) Dwight Eisenhower.
3. My classmates (tells, tell) me that Eisenhower led troops in both Africa and Europe.
4. Either Germany or Italy (was, were) the main Axis power.
5. Spain and Portugal (was, were) neutral during World War II.
6. Not until later in the war (was, were) the Axis powers joined by Japan.
7. Japan and its allies (was, were) hoping to gain control of the Pacific region.
8. On Memorial Day, veterans of World War II (is, are) honored.
9. A Memorial Day parade in many towns (features, feature) veterans who fought in wars throughout the twentieth century.
10. (Where's, Where are) the beautiful floats we came to see?
11. Most of the children in town (looks, look) forward to the Memorial Day parade.
12. Each of the veterans (is, are) asked to participate.
13. Neither my neighbor nor her children (wants, want) to miss the parade.
14. Neither rain showers nor cool weather (halts, halt) the parade.
15. Marching in the parade (is, are) bands from all over the state.

Skill Check B. Choose the correct pronoun in each sentence.

16. My grandfather was sent along with (his, their) unit to fight in Europe during World War II.
17. Each person at home wrote to (his or her, their) relatives overseas.
18. Almost every woman whose husband was fighting overseas had (her, their) own deep worries about (his, their) survival.
19. Grandmother and other women worked at a munitions factory to support (her, their) families.
20. Everyone in the family tried to do (his or her, their) part to help the troops who were fighting overseas.
21. If a person had a special skill (you, he or she) used it.
22. Mother and her sister spent (her, their) free time knitting socks for soldiers.
23. Many did (his or her, their) part by collecting old pots and pans for scrap metal.
24. All who could tried (his or her, their) best to help.
25. Each of the women my grandmother knew seemed to contribute (her, his or her, their) time in a selfless way.

Answer Key

Diagnostic Test

Each item in the diagnostic test corresponds to a specific concept in the chapter on agreement. This will enable you to tailor instruction to the particular needs of your students. See "Ongoing Assessment: Diagnose" below for further details.

Skill Check A

1. was
2. was
3. tell
4. was
5. were
6. were
7. were
8. are
9. features
10. Where are
11. look
12. is
13. want
14. halts
15. are

Skill Check B

16. his
17. his or her
18. her, his
19. their
20. his or her
21. he or she
22. their
23. their
24. their
25. her

TIME SAVERS!

Answers on Transparency Use the Grammar Exercises Answers on Transparencies for Chapter 24 to have students correct their own or one another's exercises.

On-Line Exercise Bank Have students complete the exercises on computer. The Auto Check feature will grade their work for you!

PREPARE and ENGAGE

Introduce the word *agreement.* Ask students what it means to agree with someone. Explain to them that they will learn about making the words in sentences agree with one another.

Activate Prior Knowledge

Ask a volunteer to come to the chalkboard and write the present tense of the verb *sing* with each of the six subject pronouns *(I, you, he/she/it, we, you, they).* Ask which form of the verb is different from the others. *(he/she/it sings)*

TEACH

Step-by-Step Teaching Guide

Recognizing the Number of Nouns and Pronouns

1. Review with students the definitions of *singular* and *plural.* List all the singular subject and object pronouns on the chalkboard and write their plural forms beside them. Tell students to copy this list and keep it for reference.
2. Tell students that most regular nouns need only *-s* added to them: *book, books.* If the singular noun ends in a sound that would make this awkward, then *-es* is added: *wishes, churches, boxes, glasses.*

Critical Viewing

Identify Students may say the women are plural and the tool is singular.

Answer Key

Exercise 1

1. singular
2. plural
3. plural
4. singular
5. plural
6. singular
7. singular
8. plural
9. plural
10. plural

Section 24.1

Subject and Verb Agreement

Subject and verb agreement has one main rule:

KEY CONCEPT A verb must agree with its subject in number. ■

In grammar, the concept of *number* is simple. The number of a word can be either *singular* or *plural.* A singular word indicates *one.* A plural word indicates *more than one.* Only nouns, pronouns, and verbs have number.

Theme: World War II

In this section, you will learn to make verbs agree in number with their subjects. The examples and exercises are about events that occurred during World War II.

Cross-Curricular Connection: Social Studies

Recognizing the Number of Nouns and Pronouns

The difference between the singular and plural forms of most nouns and pronouns is easy to recognize. Compare the singular and plural forms of the nouns below:

NOUNS	
Singular	Plural
soldier	soldiers
bus	buses
child	children
goose	geese

Most nouns are made plural by adding *-s* or *-es* to the singular form (soldier*s*, bus*es*). Some nouns become plural in other ways (child*ren*, g*ee*se).

Section 14.2 and Chapter 23 list the singular and plural forms of the various kinds of pronouns. For example, *I, he, she, it, this,* and *anyone* are singular; *we, they, these,* and *both* are plural; and *you, who,* and *some* can be either singular or plural.

Being able to recognize the number of nouns and pronouns will help you to determine whether a subject is singular or plural.

▲ **Critical Viewing** Identify some items in the picture that are singular and some that are plural. **[Identify]**

Exercise 1 **Recognizing the Number of Nouns and Pronouns** On your paper, label each of the following words *singular* or *plural.*

EXAMPLE: mice (plural)

1. war	3. armies	5. they	7. it	9. men
2. we	4. nation	6. he	8. us	10. these

TIME AND RESOURCE MANAGER

Resources
Print: Grammar Exercise Workbook, pp. 143–144
Technology: Writing and Grammar iText, Section 24.1; On-Line Exercise Bank, Section 24.1

In-Depth Coverage	Accelerated Pace
• Work through all key concepts, pp. 554–560. • Assign and review Exercises 1–8.	• Assign pp. 554–560 for independent student review. • Assign Section Review Exercises 9–11.

Recognizing the Number of Verbs

As shown in the conjugations in Section 22.2, verbs have many forms to indicate tense. Few of these forms cause problems in agreement because most of them can be used with either singular or plural subjects (I *go*, we *go;* he *ran*, they *ran*). Problems involving the number of verbs usually occur only with third-person forms in the present tense and with forms of *be*.

The following chart shows all the basic forms of two different verbs—*send* and *go*—in the present tense.

SINGULAR AND PLURAL VERBS IN THE PRESENT TENSE		
Singular		Plural
First and Second Person	**Third Person**	**First, Second, and Third Person**
(I, you) send (I, you) go	(he, she, it) sends (he, she, it) goes	(we, you, they) send (we, you, they) go

Notice that the verb form changes only in the third-person singular column, where an *-s* or *-es* is added to the verb. Unlike nouns, which usually become *plural* when *-s* or *-es* is added, verbs with *-s* or *-es* added to them are singular.

The helping verb *be* may also indicate whether a verb is singular or plural. The following chart shows only those forms of the verb *be* that are always singular.

FORMS OF THE HELPING VERB *BE* THAT ARE ALWAYS SINGULAR			
am	is	was	has been

Exercise 2 **Recognizing the Number of Verbs** For each of the following items, choose the verb in parentheses that agrees in number with the pronoun. After each answer, write whether the verb is singular or plural.

EXAMPLE: he (begin, begins)
ANSWER: begins (singular)

1. she (leads, lead)
2. we (retreats, retreat)
3. they (was, were)
4. I (is, am)
5. it (flies, fly)

iText
Get instant feedback! Exercise 2 is available on-line or on CD-ROM.

More Practice

Grammar Exercise Workbook
- pp. 143–144

On-line Exercise Bank
- Section 24.1

Go on-line:
PHSchool.com
Enter Web Code:
eck-8002

Step-by-Step Teaching Guide

Recognizing the Number of Verbs

1. A singular subject needs a singular verb, and a plural subject needs a plural verb. These two main pieces of a sentence must match each other. If one side of the sentence equals "more than one," the other must do the same. Ask students to choose the correct verb for the following sentences.

   Philip (run, runs).

   Philip and Mary (run, runs).

   Philip, Mary, and Michael (run, runs).

2. Review that singular verbs (except forms of *be*) end in *-s* or *-es*. Plural verbs do not end in *-s* or *-es*.

Answer Key

Exercise 2

1. leads—singular
2. retreat—plural
3. were—plural
4. am—singular
5. flies—singular

ONGOING ASSESSMENT: Monitor and Reinforce

If students miss more than two items in Exercise 1 or 2, refer them to the following for additional practice.

In the Textbook	Print Resources	Technology
Section Review, Ex. 9	Grammar Exercise Workbook, pp. 143–144	On-Line Exercise Bank, Section 24.1

TIME SAVERS!

Answers on Transparency Use the Grammar Exercises Answers on Transparencies for Chapter 24 to have students correct their own or one another's exercises.

On-Line Exercise Bank Have students complete the exercises on computer. The Auto Check feature will grade their work for you!

Step-by-Step Teaching Guide

Making Verbs Agree With Singular and Plural Subjects

1. Write sample sentences on the chalkboard in which the subject is not the first word, or in which there are many words between the subject and the verb:

   Every Thursday after school, Julio (play, plays) soccer.

   Every Thursday, Julio and his friend Vinny (play, plays) soccer.

   Ask students to identify the subject of each sentence and choose the correct verb.
2. The procedure is the same for all sentences: Look for the subject, identify whether it is singular or plural, and then make sure the verb matches it. The subject is always the noun or pronoun whose action or condition the verb is describing.
3. Review prepositions and list some of the more common ones (*on, to, under, over, with, after, before,* and so on). Remind students that although the object of a preposition is always a noun or pronoun, it is never the subject of a sentence. The preposition makes the noun or pronoun part of a phrase that describes the subject.

Answer Key

Exercise 3

1. discuss
2. are
3. learn
4. marks
5. invades, declare

Integrating Vocabulary Skills

Definitions Students may be unfamiliar with the use of the word *theaters* in sentence 1 of Exercise 4. When used with the phrase *of war, theater* means "a place where events are enacted." This sentence means that the soldiers fought the war in Europe and on the Pacific islands.

24.1

Making Verbs Agree With Singular and Plural Subjects

To check subject-verb agreement, determine the number of the subject. Then, make sure the verb has the same number.

KEY CONCEPT A singular subject must have a singular verb. A plural subject must have a plural verb. ■

In the following examples, the subjects are underlined once and the verbs are underlined twice.

SINGULAR SUBJECT AND VERB:	Larry always volunteers to fight in the front line.
PLURAL SUBJECT AND VERB:	Those soldiers never arrive on time. According to the announcements, both planes are preparing to land.

KEY CONCEPT A prepositional phrase that comes between a subject and its verb does *not* affect subject-verb agreement. ■

In the following examples, the subject is *poster,* and the word *planes* is the object of the preposition *of.* Because *poster* is singular, the plural verb *fill* does not agree with it.

INCORRECT: The poster of combat planes fill the wall.
CORRECT: The poster of combat planes fills the wall.

Exercise 3 **Making Verbs Agree With Singular and Plural Subjects** For each of the following sentences, choose the correct verb in parentheses, and write it on your paper.

EXAMPLE: The books on the shelf (is, are) about World War II.
ANSWER: are

1. At conferences, historians (discusses, discuss) how World War II began.
2. The causes and effects of World War II (is, are) the focus of our social studies class.
3. When children in elementary school (learns, learn) about war, the subject may frighten them.
4. The date, September 1, 1939, (marks, mark) the start of World War II.
5. Once Germany (invades, invade) Poland on that date, several European countries (declares, declare) war on Germany.

More Practice

Grammar Exercise Workbook
- pp. 145–148

On-line Exercise Bank
- Section 24.1

Go on-line: PHSchool.com *Enter Web Code:* eck-8002

iText

Get instant feedback! Exercise 3 is available on-line or on CD-ROM.

Making Verbs Agree With Compound Subjects

A compound subject is two or more subjects that are joined by a conjunction, usually *and, or,* or *nor.*

KEY CONCEPT A compound subject joined by *and* is usually plural and must have a plural verb. Exceptions occur when the parts of the compound subject equal one thing or when the word *each* or *every* is used before the compound subject. ■

EXAMPLES: The soldier and the sergeant are ready for combat.
Franks and beans is a popular army dish.
Every soldier and sergeant is ready for combat.

KEY CONCEPT Two or more singular subjects joined by *or* or *nor* must have a singular verb. ■

EXAMPLE: Either Alice *or* Mike is going to help us study.

In the example, *or* joins two singular subjects. Although two names make up the compound subject, the subject does not take a plural verb. Either Alice or Mike will help us study, not both of them.

Exercise 4 **Making Verbs Agree With Compound Subjects** On your paper, write the correct verb from each pair in parentheses.

EXAMPLE: Every plane and tank (has, have) been inspected.
ANSWER: has

1. During World War II, Europe and the Pacific (was, were) the two main theaters of war.
2. Any soldier or civilian who (was, were) involved in the war often faced a life-threatening situation.
3. Either Belgium or Holland (was, were) chosen by the Germans for an early attack.
4. Because their grandparents fought in World War II, Carl and Robert (has, have) conducted interviews with them.
5. Each girl and boy in my class (agrees, agree) that civilians in Europe suffered terribly during World War II.

A memorial to the brave Marines who raised the flag on Iwo Jima.

▲ Critical Viewing
Based on the picture, complete two sentences that begin: *All of the Marines . . .* and *Each of the Marines . . .* Which sentence needs a singular verb, and which needs a plural verb? **[Analyze]**

Step-by-Step Teaching Guide

Making Verbs Agree With Compound Subjects

1. When in doubt about whether a compound subject joined by *and* takes a singular or plural verb, students can try substituting a pronoun or prepositional phrase. If the pronoun is plural, the verb should be plural; if singular, the verb should be singular. In the first example sentence, *The soldier and the sergeant* can be replaced by the pronoun *they* because there is more than one independent person. Therefore, the verb is plural. In the third sentence, *Every soldier and sergeant* can be replaced by the singular pronoun *everyone.* Therefore, the verb is singular.
2. Go over the key concept about compound subjects with singular subjects joined by *or* and *nor.* Explain that *or* always offers a choice between the two parts of the subject. The verb describes an action taken by or a condition of one of them, not both. That is why the verb is singular.

Answer Key

Exercise 4

1. were
2. was
3. was
4. have
5. agrees

Critical Viewing

Analyze Students may write sentences that begin "All of the Marines are raising ..." (plural) and "Each of the Marines is holding ..." (singular), or the like.

STANDARDIZED TEST PREPARATION WORKSHOP

Grammar and Usage Standardized tests often ask students to identify which sentence in a passage contains a certain kind of grammatical error. Ask students which sentence in the following paragraph contains an error in subject-verb agreement.

(A) Young Winston Churchill and his little brother Jack spends hours playing with their many toy soldiers. (B) Winston wants to impress their father by showing how much he knows about military history. (C) Randolph Churchill, though, is too ill and tired to pay much attention to his sons. (D) Winston's grades at school are so poor that Randolph believes his son will never amount to anything.

Students should choose sentence **A.** The compound subject *Winston and Jack* is plural, so it requires the plural verb *spend.*

TIME SAVERS!

Answers on Transparency
Use the Grammar Exercises Answers on Transparencies for Chapter 24 to have students correct their own or one another's exercises.

On-Line Exercise Bank
Have students complete the exercises on computer. The Auto Check feature will grade their work for you!

Answer Key

Exercise 5

1. was
2. were
3. know
4. were
5. was

Exercise 6

We students and our teacher are reading about Nazi Germany this term. Either Emily or Sharon has been assigned to do a report on Adolf Hitler. She learned that neither Great Britain nor its allies were willing to stop Hitler from taking over Austria and Czechoslovakia in 1938. Hitler and Benito Mussolini in Italy were hoping to take over all of Europe. Every act and order of the two dictators was designed to further that goal. The Nazi army and air force were set to attack Poland on September 1, 1939. Either Great Britain or France was planning to declare war on Germany should the attack take place. Neither Hitler nor his generals were concerned. The generals and Hitler were certain that Germany would be victorious. Within months, Great Britain and France were facing their own attacks by German forces.

Customize for *Gifted/Talented Students*

Have students select any aspect of World War II that interests them. Have them do some research and write paragraphs giving details about their topics. Have partners check each other's work for correct subject-verb agreement.

Integrating Speaking Skills

Pronouncing Foreign Words
Pronounce the word *Nazi.* Explain that a *z* in a German word is pronounced similar to *ts* in English. Have students pronounce the name *Mozart.*

One situation that sometimes causes confusion involves a compound subject in which a singular subject and a plural subject are joined by *or* or *nor.* In that situation, the verb agrees in number with the subject that is closer to it.

KEY CONCEPT When singular and plural subjects are joined by *or* or *nor,* the verb must agree with the subject closer to the verb. ■

SINGULAR SUBJECT CLOSER:	Neither the students nor their teacher has seen the World War II film.
PLURAL SUBJECT CLOSER:	Neither the teacher nor the students have seen the World War II film.

Exercise 5 **Recognizing Subjects and Verbs That Agree**
For each of the following sentences, choose the correct verb in parentheses, and write it on your paper.

1. Either D-Day or the Battle of Stalingrad (was, were) a key to Germany's military downfall.
2. Marines and paratroopers from the United States (was, were) landing in France on D-Day in 1944.
3. Neither Emily nor her sisters (knows, know) much about the Battle of Stalingrad in 1942.
4. Emily, her sister, and her father (was, were) looking for books on World War II at the library.
5. They read that fish and chips (was, were) a favorite of many American soldiers based in England during the war.

Exercise 6 **Revising for Subject-Verb Agreement** On your paper, revise the paragraph below so that each verb agrees with its subject. Some sentences may be correct.

We students and our teacher is reading about Nazi Germany this term. Either Emily or Sharon have been assigned to do a report on Adolf Hitler. They learned that neither Great Britain nor its allies were willing to stop Hitler from taking over Austria and Czechoslovakia in 1938. Hitler and Benito Mussolini in Italy was hoping to take over all of Europe. Every act and order of the two dictators were designed to further that goal. The Nazi army and air force was set to attack Poland on September 1, 1939. Either Great Britain or France were planning to declare war on Germany should the attack take place. Neither Hitler nor his generals was concerned. The generals and Hitler were certain that Germany would be victorious. Within months, Great Britain and France was facing their own attacks by German forces.

ONGOING ASSESSMENT: Monitor and Reinforce

If students miss more than two items in Exercises 4–6, refer them to the following for additional practice.

In the Textbook	Print Resources	Technology
Section Review, Ex. 10, p. 561	Grammar Exercise Workbook, pp. 147–148	On-Line Exercise Bank, Section 24.1

Checking for Problems With Subject-Verb Agreement

Agreement in Inverted Sentences

In most sentences, the subject comes before the verb. Sometimes, however, this order is inverted, or turned around.

KEY CONCEPT When a subject comes after the verb, the subject and verb still must agree with each other in number. ■

In the following example, the plural verb *were* agrees with the plural subject *soldiers*. The singular noun *shore* is the object of a preposition.

EXAMPLE: Waiting along the shore were many nervous soldiers.

Sentences beginning with *there* or *here* are nearly always in inverted word order. Many questions are in inverted word order, such as, "Where's the newspaper?" Also, note that the contractions *there's* and *here's* contain the singular verb *is*: *there is*, *here is*. Do not use these contractions with plural subjects.

EXAMPLES: There were many soldiers waiting along the shore.
Here's the relief unit that we were promised.
Where are the relief units you promised me?
Here are the relief units I promised you.

▼ **Critical Viewing** Think of three question about this memorial. What is the subject and verb in each question? Do they agree with each other in number? **[Analyze]**

USS *Arizona* Memorial at Pearl Harbor in Hawaii

Exercise 7 **Checking Agreement in Sentences with Inverted Word Order** Write the subject of each sentence below. Then, choose the correct verb in parentheses, and write it next to the subject.

EXAMPLE: There (is, are) the enemy troops.
ANSWER: troops (are)

1. It is December 7, 1941, and there (is, are) a surprise attack on Pearl Harbor, Hawaii.
2. Beyond the horizon (looms, loom) 350 Japanese airplanes.
3. Docked at Pearl Harbor (is, are) the U.S. Pacific fleet.
4. Many Americans ask themselves, "Why (is, are) Japan attacking the United States?"
5. Today, there (is, are) various memorials commemorating the bombing of Pearl Harbor.

More Practice

Grammar Exercise Workbook
• pp. 149–150

On-line Exercise Bank
• Section 24.1

Go on-line:
PHSchool.com
Enter Web Code:
eck-8002

Step-by-Step Teaching Guide

Checking for Problems With Subject-Verb Agreement

1. Remind students that *there* and *here* are adverbs that answer the question *Where?* An adverb is never the subject of a sentence, even if it begins the sentence.
2. When students see sentences starting with *Here* or *There,* they should reorder the sentence to make the subject more obvious.
3. These are reorderings of the example sentences, with the subjects underlined:

   Many soldiers were waiting along the shore.

   The relief unit we were promised is here.

   The relief units you promised me are where?

   The relief units I promised you are here.

   The verb can now easily be made to agree with the subject.

Answer Key

Exercise 7

1. attack is
2. airplanes loom
3. fleet is
4. Japan is
5. memorials are

Critical Viewing

Analyze Have students work with a partner to assess each other's subject-verb agreement.

ONGOING ASSESSMENT: Prerequisite Skills

If students have difficulty with special agreement problems, you may find it necessary to review the following to ensure coverage of prerequisite knowledge.

In the Textbook	Print Resources	Technology
Basic Sentence Parts, pp. 416–425	Grammar Exercise Workbook, pp. 55–58	On-Line Exercise Bank, Section 19.4

TIME SAVERS!

Answers on Transparency Use the Grammar Exercises Answers on Transparencies for Chapter 24 to have students correct their own or one another's exercises.

On-Line Exercise Bank Have students complete the exercises on computer. The Auto Check feature will grade their work for you!

Step-by-Step Teaching Guide

Agreement With Indefinite Pronouns

1. Go over the list of singular indefinite pronouns. Students may object that *everyone* and *everybody* mean "all people" and therefore should logically be plural. Explain that both *one* and *body,* by themselves, are singular pronouns.

   When one is wrong, one should apologize.

   A body can't depend too much on others.

   When either of these words ends a compound pronoun such as *someone* or *anybody,* that pronoun is always singular.

2. Remind students that indefinite pronouns are almost all words that indicate a certain number or quantity of people or things. Students should look at an indefinite pronoun, think about whether it means only one or more than one, and make the verb agree with their conclusion.

Answer Key

Exercise 8

1. were
2. were
3. hopes
4. are
5. reach

Integrating Vocabulary Skills

Words from Other Languages *U-boat* (Exercise 8) is an abbreviation for the German word *unterseeboot,* which means "undersea boat" or "submarine."

24.1

Agreement With Indefinite Pronouns

When used as subjects, indefinite pronouns can also cause problems.

KEY CONCEPT Either a singular verb or a plural verb can agree with an indefinite pronoun, depending on the pronoun's form and meaning. ■

Look again at the list of indefinite pronouns in Section 14.2. Some of the pronouns are always singular. Included here are those ending in *-one* (*anyone, everyone, someone*), those ending in *-body* (*anybody, everybody, somebody*), and those that imply one (*each, either, every*). Other indefinite pronouns are always plural: *both, few, many, others,* and *several.* A few can be either singular or plural: *all, any, more, most, none, some.*

ALWAYS SINGULAR:	One of the submarines is equipped with radar. Everybody on the submarine was frightened by thoughts of attack. Neither of the strategies seems workable.
ALWAYS PLURAL:	Many of the soldiers are fighting on the war's front lines. Others are working to supply them with food and ammunition. Several contribute by working as code breakers.
EITHER SINGULAR OR PLURAL:	Most of the war has been fought. Most of the battles have been fought.

Exercise 8 **Checking Agreement With Indefinite Pronouns** For each of the following sentences, choose the correct verb in parentheses, and write it on your paper.

EXAMPLE: All of the flags on the battleship (was, were) waving in the wind.
ANSWER: were

1. Many of the ships that crossed the Atlantic Ocean during World War II (was, were) filled with supplies.
2. Most of the vessels (was, were) carrying vital supplies from the United States to Great Britain.
3. Everyone (hopes, hope) that the ships get to their destinations safely.
4. Several (is, are) sunk by German submarines, called U-boats.
5. Some (reaches, reach) Britain to deliver their cargoes.

Section 24.1 **Section Review**

GRAMMAR EXERCISES 9–14

Exercise 9 **Choosing the Verb That Agrees With Its Subject** For each sentence below, choose the correct verb in parentheses, and write it on your paper. After each answer, write whether the subject and verb are singular or plural.

1. During World War II, U.S. troops in the Pacific (is, are) locked in battle with Japanese troops.
2. There (is, are) new strategies developed by U.S. leaders, such as *island hopping.*
3. An island or group of islands controlled by the Japanese (is, are) selected for attack.
4. Only key islands (is, are) captured to be used as steppingstones for U.S. troops to "hop" to the next island.
5. Over a period of two years, either island hopping or other strategies (is, are) used by the United States to gain control of the Pacific.

Exercise 10 **Revising Verbs to Agree With Compound Subjects** Revise the sentences below so that each verb agrees with its subject. If a sentence is correct, write *correct.*

1. Sam and his brothers has always wondered why Nazi Germany carried out the Holocaust.
2. Neither his mother nor his father have been able to explain the tragic events.
3. Perhaps callousness or fear are to blame, they suggested.
4. Sam read a story in which a mother and her child was executed by Nazi troops.
5. Neither the story nor a movie that Sam later saw adequately describes the horrors suffered by concentration camp victims.

Exercise 11 **Revising to Eliminate Special Problems in Agreement** Revise the sentences below so that each verb agrees with its subject. If a sentence is correct, write *correct.*

1. Many who come to Amsterdam visits the Anne Frank House.
2. There are visitors to the house who do not know about the Franks' life there.
3. Invading Nazis were hunting down Jews in Holland, and most was forced to leave their homes.
4. Nearly every one of the captured Jews were sent to a concentration camp.
5. Everyone visiting the museum learn that Anne Frank's family was forced to leave their home to go into hiding.

Exercise 12 **Find It in Your Reading** Find one singular indefinite pronoun and one plural indefinite pronoun in this excerpt from *The Diary of Anne Frank.* List each pronoun and the verb it takes.

Everyone is listening, hardly breathing. MR. FRANK *starts quietly down the steps to the door.* DUSSEL *and* PETER *follow him. The others stand rigid, waiting, terrified.*

Exercise 13 **Find It in Your Writing** Choose a piece of writing from your portfolio. Copy five of the sentences. Circle the subjects and verbs, and label them *singular* or *plural.* Rewrite any sentences in which the subject and verb do not agree.

Exercise 14 **Writing Application** Write a paragraph about a book, television program, or film that deals with a war. Include several sentences with compound subjects joined by *or* or *nor.*

ASSESS and CLOSE

Section Review

Each of these exercises correlates to a concept in the section on subject and verb agreement, pages 554–560. The exercises may be used for more practice, for reteaching, or for review of the Key Concepts presented.

Answer Key

Exercise 9

1. are—plural
2. are—plural
3. is—singular
4. are—plural
5. are—plural

Exercise 10

1. have
2. has
3. is
4. were
5. correct

Exercise 11

1. visit
2. correct
3. were
4. was
5. learns

Exercise 12

Find It in Your Reading
Everyone is;
others stand

Exercise 13

Find It in Your Writing
Students also should check for subject-verb agreement.

Exercise 14

Writing Application
Ask students to explain to a partner how the verb might change if one or more of the subjects were plural.

TIME SAVERS!

Answers on Transparency Use the Grammar Exercises Answers on Transparencies for Chapter 24 to have students correct their own or one another's exercises.

On-Line Exercise Bank Have students complete the exercises on computer. The Auto Check feature will grade their work for you!

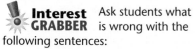

PREPARE and ENGAGE

Interest GRABBER Ask students what is wrong with the following sentences:

The collie wagged their tail.

Did Pierre like its birthday present?

Activate Prior Knowledge

Write some nouns in one column and some personal pronouns in another. Ask students to mix and match correctly (they can use more than one noun at a time).

TEACH

Step-by-Step Teaching Guide

Making Personal Pronouns and Antecedents Agree

1. A pronoun must always have an antecedent, either in the same sentence or in an earlier one:

   Dennis took a deep breath. He walked to the batter's box. He swung and missed. Strike one!

   Both *he*'s refer to Dennis.

2. If there is an intervening event, or someone else enters the scene, the subject, *Dennis,* may need to be repeated:

   Dennis took a deep breath. He walked to the batter's box. He swung and missed. Strike one! The pitcher hitched up his pants before throwing the ball. Dennis missed again. Strike two!

Answer Key

Exercise 15

1. The students are going on their first trip to the fire station. (arrow from *their* to *students*)
2. Julia and Sara brought their notebooks on the trip. (arrow from *their* to *Julia and Sara*)
3. Sam remembered to bring his lunch money. (arrow from *his* to *Sam*)
4. The class listened as the firefighters explained how they use special equipment to put out fires. (arrow from *they* to *firefighters*)
5. Each piece of equipment has its own special function. (arrow from *its* to *piece*)

Section 24.2

Agreement Between Pronouns and Antecedents

Making Personal Pronouns and Antecedents Agree

An antecedent is the word or group of words for which a pronoun stands. Sometimes, a pronoun's antecedent is a single noun. At other times, the antecedent is a group of words acting as a noun or even another pronoun.

Personal pronouns should agree with their antecedents in two ways—person and number.

KEY CONCEPT A personal pronoun must agree with its antecedent in both person and number. ■

Person indicates whether a pronoun refers to the person speaking (first person), the person spoken to (second person), or the person, place, or thing spoken about (third person). *Number* indicates whether a pronoun is singular or plural.

EXAMPLE: *Lisa* presented *her* report on careers in firefighting to the class yesterday.

In the example, the pronoun *her* is third person and singular. It agrees with its antecedent *Lisa*, which is also third person and singular.

Exercise 15 **Making Pronouns and Antecedents Agree** Rewrite each of the following sentences, filling in the blank with an appropriate pronoun. Draw an arrow from the pronoun to its antecedent.

EXAMPLE: Sometimes, a fire seems to have a life of __?__ own.

ANSWER: Sometimes, a fire seems to have a life of its own.

1. The students are going on __?__ first trip to the fire station.
2. Julia and Sara brought __?__ notebooks on the trip.
3. Sam remembered to bring __?__ lunch money.
4. The class listened as the firefighters explained how __?__ use special equipment to put out fires.
5. Each piece of equipment has __?__ own special function.

Theme: Dangerous Occupations

In this section, you will learn how to make pronouns agree with their antecedents in number and person. The examples and exercises are about jobs that can be dangerous.

Cross-Curricular Connection: Social Studies

▼ **Critical Viewing** Think of a sentence about this picture that includes the words *firefighters, fire, it,* and *them.* What is the number and person of each pronoun and antecedent? **[Analyze; Identify]**

TIME AND RESOURCE MANAGER

Resources
Print: Grammar Exercise Workbook, pp. 151–152; Hands-on Grammar Activity Book Chapter 24
Technology: Writing and Grammar iText, Section 24.2; On-Line Exercise Bank, Section 24.2

In-Depth Coverage	Accelerated Pace
• Work through all key concepts, pp. 562–565. • Assign and review Exercises 15–18.	• Assign pp. 562–565 for independent student review. • Assign Section Review Exercise 19.

Avoiding Shifts in Person A common error in agreement occurs when a personal pronoun does not have the same person as its antecedent. This error usually involves the careless use of *you* with a noun in the third person.

INCORRECT: *Alexander* is practicing climbing, a skill *you* need to master if *you* want to be a firefighter.

CORRECT: *Alexander* is practicing climbing, a skill *he* needs to master if *he* wants to be a firefighter.

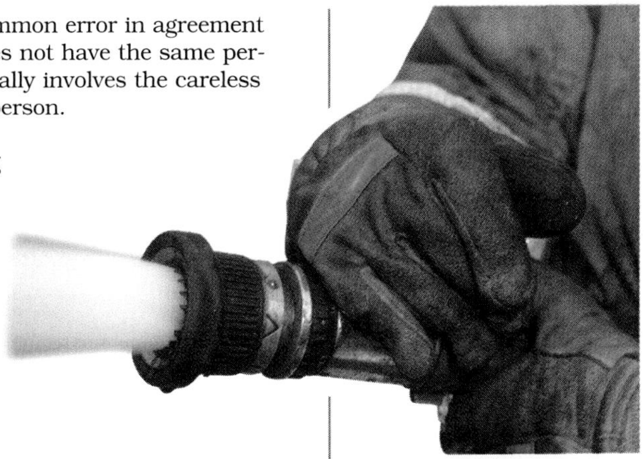

▲ **Critical Viewing** If you shift the subject of a sentence about this picture from *firefighter* to *firefighters*, how does that affect a pronoun that stands for the subject later in the sentence? **[Infer]**

KEY CONCEPT Use a singular personal pronoun to refer to two or more singular antecedents joined by *or* or *nor.* ■

Two or more singular antecedents joined by *or* or *nor* must have a singular pronoun, just as they must have a singular verb. When a compound antecedent is joined by *and,* a plural personal pronoun is used.

EXAMPLES: Either *Bob* or *Jim* is bringing *his* camera to the fire station.
Andrea and *Jane* brought *their* helmets.

Exercise 16 **Revising to Avoid Shifts in Person and Number** Revise each sentence below to correct an error in pronoun-antecedent agreement. Underline the pronoun that you have substituted and its antecedent.

EXAMPLE: Bill wants to know where you can go to study to become a police officer.

ANSWER: <u>Bill</u> wants to know where <u>he</u> can go to study to become a police officer.

1. A police officer is highly trained to perform their duties.
2. Neither Caroline nor Jessica has decided whether they will become a police officer.
3. Both Andrew and Matthew think that he can become law enforcement officials.
4. Jim found out that to become a police officer you must be eighteen.
5. Each police agency has their own age and education requirements.

More Practice

Grammar Exercise Workbook
- pp. 151–152

On-line Exercise Bank
- Section 24.2

Go on-line:
PHSchool.com
Enter Web Code:
eck-8002

ONGOING ASSESSMENT: Monitor and Reinforce

If students miss more than two items in Exercises 15–18, refer them to the following for additional practice.

In the Textbook	Print Resources	Technology
Section Review, Ex. 19–21, p. 567	Grammar Exercise Workbook, pp. 151–152	On-Line Exercise Bank, Section 24.2

Step-by-Step Teaching Guide

Avoiding Shifts in Person

1. Explain that collective nouns are words such as *team, herd,* and *crowd*—words that represent single entities made up of more than one item or person.
2. Note that when the members of these entities act as one, the entities are singular, so the pronoun *it,* not *they,* is used.

   The audience rose to <u>its</u> feet and cheered.

Answer Key

Exercise 16

1. A police <u>officer</u> is highly trained to perform <u>his</u> or <u>her</u> duties.
2. Neither <u>Caroline</u> nor <u>Jessica</u> has decided whether <u>she</u> will become a police officials.
3. Both <u>Andrew</u> and <u>Matthew</u> think that <u>they</u> can become law enforcement officials.
4. <u>Jim</u> found out that to become a police officer <u>he</u> must be eighteen.
5. Each police <u>agency</u> has <u>its</u> own age and education requirements.

Customize for *Verbal/Linguistic Learners*

Challenge students to add to the list of collective nouns above. (Possible answers: *mob, pack, gang, band, gaggle, flock, army*) Have them define each word and use the correct pronoun to replace it in a sentence.

Critical Viewing

Infer Students may suggest that the pronouns *he* and *she* would be used for *firefighter* and the pronoun *they* for *firefighters.*

PRENTICE HALL
Everyday Spelling

If you have taught the spelling skills in *Prentice Hall Everyday Spelling,* Grade 8, Chapter 28, in conjunction with this *Writing and Grammar* chapter, review and assess students' mastery of the skills before concluding the chapter.

Step-by-Step Teaching Guide

Agreement Between Personal Pronouns and Indefinite Pronouns

1. Review indefinite pronouns, using page 560. Indefinite pronouns ending in *-one* or *-body* can refer only to people; these antecedents can never take the pronouns *it* or *its.*
2. *Neither* and *each* cause confusion. *Neither of the puppies is awake* means neither *one* of the puppies; *is* is the correct verb. *Each of the puppies is awake* means each *one* of the puppies. Again, *is* agrees with the understood *one.*

Answer Key

Exercise 17

1. our
2. his
3. its
4. his or her
5. his or her

Find It in Your Writing

Have students look through their portfolios for the incorrect use of *their,* such as *Each of the children washed their hands.* Ask students to rewrite the sentences using correct pronouns.

Language Highlight

Suffixes in English have begun to reflect the variety of jobs at which women work alongside men. Traditionally, the suffix *-man* indicated a worker: *cameraman, garbageman, congressman,* and so on. Today, the suffix *-person* is often used instead. However, *cameraperson* and *garbageperson* sound silly. *Camera operator* and *garbage collector* sound better.

TIME SAVERS!

Answers on Transparency Use the Grammar Exercises Answers on Transparencies for Chapter 24 to have students correct their own or one another's exercises.

On-Line Exercise Bank Have students complete the exercises on computer. The Auto Check feature will grade their work for you!

Making Personal Pronouns and Indefinite Pronouns Agree

Indefinite pronouns (listed in Section 14.2) are words such as *each, everyone, neither,* and *one.* Pay special attention to the number of a personal pronoun when the antecedent is a singular indefinite pronoun.

KEY CONCEPT Generally, use a singular personal pronoun when its antecedent is a singular indefinite pronoun. ■

In making a personal pronoun agree with an indefinite pronoun, ignore the object of any prepositional phrase that might fall between them. In the two incorrect examples below, the pronoun *their* mistakenly agrees with *EMTs* and *instruments* rather than the singular indefinite pronouns *neither* and *each.*

INCORRECT: *Neither* of the EMTs has completed *their* training.
Put each of the instruments in *their* place.

CORRECT: *Neither* of the EMTs has completed *her* training.
Put each of the instruments in *its* place.

You may use one of three methods to make pronouns agree when you don't know the gender of the antecedent. Traditionally, the masculine pronouns *he* and *his* have been used to stand for both males and females. Now, using *he or she* and *him or her* is preferred. If those seem awkward, you may rewrite the sentence.

EXAMPLES: Each of the crew members checked *his* equipment.
Each of the crew members checked *his or her* equipment.
All of the crew members checked *their* equipment.

Exercise 17 Making Personal Pronouns and Indefinite Pronouns Agree For each of the following sentences, select the correct pronoun in parentheses, and write it on your paper.

EXAMPLE: Each of the students has (his or her, their) own first-aid kit.
ANSWER: his or her

1. All of us can give some of (our, their) time to volunteering.
2. One of my friends volunteers (his, their) time to work on the ambulance squad.
3. Each squad has openings on (their, its) night shift.
4. Every emergency medical technician (EMT) needs to use (his or her, their) skills to save lives.
5. Only one of the EMTs had (his or her, their) driver's license.

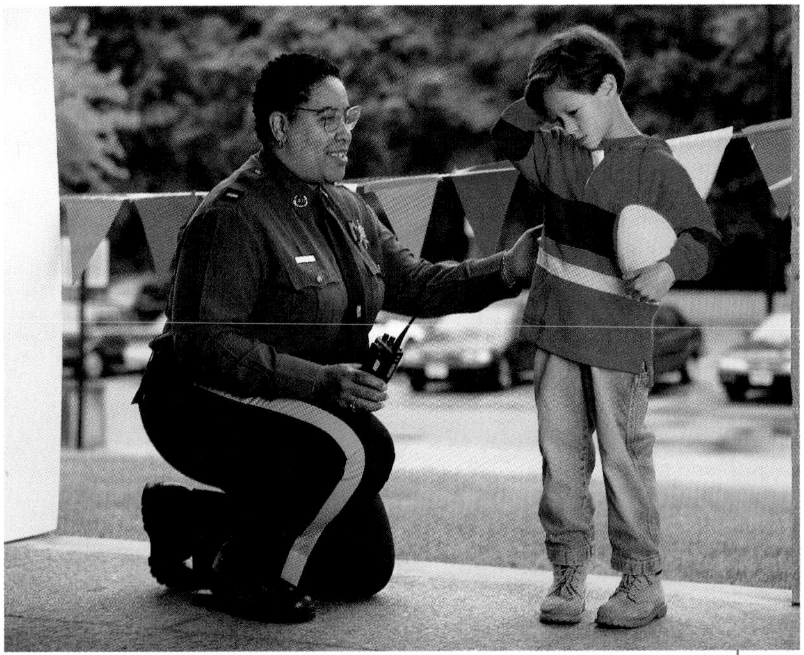

▲ Critical Viewing
Identify an antecedent in the picture to agree with each of these pronouns: *his*, *her*, *its*, and *their*. **[Identify]**

Exercise 18 **Revising for Agreement Between Pronouns and Antecedents** Rewrite the sentences below that contain errors in pronoun-antecedent agreement. If a sentence contains no errror, write *correct*.

EXAMPLE: Neither of the girls told their parents of their desire to be an astronaut.

ANSWER: Neither of the girls told her parents of her desire to be an astronaut.

1. Max is learning skills that you need to be an astronaut.
2. Some of my friends wrote to NASA in his spare time to find out how to become an astronaut.
3. Many astronauts began their careers in the military.
4. Either civilians or military personnel may begin his or her training while in college.
5. Every astronaut spends most of their time on the ground.
6. The space shuttle offers their crew the latest technology.
7. Before a shuttle mission, an astronaut will practice at least one of his or her maneuvers underwater.
8. Either Pam or Sally wants to spend their life flying in space.
9. One of Pam's parents is reluctant to give their support to the decision.
10. Few fathers and mothers would willingly allow his or her daughters to fly into space.

Critical Viewing

Identify Students may suggest "The boy is holding *his* football," "The *policewoman* is wearing *her* uniform," and so on.

Answer Key

Exercise 18

1. Max is learning skills that he needs to be an astronaut.
2. Some of my friends wrote to NASA in their spare time to find out how to become an astronaut.
3. correct
4. Either civilians or military personnel may begin their training while in college.
5. Every astronaut spends most of his or her time on the ground.
6. The space shuttle offers its crew the latest technology.
7. correct
8. Either Pam or Sally wants to spend her life flying in space.
9. One of Pam's parents is reluctant to give his or her support to the decision.
10. Few fathers and mothers would willingly allow their daughters to fly into space.

Customize for *ESL Students*

Use Exercise 18 to give students extra practice with pronoun-antecedent agreement. Ask students to underline each pronoun, circle its antecedent, and identify its gender and number. Gather students into a small group and go over sentences with them, asking each student to take a turn explaining and correcting one sentence.

Step-by-Step Teaching Guide

Pronoun Memory Game

Teaching Resources: Hands-on Grammar Activity Book, Chapter 24

1. Have students refer to their Hands-on Grammar Activity Book or give them copies of relevant pages for this activity.
2. Make sure students can distinguish personal pronouns from indefinite pronouns.

Find It in Your Reading

Have students underline the pronouns in the sentences they write. Above each pronoun, have them identify whether it is singular or plural.

Find It in Your Writing

Have students work with a partner after they have written their sentences. Each partner can assess the usage of both indefinite and personal pronouns.

24.2

Hands-on Grammar

Pronoun Memory Game

To practice identifying which personal pronouns agree with which indefinite pronouns, create a pronoun memory game. Write each of the following *indefinite* pronouns on its own index card: *each, all,* and *both.* Make two additional sets of indefinite pronoun cards. Then, create three cards with the pronoun pair *his or her.* Create three cards that say *their.* Finally, create three cards that say *its* and *their* on the same card. Turn all the cards face down.

As you would in the game Memory, alternate with other players in turning over two cards to show the words listed. If you turn over an indefinite pronoun and a personal pronoun that agree in number, you can keep the pair. Cards with indefinite pronouns that can be singular or plural count as agreeing only with cards that show both *its* and *their.* (If you allow them to agree with cards that have only singular or only plural pronouns, you will run out of matches before you run out of cards.) Use the chart on page 322 to check that you and the other players are correctly identifying the number of each indefinite pronoun.

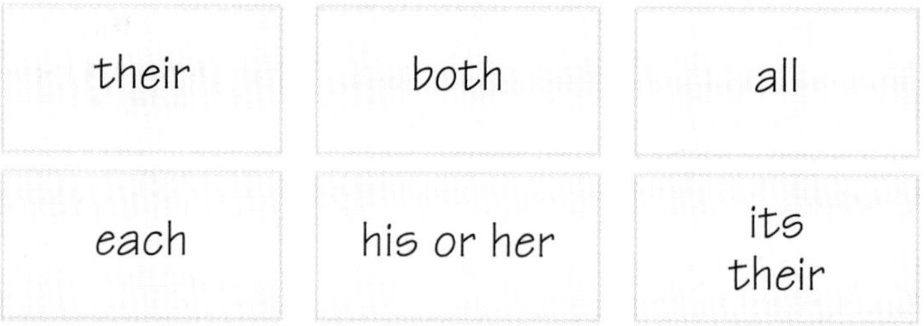

Find It in Your Reading In your reading, find examples of sentences that contain indefinite pronouns used as subjects. Write the sentences on your paper, and indicate whether the pronouns are singular or plural.

Find It in Your Writing Write sentences using the pairs matched during the game. (Choose from among all the pairs, not just the ones you matched.) Ask your teacher to check that you are correctly using indefinite and personal pronouns that agree.

TIME SAVERS!

Hands-on Grammar Book Use the Hands-on Grammar activity sheet for Chapter 24 to facilitate this activity.

ONGOING ASSESSMENT: Assess Mastery

Use the following resources to assess students' mastery of pronoun-antecedent agreement.

In the Textbook	Technology
Chapter Review, Ex. 28–30, p. 569 Standardized Test Preparation Workshop, pp. 570–571	On-Line Exercise Bank, Section 24.2

Section 24.2 **Section Review**

GRAMMAR EXERCISES 19–24

Exercise 19 **Supplying Pronouns That Agree With Antecedents** Rewrite each of the following sentences, filling in the blank with an appropriate pronoun.

1. Wilderness firefighters spend __?__ time fighting forest fires.
2. Each of these firefighters must be aware of the dangers __?__ faces.
3. All learn the importance of working closely with __?__ team members.
4. John told __?__ parents that he is planning to study firefighting.
5. John's parents responded to __?__ son's statement by wishing him luck.
6. Rachel said that in __?__ opinion, smoke jumping is very dangerous.
7. Smoke jumpers perform __?__ duties by parachuting near a forest fire.
8. Despite the dangers, Rachel says that smoke jumping is __?__ chosen career.
9. Neither John nor Rachel feels uncertain about __?__ career choice.
10. Both plan to enter __?__ careers after receiving __?__ college diplomas.

Exercise 20 **Revising to Eliminate Shifts in Person and Number** Rewrite the sentences below, correcting any errors in pronoun-antecedent agreement.

1. Henry wants to study biology because that is a subject you need to know to become a paramedic.
2. An ambulance is equipped with all of the supplies their staff needs.
3. Sometimes ambulances are stationed near an area where it might be needed.
4. In some crowded cities, a paramedic drives a specially equipped motorcycle to reach their destination quickly.
5. For accidents that occur at sea, a paramedic uses marine ambulances to rush their equipment to the scene.

Exercise 21 **Revising to Eliminate Problems in Pronoun-Antecedent Agreement** Rewrite the paragraph below, correcting problems in pronoun-antecedent agreement.

(1) Sarah, one of my friends, is considering police work as their profession. (2) She and her sister have submitted her applications for the police academy. (3) Either hopes they will join a SWAT team in the future. (4) The girls know so much about police work because her uncle is a police officer. (5) Sarah has been working out in the gym because you have to pass a physical test to get into the police academy.

Exercise 22 **Find It in Your Reading** Identify the antecedents for *they'll* and *them* in this excerpt from *The Diary of Anne Frank.*

". . . he'll make a bargain with the Green Police . . . if they'll let him off, he'll tell them where some Jews are hiding!"

Exercise 23 **Find It in Your Writing** Choose a piece of writing from your portfolio that contains personal or indefinite pronouns. Underline the pronouns and antecedents, and correct any mistakes in person or number.

Exercise 24 **Writing Application** Write a paragraph about people who have difficult jobs. Try to include at least two personal and two indefinite pronouns in your writing. Make sure the pronouns agree with their antecedents.

ASSESS and CLOSE

Section Review

Each of these exercises correlates to a concept in the section on agreement between pronouns and antecedents, pages 562–565. The exercises may be used for more practice, for reteaching, or for review of the Key Concepts presented. Answers for all chapter exercises are available in *Grammar Exercises Answers on Transparencies* in your teaching resources.

Answer Key

Exercise 19

1. Wilderness firefighters spend their time fighting forest fires.
2. Each of these firefighters must be aware of the dangers he or she faces.
3. All learn the importance of working closely with their team members.
4. John told his parents that he is planning to study fire fighting.
5. John's parents responded to their son's statement by wishing him luck.
6. Rachel said that in her opinion, smoke jumping is very dangerous.
7. Smoke jumpers perform their duties by parachuting near a forest fire.
8. Despite the dangers, Rachel says that smoke jumping is her chosen career.
9. Neither John nor Rachel feels uncertain about his or her career choice.
10. Both plan to enter their careers after receiving their college diplomas.

Exercise 20

1. Henry wants to study biology because that is a subject he needs to know to become a paramedic.
2. An ambulance is equipped with all the supplies its staff needs.
3. Sometimes ambulances are stationed near an area where they might be needed.
4. In some crowded cities, a paramedic drives a specially equipped motorcycle to reach his or her destination quickly.

continued

Answer Key continued

5. For accidents that occur at sea, paramedics use marine ambulances to rush their equipment to the scene.

Exercise 21

1. her
2. their
3. she
4. their
5. she has

Exercise 22

Find It in Your Reading
the Green Police

Exercise 23

Find It in Your Writing
Ask students if the changes improve the sentences, harm them, or have no effect.

Exercise 24

Ask students to work with partners to check each other's pronouns and antecedents.

CHAPTER REVIEW

Each of these exercises correlates to a concept in the chapter on agreement, pages 552–566. The exercises may be used for more practice, for reteaching, or for review of the Key Concepts presented.

Answer Key

Exercise 25

1. happen
2. use
3. is
4. operate
5. are
6. rely
7. are
8. leap
9. speeds
10. are

Exercise 26

1. occurs
2. panics
3. no errors
4. is
5. help
6. is
7. are
8. no errors
9. no errors
10. are

Exercise 27

1. undergoes
2. are
3. are
4. has
5. is
6. occur
7. Does
8. are
9. is
10. does

TIME SAVERS!

Answers on Transparency Use the Grammar Exercises Answers on Transparencies for Chapter 24 to facilitate corrections by students.

On-Line Exercise Bank Have students complete the exercises on computer. The Auto Check feature will grade their work for you!

Chapter 24 Chapter Review

GRAMMAR EXERCISES 25–32

Exercise 25 **Making Verbs Agree With Singular, Plural, and Compound Subjects** For each of the following sentences, choose the correct verb in parentheses, and write it on your paper.

1. Disasters at sea often (happens, happen) in bad weather conditions.
2. Rescue workers (uses, use) a special lifeboat to save victims of capsized boats.
3. One of the largest and newest lifeboats in Britain (is, are) the *Severn 7*.
4. A trained rescue worker or his or her instructors (operates, operate) the *Severn 7* during a mission.
5. Major rescue missions at sea (is, are) complex.
6. Victims of a boating accident (relies, rely) on the skill of lifeboat crews.
7. Each crew member and the pilot of a lifeboat (is, are) expected to react quickly in emergencies.
8. As soon as a distress signal comes over the radio, the crew members (leaps, leap) into action.
9. The lifeboat operated by emergency workers (speeds, speed) to the scene.
10. Quickly rescued from the water or from a damaged boat (is, are) the victims of the accident.

Exercise 26 **Revising to Eliminate Errors in Subject-Verb Agreement** Rewrite the following paragraph, correcting errors in subject-verb agreement. Some sentences will contain no errors.

(1) Sometimes an accident occur on an underwater submarine. (2) Because of training, neither the victims nor a rescue worker panic when disaster strikes. (3) A pilot operates a Deep Submergence Rescue Vehicle (DSRV) that rushes toward the scene of the accident. (4) Either sonar or radar are used by the DSRV crew to find the stricken submarine. (5) Then, cameras and other equipment helps the rescue team figure out how to approach the submarine. (6) Neither time nor effort are wasted during the rescue attempt. (7) Once victims of the accident is located, rescue operations can begin. (8) A combination clamp and hoist connected to the underwater rescue vehicle is attached to the disabled submarine. (9) Those inside the damaged sub are evacuated immediately. (10) It is clear that speed and skill is essential to bring victims to the surface.

Exercise 27 **Correcting Special Problems in Agreement** For each of the following sentences, choose the correct verb in parentheses, and write it on your paper.

1. Every underwater rescue worker (undergoes, undergo) hours of training.
2. There (is, are) special training programs for divers who wish to become rescue workers.
3. All of the divers (is, are) careful as they plunge into deep waters.
4. One of our neighbors (has, have) invented a special robot used to perform tasks that humans cannot do.
5. Soon after an airplane crashes into the ocean, what we see (is, are) rescue workers arriving on the scene.
6. Luckily, few crashes (occurs, occur).
7. (Does, Do) either of these rescue situations require mechanical assistance?
8. Most of the deep-sea divers (is, are) trained to handle these situations.
9. There (is, are) at least one accident a year that troubles rescue workers.
10. How often (does, do) it happen that rescue workers cannot help people?

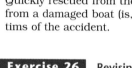

Exercise 28 **Supplying Pronouns That Agree With Antecedents** Rewrite each of the following sentences, filling in the blank with an appropriate pronoun.

1. Some rescue workers use helicopters to help ___?___ reach victims.
2. When a victim who has been stranded on a mountain sees a rescue helicopter, ___?___ waves to catch the pilot's attention.
3. Helicopter pilots must keep ___?___ eyes on both the control panel and the water when searching for victims.
4. The helicopter hovers in the air, and ___?___ rotor blades continue to spin.
5. The victim is grateful that ___?___ life has been saved.

Exercise 29 **Revising Sentences to Eliminate Errors in Pronoun-Antecedent Agreement** Rewrite any sentences below that contain pronoun-antecedent agreement errors. If a sentence is correct, write *correct.*

1. Every boy in my class seems to want to get their airplane pilot's license.
2. Many of the girls are interested in taking a test so they can become test pilots.
3. Each test pilot is responsible for flying new or experimental aircraft and giving their opinion about the craft.
4. Most have his or her college degrees.
5. After attending flight school, each pilot needs to complete as many hours of flying as they can.
6. Once a pilot gets a license, you must search for a flying job.
7. Farmers may hire a pilot to spray chemicals over his crops to control insects.
8. Large corporations maintain private planes to transport its executives.
9. Television newscasters use helicopter pilots when they need to report rush-hour traffic jams.
10. Whatever job a pilot performs, it must be well trained.

Exercise 30 **Supplying Verbs and Pronouns That Agree** Rewrite the following paragraph, filling in the blanks with logical verbs and pronouns. All verbs should be in the present or present perfect tense.

Mike and his friend Tom ___?___ playing a computer game, when suddenly ___?___ hear a loud noise. Each of the boys ___?___ out the window and ___?___ that two cars ___?___ crashed near the house. Mike rushes to the phone in ___?___ bedroom and ___?___ 911. By then, the drivers ___?___ gotten out of ___?___ cars; ___?___ seem to be discussing the damage. Soon, the emergency team ___?___. The EMTs hurry from ___?___ ambulance to see if there ___?___ injuries. Mike can see that each EMT ___?___ very serious about ___?___ job.

Exercise 31 **Writing Application** Imagine you are flying a helicopter above your city of town. Describe what you see below. Include singular and plural subjects and personal and indefinite pronouns in your description. Proofread to make sure you have no agreement errors.

Exercise 32 **CUMULATIVE REVIEW** **Verb Tense and Pronoun Usage** Rewrite the paragraph below, correcting errors in verb tense and form, as well as in pronoun usage.

(1) Anne Frank keep a diary while she hided from the Nazis during World War II. (2) Her and her sister was born in Frankfurt, Germany. (3) Her family will have moved to Holland in 1933 after the Nazis begun to persecute Jews. (4) In 1942, during the Nazi occupation of Holland, Anne's father brung the family to hide in the attic of his place of business. (5) There, Anne will record its life-threatening experiences in a diary.

Exercise 28

1. them
2. he or she
3. their
4. its
5. his or her

Exercise 29

1. his
2. correct
3. his or her
4. their
5. he or she
6. he or she
7. their
8. their
9. correct
10. he or she

Exercise 30

Mike and his friend Tom are playing a computer game, when suddenly they hear a loud noise. Each of the boys looks out the window and sees that two cars have crashed near the house. Mike rushes to the phone in his bedroom and dials 911. By then, the drivers have gotten out of their cars; they seem to be discussing the damage. Soon, the emergency team arrives. The EMTs hurry from their ambulance to see if there are injuries. Mike can see that each EMT is very serious about his or her job.

Exercise 31

Writing Application
Ask volunteers to read their descriptions to the class and ask for feedback.

Exercise 32

Cumulative Review
(1) Anne Frank kept a diary while she hid from the Nazis during World War II. (2) She and her sister were born in Frankfurt, Germany. (3) Her family moved to Holland in 1933 after the Nazis began to persecute Jews. (4) In 1942, during the Nazi occupation of Holland, Anne's father brought the family to hide in the attic of his place of business.
(5) There, Anne recorded her life-threatening experiences in a diary.

Lesson Objectives

- To identify errors in subject-verb agreement.

Step-by-Step Teaching Guide

Standard English Usage: Agreement

Teaching Resources: Standardized Test Preparation Workbook, pp.47–48

1. Have students underline each subject once and each verb twice in the passages.
2. Students then can check to see that the subject and verb in each sentence agree.
3. Remind students to review the rules for agreement regarding special cases.

Standardized Test Preparation Workshop

Standard English Usage: Agreement

Standardized tests frequently test your knowledge of the rules of subject and verb agreement. When checking a sentence for errors, first identify the subject. Next, identify the type of subject: *singular, plural,* or *compound.* Then, apply the rules of agreement to make sure that the verb in the sentence agrees with the subject.

The following questions will give you practice with different formats used for items that test knowledge of subject-verb agreement.

Test Tips

- If you are having trouble with a sentence revision, eliminate any answer choices in which the subject and verb clearly do not agree.
- Try reading the sentence to be revised silently to yourself to help you recognize when a subject and verb do not agree.

Sample Test Items	Answers and Explanations
Identify the underlined word or phrase that contains an error in the following sentence. Either Emily or Luke (A) walk the dog (B) every morning (C) before school. (D) No error. (E)	The correct answer is *B.* The compound subject of the sentence is *Either Emily or Luke.* When two singular subjects are joined by *or* or *nor*, the verb must be singular. In this case, the singular verb *walks* should be used in the sentence.
Choose the revised version of the following sentence that eliminates all errors in grammar, usage, and mechanics. Either Emily or Luke walk the dog every morning before school. **A** Either Emily, or Luke, walk the dog every morning before school. **B** Both Emily and Luke walk the dog every morning before school. **C** Neither Emily nor Luke walks the dog every morning before school. **D** Either Emily or Luke walks the dog every morning before school.	The correct answer is *D.* The compound subject of the original sentence is *Either Emily or Luke.* When two singular subjects are joined by *or* or *nor*, the verb must be singular. In this case, the singular verb *walks* should be used in the sentence. Notice that answers *B* and *C* are both grammatically correct, but they change the meaning of the original sentence.

TEST-TAKING TIP

Draw students' attention to the Test Tip above. Remind them that eliminating any incorrect answers will make choosing the correct answer easier and will help them to avoid any unnecessary mistakes.

Practice 1 **Directions:** Identify the underlined word or phrase that contains an error in each of the following sentences.

1 My brother and I (A) shares the responsibility (B) of taking care of (C) our pet dog (D). No error (E).

2 Each of us take (A) turns brushing (B) her long (C) sandy-colored hair (D). No error (E).

3 We and our dog Ginger (A) is attending (B) obedience training (C) on Saturday mornings (D). No error (E).

4 Here are (A) the books (B) that we is using (C) to teach us about our dog (D). No error (E).

5 Neither my mother nor my father (A) mind when we (B) let Ginger sleep in one (C) of our rooms (D). No error (E).

Practice 2 **Directions:** Choose the revised version of each sentence that eliminates all errors in grammar, usage, and mechanics.

1 Taking care of pets are an awesome responsibility, and not everybody are cut out to be a pet owner.

A Taking care of pets is an awesome responsibility, and not everybody is cut out to be a pet owner.

B Taking care of pets are awesome responsibilities, and not everybody are cut out to be a pet owner.

C Taking care of pets are an awesome responsibility, and not everybody is cut out to be a pet owner.

D Taking care of pets is an awesome responsibility, and not everybody are cut out to be a pet owner.

2 A wise potential owner of a dog first speak to either another dog owner or a trainer and learn the difficulties and joys of owning a dog. This helps the potential owner decide if he or she are ready to face the responsibilities of dog ownership.

A A wise potential owner of a dog first speak to either another dog owner or a trainer and learns the difficulties and joys of owning a dog. This help the potential owner decide if he or she is ready to face the responsibilities of dog ownership.

B A wise potential owner of a dog first speaks to either another dog owner or a trainer and learn the difficulties and joys of owning a dog. This helps the potential owner decide if he or she is ready to face the responsibilities of dog ownership.

C A wise potential owner of a dog first speaks to either another dog owner or a trainer and learns the difficulties and joys of owning a dog. This helps the potential owner decide if he or she is ready to face the responsibilities of dog ownership.

D A wise potential owner of a dog first speaks to either another dog owner or a trainer and learns the difficulties and joys of owning a dog. This helps the potential owner decide if he or she are ready to face the responsibilities of dog ownership.

Answer Key

Practice 1

1. B
2. A
3. B
4. C
5. B

Practice 2

1. A
2. C

Chapter 25 Time and Resource Manager

In-Depth Lesson Plan

	LESSON FOCUS	PRINT AND MEDIA RESOURCES
DAY 1	**Adjectives and Adverbs** Students work with comparative and superlative degrees of adjectives and adverbs. They learn when to change the ending of a modifier and when to use *more* or *most.* They complete a Hands-on Grammar activity (pp. 572–583).	**Teaching Resources** *Grammar Exercise Workbook,* pp. 153–160; *Grammar Exercises Answers on Transparencies,* Ch. 25; *Hands-on Grammar Activity Book,* Ch. 25 ***Writing and Grammar iText* (Interactive Text),** Section 25.1; ***On-line Exercise Bank,*** Section 25.1
DAY 2	**Troublesome Modifiers** Students work with the irregular comparative and superlative degrees of the adjectives *bad* and *good* and the adverbs *badly* and *well* (pp. 584–587).	**Teaching Resources** *Grammar Exercise Workbook,* pp. 161–162; *Grammar Exercises Answers on Transparencies,* Ch. 25 ***Writing and Grammar iText* (Interactive Text),** Section 25.2; ***On-line Exercise Bank,*** Section 25.2
DAY 3	**Review and Assess** Students review the chapter and demonstrate mastery of comparative and superlative degrees. They also complete a cumulative review (pp. 588–593).	**Teaching Resources** *Formal Assessment,* Ch. 25; *Grammar Exercises Answers on Transparencies,* Ch. 25 ***Writing and Grammar iText* (Interactive Text),** Ch. 25, Chapter Review

Accelerated Lesson Plan

	LESSON FOCUS	PRINT AND MEDIA RESOURCES
DAY 1	**Using Modifiers** Students review and work with comparative and superlative degrees of adjectives and adverbs, including the irregular modifiers *bad, badly, good,* and *well* (pp. 572–587).	**Teaching Resources** *Grammar Exercise Workbook,* pp. 153–162; *Grammar Exercises Answers on Transparencies,* Ch. 25 ***Writing and Grammar iText* (Interactive Text),** Sections 25.1–2; ***On-line Exercise Bank,*** Sections 25.1–2
DAY 2	**Review and Assess** Students review the chapter and demonstrate mastery of comparative and superlative degrees. They also complete a cumulative review (pp. 588–593).	**Teaching Resources** *Formal Assessment,* Ch. 25; *Grammar Exercises Answers on Transparencies,* Ch. 25; *Hands-on Grammar Activity Book,* Ch. 25 ***Writing and Grammar iText* (Interactive Text),** Ch. 25, Chapter Review

Options for Adapting Lesson Plans

HOMEWORK

Have students complete any stage of the lesson for homework.

SPELLING

To teach spelling skills in conjunction with grammar, mechanics, and usage, work through *Prentice Hall Everyday Spelling,* Grade 8, Chapter 29, as you cover this *Writing and Grammar* chapter.

TECHNOLOGY

Students can use *Writing and Grammar iText* to complete the exercises interactively on computer. They can complete additional exercises in the *On-line Exercise Bank:* The Auto Check feature will grade their work. Go online: PHSchool.com Use Web code: eck-8002

FEATURES

Extend coverage with the Grammar in Literature features (pp. 577, 585) and the Standardized Test Preparation Workshop (pp. 590-591).

INTEGRATED SKILLS COVERAGE

Grammar in Literature
SE pp. 577, 585

Reading
Find It in Your Reading, SE pp. 582, 587

Writing
Find It in Your Writing, SE pp. 582, 583, 587
Writing Application, SE pp. 583, 587, 589, 593

Viewing and Representing
Critical Viewing, SE pp. 572, 579, 580, 584, 586

Speaking and Listening
Fewer and *Less,* ATE p. 584

Real-World Connection
ATE p. 578

Workplace Skills
Clear Comparisons, ATE p. 581

Language Highlight
ATE p. 585

ASSESSMENT SUPPORT

Standardized Test Preparation Workshop SE pp. 590–591; ATE p. 576

Standardized Test Preparation Workbook, pp. 49–50

Formal Assessment, Ch. 25

MEETING INDIVIDUAL NEEDS

Less Advanced Students ATE p. 576. See also Ongoing Assessments ATE pp. 575, 577, 579, 581, 582, 586.

ESL Students ATE p. 575

BLOCK SCHEDULING

Pacing Suggestions
For 90-minute Blocks
- Administer the Diagnostic Test to students to determine instructional coverage.
- Have students complete the necessary exercises in class. Use the Hands-on Grammar Activity to provide a change of pace.

Resources for Varying Instruction
- ***Writing and Grammar iText* (Interactive Text)** A 90-minute block provides an ideal opportunity for students to work on computer.

Professional Development Support
- ***How to Manage Instruction in the Block*** This teaching resource provides management and activity suggestions.

MEDIA AND TECHNOLOGY

For the Student
- ***Writing and Grammar iText* (Interactive Text),** Ch. 25
- ***On-line Exercise Bank,*** Sections 25.1–2

For the Teacher
- ***Resource Pro* CD-ROM**

WRITING AND GRAMMAR ON-LINE

iText Interactive Text (On-line or on CD-ROM)
- Easily navigable instruction with on-line supporting resources
- Self-scoring exercises and diagnostic tests

Companion Web Site PHSchool.com
- On-line Exercise Bank (use Web Code eck-8002)

See the Go On-line! feature, SE p. iii.

LITERATURE CONNECTIONS

Grammar in Literature selections from *Prentice Hall Literature: Timeless Voices, Timeless Themes,* Silver:

from "The Wreck of the Hesperus," Henry Wadsworth Longfellow, SE p. 577

from "The Centaur," May Swenson, SE p. 585

Lesson Objectives

1. To understand how to form the comparative and superlative degrees of one- or two-syllable modifiers.
2. To use *more* and *most* to form comparative and superlative forms of modifiers of three or more syllables.
3. To memorize comparative and superlative forms of irregular modifiers.
4. To understand the rules for using the comparative and superlative degrees.
5. To understand the rules of balanced comparisons.
6. To understand the rule of using *other* and *else* in comparing a member of a group to the rest of the group.
7. To demonstrate knowledge of forms of troublesome adjectives and adverbs.

Critical Viewing

Describe Students' comparisons of the two ships should include both adjectives and adverbs.

Chapter 25 Using Modifiers

▲ **Critical Viewing** Use adjectives and adverbs to compare the two ships in this photograph. **[Describe]**

Shipwrecks and other disasters are major events that leave their mark on the people who experience them. When people speak about such events, they may use descriptive words, such as *horrible* and *violently*, to convey their emotions. These words are adjectives and adverbs.

Adjectives and **adverbs** can be used to compare two or more people, places, or things that share the same basic qualities. These two parts of speech have different forms, or degrees, depending on the kind of comparison that is being made.

The first section in this chapter will explain how the three degrees are formed and will show you how the different degrees should be used. The second section will discuss troublesome adjectives and adverbs, as well as provide practice in using them correctly.

ONGOING ASSESSMENT: Diagnose

If students miss more than one item in any category, direct them to the relevant pages of the text and assign exercises for practice and review.

Modifiers	Diagnostic Test Items	Teach	Practice	Section Review	Chapter Review
Skill Check A					
Identifying Comparative and Superlative Degree	A 1–10	pp. 574–577	Ex. 1–5	Ex. 9	Ex. 25
Skill Check B					
Using Comparative and Superlative Degree	B 11–15	pp. 578–579	Ex. 6	Ex. 10	Ex. 26, 29

Diagnostic Test

Directions: Write all answers on a separate sheet of paper.

Skill Check A. Write the comparative and superlative degrees of the following modifiers. If the degrees can be formed in two ways, write the *-er* and *-est* forms.

1. eager
2. happily
3. sharp
4. delicious
5. well
6. quietly
7. priceless
8. strong
9. famous
10. bad

Skill Check B. Choose the word or phrase in parentheses that correctly completes each sentence.

11. Shipwrecks used to be a (more common, most common) occurrence.
12. Of the two ships, that one is the (more, most) seaworthy.
13. The captain is the (more, most) experienced of the two.
14. Modern-day wrecks can be (worse, more worse) than those of previous eras because modern ships can carry more passengers.
15. That ship's cargo is the (heaviest, most heaviest) it has ever carried.

Skill Check C. Rewrite each of the following sentences, correcting the illogical comparisons by making them balanced or by adding *other* or *else*.

16. This ship's hull is larger than that ship.
17. The ship weathered more hurricanes than any ship.
18. That storm was worse than any storm.
19. The captain was more scared than anyone when the ship went down.
20. The shipping company's loss was worse than the other shipping company.

Skill Check D. Choose the word or phrase in parentheses that correctly completes each sentence.

21. The ship foundered (bad, badly) in the rough seas.
22. After the helmsman was injured, (only the captain could, the captain could only) steer them to safety.
23. The ship (just needed, needed just) one large wave to push it over the shoal.
24. The crew had (fewer, less) fear of sinking than of facing the captain's wrath.
25. After they had weathered the storm, the captain praised the crew for performing so (good, well).

ONGOING ASSESSMENT: Diagnose *continued*

Modifiers	Diagnostic Test Items	Teach	Practice	Section Review	Chapter Review
Skill Check C					
Using Balanced Comparisons	C 16–20	pp. 579–581	Ex. 7–8	Ex. 11	Ex. 27
Skill Check D					
Using Irregular and Troublesome Modifiers	D 21–25	pp. 584–586	Ex. 16–17	Ex. 18–21	Ex. 28
Cumulative Reviews and Applications				Ex. 13–15 Ex. 22–24	Ex. 32

Answer Key

Diagnostic Test

Each item in the diagnostic test corresponds to a specific concept in the chapter on using modifiers. This will enable you to tailor instruction to the particular needs of your students. See "Ongoing Assessment" below for further details.

Skill Check A

1. more eager, most eager
2. more happily, most happily
3. sharper, sharpest
4. more delicious, most delicious
5. better, best
6. more quietly, most quietly
7. more priceless, most priceless
8. stronger, strongest
9. more famous, most famous
10. worse, worst

Skill Check B

11. more common
12. more
13. more
14. worse
15. heaviest

Skill Check C

16. This ship's hull is larger than that ship's hull.
17. The ship weathered more hurricanes than any other ship.
18. That storm was worse than any other storm.
19. The captain was more scared than anyone else when the ship went down.
20. The shipping company's loss was worse than the other shipping company's loss.

Skill Check D

21. badly
22. only the captain could
23. needed just
24. less
25. well

TIME SAVERS!

Answers on Transparency Use the Grammar Exercises Answers on Transparencies for Chapter 25 to facilitate correction by students.

On-Line Exercise Bank Have students complete the Diagnostic Test on computer. The Auto Check feature will grade their work for you!

PREPARE and ENGAGE

Interest GRABBER Ask students to think of a favorite actor, athlete, or singer. Have some students choose any two similar people (two baseball players, two country singers) and compare them, describing how they look, move, sound, and so on. Then have other students choose any three similar people and compare them.

Activate Prior Knowledge

Ask students to recall some of the comparison words used in their Interest Grabber responses. Remind them that these are comparatives and superlatives. Ask volunteers to take sentences from the Interest Grabber in which comparatives were used and turn them into sentences with superlatives. For example, "Cal Ripkin is a better ballplayer than Sammy Sosa," might become, "Cal Ripkin is the best ballplayer of the last twenty-five years."

TEACH

Step-by-Step Teaching Guide

Using Modifiers of One or Two Syllables

1. Review with students the fact that modifiers, like verbs, are either regular or irregular. Rules apply only to regular modifiers.
2. For most modifiers with one or two syllables, the comparative degree is formed using *-er* and the superlative degree is formed by adding *-est.*
3. Write the following chart on the board for additional practice:

Modifier	Comparative	Superlative
sweet	sweeter	sweetest
sharp	sharper	sharpest
funny	funnier	funniest

4. Review the rules for forming comparative and superlative degrees for modifiers ending in *-y* or in a single consonant preceded by a single vowel.
5. With some one- and two-syllable modifiers, and for most adverbs ending in *-ly,* the comparative and superlative degrees are formed by adding *more* and *most.*

Modifier	Comparative	Superlative
sweetly	more sweetly	most sweetly
eager	more eager	most eager

Section 25.1

Comparisons Using Adjectives and Adverbs

Like verbs, adjectives and adverbs can be either *regular* or *irregular.* Two rules govern *regular* modifiers. The first covers adjectives and adverbs of one or two syllables. The second concerns adjectives and adverbs of three or more syllables.

Using Modifiers of One or Two Syllables

KEY CONCEPT Use *-er* or *more* to form the comparative degree and *-est* or *most* to form the superlative degree of most one- and two-syllable modifiers. ■

The most common way to form these degrees is by adding *-er* or *-est.*

COMPARATIVE AND SUPERLATIVE DEGREES FORMED WITH *-ER* AND *-EST*

Positive	Comparative	Superlative
deep	deeper	deepest
hard	harder	hardest
salty	saltier	saltiest
slimy	slimier	slimiest

More and *most* can also be used to form the comparative and superlative degrees of most one- and two-syllable modifiers. They should not be used, however, when their use would sound awkward, as in "The water is *more deep* in the ocean." Notice in the following chart that two of the modifiers from the preceding chart, *salty* and *slimy,* can use *more* and *most* to form the comparative and superlative degrees. *More* and *most* are used with most adverbs ending in *-ly* and with one- and two-syllable modifiers that would sound awkward with *-er* and *-est.* If you are in doubt about which form to use, consult a dictionary.

COMPARATIVE AND SUPERLATIVE DEGREES FORMED WITH *MORE* AND *MOST*

Positive	Comparative	Superlative
salty	more salty	most salty
slimy	more slimy	most slimy
quickly	more quickly	most quickly
often	more often	most often

Theme: Sailing Ships

In this section, you will learn how the comparative and superlative degrees of adjectives and adverbs are formed. The examples and exercises are about sailing ships and shipwrecks.

Cross-Curricular Connection: Social Studies

Spelling Tip

Words that end in *y* exchange the *y* for an *i* when the endings for the comparative and superlative degrees are added.

TIME AND RESOURCE MANAGER

Resources
Print: Grammar Exercise Workbook, pp. 153–160; Hands-on Grammar Activity Book, Chapter 25
Technology: Writing and Grammar iText, Section 25.1; On-Line Exercise Bank, Section 25.1

In-Depth Coverage	Accelerated Pace
• Work through all key concepts, pp. 574–581. • Assign and review Exercises 1–8. • Read and discuss Grammar in Literature, p. 577.	• Assign pp. 574–581 for independent student review. • Review *other* and *else* in Comparisons and assign Exercise 8. • Assign Section Review Exercises 9–10.

▶ **Exercise 1** Forming the Comparative and Superlative Degrees of One- and Two-Syllable Modifiers On your paper, write the comparative and superlative degrees of the following modifiers. If the degrees can be formed in two ways, write the -er and -est forms.

1. high
2. friendly
3. fully
4. low
5. steep
6. painful
7. early
8. small
9. brisk
10. near

Using Modifiers of Three or More Syllables

▶ **KEY CONCEPT** Use *more* and *most* to form the comparative and superlative degrees of all modifiers of three or more syllables. ■

DEGREES OF MODIFIERS WITH THREE OR MORE SYLLABLES		
Positive	Comparative	Superlative
gracefully	more gracefully	most gracefully
poisonous	more poisonous	most poisonous
flexible	more flexible	most flexible

Less and *least*, which mean the opposite of *more* and *most*, can be used to form the comparative and superlative degrees of any of the modifiers in the chart. *Less* and *least* can also be used with modifiers of one or two syllables.

EXAMPLES:
gracefully	less gracefully	least gracefully
poisonous	less poisonous	least poisonous

▶ **Exercise 2** Forming the Comparative and Superlative Degrees of Modifiers With Three or More Syllables Write the comparative and superlative degrees of the following modifiers. Use *more* and *most* and then *less* and *least* for each.

EXAMPLE: carefully
ANSWER: more carefully most carefully
 less carefully least carefully

1. rapidly
2. powerful
3. suddenly
4. eagerly
5. acceptable

More Practice

Grammar Exercise Workbook
• pp. 86–89
On-line Exercise Bank
• Section 25.1
Go on-line:
PHSchool.com
Enter Web Code:
eck-8002

iText

Get instant feedback! Exercises 1 and 2 are available on-line or on CD-ROM.

Answer Key

▶ **Exercise 1**

1. higher, highest
2. friendlier, friendliest
3. more fully, most fully
4. lower, lowest
5. steeper, steepest
6. more painful, most painful
7. earlier, earliest
8. smaller, smallest
9. brisker, briskest
10. nearer, nearest

Step-by-Step Teaching Guide

Modifiers of Three or More Syllables

1. Modifiers of three or more syllables use *more* or *most*, or *less* or *least,* to form the comparative and superlative degrees.

2. Write the following examples on the board for more practice:

Modifier	Comparative
wonderful	more wonderful
ridiculous	less ridiculous
stupidly	more stupidly

Superlative
most wonderful
least ridiculous
most stupidly

Answer Key

▶ **Exercise 2**

1. more rapidly, most rapidly; less rapidly, least rapidly
2. more powerful, most powerful; less powerful, least powerful
3. more suddenly, most suddenly; less suddenly, least suddenly
4. more eagerly, most eagerly; less eagerly, least eagerly
5. more acceptable, most acceptable; less acceptable, least acceptable

Customize for
ESL Students

Native English speakers can use the "sounds funny" rule to reject words such as *poisonouser.* But to students learning English, many words sound funny simply because they are new. Review with students how to find forms of words in the dictionary. Students must know and then look up the base word, *happy,* to find *happier, happiest,* and so on.

☑ ONGOING ASSESSMENT: Prerequisite Skills

If students have difficulty with the concept of modifiers in general, you may find it necessary to review the following to ensure coverage of prerequisite knowledge.

In the Textbook	Print Resources	Technology
Adjectives and Adverbs, pp. 346–369	Grammar Exercise Workbook, pp. 23–38	Writing and Grammar iText, Sections 16.1–2; On-Line Exercise Bank, Sections 16.1–2

Answer Key

Exercise 3

1. more fully, most fully; less fully, least fully
2. more difficult, most difficult; less difficult, least difficult
3. more slippery, most slippery; less slippery, least slippery
4. more playful, most playful; less playful, least playful
5. more favorable, most favorable; less favorable, least favorable

Step-by-Step Teaching Guide

Memorizing Irregular Adjectives and Adverbs

Irregular modifiers do not follow any rules in forming degrees of comparison. They must be memorized. Remind students that the best way to memorize them is through practice and regular usage.

Answer Key

Exercise 4

1. positive
2. superlative
3. comparative
4. comparative
5. superlative

Customize for *Less Advanced Students*

Work with students individually or in small groups to practice using irregular adjectives and adverbs. Students may invent their own dialogues or skits, using the irregular modifiers from the list as they practice degrees of comparison.

25.1

Exercise 3 **Forming the Comparative and Superlative Degrees of Regular Modifiers** Write the comparative and superlative degrees of the following modifiers. Use *more* and *most* and then *less* and *least* when necessary.

1. fully
2. difficult
3. slippery
4. playful
5. favorable

Memorizing Irregular Adjectives and Adverbs

The comparative and superlative degrees of a few adjectives and adverbs are *irregular* in form. The only way to learn them is to memorize them.

KEY CONCEPT Memorize the comparative and superlative forms of certain irregular adjectives and adverbs. ■

The chart below lists the most common irregular modifiers.

DEGREES OF IRREGULAR ADJECTIVES AND ADVERBS

Positive	Comparative	Superlative
bad	worse	worst
badly	worse	worst
far (distance)	farther	farthest
far (extent)	further	furthest
good	better	best
well	better	best
many	more	most
much	more	most

Exercise 4 **Recognizing the Degree of Irregular Modifiers** Identify the degree of the underlined word in each sentence.

EXAMPLE: The worst shipwrecks are described in this book.
ANSWER: superlative

1. For many thousands of years, people have feared shipwrecks.
2. Sailors did their best to avoid these costly disasters.
3. The farther from shore a ship traveled, the less chance it had to receive aid.
4. Better charts and navigation methods allowed captains to steer clear of trouble spots.
5. The best advances came with the invention of new technology, such as radio waves and satellites.

STANDARDIZED TEST PREPARATION WORKSHOP

Grammar and Usage Many standardized tests require students to identify errors in sentences, including incorrect degrees of comparison. Ask students to identify and correct the error in the following sentence.

Raul made the worse error of the game.

A Change *worse* to *bad*

B Change *worse* to *worst*

C Change *worse* to *more worse*

D Change *worse* to *most worse*

Item B is correct because the sentence requires the superlative form. Item A is not a comparative or a superlative. Items C and D use incorrect comparatives and superlatives.

GRAMMAR IN LITERATURE

from The Wreck of the Hesperus

Henry Wadsworth Longfellow

The poet has used the comparative degree of cold *to describe how the wind blew.*

Colder and colder blew the wind,
A gale from the Northeast,
The snow fell hissing in the brine,
And the billows frothed like yeast.

Exercise 5 **Supplying the Comparative and Superlative Degrees of Irregular Modifiers** Copy each sentence below, supplying the form of the modifier indicated in parentheses.

EXAMPLE: People on shore did their (good—superlative) to rescue the crew of the sinking ship.
ANSWER: best

1. Shipwrecks often occur during the (bad—superlative) weather conditions.
2. They may happen (far—comparative) out to sea than a person could possibly swim.
3. (Many—superlative) crew members could not reach land.
4. Surf boats are one of the (good—superlative) methods for rescuing crew members.
5. The boats are (much—comparative) useful for retrieving cargo that would otherwise sink with the ship.
6. In a mild storm, surf boats can reach the ship, but in (bad—comparative) weather, even these boats will overturn.
7. Helicopters work (well—comparative) in calmer weather.
8. Rescue teams developed a new method to overcome the (bad—superlative) weather conditions.
9. It seemed a (good—comparative) idea to shoot a rope out of a cannon in the direction of the ship; the crew would then secure the rope to the ship's mast.
10. The rescue team then used pulleys to bring people to shore before (far—comparative) damage could be done to the ship.

More Practice

Grammar Exercise Workbook
• pp. 86–89
On-line Exercise Bank
• Section 25.1
Go on-line: PHSchool.com
Enter Web Code: eck-8002

iText

Get instant feedback! Exercise 5 is available on-line or on CD-ROM.

ONGOING ASSESSMENT: Monitor and Reinforce

If students miss more than two items in Exercises 1–5, refer them to the following for additional practice.

In the Textbook	Print Resources	Technology
Section Review, Ex. 9	Grammar Exercise Workbook, pp. 153–156	On-Line Exercise Bank, Section 25.1

Step-by-Step Teaching Guide

Grammar in Literature

1. Have a volunteer read aloud the Longfellow passage.
2. Discuss how the poet uses repetition of the comparative degree to produce a gathering or accumulating effect. Ask if *cold* and *colder* would work as well. (no) *Colder* and *coldest?* (no)

More About the Author

Henry Wadsworth Longfellow (1807–1882) was one of the most acclaimed American poets of the nineteenth century. Longfellow was born in Maine and lived in Boston, where he taught at Harvard. Besides *The Wreck of the Hesperus* (1841), some other famous poems of his are *Paul Revere's Ride* (1863) and the long narrative poems *Evangeline* (1847), *The Song of Hiawatha* (1855), and *The Courtship of Miles Standish* (1858). Generations of American students have had to memorize Longfellow's verses in school.

Answer Key

Exercise 5

1. Shipwrecks often occur during the worst weather conditions.
2. They may happen farther out to sea than a person could possibly swim.
3. Most crew members could not reach land.
4. Surf boats are one of the best methods for rescuing crew members.
5. The boats are more useful for retrieving cargo that would otherwise sink with the ship.
6. In a mild storm, surf boats can reach the ship, but in worse weather, even these boats will overturn.
7. Helicopters work better in calmer weather.
8. Rescue teams developed a new method to overcome the worst weather conditions.
9. It seemed a better idea to shoot a rope out of a cannon in the direction of the ship; the crew would then secure the rope to the ship's mast.
10. The rescue team then used pulleys to bring people to the shore before further damage could be done to the ship.

Step-by-Step Teaching Guide

Using Comparative and Superlative Degrees

1. The basic rule of degrees of comparison is that the comparative degree is used to compare two items, and the superlative is used for three or more items.
2. Often the number of items is not directly stated. In the sentence *I think I did better on this test,* it can be inferred that the comparison is to a previous test. In the sentence *I did best on this test,* the meaning is either in comparison to other students or to several previous tests.
3. Tell students that they are telling a listener or reader how many items, up to three or more, are being referred to by their choice of degrees. Use this example sentence:

   Considering the Nunez girls, it is clear that Jacqui is the taller one.

   From this, everyone knows there are just two Nunez sisters and not three or more.
4. Double comparisons are a common error, and there are two ways to avoid them. First, pay attention to the rules of degrees of comparison explained here. Second, read a sentence aloud. The clumsiness of the construction should signal that it is wrong.

Real-World Connection

Ask students to look in newspaper or magazine articles to find examples of balanced comparisons.

25.1

Using Comparative and Superlative Degrees

Keep two rules in mind when you use the comparative and superlative degrees:

KEY CONCEPTS Use the **comparative degree** to compare *two* people, places, or things. Use the **superlative degree** to compare *three or more* people, places, or things. ■

Usually, you do not need to mention specific numbers when you are making a comparison. The other words in the sentence should help make it clear whether you are comparing two items or three or more items.

EXAMPLES: The captain felt *better* once all the crew was safely on shore.
The rescue team completed the practice session in their *best* time.

Pay particular attention to the modifiers you use when you are comparing just two items. Do not make the mistake of using the superlative degree.

INCORRECT: Of their two practice runs, that one was *best.*
CORRECT: Of their two practice runs, that one was *better.*

INCORRECT: They were the *fastest* of the two teams competing.
CORRECT: They were the *faster* of the two teams competing.

Do not make *double comparisons.* You should never use both *-er* and *more* to form the comparative degree or both *-est* and *most* to form the superlative degree. Also, be sure not to use *-er* or *more* and *most* with an irregular modifier.

INCORRECT: That ship sank the *most fastest.*
CORRECT: That ship sank the *fastest.*

INCORRECT: The disaster was *more worse* than the sinking last summer.
CORRECT: The disaster was *worse* than the sinking last summer.

More Practice

Grammar Exercise Workbook
- pp. 86–89

On-line Exercise Bank
- Section 25.1

Go on-line:
PHSchool.com
Enter Web Code:
eck-8002

Exercise 6 Revising Sentences to Correct Errors in Degree
On your paper, rewrite the following sentences to correct errors in the degree of modifiers. If a sentence contains no errors, write *correct.*

1. Originally, lifesaving services were run by private organizations that tried to help the sinking ships most closest to shore.
2. American shipping magnates knew that their crew and cargo could be saved if help could get to them sooner.
3. Some critics claimed that of the crew and cargo, the magnates would miss the cargo the most.
4. By the late 1840's, Congress agreed to fund the construction of lifesaving stations to guard the worse areas of the shoreline.
5. Which of these two stations is closest to the ship in distress?

▼ Critical Viewing
Compare this sixteenth-century ship to one you might take a cruise on today. Make logical comparisons in your sentences. **[Compare and Contrast]**

Making Logical Comparisons

In most situations, you will have no problems forming the degrees of modifiers and using them correctly in sentences. Sometimes, however, you may find that the way you have phrased a sentence makes your comparison unclear. You will then need to think about the words you have chosen, and revise your sentence, making sure that your comparison is logical.

Balanced Comparisons Most comparisons make a statement or ask a question about the way in which basically similar things are either alike or different.

EXAMPLE: Is Chesapeake Bay deeper than Puget Sound?

Because the sentence compares depth to depth, the comparison is *balanced.* Problems can occur, however, when a sentence compares basically dissimilar things. For example, it would be illogical to compare the *depth* of one bay to the *shape* of another bay. Depth and shape are not basically similar things and cannot be compared meaningfully.

ONGOING ASSESSMENT: Monitor and Reinforce

If students miss more than two items in Exercises 4–6, refer them to the following for additional practice.

In the Textbook	Print Resources	Technology
Section Review, Ex. 10	Grammar Exercise Workbook, pp. 86–89	On-Line Exercise Bank, Section 25.1

Answer Key

Exercise 6

1. Originally, lifesaving services were run by private organizations that tried to help the sinking ships closest to shore.
2. American shipping magnates knew that their crew and cargo could be saved if help could get to them soon.
3. Some critics claimed that of the crew and cargo, the magnates would miss the cargo more.
4. By the late 1840's, Congress agreed to fund the construction of lifesaving stations to guard the worst areas of the shoreline.
5. Which of these two stations is closer to the ship in distress?

Step-by-Step Teaching Guide

Making Logical Comparisons

1. Comparisons make little sense if they are not logical.
2. In conversation, we use comparison all the time. To illustrate illogical comparison, use the following examples:

   This snake is longer.

   Longer than the other snake? Longer than a garden hose? These are important questions when dealing with snakes.

   This house's yard is bigger than that house.

   Is this yard bigger than that whole house? Or is this house's yard bigger than the yard of that house? The sentence is not clear.

Critical Viewing

Compare and Contrast Have students work in pairs to assess the accuracy of each other's logical comparisons.

Critical Viewing

Compare and Contrast Students might use balanced comparisons that refer to both the size and shape of the two craft.

Step-by-Step Teaching Guide

Balanced Comparisons

1. Reinforce the basic point: Compare only items of a similar kind.
2. Write the following example on the board and ask students to correct it to create a balanced comparison:

   The school's flagpole is taller than that school. (The school's flagpole is taller than that school's flagpole.)

Answer Key

Exercise 7

1. That crew is more experienced than the crew of the other ship.
2. The gusts of wind at the center of the storm are stronger than the gusts at the edge.
3. Ships with larger sails are more likely to capsize than are ships with smaller sails.
4. A ship with a smaller sail than that ship's sail could weather the storm better.
5. The distance of that ship to the barrier reef is greater than the other ship's distance.

TIME SAVERS!

Answers on Transparency Use the Grammar Exercise Answers on Transparencies for Chapter 25 to facilitate corrections by students.

On-Line Exercise Bank Have students complete the exercises on computer. The Auto Check feature will grade their work for you!

25.1

KEY CONCEPT Make sure that your sentences compare only similar items. ■

An unbalanced comparison is usually the result of carelessness. The writer generally has simply left something out. Read the following incorrect sentences carefully.

INCORRECT: This ship's sail is bigger than that ship.

The number of shipwrecks off the east coast is larger than the west coast.

In the first sentence, a sail is mistakenly compared to an entire ship. In the second sentence, events are compared to a place. Both sentences can easily be corrected to make the comparisons balanced.

CORRECT: This ship's sail is bigger than that ship's sail.

The number of shipwrecks off the east coast is larger than the number off the west coast.

▲ **Critical Viewing** In sentences using balanced comparisons, compare the small boat to the sailing ship. **[Compare and Contrast]**

Exercise 7 **Revising Sentences to Make Balanced Comparisons** Revise each of the following sentences, making the illogical comparisons more balanced.

EXAMPLE: This ship's hull is longer than that ship.
ANSWER: This ship's hull is longer than that ship's hull.

1. That crew is more experienced than the other ship.
2. The gusts of wind at the center of the storm are stronger than the edge.
3. Ships with larger sails are more likely to capsize than smaller sails.
4. A ship with a smaller sail than that ship could weather the storm better.
5. The distance of that ship to the barrier reef is greater than the other ship.

Other and *Else* in Comparisons

Another common error in writing comparisons is to compare something with itself.

KEY CONCEPT When comparing one of a group with the rest of the group, make sure your sentence contains the word *other* or *else*. ■

Adding *other* or *else* in such situations helps make the comparison clear. For example, because the United States is itself a country, it cannot logically be compared to *all* countries. It must be compared to all *other* countries.

Problem Sentences	Corrected Sentences
A salvor is someone who returns an abandoned or sunken ship to shore before anyone.	A salvor is someone who returns an abandoned or sunken ship to shore before anyone else.
U.S. laws may allow a salvor to collect a larger reward than any country's laws.	U.S. laws may allow a salvor to collect a larger reward than any other country's laws.

Exercise 8 **Revising Sentences to Make Logical Comparisons** Rewrite each of the following sentences, adding *other* or *else* to make the comparisons more logical.

EXAMPLE: Because there are no limits on salvage rewards in the United States, a salvor could conceivably earn more money in U.S. waters than anywhere.

ANSWER: Because there are no limits on salvage rewards in the United States, a salvor could conceivably earn more money in U.S. waters than anywhere else.

1. That salvor has rescued more ships than anyone.
2. The salvor is given cash more often than any type of payment.
3. The salvor's job may be more dangerous than any job on the high seas.
4. The master of the salvage ship receives a larger payment than anyone on board.
5. The amount of salvage retrieved from the British cruiser the *Edinburgh* was larger than any amount of salvage.

More Practice

Grammar Exercise Workbook
- pp. 86–89

On-line Exercise Bank
- Section 25.1

Go on-line: PHSchool.com
Enter Web Code: eck-8002

iText

Get instant feedback! Exercise 8 is available on-line or on CD-ROM.

ONGOING ASSESSMENT: Monitor and Reinforce

If students miss more than one item in Exercises 7–8, refer them to the following for additional practice.

In the Textbook	Print Resources	Technology
Section Review, Ex. 11	Grammar Exercise Workbook, pp. 157–160	On-Line Exercise Bank, Section 25.1

Step-by-Step Teaching Guide

Other and *Else* in Comparisons

1. Comparing something to itself is another common error in using the comparative and superlative degrees. Review the rule of including *other* or *else* when comparing one of a group with the rest of the group.
2. Write the following sentences on the board for additional practice and have students correct them by adding *other* or *else:*

   The catcher is more involved in the flow of the game than anyone (else).

   Our manager uses the hit-and-run play more than any (other) manager.

Integrating Workplace Skills

Clear and helpful comparisons are important in all kinds of work. If a car manufacturer announces that "the Neptune sedan is safer," what does that mean? Safer than it was last year? Safer than the least safe car on the road? Safer than any other car? How do you decide whether to order a sandwich that has "fewer calories"? Does it have fewer calories than another sandwich, than a burger, or than a salad?

Answer Key

Exercise 8

1. That salvor has rescued more ships than anyone else.
2. The salvor is given cash more often than any other type of payment.
3. The salvor's job may be more dangerous than any other job on the high seas.
4. The master of the salvage ship receives a larger payment than anyone else on board.
5. The amount of salvage retrieved from the British cruiser the *Edinburgh* was larger than any other amount of salvage.

Step-by-Step Teaching Guide

Comparison Balance

Teaching Resources: Hands-on Grammar Activity Book, Chapter 25

1. Have students refer to their *Hands-on Grammar* activity books or give them copies of relevant pages for this activity.
2. Make sure students understand how the comparison balance is relevant to the comparisons they write in sentences.

Find It in Your Reading

Allow time for this activity in the classroom each day that you work on the relevant section in the chapter.

Find It in Your Writing

Ask volunteers to write some of their corrected sentences on the board for comment by the class.

25.1

Hands-on Grammar

Comparison Balance

In this exercise, you will learn how to form balanced comparisons using the comparison balance as a guide.

Cut two triangles of equal size out of lightweight cardboard and make slots in them as shown in the first illustration. Fit the triangles together so that they stand up, and tape them together. Cut a balance beam out of cardboard, and put it in the slot at the top of the standing triangle. You can use a paper clip to hold your comparative in the center of the balance. You now need some sentences to balance. Cut some strips of paper and fold one edge over so that the paper will hang on your balance beam.

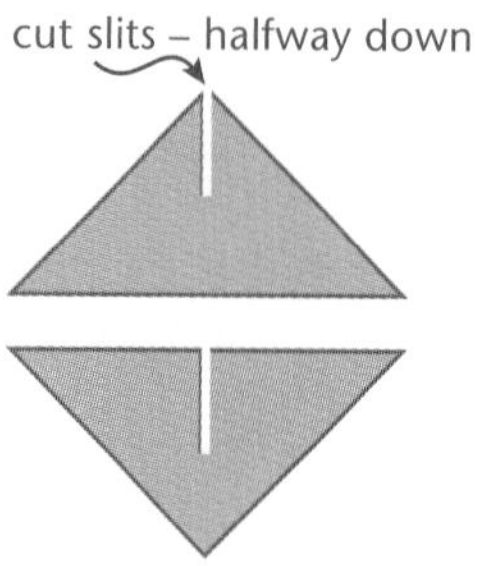

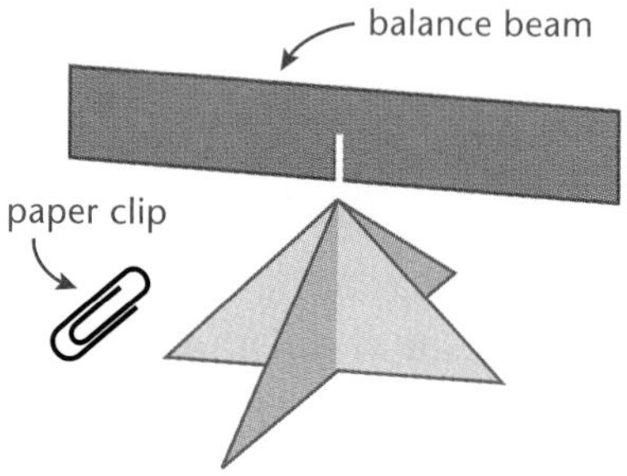

In the third illustration, you will see that the sample sentence used is *This ship's sail is bigger than that ship.* You should notice that the sentence is *not* balanced. The slip of paper that says *that ship's sail* would balance the sentence if hung on the beam. Use the sentence *This dog's coat is shinier than that dog,* and *This dog's coat is shinier than that dog's coat.* Which is the balanced sentence? Work with a partner to correct other sentences.

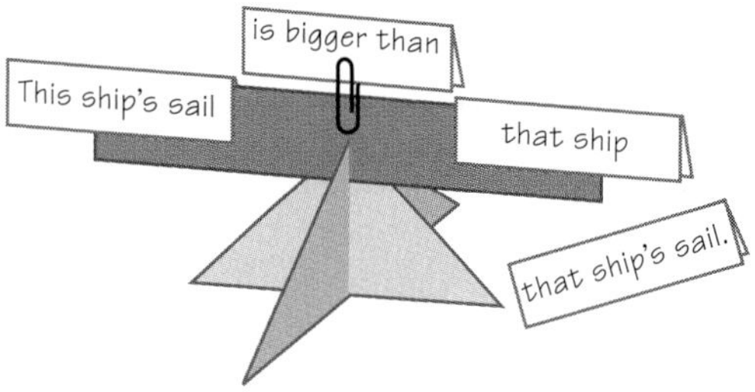

Find It in Your Reading In a short story or in a textbook, pick out examples of comparative sentences. Put them on strips of paper, and hang them on your balance.

Find It in Your Writing Look through your portfolio to find examples of comparatives. Make sure that they are balanced. If they are not, rewrite them correctly.

TIME SAVERS!

Hands-on Grammar
Use the Hands-on Grammar activity sheet for Chapter 25 to facilitate this activity.

ONGOING ASSESSMENT: Assess Mastery

Use the following resources to assess mastery of degrees of comparison.

In the Textbook	Technology
Chapter Review, Ex. 25–27 Standardized Test Preparation Workshop, pp. 490–491	Writing and Grammar iText, Section 25.1, Section Review; On-Line Exercise Bank, Section 25.1

Section 25.1 **Section Review**

GRAMMAR EXERCISES 9–15

Exercise 9 Forming the Comparative and Superlative Degrees Write the comparative and superlative of each modifier below.

1. faintly
2. sympathetic
3. firm
4. wryly
5. badly
6. pale
7. physically
8. many
9. fabulous
10. good

Exercise 10 Revising Sentences to Correct Errors in Degree Rewrite the sentences below, correcting the errors in modifiers.

1. More people who discover shipwrecks are professional treasure hunters.
2. Their searches are most likely to be successful if they consult old records than if they search randomly.
3. The treasure of the *Nuestra Señora de Atocha* is one of the most largest treasures ever recovered.
4. The *Titanic* is probably the more famous shipwreck today.
5. This is the most valuable of the two bells found on that ship.

Exercise 11 Revising Sentences to Make Logical Comparisons Rewrite each of the following sentences. Correct the illogical comparisons by balancing them or by adding *other* or *else*.

1. The professional reputation of underwater archaeologists is more respected than treasure hunters.
2. However, until the 1960's, underwater archaeologists were more apt to be shunned than any archaeologists.
3. Before then, exploration of shipwrecks was considered a field more appropriate for adventurers than for anyone.
4. The explorations of archaeologists were more systematic than adventurers.
5. Bob Ballard, head of the American part of the *Titanic* excavation team, is probably more famous than anyone in the business of underwater archaeology.

Exercise 12 Writing Logical Comparisons On your paper, write a sentence that makes the comparison specified in each of the following items.

1. Compare a sail boat to a speed boat.
2. Compare one city with all the rest.
3. Compare winter with other seasons.
4. Compare a sail boat to all other boats.
5. Compare a blizzard with a thunderstorm.

Exercise 13 Find It in Your Reading Write the adjective from these lines from "The Wreck of the Hesperus," and identify its degree.

For I can weather the roughest gale,
That ever wind did blow.

Exercise 14 Find It in Your Writing Look through your writing portfolio. Find two adjectives in the comparative degree and two in the superlative degree. Check to make sure that your comparisons are clear and logical.

Exercise 15 Writing Application Imagine that you are caught at sea during a fierce storm. Write a brief narrative describing your experience. Use at least two comparative degrees and two superlative degrees of adjectives.

Section Review

Each of these exercises correlates to a concept in the section on regular adjectives and adverbs, pages 574–582. These exercises may be used for more practice, for reteaching, or for review of the Key Concepts presented.

Answer Key

Exercise 9

1. more faintly, most faintly
2. more sympathetic, most sympathetic
3. firmer, firmest
4. more wryly, most wryly
5. worse, worst
6. paler, palest
7. more physically, most physically
8. more, most
9. more fabulous, most fabulous
10. better, best

Exercise 10

1. Most people who discover shipwrecks are professional treasure hunters.
2. Their searches are more likely to be successful if they consult old records than if they search randomly.
3. The treasure of the *Nuestra Señora de Atocha* is one of the largest treasures ever recovered.
4. The *Titanic* is probably the most famous shipwreck today.
5. This is the more valuable of the two bells found on that ship.

Exercise 11

1. The professional reputation of underwater archaeologists is more respected than the reputation of treasure hunters.
2. However, until the 1960's, underwater archaeologists were more apt to be shunned than any other archaeologists.
3. Before then, exploration of shipwrecks was considered a field more appropriate for adventurers than for anyone else.
4. The explorations of archaeologists were more systematic than the explorations of adventurers.
5. Bob Ballard, head of the American part of the *Titanic* excavation team, is probably more famous than anyone else in the business of underwater archaeology.

continued

Answer Key continued

Exercise 12

Sentences will vary.

Exercise 13

Find It in Your Reading
roughest—superlative

Exercise 14

Find It in Your Writing
If the comparisons are not clear or logical, students should correct them.

Exercise 15

Writing Application
Students can read aloud their narratives to practice speaking and listening skills.

PREPARE and ENGAGE

Interest GRABBER Write the following sentences on the chalkboard and ask students to choose the correct word in parentheses:

The armadillo behaved (bad/badly) when it tracked mud into the house.

Petting an armadillo does not feel (good/well).

Activate Prior Knowledge

Ask students to identify the part of speech of the following words:

good (adjective)

well (adverb or adjective)

bad (adjective)

badly (adverb)

Critical Viewing

Apply Have students correct a partner's sentences.

TEACH

Step-by-Step Teaching Guide

Troublesome Modifiers

1. How things sound is not reliable for determining correct usage. Tell students that understanding the function of each modifier will help them choose correctly.
2. Modifiers that follow linking verbs are adjectives. In *Benita sang loudly, loudly* is an adverb modifying the action verb *sang.* In *That song was loud, loud* is an adjective modifying the noun *song. Was* is a linking verb.
3. *Less* and *fewer* are both adjectives, but they answer different questions.

   There was (fewer/less) rain this month. (less—answers How much?)

   I made (fewer/less) mistakes in the dance today. (fewer—answers How many?)

Integrating Speaking and Listening Skills

Fewer and Less Have students read to each other the examples above to get used to speaking and hearing the correct usage.

Section 25.2

Troublesome Modifiers

Certain commonly used adjectives and adverbs can cause problems, both in speaking and in writing. As you read through the following list, make a note of those words that have puzzled you in the past, and use the exercises to test your understanding. When you are writing and revising a composition, refer to this section to check your work.

(1) *bad, badly* *Bad* is an adjective; *badly* is an adverb. Use *bad* after linking verbs, such as *appear, feel, look,* and *sound.* Use *badly* after action verbs, such as *act, behave, do,* and *perform.*

INCORRECT: She felt (LV) *badly* all winter long.

CORRECT: She felt (LV) *bad* all winter long.

INCORRECT: She coughed (AV) *bad* because of her cold.

CORRECT: She coughed (AV) *badly* because of her cold.

(2) *fewer, less* The adjective *fewer* answers the question *How many?* Use it to modify things that can be counted. The adjective *less* answers the question *How much?* Use it to modify amounts that cannot be counted.

HOW MANY: *fewer* snowmen, *fewer* green leaves, *fewer* warm nights

HOW MUCH: *less* snow, *less* foliage, *less* heat

(3) *good, well* *Good* is an adjective. *Well* can be either an adjective or an adverb. Most mistakes in the use of these modifiers occur when *good* is placed after an action verb. Use the adverb *well* instead.

INCORRECT: Caroline makes (AV) snow forts *good.*

CORRECT: Caroline makes (AV) snow forts *well.*

As adjectives, these words have slightly different meanings. *Well* is usually used to refer to a person's health.

Theme: Winter

In this section, you will learn how to use troublesome modifiers correctly. The examples and exercises are about winter and winter activities.

Cross-Curricular Connection: Humanities

▼ **Critical Viewing** Use *good* in one sentence about this picture. Use *well* in another sentence about the picture. **[Apply]**

TIME AND RESOURCE MANAGER

Resources
Print: Grammar Exercise Workbook, pp. 161–162
Technology: Writing and Grammar iText, Section 25.2; On-Line Exercise Bank, Section 25.2

In-Depth Coverage	Accelerated Pace
• Cover pp. 584–586 in class. • Assign and review Exercise 16.	• Assign pp. 584–586 for independent student review. • Assign Section Review Exercises 19–21.

EXAMPLES: John feels *good* after playing outside in the snow.
The snowfall this year is especially *good*.
Selena wasn't *well* enough to play outside in the snow.

(4) *just* As an adverb, *just* often means "no more than." When *just* has this meaning, make sure it is placed immediately before the word it logically modifies.

INCORRECT: Tim *just* wanted one last ride on his sled.

CORRECT: Tim wanted *just* one last ride on his sled.

(5) *only* The position of *only* in a sentence sometimes affects the entire meaning of the sentence. Consider the meaning of the following sentences:

EXAMPLES: *Only* expert skiers go down that slope. (Nobody else goes down that slope.)
Expert skiers *only* go down that slope. (They do nothing else on that slope.)
Expert skiers go down *only* that slope. (They don't go down any other slopes.)

Problems can occur when *only* is placed in a sentence in such a way that it makes the meaning imprecise.

IMPRECISE: *Only* wear warm clothes in the winter.
BETTER: Wear warm clothes *only* in the winter.

GRAMMAR IN LITERATURE

from The Centaur

May Swenson

In the first stanza of this poem, the modifier only *is in blue italics. It modifies the word* one.

The summer that I was ten—
Can it be there was *only* one
summer that I was ten? . . .

Grammar and Style Tip

Deciding where to put these modifiers can be tricky. Try to keep the modifier close to the word it is modifying.

Step-by-Step Teaching Guide

Troublesome Modifiers

1. Remind students that action verbs are modified by adverbs. *Good* is an adjective so it never can modify an action verb.
2. *Well* is trickier because it can be both an adjective and adverb. Write the following examples on the board, asking students to choose the correct answers:

   He ran a (good/well) race. (good—adjective modifies the noun *race)*

   She skis (good/well). (well—adverb modifies the verb *skis)*

   He is (good/well) now that his leg has healed. (well—adjective modifies the noun *He)*
3. Errors with *just* usually involve placement. *Just* needs to immediately precede the word it modifies, as in *You need to answer just one question.*
4. Errors with *only* also involve placement. Students need to pay attention to their intended meaning and place the word accordingly.

Language Highlight

The word *good* is a commonly used word in English with over a dozen shades of meaning. It is believed to have developed from the Sanskrit word *gadh*, meaning "to hold fast, uniting, fitting" and the Old High German word *bigaton*, meaning "to fit together."

Answer Key

Exercise 16

1. correct
2. The hemisphere that is farther from the sun receives less sunlight, so it is colder and darker.
3. In December, January, February, and March, the Northern Hemisphere is farther from the sun, which thus cannot warm it well.
4. correct
5. The term *winter* is used to indicate just one climatic season.
6. Winter comes only once a year in each hemisphere.
7. Some people react badly to the shorter days and weaker sunlight of winter.
8. Because areas near the equator are nearly always the same distance from the sun, they have fewer cold days than anywhere else.
9. If you time your travel plans well, you can arrange to be in summer all year round.
10. correct

Exercise 17

Sentences will vary.

Critical Viewing

Compare and Contrast Ask volunteers to write their sentences on the board for class feedback.

PRENTICE HALL
Everyday Spelling

If you have taught the spelling skills in *Prentice Hall Everyday Spelling,* Grade 8, Chapter 29, in conjunction with this *Writing and Grammar* chapter, review and assess students' mastery of the skills before concluding the chapter.

Exercise 16 **Revising Sentences With Troublesome Adjectives and Adverbs** On your paper, rewrite the following sentences that contain errors in the use of modifiers. Write *correct* if a sentence contains no errors.

EXAMPLE: Carla's winter jacket from last year no longer fits good.

ANSWER: Carla's winter jacket from last year no longer fits well.

1. Winter visits only one hemisphere, northern or southern, at a time.
2. The hemisphere that is farther from the sun receives fewer sunlight, so it is colder and darker.
3. In December, January, February, and March, the Northern Hemisphere is farther from the sun, which thus cannot warm it good.
4. Therefore, winter comes to just the Northern Hemisphere then.
5. The term *winter* is used just to indicate one climatic season.
6. Winter only comes once a year in each hemisphere.
7. Some people react bad to the shorter days and weaker sunlight of winter.
8. Because areas near the equator are nearly always the same distance from the sun, they have less cold days than anywhere else.
9. If you time your travel plans good, you can arrange to be in summer all year round.
10. Of course, some people would consider year-round summer to be a bad idea.

Exercise 17 **Writing Sentences With Troublesome Adjectives and Adverbs** Write sentences demonstrating the proper use of the modifiers listed below.

1. bad, badly
2. good, well
3. just
4. *only* modifying *go*
5. *only* modifying *seven*

▶ **Critical Viewing** Is this what winter looks like where you live? Use the comparative or superlative degree of the troublesome modifiers *bad* and *good* correctly in the sentences of your response. **[Compare and Contrast]**

More Practice

Grammar Exercise Workbook
- p. 90

On-line Exercise Bank
- Section 25.2

Go on-line: PHSchool.com *Enter Web Code:* eck-8002

TIME SAVERS!

Answers on Transparency Use the Grammar Exercises Answers on Transparencies for Chapter 25 to have students correct their own or one another's exercises.

On-Line Exercise Bank Have students complete the exercises on computer. The Auto Check feature will grade their work for you!

ONGOING ASSESSMENT: Assess Mastery

Use the following resources to assess mastery of troublesome adjectives and adverbs.

In the Textbook	Print Resources	Technology
Chapter Review, Ex. 28	Grammar Exercise Workbook, pp. 161–162	Writing and Grammar iText, Section 25.2, Section Review; On-Line Exercise Bank, Section 25.2

Section 25.2 **Section Review**

GRAMMAR EXERCISES 18–24

Exercise 18 **Using Troublesome Adjectives and Adverbs Correctly** For each of the following words, choose the correct modifier in parentheses.

1. verb—play (bad, badly)
2. verb—shovels (good, well)
3. noun—(fewer, less) darkness
4. noun—(good, well) snowman
5. verb—feels (bad, badly)
6. noun—(fewer, less) sleds
7. verb—skis (bad, badly)
8. noun—(bad, badly) fall
9. noun—(good, well) home
10. noun—(fewer, less) snowballs

Exercise 19 **Revising Sentences With Troublesome Modifiers** Rewrite the sentences below that contain errors in the use of modifiers. Write *correct* if a sentence contains no errors.

1. During the winter, there are less hours of daylight than in the summer.
2. The drop in temperature affects some animals bad.
3. Many animals only can live in warm temperatures.
4. Coldblooded animals cannot perform good in the cold.
5. It is not only coldblooded animals that experience difficulties in the cold weather.

Exercise 20 **Revising a Paragraph With Troublesome Modifiers** Rewrite the following paragraph, correcting all errors caused by troublesome modifiers.

Rose performs good in all winter sports. There isn't any game or athletic feat she does not do good. Her brother, Jorge, on the other hand, is very bad at sports. Snowshoeing only is the winter sport he likes. He just needs his snowshoes and a set of poles to be happy all afternoon. Rose has time for fewer sports this season. It is hard for her to just concentrate on one activity. She only competes in skating; the other sports are for fun. At her last competition, she had a bad fall, but she got right up again. Overall, she did very good, earning a bronze medal.

Exercise 21 **Writing Sentences With Troublesome Modifiers** Use each of the following modifiers correctly in a sentence.

1. fewer
2. less
3. just
4. only
5. badly

Exercise 22 **Find It in Your Reading** Look for an article on a seasonal sport in a newspaper or magazine. Find examples of at least three of the following modifiers: *good, well, bad, badly, fewer,* and *less.* Explain why the form used is the correct one in each case.

Exercise 23 **Find It in Your Writing** Look through your writing portfolio to find examples of at least three of the troublesome modifiers discussed in this section. Check to make sure that you have used each modifier correctly.

Exercise 24 **Writing Application** Write a short essay about your favorite aspect of winter. Include four of the following modifiers: *bad, badly, fewer, less, good, well, just,* and *only.*

ASSESS and CLOSE

Section Review

Each of these exercises correlates to a concept in the section on troublesome modifiers, pages 584–586. These exercises may be used for more practice, for reteaching, or for review of the Key Concepts presented.

Answer Key

Exercise 18

1. badly
2. well
3. less
4. good
5. bad
6. fewer
7. badly
8. bad
9. good
10. fewer

Exercise 19

1. During the winter, there are fewer hours of daylight than in the summer.
2. The drop in temperature affects some animals badly.
3. Many animals can live only in warm temperatures.
4. Coldblooded animals cannot perform well in the cold.
5. correct

Exercise 20

(1) Rose performs well in all winter sports. (2) There isn't any game or athletic feat she does badly. (3) Her brother, Jorge, on the other hand, is very bad at sports. (4) Snowshoeing is the only winter sport he likes. (5) He needs just his snowshoes and a set of poles to be happy all afternoon long. (6) Rose has time for fewer sports this season. (7) It is hard for her to concentrate on just one activity. (8) She competes only in skating; the other sports are for fun. (9) At her last competition, she had a bad fall, but she got right up again. (10) Overall, she did very well, earning a bronze medal.

Exercise 21

Sentences will vary.

continued

Answer Key continued

Exercise 22

Find It in Your Reading
Encourage students to share their examples with the class.

Exercise 23

Find It in Your Writing
If students have not used modifiers correctly, they should correct their papers.

Exercise 24

Writing Application
Students can trade papers with a partner to check.

CHAPTER REVIEW

Each of these exercises correlates to a concept in the chapter on using modifiers, pages 572–586. These exercises may be used for more practice, for reteaching, or for review of the Key Concepts presented.

Answer Key

Exercise 25

1. more luxurious, most luxurious
2. more careful, most careful
3. more frantically, most frantically
4. faster, fastest
5. worse, worst
6. more boldly, most boldly
7. more fantastic, most fantastic
8. slicker, slickest
9. more, most
10. more hopeless, most hopeless

Exercise 26

1. Of spring and winter, I like spring better.
2. The weather begins to turn warmer at this time.
3. correct
4. Spring may also bring the worst rain showers.
5. Plants need the rain to grow well.
6. Spring is the best of the four seasons for planting crops.
7. The colors of spring could not be better.
8. Of the two seasons, spring is the more colorful.
9. Some flowers bloom earlier in the year than others.
10. Daffodils and tulips are among the hardiest of spring flowers.

Exercise 27

1. Summer temperatures are higher than spring temperatures.
2. Daylight hours extend longer than winter hours.
3. Summer clothing is made of lighter fabrics than any other clothing.
4. Many students think summer is better than any other season.
5. Jeffrey works harder during the summer than any other season.
6. He works longer than anyone else.
7. During the summer, crops that were planted in the spring grow bigger and stronger than at any other time.
8. Because of this year's dry climate, harvests will be smaller than harvests last year.

Chapter 25 Chapter Review

GRAMMAR EXERCISES 25–32

Exercise 25 Forming the Comparative and Superlative Degrees Write the comparative and superlative degrees of the following modifiers.

1. luxurious
2. careful
3. frantically
4. fast
5. bad
6. boldly
7. fantastic
8. slick
9. much
10. hopeless

Exercise 26 Correcting Errors in Degree Rewrite the following sentences that contain errors in degree. Write *correct* if the sentence contains no errors.

1. Of spring and winter, I like spring best.
2. The weather begins to turn warmest at this time.
3. The warmth allows hibernating animals to awaken more easily.
4. Spring may also bring the most worst rain showers.
5. Plants need the rain to grow best.
6. Spring is the better of the four seasons for planting crops.
7. The colors of spring could not be more better.
8. Of the two seasons, spring is the most colorful.
9. Some flowers bloom more earlier in the year than others.
10. Daffodils and tulips are among the most hardiest of spring flowers.

Exercise 27 Making Logical Comparisons Rewrite each of the following sentences. Correct the illogical comparisons by balancing them or by adding *other* or *else* to make them logical.

1. Summer temperatures are higher than spring.
2. Daylight hours extend longer than winter.
3. Summer clothing is made of lighter fabrics than any clothing.
4. Many students think summer is better than any season.
5. Jeffrey works harder during the summer than any season.
6. He works longer than anyone.
7. During summer, crops that were planted in the spring grow bigger and stronger than at any time.
8. Because of this year's dry climate, harvests will be smaller than last year.
9. Baseball is more popular than any summer sport.
10. Some people think Babe Ruth played the game better than anyone.

Exercise 28 Correcting Errors Caused by Troublesome Modifiers Rewrite the following sentences that contain errors involving troublesome modifiers. Write *correct* if a sentence contains no errors.

1. In the fall, the days begin to shorten and there are less hours of daylight.
2. Who can feel badly on a brisk, clear day?
3. Crops that have grown good can be harvested.
4. In the winter, there is fewer food for the animals to find.
5. At this time, many animals prepare good for the winter.
6. These animals collect food to eat during the winter, but some other animals prepare bad.
7. They just rely on the chance of a mild winter with plenty of food.
8. Some animals just stockpile enough food to survive the winter.

9. Baseball is more popular than any other summer sport.
10. Some people think Babe Ruth played the game better than anyone else.

Exercise 28

1. In the fall, the days begin to shorten and there are fewer hours of daylight.
2. Who can feel bad on a brisk, clear day?
3. Crops that have grown well can be harvested.
4. In the winter, there is less food for the animals to find.
5. At this time, many animals prepare well for the winter.
6. These animals collect food to eat during the winter, but some other animals prepare badly.
7. They rely on just the chance of a mild winter with plenty of food.
8. Some animals stockpile just enough food to survive the winter.
9. Other animals spend only part of the winter awake.
10. They will need fewer calories because they hibernate for part of the year.

9. Other animals only spend part of the winter awake.
10. They will need less calories because they hibernate for part of the year.

Exercise 29 **Supplying the Comparative and Superlative Forms of Modifiers** Rewrite the sentences below, supplying the needed comparative or superlative forms of the modifiers in parentheses.

1. The tropics have seasons that are (dry) or (wet) than other places.
2. In the tropics, the areas (close) to the equator receive large amounts of rainfall, and many rain forests are found there.
3. Areas (far) from the equator have (few) inches of rain and are likely to have a dry season.
4. These regions have forests with trees that lose their leaves during the (dry) time of year.
5. Places (near) to sea level are (warm) than places (high) up in the mountains.

Exercise 30 **Revising a Passage With Modifiers** Rewrite the following paragraph, correcting mistakes in the usage of modifiers.

Some places on Earth just experience one season all year round. Only the North and South poles have a winter season. When a pole is at its farther point from the sun, it goes through a polar winter. Although it is always cold and snowy at the poles, it gets more cold during this time. At this point, the pole receives less hours of daylight, sometimes none at all. At the South Pole, scientists have set up a center for studying such things as global warming and astronomy because there they can work farther away from electric lights and pollution than anywhere. No one can reach the scientists for nine months out of the year because the conditions for airplanes are the worser then. When the pole reaches its closer point to the sun, it warms up considerably, but it is still cold. The pole then receives its greater amount of sunlight—sometimes without any interruption. You might think the climate at the poles is more constant than anywhere on Earth. However, just the climate in some areas of the tropics is as constant. The tropics are the warmest of the two regions. Of course, the colors of the tropical landscape are richer than the poles. There are more plants and animals here than in any area. Some places are so dry that few kinds of plants do good.

Exercise 31 **Writing Sentences With Modifiers** Write five sentences using each of the following modifiers in the degree indicated.

1. many (comparative)
2. good (superlative)
3. slippery (superlative)
4. far (comparative)
5. badly (comparative and superlative)

Exercise 32 **Writing Application** Write an essay comparing two seasons in the area where you live. Include three comparative degrees and three superlative degrees of modifiers. Check to make sure that your comparisons are balanced and logical. Use each of the following items correctly in a sentence.

1. more logical
2. farther
3. happiest
4. than anyone else
5. than any other
6. bad
7. less
8. better
9. just
10. only

Exercise 29

1. The tropics have seasons that are drier or wetter than other places.
2. In the tropics, the areas closest to the equator receive large amounts of rainfall, and many rain forests are found there.
3. Areas farther from the equator have fewer inches of rain and are likely to have a dry season.
4. These regions have forests with trees that lose their leaves during the driest time of year.
5. Places nearer to sea level are warmer than places higher up in the mountains.

Exercise 30

(1) Some places on Earth experience just one season all year round. (2) The North and South poles have only a winter season. (3) When a pole is at its farthest point from the sun, it goes through a polar winter. (4) Although it is always cold and snowy at the poles, it gets colder during this time. (5) At this point, the pole receives fewer hours of daylight, sometimes none at all. (6) At the South Pole, scientists have set up a center for studying such things as global warming and astronomy because there they can work farther away from electric lights and pollution than anywhere else. (7) No one can reach the scientists for nine months out of the year, because the conditions for airplanes are worst then. (8) When the pole reaches its closest point to the sun, it warms up considerably, but it is still cold. (9) The pole then receives its greatest amount of sunlight—sometimes without any interruption. (10) You might think the climate at the poles is more constant than anywhere else on Earth. (11) However, the climate in some areas of the tropics is just as constant. (12) The tropics are the warmer of the two regions. (13) Of

continued

Answer Key continued

course, the colors of the tropical landscape are richer than the colors at the poles. (14) There are more plants and animals here than in any other area. (15) Some places are so dry that few kinds of plants do well.

Exercise 31

Sentences will vary.

Exercise 32

Answers will vary.

TIME SAVERS!

Answers on Transparency
Use the Grammar Exercise Answers on Transparencies for Chapter 25 to facilitate corrections by students.

On-Line Exercise Bank
Have students complete the exercises on computer. The Auto Check feature will grade their work for you!

Lesson Objectives

- To use modifiers correctly.

Step-by-Step Teaching Guide

Standard English Usage: Using Modifiers

Teaching Resources: Standardized Test Preparation Workbook, pp. 49–50

1. Review the bulleted information with students. Suggest that students highlight the items being compared to make sure of their number.
2. Remind students that they can eliminate choices once they determine if an adjective or adverb is needed to complete the sentence.

Standardized Test Preparation Workshop

Standard English Usage: Using Modifiers

To succeed on standardized tests of grammar and usage, you must understand and be able to use modifiers. You will be given a written passage with numbered blanks. After reading the passage, you will be given a choice of several modifiers. Often, the correct choice will depend on the form the modifier should take or the degree of comparison.

- Decide whether the comparison is being made between two items or more items, than two items.
- Be especially careful to avoid choosing a double comparison, in which *more* or *most* is used with a modifier that is already in the comparative or superlative degree.

The following sample test item will give you practice with questions that test your ability to choose the correct modifier.

Test Tip

When two or more of the choices seem very similar, identify the way in which they are different before choosing one of them as your answer. This difference is the key to the answer.

Sample Test Item	Answer and Explanation
Read the passage, and choose the letter of the word or group of words that belongs in the space. The spring garden tour provides a rare glimpse of the __(1)__ public gardens and homes in all of Charleston. 1 A more lovely B lovelier C most loveliest D loveliest	The correct answer is *D*. The gardens and homes being shown are compared to all the others in Charleston, so the superlative degree should be used. Choices *A* and *B* are incorrect because they are comparative degrees. *C* is incorrect because it is a double comparison—it uses *most* with a modifier that ends with *-est*.

TEST-TAKING TIP

Encourage students to read the sentence with their choice in place before making a final decision. Hearing the choice in the context of the sentence may help them avoid unnecessary mistakes.

Practice 1 **Directions:** Read the passage, and choose the letter of the word or group of words that belongs in each space.

The children's choir is a __(1)__ musical group. The children sing __(2)__ under the direction of Mrs. Lacey Whaley. After practicing each member sings __(3)__ than when he or she first joined. Some songs are __(4)__ to learn than others. Even the __(5)__ melodies sound beautiful when sung by the children's choir.

1 **A** wonderful
B more wonderful
C wonderfuler
D more wonderfuler

2 **F** good
G well
H better
J bad

3 **A** good
B well
C better
D best

4 **F** easy
G more easy
H easier
J most easy

5 **A** simpler
B more simpler
C simplest
D most simplest

Practice 2 **Directions:** Read the passage, and choose the letter of the word or group of words that belongs in each space.

Learning to ski was one of the __(1)__ difficult things I have ever done. It was, however, also one of the __(2)__ . My sister has been skiing __(3)__ than I have, so she helped me manage the lift. Although I tried some slopes that were __(4)__ than the beginner slopes, I avoided the __(5)__ slopes of all.

1 **A** difficult
B more difficult
C difficultest
D most difficult

2 **F** funner
G more fun
H most fun
J most funnest

3 **A** long
B longer
C more long
D longest

4 **F** challenging
G more challenging
H most challenging
J most challengingest

5 **A** high
B higher
C highest
D most highest

Answer Key

Practice 1

1. A
2. G
3. C
4. H
5. C

Practice 2

1. D
2. H
3. B
4. G
5. C

Answer Key

Exercise A

1. done; done (past perfect)
2. set; set (past perfect)
3. seen; seen (present perfect)
4. played; played (present perfect)
5. gone; gone (present perfect)
6. traveled; traveled (present perfect)
7. continue; continue (future)
8. says; says (present)
9. measuring; measuring (past progressive)
10. passes; passes (present)

Exercise B

1. their—possessive
2. they—subject
3. its—possessive
4. it—objective
5. him—objective
6. They—subject
   who—subject
7. its—possessive
   they—subject
8. them—objective
9. who—subject
10. his—possessive

Exercise C

1. thrive
2. them
3. forms
4. It is
5. grow
6. them
7. constitute
8. its
9. they
10. links

Cumulative Review

USAGE

Exercise A **Using Verbs** Choose the verb or verb phrase that makes each sentence correct. Identify its principal part and tense.

1. The digging of the Mississippi River was (did, done) by glaciers during the last Ice Age.
2. Several Native American groups had (set, sat) their communities on the banks of the Mississippi.
3. If we had lived in earlier times, we would have (saw, seen) a different landscape from the one we see today.
4. The Mississippi River has (play, played) a central role in the development of North America.
5. A major portion of freight shipments have (gone, went) down this river.
6. More freight has (traveling, traveled) on the Mississippi than on any other inland waterway in North America.
7. The river will (continue, continues) to be of great economic importance to cities from Saint Paul to New Orleans.
8. The teacher (says, said) that if measured from Lake Itasca, the Mississippi River is 2,540 miles long.
9. However, if one was (measured, measuring) the river from the headwaters of the Missouri River, a major tributary, its length totals 3,710 miles.
10. After it (passes, passed) New Orleans, the river branches into smaller channels in the delta.

Exercise B **Identifying the Case of Pronouns** Identify the case of each pronoun in the following sentences as *subject*, *objective*, or *possessive*.

1. The Ojibwa, Natchez, and Choctaw made (them, their) homes along the Mississippi River.
2. As settlers moved in, the Native Americans and (they, them) briefly shared this territory.
3. The Algonquin word *missisipioui*, meaning "big water," gave the river (their, its) name.
4. Exploring the landscape in 1541, Hernando de Soto was the first European to see (its, it).
5. French explorers Louis Jolliet and Jacques Marquette followed (he, him) in 1673.
6. (They, Their) were succeeded by La Salle, (who, whom) claimed the entire Mississippi Valley for France.
7. The French gave the Mississippi (their, its) first European settlements when (it, they) founded New Orleans, St. Louis, and other cities in the early eighteenth century.
8. By the 1830's, farmers and settlers encouraged the steamboat trade because it made (they, them) more prosperous.
9. The golden age of steamboats attracted those (who, whom) wanted to serve as a boat captain or pilot.
10. Mark Twain wrote about (him, his) own experiences on and around the Mississippi River.

Exercise C **Making Verbs Agree With Subjects** Choose the correct word or words from the choices in parentheses, and write them on your paper.

1. Several species of fish, especially catfish, (thrive, thrives) in the Mississippi River.
2. Commercial fishermen harvest (it, them) very successfully.
3. The flood plain in the delta area (form, forms) an extensive wetlands area.

4. (They are, It is) an important habitat for migratory birds.
5. Grains, soybeans, cotton, and rice (grow, grows) in the flood plains.
6. The rich soil from periods of erosion and deposition supports (it, them).
7. Coal, sand, gravel, and other bulk products (constitutes, constitute) the important cargoes that travel the river.
8. The region north of Saint Paul, due to (its, their) Falls of Saint Anthony, is not navigable.
9. Dams or locks have been built, so (they, it) provide a navigation channel from Saint Paul to St. Louis.
10. St. Louis, near the junction of the Missouri River, (link, links) the Mississippi with the Great Plains.

Exercise D **Using Modifiers** Write the form of the adjective or adverb indicated in parentheses.

1. The Missouri River is the Mississippi's (long—superlative) tributary.
2. (Initially—positive), the Mississippi River begins at Lake Itasca in Minnesota.
3. There, it is (only—positive) twelve feet wide and (barely—positive) two feet deep.
4. Much of the river is now (navigable—comparative) than before due to dredging and engineering efforts.
5. There are now (few—comparative) hazards for large vessels.
6. Barge traffic increased (steadily—positive) during the twentieth century.
7. At the delta area, the river splits into (small—comparative) channels called distributaries before entering the gulf.
8. The Mississippi River system is the (large—superlative) drainage system in North America.
9. There is a (vast—positive) network of levees built to limit the river's flooding.
10. However, there is concern that the levees may have caused (great—comparative) damage in 1993.

Exercise E **Revising Sentences to Eliminate Usage Errors** Rewrite the following sentences, correcting any usage errors.

1. The Monongahela River and the Allegheny River joins together at Pittsburgh, forming the Ohio River.
2. It provides slightly fewer than half of the Mississippi River's water.
3. The Ohio River winds southeast where they borders on five different states.
4. Cities like Pittsburgh, Cincinnati, and Louisville lay alongside the river.
5. They owed much of their growth to it proximity.
6. Now, there was little shipping conducted out of these cities.
7. Currently, bulk products like coal are just shipped on the Ohio River.
8. A series of thirteenth dams and locks ensure the passage of commercial vessels.
9. The products are loaded onto barges, which carry it to nearby electric plants along the river.
10. The river is frequented by local residents whom use it for recreational activities.

Exercise F **Writing Application**

Write a short description of a trip you have taken on or near a body of water. Be sure that the words in your sentences follow the rules of agreement and that your modifiers are used correctly. Then, list your verbs and verb phrases, identifying their tense. Make a list of the personal pronouns, and label the case of each one.

Exercise D

1. longest
2. Initially
3. only, barely
4. more navigable
5. fewer
6. steadily
7. smaller
8. largest
9. vast
10. greater

Exercise E

1. The Monongahela River and the Allegheny River join at Pittsburgh, forming the Ohio River.
2. The Ohio provides slightly less than half of the Mississippi River's water.
3. The Ohio River winds southeast where it borders on five different states.
4. Cities like Pittsburgh, Cincinnati, and Louisville lie alongside the river.
5. They owe much of their growth to its proximity.
6. Now there is little shipping conducted from these cities.
7. Currently, bulk products like coal are shipped just on the Ohio River.
8. A series of thirteen dams and locks ensures the passage of commercial vessels.
9. The products are loaded onto barges, which carry them to nearby electric plants along the river.
10. The river is frequented by local residents who use it for recreational activities.

Exercise F

Ask volunteers to list some of their verbs, tenses, and cases on the board and have the class check them for accuracy.

Chapter 26 Time and Resource Manager

In-Depth Lesson Plan

	LESSON FOCUS	PRINT AND MEDIA RESOURCES
DAY 1	**End Punctuation** Students learn to use periods, question marks, and exclamation marks at the ends of sentences (pp. 596–599).	**Teaching Resources** *Grammar Exercise Workbook,* pp. 163–164; *Grammar Exercises Answers on Transparencies,* Ch. 26 ***Writing and Grammar iText* (Interactive Text),** Section 26.1
DAY 2	**Commas** Students learn to use commas between clauses, in series, with adjectives, after introductory and parenthetical phrases, with dates and geographical names, and in letters (pp. 600–609).	**Teaching Resources** *Grammar Exercise Workbook,* pp. 165–172; *Grammar Exercises Answers on Transparencies,* Ch. 26 ***Writing and Grammar iText* (Interactive Text),** Section 26.2
DAY 3	**Other Punctuation Marks** Students review semicolons and colons, the proper format for the titles of works, and quotation marks (pp. 610–622).	**Teaching Resources** *Grammar Exercise Workbook,* pp. 173–182; *Grammar Exercises Answers on Transparencies,* Ch. 26 ***Writing and Grammar iText* (Interactive Text),** Sections 26.3–4
DAY 4	**Hyphens and Apostrophes** Students work with hyphens and apostrophes. They also complete a Hands-on Grammar activity (pp. 623–631).	**Teaching Resources** *Grammar Exercise Workbook,* pp. 183–188; *Grammar Exercises Answers on Transparencies,* Ch. 26; *Hands-on Grammar Activity Book,* Ch. 26 ***Writing and Grammar iText* (Interactive Text),** Section 26.5
DAY 5	**Review and Assess** Students review the chapter and demonstrate mastery of punctuation marks (pp. 632–635).	**Teaching Resources** *Formal Assessment,* Ch. 26; *Grammar Exercises Answers on Transparencies,* Ch. 26 ***Writing and Grammar iText* (Interactive Text),** Ch. 26, Chapter Review

Accelerated Lesson Plan

	LESSON FOCUS	PRINT AND MEDIA RESOURCES
DAY 1	**End Punctuation and Commas** Students review the use of periods, question marks, and exclamation points (pp. 596–599) and of commas (pp. 600–609).	**Teaching Resources** *Grammar Exercise Workbook,* pp. 163–172; *Grammar Exercises Answers on Transparencies,* Ch. 26 ***Writing and Grammar iText* (Interactive Text),** Section 26.1–2
DAY 2	**Other Punctuation Marks** Students review semicolons and colons, the proper format for the titles of works, quotation marks, and hyphens and apostrophes (pp. 610–631).	**Teaching Resources** *Grammar Exercise Workbook,* pp. 173–188; *Grammar Exercises Answers on Transparencies,* Ch. 26; *Hands-on Grammar Activity Book,* Ch. 26 ***Writing and Grammar iText* (Interactive Text),** Sections 26.3–5
DAY 3	**Review and Assess** Students review the chapter and demonstrate mastery of punctuation marks (pp. 632–635).	**Teaching Resources** *Formal Assessment,* Ch. 26; *Grammar Exercises Answers on Transparencies,* Ch. 26 ***Writing and Grammar iText* (Interactive Text),** Ch. 26, Chapter Review; ***On-line Exercise Bank,*** Sections 26.1–5

Options for Adapting Lesson Plans

HOMEWORK

Have students complete any stage of the lesson for homework.

SPELLING

To teach spelling skills in conjunction with grammar, mechanics, and usage, work through *Prentice Hall Everyday Spelling,* Grade 8, Chapter 31, as you cover this *Writing and Grammar* chapter.

TECHNOLOGY

Students can use *Writing and Grammar iText* to complete the exercises interactively on computer. They can complete additional exercises in the *On-Line Exercise Bank:* The Auto Check feature will grade their work. Go on-line: PHSchool.com Use Web Code: eck-8002

INTEGRATED SKILLS COVERAGE

Grammar in Literature
SE p. 611

Writing
Find It in Your Writing, SE pp. 599, 609, 613, 622, 630, 631
Writing Application, SE pp. 599, 609, 613, 622, 631, 633

Viewing and Representing
Critical Viewing, SE pp. 594, 597, 601, 602, 605, 607, 611, 615, 616, 618, 621, 623, 626

Speaking and Listening
Reading Aloud, ATE p. 603

Vocabulary
Varying Verbs, ATE p. 618

Real-World Connection
ATE pp. 619, 620

ASSESSMENT SUPPORT

Standardized Test Preparation Workshop, SE pp. 634–635; ATE p. 606

Standardized Test Preparation Workbook, pp. 51–52

Formal Assessment, Ch. 26

MEETING INDIVIDUAL NEEDS

Less Advanced Students ATE p. 615. See Ongoing Assessments ATE pp. 598, 602, 607, 608, 612, 617, 618, 620, 621, 625, 628, 630.

ESL Students ATE pp. 598, 606

More Advanced Students ATE p. 604

BLOCK SCHEDULING

Pacing Suggestions
For 90-minute Blocks
- Administer the Diagnostic Test to students to determine instructional coverage.
- Have students complete the necessary exercises in class. Use the Hands-on Grammar Activity to provide a change of pace.

Resources for Varying Instruction
- ***Writing and Grammar iText* (Interactive Text)** A 90-minute block provides an ideal opportunity for students to work on computer.

Professional Development Support
- ***How to Manage Instruction in the Block*** This teaching resource provides management and activity suggestions.

MEDIA AND TECHNOLOGY

For the Student
- ***Writing and Grammar iText* (Interactive Text),** Ch. 26
- ***On-line Exercise Bank,*** Sections 26.1–5

For the Teacher
- ***Resource Pro* CD-ROM**

WRITING AND GRAMMAR ON-LINE

iText Interactive Text (On-line or on CD-ROM)
- Easily navigable instruction with on-line supporting resources
- Self-scoring exercises and diagnostic tests

Companion Web Site PHSchool.com
- On-line Exercise Bank (use Web Code eck-8002)

See the Go On-line! feature, SE p. iii.

CHAPTER 26
PUNCTUATION

Lesson Objectives

1. To understand the correct usage of end marks, including periods, question marks, and exclamation points.
2. To understand the correct usage of commas, semicolons, and colons.
3. To understand the correct usage of quotation marks, underlining, and italics.
4. To understand the correct usage of hyphens and apostrophes.
5. To capitalize and punctuate correctly to clarify and enhance meaning such as capitalizing titles, using hyphens, semicolons, colons, possessives, and sentence punctuation.
6. To write with increasing accuracy when using apostrophes in contractions and possessives.

Critical Viewing

Analyze Students should be encouraged to use different end punctuation marks. For example, Do you think this coyote pup is cute? I would really like to photograph it. I wouldn't want to be too close!

Chapter 26 Punctuation

Punctuation marks act as signals to readers. They tell readers when to pause or stop, when to read with a questioning tone, and when to read with excitement. Punctuation marks also connect ideas or set ideas apart. **Punctuation** is a commonly accepted set of symbols used to convey specific directions to the reader. This chapter will help you become more familiar with punctuation marks and the rules for using them.

▲ Critical Viewing How would you describe this photograph of a coyote pup? Write a three-sentence description. Then, review the punctuation marks you used. **[Analyze]**

ONGOING ASSESSMENT: Diagnose

If students miss more than one item in each category, direct them to the relevant pages of the text and assign exercises for practice and review.

Punctuation	Diagnostic Test Items	Teach	Practice	Section Review	Chapter Review
Skill Check A					
End Marks	A 1–5	pp. 596–598	Ex. 1–3	Ex. 4–7	Ex. 57
Skill Check B					
Commas, Colons, and Semicolons	B 6–10	pp. 600–612	Ex. 11–18, 25–26	Ex. 19–21, 27–29	Ex. 57–59

Diagnostic Test

Directions: Write all answers on a separate sheet of paper.

Skill Check A. Write the end marks that belong in the following sentences.

1. What factors are responsible for the temperature of a desert
2. I read that latitude and longitude determine temperature
3. Wow some deserts are *so* hot
4. Weren't you surprised to learn that the base elevation of the Great Basin Desert is as high as many mountains
5. The Sonoran Desert has a low base elevation, and it is the warmest desert in the United States

Skill Check B. Copy the following sentences, adding commas, colons, and semicolons where needed.

6. The Mojave Desert has the lowest elevation but its latitude is relatively high.
7. The Sonoran Desert is south of the Mojave but the Mojave has lower average temperatures.
8. The elevation of the Great Basin Desert is almost 5000 feet at its lowest point.
9. Generally high temperatures and a lack of water make desert air drier this affects our perception of the actual temperature.
10. Arizona's heat is drier than the moist heat of some other areas Florida Georgia and Washington D.C.

Skill Check C. Copy the following sentences, adding quotation marks, commas, end punctuation, and underlining where needed. If the sentence needs no added punctuation, write *correct*.

11. Wasn't there a television program about the Mojave Desert asked Anne.
12. Yes answered Martha It was called Death Valley Days.
13. Anne remembered that the program was hosted by former President Ronald Reagan.
14. I think said Martha the space shuttle landed in the desert
15. Anne asked Wasn't there a movie called Death Valley that was filmed in Death Valley

Skill Check D. Copy the following sentences, adding hyphens and apostrophes where needed.

16. Desert animals survival is related to special behavior and physical features.
17. By midmorning, most desert animals have found shelter from the all powerful heat.
18. In the southwestern deserts sprawl, the coyotes dig their own dens or enlarge the dens of smaller animals.
19. The coyotes sense of smell is excellent.
20. The coyote senses its prey and then stalks it for almost 35 minutes before pouncing.

ONGOING ASSESSMENT: Diagnose *continued*

Punctuation	Diagnostic Test Items	Teach	Practice	Section Review	Chapter Review
Skill Check C					
Quotation Marks, Commas, End Punctuation, and Underlining	C 11–15	pp. 614–621	Ex. 33–38	Ex. 39–41	Ex. 57–60
Skill Check D					
Hyphens and Apostrophes	D 16–20	pp. 623–629	Ex. 45–50	Ex. 51–53	Ex. 61–63
Cumulative Reviews and Applications				Ex. 8–10 Ex. 22–24 Ex. 30–32 Ex. 42–44 Ex. 54–56	Ex. 64–65

Answer Key

Diagnostic Test

- Each item in the diagnostic test corresponds to a specific concept in the chapter on punctuation. This will enable you to tailor instruction to the particular needs of your students. See "Ongoing Assessment: Diagnose" on the bottom of pages 594–595 for further details.
- Answers for the Diagnostic Test and all chapter exercises are available in *Grammar Exercise Answers on Transparencies* in your teaching resources.

Skill Check A

1. ?
2. .
3. !
4. ?
5. .

Skill Check B

6. elevation, but
7. Mojave, but
8. 5,000
9. Generally, drier; this
10. areas: Florida, Georgia, or Washington, D.C.

Skill Check C

11. "Wasn't there a television program about the Mojave Desert?" asked Anne.
12. "Yes," answered Martha. "It was called <u>Death Valley Days</u>."
13. correct
14. "I think," said Martha, "the space shuttle landed in the desert."
15. Anne asked, "Wasn't there a movie called <u>Death Valley</u> that was filmed in Death Valley?"

Skill Check D

16. Desert animals' survival is related to special behavior and physical features.
17. By midmorning, most desert animals have found shelter from the all-powerful heat.
18. In the southwestern desert's sprawl, the coyotes dig their own dens or enlarge the dens of smaller animals.
19. The coyote's sense of smell is excellent.
20. The coyote senses its prey and then stalks it for almost 35 minutes before pouncing.

PREPARE and ENGAGE

Interest GRABBER Write the following sentences on the chalkboard:

Pythons live in Africa, Asia, Australia, and the South Pacific islands

Did you know they can grow to more than 30 feet long

That's scary

Ask students what is wrong with these sentences (They are missing end punctuation). Have students add the correct punctuation.

Activate Prior Knowledge

Ask students to suggest a declarative sentence, a question, and an exclamation about big, scary snakes. Ask volunteers to write and punctuate these sentences.

TEACH

Step-by-Step Teaching Guide

End Marks

1. The period has two basic uses: to end most sentences and to end most abbreviations.
2. Review each of the four sentence types: statements of fact, opinion, direct command, and indirect quotation. Tell students that most sentences end in a period, the exceptions being interrogatory sentences and exclamations.
3. Review that a period is *not* used following U.S. Postal Service abbreviations for states.

MA	*Mass.*	*Massachusetts*
CA	*Calif.*	*California*

Students can use an almanac or Web site to produce a chart with the names of all fifty states and the two-letter abbreviations for them.

Answer Key

Exercise 1

1. A. V.
2. deserts.
3. correct
4. pressure.
5. correct
6. Mr., Mrs., St., Mo.
7. correct
8. correct
9. correct
10. Calif.

Section 26.1

End Marks

End marks signal the end or conclusion of a sentence, word, or phrase. There are three end marks: the period (.), the question mark (?), and the exclamation mark (!).

Theme: Deserts

In this section, you will learn about the proper use of periods, question marks, and exclamation marks. The examples and exercises are about deserts.

Cross-Curricular Connection: Geography

Using Periods

The period is the most frequently used of all the end marks.

KEY CONCEPT Use a period to end a declarative sentence, a mild imperative, or an indirect question. ■

A *declarative sentence* is a statement of fact or opinion. An *imperative sentence* is a direction or command. An *indirect question* restates a question in a declarative sentence.

STATEMENT OF FACT:	Death Valley is the lowest point in the Western Hemisphere.
STATEMENT OF OPINION:	This is a beautiful park.
DIRECTION:	Turn left at the next intersection.
COMMAND:	Come here.
INDIRECT QUESTION:	Jackie asked what time it was.

KEY CONCEPT Use a period to end most abbreviations. ■

INITIALS:	L. J. Fergusson			
TITLES:	Mr.	Mrs.	Dr.	Gen.
PLACE NAMES:	St.	Mt.	Calif.	Mass.

When a sentence ends with an abbreviation that makes use of a period, it is not necessary to put a second period at the end.

iText

Get instant feedback! Exercise 1 is available on-line or on CD-ROM.

Exercise 1 **Supplying Periods to Sentences** Copy each of the sentences below, adding periods as needed. If the sentence is correct, write *correct.*

1. A V Humboldt helped to develop geography as a science.
2. Today, one wonders how geographers categorize deserts
3. He asked how deserts form.
4. Some develop in regions of persistent high atmospheric pressure
5. Some form behind large mountain ranges.
6. During their cross-country drive, Mr and Mrs Lynch stopped in St Louis, Mo, as they drove west.
7. They also drove through the Mojave Desert in California.
8. The Lynches found the desert beautiful.
9. They wondered how it would be to live there year round.
10. Next year, they plan on visiting Death Valley, Calif

More Practice

Grammar Exercise Workbook
- pp. 163–164

On-line Exercise Bank
- Section 26.1

Go on-line: PHSchool.com *Enter Web Code:* eck-8002

TIME AND RESOURCE MANAGER

Resources
Print: Grammar Exercise Workbook, pp. 163–164
Technology: Writing and Grammar iText, Section 26.1; On-Line Exercise Bank, Section 26.1

In-Depth Coverage	Accelerated Pace
• Work through all key concepts, pp. 596–598. • Assign and review Exercises 1–3.	• Assign pp. 596–598 for independent student review. • Assign Section Review Exercises 4–6.

Using Question Marks

KEY CONCEPT Use a question mark to end an interrogative sentence—a direct question. ■

INTERROGATIVE SENTENCES: Where are you staying in the desert?
Was there a valid reason for her absence?

Do not confuse an interrogative sentence, which is a direct question, with an indirect question. An indirect question requires no answer and should end with a period.

Sometimes a single word or phrase is used to ask a question. Use a question mark to end an incomplete question in which the rest of the question is understood.

EXAMPLE: Of course, I will meet you. When?

A question that shows surprise is sometimes phrased as a declarative sentence. Use a question mark to indicate that the sentence is a question.

KEY CONCEPT Use a question mark to end a statement that is intended as a question. ■

EXAMPLES: There is no electricity?
You invited him for dinner?

▲ **Critical Viewing** Write three to five questions you would like answered about the cactus in this photograph. Be sure to use question marks correctly. **[Analyze]**

Exercise 2 **Supplying Question Marks and Periods** Each of the following sentences is either a direct question, an indirect question, or a statement intended as a question. Copy each sentence onto your paper, adding the correct end mark.

EXAMPLE: How are deserts formed
ANSWER: How are deserts formed?

1. I just had to ask why deserts are hot and dry
2. Don't deserts form in areas of high atmospheric pressure
3. Deserts are formed because of large-scale climatic patterns
4. Why might deserts form behind mountain ranges
5. Mountain ranges create a rain shadow effect Where did you learn that

More Practice

Grammar Exercise Workbook
- pp. 163–164

On-line Exercise Bank
- Section 26.1

Go on-line: PHSchool.com
Enter Web Code: eck-8002

Step-by-Step Teaching Guide

Using Question Marks

1. A question mark ends a direct question or a statement intended as a question.
2. Write the following examples on the board and ask students to identify each as a direct or indirect question and supply the correct punctuation.

   She wants to know what the question is (. indirect)

   What is the question (? direct)

   Why are you going (? direct)

   I need to know why you are going (. indirect)

Critical Viewing

Analyze Students may suggest questions like these:

Where do these plants grow? Do they have a name? Could I grow them in my yard?

Answer Key

Exercise 2

1. I just had to ask why deserts are hot and dry.
2. Don't deserts form in areas of high atmospheric pressure?
3. Deserts are formed because of large-scale climatic patterns.
4. Why might deserts form behind mountain ranges?
5. Mountain ranges create a rain shadow effect. Where did you learn that?

TIME SAVERS!

Answers on Transparency Use the Grammar Exercises Answers on Transparencies for Chapter 26 to have students correct their own or one another's exercises.

On-Line Exercise Bank Have students complete the exercises on computer. The Auto Check feature will grade their work for you!

Step-by-Step Teaching Guide

Using Exclamation Marks

1. An exclamation mark ends a statement showing strong emotion. Both strong commands and exclamatory statements require an exclamation mark.
2. Review the situations requiring usage of an exclamation mark. To illustrate the danger of overuse of exclamation marks, write the following on the chalkboard:

   Run! Get moving! Way to go! Wow! You did it! Fantastic!
3. Write the following sentences on the board. Ask students to punctuate and tell why each requires an exclamation mark.

   Oh no (! interjection) I really did it (! exclamation)

   Stop right now (! urgent command)

Answer Key

Exercise 3

1. I *hate* being lost in a desert! exclamatory sentence
2. I want water! exclamatory sentence
3. Yippee! It's going to rain! interjection, exclamatory sentence
4. Oh, no! It's a flash flood! interjection, exclamatory sentence
5. Get to high ground! imperative sentence
6. Hurry! The water is rising quickly. imperative sentence, declarative sentence
7. That was close! exclamatory sentence
8. What a frightening sight that is! exclamatory sentence
9. Whew! Let's go home! interjection, imperative sentence
10. I can't wait to tell my friends! exclamatory sentence

Customize for *ESL Students*

Spanish uses question and exclamation marks before and after the sentence. In English, these marks appear only once, at the end.

26.1

Using Exclamation Marks

KEY CONCEPT Use an exclamation mark to end an exclamatory sentence—a statement showing strong emotion. ■

EXAMPLES: I finally understand the problem!
That was a terrifying experience!

The exclamation mark may also be used to end an urgent imperative sentence.

KEY CONCEPT Use an exclamation mark after an imperative sentence if the command is urgent and forceful. ■

EXAMPLE: Run for your life!

In addition, an exclamation mark often follows an interjection.

KEY CONCEPT Use an exclamation mark after an interjection expressing strong emotion. ■

EXAMPLE: Oh! You've ruined the surprise!

Note About *Using Exclamation Marks*: Exclamation marks should not be used too often. Overusing them makes writing too emotional and less effective.

Exercise 3 **Supplying Exclamation Marks to Sentences** Copy the items below, adding exclamation marks as needed. Then, label each item an *exclamatory sentence*, an *imperative sentence*, or an *interjection*.

EXAMPLE: I am *hot*
ANSWER: I am *hot!* (exclamatory sentence)

1. I *hate* being lost in a desert
2. I want water
3. Yippee It's going to rain.
4. Oh, no It's a flash flood
5. Get to high ground
6. Hurry The water is rising quickly
7. That was close
8. What a frightening sight that is
9. Whew Let's go home
10. I can't wait to tell my friends

More Practice

Grammar Exercise Workbook
- pp. 163–164

On-line Exercise Bank
- Section 26.1

Go on-line: PHSchool.com
Enter Web Code: eck-8002

ONGOING ASSESSMENT: Monitor and Reinforce

If students miss more than two items in Exercises 1–3, refer them to the following for additional practice.

In the Textbook	Print Resources	Technology
Chapter Review, Ex. 57, p. 632	Grammar Exercise Workbook, pp. 163–164	On-Line Exercise Bank, Section 26.1

Section 26.1 Section Review

GRAMMAR EXERCISES 4–10

Exercise 4 **Supplying Periods and Question Marks** Copy each of the sentences below, adding the correct punctuation mark.

1. What does a desert look like
2. Isn't a desert mostly a barren area of rock, soil, and sand
3. Luella asked if the nights were cool
4. Is it true that we can get lost in the desert
5. You will take your camera

Exercise 5 **Revising Sentences Using the Exclamation Mark** Copy each of the following items, adding exclamation marks as needed. Label each an *exclamatory sentence*, an *imperative sentence*, or an *interjection*.

1. The desert is beautiful
2. Man Is it hot
3. What You didn't bring water
4. I have got to find water
5. Wow See all that blowing sand

Exercise 6 **Supplying End Marks** Copy the following items, adding the correct end marks.

1. How would you describe a desert
2. Hot *Very* hot
3. Are you sure of your answer
4. Were you aware that not all regions defined as deserts are in warm climates
5. Imagine Deserts can be found in some regions of the North and South poles
6. They are called deserts because moisture freezes and plant life cannot grow
7. I must ask whether you would like to learn more about these frozen deserts
8. Well, use library resources to answer all your questions
9. Good luck
10. Tom wondered where he could find books

Exercise 7 **Proofreading for End Marks in a Paragraph** Copy the following paragraph on a separate sheet of paper, revising end marks where necessary. (Some sentences are correct as is.)

The Sahara is the largest desert in the world. Wow It's even larger than the United States? Did you know that not all of the Sahara is dry wasteland. There are lush oases scattered throughout the region? Are these areas inhabited! You bet.

Exercise 8 **Find It in Your Reading** Find a magazine or encyclopedia article on desert life. Locate sentences ending with a period, with a question mark, or with an exclamation point. Find three examples of each. Explain why the author uses each.

Exercise 9 **Find It in Your Writing** Look through your portfolio, and find examples of sentences ending with a period, a question mark, and an exclamation point. Explain why you used each mark.

Exercise 10 **Writing Application** Write a brief paragraph about a landform or landmark that has impressed you. Include a variety of sentence types and use end marks correctly. Then, label each sentence *declarative*, *imperative*, *indirect*, *interrogative*, or *exclamatory*.

ASSESS and CLOSE

Section Review

Each of these exercises correlates to a concept in the section on end marks, pages 596–598. These exercises may be used for more practice, for reteaching, or for review of the Key Concepts presented. Answers for all chapter exercises are available in *Grammar Exercises Answers on Transparencies* in your teaching resources.

Answer Key

Exercise 4

1. What does a desert look like?
2. Isn't a desert mostly a barren area of rock, soil, and sand?
3. Luella asked if the nights were cool.
4. Is it true that we can get lost in the desert?
5. You will take your camera.

Exercise 5

1. The desert is beautiful! exclamatory sentence
2. Man! Is it hot! interjection, exclamatory sentence
3. What! You didn't bring water! interjection, exclamatory sentence
4. I have got to find water! exclamatory sentence
5. Wow! See all that blowing sand! interjection, imperative sentence

Exercise 6

1. How would you describe a desert?
2. Hot! Very hot!
3. Are you sure of your answer?
4. Were you aware that not all regions defined as deserts are in warm climates?
5. Imagine! Deserts can be found in some regions of the North and South poles.
6. They are called deserts because moisture freezes and plant life cannot grow.
7. I must ask whether you would like to learn more about these frozen deserts.
8. Well, use library resources to answer all your questions.
9. Good luck!
10. Tom wondered where he could find books.

continued

Answer Key continued

Exercise 7

The Sahara is the largest desert in the world. Wow! It's even larger than the United States. Did you know that not all of the Sahara is dry wasteland? There are lush oases scattered throughout the region. Are these areas inhabited? You bet!

Exercise 8

Find It in Your Reading
Ask students why they think they found question marks and exclamation points in magazines but not (or rarely) in encyclopedias.

Exercise 9

Find It in Your Writing
Students can explain to a partner why they used each end mark.

Exercise 10

Writing Application
Students may want to use books or the Internet to find details about their topic.

PREPARE and ENGAGE

Interest GRABBER Write the following sentence on the board and ask students to provide the missing commas.

In the beginning Henry LaShonda Steve the kid next door the brilliant but boastful Gail from Buffalo New York and Luis all remembered their lines. (In the beginning, Henry, LaShonda, Steve, the kid next door, the brilliant but boastful Gail from Buffalo, New York, and Luis all remembered their lines.)

Activate Prior Knowledge

Ask students to explain in their own words when they use commas. (Possible responses: to separate a list; to separate different parts of a sentence, with *and* or *but;* in dates; between city and state)

TEACH

Step-by-Step Teaching Guide

Commas

1. Use commas to separate the independent clauses of a compound sentence. Follow the comma by a coordinating conjunction, such as *and, but,* or *or.*
2. Students should not take this as a rule that a comma always precedes a coordinating conjunction.

   Do you want pizza or a sandwich?

   I like cats and dogs.

Answer Key

Exercise 11

1. The Thar Desert spans India and Pakistan, and it is one of the world's harshest areas.
2. correct
3. You can take a bus tour, or you can join a camel safari.
4. correct
5. You won't be disappointed, nor will you ever forget your visit.

Section 26.2

Commas

A *comma* (,) in a sentence signals the reader to pause briefly. Often, writers either neglect commas or overuse them. If you use a comma only when you have a specific rule in mind, your writing will be smoother and clearer.

Using Commas With Compound Sentences

A compound sentence consists of two or more independent clauses that are joined by a coordinating conjunction, such as *and, but, for, nor, or, so,* or *yet.*

KEY CONCEPT Use a comma before the conjunction to separate two independent clauses in a compound sentence. ■

COMPOUND SENTENCES: The Thar Desert has little rain or vegetation, and the herders must collect the leaves from the tops of trees for their flocks.

Use a comma before a conjunction only when there are complete sentences on both sides of the conjunction. If the conjunction joins single words, phrases, or subordinate clauses, do not use a comma.

SINGLE WORDS: **Heat and sand are common desert features.**

PHRASES: Deserts are found north and south of the equator.

SUBORDINATE CLAUSES: They have decided that you should study more and that you should watch less television.

Exercise 11 **Revising Compound Sentences Using Commas** Rewrite the sentences below, inserting commas where they are needed. If no comma is needed, write *correct.*

EXAMPLE: Clouds appeared but there was no rain.

ANSWER: Clouds appeared, but there was no rain.

1. The Thar Desert spans India and Pakistan and it is one of the world's harshest areas.
2. However, a rich desert culture and colorful people can be found in the Thar.
3. You can take a bus tour or you can join a camel safari.
4. You'll have a great time visiting the villages and exploring the markets.
5. You won't be disappointed nor will you ever forget your visit.

Theme: Deserts

In this section, you will learn the many uses of commas. The examples and exercises are about deserts.

Cross-Curricular Connection: Geography

iText

Get instant feedback! Exercise 11 is available on-line or on CD-ROM.

More Practice

Grammar Exercise Workbook
- pp. 165–166

On-line Exercise Bank
- Section 26.2

Go on-line: PHSchool.com
Enter Web Code: eck-8002

TIME AND RESOURCE MANAGER

Resources
Print: Grammar Exercises Workbook, pp. 165–172
Technology: Writing and Grammar iText, Section 26.2; On-Line Exercise Bank, Section 26.2

In-Depth Coverage	Accelerated Pace
• Work through all key concepts, pp. 600–608. • Assign and review Exercises 11–18.	• Assign pp. 600–608 for independent student review. • Assign Section Review Exercises 19–21.

Using Commas Between Items in a Series

A series consists of three or more similar items.

KEY CONCEPT Use commas to separate three or more words, phrases, or clauses in a series. ■

Notice that the number of commas used is one fewer than the number of items in the series.

SERIES OF WORDS: The desert animals included *camels*, *toads*, *gerbils*, and *insects*.

SERIES OF PHRASES: The treasure map directed them *over the dunes*, *into the oasis*, and *past the palm tree*.

SERIES OF CLAUSES: The house was rather quiet *before she arrived*, *before her luggage was piled up in the hall*, and *before her three poodles took over*.

When each item is joined to the next by a conjunction, no commas are necessary.

EXAMPLE: For this journey, you will need two camels *and* a guide *and* a canteen.

A second exception to the rule concerns words that are considered to be one item.

EXAMPLE: Every table in the diner was set with *a knife and fork*, *a cup and saucer*, and *salt and pepper*.

▲ **Critical Viewing** Write a description of the rabbit in this photograph. Include at least one sentence using items in a series separated correctly with commas. **[Classify]**

Exercise 12 **Proofreading for Commas to Separate Items in a Series** Copy each of the following sentences onto your paper, adding commas as needed.

1. The surface of a desert may be covered with sand gravel or polished stones.
2. An oasis is a place where ground water pools plant growth flourishes and animals begin to feed.
3. The location of deserts is determined by ocean currents the location of mountains and prevailing wind patterns.
4. Most deserts are located near and between the Tropic of Cancer the equator and the Tropic of Capricorn.
5. The Gobi and the Takla Makan and the Kyzyl Kum are some Asian deserts.

More Practice

Grammar Exercise Workbook
- pp. 165–166

On-line Exercise Bank
- Section 26.2

Go on-line:
PHSchool.com
Enter Web Code:
eck-8002

Step-by-Step Teaching Guide

Commas Between Items in a Series

1. Separating items in a series with commas is a natural way to distinguish between the items. Read the following example first with no pauses or changes in inflections. Then read it as it is written, with a slight pause between the items in a series.

   The sky was a mix of blue, pink, yellow, and orange.

2. Review the different situations in which commas are used, seeing that students understand that the common thread is a series of like items—words, phrases, or clauses.
3. Students need to read sentences carefully to identify the different items.

   The breakfast choices are cereal and milk, bacon and eggs, or muffins and jam.

   This sentence would be grammatically correct as follows—but it would not be a very tasty meal!

   The breakfast choices are cereal, milk, bacon, eggs, muffins, or jam.

Critical Viewing

Classify Students may state that the rabbit has huge ears, large eyes, a fur coat, and a long nose.

Answer Key

Exercise 12

1. The surface of a desert may be covered with sand, gravel, or polished stones.
2. An oasis is a place where ground water pools, plant growth flourishes, and animals begin to feed.
3. The location of deserts is determined by ocean currents, the location of mountains, and prevailing wind patterns.
4. Most deserts are located near and between the Tropic of Cancer, the equator, and the Tropic of Capricorn.
5. correct

Step-by-Step Teaching Guide

Commas Between Adjectives

1. A comma is used to separate only adjectives of equal rank. When adjectives are used in a specific sequence, no comma is needed.
2. See that students understand the idea of adjectives of equal rank. One test is if the adjectives can be used in reverse order.

   You sent a sweet, kind note. (You sent a kind, sweet note.)
3. A comma should never come between an adjective and the noun it modifies: This can get tricky, so students need to read sentences carefully for sense: *Maura is a red-haired, green-eyed teenage girl.* Here, the adjectives *red-haired* and *green-eyed* modify *teenage girl.*

Answer Key

Exercise 13

1. The long, dry stretches of sand were mesmerizing.
2. Two small goats were grazing.
3. A large, threatening vulture circled overhead.
4. The white, fluffy clouds were an illusion.
5. The few hard rocks we found were cracked.

Critical Viewing

Analyze Students may state that the camel looks alert, amused, and ready-to-go.

26.2

Using Commas Between Adjectives

Sometimes, two or more adjectives are placed before the noun they describe. Use the following rule to determine whether to use a comma between them.

▲ **Critical Viewing** What adjectives come to mind when you look at this camel? Write a sentence using adjectives of equal rank separated by commas. **[Analyze]**

KEY CONCEPT Use commas to separate adjectives of *equal* rank. ■

If the word *and* can be placed between the adjectives without changing the meaning of the sentence, the adjectives are of equal rank. If the order of the adjectives can be changed, then they are of equal rank.

EXAMPLES: She left *detailed, precise* instructions for the substitute.
A *smooth, round* stone was cupped in her hand.

KEY CONCEPT *Do not* use commas to separate adjectives that must stay in a specific order. ■

In the following examples, you can see that either adding *and* or changing the order of the adjectives would result in a sentence that makes no sense.

EXAMPLES: *Three brief* hours will be enough to reach the mountains.
An *experienced desert* guide led us into the Sahara.

Note About *Commas With Adjectives:* Never use a comma to separate the last adjective in a series from the noun it modifies.

INCORRECT: A large, gentle-looking, camel sat by the road.
CORRECT: A large, gentle-looking camel sat by the road.

Exercise 13 **Supplying Commas Between Adjectives** Copy the following sentences onto your paper, adding commas between the underlined adjectives as needed.

1. The long dry stretches of sand were mesmerizing.
2. Two small goats were grazing.
3. A large threatening vulture circled overhead.
4. The white fluffy clouds were an illusion.
5. The few hard rocks we found were cracked.

More Practice

Grammar Exercise Workbook
• pp. 165–166
On-line Exercise Bank
• Section 26.2
Go on-line:
PHSchool.com
Enter Web Code:
eck-8002

TIME SAVERS!

Answers on Transparency Use the Grammar Exercises Answers on Transparencies for Chapter 26 to have students correct their own or one another's exercises.

On-Line Exercise Bank Have students complete the exercises on computer. The Auto Check feature will grade their work for you!

ONGOING ASSESSMENT: Monitor and Reinforce

If students miss more than two items in Exercises 11–13, refer them to the following for additional practice.

In the Textbook	Print Resources	Technology
Chapter Review, Ex. 57–58, p. 632	Grammar Exercise Workbook, pp. 165–166	On-Line Exercise Bank, Section 26.2

Using Commas After Introductory Material

Commas are often used to set off information at the beginning of a sentence.

KEY CONCEPT Use a comma after most introductory words, phrases, or clauses. ■

KINDS OF INTRODUCTORY MATERIAL	
Introductory Words	*No,* we don't need any. *Hey,* give me your camera quickly before the kangaroo rat moves. *Smiling,* the flight attendant greeted the passengers.
Introductory Phrases	*Storing water in their roots,* succulent desert plants survive dry periods. *Protected by thorns,* other plants keep their water supply from animals. *To conserve water,* some plants drop their leaves.
Introductory Adverb Clauses	*When the wind blows constantly,* rocks are eroded into unusual shapes. *Although the alarm had gone off,* the police arrived too late.

Exercise 14 Using Commas After Introductory Material For the sentences below, write the introductory word or words, the comma, and the word following the comma.

EXAMPLE: Shocked you see a huge spider with long, hairy legs.
ANSWER: Shocked, you

1. Fearsome looking the desert tarantula is three inches long.
2. Shrinking back you might think it will jump and bite you.
3. However they can jump only a few inches.
4. For the most part they are harmless creatures.
5. Even if you are bitten the venom is not fatal.
6. When attacked the tarantula will raise its front legs.
7. Looking for a meal desert tarantulas often feed on lizards.
8. Although desert tarantulas are large the largest tarantulas live in South America.
9. Known as bird eaters they often have ten-inch leg spans.
10. The largest spiders in the world they are known to attack small birds.

More Practice

Grammar Exercise Workbook
- pp. 167–168

On-line Exercise Bank
- Section 26.2

Go on-line: PHSchool.com
Enter Web Code: eck-8002

iText

Get instant feedback! Exercise 14 is available on-line or on CD-ROM.

Step-by-Step Teaching Guide

Commas After Introductory Material

1. Commas are used after three types of introductory material: words, phrases, and adverbial clauses. Review the chart on the page with students.
2. Read aloud the sentences for introductory words, pausing at the comma. Follow with the phrase and adverb clause sentences.

Integrating Speaking/Listening Skills

Have students work in pairs. One student reads aloud a paragraph of a newspaper article while the partner writes it down, paying particular attention to the use of commas. Readers should read slowly and distinctly but take care not to overly exaggerate pauses.

Answer Key

Exercise 14

1. Fearsome looking, the
2. Shrinking back, you
3. However, they
4. For the most part, they
5. Even if you are bitten, the
6. When attacked, the
7. Looking for a meal, desert
8. Although desert tarantulas are large, the
9. Known as bird eaters, they
10. The largest spiders in the world, they

Step-by-Step Teaching Guide

Commas with Parenthetical Expressions

1. Commas are used to set off parenthetical expressions—words or phrases not essential to the meaning of a sentence. The best way to identify a parenthetical expression is to omit it and read the sentence. The sentence retains its meaning.
2. Have volunteers read the sentences with names of people being addressed, first as written and then with the names omitted. Point out how the parenthetical expression is not essential to the meaning but just adds detail to the sentence.
3. Adverbs such as *therefore, however,* and *thus* are set off by commas.
4. Common expressions such as *I think, of course,* and the ubiquitous and dreaded *you know* are set off by commas. Oral reading of the sentences will demonstrate how the comma sets the expression off from the rest of the sentence.
5. Read the contrasting expressions and the sentences aloud so students can hear how these are set off from the rest of the sentence.

Customizing for *More Advanced Students*

Have students review a selection from their portfolio for use of commas with parenthetical expressions and introductory material. If they do not find any, have them write a short paragraph in which they use each type of parenthetical expressions shown on this page.

26.2

Using Commas With Parenthetical Expressions

A *parenthetical expression* is a word or phrase that is not essential to the meaning of the sentence.

KEY CONCEPT Use commas to set off parenthetical expressions. ■

A parenthetical expression in the middle of a sentence needs two commas. A parenthetical expression at the end of a sentence needs only one.

KINDS OF PARENTHETICAL EXPRESSIONS	
Names of People Being Addressed	Listen carefully, *Bob and Lucinda,* while I explain. That's a logical conclusion, *Pete.*
Certain Adverbs	The other sand dune, *therefore,* is several meters higher. Roberta will not be able to go with us, *however.*
Common Expressions	The sand, *I think,* is scarce on Peruvian deserts. They believe in her ability, *of course.*
Contrasting Expressions	These dunes, *not those,* resemble crescents. The decision should be mine, *not yours.*

Exercise 15 **Proofreading Sentences for Commas With Parenthetical Expressions** Copy the following sentences on a separate sheet of paper, adding commas as needed to set off the parenthetical expressions.

1. The position of Earth's deserts is explainable not accidental.
2. Without a doubt Jason Earth's tilt on its axis contributes to the desert climates.
3. Different areas of Earth as we know are angled toward the sun at specific times each year.
4. The same areas of course do not receive as much sunlight at other times.
5. This tilt of Earth therefore causes the four seasons.

iText

Get instant feedback! Exercise 15 is available on-line or on CD-ROM.

More Practice

Grammar Exercise Workbook
- pp. 167–168

On-line Exercise Bank
- Section 26.2

Go on-line: PHSchool.com
Enter Web Code: eck-8002

Answer Key

Exercise 15

1. The position of Earth's deserts is explainable, not accidental.
2. Without a doubt, Jason, Earth's tilt on its axis contributes to the desert climates.
3. Different areas of Earth, as we know, are angled toward the sun at specific times each year.
4. The same areas, of course, do not receive as much sunlight at other times.
5. This tilt of Earth, therefore, causes the four seasons.

Using Commas With Nonessential Expressions

To determine when a phrase or clause should be set off with commas, decide whether the phrase or clause is *essential* or *nonessential* to the meaning of the sentence.

KEY CONCEPT Use commas to set off nonessential expressions. ■

Appositives and Appositive Phrases

ESSENTIAL: The 1943 movie *Sahara* takes place in North Africa.

NONESSENTIAL: *Sahara*, a 1943 movie, takes place in North Africa.

Participial Phrases

ESSENTIAL: The man *waiting in the van* is our guide.

NONESSENTIAL: Pat, *waiting in the van*, asked us to hurry.

Adjective Clauses

ESSENTIAL: We need someone *who can lead us to the oasis.*

NONESSENTIAL: We cheered enthusiastically for Darius, *who could lead us to the oasis.*

▼ Critical Viewing
Compare and contrast this ostrich with the bird pictured on page 607. As you revise, make sure you have used commas correctly. **[Compare and Contrast]**

Exercise 16 **Using Commas With Nonessential Expressions** Read each of the sentences below carefully to determine whether the underlined expression is essential or not essential. If the material is essential, write *E*. If the material is not essential, copy the sentence onto your paper, adding any commas that are needed.

EXAMPLE: The Joshua tree a desert plant has thin leaves to slow water loss.

ANSWER: The Joshua tree, a desert plant, has thin leaves to slow water loss.

1. The baboon eating the baobab fruit belongs to the zoo.
2. Desert insects dormant for most of the year appear when rain causes flowers to bloom.
3. Ostriches are large African birds that lay eggs with very hard shells.
4. The roadrunner racing by our car could fly if it had to.
5. The desert tortoise a reptile stores fluid in sacs under its shell.

More Practice

Grammar Exercise Workbook
- pp. 169–170

On-line Exercise Bank
- Section 26.2

Go on-line:
PHSchool.com
Enter Web Code:
eck-8002

Step-by-Step Teaching Guide

Commas with Nonessential Expressions

1. Commas are used to set off the three types of nonessential expressions: appositives and appositive phrases, participial phrases, adjective clauses. Nonessential expressions rename the noun they modify. They are nonessential because the sentence retains its meaning when they are omitted.
2. Appositives can be either essential or nonessential. Only a nonessential appositive is set off by a comma.
3. Review the examples of nonessential participial phrases and adjective clauses. Be sure that students can identify the nonessential examples.
4. Write the following examples on the board and ask students to explain why each is a nonessential expression.

   The goalie, Sarah, had a great game. (nonessential appositive)

   Sarah, standing in the goal, had 23 saves. (nonessential participial phrase)

   The crowd cheered for Sarah, who led a great defensive effort. (nonessential adjective clause)

Answer Key

Exercise 16

1. E
2. Desert insects, dormant for most of the year, appear when rain causes flowers to bloom.
3. E
4. The roadrunner, racing by our car, could fly if it had to.
5. The desert tortoise, a reptile, stores fluid in sacs under its shell.

Critical Viewing

Compare and Contrast Students may state that the ostrich is much larger than the other bird, looks more interesting, and seems to be more alert.

Step-by-Step Teaching Guide

Using Commas with Dates and Geographical Names

1. Be sure students understand that a comma is needed in dates with two or more parts except for a month followed by a day (September 17) or a date with only a month and year (August 2004).
2. Geographical names made up of two or more parts require a comma. (San Antonio, Texas)

Customize for *ESL Students*

Students can practice using commas in dates and places by writing sentences about their home cultures or countries. For example: *This year Cinco de Mayo will be celebrated on Tuesday, May 5. I was born in Havana, Cuba, in 1986.*

Answer Key

Exercise 17

1. There was no reason to go to New Delhi, India, in June.
2. correct
3. However, by January 6, 2000, we'd left for home.
4. Amman, Jordan, is the capital of that mostly arid country.
5. You'll find Eilat, Israel, bordering Aqaba, Jordan, at the southern tip of the Negev Desert.

26.2

Using Commas With Dates and Geographical Names

Dates usually have several parts, including months, days, and years. Commas prevent such dates from being unclear.

KEY CONCEPT When a date is made up of two or more parts, use a comma after each item except in the case of a month followed by a day. ■

EXAMPLES: Saturday, July 20, is their anniversary.
January 1, 1945, was the beginning of an exciting year.
September 7, 1999, was my first day of school.

When dates contain only months and years, commas are unnecessary.

EXAMPLE: It wasn't until July 1999 that records were kept for that part of the Sahara.

Geographical names may also consist of more than one part. Again, commas help prevent confusion.

KEY CONCEPT When a geographical name is made up of two or more parts, use a comma after each item. ■

EXAMPLES: Amos moved from Tripoli, Libya, to Fez, Morocco.
Many antiquities were stolen from Cairo, Egypt, and shipped to Paris, France.

Exercise 17 **Using Commas With Dates or Geographical Names** Copy each of the following sentences onto your paper, adding commas where they are needed. Write *correct* if no commas are needed.

EXAMPLE: They began their cruise on the Nile near Alexandria Egypt in June.
ANSWER: They began their cruise on the Nile near Alexandria, Egypt, in June.

1. There was no reason to go to New Delhi India in June.
2. We were in India in August 1999; the monsoon affected our journey.
3. However by January 6 2000 we'd left for home.
4. Amman Jordan is the capital of that mostly arid country.
5. You'll find Eilat Israel bordering Aqaba Jordan at the southern tip of the Negev Desert.

More Practice

Grammar Exercise Workbook
• pp. 171–172
On-line Exercise Bank
• Section 26.2
Go on-line: PHSchool.com
Enter Web Code: eck-8002

iText

Get instant feedback! Exercise 17 is available on-line or on CD-ROM.

TIME SAVERS!

Answers on Transparency Use the Grammar Exercises Answers on Transparencies for Chapter 26 to have students correct their own or one another's exercises.

On-Line Exercise Bank Have students complete the exercises on computer. The Auto Check feature will grade their work for you!

STANDARDIZED TEST PREPARATION WORKSHOP

Grammar and Usage Many standardized tests require students to use correct punctuation. Ask students which sentence uses commas correctly.

A On December 7 1941 the Japanese attacked Pearl Harbor Hawaii.
B On December 7, 1941 the Japanese attacked Pearl Harbor, Hawaii.
C On December 7, 1941, the Japanese attacked Pearl Harbor Hawaii.
D On December 7, 1941, the Japanese attacked Pearl Harbor, Hawaii.

Item **D** correctly punctuates the date and location.

Other Uses of the Comma

The following rules govern the use of commas in addresses, letter salutations and closings, numbers, and quotations. A final rule concerns using commas to avoid misunderstandings.

KEY CONCEPT Use a comma after each item in an address made up of two or more parts. ■

As you can see in the following example, commas are placed after the name, street, and city. No comma separates the state from the ZIP Code.

EXAMPLE: Write to Maxwell Hunnicutt, 54 Monmouth Avenue, Dallas, Texas 75243.

Fewer commas are needed when an address is stacked, such as in a letter or on an envelope.

EXAMPLE: Maxwell Hunnicutt
54 Monmouth Avenue
Dallas, Texas 75243

KEY CONCEPT Use a comma after the salutation in a personal letter and after the closing in all letters. ■

SALUTATIONS: Dear Bill, Dear Aunt Harriet and Uncle Bill,
CLOSINGS: Sincerely, Best wishes, Yours truly,

KEY CONCEPT With numbers of more than three digits, insert a comma before every third digit, counting from the right. ■

EXAMPLES: 1,750 feet
3,608,787 square miles

Note About *Commas With Numbers*: Do not use commas with ZIP Codes, telephone numbers, page numbers, or serial numbers.

ZIP CODE: Niagara Falls, New York 14301
TELEPHONE NUMBER: (212) 555-2473
PAGE NUMBER: on page 1022
SERIAL NUMBER: 059 94 6106

▼ Critical Viewing How do you think this bird is able to perch on this spiny cactus? How do you suppose it survives in the desert? Write answers to these questions. Be sure to use commas correctly. **[Speculate]**

Step-by-Step Teaching Guide

Other Uses of the Comma

1. A comma separates each item in an address written in sentence form.
2. When an address is used on an envelope, the items are written on a separate line and no commas are needed to separate them.
3. Commas are used after letter salutations and closings. You might want to tell students the exception: in business letters, a colon is used after the salutation.
4. Point out the usefulness of using commas with four-digit and larger numbers. Write the following numbers on the board and ask students to read them first without and then with commas.

   236783 *236,783*
   37289 *37,289*
   4231846 *4,231,846*
5. Point out the exceptions. Commas are not used with ZIP Codes, telephone numbers, page numbers, and serial numbers.

Critical Viewing

Speculate Encourage students to suggest ways a bird could balance on the cactus and survive in the desert. Have students verify their ideas using research materials.

ONGOING ASSESSMENT: Monitor and Reinforce

If students miss more than two items in Exercises 14–18, refer them to the following for additional practice.

In the Textbook	Print Resources	Technology
Chapter Review, Ex. 58, p. 632	Grammar Exercise Workbook, pp. 169–170	On-Line Exercise Bank, Section 26.2

Step-by-Step Teaching Guide

Other Uses of the Comma

1. Review the use of commas to set off direct quotations. Before the quote, the comma is outside the quotation marks, and at the end, it is inside the quotation marks.
2. Write the following examples on the board and ask students to insert commas correctly:

   LuAnn said(,) "There is a test tomorrow."

   "I am not ready(,)" Shari moaned.

   "Don't worry(,)" LuAnn assured her, "I'll help you study."
3. Review the examples in which a comma helps clarify the sentence and prevents confusion. There are no rules for these situations. But students need to read their sentences carefully to make sure a reader will understand the meaning. If the meaning is unclear, a comma should be used to clarify.

Answer Key

Exercise 18

1. Kayla said, "Two kinds of camels live in the desert."
2. Nearby, the one-humped dromedary waited patiently.
3. Most camels used for caravans are dromedaries, or one-humped camels.
4. Often called "the ships of the desert," camels have flat feet that are well suited for walking on sand.
5. "Camels store food in their humps and in parts of their stomachs," he said, "so they can go a long time without food or drink."
6. The area of Mongolia where many camels live, the harsh Gobi, is 604,800 square miles.
7. Protecting themselves from the unfriendly desert, people wear clothes that cover them completely.
8. "Our heads are never left uncovered in the sun," said the desert nomad.
9. To find out more, write the Camel Cruise Corporation, 1035 Camelback Way, New Found City, Hawaii 99900.
10. "We went on a camel cruise last year," she told us excitedly.

KEY CONCEPT Use commas to set off a direct quotation from the rest of a sentence. ■

As you read the following examples, notice that the correct location of the commas depends upon the "he said/she said" part of the sentence. (See Section 27.4 for more information about the punctuation used with quotations.)

EXAMPLES:	Bret said, "Hold the door open."
	"I can't," Lorna replied, "because my arms are full of books."

KEY CONCEPT Use a comma to prevent a sentence from being misunderstood. ■

Without commas, the following sentences are confusing. The addition of commas clarifies the meaning.

UNCLEAR:	Beyond the mountains were clearly visible.
CLEAR:	Beyond, the mountains were clearly visible.
UNCLEAR:	After watching Zack asked to join the game.
CLEAR:	After watching, Zack asked to join the game.

Exercise 18 **Proofreading for Commas in Other Situations** Copy each item below onto your paper, adding commas as needed.

1. Kayla said "Two kinds of camels live in the desert."
2. Nearby the one-humped dromedary waited patiently.
3. Most camels used for caravans are dromedaries or one-humped camels.
4. Often called "the ships of the desert" camels have flat feet that are well suited for walking on sand.
5. "Camels store food in their humps and in parts of their stomachs" he said "so they can go a long time without food or drink."
6. The area of Mongolia where many camels live the harsh Gobi is 604800 square miles.
7. Protecting themselves from the unfriendly desert people wear clothes that cover them completely.
8. "Our heads are never left uncovered in the sun" said the desert nomad.
9. To find out more write the Camel Cruise Corporation 1035 Camelback Way New Found City Hawaii 99900.
10. "We went on a camel cruise last year" she told us excitedly.

More Practice

Grammar Exercise Workbook
- pp. 169–170

On-line Exercise Bank
- Section 26.2

Go on-line: PHSchool.com
Enter Web Code: eck-8002

iText

Get instant feedback! Exercise 18 is available on-line or on CD-ROM.

ONGOING ASSESSMENT: Assess Mastery

Use the following resources to assess mastery of using commas.

In the Textbook	Technology
Chapter Review, Ex. 57–58, p. 632	Writing and Grammar iText, Section 26.2, Section Review; On-Line Exercise Bank, Section 26.2

Section 26.2

Section Review

GRAMMAR EXERCISES 19–24

Exercise 19 **Using Commas to Separate Basic Elements in a Sentence** Write the following sentences on your paper, adding commas where needed. If no commas are needed, write *correct*.

1. Scientists are determined to help desert people prevail so they have made careful studies of the desert environment.
2. Their work has not been limited to plants and animals.
3. The situation remains urgent yet it takes time to understand the effects of soil depletion.
4. China limited the size of sheep herds and protected oases from overuse.
5. The land was rejuvenated and vegetation animals and people thrived.

Exercise 20 **Using Commas With Series and Introductory Elements** Write the sentences below on your paper, inserting commas where needed.

1. In the United States deserts were restored to health through the careful management of grazing lands.
2. Areas were fenced off plowed clear or burned off so new grass could grow.
3. Now struggling crops will have a better chance to grow.
4. Although the trees provide shade other benefits are also seen.
5. First of all the root system of the trees will help the desert soil hold moisture.

Exercise 21 **Using Commas With Added Elements** Write the sentences that follow on your paper, using commas as needed to set off parenthetical expressions. If no commas are needed, write *correct*.

1. The Nile River which flows through Egypt is a source of irrigation water.
2. The Nile flood waters covering the fields left important nutrients.
3. When the flood waters subsided the ground was useless however.
4. The farmers needed a system that would trap the waters for later use.
5. "The solution" Russell said "was to build canals to hold the water."

Exercise 22 **Find It in Your Reading** Read this excerpt from *The World Almanac* about Egypt. On your paper, rewrite the sentences, adding commas where necessary.

The Aswan High Dam completed in 1971 provides irrigation for more than a million acres of land. Artesian wells drilled in the Western Desert reclaimed 43000 acres from 1960–1966.

Exercise 23 **Find It in Your Writing** Look through your portfolio for at least one example of each of the following uses of commas:

- compound sentences
- commas between items in a series
- nonessential expressions

Exercise 24 **Writing Application** Write a short letter to a friend describing an imaginary trip across the desert. Include the following elements:

- address, date, and greeting
- one sentence with a series of four items
- one sentence with two equal adjectives and a contrasting expression
- one sentence with an introductory phrase

ASSESS and CLOSE

Section Review

Each of these exercises correlates to a concept in the section on commas, pages 600–608. These exercises may be used for more practice, for reteaching, or for review of the Key Concepts presented. Answers for all chapter exercises are available in *Grammar Exercises Answers on Transparencies* in your teaching resources.

Answer Key

Exercise 19

1. Scientists are determined to help desert people prevail, so they have made careful studies of the desert environment.
2. correct
3. The situation remains urgent, yet it takes time to understand the effects of soil depletion.
4. correct
5. The land was rejuvenated, and vegetation, animals, and people thrived.

Exercise 20

1. In the United States, deserts were restored to health through the careful management of grazing lands.
2. Areas were fenced off, plowed clear, or burned off so new grass could grow.
3. Now, struggling crops will have a better chance to grow.
4. Although the trees provide shade, other benefits are also seen.
5. First of all, the root system of the trees will help the desert soil hold moisture.

Exercise 21

1. The Nile River, which flows through Egypt, is a source of irrigation water.
2. correct
3. When the flood waters subsided, the ground was useless, however.
4. correct
5. "The solution," Russell said, "was to build canals to hold the water."

continued

Answer Key continued

Exercise 22

Find It in Your Reading
The Aswan High Dam, completed in 1971, provides irrigation for more than a million acres of land. Artesian wells drilled in the Western Desert reclaimed 43,000 acres from 1960–1966.

Exercise 23

Find It in Your Writing
Students can trade papers with partners to check for correct punctuation in the sentences.

Exercise 24

Writing Application
Encourage students to mail or e-mail their letters.

PREPARE and ENGAGE

Interest GRABBER Write the following sentences on the board and ask students what is wrong with the punctuation.

I hate studying grammar: it gives me a headache. (Colon should be semicolon.)

There are worse things to study; algebra, geometry, and calculus. (Semicolon should be colon.)

Activate Prior Knowledge

Ask students to tell in their own words what commas and periods do. (Possible response: Commas show a pause. Periods show a stop or separate different ideas.)

TEACH

Step-by-Step Teaching Guide

Using Semicolons

1. A semicolon is used to link two independent clauses not joined by a coordinating conjunction. A semicolon signals a longer pause than a comma, but not the full stop of a period. It is an "in between" punctuation mark.
2. Review the examples with students. Point out that in each case, the clauses are closely linked. Emphasize that a semicolon is correct only when there is a close relationship between the clauses.

   Incorrect: The house was dark; it was Friday.

   Correct: The house was dark; the darkness was a little spooky.
3. Review the list of conjunctive adverbs and transitional expressions. Point out the comma that follows the conjunctive adverb or transitional expression. Show students how the same principle is at work here as in the previous key concept: The clauses are closely linked.
4. Semicolons are also used to separate items in which commas already appear, such as dates and geographic locations, to avoid confusion.

   On December 7, 1941, the Japanese attacked Pearl Harbor, Hawaii; on September 2, 1945, they surrendered to the United States in Tokyo, Japan.

Section 26.3

Semicolons and Colons

The *semicolon* looks like a period above a comma (;). It joins related independent clauses and takes the place of a comma or a period.

Using Semicolons

KEY CONCEPT Use a semicolon to join related independent clauses that are not already joined by the conjunctions *and, or, nor, for, but, so,* or *yet.* ■

TWO INDEPENDENT CLAUSES:	The fire began with a tossed match. Jamestown was burned in 1676.
CLAUSES WITH SEMICOLONS:	The fire began with a tossed match; in that one moment in 1676, all of Jamestown began to burn.
	Marianne's report was about Christopher Newport; Dave's was about General George McClellan.

Note that when a sentence contains three or more related independent clauses, they may still be separated with semicolons.

EXAMPLE:	The birds vanished; the sky grew dark; the little pond was still.

KEY CONCEPT Use a semicolon to join independent clauses separated by either a conjunctive adverb or a transitional expression. ■

CONJUNCTIVE ADVERBS:	also, besides, furthermore, however, indeed, instead, moreover, nevertheless, otherwise, then, therefore, thus
TRANSITIONAL EXPRESSIONS:	as a result, at this time, consequently, first, for instance, in fact, on the other hand, second, that is
EXAMPLE:	We were very impressed with the child's knowledge of history; *indeed*, she was remarkably well informed about the first English settlement.

Remember to place a comma after the conjunctive adverb or transitional expression. The comma sets off the conjunctive adverb or transitional expression, which acts as an introductory expression to the second clause.

Theme: Virginia

In this section, you will learn about using semicolons to join clauses and to avoid confusion, as well as the special uses of colons. The examples and exercises are about historic Virginia.

Cross-Curricular Connection: Social Studies

TIME AND RESOURCE MANAGER

Resources
Print: Grammar Exercises Workbook, pp. 173–176
Technology: Writing and Grammar iText, Section 26.3; On-Line Exercise Book, Section 26.3

In-Depth Coverage	Accelerated Pace
• Work through all key concepts, pp. 610–612. • Assign and review Exercises 25–26. • Read and discuss Grammar in Literature, p. 611.	• Assign pp. 610–612 for independent student review. • Assign Section Review Exercises 27–29.

GRAMMAR IN LITERATURE

from The Man Without a Country

Edward Everett Hale

In this excerpt, the author has used semicolons (in blue) to join a series of independent clauses

. . . He says, "Take us home; take us to our own country; take us to our own house; take us to our own children and our own women."

More Practice

Grammar Exercise Workbook
- pp. 173–174

On-line Exercise Bank
- Section 26.3

Go on-line:
PHSchool.com
Enter Web Code:
eck-8002

KEY CONCEPT Consider the use of a semicolon to avoid confusion when independent clauses or items in a series already contain commas. ■

EXAMPLE: Three important dates in Jamestown history are April 30, 1607; September 10, 1607; and January 7, 1608.

Exercise 25 **Revising Sentences Using Semicolons to Join Independent Clauses and to Avoid Confusion** Rewrite each sentence below, replacing commas with semicolons where necessary.

1. English investors supported the Jamestown settlement, therefore, Virginia became a popular destination.
2. The desire to acquire land inspired the colonists, indeed, many Virginians joined in the westward expansion.
3. It was not an easy voyage, the immigrants traveled on small ships for many months.
4. The cities of Williamsburg, Virginia, New Bern, North Carolina, Charleston, South Carolina, and Savannah, Georgia, became centers of commerce.
5. In Williamsburg, particularly, there were wig makers, who provided wigs for successful men and women, saddlers, who made saddles and other horse equipment, and cabinet makers, who produced fine furniture.

▼ Critical Viewing
Describe the picture below in a sentence that includes two independent clauses joined by a semicolon. **[Analyze]**

Step-by-Step Teaching Guide

Grammar in Literature

1. Have a volunteer read aloud the passage from *The Man Without a Country.*
2. Discuss the close relationship of the clauses linked by semicolons. Point out how the use of semicolons emphasizes the parallel construction and rhythmic momentum gained from the repetitive use of *take us.*

More About the Author

Edward Everett Hale (1822–1909) was a Boston clergyman and writer. Hale was a leading abolitionist and the author of more than 70 books. *The Man Without a Country* is his best-known work and was written in 1863 to inspire support for the Union cause during the Civil War.

Critical Viewing

Analyze Students may suggest:

The man seems to enjoy what he is doing; the horse does not.

Answer Key

Exercise 25

1. English investors supported the Jamestown settlement; therefore, Virginia became a popular destination.
2. The desire to acquire land inspired the colonists; indeed, many Virginians joined in the westward expansion.
3. It was not an easy voyage; the immigrants traveled on small ships for many months.
4. The cities of Williamsburg, Virginia; New Bern, North Carolina; Charleston, South Carolina; and Savannah, Georgia, became centers of commerce.
5. In Williamsburg, particularly, there were wigmakers, who provided wigs for successful men and women; saddlers, who made saddles and other horse equipment; and cabinet makers, who produced fine furniture.

Step-by-Step Teaching Guide

Uses of the Colon

1. Colons are used in the following manner: for lists of items, to separate hours and minutes, for salutations in business letters, and to signal important information.
2. Review each use of a colon. Point out that a colon is used if a list is written in sentence form or is itemized with bullets.

Answer Key

Exercise 26

1. backgrounds: Amish, Lutherans, and Mennonites.
2. Caution: Deer Crossing
3. woods: two bucks,
4. Dear Mr. Connolly:
5. Notice: Classes Canceled
6. Gentlemen: This is
7. 2:00 P.M. not 3:30 P.M.
8. topics: schedule
9. 8:30 or 9:00
10. Wanted: Full-

26.3

Using Colons

The *colon* looks like one period placed above another (:). This mark directs attention to the information that follows it.

KEY CONCEPT Use a colon before a list of items following an independent clause. ■

EXAMPLE: You can visit these historic places in Virginia: the Jamestown Archaeological Laboratory, Jamestown Festival Park, and James Fort.

KEY CONCEPT A colon is used to indicate time with numerals, to end salutations in business letters, and to signal important ideas. ■

The following examples show special uses of the colon.

NUMERALS GIVING THE TIME:	3:04 P.M. 5:00 A.M.
SALUTATIONS IN BUSINESS LETTERS:	Dear Ms. Langly:
LABELS:	Notice: Shop is closed for repairs.

Exercise 26 **Revising Sentences Using Colons** Rewrite each item below, inserting the missing colon.

EXAMPLE: The settler wanted three things a horse, a saddle, and boots.
ANSWER: The settler wanted three things: a horse, a saddle, and boots.

1. Settlers in Virginia during the early eighteenth century included German settlers of many religious backgrounds Amish, Lutherans, and Mennonites.
2. Caution Deer Crossing
3. We saw several deer in the woods two bucks, five does, and three fawns.
4. Dear Mr. Connolly
5. Notice Classes Canceled
6. Gentlemen This is to inform you of a change in schedule.
7. The meeting will be held today at 200 P.M., not 330 P.M.
8. The meeting will cover these topics schedule, budget, guidelines, and goals.
9. Does your flight arrive at 830 or 900?
10. Help Wanted Full- or Part-Time

More Practice

Grammar Exercise Workbook
- pp. 175–176

On-line Exercise Bank
- Section 26.3

Go on-line: PHSchool.com
Enter Web Code: eck-8002

iText

Get instant feedback! Exercise 26 is available on-line or on CD-ROM.

TIME SAVERS!

Answers on Transparency Use the Grammar Exercises Answers on Transparencies for Chapter 26 to have students correct their own or one another's exercises.

On-Line Exercise Bank Have students complete the exercises on computer. The Auto Check feature will grade their work for you!

ONGOING ASSESSMENT: Monitor and Reinforce

If students miss more than two items in Exercises 25–26, refer them to the following for additional practice.

In the Textbook	Print Resources	Technology
Chapter Review, Ex. 59, p. 632	Grammar Exercise Workbook, pp. 173–176	On-Line Exercise Bank, Section 26.3

Section 26.3 **Section Review**

GRAMMAR EXERCISES 27–32

Exercise 27 **Using Semicolons in Independent Clauses** Some of the sentences below need semicolons to join related independent clauses. On your paper, write the word before the semicolon, the semicolon, and the word that follows.

1. Many educated people in Virginia knew slavery was wrong they believed that the custom should be abolished.
2. In the late eighteenth century, James Monroe offered plans to free the slaves however, few were actually returned to their homeland.
3. Abolitionist John Brown took control of Harper's Ferry in 1859 his planned revolt failed without the support of the slaves.
4. Brown was captured by Robert E. Lee consequently, he was tried for treason.
5. There was talk of Virginia's seceding nevertheless, it stayed with the Union until later.

Exercise 28 **Using Colons** Some of the items below should have colons. On your paper, write the word before the colon, the colon, and the word that follows, if applicable. If no colon is needed, write *correct*.

1. Dear President Lincoln
2. During Reconstruction, several forms of travel were available rail, boat, and wagon.
3. General Billy Malone helped provide these things for Virginia funding of public education, abolishment of the poll tax, and establishment of a college for African American teachers.
4. The polls in Richmond will be open from 8:00 A.M. to 9:00 P.M.
5. Please Note No campaigning is allowed near the polls.

Exercise 29 **Revising With Semicolons and Colons** Rewrite the letter below, supplying semicolons and colons where necessary.

Dear Madam

I've learned that you provide assistance to new residents. Therefore, I am asking for your help in obtaining these things part-time computer work, in which I am skilled an apartment near town and information about your adult school, where I might take a car-maintenance course.

Sincerely,
Louise Casella

Exercise 30 **Find It in Your Reading** Read the labels of at least three common household products. On your paper, explain the use of colons and semicolons on the labels.

Exercise 31 **Find It in Your Writing** Review your writing portfolio. Find examples of sentences that could be combined by using colons or semicolons. On your paper, write the new sentences, and explain how the colons or semicolons are used correctly.

Exercise 32 **Writing Application** Write a paragraph about a historic time that interests you. Include at least three of the following in your sentences:

1. colon to introduce a series of items
2. semicolon to avoid confusion
3. semicolon before a conjunctive adverb
4. transitional expression
5. semicolon before items in a series that already contain commas

ASSESS and CLOSE

Section Review

Each of these exercises correlates to a concept in the section on semicolons and colons, pages 610–612. These exercises may be used for more practice, for reteaching, or for review of the Key Concepts presented. Answers for all chapter exercises are available in *Grammar Exercises Answers on Transparencies* in your teaching resources.

Answer Key

Exercise 27

1. wrong; they
2. slaves; however
3. 1859; his
4. Lee; consequently
5. seceding; nevertheless

Exercise 28

1. Lincoln:
2. available: rail
3. Virginia: funding
4. correct
5. Note: No

Exercise 29

Dear Madam:

I've learned that you provide assistance to new residents. Therefore, I am asking your help in obtaining these things: part-time computer work, in which I am skilled; an apartment near town; and information about your adult school, where I might take a car-maintenance course.

Sincerely,

Louise Casella

Exercise 30

Find It in Your Reading
Students may not find semicolons. They will find colons after *Ingredients, Directions, Warning,* and the like. Colons are used because a list follows.

Exercise 31

Find It in Your Writing
Students can make their explanations orally to partners.

Exercise 32

Writing Application
You might want to challenge students to use all five sentence formations.

PREPARE and ENGAGE

Interest GRABBER Write the following paragraph from Poe's "The Tell-Tale Heart" on the board and have a volunteer read it with as much gusto as possible.

"Villains!" I shrieked, "dissemble no more! I admit the deed!—tear up the planks!—here, here!—it is the beating of his hideous heart!"

Ask students why Poe used quotation marks.

Activate Prior Knowledge

Ask students whether the following sentences require quotation marks. Why or why not?

My mother always nags me to wash my hands.

Wash your hands, my mother nagged.

TEACH

Step-by-Step Teaching Guide

Quotation Marks

Direct quotations represent a person or character's exact speech and require quotation marks.

An indirect quotation is a summary or gives the general meaning. It is not a quotation, so it does not require quotation marks.

Answer Key

Exercise 33

1. D
2. I
3. D
4. I
5. D

Section 26.4

Quotation Marks and Underlining

There are many reasons for using quotation marks. Sometimes, you may want to show that you are repeating the exact words spoken by a person or printed in a book. At other times, you may want your characters to reveal themselves in their own words or to show action through dialogue.

Using Direct and Indirect Quotations

There are two types of quotations: *direct* and *indirect.* A direct quotation requires the use of special punctuation.

KEY CONCEPT A **direct quotation** represents a person's exact speech or thoughts and is enclosed in quotation marks (" "). ■

EXAMPLES: Kate said, "Williamsburg had the first theater."
"What play was presented?" Dorothy wondered.

KEY CONCEPT An **indirect quotation** reports the general meaning of what a person said or thought and does not require quotation marks. ■

EXAMPLES: Margo said that she would do it for me.
Don wondered why she hadn't called him.

Exercise 33 **Distinguishing Between Direct and Indirect Quotations** If a sentence below contains a direct quotation, write *D* on your paper. If it contains an indirect quotation, write *I.* (Notice that quotation marks have been intentionally omitted.)

EXAMPLE: Governor Alexander Spotswood negotiated with the Indians, said Ruby.
ANSWER: D

1. Cheryl said *Assaragoa* means 'long knife' in Iroquois.
2. Peter said that Governor Spotswood made a good treaty with the Iroquois.
3. Many of the immigrants who benefited from that treaty were German Karen added.
4. The teacher said that two leaders of German immigration were Joist Hite and Jacob Stover.
5. Many Germans said Cheryl moved westward to farm.

Theme: Virginia

In this section, you will learn various uses for quotation marks and underlining. The examples and exercises are about historic Virginia.

Cross-Curricular Connection: Social Studies

More Practice

Grammar Exercise Workbook
- pp. 177–178

On-line Exercise Bank
- Section 26.4

Go on-line: PHSchool.com
Enter Web Code: eck-8002

iText

Get instant feedback! Exercise 33 is available on-line or on CD-ROM.

TIME SAVERS!

Answers on Transparency Use the Grammar Exercises Answers on Transparencies for Chapter 26 to have students correct their own or one another's exercises.

On-Line Exercise Bank Have students complete the Diagnostic Test on computer. The Auto Check feature will grade their work for you!

TIME AND RESOURCE MANAGER

Resources
Print: Grammar Exercises Workbook, pp. 177–182
Technology: Writing and Grammar iText, Section 26.4; On-Line Exercise Bank, Section 26.4

In-Depth Coverage	Accelerated Pace
• Work through all key concepts, pp. 614–621. • Assign and review Exercises 33–38.	• Assign pp. 614–621 for independent student review. • Assign Section Review Exercises 39–41.

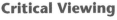

Using Direct Quotations With Introductory, Concluding, and Interrupting Expressions

A writer will generally identify a speaker by using words such as *he asked* or *she said* with a quotation. These expressions can introduce, conclude, or interrupt a quotation.

KEY CONCEPT When an introductory expression precedes a direct quotation, place a comma after the introductory expression and write the quotation as a full sentence. ■

EXAMPLES: The guide explained, "All historical buildings should be treated with respect."
Barney asked, "Is it difficult to identify artifacts?"

KEY CONCEPT When a concluding expression follows a direct quotation, write the quotation as a full sentence ending with a comma, question mark, or exclamation mark inside the quotation mark. Then, write the concluding expression. ■

EXAMPLES: "That depends on several factors," the guide replied.
"Could you show us one of the houses?" interrupted Barney.
"Please!" everyone chorused.

Notice also that the concluding expressions do not begin with capitals.

KEY CONCEPT When the direct quotation of one sentence is interrupted, end the first part of the direct quotation with a comma and a quotation mark. Place a comma after the interrupting expression, and then use a new set of quotation marks to enclose the rest of the quotation. ■

EXAMPLES: "This," the trainer said, "is Carter's Grove Plantation, a mid-eighteenth-century mansion."
"What would we have done," asked Corrina, "if we had lived there?"

▲ Critical Viewing Write several lines of dialogue between the two figures in this photograph. As you revise, check to make sure you have used quotation marks correctly. **[Analyze]**

Critical Viewing

Analyze Students may suggest a possible answer: "What an interesting old boat that is!" said the person on the left.

"I think it came from the Parade of Ships," replied the friend.

"I wish we could sail on it," replied the first speaker. "It would be great fun."

Step-by Step Teaching Guide

Direct Quotations with Introductory, Concluding, and Interrupting Expressions

1. A comma is used between an introductory expression and a direct quotation. The purpose of the comma is to set the quote off from the introductory expression. Point out that the quotation begins with a capital letter as if it were the beginning of a sentence.
2. Punctuation in closing expressions is trickier than in introductory expressions. Review the rule that the quotation ends with a punctuation mark. If it is a declarative sentence, end the quotation with a comma inside the quotation marks. A question mark or exclamation mark for a question or an exclamation also goes inside the quotation marks, before proceeding with the concluding expression.
3. Punctuating interrupting expressions works the same way, ending with a comma inside the quotation marks before the interrupting expression. The second part of the quotation does not begin with a capital letter unless it is the beginning of a new sentence.

Customize for *Less Advanced Students*

The rules for punctuating quotations are fairly consistent. Punctuation marks go inside quotation marks. The hard one for students to remember might be the use of the comma as an end mark for a complete sentence quotation.

Step-by-Step Teaching Guide

Direct Quotations with Introductory, Concluding, and Interrupting Expressions *(continued)*

1. Review the rule for an interrupted quotation that is in two sentences: place an end mark inside the quotation marks and then a period at the end of the first sentence. The second sentence is placed in quotation marks with the end mark placed inside the quotation marks.
2. Write the following sentences on the board and ask students to supply the punctuation.

   (")I am going to the store(,") Mark said. (")We need food for dinner(.")

Answer Key

Exercise 34

1. Mark said, "The College of William and Mary was built in Williamsburg."
2. "Yes," Garth agreed, "and do you know what was taught there?"
3. "I do know one subject," Jenny added. "They taught religion."
4. "Didn't they teach science, literature, and philosophy also?" asked Mark.
5. "Of course," Garth assured him. "William and Mary had many fine professors."
6. "One of their science professors was William Barton Rogers," Jenny said. "He founded the Massachusetts Institute of Technology."
7. "The college was, however," noted Jenny, "slow to educate women."
8. "What exactly do you mean by that?" Mark asked.
9. "She's talking about the educational needs of women," Garth explained. "Women weren't admitted to the college until 1918."
10. "Although," Jenny said, "a few women did attend some classes as early as the 1830's."

KEY CONCEPT When two sentences in a direct quotation are separated by an interrupting expression, end the first quoted sentence with a comma, question mark, or exclamation mark and a quotation mark. Place a period after the interrupter, and then write the second quoted sentence as a full quotation. ■

EXAMPLES: "That would be exciting," the guide explained. "Plantation owners were very rich."
"Did you see those rooms?" asked Mark. "I can't imagine having such a large house."

Exercise 34 **Using Direct Quotations With Introductory, Concluding, and Interrupting Expressions** Copy each of the following sentences onto your paper, making the necessary corrections.

EXAMPLE: Elena said we will need at least two hours to see the museum.
ANSWER: Elena said, "We will need at least two hours to see the museum."

1. Mark said the College of William and Mary was built in Williamsburg
2. Yes Garth agreed and do you know what was taught there
3. I do know one subject Jenny added they taught religion
4. Didn't they teach science, literature, and philosophy also asked Mark
5. Of course Garth assured him William and Mary had many fine professors
6. One of their science professors was William Barton Rogers Jenny said he founded the Massachusetts Institute of Technology
7. The college was however noted Jenny slow to educate women
8. What exactly do you mean by that Mark asked
9. She's talking about the educational needs of women Garth explained women weren't admitted to the college until 1918
10. Although Jenny said a few women did attend some classes as early as the 1830's

More Practice

Grammar Exercise Workbook
- pp. 177–178

On-line Exercise Bank
- Section 26.4

Go on-line: PHSchool.com
Enter Web Code: eck-8002

▶ Critical Viewing Use direct quotations with interrupting expressions in a dialogue between two or more of the figures in this photograph. **[Analyze]**

Critical Viewing

Analyze Possible student response: "I would like to live here," said one visitor, "and go to college."

Using Quotation Marks With Other Punctuation Marks

Sometimes, it may be hard to decide whether to place another punctuation mark inside or outside a quotation mark. You have seen that a comma or period used with a direct quotation goes inside the final quotation mark. In some cases, however, an end mark comes after the quotation mark. The following rules can help you choose the correct placement.

KEY CONCEPT Always place a comma or a period inside the final quotation mark. ■

EXAMPLES: "This area needs attention," Mrs. Finch said.
She added, "It looks like a junkyard."

KEY CONCEPT Place a question mark or an exclamation mark inside the final quotation mark if the end mark is part of the quotation. Do not use an additional end mark. ■

EXAMPLES: Joseph asked, "Didn't I already clear that rubble?" Salvatore, his brother, protested loudly, "I helped rebuild three buildings last summer!"

INCORRECT: Rodney asked, "Will you stop arguing?".

CORRECT: Rodney asked, "Will you stop arguing?"

KEY CONCEPT Place a question mark or exclamation mark outside the final quotation mark if the end mark is part of the entire sentence, not part of the quotation. ■

EXAMPLES: Did anyone say, "You have been negligent"?
Mary said, "I'm not responsible"!

Exercise 35 **Using End Marks With Direct Quotations** Decide whether the missing end mark in each sentence below should be placed inside or outside the quotation marks. Copy the sentences, and include the necessary end mark.

1. Does anyone remember hearing the guide say, "Now I'll tell you the name of the first religious order in Virginia"
2. I can't believe he just shouted out, "There was no real education system in Virginia until 1870"
3. Cathy asked, "What constitutes a real education system"
4. Did he say, "The lawn of the University of Virginia was *planted* by Thomas Jefferson"
5. No, he said, "The lawn of the University of Virginia was *planned* by Thomas Jefferson"

Grammar and Style Tip

Ellipsis marks (. . .) can be used to indicate that words have been omitted. They can be used at the beginning, middle, or end of a quotation. A period or other end mark is added to the ellipsis marks at the end of a sentence. For example: ". . . and then we visited Colonial Williamsburg," continued Sarah. "We drove from Washington, D.C., to . . . Colonial Williamsburg," Sarah added. Sarah said, "After the plane landed, we were on our way. . . ."

More Practice

Grammar Exercise Workbook
• pp. 179–180

On-line Exercise Bank
• Section 26.4

Go on-line:
PHSchool.com
Enter Web Code:
eck-8002

Step-by-Step Teaching Guide

Quotation Marks with Other Punctuation Marks

1. Explain that, in most cases, end marks go inside quotation marks. The end mark belongs inside quotation marks when it concludes both the quotation and the sentence. An additional end mark is not required, as shown in the text examples.
2. Explain that the only exceptions occur when a question mark or an exclamation point is not part of the quotation but is used to conclude the writer's own sentence. Use the examples on page 617 to illustrate this exception.

Answer Key

Exercise 35

1. Does anyone remember hearing the guide say, "Now I'll tell you the name of the first religious order in Virginia"?
2. I can't believe he just shouted out, "There was no real education system in Virginia until 1870!"
3. Cathy asked, "What constitutes a real education system?"
4. Did he say, "The lawn of the University of Virginia was *planted* by Thomas Jefferson"?
5. No, he said, "The lawn of the University of Virginia was *planned* by Thomas Jefferson."

ONGOING ASSESSMENT: Monitor and Reinforce

If students miss more than two items in Exercises 33–35, refer them to the following for additional practice.

In the Textbook	Print Resources	Technology
Chapter Review, Ex. 60, p. 632	Grammar Exercise Workbook, pp. 177–180	On-Line Exercise Book, Section 26.4

TIME SAVERS!

Answers on Transparency Use the Grammar Exercises Answers on Transparencies for Chapter 26 to have students correct their own or one another's exercises.

On-Line Exercise Bank Have students complete the Diagnostic Test on computer. The Auto Check feature will grade their work for you!

Step-by-Step Teaching Guide

Quotation Marks for Dialogue

1. In addition to a new set of quotation marks for each speaker, a new paragraph indicates a change in speaker. Both are necessary.
2. In a long written conversation, students do not need to add "he said," "she replied" on every line. That is distracting. At the same time, a reader can lose track if dialogue goes on for a page or more without a reminder of who is speaking.

Integrating Vocabulary

In written dialogue, the reader quickly becomes bored with a long series of "he said," "she said." Encourage students to vary the verb, using a thesaurus if necessary. *Asked, answered, shouted, whispered, muttered, barked, mumbled, wailed,* and so on are all good replacements for *said.*

Answer Key

Exercise 36

"Thomas Jefferson," commented Ray, "was eleven years younger than Washington."

"Also," said Mary, "he was somewhat more artistic and liberal in his politics."

"Yes, and like Washington, he was buried near his home," Ray said.

Mary wondered, "Was that a common tradition in Virginia?"

"I don't know," said Ray, "but I will try to find the answer."

Critical Viewing

Describe Possible student response: "Tom, old boy, why are you wearing a wig?" I asked.

"It is the fashion of the times for gentlemen," he replied. "I wear a ruffled shirt, too."

26.4

Using Quotation Marks for Dialogue

Dialogue is a direct conversation between two or more people.

KEY CONCEPT When writing dialogue, begin a new paragraph with each change of speaker. ■

EXAMPLE: "Will you be going with us on the family trip this summer?" Noreen asked her cousin.

Gwen hesitated before answering. "I'm afraid so. My parents think I enjoy the experience."

"You fooled me, too," Noreen replied. "Maybe the trip will be better this year."

"Well, at least it can't be any worse," sighed Gwen. "On the last trip, we waited in line at three different historic homes in one day!"

Notice that each sentence is punctuated according to the rules discussed earlier in this section. When writing dialogue, you also need to remember to indent whenever a new speaker talks.

Exercise 36 **Revising Using Quotation Marks and Paragraph Indentations With Dialogue** The following selection is a dialogue. However, it is missing some punctuation marks and paragraph indentations. Decide where quotation marks, other punctuation marks, and indentations are needed. Then, copy the dialogue onto your paper, making the necessary changes.

Thomas Jefferson, commented Ray was eleven years younger than Washington. Also said Mary he was somewhat more artistic and liberal in his politics. Yes, and like Washington he was buried near his home, Ray said. Mary wondered Was that a common tradition in Virginia I don't know said Ray but I will try to find the answer

More Practice

Grammar Exercise Workbook
- pp. 179–180

On-line Exercise Bank
- Section 26.4

Go on-line: PHSchool.com
Enter Web Code: eck-8002

◀ **Critical Viewing** Write a three-line dialogue between Thomas Jefferson and you about what he is wearing in this picture. Punctuate carefully. **[Describe]**

ONGOING ASSESSMENT: Monitor and Reinforce

If students miss more than two items in Exercises 33–36, refer them to the following for additional practice.

In the Textbook	Print Resources	Technology
Chapter Review, Ex. 60, p. 632	Grammar Exercise Workbook, pp. 177–180	On-Line Exercise Bank, Section 26.4

Using Underlining, Italics, and Quotation Marks

Underlining, italics, and quotation marks help make titles and other special words and names stand out in your writing.

KEY CONCEPT Underline or italicize the titles of long written works and the titles of publications that are published as a single work. ■

WRITTEN WORKS THAT ARE UNDERLINED	
Title of a Book	The Adventures of Tom Sawyer
Title of a Play	A Raisin in the Sun
Title of a Long Poem	Paradise Lost
Title of a Magazine	The William and Mary Quarterly
Title of a Newspaper	The New York Times

KEY CONCEPT Underline or italicize the titles of movies, television and radio series, long works of music, and art. ■

ARTISTIC WORKS THAT ARE UNDERLINED	
Title of a Movie	Notting Hill
Title of a Television Series	Friends
Title of a Long Work of Music	Surprise Symphony
Title of a Compact Disc	Elton John's Greatest Hits
Title of a Painting	Christina's World
Title of a Sculpture	The Thinker

KEY CONCEPT Underline or italicize the names of individual air, sea, space, and land craft. ■

AIR: the Kitty Hawk — SPACE: Gemini 5
SEA: the Titanic — LAND: the Tom Thumb

KEY CONCEPT Underline or italicize words, letters, or numbers used as names for themselves. ■

EXAMPLE: The word maybe is not part of her vocabulary.

Technology Tip

Underlining is used only in handwritten and typed work. In work done on a word processor and in printed materials, italics take the place of underlining.

Step-by-Step Teaching Guide

Underlining, Italics, and Quotation Marks

1. Underlining is done only when writing by hand or on a typewriter. On a computer, all underlining appears as italics.
2. The general rule is that titles of longer items get underlined; shorter ones that form the contents of longer ones such as chapters in a book or songs in a show or on a CD get quotation marks, as is covered on pages 619–621.

Real-World Connection

Have students work together and add new titles for each example in the charts on this page.

Answer Key

Exercise 37

1. The Tempest
2. u, Iroquois
3. Generall Historie of Virginia, New England, and the Summer Isles
4. generall, historie
5. Virginia, i
6. Gone With the Wind
7. Touched by an Angel
8. Mayflower
9. seven
10. c, necessary

Real-World Connection

Ask students to add real short stories, book chapters, short poems, and articles to their list of titles.

Step-by-Step Teaching Guide

Use Quotation Marks

1. Remind students that quotation marks are used for short works such as a short story and parts of a longer work such as a chapter in a book.
2. Have students look in *Prentice Hall Literature: Timeless Voices, Timeless Themes,* Silver for examples of the use of quotations for shorter works.

Exercise 37 **Underlining Titles, Names, and Words** Each of the following sentences contains a title, name, or word that needs underlining. Write the items that require underlining on your paper, and underline them.

EXAMPLE: The Lusitania sank in 1915 off the coast of Ireland.
ANSWER: Lusitania

1. William Shakespeare wrote The Tempest, a play about a shipwreck off the coast of Virginia.
2. Sue frequently leaves the u out of Iroquois.
3. John Smith of early Jamestown wrote Generall Historie of Virginia, New England, and the Summer Isles.
4. The spelling of the words generall and historie are correct for that era.
5. Also, Virginia was sometimes spelled without the third i.
6. My favorite book is Gone With the Wind.
7. Have you ever seen Touched by an Angel on television?
8. The pilgrims sailed across the Atlantic in the Mayflower.
9. The number seven is considered lucky by many.
10. I often add a second c in necessary.

More Practice

Grammar Exercise Workbook
- pp. 181–182

On-line Exercise Bank
- Section 26.4

Go on-line: PHSchool.com
Enter Web Code: eck-8002

iText

Get instant feedback! Exercise 37 is available on-line or on CD-ROM.

When to Use Quotation Marks

In general, quotation marks are used for short works and works that are part of a longer work.

KEY CONCEPT Use quotation marks to enclose the titles of short written works. ■

The following chart contains examples of titles that should be enclosed in quotation marks.

WRITTEN WORKS THAT TAKE QUOTATION MARKS	
Title of a Short Story	"The Gift of the Magi"
Chapter From a Book	"The Test Is in the Tasting" from *No-Work Garden Book*
Title of a Short Poem	"Lucy"
Title of an Article	"How to Build a Birdhouse"

KEY CONCEPT Use quotation marks around the titles of episodes in a series, songs, and parts of a long musical composition. ■

TIME SAVERS!

Answers on Transparency Use the Grammar Exercises Answers on Transparencies for Chapter 26 to have students correct their own or one another's exercises.

On-Line Exercise Bank Have students complete the exercises on computer. The Auto Check feature will grade their work for you!

ONGOING ASSESSMENT: Monitor and Reinforce

If students miss more than two items in Exercises 37–38, refer them to the following for additional practice.

In the Textbook	Print Resources	Technology
Chapter Review, Ex. 65, p. 633	Grammar Exercise Workbook, pp. 181–182	On-Line Exercise Bank, Section 26.4

KEY CONCEPT Use quotation marks around the title of a work that is mentioned as part of a collection. ■

The title of the play *Uncle Vanya* normally is underlined or italicized. In the following example, however, the title is placed in quotation marks because it is cited as part of a larger work.

EXAMPLE: "Uncle Vanya" in *Eight Great Comedies*

Exercise 38 Using Quotation Marks With Titles Each of the following sentences contains a title that needs quotation marks. Some of the sentences also contain titles that need underlining. Copy the titles onto your paper, either enclosing them in quotation marks or underlining them.

EXAMPLE: My favorite song is Getting to Know You from The King and I.

ANSWER: "Getting to Know You"; <u>The King and I</u>

1. John Brown's Body is a short poem written about the abolitionist leader.
2. Pygmalion, by George Bernard Shaw, can be found in the collection Masterpieces of Drama.
3. Michael Drayton, England's poet laureate in 1606, wrote Ode to the Virginian Voyage, a long poem.
4. I read about Virginia in The Virginia Magazine of History and Biography.
5. In 1903, a train wreck in Danville inspired the folk song The Wreck of the Old '97.
6. My favorite Greek myth is Perseus, which can be found in the collection Classic Greek Myths and Legends.
7. We found a great article entitled Discovering Virginia's Heritage in Travel Virginia magazine.
8. My favorite short poem is Mending Wall by Robert Frost.
9. For homework, we were assigned to read Chapter 13, The Southern Colonies, in our history book.
10. Have you ever heard the song Whatever Became of Delilah?

▲ **Critical Viewing** Write the titles of your favorite novel, short story, and song. Use quotation marks and underlining as needed. **[Apply]**

More Practice

Grammar Exercise Workbook
• pp. 181–182
On-line Exercise Bank
• Section 26.4

Go on-line: PHSchool.com
Enter Web Code: eck-8002

Answer Key

Exercise 38

1. "John Brown's Body"
2. "Pygmalion," <u>Masterpieces of Drama</u>
3. <u>Ode to the Virginian Voyage</u>
4. <u>The Virginia Magazine of History and Biography</u>
5. "The Wreck of the Old '97"
6. "Perseus", <u>Classic Greek Myths and Legends</u>
7. "Discovering Virginia's Heritage," <u>Travel Virginia</u>
8. "Mending Wall"
9. "The Southern Colonies"
10. "Whatever Became of Delilah?"

Critical Viewing

Apply Students' answers will vary. Be sure they are correctly marked with quotation marks and underlining. Sample answer: <u>The Adventures of Tom Sawyer</u>

"The Pit and the Pendulum"

"New York, New York"

ONGOING ASSESSMENT: Assess Mastery

Use the following resources to assess mastery of underlining and quotation marks.

In the Textbook	Technology
Chapter Review, Ex. 65, p. 633 Standardized Test Preparation Workshop, pp. 634–635	Writing and Grammar iText, Section 26.4, Section Review; On-Line Exercise Bank, Section 26.4

ASSESS and CLOSE

Section Review

Each of these exercises correlates to a concept in the section on quotation marks and underlining, pages 614–621. These exercises may be used for more practice, for reteaching, or for review of the Key Concepts presented. Answers for all chapter exercises are available in *Grammar Exercises Answers on Transparencies* in your teaching resources.

Answer Key

Exercise 39

1. Buck told us, "On April 9, 1865, General Lee surrendered at Appomattox."
2. "The time after the war during which the South was recovering is called the Reconstruction," Buck recalled.
3. Sally sighed, "Some in Congress were determined to treat the South like a conquest."
4. I
5. "It was, I believe," Robert said, "in 1870 before Virginia was back in Congress."

Exercise 40

1. "Have you ever visited Colonial Williamsburg?" asked Keesha.
2. "Not since I was in second grade," I answered.
3. Keesha said she'd been there during spring vacation.
4. "So much history!" she exclaimed. "It's called the largest living museum in the world."
5. She went on, "We were able to experience first-hand how people in colonial times lived."

Exercise 41

1. <u>Susan Constant</u>, <u>Goodspeed</u>, <u>Discovery</u>
2. <u>Pocahontas</u>
3. <u>American Journey</u>
4. "Shenandoah"
5. <u>Gazette</u>

Section 26.4

Section Review

GRAMMAR EXERCISES 39–44

Exercise 39 **Revising Sentences Using Quotation Marks** Write the following sentences on your paper, capitalizing correctly and placing commas and quotation marks in the proper places. If the quotation is indirect, write *I* on your paper.

1. Buck told us, on April 9, 1865, General Lee surrendered at Appomattox.
2. The time after the war during which the South was recovering is called the Reconstruction Buck recalled.
3. Sally sighed some in Congress were determined to treat the South like a conquest.
4. Sally asked when it was that Virginia was able to return to the Union.
5. It was I believe Robert said in 1870 before Virginia was back in Congress.

Exercise 40 **Supplying Punctuation and Capitalization for Quotations** Copy these sentences onto your paper. Insert quotation marks, end marks, and capitalization as needed.

1. Have you ever visited Colonial Williamsburg asked Keesha
2. Not since I was in second grade I answered
3. Keesha said that she'd been there during spring vacation
4. So much history she exclaimed it's called the largest living museum in the world
5. She went on we were able to experience firsthand how people in colonial times lived

Exercise 41 **Using Underlining and Quotation Marks With Titles** Write the titles from the following sentences, using underlining or quotation marks.

1. The first ships to arrive in Virginia were the Susan Constant, the Goodspeed, and the Discovery.
2. Pocahontas is a movie about a Powhatan woman who married a settler, John Rolfe.
3. I read about Virginia history in David Goldfield's American Journey.
4. Shenandoah is a song about the Shenandoah River valley in Virginia.
5. The first newspaper in Williamsburg was the Gazette, started in 1736.

Exercise 42 **Find It in Your Reading** Copy the following paragraph onto a separate sheet of paper. Then, insert the proper underlining and quotation marks.

Carla reported The Drummer Boy of Shiloh by Ray Bradbury tells the story of a boy on the eve of his first Civil War battle. Sean asked if it was exciting to read. Dion exclaimed It is better than the movie The Red Badge of Courage.

Exercise 43 **Find It in Your Writing** Look through your writing portfolio for a piece of writing that uses quotation marks. Check to make sure you have used quotation marks correctly. Then, challenge yourself to add six more sentences using quotation marks in dialogue, titles, special words, or names.

Exercise 44 **Writing Application** Write ten sentences of dialogue between two students and their teacher about a history lesson. Use question marks and other punctuation marks to show the questions and answers that these three characters share.

Exercise 42

Find It in Your Reading

Carla reported, "<u>The Drummer Boy of Shiloh</u> by Ray Bradbury tells the story of a boy on the eve of his first Civil War battle."

Sean asked if it was exciting to read. Dion exclaimed, "It is better than the movie <u>The Red Badge of Courage</u>."

Exercise 43

Find It in Your Writing

Have students work with partners and check each other's work.

Exercise 44

Writing Application

Remind students to indent in their dialogues when speakers change.

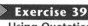

Section 26.5

Hyphens and Apostrophes

The *hyphen* is used to combine numbers and word parts, to join certain compound words, and to show that a word has been broken between syllables at the end of a line.

Theme: The Yukon

In this section, you will learn several purposes for hyphens and apostrophes. The examples and exercises are about the Yukon and the gold rush in the Klondike.

Cross-Curricular Connection: Social Studies

Using Hyphens

KEY CONCEPT Use a hyphen when writing out two-word numbers from twenty-one through ninety-nine. ■

EXAMPLES: There were *thirty-four* people panning for gold.

KEY CONCEPT Use a hyphen when writing fractions that are used as adjectives. ■

EXAMPLE: A *four-fifths* majority wanted to head west.

Notice, however, that a fraction used as a noun, rather than as an adjective, does not need a hyphen.

EXAMPLE: *Two thirds* of the ore had been placed in the cart.

KEY CONCEPT Use a hyphen after a prefix that is followed by a proper noun or adjective. ■

The following prefixes are often used before proper nouns: *ante-*, *anti-*, *mid-*, *post-*, *pre-*, *pro-*, and *un-*.

EXAMPLE: Many settlers moved west in the *post-Revolutionary* years.

▼ Critical Viewing
Use *pre-* or *post-* as a prefix in a description of this picture. **[Apply]**

KEY CONCEPT Use a hyphen in words with the prefixes *all-*, *ex-*, and *self-* and with the suffix *-elect*. ■

EXAMPLES: all-powerful
self-determined
ex-leader
governor-elect

KEY CONCEPT Use a hyphen to connect two or more nouns that are used as one word, unless the dictionary gives a different spelling. ■

EXAMPLES: lady-in-waiting, great-grandfather, cave-in, secretary-treasurer

PREPARE and ENGAGE

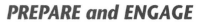

Interest GRABBER Write the following sentences on the board and ask students why some have hyphens and some do not.

I have three quarters in my pocket.

The bottle of juice is three-quarters full.

Jake is a great grandfather to his grandchildren.

Jake is my great-grandfather.

The cave-in buried the explorer.

There is a cave in that mountain.

Activate Prior Knowledge

Ask students to form the possessive of the following nouns.

shark (shark's)	*sharks (sharks')*
man (man's)	*men (men's)*
he (his)	*they (their, theirs)*

TEACH

Step-by-Step Teaching Guide

Hyphens and Apostrophes

1. Some hyphen rules have exceptions. The only way to know if a hyphen is needed is to use a dictionary. For example, *Atlantic* is a proper adjective, but *transatlantic* is not hyphenated and the *a* is lowercase.
2. Compound words must be looked up too. The only way to know if *hot dog* is one word, two words, or hyphenated is to use the dictionary.
3. After determining that *hot dog* is two words, students cannot assume that all words beginning with *hot* also are two words: *hotcake, hot-wire.*

Critical Viewing

Apply Students may suggest: I'd like to preview a movie on this event.

TIME AND RESOURCE MANAGER

Resources
Print: Grammar Exercises Workbook, pp. 183–188; Hands-on Grammar Activity Book, Ch. 26
Technology: Writing and Grammar iText, Section 26.5; On-Line Exercise Bank, Section 26.5

In-Depth Coverage	Accelerated Pace
• Work through all key concepts, pp. 623–629. • Assign and review Exercises 45–50. • Do the Hands-on Grammar Activity, p. 630.	• Assign pp. 623–629 for independent student review. • Assign Section Review Exercises 51–53.

Answer Key

Exercise 45

1. correct
2. correct
3. Franklin was a self-confident man.
4. He first reached the Yukon from the Arctic side, a once-in-a-lifetime accomplishment.
5. In 1841, Robert Campbell explored the Yukon, thirty-four years after The Hudson Bay Company navigated the area.

26.5

KEY CONCEPT Use a hyphen to connect a compound modifier that comes before a noun. ■

EXAMPLE: Cass was a *big-hearted* miner.

No hyphen is necessary when a compound modifier follows the noun it describes.

BEFORE: The settlers moved in an *east-to-west* direction.
AFTER: They moved in the direction *east to west.*
BEFORE: They traveled in *well-equipped* wagons.
AFTER: They traveled in wagons that were *well equipped.*

However, if a dictionary spells a word with a hyphen, the word must always be hyphenated, even when it follows a noun.

EXAMPLES: This *poor-spirited* man will never find gold.
This man is *poor-spirited.*

KEY CONCEPT Do *not* use a hyphen with a compound modifier that includes a word ending in *-ly* or in a compound proper adjective. ■

INCORRECT: clearly-written
CORRECT: clearly written
INCORRECT: West-Indian music
CORRECT: West Indian music

Spelling Tip

Plurals of compound nouns that are written with hyphens are frequently formed by making the first word plural:

lady-in-waiting
ladies-in-waiting

mother-in-law
mothers-in-law

jack-of-all-trades
jacks-of-all-trades

Exercise 45 **Proofreading for Hyphens in Numbers, Word Parts, and Compound Words** Rewrite the sentences below, adding hyphens where needed. If an item does not require a hyphen, write *correct.*

EXAMPLE: Freshly fallen snow covered the area.
ANSWER: correct

1. Sir John Franklin was the first nonnative to see any part of the Yukon Territory.
2. This part of Canada was not a clearly mapped region.
3. Franklin was a self confident man.
4. He first reached the Yukon from the Arctic side, a once in a lifetime accomplishment.
5. In 1841, Robert Campbell explored the Yukon, thirty four years after The Hudson Bay Company navigated the area.

More Practice

Grammar Exercise Workbook
• pp. 183–184
On-line Exercise Bank
• Section 26.5
Go on-line:
PHSchool.com
Enter Web Code:
eck-8002

TIME SAVERS!

Answers on Transparency Use the Grammar Exercises Answers on Transparencies for Chapter 26 to have students correct their own or one another's exercises.

On-Line Exercise Bank Have students complete the exercises on computer. The Auto Check feature will grade their work for you!

Rules for Dividing Words at the End of a Line

Avoid dividing words at the end of a line whenever possible. If a word must be divided, divide it between syllables.

EXAMPLE: You must not feel that your contribution was insignificant.

KEY CONCEPT Do *not* divide one-syllable words even if they seem long or sound like words with two syllables. ■

INCORRECT:	sch-ool	bru-ised	thro-ugh
CORRECT:	school	bruised	through

KEY CONCEPT Do *not* divide a word so that a single letter stands alone. ■

INCORRECT:	a-mid	ver-y	o-kay
CORRECT:	amid	very	okay

Avoid placing *-ed* at the beginning of a new line.

INCORRECT: halt-ed
CORRECT: halted

KEY CONCEPT Divide a hyphenated word or phrase only after the hyphen. ■

INCORRECT: During the gold rush, many prospec-
tor-friendly towns popped up.

CORRECT: During the gold rush, many prospector-
friendly towns popped up.

Exercise 46 **Using Hyphens to Divide Words** Decide whether you can hyphenate each of the following words. If you can divide the word, write it with a hyphen at each point that it can be divided. If it cannot be divided, write the whole word. If you are not sure how a word should be divided, check a dictionary.

1. counter
2. empty-handed
3. engage
4. snowfall
5. tent
6. regroup
7. overrun
8. farther
9. digging
10. queen

Technology Tip

Many word-processing programs include the option of automatically dividing words as you type them.

iText

Get instant feedback! Exercise 46 is available on-line or on CD-ROM.

More Practice

Grammar Exercise Workbook
• pp. 183–184
On-line Exercise Bank
• Section 26.5
Go on-line:
PHSchool.com
Enter Web Code:
eck-8002

Find It In Your Writing

Have students review a selection from their portfolio for hyphen use. Have them correct any mistakes they find.

Answer Key

Exercise 46

1. coun-ter
2. empty-handed
3. en-gage
4. snow-fall
5. tent
6. re-group
7. over-run
8. far-ther
9. dig-ging
10. queen

ONGOING ASSESSMENT: Monitor and Reinforce

If students miss more than two items in Exercises 45–46, refer them to the following for additional practice.

In the Textbook	Print Resources	Technology
Chapter Review, Ex. 61, p. 633	Grammar Exercise Workbook, pp. 183–184	On-Line Exercise Bank, Section 26.5

Step-by-Step Teaching Guide

Apostrophes with Possessive Nouns

1. Apostrophe *-s* is added to nouns to show possession. Point out the choice of adding an *-s* to nouns already ending in *-s.*
2. Show students that for plural nouns ending in *-s* or *-es,* only an apostrophe is added to form the possessive.

   dogs dogs'

   buildings buildings'
3. There are two special cases. The Biblical names, such as Jesus and Moses, take only an apostrophe to form the possessive. Proper names with the final syllable pronounced *eez,* such as Euripides and Aristophanes, also take only an apostrophe.

Critical Viewing

Apply Students may suggest: Max the moose's photograph is interesting.

The moose's antlers are large.

Its antlers' prongs look dangerous.

26.5

Using Apostrophes With Possessive Nouns

Apostrophes are used with nouns to show ownership or possession.

KEY CONCEPT Add an apostrophe and -*s* to show the possessive case of most singular nouns. ■

EXAMPLE: The role *of the parent* becomes the *parent's* role.

Even when a singular noun already ends in -*s*, you can usually add an apostrophe and -*s* to show possession.

EXAMPLE: The color *of an iris* becomes an *iris's* color.

In classical or ancient names that end in -*s*, such as Odysseus or Democritus, it is common practice to leave the final -*s* off for ease of pronunciation.

EXAMPLE: *Odysseus'* voyages were dangerous.

KEY CONCEPT Add just an apostrophe to show the possessive case of plural nouns ending in -*s* or -*es*. ■

EXAMPLES: The mother of the *bears* becomes the *bears'* mother.
The belief of the *multitudes* becomes the *multitudes'* belief.

◀ **Critical Viewing** Use possessive nouns in three sentences about the moose in this photograph. Be sure to place apostrophes correctly. **[Apply]**

Exercise 47 **Supplying Apostrophes to Plural Possessive Nouns** Write the possessive case of the plural nouns in the sentences below, adding apostrophes as needed.

1. The gold seekers need for money led them to the Yukon.
2. At that time, many countries economies were suffering.
3. The prospectors haste to reach the Yukon began in 1896.
4. It was many travelers belief that they could find gold.
5. Fifteen hundred adventurers dreams were lost.
6. The prospectors preferred method of travel was by dog sled.
7. The dogs lives were not altogether unpleasant, although they worked hard.
8. The dog teams task was to pull heavily loaded sleds through the snow.
9. The sleds loads were often hundreds of pounds.
10. The dogs and the prospectors comfort was less important than hauling enough supplies to survive in the cold.

KEY CONCEPT Add an apostrophe and *-s* to show the possessive case of plural nouns that do not end in *-s* or *-es*. ■

EXAMPLE: The trek *of the men* becomes the *men's* trek.

KEY CONCEPT Add an apostrophe and *-s* (or just an apostrophe if the word is a plural ending in *-s)* to the last word of a compound noun to form the possessive. ■

EXAMPLES: the *Girl Scouts'* cookie sale
my *sister-in-law's* car

Exercise 48 **Using Apostrophes to Form the Possessives of Nouns** Copy each underlined noun below onto your paper, putting it into the possessive form by adding an apostrophe and *-s* as needed.

EXAMPLE: The region museums of the gold rush have been a great success.
ANSWER: region's

1. Many prospectors would seek a guide assistance.
2. Explorers depended on the native peoples knowledge.
3. Settlers lives were eased by friendships with the Chinook people.
4. The Hudson Bay traders ingenuity led them to create a common language with the Chinook.
5. The Chinooks home was along the Columbia River.

More Practice

Grammar Exercise Workbook
• pp. 185–186
On-line Exercise Bank
• Section 26.5
Go on-line:
PHSchool.com
Enter Web Code:
eck-8002

iText

Get instant feedback! Exercises 47 and 48 are available on-line or on CD-ROM.

Answer Key

Exercise 47

1. gold seekers'
2. countries'
3. prospectors'
4. travelers'
5. adventurers'
6. prospectors'
7. dogs'
8. teams'
9. sleds'
10. dogs', prospectors'

Exercise 48

1. guide's
2. people's
3. Settlers'
4. traders'
5. Chinooks'

TIME SAVERS!

Answers on Transparency Use the Grammar Exercises Answers on Transparencies for Chapter 26 to have students correct their own or one another's exercises.

On-Line Exercise Bank Have students complete the exercises on computer. The Auto Check feature will grade their work for you!

Step-by-Step Teaching Guide

Apostrophes with Pronouns

1. Students are frequently confused by how to treat possessive personal pronouns. They apply the rule add *'s* and end up with *hers's* and *his's.* Remind students that possessive pronouns are already possessive, so they never take *'s.*
2. Contractions are covered on page 629. When students confuse *its/it's* and *their/there/they're,* it is usually the result of haste rather than not knowing which is which.

Answer Key

Exercise 49

1. correct
2. another's
3. yours
4. everyone's
5. correct

26.5

Using Apostrophes With Pronouns

Both indefinite and personal pronouns can show possession.

KEY CONCEPT Use an apostrophe and -*s* with indefinite pronouns to show possession. ■

EXAMPLES: another's preference
nobody else's business

KEY CONCEPT Do not use an apostrophe with possessive personal pronouns. ■

None of the following personal pronouns needs an apostrophe to show possession: *my, mine, your, yours, his, her, hers, its, our, ours, their,* and *theirs.*

Some of these pronouns act as adjectives.

EXAMPLES: The spider caught a fly in *its* web.
Our house is for sale.

Others act as subjects, objects, and subject complements.

EXAMPLES: *Mine* is the yellow crayon.
Someone broke *yours.*
The red one is *his.*

Exercise 49 **Proofreading for Apostrophes With Pronouns** The following sentences contain possessive pronouns. If a possessive is written incorrectly, rewrite it to make it correct. If all pronouns in a sentence are used correctly, write *correct.*

EXAMPLE: In the new claim, the lake was <u>his</u> and the island was <u>their's</u>.
ANSWER: theirs

1. Once prospectors reached the Klondike, they had only to find open land and stake their claims.
2. If a prospector took anothers claim, it was called "claim jumping."
3. Imagine the disappointment of surviving the trip to the Klondike only to lose what was yours' to claim jumping!
4. Finally, the Miners' Association was formed to protect everyones legal claims.
5. The association had its first building in Discovery, the tent city on the Pine Creek.

More Practice

Grammar Exercise Workbook
- pp. 185–186

On-line Exercise Bank
- Section 26.5

Go on-line:
PHSchool.com
Enter Web Code:
eck-8002

iText

Get instant feedback! Exercise 49 is available on-line or on CD-ROM.

ONGOING ASSESSMENT: Monitor and Reinforce

If students miss more than two items in Exercises 47–49, refer them to the following for additional practice.

In the Textbook	Print Resources	Technology
Chapter Review, Ex. 62, p. 633	Grammar Exercise Workbook, pp. 185–186	On-Line Exercise Bank, Section 26.5

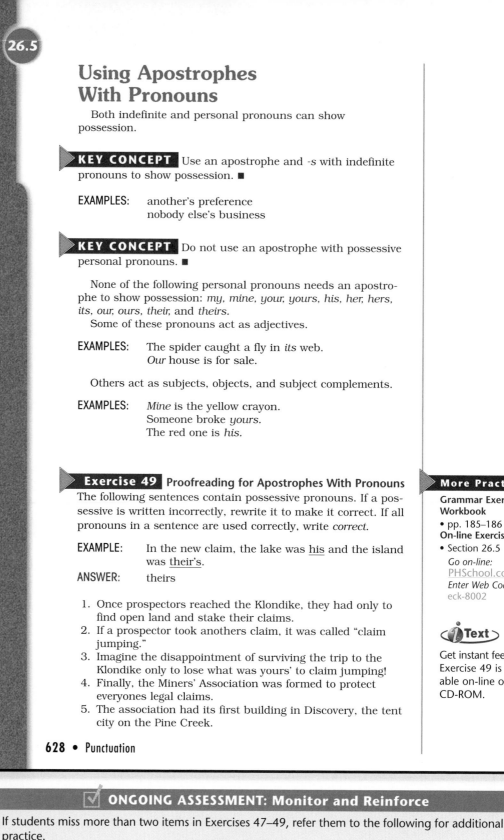

Using Apostrophes With Contractions

Contractions are shortened forms of words or phrases.

KEY CONCEPT Use an apostrophe in a contraction to indicate the position of the missing letter or letters. ■

COMMON CONTRACTIONS WITH VERBS		
Verb + *not*	are not (aren't) is not (isn't) was not (wasn't) were not (weren't) cannot (can't)	could not (couldn't) did not (didn't) do not (don't) should not (shouldn't) would not (wouldn't)
Pronoun + the Verb *will*	I will (I'll) you are (you'll) he will (he'll) she will (she'll)	we will (we'll) they will (they'll) who will (who'll)
Pronoun or Noun + the Verb *be*	I am (I'm) you are (you're) he is (he's) she is (she's) it is (it's)	we are (we're) they are (they're) who is (who's) where is (where's) Lee is (Lee's)
Pronoun or Noun + the Verb *would*	I would (I'd) you would (you'd) he would (he'd) she would (she'd)	we would (we'd) they would (they'd) who would (who'd) Nancy would (Nancy'd)

An apostrophe is also used to form contractions of years.

EXAMPLE: the 2001 yearbook (the *'01* yearbook)

Exercise 50 **Using Contractions in Informal Writing** On your paper, write the contractions possible in each sentence below.

EXAMPLE: Where is the new history book?
ANSWER: Where's

1. Yukon life was not without heartache.
2. The majority of prospectors did not find their fortune.
3. Often, a gold seeker's family would not hear of his fate.
4. After the gold rush ended, a woman could move to the Yukon if she thought she would find work.
5. One German prospector sent for his wife— "If she will make the voyage," he said.

iText

Get instant feedback! Exercise 50 is available on-line or on CD-ROM.

More Practice

Grammar Exercise Workbook
- pp. 187–188

On-line Exercise Bank
- Section 26.5

Go on-line:
PHSchool.com
Enter Web Code:
eck-8002

Step-by-Step Teaching Guide

Apostrophes with Contractions

1. Contractions are a convenient way of shortening expressions. Advise students that they are fine for informal writing, but that in formal writing contractions should be avoided.
2. Review the contraction chart with students, going through each example individually.

Answer Key

Exercise 50

1. wasn't
2. didn't
3. wouldn't
4. she'd
5. she'll

PRENTICE HALL
Everyday Spelling

If you have taught the spelling skills in *Prentice Hall Everyday Spelling,* Grade 8, Chapter 31, in conjunction with this *Writing and Grammar* chapter, review and assess students' mastery of the skills before concluding the chapter.

TIME SAVERS!

Answers on Transparency Use the Grammar Exercises Answers on Transparencies for Chapter 26 to have students correct their own or one another's exercises.

On-Line Exercise Bank Have students complete the exercises on computer. The Auto Check feature will grade their work for you!

Step-by-Step Teaching Guide

Contractions-Fold

Teaching Resources: Hands-on Grammar Activity Book, Chapter 26

1. Have students refer to their Hands-on Grammar activity books or give them copies of the relevant pages for this activity.
2. If students have trouble with this activity have them make a list and write the proper contraction for each word before they begin folding.

Find It in Your Reading

Have students compare their results from this activity to see whether a pattern emerges.

Find It in Your Writing

Have students work in pairs and check each other's contractions.

26.5

Hands-on Grammar

Contractions-Fold

To review which letters are dropped and where apostrophes belong in common contractions, try this contractions-fold activity. Start by cutting out fifteen strips of paper. Each strip should be 1" wide and 3 1/4" long. On each strip, print one of the following words exactly as they appear below. Write each word in capital letters and as large as possible on the strip.

ISNOT	IHAVE	IWOULD
ARENOT	SHEWILL	YOUWOULD
DIDNOT	WEHAVE	HEWOULD
WERENOT	YOUARE	WEWOULD
CANNOT	YOUWILL	THEYWOULD

Place the completed strips of paper into an envelope or some other receptacle from which they can be chosen at random. Working alone or with a group, select strips of paper from the envelope. Look at the word you selected and decide the proper form of its contraction. Fold the strip of paper in such a way as to cover up the letters to be replaced by an apostrophe. To do this, fold the paper once in the middle of the letters you want to cover and again next to the first letter to the right of where the apostrophe should be placed.

After you have correctly folded the strip of paper to show the proper form of the contraction, use it in a sentence.

Find It in Your Reading Review several nonfiction articles from your literature textbook or from newspapers and magazines. Note the types of contractions used and their frequency. Then, analyze how formal each nonfiction article is, and determine whether there is a correlation between how formal the writing is and how many contractions are used.

Find It in Your Writing Review your writing portfolio, and select a piece of writing in which you have used contractions. Make sure you have used contractions correctly in the piece. If not, revise your writing.

630 • Punctuation

TIME SAVERS!

Hands-on Grammar
Use the Hands-on Grammar activity sheet for Chapter 26 to facilitate this activity.

ONGOING ASSESSMENT: Assess Mastery

Use the following resources to assess mastery of using hyphens and apostrophes.

In the Textbook	Technology
Chapter Review, Ex. 62, p. 633 Standardized Test Preparation Workshop, pp. 634–635	On-Line Exercise Bank, Section 26.5

Section 26.5 Section Review

GRAMMAR EXERCISES 51–56

Exercise 51 **Supplying Hyphens in Numbers, Word Parts, and Compound Words** On your paper, write the hyphenated word, compound word, or number that needs a hyphen in the sentences below. If no hyphen is needed, write *correct.*

1. Strong bonds were formed between the adventurers during the two year rush to the Yukon.
2. The native peoples were open to newly formed friendships.
3. Each person in an exploration party had three much needed items.
4. It was an unheard of occurrence to leave civilization without a compass.
5. Equally important was a fairly high quality magnifying glass.

Exercise 52 **Indicating Where Hyphens Divide Words and Compound Words at the End of a Line** Copy each word or phrase below, drawing a vertical line at each point where it could be divided. (Not every item can be divided.) If you are unsure of a word, use a dictionary.

1. constructive
2. Europe
3. all-powerful
4. to-and-fro
5. Yukon
6. strummed
7. tomorrow
8. above
9. turkey
10. compass

Exercise 53 **Supplying Apostrophes With Plural and Singular Nouns to Form Possessives of Words Ending in *-s* or *-es*** Each of the following sentences needs at least one apostrophe to form the possessive case. Write the word or words with the apostrophe.

1. During the gold rush, the Yukon Rivers largest settlement was Dawson.
2. In 1899, the inhabitants homes were tents and quickly built cabins.
3. Dawsons population was an astonishing 25,000 people.
4. The womens lives were difficult, as were the mens.
5. The people of Dawson always depended on one anothers kindness.

Exercise 54 **Find It in Your Reading** Find a textbook or encyclopedia article about the Yukon Territory. Find examples of apostrophes used with possessive nouns and pronouns and hyphens used to divide words. Write down at least one example of each.

Exercise 55 **Find It in Your Writing** Choose a paragraph of writing from your portfolio. Imagine that you have been asked to narrow the right-hand margin of your paper; therefore, you have to decide whether to hyphenate the words at the end of each line or to write the complete word on the next line. If you can divide the word, write the part of the word that would appear at the end of the first line on your paper. If you cannot divide the word, write the complete word.

Exercise 56 **Writing Application** Write a brief narrative about an exciting adventure you or someone you know has experienced. Include at least three of the following in your narrative:

1. hyphenated number
2. apostrophe to show possession
3. apostrophe to form a contraction
4. contraction of *he is* or *she is*
5. hyphen at the end of a line

ASSESS and CLOSE

Section Review

Each of these exercises correlates to a concept in the section on hyphens and apostrophes, pages 623–629. These exercises may be used for more practice, for reteaching, or for review of the Key Concepts presented. Answers for all chapter exercises are available in *Grammar Exercises Answers on Transparencies* in your teaching resources.

Answer Key

Exercise 51

1. two-year
2. correct
3. much-needed
4. unheard-of
5. high-quality

Exercise 52

1. con|struc|tive
2. Eu|rope
3. all-|powerful
4. to-|and-|fro
5. Yu|kon
6. strummed
7. to|mor|row
8. above
9. tur|key
10. com|pass

Exercise 53

1. River's
2. inhabitants'
3. Dawson's
4. women's, men's
5. another's

Exercise 54

Find It in Your Reading
Ask students to tell whether the apostrophes show singular or plural possessives.

continued

Answer Key continued

Exercise 55

Find It in Your Writing
Encourage students to use the dictionary to be sure of correct hyphenations.

Exercise 56

Writing Application
Students can also describe an adventure they would like to have, such as traveling to Neptune or to the center of a volcano.

TIME SAVERS!

Answers on Transparency Use the Grammar Exercises Answers on Transparencies for Chapter 26 to have students correct their own or one another's exercises.

On-Line Exercise Bank Have students complete the exercises on computer. The Auto Check feature will grade their work for you!

CHAPTER REVIEW

Each of these exercises correlates to a concept in the chapter on punctuation, pages 596–629. These exercises may be used for more practice, for reteaching, or for review of the Key Concepts presented. Answers for all exercises are available in *Grammar Exercises Answers on Transparencies* in your teaching resources.

Answer Key

Exercise 57

1. Was the Yukon gold rush the only one in North America?
2. Wow! Nothing could be more exciting than finding gold.
3. The Yukon rush was dramatic because conditions were so severe, yet the rush was not North America's first.
4. A Swiss immigrant named Sutter founded a town in central California, and he tried to build a trading fortune there.
5. In 1848, a tiny piece of gold was found in the tailrace of his sawmill, but that was enough evidence to begin a wild stampede.

Exercise 58

1. John Sutter lost everything in the gold rush, including his buildings, property, and livestock.
2. The more than 80,000 would-be millionaires lived in hastily constructed shacks, in crowded tents, and on the trampled ground.
3. Sutter left Sutter's Mill and California in 1851, bankrupt, bitter, and regretful.
4. Unfortunately, the main deposits of gold, or Mother Lode, had dwindled away quickly.
5. Once thriving and bustling, the boom towns became deserted ghost towns overnight.

Exercise 59

1. The Alaskan gold rush began in 1886; the site was Fortymile Creek on the Yukon River.

Chapter 26

Chapter Review

GRAMMAR EXERCISES 57–65

Exercise 57 **Proofreading Sentences for End Marks and Commas** Write the sentences below on your paper, inserting end marks and commas as necessary.

1. Was the Yukon gold rush the only one in North America
2. Wow Nothing could be more exciting than finding gold
3. The Yukon gold rush was dramatic because conditions were so severe yet the rush was North America's first
4. A Swiss immigrant named Sutter founded a town in central California and he tried to build a trading fortune there
5. In 1848 a tiny piece of gold was found in the tailrace of his sawmill but that was enough evidence to begin a wild stampede

Exercise 58 **Proofreading Sentences for Commas** Write the sentences below on your paper, inserting commas as necessary. If the sentence needs no comma, write *correct.*

1. John Sutter lost everything in the gold rush, including his buildings property and livestock.
2. The more than 80000 would-be millionaires lived in hastily constructed shacks in crowded tents and on the trampled ground.
3. Sutter left Sutter's Mill and California in 1851, bankrupt bitter and regretful.
4. Unfortunately the main deposits of gold or mother lode had dwindled away quickly.
5. Once thriving and bustling the boom towns became deserted ghost towns overnight.

Exercise 59 **Revising Sentences Using Semicolons and Colons** Copy the sentences below, inserting semicolons or colons as necessary.

1. The Alaskan gold rush began in 1886 the site was Fortymile Creek on the Yukon River.
2. There has always been some confusion involved with the Yukon and Alaska gold rushes both stampedes started on the Yukon River, which flows through Alaska and Canada's Yukon Territory.
3. Ten years later, the Canadian rush began however, the Alaskan rush was longer and more profitable.
4. Life was tough in winter, there was daylight only from about 11:00 A.M. to 2:00 P.M.
5. There were some things he forgot to bring bacon, gloves, and matches.

Exercise 60 **Identifying and Revising Direct and Indirect Quotations** On your paper, rewrite the direct quotations with the proper punctuation. If the sentence is an indirect quotation, write *I* on your paper.

1. Many of the descendants of prospectors who joined the Yukon gold rush still live there said Martin.
2. Chloe recalled that as a child her mother had visited the Yukon Territory.
3. The Yukon gold rush said Jake took place in Canada.
4. Why asked Meredith do you make that statement?
5. Jake replied that many people still think that the Yukon Territory is in Alaska.

2. There has always been some confusion involved with the Yukon and Alaska gold rushes; both stampedes started on the Yukon River, which flows through Alaska and Canada's Yukon Territory.
3. Ten years later, the Canadian rush began; however, the Alaskan rush was longer and more profitable.
4. Life was tough in the winter; there was daylight only from about 11:00 A.M. to 2:00 P.M.
5. There were some things he forgot to bring: bacon, gloves, and matches.

Exercise 60

1. "Many of the descendants of prospectors who joined the Yukon gold rush still live there," said Martin.
2. I
3. "The Yukon gold rush," said Jake, "took place in Canada."
4. "Why," asked Meredith, "do you make that statement?"
5. I

Exercise 61 **Dividing Words at the End of a Line** Decide whether you can hyphenate each of the following words. If you can, write the word with a hyphen to indicate where the word could break at the end of a line.

1. interesting
2. whitewater
3. pell-mell
4. rented
5. Alaska

Exercise 62 **Proofreading for Apostrophes With Possessive Nouns and Pronouns** Copy the following sentences on your paper, inserting apostrophes in the proper places or removing them if they are used incorrectly.

1. Kathleen said that many peoples dreams were lost in the gold rushes.
2. However, it is nobody elses business how one chooses to seek his or her fortune.
3. My choice would not be the same as yours'.
4. Prospectors families hoped that their's would be the claim that paid off.
5. Often, the childrens lives were least affected by the rush, as their job was simply to go to school.

Exercise 63 **Proofreading for Punctuation** Revise the following paragraph, correcting all errors in the use of end marks, commas, colons, semicolons, hyphens, apostrophes, and quotation marks.

You know said Zoe there were as many disappointments during Californias gold rush as there were in the Yukons Then she told this tale

It was up in California around June 15 1849 and two prospectors Bill and Jeb were about to have their first gold washing experience At the break of dawn they set up a pump by the river Jeb fed the machine Bill shoveled the accumulated dirt Near sundown the mens' backs began to ache However Bills eagerness kept them working They started washing the dirt with a half circular swinging motion in the water After straining the last of the dirt they looked at each other and asked Where is the gold Alas After a whole days labor they had only one tiny piece worth perhaps half a dollar

Exercise 64 **CUMULATIVE REVIEW** **Capitalization and Punctuation** Rewrite the following paragraph on your paper, inserting the necessary punctuation and capitalization.

(1) todays economy enjoys many positive effects as the result of the gold rush period in north america (2) in fact if it werent for peoples desire to conquer natures difficulties much of alaska and the yukon territory probably would not have been explored so soon (3) the then newly discovered treasures of oil timber wildlife and tourism continue to be assets of the area (4) alaskas oil pipeline is one of this countrys greatest accomplishments it perhaps would not exist had it not been for the less successful rush for gold (5) it might have taken both the united states and canada years longer to make use of the yukon's resources

Exercise 65 **Writing Application** Write a narrative about a trip to a beach. Include dialogue between two or more people. Include the following items in your narrative, and be sure to punctuate and capitalize correctly.

1. title of a book
2. possessive plural noun that ends in *-s* or *-es*.
3. hyphenated word
4. semicolon to connect two ideas
5. colon to introduce items in a series

Answer Key continued

4. Alaska's oil pipeline is one of this country's greatest accomplishments. It perhaps would not exist had it not been for the less-successful rush for gold.
5. It might have taken both the United States and Canada years longer to make use of the Yukon's resources.

Exercise 65

Writing Application
Partners may want to work together on the dialogue, each responsible for one person's words but collaborating on the rest.

Exercise 61

1. in-ter-est-ing
2. white-water
3. pell-mell
4. rented
5. Alas-ka

Exercise 62

1. Kathleen said that many people's dreams were lost in the gold rushes.
2. However, it is nobody else's business how one chooses to seek his or her fortune.
3. My choice would not be the same as yours.
4. Prospectors' families hoped that theirs would be the claim that paid off.
5. Often, the children's lives were least affected by the rush, as their job was simply to go to school.

Exercise 63

"You know," said Zoe, "there were as many disappointments during California's gold rush as there were in the Yukon's." Then she told me this tale:

"It was up in California around June 15, 1849, and two prospectors, Bill and Jeb, were about to have their first gold-washing experience. At the break of dawn they set up a pump by the river. Jeb fed the machine. Bill shoveled the accumulated dirt. Near sundown the men's backs began to ache; however, Bill's eagerness kept them working. They started washing the dirt with a half-circular swinging motion in the water. After straining the last of the dirt, they looked at each other and asked, 'Where is the gold?' Alas! After a whole day's labor, they had only one tiny piece, worth perhaps half a dollar."

Exercise 64

Cumulative Review

1. Today's economy enjoys many positive effects as the result of the gold rush period in North America.
2. In fact, if it weren't for people's desire to conquer nature's difficulties, much of Alaska and the Yukon Territory probably would not have been explored so soon.
3. The then newly discovered treasures of oil, timber, wildlife, and tourism continue to be assets of the area.

continued

Lesson Objectives

- To proofread passages for errors in punctuation.

Step-by-Step Teaching Guide

Proofreading

Teaching Resources: Standardized Test Preparation Workbook, pp. 51–52

1. Remind students to look at the exercises carefully to see what part of the sentence each number covers.
2. Sample 2 is an example of an item requiring more than one correction. Be sure to have students check each item for this possibility.

Standardized Test Preparation Workshop

Proofreading

To evaluate your mastery of punctuation rules, standardized tests often require you to proofread a passage for errors and choose from several possible revisions of each underlined section.

The following sample items will give you practice with identifying punctuation errors.

Test Tip

Look carefully at all the punctuation in each passage. There may be more than one error in a given passage. Choose the answer that corrects all the errors.

Sample Test Items	Answers and Explanations
Choose the best way to write each underlined section. If the underlined section needs no change, mark the choice "Correct as is." Mr Harrison asked the neighbors to (1) "help him collect money." for the new (2) homeless shelter downtown	
1 A Mr, Harrison asked the neighbors **B** Mr. Harrison asked the neighbors **C** M.r. Harrison asked, the neighbors **D** Correct as is	The correct answer for item 1 is *B*. The title *Mr.* requires a period.
2 F "help him collect money," for the new homeless shelter downtown? **G** "help him collect money." for the new homeless shelter downtown. **H** help him collect money for the new homeless shelter downtown. **J** Correct as is	The correct answer for item 2 is *H*. There is no direct quotation; therefore, no quotation marks are needed. The sentence also requires an end mark—for this declarative sentence, a period is needed.

TEST-TAKING TIP

Suggest to students that it is a good idea to correct the errors in their own minds before looking at possible answers. Students can correct the errors in each passage and then use this information to select the correct answer.

Practice **Directions:** Choose the best way to write each underlined section. If the underlined section needs no change, mark the choice "Correct as is."

Two years ago my sister and I took a tour (1) of Civil War historic sites? We began our (2) trip at Manassas, Virginia, and ended it at Appomattox Courthouse, also in Virginia. In order to visit four different states in two (3) weeks, we arose every morning by 6:00 AM. My sister, who rarely complains, said, (4) I can't believe we are getting up before the sun on our vacation! Mrs. Sherman, who (5) publishes travel articles for our local paper The Traveler, prepared our itinerary. The. (6) most compelling stop was Andersonville prison, near Americus, Georgia.

1 **A** Two years ago, my sister, and I took a tour of Civil War historic sites?
B Two years ago my sister and I took a tour of Civil War historic sites.
C Two years ago my sister and I took a tour of Civil War historic sites;
D Correct as is

2 **F** We began our trip at Manassas VA, and ended it at Appomattox Courthouse, also in Virginia.
G We began our trip at Manassas V.A., and ended it at Appomattox Courthouse, also in Virginia?
H We began our trip at Manassas, VA, and ended it at Appomattox Courthouse, also in Virginia.
J Correct as is

3 **A** In order to visit four different states in two weeks, we arose every morning by 6:00 A.M.
B In order to visit four different states in two weeks, we arose every morning by 6:00: A.M.
C In order to visit four different states in two weeks, we arose every morning by 6:00 Am.
D Correct as is

4 **F** My sister, who rarely complains, said, "I can't believe we are getting up before the sun on our vacation!".
G My sister, who rarely complains said I can't believe we are getting up before the sun on our vacation!
H My sister, who rarely complains, said, "I can't believe we are getting up before the sun on our vacation!"
J Correct as is

5 **A** Mrs. Sherman, who publishes travel articles for our local paper, The Traveler, prepared our itinerary.
B Mrs Sherman, who publishes travel articles for our local paper, The Traveler prepared our itinerary.
C Mrs. Sherman, who publishes travel articles for our local paper, The Traveler prepared our itinerary?
D Correct as is

6 **F** The most compelling stop was Andersonville prison near Americus: Georgia.
G The most compelling stop was Andersonville prison near Americus, Georgia.
H The most compelling "stop" was Andersonville prison near Americus. Georgia!
J Correct as is

Answer Key

Practice

1. B
2. J
3. A
4. H
5. A
6. G

Chapter

27 Time and Resource Manager

In-Depth Lesson Plan

	LESSON FOCUS	PRINT AND MEDIA RESOURCES
DAY 1	**Using Capitals** Students capitalize the first word of a sentence, the pronoun *I*, and all proper nouns (pp. 636–646).	**Teaching Resources** *Grammar Exercise Workbook,* pp. 189–194; *Grammar Exercises Answers on Transparencies,* Ch. 27 ***Writing and Grammar iText* (Interactive Text),** Ch. 27; ***On-Line Exercise Bank,*** Ch. 27
DAY 2	**Using Capitals** *(continued)* Students capitalize proper adjectives, titles, and certain words in friendly letters. They also complete a Hands-on Grammar activity (pp. 646–651).	**Teaching Resources** *Grammar Exercise Workbook,* pp. 195–200; *Grammar Exercises Answers on Transparencies,* Ch. 27; *Hands-on Grammar Activity Book,* Ch. 27 ***Writing and Grammar iText* (Interactive Text),** Ch. 27; ***On-line Exercise Bank,*** Ch. 27
DAY 3	**Review and Assess** Students review the chapter and demonstrate mastery of capitalization (pp. 652–653).	**Teaching Resources** *Formal Assessment,* Ch. 27; *Grammar Exercises Answers on Transparencies,* Ch. 27 ***Writing and Grammar iText* (Interactive Text),** Ch. 27, Chapter Review; ***On-line Exercise Bank,*** Ch. 27

Accelerated Lesson Plan

	LESSON FOCUS	PRINT AND MEDIA RESOURCES
DAY 1	**Using Capitals** Students capitalize the first word of a sentence, the pronoun *I*, all proper nouns, proper adjectives, titles, and certain words in friendly letters (pp. 636–651).	**Teaching Resources** *Grammar Exercise Workbook,* pp. 189–200; *Grammar Exercises Answers on Transparencies,* Ch. 27; *Hands-on Grammar Activity Book,* Ch. 27 ***Writing and Grammar iText* (Interactive Text),** Ch. 27, Chapter Review; ***On-line Exercise Bank,*** Ch. 27
DAY 2	**Review and Assess** Students review the chapter and demonstrate mastery of capitalization (pp. 652–653).	**Teaching Resources** *Formal Assessment,* Ch. 27; *Grammar Exercises Answers on Transparencies,* Ch. 27 ***Writing and Grammar iText* (Interactive Text),** Ch. 27, Chapter Review; ***On-line Exercise Bank,*** Ch. 27

Options for Adapting Lesson Plans

HOMEWORK

Have students complete any stage of the lesson for homework.

SPELLING

To teach spelling skills in conjunction with grammar, mechanics, and usage, work through *Prentice Hall Everyday Spelling,* Grade 8, Chapter 32, as you cover this *Writing and Grammar* chapter.

TECHNOLOGY

Students can use *Writing and Grammar iText* to complete the exercises interactively on computer. They can complete additional exercises in the *On-line Exercise Bank:* The Auto Check feature will grade their work. Go on-line: PHSchool.com Use Web Code: eck-8002

FEATURES

Extend coverage with the Grammar in Literature features (p. 641) and the Standardized Test Preparation Workshop (pp. 654–655).

INTEGRATED SKILLS COVERAGE

Grammar in Literature
SE p. 641

Reading
Find It in Your Reading, SE p. 651

Writing
Find It in Your Writing, SE p. 651
Writing Application, SE pp. 653, 657

Viewing and Representing
Critical Viewing, SE pp. 636, 638, 639, 641, 642, 644, 647, 648

Speaking and Listening
ATE p. 639

Workplace Skills
ATE p. 648

Real-World Connection
ATE p. 644

Spelling
SE p. 650

ASSESSMENT SUPPORT

Standardized Test Preparation Workshop SE pp. 654–655, ATE p. 640

Standardized Test Preparation Workbook, pp. 53–54

Formal Assessment, Ch. 27

MEETING INDIVIDUAL NEEDS

Less Advanced Students ATE p. 642. See also Ongoing Assessments ATE pp. 644, 647.

ESL Students ATE pp. 638, 647

Gifted/Talented Learners ATE p. 649

BLOCK SCHEDULING

Pacing Suggestions
For 90-minute Blocks
- Administer the Diagnostic Test to students to determine instructional coverage.
- Have students complete the necessary exercises in class. Use the Hands-on Grammar Activity to provide a change of pace.

Resources for Varying Instruction
- ***Writing and Grammar iText* (Interactive Text)** A 90-minute block provides an ideal opportunity for students to work on computer.

Professional Development Support
- ***How to Manage Instruction in the Block*** This teaching resource provides management and activity suggestions.

MEDIA AND TECHNOLOGY

For the Student
- ***Writing and Grammar iText* (Interactive Text),** Ch. 27
- ***On-line Exercise Bank,*** Ch. 27

For the Teacher
- ***Resource Pro* CD-ROM**

WRITING AND GRAMMAR ON-LINE

***iText* Interactive Text (On-line or on CD-ROM)**
- Easily navigable instruction with on-line supporting resources
- Self-scoring exercises and diagnostic tests

Companion Web Site PHSchool.com
- On-line Exercise Bank (use Web Code eck-8002)

See the Go On-line! feature, SE p. iii.

CHAPTER 27
USING CAPITALS

Lesson Objectives

1. To understand the rules of capitalizing the first word in sentences.
2. To capitalize the first word in a quotation.
3. To capitalize the pronoun *I*.
4. To capitalize all proper nouns.
5. To capitalize each part of a person's full name.
6. To capitalize geographical names.
7. To capitalize the names of specific events and times.
8. To capitalize the names of various organizations, nationalities, and languages.
9. To capitalize religious references.
10. To capitalize most proper adjectives.
11. To capitalize a person's title.
12. To capitalize the first word and all other important words in titles of works.
13. To capitalize titles of school courses.
14. To capitalize the first word in letter salutations and closings.

Critical Viewing

Speculate Students should say that the specific name of the mountains, the road name, and possibly the park name, town, or state should be capitalized.

Chapter 27 Capitalization

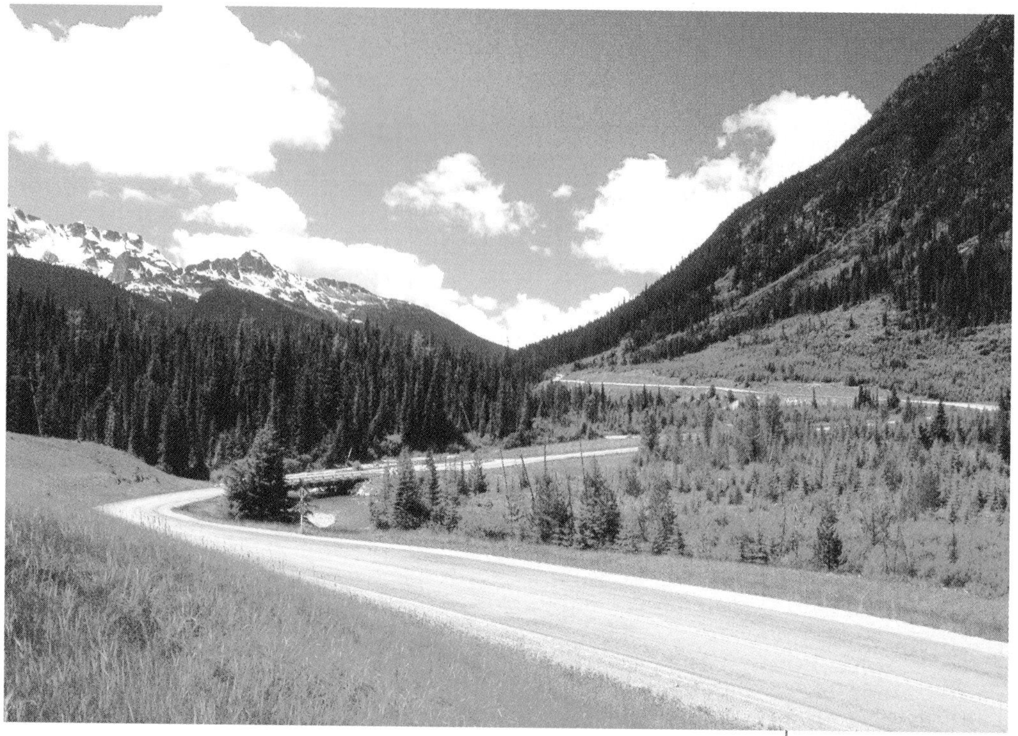

▲ Critical Viewing What features of this picture would be named by words that begin with capital letters? Why? **[Speculate]**

If you were to travel across the country, you would pass many geographical locations and landmarks. You might start a journal to keep track of the interesting sites you visit along the way. When you write about your adventures, you will need to capitalize the names of towns, rivers, landmarks, and buildings, among other things. *Capital letters* may signal the beginning of a sentence, an important word within a sentence, or a proper noun.

A sentence written without capitals is confusing: *mr. bailey traveled with the band from youngstown to visit the birthplace of john philip sousa.* With the addition of capitals, the same sentence is easier to read: *Mr. Bailey traveled with the band from Youngstown to visit the birthplace of John Philip Sousa.*

The meaning of a sentence is clearer when words are capitalized correctly.

ONGOING ASSESSMENT: Diagnose

If students miss more than one item in each category, direct them to the relevant pages of the text and assign exercises for practice and review.

Capitalization	Diagnostic Test Items	Teach	Practice	Chapter Review
Skill Check A				
Capitalizing Initial Words of Sentences, Quotations, *I*, and Proper Nouns	A 1–5	pp. 638–640	Ex. 1–4	Ex. 13, 15
Skill Check B				
Capitalizing Geographical Places and Proper Nouns	B 6–10	pp. 641–643	Ex. 4–5	Ex. 13, 15

Diagnostic Test

Directions: Write all answers on a separate sheet of paper.

Skill Check A. Copy the following sentences onto your paper, adding the missing capitals.

1. i have never been to West Virginia, but i would like to go there.
2. "where is West Virginia," asked Charlotte, "in relation to Ohio?"
3. ohio and Virginia are two states that border West Virginia.
4. what beautiful foliage in the fall!
5. "driving through the mountains is fun to do," said Hector.

Skill Check B. On your paper, write each name, geographical place, or other proper noun that you find in the following sentences, adding the missing capitals.

6. rebecca told me that white sulphur springs boasts a house made of 30 tons of coal.
7. When the o'connel family went to west virginia, they visited the beckley exhibition coal mine in beckley.
8. When samuel drives to valley falls, west virginia, he is going to take route 79 from charleston.
9. We drove down a winding road to get to stonewall jackson lake.
10. tomorrow, we will visit the seneca caverns in sendleton county.

Skill Check C. Complete each of the following sentences by supplying a proper adjective that is correctly capitalized.

11. The Statue of Liberty is an __?__ symbol.
12. If you mentioned the Eiffel Tower, anyone would know that you were referring to a __?__ structure.
13. The Leaning Tower of Pisa represents __?__ architecture.
14. The __?__ pyramids are one of the Wonders of the World.
15. Tortillas are a staple item in __?__ cuisine.

Skill Check D. On your paper, write each title or family name that you find in the following sentences, adding all the capitals that are missing.

16. president Jimmy Carter was given a 10-foot-tall peanut in 1977.
17. Yesterday, aunt Jane said that it was made in Evanston, Illinois.
18. My other aunt, professor Deirdre Thomas, told me that the peanut sits in Plains, Georgia, now.
19. Come meet uncle Rodney, a retired navy captain who now lives in Plains, Georgia.
20. He met the president when carter was home for a visit.

Skill Check E. Write each title of the works of art and courses correctly, adding all the capitals that are missing.

21. I am taking biology 201 next semester.
22. In english, we read <u>bearstone</u> and <u>the pearl</u>.
23. I took art 160 so that I could learn about Van Gogh.
24. When Jack was in a humanities class, he had to study selections from <u>swan lake</u> and <u>the nutcracker</u>.
25. The spanish 201 class is reading <u>don quixote de la mancha</u>.

Answer Key

Diagnostic Test

Each item in the diagnostic test corresponds to a specific section in the using capitalization chapter. This will enable you to tailor instruction to the particular needs of your students. See "Ongoing Assessment: Diagnose" on the bottom of page 636 for further details.

Skill Check A

1. I have never been to West Virginia, but I would like to go there.
2. "Where is West Virginia," asked Charlotte, "in relation to Ohio?"
3. Ohio and Virginia are two states that border West Virginia.
4. What beautiful foliage in the fall!
5. "Driving through the mountains is fun to do," said Hector.

Skill Check B

6. Rebecca, White Sulphur Springs
7. O'Connel, West Virginia, Beckley Exhibition Coal Mine, Beckley
8. Samuel, Valley Falls, West Virginia, Route, Charleston
9. Stonewall Jackson Lake
10. Tomorrow, Seneca Caverns, Sendleton County

Skill Check C

11. American
12. French
13. Italian
14. Egyptian
15. Mexican

Skill Check D

16. President
17. Aunt
18. Professor
19. Uncle
20. Carter

Skill Check E

21. Biology 201
22. English, <u>Bearstone</u>, <u>The Pearl</u>
23. Art 160
24. <u>Swan Lake</u>, <u>The Nutcracker</u>
25. Spanish 201, <u>Don Quixote de la Mancha</u>

ONGOING ASSESSMENT: Diagnose *continued*

Capitalization	Diagnostic Test Items	Teach	Practice	Chapter Review
Skill Check C				
Capitalizing Proper Adjectives	C 11–15	p. 646	Ex. 7	Ex. 13, 15
Skill Check D				
Capitalizing Titles and Family Names	D 16–20	pp. 647–649	Ex. 8–9	Ex. 14, 15
Skill Check E				
Capitalizing Course Titles and Works of Art	E 21–25	pp. 649–650	Ex. 10–12	Ex. 14, 15

PREPARE and ENGAGE

Interest GRABBER Write the following sentences on the chalkboard and ask students to capitalize them correctly:

david owns an acre of land in acre, israel.

alice spent last spring in alice springs, australia.

should ann create an arbor in ann arbor, michigan?

Activate Prior Knowledge

Ask students to write the following information: their name, home town, school, teacher's name, month, current season, favorite movie or TV show, favorite sports team. Ask them how they knew which words to capitalize.

TEACH

Step-by-Step Teaching Guide

Capitals for First Words

1. The easiest rule of capitalization is always to capitalize the first word of a sentence.
2. Review each sentence type. Tell them this is one rule with no exceptions.

Customize for *ESL Students*

Other languages may have different rules of capitalization. Tell students that they will learn several rules of capitalization in this chapter which may differ from the rules of their home language.

Answer Key

Exercise 1

1. Tomorrow
2. Bring
3. Will
4. That
5. How

Critical Viewing

Describe Students should say that it is the Statue of Liberty. They may add that it is located in New York City.

27

Using Capitals for First Words

Capital letters are used for the first words in all sentences and in many quotations. They are also used for the word *I*, whatever its position in a sentence.

Sentences

One of the most common uses of a capital is to signal the beginning of a sentence.

KEY CONCEPT Capitalize the first word in declarative, interrogative, imperative, and exclamatory sentences. ■

DECLARATIVE:	Strong gusts of wind made it dangerous to drive on the bridge.
INTERROGATIVE:	Who found the clue leading to the suspect's arrest?
IMPERATIVE:	Think carefully before you decide.
EXCLAMATORY:	What an amazing coincidence this is!

Sometimes only part of a sentence is written out. The rest of the sentence is understood. In these cases, a capital is still needed for the first word.

EXAMPLES: When? Why not? Certainly!

Exercise 1 **Using Capitals to Begin Sentences** Copy the following sentences onto your paper, adding the missing capitals.

EXAMPLE: great! when do we leave?
ANSWER: Great! When do we leave?

1. tomorrow, we will begin our road trip across the country.
2. bring your camera.
3. will you be ready to make many stops along the way?
4. that roadside scene is amazing!
5. how big do you think that lake is?

Theme: Tourist Attractions

In this chapter, you will learn the many instances in which you must use capital letters. The examples and exercises are about quaint and unusual tourist attractions.

Cross-Curricular Connection: Social Studies

▼ Critical Viewing
Describe this famous American landmark, making sure to use capitalization correctly. **[Describe]**

TIME AND RESOURCE MANAGER

Resources
Print: Grammar Exercise Workbook, pp. 189–200; Hands-on Grammar Activity Book, Ch. 27
Technology: Writing and Grammar iText, Ch. 27; On-Line Exercise Bank, Ch. 27

In-Depth Coverage	Accelerated Pace
• Work through all key concepts, pp. 638–650. • Assign and review Exercises 1–12. • Do the Hands-on Grammar Activity on p. 651.	• Assign pp. 638–651 for independent student review.

Quotations

A capital letter also signals the first word in a quotation.

KEY CONCEPT Capitalize the first word in a quotation if the quotation is a complete sentence. ■

In each of the following examples, the first word of the quotation is capitalized because it begins a complete sentence.

EXAMPLES: Several people shouted, "Stop the bus!"
"She really wants to skip that monument," Arlene confided.

When a quotation consists of one complete sentence in two parts, only one capital is needed.

EXAMPLE: "How much longer," asked Brian, "until we reach the next attraction?"

If a quotation contains more than one sentence, capitalize the first word of each sentence.

EXAMPLE: "Please distribute these maps to everyone," said the director. "They show the location of each exhibit."

Exercise 2 **Using Capitals for Quotations** Copy each of the following sentences onto your paper, adding the missing capitals.

EXAMPLE: "isn't this an incredible place?" he asked.
ANSWER: "Isn't this an incredible place?" he asked.

1. Charles said, "my little brothers like the cows the best."
2. "there is no way that a mosquito that big can be real!" exclaimed Roberta.
3. "if you will look to your right," directed the tour guide, "you will see the jackalope."
4. "do not pet the mastodon," said their mother. "its coat is made of polyester and fiberglass."
5. "if we can't stop here," whined the twins, "can we go sightseeing in the next town?"

More Practice

Grammar Exercise Workbook
• pp. 189–190
On-line Exercise Bank
• Chapter 27
Go on-line:
PHSchool.com
Enter Web Code:
eck-8002

▼ Critical Viewing
What words would be capitalized in a sentence describing this scene?
[Analyze]

Step-by-Step Teaching Guide

Quotations

1. The first word of a quotation, when it starts a sentence, is always capitalized. Review the examples given, making sure that students also understand the punctuation of quotations.
2. Write the following examples on the chalkboard for additional practice:

   Every parent dreads hearing, "Are we there yet?" coming from the backseat.

   We were riding along enjoying the scenery when Helen wailed, "We're lost."

Answer Key

Exercise 2

1. Charles said, "My little brothers like the cows the best."
2. "There is no way that a mosquito that big can be real!" exclaimed Roberta.
3. "If you will look to your right," directed the tour guide, "you will see the jackalope."
4. "Do not pet the mastodon," said their mother. "Its coat is made of polyester and fiberglass."
5. "If we can't stop here," whined the twins, "can we go sightseeing in the next town?"

Integrating Speaking Skills

When reading aloud literature that contains quotations, there is no set way to indicate the quoted material. However, the reader can mark the beginning and end of quotations, in the form of dialogue, by changing the tone or pitch of his or her voice. Have students select an excerpt from something they have read recently (with quotations) and practice reading aloud the material.

Critical Viewing

Analyze Students should suggest that at least the first word should be capitalized.

Step-by-Step Teaching Guide

Capitalizing the Word *I*

1. Tell students that in grammar almost every rule has exceptions. Only in capitalization do we find basic simple rules like this one that never ever change: Always capitalize the pronoun *I* regardless of where it appears in the sentence.
2. Write the following examples on the chalkboard and ask students to comment:

   He said I was wrong.

   You did not dot the i.

   See that students understand that the *i* in the second example is not the pronoun *I* and therefore does not get capitalized.

Answer Key

Exercise 3

1. While traveling through Ohio, I stopped in the quaint town of Dresden.
2. I saw the World's Largest Basket there.
3. When I arrived in Wilmot, I stopped at the World's Largest Cuckoo Clock.
4. Because I was there when the clock struck the hour, I got to see the animated figures come to life.
5. I was amazed that a clock could be twenty-three feet tall.

Step-by-Step Teaching Guide

Capitals for Proper Nouns

1. The rule is to capitalize all proper nouns, including all parts of a person's name.
2. Remind students that a proper noun is the name of a person, place, or thing:

   Franklin Delano Roosevelt

   South Dakota

   Golden Gate Bridge

   Lake Champlain

   Pennsylvania Turnpike

   Galveston, Texas

   Green Bay Packers

27

Capitalizing the Word *I*

The pronoun *I* is always written as a capital.

KEY CONCEPT Capitalize the word *I* wherever it appears in a sentence. ■

EXAMPLE: I worked for two years as a clerk before I received the promotion.

Exercise 3 **Capitalizing the Pronoun *I*** Copy the following sentences onto your paper, adding the missing capitals.

EXAMPLE: she and i were the last to arrive.
ANSWER: She and I were the last to arrive.

1. While traveling through Ohio, i stopped in the quaint town of Dresden.
2. i saw the World's Largest Basket there.
3. When i arrived in Wilmot, i stopped at the World's Largest Cuckoo Clock.
4. Because i was there when the clock struck the hour, i got to see the animated figures come to life.
5. i was amazed that a clock could be twenty-three feet tall.

Using Capitals for Proper Nouns

A proper noun is capitalized because it names a specific person, place, or thing.

KEY CONCEPT Capitalize all proper nouns. ■

EXAMPLES: Joe Smyth — Joshua Tree National Monument — the Tappan Zee Bridge — the Eiffel Tower

KEY CONCEPT Capitalize each part of a person's full name. ■

EXAMPLES: Michelle T. Como — P. A. Sullivan

When a last name has two parts and the first part is *Mc, O',* or *St.*, the second part of the last name must also be capitalized.

EXAMPLES: McMurphy — O'Connor — St. John

For two-part last names that do not begin with *Mc, O',* or *St.*, the capitalization varies. Check a reliable source, such as a biographical dictionary, for the correct spelling.

STANDARDIZED TEST PREPARATION WORKSHOP

Grammar and Usage Many standardized tests require students to identify errors in capitalization. Ask students to choose the correct rewrite for the following sentence:

I took carlos to the top of the sears tower in chicago.

A I took Carlos to the top of the Sears tower in Chicago.
B I took carlos to the top of the Sears Tower in Chicago.
C I took Carlos to the top of the Sears Tower in Chicago.
D I took Carlos to the top of the sears tower in Chicago.

The correct choice is item **C**, because names of specific people, places, and things are capitalized.

Exercise 4 **Using Capitals for Names of People** On your paper, write each name that you find in the following sentences, adding the missing capitals.

EXAMPLE: Her best friend was andrea mcmahon.
ANSWER: Andrea McMahon

1. martin maurer got the idea to build the Big Duck after seeing a coffee shop shaped like a pot in California.
2. george reeve, w. collins, and s. collins built the duck to be used as a roadside stand to sell ducks and eggs.
3. In 1991, christie brinkley narrated the history of the Big Duck.
4. Martha's friend, kathleen o'rourke, came from Ireland to see this attraction.
5. d. st. john told his friend bill that he had never seen anything so funny.

More Practice

Grammar Exercise Workbook
- pp. 191–194

On-line Exercise Bank
- Chapter 27

Go on-line:
PHSchool.com
Enter Web Code:
eck-8002

GRAMMAR IN LITERATURE

from The Man Without a Country

Edward Everett Hale

In Edward Everett Hale's "The Man Without a Country," the narrator tells of a letter he once read. Titles, names of people, and names of places are capitalized.

Sir:

You will receive from Lieutenant Neale the person of Philip Nolan, late a lieutenant in the United States Army.

This person on his trial by court-martial expressed, with an oath, the wish that he might "never hear of the United States again."

▼ **Critical Viewing** Where do you think this tall ship might be going? What ocean or sea might it be sailing on? How would you capitalize the names of countries and bodies of water? **[Speculate]**

Answer Key

Exercise 4

1. Martin Maurer
2. George Reeve, W. Collins, S. Collins
3. Christie Brinkley
4. Kathleen O'Rourke
5. D. St. John, Bill

Step-by-Step Teaching Guide

Grammar in Literature

1. Have a volunteer read aloud the passage from "The Man Without a Country."
2. Point out the capitalization's of army rank when it is used as a person's title, name, organization, and country in the passage. Note that the rank *lieutenant* is not capitalized when it does not refer to a particular officer.

More About the Author

Edward Everett Hale (1822–1909) was a clergyman and writer whose patriotic short story "A Man Without a Country" (1863) brought him lasting fame. Hale was born in Boston and educated at Harvard. He was a prominent abolitionist and wrote "A Man Without a Country" to inspire support for the Union cause during the Civil War. Hale wrote more than 70 books of essays and novels. From 1903 until his death, he served as chaplain of the U.S. Senate.

Critical Viewing

Speculate Students may suggest any ocean or sea and any country. Be sure they capitalize all proper names.

TIME SAVERS!

Answers on Transparency Use the Grammar Exercises Answers on Transparencies for Chapter 27 to have students correct their own or one another's exercises.

On-Line Exercise Bank Have students complete the exercises on computer. The Auto Check feature will grade their work for you!

Step-by-Step Teaching Guide

Capitals for Geographical Names

1. All geographical names are capitalized. Review with students the categories shown.
2. All specific landforms and geographical features get capitalized. That includes swamps, rivers, lakes, bays, creeks, mountains, deserts, and so on:

   Alligators live in the swamp.

   The Okefenokee Swamp is full of alligators.

   The sheep graze on the hill.

   The sheep are grazing on Norwood Hill.
3. Geographical directions do not get capitalized unless they refer to a specific place:

   He lives northeast of here.

   The northeastern part of Vermont is called the Northeast Kingdom.

Customize for *Less Advanced Students*

Help students understand the basic concept that proper nouns, as *specific* names, places, or things, are capitalized.

Critical Viewing

Infer Students may suggest southeastern locations such as the Everglades in Florida or the swamps of Louisiana.

27

KEY CONCEPT Capitalize geographical names. ■

Any place listed on a map should be capitalized.

GEOGRAPHICAL NAMES	
Streets	First Avenue, Spencer Road
Towns and Cities	Plainfield, Los Angeles, Tokyo
Counties	Orange County, Wayne County
States and Provinces	Oklahoma, Manitoba
Nations	France, Ecuador, Saudi Arabia
Continents	South America, Africa, Asia
Valleys and Deserts	Death Valley, Mojave Desert
Mountains	Rocky Mountains, Mount Rushmore
Sections of a Country	New England, Southwest
Islands	Pitcairn Island, Long Island
Scenic Spots	Everglades, Yosemite National Park
Rivers and Falls	Colorado River, Rainbow Falls
Lakes and Bays	Lake Superior, Saginaw Bay
Seas and Oceans	Dead Sea, Indian Ocean

Compass points, such as north, southwest, or east, are considered proper nouns only when they name specific geographical locations. In those cases, they are capitalized. When they simply refer to directions, they are not.

EXAMPLES: We spent our vacation in the Southeast.
Our boat headed north on the river.

◀ **Critical Viewing** Using capitals correctly in a sentence, give the possible geographic location of this picture. **[Infer]**

Exercise 5 **Using Capitals for Geographical Places** On your paper, write each geographical place name that you find in the following sentences, adding all the missing capitals.

EXAMPLE: They had seen niagara falls in 1997.
ANSWER: Niagara Falls

1. From east to west on the north american continent, there are many roadside sites, especially in the midwest.
2. If you've ever been to moose jaw, saskatchewan, canada, you have probably seen Mac, the World's Largest Moose.
3. If you stop in jackson on your way to yellowstone national park, you will see the World's Biggest Ball of Barbed Wire.
4. There is a lighthouse in hannibal, missouri, near the mississippi river.
5. The World's Largest Kaleidoscope can be found in mt. tremper, new york, in the heart of the catskill mountains.
6. white lake is the former home port of the *Ellenwood*, a lumber schooner.
7. In 1901, after the *Ellenwood* sank in lake michigan, its nameplate drifted east across lake michigan to white lake.
8. The *Ellenwood* is now pictured on the top of the World's Largest Weather Vane in montague, michigan.
9. Several cities in minnesota are home to famous "World's Largest" attractions, such as a dog dish and an ear of corn.
10. Balls of twine in mountain springs, texas; cawker city, kansas; and darwin, minnesota, are among the world's largest.

KEY CONCEPT Capitalize the names of specific events and periods of time. ■

The following chart gives examples of events and times that are capitalized.

SPECIFIC EVENTS AND TIMES	
Historical Periods	Golden Age, Renaissance
Historical Events	Boxer Rebellion, World War I
Documents	Bill of Rights, Homestead Act
Days	Friday, Sunday
Months	March, June
Holidays	Memorial Day, New Year's Day
Religious Days	Easter, Pentecost, Muharram
Special Events	Orange Bowl, State Fair of Texas

More Practice

Grammar Exercise Workbook
- pp. 191–194

On-line Exercise Bank
- Chapter 27

Go on-line: PHSchool.com
Enter Web Code: eck-8002

iText

Get instant feedback! Exercise 5 is available on-line or on CD-ROM.

Answer Key

Exercise 5

1. North American, Midwest
2. Moose Jaw, Saskatchewan, Canada
3. Jackson, Yellowstone National Park
4. Hannibal, Missouri, Mississippi River
5. Mt. Tremper, New York, Catskill Mountains
6. White Lake
7. Lake Michigan, Lake Michigan, White Lake
8. Montague, Michigan
9. Minnesota
10. Mountain Springs, Texas, Cawker City, Kansas, Darwin, Minnesota

TIME SAVERS!

Answers on Transparency Use the Grammar Exercises Answers on Transparencies for Chapter 27 to have students correct their own or one another's exercises.

On-Line Exercise Bank Have students complete the exercises on computer. The Auto Check feature will grade their work for you!

Step-by-Step Teaching Guide

Using Capitals for Various Organizations

1. Review with students that the names of seasons do not get capitalized:

   I like summer.

   The summer of 1988 was the best one ever.

2. Review the capitalization rules for the entities stated here. Provide the following additional examples:

   Boston Symphony Orchestra

   National Education Association

   Department of Defense

   German language

   Russian people

3. Discuss with students that organizations cover a lot of ground:

   Apple Computer

   New York Yankees

   Backstreet Boys

   See that students understand that the above are specific representatives of the following general nouns: *company, sports team, rock group*. Specific, proper nouns get capitalized; general nouns do not.

Real-World Connection

Proper nouns are important in sports and news reports. Fans want to know which goalie, which team, and which city. Readers want to know in which city the earthquake occurred and who was elected president.

Critical Viewing

Analyze Students should reply that the ship is the Queen Mary and both the title and the person's name should be capitalized.

27

Even though the names of seasons represent specific times of the year, they are not capitalized.

EXAMPLES: Last winter was the coldest in a decade.
We can't wait for summer.

KEY CONCEPT Capitalize the names of various organizations, government bodies, political parties, and nationalities, as well as the languages spoken by different groups. ■

The following chart shows examples of each of these categories.

SPECIFIC GROUPS	
Clubs	Lincoln School Camera Club, Philadelphia Pioneer Track Club
Organizations	International Red Cross, Girl Scouts
Institutions	Georgia Institute of Technology, Tenakill School, Beth Israel Hospital
Government Bodies	Congress of the United States, Supreme Court, Los Angeles City Council
Political Parties	Republican Party, Democratic Party
Nationalities	Algerian, Japanese, Mexican, American
Languages Spoken by Different Groups	English, Portuguese, Arabic, Norwegian

◀ **Critical Viewing** What is the name of this ship? How would you capitalize it and why? **[Analyze]**

ONGOING ASSESSMENT: Monitor and Reinforce

If students miss more than two items in Exercises 4–5, refer them to the following for additional practice.

In the Textbook	Print Resources	Technology
Chapter Review, Ex. 13, 15, pp. 652–653	Grammar Exercise Workbook, pp. 191–194	On-Line Exercise Bank, Ch. 27

KEY CONCEPT Capitalize references to religions, deities, and religious scriptures. ■

The following chart presents a list of five of the world's major religions. Listed next to each are the words that each religion uses to refer to important religious figures and holy writings. Be sure to capitalize these in your writing. Note that the name of each religion is also capitalized.

RELIGIOUS REFERENCES	
Christianity	God, Lord, Father, Son, Holy Ghost, Bible, books of the Bible (such as Genesis, Exodus, Matthew, Mark)
Judaism	God, Lord, Father, Prophets, Torah, Talmud, Midrash
Islam	Allah, Prophet, Muhammad, Koran
Hinduism	Brahma, Bhagavad-Gita, Vedas
Buddhism	Buddha, Mahayana, Hinayana

KEY CONCEPT Capitalize the names of other special places and items. ■

This final rule applies to proper nouns such as monuments, memorials, buildings, celestial bodies, awards, names of specific vehicles, and trademarks.

The following chart shows specific examples of these other kinds of proper nouns.

OTHER SPECIAL PLACES AND ITEMS	
Monuments	Eiffel Tower, Statue of Liberty
Memorials	Tomb of the Unknown Soldier
Buildings	Museum of Natural History
Celestial Bodies (except the moon and the sun)	Spiral Galaxy, Jupiter, Orion, Earth
Awards	Pulitzer Prize, Nobel Peace Prize
Air, Sea, Space, and Land Craft	*Air Force One, Lusitania, Apollo 12,* Ford Model A
Trademarks	Krispy Crackers, Seemore Electronics

Step-by-Step Teaching Guide

Using Capitals for Religious References

1. Capitalization rules for religious references can be confusing, especially to people of different faiths from the one under discussion. Tell students to think of proper nouns. Any specific reference is capitalized.
2. Review the list with students. Tell them that any reference to the deity, prophets, holy figures, and books and chapters of religious scriptures are capitalized.
3. Special places and items also are capitalized as proper nouns.

   Washington Monument

   Lincoln Memorial

   World Trade Center

   Venus

   Most Valuable Player

   Starship Enterprise

   Corvette

   Cheerios, Swatch

Answer Key

Exercise 6

1. May
2. Utah
3. Mormon
4. Sunday, Catholic, Spanish
5. Living Traditions Festival
6. Cedar City, Old Sorrel House Monument
7. Three-Legged Dog
8. Yuma
9. Utah State University
10. Golden Spike

Step-by-Step Teaching Guide

Capitals for Proper Adjectives

1. For many proper adjectives, it is not the word but the usage that matters. *Civil War* is a proper noun. In *a Civil War battle, Civil War* is a proper adjective because it modifies the common noun *battle.*
2. Review the Grammar and Style Tip about proper nouns changing form to become proper adjectives. Go over the following list with students and ask them to add to it:

Germany	*German*
Canada	*Canadian*
Mexico	*Mexican*
Italy	*Italian*
Brazil	*Brazilian*
Egypt	*Egyptian*
China	*Chinese*
Sudan	*Sudanese*

TIME SAVERS!

Answers on Transparency Use the Grammar Exercises Answers on Transparencies for Chapter 27 to have students correct their own or one another's exercises.

On-Line Exercise Bank Have students complete the exercises on computer. The Auto Check feature will grade their work for you!

Exercise 6 **Using Capitals for Other Proper Nouns** On your paper, write all the proper nouns that do not have capitals in the following sentences.

1. While traveling through Utah last may, Naira and her friends discovered many fascinating places.
2. In Salt Lake City, they gathered at the state capitol building, where the utah legislature was in session.
3. They saw statues of the "Father of Television" Philo Farnsworth and the mormon leader Brigham Young.
4. Because they were downtown on sunday, they stopped to hear a catholic mass given in spanish.
5. In the afternoon, they spent two hours at Salt Lake's living traditions festival.
6. In cedar city, they saw the old sorrel house monument.
7. They decided to pass through Myton, the home of the grave of Sidney, the three-legged dog.
8. If they hadn't been driving a new yuma 4 × 4, they would not have reached the grave of Old Ephraim, "The Last Grizzly Bear in Utah."
9. The skull of the bear, however, was on display at the library of utah state university.
10. Naira and her friends wished they could have gone to Strasburg, Iowa, to see the 56-foot-tall golden spike.

Using Capitals for Proper Adjectives

KEY CONCEPT Capitalize proper adjectives. ■

In the following examples, notice that both proper nouns and proper adjectives are capitalized. Common nouns that are modified by proper adjectives, however, are not capitalized.

PROPER NOUNS:	World War I	Canada
PROPER ADJECTIVES:	a World War I battle	
	a Canadian flag	

A trademark, the name of a company's product, is considered a proper noun. If you use only part of the trademark, or brand name, to describe a common noun, the brand name becomes a proper adjective. In this case, capitalize only the proper adjective.

PROPER NOUN:	Healthy Grains
PROPER ADJECTIVE:	Healthy Grains cereal

More Practice

Grammar Exercise Workbook
- pp. 191–196

On-line Exercise Bank
- Chapter 27

Go on-line: PHSchool.com *Enter Web Code:* eck-8002

iText

Get instant feedback! Exercise 6 is available on-line or on CD-ROM.

Grammar and Style Tip

The names of some countries and states must be modified to be used as proper adjectives. For example, something from Kenya is Kenyan, someone from Texas is a Texan, a chair from Spain is a Spanish chair, and a building in France is a French building.

Exercise 7 **Using Capitals for Proper Adjectives** Complete each of the following sentences by supplying a proper adjective that is correctly capitalized.

EXAMPLE: Her most treasured possession was an antique __?__ sofa.
ANSWER: Victorian

1. Although Moorhead, Minnesota, is far from the home of the Vikings, you can find an exact replica of a __?__ ship there.
2. In honor of the settlers from Norway, who came to Illinois in 1835, there is a __?__ Settlers State Memorial.
3. At Florida Splendid China theme park, you can see replicas of the Great Wall of China and __?__ temples.
4. From San Diego to San Francisco, one can enjoy the beautiful __?__ scenery.
5. Holland, Michigan, has much in common with its European counterpart, including thousands of tulips, windmills, and __?__ wooden shoes.

▲ Critical Viewing Where might this windmill be located? If it is in the Netherlands, what proper adjective would you use to describe it? **[Speculate]**

Using Capitals for Titles of People

Several rules govern the use of capitals for titles of people.

Social and Professional Titles Social and professional titles may be written before a person's name or may be used when speaking directly to another person.

KEY CONCEPT Capitalize a person's title when it is followed by the person's name or when used in direct address. ■

The following chart gives examples of some of these titles.

TITLES OF PEOPLE	
Social	Mister, Madam or Madame, Miss, Sir
Business	Doctor, Professor, Superintendent
Religious	Reverend, Father, Rabbi, Bishop, Sister
Military	Private, Ensign, Captain, General, Admiral, Colonel
Government	President, Secretary of State, Ambassador, Senator, Representative, Governor, Mayor

Answer Key

Exercise 7

Answers will vary. Samples are given.

1. Viking
2. Norwegian
3. Chinese
4. California
5. Dutch

Step-by-Step Teaching Guide

Using Capitals for Titles of People

1. Review the list of titles. Tell students the title is always capitalized when used with a person's name.
2. When the title is used without a person's name, it is not capitalized.

   I asked Dr. Wisner why I couldn't stop hiccuping.

   I asked the doctor why I couldn't stop hiccuping.

Customize for *ESL Students*

Students from the same country or culture can work together to capitalize words for people, places, and things from that country. For example, Floating Gardens of Xochimilco, Temple of Angkor Wat, Great Zimbabwe, Simón Bolívar.

Critical Viewing

Speculate Students will probably suggest the Netherlands and use the adjective Dutch.

ONGOING ASSESSMENT: Monitor and Reinforce

If students miss more than two items in Exercises 6–10, refer them to the following for additional practice.

In the Textbook	Print Resources	Technology
Chapter Review, Ex. 13, 14, pp. 652–655	Grammar Exercise Workbook, pp. 191–196	On-Line Exercise Bank, Ch. 27

TIME SAVERS!

Answers on Transparency Use the Grammar Exercises Answers on Transparencies for Chapter 27 to have students correct their own or one another's exercises.

On-Line Exercise Bank Have students complete the exercises on computer. The Auto Check feature will grade their work for you!

Answer Key

Exercise 8

1. President
2. Mr.
3. correct
4. President
5. professor
6. Doctor
7. pastor
8. correct
9. Uncle
10. correct

Step-by-Step Teaching Guide

Using Capitals for Family Titles

1. Family names are capitalized when used with a name (Aunt Hilda) or when used as a direct form of address.
2. When used without a name (my aunt), the reference is general and is not capitalized.

Integrating Workplace Skills

Letter-writing is a very important part of any job search. It is the first impression you make on potential employers. Knowing how to properly capitalize people's titles in the letters you write will help you make a good impression on the people reading them.

Critical Viewing

Speculate Students may suggest Native American nations or United States army personnel traveled here.

TIME SAVERS!

Answers on Transparency Use the Grammar Exercises Answers on Transparencies for Chapter 27 to have students correct their own or one another's exercises.

On-Line Exercise Bank Have students complete the exercises on computer. The Auto Check feature will grade their work for you!

KEY CONCEPT Capitalize the titles of certain high government officials even when the titles are not followed by a person's name or used in direct address. ■

WITH A PERSON'S NAME:	Queen Victoria ruled England.
WITHOUT A PERSON'S NAME:	The President greeted the Queen.

▲ **Critical Viewing** Who might have traveled through this landscape to Echo Cliffs, Arizona? Write two sentences describing these travelers. Capitalize titles in your sentences. **[Speculate]**

The titles of other government officials may also be capitalized when there is no name given, but only when they refer to the specific person who has that title.

SPECIFIC REFERENCE:	The Mayor will speak with you now.
GENERAL REFERENCE:	The mayor of a large city works hard.

Exercise 8 **Using Capitals for Social and Professional Titles** If the title in each of these sentences is correctly capitalized, write *correct*. If it is not, rewrite the title correctly.

1. It is likely that the state of Washington is named after president George Washington.
2. A shoe of mr. Robert Wadlow is found in a collection of giant shoes in Seattle, Washington.
3. Will you please take a picture of me, Sir?
4. The president was seated in the Oval Office.
5. Because the Professor was teaching a class about chickens, the class visited the world's largest egg.
6. At the Whitman Massacre Site Interpretive Center, there are depictions of doctor Marcus Whitman and his wife.
7. If you want to visit with the Pastor of the Evangelisch Lutherisch Kirche, you will have to wait for the service.
8. Excuse me, Miss, there is room for only forty-six people in that little church.
9. When we visit uncle Fred, we always see interesting tourist attractions.
10. Josh wondered if the mayor had made a statement about the gigantic concrete troll in Fremont, Washington.

KEY CONCEPT Capitalize titles showing family relationships when the title is used with the person's name or as the person's name. ■

WITH A NAME:	We invited Aunt Rebecca to the party.
AS A NAME:	Watch out, Uncle Tom, or you'll slip. Is Grandmother going?

Exercise 9 **Using Capitals for Family Titles** Complete each of the following sentences by filling in the blank with a family title or a title with a name.

EXAMPLE: Please, __?__, take us to see the ball of twine.
ANSWER: Please, Grandfather, take us to see the ball of twine.

1. Meredith will visit __?__ in Minneapolis.
2. __?__ Paul catches big fish, but they are nothing compared to the plastic 28-foot codfish in Madison, Minnesota.
3. Will __?__ come with us to see the walleye?
4. When my __?__ took me to the mall in Bloomington, we saw Snoopy.
5. __?__ Sophia explained that the dog dish in front of Snoopy is the largest in the world.

KEY CONCEPT Capitalize the first word and all the other important words in the titles of books, periodicals, poems, stories, plays, song titles, movies, and works of art. ■

Notice the use of underlining and quotation marks in the following examples. Also, notice that no matter how short, verbs—such as *Is* in the poem title—are always capitalized.

BOOK: The Red Pony
PERIODICAL: National Geographic
POEM: "It Is a Beauteous Evening"
SHORT STORY: "The Gold Bug"
PAINTING: A Girl With a Watering Can

Exercise 10 Rewrite the titles below, adding the missing capitals.

EXAMPLE: the family in the garden at argenteuil
ANSWER: The Family in the Garden at Argenteuil

1. starry night (painting)
2. "america the beautiful" (song)
3. tarean the golden lion (movie)
4. "o captain, my captain!" (poem)
5. a wrinkle in time (book)

iText

Get instant feedback! Exercise 10 is available on-line or on CD-ROM.

More Practice

Grammar Exercise Workbook
- pp. 197–198

On-line Exercise Bank
- Chapter 27

Go on-line: PHSchool.com
Enter Web Code: eck-8002

Answer Key

Exercise 9

Answers will vary. Samples are given.
1. Aunt Edith
2. Uncle
3. Grandfather Eric
4. Great Aunt Molly
5. Aunt

Step-by-Step Teaching Guide

Using Capitals for Titles of Things

1. Review the rule for capitalizing titles of books, movies, and other artistic works. See that students understand the first word is always capitalized, along with all other words except articles, conjunctions, and short prepositions.
2. Write the following titles on the chalkboard and ask students to capitalize them:

   the adventures of tom sawyer
   return of the jedi
   beauty and the beast

Answer Key

Exercise 10

1. Starry Night
2. "America the Beautiful"
3. Tarean the Golden Lion
4. "O Captain, My Captain!"
5. A Wrinkle in Time

Customize for *Gifted/Talented Learners*

Challenge students to capitalize correctly (or as correctly as possible!) E. E. Cummings's poem "love is a place" in *Timeless Voices, Timeless Themes,* Silver.

Step-by-Step Teaching Guide

Using Capitals for Titles of Things

1. The rule for school courses follows the specific/general one. Specific courses are capitalized, general references are not. Languages are always capitalized regardless of reference.
2. Write the following examples on the chalkboard for additional practice:

   History 101

   Algebra 2

   I have history and algebra homework.

   I like French and am studying French literature.

Answer Key

Exercise 11

1. Spanish
2. English, Italian, Biology 200, literature
3. physical science, English
4. Agriculture 204
5. accounting

Step-by-Step Teaching Guide

Using Capitals for Salutations and Closings

1. Salutations and closings are other examples that do not vary. The first word of both is always capitalized.
2. Remind students that since a name or specific reference usually follows the salutation, the second word (if not the entire salutation) is capitalized.

   Dear Dr. Johnson,

   Dear Frankie,

   Dear Good Friends,

Answer Key

Exercise 12

1. To Whom It May Concern,
2. Thank you,
3. My Beloved Brothers and Sisters,
4. Dear Uncle Dave,
5. With love,

KEY CONCEPT Capitalize titles of school courses when the courses are language courses or when the courses are followed by a number. ■

EXAMPLE: My schedule includes Latin, English, and Science 101.

Although languages are always capitalized, other school subjects should not be capitalized when discussed in a general manner.

EXAMPLE: This semester I will study typing, algebra, and Spanish.

Exercise 11 **Using Capitals for Titles of Things** For each of the following, choose the correctly written course title from the choices in parentheses, and write it on your paper.

1. If you want to go to Mexico, you should take a (Spanish, spanish) class.
2. Carlos took (English, english), (Italian, italian), (Biology 200, biology 200), and (Literature, literature) during his first semester.
3. The students had to decide between (Physical Science, physical science) and (English, english).
4. There was not enough time in Martha's schedule to take (Agriculture 204, agriculture 204)
5. Paul and Connie were happy to have (Accounting, accounting) together.

KEY CONCEPT Capitalize the first word and all nouns and pronouns in letter salutations, as well as the first word in letter closings. ■

SALUTATIONS:	Dear Mr. Perkins:	Dear Aunt Maude,
CLOSINGS:	Sincerely yours,	Yours truly,

Exercise 12 **Using Capitals for Letter Salutations and Closings** Rewrite each of the following letter parts, adding the missing capitals.

1. to whom it may concern,
2. thank you,
3. my beloved brothers and sisters,
4. dear uncle dave,
5. with love,

More Practice

Grammar Exercise Workbook
- pp. 199–200

On-line Exercise Bank
- Chapter 27

Go on-line: PHSchool.com
Enter Web Code: eck-8002

iText

Get instant feedback! Exercises 11 and 12 are available on-line or on CD-ROM.

Spelling Tip

To recall the correct spelling of *sincerely*, remember that the adjective *sincere* becomes an adverb by adding *-ly*.

ONGOING ASSESSMENT: Assess Mastery

Use the following resources to assess mastery of capitalizing proper adjectives and titles.

In The Textbook	Technology
Chapter Review, Ex. 13–14, p. 652 Standardized Test Preparation Workshop, pp. 654–655	Writing and Grammar iText, Ch. 27, Chapter Review; On-Line Exercise Bank, Ch. 27

Hands-on Grammar

Proper Noun Package

Classify proper nouns into categories so that you will be able to remember to capitalize them.

Fold a piece of $6\frac{1}{2}$" x $8\frac{1}{2}$" paper in half the short way. Crease it. Open it back up, and fold each end down to the crease to form pockets, as shown in the illustration. Cut four $\frac{3}{4}$" slots in each pocket. These will hold your proper noun lists. Then, cut eight strips of paper $1\frac{3}{4}$" wide x $3\frac{1}{4}$" long. On the top of each list, put a category of proper noun, such as *desert, river, title, event, island, mountain, day, country, state.*

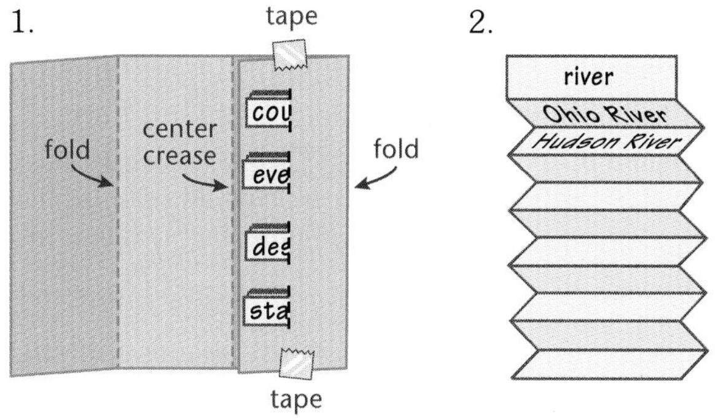

List the following proper nouns on the appropriate strip of paper: *Memorial Day, New Year's Day, Long Island, Orcas Island, Mount Rainier, Rocky Mountains, Utah, Maine, Arizona, Rose Bowl, New York State Fair, Mojave Desert, Gobi Desert, Ohio River, Hudson River, Algeria, Spain, Uncle John, Aunt Joan, Queen Anne, Admiral Nelson.* Then, for each strip, make approximately $\frac{1}{2}$" folds back and forth like an accordion or a fan, and slip it into a slot in the pocket of the package. You can fold this package in half and keep it in your notebook or desk. Add proper nouns to your lists from your daily reading.

Find It in Your Reading In your reading, find sentences with capitalized proper nouns and titles. Copy each of these words onto the appropriate list in your package. Make additional lists with other categories, if necessary.

Find It in Your Writing Look through samples of your own writing to find sentences in which you have used both proper and common nouns to see whether you have capitalized the proper nouns.

Step-by-Step Teaching Guide

Proper Noun Package

Teaching Resources: Hands-on Grammar Activity Book, Chapter 27

1. Have students refer to their Hands-on Grammar Activity Books or give them copies of the relevant pages for this activity.
2. If students have trouble making the folds model an example for them.
3. Allow interested students to make more proper noun strips.

Find It in Your Reading

Allow students to share lists to increase their packages of proper nouns.

Find It in Your Writing

Students may wish to work with partners and check each other's writings for proper capitalization.

PRENTICE HALL
Everyday Spelling

If you have taught the spelling skills in *Prentice Hall Everyday Spelling,* Grade 8, Chapter 32, in conjunction with this *Writing and Grammar* chapter, review and assess students' mastery of the skills before concluding the chapter.

TIME SAVERS!

Hands-on Grammar
Use the Hands-on Grammar activity sheet for Chapter 27 to facilitate this activity.

ASSESS and CLOSE

Chapter Review

Each of these exercises correlates to a concept in the chapter on capitalization, pages 638–650. These exercises may be used for more practice, for reteaching, or for review of the Key Concepts presented.

Answer Key

Exercise 13

1. Jefferson Davis was the president of the Confederate States of America.
2. A shrine and museum in honor of Jefferson Davis is located in Biloxi, Mississippi.
3. To see his first house, go to Woodville, Mississippi.
4. President Zachary Taylor's daughter was Davis's first wife.
5. The Fountain of Youth was discovered by Dutch colonists in 1631.
6. In the area of Washington, D.C., you will find the Fort Ward Museum.
7. It is open Tuesday through Saturday from noon to 5:00 P.M.
8. There is a replica of an American symbol, the Liberty Bell, in Dover, Delaware.
9. You can also visit Arlington National Cemetery, where more than 16,000 Union soldiers are buried.
10. There are also sections devoted to Confederate soldiers and to the residents of Freedman's Village, where freed slaves once lived.

Exercise 14

1. President
2. correct
3. correct
4. President
5. correct
6. correct
7. Doctor
8. Aunt
9. Grandma
10. Professor

Exercise 15

1. Cows
2. We've; Can't
3. I
4. To
5. I've
6. Salem Sue, the Largest Cow
7. Where
8. Harvard
9. I, Do, I
10. How
11. I, I
12. I
13. I, Cow
14. I
15. I, I

Chapter 27

Chapter Review

GRAMMAR EXERCISES 13–19

Exercise 13 **Using Capitals for Proper Nouns and Proper Adjectives** Copy each of the following sentences onto your paper, adding the missing capitals.

1. jefferson davis was the president of the confederate states of america.
2. A shrine and museum in honor of jefferson davis is located in biloxi, mississippi.
3. To see his first house, go to woodville, mississippi.
4. President zachary taylor's daughter was davis's first wife.
5. The fountain of youth was discovered by dutch colonists in 1631.
6. In the area of washington, d.c., you will find the fort ward museum.
7. It is open tuesday through saturday from noon to 5:00 P.M.
8. There is a replica of an american symbol, the liberty bell, in dover, delaware.
9. You can also visit arlington national cemetery, where more than 16,000 union soldiers are buried.
10. There are also sections devoted to confederate soldiers and to the residents of freedman's village, where freed slaves once lived.

Exercise 14 **Using Capitals for Titles** Rewrite the following sentences on your paper, adding capitals as needed. If no capitals are needed, write *correct.*

1. A 30-foot-tall statue in Springfield, Illinois, denotes the birthplace of president Abraham Lincoln.
2. Your cousin can take us to the corner of 144th Street and West Dodge Road.
3. Julian's grandfather was part of the Boys Town Stamp Collecting Club.
4. It would be a demanding job to be the president of the United States.
5. Their aunt is a stamp collector.
6. The doctors at Southern Illinois University promote health awareness at the Pearson Museum.
7. When I had an ear infection, doctor Thompson gave me a prescription for antibiotics.
8. Will aunt Mary know how to get there?
9. After school, grandma told me stories about the 1950's.
10. My brother learned about old medical techniques from professor Mill.

Exercise 15 **Using All the Rules of Capitalization** Rewrite the following sentences, adding the missing capitals.

1. cows are important to the economy of many small towns.
2. "we've already seen three of the largest cow statues in the world," complained the young boy. "can't we go to an amusement park?"
3. Do you think i should go to Berlin, Ohio, to see the Largest Real Cheese Block?
4. to see a cow in a cheesehead hat, I would have to go to Janesville, Wisconsin.
5. "i've seen more statues of cows than of any other animal across the country," declared Connie.
6. "salem Sue, the largest cow," explained their aunt, "stands on School Hill in North Dakota."
7. where is the milk center of the world?
8. harvard claims to be the milk center of the world.
9. "i have never heard of a 38-foot-tall cow!" exclaimed Peter. "do you think i could see it from the highway?"
10. "how much more time," asked Suzie, "until I get to see Chatty Belle, the World's Largest Talking Cow?"

11. i heard that the World's Largest Replica Cheese replaced the real one in 1965 before i was born.
12. When i saw the replica, it was inside the Cheesemobile in Wisconsin.
13. i have heard that Harmilda the cow is the mascot there.
14. You know, i can see The World's Largest Talking Cow and The World's Largest Replica Cheese in one stop.
15. i wish i could have tried some of the World's Largest Cheese.

Exercise 16 **Writing Sentences With Capitals** Write a sentence about each of the following, using capitals correctly.

1. the governor of your state
2. a local historic site
3. the nearest college or university
4. your favorite vacation spot
5. a club you belong to
6. your best friend
7. your favorite movie star
8. a movie you saw recently
9. a piece of literature you enjoy
10. a work of art you have seen
11. a museum you have visited
12. your state capital
13. the biggest city you have visited
14. a national park
15. a body of water near your home

Exercise 17 **Proofreading Sentences for Capitalization** Rewrite each of the following sentences, adding capitals where necessary.

1. during the depression, an austrian immigrant got the idea to open a jungle for tourists.
2. parrot jungle features bird shows, monkeys, alligators, and flamingos.
3. jared and his uncle are going to see the shows on thursday, july 21.
4. then, they will join the rest of the family on a cruise on the u.s.s. atlantic.
5. jared is worried that the ship will go through the bermuda triangle, one of the most dangerous places in the atlantic ocean.

Exercise 18 **Proofreading Paragraphs for Capitalization** Copy the following paragraph onto your paper, adding the missing capitals.

if "matters of the heart" are important to you, you will find many amusing stops in your travels through the united states. start with a stroll through the heart of America. First, you can stop at the museum of science and industry in chicago, illinois; the franklin institute in philadelphia, pennsylvania; or the oregon museum of science and industry in portland, oregon. For a romantic outing, take your special sweetheart to the heart-shaped pond at the funny farm in bend, oregon. A good day for this outing would be valentine's day, february 14. For a special treat, you may need to cross the allegheny mountains to find a kiss in hershey, pennsylvania. if you are traveling with the greatest love of your life, take her or him to dinosaur world in ossineke, michigan. there you will find "the greatest heart." You'll find many sites in john margolies's book fun along the road: american tourist attractions.

Exercise 19 **Writing Application** Imagine that you are going on a trip across the country. Write a paragraph about the places that you see, including dates, geographical features, monuments, and buildings. Be sure to use correct capitalization.

Answer Key continued

the Allegheny Mountains to find a kiss in Hershey, Pennsylvania. If you are traveling with the greatest love of your life, take her or him to Dinosaur World in Ossineke, Michigan. There you will find "the Greatest Heart." You'll find many sites in John Margolies book Fun Along the Road: American Tourist Attractions.

Exercise 19

Writing Application
Students may want to access the Web sites of some of these places to learn more about them.

Exercise 16

Answers will vary. Samples are given.

1. The governor of my state is George Pataki.
2. Federal Hall is a local historical site.
3. New York University is the closest university.
4. My favorite vacation spot is White Roe Lake.
5. I belong to the school Chess Club.
6. My best friend is named Joan.
7. My favorite movie star is Mel Gibson.
8. I saw the movie Mansfield Park recently.
9. My favorite book is The Hobbit.
10. I saw Monet's Water Lilies.
11. I saw the painting at the Museum of Modern Art.
12. Albany is the capital of my state.
13. New York City is the biggest city I have visited.
14. Denali National Park is in Alaska.
15. The East River is two blocks away from my home.

Exercise 17

1. During the Depression, an Austrian immigrant got the idea to open a jungle for tourists.
2. Parrot Jungle features bird shows, monkeys, alligators, and flamingos.
3. Jared and his uncle are going to see the shows on Thursday, July 21.
4. Then they will join the rest of the family on a cruise on the U.S.S. Atlantic.
5. Jared is worried that the ship will go through the Bermuda Triangle, one of the most dangerous places in the Atlantic Ocean.

Exercise 18

If "matters of the heart" are important to you, you will find many amusing stops in your travels through the United States. Start with a stroll through the heart of America. First, you can stop at the Museum of Science and Industry in Chicago, Illinois; the Franklin Institute in Philadelphia, Pennsylvania; or the Oregon Museum of Science and Industry in Portland, Oregon. For a romantic outing, take your special sweetheart to the heart-shaped pond at the Funny Farm in Bend, Oregon. A good day for this outing would be Valentine's Day, February 14. For a special treat, you may need to cross

Lesson Objectives

- To proofread a passage for errors in mechanics.

Step-by-Step Teaching Guide

Proofreading for Errors in Capitalization, Spelling, and Punctuation

Teaching Resourses: Standardized Test Preparation Workbook, pp. 53–54

1. Although the choices for both samples are given in the same order, remind students that this is not always the case on tests.
2. In items like these, be sure students understand that they need only identify errors in the underlined part of the passage for each question.
3. Many times, students read the passages too quickly and overlook errors. This is especially true for errors in punctuation and spelling errors involving homophones. Tell students to read slowly and carefully.

Standardized Test Preparation Workshop

Proofreading for Errors in Capitalization, Spelling, and Punctuation

Many standardized tests measure your ability to proofread a passage and identify the type of error contained in a given section. The following sample items will allow you to practice this skill.

Test Tip

Although "No error" is sometimes the correct choice, do not choose this option too quickly. Always double-check the test item to make sure you haven't missed an error.

Sample Test Item	Answers and Explanations
Read the passage, and decide which type of error, if any, appears in each underlined section. This summer our Youth Group will be (1) taking a tour of the united states. (2)	
1 **A** Spelling error **B** Capitalization error **C** Punctuation error **D** No error	The correct answer for item 1 is *B*. *Youth Group* is not a proper noun and should not be capitalized.
2 **F** Spelling error **G** Capitalization error **H** Punctuation error **J** No error	The correct answer for item 2 is *G*. The names of nations, such as the United States, are always capitalized.

TEST-TAKING TIP

Encourage students to mark the passages as they read, identifying only errors in mechanics. They can use this information to answer the questions.

Practice 1 **Directions:** Read the passage, and decide which type of error, if any, appears in each underlined section.

Before we begin our trip, I am going to read Travels with charley by John Steinbeck. (1) This work describes Steinbeck's travels around (2) the Country (3) with his dog. One place he visited was the badlands (4) in south Dakota (5).

1 **A** Spelling error
B Capitalization error
C Punctuation error
D No error

2 **F** Spelling error
G Capitalization error
H Punctuation error
J No error

3 **A** Spelling error
B Capitalization error
C Punctuation error
D No error

4 **F** Spelling error
G Capitalization error
H Punctuation error
J No error

5 **A** Spelling error
B Capitalization error
C Punctuation error
D No error

Practice 2 **Directions:** Read the passage, and decide which type of error, if any, appears in each underlined section.

We will visit the badlands national monument (1), and then mount Rushmore (2). My Aunt has been (3) to each monument and has assured me that both will be very intresting and worth the visit. (4) My history teacher Mrs Shaw will also be our group leader (5). I'm sure she knows a lot about both places.

1 **A** Spelling error
B Capitalization error
C Punctuation error
D No error

2 **F** Spelling error
G Capitalization error
H Punctuation error
J No error

3 **A** Spelling error
B Capitalization error
C Punctuation error
D No error

4 **F** Spelling error
G Capitalization error
H Punctuation error
J No error

5 **A** Spelling error
B Capitalization error
C Punctuation error
D No error

Answer Key

Practice 1

1. B
2. J
3. B
4. G
5. B

Practice 2

1. B
2. G
3. B
4. F
5. C

Answer Key

Exercise A

1. Cocoa beans grow in a specific location: hot, humid, climates.
2. After harvesting and roasting the cocoa beans, what is the next step for making chocolate?
3. The beans are crushed into an unsweetened substance; consequently, sugar may be added to the mixture.
4. Emulsifiers are included for smoothness, and cocoa butter is added or removed.
5. Most American companies make one kind of chocolate: milk chocolate.
6. Other types of chocolate include: baking chocolate, cocoa powder, and eating chocolate.
7. Hey! White chocolate isn't really chocolate.
8. Did you know that no part of the cocoa bean is used in making white chocolate?
9. It still tastes really good.
10. The original cocoa bean mash in its ingredients is called unsweetened chocolate; it is also called baking chocolate.

Exercise B

1. Did you know that butter is made out of cream?
2. It is skimmed off the top of whole milk with a cream ladle, a large spoon with holes in it.
3. The milk runs through the holes, but the cream won't.
4. The cream is chilled and soured; next, the mixture needs to reach room temperature.
5. Then, it is poured into the most well-known piece of equipment, the churn.
6. Wow! My hands got tired separating the butter from the buttermilk.
7. Grandmother said, "It can take from one-half hour to forever to separate."
8. We work the butter with a butter paddle, and we use clean water to wash it.
9. Before putting it in the molds, we sprinkle in some salt.
10. In the book, <u>Little House in the Big Woods</u>, Laura Ingalls Wilder writes about making butter.

Cumulative Review

MECHANICS

Exercise A **Using End Marks, Commas, Semicolons, and Colons** Copy the following sentences, inserting the appropriate end marks, commas, semicolons, and colons.

1. Cocoa beans grow in a specific location hot humid climates
2. After harvesting and roasting the cocoa beans what is the next step for making chocolate
3. The beans are crushed into an unsweetened substance consequently sugar may be added to the mixture
4. Emulsifiers are included for smoothness and cocoa butter is added or removed
5. Most American companies make one kind of chocolate milk chocolate
6. Other types of chocolate include baking chocolate cocoa powder and eating chocolate
7. Hey White chocolate isn't really chocolate
8. Did you know that no part of the cocoa bean is used in making white chocolate
9. It still tastes really good
10. The original cocoa bean mash in its ingredients is called unsweetened chocolate it is also called baking chocolate

Exercise B **Using All the Rules of Punctuation** Copy the following sentences, inserting the appropriate end marks, commas, semicolons, colons, quotation marks, underlining, hyphens, and apostrophes. All quoted material is underlined.

1. Did you know that butter is made out of cream
2. It is skimmed off the top of whole milk with a cream ladle a large spoon with holes in it
3. The milk runs through the holes but the cream wont
4. The cream is chilled and soured next the mixture needs to reach room temperature
5. Then it is poured into the most well known piece of equipment the churn
6. Wow My hands got tired separating the butter from the buttermilk
7. Grandmother said <u>It can take from one-half hour to forever to separate</u>
8. We work the butter with a butter paddle, and we use clean water to wash it
9. Before putting it in the molds we sprinkle in some salt
10. In the book Little House in the Big Woods Laura Ingalls Wilder writes about making butter

Exercise C **Using Capitalization** Copy the following sentences, capitalizing letters where appropriate.

1. christopher columbus, who sailed for queen isabella in 1492, discovered chili peppers.
2. Columbus found these popular in south america and mexico, and so he brought them to spain.
3. colombus's discovery influenced cooking worldwide.
4. indian, thai, and japanese cooking quickly embraced these peppers.
5. also, szechwan-style chinese cooking is spicy and uses peppers.
6. even colonists in the americas began using chili peppers.
7. however, it wasn't until the twentieth century that people in the united states began exploring chilies.
8. in 1975, the <u>hellfire cookbook</u> was published, which contained only hot and spicy recipes.
9. the <u>chili pepper encyclopedia</u> explains

656 • Mechanics

Exercise C

1. Christopher Columbus, who sailed for Queen Isabella in 1492, discovered chili peppers.
2. Columbus found these popular in South America and Mexico, and so he brought them to Spain.
3. Columbus's discovery influenced cooking worldwide.
4. Indian, Thai, and Japanese cooking quickly embraced these peppers.
5. Also, Szechwan-style Chinese cooking is spicy and uses peppers.
6. Even colonists in the Americas began using chili peppers.
7. However, it wasn't until the twentieth century that people in the United States began exploring chilies.
8. In 1975, the <u>Hellfire Cookbook</u> was published, which contained only hot and spicy recipes.
9. <u>The Chili Pepper Encyclopedia</u> explains that there are many different levels of spiciness.
10. People are not aware of the variety of peppers and their flavors.

continued

that there are many different levels of spiciness.

10. people are not aware of the variety of peppers and their flavors.
11. the habanero chile is native to the yucatan peninsula and the caribbean islands.
12. it is fifty times hotter than the jalapeno, which is used throughout the united states in nachos.
13. the serrano is a mexican-grown pepper that turns from green to red to yellow as it grows.
14. in the american southwest, it is used in several popular snacks.
15. the poblana chile is a dark-green, triangular–shaped chile used in *mole* sauces.

Exercise D Using Capitalization and Punctuation Copy the following dialogue, inserting the appropriate capitalization, punctuation, and indentation.

1. rob what kind of salad dressing do you want on your salad asked karin
2. rob answered i usually choose italian or creamy italian
3. have you ever tried plain oil and vinegar its a distinct taste, but very good
4. well, what kind of oil do they mean asked rob
5. olive oil is the best choice for salads It has a distinct flavor and is very smooth karin answered
6. wait just a second is it really made out of olives
7. karin responded yes countries like italy greece and spain have been making and using olive oil for thousands of years.
8. ive seen olive oils in the stores said rob sometimes it is very dark, and sometimes it looks much lighter
9. the book the joy of cooking explained that it can depend on the type of olive that was used and also on how pure the oil really is karin explained
10. then rob asked does that affect the taste of the oil
11. many factors affect the taste replied karin from the number of times it was pressed to how long it has mellowed
12. well karin how does one choose an oil to use on salad
13. it is important to look for oil that has been cold pressed and contains little acid
14. i think i would be interested in trying some it is such a historical product said rob
15. youve made a good choice here drizzle this on your salad and then ill use it

Exercise E Proofreading for Errors in Punctuation and Capitalization
Read the following passage. Then, rewrite it, correcting all errors in punctuation and capitalization.

Cooking is a fun, and useful hobby. Whether you cook fancy meals or simple ones, you can enjoy the results of your work. If you are interested in getting started i have several helpful books "the joy of cooking" "meals on a budget" and "market fresh meals". Are you interested in borrowing any of them. Start with simple meals then move on to the more complicated ones.

Exercise F Writing Application
Write a short dialogue between you and a friend about your favorite foods. Be sure to use correct capitalization and punctuation.

Answer Key continued

Exercise C continued

11. The harbanero chile is native to the Yucatan Peninsula and the Caribbean Islands
12. It is fifty times hotter than the jalapeno, which is used throughout the United States in nachos.
13. The serrano is a Mexican-grown pepper that turns from green to red to yellow as it grows.
14. In the American Southwest, it is used in several popular snacks.
15. The poblana chile is a dark-green, triangular-shaped chile used in *mole* sauces.

Exercise D

1. "Rob, what kind of salad dressing do you want on your salad?" asked Karin.
2. Rob answered, "I usually choose Italian or creamy Italian."
3. "Have you ever tried plain oil and vinegar? It's a distinct taste, but very good."
4. "Well, what kind of oil do they mean?" asked Rob.
5. "Olive oil is the best choice for salads. It has a distinct flavor and is very smooth," Karin answered.
6. "Wait just a second! Is it really made out of olives?"
7. Karin responded, "Yes, countries like Italy, Greece, and Spain have been making and using olive oil for thousands of years."
8. "I've seen olive oils in the stores," said Rob. "Sometimes, it is very dark, and sometimes, it looks much lighter."
9. "The book, *The Joy of Cooking*, explained that it can depend on the type of olive that was used, and also on how pure the oil really is," Karin explained.
10. Then Rob asked, "Does that affect the taste of the oil?"
11. "Many factors affect the taste," replied Karin, "from the number of times it was pressed to how long it has mellowed."
12. "Well, Karin, how does one choose an oil to use on salad?"
13. "It is important to look for oil that has been cold pressed and contains little acid."
14. "I think I would be interested in trying some. It is such a historical product," said Rob.
15. "You've made a good choice. Here, drizzle this on your salad, and then I'll use it."

Exercise E

Cooking is a fun and useful hobby. Whether you cook fancy meals or simple ones, you can enjoy the results of your work. If you are interested in getting started I have several helpful books: *The Joy of Cooking, Meals on a Budget,* and *Market Fresh Meals.* Are you interested in borrowing any of them? Start with simple meals, then move on to the more complcated ones.

Exercise F

You may wish to have students work in pairs and check each other's dialogues for capitalization and punctuation.

continued

Answer Key

Exercise 1

1.
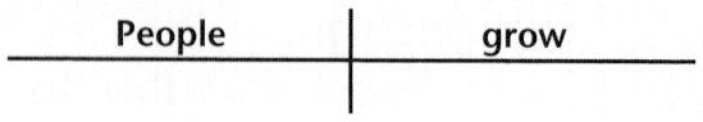

2.
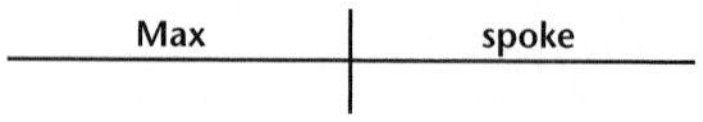

3.
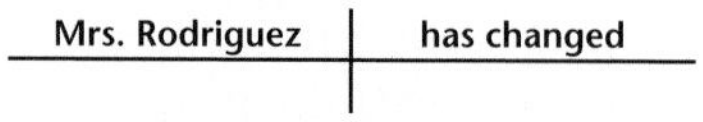

4.
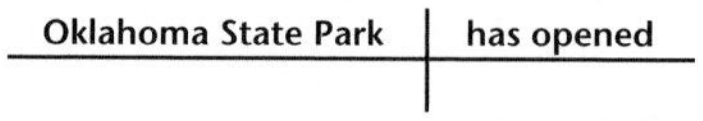

5.
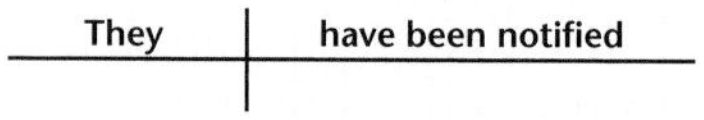

Sentence Diagraming Workshop

Diagraming is a visual way to explain how parts of a sentence are related. In a diagram, the words from a sentence are positioned on horizontal, vertical, and slanted lines. Each line stands for something different. This section will explain how you can draw diagrams for each of the sentence parts that you learned about in Chapter 19.

Subjects and Verbs

The basic parts of any sentence are the subject and its verb. In a diagram, both the subject and the verb are placed on a horizontal line. They are separated by a vertical line, with the subject on the left and the verb on the right.

EXAMPLE: Cars (S) race (V).

Names and compound nouns are diagramed in the same way as *cars* in the preceding example. Verb phrases are diagramed in the same way as the verb *race* above.

EXAMPLE: Elizabeth Wilson (S) has been called (V).

Exercise 1 **Diagraming Subjects and Verbs** Diagram each sentence below, using the preceding examples as models.

1. People grow.
2. Max spoke.
3. Mrs. Rodriguez has changed.
4. Oklahoma State Park has opened.
5. They have been notified.

Adjectives, Adverbs, and Conjunctions

Most sentences contain more than a subject and a verb. Here are the ways to add adjectives, adverbs, and conjunctions to your basic diagrams.

Adding Adjectives Adjectives are placed on slanted lines directly below the nouns or pronouns they modify.

S V

EXAMPLE: A *strong, icy* wind appeared.

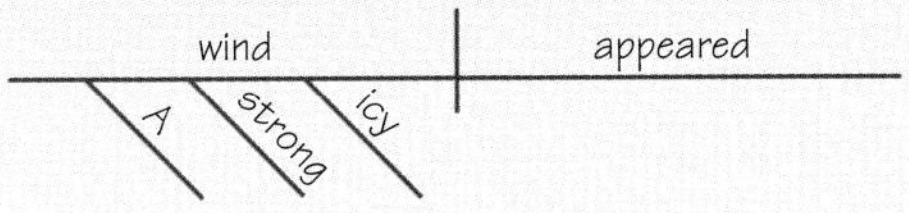

Adding Adverbs Adverbs are also placed on slanted lines. They go directly under the verbs, adjectives, or adverbs they modify.

ADJ S V

EXAMPLE: *Quite* nervous, Frank spoke *very hesitantly.*

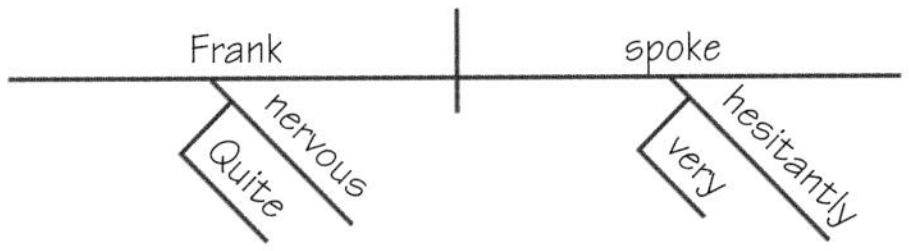

Adding Conjunctions Conjunctions are diagramed on dotted lines drawn between the words they connect.

ADJ ADJ S V ADV

EXAMPLE: The warm and friendly nurse spoke softly but

ADV

firmly.

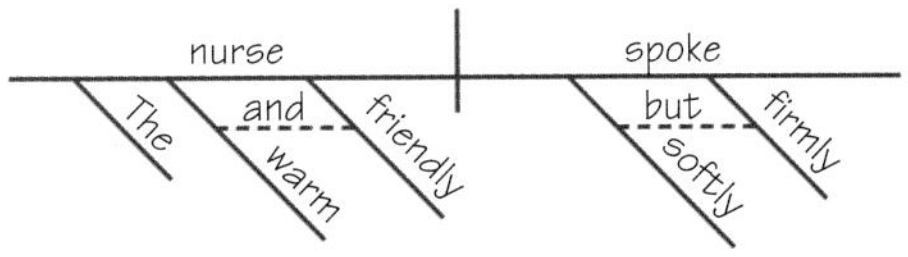

Answer Key

Exercise 2

1.
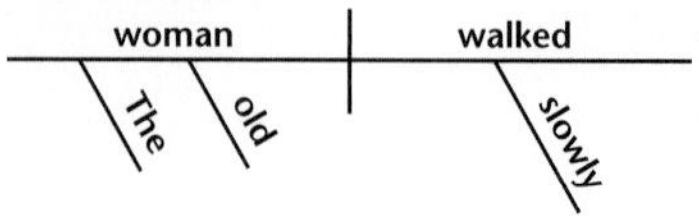

2.
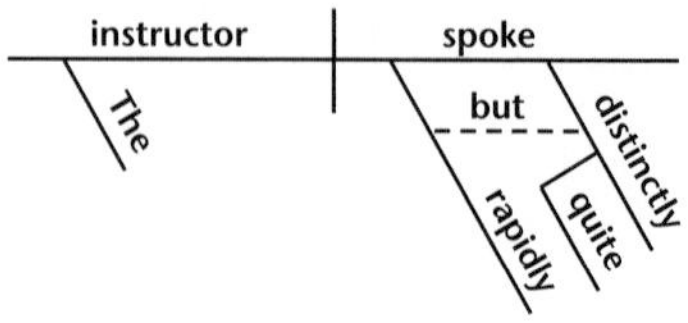

3.
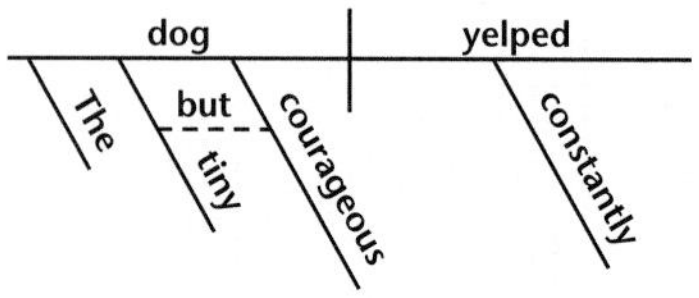

4.
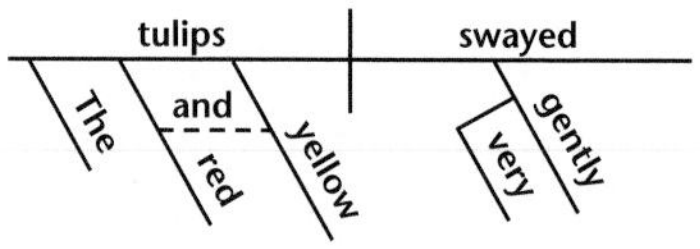

5.
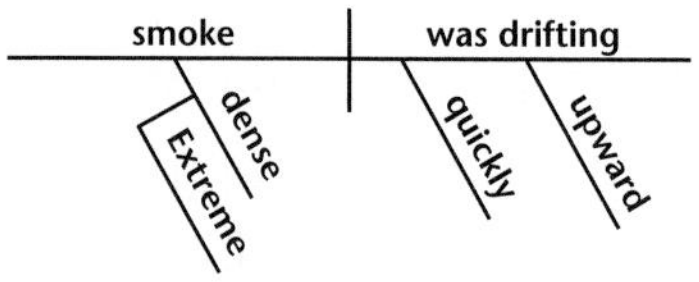

Exercise 2 **Diagraming Subjects and Verbs With Modifiers and Conjunctions** In addition to subjects and verbs, the following sentences contain adjectives, adverbs, and conjunctions. Diagram each sentence.

1. The old woman walked slowly.
2. The instructor spoke rapidly but quite distinctly.
3. The tiny but courageous dog yelped constantly.
4. The red and yellow tulips swayed very gently.
5. Extremely dense smoke was quickly drifting upward.

Compound Subjects and Verbs

It is necessary to split the horizontal line in order to diagram a sentence with either a compound subject or a compound verb.

Compound Subjects A sentence with a compound subject has its subject diagramed on two levels.

EXAMPLE: Father (S) and Mother (S) are arriving (V).

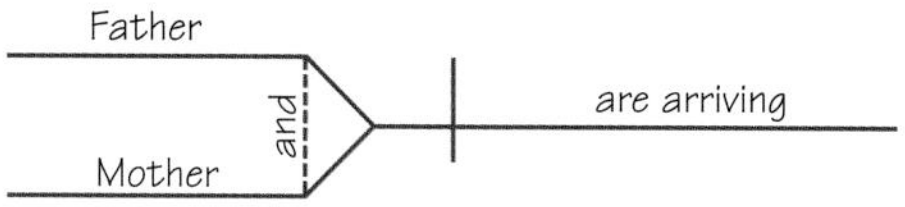

In diagraming compound subjects, place any adjective directly under the word it modifies. If an adjective modifies the entire compound subject, place it under the main line of the diagram. In the following example, *several* modifies the entire compound subject. *Red* and *blue* modify separate subjects.

EXAMPLE: *Several red* balloons (S) and *blue* kites (S) floated (V) overhead.

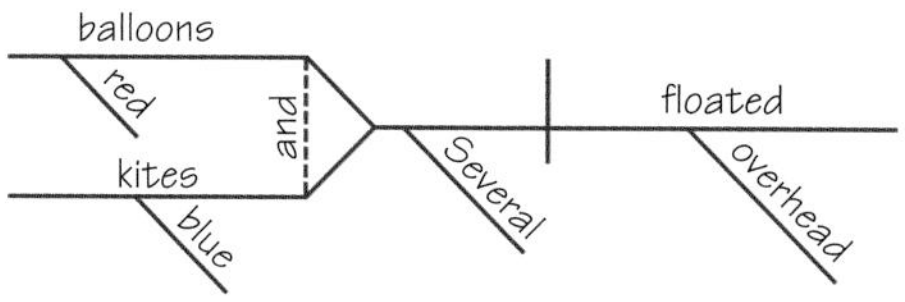

Compound Verbs Sentences with compound verbs are diagramed similarly. In the following example, the adverb *magnificently* modifies both parts of the compound verb.

S V V

EXAMPLE: Jeffrey acts and sings magnificently.

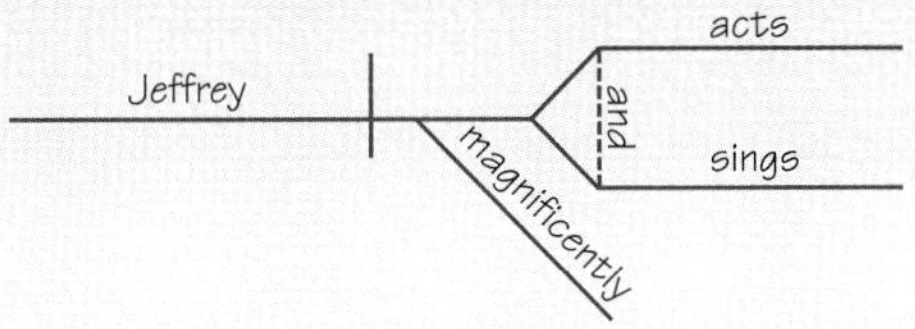

If the parts of a compound verb share a helping verb, the helping verb is placed on the main line of the diagram. If each part of the compound verb has its own helping verb, then each helping verb is placed on the line with its own verb.

HV

EXAMPLE: Betty will win or lose.

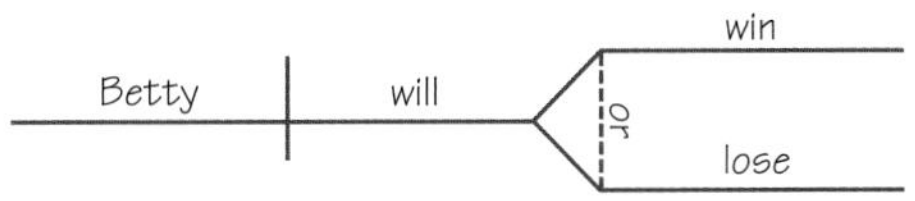

HV HV

EXAMPLE: This project must grow or must shrink.

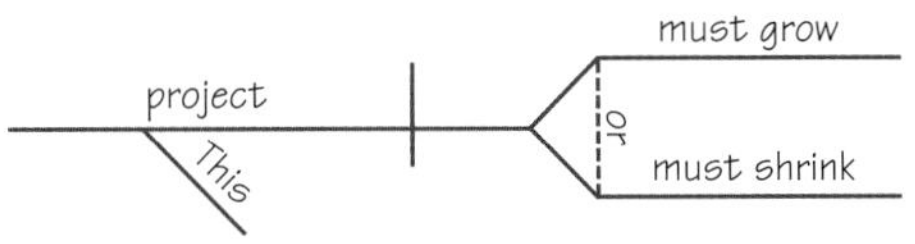

Exercise 3 **Diagraming Compound Subjects and Compound Verbs** Correctly diagram each sentence below.

1. Apples and grapes were served.
2. They can come or can stay.
3. The players, coaches, and parents cheered wildly.
4. The noisy crowd cheered, whistled, and applauded.
5. My brother and sister arrived early and left late.

Answer Key

Exercise 3

1.
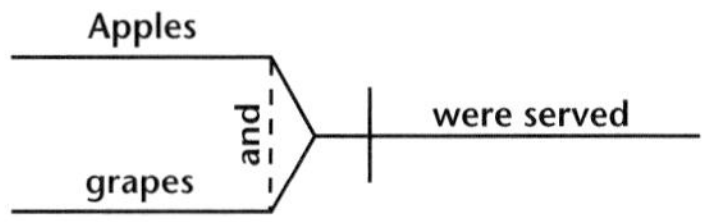

2.
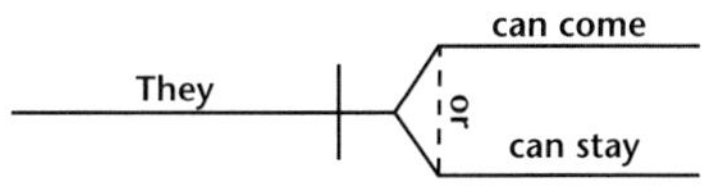

3.
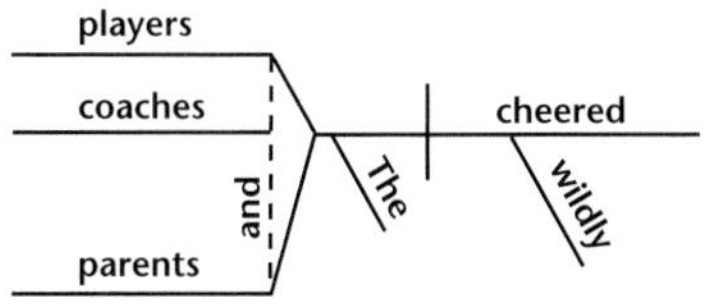

4.
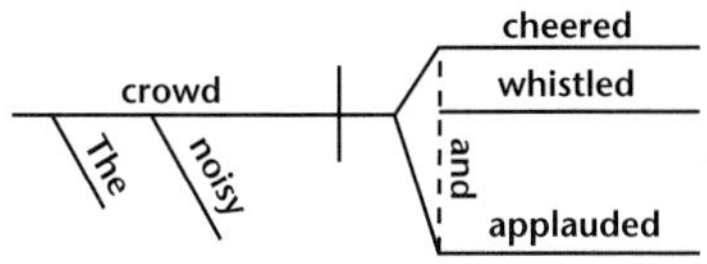

5.
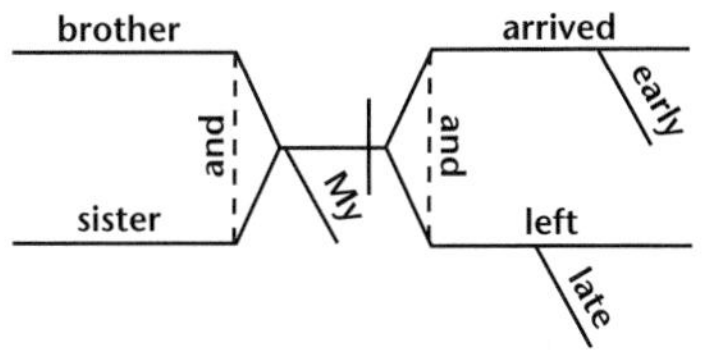

Orders, Sentences Beginning With *There* or *Here,* and Interjections

Orders, sentences beginning with *there* or *here,* and interjections all follow special forms.

Orders The subject of an order is usually understood to be *you.* The understood subject *you* is diagramed in the regular subject position, but in parentheses.

EXAMPLE: Stop (V) now.

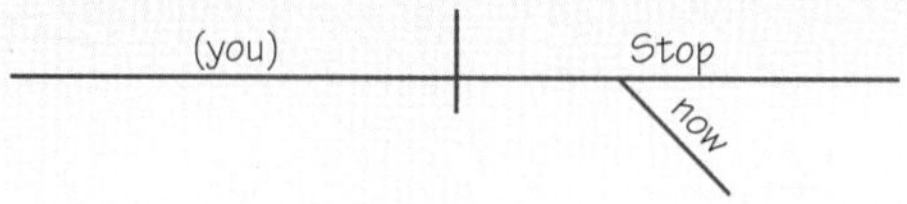

Sentences Beginning With *There* or *Here* *There* and *here* sometimes appear at the beginning of sentences and are mistaken for subjects. They are usually adverbs that modify the verb.

EXAMPLE: *Here* is (V) your watch.

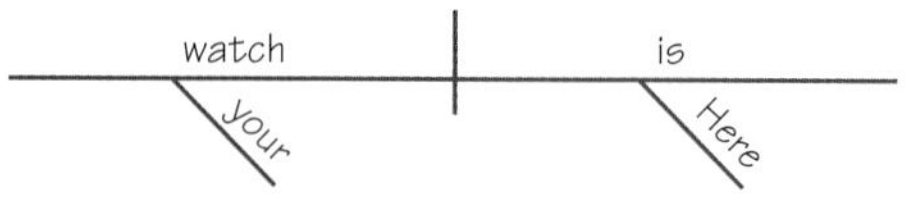

When *there* is used simply to start a sentence, it has no grammatical link to the rest of the sentence. It is therefore placed on a short line above the subject.

EXAMPLE: *There* is (V) an important meeting (S) now.

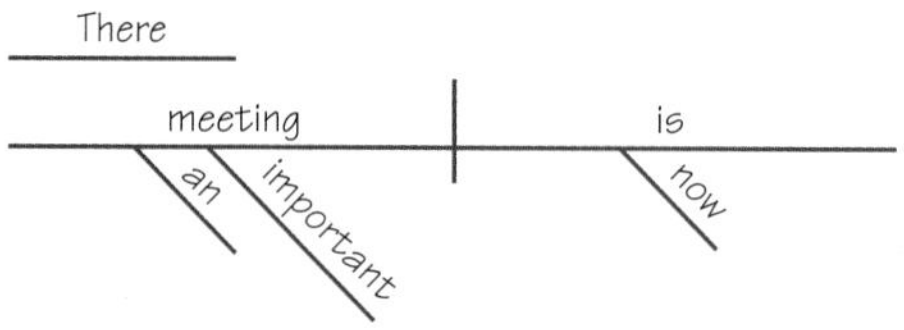

Interjections Like the word *there* when it is used simply to start a sentence, interjections have no grammatical link to the other words in a sentence. For this reason, interjections are also placed on a short line above the subject.

EXAMPLE: Wow! I won. (S = I, V = won)

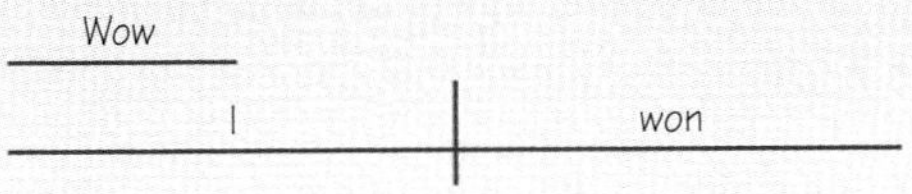

Exercise 4 **Diagraming Orders, Sentences Beginning With *There* or *Here*, and Interjections** Diagram each of the following sentences.

1. Begin now.
2. Here is my homework.
3. There once was a snake.
4. Whew! That hurt.
5. Gee! Watch out.

Answer Key

Exercise 4

1.
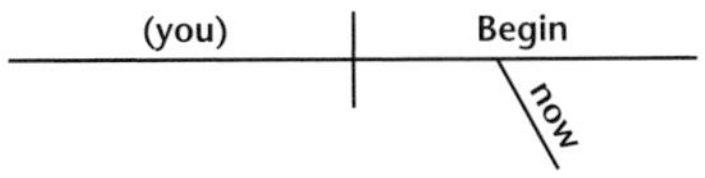

2.
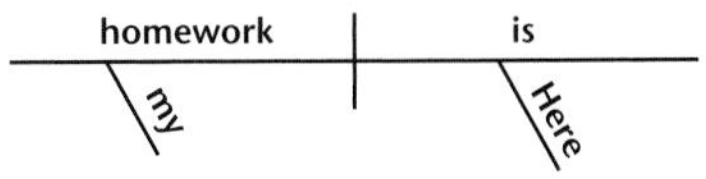

3.
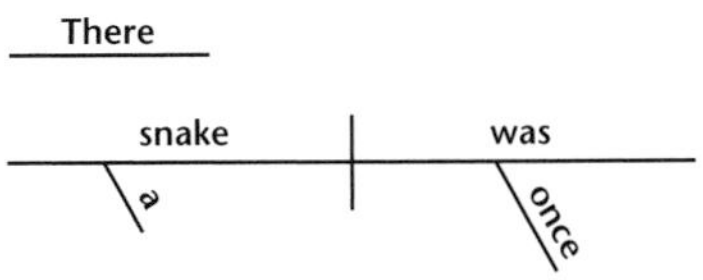

4.
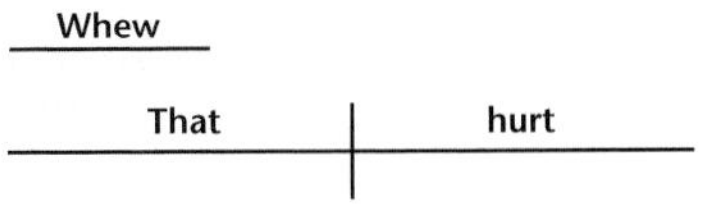

5.
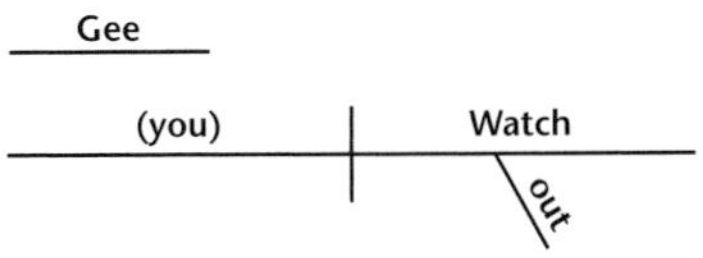

Complements

Direct objects, indirect objects, and subject complements are diagramed in three different ways.

Direct Objects A direct object is placed on the same line as the subject and verb. The direct object follows the verb and is separated from it by a short vertical line.

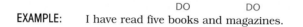

EXAMPLE: Children drink milk. (DO: milk)

A compound direct object is diagramed in a way similar to that used for compound subjects and verbs. An adjective modifying both parts of the compound direct object is placed under the main line of the diagram. Otherwise, the adjective is placed directly under the word it modifies.

EXAMPLE: I have read five books and magazines. (DO: books; DO: magazines)

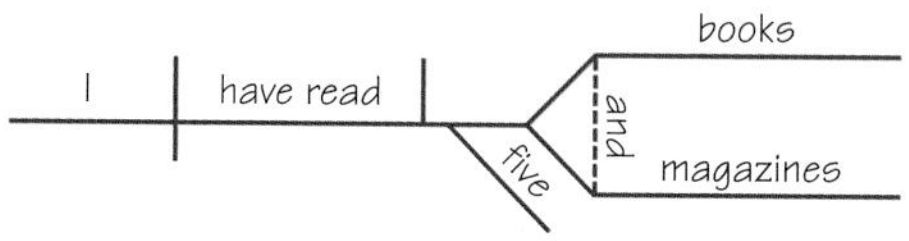

Indirect Objects The indirect object is placed on a short horizontal line extending from a slanted line drawn directly directly below the verb.

EXAMPLE: The teacher gave them the good news. (IO: them)

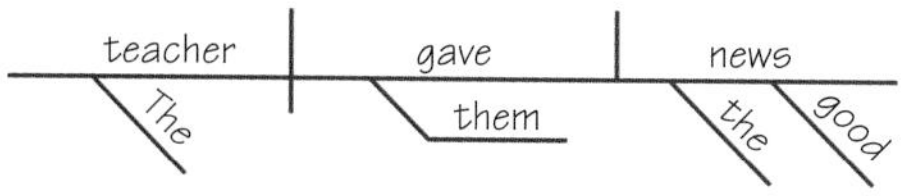

A sentence with a compound indirect object is diagramed in the following way.

EXAMPLE: Mother bought Billy (IO) and me (IO) new gloves.

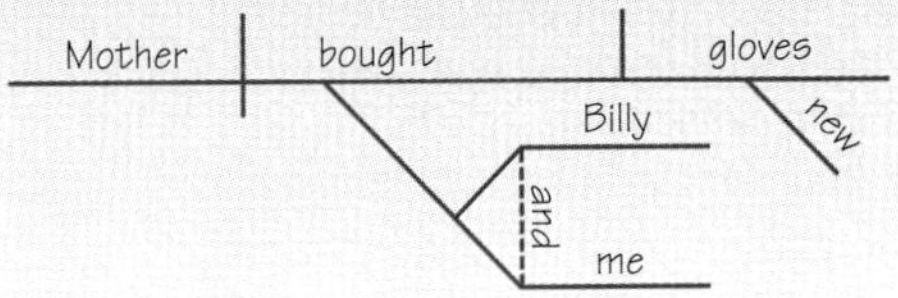

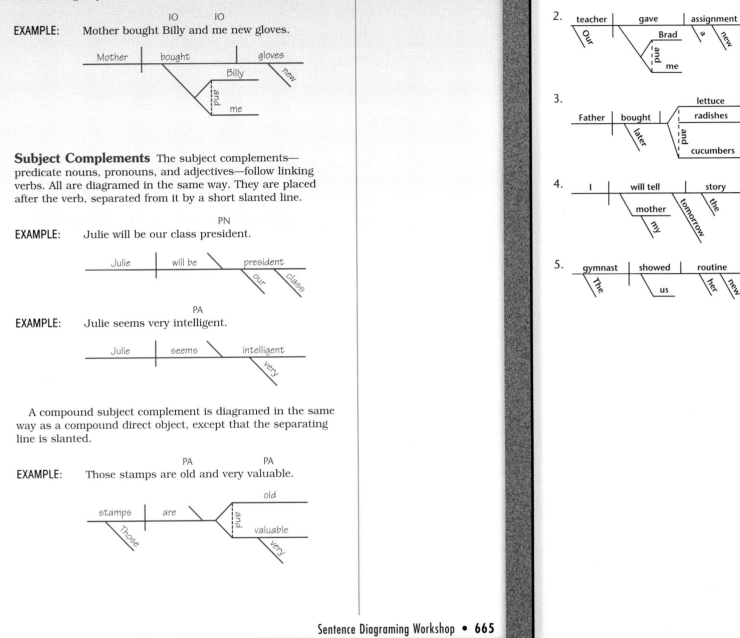

Subject Complements The subject complements—predicate nouns, pronouns, and adjectives—follow linking verbs. All are diagramed in the same way. They are placed after the verb, separated from it by a short slanted line.

EXAMPLE: Julie will be our class president (PN).

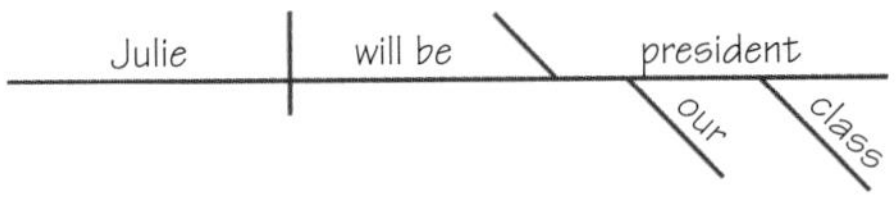

EXAMPLE: Julie seems very intelligent (PA).

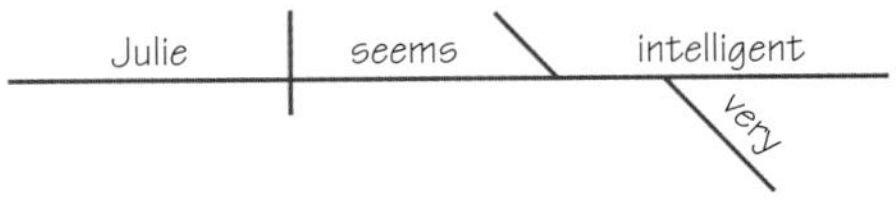

A compound subject complement is diagramed in the same way as a compound direct object, except that the separating line is slanted.

EXAMPLE: Those stamps are old (PA) and very valuable (PA).

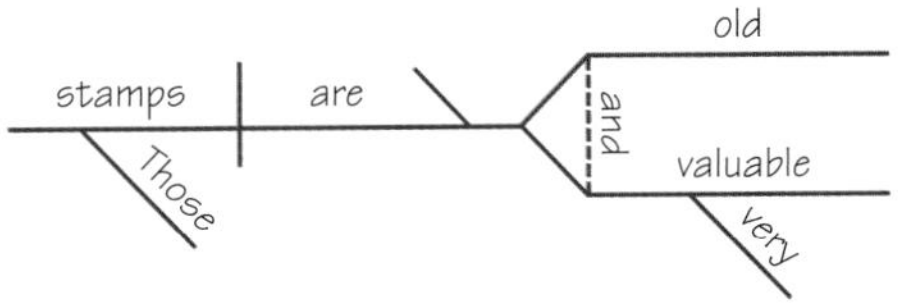

Answer Key

Exercise 5 *(page 666)*

1.
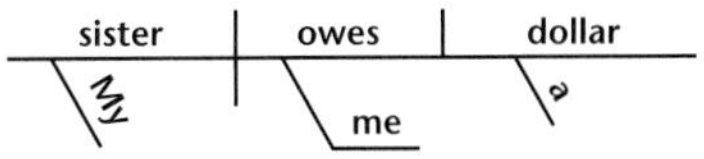

2.
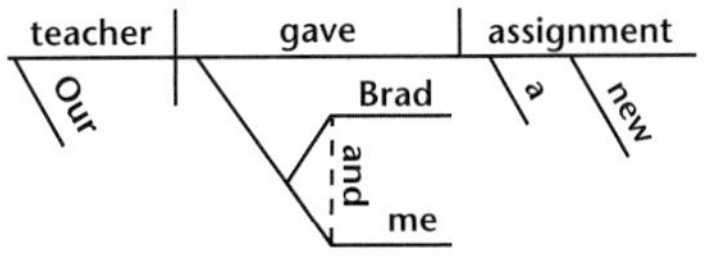

3.
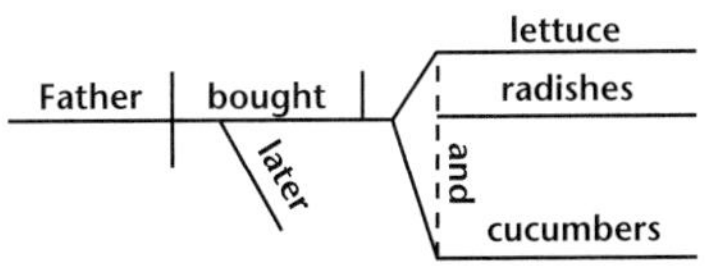

4.
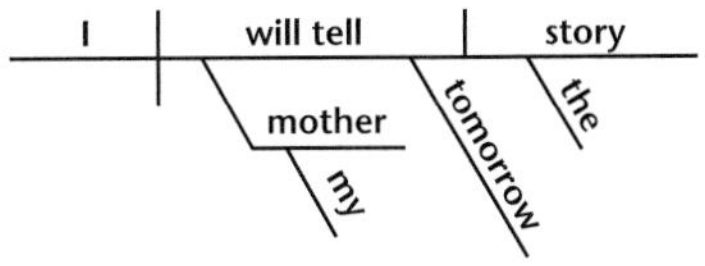

5.
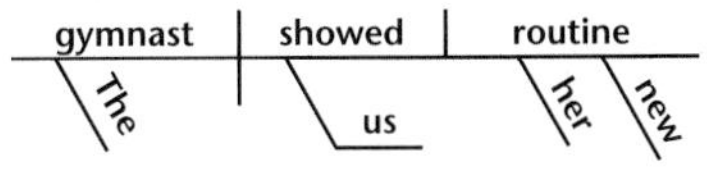

Answer Key

Exercise 6

1.

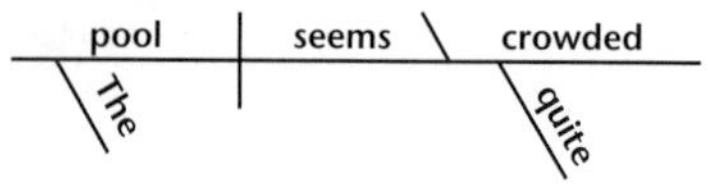

2.

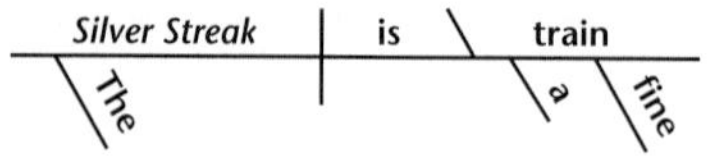

3.

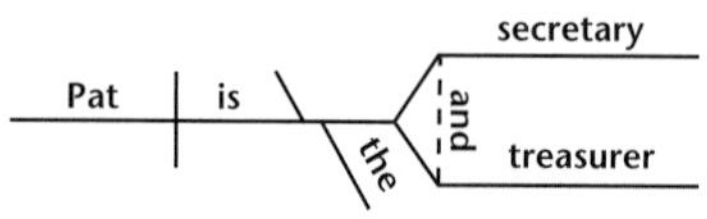

4.

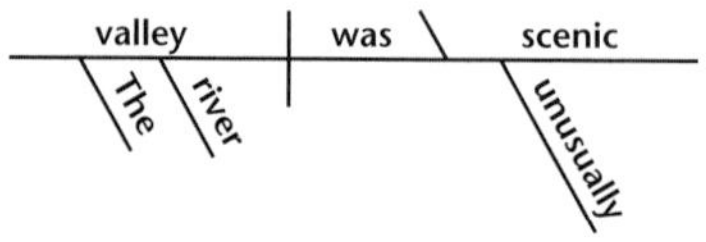

5.

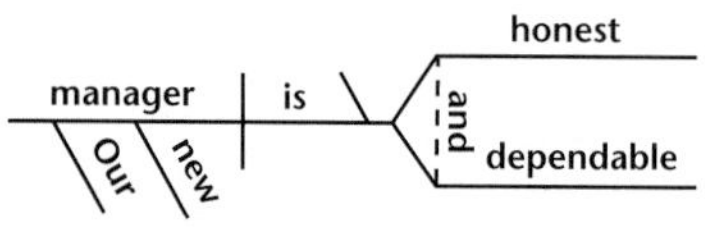

Exercise 7

Sample answers are given.

1. My new car does not function properly.

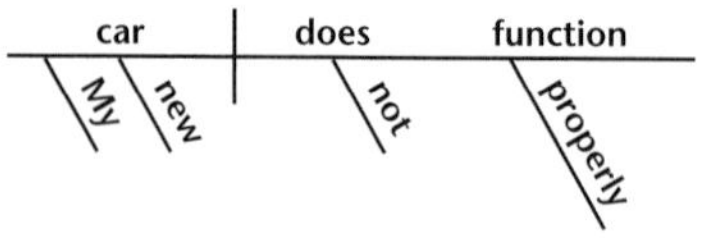

2. Both Josh and Lisa ski and snowboard.

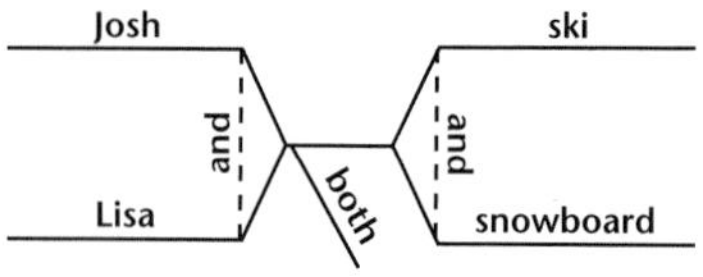

3. Leave him alone!

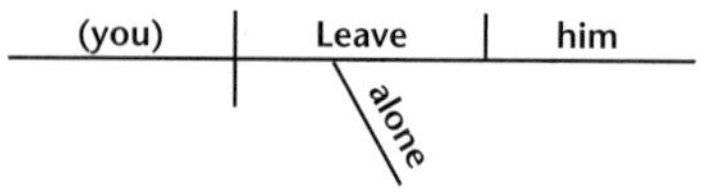

4. Teachers check homework.

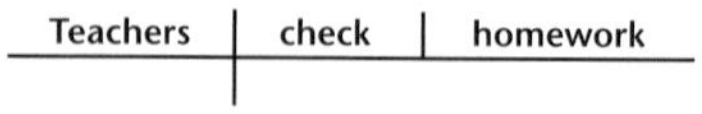

5. His wife is pleasant and graceful.

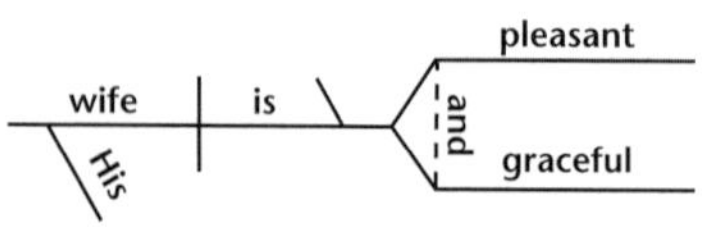

Exercise 5 **Diagraming Direct Objects and Indirect Objects** Diagram the following sentences. Note that some of the objects are compound.

1. My sister owes me a dollar.
2. Our teacher gave Brad and me a new assignment.
3. Father later bought lettuce, radishes, and cucumbers.
4. I will tell my mother the story tomorrow.
5. The gymnast showed us her new routine.

Exercise 6 **Diagraming Subject Complements** Diagram the following sentences. Note that some of the complements are compound.

1. The pool seems quite crowded.
2. The *Silver Streak* is a fine train.
3. Pat is the secretary and treasurer.
4. The river valley was unusually scenic.
5. Our new manager is honest and dependable.

Exercise 7 **Writing and Diagraming Sentences** Follow the instructions below to write five sentences of your own. Then, correctly diagram each sentence. Keep your sentences simple.

EXAMPLE: Write a sentence that contains a direct object.
The actor memorized the entire script.

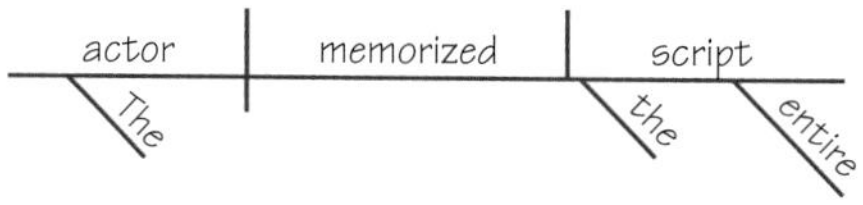

1. Write a sentence that contains at least one adjective and one adverb.
2. Write a sentence with a compound subject and compound verb.
3. Write a sentence that gives an order.
4. Write a sentence that contains a direct object.
5. Write a sentence with a compound subject complement.

Exercise 8 *(page 667)*

1.

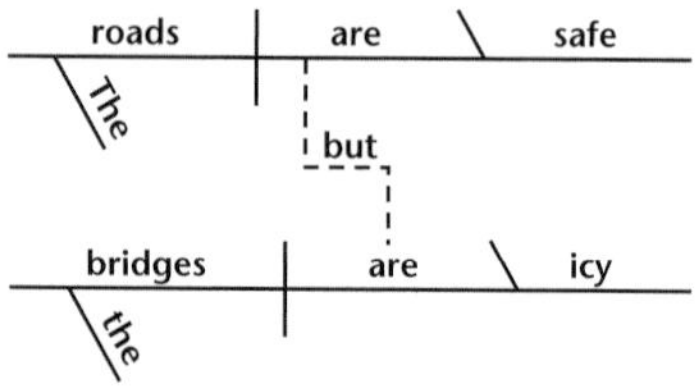

2.

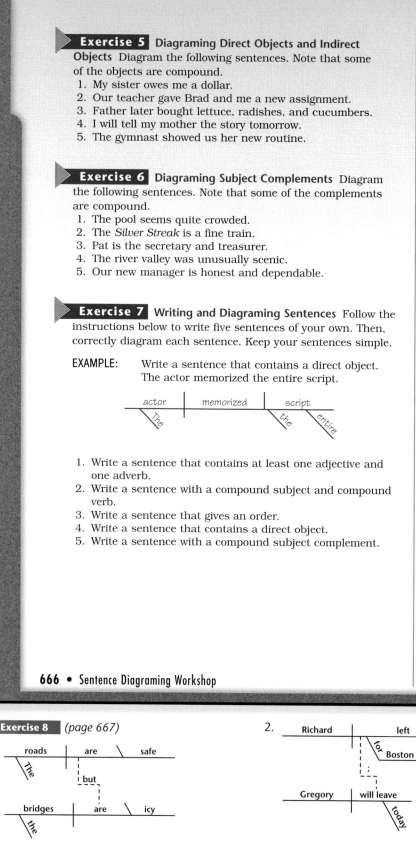

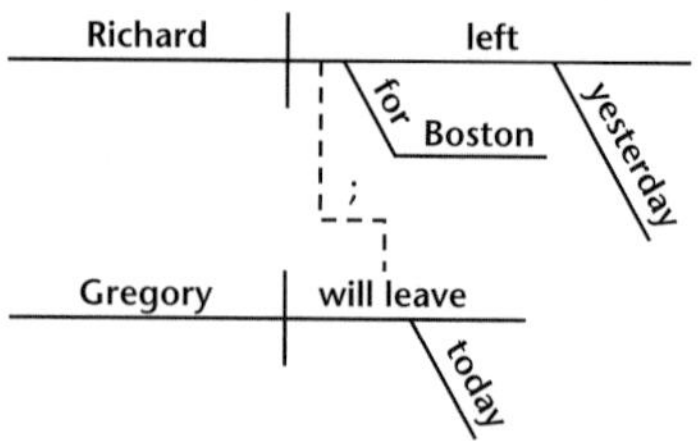

continued

Diagraming Clauses

The previous sections on diagraming dealt with different forms of simple sentences. This section will introduce diagrams for clauses in compound and complex sentences.

Compound Sentences

A compound sentence is a combination of two or more independent clauses. To diagram a compound sentence, begin by diagraming each clause separately, one above the other. Then, join the clauses at the verbs using a dotted line shaped like a step. Place the conjunction or semicolon on the horizontal part of the step.

EXAMPLE: Mary (S) slowly opened (V) the package, and then she (S) smiled (V) happily.

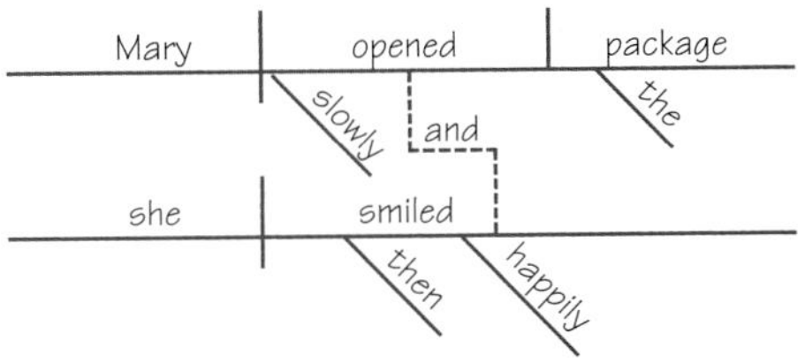

Exercise 8 **Diagraming Compound Sentences** On your paper, diagram each of the following compound sentences.

1. The roads are safe, but the bridges are icy.
2. Richard left for Boston yesterday; Gregory will leave today.
3. She wrote herself a note, yet she still forgot her appointment.
4. We must paint the fence; otherwise, it may rot.
5. We will give him three guesses; she will then tell him the answer.
6. Mary read the assignment, but she had trouble with the vocabulary.
7. Last winter, we had a great deal of snow; this year, we had very little.
8. She enjoyed the movie, and she recommended it to her friends.
9. We waited for Tom, but he didn't show up.
10. Frances was pleased with the results; everything went according to the plan.

Answer Key continued

3.
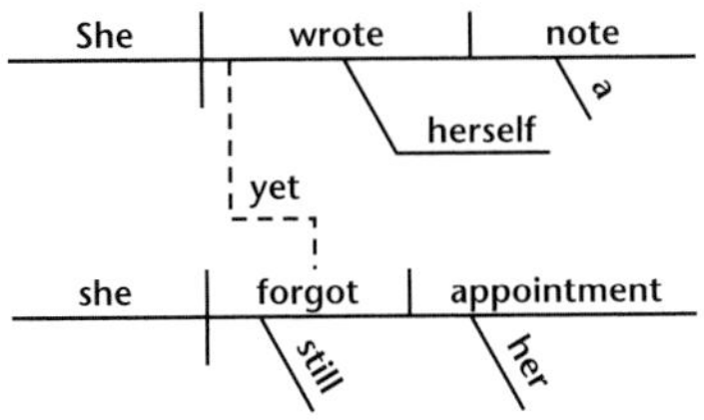

4.
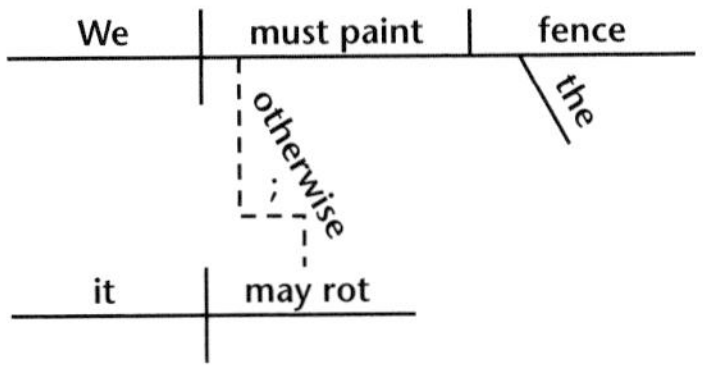

5.
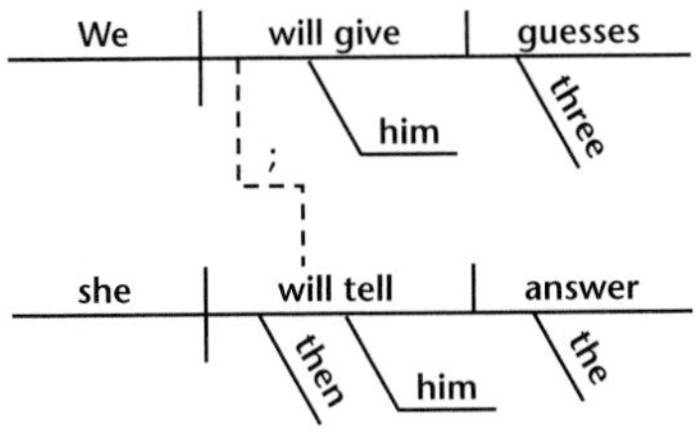

6.
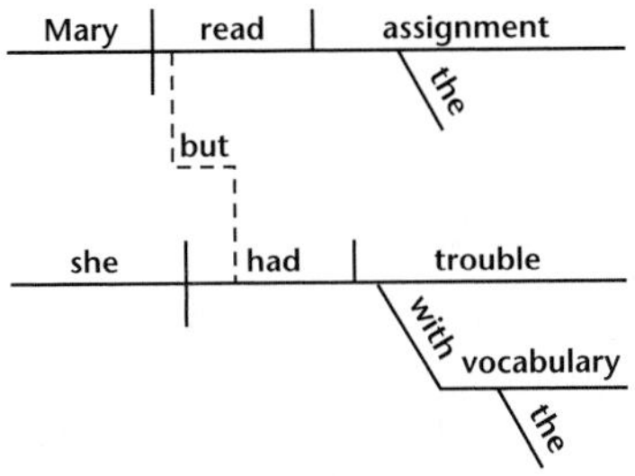

7.
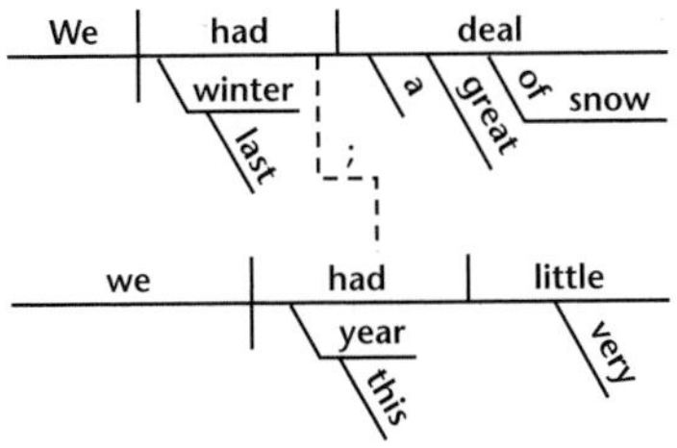

8.
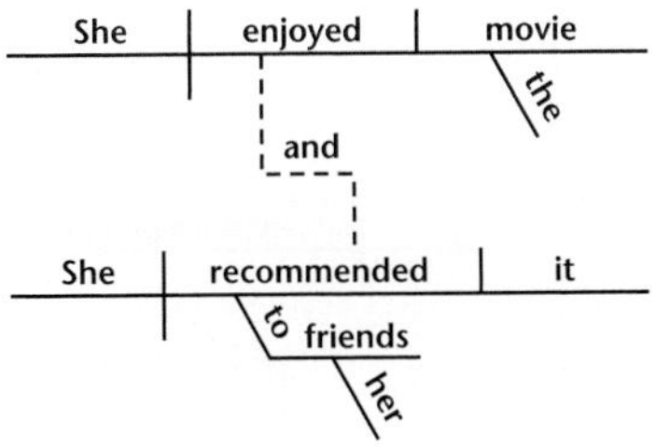

continued

Answer Key continued

9.
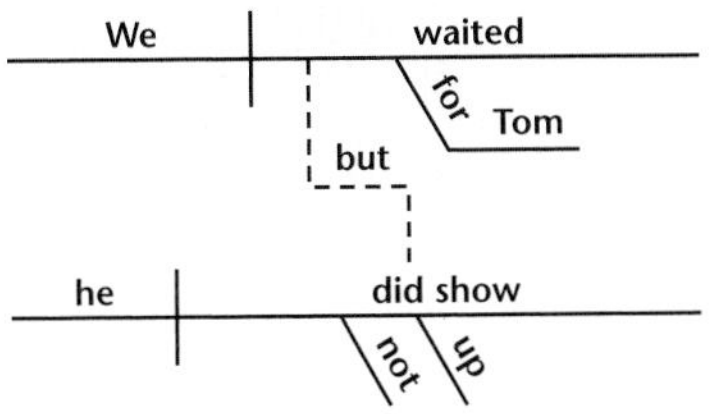

10.
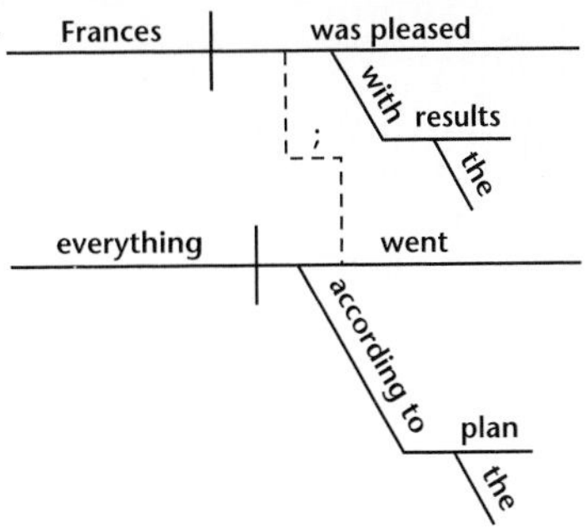

Answer Key

Exercise 9

1.
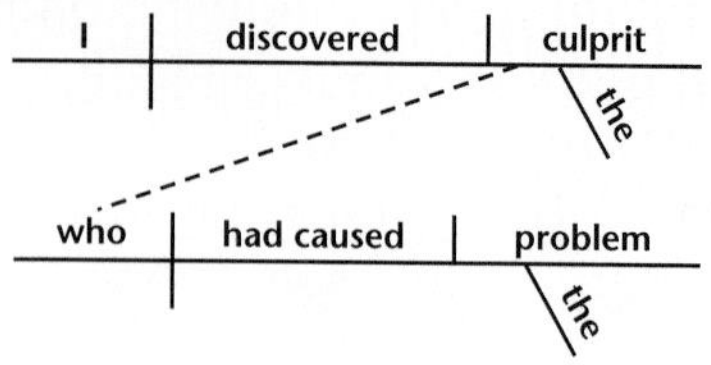

2.
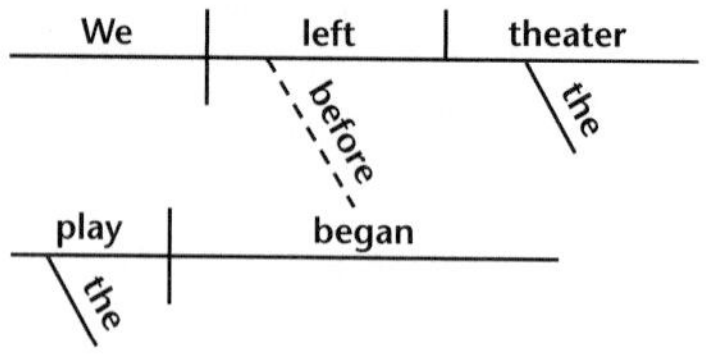

3.
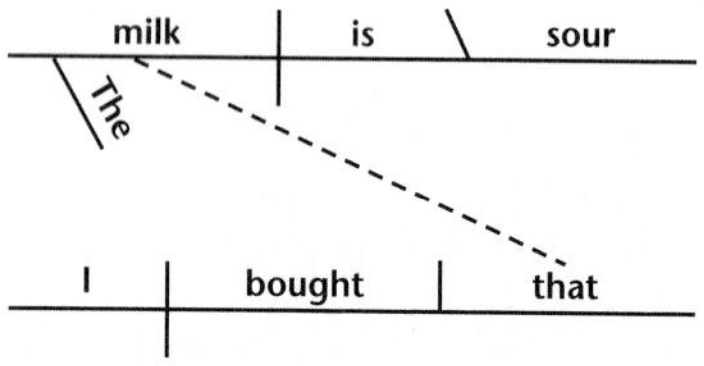

4.
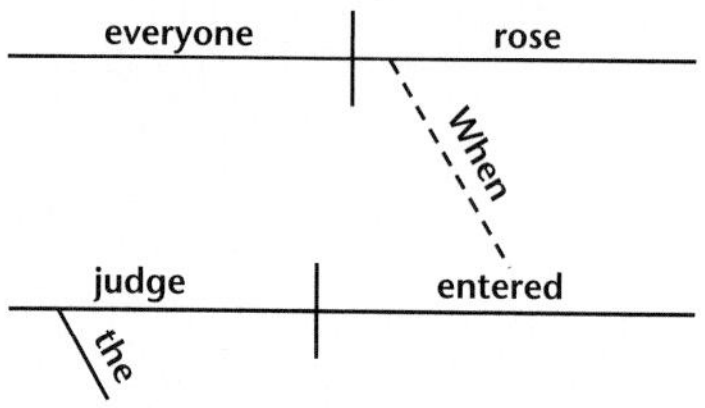

5.
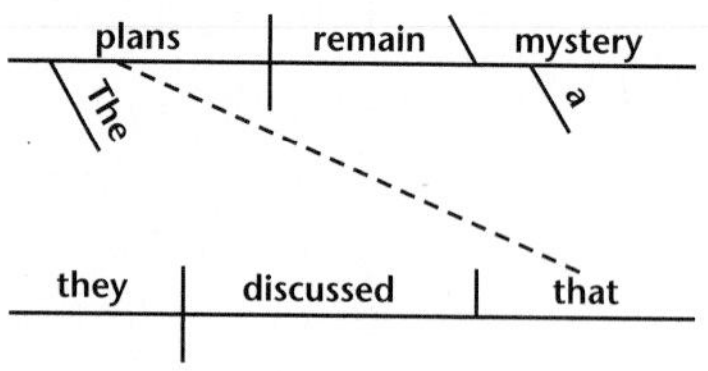

6.
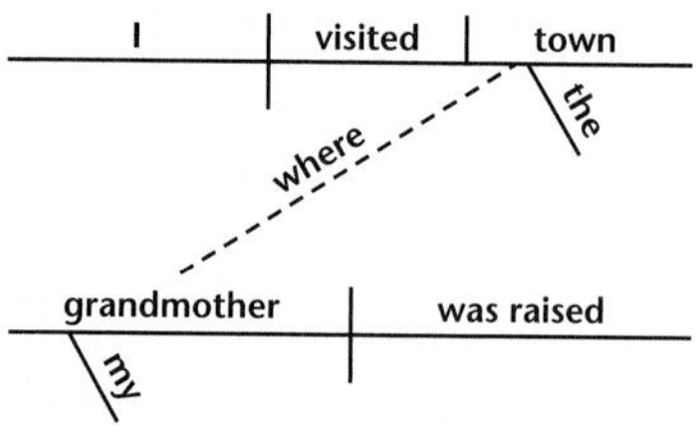

7.
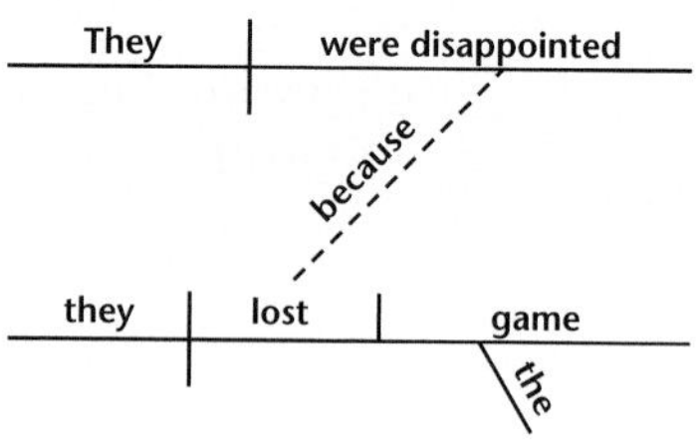

8.
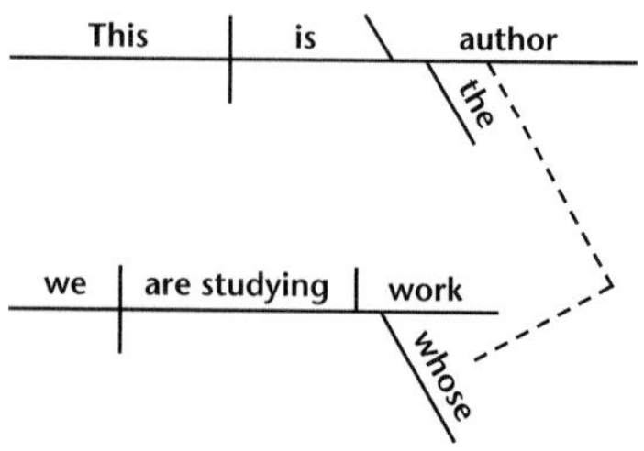

Subordinate Clauses

A complex sentence contains one independent clause and one or more subordinate clauses. In a diagram of a complex sentence, each clause is placed on a separate horizontal line.

Adjective Clauses A subordinate adjective clause is placed on a horizontal line of its own beneath the independent clause. The two clauses are then connected by a dotted line. This dotted line connects the noun or pronoun being modified in the independent clause with the relative pronoun in the adjective clause.

S S V V

EXAMPLE: The person *whom you described* is the principal.

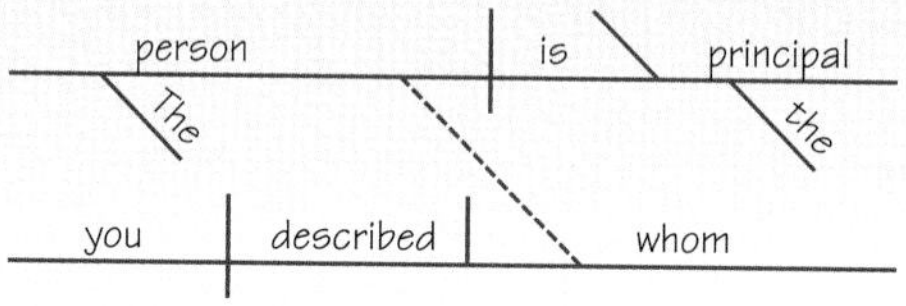

S V S V

EXAMPLE: This is the man *whose car was stolen.*

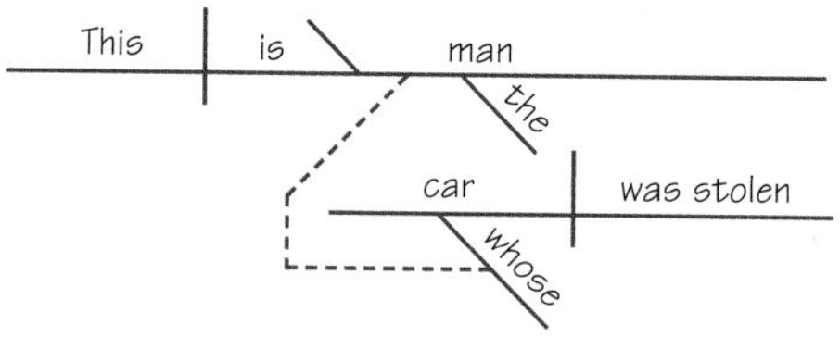

Adverb Clauses A subordinate adverb clause is diagramed in the same way a subordinate adjective clause is. The adverb clause is also written on a horizontal line of its own beneath the independent clause. In a diagram of an adverb clause, however, the subordinating conjunction is written along the dotted line. This line extends from the modified verb, adverb, or adjective in the independent clause to the verb in the adverb clause.

9.
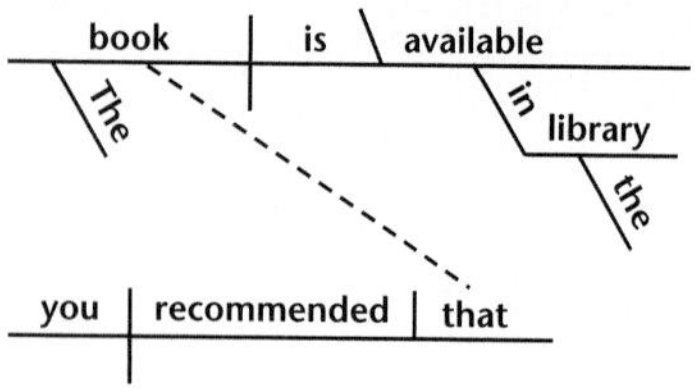

10.
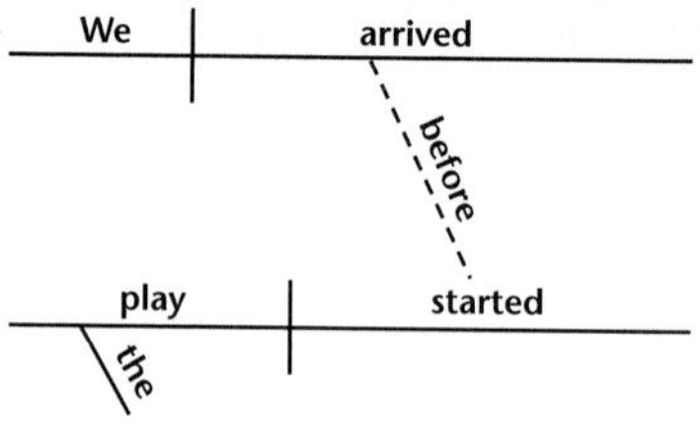

EXAMPLE: They left *before the parade began.* (S V ... S V)

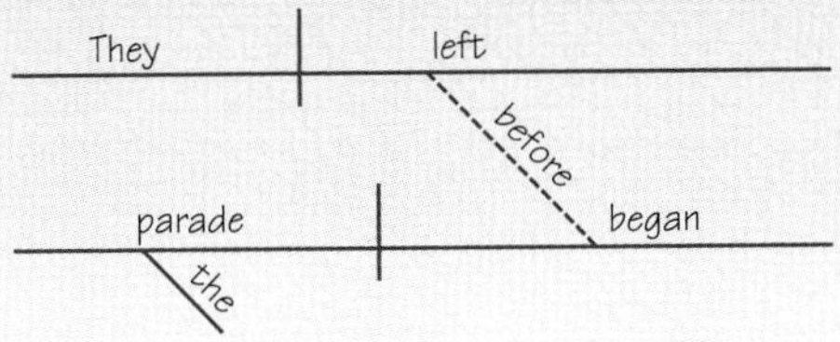

Exercise 9 **Diagraming Subordinate Clauses** Diagram the following sentences, each of which contains an adjective or an adverb clause.

1. I discovered the culprit who had caused the problem.
2. We left the theater before the play began.
3. The milk that I bought is sour.
4. When the judge entered, everyone rose.
5. The plans that they discussed remain a mystery.
6. I visited the town where my grandmother was raised.
7. They were disappointed because they lost the game.
8. This is the author whose work we are studying.
9. The book that you recommended is available in the library.
10. We arrived before the play started.

Exercise 10 **Writing and Diagraming Compound and Complex Sentences** Start with this simple sentence: *Rain fell for two hours.* Expand the simple sentence according to the instructions below to form compound and complex sentences. Then, diagram each new sentence.

EXAMPLE: Form a compound sentence by adding *but* and a second independent clause.
Rain fell for two hours, but we finished the game.

1. Form a compound sentence by adding *so* and another independent clause.
2. Form a compound sentence by adding a semicolon and another independent clause.
3. Add an adverb clause at the beginning to form a complex sentence.
4. Add an adverb clause at the end to form a complex sentence.
5. Add an adjective clause after *Rain* to form a complex sentence.

Answer Key

Exercise 10

Sample answers are given.

1. Rain fell for two hours, so we stayed inside.

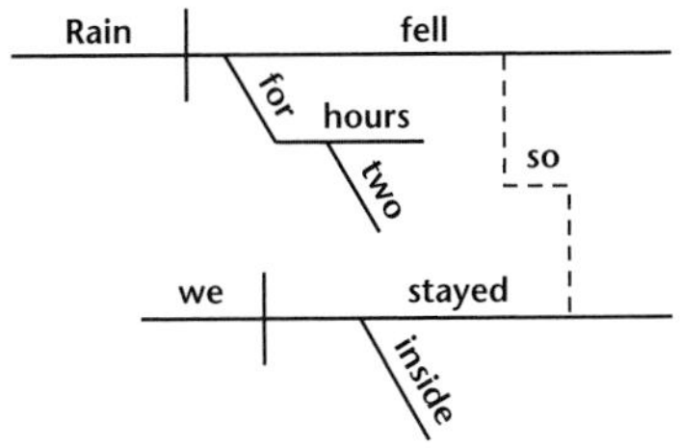

2. Rain fell for two hours; it rained hard.

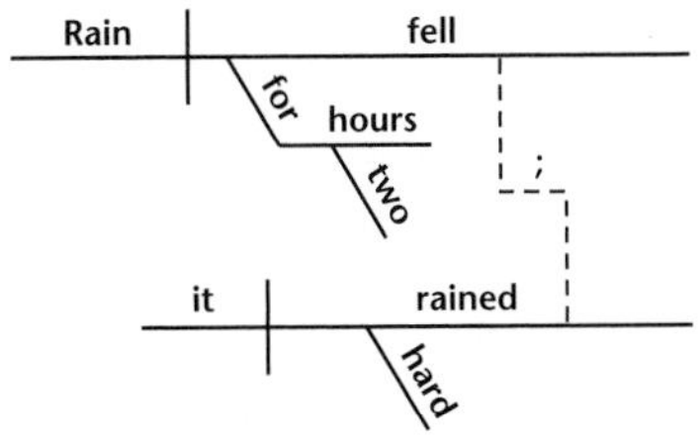

3. Before the play began, rain fell for two hours.

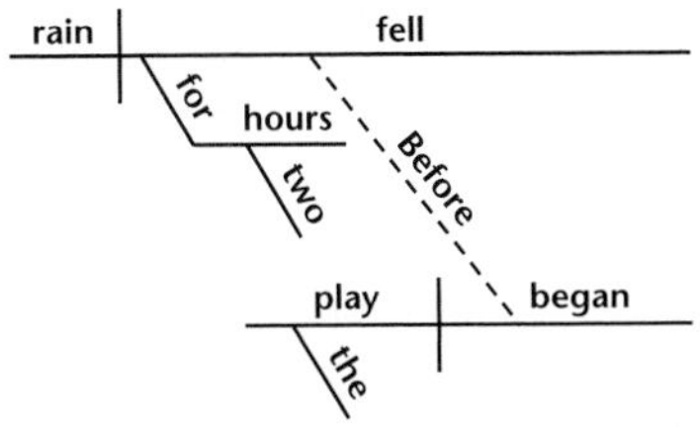

4. Rain fell for two hours while my mother was sleeping.

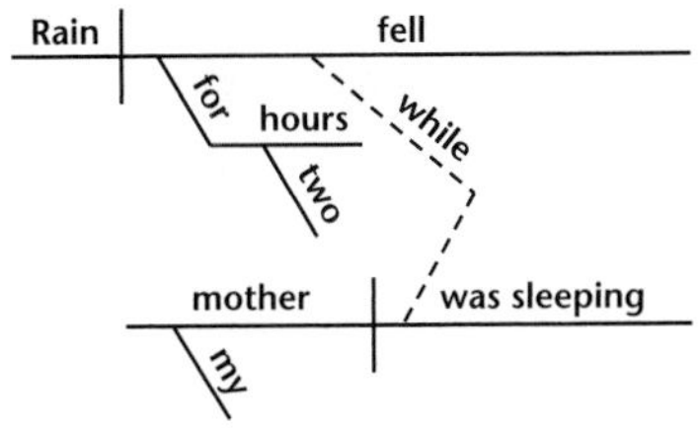

5. Rain, which was most welcome, fell for two hours.

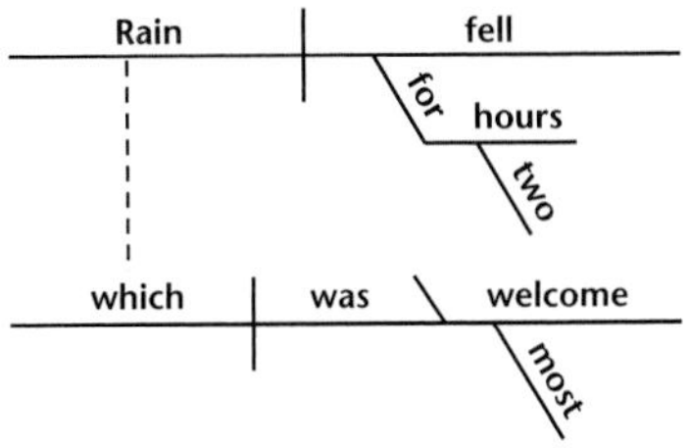

PART 3

ACADEMIC AND WORKPLACE SKILLS

Lesson Objectives

1. To develop critical listening and effective speaking skills and apply them to various types of presentations
2. To understand and evaluate visual images and messages in a variety of media
3. To produce visual images, messages, and meanings that communicate with others
4. To expand vocabulary through reading and listening and by developing skills in using context, word structure, word origins, and reference tools to determine word meanings
5. To develop and apply reading strategies for a variety purposes and texts
6. To develop study and research skills and become familiar with reference tools and the resources of libraries and the Internet
7. To develop skills in taking tests in various formats
8. To learn and apply specific communication and procedural skills of the workplace, including the problem-solving and managing time and money

Emblems, Roger De La Fresnaye, The Phillips Collection, Washington, DC

PART 3

Academic and Workplace Skills

Step-by-Step Teaching Guide

Responding to Fine Art

Emblems
by Roger De La Fresnaye

Use this painting to start a discussion about the definition of academic and workplace skills.

1. Have students examine the painting on pages 670–671. You might use the following questions to prompt discussion:

   Describe some of the objects you see in the painting. What do you think this painting depicts? Where do you think this scene takes place? What kinds of books do you think these are? Why are books so important to the places you mentioned?

2. Ask students to name workplace environments in which they would expect to find books and other types of writing. Have students discuss why writing and other communication skills are important to the workplaces they identified.

Chapter 28

Time and Resource Manager

In-Depth Lesson Plan

	LESSON FOCUS	PRINT AND MEDIA RESOURCES
DAY 1	**Speaking and Listening Skills** Students discuss and practice formal and informal speaking skills. They practice listening effectively and critically (pp. 672–679).	**Teaching Resources** *Academic and Workplace Skills Activity Book*, pp. 1–5
DAY 2	**Viewing Skills** Students interpret maps, graphs, and fine art. They learn to question and criticize television news programs and other media (pp. 680–685).	**Teaching Resources** *Academic and Workplace Skills Activity Book*, pp. 6–9
DAY 3	**Representing Skills** Students create visual aids for their papers, reports, and presentations. They experiment with computer graphics and various types of visual media. They work together on videos and dramatic performances (pp. 686–691).	**Teaching Resources** *Academic and Workplace Skills Activity Book*, pp. 10–16

Accelerated Lesson Plan

	LESSON FOCUS	PRINT AND MEDIA RESOURCES
DAY 1	**Speaking and Listening Skills** Students review and practice formal and informal speaking skills and work to listen critically and effectively (pp. 672–679).	**Teaching Resources** *Academic and Workplace Skills Activity Book*, pp. 1–5
DAY 2	**Viewing and Representing Skills** Students interpret maps, graphs, and fine art. They watch and evaluate documentaries and broadcasts. They create their own visual aids (pp. 680–691).	**Teaching Resources** *Academic and Workplace Skills Activity Book*, pp. 6–16

Options for Adapting Lesson Plans

HOMEWORK

Have students complete any stage of the lesson for homework.

FEATURES

Extend coverage with the Standardized Test Preparation Workshop (pp. 692–693).

TECHNOLOGY

Students can complete any stage of the lesson on computer. Have them print out their completed work.

SPELLING

To teach spelling skills in conjunction with academic and workplace skills, work through *Prentice Hall Everyday Spelling*, Grade 8, Chapter 33, as you cover this *Writing and Grammar* chapter.

INTEGRATED SKILLS COVERAGE

Viewing and Representing
Critical Viewing, SE pp. 672, 677, 686, 690

Workplace Skills
ATE pp. 676, 682

Technology Skills
ATE p. 688; SE pp. 670, 674, 679, 687, 688

ASSESSMENT SUPPORT

Standardized Test Preparation Workshop SE pp. 692–693; ATE p. 678

Standardized Test Preparation Workbook, pp. 55–56

Writing Assessment and Portfolio Management

MEETING INDIVIDUAL NEEDS

Less Advanced Students ATE p. 680. See also Ongoing Assessments ATE pp. 675, 681, 684, 689.

ESL Students ATE p. 679

Visual/Spatial Learners ATE p. 673

Logical/Mathematical Learners ATE p. 675

BLOCK SCHEDULING

Pacing Suggestions
For 90-minute Blocks

- Have students complete the chapter in a single class period.

Professional Development Support

- ***How to Manage Instruction in the Block*** This teaching resource provides management and activity suggestions.

MEDIA AND TECHNOLOGY

For the Teacher

- ***Resource Pro*** **CD-ROM**

WRITING AND GRAMMAR ON-LINE

iText Interactive Text (On-line or on CD-ROM)

- Easily navigable instruction with interactive Revision Checkers
- Full use of e-rater™, the essay-scoring system (on-line only)

Companion Web Site PHSchool.com

- Scoring rubrics with models (use Web Code eck-8001)

See the Go On-line! feature, SE p. iii.

CHAPTER 28
SPEAKING, LISTENING, VIEWING, AND REPRESENTING

Lesson Objectives

1. Develop informal speaking skills.
2. Choose topic, audience, and purpose of formal speech.
3. Use an organized plan to prepare and present a speech.
4. Evaluate a speech for content, credibility, and delivery.
5. Practice active listening skills.
6. Learn about different types of language and verbal and nonverbal gestures.
7. Improve listening skills through self-evaluation and comparison and contrast.
8. Use critical viewing skills.
9. Interpret maps and graphs.
10. Evaluate persuasive techniques.
11. Interpret fine art.
12. Create a visual aid.
13. Use technology to format work.
14. Prepare multimedia presentation.

Critical Viewing

Analyze Students may suggest that the presentation being made is formal because the student in the photograph is standing up in front of his classmates and teacher, who are sitting and listening attentively. Moreover, the student is using a prop to illustrate or explain certain key issues of his speech.

Chapter
28 Speaking, Listening, Viewing, and Representing

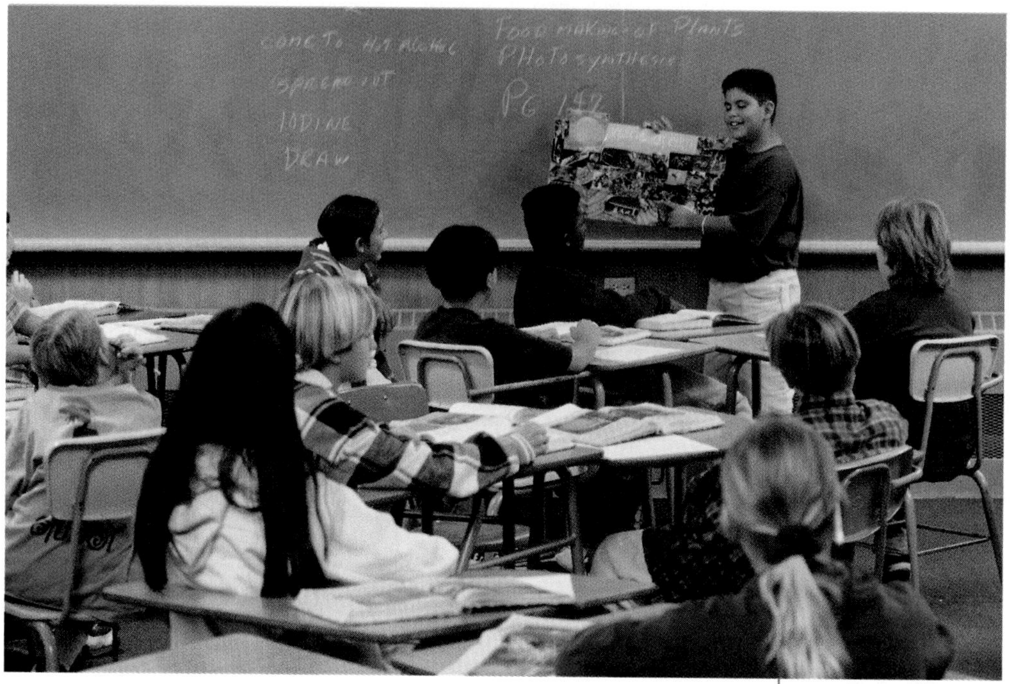

▲ **Critical Viewing** What type of presentation do you think this student is giving? Why? **[Analyze]**

In today's world, more and more information is being presented through visual media, such as television, radio, and Internet Web sites. To be an effective communicator in today's media-rich age, it is essential not only to be a strong writer but also to be a strong speaker, listener, viewer, and presenter. In this chapter, you will learn strategies for developing all of these skills.

TIME AND RESOURCE MANAGER

Resources
Print: Academic and Workplace Skills Activity Book, pp. 1–3

In-Depth Coverage	Accelerated Pace
• Cover pp. 673–676 in class. • Discuss different types of informal and formal speaking skills. • Have students prepare and deliver a formal speech. • Review Checklist for Evaluating a Speech, p. 676. • Assign Exercises 1–5.	• Assign pp. 673–676 for independent student review. • Discuss definitions and types of speaking skills. • Have students prepare and deliver a formal speech.

Section 28.1

Speaking and Listening Skills

If you speak well, you can communicate your ideas clearly. If you listen well, you can remember and understand more of what you hear. Speaking and listening require that you actively engage in thinking about how you want to express yourself and how you process what you hear.

Using Informal Speaking Skills

Every day, you practice informal speaking in the classroom, with your friends, and at home with your family. By making a conscious effort to build your informal speaking skills, you will become a more effective participant in class discussions and improve your ability to give directions.

Take Part in Class Discussions Practice and preparation are keys to improving your classroom participation.

1. Do the required homework and reading so that you are well prepared.
2. Plan the points you want to make, and review homework before the discussion begins.
3. Volunteer to contribute your ideas.
4. Listen to the discussion carefully, and make sure that your points are relevant to the discussion.
5. Ask questions about what you do not understand or would like to know more about.

Give Directions Being able to give clear and accurate directions that people can follow easily is a valuable skill.

1. Think through directions carefully before you speak.
2. Speak slowly so that your listeners can follow.
3. Choose your words carefully, being as specific as you can. Give only one step of the directions in each sentence.
4. Give the most important details, but do not confuse your listener with unnecessary information.

Exercise 1 **Improving Class Participation Skills** Set a goal for how many times per week you will participate in each of your classes, and record your contributions for one week.

Exercise 2 **Writing Directions** Write directions from one location in school to another. Read your directions aloud to a classmate, and have that person evaluate them.

Speaking and Listening Tip

A great way to build confidence for participating in class discussions is to practice your group discussion skills with friends. Hold informal group discussions about subjects you are studying in school. Make sure that everyone in the group participates.

ONGOING ASSESSMENT: Diagnose

Use one of the following options to diagnose students' current level of proficiency in speaking and listening skills.

Option 1 Try to observe as many students as possible in group discussion exercise: their speaking skills, the questions they ask, their body language, and their listening skills.

Option 2 Put students with common interests in a group and observe a structured discussion on the topic they have chosen.

PREPARE and ENGAGE

Interest GRABBER Students talk *all* the time. So ask them to recall a time they told a funny story to a group of people. Ask why they told that story. How did people react? Was the reaction what they hoped for? How did the reaction to their story make them feel?

Activate Prior Knowledge

Working in small groups, ask each student to tell a short, interesting anecdote or comment on a topic of his or her choice.

TEACH

Step-by-Step Teaching Guide

Using Informal Speaking Skills

1. Taking part in class discussions is easier for some students than others. Ask students who contribute often to tell some of the benefits (other than impressing the teacher). (Possible answers: Saying something aloud helps them remember it. They can't count on someone else to ask questions they need answered.)
2. Urge students who rarely participate to tell why. They are probably unsure of their language skills and/or afraid of asking a "stupid" question. Reassure them that stupid is *not* asking the question. And they get credit for trying. Finally, point out that the more they practice talking in class, the easier it will get.
3. Giving directions often involves the specific skill of sequencing. Suggest that students make some notes about the sequence of steps before they give the directions.

Customize for *Visual/Spatial Learners*

Speaking may not come as easily to these students as their more verbally inclined classmates. Work with students on how they can translate their sense of images and patterns into words. One suggestion might be compiling vocabulary lists and practicing to build more verbal confidence.

Answer Key

Exercise 1 *(page 673)*

Answers will vary.

Exercise 2 *(page 673)*

Answers will vary.

Step-by-Step Teaching Guide

Using Formal Speaking Skills

1. Formal speeches do not have to be boring. Much depends on the speaker and the circumstances of the presentation. Ask students to consider how the fact of being a captive audience (meaning they have no choice about whether to stay or go) can affect their reaction to a speech.
2. Though it is a subcategory of the persuasive speech, explore the motivational speech as a genre of its own. It is certainly one that students get a great deal of exposure to. Ask students to recall both good ones and bad ones they have heard. Ask what made both memorable.
3. The effectiveness of a speech depends both on content and delivery. Explore how a speaker who makes a favorable impression on listeners gets a sympathetic ear. We forgive many things if we like the speaker. If we don't feel some interest in the speaker, it is a challenge to stay involved in the speech.

Answer Key

Exercise 3

Answers will vary. Examples include the following:

Explanatory: What is modern art?/art students; How to build a bookcase/students interested in woodcraft

Persuasive: Why we need a new school gym/athletic students; The importance of eating a balanced diet/fitness-minded students

Entertaining: How to teach a cat to like a dog/animal lovers; Why snowmen get lonely in the summer/classmates

28.1

Using Formal Speaking Skills

As a student—and later, when you enter the work force—you will be called on to deliver formal speeches in front of audiences. By understanding the different types of speeches and learning strategies for preparing and delivering a speech, you can build the confidence and the skills necessary to succeed in these situations.

Recognize the Different Types of Speeches There are numerous different topics and occasions for speeches. However, virtually all speeches can be classified into one of the following categories: *explanatory, persuasive,* or *entertaining.*

- An **explanatory** speech provides information about or explanations of an idea, an object, or an event. A speech you deliver in school about information you have gathered about a historical event is an example of an explanatory speech.
- A **persuasive** speech is one in which the speaker attempts to persuade the audience to agree with a point of view or to take some course of action. Most political speeches are examples of persuasive speeches.
- An **entertaining** speech is given to amuse the audience. Speeches given at weddings and parties are most often entertaining speeches.

KEY CONCEPT Choose the kind of speech you will give by considering both the purpose of the speech and your audience. Use appropriate language when presenting your speech. ■

Exercise 3 **Listing Kinds of Speeches** Give two topic examples for each speech described above. Then, identify appropriate audiences for each.

Prepare Your Speech Thorough preparation is the key to delivering a successful speech. Follow these steps to help you choose a topic, gather information, and rehearse.

Choose Your Topic Sometimes, a topic is assigned to you—either in school or at work. When it is up to you to choose a topic, consider the kind of speech you will be giving as well as your audience, and search for a topic that will interest them. For example, if you are delivering an entertaining speech to friends at a party, think of topics that will amuse them.

Technology Tip

One of the best ways to build your speaking skills is to see and hear models of good speeches. Consult with your teacher or librarian to find examples of each type of speech on videotape, audiotape, or on the Internet.

Gather Information If your topic is an area in which you are not an expert, you will want to gather information by conducting research in the library or on the Internet.

Outline Main Points and Supporting Details Organize your information into an outline like the one to the right. Group your details under subtopics or main points. Arrange the subtopics in a logical order.

Prepare Note Cards Print the information in your outline on small index cards to which you can refer as you deliver your speech.

- Make note cards that contain your opening and closing statements.
- Create at least one note card for each subtopic. Underline the subtopic, and list the key details beneath it.
- Number your note cards to help you keep them in order.

Practice Your Speech Before you deliver your speech, rehearse, either on your own or with a family member or classmate. Don't try to memorize what you will say. Instead, use your note cards to guide you in presenting your key points. Use body language and the tone and volume of your voice to emphasize key points.

Deliver Your Speech When it is time to deliver your speech, use the following strategies:

1. Review your note cards to refresh your memory before you start.
2. Do not read to your audience. Use your note cards to help you focus on your key points, but do not read from the cards word for word.
3. Speak slowly, pronouncing each of your words clearly.
4. Make eye contact with members of the audience.
5. Use *verbal* techniques, such as altering the tone and loudness of your voice, to emphasize key points.
6. Use *nonverbal* techniques, such as your movements, posture, facial expressions, and gestures, to reinforce your ideas and to maintain the attention of your audience.

Exercise 4 **Preparing and Presenting a Speech** Prepare a short speech on a current issue about which you feel strongly or on a topic of special interest to you. Follow the steps presented in this section to plan and deliver your speech.

SAMPLE OUTLINE

Making a Terrarium

A. Selection of basic ingredients
  1. Use a fish tank or bowl
  2. Find good soil, sand, and gravel
  3. Choose plants

B. Preparation of soil
  1. Line bottom with layer of gravel
  2. Place equal amounts of sand and soil on gravel

C. Rooting of plants
  1. Dig holes and press roots into holes
  2. Add stones and bark
  3. Place near window for sunlight

Step-by-Step Teaching Guide

Deliver Your Speech

1. Using Exercise 4 as a guide, tell students that they will be preparing a three-minute speech.
2. Tell students to choose a topic they already know something about. The person who gave the terrarium speech undoubtedly had a terrarium, so was comfortable with the subject.
3. Many students will be very nervous delivering a speech that they do not have written out. On the other hand, you don't want them to read a speech. Have students construct a fairly tight outline with main ideas, supporting details, and all important statements written in note form. Build their confidence by having them practice their speech a section at a time.
4. Before students begin practicing verbal and nonverbal language, discuss the importance of using techniques that go with their overall demeanor. If a student is fairly introverted, he or she should not take on the language and gestures of a highly extroverted person. It will not look authentic.
5. The best way to learn verbal and nonverbal language is through modeling and observing. Model verbal techniques such as altering tone and pace and emphasizing and/or repeating key words and phrases. Also model using eye contact, posture, gesture, and appropriate facial expressions to underscore the points of the speech.

Customize for *Logical/Mathematical Learners*

Suggest that students organize their speech by writing each point on a self-stick note, then arranging the notes in a logical order.

Answer Key

Exercise 4

Answers will vary. Students' speeches should reflect adequate research, and their presentation should use verbal and nonverbal speaking strategies.

ONGOING ASSESSMENT: Monitor and Reinforce

If some students are having difficulty using appropriate strategies, use one of the following options.

Option 1 If resources permit, videotape students so they can see what they look like, how they are fidgeting, slouching, saying "um," and so on. Watch the tape with them and make a list of items for them to improve.

Option 2 Have students practice delivering their speech in front of a full-length mirror observing their gestures, posture, and overall demeanor.

Step-by-Step Teaching Guide

Evaluate a Speech

1. Review the items on the checklist. You might want to suggest an additional item, one that frequently is an issue with student speakers: Did the student project his or her voice? Was it easy to hear what he or she was saying? Remind students that when they speak, they need to reach not just the front row, but the back row, as well, and project their voice accordingly. This is not the same as shouting.
2. To counterbalance the checklist, acknowledge that speaking in public can be challenging for many people. When listening to others, remember the difficulty of speaking in public and respect the effort they are making.

Answer Key

Exercise 5

Answers will vary. Students' evaluations should be insightful and helpful to the speaker and should answer all or most questions from the evaluating a speech checklist.

Integrating Workplace Skills

Workers in all kinds of jobs give persuasive speeches. They try to persuade a boss to give them a raise or a promotion. They try to persuade coworkers that their idea is good. They try to persuade customers to buy their product. Have partners practice the art of persuasive speech. One student is the parent. The other gives a speech on a "hard-sell" topic—why he or she should have a later curfew, why the family really, really needs a dog, for example.

28.1

Evaluate a Speech Evaluating the speeches of others can help you improve your own speaking skills.

KEY CONCEPT When you evaluate a speech, critically examine the effectiveness of the content and the delivery. ■

Following is a checklist that will help guide you in evaluating a speech:

CHECKLIST
FOR EVALUATING A SPEECH

- ☐ Did the speech achieve its purpose? For example, did it explain thoroughly, persuade convincingly, or entertain effectively?
- ☐ Did the speaker elaborate his or her main ideas and support each with facts or appropriate details?
- ☐ Did the speaker introduce the topic clearly, develop it well, and conclude it effectively?
- ☐ Did the speaker's facial expressions, gestures, and movements reinforce the spoken message?
- ☐ Did the speaker give complete answers to audience questions?

Exercise 5 **Evaluating a Speech** Using the checklist, write an evaluation for a speech given in class. Consider the content and credibility of the information presented, as well as the speaker's delivery. Then, give a copy of your evaluation to the person who gave the speech.

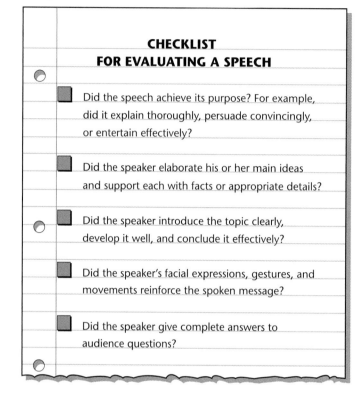

Listening Effectively

When you think about listening, you probably think of it as something you do naturally—not as a skill that you have to practice and develop. However, there is a major difference between simply hearing what is being said and effectively listening to what is being said. To be an effective listener, you have to get involved with what you are hearing and use strategies to make sure that you understand what is being said.

▲ Critical Viewing
What details in this photograph suggest that these students are listening effectively to one another? **[Analyze]**

KEY CONCEPT The keys to effective listening include setting a purpose for listening, eliminating distractions, asking questions, and taking good notes. ■

Determine Your Purpose for Listening When you determine your purpose for listening, you identify what you want to take away from what you are hearing. Your purpose will affect how you listen and how you respond to what is said. Following are possible purposes for listening:

- **To Gain Information** Listen for main ideas and major details.
- **To Solve Problems** Listen and ask questions to clarify problems so that a solution can be found.
- **To Enjoy and Appreciate** Listen for artistic elements, such as rhyme, imagery, and descriptive language.

Eliminate Barriers Prepare to listen by putting away all distracting material (books, magazines, homework). Block out all distracting noises, inside and outside the classroom, so that you can concentrate on the speaker and his or her message.

Summarize Main Ideas and Supporting Details Summarizing a speaker's message forces you to listen attentively and to make decisions about what is important. Use the suggestions below to summarize a speaker's message:

- Write down in your own words only main ideas and supporting details—the information you want to remember.
- Underline main ideas to make them easy to locate when you want to refer to them.
- Write notes in short phrases, not complete sentences.

Exercise 6 **Becoming an Active Listener** For one week, practice active listening techniques in one of your classes. Track your progress in your notebook.

Step-by-Step Teaching Guide

Listening Effectively

1. Active listening starts with connecting with the speaker. Ask students to consider how they listen to different people with varying interest and attention. To listen actively they need to care about both what is being said and who is saying it. Suggest that they put themselves in the speaker's place to help create an empathic connection.
2. There is one fact about active listening: You can't listen and do something else at the same time. You can't daydream, plan your after-school time, get a head start on homework, or anything else. Listen with full attention.
3. Note taking and summarizing are devices that foster attention. Even if the notes or summary will have little value after the speech or discussion, they serve the purpose of keeping us listening to the discussion as it happens.

Answer Key

Exercise 6

Answers will vary.

Critical Viewing

Analyze Students may note that the students who are listening to their classmate have their gaze directed towards him. Moreover, some students have pens in hand, which suggests that they are taking notes.

TIME AND RESOURCE MANAGER

Resources
Print: Academic and Workplace Skills Activity Book, pp. 4–5

In-Depth Coverage	Accelerated Pace
• Cover pp. 677–679 in class. • Discuss active and critical listening skills. • Have students evaluate their listening skills. • Assign Exercises 6–8.	• Have students read pp. 677–679 independently and do Exercises 6–8.

Step-by-Step Teaching Guide

Listening Critically

1. Critical listening is a key skill. When students listen with less than full attention, they miss much of what is said. There is also a tendency to hear only what they want or expect to hear.
2. Listening for facts is an important skill. But students need to listen for *meaningful facts,* facts that support the speaker's argument and refute counter arguments. Encourage them first to identify facts and opinions, then to ask what the significance of each is.
3. Connotative language is a subtle tool by which a speaker tries to influence listeners. Negative and positive connotation is the equivalent of stereotyping in the movies, in which the good guy and bad guy are clearly signified by dress, demeanor, lighting, and other techniques.
4. The basic requirement of critical listening is to ask and answer questions about the speech. It is a critical listener's job to ask why something is being said and said in the way it is being stated, why the gestures, and nonverbals are attached in the way they are. In other words: Do not take speeches at face value. Make the speaker pass a credibility test of fact, meaningfulness, sincerity, consistency, and fairness.

Answer Key

Exercise 7

Answers will vary. Students' summaries should be based on or supported by their examples of fact and opinion statements, denotation and connotation, and verbal and nonverbal gestures.

28.1

Listening Critically

In addition to listening effectively in order to comprehend what is said, it is important to critically evaluate the points a speaker is making.

KEY CONCEPT Become a critical listener by learning to distinguish fact from opinion, recognize persuasive language, and interpret a speaker's use of both verbal and nonverbal techniques. ■

Recognize Facts and Opinions A **fact** is something that can be verified as true. An **opinion** is something that cannot be proved to be true. Speakers must support opinions with facts before the opinions can be accepted as valid. Listen for opinions unsupported by evidence.

Analyze Persuasive Language Pay close attention to the words a speaker chooses. The **denotation** of a word is its literal or exact meaning. The **connotation** is its suggested or implied meaning. Speakers may choose words with negative connotations to present someone or something unfavorably. Positive connotations present someone or something favorably.

NEUTRAL:	He *walked* through the crowd.
NEGATIVE CONNOTATION:	He *stumbled* through the crowd.
POSITIVE CONNOTATION:	He *paraded* through the crowd.

Interpret the Speaker's Message To interpret the speaker's message, be aware of verbal and nonverbal gestures.

- **Verbal Signals** Notice how a speaker chooses to emphasize or elaborate some points over others. Pay attention to when the speaker raises or lowers, or slows down or speeds up, his or her voice.
- **Nonverbal Signals** Notice a speaker's movements, such as arm waving, head nodding, or moving closer to or farther away from the audience.

Paying careful attention to verbal and nonverbal signals can enhance your comprehension of a speaker's message and reveal the speaker's attitudes and emotions about a subject.

Technology Tip

Apply all of these strategies when you are watching political speeches and debates on television.

Exercise 7 **Listening Critically** Listen to a speech in school or on television. Record examples of fact and opinion statements, denotation and connotation, and verbal and nonverbal signals.

STANDARDIZED TEST PREPARATION WORKSHOP

Fact and Opinion Students may be asked on standardized tests to identify statements of fact and opinion. Write the following examples on the board and have students choose the correct answer.

1. Thomas Alva Edison invented the electric lightbulb.
   A Fact
   B Opinion
2. Henry Ford is credited with inventing the assembly line for factory mass production.
   A Fact
   B Opinion
3. Ford's invention was not as important as Edison's.
   A Fact
   B Opinion

Students should identify 1 and 2 as facts and 3 as opinion.

Evaluate Your Listening One way to improve your listening skills is to evaluate them, deciding which listening skills work for you and which skills need improvement.

KEY CONCEPT Improve your listening skills through self-evaluation and comparison and contrast. ■

Monitor Your Understanding You can test your understanding of the speaker's message by restating parts of it to the speaker. If your restatement is accurate, you know you have listened well. If it is inaccurate, ask questions to improve it.

Compare and Contrast Interpretations Write your interpretation of a speaker's message, and then compare and contrast it with another student's interpretation. Use a Venn diagram to list the points on which you agree and disagree. Resolve these points of disagreement through discussion.

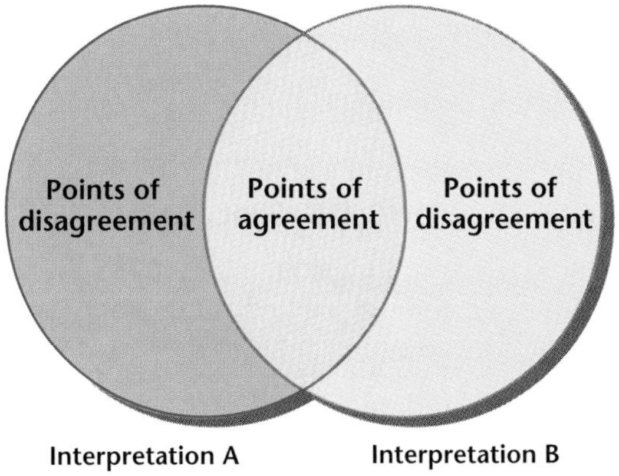

Exercise 8 **Evaluating Your Listening Skills** Work with another classmate to complete the following activities.

1. Have your classmate read a paper or present a speech to you. Have him or her pause periodically so that you can restate the information. Afterward, exchange roles.
2. With your classmate, listen to a speech in class, then write your interpretations of the speaker's message. Afterward, compare and contrast what you have written..
3. Write an evaluation of your listening skills. Identify the areas in which you excelled and those in which you need improvement.

Technology Tip

Practice your listening skills with audio books at your school or public library.

Step-by-Step Teaching Guide

Evaluate Your Listening

1. Ask students if they have ever been called on and been startled because they were not paying attention. Tell students it is easy to tune out, even when they think they are paying attention. That is why evaluating their listening skills is a good idea.
2. Note taking and summarizing are tests of attention. If, at the end of a speech, students can look at their notes and put together a plausible summary of what was said, they were paying attention.
3. The big challenge in listening is to hear what the speaker says. Too often, listeners hear the first part of an idea, fact, or message, then jump ahead with what they assume is to follow. Of course, in that leap, listeners can miss something critical that is very different from what they expected. Students need to listen as closely as possible, with both full attention and a critical mind.

Customize for *ESL Students*

Students learning English have the double challenge of understanding unfamiliar vocabulary and the ideas in a speech. On the other hand, they are likely to pay greater attention than other students. To help them understand the speaker, urge them to pay close attention to nonverbals, which can cue important phrases and emotional tone.

Answer Key

Exercise 8

Answers will vary.

Step-by-Step Teaching Guide

Interpreting Maps and Graphs

1. Ask students what maps can do. (Maps can show how to get places and provide a variety of geographical information.)
2. Examine the map in the text and note the key and the information it contains.
3. Besides the shadings and their key, ask students to point out the other detail on the map that shows the separation between the Union and the Confederacy. (Students should point out the bold line that marks the "northern" border of the Confederacy)
4. Ask students to relate the small print about Virginia and West Virginia to the map's key. Discuss how the asterisk is used in printing and writing to call attention to something about the object of discussion. In this case, the asterisk is calling attention to a footnote. Students should relate the fact that although West Virginia separated from Virginia in 1861, the year the Confederacy was formed, it did not join the Union until 1863.

Customize for *Less Advanced Students*

Some students have trouble reading maps. One tendency is to get overwhelmed with all the information presented and be unable to discriminate among bits of data. Help students look at maps a section at a time by covering all but one sector of the map and looking at each quadrant individually. Move on to looking at half the map before uncovering the entire map.

Section 28.2

Viewing and Representing Skills

Interpreting Maps and Graphs

Textbooks and other written works use an assortment of maps and graphs to convey information.

KEY CONCEPT Interpret maps and graphs to become a more informed reader. ■

Maps

Maps can do more than simply guide you to a destination. Maps can also show you historical information, indicate the borders and sizes of countries, or provide vital statistics of population or agriculture. To interpret a map: **(1)** Determine the type and purpose of the map. **(2)** Examine the map's distance scale and any symbols. **(3)** Relate the map's information to any accompanying written information.

CHOOSING SIDES IN THE CIVIL WAR

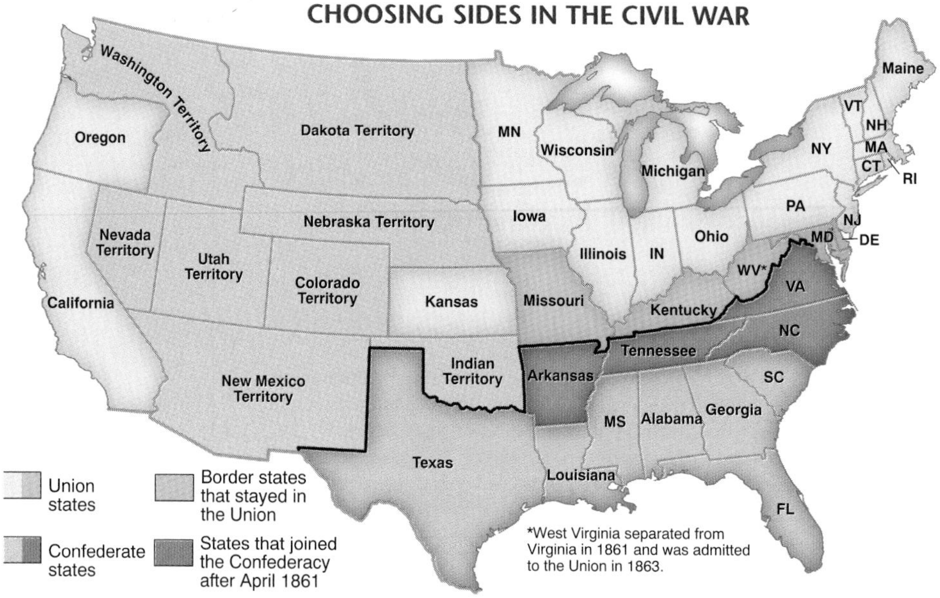

TIME AND RESOURCE MANAGER

Resources
Print: Academic and Workplace Skills Activity Book, pp. 6–9

In-Depth Coverage	Accelerated Pace
• Cover pp. 680–685 in class. • Discuss different types of viewing skills in class. • Review Interpreting Fine Art, p. 685. **Option** Have students work individually or in groups on the Viewing Skills section of the Writing Lab CD-ROM.	• Have students read pp. 680–685 independently.

Graphs

Graphs provide a visual comparison of several pieces of related information. Different kinds of graphs are used to show different kinds of information.

Pie Graph A **pie graph** shows the relationship of parts to a whole. The graph is a circle that stands for 100 percent of something. Each part stands for a certain portion, or percentage, of the whole. This pie graph shows France's Gross Domestic Product, the total output of all goods and services produced in one year. To interpret the pie graph: **(1)** Look at the numbers that go with the individual parts. **(2)** Match the individual parts with the key. **(3)** Use the numbers and parts to make comparisons.

FRANCE'S GROSS DOMESTIC PRODUCT

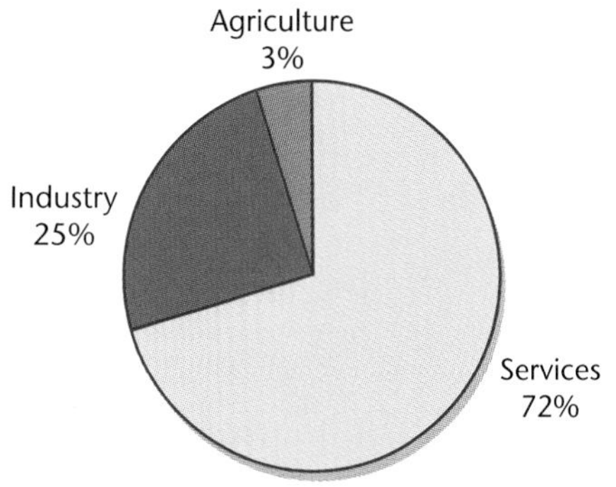

Bar Graph A **bar graph** compares and contrasts amounts. In a bar graph, you read the heights or lengths of bars to see the numbers they represent. To interpret a bar graph: **(1)** Look at the heights or lengths of the bars. **(2)** Match the subject that goes with the bar to the number the bar reaches. **(3)** Compare and contrast the heights or lengths of bars.

LEADING CHEESE-PRODUCING COUNTRIES

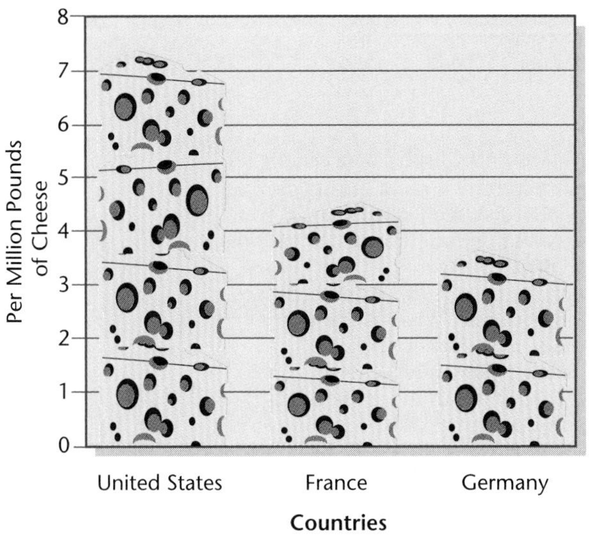

Data from *World Book Encyclopedia*

Step-by-Step Teaching Guide

Graphs

1. A pie graph is best suited to showing the relationship of parts to a whole.
2. If a pie graph is shown in percentages, what sum must the numbers be? The answer has to be 100%.
3. A bar graph is useful for comparing and contrasting amounts. Explain the information on each axis.
4. Make sure students understand the numerical shorthand of the vertical axis: The numbers stand for millions of pounds of cheese. 1 = 1 million pounds, 2 = 2 million pounds, and so on. Expressing actual numbers would take up too much space.

ONGOING ASSESSMENT: Monitor and Reinforce

If some students are having difficulty reading the graphs, use the following option.

Draw a pie graph about a concrete issue: A fictitious teenager with ten dollars to spend at a flea market. Graph the expenses in round numbers.

Step-by-Step Teaching Guide

Line Graph

1. A line graph shows change over time.
2. Ask the following questions to test students' comprehension:

   What was the approximate population of France in 1950? (40 million)

   In which two 50-year time spans did the population experience a brief decline? (1850–1900; 1900–1950)

   In which 50-year interval was the greatest population growth? (1950–2000)

Answer Key

Exercise 9

Answers may vary.

1. West Virginia
2. Industry and agriculture equal 28%. The difference between industry and agriculture and service is 44%.
3. 7 million of pounds of cheese are produced in the United States. France produces 1 million more pounds of cheese than Germany.
4. The increase in population from 1850 to 1950 is 4 million. From 1950 to 2000, 19 million. The difference is 15 million.

Integrating Workplace Skills

Making graphs is a common way data are analyzed in many businesses. Have students work in small groups to make their own series of graphs showing easily available information. Some suggested topics: percentage of students in the class with last names A–E, F–J, etc.; comparing population figures for neighboring states or cities; school attendance every day this month.

Line Graph A **line graph** shows changes over a specific period of time. It features a line that connects points. The points, which may appear as actual dots, represent numbers or amounts of something. To interpret a line graph: **(1)** Look across the horizontal and vertical lines to determine what information is shown. **(2)** Compare and contrast points. **(3)** Identify patterns of change.

FRANCE: POPULATION TRENDS IN THE 19TH AND 20TH CENTURIES

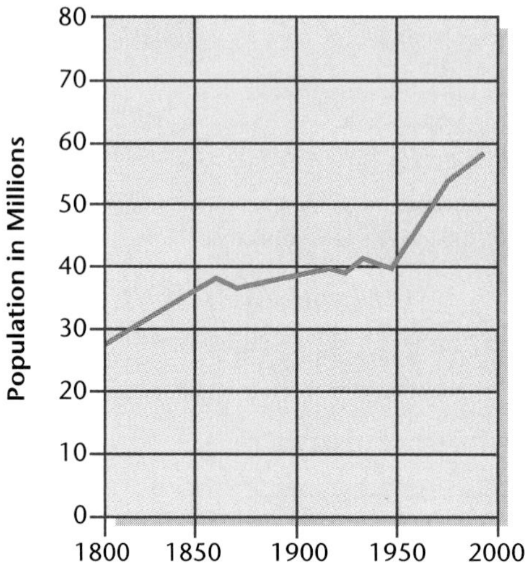

Exercise 9 **Interpreting Maps and Graphs** Answer the following questions about the map and the graphs in this section.

1. Use the Civil War map to identify which state split in two in 1861, leading to the formation of another state that was admitted to the Union in 1863.
2. Use the pie graph to determine the combined percentage of France's industry and agriculture. What is the difference between this percentage and that of services?
3. Use the bar graph to determine how much cheese is produced in the United States. How much more cheese is produced in France than in Germany?
4. Use the line graph to determine the increase in France's population from 1850 to 1950, and from 1950 to 2000. What is the difference between the two?

Viewing Information Media Critically

Since the media distribute large amounts of information, it is important to learn how to view this information critically. As a critical viewer, you will learn to evaluate the information for content, quality, and importance.

KEY CONCEPT Become a critical viewer by learning to identify and evaluate different types of visual media and images. ■

Recognize Kinds of Information Media Knowing the characteristics of various kinds of media will help you to identify them during your viewing. The following chart describes several forms of information media.

TYPES OF INFORMATION MEDIA

Television News Program	Television Newsmagazine
• Covers current news events • Gives information objectively	• Covers a variety of topics • Entertains and informs
Documentary	**Commercial**
• Focuses on one topic of social interest • Sometimes expresses controversial opinions	• Presents products, people, or ideas • Persuades people to buy or take action

Exercise 10 **Identifying Types of Information Media** Identify each of the four types of information media in your viewing. For each type, describe the topics covered, and then write down your impressions of the way the topics were presented.

Research Tip

Many television news organizations have Web sites with in-depth coverage of current events.

Step-by-Step Teaching Guide

Viewing Information Media Critically

1. Discuss the importance of understanding the source of news and the point of view or possible bias that may be represented. Be sure they recognize the difference between news programs that purport to present an objective view with editorials and columns that present an individual or collective point of view.
2. Focus on news programs and objectivity. Ask students if they think they can believe everything they read or hear in a news report. They should always watch critically, asking questions of what they read and look for possible bias that the speaker may not even be aware of. For instance, do students think that news reports about kids written and reported by adults are always done objectively? If trouble at their school was reported in the local paper, would the article accurately reflect life at their school?
3. No matter what the source of information is, students should always analyze it critically.

Answer Key

Exercise 10

Answers will vary.

Step-by-Step Teaching Guide

Evaluate Persuasive Techniques

1. Review the text information on fact and opinion, bias, and loaded language and images.
2. Make sure that students have a solid grasp of the difference between a claim about fact—something provable—and opinion. Point out that facts are not always true. For example, the statement, *Los Angeles is on the Atlantic Ocean* is a claim about a fact because it can be proved true or false.
3. Write the following statements on the board and ask students to identify them as fact or opinion:

   Luigi's Pizza is on the corner. (fact)

   Luigi's Pizza is the best. (opinion)

   Anchovies are my favorite topping. (opinion)
4. Discuss bias. Bias is often unconscious. Sometimes bias results from ignorance or being out of touch with a point of view. Here are some examples:

   Some adults have difficulty understanding teenagers' favorite music.

   Some dog-owners have difficulty understanding why cat owners love their pets.

   Some meat-eaters have difficulty understanding a vegetarian's point of view.
5. Conclude with the idea that "objectivity" is not so easily arrived at. From that conclusion, it is important for everyone to use critical judgment in analyzing information received from different media. In other words, people need to think.

28.2

Evaluate Persuasive Techniques The media sometimes use persuasive techniques to present information in a particular way. Knowledge of these techniques will help you to evaluate the credibility of information presented through the media.

Facts and opinions are important to separate when watching the media. A *fact* is a statement that can be proved to be true. An *opinion* is a viewpoint that cannot be proved to be true.

Bias is a tendency to think in a certain way. As you watch, consider whether the information is being presented in a one-sided way, or whether it takes into account all viewpoints.

Loaded language and images are emotional words and visuals used to persuade you to think a certain way.

Evaluate Information From the Media Combine your knowledge of persuasive techniques with the following strategies to increase your understanding of the messages conveyed through the media:

- Be aware of the kind of program you are watching. What is its purpose? What are its limitations?
- Sort out facts from opinions. Make sure that any opinions presented are solidly backed up with facts.
- Be aware of any loaded language or images that may cause you to react in a certain way.
- Listen for bias, and note any points of view not discussed. If you detect bias, try to gather information on other points of view that have not been presented before deciding with which point of view you agree.
- Check surprising or questionable information in other sources.
- View the complete program before reaching a conclusion. Then, develop your own views on the issues, people, and information presented.

Exercise 11 Evaluating Information From the Media
Watch a news or other informative program, including the commercials. In an essay, identify the kind of program you watched and describe the topics it covered. Also, identify what each commercial was selling and the slogans and images that were used to impress viewers. Then, evaluate the information on each topic in the program and in the commercials, using the viewing strategies on this page. Write a summary of your evaluation.

Learn More

For more information about methods of persuasion, see Chapter 7.

Answer Key

Exercise 11

Answers will vary. Students' summary should demonstrate an understanding of the different types of media and persuasive techniques used in the media.

ONGOING ASSESSMENT: Monitor and Reinforce

If some students are having difficulty with the ideas of viewing information media critically, use the following options.

Option 1 Have students watch the same news reports, take notes on everything they see and hear, and then compare their findings.

Option 2 If you are using videotaped news reports, have students watch three times: first as shown; second with the sound off; third with sound but the monitor turned off. Then have students analyze the role of speech and images.

Interpreting Fine Art

Paintings, drawings, sculptures, and photographs are all examples of fine art. When you view fine art, you have to use different standards for evaluation than when you view the media. Instead of looking for persuasive techniques, you look for artistic ones, such as shape, line, and color. Learning how to view fine art will help you to see and experience the vision of the artist.

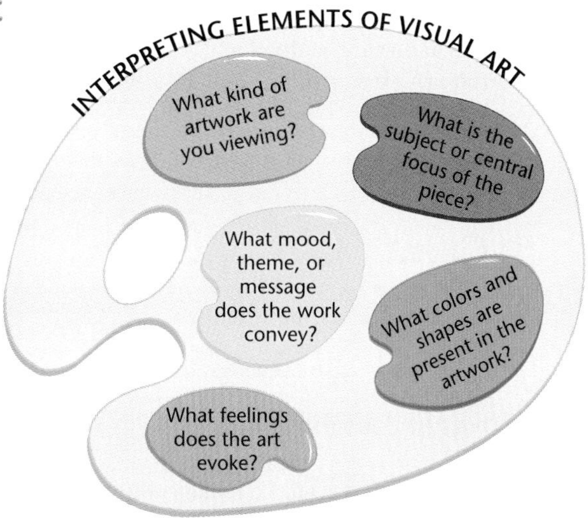

INTERPRETING ELEMENTS OF VISUAL ART
What kind of artwork are you viewing?
What is the subject or central focus of the piece?
What mood, theme, or message does the work convey?
What colors and shapes are present in the artwork?
What feelings does the art evoke?

KEY CONCEPT Enrich your enjoyment and understanding of fine art by interpreting the elements that create the work. ■

Exercise 12 **Interpreting Fine Art** Interpret the painting below—*Zinnias* by John Hollis Kaufmann—by asking the questions from the chart above. Write your answers in your notebook, along with any other observations you might care to make.

Zinnias, 1937, John Hollis Kaufmann, Private Collection

Step-by-Step Teaching Guide

Interpreting Fine Art

1. Viewers do not have to know anything about art to respond to it.
2. Using *Prentice Hall Literature: Timeless Voices, Timeless Themes,* Silver, show students several different styles of art, which you will find by paging through the book.
3. Ask volunteers to pick a work they like and tell why. Sometimes it's hard to say in words exactly why. "I like the colors" or "It makes me smile" are valid responses (though try at least to get elaboration).
4. Encourage students to put themselves in the pictures and tell how it feels.
5. Tell students that they do not have to like a painting just because experts say it is good. Some art doesn't please our eyes, or the work makes us nervous. That is all right. A response need not be positive.

Answer Key

Exercise 12

Answers will vary. Sample answers are as follows (running clockwise from the top).

1. The work is a painting.
2. The subject is a still life of flowers in a pot and a glass bottle.
3. The painting is almost shapeless, but very colorful (red, green, yellow, blue, orange).
4. The artwork evokes feelings of hopefulness, friendliness, and warmth.
5. The theme or message may be that flowers are beautiful but that beauty cannot last forever, as hinted at by the fallen flower petals encircling the pot.

Step-by-Step Teaching Guide

Creating Visual Aids

1. Visual aids can be useful tools for illustrating information. Use this book or other textbooks to illustrate the use of headings and subheadings.
2. Write the following graphic organizers on the board and give students a demonstration of each:

   Concept map

   Flow chart

   Outline

   Venn diagram
3. In teaching this section about representation skills be aware of students who do not process information visually and actually get confused by graphic organizers. Graphic organizers are a learning tools, not ends in themselves. Help those students find other learning tools that work better for them.

Critical Viewing

Analyze Students may suggest a Vern diagram, a chart, table or outline. A computer may be useful for all of these visual aids, but may be necessary for a detailed diagram or illustration.

28.2

In addition to learning how to interpret the visual information that you encounter, it is important to develop the ability to use visuals to present your own ideas. For example, you can use visual aids when delivering a speech, or you can create a report that consists entirely of multimedia elements.

▲ **Critical Viewing** What types of visual aids could you create with a pen and a piece of paper, as this girl is doing? For what types would you have to use a computer? **[Analyze]**

Creating Visual Aids

When you have technical data or important information to present, consider putting that information into a visual form that is easy to comprehend. Visual aids can also help you to organize research for a paper or to study for a test.

KEY CONCEPT To make complex information easier to understand, create a visual aid in which to organize it. ■

Use these strategies to construct your own visual aids:

Use Text Descriptions When you read a textbook or another informational text, you may notice that information is organized with headings and subheadings to indicate various sections. To help you understand all this information, create a graphic organizer, such as a concept map, to display the information visually. For text with many descriptions, you may want to create a drawing to clarify these details.

Look at Text Structure The organization or structure of a text can help you create graphic organizers. First, identify the text structure. Is it comparison-and-contrast, cause-and-effect, main-idea-and-details, or chronological order? For comparison and contrast, a Venn diagram or a comparison chart can show similarities and differences. A flowchart can help you understand cause-and-effect relationships. An outline is a good way to organize main ideas with supporting details. One way to visualize chronological order is with a timeline.

Identify Your Purpose Consider which part of the text you would like to understand better. Then, decide which type of graphic organizer will help you to communicate this information effectively. For instance, perhaps you would like to show the contrast between two characters in a story or chart the outcomes of their actions. You may also want to make an outline of a persuasive essay so that you can understand the author's main points.

Learn More

You can find several different types of graphic organizers in the chapters on writing.

TIME AND RESOURCE MANAGER

Resources

Print: Academic and Workplace Skills Activity Book, pp. 10–16

In-Depth Coverage	Accelerated Pace
• Cover pp. 686–691 in class. • Discuss different types of Representing Skills in class. • Have students prepare multimedia presentation. • Assign Exercises 13–17.	• Have students read pp. 686–691 independently. • Have students prepare a multimedia presentation.

Following are descriptions of various types of visual aids:

Charts, Graphs, and Tables To present columns of numbers or survey statistics, create a chart, graph, or table. A *chart* can be any shape or color and contain any type of information. A *graph*, such as a bar or line graph, is a good way to show changes that take place over time. *Tables* enable you to present scientific and mathematical information clearly and logically.

Diagrams and Illustrations Diagrams and illustrations are line drawings that indicate the features of something.

Maps To explain directions to your house or present geographical information about one or more regions, put that information into map form. Maps can show almost any type of information—from mountain ranges to airplane flight patterns to important monuments and landmarks. The map below shows important landmarks in Paris.

PARIS LANDMARKS

Exercise 13 **Creating Visual Aids** Complete the following:

1. Create one visual aid to illustrate a portion of a chapter from one of your textbooks. Write your reasons why this particular visual aid best represents the information.
2. Take a poll on any topic in your class, and arrange the information into a pie graph or a bar graph. Clearly label your graph, and include titles and a key, if necessary.

Technology Tip

Use a computer to make charts, graphs, and tables. Look in the computer manual or use the Help function to find out how you can draw diagrams and illustrations on the screen.

Step-by-Step Teaching Guide

Visual Aids

1. Show students examples of charts, graphs, and tables. Ask them to consider how much clearer numerical information is in these visual formats than it would be if presented in sentence form in paragraphs.
2. Ask students to draw a map of how to get from the classroom to the cafeteria and then explain and compare their maps.

Answer Key

Exercise 13

Answers will vary.

1. Students' reasons for choosing one particular visual aid over another to present information should be logical, and the visual aid itself should demonstrate this.
2. The pie or bar graph should be neatly labeled and include titles and a key, if needed.

Step-by-Step Teaching Guide

Using Formatting Features

1. Review the use of formatting. Have students point out examples of each bulleted item in the text on the babysitting flier.
2. Discuss other formatting options such as shading, borders, boxes, different fonts and point size, and design elements that can make written work more presentable.

Integrating Technology Skills

Utilize peer tutoring for students to teach others different formatting techniques.

Answer Key

Exercise 14

Answers will vary. Students' flyers or brochures should be creative and incorporate a variety of formatting techniques.

28.2

Using Formatting Features

Using basic formatting features, found on most word processors, can enhance any written work. Following are some tips for creating effective visual enhancements to your text:

- **Capital Letters** Use capital letters in heads to call out important ideas and topics.
- **Boldface or Italics** Boldface or italics can direct the reader's eyes or give special emphasis to key concepts or ideas.
- **Numbered or Bulleted Lists** When you have steps to be followed in sequence, use a numbered list. Items that can be presented in any order can go in a bulleted list.
- **Graphics and Color** Use graphics and color to attract a reader's attention and to reinforce your message.

The Babysitters
EXPERIENCED, DEPENDABLE BABYSITTERS WILL CARE FOR YOUR CHILDREN
• Excellent references
• Formal babysitter training
• Neat, clean, and careful
• Love children
• Available after school and weekends
Call or e-mail
Rhonda, Jackie, or Melanie
to set up an appointment
phone: 210-555-5182
e-mail: www.babysit.place

Exercise 14 **Using Formatting to Create a Flyer** Use the tips on formatting and design to create a flyer that promotes a student-run business. When your flyer is complete, ask a classmate to evaluate your use of formatting features.

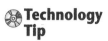

Technology Tip

Find out how to use these formatting techniques on your computer. Experiment with other formatting options, such as page borders and shading, different fonts (type styles), and special effects on type, such as outlines and shadows.

Working With Multimedia

In a multimedia presentation, the presenter gives an oral report and then uses media selections to illustrate main points. With careful planning and creativity, this kind of presentation can be informative and memorable.

KEY CONCEPT Multimedia presentations supply information through a variety of media, including text, slides, videos, music, maps, charts, and artwork. ■

Prepare and Give a Multimedia Presentation The first step in preparing a multimedia presentation is to consider the topic, the audience, and the equipment available to you. Then, follow these suggestions to create your presentation:

- Create an outline of your report, and then decide which parts to illustrate using media.
- Choose a medium that is suited to your topic. For example, if you were discussing the plays of William Shakespeare, you might use video to show scenes from the plays, music from his time period, and charts to show the order in which the plays were written.
- Evenly space the media you use within your presentation. Do not present all the media at the beginning or at the end, or their effectiveness will be diminished.
- Check to ensure that the media you've selected will be able to be seen and/or heard by everyone. Images that are too small cannot be seen by everyone, and music that is too loud will overwhelm your presentation.
- Before the presentation, check your equipment—slide projectors, overhead projectors, microphones, cassette players—to be sure that they are in working order.
- Rehearse with the equipment before the day of the presentation.
- Always have a backup plan in case anything goes wrong with the equipment.

Exercise 15 **Preparing a Multimedia Presentation** Read through some writings in your portfolio. Select one piece to prepare as a multimedia presentation. Choose appropriate forms of media to illustrate your writing. Then, outline a plan showing how you will use the media, and the order in which it will be presented. Rehearse your presentation, and then present it to your classmates.

Research Tip

Your school or public library may have slides, videos, and audiocassettes that you can use in your multimedia presentation.

ONGOING ASSESSMENT: Monitor and Reinforce

If some students are having difficulty finding a workable topic for their multimedia presentation, use the following options.

Option 1 To streamline the activity and focus it on the use of multimedia, you could select a topic that lends itself well to multimedia and have all students do their presentations on this topic.

Option 2 Have students submit both text and media usage outlines to you for approval.

Step-by-Step Teaching Guide

Working With Multimedia

1. Before beginning this exercise, make a list of the equipment available. In the interest of fairness, you may want to limit students to the equipment available to all.
2. Try to obtain a TV monitor and VCR, an overhead slide projector and screen, and an audio CD/cassette player.
3. Students will need a topic and a text, as well as different media presentations. Help them select well-defined topics that lend themselves to illustration. Sports topics that involve easily obtainable statistics could be a good starting point. Take care that students select a narrow enough, easy-to-research topic, or else this exercise could become unwieldy.
4. Have students make visual representations on overhead slides that can be shown on the projector. If you have a computer that has PowerPoint available, see if students can project slides directly off the computer. If not, have them print the slides (on a color printer, if possible).
5. Show students how to cue video and audio materials. Make sure they understand the need to have them cued up. No matter how effective, it is easy to lose an audience's attention while fumbling around to find the right starting point.
6. Allow students sufficient rehearsal time. Remind them strongly that although the multimedia part is the core of this assignment, in most presentations it is the illustrative material. The speaker needs to have a well-rehearsed talk prepared and be ready to integrate the talk with the multimedia presentation.

Answer Key

Exercise 15

Answers will vary. Students should demonstrate an understanding of the purpose for using multimedia, and the multimedia they use should reinforce the oral portion of their presentation.

Creating a Video

1. This activity depends on the availability of video cameras and tape.
2. If resources are available, decide on their allocation—how many cameras for how many students?
3. Next, walk students through the text materials.
4. One step you may want to add is story boarding. If students are shooting with a script, having them construct a story board will give them more control over the story and result in more efficient use of shooting time and resources.
5. You could also encourage some students to make documentary films. A documentary doesn't have a script. Without editing facilities, students will get what they shoot. What they will need is a good topic and a set of questions for doing interviews.
6. Set some goals for the activity, since the results may not be the sole indicator of the learning experience. There are several identifiable tasks students should address:
   - Project management: creating a film involves planning and organizational skills
   - Story-telling and narrative skills
   - The experience of seeing the world through a viewfinder
   - Interpersonal skills: interacting with classmates in the production process

Answer Key

Exercise 16

Answers will vary.

Critical Viewing

Analyze Students' responses will vary, but they may say that it is an informational video about skateboarding safely.

Creating a Video

Telling a story or reporting on a topic by using images, sound, and dialogue is a powerful way to communicate. A film allows your viewers to see the particular subject matter, event, or story through your eyes. A film can be informative, humorous, or dramatic.

KEY CONCEPT Create a film to communicate information, to entertain, or to do both. ■

Organization is the most essential component in making a film. Follow these basic steps:

Basic Steps

1. Write out the story or message in the form of a shooting script. A *shooting script* contains lines to be spoken, or dialogue among the characters. It also contains directions about camera angles and descriptions of settings, costumes or wardrobe, and props.
2. Create an outline of the scenes, places, and shots you want to cover. Use your outline while shooting.
3. Select locations for shooting, and get permission to use them.
4. Cast people to play the various roles, and rehearse.
5. Film the scenes. Edit the film.

Tips for Filming

- Hold the camera steady.
- Use the following filming techniques for effect:

  Pan: Move the camera to the left or right.

  Zoom: Adjust from a distant to a close shot while filming.

  Fade: Increase or reduce the intensity of a picture.

  Cut: Move directly from one shot to another.
- When in doubt, shoot more. It is easier to cut scenes than to have to reassemble the cast to refilm.
- Keep scenes simple and short.

Exercise 16 **Creating a Film** Create a three-minute film on a topic in which you are interested. Write out a script to follow while you are filming, and use your outline to ensure that you do not leave anything out. Select the location and actors for your film. Then, shoot and edit your work. Present the finished product to your classmates.

▼ Critical Viewing What type of video do you think these students are shooting? Why? **[Analyze]**

Performing and Interpreting

We have all experienced the thrill of watching a live performance in a theater or an auditorium. Actors, singers, musicians, and dancers are all performing artists.

KEY CONCEPT Performers use a variety of techniques to convey the meaning of a text. ■

Perform a Scene or Monologue Whether you are planning a performance or an original piece, the following steps can help to make your performance a success:

1. Write the text of the scene or monologue in a notebook, and highlight its most important words and ideas.
2. Read the text aloud several times, experimenting with the tone and pitch of your voice.
3. Consider selecting props, music, costumes, and settings to help express the meaning and mood of the text.
4. Rehearse, using gestures and other body language to express yourself.
5. Keep your performance simple and direct to ensure that it will have clarity and power.

Research Tip

You can learn more about how plays were performed in Shakespeare's time by doing research on the Globe Theater.

Exercise 17 **Performing a Scene From a Play** Select a scene from a play to interpret and perform, either alone or with others. Copy it, and highlight important ideas. Decide what you want to communicate, and take performance notes on setting, mood, costumes, and props. Rehearse, and then perform the scene for your class.

Reflecting on Your Speaking, Listening, Viewing, and Representing Skills

Review all the different strategies and suggestions discussed in this chapter. Write a journal entry discussing these experiences. Begin your inquiry by asking yourself these questions:

- What are my strengths and weaknesses as a speaker and as a listener? Which skills need improvement?
- What viewing experiences gave me the most information?
- What representing experiences did I find the most enjoyable?

ONGOING ASSESSMENT: Assess Mastery

Use one of the following options to assess mastery of representing skills.

Self-Assessment Ask students to reflect on their representing skills, making sure they have identified areas they feel strong in and areas they would like to improve.

Teacher Assessment Review your notes on each exercise students have performed. Also consider their basic understanding of the subject matter as evidenced by their participation in class discussions.

Step-by-Step Teaching Guide

Performing and Interpreting

1. Many people have fears about public speaking. Those fears are amplified when it comes to performing. Public speaking is an important enough skill that it is worth working hard to get over the discomfort. But performing is not necessarily for everyone. You may want to adapt this exercise, allowing some students to do speeches or serve as production assistants in a larger skit or play.
2. One way to involve reluctant students in this exercise is to let them collaborate on a comedy skit.
3. If you need to shorten the exercise, students could choose scenes from plays instead of writing their own skit or monologue.

Answer Key

Exercise 15

Answers will vary. Performance should reflect preparation and planning and include verbal and nonverbal strategies and costume(s) or other props.

PRENTICE HALL
Everyday Spelling

If you have taught the spelling skills in *Prentice Hall Everyday Spelling,* Grade 8, Chapter 33, in conjunction with this *Writing and Grammar* chapter, review and assess students' mastery of the skills before concluding the chapter.

Lesson Objectives

- To interpret graphic aids.

Step-by-Step Teaching Guide

Interpreting Graphic Aids

Teaching Resources: Standardized Test Preparation Workbook, pp. 55–56

1. Emphasize to students that their key to success in most standardized tests is for them to read the questions carefully. Remind them that some test questions will not only pertain to passages on a specific topic, but that these passages may accompany graphic aids.
2. Remind students to determine the purpose of maps by paying attention to the title, headings, keys, symbols, etc.
3. For instance, the title of the map in the textbook is "Native American Culture Areas." Students should expect to find both regions and cultural groups identified on the map. Point out that different typefaces are used to distinguish labels of regions, set in large italics (e.g., *"Southeast"*), from the names of the tribes who lived there, set in Roman (e.g., "Natchez"). Point out the correspondence between the different colors and the different region-labels.
4. Remind them that graphs function as visual aids to compare several pieces of related information. Make sure they understand the differences between a pie graph (shows the relationship of parts to a whole), a bar graph (compares and contrasts amounts), and a line graph (shows changes over a specific period of time).

Standardized Test Preparation Workshop

Interpreting Graphic Aids

Some standardized test questions evaluate your ability to gather details, draw conclusions, and interpret from the information provided in maps, charts, graphs, and other graphic aids. The following sample items will help you become familiar with these types of questions.

Test Tip

As you examine each graphic aid, ask yourself what each part of the graphic means or represents in relation to the whole.

NATIVE AMERICAN CULTURE AREAS

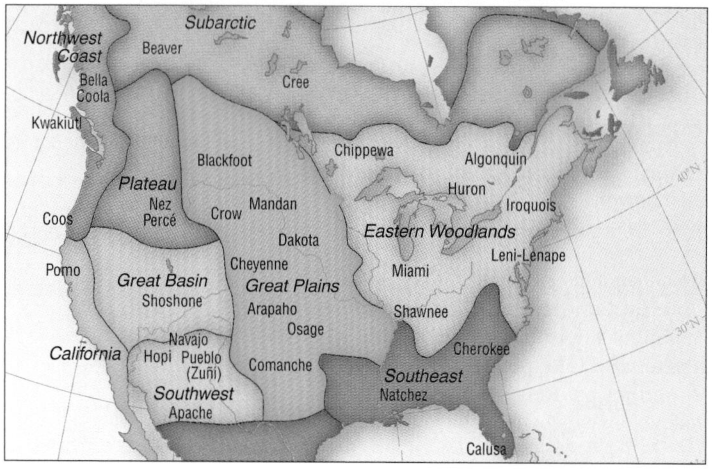

Sample Test Item	Answer and Explanation
Read the passage, and answer the questions that follow. Native American civilizations provide the longest continuous record of human habitation on the North American continent. The above map shows where different Native American culture areas developed.	
1 The section of the continent with the greatest number of culture areas was the— A Southeast B Great Plains C Eastern Woodlands D Plateau	The correct answer is *B*. The Great Plains had the largest number of tribes settle within its boundaries—eight different Native American tribes.

TEST-TAKING TIP

Encourage students to examine the given graphic aid before reading the questions that pertain to it. Once students have familiarized themselves with the information contained in the aid, they can read the questions. This will help give them a better sense of the information for which they need to look to answer the questions.

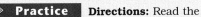

Practice **Directions:** Read the passage, and answer the questions that follow.

For thousands of years, China kept out foreign influences, but it could not keep out change forever. In the 1800's, nations such as Great Britain became involved in trade with China. Some Chinese citizens earned great wealth as a result of the trade. Many more, however, were poor and did not benefit from the interactions with other nations. Rebellions broke out beginning in the 1850's. During this time, many left China in search of a new life.

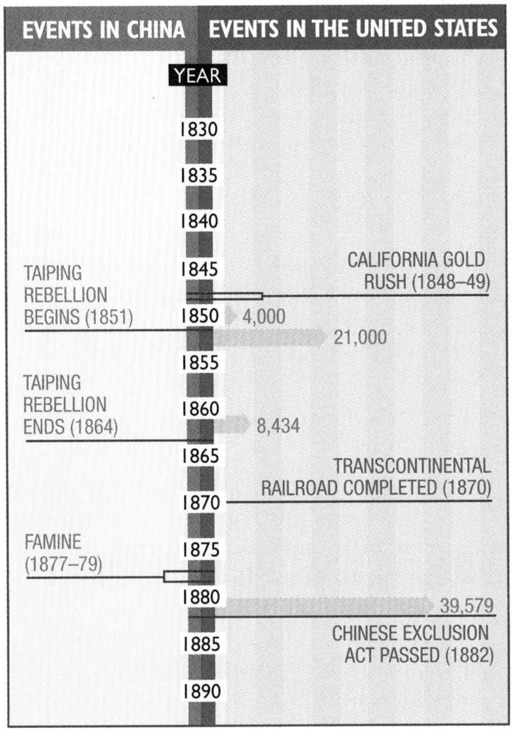

(Green arrows indicate number of Chinese people entering the United States)

1 What was occurring in China during the ten-year span when the greatest number of Chinese immigrants entered the United States?

A California Gold Rush
B Taiping Rebellion
C Famine
D Chinese Exclusion Act

2 The largest number of Chinese immigrants entered the United States in the—

F 1880's
G 1870's
H 1850's
J 1860's

3 What is the most likely reason that people would have left China in the 1870's to immigrate to the United States?

A Rebellions were dangerous.
B The gold rush promised prosperity.
C The famine caused them to leave in search of food.
D They were motivated by the Chinese Exclusion Act.

4 Based on the information in the chart, what is the most logical conclusion regarding the Chinese Exclusion Act?

F It was a law allowing more Chinese into the country.
G It was a law halting Chinese immigration.
H It was an act that prohibited foreign interference in the affairs of China.
J It was the name of certain ports through which the Chinese could enter the country.

Answer Key

Practice

1. C
2. F
3. C
4. G

Chapter 29 Time and Resource Manager

In-Depth Lesson Plan

	LESSON FOCUS	PRINT AND MEDIA RESOURCES
DAY 1	**Developing Vocabulary** Students develop vocabulary skills by listening carefully, using context clues, and studying new words in specific curriculum areas (pp. 694–698).	**Teaching Resources** *Academic and Workplace Skills Activity Book,* pp. 17–19
DAY 2	**Studying Words Systematically** Students keep vocabulary notebooks and use dictionaries and other reference sources (pp. 699–701).	**Teaching Resources** *Academic and Workplace Skills Activity Book,* pp. 20–22 ***Prentice Hall Everyday Spelling,*** Grade 8, Dictionary Handbook, pp. 246–312
DAY 3	**Studying Word Parts and Origins** Students use roots, prefixes, suffixes, and word origins to define new words (pp. 702–705).	**Teaching Resources** *Academic and Workplace Skills Activity Book,* pp. 23–25 ***Prentice Hall Everyday Spelling,*** Grade 8, Chapters 4, 9, 10, 13, 15, 20, 21, 25–27, 32, 33
DAY 4	**Improving Your Spelling** Students keep and study personal spelling lists. They apply a variety of spelling rules and look for patterns in spelling (pp. 706–715).	**Teaching Resources** *Academic and Workplace Skills Activity Book,* pp. 26–33 ***Prentice Hall Everyday Spelling,*** Grade 8, pp. 12, 38, 64, 90, 116, 142

Accelerated Lesson Plan

	LESSON FOCUS	PRINT AND MEDIA RESOURCES
DAY 1	**Developing Vocabulary; Studying Words Systematically** Students enlarge their vocabularies by listening carefully, using context clues, defining words in specific curriculum areas, and using reference aids (pp. 694–701).	**Teaching Resources** *Academic and Workplace Skills Activity Book,* pp. 17–22 ***Prentice Hall Everyday Spelling,*** Grade 8, Dictionary Handbook, pp. 246–312
DAY 2	**Studying Word Parts and Origins; Spelling** Students use roots, prefixes, suffixes, and word origins to help them define new words. They apply a variety of spelling rules (pp. 702–715).	**Teaching Resources** *Academic and Workplace Skills Activity Book,* pp. 23–33 ***Prentice Hall Everyday Spelling,*** Grade 8, pp. 12, 38, 64, 90, 116, 142

Options for Adapting Lesson Plans

HOMEWORK

Have students complete any stage of the lesson for homework.

FEATURES

Extend coverage with the Standardized Test Preparation Workshop (pp. 716–717).

TECHNOLOGY

Students can complete any stage of the lesson on computer. Have them print out their completed work.

SPELLING

To reinforce and expand on the spelling skills covered in this chapter, use *Prentice Hall Everyday Spelling,* Grade 8. (See the Lesson Plan charts above for specific suggestions.)

INTEGRATED SKILLS COVERAGE

Viewing and Representing
Critical Viewing, SE pp. 694, 698, 701, 707, 709, 710, 714

Real-World Connection
Pronunciation, ATE p. 708

Speaking and Listening
SE p. 695

Technology Skills
SE pp. 697, 705, 706, 708; ATE p. 708

BLOCK SCHEDULING

Pacing Suggestions
For 90-minute Blocks
- Have students complete the chapter in a single class period.

Professional Development Support
- ***How to Manage Instruction in the Block*** This teaching resource provides management and activity suggestions.

ASSESSMENT SUPPORT

Standardized Test Preparation Workshop SE pp. 716–717; ATE p. 701

Standardized Test Preparation Workbook, pp. 57–58

Writing Assessment and Portfolio Management

MEDIA AND TECHNOLOGY

For the Teacher
- ***Resource Pro* CD-ROM**

MEETING INDIVIDUAL NEEDS

Less Advanced Students ATE p. 714. See also Ongoing Assessments ATE pp. 697, 700, 704, 710.

ESL Students ATE p. 701

More Advanced Students ATE p. 702

Gifted/Talented Students ATE p. 714

Verbal/Linguistic Learners ATE pp. 697, 713

Bodily/Kinesthetic Learners ATE p. 700

WRITING AND GRAMMAR ON-LINE

iText Interactive Text (On-line or on CD-ROM)
- Easily navigable instruction with interactive Revision Checkers
- Full use of e-rater™, the essay-scoring system (on-line only)

Companion Web Site PHSchool.com
- Scoring rubrics with models (use Web Code eck-8001)

See the Go On-line! feature, SE p. iii.

CHAPTER 29
VOCABULARY AND SPELLING

Lesson Objectives

1. To develop vocabulary skills through listening.
2. To use context clues.
3. To study meanings in the content areas.
4. To study words systematically.
5. To use dictionaries and other reference aids.
6. To use roots, prefixes, and suffixes to define words.
7. To examine word origins.
8. To apply spelling rules.

Critical Viewing

Deduce Students might suggest that note taking will help them notice words with which they are unfamiliar and that writing unfamiliar words will help them spell these words.

Chapter 29 Vocabulary and Spelling

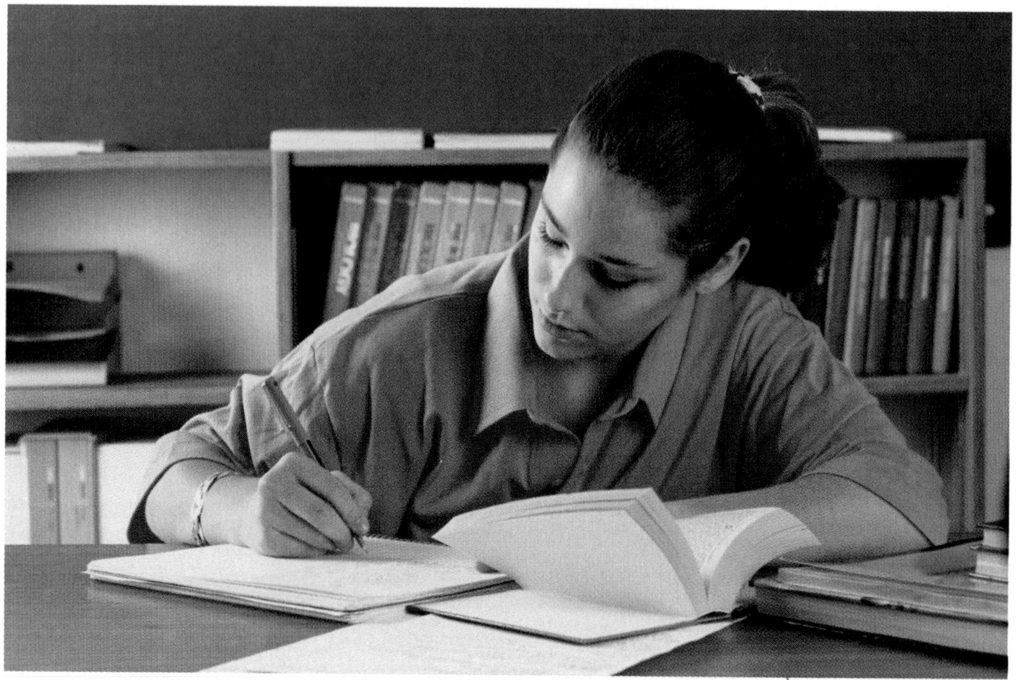

As your vocabulary and spelling improve, your pleasure in reading and writing will grow as well. You will be pleasantly surprised to see your reading comprehension become deeper as you become more knowledgeable about the meaning of a whole variety of words.

Adding to your vocabulary gives you new resources for your writing and, therefore, more ways to express yourself. Improving your spelling will help readers to form a good impression of your work and will allow them to focus on *what* you are writing, instead of being distracted by errors. Finally, as you work on both vocabulary and spelling skills, your standardized test-taking skills will improve. There are several techniques that can help you to develop your skills, and the reward is well worth the effort.

▲ **Critical Viewing** In what ways might taking notes as you read help you to increase your vocabulary and improve your spelling? **[Deduce]**

TIME AND RESOURCE MANAGER

Resources
Print: Academic and Workplace Skills Activity Book, pp. 17–19

In-Depth Coverage	Accelerated Pace
• Cover pp. 695–698 in class. • Assign and review Exercises 1–4.	• Assign pp. 695–698 for independent student review.

Section 29.1

Developing Vocabulary

Developing Your Vocabulary Through Listening

Conversation

Your vocabulary development began on the day you were born! Everyone is born with the ability to learn language. As a baby and a toddler, you soaked up words and grammar at an amazing rate. You used your listening skills to increase your vocabulary and to learn how to pronounce new words.

Now you can read and write, but one of your most important skills in language learning is still your listening skill. Throughout your life, you can (and should) learn and use new words in conversation. Whenever you talk with teachers, people from different places, and people whose interests and ideas are different from yours, listen for unfamiliar words. You can find out the meanings of the words by asking, listening for clues, and looking up the words in a dictionary.

Works Read Aloud

Listening to works of literature read aloud is another good way to build your vocabulary. Numerous books are available on audiocassette or CD, and most libraries have them. When you listen to a recorded book, you hear how unfamiliar words are pronounced, and how they are used in context. If you have a copy of the book, you may try reading along with the recording so that you can both see and hear new words.

Wide Reading

The more you read, the more new words you will encounter. When you see those words over and over again in different contexts, they will become familiar to you and part of your own vocabulary. Each time you read a word in a different context, you will increase your understanding of the word's meaning and usage. Read from a broad range of sources—books, magazines, newspapers, Internet articles—in order to encounter the widest variety of words.

Speaking and Listening Tip

Together with a partner, take turns reading a literary work aloud. Note words that are unfamiliar, and try to guess their meanings from the context in which they are used. Keep a list of the words, and check their meanings in a dictionary later.

PREPARE and ENGAGE

Interest GRABBER American writer and humorist Mark Twain once wrote a set of rules for writers. Share the first two rules with students:

The writer shall:

1. *Say* what he is proposing to say, not merely come near it.
2. Use the right word, not its second cousin.

Language is, above all else, a means of communication. No one can communicate ideas effectively without expressing them in the most precise words possible. In this chapter, students will learn to enlarge their vocabularies and to spell basic words correctly.

Activate Prior Knowledge

Write the noun *house* on the chalkboard. Ask students to list as many words as they can that mean the same or nearly the same thing. (Possible answers: *home, cottage, apartment, mansion, bungalow, teepee, igloo, treehouse, brownstone, trailer, shack, hut*) Ask students whether these words really mean the same thing, or whether they all have distinct meanings. Point out that *house* is a vague word and can describe any number of types of shelter. The other words give a much more exact idea of the type of shelter the speaker or writer is talking or writing about. Stress the importance of using precise words in speaking and writing.

TEACH

Step-by-Step Teaching Guide

Developing Vocabulary Through Listening

1. Ask students if they are familiar with reading words aloud outside the classroom setting. Have students share their experiences with the class.
2. Ask students what they usually do when they encounter unfamiliar words as they read. Explain to them that they will be learning different strategies to help them in these situations.

Step-by-Step Teaching Guide

Using Context

1. A word's context is its setting—the words that surround it. The context often gives clues that help a reader figure out the meaning of an unfamiliar word. For example, near the end of Edgar Allan Poe's story "The Fall of the House of Usher," there is the sentence, "From that chamber, and from that mansion, I fled aghast." The speaker of this sentence has just witnessed a violent death and discovered that a supposed corpse was buried alive. He is also running away from the scene. This context makes it clear that *aghast* means something like "horrified."
2. Discuss the different types of context clues readers may encounter. They include synonyms and definitions in the sentence or nearby sentences and descriptions of the unfamiliar word. Students can always begin by determining a word's part of speech; this will help them figure out its meaning. When text is spoken aloud, the speaker's tone and manner can also provide clues to the meaning of words.
3. Discuss figurative language. Point out that the word *assignment* already makes it clear that the expression "piece of cake" is not being used literally; the speaker is talking about homework, not food. Therefore, the context helps make the meaning clear.

Answer Key

Exercise 1

Answers will vary. Samples are given.

subterranean, underground
retreat, hideaway
tedious, boring
deteriorate, get worse
passively, without doing anything

29.1

Using Context

When you come across an unfamiliar word, you may not always need to use a dictionary. You might be able to figure out the meaning of the word by using clues from the author.

Recognize Context Clues

If you look carefully at the sentence or paragraph that contains the unfamiliar word, you can sometimes figure out the word's meaning.

KEY CONCEPT The **context** of a word means the group of words that surround it. ■

USING CONTEXT CLUES

1. Read the sentence, leaving out the unfamiliar word.
2. Find clues in the sentence to figure out the word's meaning.
3. Read the sentence again, substituting your possible meaning for the unfamiliar word.
4. Check your possible meaning by looking up the unfamiliar word in the dictionary. Write the word and its definition in your vocabulary notebook.

Figurative Language Figurative language is not meant to be taken literally. Many types of figurative language use words in unfamiliar ways. For example, you might read or hear the sentence, "This assignment is a piece of cake." The assignment does not literally have anything to do with making or eating cake; the comment is interpreted to mean that the assignment is easy.

Idioms An idiom is an expression used by people of a particular region or background. Sometimes, you will be unfamiliar with idioms used by people who are not from your area. When you recognize an unusual expression as an idiom, compare it to expressions that you use in similar instances.

Exercise 1 **Using Context Clues** Use context clues from the selection below to define the underlined words below.

In 1972, Michel Siffre entered a subterranean cave to experiment with living underground and alone. The cave was silent and seemed like a suitable retreat, away from society. Initially, Michel spent time reading, but after a week of the same thing, the activity became tedious. Soon, his condition began to deteriorate, and now, weak and gloomy, he sat passively, not moving for hours. He finally realized humans need companionship.

More Practice

Academic and Workplace Skills Activity Book
• pp. 19–20

Use Context Clues in All of Your Reading In any reading, whether it is fiction or nonfiction, you can often figure out the meaning of a word from its context.

Use Possible Sentences One good method for helping you to increase your vocabulary and your understanding of words in context is the possible-sentences strategy. Use it to experiment with unfamiliar words.

STEPS FOR USING POSSIBLE SENTENCES

1. Find an unfamiliar word in your reading, and try to figure out its meaning.
2. Write a sentence for the unfamiliar word in your vocabulary notebook.
3. Check the actual meaning of the word in a dictionary.
4. Evaluate your sentence to see whether you have used the word correctly.
5. Revise your sentence to make it correct.

Exercise 2 **Using the Possible-Sentences Strategy With Words in Context** Choose a book about a subject that interests you, such as music, geography, computers, or gardening. Find five words that are unfamiliar to you. Use the possible-sentences strategy to define the words. Enter the words and their correct meanings in your vocabulary notebook.

Exercise 3 **Writing Possible Sentences to Learn New Words** Use the possible-sentences strategy to define the following words.

1. phonetic
2. renown
3. tangible
4. reverie
5. configuration

Internet Tip

In an on-line encyclopedia, find a short entry on a subject of interest to you. Find three unfamiliar words, look them up in a dictionary, and add them to your notebook.

Step-by-Step Teaching Guide

Use Possible Sentences

Encourage students to follow the 5 steps in the chart to find the meaning of an unfamiliar word from a selection in *Prentice Hall Literature: Timeless Voices, Timeless Themes,* Silver

Answer Key

Exercise 2

Ask students to contribute some examples from their work to a class discussion of the strategy.

Exercise 3

Answers will vary. Samples are given.

1. phonetic, related to sound
2. renown, fame
3. tangible, able to be touched
4. reverie, daydream
5. configuration, arrangement

Customize for *Verbal/Linguistic Learners*

Students can extend Exercise 3 by looking up each word in two different abridged dictionaries and one unabridged dictionary. Have them compare and contrast the entries.

ONGOING ASSESSMENT: Monitor and Reinforce

If students are having difficulty using context to find meaning, use one of the following options.

Option 1 Have students find other examples of figurative language or idioms in their reading. Have them explain what each means.

Option 2 Find or write exercises that use unfamiliar words in sentences with in-sentence clues, such as *Recurring problems happened on my computer many times today.*

Step-by-Step Teaching Guide

Studying Meanings in the Content Areas

Organize students into small groups by subject of interest—law, social studies, music, science, art, and so on. Groups can work together to learn ten words related to their subject, then teach them to the class. You might spread this activity out over time, so that students can master one set of words before going on to study the next.

Answer Key

Exercise 4

Go over students' notebooks with them individually. Test them on a few of their listed words and ask students to explain how they grouped their words.

Critical Viewing

Infer Students may suggest that knowing the definitions of various landforms will allow this girl to use them properly in her writing, adding variety and detail to her writing.

29.1

Studying Meanings in the Content Areas

Use a Notebook and a Glossary

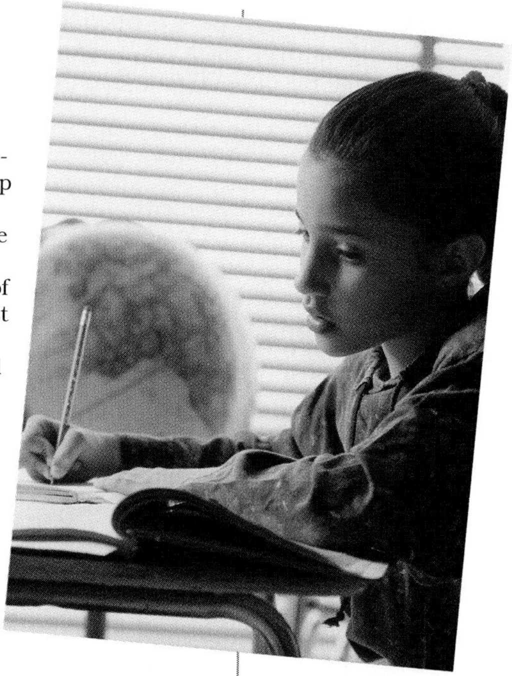

▲ Critical Viewing How will writing the definitions of various landforms help this geography student to increase her vocabulary? **[Infer]**

When you are reading in your school subjects, you can often use context clues to help you figure out the meaning of unfamiliar words. However, you should make a practice of recording and studying words that are related to the content area. Keep a section of your notebook for each subject area, and list new words and their meanings. Use the glossary at the back of your textbook to find the specific definitions of unfamiliar words.

Social Studies In your social studies classes, you will discover new words that deal with historical events, government, political activities, and physical features of an area. Use the categories that apply to your subject to group words according to what they name or describe. Look for words that name or describe related features or situations.

Science Unfamiliar words in science often have Latin origins. Categorize science words by their prefixes, suffixes, or roots. For example, you could group *ultrasonic* with *ultraviolet* because both begin with *ultra-*. Once you learn that *ultra-* means "beyond the range of," you will more easily remember the meaning of each word.

Current Events By listening to the news or reading a newspaper, you increase the chances that you will encounter the words you learn in science and social studies. The more you see and hear a word used, the better you will understand its meaning. Use current-events topics to reinforce your vocabulary building.

Exercise 4 **Studying Words in the Content Areas** With a partner, look over a chapter in your science or social studies book, and list any unfamiliar words and their definitions. You might want to write them on index cards so that you can group the words in various ways. When you have the words defined and logically grouped, record them in your notebook.

Research Tip

Choose five unfamiliar words from any textbook. Check their definitions in the book's glossary, then use a thesaurus to find a synonym for each word.

Section 29.2

Studying Words Systematically

Keeping a Vocabulary Notebook

There are a variety of methods for studying and reviewing new words. Use the method that works best for you.

KEY CONCEPT Along with a dictionary, keep a notebook available to list new words. ■

Divide the page of your notebook into three sections: List (1) the word, (2) a bridge word or hint to help you remember the meaning, and (3) its dictionary definition.

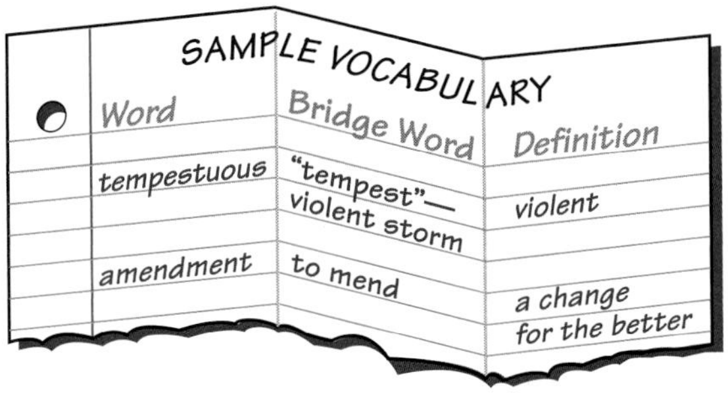

SAMPLE VOCABULARY
Word
Bridge Word
Definition
tempestuous
"tempest"— violent storm
violent
amendment
to mend
a change for the better

Exercise 5 **Setting Up a Vocabulary Notebook** Focus on a textbook that you are using in one of your classes or on a story or poem you are reading in English. As you read, list any unfamiliar words. Afterwards, look up the words in a dictionary and record their meanings in your notebook.

Studying New Words

Use Your Notebook Practice learning the meanings by covering the definition and looking only at the word and the bridge word. Then, uncover the definition, and read it. Finally, write a new sentence using the word.

Write Sentences With Vocabulary Words When you write sentences using vocabulary words, reinforce the meaning of the word by using the word's definition in the sentence.

EXAMPLE: The crowd *dispersed* quickly, *scattering in all directions* when the performance ended.

More Practice

Academic and Workplace Skills Activity Book
- p. 22

Step-by-Step Teaching Guide

Keeping a Vocabulary Notebook

For practice, have students write notebook entries for the following interesting words. Tell them it isn't always possible to find a bridge word.

caryatid
droll
faugh
gazebo
scrounge
topiary

Answer Key

Exercise 5

Go over students' notebooks with them individually. Discuss ways they can use these notebooks as aids to remember the words they write down.

TIME AND RESOURCE MANAGER

Resources
Print: Academic and Workplace Skills Activity Book, pp. 20–22
Prentice Hall Everyday Spelling, Grade 8, Dictionary Handbook, pp. 246–251

In-Depth Coverage	Accelerated Pace
• Cover pp. 699–701 in class. • Assign and review Exercises 5–7.	• Assign pp. 699–701 for independent student review.

Answer Key

Exercise 6

Flashcards: Answers will vary. Samples are given.

1. setting
2. lengthen
3. underwater telescope
4. worriedly
5. already inclined toward

Customize for *Bodily/Kinesthetic Learners*

Challenge students to share new vocabulary words by playing charades. One student thinks of a word and acts it out for the audience, sometimes syllable by syllable. The audience has to guess the word. Players take turns until they have run out of words. When new words come up during the game, players can write them down and define them in their notebooks.

29.2

Review New Words With Flashcards You can practice your vocabulary using a set of flashcards. Make a card for each word in your vocabulary notebook. On the front, write the word you want to remember. On the back, write the definition and the subject to which it relates. You can test yourself or ask others to test you.

Use a Tape Recorder Record a vocabulary word. First, pronounce the word carefully. Then, after a pause, record its definition. To review, play the tape. During the pause, recall the word's definition. Listen to the recorded definition to check yourself and to reinforce the word's meaning.

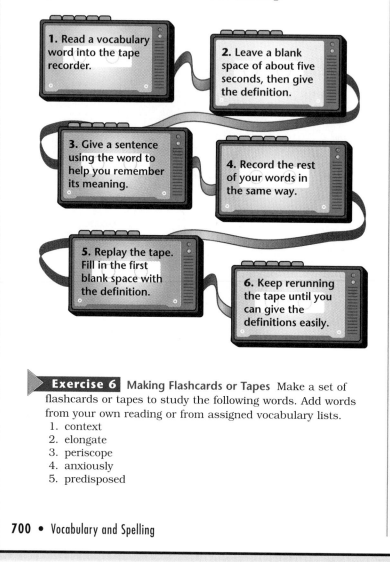

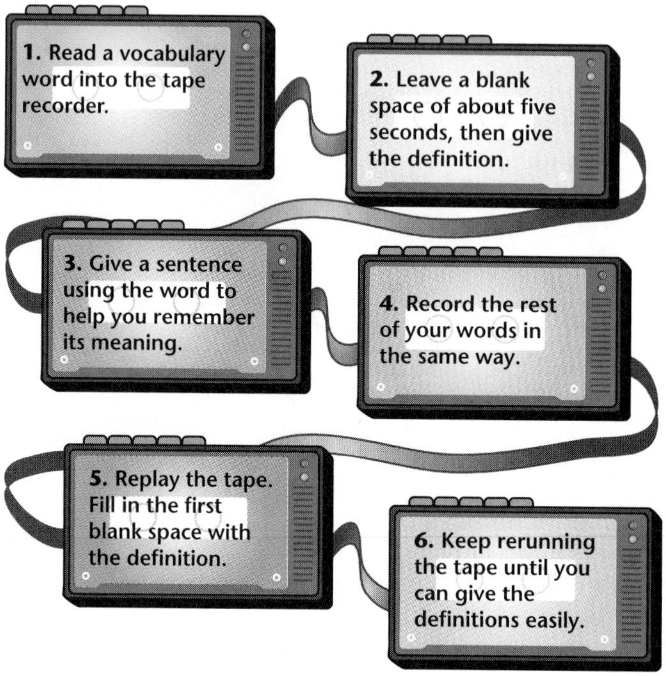

1. Read a vocabulary word into the tape recorder.
2. Leave a blank space of about five seconds, then give the definition.
3. Give a sentence using the word to help you remember its meaning.
4. Record the rest of your words in the same way.
5. Replay the tape. Fill in the first blank space with the definition.
6. Keep rerunning the tape until you can give the definitions easily.

Exercise 6 **Making Flashcards or Tapes** Make a set of flashcards or tapes to study the following words. Add words from your own reading or from assigned vocabulary lists.

1. context
2. elongate
3. periscope
4. anxiously
5. predisposed

Research Tip

Find a book about outdoor sports—mountain climbing, hiking, skiing, kayaking, and so on. Find five unfamiliar words, and guess their meanings using context clues. Check their meanings in a dictionary.

ONGOING ASSESSMENT: Monitor and Reinforce

If students are having difficulty finding meanings for unfamiliar words, use one of the following options.

Option 1 Have students work in pairs. Each student writes the words with which he or she is having difficulty on a list. Each partner goes on a "scavenger hunt" to find definitions for the other partner's words. Students should use a dictionary, thesaurus, book of synonyms.

Option 2 Have students present their lists of difficult words. Divide students into two teams and have a "meaning bee."

Using a Dictionary

A dictionary provides more than just the definitions of a word. Look in a dictionary when you want to find out a word's pronunciation, its origins, or its uses as different parts of speech and in various expressions. Note that reading the origins of a word can help you make associations with other words that share the origin. Words in a dictionary are listed in alphabetical order. Whenever you are unsure of the meaning of a word you encounter in your reading, look it up. Record the words you look up in your vocabulary notebook.

Using Other Reference Aids

Thesaurus A thesaurus lists a word's synonyms (words with similar meanings) and, sometimes, its antonyms (words with opposite meanings). Words in some thesauruses are listed alphabetically. In others, words are arranged by categories according to an alphabetical index.

▲ Critical Viewing What kinds of words would you expect to see defined in the glossary of a math book? **[Relate]**

Synonym Finder Many word-processing programs have a synonym finder or thesaurus in their menus. If you are drafting on-line, highlight a word for which you want to find a synonym, and use the synonym finder or thesaurus to check alternative words.

Glossary A glossary is a list of terms and definitions specific to a field of study. Each of your textbooks will likely have a glossary that lists the words you need to know in that subject area. Check the book's table of contents to find out where the glossary appears.

Software Like most references, dictionaries and thesauruses are available in electronic form. Some can be purchased on CD-ROM and loaded onto your hard drive, while many others are available on the Internet. Search "on-line dictionary" or "on-line thesaurus."

Exercise 7 **Using Vocabulary Reference Aids** Look up each of the following words in the references indicated. Compare and contrast the information found in both sources.

1. deciduous (science textbook glossary, dictionary)
2. topography (social studies textbook glossary, dictionary)
3. constitutes (dictionary, thesaurus)
4. carnivorous (science textbook glossary, on-line dictionary)
5. steadfast (dictionary, synonym finder)

More Practice

Academic and Workplace Skills Activity Book
- p. 22

Step-by-Step Teaching Guide

Using a Dictionary and Other Reference Aids

1. Bring in a dictionary and the other reference aids listed and give students some time to look through them.
2. Students should study how the reference aids are organized and examine the different kinds of information contained in each one.

Customize for *ESL Students*

Go over an ordinary dictionary entry with students. Point out that English dictionaries always show how a word is pronounced. This information will help students learning English, since it is not always phonetic. Glossaries sometimes show pronunciation; thesauruses do not. Encourage students to use dictionaries to help them learn to pronounce new words.

Answer Key

Exercise 7

Answers will vary. Samples are given.

1. referring to trees that lose their leaves annually; shedding leaves annually
2. configuration of a surface; study of surface features of an area
3. sets up, appoints; comprises, forms, appoints
4. meat-eating; cannibal, flesh-eating, omnivorous, hungry
5. loyal, unable to be swayed or influenced; adherent

Critical Viewing

Relate Students should suggest that mathematical operations such as *addition, subtraction, multiplication,* and *division* along with types of numbers: *whole, fraction, decimal* will be found.

STANDARDIZED TEST PREPARATION WORKSHOP

Vocabulary Standardized tests often measure students' ability to determine the meaning of a word in a passage using context clues. Ask students to choose the letter of the definition of the underlined word in the following passage:

Our trip to the Bahamas was almost ruined by intermittent rain. It would have been worse if the rain had been continuous. At least we had a few hours of sunshine each day.

A heavy **C** periodic
B constant **D** terrible

Students should see that *intermittent* means "periodic." The passage gives two clues: the rain was not continuous and there were periods of sun each day. The correct choice is item **C**.

Step-by-Step Teaching Guide

Using Roots

1. Most roots come from Latin and Greek. A root is not a word; it is a word part.
2. Use *captivate* to show students how to use roots to define words. Ask them to list other words that contain the letter combination *-cap-* or *-capt-*. (Possible answers: *capture, captive, captivity, captor*) List these words on the chalkboard, underlining the root. Define (or have students define) each word.
3. Still using *captivate,* point out that *cap* in a word does not always mean "to take or seize." In *decapitate,* for example, *cap* comes from *caput,* the Latin word for "head." *Decapitate* = "cut off the head." Over time, students will learn to recognize various roots and combinations.

Customize for *More Advanced Students*

Challenge students to find at least two more words for each root in the chart. Remind them that these words must be related in meaning; they must come from the same root, not a look-alike one with a different meaning. (Possible answers: *dictate, dictionary, dynamic, dynamite, synonym, anonymous, impose, expose, spectacles, spectacular, vertical, vertices, invisible, visor*)

Answer Key

Exercise 8

1. f
2. d
3. a
4. b
5. c

Section 29.3

Studying Word Parts and Origins

Using Roots

Learning the roots of words, their most fundamental part, will help you learn the meanings of entire groups of words. For example, if you know that the root *-script-* means "write," you have a key to the meaning of the following words: *script, manuscript, transcript, prescription, proscription,* and *postscript.*

KEY CONCEPT A **root** is the base of a word. ■

Knowing the roots of words is fundamental to developing your vocabulary. Roots have come into the English language from many sources, such as Latin and Greek (noted as L. and Gr.) or Anglo-Saxon (noted as A.S.). In the first column below, other versions of the same root are in parentheses.

SOME COMMON ROOTS		
Root and Origin	**Meaning**	**Example**
-cap- (-capt-) [L.]	to take, seize	*capt*ivate (to take hold of)
-dic- (-dict-) [L.]	to say in words	pre*dict* (to say before)
-dyna- [Gr.]	to be strong	*dyna*sty (a state of strength)
-nym- [Gr.]	to name	anto*nym* (to name as an opposite)
-pon- (-pos-) [L.]	to put, place	com*pose* (to put together)
-spec- (-spect-) [L.]	to see	*spect*ator (one who sees)
-vert- (-vers-) [L.]	to turn	in*vert* (to turn upside down)
-vid- (-vis-) [L.]	to see	*vis*ible (able to be seen)

Exercise 8 **Using Roots to Define Words** Match the words below with their definitions in the second column.

1. prospect	a. to change places
2. inversion	b. a false name
3. transpose	c. operated by the strength of water
4. pseudonym	d. a turning upside down
5. hydrodynamic	f. future outlook

TIME AND RESOURCE MANAGER

Resources
Print: Academic and Workplace Skills Activity Book, pp. 23–25
Prentice Hall Everyday Spelling, Grade 8, Chapters 4, 9, 10, 13, 15, 20, 21, 25–27, 32, 33

In-Depth Coverage	Accelerated Pace
• Cover pp. 702–705 in class. • Assign and review Exercises 8–11.	• Assign pp. 702–705 for independent student review.

Using Prefixes

KEY CONCEPT A **prefix** is one or more syllables joined to the beginning of a word to change its meaning or form a new word. ■

TEN COMMON PREFIXES		
Prefix and Origin	**Meaning**	**Example**
ad- [L.]	to, toward	*ad*here (to stick to)
dis- [L.]	away, apart	*dis*grace (to lose favor)
ex- [L.]	from, out	*ex*port (to send out)
mis- [A.S.]	wrong	*mis*lead (to lead in a wrong direction)
mono- [Gr.]	one, alone	*mono*rail (a single rail)
post- [L.]	after	*post*war (after the war)
re- [L.]	back, again	*re*view (to view again)
sub- [L.]	beneath, under	*sub*merge (to place under water)
syn- [Gr.]	with, together	*syn*onym (to name together)
un- [A.S.]	not	*un*known (unable to be determined)

As you combine prefixes with words or roots, you will see that some of them change their spellings. The root remains the same.

EXAMPLES: *ad-* ⟶ *ac-* (*ac*cept), *ap-* (*ap*ply), *as-* (*as*sume)
sub- ⟶ *suc-* (*suc*ceed), *suf-* (*suf*fix), *sup-*(*sup*port)

Exercise 9 **Using Prefixes to Form New Words** On a piece of paper, use prefixes from the chart above to create new words from the ones below. In your notebook, write the definition next to each word. Use a dictionary to check your answers.

1. syllable
2. arm
3. marine
4. place
5. read
6. thesis
7. venture
8. script
9. change
10. reliable

Challenge

With two or three of your classmates, see how many more words you can list, using the roots and prefixes on these two pages. Have a dictionary nearby to check word meanings, if necessary. Make copies of the lists for each group member to keep as a reference.

Step-by-Step Teaching Guide

Using Prefixes

1. Choose a root that can take many prefixes to form common English words, such as *pos.*
2. Write the words *compose, expose, impose, depose, suppose, repose,* and *dispose* on the chalkboard. Students have just learned that the root *pos* means "put."
3. Have them use this chart and their knowledge to define the words you have listed.
4. Challenge students to try the same thing with other roots, such as *gress.* (Possible answers: *progress, congress, egress, digress, regress*)

Answer Key

Exercise 9

1. monosyllable—a word having one syllable
2. disarm—take away weapons
3. submarine—underwater
4. misplace—put in the wrong place
5. reread—read again
6. synthesis—parts combined to make a whole
7. adventure—risky trip or undertaking
8. postscript—something added at the end of a letter or book
9. exchange—trade
10. unreliable—not dependable

Step-by-Step Teaching Guide

Using Suffixes

1. Go over the suffixes in the chart and have students give examples of other words with each suffix.
2. Explain that suffixes work the same way as prefixes to change a word's meaning; they simply come at the end of the word rather than at the beginning.

Answer Key

Exercise 10

Sample answers are given.

1. performance—act of performing; noun
2. regretful—full of regret; adjective
3. socially—in a social way; adverb
4. invention—something invented; noun
5. timidity—fear; noun

29.3

Using Suffixes

KEY CONCEPT A **suffix** is a letter, syllable, or group of syllables added to the end of a word to change its meaning or function or to form a new word. ■

TEN COMMON SUFFIXES		
Suffix and Origin	**Meaning and Example**	**Part of Speech**
-able (-ible) [L.]	capable of being: comfort*able*	adjective
-ance (-ence) [L.]	the act of: confid*ence*	noun
-cy (-acy) [Gr.]	quality of: hesitan*cy*	noun
-ful [A.S.]	full of: joy*ful*	adjective
-ist [Gr.]	a person skilled in: pian*ist*	noun
-ity [L.]	state of being: char*ity*	noun
-less [A.S.]	without, lacking: humor*less*	adjective
-ly [Gr.]	in a certain way: firm*ly*, love*ly*	adverb or adjective
-ment [L.]	result of being: amaze*ment*	noun
-tion (-ion, -sion) [L.]	state of being: ac*tion*, ten*sion*,	noun

Exercise 10 **Using Suffixes to Change Words From One Part of Speech to Another** Use the suffixes from the chart above to change the following words. Then, write a brief definition of the word you create, and include the word's new part of speech.

Original Word	New Word	Definition	Part of Speech
1. perform	?	?	?
2. regret	?	?	?
3. social	?	?	?
4. invent	?	?	?
5. timid	?	?	?

More Practice

Academic and Workplace Skills Activity Book
• pp. 23–25

ONGOING ASSESSMENT: Monitor and Reinforce

If students are having difficulty learning meanings from word parts, use one of the following options.

Option 1 Have students work in small groups to define each part of a word: root, prefix, or suffix. The group can decide on the whole word meaning after analyzing the parts.

Option 2 Have students use lists of roots, prefixes and suffixes to play a mix-and-match game. Students need to tell if the word they build is a real world and what it means.

Examining Word Origins

English is considered part of the Indo-European family of languages. Within that family, its closest relatives are other Germanic languages, such as Dutch and German. Not only is English the most widely spoken language in the Western world, it is also the most global in the number of languages from which it has borrowed. More than seventy percent of words we call English have been borrowed from other languages.

Understand Historical Influences

If English had developed in isolation, it would have fewer borrowed words. No language develops in complete isolation, however. Battles, travels, new inventions and technologies—each of these events or circumstances contributes to the growth and change of a language. In the chart below, you will see examples of new words that came into English as a result of specific historic events. What the chart does not show is the great impact of these events on the structure of English.

THE GROWTH OF ENGLISH

Events	New Words
790—Danish invasions begin	law, bylaw, window, steak, knives, happy
1066—Norman Conquest	govern, reign, court, honor, glory, army, war, battle, officer
1500's—Renaissance	describe, perfect, adventure, language, equal, color, machine

Exercise 11 **Analyzing Word Origins** Look up each of the following words in a print or electronic dictionary. Write the word on a separate sheet of paper. Then, write the language from which it comes.

1. mosquito
2. mansion
3. pork
4. squash
5. oral
6. terrestrial
7. zero
8. bungalow
9. schooner
10. balcony

Internet Tip

To find Internet sites about how other languages influenced the development of English, type "origins of English" in the query field of your search engine.

Step-by-Step Teaching Guide

Examining Word Origins

1. Read the first two paragraphs of text on this page aloud, or have students read them aloud. Discuss any questions students have.
2. Explain that Latin and Greek have also made substantial contributions to English; this is why students who are studying (or who already speak) French and Spanish will find many familiar-looking words.
3. Words from different languages that look and sound alike and mean about the same thing are called *cognates.*

Answer Key

Exercise 11

1. Latin
2. Latin
3. Latin
4. Narragansett
5. Latin
6. Latin
7. French, Italian
8. Hindi
9. origin unknown
10. Italian

Step-by-Step Teaching Guide

Starting a Personal Spelling List

1. Spelling words correctly in English is difficult for everyone, because English is not a phonetic language. Words can contain the same combination of letters but be pronounced differently. *Tough, cough, plough,* and *dough* do not rhyme, so English speakers simply have to memorize how they are spelled and pronounced.
2. Have students volunteer some words they have trouble spelling. Make sure everyone is pronouncing the words correctly. Then have students define the words and brainstorm for some memory aids for them. This class practice will help them get started on a spelling notebook like that shown in the model.

Answer Key

Exercise 12

1. laboratory
2. accidentally
3. anonymous
4. library
5. desert
6. February
7. different
8. *Separate*
9. athletes
10. allowance

Section 29.4

Improving Your Spelling

Starting a Personal Spelling List

The ability to write effectively has always been recognized as a valuable skill. One of the first steps in improving your writing is to improve your spelling. Doing so will allow people to read your work without being distracted by errors.

KEY CONCEPT Select the words you want for your personal spelling list, enter them in your notebook, and study them regularly. ■

Record Frequently Misspelled Words Set aside a special section of your notebook to list words that you frequently misspell. Look through your corrected tests, essays, and homework to find your personal problem words. Include with each word its spelling and pronunciation, a definition, and either a sentence or a memory aid.

Frequently Misspelled Words

Word	Pronunciation	Definition	Sentence/ Memory Aid
accept	ək sept′	to receive willingly	She accepts two C's.
schedule	ske′ jool	a list of times	It's a school schedule.

Technology Tip

Do an on-line search to find more "commonly misspelled words."

Exercise 12 **Adding to Your Personal Spelling List** Correct the misspelled word in each sentence below. Check your answers in a dictionary. Add any difficult words to your list.

1. Sarah loves to do experiments in the science labratory.
2. Nate accidently spilled his glass of lemonade.
3. The detective received an anonymus tip.
4. How many books did you borrow from the libary?
5. The camel is well-adapted to dessert life.
6. Every Febuary we celebrate the birthdays of presidents George Washington and Abraham Lincoln.
7. A tropical climate is very diffrent from a temperate one.
8. One book I like to recommend is *A Seperate Peace.*
9. Our best athaletes were selected for an all-star team.
10. Lily saved her allowence for a special occasion.

More Practice

Academic and Workplace Skills Activity Book
- pp. 26–30

TIME AND RESOURCE MANAGER

Resources
Print: Academic and Workplace Skills Activity Book, pp. 20–22
Prentice Hall Everyday Spelling, Grade 8, pp. 12, 38, 64, 90, 116, 142

In-Depth Coverage	Accelerated Pace
• Cover pp. 706–715 in class. • Assign and review Exercises 12–24.	• Assign pp. 706–715 for independent student review.

Studying Spelling Words

Study spelling words regularly. It helps to divide your list into small groups of five or ten words. Then, study each group for a week. As you become accustomed to the method, test yourself on larger groups of words. Include words you have already mastered and those you are in the process of learning.

KEY CONCEPT Review your spelling words each week, several times a week. ■

STEPS FOR REVIEWING PROBLEM WORDS

1. *Look* at each word carefully to notice the arrangement or pattern of the letters. Try to see the word in your mind.
2. *Pronounce* each syllable of the word to yourself.
3. *Write* the word, and check its spelling in the dictionary.
4. *Review* your list until you can write each word correctly.

Exercise 13 **Spelling Difficult Words** Write *correct* if an underlined word below is spelled correctly. If it is not, correct it. Check a dictionary. Enter misspelled words on your list.

1. Molly Pitcher was a couragous figure of the Revolution.
2. Grandma served warm apple pie for dessert.
3. Jason wrote the address on the outside of the envelope.
4. Check the calender to see when our vacation begins.
5. Dale, an expert gymnast, excels on the parallel bars.
6. The libary has a section of rare books.
7. I taught a rat to run through a maze in the labratory.
8. Those who criticize have obviously not tried it.
9. To suceed, one must keep trying.
10. We bought a used car that had low milage.

Exercise 14 **Identifying Commonly Misspelled Words** Look through your writing portfolio and tests that have been returned to you. Find words you have misspelled, and record them in your notebook. Study them. Then, have a partner test you on the words.

▶ Critical Viewing The strength of this gymnast's performance is in his good form. How does good spelling add strength to your writing? **[Relate]**

Step-by-Step Teaching Guide

Studying Spelling Words

1. Encourage students to work on their spelling with partners. They can test each other on spelling as well as definitions.
2. Urge partners to set up weekly sessions in which they work on spelling.
3. Encourage highly verbal students who are good at spelling to work with students who need more help.

Answer Key

Exercise 13

1. courageous
2. correct
3. correct
4. calendar
5. correct
6. library
7. laboratory
8. correct
9. succeed
10. mileage

Exercise 14

Keep an eye on students' work throughout the year for repeated spelling errors. Work individually with students who need help.

Critical Viewing

Relate Students may suggest that good spelling adds strength by promoting a better overall image, one that shows a careful writer.

PRENTICE HALL
Everyday Spelling

To reinforce and extend the coverage of spelling skills in this chapter, you may want to assign students lessons in *Prentice Hall Everyday Spelling*, Grade 8.

Step-by-Step Teaching Guide

Applying Spelling Rules

1. Urge students to memorize the key concept and the rules that are below it.
2. Stress a more important rule: When in doubt, use the dictionary.

Technology Tip

The spell check function on a computer will catch all *ie/ei* errors. When this happens, students also should write the words in vocabulary or spelling notebooks under a heading such as "Words I Often Misspell."

Answer Key

Exercise 15

1. ceiling
2. field
3. piece
4. hygiene
5. freight

Real-World Connection

Many people have jobs that include announcing other people's names—talk-show hosts, stadium announcers, broadcasters, and anyone presenting an award. Teachers call the roll. Learning about spelling patterns helps people understand and remember how words are pronounced. If you are unsure how a person pronounces his or her name, just ask! Everyone likes to hear his or her name spoken correctly.

29.4

Applying Spelling Rules

In addition to studying words that give you particular trouble, study rules that apply to groups of words.

Rules for *ie* and *ei*

Observing the basic rules for *ie* and *ei* words will help you. You will need to memorize certain exceptions to these rules.

KEY CONCEPTS Remember the rule: *i* before *e* except after *c* and when sounded as *ay* as in *neighbor* and *weigh*.

- When a word has a long *e* sound, use *ie*.
- When a word has a long *a* sound, use *ei*.
- When a word has a long *e* sound preceded by the letter *c*, use *ei*. ■

COMMON *ie* AND *ei* WORDS

Long *e* Sound: Use *ie*	Long *a* Sound: Use *ei*	Long *e* Sound Preceded by *c*: Use *ei*
brief	eight	ceiling
chief	freight	deceive
niece	reign	perceive
piece	sleigh	receipt
relieve	vein	receive
shield	weight	
yield		

EXCEPTIONS: either, neither, seize, science

Exercise 15 **Spelling *ie* and *ei* Words** Fill in the blanks below with either *ie* or *ei*. Check the spellings in a dictionary. Add difficult words to your personal spelling list.

1. The c _ _ ling in the room was powder blue.
2. We noticed the farmer in his f _ _ ld plowing the soil.
3. A p _ _ ce of watermelon can be very refreshing.
4. Tom is giving a nutrition report in our hyg _ _ ne class.
5. How many cars were on that fr _ _ ght train?

Technology Tip

Many word-processing programs have automatic spelling checkers that alert a writer immediately if a word is misspelled. Check to see whether your program has that function, and be sure to use it whenever you write.

More Practice

Academic and Workplace Skills Activity Book
- pp. 26–30

Adding Suffixes

Recall that a suffix is one or more syllables added to the end of a word.

KEY CONCEPT Adding a suffix often involves a spelling change in the word. ■

When adding suffixes to some words, it is necessary to change the spelling. The following summarizes the major kinds of spelling changes that can take place when a suffix is added.

Spelling changes in words ending in *y*: Use the following rules for spelling changes for words ending in *y*, paying careful attention to the rule's exceptions:

1. When adding a suffix to words ending in *y* preceded by a consonant, change *y* to *i*. Most suffixes beginning with *i* are the exception to the rule:

   ply + -able = pliable | happy + -ness = happiness
   defy + -ing = defying | cry + -ing = crying

2. For words ending in *y* preceded by a vowel, make no change when adding most suffixes. A few short words are the exceptions:

   annoy + -ance = annoyance | enjoy + -ment = enjoyment
   day + -ly = daily | pay + -ed = paid

Spelling changes in words ending in *e*: Use the following rules for spelling changes for words ending in *e*, paying careful attention to the rule's exceptions:

1. Drop the *e* when adding a suffix beginning with a vowel. The exceptions to the rule are (1) words ending in *ce* or *ge* with suffixes beginning with *a* or *o*, (2) words ending in *ee*, and (3) a few special words:

   move + -able = movable | drive + -ing = driving
   trace + -able = traceable | courage + -ous = courageous
   see + -ing = seeing | agree + -able = agreeable
   dye + -ing = dyeing | be + -ing = being

2. Make no change when adding a suffix beginning with a consonant.
   peace + -ful = peaceful | brave + -ly = bravely

   A few special words are the exceptions:
   argue + -ment = argument | judge + -ment = judgment

▲ Critical Viewing
If the *e* in *judge* is dropped in *judgment*, how might this exception to a rule apply to *acknowledge*? **[Connect]**

Step-by-Step Teaching Guide

Adding Suffixes

1. Go over the first set of sample words ending in *-y*. Go over all the examples and challenge students to volunteer more examples that follow this rule. If students give examples that don't follow the rule, ask them to explain their reasoning. Encourage students to make lists of difficult or irregular words and keep them for reference. Repeat this activity with each of the next five sets of words (they continue on to the next page).
2. Challenge students to a spelling bee. Divide the class in half and have the two teams form lines on opposite sides of the room. Beforehand, create a list of words with the suffixes shown on these two pages. Give a word to the first person on the first team. If he or she spells it correctly, the other team gets a turn. If he or she misses it, give it to the other team. Students must drop out if they miss a word. The last student left is the winner.

Critical Viewing

Connect Students may note that the *e* in *acknowledge,* which like *judge,* ends in *-dge,* may be dropped in spelling acknowledgment.

Answer Key

Exercise 16

1. valuable
2. growing
3. imaginary
4. hopeful
5. reliable
6. scarcely
7. reverence
8. business
9. beautiful
10. payment

Step-by-Step Teaching Guide

Adding Prefixes

If necessary, students can review the prefixes on page 703. Encourage them to recall what each prefix means and when to use it. Some prefixes cannot be used with certain words. Have students try following the pattern in Exercise 17 to coin words and check dictionaries to be sure they have created real words.

Answer Key

Exercise 17

1. incomplete
2. misread
3. dissolve
4. unusual
5. refill
6. disappear
7. unfortunate
8. invisible
9. disappoint
10. unnoticed

Critical Viewing

Analyze Students may suggest that playing *spelling* games in the *reference* library is a popular activity.

29.4

Doubling the final consonant before suffixes: Use the following rules for cases in which a final consonant may or may not change, paying careful attention to the rule's exceptions:

1. For words ending in a consonant + vowel + consonant in a stressed syllable, double the final consonant when adding a suffix beginning with a vowel. The exceptions to the rules are (1) words ending in *x* or *w* and (2) words in which the stress changes after the suffix is added:

mud´ + -y = mud´ dy	submit´ + -ed = submit´ ted
mix + -ing = mixing	row + -ing = rowing
refer´ + -ence = ref´ erence	confer´ + -ence = con´ ference

2. For words ending in a consonant + vowel + consonant in an unstressed syllable, make no change when adding a suffix beginning with a vowel. There are no major exceptions to this rule.

▲ Critical Viewing
Use words ending in *-ing* and *-ence* to describe the activity in this scene.
[Analyze]

Exercise 16 **Making New Words With Suffixes** Make new words by combining root words and suffixes. Check the spellings in a dictionary, and add difficult words to your list.

1. value + -able
2. grow + -ing
3. imagine + -ary
4. hope + -ful
5. rely + -able
6. scarce + -ly
7. revere + -ence
8. busy + -ness
9. beauty + -ful
10. pay + -ment

Adding Prefixes

When a prefix is added to a word, the spelling of the root word remains the same.

EXAMPLES: re- + cover = recover
un- + necessary = unnecessary
dis- + satisfied = dissatisfied

Exercise 17 **Using Prefixes** Combine the prefixes and root words below to make new words.

1. in- + complete
2. mis- + read
3. dis- + solve
4. un- + usual
5. re- + fill
6. dis- + appear
7. un- + fortunate
8. in- + visible
9. dis- + appoint
10. un- + noticed

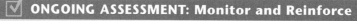

ONGOING ASSESSMENT: Monitor and Reinforce

If students are finding spelling certain words challenging, use one of the following options.

Option 1 Keep a list of words students find difficult to spell correctly. Have an "honors" spelling bee with these words.

Option 2 Start a class nonsense story. Each day add another sentence or two that includes words students find difficult. Have volunteers write each difficult word on the chalkboard.

Using Memory Aids

In English, many spelling rules do not apply, mainly because so many of our words come from different languages. Some words must be memorized. Try making up sentences to help you remember the correct spelling of difficult words.

KEY CONCEPT Use memory aids to help remember difficult spelling words. ■

You can associate the troublesome part of a word with a word you know or find a short word within a longer word.

EXAMPLES: The lib*rar*y has *rare* books.
A *rat* is in the labo*rat*ory.

Exercise 18 **Making Memory Aids** Make up a memory aid for each of the following words.

1. accidentally	3. amateur	5. attendance
2. believe	4. clothes	

Understanding the Influence of Other Languages and Cultures

Because more than 70 percent of English words are borrowed from other languages, it is very difficult to make a set of rules for spelling and pronunciation. For this reason, English uses a wide variety of letters to spell certain "silent letters." When you are writing, use a dictionary to confirm the spelling of any word about which you are unsure.

KEY CONCEPT Because other languages contribute to the spelling and pronunciation of words in English, different letters may be used in different words to spell the same sound. ■

EXAMPLES:	puff	phone	giraffe
	cough	fuel	jump

Exercise 19 **Choose the Correct Spelling** Select the correct word in each group below. Check your answers in a dictionary. Enter problem words on your personal list.

1. skuash	squash	skwash
2. filosophy	philosofy	philosophy
3. enouff	enouph	enough
4. forin	foreign	phoreign
5. sizzers	scissors	sissers

More Practice
Academic and Workplace Skills Activity Book
• pp. 26–30

Answer Key

Exercise 18

Answers will vary. Samples are given.

1. I *accidentally* spilled *all* the milk.
2. Do not *believe* a *lie.*
3. The *amateur* gymnast practiced with her *mate.*
4. *Clothes* are often made of *cloth.*
5. *At ten, dance.*

Exercise 19

1. squash
2. philosophy
3. enough
4. foreign
5. scissors

Step-by-Step Teaching Guide

Forming Plurals

1. Have students try to find additional words that follow each rule in the chart
2. Remind students to be especially careful with exceptions to the rules and with plurals that change one letter to another. (*y* to *i*, *f* to *v*)
3. Explain that even regular plurals have some irregularities. (piano and other musical instruments)
4. Explain that irregular plurals really follow no rules. Looking them up in a dictionary is best.

Integrating Dictionary Skills

The entry for *zero* in the dictionary gives two plural forms: *zeros* and *zeroes.* Both are correct, but the first spelling is preferred. Students should always choose the preferred (first) spelling of a word.

Section 29.5

Using Basic Spelling Rules

Forming Plurals

The plural form of a noun indicates "more than one." The plural forms can be either regular or irregular.

KEY CONCEPT The plural of regular nouns is formed by adding *-s* or *-es.* Most nouns have regular plural forms. ■

The spelling of some regular nouns changes in the plural form. The chart below lists some examples of words that change slightly.

FORMING REGULAR PLURALS

Word Ending	Rule	Examples
-s, -ss, -x, -z, -zz, -sh, -ch	Add *-es.*	circus, circuses dress, dresses tax, taxes wish, wishes bench, benches buzz, buzzes
-o preceded by a consonant	Add *-es.*	echo, echoes EXCEPTIONS: piano, pianos (and other musical terms)
-o preceded by a vowel	Add *-s.*	patio, patios
-y preceded by a consonant	Change *y* to *i* and add *-es.*	city, cities enemy, enemies
-y preceded by a vowel	Add *-s.*	key, keys
-ff	Add *-s.*	staff, staffs cuff, cuffs
-fe	Change *f* to *v* and add *-es.*	wife, wives knife, knives
-f	Add *-s.* OR Change *f* to *v* and add *-es.*	proof, proofs leaf, leaves wolf, wolves

Learn More

To learn more about making verbs and pronouns agree with plural nouns, turn to Chapter 24.

KEY CONCEPT Use a dictionary to look up the correct spelling of irregular plurals. Memorize them. ■

IRREGULAR PLURALS

Singular Forms	Ways of Forming Plurals	Plural Forms
ox	Add *-en.*	oxen
child	Add *-ren.*	children
tooth, mouse, woman	Change one or more letters.	teeth, mice, women
radius, focus, alumnus	Change *-us* to *-i.*	radii, foci, alumni
alumna	Change *-a* to *-ae.*	alumnae
crisis, emphasis	Change *-is* to *-es.*	crises, emphases
medium, datum, curriculum	Change *-um* to *-a.*	media, data, curricula
phenomenon, criterion	Change *-on* to *-a.*	phenomena, criteria
deer, sheep	plural form same as singular	deer, sheep
	plural form only	scissors, slacks

Most one-word compound nouns have regular plural forms. If one part of the compound noun is irregular, the plural form will also be irregular.

EXAMPLES: armchair, armchairs (regular)
snowman, snowmen (irregular)

For most compound nouns written with hyphens or as separate words, form the plural by making the modified word plural. The modified word is the word being described.

EXAMPLES: mother-in-law, mothers-in-law
field mouse, field mice

Exercise 20 **Writing Plurals** Write the plural form for each of the following words. Use a dictionary if necessary. Add any difficult words to your personal spelling list.

1. veto
2. house
3. ax
4. tariff
5. thief
6. turkey
7. crisis
8. wolf
9. activity
10. crash

More Practice

Academic and Workplace Skills Activity Book
• pp. 26–30

Customize for *Verbal/Linguistic Learners*

The chart on this page shows ten ways to form plurals. Challenge students to find other words that form their plurals in some of these ways. (Possible answers: *goose/geese, man/men, thesis/theses, memorandum/memoranda, fish/fish*)

Answer Key

Exercise 20

1. vetoes
2. houses
3. axes
4. tariffs
5. thieves
6. turkeys
7. crises
8. wolves
9. activities
10. crashes

Step-by-Step Teaching Guide

Spelling Homophones

1. Go over the four groups of homophones and their definitions with students.
2. Encourage students to memorize them so as to avoid making careless errors.

Customize for *Less Advanced Students*

Have students make a set of flashcards. Each card should have a homophone such as *whose* or *two* on one side and its definition on the other. The cards can be kept in class for everyone's use. Students can choose partners and use the cards to practice.

Customize for *Gifted/Talented Students*

Explain that homonyms are words that are spelled the same but have different meanings, such as *clog:* a wooden shoe and something stuck in a drain. Challenge a group of students to make a list of possible homonyms.

Answer Key

Exercise 21

1. their
2. pair
3. through
4. two, to
5. Who's

Exercise 22

Answers will vary. Samples are given.

1. **a.** Sew on the button.
   b. Use the potholder, so you won't burn your hands.
2. **a.** Be careful where you walk when your feet are bare.
   b. The bear is a large mammal.
3. **a.** Let's go for a sail in my new boat.
   b. Let's go to the sale and pick up a bargain.
4. **a.** It's dark outside at night.
   b. The knight wears armor.
5. **a.** The sum of 5 + 6 = 11.
   b. Some of my best friends will be at the party.

29.5

Spelling Homophones

KEY CONCEPT **Homophones** are words that sound the same but have different meanings and may have different spellings. ■

Learn the homophones below, and be careful to spell and use them correctly in your writing.

EXAMPLES:

their: a possessive pronoun that means "belonging to them"
they're: a contraction for *they are*
there: a place word or sentence starter, as in "There are five cookies"

threw: past tense of the verb *throw,* meaning "to cause to fly through the air"
through: a preposition that means "in one side and out the other"

who's: a contraction for *who is*
whose: a possessive pronoun that means "that or those belonging to whom"

to: begins a prepositional phrase or an infinitive
too: also
two: a number

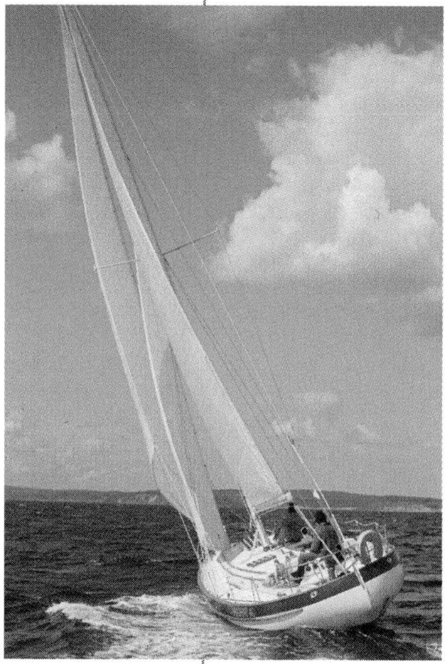

▲ Critical Viewing *The boat was on sale.* If you were to rewrite this sentence, changing *on* to *in full,* what else would change? **[Apply]**

Exercise 21 **Spelling Homophones** Select the correct word from each pair in parentheses below. Check your answers in a dictionary.

1. Are you going to (their, they're) party?
2. I would like a (pear, pair) of blue shoes.
3. The ball flew (threw, through) the window.
4. I have (to, two, too) sisters who like (to, two, too) help our mother.
5. (Who's, Whose) going to clean up the mess?

Exercise 22 **Writing Sentences With Homophones** Write a sentence for each lettered word in each numbered pair below. Check a dictionary to make sure that you are spelling and using each word correctly.

1. (a) sew (b) so
2. (a) bare (b) bear
3. (a) sail (b) sale
4. (a) night (b) knight
5. (a) sum (b) some

More Practice

Academic and Workplace Skills Activity Book
- pp. 31–32

Critical Viewing

Apply Most students will recognize the difference between "on sale" (available to buy) and "in full sail" (all sails open to catch the wind).

Proofreading and Using References

Proofread all your written work to make sure that you have eliminated all spelling errors. If you are unsure whether you have spelled a word correctly, double-check it in a reference.

KEY CONCEPT Use dictionaries, electronic spell-checkers, and glossaries to check spellings. ■

Exercise 23 **Proofreading Sentences** Copy and proofread the following sentences. Correct any words that are written incorrectly. Use a dictionary, spell-checker, or glossary to confirm the spelling of any words about which you are unsure. If a sentence contains no errors, write *correct.*

1. Nate accidently spilled his glass of milk.
2. Our teacher was absent, so we had a substatute.
3. I wonder wheather Jennifer will win the race.
4. What foriegn languages can you speak?
5. The captain of the ship wore a blue uniform.

Exercise 24 **Proofreading a Paragraph** Copy and proofread the following paragraph. Correct any words that are written incorrectly. Check the spelling of any words about which you are unsure.

For Joanna's fiffteenth brithday, she hoped to have a skating party. All of her freinds had there own skates. Sum of them had taken lesons with a perfesional skater. Jennifer was very exsited. Her mother had asksed her friends to meat at the rink. She beleived that everone new where the rink was. By five o'clock nowon was there. She desided to call her best friend, Martha. Martha ansered the fone on the second ring. "Hi, Joanna!" Martha said, "I can't weight for you're party tomorrow." Joanna realised that she had come to her own party a hole day early!

Reflecting on Your Vocabulary and Spelling Skills

Think about what you have learned by answering the following questions:

- Which of these techniques do you find most effective for studying spelling words?
- Which do you find most helpful for studying vocabulary words?
- What do these techniques have in common? How are they different?

Step-by-Step Teaching Guide

Proofreading and Using References

1. Students may complain, "How can we look up a word when we don't know how to spell it?" Encourage them to sound out the word carefully and make their best guess. Sometimes they will have to try two or three different pages in the dictionary before they find the word. One way to be sure is to check the definition.
2. Encourage students to pay attention to patterns in spelling and sound. For instance, a single *c* can be hard or soft, but a *cc* is always pronounced *ks (success).* If the letter combination *gn* occurs within a syllable, the *g* is silent *(foreign, bologna);* if there is a break between syllables between these two letters, it is pronounced the way it looks *(magnet).*
3. Remind students that electronic spell-checkers won't catch every mistake. It will not correct *The seventeen-inning game took almost all knight* because although the wrong homophone was used, it is a correctly spelled English word. Encourage students to read over their work; their human eyes and brains can catch mistakes no computer will notice.

Answer Key

Exercise 23

1. Nate accidentally spilled his glass of milk.
2. Our teacher was absent, so we had a substitute.
3. I wonder whether Jennifer will win the race.
4. What foreign languages can you speak?
5. correct as is

continued

Answer Key continued

Exercise 24

For Joanna's fifteenth birthday, she hoped to have a skating party. All of her friends had their own skates. Some of them had taken lessons with a professional skater. Joanna was very excited. Her mother had asked her friends to meet at the rink. She believed that everyone knew where the rink was. By five o'clock no one was there. She decided to call her best friend, Martha. Martha answered the phone on the second ring. "Hi, Joanna!" Martha said. "I can't wait for your party tomorrow." Joanna realized that she had come to her own party a whole day early!

Lesson Objectives

- To use context clues to determine the meaning of words.

Step-by-Step Teaching Guide

Using Context to Determine Word Meaning

Teaching Resources: Standardized Test Preparation Workbook, pp. 57–58

1. Review with students the strategies on page 696 that they can use to determine the meaning of a word from its context.
2. Draw students' attention to the Test Tip. Remind them to always determine the meaning of a word as it is used in the given passage, and not just to assume they know the meaning of the word. Some words have multiple meanings. Sample 2 is a good example of this.

Standardized Test Preparation Workshop

Using Context to Determine Word Meaning

The questions on standardized tests often require you to discern the meaning of a word using its context. Using the group of words surrounding an underlined term or phrase will help you determine the meaning of idioms, expressions, words with multiple meanings, figurative language, and specialized and technical terms.

The following sample test items will provide practice answering these types of questions.

Test Tip

Although you may recognize an underlined word, it does not necessarily mean you know its definition. Some words have multiple meanings. Read the passage carefully and choose a word that *best defines* the underlined word in the context of the passage.

Sample Test Items	Answers and Explanations
Directions: Read the passage. Then, read each question that follows the passage. Decide which is the best answer to each question. Making collages, art students study proportion. They do so by comparing items in the collage in relation to their size and number. 1 In this passage, the word proportion means— A equality between ratios B relationship between sizes of items C similarity D relationship between colors	The correct answer to item 1 is *B, relationship between sizes of items*. The second sentence provides a context clue for the definition of *proportion* by explaining how students study it.
2 The word relation in this passage means— F family member G narration or telling H connection J opposition	The correct answer to item 2 is *H, connection*. Although two of the other definitions are correct meanings of the word, they are not appropriate in this sentence. The words *comparing items* provide a context clue for the definition of *proportion*.

TEST-TAKING TIP

Remind students not to choose the definition of a word without checking the context. In sample 2, they might choose F in error.

Practice 1 **Directions:** Read the passage. Then, read each question that follows the passage. Decide which is the best answer to each question.

You know this old adage: "Every cloud has a silver lining." These words mean that from an apparent disaster, good things may result. The veracity of this is shown by the benefits that came from what seemed to be a monumental disaster—the Great Fire of London!

1 The word adage in this passage means—
- **A** poem
- **B** an accepted saying
- **C** old person
- **D** signature

2 In this passage, the term apparent means—
- **F** seeming
- **G** family
- **H** unnecessary
- **J** unimportant

3 The word veracity in this passage means—
- **A** large metropolitan area
- **B** confusion
- **C** error
- **D** truth

4 The word monumental in this passage means—
- **F** frightening
- **G** huge
- **H** high
- **J** honoring

Practice 2 **Directions:** Read the passage. Then, read each question that follows the passage. Decide which is the best answer to each question.

My favorite Impressionist artist is Mary Cassatt. With short strokes of color, she captured the way light affects a subject. Mother and child appear soft and gentle in her renderings.

1 In this passage, the term Impressionist means—
- **A** type of painter
- **B** cartoonist
- **C** one who copies
- **D** impressive

2 The word strokes in this passage means—
- **F** blows
- **G** marks made by a tool
- **H** flatteries
- **J** rowing

3 In this passage, the term subject means—
- **A** course of study
- **B** under authority or control
- **C** main topic or theme of a work
- **D** perception

4 The word renderings in this passage means—
- **F** submissions
- **G** paintings
- **H** declarations
- **J** translation

Answer Key

Practice 1

1. B
2. F
3. D
4. G

Practice 2

1. A
2. G
3. C
4. G

Chapter 30 Time and Resource Manager

In-Depth Lesson Plan

	LESSON FOCUS	PRINT AND MEDIA RESOURCES
DAY 1	**Reading Methods and Tools** Students vary their approaches to reading depending on the text and purpose. They experiment with different ways of organizing notes on what they read (pp. 718–724).	**Teaching Resources:** *Academic and Workplace Skills Activity Book,* pp. 34–37
DAY 2	**Reading Nonfiction Critically** Students learn to question, interpret, and comprehend nonfiction (pp. 725–730).	**Teaching Resources:** *Academic and Workplace Skills Activity Book,* pp. 38–43
DAY 3	**Reading Literary Writings** Students become active readers of fiction, poetry, drama, and tales (pp. 731–735).	**Teaching Resources:** *Academic and Workplace Skills Activity Book,* pp. 44–50
DAY 4	**Reading From Varied Sources** Students discuss a variety of texts and possible purposes for and methods of reading them (pp. 736–737).	**Teaching Resources:** *Academic and Workplace Skills Activity Book,* p. 51

Accelerated Lesson Plan

	LESSON FOCUS	PRINT AND MEDIA RESOURCES
DAY 1	**Reading Methods and Tools** Students vary their approaches to reading depending on the text and purpose. They experiment with different ways of organizing notes on what they read (pp. 718–724).	**Teaching Resources:** *Academic and Workplace Skills Activity Book,* pp. 34–37
DAY 2	**Reading Nonfiction Critically** Students learn to question, comprehend, and interpret nonfiction (pp. 702–715).	**Teaching Resources:** *Academic and Workplace Skills Activity Book,* pp. 38–43
DAY 3	**Reading Literary Writings and Texts From Varied Sources** Students become active readers of fiction, drama, poetry, and tales. They discuss a variety of texts and approaches to reading them (pp. 731–737).	**Teaching Resources:** *Academic and Workplace Skills Activity Book,* pp. 44–51

Options for Adapting Lesson Plans

HOMEWORK
Have students complete any stage of the lesson for homework.

FEATURES
Extend coverage with the Standardized Test Preparation Workshop (pp. 738–739).

TECHNOLOGY
Students can complete any stage of the lesson on computer. Have them print out their completed work.

SPELLING
To teach spelling skills in conjunction with academic and workplace skills, work through *Prentice Hall Everyday Spelling,* Grade 8, Chapter 34, as you cover this *Writing and Grammar* chapter.

INTEGRATED SKILLS COVERAGE

Viewing and Representing
Critical Viewing, SE pp. 718, 727, 731, 735, 737

Speaking and Listening
SE p. 729; Listening to Poetry, ATE p. 733

Vocabulary
Derivations, ATE p. 724

Technology
SE pp. 722, 723, 732

Workplace Skills
Reading Various Texts, ATE p. 737

ASSESSMENT SUPPORT

Standardized Test Preparation Workshop, SE pp. 738–739

Standardized Test Preparation Workbook, pp. 59–60

Writing Assessment and Portfolio Management

MEETING INDIVIDUAL NEEDS

Less Advanced Students See Ongoing Assessments ATE pp. 724, 729, 735

More Advanced Students ATE p. 729

Visual/Spatial Learners ATE p. 723

BLOCK SCHEDULING

Pacing Suggestions
For 90-minute Blocks
- Have students complete the chapter in a single class period.

Professional Development Support
- ***How to Manage Instruction in the Block*** This teaching resource provides management and activity suggestions.

MEDIA AND TECHNOLOGY

For the Teacher
- ***Resource Pro*** **CD-ROM**

WRITING AND GRAMMAR ON-LINE

***iText* Interactive Text (On-line or on CD-ROM)**
- Easily navigable instruction with interactive Revision Checkers
- Full use of e-rater™, the essay-scoring system (on-line only)

Companion Web Site PHSchool.com
- Scoring rubrics with models (use Web Code eck-8001)

See the Go On-line! feature, SE p. iii.

CHAPTER 30
READING SKILLS

Lesson Objectives

1. To learn how to use sections and features of textbooks.
2. To use reading strategies.
3. To interpret graphic organizers.
4. To comprehend nonfiction.
5. To distinguish fact from opinion.
6. To identify the author's purpose.
7. To apply forms of reasoning.
8. To analyze the text.
9. To apply reading strategies to fiction, drama, poetry, and tales from the oral tradition.
10. To learn how to read various sources.

Critical Viewing

Analyze Students may suggest that the natural setting, with its silence and direct sunlight, might make reading an enjoyable experience.

Chapter 30 Reading Skills

▲ Critical Viewing What details in this photograph make reading look like an appealing and enjoyable experience? **[Analyze]**

Reading in Everyday Life

Knowing how to read well is important to success in school and in life. Being a good reader means more than simply finding and remembering facts in books. It also means applying critical thinking skills to what you read. This chapter will help you to improve your skills in reading all kinds of books.

TIME AND RESOURCE MANAGER

Resources
Print: Academic and Workplace Skills Activity Book, pp.34–37

In-Depth Coverage	Accelerated Pace
• Cover pp. 719–724 in class. • Assign and review Exercises 1–5.	• Assign pp. 719–724 for independent student review.

Section 30.1

Reading Methods and Tools

Many books—particularly textbooks—have a number of features that provide important information related to the main content of the book. Learning to use these features effectively will help you to improve your understanding of the content.

Using Sections in Textbooks

Most textbooks have a number of special sections located at the front and back of the book. Learn what these sections are and how to use them so that you take full advantage of the material in your textbooks.

KEY CONCEPT Use the special sections of your textbook to become familiar with its contents. ■

Table of Contents The table of contents is at the front of your textbook. It lists the units, chapters, and sections of the book, as well as the pages where each one begins.

Table of Contents

UNIT ONE: MATTER: BUILDING BLOCKS of the UNIVERSE..2

CHAPTER 1 Exploring Physical Science..........................4

1–1 Science—Not Just for Scientists...........6

1–2 The Scientific Method—A Way of Problem Solving............................11

1–3 The Metric System............................20

1–4 Tools of Measurement.......................26

1–5 Safety in the Science Laboratory..........31

Chapter Introduction and Summary A chapter introduction tells you the main ideas of the chapter. The chapter summary, appearing at the end of the chapter, reviews the main points and other important information.

Glossary The glossary, located at the back of the book, is a list of terms with definitions. Generally, the glossary includes specialized terms that are used within the textbook. These terms are listed alphabetically.

Appendix The appendix is also found at the back of the textbook. It contains useful additional or supplementary material. Some materials that may be found in an appendix include charts, maps, formulas, timelines, essays, and biographical or historical information.

Index This is the final section of the textbook. The index lists alphabetically all the subjects covered in the book and tells on which pages the information can be found.

PREPARE and ENGAGE

Interest GRABBER Ask students what kinds of things they read for fun and why. List their answers on the chalkboard. Ask why no one mentioned a textbook.

Activate Prior Knowledge

Display on an overhead projector textbook pages that contain many different elements. Ask students to identify as many as they can. They do not need to know formal terminology, such as running foot. "Line at the bottom that tells what chapter" is fine.

TEACH

Step-by-Step Teaching Guide

Using Sections in Textbooks

Using this textbook as an example, ask students to locate and point out the various sections. Remind students that not all textbooks have every section listed here. This is simply a general indication of what students can expect from a textbook.

Step-by-Step Teaching Guide

Using Features of Textbooks

1. Ask students to close their books, keeping their place. Then have them reopen the books and look at these two pages for ten seconds before they close the books again. Ask students what the two pages were about and how they know. (Students should recall some of the main headings and subheads, because their large, bold type makes them stand out on the page and grab the attention.) Point out that the heads clearly indicate the contents of each section of the page.
2. Have students skim this chapter for exercises and illustrations. Point out that these can occur anywhere in a textbook. Exercises may be placed at the end of a chapter, or they may be placed throughout the section, after each skill as it is taught.
3. Emphasize the usefulness of reading captions. Show students a history textbook, in which portraits of key people and works of fine art may illustrate points being made in the text. Without reading the captions, students would not know who the people were or what the artworks had to do with the period being discussed in the text.

Answer Key

Exercise 1

Answers will vary depending on textbook choice.

Exercise 2

Answers will vary depending on textbook choice.

30.1

Using Features of Textbooks

In addition to using the special sections of your textbooks, you should use the textbook's special features to help you read and study the material.

KEY CONCEPT Use the special features of your textbook to aid your reading and studying. ■

Titles, Headings, and Subheadings Most titles, headings, and subheadings are printed in large, heavy type and give you an idea of what the material is about. They also divide the material into sections so you can learn it more easily.

Questions and Exercises Located at the end of the chapter, questions and exercises help you to retain the information you have read.

Pictures and Captions Pictures can make a confusing idea clearer. A caption next to a picture provides information describing the picture.

Exercise 1 **Examining the Sections of a Textbook** Look at one of your textbooks, and follow the directions given below.

1. Read the table of contents. How many units and chapters does the textbook contain?
2. Does your textbook have a glossary? If so, write the definitions of three unusual words.
3. If there is an appendix, tell what information it contains.
4. Pick one subject covered in the textbook. Then, list all the information covered on this topic by using the index.
5. Pick one chapter in the book. Read the introduction, and list the main points that will be made in the chapter.

More Practice

Academic and Workplace Skills Activity Book
• p. 35

Exercise 2 **Examining the Features of a Textbook** Look at one of your textbooks, and answer the following questions.

1. How many headings and subheadings does the first chapter contain? Describe their sizes and colors.
2. How does the size of the headings help you figure out the relationships between topics?
3. Is there a chapter introduction or a chapter summary? What information can be learned from these?
4. Does the chapter have questions and exercises? What can you learn from these?
5. Find three pictures in the textbook that have captions. Describe how the captions explain the pictures. What information in the text does each picture help to explain?

Using Reading Strategies

Three strategies you can use to increase your understanding of the material you read are varying your reading style, learning Question-Answer Relationships, and using the SQ4R method.

KEY CONCEPT Use reading strategies to help you get a better understanding of the material you read. ■

Varying Your Reading Style The three reading styles are *skimming, scanning,* and *close reading*—each used for different purposes. Choose the reading style that best suits your purpose.

Skimming a text means looking it over quickly to get a general idea of its contents. When you skim, look for highlighted or bold type, headings, and topic sentences.

Scanning involves looking the text over to find specific information. When you scan, look for words related to your topic or purpose for reading.

Close reading is reading the material carefully to understand and remember its ideas, to find relationships between the ideas, and to draw conclusions about what you read.

Use Question-Answer Relationships (QARs) There are four general types of questions that you should learn how to answer properly. By getting into the habit of asking and answering these four types of questions, you will also improve your reading skills.

FOUR QUESTION-ANSWER RELATIONSHIPS

RIGHT THERE
The answer is right there in the text, usually in one or two sentences. To answer this question, scan the text to locate specific information.

THINK AND SEARCH
The answer is in the text, but you need to think about the question's answer and then search the text for the evidence to support it.

AUTHOR AND YOU
The answer is not just in the text. To answer this question, think about what the author has said, what you already know, and how these fit together.

ON YOUR OWN
The answer is, for the most part, not in the text. To answer this question, you need to draw from your own experiences. You can, however, revise or expand your answer based on your reading.

Step-by-Step Teaching Guide

Using Reading Strategies

1. Point out the relationship between reading style and purpose. A student using an encyclopedia to write a report on national parks would read closely. To find out about Yellowstone, he or she would skim, looking for a subhead. Then, to find out Yellowstone's area, he or she would scan the text for numbers.
2. Choose a story that all students have read, such as Garrison Keillor's "Something From the Sixties." Have students suggest questions that will fit into each of the four categories described. (Possible questions: Right there: Who are the main characters? Think and search: What is the son's problem, and how do you know? Author and you: Did the author enjoy the sixties? Support your answer with evidence from the text. On your own: What have you saved from when you were younger? Why?)

continued

Step-by-Step Teaching Guide continued

3. The SQ4R method is useful for a book that students are reading for study or research. When studying or researching, it is not necessary to read an entire book closely, because not every section of it will be relevant to the topic. Students need to use the first two steps to determine whether a book will be useful to them. The next four steps will help them get what they need out of the book.

Answer Key

Exercise 3

Answers may vary.

Exercise 4

Answers will vary.

30.1

Use the SQ4R Method Once you have identified and examined the special sections and features of your textbooks, you can use this knowledge to help you study better. In the SQ4R method described below, you Survey, Question, Read, Record, Recite, and Review. Use this method to help you focus on your reading and to assist you in recalling information.

THE SIX STAGES OF SQ4R

Survey	Look over the material you are going to read for these features: chapter titles, headings, subheadings, introduction, summary, and questions or exercises.
Question	Ask questions about what information might be covered under each heading. Ask the questions *Who? What? When? Where?* and *Why?*
Read	Search for the answers to the questions you asked in the previous step.
Record	Take notes to remember the information better. List the main ideas and major details.
Recite	Aloud or silently, recall the questions and their related answers.
Review	Review the material on a regular basis, using some or all of the steps above.

Exercise 3 **Writing QAR Questions and Using Reading Styles to Answer Them** Using the QAR method described on page 721, write and answer the four general types of questions for your next reading assignment. Use the various reading styles: *Scan* the text to answer the Right There question. *Skim* the text to answer the Think and Search question, and *closely read* the text to prepare your answer for the Author and You question.

Exercise 4 **Using the SQ4R Method** Use the SQ4R method to study a chapter or section of a textbook. Then, write a brief summary describing how the SQ4R method helped you to learn and remember the information.

Technology Tip

If you are reading an article on-line, you can use the software's search feature to find key words in the text.

More Practice

Academic and Workplace Skills Activity Book
- p. 36

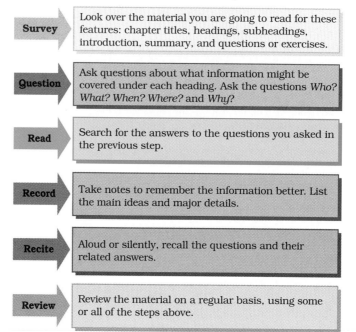

Using Graphic Organizers

A graphic organizer is used to summarize information and to show relationships among ideas or details. Because the information is organized in a chart or diagram, the graphic organizer gives a quick snapshot of the subject. Before you make a graphic organizer, think about the subject. How are its parts related? Choose a format that will show those relationships.

KEY CONCEPT Use graphic organizers to help you understand the relationships among the ideas in a text. ■

Timeline A timeline shows when events occurred. This graphic organizer is a good way to perceive the time between events and the order in which they occurred. Start your timeline by writing the beginning event in the box at the top. The final event is written at the bottom. The horizontal lines are for the events that have occurred between the initial and the final events. On the left, write the events. On the right, record the dates or times when the events took place. In the box at the top, give the unit of time you are using (years, days, minutes).

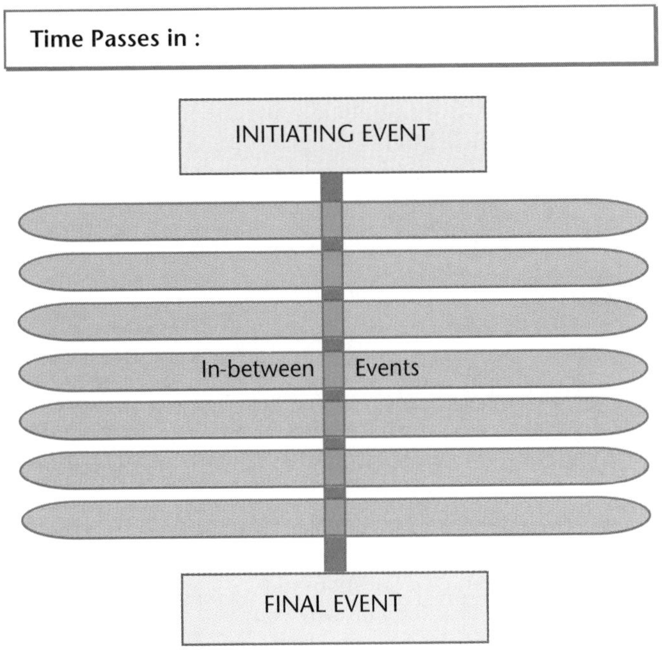

Technology Tip

Some computer applications will create graphic organizers for you.

Step-by-Step Teaching Guide

Using Graphic Organizers

Have students look through this chapter at the various graphic organizers—charts, diagrams, and so on. Ask students to pick some at random and describe their purposes. Have students discuss how a graphic representation differs from a verbal description of the same concept and what it can tell or show them that a verbal explanation cannot.

Customize for *Visual/Spatial Learners*

Have each student go through this chapter and select any concept not illustrated with a graphic organizer. Challenge them to design their own graphic organizer to teach the concept they have chosen. Students can draw their diagrams or tables by hand, or they can use computers. Remind them to include any text needed to explain the graphic organizer. It can include sections to be filled out, or it can be a complete illustration of the concept. Finally, students can use their graphic organizers to teach the concepts to small groups of classmates.

Integrating Vocabulary Skills

Herringbone The herringbone organizer gets its name from the skeleton of a herring, which has two sets of bones slanting away from its spinal column. Students have probably seen the herringbone pattern in woven woolen fabrics like tweeds and in brickwork.

Answer Key

Exercise 5

Answers will vary.

30.1

Herringbone Organizer

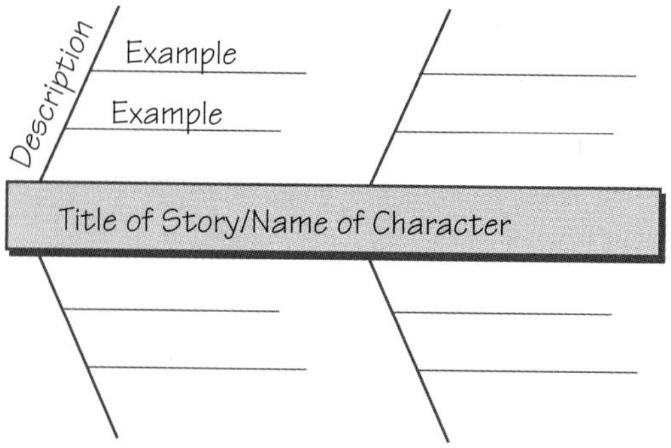

Use a herringbone organizer to organize details around a central idea, such as character development, or to show the multiple causes of a complex event. If you were going to track development, you could use the herringbone this way: Write the name of the character on the center line. Next, on the top left diagonal spine, write a statement that describes a quality of the character. Then, in the attached horizontal lines, record examples of actions or feelings that demonstrate this quality. Continue the process by examining another quality of the character.

Question-and-Answer Chart Use this graphic organizer to help you identify important ideas in your reading by asking questions such as: *Who* is the main character in the piece? *What* is the relationship between two events? *When* and *where* does an action take place? *Why* did a character do or say that? To make your question-and-answer chart, write the subject you want to learn more about in the center. Then, in the surrounding boxes, write the answers to your questions.

QUESTION-AND-ANSWER CHART

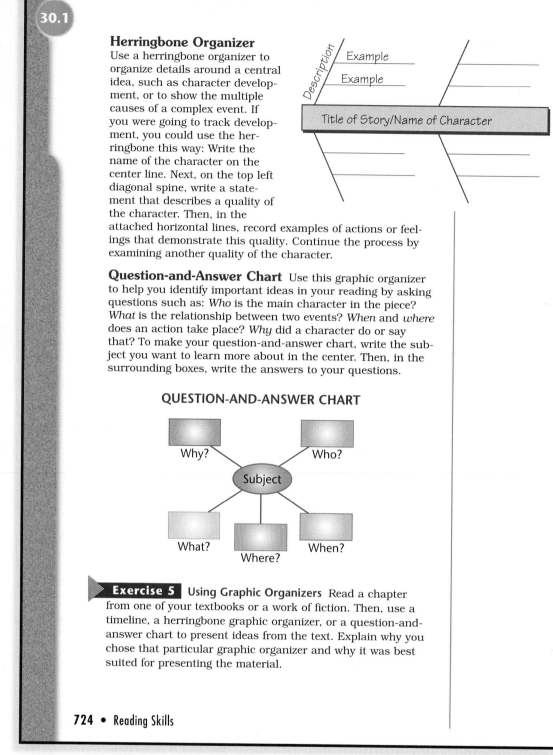

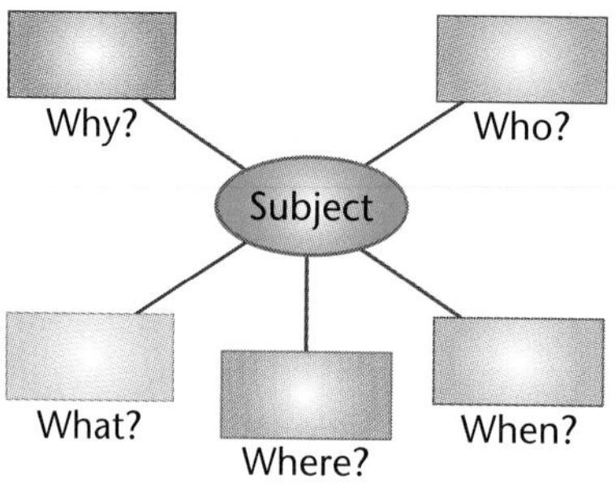

Exercise 5 **Using Graphic Organizers** Read a chapter from one of your textbooks or a work of fiction. Then, use a timeline, a herringbone graphic organizer, or a question-and-answer chart to present ideas from the text. Explain why you chose that particular graphic organizer and why it was best suited for presenting the material.

ONGOING ASSESSMENT: Monitor and Reinforce

If students have trouble using reading strategies or constructing graphic organizers, try one of the following options.

Option 1 Assign a short reading and have them apply the QAR method. Have the students write out the questions and then answers. Then have the students pair up to check each other's answers.	**Option 2** Using the same short reading, have students identify important ideas in the text by constructing a Question-and-Answer Chart. You may want to put the students into groups to discuss their findings.

Section 30.2

Reading Nonfiction Critically

When you read nonfiction critically, you examine and question the ideas the author presents in the text. You learn to distinguish between fact and opinion, to identify the author's purpose, and to recognize when language is being used to distort your understanding of the text.

Comprehending Nonfiction

The first step in reading a text critically is to gain a general understanding of the material. To do so, you need to find and interpret key information, determine the author's purpose, and consider the relationship of the material to the topic you're studying.

KEY CONCEPT Comprehending nonfiction involves understanding the author's purpose as well as the information presented in the writing. ■

These strategies will help you comprehend nonfiction works:

Identify Main Points and Details The main points are the most important ideas in the work. Details are the facts and examples the author uses to support each point.

Interpret What You Read Use the main ideas and major details to help you paraphrase, or state in your own words, the information in the text. Restating the information will help you to remember how ideas relate to one another.

Identify the Author's Purpose in Writing Once you have a general idea of the content of the text, the next step is to determine the author's purpose. You can do this by examining the writer's choice of words and details (how things are said, and what is described). As you continue to read, look for additional clues that support this purpose.

Respond to What You Have Read Think about your own feelings about the topic. Consider how the information relates to the subject you are studying. Consider how you might apply this new knowledge to your life.

Exercise 6 **Comprehending Nonfiction** Use the strategies mentioned above to read a chapter from one of your textbooks. What main points and major details did you find? What was the author's purpose? What points helped you identify it? What is the significance of the information you read?

More Practice

Academic and Workplace Skills Activity Book
- pp. 37–39

Step-by-Step Teaching Guide

Comprehending Nonfiction

1. Ask students which they prefer reading, fiction or nonfiction.
2. Point out that some people prefer nonfictions because it is more useful. Others may prefer fiction. They say it is easier or more interesting. The two genres are really not so different. A history book and a novel both contain characters, a setting, and a plot. History contains problems to solve, as does a good novel.
3. The main difference is that, if the nonfiction is a textbook, students have to pay attention to dates and names of people, places, and things that are hard to spell and pronounce. Everything they read may be "on the quiz."
4. Ask students to relate the difference for them between reading nonfiction in a textbook and in reading, for example, nonfiction in a celebrity profile or magazine related to a favorite hobby or other interest.
5. Have small groups choose a section from their science textbook. Ask them to use the four strategies to understand the section.
6. You may want to repeat this exercise with a newspaper article.

Answer Key

Exercise 6

Answers will vary.

TIME AND RESOURCE MANAGER

Resources
Print: Academic and Workplace Skills Activity Book, pp.38–43

In-Depth Coverage	Accelerated Pace
• Cover pp. 725–730 in class. • Assign and review Exercises 6–12.	• Assign pp. 725–730 independent student review.

Step-by-Step Teaching Guide

Distinguishing Fact From Opinion

1. Point out that it is often easy to tell a fact from an opinion. For example: *A banana is a fruit* (fact); *I like bananas best of all* (opinion).
2. Explain that sometimes it is not so easy to distinguish between facts and opinions. Some writers state opinions as if they were facts. That is why it is important to check things they read if they are not familiar with the facts, or be sure to read reliable sources.
3. Students cannot disagree with a true fact. A banana *is* a fruit. They can, however, disagree with any opinion.
4. Have students offer opinions about things that interest them—food, music, sports, actors, anything. Then have them support their opinions.

Answer Key

Exercise 7

1. fact; false
2. opinion; invalid
3. fact; true
4. opinion; invalid
5. opinion; valid

30.2

Distinguishing Fact From Opinion

When you read critically, you should learn to separate fact statements from opinion statements.

Fact Statements A statement of fact can be verified or proved to be true by consulting a written source—such as an atlas, an encyclopedia, an almanac, or other reference book—a human authority, or by personally observing something directly.

STATEMENTS OF FACT:	Earth revolves around the sun approximately every 365 days. (true) Earth is the center of the solar system. (false)

The first fact statement is *true* because it can be verified by consulting a written authority, such as an encyclopedia or science textbook. The second fact statement is *false* because these same sources tell us that the sun, and not Earth, is the center of the solar system.

Opinion Statements An opinion statement expresses a person's feelings, judgments, or predictions about a given situation. An opinion statement cannot be proved to be true. It can, however, be a valid statement if it is supported by evidence, such as related facts or an authority.

SUPPORTED OPINION:	According to scientists at the university, an excessive amount of sunlight can lead to skin cancer. (valid)
UNSUPPORTED OPINION:	The sun is bad for you. (invalid)

The first opinion statement is *valid* because it is based on related facts given by an authority. The second opinion statement, however, is *invalid* because it contains no facts and is not given by an authority.

Learn More

To learn more about distinguishing fact from opinion, see Chapter 7.

Exercise 7 Evaluating Fact and Opinion Statements

Identify each statement below as *fact* or *opinion*. If the statement is a fact, tell whether it is *true* or *false*. If the statement is an opinion, tell whether it is *valid* or *invalid*. Consult a reference book if necessary.

1. John Steinbeck wrote *Romeo and Juliet*.
2. Donna has been training hard all year. She will win first place in the track competition.
3. There are nine planets in the solar system.
4. Broccoli tastes terrible.
5. Because his plays and poetry form a respected part of English literature, William Shakespeare is a great author.

More Practice

Academic and Workplace Skills Activity Book
- pp. 40–42

Identifying the Author's Purpose

A crucial step in becoming a critical reader is determining the author's purpose—why he or she is writing. As you read, remember to look for clues that help you identify the author's purpose. When you think you know the author's purpose, confirm your conclusion by linking it to details in the text.

KEY CONCEPT Learn to identify the author's purpose by using clues found in the text. ■

The list below describes common purposes of authors. Use these definitions as clues to help you identify the author's purpose in your reading.

- **To inform**—a series of factual statements
- **To instruct**—a step-by-step explanation of an idea or a process
- **To offer an opinion**—presentation of a topic with a certain point of view
- **To sell**—persuasive techniques designed to sell a product
- **To entertain**—narration of an event in a humorous way, often used to lighten a serious topic

▲Critical Viewing Assuming each of five authors writes for a different purpose, how might they write about this Civil War scene? **[Speculate]**

Exercise 8 **Determining the Author's Purpose** Read each of the following sentences, and determine the author's purpose. Explain your answer.

1. This booklet will tell you, in three easy steps, how to properly bait a hook for freshwater fishing.
2. The American Civil War ended on April 9, 1865, at Appomattox.
3. I think everyone should go to college, and here are my reasons.
4. If you are looking for the very best prices on the Web, shop at **iluvadiscount.com.**
5. My brother's dream is to be a rock star, but the only instrument he can play is the triangle.

Step-by-Step Teaching Guide

Identifying the Author's Purpose

1. Unless the title of a work makes it obvious—"How to make an Apple Pie," "School Uniforms? Forget About It!," "My Funniest Experience Ever"—readers have to infer the author's purpose as they read.
2. Ask students to choose two purposes and tell how they would read an example of each differently.
3. Have students look through their portfolios to find an example of writing for each purpose.

Critical Viewing

Speculate Answers will vary. Discuss the details of the photograph with your students.

Answer Key

Exercise 8

1. To instruct; author states this purpose directly
2. To inform; author states a fact
3. To offer an opinion; author uses the words "I think"
4. To sell; author mentions "best prices"
5. To inform or entertain; sentence tells about brother's life in a humorous way

Step-by-Step Teaching Guide

Applying Forms of Reasoning

1. Give students the familiar example of the actor Christopher Reeve becoming paralyzed after a horseback-riding accident. Students could infer from this that horseback riding can result in accidents or that these accidents can be serious. Those are valid inferences.
2. Generalize from the example that many people who ride horses fall off, that all falls are serious, and that most falls cause paralysis. These are all invalid generalizations because there are no facts to back them up.

Answer Key

Exercise 9

1. inference; invalid
2. generalization; invalid
3. inference; invalid
4. generalization; valid
5. inference; valid

30.2

Applying Forms of Reasoning

Once you have learned how to evaluate the material you read, you are ready to draw your own conclusions about the work. Learn to apply forms of reasoning—logical ways of thinking—to get the fullest meaning from your reading.

KEY CONCEPT Examine the details of the material you read to help you make inferences and generalizations. ■

Make Inferences In your reading, you won't always find the author's main ideas stated directly. Sometimes, the main ideas are implied, or stated indirectly. When you make inferences, you put details together to figure out what they mean. Use an inference map like the one below to help you organize details and make inferences that will lead you to conclusions.

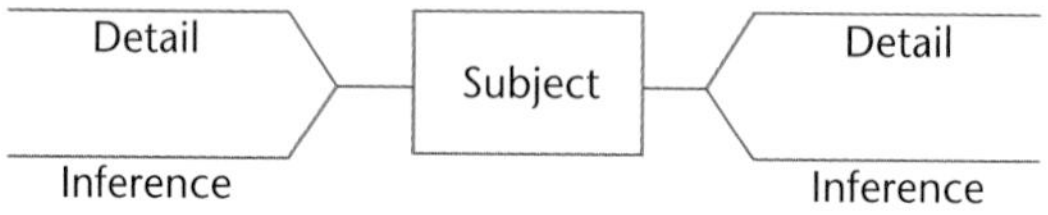

Make Generalizations A generalization is a statement based on facts or examples. A generalization is *valid* when it is based on a large number of examples. A generalization is *invalid* when it is based on too few examples. Use the following questions to make a valid generalization.

- What facts are provided to justify the generalization?
- Will the generalization hold true in all or most cases? Are there exceptions to the generalization?
- Are enough cases given to make the generalization valid?

Exercise 9 **Evaluating Inferences and Generalizations** One way to learn how to make good inferences and generalizations is by learning to identify them. Read the following sentences. Identify each as an *inference* or a *generalization*. Then, explain whether each conclusion is *valid* or *invalid*.

1. Dan plays the piano well; he will become a concert pianist.
2. My father's car got stuck in the snow last winter, so no one should drive during snowy weather.
3. Since the governor was elected, the state population has dramatically declined. Therefore, he should not be re-elected.
4. Studies conducted over the last five years tell us that seatbelts save lives, so all drivers should wear them.
5. Susan has studied a great deal about the Middle Ages; she must know everything about castles.

More Practice

Academic and Workplace Skills Activity Book
- pp. 40–42

Analyzing Text

When you analyze text, you examine how language is used to express thoughts and feelings, and you examine the text's structure to aid your comprehension of the material.

KEY CONCEPT Identify and understand the purposes of the different uses of language and text structure. ■

Examine an Author's Language Authors sometimes use language in ways that can suggest how you should feel about a particular subject or issue. *Denotation, connotation,* and *jargon* are three ways that authors use language to affect your opinions and ideas about what you are reading.

Denotation and Connotation When words are used in a *denotative* way, they describe a situation in a neutral tone. Words used in a *connotative* way are value-laden. Connotations imply a particular point of view in a positive or negative tone.

Jargon *Jargon* is the use of words with specialized meanings intended for a particular trade or profession. Jargon is meant to have very precise meaning, but it often hides rather than reveals meaning. The opposite of jargon is *direct language.*

Exercise 10 **Analyzing Uses of Language** Identify the pairs of sentences below for the use of *denotation/connotation* or *jargon/direct language.*

1. The girl wore a pink and yellow dress.
   The young girl was dressed in shades of rose and lemon.
2. In preschool, children interface with their peer group.
   In preschool, children play with their classmates.
3. The senator's petty questioning dragged on interminably.
   The senator's interrogation lasted for two hours.
4. The candy has a cloying, sickly sweet taste.
   The candy is too sweet.
5. Declining sales had a negative impact on our financial depository.
   Lower sales caused us to lose money.

Exercise 11 **Identifying Uses of Language** Look through magazines and newspapers. Find three examples of words with positive connotations, three examples of words with negative connotations, and three examples of jargon.

Speaking and Listening Tip

Explore the effects of words with positive and negative connotations. Join with two or three of your classmates, and take turns reading the examples you found for Exercise 11. As you read and listen, be aware of the feelings the words convey.

ONGOING ASSESSMENT: Monitor and Reinforce

If students are having trouble reading initially, try one of the following options.

Option 1 Write these four sentences:

Robert Frost was an American poet.

Robert Frost was born and raised in Rome, Italy.

Because numerous books on his life and works are still being published today, Robert Frost is a great poet.

Robert Frost is the greatest American poet ever to have lived.

The first sentence is a true fact, the second a false fact, the third valid or supported opinion, and the fourth an invalid or unsupported opinion.

Option 2 Write these two sentences:

Sally broke her ankle rollerblading in Central Park so no one should ever rollerblade in Central Park.

Bill can point out almost every constellation in the sky; he will become an astronomer when he goes to college.

Sentence one is an invalid generalization, and sentence two is an invalid inference. Challenge them to come up with both valid inferences and generalizations.

Step-by-Step Teaching Guide

Analyzing Text

1. Denotation is neutral and impartial. It states facts without making a judgment. For example, "During Tom Robinson's trial, Atticus Finch worked long hours at his law office."
2. A connotation makes a subtle implication by using positive or negative language. "During Tom Robinson's trial, Atticus Finch was so busy at work that he ignored his children." "Atticus Finch was a dedicated lawyer who worked hard to get his innocent client acquitted."
3. The purpose of language is to communicate ideas, and direct language does this much better than jargon. Jargon is usually used to hide the truth or make something sound better than it is: *downsized* vs. *fired; equipment supervisor* vs. *batboy.*

Answer Key

Exercise 10

1. denotation, connotation
2. jargon, direct language
3. connotation, denotation
4. connotation, denotation
5. jargon, direct language

Exercise 11

Answers will vary.

Customize for *More Advanced Students*

Have students exchange examples from materials they located for Exercise 11. Challenge them to rewrite each example of connotative language in denotative language, and each example of jargon in direct language. Students can compare the rewrites to the originals and discuss which versions they think are better and why.

Step-by-Step Teaching Guide

Identify Text Structure

1. Discuss the three types of text structure.
2. Have students suppose that they have to write an essay about the sinking of the *Titanic*. Ask which of the three types of text structure students would use and why. (Possible answers: Cause and effect, because the most interesting question is why the ship sank; comparison and contrast to discuss the fates of the first-, second-, and third-class passengers; chronological order, because telling the story from beginning to end preserves the suspense.)
3. Point out that each kind of structure can illuminate a different aspect of the same topic.

Answer Key

Exercise 12

Answers may vary.

Identify Text Structure Authors arrange their writing so that they can communicate their ideas in a clear and effective way. Learn to recognize how an author structures the text so that you can understand the relationships among ideas and locate information more easily.

KEY CONCEPT Learn how an author structures his or her text to understand ideas and locate information more easily. ■

Cause and Effect A *cause* is the reason that something happens. An *effect* is the outcome. Together, they form an *event*. A cause-and-effect structure shows a series of events. Also, note that most effects in turn act as a cause for something else, thereby continuing the series of events. Some word clues identifying cause and effect are listed in the following illustration.

CAUSE + EFFECT = EVENT

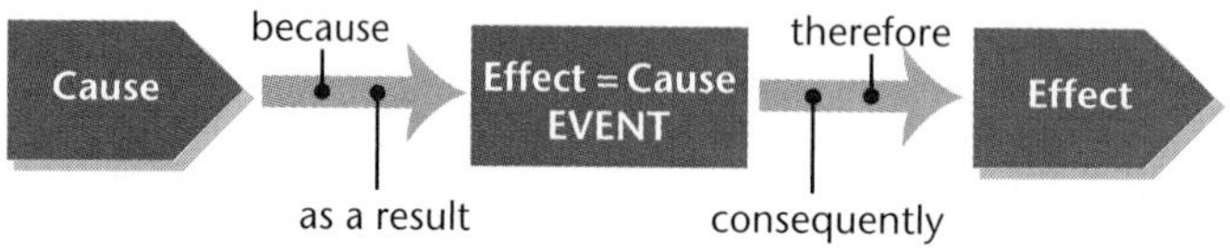

Comparison and Contrast An author uses this text structure to describe similarities and differences between two or more items, either feature by feature or subject by subject. The following words often signal a comparison: *like, similarly, both, in the same way*. The words *but, yet, in spite of, on the other hand, although, nevertheless, in contrast, whereas*, and *unlike* often signal a contrast.

Chronological Order An author uses chronological order when he or she wants to show the arrangement of events in the order in which they occurred during a period of time. Words such as *next, then, later*, and *soon* show the order of events as well as the passing of time.

Exercise 12 **Analyzing Text Structure** Go back to the cause-and-effect professional or student model in Chapter 9, and identify a cause and effect in the essay. Show the details that support your answer. Turn to the comparison-and-contrast professional or student model in Chapter 8, and tell which two items or features are being contrasted. Name two of their similarities and two of their differences.

More Practice

Academic and Workplace Skills Activity Book
- pp. 43–46

Section 30.3

Reading Literary Writings

Fiction, drama, poetry, and tales from the oral tradition are all types of literary writing. While reading literary writing, you use your mind, your emotions, and your imagination. You can also use the following strategies to increase your understanding and appreciation of literary writing.

Reading Fiction

Short stories are brief works of fiction, whereas novels are longer fictional works.

Determine the Point of View The point of view is the vantage point from which the author or narrator tells a story. Three commonly used points of view are omniscient third person, limited third person, and first person.

- In *omniscient third-person point of view*, the narrator has complete knowledge of all the characters and tells what they feel and think.
- In *limited third-person point of view*, the narrator has knowledge of the thoughts and feelings of only one character, and everything is viewed from this character's vantage point.
- In *first-person point of view*, the narrator is a character in the story, referring to himself or herself with the first-person pronoun *I*.

Envision the Action and Setting As you read, allow yourself to create mental pictures of the action, setting, and characters. Look for these kinds of words:

- Action words
- Adverbs—words that tell how an action is performed
- Sensory words—words that tell how things look, feel, taste, smell, and sound

Identify the Conflict Most plots—what happens in a story—develop from conflict, the struggle between opposing forces. There are two kinds of conflict: internal and external. An *internal conflict* is a mental struggle within a character. An *external conflict* is a struggle between the character and an outside force.

Exercise 13 **Reading Fiction** Read a short story or the first chapter of a novel. Then, list experiences or qualities you share with the main character. Make a prediction about what might happen. Find at least two action words, and describe the action taking place.

▼ **Critical Viewing** Explain the kind of conflict depicted in this photograph, and give one action word, one adverb, and one sensory word that you might use to describe the conflict. **[Analyze]**

Step-by-Step Teaching Guide

Reading Fiction

1. Give students examples of the three points of view.

   omniscient third person: Jack London's "Up the Slice"

   limited third person: Shirley Jackson's "Charles"

   first person: Daniel Keyes's "Flowers for Algernon"

2. Each point of view has its benefits and drawbacks. Third person gives readers a more complete picture of all the characters. First person gives readers a close-up view of one character's feelings.
3. Review conflict. It is what makes a work interesting and makes readers care what happens. Ask students to name stories or books they enjoyed and briefly state the conflict(s). Most works of fiction contain both internal and external conflicts.

Answer Key

Exercise 13

Answers will vary.

Critical Viewing

Analyze Students may suggest action words, such as *charging*, *lunging*, and *ramming*, adverbs such as *fiercely*, *hotly*, and *wildly*, and sensory words such as *wild*, *intense*, and *exciting*.

TIME AND RESOURCE MANAGER

Resources
Print: Academic Workplace Skills and Activity Book, pp. 44–50

In-Depth Coverage	Accelerated Pace
• Cover pp. 731–735 in class. • Assign and review Exercises 13–16.	• Assign pp. 731–735 for independent student review.

Step-by-Step Teaching Guide

Reading Drama

1. Unlike a novel, which is full of description, a play contains only dialogue. Readers have to imagine what the characters look like, what the setting looks like, and how the characters feel.
2. Have students look at *The Diary of Anne Frank* (*Prentice Hall Literature: Timeless Voices, Timeless Themes,* Silver). The lengthy stage directions (everything in italic type) help readers visualize the setting, actions, and emotions.

30.3

Reading Drama

Drama is a story designed to be performed on the stage. It is told mostly through what the actors say and do. Stage directions in the script contain instructions about how actors should move and how they should speak their lines. Sometimes, these stage directions contain information about the sets, costumes, lighting, and sound effects. Use the following strategies to increase your understanding of drama:

Read the Cast of Characters Before the play begins, there is usually a list of the characters that take part in the action. Reading this list can tell you the various relationships among the characters. It may also give a brief description of the characters to help you imagine who they are.

Use Stage Directions to Envision the Play As you read, use your imagination to mentally "stage" what is happening in the play.

- Use the stage directions to picture in your mind what the characters look like and how they behave.
- To get more involved in the play, imagine conversations among the characters. You may find it helpful to read these conversations aloud or with a friend.
- If the play does not take place in the present, don't forget to consider what you already know about the time in history when it took place.

Predict After you have read the first act or scene of the play, try to predict, or figure out, what characters will do or which events will happen in the next act or scene. Look for clues in what the characters say or do to help you make your prediction.

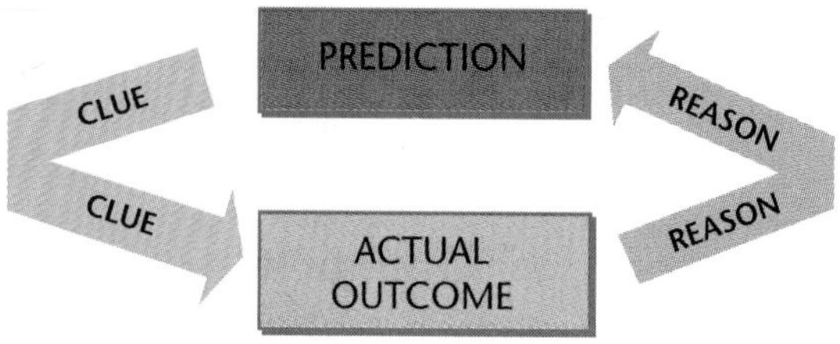

Question A good way to learn more about characters and events is to ask questions. By asking questions, you can also find new relationships between the characters and events within the work. As you continue to read, search the story for the answers to your questions.

Technology Tip

Try looking up famous characters from literature on the Internet. You may find descriptions that help you get involved in the story.

QUESTIONING TO LEARN MORE ABOUT DRAMA

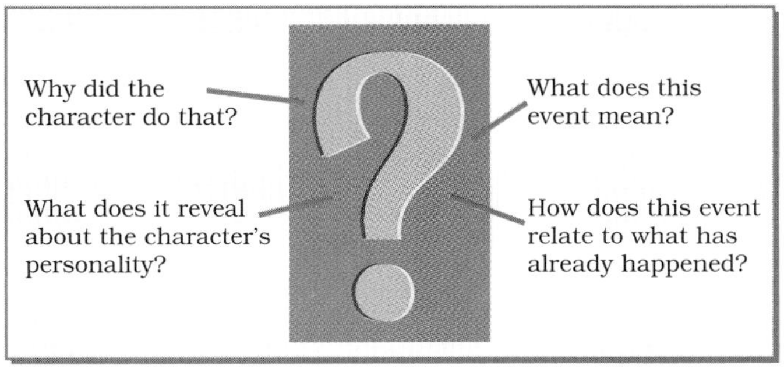

Why did the character do that?
What does this event mean?
What does it reveal about the character's personality?
How does this event relate to what has already happened?

Summarize Dramas are usually broken into parts called acts. Acts are broken into scenes. At the end of an act or a scene, repeat to yourself what has happened to that point.

Exercise 14 **Reading Drama** Read the beginning of a play—a first act or scene. As you read, answer these questions:

1. What do you learn about the characters and setting from reading the cast list and opening stage directions?
2. How do stage directions contribute to your understanding of a mood, an action, or a character?
3. What do you predict will happen in the play? Pick a character, and tell what you think will happen to him or her.

More Practice
Academic and Workplace Skills Activity Book
• pp. 47–48

Reading Poetry

In poetry, the language does more than describe events and characters. It evokes a mood and creates its own reality with sounds, rhythms, and multiple meanings. Poets treat words with reverence. Give every word in the poem the attention it deserves. Here are some strategies to use:

Read Lines According to Punctuation Because lines of poetry are usually short, a single thought or image may continue for several lines. Therefore, instead of pausing in your reading at the end of each line, be aware of the punctuation, and pause only where a comma or an end mark signals a pause.

- Pause slightly for commas and a bit longer for semicolons or dashes.
- Make the longest stops for end marks, such as periods, exclamation marks, and question marks.
- Don't stop at the ends of lines if there is no punctuation.

Answer Key

Exercise 14

Answers will vary. You may wish to assign your students a first act or scene from a play that you have or will discuss.

Step-by-Step Teaching Guide

Reading Poetry

1. Remind students that when they read prose, they pause at the punctuation, not at the end of each line. The same process applies to reading poetry.
2. Students may need to read a poem several times, until they can read it in "sentences" rather than in lines.

continued

Integrating Listening Skills

It can be easier for students to hear poetry than to read it, so they are not distracted by the unusual look of the words on the page. All of the poems in *Timeless Voices, Timeless Themes* are available on the Listening to Literature Audiocassettes. Encourage students to listen to poems they find hard to understand. Also urge them to listen to their favorite poems.

Step-by-Step Teaching Guide continued

3. Read aloud the following lines of poetry and ask students to identify simile, metaphor, and personification.

   Her cheeks like the dawn of day (simile)

   [The storm] shuddered and paused (personification)

   Life is but a toy that swings on a bright gold chain (metaphor)

   A poem must be . . . musical as a sea gull (simile)

   I encountered Death . . . thin as a scythe he stood there (simile, personification)

   Life is a broken-winged bird that cannot fly (metaphor)

Answer Key

Exercise 15

Answers will vary. You may wish to assign your students a poem that you have or will discuss.

Identify the Speaker The poet is not always the speaker in the poem. The speaker is the voice that "says" the words. Listen for clues about who the speaker is.

ANALYZING THE SPEAKER

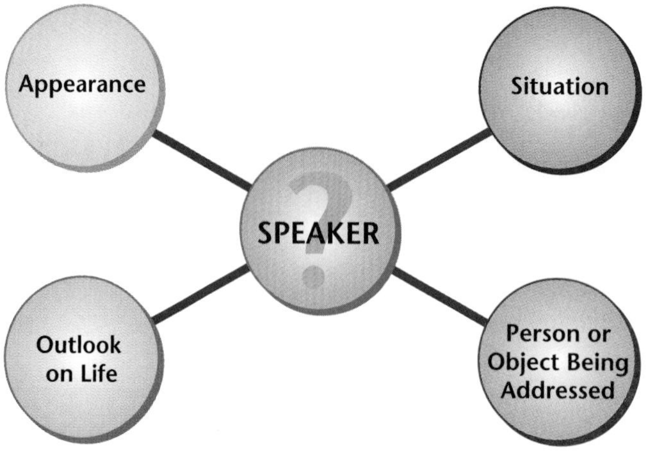

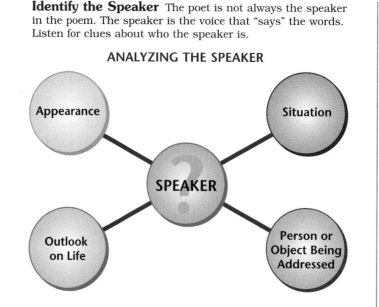

Paraphrase the Lines When reading poetry, pause every stanza or every few lines to paraphrase—or restate in your own words—the poet's ideas. By putting the poet's ideas in your own words, you'll not only be able to understand the poem better, but you'll remember it better, too.

Understand Figurative Language Language that is used to make you see and feel things in a new way is called *figurative language*. Listed below are three types of figurative language:

- **Simile** uses the words *like* or *as* to compare apparently unlike things: *The eagle dives like a thunderbolt.*
- **Metaphor** compares apparently unlike things by describing one item as though it were another without using *like* or *as: Life is a broken-winged bird that cannot fly.*
- **Personification** gives human qualities to nonhuman objects: *Sorrow knocked at my door, but I was afraid to answer.*

Exercise 15 **Reading Poetry** Read a one- or two-page poem. Number the lines that require pauses at the ends of them. Identify the speaker in the poem, if possible. Give two or three images from the poem, and name the senses to which they appeal. Paraphrase one complete thought in the poem.

More Practice

Academic and Workplace Skills Activity Book
- pp. 49–50

Reading Tales From the Oral Tradition

Folk tales, legends, and myths were originally told orally. They sometimes contain a lot of repetition, which made them easier to remember. To better understand one of these stories, a reader needs to know about the culture or the region from which the story came.

Understand the Culture When you read a folk tale, it helps to know something about the setting of the story and its origins. When was it told and written down? Where did its tellers live? Were they farmers, nomads, or city dwellers? What were their beliefs and social customs?

Recognize the Storyteller's Purpose Some of the reasons folk tales were told include providing entertainment, teaching a lesson, transmitting beliefs, or explaining natural occurrences, such as the rising of the sun or the mystery of birth.

Know What to Expect In folk tales, myths, and legends, there are often special elements you should look for, such as strong moral messages, supernatural events, magic transformations, and animals acting like people.

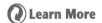

Learn More

To learn about other ways of responding to literature, see Chapter 12.

Exercise 16 Reading Myths, Legends, and Folk Tales Choose a myth, legend, or folk tale from your textbook, and answer the following questions:

1. What three things can you tell about the culture from which your folk tale, myth, or legend comes?
2. What is the storyteller's purpose in writing this tale?
3. What special elements did you find?

▶ Critical Viewing In what ways are stories that children tell around a campfire similar to many legends and folk tales? **[Relate]**

ONGOING ASSESSMENT: Monitor and Reinforce

If students are having trouble reading the various types of literary texts, try the following option.

Assign your students a short reading, such as a short story or scene from a play. Have them form small groups and discuss the various elements of the work. If it is a short story, have them determine the point of view and setting and identify the main conflict. If it is a scene or act from a play, have them discuss the characters' motivations. Then, have them present their findings to the class.

Step-by-Step Teaching Guide

Reading Tales from the Oral Tradition

Explain the difference among folktales, legends, and myths.

A folktale is an entertaining story that is passed from person to person. Example: "Brer Possum's Dilemma"

A legend is a story about the past that may or may not be true. Example: "The Girl Who Hunted Rabbits"

A myth is a fictional tale that tries to explain nature or the actions of gods and goddesses. Example: "Coyote Steals the Sun and Moon"

Critical Viewing

Relate Students may suggest that the stories are often scary, but have been heard before. Like legends and folktales, campfire stories are entertaining, passed on from person to person, and often make claims of being true.

Answer Key

Exercise 16

Answers will vary. You may wish to assign your students a myth, legend, or folktale that you have or will discuss.

Step-by-Step Teaching Guide

Reading From Varied Sources

1. Ask students why they would read materials in each category. Then ask them to describe how they would read them. For instance, a student reading a newspaper would probably turn the pages quickly, reading only the headlines, to find an article he or she wanted to read. The student would then read the article carefully.
2. Warn students of the dangers of reading or researching on the Internet. Because anyone can post anything on the Internet, sources may not be reliable. Students should use caution.
3. Emphasize the need to read instructions all the way through before beginning to install a new computer game or put a bicycle together. Ask how many students have realized halfway through a project that they have made crucial mistakes simply because they failed to read the directions carefully.

Section 30.4

Reading From Varied Sources

Obviously, much of the reading you do involves materials other than textbooks and literary works. You can read from a wide selection of magazines, newspapers, Web pages, advertisements, anthologies, and various manuals and handbooks. What you read depends on why you are reading. Select material that is best suited to your purpose for reading.

Reading Forms and Applications Filling out forms and applications is probably one of the most practical purposes for reading. You should read these carefully so that you understand the information that is being requested. Doing so will help you to fill out forms accurately, which leads to quicker results than if the form must be resubmitted with revised information.

Reading Newspapers Newspapers keep you informed about what is going on in your community and the world. There are many different kinds of newspapers available to you, depending on what your interest is. Local newspapers focus on events that affect a town, city, county, or region. National newspapers cover events and issues that affect the entire country. There are financial newspapers, foreign language newspapers, and newspapers for many different organizations. You can choose the newspaper that will give the most thorough coverage of the type of events that interest you. Except for sections that are intended to offer a viewpoint, such as the editorial page, newspapers should report the news objectively, without adding opinions or viewpoints.

Reading Magazines Magazines exist for almost every interest. When you want to read about something specific, you can usually find the information in a magazine. Some magazines deal with current events, but many magazines are focused on attracting a specific audience with specific interests. You can find magazines on fashion, movies, music, gardening, travel, science, computers, art, and architecture, among many other topics. Unlike newspapers, magazines usually offer an opinion or point of view on the topic they present. Even magazines that cover current events or celebrities set a tone or show an attitude toward the subjects they cover.

Reading Anthologies Perhaps you like to read a particular type of literature, or literature of a certain time period. If so, you might select an anthology, which is a collection of varied works, usually by many different authors. If you want to focus on the work of a single author, look for a collection of that author's writings, often entitled *The Collected Works of . . . .*

TIME AND RESOURCE MANAGER	
Resources **Print:** Academic and Workplace Skills Activity Book, p. 51	
In-Depth Coverage	**Accelerated Pace**
• Cover pp. 736–737 in class.	• Assign pp. 736–737, for independent student review.

Reading Electronic Texts

Articles and information that you can read on Web pages cover a wide range of topics. The information may be objective, or it may present one person's point of view on a topic. Because Web pages comes from such a wide variety of sources, it is very important that you evaluate the authority and the background of the source before using or accepting any of the information presented. Some electronic texts are provided by retailers—companies that want to sell you something—and should be viewed as advertisements rather than as informational texts.

Reading Manuals Whether you are installing a new computer game or putting together a bicycle, you will be more successful if you read the directions. Many new products come with an owner's manual, which has detailed directions and important information that will help you put together and use a product correctly. It is important to read the owner's manual for necessary safety instructions, as well.

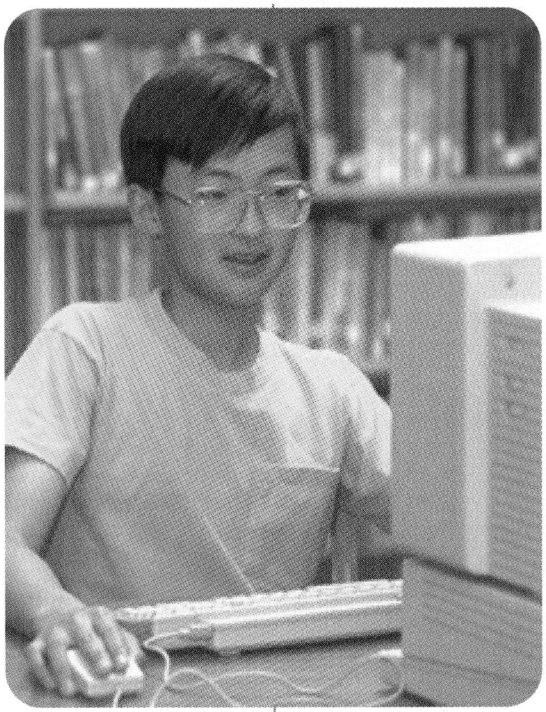

▲ Critical Viewing What might this student do to judge whether the information he has found on-line is valid? **[Apply]**

Reflecting on Your Reading

After a week of practicing your reading skills, write a paragraph about your progress. Use the following questions to get you started:

- Which sections of my textbooks do I use on a regular basis?
- How does varying my reading style help me to find information and to study?
- Which reading strategies do I find most useful?
- How am I, in general, a more careful and reflective reader?

Integrating Workplace Skills

On the job, people have to read every kind of texts mentioned here and other kinds as well. Correspondence, memos, and reports make up daily office reading for many people. Readers need to apply the reading skills taught in this chapter to understand all these different texts.

Critical Viewing

Apply Students may suggest checking the source of the Web page.

PRENTICE HALL

Everyday Spelling

If you have taught the spelling skills in *Prentice Hall Everyday Spelling,* Grade 8, Chapter 34, in conjunction with this *Writing and Grammar* chapter, review and assess students' mastery of the skills before concluding the chapter.

Lesson Objectives

- To make inferences and predictions.

Step-by-Step Teaching Guide

Making Inferences and Predictions

Teaching Resources: Standardized Test Preparation Workbook, pp.59–60

1. Emphasize to students that their key to success in most standardized tests, whether essay or multiple choice, is for them to address the question being asked. Remind them that reading test questions often involves making inferences, or putting details together to piece together the implied meaning.
2. Remind students that whether they are reading nonfiction or fiction, they can make proper inferences by isolating certain words or phrases in the text, and that these words and phrases are like clues that can help them anticipate future actions or outcomes from the material they have read.
3. Assign a reading accompanied by two questions, one in essay format and one as a multiple choice. Go over the reading and the questions with your students, taking care to point out all significant words and phrases that will help them to understand the process of making inferences about text.

Standardized Test Preparation Workshop

Making Inferences and Predictions

Reading questions on standardized tests often measure your ability to make inferences. You can make inferences—draw logical conclusions—about what you have read and about characters and stories, or you can make them about the author's purpose or point of view. You can also make predictions or anticipate future actions or outcomes from the material you have read. Reading questions may have a multiple-choice or essay format.

The following sample test items will help you prepare for answering these types of questions on standardized tests.

Test Tip

When a test calls for a written response, read the question first. Then, read the passage, keeping in mind the type of response you will draft.

Sample Test Items	Answers and Explanations
Read each passage. Then, answer the questions that follow the passage. from "Average Waves in Unprotected Waters" by Anne Tyler Like any other nine-year-old, he wore a striped shirt and jeans, but the shirt was too neat and the jeans too blue, unpatched and unfaded, and would stay that way till he outgrew them. 1 The boy is— A just like any other nine-year-old B not physically active C very active D not growing	The answer for item 1 is *B*. The narrator describes the boy's clothes as unusual for a nine-year-old. Because his clothes are neater and less worn than those of other boys, you can infer that he does not engage in physical activity that would cause wear and tear.
Answer the following question. Base your answer on "Average Waves in Unprotected Waters." How does the narrator evoke a sense of sympathy for the boy?	Your answer should consist of a paragraph that includes a topic sentence and details from the passage that support it. The following is part of a possible response: *The narrator creates a visual image of a little boy who does not, or cannot, play and run and do the things that would wear out his clothes. This image evokes sympathy in the reader.*

TEST-TAKING TIP

Remind students that when they make inferences, they must often "read between the lines" to draw conclusions about information the author does not directly state. They will have to carefully evaluate details about characters, as well as the author's tone, in order to make these inferences.

Practice 1 **Directions:** Read the passage. Then, answer the questions that follow the passage.

The following excerpt from "Dust Tracks on a Road" by Zora Neale Hurston, who attended an all-black school in rural Florida, describes an incident from her youth.

When school let out at three o'clock, Mr. Calhoun told me to wait. When everybody had gone, he told me I was to go to the Park House, that was the hotel in Maitland, the next afternoon to call upon Mrs. Johnstone and Miss Hurd. I must tell Mama to see that I was clean and brushed from head to feet, and I must wear clean shoes and stockings. The ladies liked me, he said, and I must be on my best behavior . . .

First thing, the ladies gave me strange things like stuffed dates and preserved ginger, and encouraged me to eat all that I wanted. Then they showed me their Japanese dolls and just talked. I was then handed a copy of *Scribner's Magazine*, and asked to read a place that was pointed out to me. After a paragraph or two, I was told with smiles that that would do.

1 Hurston writes the story in first person—

A to share her thoughts and feelings

B to use a traditional story form

C to keep the reader guessing

D to create suspense

2 The author wants the reader to know—

F that African Americans suffered greatly in the rural south

G that African American children were not well groomed

H that African Americans attended excellent schools

J that white ladies were not usually so kind to African American children in Florida at that time

3 What attitude do Mrs. Johnstone and Miss Hurd have toward Zora?

A They dislike her.

B They greatly admire her.

C They believe she is inferior.

D They see her as a curiosity.

4 What kind of future would you predict for Zora Neale Hurston?

F Her chances for higher education would be limited by her race.

G Because she is intelligent and strives to be educated, she will accomplish many things.

H She will be unable to go beyond the local school.

J She will become bitter and resentful.

5 Why did the ladies ask Zora to read from a literary magazine?

A They wanted to impress her with their good taste.

B They wanted to expose her to quality literature.

C They wanted to see how well she could read.

D They wanted to hear her Southern accent.

Practice 2 **Directions:** Answer the following question. Base your answer on "Dust Tracks on a Road."

READ, THINK, EXPLAIN How can you tell that visiting the white ladies made an impression on Hurston? Use details from the passage to explain your answer.

Answer Key

Practice 1

1. A
2. H
3. D
4. J
5. C

Practice 2

Answers will vary. Make sure students support their ideas with details from the passage.

Chapter 31 Time and Resource Manager

In-Depth Lesson Plan

	LESSON FOCUS	PRINT AND MEDIA RESOURCES
DAY 1	**Basic Study Skills** Students practice such basic study skills as developing study plans, developing assignment books, and taking notes (pp. 740–743).	**Teaching Resources:** *Academic and Workplace Skills Activity Book,* pp. 52–53
DAY 2	**Reference Skills** Students discuss how to find different types of books in libraries (pp. 744–747).	**Teaching Resources:** *Academic and Workplace Skills Activity Book,* pp. 54–58
DAY 3	**Reference Skills** ***(continued)*** Students practice using conventional and electronic card catalogs, periodicals and indexes, various reference books, and the Internet (pp. 748–754).	**Teaching Resources:** *Academic and Workplace Skills Activity Book,* pp. 54–58
DAY 4	**Test-Taking Skills** Students discuss and practice strategies for answering different types of test questions (pp. 755–759).	**Teaching Resources:** *Academic and Workplace Skills Activity Book,* pp. 59–60

Accelerated Lesson Plan

	LESSON FOCUS	PRINT AND MEDIA RESOURCES
DAY 1	**Basic Study Skills** Students practice such basic study skills as developing study plans, developing assignment books, and taking notes (pp. 740–743).	**Teaching Resources:** *Academic and Workplace Skills Activity Book,* pp. 52–53
DAY 2	**Reference Skills** Students discuss how to find different types of books in libraries. They practice using conventional and electronic card catalogs, periodicals and indexes, various reference books, and the Internet (pp. 744–754).	**Teaching Resources:** *Academic and Workplace Skills Activity Book,* pp. 54–58
DAY 3	**Test-Taking Skills** Students discuss and practice strategies for answering different types of test questions (pp. 755–759).	**Teaching Resources:** *Academic and Workplace Skills Activity Book,* pp. 59–60

Options for Adapting Lesson Plans

HOMEWORK

Have students complete any stage of the lesson for homework.

FEATURES

Extend coverage with the Standardized Test Preparation Workshop (pp. 760–761).

TECHNOLOGY

Students can complete any stage of the lesson on computer. Have them print out their completed work.

SPELLING

To teach spelling skills in conjunction with academic and workplace skills, work through *Prentice Hall Everyday Spelling,* Grade 8, Chapter 35, as you cover this *Writing and Grammar* chapter.

INTEGRATED SKILLS COVERAGE

Viewing and Representing

Critical Viewing, SE pp. 740, 742, 754, 756

Technology Tip SE pp. 745, 747, 748, 749, 752

ASSESSMENT SUPPORT

Standardized Test Preparation Workshop, SE pp. 760–761; ATE p. 757

Standardized Test Preparation Workbook, pp. 61–62

Writing Assessment and Portfolio Management

MEETING INDIVIDUAL NEEDS

Less Advanced Students ATE p. 746. See also Ongoing Assessments ATE pp. 742, 743, 747, 750, 753, 756.

ESL Students ATE pp. 746, 749

More Advanced Students ATE p. 743

BLOCK SCHEDULING

Pacing Suggestions

For 90-minute Blocks

- Have students complete the chapter in a single class period.

Professional Development Support

- ***How to Manage Instruction in the Block*** This teaching resource provides management and activity suggestions.

MEDIA AND TECHNOLOGY

For the Teacher

- ***Resource Pro*** **CD-ROM**

WRITING AND GRAMMAR ON-LINE

iText Interactive Text (On-line or on CD-ROM)

- Easily navigable instruction with interactive Revision Checkers
- Full use of e-rater™, the essay-scoring system (on-line only)

Companion Web Site PHSchool.com

- Scoring rubrics with models (use Web Code eck-8001)

See the Go On-line! feature, SE p. iii.

Lesson Objectives

1. To develop a study plan.
2. To take good notes.
3. To use the library.
4. To use periodicals and periodical indexes.
5. To use dictionaries and other reference works.
6. To use the Internet.
7. To answer objective test questions.
8. To answer short-answer and essay questions.

Critical Viewing

Analyze Students may suggest that the students in the photograph are learning how to use reference material, such as a dictionary or encyclopedia. The open book on the desk, the teacher's explanatory gestures, and the students' attentiveness lend evidence to this analysis.

Chapter 31

Study, Reference, and Test-Taking Skills

▲ Critical Viewing What study skills do you think the students in this photograph are using? Explain. **[Analyze]**

You can build a solid foundation for learning by becoming better at studying, researching, and taking tests. In this chapter, you will learn the best ways to use your study time. You will also learn how to find information more quickly in the library and on the Internet and how to use a variety of reference sources. In addition, you will learn strategies to help improve your performance on tests.

TIME AND RESOURCE MANAGER

Resources
Print: Academic and Workplace Skills Activity Book, pp. 52–53

In-Depth Coverage	Accelerated Pace
• Cover pp. 740–743 in class. • Assign and review Exercises 1–5.	• Assign pp. 740–743 for independent student review.

Section 31.1 Basic Study Skills

Developing a Study Plan

Create an effective study plan by establishing a study area that works well for you and scheduling regular periods of time for studying.

Find a Suitable Study Area You may not realize it, but the place where you choose to study has a major impact on how well you study. Find a study area that is

- free of distractions.
- comfortable.
- well-lit.
- organized.
- equipped with all the necessary supplies, such as pencils, paper, erasers, a stapler and staples, index cards, a dictionary, and a ruler.

Create a Study Schedule It is also important to schedule set time periods in which to study. Create a study schedule that fits your personal needs. Vary the amount of time you spend on each subject, depending on upcoming tests and long-term projects. Set aside extra time for those subjects that give you the most problems.

SAMPLE STUDY SCHEDULE

	4:30–5:00	5:00–5:30	5:30–6:00	7:00–7:30	7:30–8:00	8:00–8:30
Mon	daily assignments		review for ss test Weds	work on science report	study for math test	
Tues	daily assignments		work on science report	study for ss test		
Wed	daily assignments		finish science report		review for Lit test Fri	

Exercise 1 **Planning Your Study Schedule** Create your own study schedule, using the sample above as a model. Follow your schedule for one week, and then evaluate it. Did it help you complete your work on time? Did you follow it every day? Revise the schedule based on your evaluation. Keep a copy of your revised schedule in your notebook, and try to follow it.

Research Tip

In the library and on the Internet, you can find books and articles that offer additional suggestions for improving your study habits.

PREPARE and ENGAGE

Interest GRABBER Announce that there will be a surprise quiz on a topic you know students don't remember, say pronoun-antecedent agreement. After the panic subsides, say you were kidding. Instead the quiz will be about what actors are starring in current movies. After the cheering subsides, ask why students reacted differently to the quizzes. If they spent half the time thinking about schoolwork as they spend thinking about movies, they could relax. This chapter will give them some tips.

Activate Prior Knowledge

Have students share a few study strategies they use. Do they take notes and go over them? Study with partners or in groups? Stay up late going over material the night before a test? Have students give examples of strategies that work well for them and others that don't.

TEACH

Step-by-Step Teaching Guide

Developing a Study Plan

1. Ask students whether they set aside a particular time of day for study. Classes, extracurricular activities, part-time jobs, and many other events happen at regular times every day or every week. Ask what benefits students see in following a regular schedule.
2. Because family obligations, special events, and emergencies frequently come up, study schedules should be flexible. As they set up their schedules, students should try to be realistic about what they can accomplish in a given amount of time. They should also think carefully about priorities. Students have many demands on their time and need to give the most time to the most important responsibilities.

Answer Key

Exercise 1

Have a whole-class discussion of the results of one week's attempt to follow the study schedule. Have students share obstacles they faced in sticking to their study plans, and also success stories. Have students adjust their plans as needed and try again for another week.

Step-by-Step Teaching Guide

Keeping an Assignment Book

1. There is no point creating an assignment book if it gets forgotten at the bottom of a backpack. Students need to record assignments and refer to the book every day.
2. Students can choose an assignment buddy and remind each other every day in school to note work to do.
3. What is the first thing students do when they get home from school? If it is head for the refrigerator, they can stick a large note on the door saying CHECK ASSIGNMENT BOOK.

Critical Viewing

Evaluate Students may say that the comfortable work environment—perhaps, his dining room table—the open books, and notetaking suggests that the boy in the photograph has good study habits.

Answer Key

Exercise 2

At the end of the week, ask students how useful they found this exercise. Ask students to share ideas about how it might be more useful.

31.1

Keeping an Assignment Book

Instead of trusting your memory to recall homework assignments and long-term projects, write them down in an assignment book that makes the due dates clear.

KEY CONCEPT Use an assignment book to record homework and long-term projects and their due dates. ■

One simple way to set up your assignment book is to make five columns on each page. Put the date in the first column. In the second column, list your school subjects. In the third, provide details about your assignments. In the fourth column, list the dates when your assignments are due. In the fifth, check off assignments as they are completed. The sample page below lists two overnight homework assignments and a long-term science project. Notice how the long-term project is divided into a series of steps.

Date	Subject	Assignment	Due	Completed
11/19	English	Read pages 126-136	11/20	✓
11/19	Math	Study for test on decimals	11/20	
11/20	Science	Report on fruit flies	11/30	
		—Research	(11/23)	
		—Drafting	(11/25)	
		—Revising	(11/27)	
		—Final draft	(11/30)	

▼ Critical Viewing What can you conclude about this student's study habits, based on this photograph? **[Evaluate]**

Exercise 2 Setting Up an Assignment Book

In the back of your notebook or in a separate notebook, set up an assignment book. Date each page, and record your assignments using the sample above as a model. Use your assignment book for two weeks. Then, decide whether you need to revise it. For example, you might need to provide more room for writing assignments, or use colored pencils to code the due dates of tests or reports.

ONGOING ASSESSMENT: Monitor and Reinforce

If students are having difficulty setting up and using assignment books, use one of the following options.

Option 1 Have students follow the model shown on the textbook page. Meet with students individually for a minute or two each day, asking what they had planned to accomplish last night and whether they were able to finish it. As time goes on, students should begin to be able to manage on their own.

Option 2 Have students choose just one subject, such as English or science, and keep track of assignment for only that subject for the first two days. On the third day, students can add one more subject, and so on until all subjects of study are covered in the assignment book.

Taking Notes

Taking notes is one of the best ways to remember what you have learned. Organize your notebook by school subject. Then, take notes on what you hear in class and what you read in textbooks. Remember that notes should cover the most important information. You don't have to write down everything.

Use a Modified Outline A modified outline can help you take notes or organize ideas for writing assignments. List main ideas along the margin, indent to show major details, and indent further to show supporting details.

Many Parts of Human Eye — Main idea
1. Iris — Major details
Colored part / *Filters light* — Supporting details
2. Pupil
Black spot
Hole opens wider or closes as more or less light comes in
3. Cornea and Lens
Help focus light
Project upside-down image on retina
4. Retina
Like movie screen
Nerves transmit image to brain, which interprets it

Use Summaries Summaries are an excellent tool to help you review your notes or the chapters you have read. Create a summary by stating in your own words the main ideas and major details of what you have learned.

Exercise 3 **Writing a Paragraph From a Modified Outline** Using the modified outline above, create a paragraph based on the details in it. Examine your paragraph, and ask yourself whether it covers most of the important information.

Exercise 4 **Taking Notes in Outline Form** Create a modified outline based on a chapter in your science textbook.

Exercise 5 **Creating a Summary** Write a summary of a chapter or section of your social studies book.

Learn More

For more information on creating models and taking notes, see Chapter 11, Research.

ONGOING ASSESSMENT: Monitor and Reinforce

If test performance shows that students are probably not taking good notes, try the following option.

Challenge each student to talk to you for a few minutes about any topic with which he or she is familiar. Take notes during the student's talk. Then share your notes with the student, explaining exactly how you organized them and how you can use them to reconstruct the lecture. Then reverse roles, giving the student a chance to try taking notes while you lecture. Go over the student's notes, giving guidance or suggestions for improvement.

Step-by-Step Teaching Guide

Taking Notes

1. Students may want to keep a separate notebook for each class. You might suggest that they use notebooks with different-colored covers, so that there is less chance of grabbing the wrong notebook on the way to class.
2. When taking notes, listeners never write down every word. Writing takes much longer than speaking, and no listener can possibly catch every word. Students should write only main points and should not try to write in complete sentences.

Customize for *More Advanced Students*

Give students a two- or three-minute talk on any subject with which you are very familiar and have them take notes while you are talking. Then challenge them to reconstruct your talk from their notes. They need not attempt to repeat your talk word for word, but they should be able to give the same basic information and take about the same amount of time you took.

Answer Key

Exercise 3

Answers will vary. You may wish to have students check each other's work.

Exercise 4

Answers will vary. You may wish to assign a particular chapter from their science textbook.

Exercise 5

Answers will vary. You may wish to assign a particular chapter or section from their social studies book.

Step-by-Step Teaching Guide

Using the Library

1. You may want to teach this part of the lesson in the school library, so that students can see different sections and elements of the library as you discuss how to use them. Enlist a school librarian to participate in this lesson.
2. The catalog is a complete list of the library's holdings—books, periodicals (magazines), and audiovisual materials.
3. Different libraries alphabetize names by different rules. Students may have to check under both *V* and *B* for Ludwig van Beethoven, and the like.

continued

Section 31.2

Reference Skills

Today, more information is available to people than ever before. Because there is so much information, however, it is essential to develop strong research skills.

Using the Library

Even though there is now a wealth of information available on the Internet, the library is still the best place to begin a research project. To use libraries effectively, it is important to learn the main features of a library and to understand how libraries organize their resources.

Understanding How Resources Are Organized When searching for library resources, be aware that libraries use word-by-word alphabetizing.

- *A, an,* and *the* at the beginning of an entry are not used in alphabetizing. *The Enemy* would be alphabetized under *E.*
- Abbreviations and numbers are read as if they were spelled out. *Dr.* is treated as *Doctor* and *100* as *one hundred.*
- All *Mc* and *Mac* words are alphabetized as if they were *Mac.*

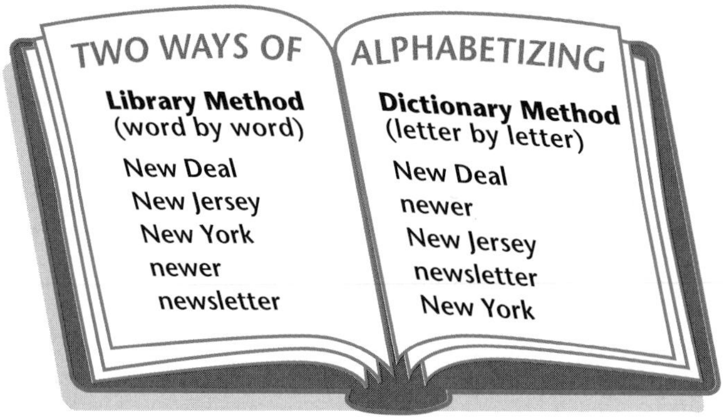

Using the Library Catalog The above methods are used for alphabetizing the resources listed in the library catalog. The library catalog is the starting place for finding most resources in a library. The catalog can be in one of three forms:

Card Catalog This system lists books on index cards, with a separate *author card* and *title card* for each book. If the book is nonfiction, it also has a subject card. Author cards are alphabetized by last names, and title cards, by the title's first word. Look at the sample on the next page.

TIME AND RESOURCE MANAGER

Resources
Print: Academic and Workplace Skills Activity Book, pp. 54–58

In-Depth Coverage	Accelerated Pace
• Cover pp. 744–754 in class. • Assign and review Exercises 6–14.	• Assign pp. 744–754 for independent student review.

CARD CATALOG (AUTHOR CARD)

call number/ author	**909.0492B Banks, Lynne Reid**
title	**Letters to my Israeli sons: the story of Jewish survival**
city of publication	**New York:**
publisher,/ publication date	**F. Watts, 1980**
number of pages /special features	**276 p; maps**
subjects	**1. Jews—history 2. Zionism 3. Palestine**

Printed Catalog This catalog lists books in printed booklets, with each book listed alphabetically by author, by title, and—if nonfiction—by subject.

PRINTED CATALOG (TITLE LISTING)

title	author	
LETTERS TO MY ISRAELI SONS: THE STORY OF JEWISH SURVIVAL	Lynne Reid Banks	
city of publication	publisher	publication date
New York:	F. Watts,	1980.
number of pages/illustrations	size of book	
276p. maps	25cm.	
subject	call number	
Jews; Zionism; Palestine	909.0492 B	

Electronic Catalog This catalog lists books in a CD-ROM or on-line database. Using a library computer, you can find a book's catalog entry by typing in its title, key words in the title, the author's name, or, for nonfiction, a related subject.

ELECTRONIC CATALOG

Author:	Banks, Lynne Reid
Title:	Letters to my Israeli sons: the story of Jewish survival.
Published:	New York: F. Watts, 1980
Description:	276p.; maps.; 25 cm.
Subject:	Jews; Zionism; Palestine
Call No.:	909.0492 B
Status:	On shelf.

Technology Tip

Some library catalogs can be accessed remotely from home computers. Ask your librarian whether this feature is available.

Step-by-Step Teaching Guide continued

4. Go through the descriptions of the three types of catalogs with students. Most libraries have converted their card catalogs to electronic catalogs. Electronic catalogs take up less space and provide certain conveniences in searching that card catalogs did not. Many times, small special collections in large libraries will still have card catalogs.
5. A card catalog is a series of cabinets with drawers just the right size to hold long rows of index cards. Each drawer is labeled with the letters of the first and last card contained in the drawer, for example, ARB–ASC. The drawers are arranged in alphabetical order. Cards for authors, titles, and subjects are all interfiled in one large alphabetical run. In other words, cards for the author Laurence **Yep,** the subject **Yemen,** and the title *The* **Year** *the Yankees Lost the Pennant* will all be in the same drawer of the card catalog.

Answer Key

Exercise 6

1. Answers may vary.
2. Rachel Carson; nonfiction
3. Answers may vary.
4. Answers may vary.
5. Answers may vary.

Step-by-Step Teaching Guide

Finding the Book You Want

1. For locating works of fiction, all students have to do is know how to spell the author's name. Works of poetry, drama, and children's fiction are also filed alphabetically by the author's last name.
2. Go over the sections of the Dewey Decimal System. Some libraries use the Library of Congress system. Although it assigns call numbers on a different basis from the Dewey Decimal system, it also shelves books in call-number order.
3. Reference books labeled R or REF are set aside for use in the library only. These books, such as encyclopedias, dictionaries, and atlases, cannot be borrowed.

continued

Customize for *ESL and Less Advanced Students*

Urge students not to hesitate to ask the librarian questions, even if students think they are "stupid" questions. Librarians love to help—that's what they are there for.

Exercise 6 **Using the Library Catalog** Visit your school or local library, and find the answers to the following questions:

1. What kind of catalog does the library use—card, printed, or electronic? Where is it located?
2. Who wrote *Silent Spring*? Is it fiction or nonfiction?
3. What are the titles, subjects, and call numbers of two books your library carries by author Diane Ackerman?
4. What are the titles, authors, and call numbers of three books about snakes published since 1985?
5. What are the titles, authors, and call numbers of two books about rock climbing that are more than 100 pages long?

Finding the Book You Want Usually, a library divides and shelves books according to whether they are *fiction* (stories and novels) or *nonfiction* (factual information). Nonfiction also includes two smaller groups that are often shelved separately: *biographies* and *reference books.*

KEY CONCEPT Fiction and nonfiction books are shelved separately in the library, with each following a different method of organization. ■

Fiction Books If you know the author's last name, you can go to the fiction section and look for your book by author. If you do not know the author, look up the book under its title in the library catalog. If there are two or more books by a particular author on the shelf, they will be alphabetized by title.

Nonfiction Books Nonfiction books are arranged according to a *call number*, a combination of a number and one or more letters. It is found on the upper left corner of a catalog card and on the spine (side) of the book. Books are arranged in number-letter order on the shelves—for example, 541.1, 541.2, 541.21A, 541.21C, 541.3. To find a nonfiction book, look it up in the library catalog, find its call number, and then follow number-letter order to locate it on the shelves.

Most school and public libraries use the **Dewey Decimal System** to classify books. In this system, all knowledge is divided into ten main classes, numbered from 000 to 999 (see the chart at the top of the next page). The first digit indicates the general subject of the book. The other digits represent subgroupings of the general subject. To help you find books using the Dewey Decimal System, note that

- libraries display call numbers on each stack of shelves. For example, if you wanted a book with the call number 974.2T, you would go to the shelves labeled "972–979."
- you can find more books on a subject by looking at books with the same call number.

Understanding the main classes of the Dewey Decimal System will also help you find books more quickly.

Main Classes of the Dewey Decimal System

000-099	General Works
100-199	Philosophy
200-299	Religion
300-399	Social Sciences
400-499	Languages
500-599	Pure Sciences
600-699	Technology
700-799	The Arts
800-899	Literature
900-999	History

Finding Special Materials In addition to the fiction and nonfiction sections, libraries usually have other sections that contain specialized books, such as the following:

Biographies Many libraries have a section for biographies. The call number is usually *B* or 92, followed by the first few letters of the subject of the book. For example, *Kit Carson: Trail Blazer and Scout,* by Shannon Garst, would be labeled *B* for biography and *Car* for Carson.

Reference Books Reference works may also be shelved in a special section. Books in the reference section are often labeled *R* or *REF.* A call number follows the abbreviation. If a book you look up in the library catalog has *REF* before its call number, go first to the library's reference section. Then, use the call number to find the book.

Young Adult Books Some libraries also have a section for young adult books. These are books written for teenagers.

Exercise 7 **Locating Fiction Books** Arrange the following fiction books in library-shelf order:

1. *Mystery at Crane's Landing* by Marcella Thum
2. *The Martian Chronicles* by Ray Bradbury
3. *Sea Glass* by Laurence Yep
4. *Something Wicked This Way Comes* by Ray Bradbury
5. *Summer of the Swans* by Betsy Byars

Exercise 8 **Locating Nonfiction Books** Arrange the following call numbers in library-shelf order. Then, identify the general subject area of each book.

1. 150.1 G
2. 629 M
3. 301.42 A
4. 301.415 F
5. 629 B

Technology Tip

Print the search results from an electronic catalog to search efficiently for several sources in one trip to the shelves.

Step-by-Step Teaching Guide continued

4. Encourage students to browse library shelves. Books on similar subjects are shelved close together, and glancing through the contents of the shelves will often show students books they did not come across in their catalog searches. If the particular book they wanted is missing, they can find another book that covers the same information.

Answer Key

Exercise 7

1. *The Martian Chronicles* by Ray Bradbury
2. *Something Wicked This Way Comes* by Ray Bradbury
3. *Summer of the Swans* by Betsy Byars
4. *Mystery at Crane's Landing* by Marcella Thum
5. *Sea Glass* by Laurence Yep

Exercise 8

150.1 G, philosophy; 301.415 F, social sciences; 301.42 A, social sciences; 629 B, technology; 629 M, technology

ONGOING ASSESSMENT: Monitor and Reinforce

If students are having trouble using the library, try the following option.

Assign your students two or three classes from the Dewey Decimal System. Have them find the particular section in the library that contains these classes. Choose one book for each class, and write down the author, title, call number, and the amount of pages contained in the book. Remind them that they may have to go to different sections of the library to find the books, as the classes may differ greatly.

Step-by-Step Teaching Guide

Using Periodicals and Periodical Indexes

1. A periodical is a magazine, journal, or newspaper that is published in a given period, such as weekly or monthly.
2. Some periodicals come out so often that they have their own indexes. Major daily newspapers such as *The New York Times* and *The Washington Post* publish annual indexes of all the articles in every issue of the paper. Articles are indexed by subject. Many libraries have major newspapers on microfilm, since newspaper deteriorates rapidly and cannot be handled without damage.

Answer Key

Exercise 9

Answers may vary.

Using Periodicals and Periodical Indexes

Periodicals are printed materials, such as newspapers and magazines, that are published on a regular basis.

KEY CONCEPT Use magazines, journals, and newspapers to find concise, current information. Use periodical indexes to find articles in periodicals. ■

Periodical Indexes When you are researching a topic, use periodical indexes to locate articles on that topic. Use the subject index to find *citations*, or listings that tell you when and where articles were published on your topic. Some periodical indexes also include *abstracts*, or brief summaries of articles.

Some periodical indexes cover articles from many printed sources; others cover articles from only one source. The periodical index that you will probably use the most is the *Readers' Guide to Periodical Literature*. It lists, by subject, articles that have appeared in most magazines within a specific time frame.

ENTRY FROM THE *READERS' GUIDE*

Labels: Main subject heading; Cross-references; Title of article; Magazine title; Author of article; Volume: page numbers and date; Illustrated; Subheading

Solar radiation
See also
Solar flares
Solar wind
Sunspots
Ultraviolet rays
The inconstant solar constant [Solar Max data] R. C. Willson and others. il *Sky Telesc* 67:501-3 Je '84
Liquid droplets on high [water in cirus clouds: research by Kenneth Sassen and Kuo-Nan Liou] C. Simon. *Sci News* 125:406 Je 30 '84
Radiation satellite designed for shuttle [Earth Radiation on climate] C. Covault. il *Aviat Week Space Technol* 121:41-3+ S 17 '84
Solar irradiance observations [solar constant; Spacelab data] D. Crommelynck and V. Domingo. bibl f il *Science* 225:180-1 Jl 13 '84
Physiological effects
See also
Seasonal affect disorder
Suntan

Exercise 9 **Using the *Readers' Guide*** Use a recent volume of the *Readers' Guide* to locate two articles on earthquakes. For each article, note the periodical, the title of the article, its author, volume, date, and page number(s).

Technology Tip

Most periodical indexes are now available electronically, either on CD-ROM or on the Internet. Use the keyword search feature to access citations of articles on your topic. You will find that some electronic indexes include complete articles on some topics.

Finding Periodicals Once you've used a periodical index to identify appropriate articles, enlist the help of your librarian to locate the articles. Often, past editions of magazines are stored by a library on a database, on microfilm, or on CD-ROMs. Your librarian can show you how to use these resources.

Using Vertical Files In addition to information stored on shelves, on CD-ROMs, and on microfilm, many libraries have vertical files—file cabinets with large drawers where they store pamphlets on a wide variety of topics. For example, your library might have pamphlets about your local government. Such pamphlets can be a valuable research aid. Ask your librarian about the type of information stored in your library's vertical files.

Using Dictionaries

A *dictionary* is a collection of words and their meanings. A dictionary explains how words are spelled, how they are pronounced, and how they are used in a sentence. Dictionaries also provide information about a word's history, or *etymology*.

KEY CONCEPT Dictionaries contain a great deal of useful information about words. ■

Using Your Dictionary to Check Spelling The English language can have many spellings for one sound.

KEY CONCEPT Become familiar with the different spelling patterns of sounds in English words. ■

You can usually find the word you want if you guess at the first few letters. *Webster's New World Dictionary* (student edition) has charts like the one below that can help you locate words with tricky sounds.

WORD FINDER CHART

If the sound is like the...	try also the spelling...	as in the words...
a in fat	ai, au	plaid, draught
a in lane	ai, ao, au, ay, ea, ei, eigh, et, ey	rain, gaol, gauge, ray, break, rein, weigh, sachet, they
a in care	ai, ay, e, eu, ei	air, prayer, there, wear, their
a in father	au, e, ea	gaunt, sergeant, hearth
a in ago	e, i, o, u	agent, sanity, comply, focus
ch in chin	tch, ti, tu	catch, question, nature
e in get	a, ae, ai, ay	any, aesthete, said, says

Internet Tip

Today, most magazines have Web sites. Utilize these Web sites to help you find the articles you've identified in periodical indexes.

Step-by-Step Teaching Guide

Using Dictionaries

1. Display an unabridged dictionary and show students some of its special sections. Besides the A–Z entries of words, dictionaries often include illustrations of certain entries; tables; maps; gazetteers; lists of personal names and what they mean; lists of abbreviations; a section of rhyming words; and other special information.
2. As a homework assignment, have students spend ten minutes looking through an unabridged dictionary. Have them turn over its pages, look at the special sections in the front and back, read a few entries that catch their eye, look at some of the illustrations, and so on. Next day in class, have students share what they learned about dictionaries.

continued

Customize for *ESL Students*

Students whose home language is not English may be puzzled by phonetic spellings in English dictionaries. In languages such as Spanish, Italian and Swahili, words are pronounced the way they are spelled. Dictionaries of these languages do not show phonetic spellings—it isn't necessary. Encourage students to pay attention to the pronunciations when they look up English words. This will help them learn the language.

Step-by-Step Teaching Guide continued

3. Many dictionaries are thumb-indexed to make finding words easier. Students should look at these tabs to find the first letter of the word they are looking up.
4. Some dictionaries do not include geographical names within the alphabetical entries. Instead, they have a separate section of all place names in alphabetical order. This listing is called a gazetteer. Names of prominent historical figures may be in another separate alphabetical listing.

Answer Key

Exercise 10

1. Rip Van Winkle
2. ripe
3. ripen
4. ripple
5. riptide

Exercise 11

Answers will vary.

1. S–Z, tolerability/tomfool
2. E–L, impart/imperialistically
3. M–R, parachutist/parallel
4. M–R, ringneck snake/riptide
5. S–Z, Sherwood/shine

31.2

Finding Words Quickly in a Dictionary Use the three-step process to help you find words quickly in a dictionary.

1. Step One: Take a Four-Section Approach Mentally divide the dictionary into four sections:

ABCD EFGHIJKL MNOPQR STUVWXYZ

These sections seem unequal, but there are as many English words that start with A–D as with S–Z. Here is how to use this approach: If you are looking for the word *catastrophic*, you know it will be in the first quarter of the dictionary. Similarly, the word *noxious* will be near the middle.

2. Step Two: Use the Guide Words At the top of each page are *guide words*. The guide word on the left tells the first word on the page. The guide word on the right tells the last word on the page. Look for the pair of guide words that come before and after your word.

3. Step Three: Follow Letter-by-Letter Alphabetical Order To locate your word on the page, remember that the entries are in *strict alphabetical order*. This rule holds true even if the entry has more than one word. (For example, *okra* comes before *Olaf*, *Olaf* before *olden*, and *olden* before *old hand*.)

Exercise 10 **Alphabetizing Words** List the following words in the order you would find them in a dictionary.

1. ripen
2. riptide
3. ripple
4. Rip Van Winkle
5. ripe

Exercise 11 **Finding Words Quickly** Use the three steps listed above to find these words quickly. Identify the dictionary section and the guide words for the page on which you find each word.

1. tomahawk
2. impassive
3. paradox
4. ripe
5. shilling

Understanding Dictionary Entries The words that make up a dictionary are called *entry words*. An entry word, with all of the information about it, is called a *main entry*. Entry words include not only single words but also compound words (two or more words acting as one, such as *national bank*), abbreviations (*nat.*), prefixes (*re-*), suffixes (*-ent*), and the names of significant persons and places (*Nigeria*).

Look at the sample main entry on the next page.

Technology Tip

When using an electronic dictionary, you can find a word by typing in its first few letters. Doing so will take you to a list of words with similar beginnings from which you can choose the word for which you are looking.

ONGOING ASSESSMENT: Monitor and Reinforce

If written work shows that students are weak in vocabulary and spelling, use one of the following options.

Option 1 Students should go over the corrections marked on their written assignments, looking for misused and misspelled words. Students should check each word in a dictionary, noting its correct meaning and spelling. Students can copy the words and definitions into vocabulary notebooks.

Option 2 Have students who have difficulty with reading comprehension work together on reading assignments. At the end of each chapter or section of text, partners can go over new or unfamiliar words. They should check the meaning of each in a dictionary. Periodically, partners can test each other on these words.

MAIN ENTRY IN A DICTIONARY

Pronunciation — Primary Stress — Main Entry — Syllabification — Part of Speech — Etymology — Field Label — Numbered Definitions — Usage Label — Idiom — Part of Speech — Derived Word

wid•ow (wid´ō) ***n.*** **[**ME. *widwe* < OE. *widewe,* akin to G. *witwe* < IE. **widhewo-*, separated < **weidh-*, to separate, whence G. *waise,* orphan, L. *vidua,* a widow, (*di*)videre, to DIVIDE**]** **1.** a woman who has outlived the man to whom she was married at the time of his death; esp., such a woman who has not remarried **2.** *Cards* a number of cards dealt into a separate pile, typically for the use of the highest bidder **3.** [Colloq.] a) *short for* GRASS WIDOW b) a woman whose husband is often away indulging a specified hobby, sport, etc. [a golf *widow*] —***vt.*** **1.** to cause to become a widow: usually in the past participle [*widowed* by the war] —**wid´ow•hood´** ***n.***

- **Syllabification** Dots, spaces, or slashes (/) show how a word is divided into syllables. This can help you when you need to break a word at the end of a line in your writing.
- **Pronunciations** Symbols show how to say a word and indicate which syllable to stress. A heavy mark (´) shows the syllable emphasized most (*primary stress*), and a lighter mark (ˊ) shows one with less emphasis (*secondary stress*).
- **Parts-of-Speech Labels** These labels are abbreviated. They show how a word can be used in a sentence—whether it functions as a noun, a verb, or some other part of speech. Different meanings may fit different uses.
- **Etymology** Etymology is defined as the origin and history of a word. This useful information is provided in brackets after the definition. The etymological abbreviations and symbols are explained at the beginning of a dictionary.
- **Definitions** If there is more than one meaning for a word, each is listed by number. Multiple meanings are often used in a phrase or sentence for clarification.
- **Special Labels** *Usage labels*—such as *slang, dialect,* and *colloquial*—tell you that a certain meaning is not used in formal English. *Field labels,* such as *Bio* (for Biology), show that a meaning is limited in its usage.
- **Idioms** *Idioms* are expressions that contain the entry word, such as *down at the heels.* These may need to be explained because they do not mean exactly what their words say.
- **Derived Words** Words formed by adding a suffix (*-ly, -ness*) are listed at the end of the main entry.

Spelling Tip

Be aware that some words have more than one accepted spelling. All acceptable spellings are listed in dictionaries.

Step-by-Step Teaching Guide

Understanding Dictionary Entries

1. If students cannot remember what all the pronunciation symbols mean, they can use the key in the dictionary. It usually appears at the bottom of every right-hand page.
2. Go over the etymology of *widow* item by item. The < symbol traces the word back from Middle English to Old English to German to Indo-European to Latin.

Answer Key

Exercise 12

1. fourth syllable
2. from the French *charrar,* meaning "to gossip, chatter"
3. pleasurable excitement, thrill
4. off the peg, peg away at, round peg in a square hole, square peg in a round hole, take down a peg
5. to shut up in a private room for a confidential discussion

Step-by-Step Teaching Guide

Using Other Reference Works

1. In addition to general encyclopedias such as *World Book,* there are many smaller, more specialized encyclopedias. These can be several volumes or sometimes just one. Small encyclopedias focus on a particular subject and give greater detail about it. Examples include *The African American Encyclopedia* and *The Baseball Encyclopedia.* When students research a topic in depth, these specialized encyclopedias can be very helpful.
2. Introduce students to some of the major biographical references, such as *Who's Who in the United States* and *The Dictionary of American Biography.* Libraries contain many specialized biographical references that deal with a particular category of people. One example is the *Dictionary of Literary Biography,* a multivolume work that gives detailed biographies of writers.

continued

Exercise 12 **Working With Main Entries** Answer the following questions by using a dictionary.

1. Which syllable in *characteristic* has the primary stress?
2. Give the etymology of the word *charade.*
3. Find a slang definition for the word *charge.*
4. Find an idiom for the word *peg.*
5. What is the meaning of *closet* used as a verb?

Using Other Print and Electronic References

In addition to nonfiction books, dictionaries, and periodicals, there is a wide range of other print and electronic references you can use.

Using Encyclopedias Encyclopedias contain facts on a great many subjects. They provide basic information to help you start researching a topic.

KEY CONCEPT Use encyclopedias for basic facts, background information, and suggestions for additional research. ■

Volumes and Articles Are Arranged Alphabetically The volumes of an encyclopedia are arranged in alphabetical order. The pages have guide words to show you the first and last subjects covered on each page.

Major Encyclopedias Have an Index Most encyclopedias have an index to help you locate articles. The encyclopedia index entry shown below directs you to the volume and page number of the article. Related articles are also listed.

ENCYCLOPEDIA INDEX ENTRY

Volume
Page Number

Space travel So:560 *with pictures and maps*
See also the reading and study guide on this topic
Air Force, United States (The Air Force in Space) A:185
Altitude A:372b
Astronomy (Space Exploration) A:813
Computer (In Engineering) Ci:742 *with picture*
Cosmic Rays (Effect of Cosmic Rays) Ci:857

Using Biographical References These books provide brief life histories of famous people in many different fields. Biographical references may offer short entries similar to those in dictionaries or longer articles more like those in encyclopedias. Most contain an index to help you locate entries.

Technology Tip

There is a wide range of multimedia encyclopedias on CD-ROM. In addition to articles, photographs, maps, and charts, these CD-ROMs offer audio and video on certain subjects. To use a CD-ROM encyclopedia, type your subject into the keyword search feature.

Using Almanacs Almanacs are published annually. They contain facts and statistics about many subjects, including government, world history, geography, entertainment, business, and sports. To find a subject in a printed almanac, refer to the index in the front or back. In an *electronic almanac*, you can usually find information by typing a subject or key word.

Using Atlases and Electronic Map Collections *Atlases* and *electronic map collections* contain maps and information based on them, such as facts about cities, bodies of water, mountains, and landmarks. Some also supply statistics about population, climate, products, and natural resources. In *printed atlases*, use an index to learn on which map to look for a particular place. In electronic atlases or map collections, you usually type in the place name, and the computer searches a database for the appropriate map.

Using Thesauruses A thesaurus gives *synonyms* (words with similar meanings) and may list *antonyms* (words with opposite meanings). It is especially useful for writing, when you need to find a substitute for a word. Many *printed thesauruses* arrange words alphabetically. Others arrange words on the basis of themes; you must look up the word in an index to learn where to find its synonyms. With *electronic thesauruses* (included with most word-processing programs), you usually type in or highlight a word, and the computer searches a database.

Using Electronic Databases Available on CD-ROMs or on-line, electronic databases provide quick access to a wealth of information on a broad topic. For example, you could use an electronic database to look at information on a stock's performance over the past several years. Using a search feature, you can easily access any type of data, piece together related information, or look at the information in different ways.

Exercise 13 **Using Reference Sources** Supply information for each item below, and list the type of reference you used.

1. average temperature of Phoenix, Arizona, in March
2. states that border Lake Erie
3. birthdate of the cartoonist who created Charlie Brown
4. three accomplishments of Harriet Tubman
5. information about malaria
6. three synonyms for the word *inflexible*
7. Ray Bradbury's first published novel
8. two antonyms for the word *discomfort*
9. American League baseball's Most Valuable Player for 1999
10. five states with towns or cities named *Augusta*

Technology Tip

You can use electronic maps to examine a historical journey, plan the route for a trip, or give local directions.

Step-by-Step Teaching Guide continued

3. An almanac is full of more interesting information than the exports of Uruguay and the capital of Mozambique. An almanac tells the members of the Baseball Hall of Fame, Academy Award winners, the longest snake, the fastest animal, and the worst volcanic eruption ever.
4. Make sure students understand the difference between a dictionary and a thesaurus. A dictionary defines words; a thesaurus does not. It provides synonyms for thousands of words. It can be a writer's best friend.

Answer Key

Exercise 13

Some answers will vary. Samples are given.

1. 58°F
2. New York, Pennsylvania, Ohio, Michigan—atlas
3. 1922—encyclopedia
4. conductor on Underground Railroad, abolitionist, Union nurse in Civil War—encyclopedia
5. infectious disease transmitted by *Anopheles* mosquito; treated with quinine; common in Central and South America, Mediterranean countries, Asia, Pacific Islands—encyclopedia
6. stubborn, adamant, determined—thesaurus
7. *Fahrenheit 451* (1953)
8. uneasiness, inconvenience, distress—dictionary
9. Ivan Rodriguez
10. Arkansas, Georgia, Illinois, Kentucky, Maine, Michigan, Montana, New Jersey, Wisconsin—atlas

ONGOING ASSESSMENT SYSTEM: Monitor and Reinforce

If students are having trouble using reference sources, try one of the following options.

Option 1 List five words on the chalkboard, such as effusion, fence, mercurial, scurf, and ubiquity. Using the example of a Main Entry in a Dictionary on p. 751, have students write down the various elements — etymology, part of speech, definition, etc. — that are present in the entries for these words. Then have them use a thesaurus to write down the synonyms and antonyms for the list of words.

Option 2 Have students consult an almanac and atlas for pertinent information concerning their birthplace. Have them write down any facts and statistics concerning population, climate, city history, geography, etc. Make sure that they indicate whether the information has come from an almanac or atlas. Then have students pair up and check each other's answers.

Step-by-Step Teaching Guide

Using the Internet

1. Some students may have a great deal of experience with computers and the Internet. Have them share information with those students who are less experienced.
2. Warn all students to use the Internet with caution. Since anyone can post anything on the Internet, it contains a great deal of unreliable information. If students have any doubts about information they find on the Internet, they should check it against a reference book on the appropriate topic.

Answer Key

Exercise 14

1. the creator and host of the television comedy show, *Candid Camera*
2. five
3. Answers will vary.
4. John Kague
5. Answers will vary.

Critical Viewing

Connect Students may say that another person can think of different ways to search for information.

31.2

Using the Internet

The *Internet* is a worldwide network, or Web, of computers connected over phone and cable lines. When you go *on-line*, or hook up with the Internet, you can access millions of Web sites where an amazing amount of information can be found. Each Web site has its own address, or *URL* (Universal Resource Locator). It usually consists of several Web pages of text, graphics, and sometimes audio or video displays.

A number of *search engines* have been established to help you locate a potentially useful Web site. A search engine such as **www.yahoo.com** is a good place to search for broad categories of information.

▲ Critical Viewing How can working with another student make it easier to gather information on the Internet? **[Connect]**

KEY CONCEPT Use the Internet to locate many types of information, but judge Web sites for reliability. ■

The Internet is an excellent resource, but it contains Web sites that have not been thoroughly researched or that may contain slanted opinions instead of factual information. Here are some tips for finding reliable information on the Internet:

- If you know a reliable Web site and its address (URL), simply type in the address on your Web browser.
- Consult Internet coverage in library journals (such as *Library Journal*) for lists of reliable Web sites.
- Remember to "bookmark" (or save) interesting and reliable sites that you find while searching the Web.
- Identify the organization or person that set up the site. Is that organization or person likely to have a bias?
- Identify the source of the information. Does the information come from authorities on the topic? Is it backed up by research?
- Is the information up-to-date?

Learn More

For extensive information on using the Internet and critically evaluating Internet sites, see the Internet Handbook on page 769.

Exercise 14 **Using the Internet** On a library, school, or home computer, use the Internet to answer these questions.

1. Who was Allen Funt?
2. How many MTV Awards did Lauryn Hill win in 1999?
3. What are the URLs of four Web sites with information on Lyme disease?
4. Who won the 1998 New York Marathon?
5. What is the URL of a site with a map of Detroit, Michigan?

Section 31.3 Test-Taking Skills

This section provides some tips to help you improve your performance on tests by helping you answer the different kinds of questions they contain.

Strategies for Taking Tests

When you prepare for a test, carefully study the material that the test will cover, and be sure to come to the test on time with all the equipment you have been told to bring—pens, pencils, books, and so on. When you take the test, plan how you will use your time.

KEY CONCEPT Divide your time among previewing the test, answering the questions, and proofreading your answers. ■

LOOK OVER THE TEST (no more than 25% of time)

1. Put your name on your paper.
2. Skim the test to look over the different kinds of questions.
3. Decide how much time you will spend on each section.
4. Allow time for difficult or high-point questions.

ANSWER THE QUESTIONS (allow at least 50% of time)

1. If you can, use scratch paper to jot down your ideas.
2. Answer the easy questions first.
3. For harder items, concentrate on one question at a time.
4. Be sure to follow the directions completely.

PROOFREAD ANSWERS (no more than 25% of time)

1. Check that you have followed directions.
2. Reread test questions and answers.
3. Make sure that you have answered all of the questions.

Exercise 15 **Evaluating Your Test-Taking Skills** Answer these questions about a test you have taken recently.

1. Did you give yourself enough time to study beforehand?
2. Did you focus on the information you needed for the test?
3. Did you look over the test carefully before you began writing?
4. Did you answer all of the easy questions first?
5. Did you allow enough time for the difficult questions or for questions that were worth more points?

Step-by-Step Teaching Guide

Strategies for Taking Tests

1. If there is no penalty for wrong answers, then students must answer every question, even if they take a wild guess.
2. If there is a penalty, students should try to eliminate answer choices they know are wrong. If they can eliminate two of four choices, then they should guess. If they can eliminate only one choice, guessing is not a good option. Leave the answer blank.
3. Have students share various test-taking experiences. Encourage them to describe study techniques that worked well for them.

Answer Key

Exercise 15

Answers will vary.

TIME AND RESOURCE MANAGER

Resources
Print: Academic and Workplace Skills Activity Book, pp. 59–60

• Cover pp. 755–759 in class. • Assign and review Exercises 15–17.	• Assign pp. 755–759 for independent student review.

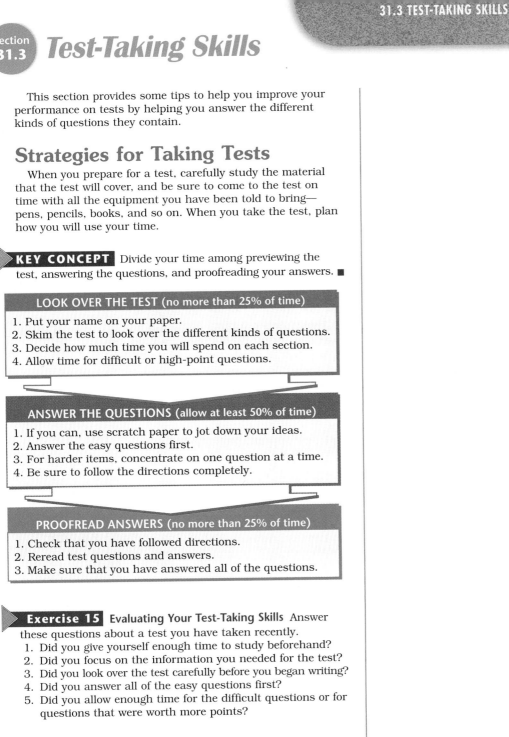

Step-by-Step Teaching Guide

Answering Different Types of Questions

1. Work through the multiple-choice example, assuming that no one knows the meaning of *martial.* It asks for the opposite. The opposite of choice a, *sad,* is *happy.* Does *martial* mean "happy"? That doesn't feel right. The opposite of choice b would be *warlike.* Does *martial* mean "warlike"? That's possible. Continue with choices c and d. By process of elimination only choice b works.
2. Point out that in both multiple-choice and matching questions on grammar tests, the part of speech of each choice is a good clue to the correct answer. Choice c, *dig,* is a verb. So it can't match 2 or 3, which are both adjectives.

continued

Critical Viewing

Analyze Students may suggest that the woman in the photograph is answering a question or questions concerning material in the open book. Therefore, one may surmise that the student is preparing for a test.

31.3

Answering Different Types of Questions

If you are familiar with the different kinds of questions that are frequently asked on tests, you may be able to improve your performance on the tests.

KEY CONCEPT Know the different kinds of objective questions and the strategies for answering them. ■

Multiple-Choice Questions This kind of question asks you to choose from several possible responses.

EXAMPLE: The opposite of *martial* is ____.

a. sad	c. enthusiastic
b. peaceful	d. hostile

In the preceding example, the answer is *b.* Follow these strategies to answer multiple-choice questions:

- Try answering the question before looking at the answer choices. If your answer is one of the choices, select that one.
- Eliminate the obviously incorrect answers, crossing them out if you are allowed to write on the test paper.
- Read all of the choices before answering. For multiple-choice items, there are often two *possible* answers, but only one *best* answer.

Matching Questions Matching questions require you to match items in one group with items in another.

EXAMPLE:

____ 1. dredge	a. shy
____ 2. introverted	b. refined
____ 3. genteel	c. dig

In the preceding example, the answers are 1.*c,* 2.*a,* 3.*b.* Follow these strategies to answer matching questions:

- Count each group to see whether items will be left over. Check the directions to see whether items can be used more than once.
- Read all of the items before you start matching.
- Match the items you know first.
- Match the remaining items of which you are less certain.

▼ Critical Viewing Do you think this student is preparing for a test or taking a test? Why? **[Analyze]**

ONGOING ASSESSMENT SYSTEM: Monitor and Reinforce

If test scores show that students are having trouble, use one of the following options.

Option 1 Have students take practice tests once a week. You may want to develop these tests, or students can use the practice tests in one of the many test-prep publications. Emphasize that the purpose is to accustom students to the format of the various types of test questions.

Option 2 Meet with students individually and discuss any difficulties they have with test formats. If a student has a particular area of difficulty, develop practice questions that will give him or her extra practice in that area. Monitor students' progress during the year.

True/False Questions True/false questions require you to determine whether a statement is accurate.

EXAMPLE: ____ Earth is the closet planet to the sun in our solar system.
____ An astronomer is someone who studies stars.
____ A telescope is not used to study the stars.

In the preceding example, the answers are *F, T, F.* Follow these strategies to answer true/false questions:

- If a statement seems true, be sure the entire sentence is true.
- Pay special attention to the word *not*, which often changes the entire meaning of a statement.
- Pay special attention to the words *all, always, never, no, none,* and *only.* They often make a statement false.
- Pay special attention to the words *generally, much, many, most, often, some,* and *usually.* They often make a statement true.

Fill-in Questions Fill-in questions ask you to supply an answer in your own words. The answer may complete a statement or may simply answer a question.

EXAMPLE: Presidential elections are held every ____ years.

In the preceding example, the answer is *four.* Follow these strategies to answer fill-in questions:

- Read the question or incomplete statement carefully.
- If you are answering a question, change it into a statement by inserting your answer, and see whether it makes sense.

Analogies An analogy asks you to find pairs of words with a similar relationship.

EXAMPLE: CEILING : ROOM ::
a. wall : floor c. roof : house
b. foundation : cement d. wall : paper

In the preceding example, the answer is *c.* The relationship is *part to whole.* The ceiling is part of a room, and the roof is part of a house. Once you understand analogy relationships (see the chart on the next page), you can use the strategies below to answer the questions.

- Identify how the first pair of words relate.
- If more than one choice seems correct, go back to the first pair, and redefine its relationship.
- If you cannot find an equal relationship between the first pair and a second pair, consider other possible word meanings.

Step-by-Step Teaching Guide continued

3. Stress the importance of reading questions carefully. If students skim the third true/false question, they are likely to miss *not* and so choose the wrong answer.
4. If students don't know the answer to a fill-in question, they can try to narrow down the possibilities.

STANDARDIZED TEST PREPARATION WORKSHOP

Analogies Standardized tests contain all of the types of objective questions shown on these two pages. Ask students to choose the word that best completes the following analogy.

BAT : BASEBALL :: HAMMER : ___

A screwdriver **B** nail
C horseshoe **D** strike

The correct answer is **B**. A baseball hits a bat; a hammer hits a nail.

Step-by-Step Teaching Guide

Answering Analogies

Go over the answers to Exercise 16. Ask students to explain how they made their choices. For example, for question 7: "You stretch before you run, and you chew before you swallow."

Answer Key

Exercise 16

1. synonyms; a
2. type; c
3. cause and effect; c
4. specific to general; a
5. antonyms; c
6. part to whole; a
7. cause-effect; b
8. type; c
9. synonyms; b
10. antonyms; a

Exercise 17

Answers will vary.

31.3

COMMON ANALOGY RELATIONSHIPS

Relationship	Example
synonym (same meaning)	carousel : merry-go-round
antonym (opposite meaning)	enlarge : shrink
function	chauffeur : drive
part to whole	page : book
cause-effect	veterinarian : heal
type	mongoose : mammal

Exercise 16 **Answering Analogies** Identify the relationship between the words in each first pair below. Then, complete each second pair (the first part of it has been provided).

1. NOTIFY : TELL :: SPECULATE : __?__
   a. guess b. invest c. insult
2. SURGEON : DOCTOR :: SEDAN : __?__
   a. drive b. accident c. automobile
3. SHOVEL : HOLE :: GLUE : __?__
   a. loosen b. sticky c. attachment
4. PHARAOH : RULER :: TORNADO : __?__
   a. storm b. hurricane c. summer
5. PERMANENT : TEMPORARY :: PURIFIED : __?__
   a. water b. safe c. polluted
6. HANDLE : CUP :: WINDSHIELD : __?__
   a. car b. protect c. wind
7. STRETCH : RUN :: CHEW : __?__
   a. cook b. swallow c. bite
8. DRIZZLE : DOWNPOUR :: TAP : __?__
   a. drink b. dance c. wallop
9. PILFER : STEAL :: ANTAGONIZE : __?__
   a. remove b. anger c. befriend
10. EMINENT : UNKNOWN :: OBVIOUS : __?__
    a. unclear b. unsafe c. unhappy

Exercise 17 **Answering Test Items** Using a topic you are studying in science class, prepare a short test on the material. Write five multiple-choice questions, five matching questions, five true/false questions, and five fill-in questions. Exchange tests with a classmate, and take the other student's test.

Learn More

To learn more about analogies, see Chapter 30.

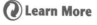

Answering Short-Answer and Essay Questions

Some test questions require you to supply an answer, rather than simply identify a correct answer. Identify these questions when you preview the test. Allow time to write complete, accurate answers.

KEY CONCEPT Allow time and space to respond to short-answer and essay questions. ■

Follow these strategies to respond to short-answer and essay questions:

Identify Key Words Whether you are responding to a short-answer question or an essay topic, identify the key words in the test item. Look for words such as *discuss*, *explain*, *identify*, and any numbers or restrictions. If the question asks for three causes, make sure you supply three.

Check Your Space On some tests, you will be given a certain number of lines on which to write your answer. Make sure that you understand whether you are limited to that space or whether you can use more paper. If your space is limited, use it for the most important information that fits the topic.

Stick to the Point Do not put down everything you know about a topic. If the question asks you to identify three kinds of clouds and explain how to recognize them, you will not get extra credit for explaining how tornados move. In fact, including unrelated information may cause you to lose points.

Learn More

Chapter 13, Writing for Assessment, provides in-depth guidance and practice in writing essays for tests.

Reflecting on Your Study, Reference, and Test-Taking Skills

Answer the following questions to consider what you have learned about your study, reference, and test-taking habits and skills.

- Which strategies seem new or unusual? How can using these strategies help me improve my academic performance?
- Which strategies do I already use? Why do I find these most comfortable and useful?

Step-by-Step Teaching Guide

Answering Short-Answer and Essay Questions

1. Go over the essay tips with students. Remind them that teachers don't expect perfection when a student's time is limited. Students should not hold their writing to the same standards on an essay test as they would on a piece of writing they are allowed to draft, revise, proofread, and so on. However, students should reread test essays and revise them if time permits. Essays on tests should stick to the point, answer the question asked, and contain as few grammatical errors as possible. Most important, they should be legible. An essay that is 100% correct will receive a low score if the person scoring it can't read the handwriting.
2. Sometimes, essay tests are given as take-home tests. In this case, students may not be given strict time limits as they would be in a classroom. Remind them to use their time to proofread, revise, tighten, and sharpen their essays so that they answer the questions as thoroughly and accurately as possible.

PRENTICE HALL
Everyday Spelling

If you have taught the spelling skills in *Prentice Hall Everyday Spelling,* Grade 8, Chapter 35, in conjunction with this *Writing and Grammar* chapter, review and assess student's mastery of the skills before concluding the chapter.

Lesson Objectives

- To construct meaning from informational text.

Step-by-Step Teaching Guide

Constructing Meaning From Informational Texts

Teaching Resources: Standardized Test Preparation Workbook, pp.61–62

1. Emphasize to the students that their key to success in correctly answering questions dealing with informational passages is to read the passage very carefully.
2. Remind students to underline facts such as names of people and places, and dates. This will help them to save time when answering questions concerning the main idea of a passage, or questions that deal with the identification of the best summary for a passage.
3. Remind students that they should look for context clues to distinguish between fact and opinion. Words that express emotions are almost always opinions.

Standardized Test Preparation Workshop

Constructing Meaning From Informational Texts

When you take a standardized test, you often must demonstrate your ability to construct meaning from an informational passage. You will be given a passage to read, followed by several multiple-choice questions. These types of questions require you to identify a main idea, distinguish between the facts and opinions in the passage, identify the author's purpose for writing, and identify the best summary, or restating of the key points of the passage.

The following sample test item will give you practice answering these types of questions.

Test Tip

Look for context clues to identify opinions in written passages. Words like *felt* and *wanted,* or other words that express feelings or emotions, are almost always opinions.

Sample Test Item	Answer and Explanation
Directions: Read the passage. Then, read the question that follows the passage. Decide which is the best answer to the question. Before the reign of Elizabeth I, theater companies traveled about the country putting on plays wherever they could find an audience, often performing in the open courtyards of inns. Spectators watched either from the ground or from balconies or galleries above.	
1 What is the main idea of this passage? A Theater companies loved to travel. B Before Elizabeth I, theater companies performed outside. C Instead of performing in theaters, early companies of actors traveled and performed wherever an audience could gather. D Spectators watched from balconies.	The correct answer is C. This is the only statement that includes all of the relevant information from the passage.

TEST-TAKING TIP

Encourage students to use a process of elimination when dealing with multiple choice questions. Remind them to eliminate the obviously incorrect answers.

Practice 1 **Directions:** Read the passage. Then, read each question that follows the passage. Decide which is the best answer to each question.

Richard III ruled England during a period of unrest known as the War of the Roses—a series of confrontations between the noble houses of York and Lancaster. The emblems of the families were a white rose for York and a red rose for Lancaster. That is how the war got its name. Richard was a power-hungry man, believed to have killed two nephews to assure his right to the throne. When Henry Tudor defeated Richard at the Battle of Bosworth in 1485, he became king and ended the turbulent period in England.

1 What is the main idea of this passage?
A The War of the Roses was between the houses of York and Lancaster.
B Richard III was a bad English king.
C Richard III ruled England during the Battle of the Roses, a turbulent time.
D Henry Tudor defeated Richard III at the Battle of Bosworth in 1485.

2 Which of the following is an OPINION expressed in the passage?
F Richard III ruled England during the Battle of the Roses.
G Richard was power-hungry.
H Henry Tudor defeated Richard in 1485.
J The York emblem was a white rose.

3 Which of the following is the best summary of this passage?
A Richard III grabbed power near the end of the War of the Roses and was defeated by Henry Tudor in 1485, ending a period of unrest in England.
B Richard III was a power-hungry ruler of England during a difficult period.
C The War of the Roses was finally ended when Richard was defeated.
D Richard III was king during the War of the Roses and was defeated in 1485.

Practice 2 **Directions:** Read the passage. Then, read each question that follows the passage. Decide which is the best answer to each question.

One of William Shakespeare's best-known tragedies deals with the life and death of Richard III. In Shakespeare's play, Richard starts out telling the audience about his plans to have his brother killed so he can take over the throne. He presents his plans during a famous monologue that begins, "Now is the winter of our discontent." Throughout the play, Richard is portrayed as evil. Audiences are probably happy when he is killed at the end.

1 What is the main idea of the passage?
A Shakespeare portrays Richard III as evil during a famous tragedy.
B Richard III opens Shakespeare's play with a monologue that begins, "Now is the winter of our discontent."
C Shakespeare wrote a famous play about Richard III.
D Audiences are happy when Richard dies at the end of Shakespeare's play.

2 Which of the following is an OPINION expressed in the passage?
F Shakespeare wrote a play about Richard III.
G Richard starts with a monologue.
H The monologue begins, "Now is the winter of our discontent."
J Audiences are probably happy when Richard is killed at the end.

3 Which of the following explains the author's main purpose in the passage?
A The author wants to persuade readers to see the play.
B The author wants to present an entertaining anecdote.
C The author wants to inform readers about Shakespeare's play.
D The author wants to review a performance of the play *Richard III.*

Answer Key

Practice 1
1. C
2. G
3. D

Practice 2
1. A
2. J
3. C

Styles for Business and Friendly Letters

Business Letters

From a letter requesting information about a product to a letter asking for charitable donations, business letters are a common form of formal writing, writing intended for readers with whom the writer is not personally acquainted. Whatever the subject, an effective business letter

- includes six parts: the heading, the inside address, the salutation or greeting, the body, the closing, and the signature.
- follows one of several acceptable forms: In *block format,* each part of the letter begins at the left margin; in *modified block format,* the heading, the closing, and the signature are indented to the center of the page.
- uses formal language to communicate respectfully, regardless of the letter's content.

The **heading** indicates the address and business affiliation of the writer. It also includes the date the letter was sent.

Model Business Letter

In this letter, Yolanda Dodson uses modified block format to request information.

Students for a Cleaner Planet
c/o Memorial High School
333 Veterans' Drive
Denver, Colorado 80211

January 25, 20 – –

The **inside address** indicates where the letter will be sent.

Steven Wilson, Director
Resource Recovery Really Works
300 Oak Street
Denver, Colorado 80216

A **salutation** is punctuated by a colon. When the specific addressee is not known, use a general greeting such as "To whom it may concern:"

Dear Mr. Wilson:

The **body** of the letter states the writer's purpose. In this case, the writer is requesting information.

Memorial High School would like to start a branch of your successful recycling program. We share your commitment to reclaiming as much reusable material as we can. Because your program has been successful in other neighborhoods, we're sure that it can work in our community. Our school includes grades 9–12 and has about 800 students.

Would you send us some information about your community recycling program? For example, we need to know what materials can be recycled and how we can implement the program.

At least fifty students have already expressed an interest in getting involved, so I know we'll have the people power to make the program work. Please help us get started.

Thank you in advance for your time and consideration.

The **closing** "Sincerely" is common, but "Yours truly" or "Respectfully yours" are also acceptable. To end the letter, the writer types her name and provides a **signature**.

Sincerely,

Yolanda Dodson

Yolanda Dodson

Friendly Letters and Social Notes

When you write a letter telling news to a friend or thanking a relative for a gift, you are writing a friendly letter or a social note. A friendly letter is any informal letter you write that is based on a personal relationship with the reader. A social note includes a semiformal thank-you note written to someone you do not know quite well. Friendly letters and social notes typically feature the following elements:

- a heading, a salutation or greeting, a body, a closing, and a signature; they generally do not include an inside address
- a comma after the greeting
- paragraphs with indented first lines
- the use of a version of semiblock style, in which the heading, closing, and signature align to the right of the center of the page
- informal or semiformal language, often featuring the lively expression of feelings or amusement

How careful you need to be in following appropriate format depends on your relationship with the reader: The less well you know the person, the more careful you should be to follow the correct format. Consult the model below for proper formatting.

The **heading, closing,** and **signature** are aligned, semiblock style, to the right of the center of the page. (In very informal letters, writers may choose to omit their own address in the heading.)

1111 Main St.
Mayfair, OH
November 11, 20 - -

A comma is used after the **greeting;** Mayra addresses her reader semiformally.

Dear Aunt Margie,

The first line of each paragraph in the **body** is indented. The writer uses informal language and gives details that are of personal interest.

Well, as you predicted, the trip to the amusement park was a lot of fun. I had a great time! The rides were more thrilling than any I've ever been on before. Even the twins were impressed—I don't think they had a single fight during the entire trip, and you know that's saying a lot!

The only part I wouldn't visit again was the spooky House of Chills. Ugh! I didn't mind the visuals: skeletons, scary pirates, and that sort of thing. But there's one part of the ride that takes place in complete darkness, with very quiet sound effects, and while you sit there wondering what will happen next, a cold, clammy THING runs slithering across your back or your hand! I nearly jumped out of my skin. I wasn't that frightened even when we told scary stories the night the lights went out at your house.

The writer's **purpose** in writing is clearly expressed here: She is writing to thank her aunt for the gift of tickets.

Thanks very much for the tickets and the fun day. We all loved the trip. I hope you'll come to visit again soon.

Your tallest niece,
Mayra

A friendly letter may use or adapt a **closing** such as "Love," "Yours," and "Best," followed by a comma. As is customary when writer and reader know each other well, Mayra signs her first name only and does not add her name written out.

Citing Sources and Preparing Manuscript

The presentation of your written work is important. Your work should be neat, clean, and easy to read. Follow your teacher's directions for placing your name and class, along with the title and date of your work, on the paper.

For handwritten work:

- Use cursive handwriting or manuscript printing, according to the style your teacher prefers. The penmanship reference below shows the accepted formation of letters in cursive writing.
- Write or print neatly.
- Write on one side of lined 8 $^{1}/_{2}$" x 11" paper with a clean edge. (Do not use pages torn from a spiral notebook.)
- Indent the first line of each paragraph.
- Leave a margin, as indicated by the guidelines on the lined paper. Write in a size appropriate for the lines provided. Do not write so large that the letters from one line bump into the ones above and below. Do not write so small that the writing is difficult to read.
- Write in blue or black ink.
- Number the pages in the upper right corner.
- You should not cross out words on your final draft. Recopy instead. If your paper is long, your teacher may allow you to make one or two small changes by neatly crossing out the text to be deleted and using a caret [^] to indicate replacement text. Alternatively, you might make one or two corrections neatly with correction fluid. If you find yourself making more than three corrections, consider recopying the work.

PENMANSHIP REFERENCE

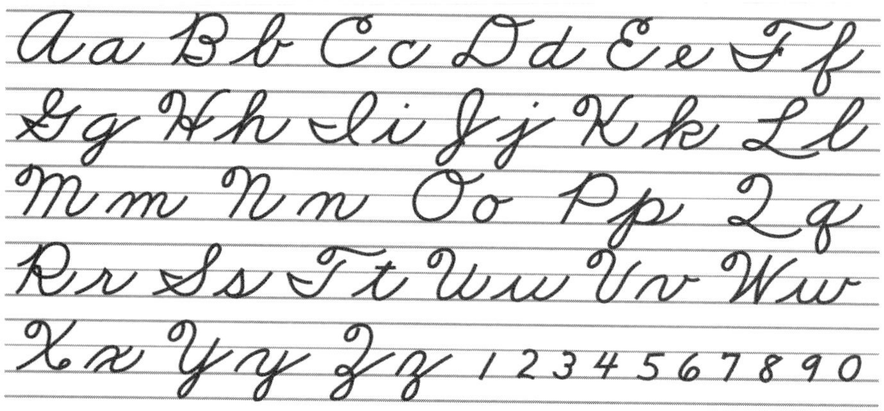

For word-processed or typed documents:

- Choose a standard, easy-to-read font.
- Type or print on one side of unlined $8\,^1/_2$" x 11" paper.
- Set the margins for the side, top, and bottom of your paper at approximately one inch. Most word-processing programs have a default setting that is appropriate.
- Double-space the document.
- Indent the first line of each paragraph.
- Number the pages in the upper right corner. Many word-processing programs have a header feature that will do this for you automatically.
- If you discover one or two errors after you have typed or printed, use correction fluid if your teacher allows such corrections. If you have more than three errors in an electronic file, consider making the corrections to the file and reprinting the document. If you have typed a long document, your teacher may allow you to make a few corrections by hand. If you have several errors, however, consider retyping the document.

For research papers:

Follow your teacher's directions for formatting formal research papers. Most papers will have the following features:

- Title page
- Table of Contents or Outline
- Works-Cited List

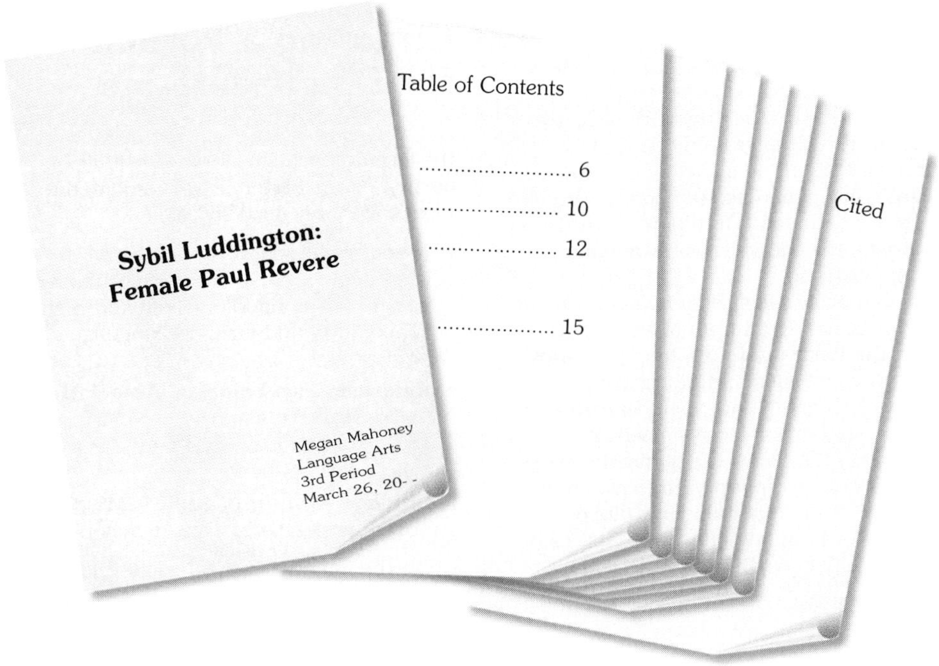

Incorporating Ideas From Research

Below are three common methods of incorporating the ideas of other writers into your work. Choose the most appropriate style by analyzing your needs in each case. In all cases, you must credit your source.

- **Direct Quotation:** Use quotation marks to indicate the exact words.
- **Paraphrase:** To share ideas without a direct quotation, state the ideas in your own words. While you haven't copied word-for-word, you still need to credit your source.
- **Summary:** To provide information about a large body of work—such as a speech, an editorial, or a chapter of a book—identify the writer's main idea.

Avoiding Plagiarism

Whether you are presenting a formal research paper or an opinion paper on a current event, you must be careful to give credit for any ideas or opinions that are not your own. Presenting someone else's ideas, research, or opinion as your own—even if you have rephrased it in different words—is *plagiarism*, the equivalent of academic stealing, or fraud.

You can avoid plagiarism by synthesizing what you learn: Read from several sources and let the ideas of experts help you draw your own conclusions and form your own opinions. Ultimately, however, note your own reactions to the ideas presented.

When you choose to use someone else's ideas or work to support your view, credit the source of the material. Give bibliographic information to cite your sources of the following information:

- Statistics
- Direct quotations
- Indirectly quoted statements of opinions
- Conclusions presented by an expert
- Facts available in only one or two sources

Crediting Sources

When you credit a source, you acknowledge where you found your information and you give your readers the details necessary for locating the source themselves. Within the body of the paper, you provide a short citation, a footnote number linked to a footnote, or an endnote number linked to an endnote reference. These brief references show the page numbers on which you found the information. To make your paper more formal, prepare a reference list at the end of the paper to provide full bibliographic information on your sources. These are two common types of reference lists:

- A **bibliography** provides a listing of all the resources you consulted during your research.
- A **works-cited list** indicates the works you have referenced in your paper.

Choosing a Format for Documentation

The type of information you provide and the format in which you provide it depend on what your teacher prefers. These are the most commonly used styles:

- **Modern Language Association (MLA) Style** This is the style used for most papers at the middle-school and high-school level and for most language arts papers.
- **American Psychological Association (APA) Style** This is used for most papers in the social sciences and for most college-level papers.
- ***Chicago Manual of Style* (CMS) Style** This is preferred by some teachers.

On the following pages, you'll find sample citation formats for the most commonly cited materials. Each format calls for standard bibliographic information. The difference is in the order of the material presented in each entry and the punctuation required.

MLA Style for Listing Sources

Book with one author	Pyles, Thomas. *The Origins and Development of the English Language.* 2nd ed. New York: Harcourt Brace Jovanovich, Inc., 1971.
Book with two or three authors	McCrum, Robert, William Cran, and Robert MacNeil. *The Story of English.* New York: Penguin Books, 1987.
Book with an editor	Truth, Sojourner. *Narrative of Sojourner Truth.* Ed. Margaret Washington. New York: Vintage Books, 1993.
Book with more than three authors or editors	Donald, Robert B., et al. *Writing Clear Essays.* Upper Saddle River, NJ: Prentice-Hall, Inc., 1996.
A single work from an anthology	Hawthorne, Nathaniel. "Young Goodman Brown." *Literature: An Introduction to Reading and Writing.* Ed. Edgar V. Roberts and Henry E. Jacobs. Upper Saddle River, NJ: Prentice-Hall, Inc., 1998. 376–385. [Indicate pages for the entire selection.]
Introduction in a published edition	Washington, Margaret. Introduction. *Narrative of Sojourner Truth.* By Sojourner Truth. New York: Vintage Books, 1993, pp. v–xi.
Signed article in a weekly magazine	Wallace, Charles. "A Vodacious Deal." *Time* 14 Feb. 2000: 63.
Signed article in a monthly magazine	Gustaitis, Joseph. "The Sticky History of Chewing Gum." *American History* Oct. 1998: 30–38.
Unsigned editorial or story	"Selective Silence." Editorial. *Wall Street Journal* 11 Feb. 2000: A14. [If the editorial or story is signed, begin with the author's name.]
Signed pamphlet	[Treat the pamphlet as though it were a book.]
Pamphlet with no author, publisher, or date	*Are You at Risk of Heart Attack?* n.p. n.d. [n.p. n.d. indicates that there is no known publisher or date]
Filmstrips, slide programs, and videotape	*The Diary of Anne Frank.* Dir. George Stevens. Perf. Millie Perkins, Shelley Winters, Joseph Schildkraut, Lou Jacobi, and Richard Beymer. Twentieth Century Fox, 1959.
Radio or television program transcript	"The First Immortal Generation." *Ockham's Razor.* Host Robyn Williams. Guest Damien Broderick. National Public Radio. 23 May 1999. Transcript.
Internet	*National Association of Chewing Gum Manufacturers.* 19 Dec. 1999 <http://www.nacgm.org/consumer/funfacts.html> [Indicate the date you accessed the information. Content and addresses at Web sites change frequently.]
Newspaper	Thurow, Roger. "South Africans Who Fought for Sanctions Now Scrap for Investors." *Wall Street Journal* 11 Feb. 2000: A1+ [For a multipage article, write only the first page number on which it appears, followed by a plus sign.]
Personal interview	Smith, Jane. Personal interview. 10 Feb. 2000.
CD (with multiple publishers)	Simms, James, ed. *Romeo and Juliet.* By William Shakespeare. CD-ROM. Oxford: Attica Cybernetics Ltd.; London: BBC Education; London: HarperCollins Publishers, 1995.
Article from an encyclopedia	Askeland, Donald R. (1991). "Welding." *World Book Encyclopedia.* 1991 ed.

Sample Works-Cited List (MLA)

Carwardine, Mark, Erich Hoyt, R. Ewan Fordyce, and Peter Gill. *The Nature Company Guides: Whales, Dolphins, and Porpoises.* New York: Time-Life Books, 1998.

Ellis, Richard. *Men and Whales.* New York: Knopf, 1991.

Whales in Danger. "Discovering Whales." 18 Oct. 1999. <http://whales.magna.com.au/DISCOVER>

Sample Internal Citations (MLA)

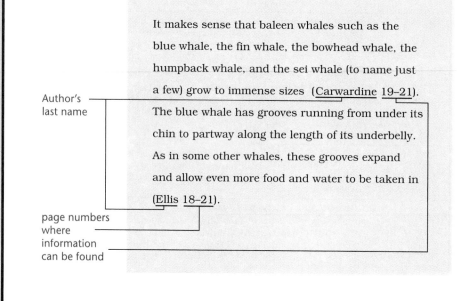

It makes sense that baleen whales such as the blue whale, the fin whale, the bowhead whale, the humpback whale, and the sei whale (to name just a few) grow to immense sizes (Carwardine 19–21). The blue whale has grooves running from under its chin to partway along the length of its underbelly. As in some other whales, these grooves expand and allow even more food and water to be taken in (Ellis 18–21).

Author's last name

page numbers where information can be found

Introduction to the Internet

The Internet is a series of networks that are interconnected all over the world. The Internet allows users to have almost unlimited access to information stored on the networks. Dr. Berners-Lee, a physicist, created the Internet in the 1980's by writing a small computer program that allowed pages to be linked together using key words. The Internet was mostly text-based until 1992, when a computer program called the NCSA Mosaic (National Center for Supercomputing Applications at the University of Illinois) was created. This program was the first Web browser. The development of Web browsers greatly eased the ability of the user to navigate through all the pages stored on the Web. Very soon, the appearance of the Web was altered as well. More appealing visuals were added, and sound was also implemented. This change made the Web more user-friendly and more appealing to the general public.

Using the Internet for Research

Key Word Search

Before you begin a search, you should identify your specific topic. To make searching easier, narrow your subject to a key word or a group of key words. These are your search terms, and they should be as specific as possible. For example, if you are looking for the latest concert dates for your favorite musical group, you might use the band's name as a key word. However, if you were to enter the name of the group in the query box of the search engine, you might be presented with thousands of links to information about the group that is unrelated to your needs. You might locate such information as band member biographies, the group's history, fan reviews of concerts, and hundreds of sites with related names containing information that is irrelevant to your search. Because you used such a broad key word, you might need to navigate through all that information before you find a link or subheading for concert dates. In contrast, if you were to type in "Duplex Arena and [band name]" you would have a better chance of locating pages that contain this information.

How to Narrow Your Search

If you have a large group of key words and still don't know which ones to use, write out a list of all the words you are considering. Once you have completed the list, scrutinize it. Then, delete the words that are least important to your search, and highlight those that are most important.

These **key search connectors** can help you fine-tune your search:

AND: narrows a search by retrieving documents that include both terms. For example: *baseball AND playoffs*

OR: broadens a search by retrieving documents including any of the terms. For example: *playoffs OR championships*

NOT: narrows a search by excluding documents containing certain words. For example: *baseball NOT history of*

Tips for an Effective Search

1. Keep in mind that search engines can be case-sensitive. If your first attempt at searching fails, check your search terms for misspellings and try again.
2. If you are entering a group of key words, present them in order, from the most important to the least important key word.
3. Avoid opening the link to every single page in your results list. Search engines present pages in descending order of relevancy. The most useful pages will be located at the top of the list. However, read the description of each link before you open the page.
4. When you use some search engines, you can find helpful tips for specializing your search. Take the opportunity to learn more about effective searching.

Other Ways to Search

Using On-line Reference Sites *How* you search should be tailored to *what* you are hoping to find. If you are looking for data and facts, use reference sites before you jump onto a simple search engine. For example, you can find reference sites to provide definitions of words, statistics about almost any subject, biographies, maps, and concise information on many topics. Some useful on-line reference sites:

- On-line libraries
- On-line periodicals
- Almanacs
- Encyclopedias

You can find these sources using subject searches.

Conducting Subject Searches As you prepare to go on-line, consider your subject and the best way to find information to suit your needs. If you are looking for general information on a topic and you want your search results to be extensive, consider the subject search indexes on most search engines. These indexes, in the form of category and subject lists, often appear on the first page of a search engine. When you click on a specific highlighted word, you will be presented with a new screen containing subcategories of the topic you chose. In the screen shots below, the category *Sports & Recreation* provided a second index for users to focus a search even further.

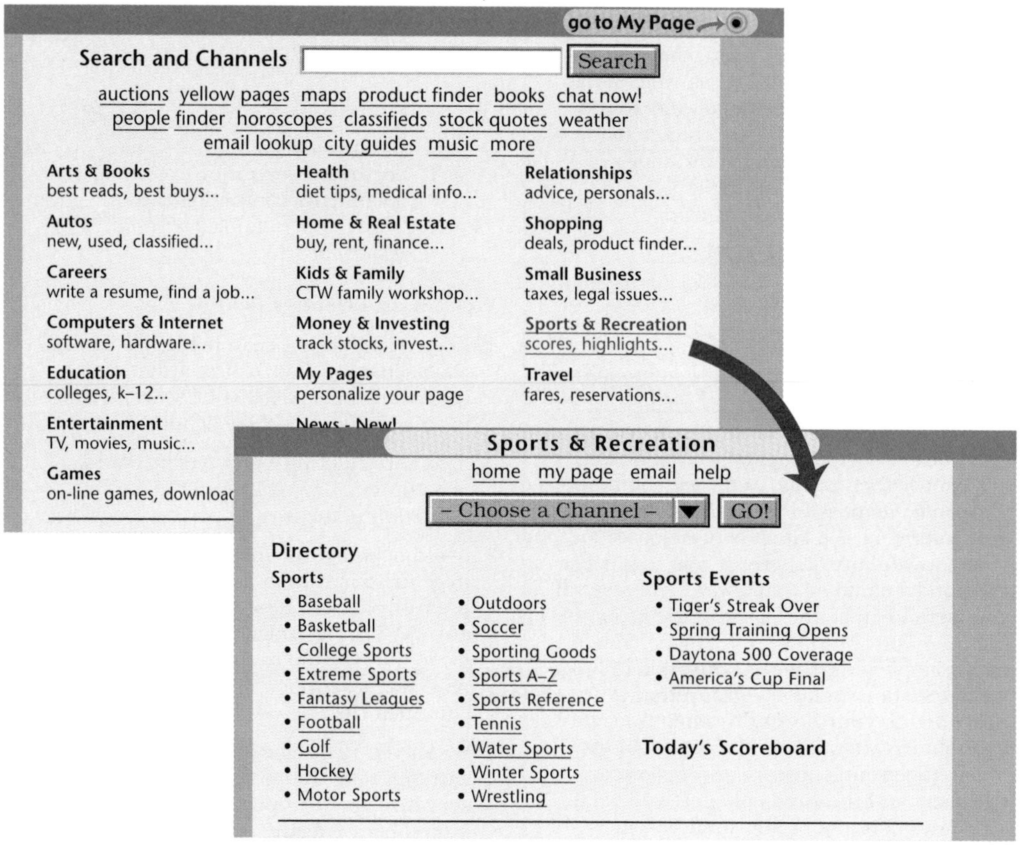

Evaluating the Reliability of Internet Resources Just as you would evaluate the quality, bias, and validity of any other research material you locate, check the source of information you find on-line. Compare these two sites containing information on the poet and writer Langston Hughes:

Site A is a personal Web site constructed by a college student. It contains no bibliographic information or links to sites that he used. Included on the site are several poems by Langston Hughes and a student essay about the poet's use of symbolism. It has not been updated in more than six months.

Site B is a Web site constructed and maintained by the English Department of a major university. Information on Hughes is presented in a scholarly format, with a bibliography and credits for the writer. The site includes links to other sites and indicates new features that are added weekly.

For your own research, consider the information you find on Site B to be more reliable and accurate than that on Site A. Because it is maintained by experts in their field who are held accountable for their work, the university site will be a better research tool than the student-generated one.

Tips for Evaluating Internet Sources

1. Consider who constructed and who now maintains the Web page. Determine whether this author is a reputable source. Often, the URL endings indicate a source.
   - Sites ending in *.edu* are maintained by educational institutions.
   - Sites ending in *.gov* are maintained by government agencies (federal, state, or local).
   - Sites ending in *.org* are normally maintained by nonprofit organizations and agencies.
   - Sites with a *.com* ending are commercially or personally maintained.
2. Skim the official and trademarked Web pages first. It is safe to assume that the information you draw from Web pages of reputable institutions, on-line encyclopedias, on-line versions of major daily newspapers, or government-owned sites produce information as reliable as the material you would find in print. In contrast, unbranded sites or those generated by individuals tend to borrow information from other sources without providing documentation. As information travels from one source to another, the information has likely been muddled, misinterpreted, edited, or revised.
3. You can still find valuable information in the less "official" sites. Check for the writer's credentials and then consider these factors:
   - Don't let official-looking graphics or presentations fool you.
   - Make sure the information is updated enough to suit your needs. Many Web pages will indicate how recently they have been updated.
   - If the information is borrowed, see whether you can trace it back to its original source.

Respecting Copyrighted Material

Because the Internet is a relatively new and quickly growing medium, issues of copyright and ownership arise almost daily. As laws begin to govern the use and reuse of material posted on-line, they may change the way that people can access or reprint material.

Text, photographs, music, and fine art printed on-line may not be reproduced without acknowledged permission of the copyright owner.

Glossary of Internet Terms

attached file: a file containing information, such as a text document or GIF image, that is attached to an e-mail message; reports, pictures, spreadsheets, and so on transmitted to others by attaching these to messages as files

bandwidth: the amount of information, mainly compressed in bits per second (bps), that can be sent through a connection within a specific amount of time; depending on how fast your modem is, 15,000 bits (roughly one page of text) can be transferred per second

bit: a binary digit of computerized data, represented by a single digit that is either a 1 or a 0; a group of bits constitutes a byte

bookmark: a feature of your Web browser that allows you to place a "bookmark" on a Web page to which you wish to return at a later time

browser: software designed to present material accessed on the Web

bulletin-board system: a computer system that members access in order to join on-line discussion groups or to post announcements

case-sensitivity: the quality of a search engine that causes it to respond to upper- or lowercase letters in different ways

chat room: informal on-line gathering sites where people share conversations, experiences, or information on a specific topic; many chat rooms do not require users to provide their identity, so the reliability or safety of these sites is uncertain

cookie: a digitized piece of information that is sent to a Web browser by a Web server, intended to be saved on a computer; cookies gather information about the user, such as user preferences, or recent on-line purchases; a Web browser can be set to either accept or reject cookies

cyberspace: a term referring to the electronic environment connecting all computer network information with the people who use it

database: a large collection of data that have been formatted to fit a certain user-defined standard

digerati: a slang term to describe Internet experts; an offshoot of the term *literati*

download: to copy files from the Internet onto your computer

e-mail: electronic mail, or the exchange of messages via the Internet; because it is speedier than traditional mail and offers easier global access, e-mail has grown in popularity; e-mail messages can be sent to a single person or in bulk to a group of people

error message: a displayed communication or printout that reports a problem with a program or Web page

FTP site (file transfer protocol): a password-protected server on the Internet that allows the transfer of information from one computer to another

GIF (Graphic Interchange Format): a form of graphics used on the Web

graphics: information displayed as pictures or images instead of text

hits: items retrieved by a key word search; the number tracking the volume of visits to a Web site

home page: the main Web page for an individual or an organization, containing links to subpages within

HTML (HyperText Markup Language): the coding text that is the foundation for creating Web pages

interactivity: a quality of some Web pages that encourages the frequent exchange of information between user and computer

Internet: a worldwide computer network that supports services such as the World Wide Web, e-mail, and file transfer

JPEG (Joint Photo Experts Group, the developers)**:** a file format for graphics especially suited to photographs

K: a measurement of file size or memory; short for "Kilobyte," 1,000 bytes of information (see *bit*)

key word: search term entered into the query box of a search engine to direct the results of the search

link: an icon or word on a Web page that, when clicked, transfers the user to another Web page or to a different document within the same page

login: the procedure by which users gain access to a server or a secure Web site; usually the user must enter a specific user name and password

modem: a device that transfers data to a computer through a phone line. A computer's modem connects to a server, which then sends information in the form of digital signals. The modem converts these signals into waves, for the purpose of information reception. The speed of a modem affects how quickly a computer can receive and download information

newbie: jargon used to describe Internet novices

newsgroup: an on-line discussion group, where users can post and respond to messages; the most prevalent collection of newsgroups is found on USENET

query box: the blank box in a search engine where your search terms are input

relevance ranking: the act of displaying the results of a search in the order of their relevance to the search terms

search engines: tools that help you navigate databases to locate information; search engines respond to a key word search by providing the user with a directory of multiple Web pages about the key word or containing the key word

server: a principal computer that provides services, such as storing files and providing access to the Internet, to another computer

signature: a preprogrammed section of text that is automatically added to an e-mail message

surfing: the process of reading Web pages and of moving from one Web site to another

URL (Uniform Resource Locator): a Web page's address; a URL can look like this:

http://www.phwg.phschool.com or *http://www.senate.gov/~appropriations/labor/testimony*

usenet: a worldwide system of discussion groups, or newsgroups

vanity pages: Web sites placed on-line by people to tell about themselves or their interests; vanity pages do not have any commercial or informational value

virus: a set of instructions, hidden in a computer system or transferred via e-mail or electronic files, that can cause problems with a computer's ability to perform normally

Web page: a set of information, including graphics, text, sound, and video, presented in a browser window; a Web page can be found by its URL once it is posted on the World Wide Web

Web site: a collection of Web pages that are linked together for posting on the World Wide Web

W3: a group of Internet experts, including networking professionals, academics, scientists, and corporate interests, who maintain and develop technologies and standards for the Internet

WWW (World Wide Web): a term referring to the multitude of information systems found on the Internet; this includes FTP, Gopher, telnet, and http sites

zip: the minimizing of files through compression; this function makes for easier transmittal over networks; a receiver can then open the file by "unzipping" it

Commonly Overused Words

When you write, use the most precise word for your meaning, not the word that comes to mind first. Consult this thesaurus to find alternatives for some commonly overused words. Consult a full-length thesaurus to find alternatives to words that do not appear here. Keep in mind that the choices offered in a thesaurus do not all mean exactly the same thing. Review all the options, and choose the one that best expresses your meaning.

about approximately, nearly, almost, approaching, close to

absolutely unconditionally, perfectly, completely, ideally, purely

activity action, movement, operation, labor, exertion, enterprise, project, pursuit, endeavor, job, assignment, pastime, scheme, task

add attach, affix, join, unite, append, increase, amplify

affect adjust, influence, transform, moderate, incline, motivate, prompt

amazing overwhelming, astonishing, startling, unexpected, stunning, dazzling, remarkable

awesome impressive, stupendous, fabulous, astonishing, outstanding

bad defective, inadequate, poor, unsatisfactory, disagreeable, offensive, repulsive, corrupt, wicked, naughty, harmful, injurious, unfavorable

basic essential, necessary, indispensable, vital, fundamental, elementary

beautiful attractive, appealing, alluring, exquisite, gorgeous, handsome, stunning

begin commence, found, initiate, introduce, launch, originate

better preferable, superior, worthier

big enormous, extensive, huge, immense, massive

boring commonplace, monotonous, tedious, tiresome

bring accompany, cause, convey, create, conduct, deliver, produce

cause origin, stimulus, inspiration, motive

certain unquestionable, incontrovertible, unmistakable, indubitable, assured, confident

change alter, transform, vary, replace, diversify

choose select, elect, nominate, prefer, identify

decent respectable, adequate, fair, suitable

definitely unquestionably, clearly, precisely, positively, inescapably

easy effortless, natural, comfortable, undemanding, pleasant, relaxed

effective powerful, successful

emphasize underscore, feature, accentuate

end limit, boundary, finish, conclusion, finale, resolution

energy vitality, vigor, force, dynamism

enjoy savor, relish, revel, benefit

entire complete, inclusive, unbroken, integral

excellent superior, remarkable, splendid, unsurpassed, superb, magnificent

exciting thrilling, stirring, rousing, dramatic

far distant, remote

fast swift, quick, fleet, hasty, instant, accelerated

fill occupy, suffuse, pervade, saturate, inflate, stock

finish complete, conclude, cease, achieve, exhaust, deplete, consume

funny comical, ludicrous, amusing, droll, entertaining, bizarre, unusual, uncommon

get obtain, receive, acquire, procure, achieve

give bestow, donate, supply, deliver, distribute, impart

go proceed, progress, advance, move

good satisfactory, serviceable, functional, competent, virtuous, striking

great tremendous, superior, remarkable, eminent, proficient, expert

happy pleased, joyous, elated, jubilant, cheerful, delighted

hard arduous, formidable, complex, complicated, rigorous, harsh

help assist, aid, support, sustain, serve

hurt injure, harm, damage, wound, impair

important significant, substantial, weighty, meaningful, critical, vital, notable

interesting absorbing, appealing, entertaining, fascinating, thought-provoking

job task, work, business, undertaking, occupation, vocation, chore, duty, assignment

keep retain, control, possess

kind type, variety, sort, form

know comprehend, understand, realize, perceive, discern

like (adj) similar, equivalent, parallel

like (verb) enjoy, relish, appreciate

main primary, foremost, dominant

make build, construct, produce, assemble, fashion, manufacture

mean plan, intend, suggest, propose, indicate

more supplementary, additional, replenishment

new recent, modern, current, novel

next subsequently, thereafter, successively

nice pleasant, satisfying, gracious, charming

old aged, mature, experienced, used, worn, former, previous

open unobstructed, accessible

part section, portion, segment, detail, element, component

perfect flawless, faultless, ideal, consummate

plan scheme, design, system, plot

pleasant agreeable, gratifying, refreshing, welcome

prove demonstrate, confirm, validate, verify, corroborate

quick brisk, prompt, responsive, rapid, nimble, hasty

really truly, genuinely, extremely, undeniably

regular standard, routine, customary, habitual

see regard, behold, witness, gaze, realize, notice

small diminutive, miniature, minor, insignificant, slight, trivial

sometimes occasionally, intermittently, sporadically, periodically

take grasp, capture, choose, select, tolerate, endure

terrific extraordinary, magnificent, marvelous

think conceive, imagine, ponder, reflect, contemplate

try attempt, endeavor, venture, test

use employ, operate, utilize

very unusually, extremely, deeply, exceedingly, profoundly

want desire, crave, yearn, long

Commonly Misspelled Words

The list on these pages presents words that cause problems for many people. Some of these words are spelled according to set rules, but others follow no specific rules. As you review this list, check to see how many of the words give you trouble in your own writing. Then, read the instruction in the "Vocabulary and Spelling" chapter in the book for strategies and suggestions for improving your own spelling habits.

abbreviate
absence
absolutely
abundance
accelerate
accidentally
accumulate
accurate
ache
achievement
acquaintance
adequate
admittance
advertisement
aerial
affect
aggravate
aggressive
agreeable
aisle
all right
allowance
aluminum
amateur
analysis
analyze
ancient
anecdote
anniversary
anonymous
answer
anticipate
anxiety
apologize
appall
appearance
appreciate
appropriate
architecture
argument
associate

athletic
attendance
auxiliary
awkward
bandage
banquet
bargain
barrel
battery
beautiful
beggar
beginning
behavior
believe
benefit
bicycle
biscuit
bookkeeper
bought
boulevard
brief
brilliant
bruise
bulletin
buoyant
bureau
bury
buses
business
cafeteria
calendar
campaign
canceled
candidate
capacity
capital
capitol
captain
career
carriage
cashier

catastrophe
category
ceiling
cemetery
census
certain
changeable
characteristic
chauffeur
chief
clothes
coincidence
colonel
column
commercial
commission
commitment
committee
competitor
concede
condemn
congratulate
connoisseur
conscience
conscientious
conscious
contemporary
continuous
controversy
convenience
coolly
cooperate
cordially
correspondence
counterfeit
courageous
courteous
courtesy
criticism
criticize
curiosity

curious
cylinder
deceive
decision
deductible
defendant
deficient
definitely
delinquent
dependent
descendant
description
desert
desirable
dessert
deteriorate
dining
disappointed
disastrous
discipline
dissatisfied
distinguish
effect
eighth
eligible
embarrass
enthusiastic
entrepreneur
envelope
environment
equipped
equivalent
especially
exaggerate
exceed
excellent
exercise
exhibition
existence
experience
explanation

extension
extraordinary
familiar
fascinating
February
fiery
financial
fluorescent
foreign
forfeit
fourth
fragile
gauge
generally
genius
genuine
government
grammar
grievance
guarantee
guard
guidance
handkerchief
harass
height
humorous
hygiene
ignorant
illegible
immediately
immigrant
independence
independent
indispensable
individual
inflammable
intelligence
interfere
irrelevant
irritable
jewelry
judgment
knowledge
laboratory
lawyer
legible
legislature
leisure
liable
library
license
lieutenant
lightning
likable
liquefy
literature
loneliness
magnificent
maintenance
marriage
mathematics
maximum
meanness
mediocre
mileage
millionaire
minimum
minuscule
miscellaneous
mischievous
misspell
mortgage
naturally
necessary
negotiate
neighbor
neutral
nickel
niece
ninety
noticeable
nuclear
nuisance
obstacle
occasion
occasionally
occur
occurred
occurrence
omitted
opinion
opportunity
optimistic
outrageous
pamphlet
parallel
paralyze
parentheses
particularly
patience
permanent
permissible
perseverance
persistent
personally
perspiration
persuade
phenomenal
phenomenon
physician
pleasant
pneumonia
possess
possession
possibility
prairie
precede
preferable
prejudice
preparation
prerogative
previous
primitive
privilege
probably
procedure
proceed
prominent
pronunciation
psychology
publicly
pursue
questionnaire
realize
really
recede
receipt
receive
recognize
recommend
reference
referred
rehearse
relevant
reminiscence
renowned
repetition
restaurant
rhythm
ridiculous
sandwich
satellite
schedule
scissors
secretary
siege
solely
sponsor
subtle
subtlety
superintendent
supersede
surveillance
susceptible
tariff
temperamental
theater
threshold
truly
unmanageable
unwieldy
usage
usually
valuable
various
vegetable
voluntary
weight
weird
whale
wield
yield

Abbreviations Guide

Abbreviations, shortened versions of words or phrases, can be valuable tools in writing if you know when and how to use them. They can be very helpful in informal writing situations, such as taking notes or writing lists. However, only a few abbreviations can be used in formal writing. They are: *Mr., Mrs., Miss, Ms., Dr., A.M., P.M., A.D., B.C., M.A, B.A., Ph.D.,* and *M.D.*

The following pages provide the conventional abbreviations for a variety of words.

Abbreviations of Common Titles

Ambassador	Amb.	Lieutenant	Lt.
Attorney	Atty.	Major	Maj.
Brigadier-General	Brig. Gen.	President	Pres.
Brother	Br.	Professor	Prof.
Captain	Capt.	Representative	Rep.
Colonel	Col.	Reverend	Rev.
Commander	Cmdr.	Secretary	Sec.
Commissioner	Com.	Senator	Sen.
Corporal	Cpl.	Sergeant	Sgt.
Doctor	Dr.	Sister	Sr.
Father	Fr.	Superintendent	Supt.
Governor	Gov.	Treasurer	Treas.
Honorable	Hon.	Vice Admiral	Vice Adm.

Abbreviations of Academic Degrees

Bachelor of Arts	B.A. (or A.B.)	Esquire (lawyer)	Esq.
Bachelor of Science	B.S. (or S.B.)	Master of Arts	M.A. (or A.M.)
Doctor of Dental Surgery	D.D.S.	Master of Business Administration	M.B.A.
Doctor of Divinity	D.D.		
Doctor of Education	Ed.D.	Master of Fine Arts	M.F.A.
Doctor of Laws	LL.D.	Master of Science	M.S. (or S.M.)
Doctor of Medicine	M.D.	Registered Nurse	R.N.
Doctor of Philosophy	Ph.D.		

Abbreviations of States

State	Traditional	Postal Service	State	Traditional	Postal Service
Alabama	Ala.	AL	Montana	Mont.	MT
Alaska	Alaska	AK	Nebraska	Nebr.	NE
Arizona	Ariz.	AZ	Nevada	Nev.	NV
Arkansas	Ark.	AR	New Hampshire	N.H.	NH
California	Calif.	CA	New Jersey	N.J.	NJ
Colorado	Colo.	CO	New Mexico	N.M.	NM
Connecticut	Conn.	CT	New York	N.Y.	NY
Delaware	Del.	DE	North Carolina	N.C.	NC
Florida	Fla.	FL	North Dakota	N.Dak.	ND
Georgia	Ga.	GA	Ohio	O.	OH
Hawaii	Hawaii	HI	Oklahoma	Okla.	OK
Idaho	Ida.	ID	Oregon	Ore.	OR
Illinois	Ill.	IL	Pennsylvania	Pa.	PA
Indiana	Ind.	IN	Rhode Island	R.I.	RI
Iowa	Iowa	IA	South Carolina	S.C.	SC
Kansas	Kans.	KS	South Dakota	S.Dak.	SD
Kentucky	Ky.	KY	Tennessee	Tenn.	TN
Louisiana	La.	LA	Texas	Tex.	TX
Maine	Me.	ME	Utah	Utah	UT
Maryland	Md.	MD	Vermont	Vt.	VT
Massachusetts	Mass.	MA	Virginia	Va.	VA
Michigan	Mich.	MI	Washington	Wash.	WA
Minnesota	Minn.	MN	West Virginia	W. Va	WV
Mississippi	Miss.	MS	Wisconsin	Wis.	WI
Missouri	Mo.	MO	Wyoming	Wyo.	WY

Common Geographical Abbreviations

Apartment	Apt.	National	Natl.
Avenue	Ave.	Park, Peak	Pk.
Block	Blk.	Peninsula	Pen.
Boulevard	Blvd.	Point	Pt.
Building	Bldg.	Province	Prov.
County	Co.	Road	Rd.
District	Dist.	Route	Rte.
Drive	Dr.	Square	Sq.
Fort	Ft.	Street	St.
Island	Is.	Territory	Terr.
Mountain	Mt.		

Abbreviations of Traditional Measurements

inch(es)	in.	ounce(s)	oz.
foot, feet	ft.	pound(s)	lb.
yard(s)	yd.	pint(s)	pt.
mile(s)	mi.	quart(s)	qt.
teaspoon(s)	tsp.	gallon(s)	gal.
tablespoon(s)	tbsp.	Fahrenheit	F.

Abbreviations of Metric Measurements

millimeter(s)	mm	liter(s)	L
centimeter(s)	cm	kiloliter(s)	kL
meter(s)	m	milligram(s)	mg
kilometer(s)	km	centigram(s)	cg
milliliter(s)	mL	gram(s)	g
centiliter(s)	cL	Celsius	C

Other Commonly Used Abbreviations

about (used with dates)	c., ca., circ.	manager	mgr.
and others	et al.	manufacturing	mfg.
anonymous	anon.	market	mkt.
approximately	approx.	measure	meas.
associate, association	assoc., assn.	merchandise	mdse.
auxiliary	aux., auxil.	miles per hour	mph
bibliography	bibliog.	miscellaneous	misc.
boxes	bx(s).	money order	M.O.
bucket	bkt.	note well; take notice	N.B.
bulletin	bull.	number	no.
bushel	bu.	package	pkg.
capital letter	cap.	page	p., pg.
cash on delivery	C.O.D.	pages	pp.
department	dept.	pair(s)	pr(s).
discount	disc.	parenthesis	paren.
dozen(s)	doz.	Patent Office	pat. off.
each	ea.	piece(s)	pc(s).
edition, editor	ed.	poetical, poetry	poet.
equivalent	equiv.	private	pvt.
established	est.	proprietor	prop.
fiction	fict.	pseudonym	pseud.
for example	e.g.	published, publisher	pub.
free of charge	grat., gratis	received	recd.
General Post Office	G.P.O.	reference, referee	ref.
government	gov., govt.	revolutions per minute	rpm
graduate, graduated	grad.	rhetorical, rhetoric	rhet.
Greek, Grecian	Gr.	right	R.
headquarters	hdqrs.	scene	sc.
height	ht.	special, specific	spec.
hospital	hosp.	spelling, species	sp.
illustrated	ill., illus.	that is	i.e.
including, inclusive	incl.	treasury, treasurer	treas.
introduction, introductory	intro.	volume	vol.
italics	ital.	weekly	wkly
karat, carat	k., kt.	weight	wt.
left	L.		

Proofreading Symbols Reference

Proofreading symbols make it easier to show where changes are needed in a paper. When proofreading your own or a classmate's work, use these standard proofreading symbols.

insert	I proofred. (a)
delete	Ip proofread.
close up space	I proof read.
delete and close up space	I proofreade.
begin new paragraph	¶ I proofread.
spell out	I proofread (10) papers. (sp)
lowercase	I Proofread. (lc)
capitalize	i proofread. (cap)
transpose letters	I proofraed. (tr)
transpose words	I only proofread her paper. (tr)
period	I will proofread ⊙
comma	I will proofread ^ and she will help.
colon	We will proofread for the following errors ^ :
semicolon	I will proofread ^ she will help. ;
single quotation marks	She said, "I enjoyed the story ^ The Invalid. ^ " ‘ ’
double quotation marks	She said, ^ I enjoyed the story. ^ “ ”
apostrophe	Did you borrow Sylvias book? ’
question mark	Did you borrow Sylvia's book ^ ?/
exclamation point	You're kidding ^ !/
hyphen	online /=/
parentheses	William Shakespeare ^ 1564–1616 ^ ( )

Student Publications

To share your writing with a wider audience, consider submitting it to a local, state, or national publication for student writing. Following are several magazines and Web sites that accept and publish student work.

Periodicals

Creative Kids P.O. Box 8813, Waco TX 76714-8813

Merlyn's Pen merlynspen.org

Skipping Stones P.O. Box 3939, Eugene, OR 97403 http://www.skippingstones.org

Teen Ink Box 30, Newton, MA 02461 teenink.com

On-line Publications

Kid Pub http://www.kidpub.org

MidLink Magazine http://www.ncsu.edu/midlink

Stone Soup http://www.stonesoup.com

Contests

Annual Poetry Contest National Federation of State Poetry Societies, Contest Chair, Kathleen Pederzani, 121 Grande Boulevard, Reading, PA 19608-9680. http://www.nfsps.com

Paul A. Witty Outstanding Literature Award International Reading Association, Special Interest Group for Reading for Gifted and Creative Students, c/o Texas Christian University, P.O. Box 297900, Fort Worth, TX 76129

***Seventeen* Magazine Fiction Contest** *Seventeen* Magazine, 1440 Broadway 13th Floor, New York, NY 10018

The Young Playwrights Festival National Playwriting Competition Young Playwrights Inc. Dept WEB, 306 West 38th Street #300, New York, NY 10018 or webmaster@youngplaywrights.org

Glossary

A

accent: the emphasis on a syllable, usually in poetry

action verb: a word that tells what action someone or something is performing (*See* linking verb.)

active voice: the voice of a verb whose subject performs an action (*See* passive voice.)

adjective: a word that modifies a noun or pronoun by telling *what kind* or *which one*

adjective clause: a subordinate clause that modifies a noun or pronoun

adjective phrase: a prepositional phrase that modifies a noun or pronoun

adverb: a word that modifies a verb, an adjective, or another adverb

adverb clause: a subordinate clause that modifies a verb, an adjective, an adverb, or a verbal by telling *where, when, in what way, to what extent, under what condition,* or *why*

adverb phrase: a prepositional phrase that modifies a verb, an adjective, or an adverb

allegory: a literary work with two or more levels of meaning—a literal level and one or more symbolic levels

alliteration: the repetition of initial consonant sounds in accented syllables

allusion: an indirect reference to a well-known person, place, event, literary work, or work of art

annotated bibliography: a research writing product that provides a list of materials on a given topic, along with publication information, summaries, or evaluations

apostrophe: a punctuation mark used to form possessive nouns and contractions

appositive: a noun or pronoun placed after another noun or pronoun to identify, rename, or explain the preceding word

appositive phrase: a noun or pronoun with its modifiers, placed next to a noun or pronoun to identify, rename, or explain the preceding word

article: one of three commonly used adjectives: *a, an,* and *the*

assonance: the repetition of vowel sounds in stressed syllables containing dissimilar consonant sounds

audience: the reader(s) a writer intends to reach

autobiographical writing: narrative writing that tells a true story about an important period, experience, or relationship in the writer's life

B

ballad: a song that tells a story (often dealing with adventure or romance) or a poem imitating such a song

bias: the attitudes or beliefs that affect a writer's ability to present a subject objectively

bibliography: a list of the sources of a research paper, including full bibliographic references for each source the writer consulted while conducting research (*See* works-cited list.)

biography: narrative writing that tells the story of an important period, experience, or relationship in a person's life, as reported by another

blueprinting: a prewriting technique in which a writer sketches a map of a home, school, neighborhood, or other meaningful place in order to spark memories or associations for further development

body paragraph: a paragraph in an essay that develops, explains, or supports the key ideas of the writing

brainstorming: a prewriting technique in which a group jots down as many ideas as possible about a given topic

C

case: the form of a noun or pronoun that indicates how it functions in a sentence

cause-and-effect writing: expository writing that examines the relationship between events, explaining how one event or situation causes another

character: a person (though not necessarily a human being) who takes part in the action of a literary work

characterization: the act of creating and developing a character through narration, description, and dialogue

citation: in formal research papers, the acknowledgment of ideas found in outside sources

classical invention: a prewriting technique in which writers gather details about a topic by analyzing the category and subcategories to which the topic belongs

clause: a group of words that has a subject and a verb

climax: the high point of interest or suspense in a literary work

coherence: a quality of written work in which all the parts flow logically from one idea to the next

colon: a punctuation mark used before an extended quotation, explanation, example, or series and after the salutation in a formal letter

comma: a punctuation mark used to separate words or groups of words

comparison-and-contrast writing: expository writing that describes the similarities and differences between two or more subjects in order to achieve a specific purpose

complement: a word or group of words that completes the meaning of a verb

compound sentence: a sentence that contains two or more independent clauses with no subordinate clauses

conclusion: the final paragraph(s) of a work of writing in which the writer may restate a main idea, summarize the points of the writing, or provide a closing remark to end the work effectively (*See* introduction, body paragraph, topical paragraph, functional paragraph.)

conflict: a struggle between opposing forces

conjugation: a list of the singular and plural forms of a verb in a particular tense

conjunction: a word used to connect other words or groups of words

connotation: the emotional associations that a word calls to mind (*See* denotation.)

consonance: the repetition of final consonant sounds in stressed syllables containing dissimilar vowel sounds

contraction: a shortened form of a word or phrase that includes an apostrophe to indicate the position of the missing letter(s)

coordinating conjunctions: words such as *and, but, nor,* and *yet* that connect similar words or groups of words

correlative conjunctions: word pairs such as *neither . . . nor, both . . . and,* and *whether . . . or* used to connect similar words or groups of words

couplet: a pair of rhyming lines written in the same meter

cubing: a prewriting technique in which a writer analyzes a subject from six specified angles: description; association; application; analysis; comparison and contrast; and evaluation

D

declarative sentence: a statement punctuated with a period

demonstrative pronouns: words such as *this, that, these,* and *those* used to single out specific people, places, or things

denotation: the objective meaning of a word; its definition independent of other associations the word calls to mind (*See* connotation.)

depth-charging: a drafting technique in which a writer elaborates on a sentence by developing a key word or idea

description: language or writing that uses sensory details to capture a subject

dialect: the form of a language spoken by people in a particular region or group

dialogue: a direct conversation between characters or people

diary: a personal record of daily events, usually written in prose

diction: a writer's word choice

direct object: a noun or a pronoun that receives the action of a transitive verb

direct quotation: a drafting technique in which writers indicate the exact words of another by enclosing them in quotation marks

documentary: nonfiction film that analyzes news events or another focused subject by combining interviews, film footage, narration, and other audio/visual components

documented essay: research writing that includes a limited number of research sources, providing full documentation parenthetically within the text

drafting: a stage of the writing process that follows prewriting and precedes revising in which a writer gets ideas on paper in a rough format

drama: a story written to be performed by actors and actresses

E

elaboration: a drafting technique in which a writer extends his or her ideas through the use of facts, examples, descriptions, details, or quotations

epic: a long narrative poem about the adventures of a god or a hero

essay: a short nonfiction work about a particular subject

etymology: the history of a word, showing where it came from and how it has evolved into its present spelling and meaning

exclamation mark: a punctuation mark used to indicate strong emotion

exclamatory sentence: a statement that conveys strong emotion and ends with an exclamation mark

exposition: writing to inform, addressing analytic purposes such as problem and solution, comparison and contrast, how-to, and cause and effect

extensive writing: writing products generated for others and from others, meant to be shared with an audience and often done for school assignments (*See* reflexive writing.)

F

fact: a statement that can be proved true (*See* opinion.)

fiction: prose writing about imaginary characters and events

figurative language: writing or speech not meant to be interpreted literally

firsthand biography: narrative writing that tells the story of an important period, experience, or relationship in a person's life, reported by a writer who knows the subject personally

five *W*'s: a prewriting technique in which writers gather details about a topic by generating answers to the following questions: *Who? What? Where? When?* and *Why?*

fragment: an incomplete idea punctuated as a complete sentence

freewriting: a prewriting technique in which a writer quickly jots down as many ideas on a topic as possible

functional paragraph: a paragraph that performs a specific role in composition, such as to arouse or sustain interest, to indicate dialogue, to make a transition (*See* topical paragraph.)

G

generalization: a statement that presents a rule or idea based on particular facts

gerund: a noun formed from the present participle of a verb (ending in *-ing*)

gerund phrase: a group of words containing a gerund and its modifiers or complements that function as a noun

grammar: the study of the forms of words and the way they are arranged in phrases, clauses, and sentences

H

helping verb: a verb added to another verb to make a single verb phrase that indicates the time at which an action takes place or whether it actually happens, could happen, or should happen

hexagonal writing: a prewriting technique in

which a writer analyzes a subject from six angles: literal level, personal allusions, theme, literary devices, literary allusions, and evaluation

homophones: pairs of words that sound the same as each other yet have different meanings and different spellings, such as *hear/here*

how-to writing: expository writing that explains a process by providing step-by-step directions

humanities: forms of artistic expression including, but not limited to, fine art, photography, theater, film, music, and dance

hyperbole: a deliberate exaggeration or overstatement

hyphen: a punctuation mark used to combine numbers and word parts, to join certain compound words, and to show that a word has been broken between syllables at the end of a line

I

I-Search report: a research paper in which the writer addresses the research experience in addition to presenting the information gathered

image: a word or phrase that appeals to one or more of the senses—sight, hearing, touch, taste, or smell

imagery: the descriptive language used to re-create sensory experiences, set a tone, suggest emotions, and guide readers' reactions

imperative sentence: a statement that gives an order or a direction and ends with either a period or an exclamation mark

indefinite pronoun: a word such as *anyone, each,* or *many* that refers to a person, place, or thing, without specifying which one

independent clause: a group of words that contains both a subject and a verb and that can stand by itself as a complete sentence

indirect quotation: reporting only the general meaning of what a person said or thought; quotation marks are not needed

infinitive: the form of a verb that comes after the word *to* and acts as a noun, adjective, or adverb

infinitive phrase: a phrase introduced by an infinitive that may be used as a noun, an adjective, or an adverb

interjection: a word or phrase that expresses feeling or emotion and functions independently of a sentence

interrogative pronoun: a word such as *which* and *who* that introduces a question

interrogative sentence: a question that is punctuated with a question mark

interview: an information-gathering technique in which one or more people pose questions to one or more other people who provide opinions or facts on a topic

intransitive verb: an action verb that does not take a direct object (*See* transitive verb.)

introduction: the opening paragraphs of a work of writing in which the writer may capture the readers' attention and present a thesis statement to be developed in the writing (*See* body paragraph, topical paragraph, functional paragraph, conclusion.)

invisible writing: a prewriting technique in which a writer freewrites without looking at the product until the exercise is complete; this can be accomplished at a word processor with the monitor turned off or with carbon paper and an empty ballpoint pen

irony: the general name given to literary techniques that involve surprising, interesting, or amusing contradictions

itemizing: a prewriting technique in which a writer creates a second, more focused, set of ideas based on an original listing activity. (*See* listing.)

J

jargon: the specialized words and phrases unique to a specific field

journal: a notebook or other organized writing system in which daily events and personal impressions are recorded

K

key word: the word or phrase that directs an Internet or database search

L

layering: a drafting technique in which a writer elaborates on a statement by identifying and then expanding upon a central idea or word

lead: the opening sentences of a work of writing meant to grab the reader's interest, accomplished through a variety of methods, including providing an intriguing quotation, a surprising or provocative question or fact, an anecdote, or a description

learning log: a record-keeping system in which a student notes information about new ideas

legend: a widely told story about the past that may or may not be based in fact

legibility: the neatness and readability of words

linking verb: a word that expresses its subject's state of being or condition (*See* action verb.)

listing: a prewriting technique in which a writer prepares a list of ideas related to a specific topic. (*See* itemizing.)

looping: a prewriting activity in which a writer generates follow-up freewriting based on the identification of a key word or central idea in an original freewriting exercise

lyric poem: a poem expressing the observations and feelings of a single speaker

M

main clause: a group of words that has a subject and a verb and can stand alone as a complete sentence

memoir: autobiographical writing that provides an account of a writer's relationship with a person, event, or place

metaphor: a figure of speech in which one thing is spoken of as though it were something else

meter: the rhythmic pattern of a poem

monologue: a speech or performance given entirely by one person or by one character

mood: the feeling created in the reader by a literary work or passage

multimedia presentation: a technique for sharing information with an audience by enhancing narration and explanation with media, including video images, slides, audiotape recordings, music, and fine art

N

narration: writing that tells a story

narrative poem: a poem that tells a story in verse

nominative case: the form of a noun or pronoun used as the subject of a verb, as a predicate nominative, or as the pronoun in a nominative absolute (*See* objective case, possessive case.)

noun: a word that names a person, place, or thing

noun clause: a subordinate clause that acts as a noun

novel: an extended work of fiction that often has a complicated plot, many major and minor characters, a unifying theme, and several settings

O

objective case: the form of a noun or pronoun used as the object of any verb, verbal, or preposition, or as the subject of an infinitive (*See* nominative case, possessive case.)

observation: a prewriting technique involving close visual study of an object; a writing product that reports such a study

ode: a long formal lyric poem with a serious theme

onomatopoeia: words such as *buzz* and *plop* that suggest the sounds they name

open-book test: a form of assessment in which students are permitted to use books and class notes to respond to test questions

opinion: beliefs that can be supported but not proved to be true (*See* fact.)

oral tradition: the body of songs, stories, and poems preserved by being passed from generation to generation by word of mouth

outline: a prewriting or study technique that allows writers or readers to organize the presentation and order of information

oxymoron: a figure of speech that fuses two contradictory or opposing ideas, such as "freezing fire" or "happy grief"

P

parable: a short, simple story from which a moral or religious lesson can be drawn

paradox: a statement that seems to be contradictory but that actually presents a truth

paragraph: a group of sentences that share a common topic or purpose and that focus on a single main idea or thought

parallelism: the placement of equal ideas in words, phrases, or clauses of similar types

paraphrase: restating an author's idea in different words, often to share information by making the meaning clear to readers

parentheses: punctuation marks used to set off asides and explanations when the material is not essential

participial phrase: a group of words made up of a participle and its modifiers and complements that acts as an adjective

participle: a form of a verb that can act as an adjective

passive voice: the voice of a verb whose subject receives an action (*See* active voice.)

peer review: a revising technique in which writers meet with other writers to share focused feedback on a draft

pentad: a prewriting technique in which a writer analyzes a subject from five specified points: actors, acts, scenes, agencies, and purposes

period: a punctuation mark used to end a declarative sentence, an indirect question, and most abbreviations

personal pronoun: a word such as *I, me, you, we, us, he, him, she, her, they,* and *them* that refers to the person speaking; the person spoken to; or the person, place, or thing spoken about

personification a figure of speech in which a nonhuman subject is given human characteristics

persuasion: writing or speaking that attempts to convince others to accept a position on an issue of concern to the writer

phrase: a group of words without a subject and verb that functions as one part of speech

plot: the sequence of events in narrative writing

plural: the form of a word that indicates more than one item is being mentioned

poetry: a category of writing in which the final product may make deliberate use of rhythm, rhyme, and figurative language in order to express deeper feelings than those conveyed in ordinary speech (*See* prose, drama.)

point of view: the perspective, or vantage point, from which a story is told

portfolio: an organized collection of writing projects, including writing ideas, works in progress, final drafts, and the writer's reflections on the work

possessive case: the form of a noun or pronoun used to show ownership (*See* objective case, nominative case.)

prefix: one or more syllables added to the beginning of a word root (*See* root, suffix.)

preposition: a word that relates a noun or pronoun that appears with it to another word in the sentence to indicate relations of time, place, causality, responsibility, and motivation

prepositional phrase: a group of words that includes a preposition and a noun or pronoun

presenting: a stage of the writing process in which a writer shares a final draft with an audience through speaking, listening, or representing activities

prewriting: a stage of the writing process in which writers explore, choose, and narrow a topic and then gather necessary details for drafting

problem-and-solution writing: expository writing that examines a problem and provides a realistic solution

pronoun: a word that stands for a noun or for another word that takes the place of a noun

prose: a category of written language in which the end product is developed through sentences and paragraphs (*See* poetry, drama.)

publishing: a stage of the writing process in which a writer shares the written version of a final draft with an audience

punctuation: the set of symbols used to convey specific directions to the reader

purpose: the specific goal or reason a writer chooses for a writing task

Q

question mark: a punctuation mark used to end an interrogative sentence or an incomplete question

quicklist: a prewriting technique in which a writer creates an impromptu, unresearched list of ideas related to a specific topic

quotation mark: a punctuation mark used to indicate the beginning and end of a person's exact speech or thoughts

R

ratiocination: a systematic approach to the revision process that involves color-coding elements of writing for evaluation

reflective essay: autobiographical writing in which a writer shares a personal experience and then provides insight about the event

reflexive pronoun: a word that ends in *-self* or *-selves* and names the person or thing receiving an action when that person or thing is the same as the one performing the action

reflexive writing: writing generated for oneself and from oneself, not necessarily meant to be shared, in which the writer makes all decisions regarding form and purpose (*See* extensive writing.)

refrain: a regularly repeated line or group of lines in a poem or song

relative pronoun: a pronoun such as *that, which, who, whom,* or *whose* that begins a subordinate clause and connects it to another idea in the sentence

reporter's formula: a prewriting technique in which writers gather details about a topic by generating answers to the following questions: *Who? What? Where? When?* and *Why?*

research: a prewriting technique in which writers gather information from outside sources such as library reference materials, interviews, and the Internet

research writing: expository writing that presents and interprets information gathered through an extensive study of a subject

response to literature writing: persuasive, expository, or narrative writing that presents a writer's analysis of or reactions to a published work

revising: a stage of the writing process in which a writer reworks a rough draft to improve both form and content

rhyme: the repetition of sounds at the ends of words

rhyme scheme: the regular pattern of rhyming words in a poem or stanza

rhythm: the form or pattern of words or music in which accents or beats come at certain fixed intervals

root: the base of a word (*See* prefix, suffix.)

rubric: an assessment tool, generally organized in a grid, to indicate the range of success or failure according to specific criteria

run-on sentence: two or more complete sentences punctuated incorrectly as one

S

salutation: the greeting in a formal letter

satire: writing that ridicules or holds up to contempt the faults of individuals or of groups

SEE method: an elaboration technique in which a writer presents a statement, an extension, and an elaboration to develop an idea

semicolon: a punctuation mark used to join independent clauses that are not already joined by a conjunction

sentence: a group of words with a subject and a predicate that expresses a complete thought

setting: the time and place of the action of a piece of narrative writing

short story: a brief fictional narrative told in prose

simile: a figure of speech in which *like* or *as* is used to make a comparison between two basically unrelated ideas

sonnet: a fourteen-line lyric poem with a single theme

speaker: the imaginary voice assumed by the writer of a poem

stanza: a group of lines in a poem, seen as a unit

statistics: facts presented in numerical form, such as ratios, percentages, or summaries

subject: the word or group of words in a sentence that tells whom or what the sentence is about

subordinate clause: a group of words containing both a subject and a verb that cannot stand by itself as a complete sentence

subordinating conjunction: a word used to join two complete ideas by making one of the ideas dependent on the other

suffix: one or more syllables added to the end of a word root (*See* prefix, root.)

summary: a brief statement of the main ideas and supporting details presented in a piece of writing

symbol: something that is itself and also stands for something else

T

theme: the central idea, concern, or purpose in a piece of narrative writing, poetry, or drama

thesis statement: a statement of an essay's main idea; all information in the essay supports or elaborates this idea

tone: a writer's attitude toward the readers and toward the subject

topic sentence: a sentence that states the main idea of a paragraph

topic web: a prewriting technique in which a writer generates a graphic organizer to identify categories and subcategories of a topic

topical paragraph: a paragraph that develops, explains, and supports the topic sentence related to an essay's thesis statement

transition: words, phrases, or sentences that smooth writing by indicating the relationship among ideas

transitive verb: an action verb that takes a direct object (*See* intransitive verb.)

U

unity: a quality of written work in which all the parts fit together in a complete, self-contained whole

V

verb: a word or group of words that expresses an action, a condition, or the fact that something exists while indicating the time of the action, condition, or fact

verbal: a word derived from the verb but used as a noun, adjective, or adverb (*See* gerund, infinitive, participle.)

vignette: a brief narrative characterized by precise detail

voice: the distinctive qualities of a writer's style, including diction, attitude, sentence style, and ideas

W

works-cited list: a list of the sources of a research paper, including full bibliographic references for each source named in the body of the paper (*See* bibliography.)

Index

Note: **Bold numbers** show pages on which basic definitions appear.

A

D

F

G

J

K

L

T

U

V

W

Y

Z

The program authors would like to acknowledge the work of the following writers whose ideas have influenced the writing strategies presented in this series.

Brock, Paula. "Help Me, Quick." *R&E Journal 2* (1998): 14-16.

Burke, Kenneth. *A Grammar of Motives.* Berkeley: University of California Press, 1969.

Cooper, Charles R., and Lee Odell. *Evaluating Writing: Describing, Measuring, Judging.* Urbana, IL: National Council of Teachers of English, 1977.

Corbett, Edward P. J., and Robert J. Connors. *Classical Rhetoric for the Modern Student.* New York: Oxford University Press, Inc., 1998.

Cowan, Gregory, and Elizabeth Swan. *Writing.* New York: John Wiley, 1980.

Elbow, Peter. *Writing Without Teachers.* New York: Oxford University Press, 1973.

Emig, Janet. *The Composing Process of Twelfth Graders.* Urbana, IL: National Council of Teachers of English, 1971.

Lane, Barry. *After the End: Teaching and Learning Creative Revision.* Portsmouth, NH: Heinemann Educational Books, Inc., 1993.

Rico, Gabriele Lusser. *Writing the Natural Way.* Los Angeles: J.P. Tarcher, 1983.

Rief, Linda. *Seeking Diversity.* Portsmouth, NH: Heinemann Educational Books, 1992.

Stillman, Peter R. *Families Writing.* Cincinnati, OH: Writer's Digest Books, 1989.

Acknowledgments

Staff Credits
The people who made up the *Prentice Hall Writing and Grammar: Communication in Action* team—representing design services, editorial, editorial services, electronic publishing technology, manufacturing & inventory planning, marketing, marketing services, market research, online services & multimedia development, product planning, production services, project office, and publishing processes—are listed below. Bold type denotes the core team members.

Betsy Bostwick, Evonne Burgess, **Louise B. Capuano, Sarah Carroll, Megan Chill,** Katherine Clarke, Rhett Conklin, Martha Conway, Harold Crudup, **Harold Delmonte,** Libby Forsyth, Ellen Goldblatt, Elaine Goldman, Jonathan Goldson, **Rebecca Graziano, Diana Hahn,** Rick Hickox, Kristan Hoskins, Raegan Keida, Carol Lavis, **George Lychock, Gregory Lynch,** William McAllister, Loretta Moser, Margaret Plotkin, Maureen Raymond, Gerry Schrenk, **Melissa Shustyk,** Annette Simmons, Robin Sullivan, Julie Tomasella, **Elizabeth Torjussen, Doug Utigard**

Additional Credits
Ernie Albanese, Diane Alimena, Susan Andariese, Michele Angelucci, Penny Baker, Cynthia Clampitt, Ken Dougherty, Angelo Focaccia, Kathy Gavilanes, Beth Geschwind, Michael Goodman, Jennifer Harper, Evan Holstrom, Leanne Korszoloski, Sue Langan, Rebecca Lauth, Dave Liston, Maria Keogh, Vicki Menanteaux, Gail Meyer, Artur Mkrtchyan, LaShonda Morris, Karyl Murray, Omni-Photo Communications, Kim Ortell, Brenda Sanabria, Carolyn Sapontzis, Slip Jig Image Research Services, Sunnyside, NY, Debi Taffet

Grateful acknowledgment is made to the following for permission to reprint copyrighted material:

Richard Curtis Associates, Inc.
"Be Not the First" by Emily Hahn. Used by permission of Richard Curtis Associates, Inc.

Richard Curtis Associates, Inc.
"Be Not the First" by Emily Hahn. Used by permission of Richard Curtis Associates, Inc.

Farrar, Straus & Giroux
Excerpt from "Are Animals Smart?" from *Nature by Design* by Bruce Brooks. Copyright © 1991 by Educational Broadcasting Corporation and Bruce Brooks. Reprinted by permission of Farrar, Straus & Giroux, LLC.

Harvard University Press
"If I can stop one Heart from Breaking" by Emily Dickinson from *The Poems of Emily Dickenson,* Thomas H. Johnson, ed., Cambridge, Mass.: The Bellknap Press of Harvard University Press. Copyright © 1951. 1955, 1979, 1983 by the President and Fellows of Harvard University. Reprinted by permission of the publishers and trustees of Amherst College.

Henry Holt and Company, LLC
"The Freedom of the Moon" by Robert Frost from *The Poetry of Robert Frost,* edited by Edward Connery Lathem. Copyright © 1928, © 1969 by Henry Holt and Co., © 1956 by Robert Frost. Reprinted by permission of Henry Holt and Company, LLC.

Holiday House, Inc.
"January" from *A Child's Calendar* by John Updike. Copyright © 1965, 1999 by John Updike. All rights reserved. Reprinted by permission of Holiday House, Inc.

The New York Times
"Darkness at Noon" by Harold Krents from *The New York Times,* May 5, 1978. Reprinted by permission.

Robert W. Peterson
Excerpt from *Riding the Underground Railroad* by Robert W. Peterson. Reprinted by permission of the author.

Quintet Publishing
"A Simple Shadow Puppet" from *The Encyclopedia of Origami and Papercraft Technique* by Emma Callery, ed. Used by permission.

Reader's Digest Association, Inc.
"Why is the sea blue?" from *Why in the World?,* copyright © 1994 The Reader's Digest Association Limited. Used by permission of The Reader's Digest Association, Inc.

Mary Harris Russell
Excerpt from "Welcome Back" by Mary Harris Russell, *The New York Times,* November 21, 1999. Reprinted by permission of the author.

Scholastic Inc.
"Accounts Settled" by Paul Annixter from *Scholastic Teacher,* February 25, 1996, issue. Copyright © 1966 by Scholastic Inc. Reprinted by permission of Scholastic Inc.

Note: Every effort has been made to locate the copyright owner of material reprinted in this book. Omissions brought to our attention will be corrected in subsequent editions.

Photo Credits

Cover: Stamp design ©United States Postal Service, All Rights Reserved; Ron Dahlquist/Super-Stock; **iii:** Getty Images, Inc.; **vi:** (top) Corel Professional Photos CD-ROM™; (bottom) *House by the Railroad,* Edward Hopper, AKG Berlin/SuperStock; **vii:** (top) Corel Professional Photos CD-ROM™; (bottom) ©The Stock Market/Lance Nelson; **ix:** Bruce Forster/Tony Stone Images; **x:** Mary Ellen Lepionka; **xi:** *Will O' the Wisp,* ca. 1900, oil on canvas (triptych), 27x44 in.; Elizabeth Adela Stanhope Forbes, The National Museum of Women in the Arts, On loan from the Wallace and Wilhelmina Holladay Collection; **xii:** AP/Wide World Photos/Joel Rennich; **xiii:** ©1999 Richard Laird/FPG International Corp.; **xiv:** Paul A. Souders/CORBIS; **xv:** *Strike,* 1992, Red Grooms, Marlborough Gallery, ©2001 Red Grooms/Artists Rights Society (ARS), New York; **xvi:** Kate DeWitt; **xvii:** M.C. Escher, *Day and Night* © 1998, Cordon Art B.V.-Baarn-Holland. All Rights Reserved; **xviii:** © Francis G. Mayer/CORBIS; **xix:** Corel Professional Photos CD-ROM™; **xx:** (top) Corel Professional Photos CD-ROM™; (bottom) Corel Professional Photos CD-ROM™; **xxi:** (top) Corel Professional Photos CD-ROM™; (bottom) Courtesy of Megan Chill; **xxii:** Corel Professional Photos CD-ROM™; **xxiii:** (top) Corel Professional Photos CD-ROM™; (bottom) New York Convention and Visitors Bureau; **xxiv:** (top) *Zinnias,* 1937, John Hollis Kaufmann, Private Collection/SuperStock; (bottom) Corel Professional Photos CD-ROM™; **xxv:** Corel Professional Photos CD-ROM™; **xxii:** (top) Corel Professional Photos CD-ROM™; (bottom) ©The Stock Market/Tom Stewart; **1:** *Orange Sweater,* 1955, Elmer Bischoff, San Francisco Museum of Modern Art, Gift of Mr. and Mrs. Mark Schorer; **2:** Peter Cade/Tony Stone Images; **4:** ©1996, Ron Chappel/FPG International Corp.; **6:** Tom McCarthy/PhotoEdit; **8:** SEF/Art Resource, NY; **12:** PhotoEdit; **24:** Photofest; **28:** Mark Richards/ PhotoEdit; **30:** Bettmann/CORBIS; **31:** (top), (bottom) Getty Images; **35:** Esbin/Anderson/Omni-Photo Communications, Inc.; **37:** PhotoDisc/Getty Images, Inc.; **43:** PhotoDisc/Getty Images, Inc.; **44:** Manuel Alvarez Bravo; **48:** Phil Schermeister/CORBIS; **50:** Kathi Lamm/Tony Stone Images; **51:** Bruce Forster/Tony Stone Images; **52:** Bob Daemmrich/The Image Works; **53:** Paul A. Souders/COR-BIS; **55:** *Self-Portrait,* Emily Childers, Leeds Museums and Galleries (City Art Gallery) U.K./Bridgeman Art Library; **57:** Bachmann/PhotoEdit; **60:** Raymond Gehman/CORBIS; **62:** David Young-Wolff/PhotoEdit; **68–69:** Rene Ritler/AP Wide World Photos; **70:** Mitchell Gerber/COR-BIS; **72:** Erich Lessing/Art Resource, NY; **76:** Illustration for the poem "Fog" by Carl Sandburg by John English; **78:** Lake County Museum/ CORBIS; **80:** "The Bloomer Costume", 1776–1850. Courtesy of Harry T. Peters Collection, Museum of the City of New York. Courtesy of Sears, Roebuck & Co.; **82:** Myrleen Cate/PhotoEdit; **85:** *The Dory,* Edward Hopper, The Nelson-Atkins Museum of Art, Kansas City, Missouri, Gift of Mrs. Louis Sosland; **86:** Mary Ellen Lepionka; **94:** (top) Rhoda Sidney/Photo-Edit; (bottom) Michael Newman/ PhotoEdit; **97:** *House by the Railroad,* Edward Hopper, AKG Berlin/SuperStock; **98:** ©The Stock Market/Mug Shots; **102:** Culver Pictures, Inc.; **106:** *Little Blue Horse,* 1912, Franz Marc, Giraudon/Art Resource, NY; **108:** Peter L. Kresan Photography; **111:** CORBIS; **113:** Van Nuys, Peter Alexander, Courtesy of artist; **117:** ©The Stock Market/ Jon Feingersh; **118:** David Young-Wolff/PhotoEdit; **126:** ©1992, Color Box/FPG International Corp.; **130:** (top) *Will O' the Wisp,* ca. 1900, oil on canvas (triptych), 27x44 in., Elizabeth Adela Stanhope Forbes, The National Museum of Women in the Arts, on loan from the Wallace and Wilhelmina Holladay Collection; (bottom) Jack Vartoogian; **134:** *Signing of the Constitution,* Helen Clark Chandler, Art Resource, NY **136:** ©1998 Arthur Tilley/FPG International Corp.; **138:** AP/Wide World Photos/Joel Rennich; **139:** Bob Rowan; Progressive Image/ CORBIS; **141:** *Untitled (Heard),* Barbara Kruger, National Museum of American Art, Washington, DC/Art Resource, NY/Courtesy: Mary Boone Gallery, New York; **142:** Bettmann/CORBIS; **149:** Horace Bristol/CORBIS; **153:** AP/Wide World Photos/Kevin Winter; **155:** Warren Morgan/ CORBIS; **156:** AP/Wide World Photos/Secretary of Education; **158:** The Granger Collection, New York; **162:** *The Empire of Light II,* 1950, René Magritte, The Museum of Modern Art, New York. Gift of D. and J. de Menil. Photograph ©1999 The Museum of Modern Art, New York. ©2001 C. Herscovici, Brussels/Artists Rights Society (ARS), New York; **164:** (top) ©Art Wolfe/Allstock/ PictureQuest; (bottom) ©The Stock Market/Jose L. Pelaez; **165:** ©1999 Patti Murray/Animals Animals; **167:** (top) *Mexican Men with Burro Carrying Sticks,* Joan Marron-LaRue/Omni-Photo Communications, Inc.; (bottom) Empire State, Tom Christopher, Vicki Morgan Associates; **168:** Michael Newman/PhotoEdit; **170:** (left) Steve Hensen/Stock, Boston/ PictureQuest; (right) Alon Reininger/Contact Press Images/ PictureQuest; **178:** Monkmeyer; **179:** ©1999 Richard Laird/FPG International Corp.; **180:** Michael Newman/PhotoEdit; **182:** (top)

I Saw the Figure 5 in Gold, Charles Demuth, SuperStock; (bottom left) Photofest; (bottom right) Philippe Renault/Liaison Agency; **186:** AP/Wide World Photos/Mark Lennihan; **188–189:** Douglas Peebles/CORBIS; **191:** *Pittsburgh,* 1927, Elsie Driggs, Collection of Whitney Museum of American Art, NYC, Gift of Gertrude Vanderbilt Whitney; **195:** Paul A. Souders/CORBIS; **196:** ©The Stock Market/Bob Shaw; **200–203:** AP/Wide World Photos; **204:** Courtesy of the Library of Congress; **205:** Paul W. Liebhardt; **206:** Culver Pictures, Inc.; **207:** Magnum Photos, Inc. ©1951 Henri Cartier-Bresson; **210:** ©The Stock Market; **212–213:** Quintet Publishing Ltd., London; **215:** *Strike,* 1992, Red Grooms, Marlborough Gallery, ©2001 Red Grooms/Artists Rights Society (ARS), New York; **217:** ©The Stock Market/C/B Productions; **221:** David Young-Wolff/PhotoEdit; **224:** Hunter Freeman/Tony Stone Images; **227:** Courtesy of Katherine Ann Roshani Stewart; **229:** PhotoEdit; **230:** (top) Photofest; (bottom) Male Dancer with Blue from *Le Tumulte Noir,* Paul Colin, National Portrait Gallery, Smithsonian Institution/Art Resource, NY, ©2001 Artists Rights Society (ARS), New York/ADAGP, Paris; **234:** CORBIS/Medford Historical Society Collections; **236:** *A Ride for Liberty—The Fugitive Slaves,* Eastman Johnson, The Brooklyn Museum of Art, Gift of Miss Gwendolyn O.L. Conkling; **237:** (left) (right) ©2000 Louis Psihoyos/National Geographic Society; **239:** *Miners in the Sierras,* Charles Christian Nahl, National Museum of American Art, Washington DC/Art Resource, NY; **242–253:** CORBIS/ Bettmann; **255:** Charles Gupton/ Stock, Boston, Inc./PictureQuest; **256:** (top) Photofest; (bottom) Kate DeWitt; **260:** Joanna Calabro, *Mask Maker, Venice,* 24" x 30" oil on linen. Courtesy of the artist; **262:** Wayne R. Bilenduke/Tony Stone Images; **265:** *The Girl I Left Behind Me,* Eastman Johnson, National Museum of American Art, Washington, DC/Art Resource, NY; **267:** CORBIS/Bettmann; **269:** ©Team Russell/Adventure Photo; **271:** M.C. Escher, *Day and Night* ©1998, Cordon Art B.V.-Baarn-Holland. All Rights Reserved; **272:** North Wind Picture Archives; **277:** Robin L. Sachs/PhotoEdit; **280:** ©1999 Dick Luria/FPG International Corp.; **282:** Tony Stone Images; **284:** Photofest; **288:** *Girl Writing,* 1908, Pierre Bonnard, Barnes Foundation, Merion, Pennsylvania/SuperStock; **289:** PhotoDisc/Getty Images, Inc.; **295:** Dale Spartas/Tony Stone Images; **298:** *King George III of England,* c. 1767, Allan Ramsay, Scottish National Portrait Gallery; **299:** Kevin Fleming/CORBIS; **300:** Will Hart; **302:** © Francis G. Mayer/CORBIS; **307:** *Snoopy-Early Sun Display on Earth,* 1970, Alma Woodsey Thomas, National Museum of American Art, Washington, DC/Art Resource, NY; **308:** Corel Professional Photos CD-ROM™; **310:** Heath Robbins/Getty Images-Taxi; **312:** Courtesy of the Library of Congress; **316–319:** Pearson Education; **328–336:** Courtesy of the Library of Congress; **346–348:** Pearson Education; **350–370:** Corel Professional Photos CD-ROM™; **373:** Pearson Education; **375:** Corel Professional Photos CD-ROM™; **376:** Rudi Von Briel/PhotoEdit; **380–411:** Corel Professional Photos CD-ROM™; **412:** Pearson Education; **416–421:** Corel Professional Photos CD-ROM™; **430–440:** Courtesy of Megan Chill; **444:** Corel Professional Photos CD-ROM™; **445:** Pearson Education; **449–472:** Corel Professional Photos CD-ROM™; **478:** Pearson Education; **482–496:** Corel Professional Photos CD-ROM™; **504:** PhotoDisc/Getty Images, Inc.; **508–513:** Pearson Education; **514:** American Foundation for the Blind, Inc.; **519:** Mary Kate Denny/PhotoEdit; **528:** Courtesy of the Library of Congress; **530:** Corel Professional Photos CD-ROM™; **538:** Pearson Education; **541:** Silver Burdett Ginn; **544–552:** Corel Professional Photos CD-ROM™; **554:** Courtesy of the Library of Congress; **557:** Corel Professional Photos CD-ROM™; **559:** Pearson Education; **562–563:** Corel Professional Photos CD-ROM™; **565** Pearson Education; **572–618:** Corel Professional Photos CD-ROM™; **621:** Pearson Education; **623:** Courtesy of the Library of Congress; **626–636:** Corel Professional Photos CD-ROM™; **638:** New York Convention and Visitors Bureau; **639–648:** Corel Professional Photos CD-ROM™; **671:** *Emblems,* Roger De La Fresnaye, The Phillips Collection, Washington, DC; **672:** David Young-Wolff/PhotoEdit; **677:** Stephen McBrady/PhotoEdit; **685:** *Zinnias,* 1937, John Hollis Kaufmann, Private Collection/SuperStock; **686–690:** David Young-Wolff/PhotoEdit; **694:** Ken Karp/PH photo; **698:** ©The Stock Market/Mug Shots; **701–707:** Tony Freeman/PhotoEdit; **709:** Bruce Ayres/Tony Stone Images; **710:** Tony Freeman/PhotoEdit; **714:** Corel Professional Photos CD-ROM™; **718:** ©The Stock Market/Lance Nelson; **727:** Pinkerton Security and Investigation Services; **731:** Corel Professional Photos CD-ROM™; **735:** Pearson Education; **737:** David Young-Wolff/PhotoEdit/PictureQuest; **740:** Mary Kate Denny/Tony Stone Images; **742:** Tony Freeman/PhotoEdit; **754:** David Young-Wolff/PhotoEdit; **756:** ©The Stock Market/Tom Stewart